OXFORD

ESSENTIAL
WORLD
ATLAS

WORLD CITIES
Cartography by Philip's

Page 11, Dublin. Based on Ordnance Survey Ireland by permission of the Government Permit No. 7336. © Government of Ireland

Page 15, London. Based upon the Ordnance Survey Maps with the permission of the Controller of Her Majesty's Stationery Office. © Crown copyright 2001. All rights reserved. Licence No. 339817

Vector data: Courtesy of Gräfe and Unser Verlag GmbH, München, Germany (city center maps of Bangkok, Beijing, Cape Town, Jerusalem, Mexico City, Moscow, Singapore, Sydney, Tokyo and Washington D.C.)

All satellite images in this section courtesy of NPA Group Limited, Edenbridge, Kent, UK (www.satmaps.com)

George Philip Limited,
a division of Octopus Publishing Group Limited,
2– 4 Heron Quays, London E14 4JP

Cartography by Philip's

Published in North America by
Oxford University Press, Inc.,
198 Madison Avenue,
New York, N.Y. 10016

www.oup-usa.org/atlas

Oxford is a registered trademark of Oxford University Press

Library of Congress Cataloging-in-Publication Data available

ISBN 0–19–521790–X

Printing (last digit):
9 8 7 6 5 4 3 2 1

Printed in Hong Kong

OXFORD

ESSENTIAL
WORLD
ATLAS

THIRD EDITION

Contents

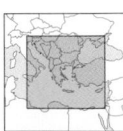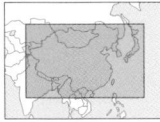

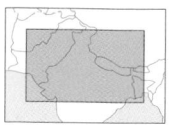
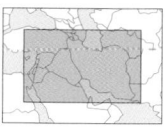

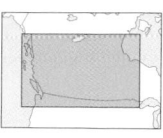

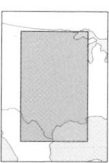
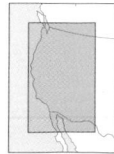

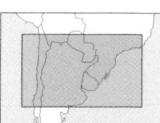

V

World Statistics: Countries

This alphabetical list includes all the countries and territories of the world. If a territory is not completely independent, the country it is associated with is named. The area figures give the total area of land, inland water and ice. The population figures are 2000 estimates. The annual income is the Gross National Product per capita in US dollars. The figures are the latest available, usually 1999 estimates.

Country/Territory	Area km² Thousands	Area miles² Thousands	Population Thousands	Capital	Annual Income US $
Afghanistan	652	252	26,511	Kabul	800
Albania	28.8	11.1	3,795	Tirana	870
Algeria	2,382	920	32,904	Algiers	1,550
American Samoa (US)	0.20	0.08	39	Pago Pago	2,600
Andorra	0.45	0.17	49	Andorra La Vella	18,000
Angola	1,247	481	13,295	Luanda	220
Anguilla (UK)	0.1	0.04	8	The Valley	6,800
Antigua & Barbuda	0.44	0.17	79	St John's	8,520
Argentina	2,767	1,068	36,238	Buenos Aires	7,600
Armenia	29.8	11.5	3,968	Yerevan	490
Aruba (Netherlands)	0.19	0.07	58	Oranjestad	22,000
Australia	7,687	2,968	18,855	Canberra	20,050
Austria	83.9	32.4	7,613	Vienna	25,970
Azerbaijan	86.6	33.4	8,324	Baku	550
Azores (Portugal)	2.2	0.87	238	Ponta Delgada	–
Bahamas	13.9	5.4	295	Nassau	20,100
Bahrain	0.68	0.26	683	Manama	7,640
Bangladesh	144	56	150,589	Dhaka	370
Barbados	0.43	0.17	265	Bridgetown	7,890
Belarus	207.6	80.1	10,697	Minsk	2,630
Belgium	30.5	11.8	9,832	Brussels	24,510
Belize	23	8.9	230	Belmopan	2,730
Benin	113	43	6,369	Porto-Novo	380
Bermuda (UK)	0.05	0.02	62	Hamilton	35,590
Bhutan	47	18.1	1,906	Thimphu	510
Bolivia	1,099	424	9,724	La Paz/Sucre	1,010
Bosnia-Herzegovina	51	20	4,601	Sarajevo	1,720
Botswana	582	225	1,822	Gaborone	3,240
Brazil	8,512	3,286	179,487	Brasília	4,420
Brunei	5.8	2.2	333	Bandar Seri Begawan	24,630
Bulgaria	111	43	9,071	Sofia	1,380
Burkina Faso	274	106	12,092	Ouagadougou	240
Burma (= Myanmar)	677	261	51,129	Rangoon	1,200
Burundi	27.8	10.7	7,358	Bujumbura	120
Cambodia	181	70	10,046	Phnom Penh	260
Cameroon	475	184	16,701	Yaoundé	580
Canada	9,976	3,852	28,488	Ottawa	19,320
Canary Is. (Spain)	7.3	2.8	1,494	Las Palmas/Santa Cruz	–
Cape Verde Is.	4	1.6	515	Praia	1,330
Cayman Is. (UK)	0.26	0.10	35	George Town	20,000
Central African Republic	623	241	4,074	Bangui	290
Chad	1,284	496	7,337	Ndjaména	200
Chile	757	292	15,272	Santiago	4,740
China	9,597	3,705	1,299,180	Beijing	780
Colombia	1,139	440	39,397	Bogotá	2,250
Comoros	2.2	0.86	670	Moroni	350
Congo	342	132	3,167	Brazzaville	670
Congo (Dem. Rep. of the)	2,345	905	49,190	Kinshasa	110
Cook Is. (NZ)	0.24	0.09	17	Avarua	900
Costa Rica	51.1	19.7	3,711	San José	2,740
Croatia	56.5	21.8	4,960	Zagreb	4,580
Cuba	111	43	11,504	Havana	1,560
Cyprus	9.3	3.6	762	Nicosia	11,960
Czech Republic	78.9	30.4	10,500	Prague	5,060
Denmark	43.1	16.6	5,153	Copenhagen	32,030
Djibouti	23.2	9	552	Djibouti	790
Dominica	0.75	0.29	87	Roseau	3,170
Dominican Republic	48.7	18.8	8,621	Santo Domingo	1,910
Ecuador	284	109	13,319	Quito	1,310
Egypt	1,001	387	64,210	Cairo	1,400
El Salvador	21	8.1	6,739	San Salvador	1,900
Equatorial Guinea	28.1	10.8	455	Malabo	1,170
Eritrea	94	36	4,523	Asmara	200
Estonia	44.7	17.3	1,647	Tallinn	3,480
Ethiopia	1,128	436	61,841	Addis Ababa	100
Faroe Is. (Denmark)	1.4	0.54	49	Tórshavn	16,000
Fiji	18.3	7.1	883	Suva	2,210
Finland	338	131	5,077	Helsinki	23,780
France	552	213	58,145	Paris	23,480
French Guiana (France)	90	34.7	130	Cayenne	6,000
French Polynesia (France)	4	1.5	268	Papeete	18,050
Gabon	268	103	1,612	Libreville	3,350
Gambia, The	11.3	4.4	1,119	Banjul	340
Georgia	69.7	26.9	5,777	Tbilisi	620
Germany	357	138	76,962	Berlin	25,350
Ghana	239	92	20,564	Accra	390
Gibraltar (UK)	0.007	0.003	32	Gibraltar Town	5,000
Greece	132	51	10,193	Athens	11,770
Greenland (Denmark)	2,176	840	60	Nuuk (Godthåb)	16,100
Grenada	0.34	0.13	83	St George's	3,450
Guadeloupe (France)	1.7	0.66	365	Basse-Terre	9,200
Guam (US)	0.55	0.21	128	Agana	19,000
Guatemala	109	42	12,222	Guatemala City	1,660
Guinea	246	95	7,830	Conakry	510
Guinea-Bissau	36.1	13.9	1,197	Bissau	160
Guyana	215	83	891	Georgetown	760
Haiti	27.8	10.7	8,003	Port-au-Prince	460
Honduras	112	43	6,846	Tegucigalpa	760
Hong Kong (China)	1.1	0.40	6,336	–	23,520
Hungary	93	35.9	10,531	Budapest	4,650
Iceland	103	40	274	Reykjavik	29,280
India	3,288	1,269	1,041,543	New Delhi	450
Indonesia	1,905	735	218,661	Jakarta	580
Iran	1,648	636	68,759	Tehran	1,760
Iraq	438	169	26,339	Baghdad	2,400
Ireland	70.3	27.1	4,086	Dublin	19,160
Israel	27	10.3	5,321	Jerusalem	17,450
Italy	301	116	57,195	Rome	19,710
Ivory Coast (Côte d'Ivoire)	322	125	17,600	Yamoussoukro	710
Jamaica	11	4.2	2,735	Kingston	2,330
Japan	378	146	128,470	Tokyo	32,230
Jordan	89.2	34.4	5,558	Amman	1,500
Kazakstan	2,717	1,049	19,006	Astana	1,230
Kenya	580	224	35,060	Nairobi	360
Kiribati	0.72	0.28	72	Tarawa	910
Korea, North	121	47	26,117	Pyŏngyang	1,000
Korea, South	99	38.2	46,403	Seoul	8,490
Kuwait	17.8	6.9	2,639	Kuwait City	22,700
Kyrgyzstan	198.5	76.6	5,403	Bishkek	300
Laos	237	91	5,463	Vientiane	280
Latvia	65	25	2,768	Riga	2,470
Lebanon	10.4	4	3,327	Beirut	3,700
Lesotho	30.4	11.7	2,370	Maseru	550
Liberia	111	43	3,575	Monrovia	1,000
Libya	1,760	679	6,500	Tripoli	6,700
Liechtenstein	0.16	0.06	28	Vaduz	50,000
Lithuania	65.2	25.2	3,935	Vilnius	2,620
Luxembourg	2.6	1	377	Luxembourg	44,640
Macau (China)	0.02	0.006	656	Macau	16,000
Macedonia (F.Y.R.O.M.)	25.7	9.9	2,157	Skopje	1,690
Madagascar	587	227	16,627	Antananarivo	250
Madeira (Portugal)	0.81	0.31	253	Funchal	–
Malawi	118	46	12,458	Lilongwe	190
Malaysia	330	127	21,983	Kuala Lumpur	3,400
Maldives	0.30	0.12	283	Malé	1,160
Mali	1,240	479	12,685	Bamako	240
Malta	0.32	0.12	366	Valletta	9,210
Marshall Is.	0.18	0.07	70	Dalap-Uliga-Darrit	1,560
Martinique (France)	1.1	0.42	362	Fort-de-France	10,700
Mauritania	1,030	412	2,702	Nouakchott	380
Mauritius	2.0	0.72	1,201	Port Louis	3,590
Mayotte (France)	0.37	0.14	141	Mamoundzou	1,430
Mexico	1,958	756	107,233	Mexico City	4,400
Micronesia, Fed. States of	0.70	0.27	110	Palikir	1,810
Moldova	33.7	13	4,707	Chişinău	370
Monaco	0.002	0.0001	30	Monaco	25,000
Mongolia	1,567	605	2,847	Ulan Bator	350
Montserrat (UK)	0.10	0.04	13	Plymouth	4,500
Morocco	447	172	31,559	Rabat	1,200
Mozambique	802	309	20,493	Maputo	230
Namibia	825	318	2,437	Windhoek	1,890
Nauru	0.02	0.008	10	Yaren District	10,000
Nepal	141	54	24,084	Katmandu	220
Netherlands	41.5	16	15,829	Amsterdam/The Hague	24,320
Netherlands Antilles (Neths)	0.99	0.38	203	Willemstad	11,500
New Caledonia (France)	18.6	7.2	195	Nouméa	11,400
New Zealand	269	104	3,662	Wellington	13,780
Nicaragua	130	50	5,261	Managua	430
Niger	1,267	489	10,752	Niamey	190
Nigeria	924	357	105,000	Abuja	310
Northern Mariana Is. (US)	0.48	0.18	50	Saipan	9,300
Norway	324	125	4,331	Oslo	32,880
Oman	212	82	2,176	Muscat	7,900
Pakistan	796	307	162,409	Islamabad	470
Palau	0.46	0.18	18	Koror	8,800
Panama	77.1	29.8	2,893	Panama City	3,070
Papua New Guinea	463	179	4,845	Port Moresby	800
Paraguay	407	157	5,538	Asunción	1,580
Peru	1,285	496	26,276	Lima	2,390
Philippines	300	116	77,473	Manila	1,020
Poland	313	121	40,366	Warsaw	3,960
Portugal	92.4	35.7	10,587	Lisbon	10,600
Puerto Rico (US)	9	3.5	3,836	San Juan	8,200
Qatar	11	4.2	499	Doha	17,100
Réunion (France)	2.5	0.97	692	Saint-Denis	4,800
Romania	238	92	24,000	Bucharest	1,520
Russia	17,075	6,592	155,096	Moscow	2,270
Rwanda	26.3	10.2	10,200	Kigali	250
St Kitts & Nevis	0.36	0.14	44	Basseterre	6,420
St Lucia	0.62	0.24	177	Castries	3,770
St Vincent & Grenadines	0.39	0.15	128	Kingstown	2,700
Samoa	2.8	1.1	171	Apia	1,060
San Marino	0.06	0.02	25	San Marino	20,000
São Tomé & Príncipe	0.96	0.37	151	São Tomé	270
Saudi Arabia	2,150	830	20,697	Riyadh	6,910
Senegal	197	76	8,716	Dakar	510
Seychelles	0.46	0.18	75	Victoria	6,540
Sierra Leone	71.7	27.7	5,437	Freetown	130
Singapore	0.62	0.24	3,000	Singapore	29,610
Slovak Republic	49	18.9	5,500	Bratislava	3,590
Slovenia	20.3	7.8	2,055	Ljubljana	9,890
Solomon Is.	28.9	11.2	429	Honiara	750
Somalia	638	246	9,736	Mogadishu	600
South Africa	1,220	471	43,666	C. Town/Pretoria/Bloem.	3,160
Spain	505	195	40,667	Madrid	14,000
Sri Lanka	65.6	25.3	19,416	Colombo	820
Sudan	2,506	967	33,625	Khartoum	330
Surinam	163	63	497	Paramaribo	1,660
Swaziland	17.4	6.7	1,121	Mbabane	1,360
Sweden	450	174	8,560	Stockholm	25,040
Switzerland	41.3	15.9	6,762	Bern	38,350
Syria	185	71	17,826	Damascus	970
Taiwan	36	13.9	22,000	Taipei	12,400
Tajikistan	143.1	55.2	7,041	Dushanbe	290
Tanzania	945	365	39,639	Dodoma	240
Thailand	513	198	63,670	Bangkok	1,960
Togo	56.8	21.9	4,861	Lomé	320
Tonga	0.75	0.29	92	Nuku'alofa	1,720
Trinidad & Tobago	5.1	2	1,484	Port of Spain	4,390
Tunisia	164	63	9,924	Tunis	2,100
Turkey	779	301	66,789	Ankara	2,900
Turkmenistan	488.1	188.5	4,585	Ashkhabad	660
Turks & Caicos Is. (UK)	0.43	0.17	12	Cockburn Town	5,000
Tuvalu	0.03	0.01	11	Fongafale	600
Uganda	236	91	26,958	Kampala	320
Ukraine	603.7	233.1	52,558	Kiev	750
United Arab Emirates	83.6	32.3	1,951	Abu Dhabi	17,870
United Kingdom	243.3	94	58,393	London	22,640
United States of America	9,373	3,619	266,096	Washington, DC	30,600
Uruguay	177	68	3,274	Montevideo	5,900
Uzbekistan	447.4	172.7	26,044	Tashkent	720
Vanuatu	12.2	4.7	206	Port-Vila	1,170
Venezuela	912	352	24,715	Caracas	3,670
Vietnam	332	127	82,427	Hanoi	370
Virgin Is. (UK)	0.15	0.06	15	Road Town	–
Virgin Is. (US)	0.34	0.13	135	Charlotte Amalie	12,500
Wallis & Futuna Is. (France)	0.20	0.08	26	Mata-Utu	–
Western Sahara	266	103	228	El Aaiún	300
Yemen	528	204	13,219	Sana	350
Yugoslavia	102.3	39.5	10,761	Belgrade	2,300
Zambia	753	291	12,267	Lusaka	320
Zimbabwe	391	151	13,123	Harare	520

World Statistics: Physical Dimensions

Each topic list is divided into continents and within a continent the items are listed in order of size. The bottom part of many of the lists is selective in order to give examples from as many different countries as possible. The order of the continents is the same as in the atlas, beginning with Europe and ending with South America. The figures are rounded as appropriate.

World, Continents, Oceans

	km²	miles²	%
The World	509,450,000	196,672,000	–
Land	149,450,000	57,688,000	29.3
Water	360,000,000	138,984,000	70.7
Asia	44,500,000	17,177,000	29.8
Africa	30,302,000	11,697,000	20.3
North America	24,241,000	9,357,000	16.2
South America	17,793,000	6,868,000	11.9
Antarctica	14,100,000	5,443,000	9.4
Europe	9,957,000	3,843,000	6.7
Australia & Oceania	8,557,000	3,303,000	5.7
Pacific Ocean	179,679,000	69,356,000	49.9
Atlantic Ocean	92,373,000	35,657,000	25.7
Indian Ocean	73,917,000	28,532,000	20.5
Arctic Ocean	14,090,000	5,439,000	3.9

Ocean Depths

	m	ft
Atlantic Ocean		
Puerto Rico (Milwaukee) Deep	9,220	30,249
Cayman Trench	7,680	25,197
Gulf of Mexico	5,203	17,070
Mediterranean Sea	5,121	16,801
Black Sea	2,211	7,254
North Sea	660	2,165
Indian Ocean		
Java Trench	7,450	24,442
Red Sea	2,635	8,454
Pacific Ocean		
Mariana Trench	11,022	36,161
Tonga Trench	10,882	35,702
Japan Trench	10,554	34,626
Kuril Trench	10,542	34,587
Arctic Ocean		
Molloy Deep	5,608	18,399

Mountains

		m	ft
Europe			
Elbrus	*Russia*	5,642	18,510
Mont Blanc	*France/Italy*	4,807	15,771
Monte Rosa	*Italy/Switzerland*	4,634	15,203
Dom	*Switzerland*	4,545	14,911
Liskamm	*Switzerland*	4,527	14,852
Weisshorn	*Switzerland*	4,505	14,780
Taschorn	*Switzerland*	4,490	14,730
Matterhorn/Cervino	*Italy/Switzerland*	4,478	14,691
Mont Maudit	*France/Italy*	4,465	14,649
Dent Blanche	*Switzerland*	4,356	14,291
Nadelhorn	*Switzerland*	4,327	14,196
Grandes Jorasses	*France/Italy*	4,208	13,806
Jungfrau	*Switzerland*	4,158	13,642
Grossglockner	*Austria*	3,797	12,457
Mulhacén	*Spain*	3,478	11,411
Zugspitze	*Germany*	2,962	9,718
Olympus	*Greece*	2,917	9,570
Triglav	*Slovenia*	2,863	9,393
Gerlachovka	*Slovak Republic*	2,655	8,711
Galdhöpiggen	*Norway*	2,468	8,100
Kebnekaise	*Sweden*	2,117	6,946
Ben Nevis	*UK*	1,343	4,406
Asia		m	ft
Everest	*China/Nepal*	8,850	29,035
K2 (Godwin Austen)	*China/Kashmir*	8,611	28,251
Kanchenjunga	*India/Nepal*	8,598	28,208
Lhotse	*China/Nepal*	8,516	27,939
Makalu	*China/Nepal*	8,481	27,824
Cho Oyu	*China/Nepal*	8,201	26,906
Dhaulagiri	*Nepal*	8,172	26,811
Manaslu	*Nepal*	8,156	26,758
Nanga Parbat	*Kashmir*	8,126	26,660
Annapurna	*Nepal*	8,078	26,502
Gasherbrum	*China/Kashmir*	8,068	26,469
Broad Peak	*China/Kashmir*	8,051	26,414
Xixabangma	*China*	8,012	26,286
Kangbachen	*India/Nepal*	7,902	25,925
Trivor	*Pakistan*	7,720	25,328
Pik Kommunizma	*Tajikistan*	7,495	24,590
Demavend	*Iran*	5,604	18,386
Ararat	*Turkey*	5,165	16,945
Gunong Kinabalu	*Malaysia (Borneo)*	4,101	13,455
Fuji-San	*Japan*	3,776	12,388
Africa		m	ft
Kilimanjaro	*Tanzania*	5,895	19,340
Mt Kenya	*Kenya*	5,199	17,057
Ruwenzori (Margherita)	*Ug./Congo (D.R.)*	5,109	16,762
Ras Dashan	*Ethiopia*	4,620	15,157
Meru	*Tanzania*	4,565	14,977
Karisimbi	*Rwanda/Congo (D.R.)*	4,507	14,787
Mt Elgon	*Kenya/Uganda*	4,321	14,176
Batu	*Ethiopia*	4,307	14,130
Toubkal	*Morocco*	4,165	13,665
Mt Cameroon	*Cameroon*	4,070	13,353
Oceania		m	ft
Puncak Jaya	*Indonesia*	5,029	16,499
Puncak Trikora	*Indonesia*	4,750	15,584
Puncak Mandala	*Indonesia*	4,702	15,427
Mt Wilhelm	*Papua New Guinea*	4,508	14,790
Mauna Kea	*USA (Hawaii)*	4,205	13,796
Mauna Loa	*USA (Hawaii)*	4,169	13,681
Mt Cook (Aoraki)	*New Zealand*	3,753	12,313
Mt Kosciuszko	*Australia*	2,237	7,339
North America		m	ft
Mt McKinley (Denali)	*USA (Alaska)*	6,194	20,321
Mt Logan	*Canada*	5,959	19,551
Citlaltepetl	*Mexico*	5,700	18,701
Mt St Elias	*USA/Canada*	5,489	18,008
Popocatepetl	*Mexico*	5,452	17,887
Mt Foraker	*USA (Alaska)*	5,304	17,401
Ixtaccihuatl	*Mexico*	5,286	17,342
Lucania	*Canada*	5,227	17,149
Mt Steele	*Canada*	5,073	16,644
Mt Bona	*USA (Alaska)*	5,005	16,420
Mt Whitney	*USA*	4,418	14,495
Tajumulco	*Guatemala*	4,220	13,845
Chirripó Grande	*Costa Rica*	3,837	12,589
Pico Duarte	*Dominican Rep.*	3,175	10,417
South America		m	ft
Aconcagua	*Argentina*	6,960	22,834
Bonete	*Argentina*	6,872	22,546
Ojos del Salado	*Argentina/Chile*	6,863	22,516
Pissis	*Argentina*	6,779	22,241
Mercedario	*Argentina/Chile*	6,770	22,211
Huascaran	*Peru*	6,768	22,204
Llullaillaco	*Argentina/Chile*	6,723	22,057
Nudo de Cachi	*Argentina*	6,720	22,047
Yerupaja	*Peru*	6,632	21,758
Sajama	*Bolivia*	6,542	21,463
Chimborazo	*Ecuador*	6,267	20,561
Pico Colon	*Colombia*	5,800	19,029
Pico Bolivar	*Venezuela*	5,007	16,427
Antarctica		m	ft
Vinson Massif		4,897	16,066
Mt Kirkpatrick		4,528	14,855

Rivers

		km	miles
Europe			
Volga	*Caspian Sea*	3,700	2,300
Danube	*Black Sea*	2,850	1,770
Ural	*Caspian Sea*	2,535	1,575
Dnepr (Dnipro)	*Black Sea*	2,285	1,420
Kama	*Volga*	2,030	1,260
Don	*Black Sea*	1,990	1,240
Petchora	*Arctic Ocean*	1,790	1,110
Oka	*Volga*	1,480	920
Dnister (Dniester)	*Black Sea*	1,400	870
Vyatka	*Kama*	1,370	850
Rhine	*North Sea*	1,320	820
N. Dvina	*Arctic Ocean*	1,290	800
Elbe	*North Sea*	1,145	710
Asia		km	miles
Yangtze	*Pacific Ocean*	6,380	3,960
Yenisey–Angara	*Arctic Ocean*	5,550	3,445
Huang He	*Pacific Ocean*	5,464	3,395
Ob–Irtysh	*Arctic Ocean*	5,410	3,360
Mekong	*Pacific Ocean*	4,500	2,795
Amur	*Pacific Ocean*	4,400	2,730
Lena	*Arctic Ocean*	4,400	2,730
Irtysh	*Ob*	4,250	2,640
Yenisey	*Arctic Ocean*	4,090	2,540
Ob	*Arctic Ocean*	3,680	2,285
Indus	*Indian Ocean*	3,100	1,925
Brahmaputra	*Indian Ocean*	2,900	1,800
Syrdarya	*Aral Sea*	2,860	1,775
Salween	*Indian Ocean*	2,800	1,740
Euphrates	*Indian Ocean*	2,700	1,675
Amudarya	*Aral Sea*	2,540	1,575
Africa		km	miles
Nile	*Mediterranean*	6,670	4,140
Congo	*Atlantic Ocean*	4,670	2,900
Niger	*Atlantic Ocean*	4,180	2,595
Zambezi	*Indian Ocean*	3,540	2,200
Oubangi/Uele	*Congo (D.R.)*	2,250	1,400
Kasai	*Congo (D.R.)*	1,950	1,210
Shaballe	*Indian Ocean*	1,930	1,200
Orange	*Atlantic Ocean*	1,860	1,155
Cubango	*Okavango Swamps*	1,800	1,120
Limpopo	*Indian Ocean*	1,600	995
Senegal	*Atlantic Ocean*	1,600	995
Australia		km	miles
Murray–Darling	*Indian Ocean*	3,750	2,330
Darling	*Murray*	3,070	1,905
Murray	*Indian Ocean*	2,575	1,600
Murrumbidgee	*Murray*	1,690	1,050
North America		km	miles
Mississippi–Missouri	*Gulf of Mexico*	6,020	3,740
Mackenzie	*Arctic Ocean*	4,240	2,630
Mississippi	*Gulf of Mexico*	3,780	2,350
Missouri	*Mississippi*	3,780	2,350
Yukon	*Pacific Ocean*	3,185	1,980
Rio Grande	*Gulf of Mexico*	3,030	1,880
Arkansas	*Mississippi*	2,340	1,450
Colorado	*Pacific Ocean*	2,330	1,445
Red	*Mississippi*	2,040	1,270
Columbia	*Pacific Ocean*	1,950	1,210
Saskatchewan	*Lake Winnipeg*	1,940	1,205
South America		km	miles
Amazon	*Atlantic Ocean*	6,450	4,010
Paraná–Plate	*Atlantic Ocean*	4,500	2,800
Purus	*Amazon*	3,350	2,080
Madeira	*Amazon*	3,200	1,990
São Francisco	*Atlantic Ocean*	2,900	1,800
Paraná	*Plate*	2,800	1,740
Tocantins	*Atlantic Ocean*	2,750	1,710
Paraguay	*Paraná*	2,550	1,580
Orinoco	*Atlantic Ocean*	2,500	1,550
Pilcomayo	*Paraná*	2,500	1,550
Araguaia	*Tocantins*	2,250	1,400

Lakes

		km²	miles²
Europe			
Lake Ladoga	*Russia*	17,700	6,800
Lake Onega	*Russia*	9,700	3,700
Saimaa system	*Finland*	8,000	3,100
Vänern	*Sweden*	5,500	2,100
Asia		km²	miles²
Caspian Sea	*Asia*	371,800	143,550
Lake Baykal	*Russia*	30,500	11,780
Aral Sea	*Kazakstan/Uzbekistan*	28,687	11,086
Tonlé Sap	*Cambodia*	20,000	7,700
Lake Balqash	*Kazakstan*	18,500	7,100
Africa		km²	miles²
Lake Victoria	*East Africa*	68,000	26,000
Lake Tanganyika	*Central Africa*	33,000	13,000
Lake Malawi/Nyasa	*East Africa*	29,600	11,430
Lake Chad	*Central Africa*	25,000	9,700
Lake Turkana	*Ethiopia/Kenya*	8,500	3,300
Lake Volta	*Ghana*	8,500	3,300
Australia		km²	miles²
Lake Eyre	*Australia*	8,900	3,400
Lake Torrens	*Australia*	5,800	2,200
Lake Gairdner	*Australia*	4,800	1,900
North America		km²	miles²
Lake Superior	*Canada/USA*	82,350	31,800
Lake Huron	*Canada/USA*	59,600	23,010
Lake Michigan	*USA*	58,000	22,400
Great Bear Lake	*Canada*	31,800	12,280
Great Slave Lake	*Canada*	28,500	11,000
Lake Erie	*Canada/USA*	25,700	9,900
Lake Winnipeg	*Canada*	24,400	9,400
Lake Ontario	*Canada/USA*	19,500	7,500
Lake Nicaragua	*Nicaragua*	8,200	3,200
South America		km²	miles²
Lake Titicaca	*Bolivia/Peru*	8,300	3,200
Lake Poopo	*Bolivia*	2,800	1,100

Islands

		km²	miles²
Europe			
Great Britain	*UK*	229,880	88,700
Iceland	*Atlantic Ocean*	103,000	39,800
Ireland	*Ireland/UK*	84,400	32,600
Novaya Zemlya (N.)	*Russia*	48,200	18,600
Sicily	*Italy*	25,500	9,800
Corsica	*France*	8,700	3,400
Asia		km²	miles²
Borneo	*Southeast Asia*	744,360	287,400
Sumatra	*Indonesia*	473,600	182,860
Honshu	*Japan*	230,500	88,980
Sulawesi (Celebes)	*Indonesia*	189,000	73,000
Java	*Indonesia*	126,700	48,900
Luzon	*Philippines*	104,700	40,400
Hokkaido	*Japan*	78,400	30,300
Africa		km²	miles²
Madagascar	*Indian Ocean*	587,040	226,660
Socotra	*Indian Ocean*	3,600	1,400
Réunion	*Indian Ocean*	2,500	965
Oceania		km²	miles²
New Guinea	*Indonesia/Papua NG*	821,030	317,000
New Zealand (S.)	*Pacific Ocean*	150,500	58,100
New Zealand (N.)	*Pacific Ocean*	114,700	44,300
Tasmania	*Australia*	67,800	26,200
Hawaii	*Pacific Ocean*	10,450	4,000
North America		km²	miles²
Greenland	*Atlantic Ocean*	2,175,600	839,800
Baffin Is.	*Canada*	508,000	196,100
Victoria Is.	*Canada*	212,200	81,900
Ellesmere Is.	*Canada*	212,000	81,800
Cuba	*Caribbean Sea*	110,860	42,800
Hispaniola	*Dominican Rep./Haiti*	76,200	29,400
Jamaica	*Caribbean Sea*	11,400	4,400
Puerto Rico	*Atlantic Ocean*	8,900	3,400
South America		km²	miles²
Tierra del Fuego	*Argentina/Chile*	47,000	18,100
Falkland Is. (E.)	*Atlantic Ocean*	6,800	2,600

User Guide

Organization of the atlas

Prepared in accordance with the highest standards in cartography to provide accurate and detailed representation of the earth, the atlas is made up of four separate sections and is organized with ease of use in mind.

The first section of the atlas consists of up-to-date geographical and demographical statistics for all the countries in the world, and this user guide.

The second part of the atlas, the 48-page *World Cities* section, provides urban area and city center maps marking tourist sites for 67 of the world's largest and most important cities, backed up by a comprehensive index. In addition, full-page satellite images for nine of the cities featured give a stunning view of their locations from space.

The third and final section of the atlas, the 96-page *World Maps* section, covers the earth continent by continent in the classic sequence adopted by cartographers since the 16th century. This section begins with Europe, then Asia, Africa, Australia and Oceania, North America, and South America. For each continent, there are maps at a variety of scales: first, physical relief maps and political maps of the whole continent, then large-scale maps of the most important or densely populated areas.

The governing principle is that by turning the pages of the World Maps section, the reader moves steadily from north to south through each continent, with each map overlapping its neighbors. Immediately following the maps in the World Maps section is the comprehensive index to the maps, which contains 35,000 entries of both place names and geographical features. The index provides the latitude and longitude coordinates as well as letters and numbers, so that locating any site can be accomplished with speed and accuracy.

Map presentation

All of the maps in the atlas are drawn with north at the top (except for two maps: the map of the Arctic Ocean and the map of Antarctica). The maps in the United States Maps section and the World Maps section all contain the following information in their borders: the map title; scale; the projection used; the degrees of latitude and longitude; and on the physical relief maps, a height and depth reference panel identifying the colors used for each layer of contouring. In addition to this information, the maps in the *World Maps* section also contain locator diagrams which show the area covered, the page numbers for adjacent maps, and the letters and numbers used in the index for locating place names and geographical features.

Map symbols

Each map contains a vast amount of detail which is conveyed clearly and accurately by the use of symbols. Points and circles of varying sizes locate

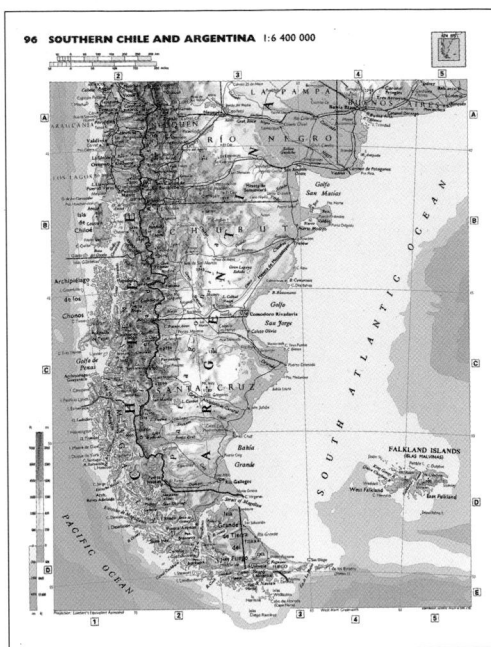

and identify the relative importance of towns and cities; different styles of type are employed for administrative, geographical and regional place names. A variety of pictorial symbols denote landscape features such as glaciers, marshes and reefs, and man-made structures including roads, railroads, airports and canals. International borders are shown by red lines. Where neighboring countries are in dispute, the maps show the *de facto* boundary between nations, regardless of the legal or historical situation. The symbols are explained on the first page of each of the map sections.

Map scales

The scale of each map is given in the numerical form known as the representative fraction. The first figure is always one, signifying one unit of distance on the map; the second figure, usually in millions, is the number by which the map unit must be multiplied to give the equivalent distance on the earth's surface. Calculations can easily be made in centimeters and kilometers, by dividing the earth units figure by 100 000 (i.e. deleting the last five 0s). Thus 1:1 000 000 means 1 cm = 10 km. The calculation for inches

LARGE SCALE		
1:1 000 000	1 cm = 10 km	1 inch = 16 miles
1:2 500 000	1 cm = 25 km	1 inch = 39.5 miles
1:5 000 000	1 cm = 50 km	1 inch = 79 miles
1:6 000 000	1 cm = 60 km	1 inch = 95 miles
1:8 000 000	1 cm = 80 km	1 inch = 126 miles
1:10 000 000	1 cm = 100 km	1 inch = 158 miles
1:15 000 000	1 cm = 150 km	1 inch = 237 miles
1:20 000 000	1 cm = 200 km	1 inch = 316 miles
1:50 000 000	1 cm = 500 km	1 inch = 790 miles
SMALL SCALE		

and miles is more laborious, but 1 000 000 divided by 63 360 (the number of inches in a mile) shows that 1:1 000 000 means about 1 inch = 16 miles.

Measuring distances

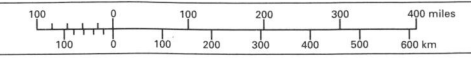

Although each map is accompanied by a scale bar, distances cannot always be measured with confidence because of the distortions involved in portraying the curved surface of the earth on a flat page. As a general rule, the larger the map scale (i.e. the lower the number of earth units in the representative fraction), the more accurate and reliable will be the distance measured. On small scale maps such as those of the world and of entire continents, measurement may only be accurate along the standard parallels, or central axes, and should not be attempted without considering the map projection.

Latitude and longitude

Accurate positioning of individual points on the earth's surface is made possible by reference to the geometrical system of latitude and longitude. Latitude parallels are drawn west–east around the earth and numbered by degrees north and south of the Equator, which is designated 0° of latitude. Longitude meridians are drawn north–south and numbered by degrees east and west of the Prime Meridian, 0° of longitude, which passes through Greenwich in England. By referring to these coordinates and their subdivisions of minutes (^{1}/60th of a degree) and seconds (^{1}/60th of a minute), any place on earth can be located to within a few hundred yards. Latitude and longitude are indicated by blue lines on the maps; they are straight or curved according to the projection employed. Reference to these lines is the easiest way of determining the relative positions of places on different maps, and for plotting compass directions.

Name forms

For ease of reference, both English and local name forms appear in the atlas. Oceans, seas and countries are shown in English throughout the atlas; country names may be abbreviated to their commonly accepted form. English conventional forms are also used for place names on the continental maps. However, local name forms are used on all large scale and regional maps, with the English form given in brackets only for important cities – the large-scale map of Russia and Central Asia thus shows Moskva (Moscow). For countries which do not use a Roman script, place names have been transcribed according to the systems adopted by the British and US Geographic Names Authorities. For China, the Pin Yin system has been used, with some more widely known forms appearing in brackets, as with Beijing (Peking). Both English and local names appear in the index.

WORLD CITIES

CITY MAPS

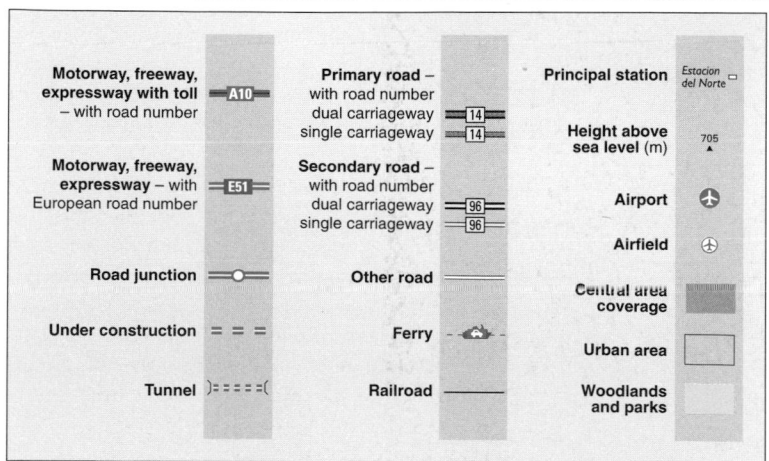

CENTRAL AREA MAPS

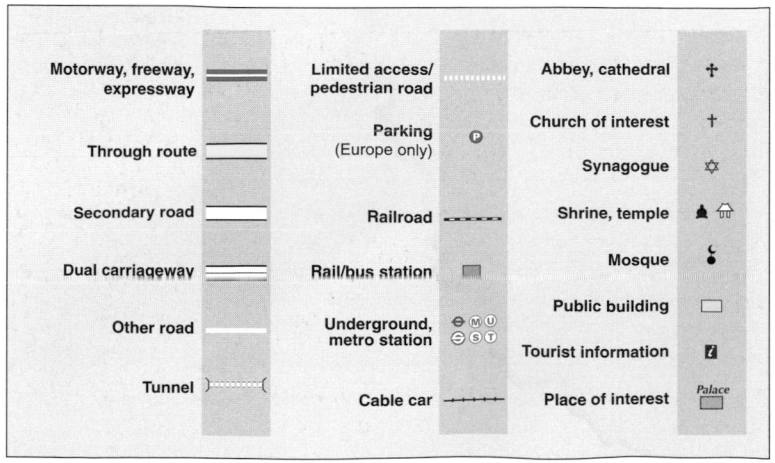

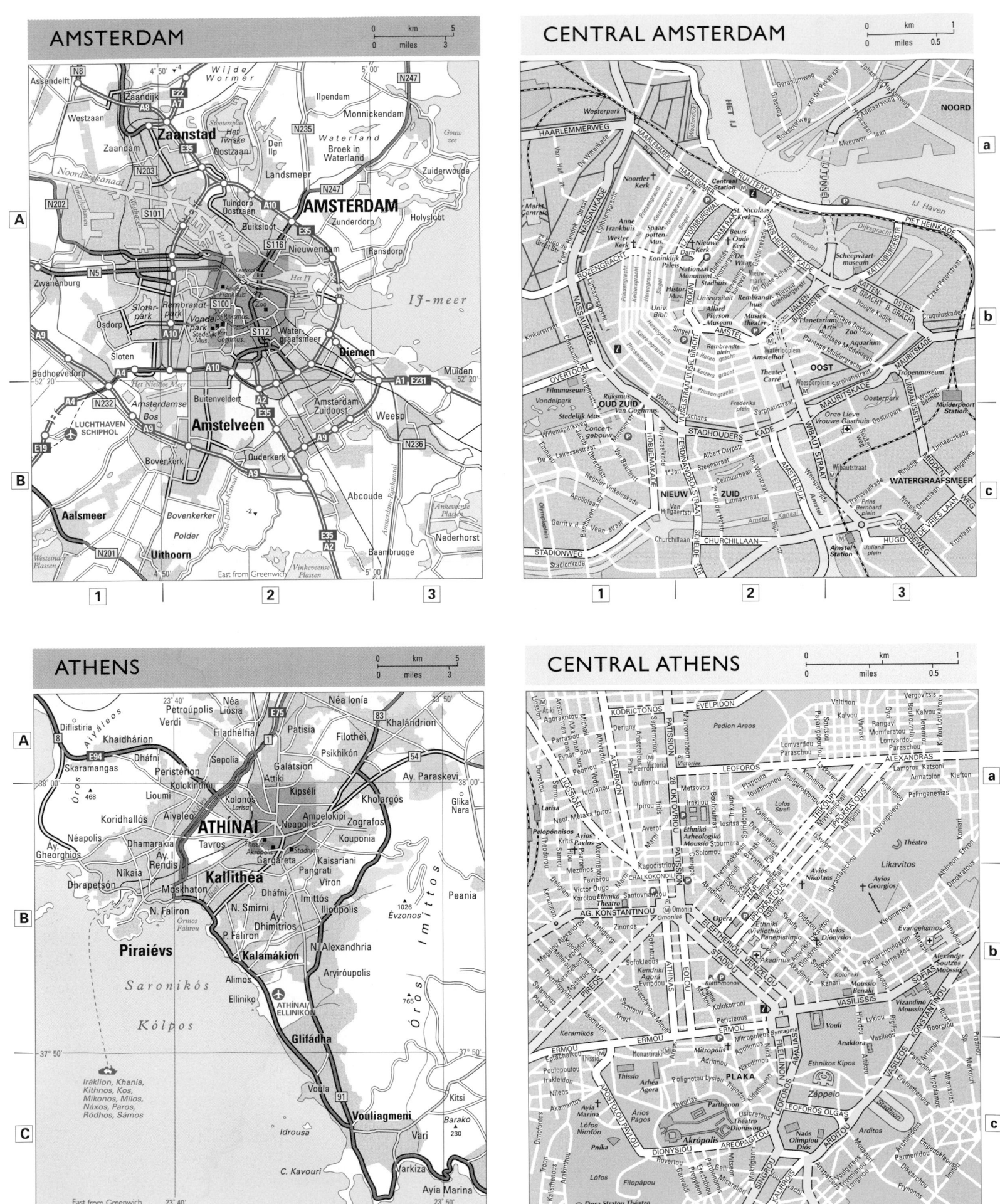
AMSTERDAM
km 0 5
miles 0 3
Assendelft
Zaandijk
Westzaan
Zaanstad
Zaandam
Ilpendam
Monnickendam
Den Ilp
Waterland
Broek in Waterland
Landsmeer
Noordzeekanaal
Zuiderwoude
Tuindorp Oostzaan
Buiksloot
AMSTERDAM
Zunderdorp
Holysloot
Nieuwendam
Ransdorp
Zwanenburg
IJ-meer
Sloterpark
Rembrandtpark
Osdorp
Vondelpark
Watergraafsmeer
Sloten
Diemen
Badhoevedorp
Muiden
Amsterdamse Bos
Buitenveldert
Amsterdam Zuidoost
Weesp
LUCHTHAVEN SCHIPHOL
Amstelveen
Bovenkerk
Ouderkerk
Abcoude
Aalsmeer
Bovenkerker Polder
Nederhorst
Baambrugge
Uithoorn
East from Greenwich
CENTRAL AMSTERDAM
km 0 1
miles 0 0.5
NOORD
HET IJ
Westerpark
HAARLEMMERWEG
Centraal Station
DE RUIJTERKADE
IJ Haven
PIET HEINKADE
Noorder Kerk
Anne Frankhuis
Wester Kerk
Nieuwe Kerk
Oude Kerk
Dam
Koninklijk Paleis
Nationaal Monument
De Waag
Scheepvaartmuseum
NASSAUKADE
Rembrandt-huis
Muziektheater
Planetarium Artis Zoo
Aquarium
AMSTEL
Amstelhof
OOST
Tropenmuseum
Theater Carré
OVERTOOM
Filmmuseum
Vondelpark
Rijksmus.
OUD ZUID
Van Goghmus.
Stedelijk Mus.
Concertgebouw
STADHOUDERSKADE
Muiderpoort Station
WATERGRAAFSMEER
NIEUW ZUID
CHURCHILLAAN
Amstel Station
STADIONWEG
ATHENS
km 0 5
miles 0 3
Néa Liósia
Petroúpolis
Néa Ionía
Khalándrion
Verdi
Filadhélfia
Patisia
Filothei
Khaidhárion
Psikhikón
Skaramangas
Peristérion
Sepolia
Galátsion
Ay. Paraskevi
Kolokinthou
Kipséli
Liouni
Kolonos
Kholargós
ATHÍNAI
Néapolis
Zografos
Koridhallós
Aiyaleo
Ampelokipi
Kouponia
Néapolis
Tavros
Ay. Gheorghios
Dhamarakia
Kaisariani
Nikaia
Kallithea
Pangrati
Viron
Dhrapetsón
Moskhaton
Dhafni
Imittós
Peania
N. Fáliron
N. Smirni
Iliúpolis
Piraiévs
P. Fáliron
Kalamákion
N. Alexandhria
Saronikós Kólpos
Alimos
Aryiróupolis
Elliniko
ATHÍNAI/ELLINIKON
Glifádha
Voula
Vouliagmeni
Kitsi
Vari
Idrousa
C. Kavouri
Varkiza
Ayía Marina
Iráklion, Khania, Kithnos, Kos, Mikonos, Milos, Náxos, Paros, Ródhos, Sámos
East from Greenwich
CENTRAL ATHENS
km 0 1
miles 0 0.5
EVELPIDON
Pedion Areos
LEOFOROS ALEXANDRAS
Larisa
Peloponnisos
Ethnikó Arheologikó Mousio
Lofos Strefi
Théatro
Likavitos
Ayios Georgios
Ayios Nikolaos
CHALKOKONDILI
Omonia
AG. KONSTANTINOU
Ethnikó Theatro
Opera
Ethnikí Vivliothiki
Panepistimio
Akadimia
Ayios Dionysios
Evangelismos
PIREOS
SOFIAS
VASILISSIS
Mousio Benaki
Vouli
Keramikós
ERMOU
Syntagma
Monastiraki
Mitropolis
PLAKA
Ethnikos Kipos
Zappeio
Stadion
Thissio
Arhea Agora
Parthenon
Akrópolis
Theatro Dionissou
Naós Olimpiou Diós
LEOFOROS OLGAS
Filopápou
Dora Stratou Théatro

ATLANTA

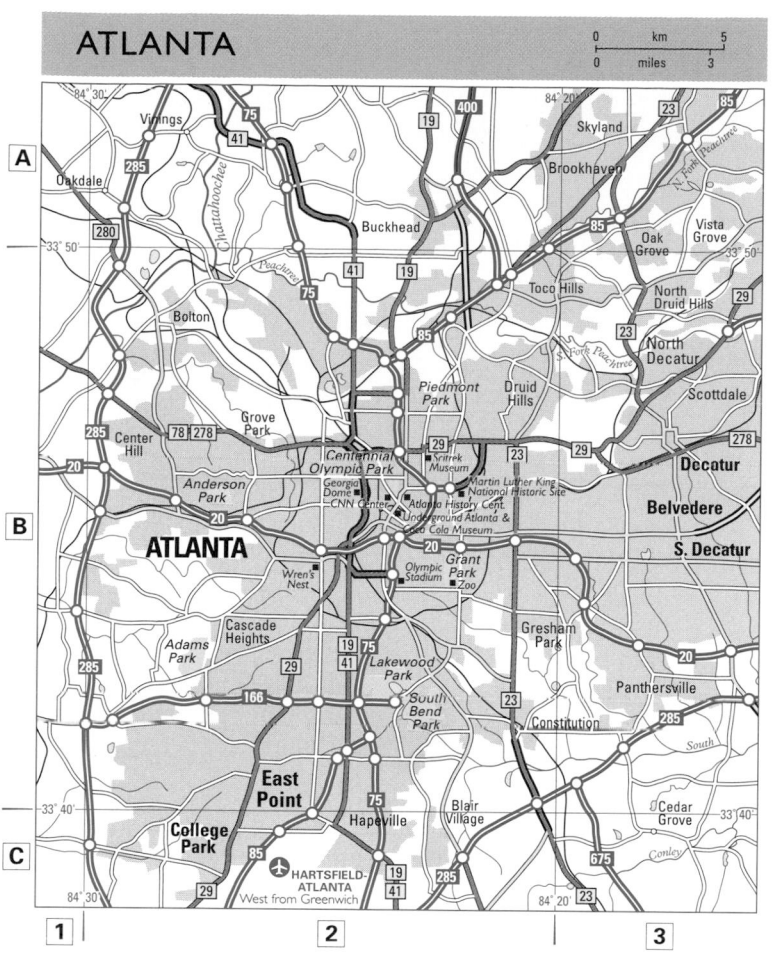

0 km 5
0 miles 3
A
B
C
1
2
3
Vinings
Oakdale
Buckhead
Skyland
Brookhaven
Oak Grove
Vista Grove
Toco Hills
North Druid Hills
North Decatur
Scottdale
Bolton
Piedmont Park
Druid Hills
Grove Park
Center Hill
Centennial Olympic Park
Decatur
Anderson Park
Belvedere
ATLANTA
S. Decatur
Wren's Nest
Grant Park
Olympic Stadium
Zoo
Cascade Heights
Adams Park
Gresham Park
Lakewood Park
South Bend Park
Panthersville
Constitution
East Point
College Park
Hapeville
Blair Village
Cedar Grove
HARTSFIELD-ATLANTA
West from Greenwich
Chattahoochee
Peachtree
South
Conley
Fernbank Museum
Georgia Dome
CNN Center
Atlanta History Cent.
Martin Luther King National Historic Site
Underground Atlanta & Coca Cola Museum
33° 50'
33° 40'
84° 30'
84° 20'

BAGHDAD

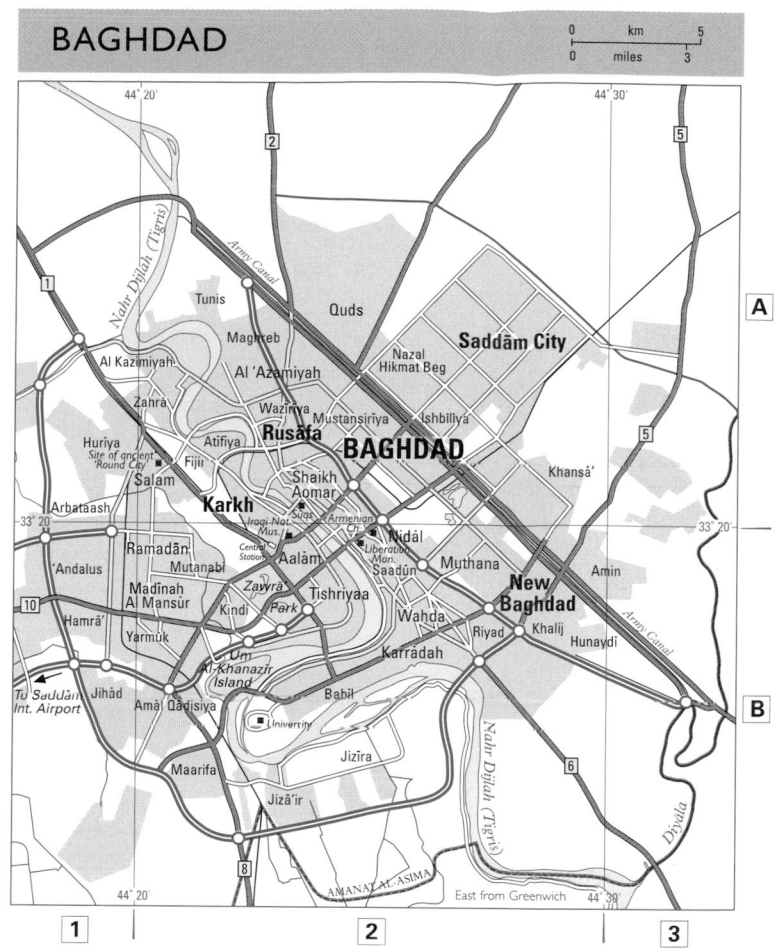

0 km 5
0 miles 3
A
B
1
2
3
44° 20'
44° 30'
33° 20'
Army Canal
Nahr Dijlah (Tigris)
Tunis
Quds
Maghreb
Saddâm City
Nazal Hikmat Beg
Al Kazimiyah
Al 'Azamiyah
Zahra
Waziriya
Mustansiriya
Ishbiliya
Huriya
Site of ancient 'Round City'
Atifiya
Rusafa
BAGHDAD
Fiji
Salam
Shaikh Aomar
Khansâ'
Karkh
Arbataash
Iraqi Nat. Mus.
Armenian Ch.
Nidâl
Liberation Mon.
Ramadân
Mutanabi
Aalâm
Sadûn
Muthana
'Andalus
Madinah Al Mansûr
Zawra Park
Tishriyaa
New Baghdad
Amin
Kindi
Hamrâ'
Yarmûk
Wahda
Riyad
Khalij
Hunaydi
Um Al-Khanazir Island
Karrâdah
To Saddâm Int. Airport
Jihâd
Amâl
Qadisiya
Babil
University
Jizîra
Maarifa
Jizâ'ir
AMANAT AL-ASIMA
East from Greenwich
Diyala

BANGKOK

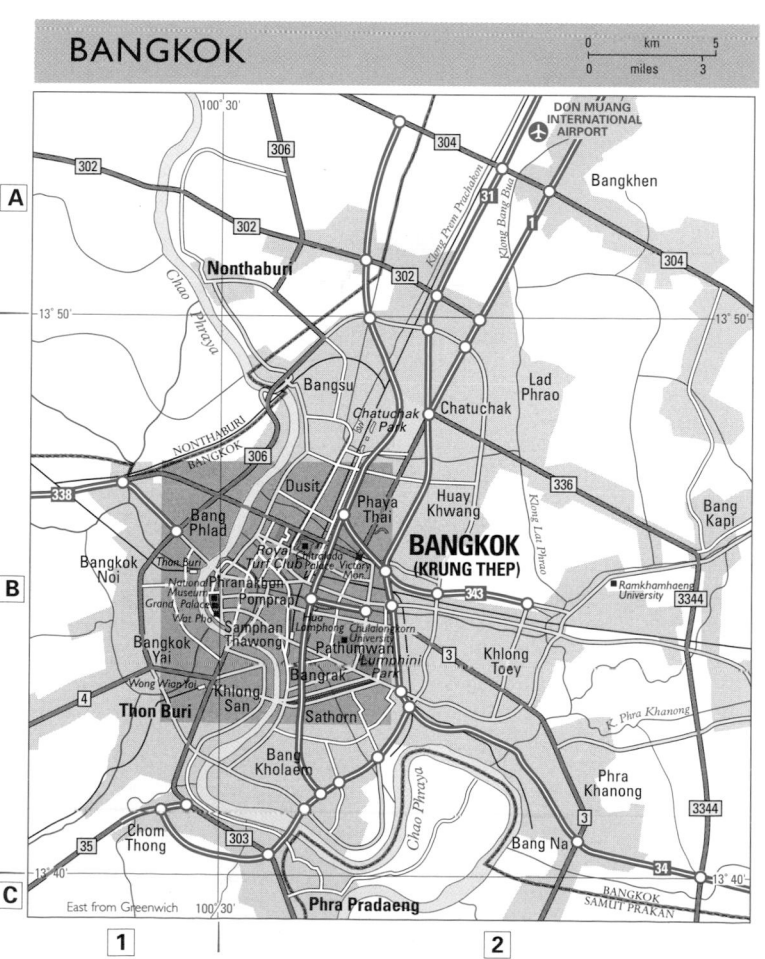

0 km 5
0 miles 3
A
B
C
1
2
DON MUANG INTERNATIONAL AIRPORT
Bangkhen
Nonthaburi
Chao Phraya
Bangsu
Lad Phrao
Chatuchak Park
Chatuchak
NONTHABURI
BANGKOK
Dusit
Phaya Thai
Huay Khwang
Bang Kapi
Bang Phlad
BANGKOK (KRUNG THEP)
Bangkok Noi
Royal Turf Club
Phranakorn
Pomprap
Ramkhamhaeng University
Samphan Thawong
Pathumwan
Lumphini Park
Khlong Toey
Bangkok Yai
Bangrak
Wong Wian Yai
Khlong San
Thon Buri
Sathorn
K. Phra Khanong
Bang Kholaem
Phra Khanong
Chom Thong
Bang Na
Phra Pradaeng
BANGKOK SAMUT PRAKAN
East from Greenwich
13° 50'
13° 40'
100° 30'

CENTRAL BANGKOK

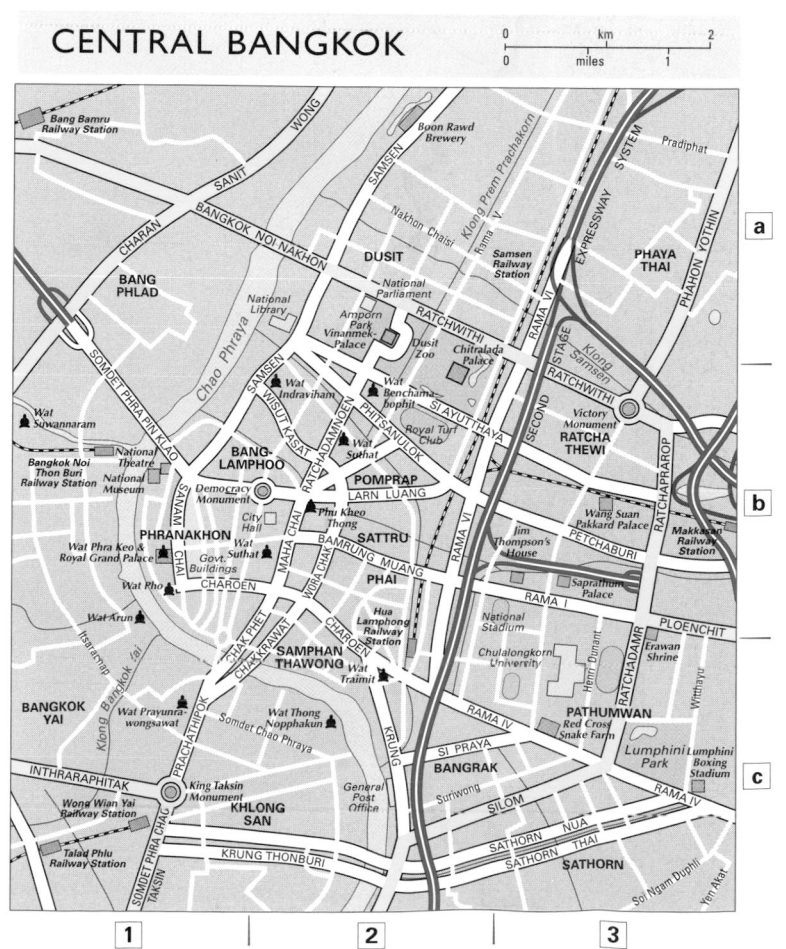

0 km 2
0 miles 1
a
b
c
1
2
3
Bang Bamru Railway Station
Boon Rawd Brewery
Pradiphat
EXPRESSWAY SYSTEM
DUSIT
Samsen Railway Station
PHAYA THAI
BANG PHLAD
National Library
National Parliament
Amporn Park
Vinanmek Palace
Dusit Zoo
Chitralada Palace
Chao Phraya
Wat Indraviharn
Wat Benchamabophit
Wat Suwannaram
Victory Monument
RATCHA THEWI
Bangkok Noi Thon Buri Railway Station
National Theatre
National Museum
BANG-LAMPHOO
Wat Suthat
Royal Turf Club
POMPRAP
Democracy Monument
LARN LUANG
City Hall
Phu Khao Thong
PHRANAKHON
Wat Phra Keo & Royal Grand Palace
Govt. Buildings
SATTRU
Wat Suthat
Jim Thompson's House
Wang Suan Pakkard Palace
Makkasan Railway Station
PETCHABURI
Wat Pho
CHAROEN
POMPRAP PHAI
Sapathum Palace
RAMA I
Wat Arun
Hua Lamphong Railway Station
National Stadium
PLOENCHIT
SAMPHAN THAWONG
Wat Traimit
Chulalongkorn University
Erawan Shrine
BANGKOK YAI
Wat Prayurawongsawat
Wat Thong Nopphakun
Red Cross Snake Farm
PATHUMWAN
RAMA IV
Lumphini Park
Lumphini Boxing Stadium
BANGRAK
INTHRARAPHITAK
King Taksin Monument
KHLONG SAN
General Post Office
Wong Wian Yai Railway Station
SILOM
SATHORN NUA
SATHORN THAI
SATHORN
Talad Phlu Railway Station
KRUNG THONBURI
SOMDET PHRA CHAO TAKSIN
Soi Ngam Duphli
Yen Akat

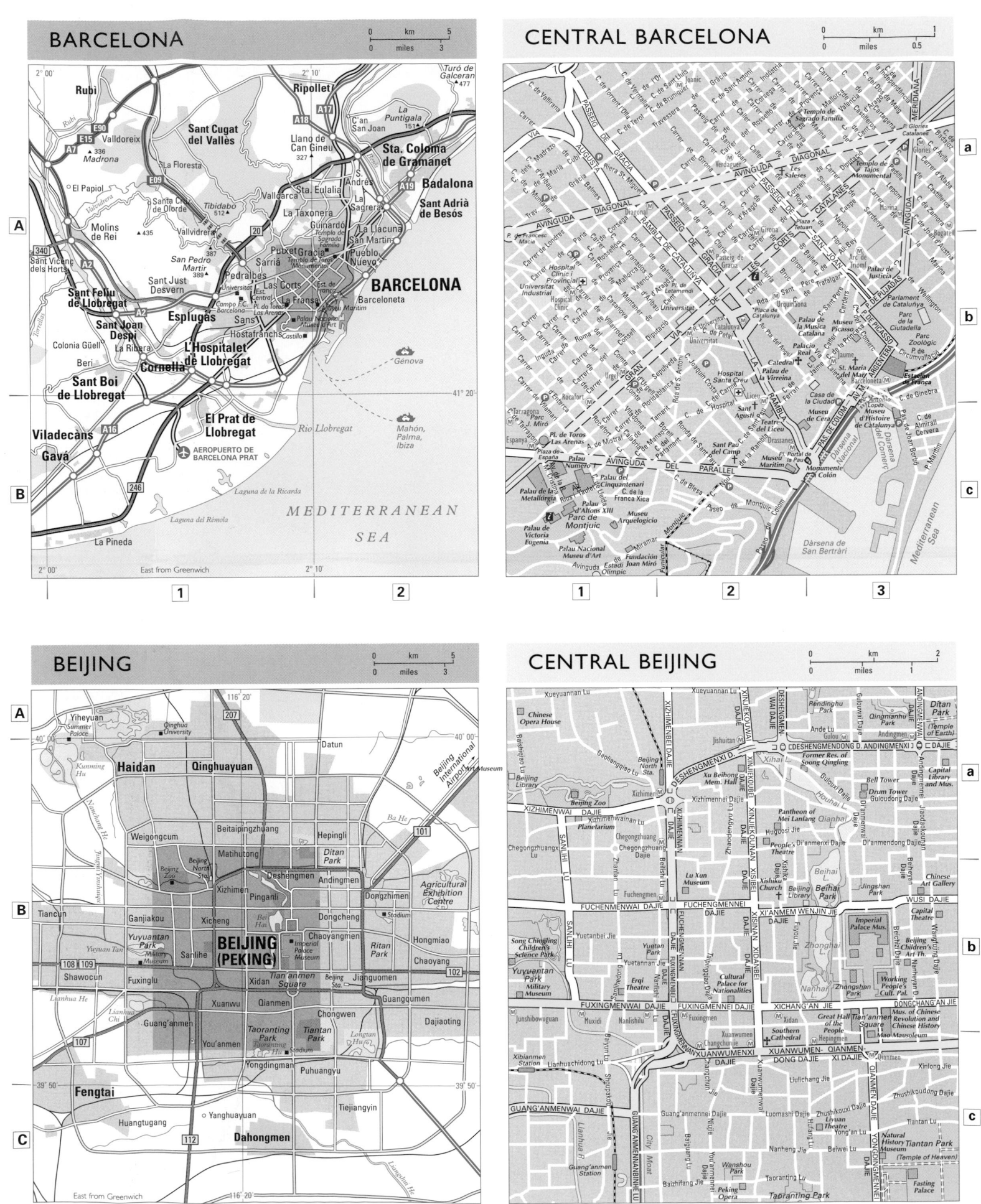
BARCELONA
0 km 5
0 miles 3
Rubi
Ripollet
Sant Cugat del Vallès
Valldoreix
Madrona
La Floresta
El Papiol
Molins de Rei
Vallvidrera
Tibidabo
Santa Creu de Olorde
Llano de Can Gineu
Sta. Coloma de Gramanet
Badalona
Sant Adrià de Besós
Vallcarca
Sta. Eulalia
La Sagrera
La Taxonera
Guinardó
La Llacuna
San Martín
Pueblo Nuevo
Putxet
Gracia
Sarrià
Pedralbes
Sant Vicenç dels Horts
San Pedro Martir
Sant Just Desvern
Las Corts
BARCELONA
Barceloneta
Sant Feliu de Llobregat
Sant Joan Despí
Esplugas
La Fransa
Sans
Hostafranchs
Colonia Güell
La Ribera
L'Hospitalet de Llobregat
Beri
Cornella
Sant Boi de Llobregat
El Prat de Llobregat
Viladecàns
Gavà
AEROPUERTO DE BARCELONA PRAT
Rio Llobregat
Génova
Mahón, Palma, Ibiza
Laguna de la Ricarda
Laguna del Rémola
MEDITERRANEAN SEA
La Pineda
East from Greenwich
2° 00'
2° 10'
41° 20'
A
B
1
2
CENTRAL BARCELONA
0 km 1
0 miles 0.5
AVINGUDA DIAGONAL
PASSEIG DE GRÀCIA
RAMBLA DE CATALUNYA
GRAN VIA DE LES CORTS CATALANES
AVINGUDA DEL PARALLEL
Templo de Sagrada Familia
Templo de Tajos Monumental
Hospital Clínic i Provincial
Universitat Industrial
Palau de la Musica Catalana
Catedral
Palau de la Virreina
Hospital Santa Creu
Palacio Real
Museu Picasso
Parlament de Catalunya
Parc de la Ciutadella
Parc Zoològic
Estacion de França
Casa de la Ciudad
Museu de Cera
Teatre del Liceu
Museu d'Histoire de Catalunya
Museu Maritim
Monumento Colón
Pl. de Toros Las Arenas
Parc J. Miró
Plaza de España
Palau de la Metallùrgia
Palau del Cinquantenari
Parc de Montjuic
Museu Arqueològico
Palau de Victoria Eugenia
Palau Nacional Museu d'Art
Fundación Joan Miró
Estadi Olimpic
Dàrsena de San Bertrári
Mediterranean Sea
a
b
c
1
2
3
BEIJING
0 km 5
0 miles 3
Yiheyuan Summer Palace
Qinghua University
Datun
Kunming Hu
Haidan
Qinghuayuan
Beijing International Airport
Art Museum
Weigongcum
Beitaipingzhuang
Hepingli
Matihutong
Ditan Park
Deshengmen
Andingmen
Xizhimen
Pinganli
Dongzhimen
Agricultural Exhibition Centre
Tiancun
Ganjiakou
Xicheng
Bei Hai
Dongcheng
Yuyuantan Park
BEIJING (PEKING)
Imperial Palace Museum
Chaoyangmen
Ritan Park
Hongmiao
Sanlihe
Chaoyang
Shawocun
Fuxinglu
Xidan
Tian'anmen Square
Beijing Sta.
Jianguomen
Guangqumen
Xuanwu
Qianmen
Chongwen
Guang'anmen
Taoranting Park
Tiantan Park
Dajiaoting
You'anmen
Yongdingman
Puhuangyu
Fengtai
Tiejiangyin
Huangtugang
Yanghuayuan
Dahongmen
East from Greenwich
116° 20'
40° 00'
39° 50'
A
B
C
1
2
CENTRAL BEIJING
0 km 2
0 miles 1
Xueyuannan Lu
Chinese Opera House
Beijing North Sta.
Beijing Library
Beijing Zoo
Planetarium
Xu Beihong Mem. Hall
Former Res. of Soong Qingling
Bell Tower
Drum Tower
Ditan Park (Temple of Earth)
Capital Library and Mus.
Pantheon of Mei Lanfang
People's Theatre
Lu Xun Museum
Xishiku Church
Beijing Library
Beihai Park
Jingshan Park
Chinese Art Gallery
Capital Theatre
Imperial Palace Mus.
Beijing Children's Art Th.
Song Chingling Children's Science Park
Yuyuantan Park
Military Museum
Erqi Theatre
Cultural Palace for Nationalities
Zhongshan Park
Working People's Cult. Pal.
Great Hall of the People
Tian'anmen Square
Mus. of Chinese Revolution and Chinese History
Mao Mausoleum
Southern Cathedral
Xibianmen Station
Liyuan Theatre
Natural History Museum
Tiantan Park (Temple of Heaven)
Fasting Palace
Wanshou Park
Peking Opera
Taoranting Park
Guang'anmen Station
City Moat
a
b
c
1
2

BERLIN

km 5
miles 3

Wandsdorf · Hennigsdorf · Haselkanal · Hermsdorf · Schulzendorf · Lübars · Blankenfelde · Schwanebeck · Birkholzaue · Löhme · Werneuchen · Rudolfshöhe
Alter Finkenkrug · Nieder Neuendorf · Siedlung Schönwalde · Heiligensee · Waidmannslust · Buchholz · Neu Buch · Birkholz · Seefeld
Waldheim · **Falkensee** · Falkenhagen · Johannesstift · Tegelort · Tegel · Wittenau · Niederschönhausen · Karow · Neu Lindenberg · Lindenberg · Blumberg · Krummensee · Wegendorf
Finkenkrug · Seegefeld · Konradshöhe · Scharfenberg · **Reinickendorf** · **Pankow** · Heinersdorf · Blankenburg · Wartenberg · Ahrensfelde · Mehrow · Paulshot · Neuhönow · Altlandsberg Nord
Dallgow · Spandau · Staaken · **Wedding** · **Weissensee** · Falkenberg · Hohenschönhausen · Marzahn · Eiche · Eiche Süd · Hönow · Seeberg · Fredersdorf Nord
Döberitz · Haselhorst · Volkspark Jungfernheide · Siemensstadt · **Tiergarten** · **Mitte** · Volkspark Friedrichshain · **Lichtenburg** · Wuhlgärten · Hellersdorf · Neuenhagen · Fredersdorf
Seeburg · **Charlottenburg** · Olympia Stadion · Deutsche Oper · **BERLIN** · Brandenburger Tor · **Friedrichshain** · Biesdorf · Kaulsdorf · Mahlsdorf · Dahlwitz-Hoppegarten · Bollensdorf · Birkenstein
Gátow · Teufelsberg · Grunewald · **Kreuzberg** · Friedrichsfelde · Karlshorst · Münchehofe · Vogelsdorf · Kleinschönebeck
Gross Glienicke · Krampnitz · Schmargendorf · **Schöneberg** · **Neukölln** · FLUGHAFEN BERLIN-TEMPELHOF · Heidemühle · Waldesruh · **Schöneiche** · Gratzwalde · Schönblick
Neu Fahrland · Kladow · Dahlem · Friedenau · **Tempelhof** · Oberschöneweide · Fichtenau · Woltersdorf
Nedlitz · Sacrow · Pfaueninsel · Nikolassee · Steglitz · Britz · Johannisthal · Aldershof · **Köpenick** · Grosse Müggelsee · Rahnsdorf · Erkner
Wannsee · **Zehlendorf** · Lichterfelde · Lankwitz · Mariendorf · Niederschöneweide · Grünau · Müggelberge · Müggelheim · Springeberg · Wilhelmshagen
Schloss Glienicke · Schwanenwerder · Buckow · Rudow · Altglienicke · Wendenschloss · Langer See
Potsdam · **Kleinmachnow** · Seehof · Osdorf · Marienfelde · Grossziethen · Bohnsdorf · FLUGHAFEN BERLIN SCHÖNEFELD · Karolinenhof · Gosen
Teltow · East from Greenwich

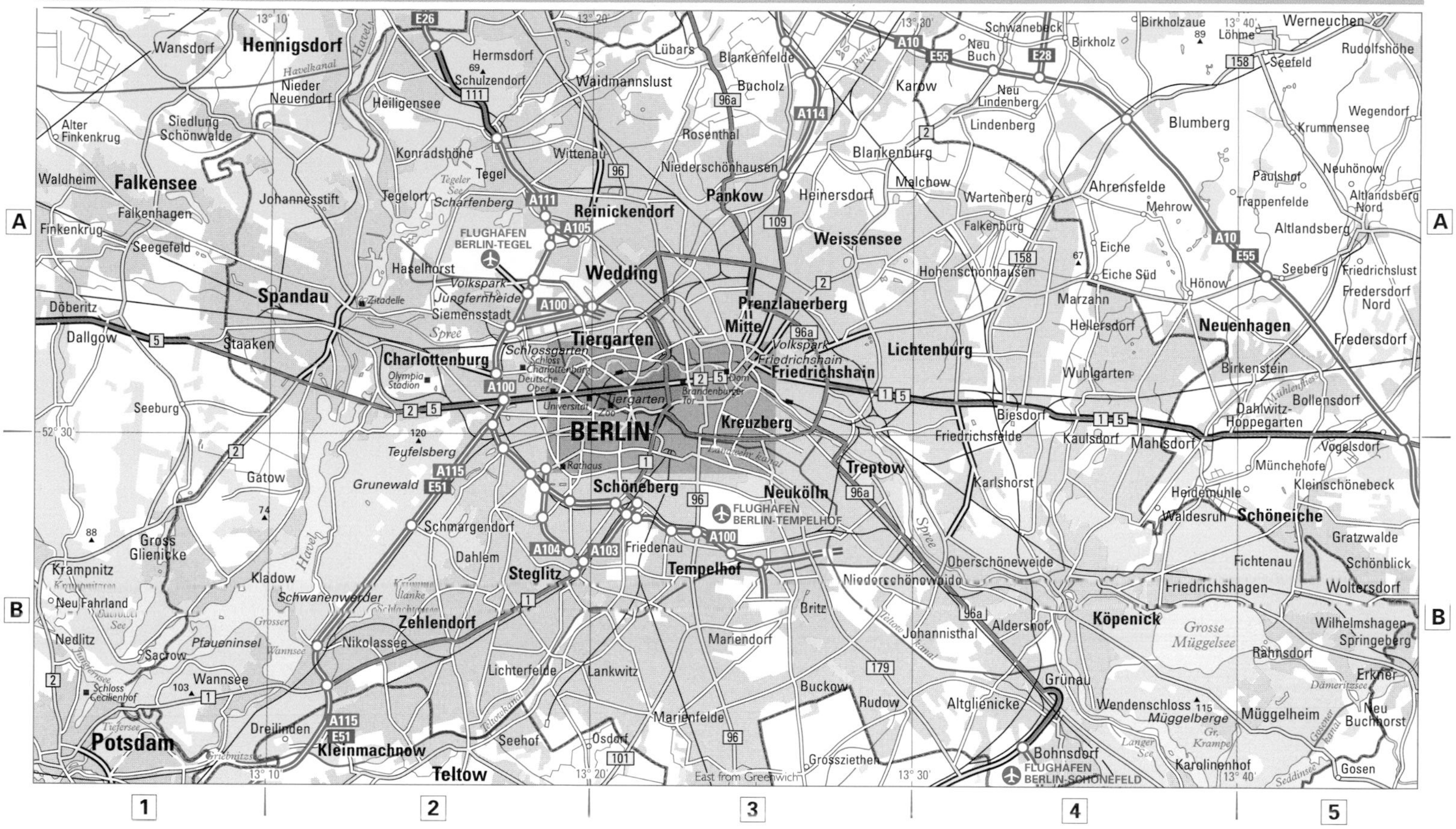

CENTRAL BERLIN

km 1
miles 0.5

CHARLOTTENBURG · **TIERGARTEN** · **MITTE**
Kaiserin Augusta Allee · Turmstrasse · St. Johannis-Kirche · Charité Krankenhaus · Deutsche Th. und Kammerspiele · Friedrichstadtpalast · Oranienburger Tor · Volksbühne
Hansatheater · Lehrter stadtbf · Invalidenstr. · Berliner Ensemble · Hackescher Mkt. · Alexander platz · Kongresshalle
Bellevue · Akad. d. Künste · Schlosspark · Schloss Bellevue · Haus der Kulturen der Welt · Platz der Republik · Reichstag · M. Gorki Th. · Pergamon mus. · National-galleries · Fernsehturm am Alexanderplatz · Dom · Schilling-strasse · Poliklinik
Staatliche Porzellanmanufaktur · Tiergarten · Siegessäule · STRASSE DES 17 JUNI · Brandenburger Tor · UNTER DEN LINDEN · Komische Oper · Staats Oper · Deutsche Staats Bibl. · Staats Bibl. · Jannowitz-brücke
Deutsche Oper · Tribünetheater · Technische Universität · Konzertsaal · Zoologischer Garten · Philharm. Halle · Kulturforum · Konzerthaus Berlin · Deutsch Dom · Spree · Märkisches Mus.
BISMARCKSTRASSE · Renaissancetheater · Ernst-Reuter-Pl. · Kaiser Wilhelm Kirche · Europa-center · KURFÜRSTENDAMM · TAUENTZIEN · KLEIST · Potsdamer Pl. · Bundesministerien · Staats Bibl. · St. Michael-Kirch
WILMERSDORF · Th. am Kurfürstendamm · Volksbühne · Nollendorfpl. · Urania · Elisabeth Krankenhaus · Anhalter Bf. · Blumenmarkt · Berlinmuseum · **KREUZBERG**
Viktoria-Luise-Pl. · BÜLOW STR. · Mus. für Verkehr und Technik · TEMPELHOFER UFER · GITSCHINER STRASSE · SKALITZER STR. · HASEN HEIDE
HOHENZOLLERNDAMM · Rathaus · Preussenpark · BERLINER STR. · GRUNE WALD STRASSE · YORCKSTRASSE · Grossgörschenstr. · Yorckstr. · GNEISENAUSTRASSE · Krankenhaus am Urban · Böckler Park · Monumenten Str.

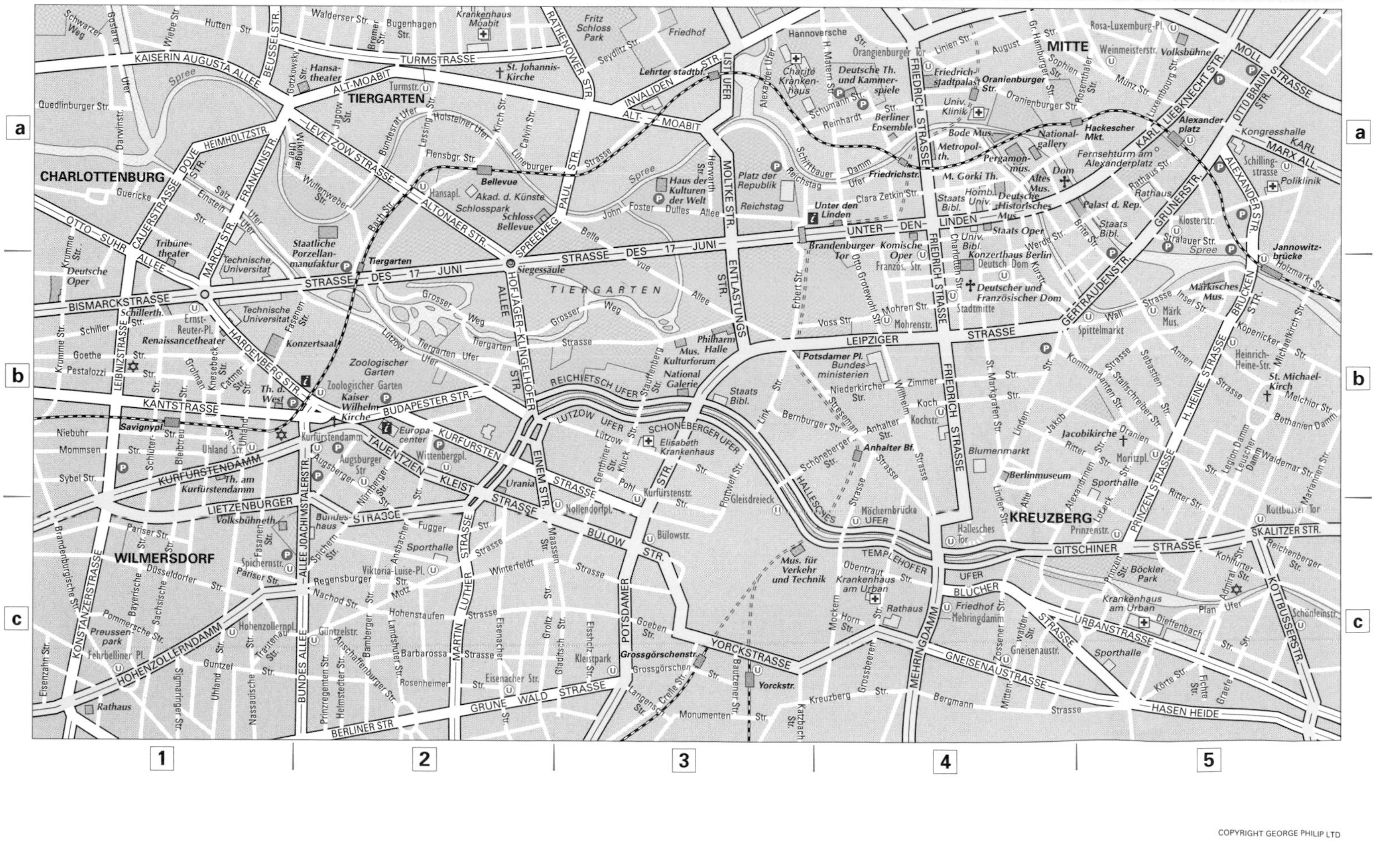

COPYRIGHT GEORGE PHILIP LTD

BOSTON

km 0 — 5
miles 0 — 3

Great Meadows Nat. Wildlife Refuge · Bedford · Burlington · Woburn · Wakefield · North Saugus Breakheart Reservation Greenwood · Marblehead · Clifton · Lynn · Swampscott

East Acton · West Bedford · Concord · LAURENCE G. HANSCOM FIELD · North Lexington · Stoneham · Walter D. Stone Mem. Zoo · Saugus · West Lynn

West Concord · Minute Man Natural History Park · Lexington · Winchester · Middlesex Fells Reservation · Melrose Mt. Hood Mem. Park · Malden · Revere · Nahant Bay · Nahant

Fairhaven Hill · Fairhaven Bay · Sandy Pond · Lincoln · East Lexington · Arlington Heights · West Medford · Medford · Everett · Chelsea · East Boston · Orient Heights · Beachmont · ATLANTIC OCEAN

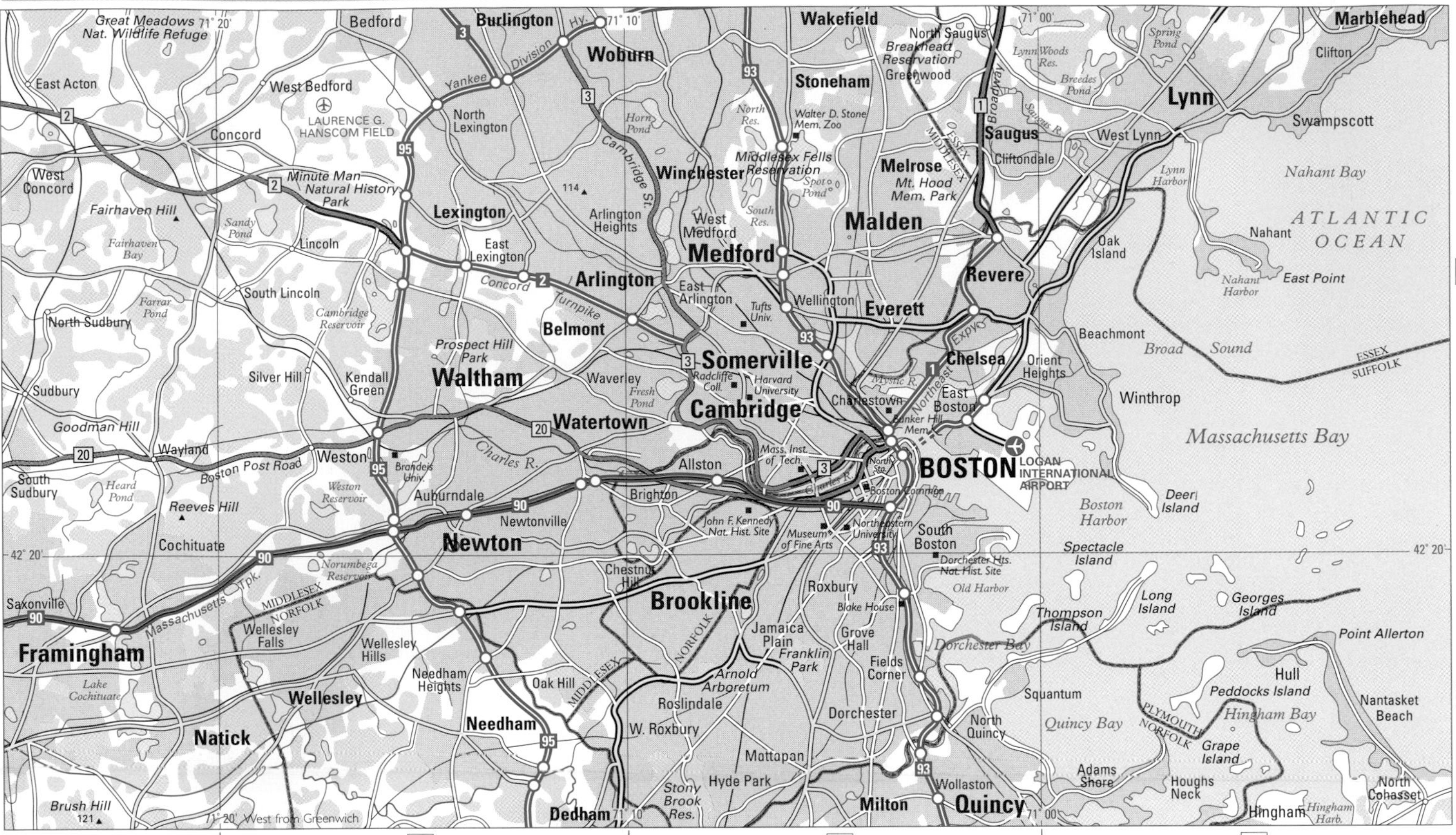

North Sudbury · Farrar Pond · South Lincoln · Cambridge Reservoir · Arlington · East Arlington · Tufts Univ. · Somerville · Charlestown · Broad Sound · Essex SUFFOLK

Sudbury · Silver Hill · Prospect Hill Park · Kendall Green · Belmont · Waverley · Radcliffe Coll. · Harvard University · Cambridge · Winthrop

Goodman Hill · Wayland · Weston · Waltham · Watertown · Fresh Pond · Allston · Mass. Inst. of Tech. · BOSTON · LOGAN INTERNATIONAL AIRPORT · Massachusetts Bay · Deer Island

South Sudbury · Heard Pond · Reeves Hill · Cochituate · Boston Post Road · Weston Reservoir · Auburndale · Brighton · John F. Kennedy Nat. Hist. Site · Northeastern University · South Boston · Boston Harbor · Spectacle Island

Sakonville · Framingham · Norumbega Reservoir · Newton · Newtonville · Chestnut · Museum of Fine Arts · Dorchester Hts. Nat. Hist. Site · Old Harbor · Thompson Island · Long Island · Georges Island · Point Allerton

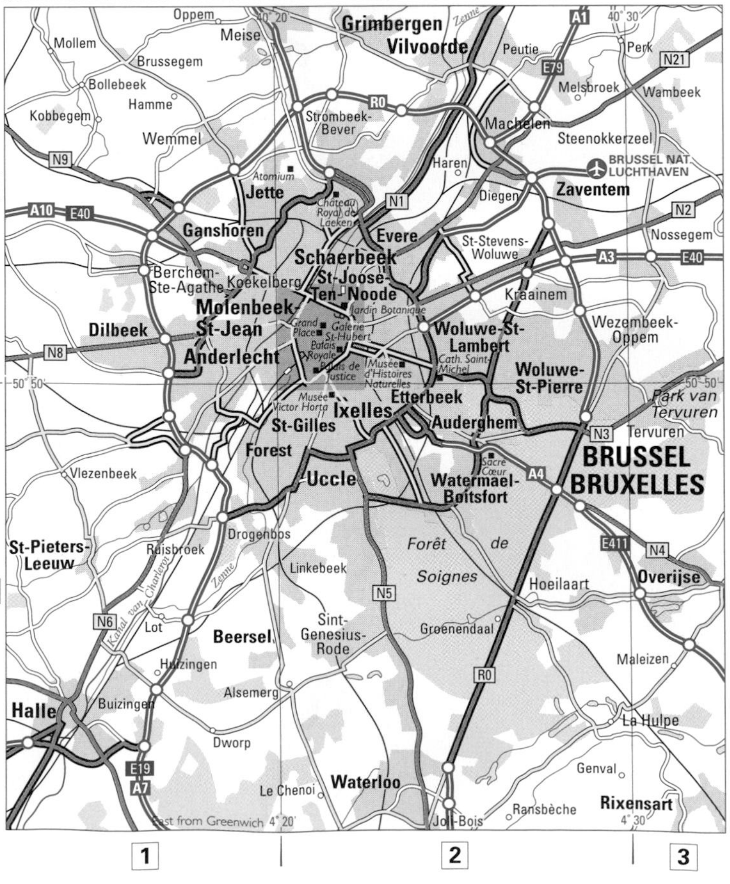

Lake Cochituate · Wellesley Falls · Wellesley Hills · Brookline · Roxbury · Blake House · Jamaica Plain Franklin Park · Grove Hall · Fields Corner · Dorchester Bay · Hull · Peddocks Island · Nantasket Beach

Natick · Needham Heights · Oak Hill · Roslindale · Dorchester · North Quincy · Quincy Bay · Squantum · Adams Shore · Houghs Neck · Grape Island · Hingham Bay

Wellesley · Needham · W. Roxbury · Mattapan · Hyde Park · Stony Brook Res. · Milton · Wollaston · Quincy · Hingham

Brush Hill · Dedham · PLYMOUTH NORFOLK · North Cohasset

1 · 2 · 3 · 4

BRUSSELS

km 0 — 5
miles 0 — 3

Oppem · Meise · Grimbergen · Vilvoorde · Peutie · Perk

Mollem · Brussegem · Bollebeek · Hamme · Wemmel · Strombeek-Bever · Machelen · Melsbroek · Wambeek

Kobbegem · Jette · Haren · BRUSSEL NAT. LUCHTHAVEN · Zaventem · Diegem · St-Stevens-Woluwe · Nossegem

Ganshoren · Berchem-Ste-Agathe · Koekelberg · Schaerbeek · Evere · Kraainem · Wezembeek-Oppem

Dilbeek · Molenbeek-St-Jean · St-Joose-Ten-Noode · Woluwe-St-Lambert · Cath. Saint-Michel · Woluwe-St-Pierre

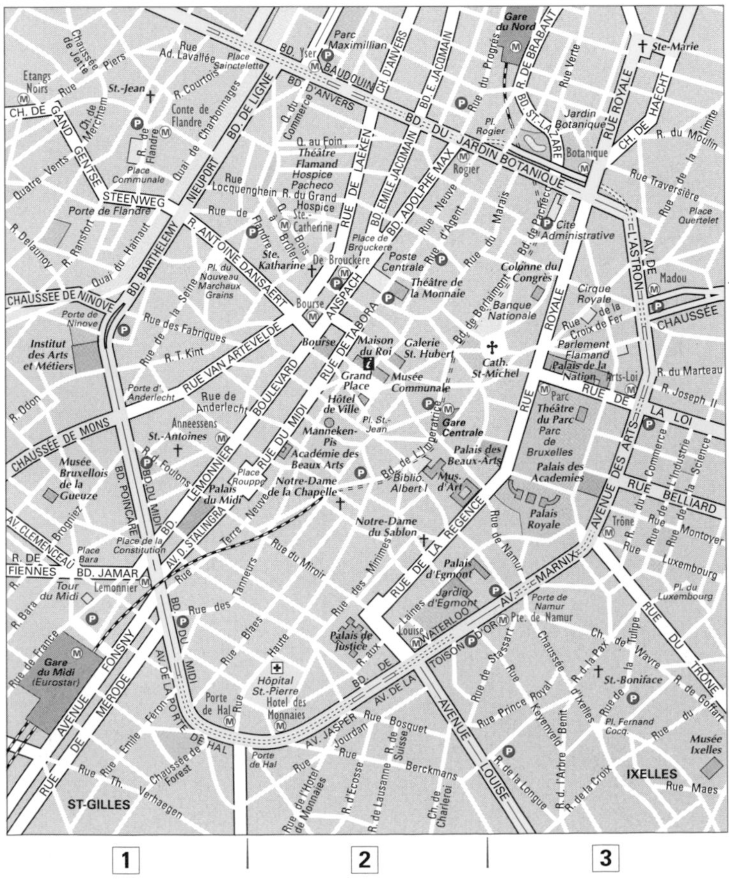

Anderlecht · Ixelles · Etterbeek · Auderghem · Park van Tervuren

St-Gilles · Forest · BRUSSEL BRUXELLES · Tervuren

St-Pieters-Leeuw · Uccle · Watermael-Boitsfort · Forêt de Soignes

Vlezenbeek · Drogenbos · Linkebeek · Hoeilaart · Overijse

Halle · Ruisbroek · Beersel · Sint-Genesius-Rode · Groenendaal

Lot · Huizingen · Alsemberg · La Hulpe

Buizingen · Dworp · Le Chenoi · Waterloo · Genval · Rixensart · Ransbèche

1 · 2 · 3

CENTRAL BRUSSELS

km 0 — 1
miles 0 — 0.5

Gare du Nord · Ste-Marie · Jardin Botanique · Botanique · Colonne du Congrès · Cirque Royale · Parlement Flamand · Palais de la Nation · Banque Nationale · Théâtre de la Monnaie · Bourse · Grand Place · Hôtel de Ville · Manneken-Pis · Académie des Beaux-Arts · Palais des Beaux-Arts · Cath. St-Michel · Notre-Dame du Sablon · Palais Royale · Palais de Justice · Gare du Midi (Eurostar) · Hôpital St-Pierre · Porte de Hal · Musée Ixelles · IXELLES · ST-GILLES

1 · 2 · 3

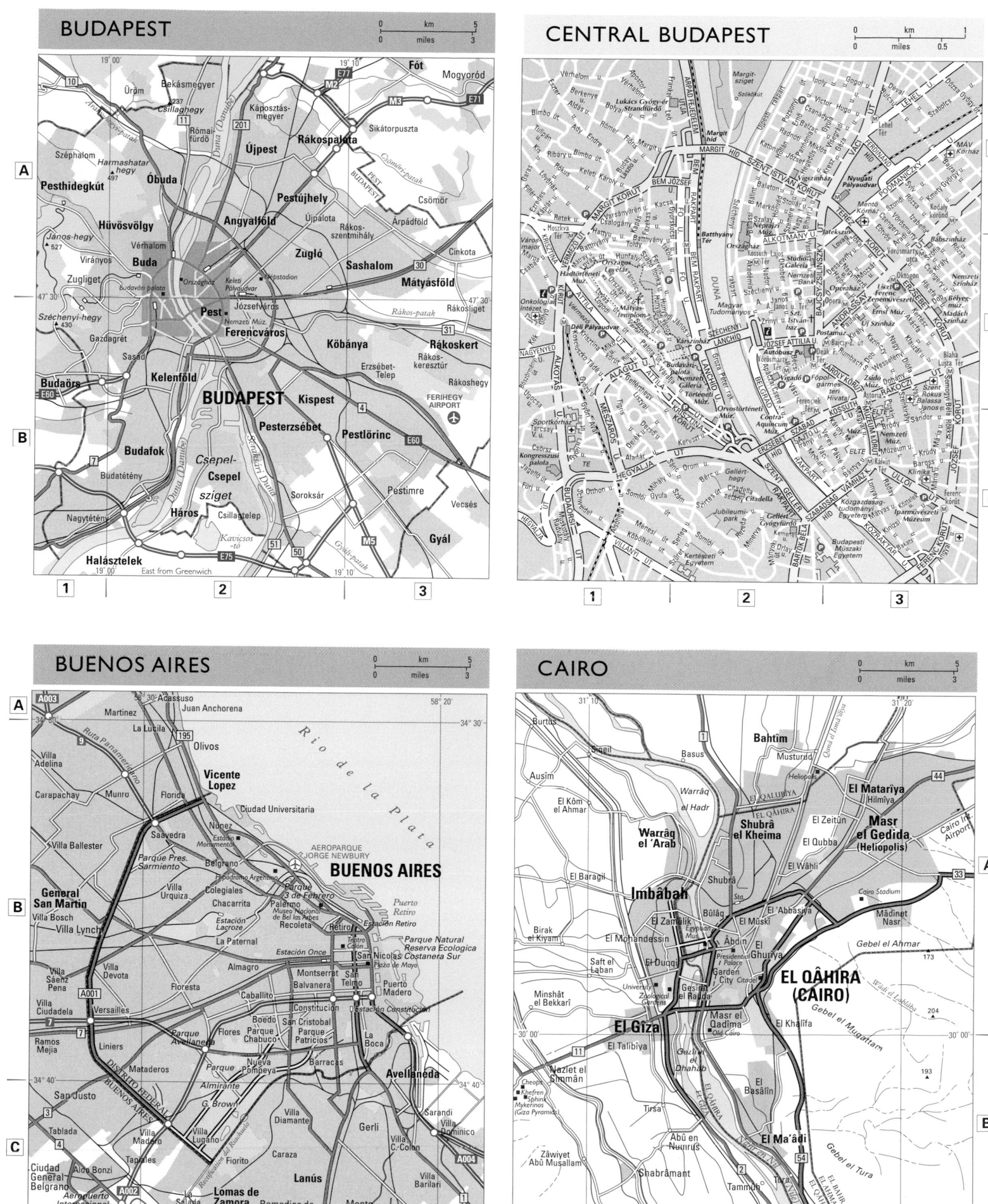
BUDAPEST
CENTRAL BUDAPEST
BUENOS AIRES
CAIRO
BUDAPEST
Újpest
Óbuda
Buda
Pest
Ferencváros
Kispest
Pesterzsébet
Csepel
Kőbánya
Zugló
Angyalföld
Rákospalota
Pestújhely
Sashalom
Mátyásföld
Rákoskert
Pestlőrinc
Budafok
Budaörs
Kelenföld
Hűvösvölgy
Pesthidegkút
Halásztelek
Gyál
FERIHEGY AIRPORT
BUENOS AIRES
Rio de la Plata
Vicente Lopez
Olivos
General San Martin
Avellaneda
Lanús
Lomas de Zamora
Belgrano
Palermo
Recoleta
Retiro
San Nicolas
La Boca
AEROPARQUE JORGE NEWBURY
Aeropuerto Internacional Ezeiza
EL QÂHIRA (CAIRO)
El Gîza
Imbâbah
Shubrâ el Kheima
Masr el Gedida (Heliopolis)
El Matarîya
El Ma'âdi
Cairo Int. Airport
East from Greenwich

CALCUTTA

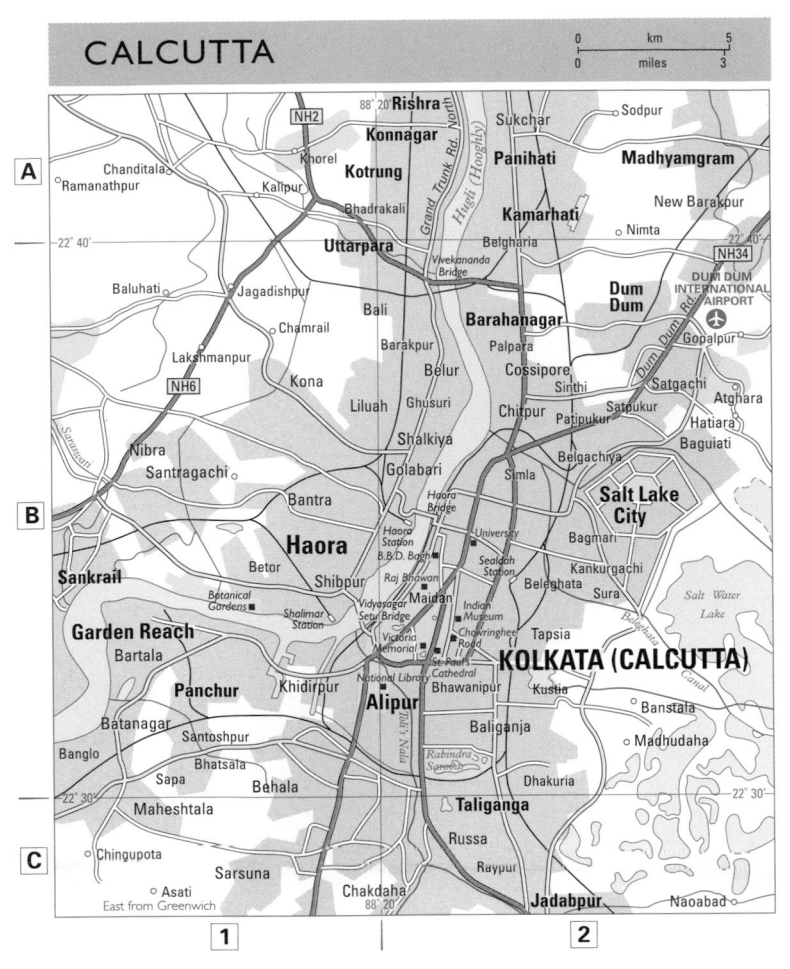
0 km 5
0 miles 3
A
B
C
1
2
88° 20'
22° 40'
22° 30'
East from Greenwich
NH2
NH6
NH34
Rishra
Sodpur
Sukchar
Konnagar
Khorel
Kotrung
Panihati
Madhyamgram
Chanditala
Ramanathpur
Kalipur
Bhadrakali
Kamarhati
New Barakpur
Nimta
Uttarpara
Belgharia
Vivekananda Bridge
Grand Trunk Rd. North
Hugli (Hooghly)
Baluhati
Jagadishpur
Bali
Dum Dum
DUM DUM INTERNATIONAL AIRPORT
Barahanagar
Gopalpur
Chamrail
Barakpur
Palpara
Lakshmanpur
Belur
Cossipore
Sinthi
Kona
Satgachi
Atghara
Liluah
Ghusuri
Chitpur
Satpukur
Patipukur
Hatiara
Baguiati
Nibra
Shalkiya
Santragachi
Golabari
Belgachiya
Simla
Salt Lake City
Bantra
Haora Bridge
Haora
Haora Station
University
Bagmari
Betor
B.B.D. Bagh
Sealdah Station
Kankurgachi
Sankrail
Shibpur
Raj Bhawan
Beleghata
Sura
Botanical Gardens
Vidyasagar Setu Bridge
Maidan
Indian Museum
Salt Water Lake
Garden Reach
Shalimar Station
Victoria Memorial
Chowringhee Road
Tapsia
Bartala
St. Paul's Cathedral
KOLKATA (CALCUTTA)
Panchur
Khidirpur
National Library
Bhawanipur
Kustia
Alipur
Banstala
Batanagar
Tolly's Nala
Baliganja
Santoshpur
Madhudaha
Banglo
Bhatsala
Rabindra Sarobar
Sapa
Behala
Dhakuria
Maheshtala
Taliganja
Chingupota
Russa
Raypur
Asati
Sarsuna
Chakdaha
Jadabpur
Naoabad

CANTON

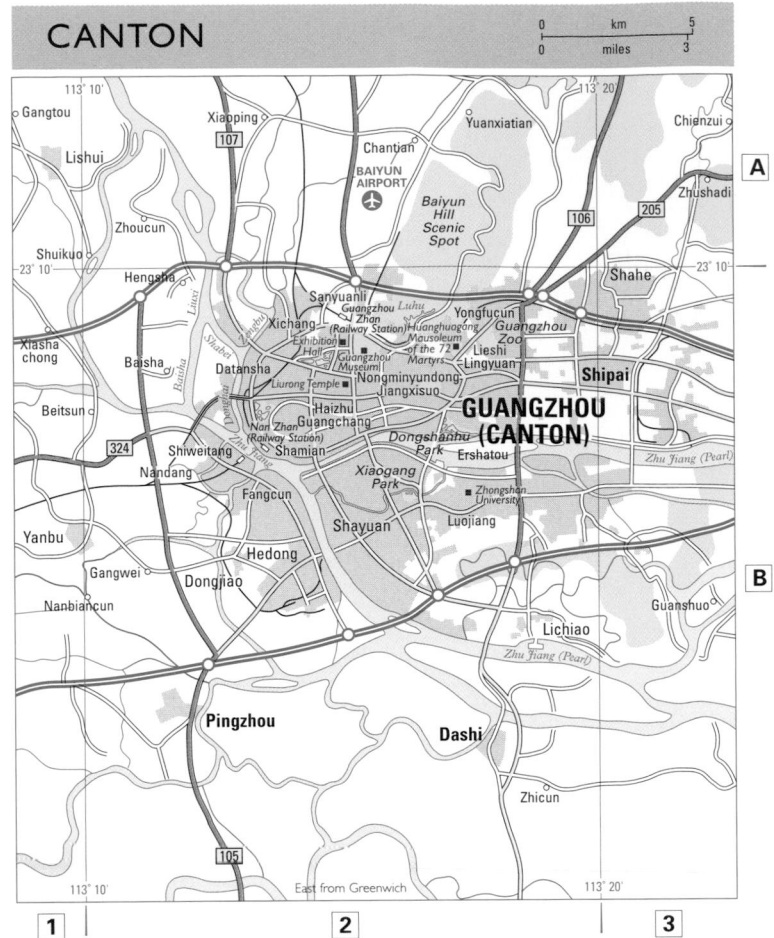
0 km 5
0 miles 3
A
B
1
2
3
113° 10'
113° 20'
23° 10'
East from Greenwich
107
106
205
324
105
Gangtou
Xiapping
Yuanxiatian
Chienzui
Lishui
Chantian
BAIYUN AIRPORT
Baiyun Hill Scenic Spot
Zhushadi
Zhoucun
Shuikou
Hengsha
Sanyuanli
Shahe
Guangzhou Zhan (Railway Station)
Luhu
Yongfucun
Xichang
Exhibition Hall
Huanghuogang Mausoleum of the 72 Martyrs
Guangzhou Zoo
Xiasha chong
Guangzhou Museum
Lieshi
Baisha
Datansha
Nongminyundong
Lingyuan
Shipai
Liurong Temple
Jiangxisuo
Beitsun
Haizhu
GUANGZHOU (CANTON)
Nan Zhan (Railway Station)
Guangchang
Dongshanhu Park
Shiweitang
Shamian
Ershatou
Zhu Jiang (Pearl)
Nandang
Xiaogang Park
Fangcun
Zhongshan University
Yanbu
Shayuan
Luojiang
Hedong
Gangwei
Dongjiao
Nanbiancun
Guanshuo
Lichiao
Pingzhou
Dashi
Zhicun

CAPE TOWN

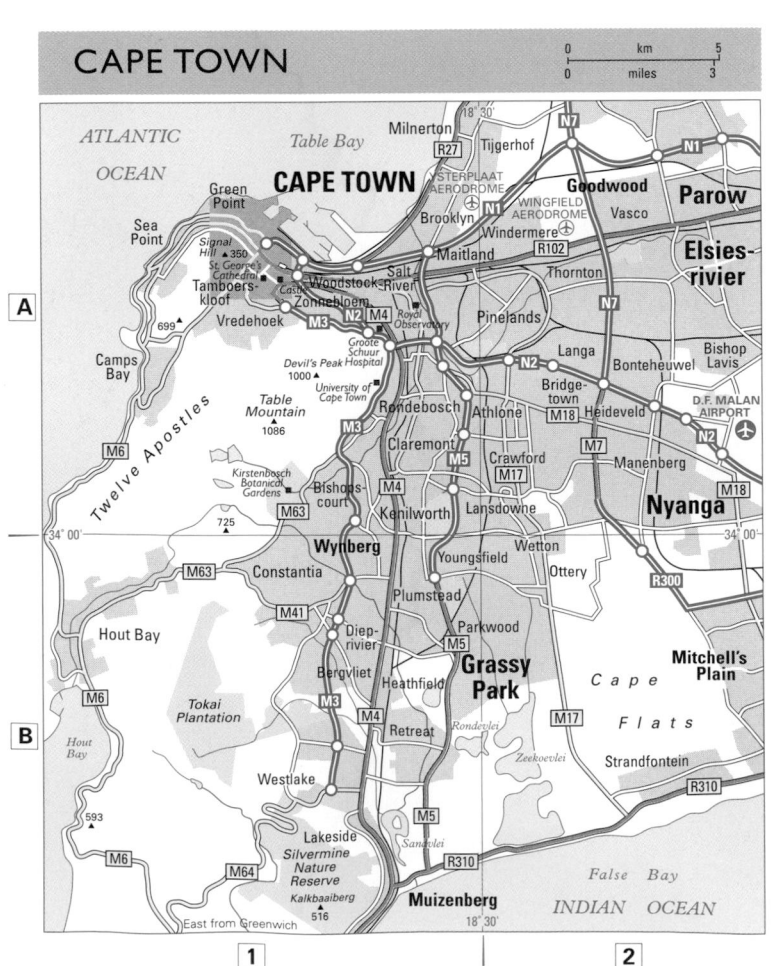
0 km 5
0 miles 3
A
B
1
2
18° 30'
34° 00'
East from Greenwich
ATLANTIC OCEAN
Table Bay
Milnerton
Tijgerhof
N7
N1
R27
CAPE TOWN
STERPLAAT AERODROME
Goodwood
Parow
Green Point
WINGFIELD AERODROME
Vasco
Sea Point
Brooklyn
Windermere
Signal Hill 350
Maitland
R102
Elsies-rivier
St. George's Cathedral
Woodstock
Salt River
Thornton
Tamboers-kloof
Zonnebloem
N2
M4
699
Vredehoek
M3
Royal Observatory
Pinelands
Groote Schuur
Langa
Bishop Lavis
Camps Bay
Devil's Peak 1000
Hospital
Bonteheuwel
University of Cape Town
Bridge-town
Table Mountain 1086
Rondebosch
Athlone
M18
Heideveld
D.F. MALAN AIRPORT
M6
Claremont
M5
Crawford
M17
Manenberg
Twelve Apostles
Kirstenbosch Botanical Gardens
Bishops-court
M63
M4
Kenilworth
Lansdowne
Nyanga
725
Wynberg
Wetton
Youngsfield
Ottery
Constantia
Plumstead
R300
M41
Hout Bay
Diep-rivier
Parkwood
Mitchell's Plain
Bergvliet
Grassy Park
Tokai Plantation
Heathfield
Cape Flats
Retreat
Rondevlei
Hout Bay
Zeekoevlei
Strandfontein
Westlake
R310
593
Lakeside
Silvermine Nature Reserve
Sandvlei
Kalkbaaiberg 516
M64
False Bay
Muizenberg
INDIAN OCEAN

CENTRAL CAPE TOWN

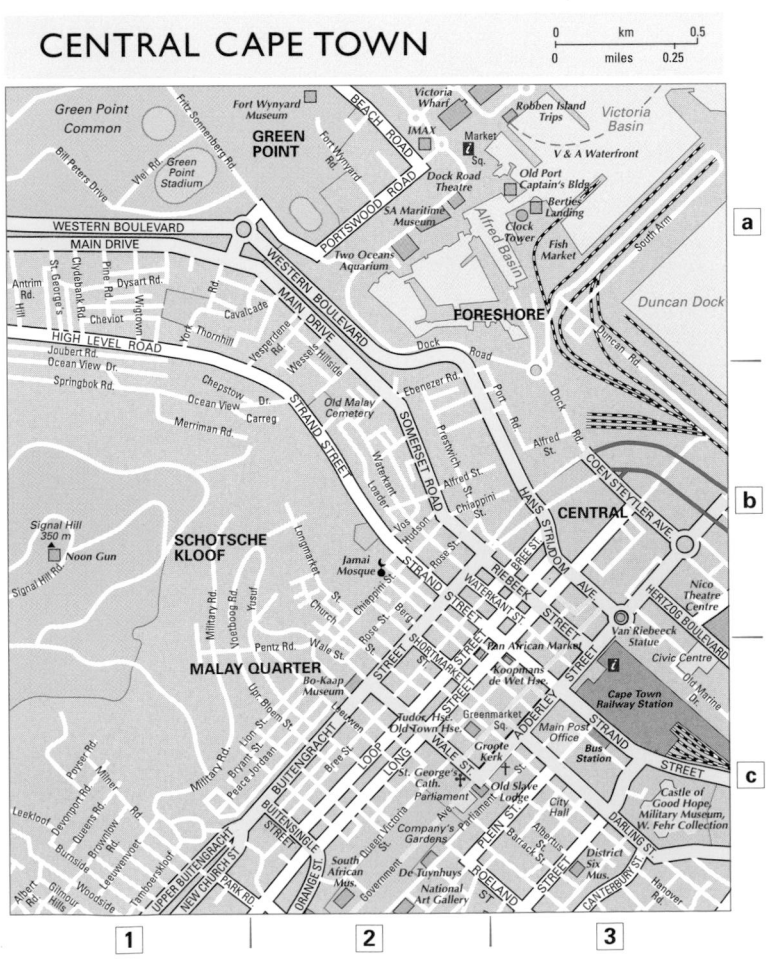
0 km 0.5
0 miles 0.25
a
b
c
1
2
3
Green Point Common
Fort Wynyard Museum
Victoria Wharf
Robben Island Trips
Victoria Basin
GREEN POINT
IMAX
Market
V & A Waterfront
Green Point Stadium
Dock Road Theatre
Old Port Captain's Bldg
Bertie's Landing
SA Maritime Museum
Alfred Basin
Clock Tower
Fish Market
South Arm
WESTERN BOULEVARD
MAIN DRIVE
PORTSWOOD ROAD
BEACH ROAD
Two Oceans Aquarium
Duncan Dock
FORESHORE
HIGH LEVEL ROAD
Cheviot
Cavalcade
Joubert Rd.
Ocean View Dr.
Springbok Rd.
Chepstow
Dock Road
Old Malay Cemetery
Merriman Rd.
STRAND STREET
SOMERSET ROAD
Ebenezer Rd.
Port Rd.
Alfred St.
COEN STEYTLER AVE.
HANS STRIJDOM AVE.
CENTRAL
Signal Hill 350 m
Noon Gun
SCHOTSCHE KLOOF
Jamai Mosque
Nico Theatre Centre
HERTZOG BOULEVARD
Van Riebeeck Statue
Civic Centre
MALAY QUARTER
Bo-Kaap Museum
Pan African Market
Koopmans de Wet Hse.
Cape Town Railway Station
Tuynhuys
Old Town Hse.
Greenmarket Sq.
Main Post Office
Bus Station
St. George's Cath.
Parliament
Old Slave Lodge
City Hall
Castle of Good Hope, Military Museum, W. Fehr Collection
Company's Gardens
South African Mus.
De Tuynhuys
National Art Gallery
District Six Mus.
BUITENGRACHT
UPPER BUITENGRACHT
NEW CHURCH ST.
ORANGE ST.
BUITENSINGEL
LONG
LOOP
ADDERLEY
PLEIN ST.
DARLING ST.
CANTERBURY ST.
STRAND
WALE ST.
BREE ST.
RIEBEEK
WATERKANT
SHORTMARKET
Leeuwen
Military Rd.
Leekloof
Devonport Rd.
Queens Rd.
Upr. Bloem St.
Rose St.
Chiappini St.

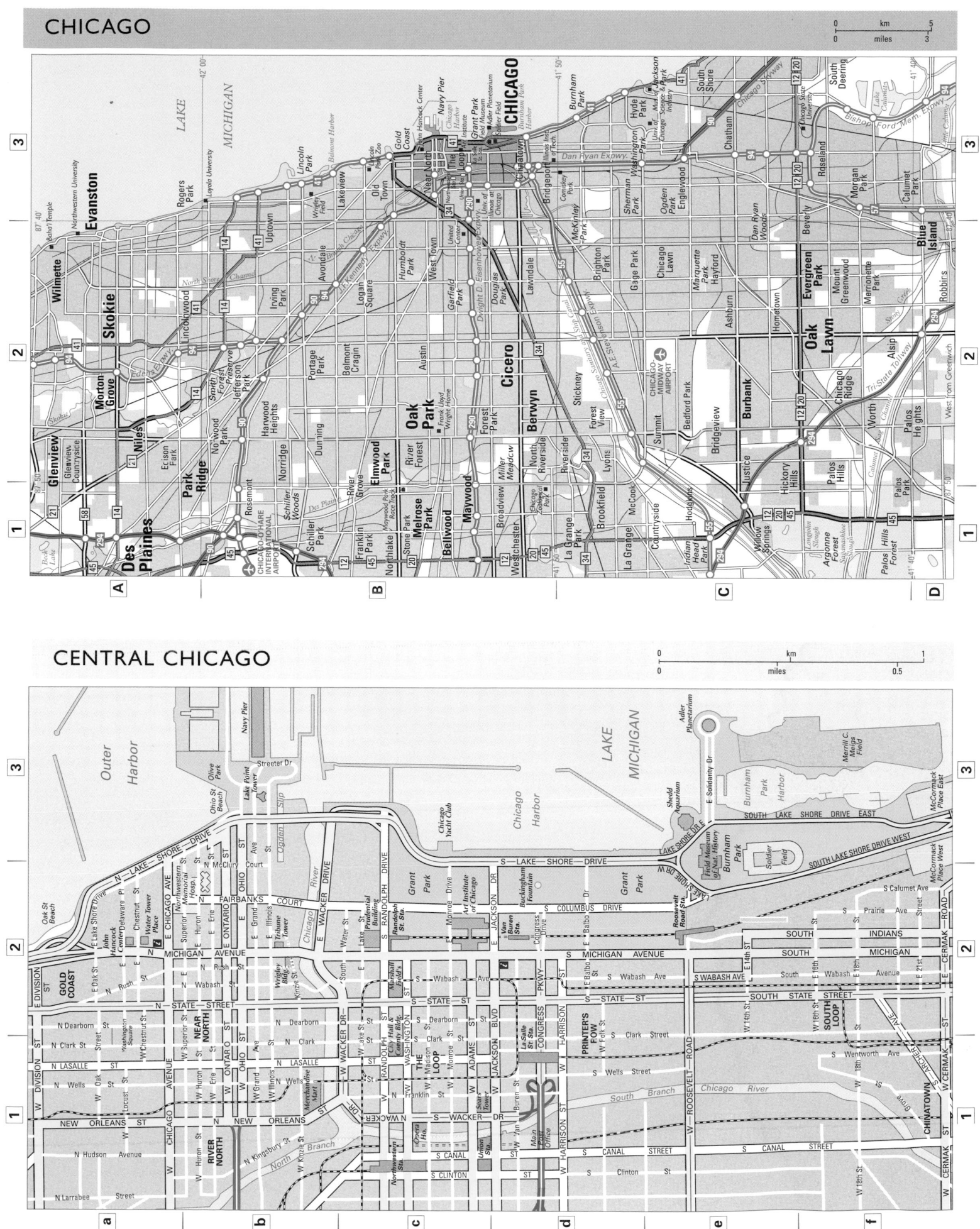

CHICAGO

CENTRAL CHICAGO

COPYRIGHT GEORGE PHILIP LTD

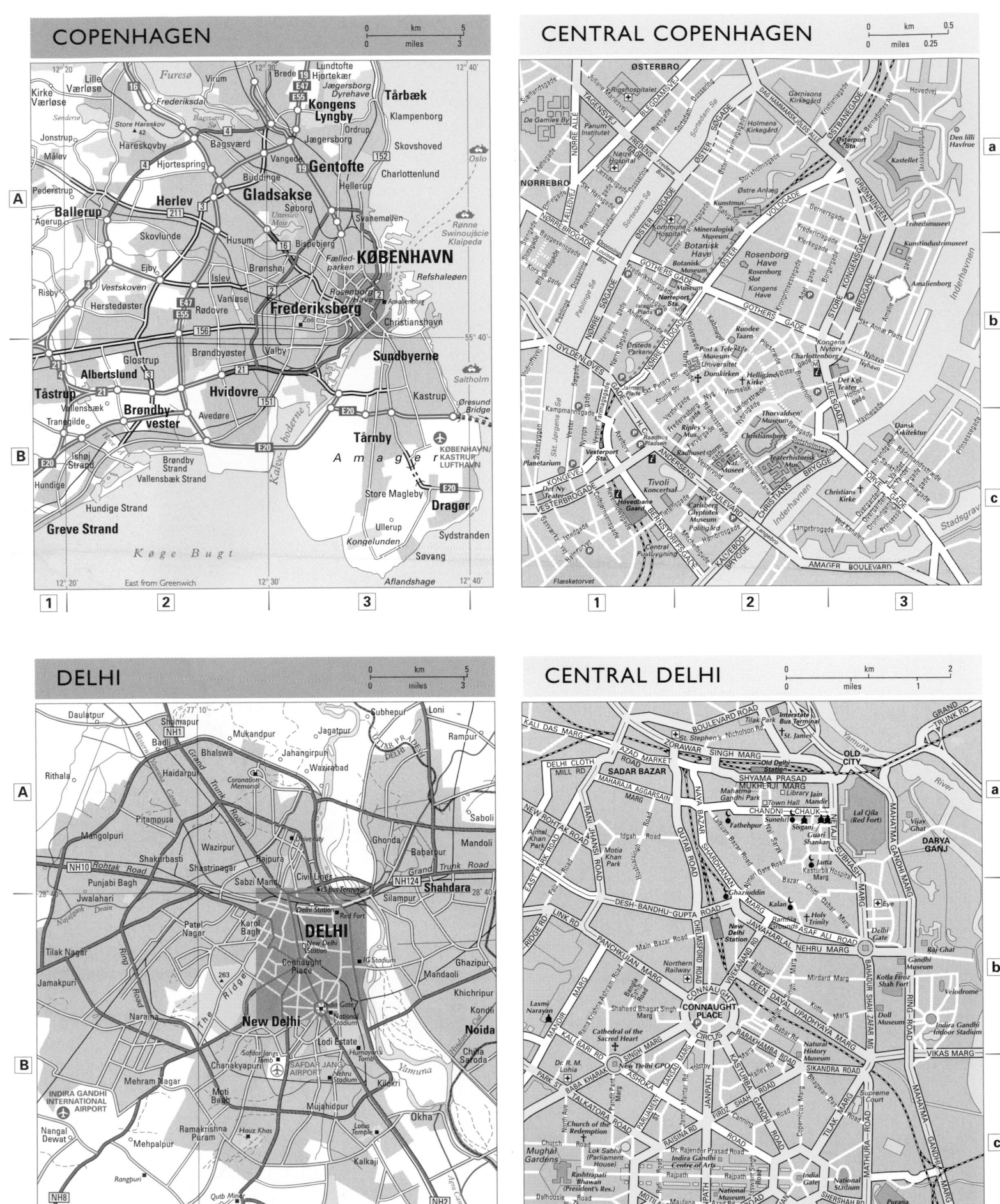
COPENHAGEN
CENTRAL COPENHAGEN
DELHI
CENTRAL DELHI
KØBENHAVN
Frederiksberg
Gentofte
Gladsakse
Herlev
Ballerup
Hvidovre
Amager
Køge Bugt
East from Greenwich
DELHI
New Delhi
Shahdara
Noida
INDIRA GANDHI INTERNATIONAL AIRPORT
OLD CITY
CONNAUGHT PLACE
SADAR BAZAR
DARYA GANJ
NEW DELHI

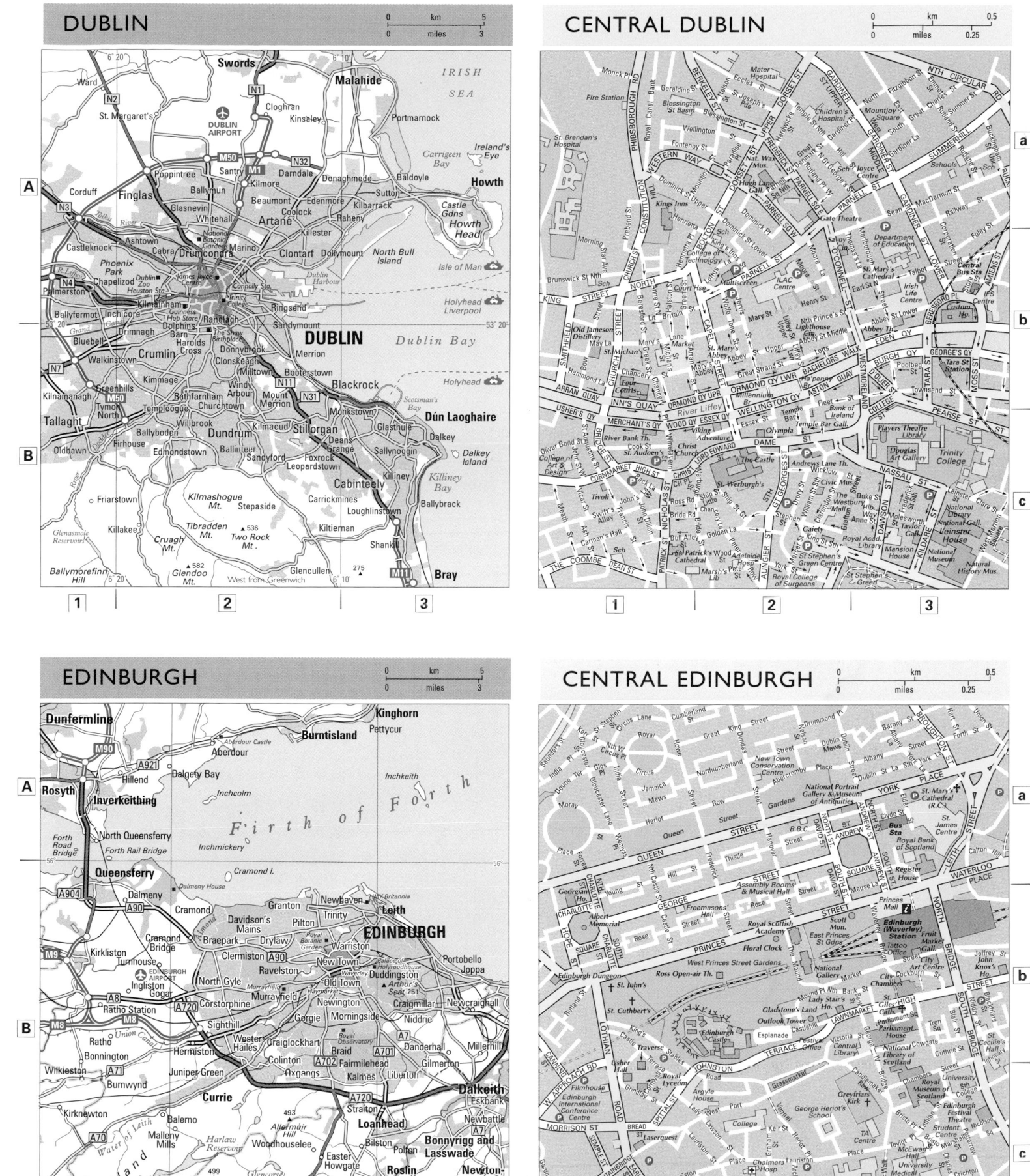
DUBLIN
0 km 5
0 miles 3
Swords
Malahide
IRISH SEA
Ward
St. Margaret's
DUBLIN AIRPORT
Cloghran
Kinsaley
Portmarnock
Carrigeen Bay
Ireland's Eye
Santry
Darndale
Donaghmede
Baldoyle
Howth
Corduff
Finglas
Poppintree
Ballymun
Kilmore
Glasnevin
Beaumont
Coolock
Edenmore
Kilbarrack
Sutton
Castle Gdns
Howth Head
Whitehall
Artane
Raheny
Castleknock
Ashtown
Killester
Cabra
Drumcondra
Marino
Clontarf
Dollymount
North Bull Island
Phoenix Park
Isle of Man
Palmerston
Chapelizod
Dublin Zoo
Heuston Sta.
Connolly Sta.
Dublin Harbour
Ballyfermot
Inchicore
Kilmainham
Trinity College
Ringsend
Holyhead
Liverpool
Bluebell
Drimnagh
Guinness Hop Store
Dolphins Barn
Ranelagh
Sandymount
DUBLIN
Dublin Bay
Crumlin
Harolds Cross
Donnybrook
Merrion
Walkinstown
Kimmage
Clonskeagh
Milltown
Booterstown
Kilnamanagh
Greenhills
Rathfarnham
Windy Arbour
Mount Merrion
Blackrock
Tymon North
Templeogue
Churchtown
Monkstown
Scotsman's Bay
Dún Laoghaire
Tallaght
Willbrook
Dundrum
Kilmacud
Stillorgan
Glasthule
Dalkey
Ballyboden
Oldbawn
Firhouse
Edmondstown
Ballinteer
Deans Grange
Sallynoggin
Dalkey Island
Sandyford
Foxrock
Leopardstown
Killiney
Killiney Bay
Cabinteely
Friarstown
Kilmashogue Mt.
Stepaside
Carrickmines
Ballybrack
Loughlinstown
Killakee
Glenasmole Reservoir
Tibradden Mt.
536
Two Rock Mt.
Kiltiernan
Cruagh Mt.
Shankill
Ballymorefinn Hill
582
Glendoo Mt.
West from Greenwich
Glencullen
275
Bray
A
B
1
2
3
CENTRAL DUBLIN
0 km 0.5
0 miles 0.25
Mater Hospital
Fire Station
Blessington St Basin
Children's Hospital
Mountjoy Square
St. Brendan's Hospital
Kings Inns
Hugh Lane Gall.
Nat. Wax Mus.
Joyce Centre
Gate Theatre
Department of Education
College of Technology
Multiscreen
ILAC Centre
St. Mary's Cathedral
Irish Life Centre
Central Bus Sta
Custom Ho.
Old Jameson Distillery
St. Michan's
Four Courts
Lighthouse Cin.
Tara St Station
River Liffey
Temple Bar
Bank of Ireland
Temple Bar Gall.
Players' Theatre Library
Viking Adventure
Olympia
Douglas Art Gallery
Trinity College
St. Audoen's
Christ Church
The Castle
College of Art & Design
St. Werburgh's
Civic Mus.
Tivoli
National Library
National Gall.
Leinster House
National Museum
Natural History Mus.
St. Patrick's Cathedral
Marsh's Lib
Gaiety
Royal Acad. Library
Mansion House
St Stephen's Green Centre
Royal College of Surgeons
St Stephen's Green
EDINBURGH
0 km 5
0 miles 3
Dunfermline
Kinghorn
Pettycur
Burntisland
Aberdour Castle
Aberdour
Dalgety Bay
Hillend
Rosyth
Inverkeithing
Inchcolm
Inchkeith
Firth of Forth
North Queensferry
Forth Road Bridge
Forth Rail Bridge
Inchmickery
Queensferry
Cramond I.
Dalmeny House
Dalmeny
Cramond
Granton
Newhaven
Leith
Davidson's Mains
Pilton
Trinity
EDINBURGH
Cramond Bridge
Braepark
Drylaw
Royal Botanic Garden
Warriston
Kirkliston
Turnhouse
EDINBURGH AIRPORT
Clermiston
New Town
Portobello
Ravelston
Palace of Holyroodhouse
Duddingston
Joppa
Ingliston
Gogar
North Gyle
Murrayfield
Old Town
Arthur's Seat 251
Ratho Station
Corstorphine
Haymarket
Newington
Craigmillar
Newcraighall
Ratho
Union Canal
Sighthill
Gorgie
Morningside
Niddrie
Bonnington
Hermiston
Wester Hailes
Craiglockhart
Royal Observatory
Danderhall
Millerhill
Braid
Wilkieston
Juniper Green
Colinton
Oxgangs
Fairmilehead
Gilmerton
Burnwynd
Kalmes
Liberton
Dalkeith
Currie
Eskbank
Kirknewton
Balerno
493
Allermuir Hill
Straiton
Loanhead
Newbattle
Malleny Mills
Harlaw Reservoir
Woodhouselee
Bilston
Bonnyrigg and Lasswade
Water of Leith
Polton
Easter Howgate
Pentland Hills
Threipmuir Reservoir
499
Glencorse Res.
Roslin
Newtongrange
Milton Bridge
Rosewell
North Esk
Harperrig Reservoir
579
Scald Law
Auchendinny
Penicuik
Silverburn
Kirkhill
Carrington
West from Greenwich
CENTRAL EDINBURGH
0 km 0.5
0 miles 0.25
Dublin Mews
New Town Conservation Centre
National Portrait Gallery & Museum of Antiquities
St. Mary's Cathedral (R.C.)
Circus
Jamaica Mews
Moray Place
Queen Street
Bus Sta
St. James Centre
Royal Bank of Scotland
Register House
Georgian Ho.
Assembly Rooms & Musical Hall
Freemasons' Hall
Princes Mall
Albert Memorial
Royal Scottish Academy
Scott Mon.
East Princes St Gdns
Edinburgh (Waverley) Station
Fruit Market Gall.
Tattoo Office
City Art Centre
Floral Clock
West Princes Street Gardens
National Gallery
Jeffrey St
John Knox's Ho.
Edinburgh Dungeon
Ross Open-air Th.
City Chambers
St. John's
St. Cuthbert's
Gladstone's Land
Lady Stair's Ho.
St. Giles Cath.
Parliament Sq
Parliament House
Edinburgh Castle
Esplanade
Outlook Tower
Castlehill
Lawnmarket
Tron Sq
St. Cecilia's Hall
Traverse
Usher Hall
Festival Office
Victoria St
Central Library
National Library of Scotland
Royal Lyceum
Filmhouse
Edinburgh International Conference Centre
Argyle House
Grassmarket
Greyfriars Kirk
Royal Museum of Scotland
University
Edinburgh Festival Theatre
George Heriot's School
Laserquest
College
TA Centre
Student Centre
McEwan Hall
University Medical Sch
Eye Hosp
Chalmers Hosp
Royal Infirmary (A & E)
Simpson Memorial Maternity Hospital
Appleton Tower
David Hume Tower
Fire Sta
Schools
Univ Lib
North Meadow Walk
Middle Meadow Walk
a
b
c
1
2
3

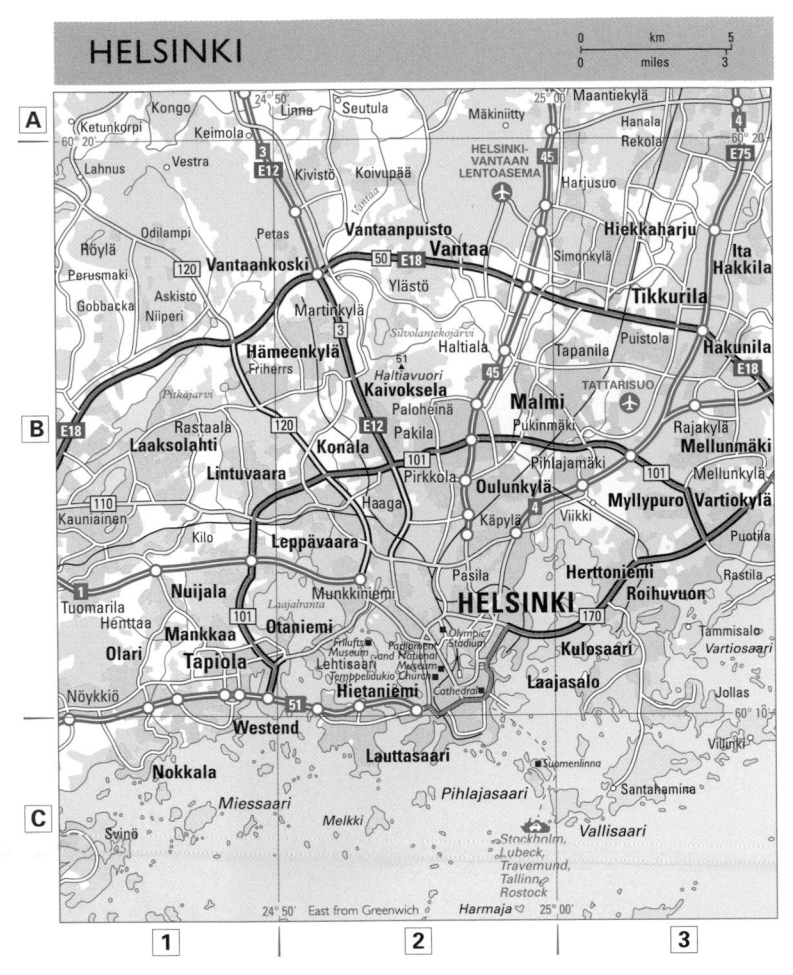
HELSINKI
0 km 5
0 miles 3
Kongo
Ketunkorpi
Keimola
Seutula
Linna
Mäkiniitty
Maantiekylä
Hanala
Rekola
HELSINKI-VANTAAN LENTOASEMA
Lahnus
Vestra
Kivistö
Koivupää
Harjusuo
Vantaanpuisto
Vantaa
Hiekkaharju
Ita Hakkila
Odilampi
Petas
Röylä
Perusmaki
Vantaankoski
Simonkylä
Tikkurila
Askisto
Niiperi
Gobbacka
Martinkylä
Ylästö
Hämeenkylä
Friherrs
Haltiala
Tapanila
Puistola
Hakunila
Kaivoksela
Paloheinä
TATTARISUO
Malmi
Pukinmäki
Rajakylä
Mellunmäki
Rastaala
Laaksolahti
Konala
Pakila
Lintuvaara
Pirkkola
Pihlajamäki
Mellunkylä
Oulunkylä
Myllypuro
Vartiokylä
Kauniainen
Haaga
Käpylä
Viikki
Kilo
Leppävaara
Puotila
Pasila
Herttoniemi
Rastila
Nuijala
Munkkiniemi
HELSINKI
Roihuvuori
Tuomarila
Henttaa
Mankkaa
Otaniemi
Tammisalo
Vartiosaari
Olari
Tapiola
Lehtisaari
Kulosaari
Hietaniemi
Laajasalo
Nöykkiö
Jollas
Westend
Lauttasaari
Villinki
Nokkala
Suomenlinna
Pihlajasaari
Santahamina
Miessaari
Melkki
Svinö
Vallisaari
Stockholm, Lubeck, Travemund, Tallinn, Rostock
Harmaja
East from Greenwich
A
B
C
1
2
3

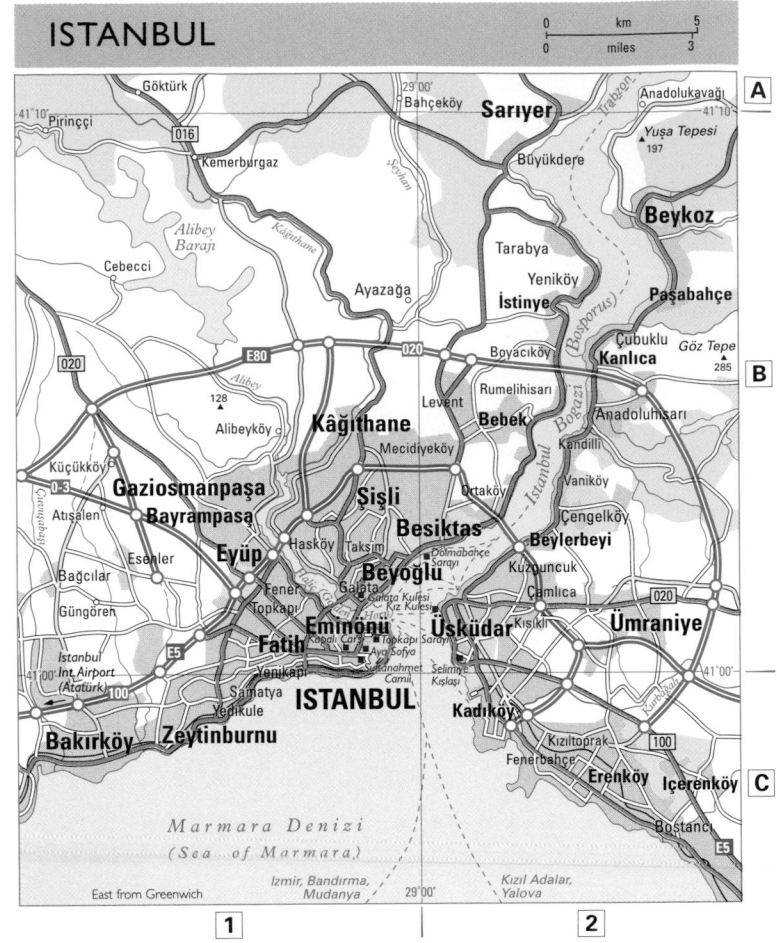
ISTANBUL
0 km 5
0 miles 3
Göktürk
Pirinççi
Bahçeköy
Sarıyer
Anadolukavağı
Yuşa Tepesi 197
Kemerburgaz
Büyükdere
Alibey Barajı
Beykoz
Tarabya
Cebecci
Yeniköy
Ayazağa
İstinye
Paşabahçe
Boyacıköy
Çubuklu
Göz Tepe 285
Kanlıca
Rumelihisarı
Levent
Bebek
Anadoluhisarı
Alibeyköy
Kâğıthane
Kandilli
Mecidiyeköy
Küçükköy
Gaziosmanpaşa
Vaniköy
Şişli
Ortaköy
Atışalen
Bayrampaşa
Besiktas
Çengelköy
Beylerbeyi
Esenler
Eyüp
Hasköy
Taksim
Dolmabahçe Sarayı
Bağcılar
Beyoğlu
Kuzguncuk
Galata
Çamlıca
Güngören
Fener
Galata Kulesi
Kız Kulesi
Topkapı
Eminönü
Üsküdar
Kısıklı
Ümraniye
Fatih
Topkapı Sarayı
Ayasofya
Sultanahmet Camii
Selimiye Kışlası
Istanbul Int. Airport (Atatürk)
Yenikapı
Samatya
Yedikule
ISTANBUL
Kadıköy
Bakırköy
Zeytinburnu
Kızıltoprak
Fenerbahçe
Erenköy
İçerenköy
Marmara Denizi
(Sea of Marmara)
Bostancı
Izmir, Bandırma, Mudanya
Kızıl Adalar, Yalova
East from Greenwich
A
B
C
1
2

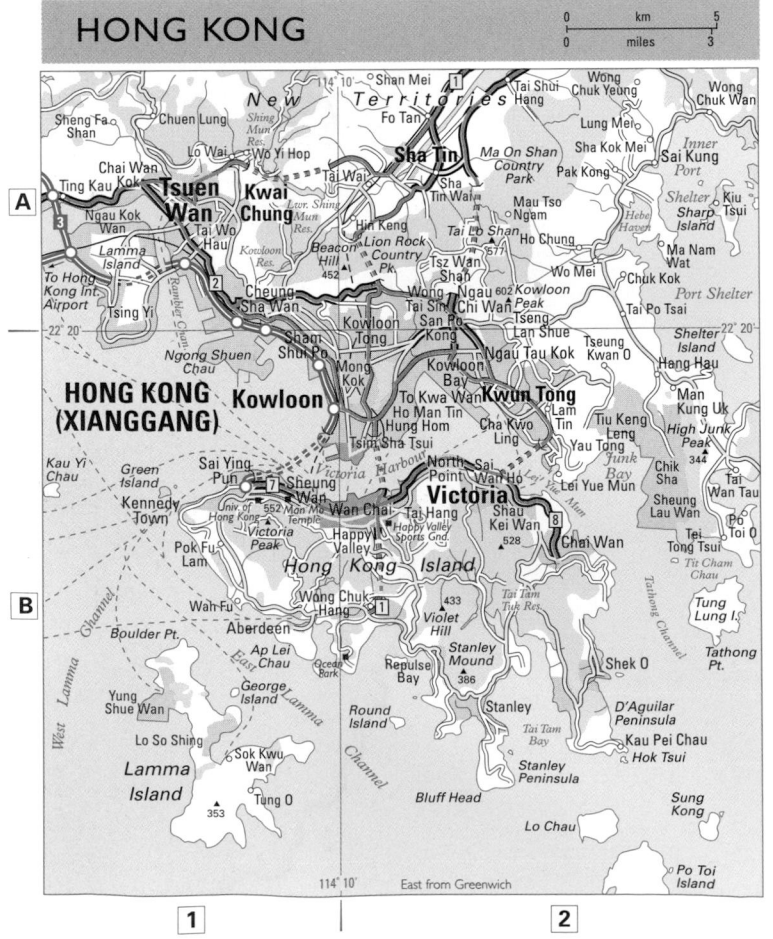
HONG KONG
0 km 5
0 miles 3
Shan Mei
Tai Shui Hang
Wong Chuk Yeung
Wong Chuk Wan
New Territories
Sheung Fa Shan
Chuen Lung
Fo Tan
Lung Mei
Shing Mun Res.
Sha Kok Mei
Inner Sai Kung Port
Chai Wan Kok
Lo Wai
Wo Yi Hop
Sha Tin
Ma On Shan Country Park
Pak Kong
Ting Kau
Tsuen Wan
Kwai Chung
Tai Wai
Sha Tin Wai
Mau Tso Ngam
Kiu Tsui
Sharp Island
Ngau Kok Wan
Tai Wo Hau
Hin Keng
Tai Lo Shan
Ho Chung
Lamma Island
Lion Rock Country Pk.
Ma Nam Wat
To Hong Kong Int. Airport
Beacon Hill 452
Tsz Wan Shan
Wo Mei
Chuk Kok
Tsing Yi
Cheung Sha Wan
Wong Tai Sin
Ngau Chi Wan
Kowloon Peak 602
Port Shelter
Tai Po Tsai
Kowloon Tong
San Po Kong
Tseng Lan Shue
Shelter Island
Ngong Shuen Chau
Sham Shui Po
Ngau Tau Kok
Tseung Kwan O
Hang Hau
Mong Kok
Kowloon Bay
HONG KONG (XIANGGANG)
Kowloon
To Kwa Wan
Kwun Tong
Man Kung Uk
Ho Man Tin
Lam Tin
Hung Hom
Cha Kwo Ling
Tiu Keng Leng
High Junk Peak 344
Tsim Sha Tsui
Yau Tong
Kau Yi Chau
Green Island
Sai Ying Pun
Victoria Harbour
North Point
Sai Wan Ho
Junk Bay
Chik Sha
Tai Wan Tau
Kennedy Town
Sheung Wan
Wan Chai
Victoria
Lei Yue Mun
Sheung Lau Wan
Victoria Peak 552
Tai Hang
Happy Valley
Shau Kei Wan 528
Tei Tong Tsui
Po Toi O
Pok Fu Lam
Hong Kong Island
Chai Wan
Tit Cham Chau
Wong Chuk Hang
Tai Tam Res.
Wah Fu
433 Violet Hill
Tung Lung I.
Boulder Pt.
Aberdeen
Ap Lei Chau
Ocean Park
Stanley Mound 386
Tathong Pt.
Repulse Bay
Shek O
George Island
Yung Shue Wan
Round Island
Stanley
D'Aguilar Peninsula
East Lamma Channel
Tai Tam Bay
Lo So Shing
Kau Pei Chau
Sok Kwu Wan
Hok Tsui
Lamma Island
Stanley Peninsula
353
Tung O
Bluff Head
Sung Kong
Lo Chau
West Lamma Channel
Tathong Channel
Po Toi Island
East from Greenwich
A
B
1
2

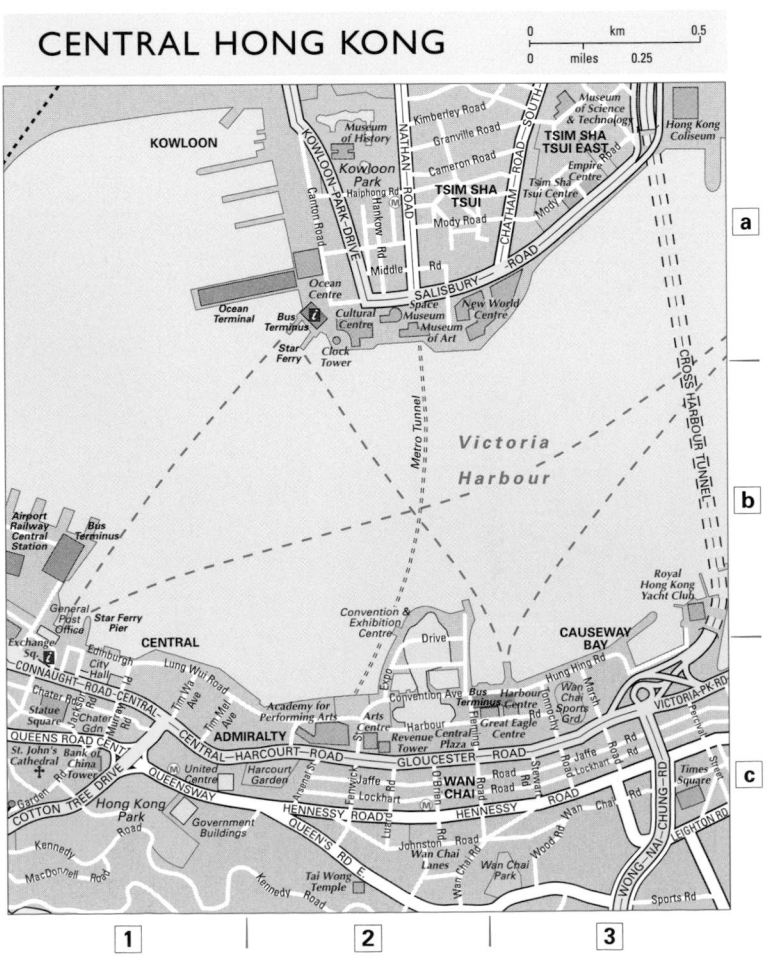
CENTRAL HONG KONG
0 km 0.5
0 miles 0.25
KOWLOON
Museum of History
Kimberley Road
Granville Road
Museum of Science & Technology
Hong Kong Coliseum
TSIM SHA TSUI EAST
Cameron Road
Kowloon Park
Haiphong Rd
TSIM SHA TSUI
Mody Road
Canton Road
KOWLOON PARK DRIVE
NATHAN ROAD
CHATHAM ROAD SOUTH
Middle Rd
SALISBURY ROAD
Ocean Centre
Ocean Terminal
Bus Terminus
Cultural Centre
Space Museum
Museum of Art
New World Centre
Star Ferry
Clock Tower
Metro Tunnel
Victoria Harbour
CROSS HARBOUR TUNNEL
Airport Railway Central Station
Bus Terminus
Royal Hong Kong Yacht Club
General Post Office
Star Ferry Pier
CENTRAL
Convention & Exhibition Centre
CAUSEWAY BAY
Exchange Sq.
City Hall
CONNAUGHT ROAD CENTRAL
Academy for Performing Arts
ADMIRALTY
Arts Centre
Harbour Centre
Great Eagle Centre
Wan Chai Sports Grd.
VICTORIA PK RD
Statue Square
Chater Gdn
QUEENS ROAD CENTRAL
St. John's Cathedral
Bank of China Tower
HARCOURT ROAD
GLOUCESTER ROAD
Revenue Tower
Central Plaza
WAN CHAI
Times Square
QUEENSWAY
United Centre
Harcourt Garden
Jaffe Road
Lockhart Road
HENNESSY ROAD
Hong Kong Park
COTTON TREE DRIVE
Government Buildings
QUEEN'S RD E.
Johnston Road
Wan Chai Lanes
Wan Chai Park
Tai Wong Temple
Kennedy Road
MacDonnell Road
WONG NAI CHUNG RD
Sports Rd
a
b
c
1
2
3

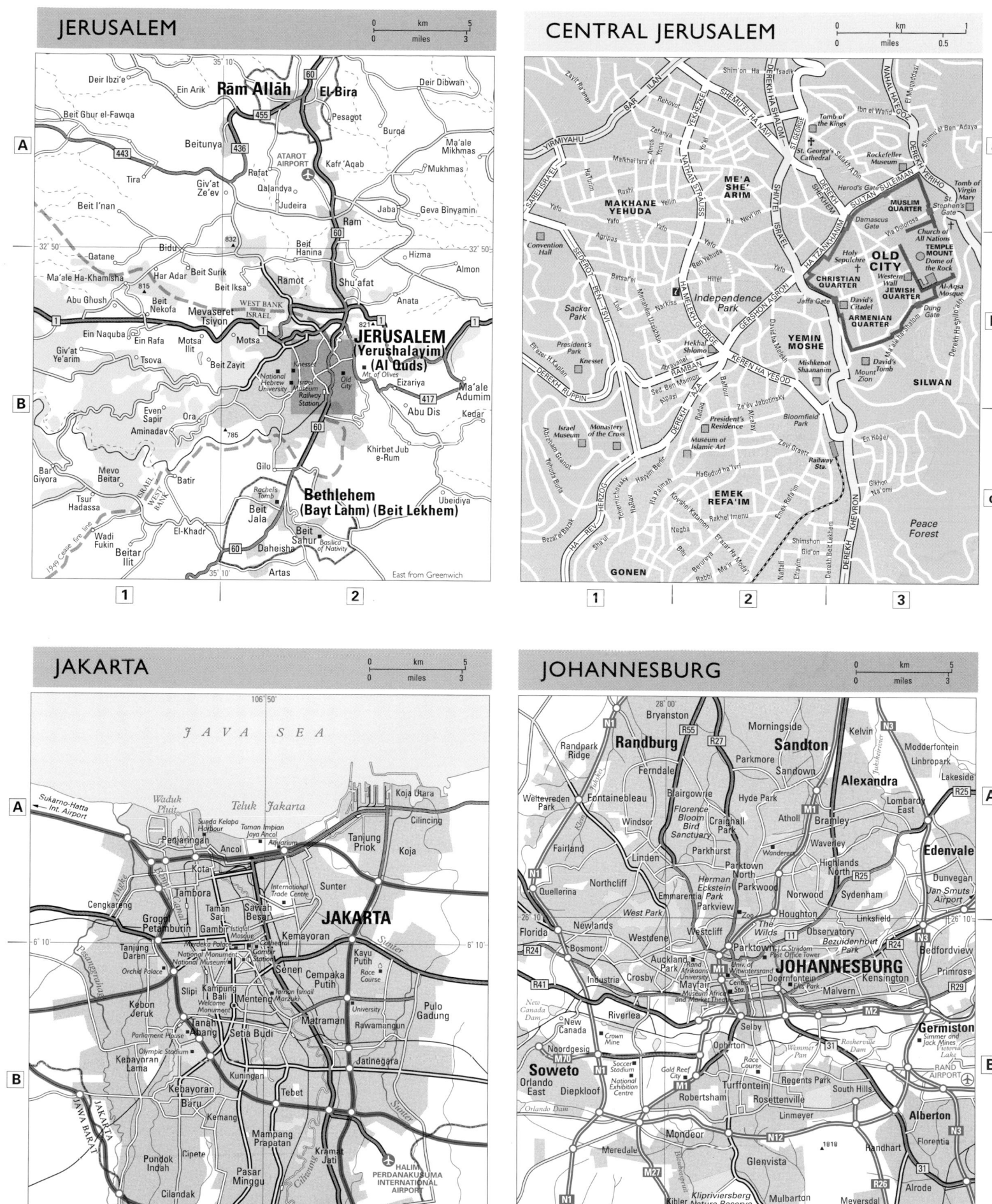
JERUSALEM
0 km 5
0 miles 3
Deir Ibzi'e
Ein Arik
Rām Allāh
El-Bira
Deir Dibwan
Beit Ghur el-Fawqa
Pesagot
Burqa
Beitunya
Ma'ale Mikhmas
ATAROT AIRPORT
Kafr 'Aqab
Mukhmas
Tira
Giv'at Ze'ev
Rafat
Qalandya
Judeira
Beit I'nan
Jaba
Geva Binyamin
Ram
Bidu
Beit Hanina
Hizma
Qatane
Almon
Ma'ale Ha-Khamisha
Har Adar
Beit Surik
Beit Iksa
Ramot
Shu'afat
Abu Ghosh
Beit Nekofa
Mevaseret Tsiyon
WEST BANK
ISRAEL
Anata
Ein Naquba
Ein Rafa
Motsa Ilit
Motsa
JERUSALEM
(Yerushalayim)
(Al Quds)
Giv'at Ye'arim
Tsova
Beit Zayit
Knesset
National Hebrew University
Israel Museum
Railway Station
Old City
Mt. of Olives
Eizariya
Ma'ale Adumim
Even Sapir
Ora
Abu Dis
Kedar
Aminadav
Khirbet Jub e-Rum
Gilo
Bar Giyora
Mevo Beitar
Batir
Rachel's Tomb
Bethlehem
(Bayt Lahm) (Beit Lekhem)
Tsur Hadassa
Beit Jala
Ubeidiya
1949 Cease-fire line
Wadi Fukin
El-Khadr
Beitar Illit
Beit Sahur
Basilica of Nativity
Daheisha
Artas
East from Greenwich
CENTRAL JERUSALEM
0 km 1
0 miles 0.5
BAR ILAN
YIRMIYAHU
SHEMU'EL HA NAVI
DEREKH HA SHALOM
Tomb of the Kings
St. George's Cathedral
Rockefeller Museum
NAHAL HA EGOZ
DEREKH YERIHO
ME'A SHE' ARIM
MAKHANE YEHUDA
Herod's Gate
SULTAN SULEIMAN
MUSLIM QUARTER
Tomb of Virgin Mary
St. Stephen's Gate
Damascus Gate
Via Dolorosa
Church of All Nations
Convention Hall
Holy Sepulchre
OLD CITY
TEMPLE MOUNT
Dome of the Rock
CHRISTIAN QUARTER
Western Wall
JEWISH QUARTER
Al-Aqsa Mosque
Independence Park
Jaffa Gate
David's Citadel
ARMENIAN QUARTER
Dung Gate
Sacker Park
President's Park
Knesset
YEMIN MOSHE
Mishkenot Shaananim
Mount Zion
David's Tomb
SILWAN
DEREKH RUPPIN
RAMBAN
KEREN HA YESOD
Israel Museum
Monastery of the Cross
President's Residence
Bloomfield Park
Museum of Islamic Art
Railway Sta.
EMEK REFA'IM
Peace Forest
HERZOG
DEREKH KHEVRON
GONEN
JAKARTA
0 km 5
0 miles 3
JAVA SEA
Sukarno-Hatta Int. Airport
Waduk Pluit
Teluk Jakarta
Koja Utara
Sunda Kelapa Harbour
Taman Impian Jaya Ancol
Aquarium
Cilincing
Penjaringan
Ancol
Tanjung Priok
Koja
Kota
International Trade Centre
Sunter
Cengkareng
Tambora
Taman Sari
Sawah Besar
JAKARTA
Grogol Petamburin
Gambir
Istiqlal Mosque
Cathedral
Kemayoran
Tanjung Duren
Merdeka Palace
National Monument
National Museum
Gambir Station
Kayu Putih
Orchid Palace
Senen
Cempaka Putih
Race Course
Slipi
Kampung Bali
Menteng
Taman Ismail Marzuki
Welcome Monument
Kebon Jeruk
University
Pulo Gadung
Tanah Abang
Parliament House
Setia Budi
Matraman
Rawamangun
Olympic Stadium
Kebayoran Lama
Jatinegara
Kuningan
Kebayoran Baru
Tebet
Kemang
Mampang Prapatan
Kramat Jati
HALIM PERDANAKUSUMA INTERNATIONAL AIRPORT
Pondok Indah
Cipete
Pasar Minggu
JAKARTA
JAWA BARAT
Cilandak
East from Greenwich
JOHANNESBURG
0 km 5
0 miles 3
Bryanston
Randpark Ridge
Randburg
Morningside
Sandton
Kelvin
Modderfontein
Linbropark
Parkmore
Sandown
Lakeside
Ferndale
Alexandra
Weltevreden Park
Fontainebleau
Blairgowrie
Hyde Park
Lombardy East
Florence Bloem Bird Sanctuary
Craighall Park
Atholl
Bramley
Windsor
Fairland
Parkhurst
Wanderers
Waverley
Edenvale
Linden
Parktown North
Highlands North
Northcliff
Herman Eckstein Park
Parkwood
Dunvegan
Quellerina
Emmarentia
Parkview
Norwood
Sydenham
Jan Smuts Airport
Zoo
Houghton
West Park
The Wilds
Linksfield
Florida
Newlands
Westdene
Westcliff
Observatory
Bezuidenhout Park
Bosmont
Parktown
J.G. Strijdom Post Office Tower
Bedfordview
Auckland Park
Rand Afrikaans University
Univ. of Witwatersrand
JOHANNESBURG
Industria
Crosby
Mayfair
Doornfontein
Ellis Park
Kensington
Primrose
Museum Africa and Market Theatre
Malvern
New Canada Dam
Riverlea
New Canada
Selby
Germiston
Crown Mine
Noordgesig
Ophirton
Wemmer Pan
Rosherville Dam
Simmer and Jack Mines
Victoria Lake
Soweto
Soccer Stadium
Gold Reef City
Race Course
RAND AIRPORT
Orlando East
Diepkloof
National Exhibition Centre
Turffontein
Regents Park
South Hills
Robertsham
Rosettenville
Orlando Dam
Linmeyer
Alberton
Mondeor
Meredale
Florentia
Randhart
Glenvista
Kibler Park
Klipriviersberg Nature Reserve
Mulbarton
Meyersdal
Alrode
East from Greenwich

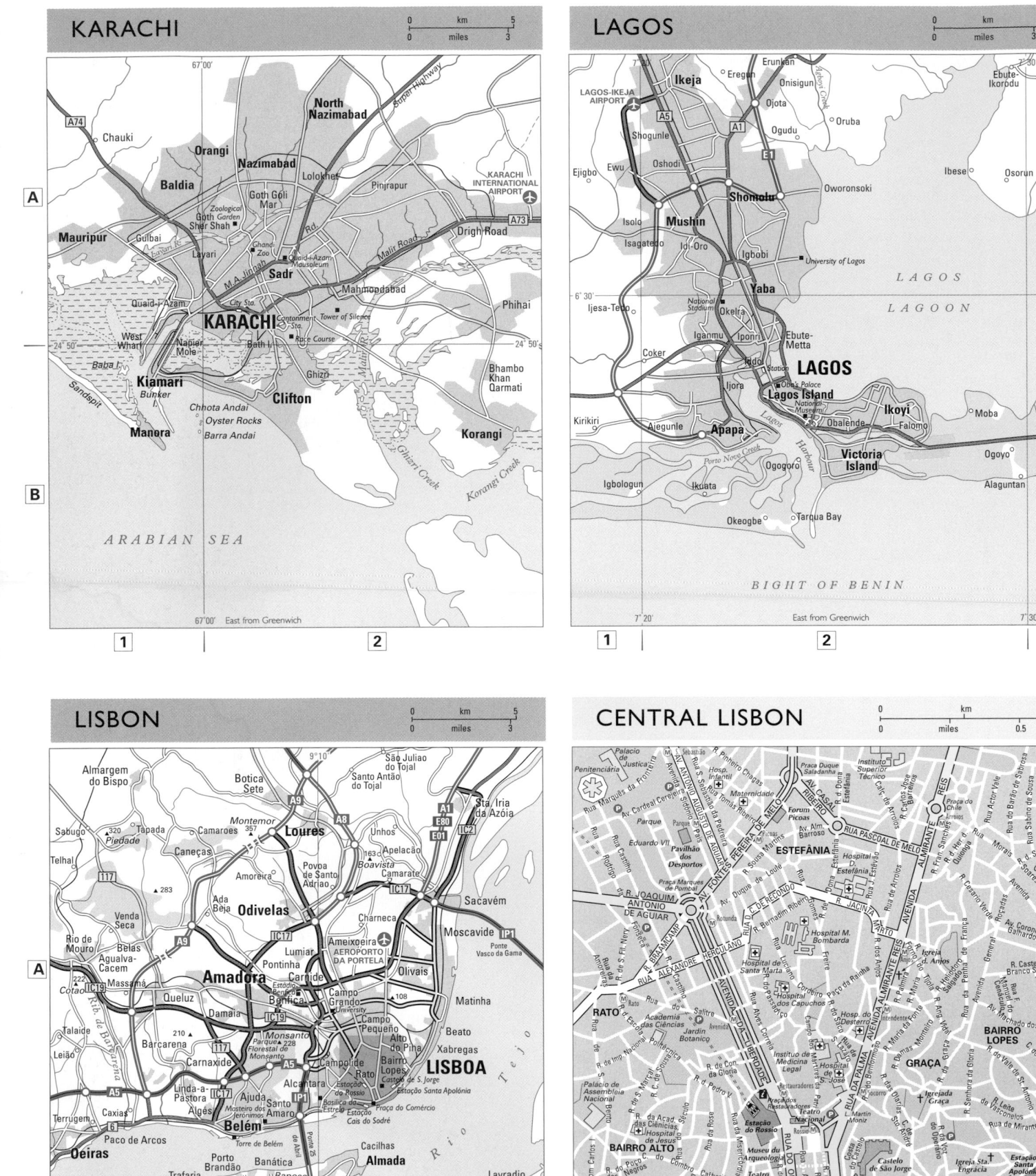

KARACHI

km 5 / miles 3

North Nazimabad, Orangi, Nazimabad, Baldia, Chauki, Mauripur, Gulbai, Goth Göli Mar, Zoological Garden, Goth Garden, Sher Shah, Layari, Lolokhet, Pinjrapur, Sadr, Ghand Zoo, Quaid-i-Azam Mausoleum, Mahmoodabad, Phihai, Malir Road, Drigh Road, City Sta., Cantonment Sta., Tower of Silence, Race Course, KARACHI, Ghizri, Bhambo Khan Qarmati, West Wharf, Napier Mole, Bath I., Baba I., Quaid-i-Azam, Kiamari, Bunker, Chhota Andai, Oyster Rocks, Barra Andai, Clifton, Korangi, Manora, Ghizri Creek, Korangi Creek, Sandspit, ARABIAN SEA

KARACHI INTERNATIONAL AIRPORT, A74, A73, Super Highway, M.A. Jinnah, 67°00', 24°50', 24°50', East from Greenwich

LAGOS

km 5 / miles 3

Erunkan, Ebute-Ikorodu, Ikeja, Eregun, Onisigun, Achori Creek, LAGOS-IKEJA AIRPORT, Ojota, Oruba, Shogunle, Ogudu, Ewu, Oshodi, Ibese, Osorun, Ejigbo, Isolo, Idi-Oro, Igbobi, University of Lagos, Shomolu, Ofin, Mushin, Oworonsoki, Isagatedo, Yaba, LAGOS LAGOON, Ijesa-Tedo, National Stadium, Okefira, Coker, Iganmu, Iponri, Ebute-Metta, Obi's Palace, Iddo, Station, LAGOS, Ijora, Lagos Island, National Museum, Ikoyi, Kirikiri, Aiegunle, Obalende, Falomo, Moba, Apapa, Harbour, Victoria Island, Ogoyo, Porto Novo Creek, Ogogoro, Igbologun, Ikuata, Alaguntan, Okeogbe, Tarqua Bay, BIGHT OF BENIN

A5, A1, E1, 7°30', 6°30', 6°30', 7°20', 7°30', East from Greenwich

LISBON

km 5 / miles 3

Almargem do Bispo, São Julião do Tojal, Santo Antão do Tojal, Botica Sete, Sta. Iria da Azóia, Sabugo, Montemor 357, Camaroes, Loures, Unhos, Apelação, Telhal, Piedade, Tapada, Caneças, Amoreira, Póvoa de Santo Adrião, Camarate, Boavista, Venda Seca, Ada Beja, Odivelas, Charneca, Moscavide, Sacavém, Rio de Mouro, Belas, Lumiar, Pontinha, Ameixoeira, AEROPORTO DA PORTELA, Ponte Vasco da Gama, Aguals-Cacem, Massamá, Carnide, Campo Grande, Olivais, Cotão, Amadora, Queluz, Benfica, Carnide, University, Matinha, Damaia, Monsanto, Campo Pequeno, Beato, Barcarena, Parque Florestal de Monsanto, Campolide, Alto do Pina, Xabregas, Carnaxide, A5, Rato, Bairro Lopes, LISBOA, Linda-a-Pastora, Ajuda, Alcântara, Castelo de S. Jorge, Algés, Santo Amaro, Estação do Rossio, Estação Santa Apolónia, Belém, Mosteiro dos Jerónimos, Praça do Comércio, Torre de Belém, Cais do Sodré, Ponte 25 de Abril, Paco de Arcos, Porto Brandão, Cacilhas, Oeiras, Trafaria, Banática, Almada, Lavradio, Terrugem, Caxias, Raposo, Cova de Piedade, Caparica, Bugio, Barreiro, Quinta de Santo António, Costa da Caparica, Sobreda, Feijó, Capuchos, Amora, Seixal, Santo André, Charneca, Cruz de Pau, Palhais, Arrentela, Rio Tejo, Corroa

A9, A8, A1, E80, E01, IC2, IC17, IP1, IC19, A5, A2, IP1, IP21, 117, 222, 320, 283, 210, 228, 125, 108, 163, 38°40', 38°40', 9°10', 9°10', West from Greenwich

CENTRAL LISBON

km 1 / miles 0.5

Palácio da Justiça, Penitenciária, Pinheiro Chaves, Praça Duque Saladanha, Instituto Superior Técnico, Rua Marquês da Fronteira, Hosp. Infantil, Parque, Maternidade, Fórum Picoas, Praça do Chile, Eduardo VII, Pavilhão dos Desportos, ESTEFÂNIA, Cemitério Alto e João, RATO, Academia das Ciências, Jardim Botânico, Hospital M. Bombarda, Hospital de Santa Marta, Instituto de Medicina Legal, BAIRRO LOPES, Palácio de Assembleia Nacional, GRAÇA, Igreja da Graça, BAIRRO ALTO, Museu do Arqueologia, Teatro San Carlos, Biblioteca Nacional, Museu de Arte Decorativas, Castelo de São Jorge, Igreja Sta. Engrácia, Estação Santa Apolónia, Sé Catedral, Museu Antoniano, ALFAMA, Museu Militar, BAIXA, Estação Cais do Sodré, Dom José I, Estação Fluvial, Rio Tejo

AV. VINTE E QUATRO DE JULHO, RUA DO ARSENAL, AV. RIBEIRA DAS NAUS, R. DA ALFÂNDEGA, DOM HENRIQUE

LONDON

0 km 5
0 miles 3

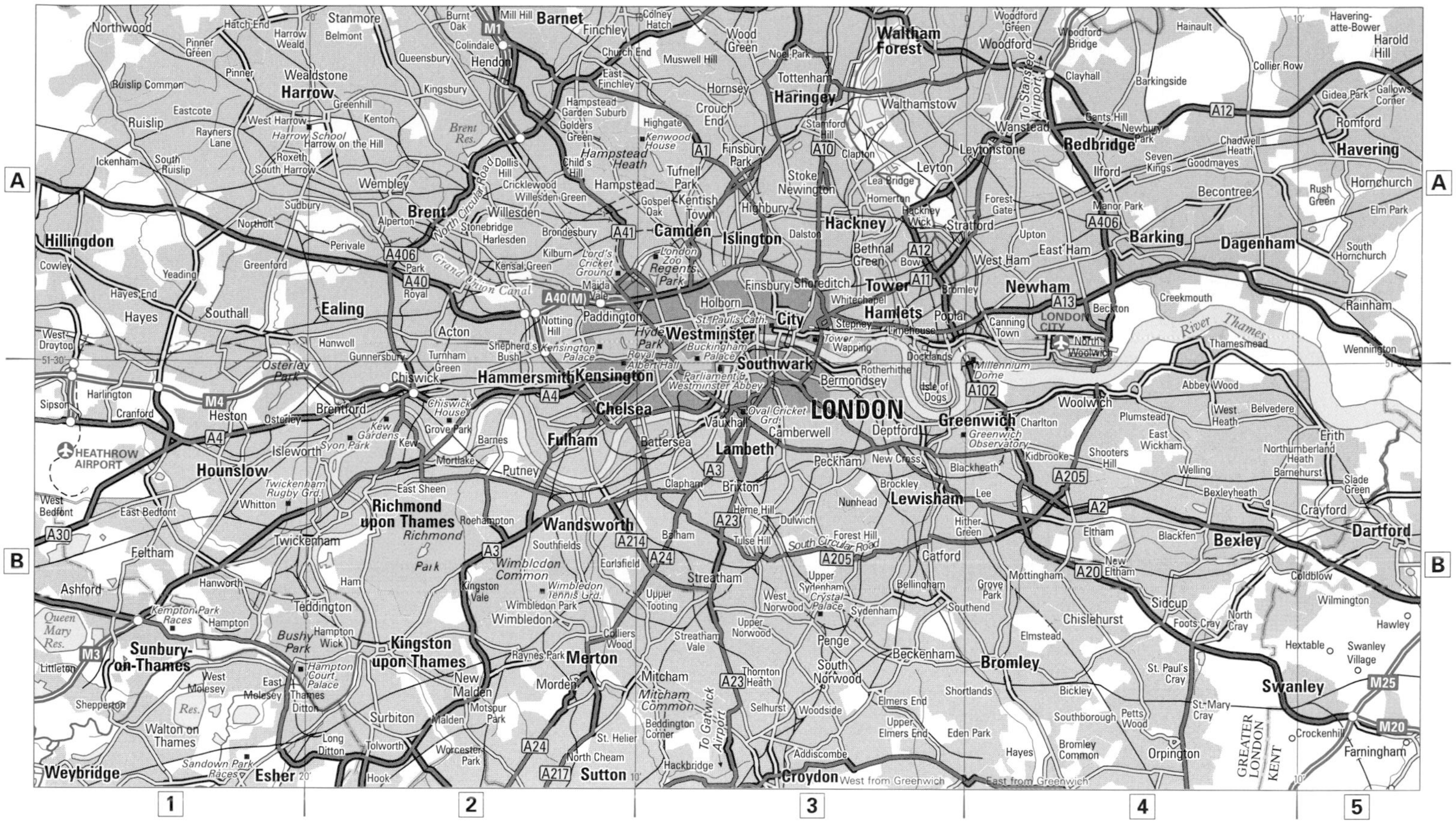

Northwood, Stanmore, Mill Hill, Barnet, Finchley, Colney Hatch, Woodford Green, Woodford, Woodford Bridge, Hainault, Havering-atte-Bower, Harold Hill, Collier Row
Pinner Green, Belmont, Burnt Oak, Church End, Muswell Hill, Wood Green, Tottenham, Chadwell Heath, Gidea Park, Romford, Gallows Corner
Ruislip Common, Eastcote, Hatch End, Harrow Weald, Queensbury, Colindale, Hendon, Hampstead Garden Suburb, Golders Green, Crouch End, Hornsey, Finsbury Park, Stoke Newington, Clapton, Leyton, Leytonstone, Wanstead, Newbury Park, Goodmayes, Elm Park, Hornchurch
Harrow, Wealdstone, Greenhill, Kenton, Kingsbury, Kentish Town, Tufnell Park, Highbury, Hackney Wick, Stratford, Upton, Manor Park, East Ham, Barkingside, Becontree
Hillingdon, Cowley, Yeading, Greenford, Perivale, Alperton, Wembley, Willesden, Kensal Green, Camden, Islington, Dalston, Homerton, West Ham, Ilford, Dagenham, South Hornchurch, Rush Green
Brent, Acton, Paddington, Holborn, St Paul's Cath., City, Shoreditch, Bethnal Green, Tower Hamlets, Poplar, Canning Town, London City, Beckton, Creekmouth, Rainham, Wennington
Ealing, Hanwell, Chiswick, Hammersmith, Kensington, Westminster, Buckingham Palace, Parliament, Westminster Abbey, Southwark, Bermondsey, Rotherhithe, Wapping, Isle of Dogs, Docklands, Millennium Dome, North Woolwich, Thamesmead
Heathrow Airport, Hounslow, Heston, Osterley, Isleworth, Brentford, Kew Gardens, Syon Park, Chelsea, Fulham, Battersea, Vauxhall, Lambeth, Camberwell, LONDON, Deptford, Greenwich, Greenwich Observatory, Charlton, Woolwich, Plumstead, Abbey Wood, West Heath, Belvedere, Erith
Hatton, Twickenham Rugby Grd., Richmond upon Thames, Richmond Park, Putney, Wandsworth, Clapham, Brixton, Herne Hill, Dulwich, Peckham, New Cross, Lewisham, Brockley, Blackheath, Kidbrooke, Eltham, Welling, Bexleyheath, Barnehurst, Northumberland Heath, Slade Green, Crayford
Feltham, Ashford, Hanworth, Teddington, Bushy Park, Hampton Wick, Wimbledon Common, Wimbledon Park, Earlsfield, Tooting, Upper Tooting, Streatham, Balham, Tulse Hill, Forest Hill, South Sydenham, Sydenham, Bellingham, Grove Park, Mottingham, New Eltham, Sidcup, Foots Cray, Chislehurst, Coldblow, Wilmington, Dartford, Bexley, Hawley
Queen Mary Res., Kempton Park Races, Hampton, East Molesey, Kingston Vale, New Malden, Motspur Park, Mitcham, Mitcham Common, Streatham Vale, Norbury, Upper Norwood, Crystal Palace, Penge, Beckenham, Elmstead, St Paul's Cray, Swanley Village, Swanley, M25
Sunbury-on-Thames, West Molesey, Thames Ditton, Long Ditton, Kingston upon Thames, Surbiton, Tolworth, Malden, Worcester Park, Morden, Merton, North Cheam, Sutton, St Helier, Beddington Corner, Thornton Heath, South Norwood, Woodside, Shortlands, Bickley, Petts Wood, Southborough, St Mary Cray, Orpington, Greater London, Kent, Crockenhill, Farningham, M20
Weybridge, Walton on Thames, Shepperton, Sandown Park Races, Esher, Hook, Chessington, A217, Croydon, Hackbridge, Selsdon, Addiscombe, To Gatwick Airport, Hayes, Eden Park, Elmers End, Upper Elmers End, Bromley Common, Bromley

West from Greenwich | East from Greenwich

CENTRAL LONDON

0 km 2
0 miles 1

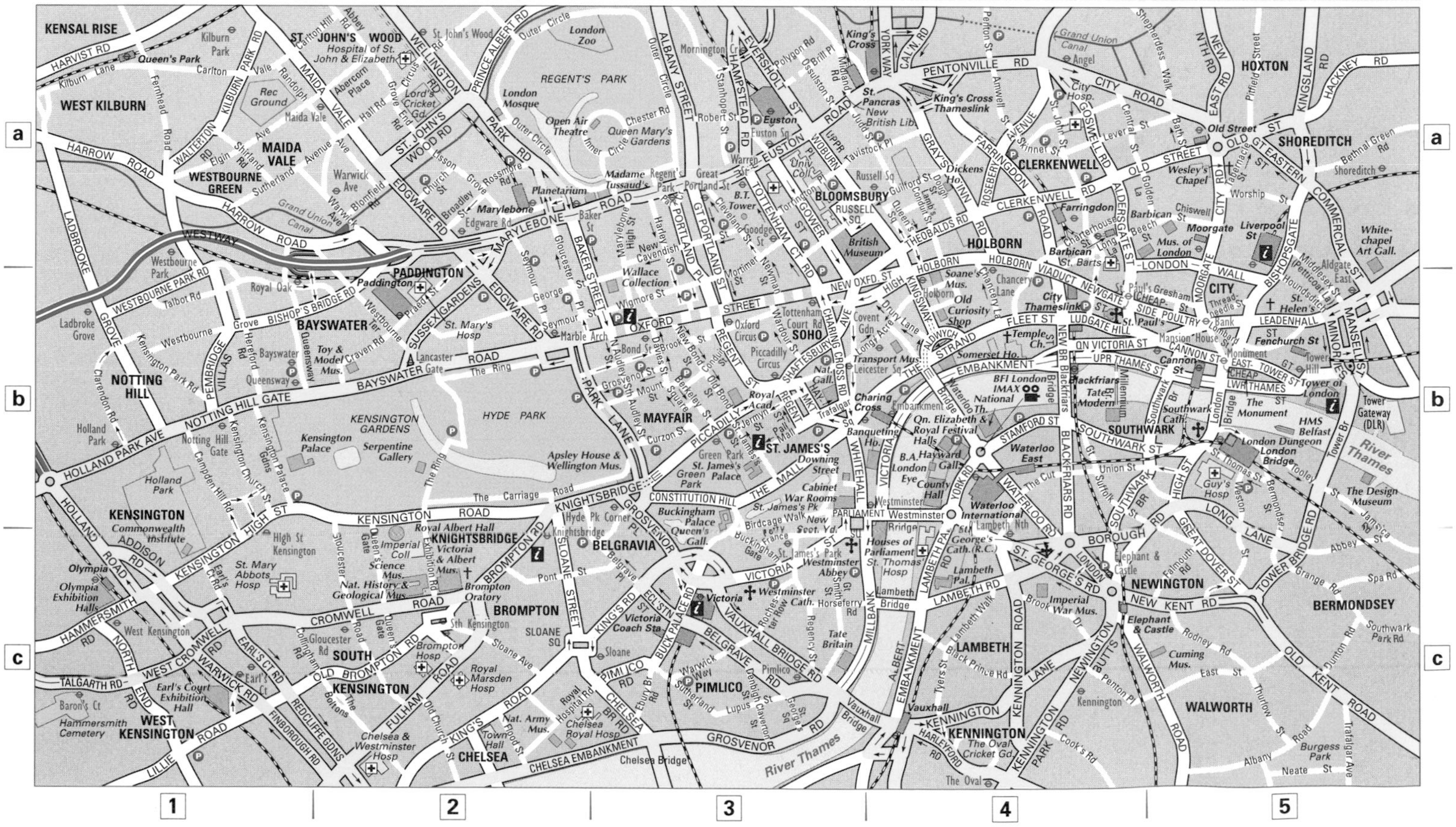

KENSAL RISE, ST. JOHN'S WOOD, London Zoo, King's Cross, HOXTON, SHOREDITCH
WEST KILBURN, Queen's Park, MAIDA VALE, REGENT'S PARK, St Pancras, King's Cross Thameslink, British Library, CLERKENWELL
WESTBOURNE GREEN, London Mosque, Queen Mary's Gardens, Open Air Theatre, Madame Tussaud's, Planetarium, Euston, BLOOMSBURY, Russell Sq., British Museum, HOLBORN, Barbican, Mus. of London, CITY, Whitechapel Art Gall.
PADDINGTON, Marylebone, Wallace Collection, Oxford Circus, SOHO, Covent Garden, Transport Mus., St Paul's, Liverpool St, Aldgate, LEADENHALL ST
BAYSWATER, NOTTING HILL, Kensington Gardens, Kensington Palace, Serpentine Gallery, HYDE PARK, MAYFAIR, PICCADILLY, ST. JAMES'S, Charing Cross, Royal Festival Halls, London Eye, SOUTHWARK, Tate Modern, The Monument, Tower of London, HMS Belfast, London Dungeon, London Bridge, Tower Bridge, River Thames, The Design Museum
HOLLAND PARK, Holland House, KENSINGTON, Royal Albert Hall, KNIGHTSBRIDGE, BELGRAVIA, Buckingham Palace, Queen's Gall., Houses of Parliament, Westminster Abbey, Westminster Cath., Lambeth Palace, Imperial War Mus., NEWINGTON, BERMONDSEY
Olympia, Commonwealth Institute, Nat. History Mus., Geological Mus., Nat. History Mus., V. & A. Mus., Science Mus., BROMPTON, SOUTH KENSINGTON, Victoria, Victoria Coach Sta., PIMLICO, Tate Britain, LAMBETH, The Oval Cricket Ground, Elephant & Castle, WALWORTH
WEST KENSINGTON, Earl's Court Exhibition Hall, Baron's Ct, Hammersmith Cemetery, Brompton Cemetery, CHELSEA, Chelsea & Westminster Hosp., Chelsea Royal Hosp., CHELSEA EMBANKMENT, Chelsea Bridge, VAUXHALL, KENNINGTON, The Oval, Burgess Park

LOS ANGELES

km 5
miles 3

Tarzana • 118° 30' • Sepulveda Flood Control Basin • Van Nuys • San Fernando Valley • 170 • North Hollywood • Burbank • Verdugo Mts. • San Rafael Hills • Altadena • San Gabriel Mts. • 34° 10' • **A**

Encino • 101 • 134 • Disney Studios • 5 • Flint Peak 575 • Rose Bowl • Pasadena • 210 • Sierra Madre • Colorado Fwy. • Monrovia

216 • Sherman Oaks • Studio City • C.B.S. Fox Studios • Warner Bros. Studios • Cahuenga Peak 555 • Glendale • 134 • Eagle Rock • California Inst. of Tech. • Arcadia

Encino Reservoir • 405 • Universal Studios • Griffith Park • Zoo • Golden State Fwy. • Glendale Galleria • 2 • South Pasadena • 110 • San Marino • 19 • Temple City

Stone Canyon Reservoir • Santa Monica Mts. • Beverly Glen • Hollywood Lake • Hollywood Bowl • Hollywood • Highland Park • Garvanza • El Sereno • Pasadena Fwy. • San Gabriel

459 • Beverly Hills • Franklin Reservoir • Hollywood Blvd. • Mann's Chinese Theatre • Sunset Blvd. • Silver Lake Reservoir • Southwest Museum • Alhambra • Rosemead • 10

Bel Air • West Hollywood • Santa Monica Blvd. • Paramount Studios • 2 • Dodger Stadium • Lincoln Heights • California State Univ. • Monterey Park • San Bernardino Fwy. • El Monte • **B**

University of California Los Angeles • Westwood Village • L.A. County Art Museum • Hollywood Fwy. • 110 • LOS ANGELES • Union Sta. • Civic Center • South San Gabriel • South El Monte • 710 • Whittier Narrows

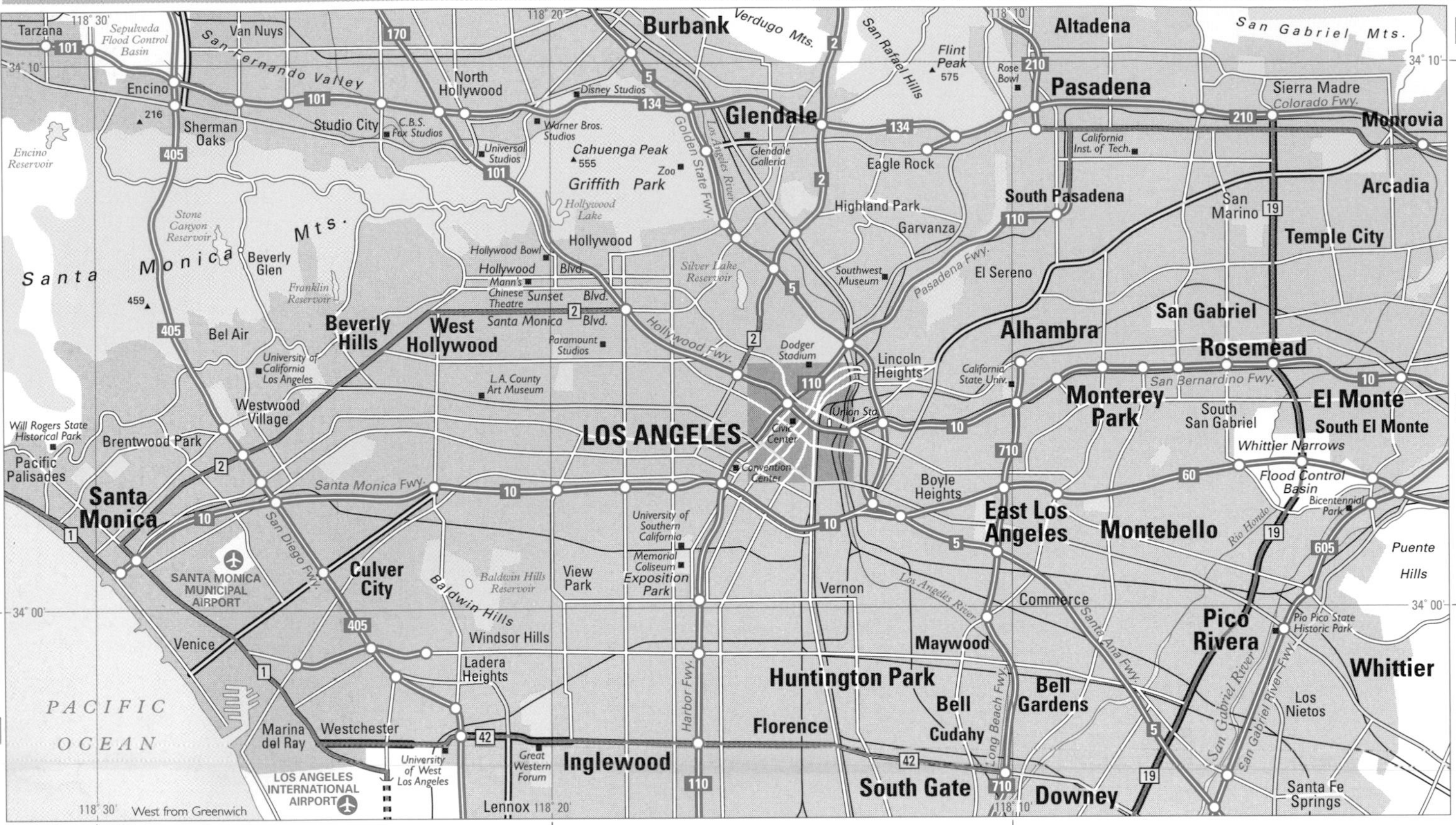

Will Rogers State Historical Park • Brentwood Park • 2 • Convention Center • Boyle Heights • 710 • 60 • Flood Control Basin • Bicentennial Park

Pacific Palisades • Santa Monica • 10 • Santa Monica Fwy. • University of Southern California • 10 • East Los Angeles • Montebello • Rio Hondo • 19 • Puente Hills • 34° 00'

San Diego Fwy. • Culver City • Memorial Coliseum Exposition Park • Los Angeles River • Commerce • Santa Ana Fwy. • 605 • Pio Pico State Historic Park

405 • Baldwin Hills Reservoir • View Park • Vernon • 5 • Pico Rivera • Whittier • **B**

Venice • Baldwin Hills • Windsor Hills • Maywood • Commerce • Los Nietos • 34° 00'

Marina del Ray • Westchester • Ladera Heights • 1 • Huntington Park • Bell • Bell Gardens • 5 • Santa Fe Springs • **C**

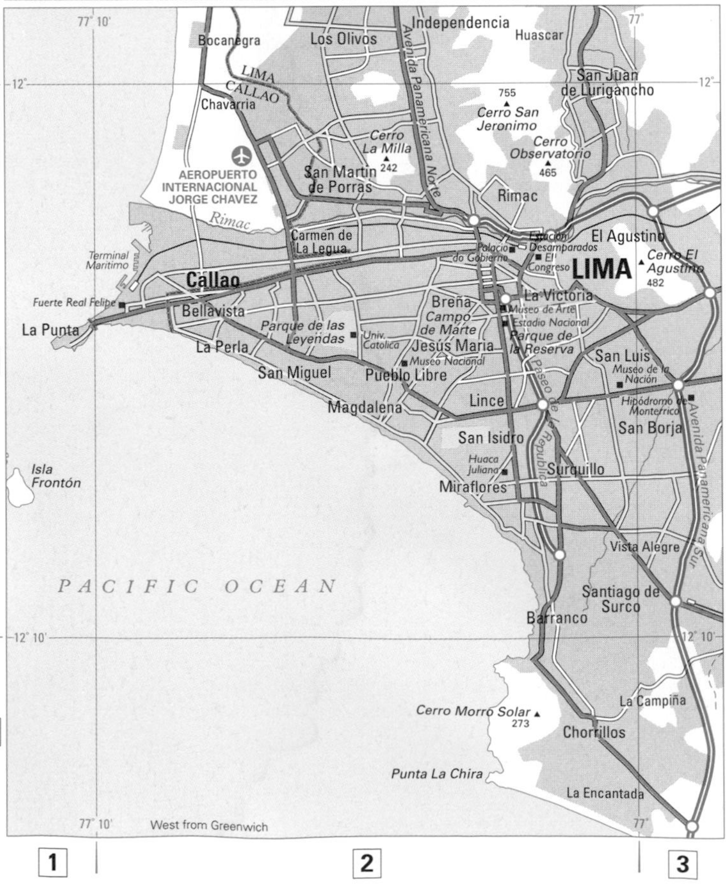

PACIFIC OCEAN • 42 • Great Western Forum • Florence • Cudahy • Long Beach Fwy.

University of West Los Angeles • Inglewood • 110 • South Gate • 710 • Downey • 19 • 118° 10'

LOS ANGELES INTERNATIONAL AIRPORT • Lennox • 118° 20' • 42 • 118° 30' West from Greenwich

1 • 2 • 3 • 4

LIMA

km 5
miles 3

Bocanegra • Los Olivos • Independencia • Huascar • San Gabriel Mts. • **A**

LIMA CALLAO • Chavarria • Avenida Panamericana Norte • San Juan de Lurigancho • 12° • 77°

Cerro La Milla 242 • Cerro San Jeronimo 755 • Cerro Observatorio 465

AEROPUERTO INTERNACIONAL JORGE CHAVEZ • San Martin de Porras • Rimac • Rimac

Terminal Maritimo • Carmen de La Legua • Estación Desamparados • Palacio de Gobierno • El Congreso • El Agustino • Cerro El Agustino 482

Callao • LIMA • La Victoria • Museo de Arte

Fuerte Real Felipe • Bellavista • Breña • Campo de Marte • Estadio Nacional • Museo Nacional • San Luis • **B**

La Punta • La Perla • Parque de las Leyendas • Univ. Catolica • Jesús Maria • Parque de la Reserva • Museo de la Nación • San Borja

San Miguel • Pueblo Libre • Lince • Huaca Juliana • Hipódromo de Monterrico

Magdalena • San Isidro • Avenida Panamericana Sur

Isla Frontón • Miraflores • Surquillo

PACIFIC OCEAN • Vista Alegre • 12° 10'

Santiago de Surco

Barranco

Cerro Morro Solar 273 • La Campiña • **C**

Chorrillos

Punta La Chira • La Encantada

77° 10' • West from Greenwich • 77°

1 • 2 • 3

CENTRAL LOS ANGELES

km 1
miles 0.5

Echo Park Ave • Elysian Park Ave • Sunset Boulevard • Dodger Stadium • Elysian Park • **a**

Echo Park Lake • W. Kensington Rd • Lilac Terr. • Stadium Way • Broadway • Ridgeway • ECHO PARK • Figueroa • Stadium Way • Bishop Rd

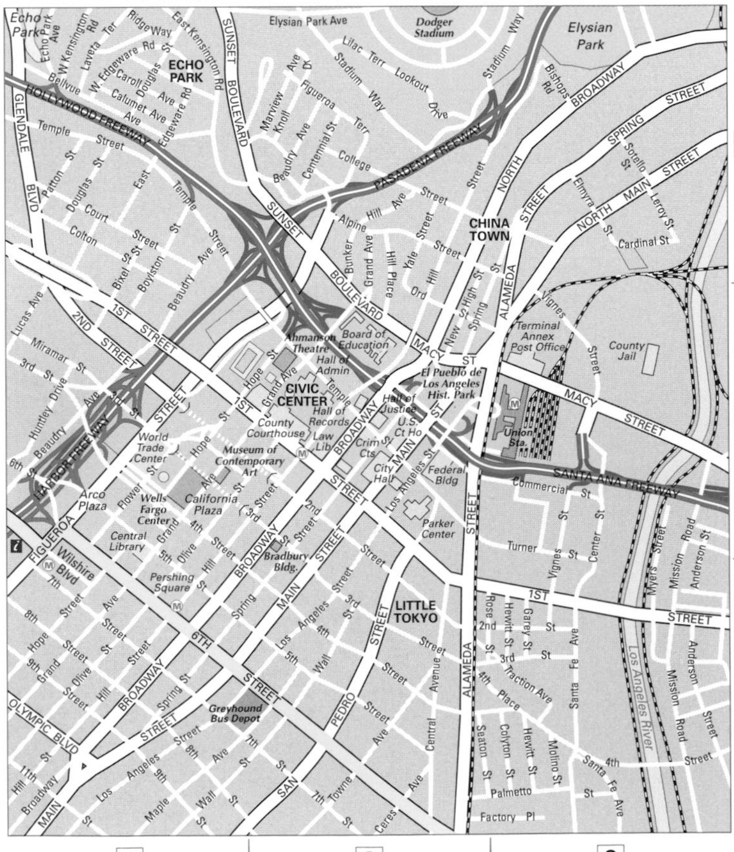

Glendale Blvd • Douglas • Temple • College • Pasadena Freeway • North Spring Street • North Main Street • a

Hollywood Freeway • Bunker Hill Ave • Alpine • Yale • Ord • CHINA TOWN • Cardinal St. • Alameda

Temple • Colton • Boylston • Figueroa • Sunset Boulevard • New High • Spring • Broadway • Terminal Annex Post Office

Ammann Theatre • Board of Education • El Pueblo de Los Angeles Hist. Park • County Jail

1st Street • 2nd Street • Harbor Freeway • Hope • Grand Ave • Hill • Civic Center • Hall of Justice • Hall of Records • U.S. Ct Ho • Union Sta. • Santa Ana Freeway • Macy St. • b

World Trade Center • County Courthouse • Law Library • Crim Cts • Federal Bldg • Commercial

Arco Plaza • Wells Fargo Center • Museum of Contemporary Art • California Plaza • City Hall • Parker Center • Turner • Vignes • Center St.

Figueroa St. • Central Library • 5th Street • 4th • Bradbury Bldg • Pershing Square • Broadway • Main • Spring • Los Angeles • 1st • Little Tokyo • Rose • Alameda • San Pedro • c

Wilshire Blvd • 7th • 6th Street • 8th • LITTLE TOKYO • 2nd • 3rd • Hewitt • Santa Fe • Traction Ave

Olympic Blvd • Hope • Olive • Broadway • Main • San Pedro • 7th • Towne • Central Ave • Palmetto • Los Angeles River

11th • Broadway • Main • Los Angeles • Wall • Stanford • Colyton • Factory Pl • Mission Rd • Anderson St.

1 • 2 • 3

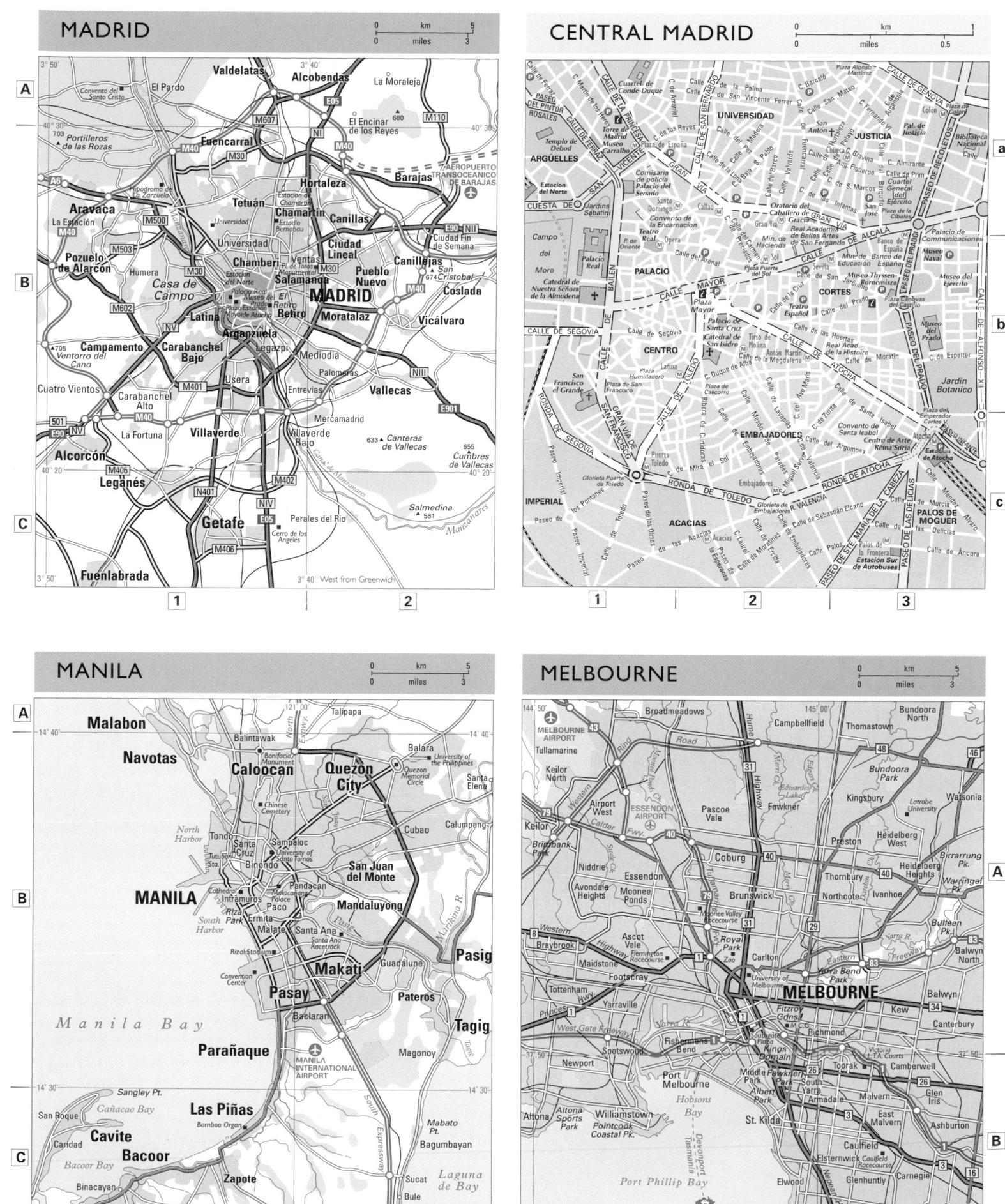
MADRID
0 km 5
0 miles 3
Valdelatas
Alcobendas
La Moraleja
El Pardo
El Encinar de los Reyes
680
Portilleros de las Rozas
703
Fuencarral
Barajas
AEROPUERTO TRANSOCEANICO DE BARAJAS
Hortaleza
Aravaca
Tetuán
Chamartín
Canillas
La Estación
Pozuelo de Alarcón
Universidad
Ciudad Lineal
Canillejas
Ciudad Fin de Semana
Humera
Chamberí
Ventas
Pueblo Nuevo
San Cristobal
Casa de Campo
Salamanca
MADRID
Coslada
Latina
Retiro
Moratalaz
Vicálvaro
Campamento
Carabanchel Bajo
Arganzuela
Legazpi
Mediodia
Ventorro del Cano
705
Usera
Palomeras
Cuatro Vientos
Carabanchel Alto
Entrevias
Vallecas
Mercamadrid
La Fortuna
Villaverde
Villaverde Bajo
Canteras de Vallecas
633
Cumbres de Vallecas
655
Alcorcón
Leganés
Getafe
Perales del Rio
Salmedina
581
Cerro de los Angeles
Fuenlabrada
3° 40' West from Greenwich
A
B
C
1
2
CENTRAL MADRID
0 km 1
0 miles 0.5
UNIVERSIDAD
JUSTICIA
ARGÜELLES
PALACIO
CORTES
CENTRO
EMBAJADORES
IMPERIAL
ACACIAS
PALOS DE MOGUER
Palacio Real
Plaza Mayor
Museo del Prado
Jardin Botanico
Estacion del Norte
Estación de Atocha
Estación Sur de Autobuses
CALLE DE ALCALA
GRAN VIA
CALLE MAYOR
CALLE DE ATOCHA
PASEO DEL PRADO
PASEO DE RECOLETOS
CALLE DE SEGOVIA
RONDA DE TOLEDO
RONDA DE ATOCHA
a
b
c
1
2
3
MANILA
0 km 5
0 miles 3
Malabon
Navotas
Caloocan
Quezon City
Balintawak
Talipapa
Balara
Tondo
Santa Cruz
Sampaloc
Cubao
Binondo
San Juan del Monte
MANILA
Intramuros
Paco
Mandaluyong
Ermita
Malate
Santa Ana
Pasig
Makati
Pasay
Guadalupe
Pateros
Baclaran
Tagig
Manila Bay
Parañaque
MANILA INTERNATIONAL AIRPORT
Magonoy
Las Piñas
Sangley Pt.
Cañacao Bay
San Roque
Cavite
Bacoor
Bacoor Bay
Zapote
Binacayan
Kawit
Sucat
Bule
Laguna de Bay
Bagumbayan
121° 00' East from Greenwich
A
B
C
1
2
MELBOURNE
0 km 5
0 miles 3
Broadmeadows
Campbellfield
Thomastown
Bundoora North
MELBOURNE AIRPORT
Tullamarine
Keilor North
Airport West
ESSENDON AIRPORT
Pascoe Vale
Fawkner
Bundoora Park
Kingsbury
Watsonia
Keilor
Coburg
Preston
Heidelberg West
Niddrie
Essendon
Thornbury
Heidelberg Heights
Avondale Heights
Moonee Ponds
Brunswick
Northcote
Ivanhoe
Braybrook
Ascot Vale
Royal Park
Carlton
Bulleen
Maidstone
Footscray
Balwyn North
Tottenham
Yarraville
MELBOURNE
Balwyn
Kew
Richmond
Canterbury
Spotswood
Fishermans Bend
Newport
Port Melbourne
Toorak
Camberwell
Hobsons Bay
Williamstown
South Yarra
Armadale
Malvern
Glen Iris
Altona
St. Kilda
East Malvern
Ashburton
Caulfield
Elsternwick
Port Phillip Bay
Elwood
Glenhuntly
Carnegie
Ormond
Oakleigh
Brighton
East from Greenwich
A
B
1
2

MEXICO CITY

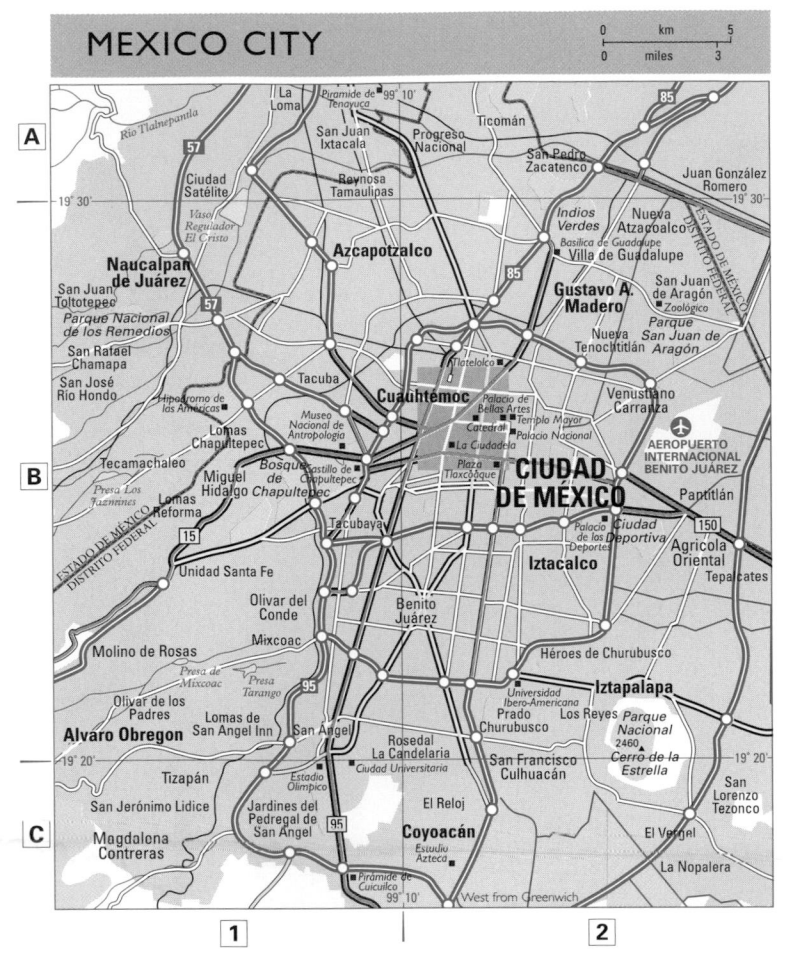
0 km 5
0 miles 3
A
B
C
1
2
La Loma
Pirámide de Tenayuca
99° 10'
Ticomán
Rio Tlalnepantla
San Juan Ixtacala
Progreso Nacional
San Pedro Zacatenco
Juan González Romero
Ciudad Satélite
Reynosa Tamaulipas
19° 30'
Vaso Regulador El Cristo
Indios Verdes
Nueva Atzacoalco
Basílica de Guadalupe
Villa de Guadalupe
ESTADO DE MÉXICO
DISTRITO FEDERAL
Naucalpan de Juárez
Azcapotzalco
San Juan Toltotepec
Parque Nacional de los Remedios
Gustavo A. Madero
San Juan de Aragón
Zoológico
Parque San Juan de Aragón
San Rafael Chamapa
San José Río Hondo
Nueva Tenochtitlán
Tlatelolco
Tacuba
Hipódromo de las Américas
Cuauhtémoc
Palacio de Bellas Artes
Templo Mayor
Catedral
Palacio Nacional
La Ciudadela
Venustiano Carranza
Museo Nacional de Antropología
Lomas Chapultepec
Tecamachaleo
Castillo de Chapultepec
Bosque de Chapultepec
Plaza Tlaxcoaque
CIUDAD DE MÉXICO
AEROPUERTO INTERNACIONAL BENITO JUAREZ
Miguel Hidalgo
Presa Los Jazmines
Lomas Reforma
Pantitlán
Tacubaya
Palacio de los Deportes
Ciudad Deportiva
Agrícola Oriental
Unidad Santa Fe
Iztacalco
Tepalcates
Olivar del Conde
Benito Juárez
Molino de Rosas
Mixcoac
Presa de Mixcoac
Presa Tarango
Héroes de Churubusco
Universidad Ibero-Americana
Iztapalapa
Olivar de los Padres
Prado Churubusco
Los Reyes
Parque Nacional
Lomas de San Angel Inn
Alvaro Obregon
San Angel
Rosedal
La Candelaria
Ciudad Universitaria
San Francisco Culhuacán
2460
Cerro de la Estrella
19° 20'
Tizapán
Estadio Olímpico
San Jerónimo Lídice
Jardines del Pedregal de San Angel
El Reloj
San Lorenzo Tezonco
Magdalona Contreras
Coyoacán
Estadio Azteca
El Vergel
La Nopalera
Pirámide de Cuicuilco
99° 10'
West from Greenwich

CENTRAL MEXICO CITY

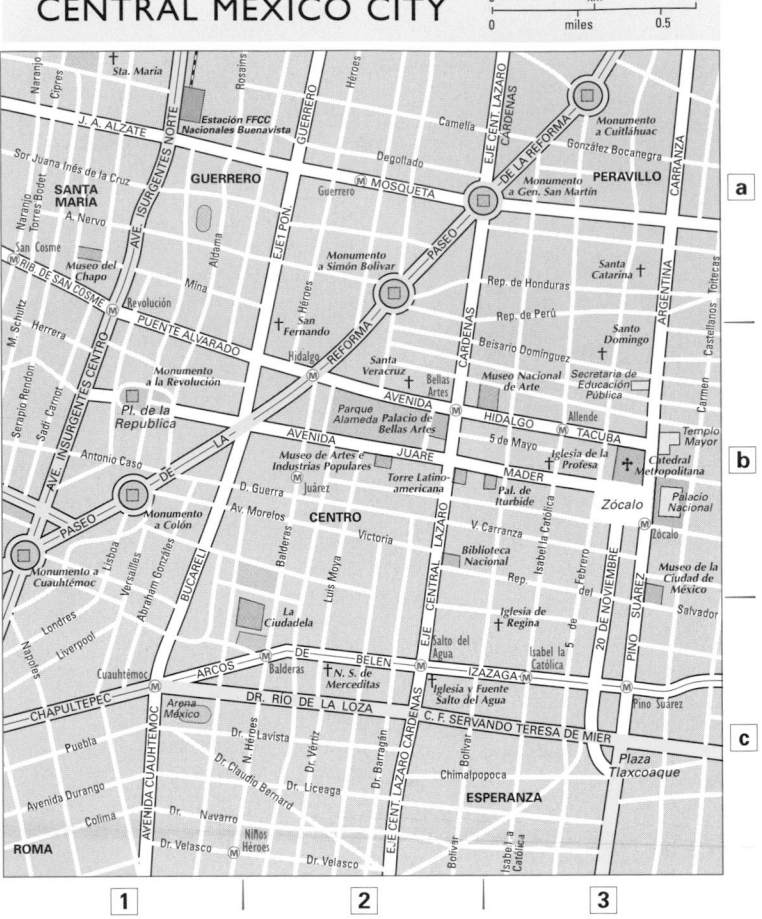
0 km 1
0 miles 0.5
a
b
c
1
2
3
Sta. María
Estación FFCC Nacionales Buenavista
J. A. ALZATE
Camelia
Monumento a Cuitláhuac
González Bocanegra
Sor Juana Inés de la Cruz
GUERRERO
Degollado
MOSQUETA
Monumento a Gen. San Martín
PERAVILLO
SANTA MARIA
Guerrero
San Cosme
Museo del Chapo
RIB. DE SAN COSME
Monumento a Simón Bolívar
Santa Catarina
Rep. de Honduras
Rep. de Perú
Revolución
PUENTE ALVARADO
San Fernando
Santo Domingo
Belisario Domínguez
Herrera
Hidalgo
REFORMA
PASEO
Santa Veracruz
Bellas Artes
Museo Nacional de Arte
Secretaría de Educación Pública
Monumento a la Revolución
Pl. de la República
AVENIDA
HIDALGO
Allende
Parque Alameda
Palacio de Bellas Artes
TACUBA
Templo Mayor
Antonio Caso
AVENIDA
5 de Mayo
Iglesia de la Profesa
Catedral Metropolitana
Museo de Artes e Industrias Populares
JUÁREZ
MADERO
Torre Latino-americana
Pal. de Iturbide
Zócalo
Palacio Nacional
D. Guerra
Juárez
Av. Morelos
CENTRO
Monumento a Colón
V. Carranza
Victoria
Biblioteca Nacional
Museo de la Ciudad de México
Monumento a Cuauhtémoc
Rep.
Salvador
Iglesia de Regina
La Ciudadela
Londres
Liverpool
Salto del Agua
Isabel la Católica
Cuauhtémoc
ARCOS DE BELEN
Balderas
N. S. de Merceditas
IZAZAGA
Iglesia y Fuente Salto del Agua
Pino Suárez
CHAPULTEPEC
DR. RIO DE LA LOZA
Arena México
C. F. SERVANDO TERESA DE MIER
Dr. Lavista
Plaza Tlaxcoaque
Puebla
Chimalpopoca
Avenida Durango
ESPERANZA
Dr. Liceaga
Colima
Dr. Navarro
ROMA
Dr. Velasco
Niños Héroes
Dr. Velasco
AVE. INSURGENTES NORTE
AVE. INSURGENTES CENTRO
BUCARELI
AVENIDA CUAUHTÉMOC
EJE CENTRAL LÁZARO CÁRDENAS
20 DE NOVIEMBRE
PINO SUÁREZ
ARGENTINA
CARRANZA

MIAMI

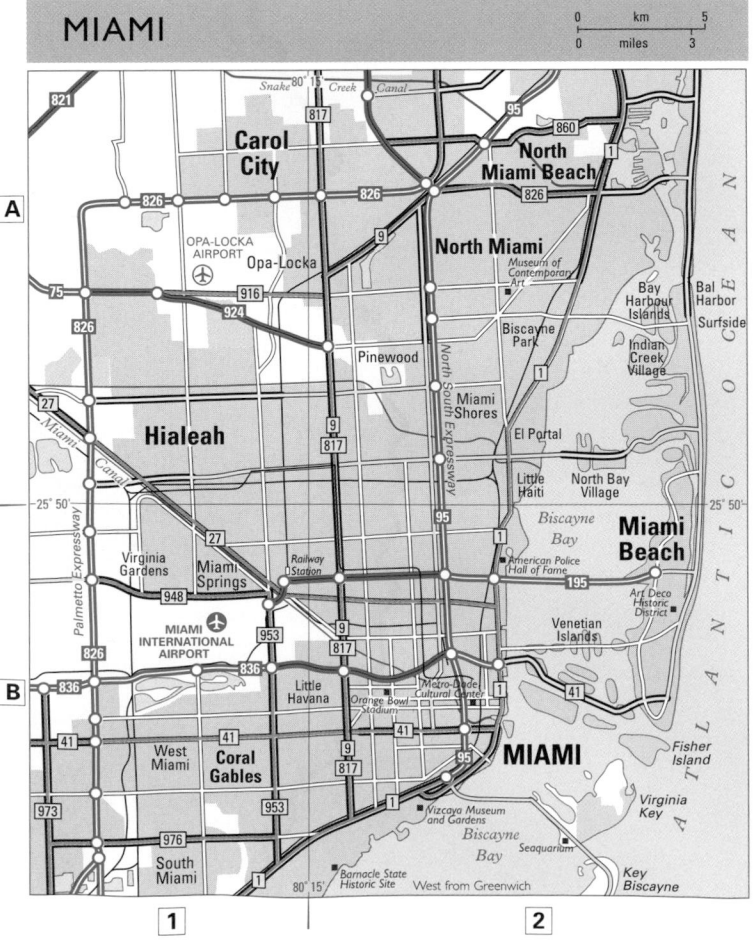
0 km 5
0 miles 3
A
B
1
2
Snake Creek Canal
80° 15'
Carol City
North Miami Beach
826
OPA-LOCKA AIRPORT
Opa-Locka
North Miami
Museum of Contemporary Art
Bay Harbour Islands
Bal Harbor
Surfside
Biscayne Park
Pinewood
Indian Creek Village
Miami Shores
North South Expressway
Hialeah
El Portal
Miami Canal
Little Haiti
North Bay Village
25° 50'
Biscayne Bay
Miami Beach
Virginia Gardens
Miami Springs
Railway Station
American Police Hall of Fame
Palmetto Expressway
MIAMI INTERNATIONAL AIRPORT
Art Deco Historic District
Venetian Islands
Little Havana
Metro-Dade Cultural Center
Orange Bowl Stadium
West Miami
Coral Gables
MIAMI
Fisher Island
Vizcaya Museum and Gardens
Virginia Key
Biscayne Bay
Seaquarium
South Miami
Barnacle State Historic Site
West from Greenwich
Key Biscayne
ATLANTIC OCEAN

MILAN

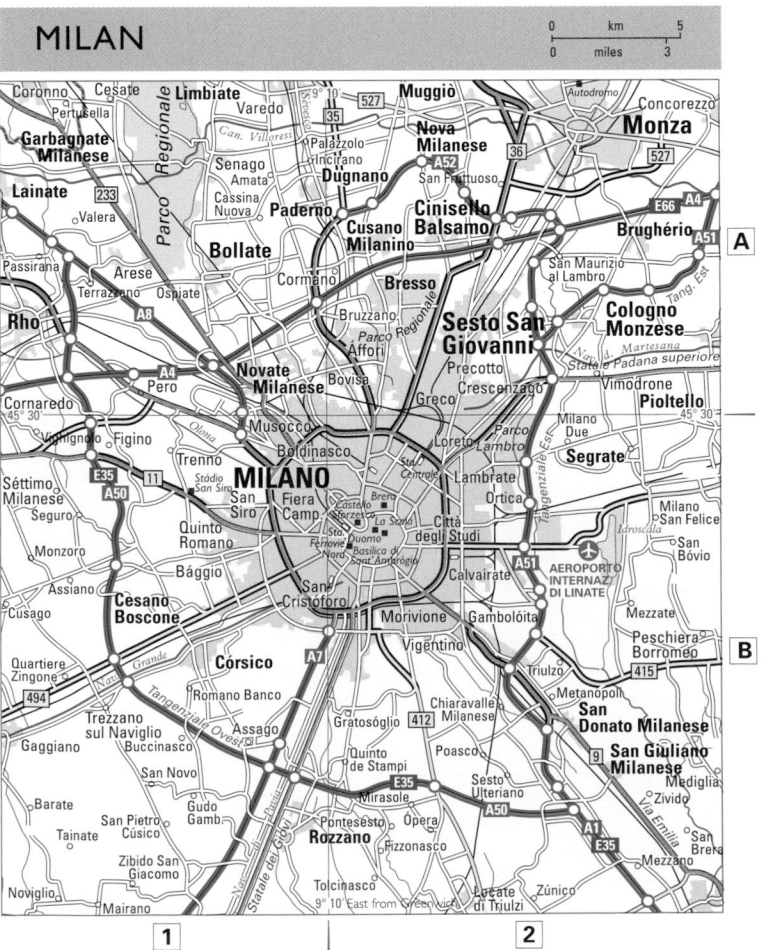
0 km 5
0 miles 3
A
B
1
2
Coronno Pertusella
Cesate
Limbiate
Varedo
9° 10'
Muggiò
Autodromo
Concorezzo
Garbagnate Milanese
Can. Villoresi
Palazzolo
Nova Milanese
Monza
Senago
Amata
Incirano
Dugnano
San Fruttuoso
Lainate
Cassina Nuova
Parco Regionale
Valera
Paderno
Cinisello Balsamo
Cusano Milanino
Brughério
Bollate
Passirana
Arese
San Maurizio al Lambro
Cormano
Bresso
Terrazzano
Ospiate
Cologno Monzese
Rho
Bruzzano
Parco Regionale
Sesto San Giovanni
Affori
Martesana
Strada Statale Padana superiore
Novate Milanese
Precotto
Pero
Bovisa
Crescenzago
Vimodrone
Cornaredo
Greco
Pioltello
45° 30'
Musocco
Loreto
Parco Lambro
Milano Due
Vighignolo
Figino
Boldinasco
Segrate
Trenno
Stazione Centrale
MILANO
Séttimo Milanese
Stádio San Siro
Brera
Lambrate
San Siro
Fiera Camp.
Castello Sforzesco
La Scala
Ortica
Milano San Felice
Seguro
Duomo
Città degli Studi
Idroscalo
Quinto Romano
Sta. Maria delle Grazie
Sta. Fermovie Nord
Basilica di Sant'Ambrogio
San Bóvio
Monzoro
Bággio
Calvairate
AEROPORTO INTERNAZ. DI LINATE
Assiano
Cesano Boscone
San Cristoforo
Mezzate
Cusago
Morivione
Gamboloita
Peschiera Borromeo
Quartiere Zingone
Córsico
Vigentino
Triulzo
Naviglio Grande
Romano Banco
Chiaravalle Milanese
Metanopoli
Trezzano sul Naviglio
Assago
Gratosóglio
San Donato Milanese
Tangenziale Ovest
Gaggiano
Buccinasco
Quinto de Stampi
Poasco
San Giuliano Milanese
San Novo
Sesto Ulteriano
Mediglia
Mirasole
Zivido
Barate
Tainate
San Pietro Cúsico
Gudo Gamb.
Pontesesto
Opera
Rozzano
Sori Brera
Zibido San Giacomo
Fizzonasco
Mezzano
Via Emilia
Noviglio
Tolcinasco
Locate di Triulzi
Zúnico
Mairano
9° 10' East from Greenwich
Statale dei Giovi
Tangenziale Est

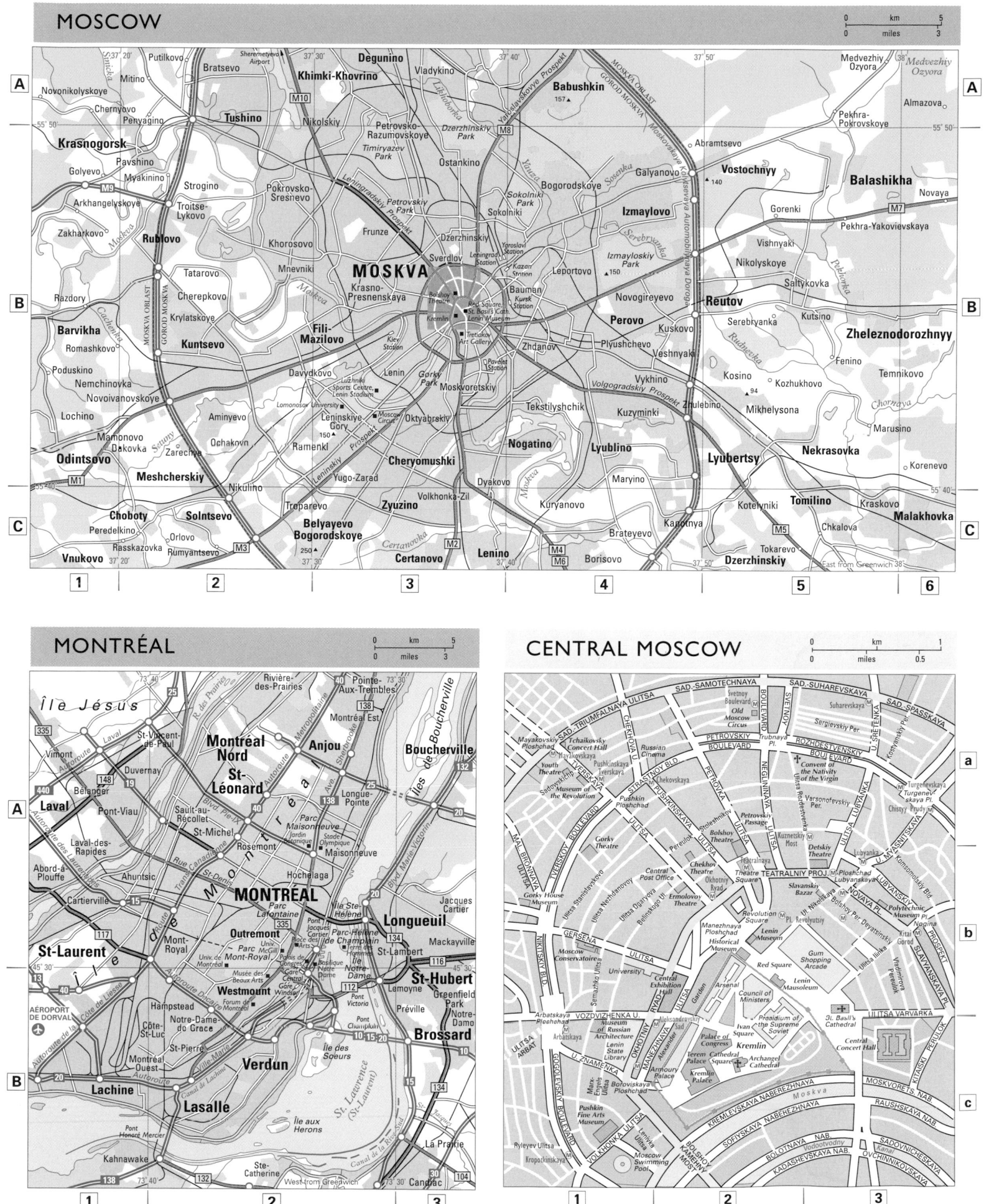

MOSCOW

| | km | | 5 |
| 0 | miles | | 3 |

Sheremetyevo Airport
Putilkovo
Novonikolyskoye
Mitino
Chernyovo
Penyagino
Bratsevo
Khimki-Khovrino
Vladykino
Deugnino
Babushkin
157
Medvezhiy Ozyora
Medvezhiy Ozyora
Almazova
Krasnogorsk
Tushino
Nikolsky
M10
Gorod Moskva
Moskva Oblast
Pekhra-Pokrovskoye
Golyevo
Pavshino
Myakinino
Strogino
Petrovsko-Razumovskoye
Dzerzhinskiy Park
M8
Abramtsevo
Vostochnyy
140
Balashikha
Novaya
Troitse-Lykovo
Pokrovsko-Sresnevo
Timiryazev Park
Ostankino
Galyanovo
Gorenki
Arkhangelyskoye
Khorosovo
Bogorodskoye
Izmaylovo
Pekhra-Yakovievskaya
Zakharkovo
Rublovo
Tatarovo
Cherepkovo
Frunze
Sokolniki Park
Izmayloskiy Park
Vishnyaki
M7
Razdory
Krylatskoye
Mnevniki
MOSKVA
Dzerzhinskiy
Leningrad Station
Kazan Station
Yaroslavl Station
Léportovo
150
Nikolyskoye
Saltykovka
Serebryanka
Barvikha
Kuntsevo
Krasno-Presnenskaya
Bolshoy Theatre
Red Square
St. Basil's Cath.
Lenin Museum
Bauman
Kursk Station
Novogireyevo
Reutov
Kutsino
Romashkovo
Fili-Mazilovo
Kremlin
Tretiakov Art Gallery
Zhdanov
Perovo
Kuskovo
Serebryanka
Zheleznodorozhnyy
Poduskino
Kiev Station
Plyushchevo
Veshnyak
Rudnevka
Fenino
Nemchinovka
Gorky Park
Moskvoretskiy
Temnikovo
Novoivanovskoye
Davydkovo
Lenin
Pavelet Station
Vykhino
Kosino
Kozhukhovo
Chornaya
Lochino
Luzhniki Sports Centre-Lenin Stadium
Leninskiye Gory
Moscow Circus
Oktyabrskiy
Tekstilyshchik
Kuzymini
Zhulebino
Mikhelysona
Mamonovo
Lomonosov University
150
Ramenkl
Yugo-Zarad
Kuryanovo
94
Marusino
Dakovka
Zarechie
Ochakovn
Cheryomushki
Nogatino
Lyublino
Lyubertsy
Nekrasovka
Korenevo
Odintsovo
Meshcherskiy
Nikulino
Dyakovo
Maryino
Tomilino
Kraskovo
M1
55° 40'
Zyuzino
Volkhonka-Zil
Kotelyniki
Choboty
Solntsevo
Treparevo
Certanovka
Kanotnya
M5
Chkalova
Malakhovka
Peredelkino
Orlovo
Belyayevo Bogorodskoye
Brateyevo
Rasskazovka
Rumyantsevo
M3
250
Certanovo
Lenino
M4
M6
Borisovo
Tokarevo
Dzerzhinskiy
East from Greenwich 38°
Vnukovo

MONTRÉAL

| | km | | 5 |
| 0 | miles | | 3 |

Île Jésus
Rivière-des-Prairies
Pointe-Aux-Trembles
Laval
St-Vincent-de-Paul
Montréal Est
Boucherville
Vimont
Duvernay
Montréal Nord
Anjou
Bélanger
Laval
Pont-Viau
St-Léonard
St-Michel
Longue-Pointe
Laval-des-Rapides
Sault-au-Récollet
Parc Maisonneuve
Jardin Botanique
Stade Olympique
Boucherville
Abord-à-Plouffe
Ahuntsic
Rosemont
Maisonneuve
Cartierville
MONTRÉAL
Hochelaga
Jacques Cartier
St-Laurent
Mont-Royal
Parc Lafontaine
Île Ste Hélène
Longueuil
Mackayville
Outremont
Parc Héléne de Champlain
St-Lambert
Hampstead
Westmount
Forum de Montréal
St-Hubert
Greenfield Park
Côte-St-Luc
Notre-Dame-do Grace
St-Pierre
Brossard
Verdun
Île des Soeurs
AÉROPORT DE DORVAL
Montréal Ouest
Lachine
Lasalle
Île aux Herons
La Prairie
Kahnawake
Ste-Catherine
Candiac
West from Greenwich

CENTRAL MOSCOW

| | km | | 1 |
| 0 | miles | | 0.5 |

SAD.-SAMOTECHNAYA
SAD.-SUHAREVSKAYA
SAD.-SPASSKAYA
Svetnoy Boulevard
Old Moscow Circus
Suharevskaya
Sergievsky Per.
SAD. TRIUMFALNAYA ULITSA
Mayakovskiy Ploshchad
Tchaikovsky Concert Hall
Russian Cinema
PETROVSKIY BOULEVARD
Trubnaya Pl.
ROZHDESTVENSKY BOULEVARD
Youth Theatre
Mayakovskaya
Pushkinskaya
Chekovskaya
Convent of the Nativity of the Virgin
Museum of the Revolution
Pushkin Ploshchad
Varsonofyevsky Per.
Turgenevskaya
Turgenevskaya Pl.
Chistiy Prudy
Gorky Theatre
Petrovsky Passage
Stoleshnikov Per.
Bolshoy Theatre
Kuznetskiy Most
Defskiy Theatre
Lubyanka
Chekhov Theatre
Theatre TEATRALNIY PROJ.
Teatralnaya
Ploshchad Lubyanskaya
NOVAYA PL.
Central Post Office
Ermolovay Theatre
Slavansky Bazar
Polytechnic Museum
Nogina
Gorky House Museum
Revolution Square
Pl. Revolyutsiy
Pl. Nikolskaya
Kitai Gorod
Moscow Conservatoire
University
Manezhnaya Ploshchad
Lenin Museum
Gum Shopping Arcade
GERSENA
Central Exhibition Hall
Historical Museum
Red Square
Lenin Mausoleum
Arsenal
Council of Ministers
Arbatskaya
VOZDVIZHENKA U.
Ploshchad
Aleksandrovsky Sad
Presidium of the Supreme Soviet
ULITSA VARVARKA
St. Basil's Cathedral
Museum of Russian Architecture
Ivan Square
Palace of Congress
Terem Palace
Cathedral Square
Archangel Cathedral
Central Concert Hall
Lenin State Library
ULITSA ARBAT
Armoury Palace
Kremlin
Marx-Engels Ulitsa
Borovitskaya Ploshchad
Pushkin Fine Arts Museum
Moskva
Ryleyev Ulitsa
VOLKHONKA ULITSA
Lenivka
KREMLEVSKAYA NABEREZHNAYA
RAUSHSKAYA NAB.
Kropotkinskaya
Moscow Swimming Pool
SOFIYSKAYA NAB.
BOLOTNAYA NAB.
Vodootvodny Canal
SADOVNICHESKAYA NAB.
OVCHINNIKOVSKAYA

MUMBAI

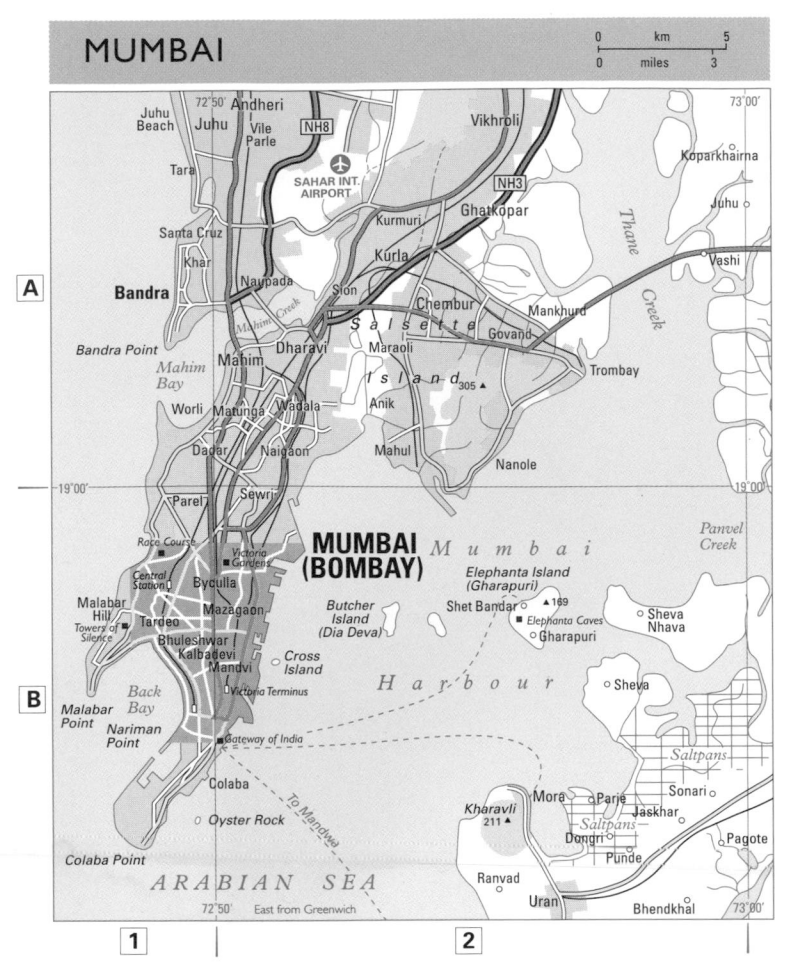
MUMBAI
km
miles
Juhu Beach
Juhu
Andheri
Vile Parle
NH8
Vikhroli
SAHAR INT. AIRPORT
NH3
Koparkhairna
Tara
Kurmuri
Ghatkopar
Juhu
Santa Cruz
Thane Creek
Khar
Kurla
Vashi
Bandra
Naupada
Sion
Chembur
Mankhurd
Mahim Creek
Govandi
Bandra Point
Mahim Bay
Mahim
Dharavi
Salsette Island
Maraoli
Trombay
Worli
Matunga
Wadala
Anik
Dadar
Naigaon
Mahul
Nanole
Parel
Sewri
MUMBAI (BOMBAY)
Mumbai Harbour
Panvel Creek
Race Course
Victoria Gardens
Central Station
Byculla
Elephanta Island (Gharapuri)
Malabar Hill
Tardeo
Mazagaon
Butcher Island (Dia Deva)
Shet Bandar
Elephanta Caves
Gharapuri
Sheva Nhava
Towers of Silence
Bhuleshwar
Kalbadevi
Mandvi
Cross Island
Victoria Terminus
Back Bay
Sheva
Malabar Point
Nariman Point
Gateway of India
Saltpans
Colaba
To Mandwa
Mora
Parje
Sonari
Kharavli
Jaskhar
Oyster Rock
Dongri
Pagote
Punde
Colaba Point
ARABIAN SEA
Ranvad
Uran
Bhendkhal
East from Greenwich

CENTRAL MUMBAI

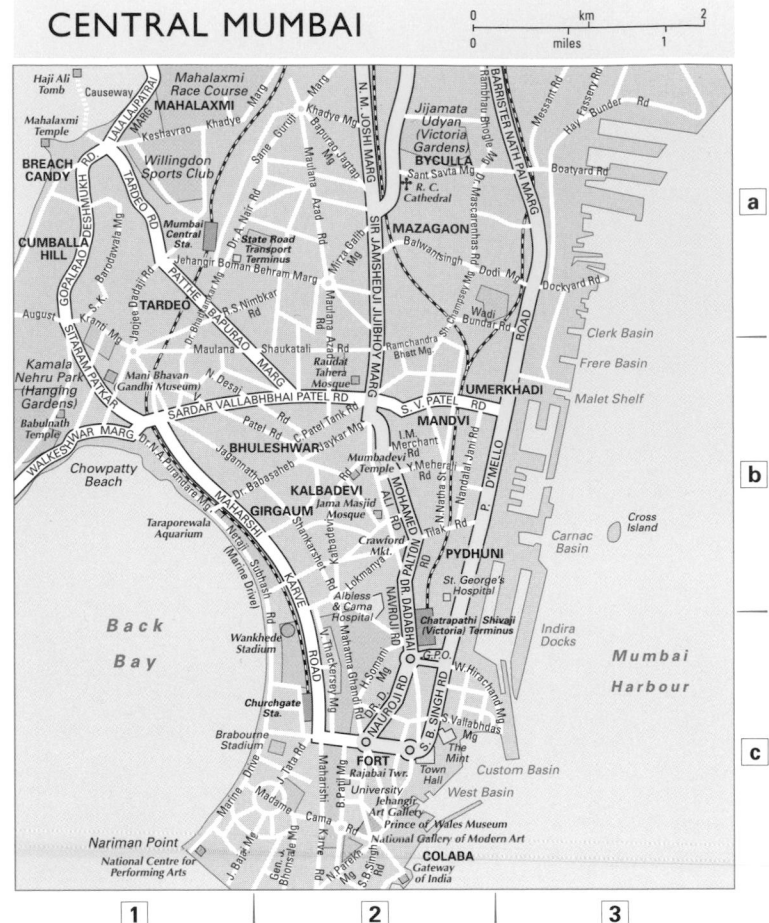
CENTRAL MUMBAI
km
miles
Haji Ali Tomb
Causeway
Mahalaxmi Race Course
MAHALAXMI
Mahalaxmi Temple
BREACH CANDY
Willingdon Sports Club
Jijamata Udyan (Victoria Gardens)
BYCULLA
St. Savta
R. C. Cathedral
Mumbai Central Sta.
State Road Transport Terminus
MAZAGAON
CUMBALLA HILL
TARDEO
Dockyard Rd
Clerk Basin
Frere Basin
Kamala Nehru Park (Hanging Gardens)
Mani Bhavan Gandhi Museum
Raudat Tahera Mosque
UMERKHADI
MANDVI
Malet Shelf
SARDAR VALLABHBHAI PATEL RD
Babulnath Temple
WALKESHWAR MARG
Chowpatty Beach
BHULESHWAR
Mumbadevi Temple
KALBADEVI
GIRGAUM
Jama Masjid Mosque
Taraporewala Aquarium
Crawford Mkt.
PYDHUNI
Cross Island
Carnac Basin
St. George's Hospital
Back Bay
Wankhede Stadium
Albless & Cama Hospital
Chatrapathi Shivaji (Victoria) Terminus
Indira Docks
Mumbai Harbour
G.P.O.
Churchgate Sta.
Brabourne Stadium
FORT
Rajabai Twr.
The Mint
Town Hall
Custom Basin
West Basin
University Jehangir Art Gallery
Prince of Wales Museum
National Gallery of Modern Art
Nariman Point
National Centre for Performing Arts
COLABA
Gateway of India

MUNICH

MUNICH
km
miles
Dachau-Ost
Flughafen München (Franz Josef Strauss)
Dachau
Obermoos Schwaige
Oberschleissheim
Fischerhäuser
Lustheim
Hochbrück
Garching
Rothschwaige
Karlsfeld
Dirnismaning
Ismaning
Gröbenried
Eschenried
Ludwigsfeld
Neuherberg
Speicher-See
Feldmoching
Am Hasenbergl
Gerberau
Allach
Freimann
Fasanerie-Nord
Gross-Lappen
Unterföhring
Untermenzing
Moosach
Milbertshofen
Aschheim
Langwald
Johanneskirchen
Lockhausen
Obermenzing
Gern
Oberföhring
Aubing
Blutenberg
Nymphenburg
Schwabing
Schloss Nymphenburg
Neuhausen
Bogenhausen
Neu Aubing
Dornach
Feldkirchen
Zamdorf
Daglfing
Riem
Freiham
Pasing
Lochham
Laim
MÜNCHEN
Haidhausen
Kirchtrudering
Gräfelfing
Gross-Hadern
Sendling
Gronsdorf
Planegg
Ramersdorf
Berg am Laim
Strasstrudering
Martinsried
Thalkirchen
Giesing
Neuperlach
Perlach
Waldtrudering
Krailling
Forstenried
Fasangarten
Solalinden
Neuried
Öden-Stockach
Maxhof
Solln
Harlaching
Waldperlach
Perlacher Forst
Unterbiberg
Warnberg
Grosshesselohe
Neubiberg
Forstenrieder Park
Geiselgasteig
Unterhaching
Westerham
Ottobrunn
Hohenbrunn
Pullach
Am Wald
Taufkirchen
Winning
Höllriegelskreuth
Grünwalder Forst
Furth
Wachterhof
Buchenhain
Grünwald
Bergham
Potzham
Oberhaching
Kirchstockbach
East from Greenwich

CENTRAL MUNICH

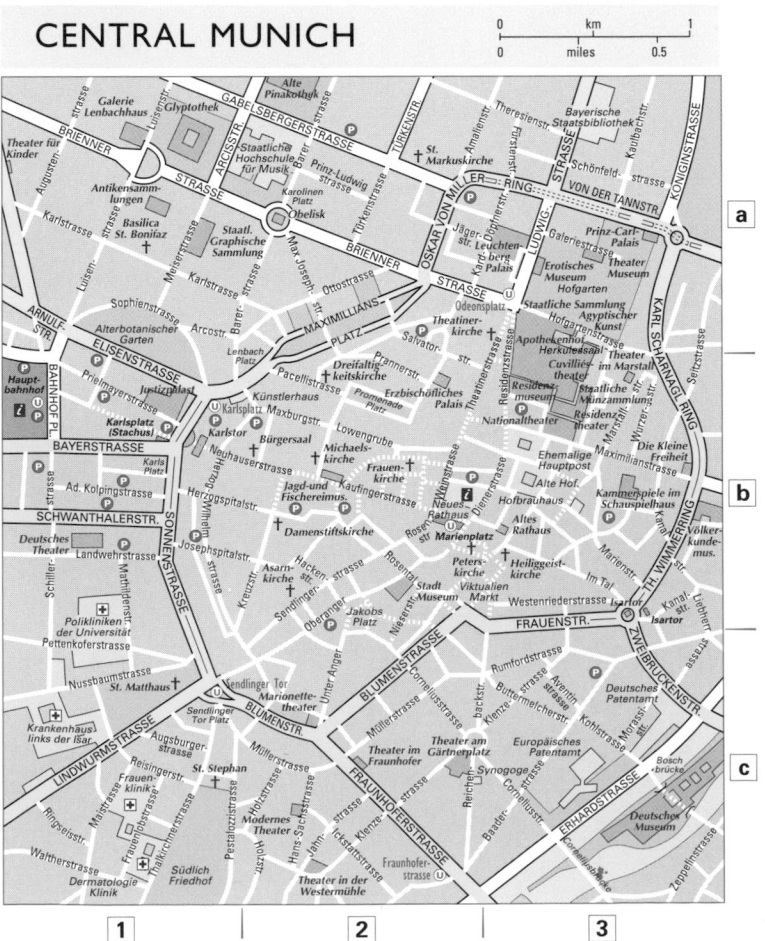
CENTRAL MUNICH
km
miles
Alte Pinakothek
Galerie Lenbachhaus
Glyptothek
GABELSBERGERSTRASSE
Bayerische Staatsbibliothek
Theater für Kinder
BRIENNER STRASSE
Staatliche Hochschule für Musik
St. Markuskirche
Antikensammlungen
Karolinen Platz
Obelisk
OSKAR VON MILLER RING
VON DER TANNSTR.
KÖNIGINSTRASSE
Basilica St. Bonifaz
Staatl. Graphische Sammlung
Prinz-Carl-Palais
Leuchtenberg Palais
Erotisches Museum
Theater Museum
Hofgarten
Staatliche Sammlung Ägyptischer Kunst
Odeonsplatz
Theatinerkirche
MAXIMILIANSPLATZ
Alterbotanischer Garten
Lenbach Platz
Apothekenhof
Herkulessaal
Cuvillies-theater
Theater im Marstall
ELISENSTRASSE
Hauptbahnhof
Dreifaltigkeitskirche
Erzbischöfliches Palais
Residenzmuseum
Staatliche Münzsammlung
Künstlerhaus
Karlsplatz (Stachus)
Karlstor
Nationaltheater
Residenztheater
Bürgersaal
Michaelskirche
Frauenkirche
Ehemalige Hauptpost
Die Kleine Freiheit
BAYERSTRASSE
Ad. Kolpingstrasse
Jagd-und Fischereimus.
Alte Hof
Kammerspiele im Schauspielhaus
SCHWANTHALERSTR.
Neues Rathaus
Hofbräuhaus
Altes Rathaus
Damenstiftskirche
Marienplatz
Deutsches Theater
Völkerkundemus.
Peterskirche
Heiliggeistkirche
Asamkirche
Stadt Museum
Viktualien Markt
Isartor
FRAUENSTR.
Poliklinken der Universität
Jakobs Platz
St. Matthaus
Sendlinger Tor
Marionettetheater
Deutsches Patentamt
Krankenhaus links der Isar
Sendlinger Tor Platz
BLUMENSTRASSE
Theater im Fraunhofer
Theater am Gärtnerplatz
Europäisches Patentamt
LINDWURMSTRASSE
St. Stephan
Synogoge
Frauenklinik
Modernes Theater
FRAUNHOFERSTRASSE
ERHARDSTRASSE
Deutsches Museum
Südlich Friedhof
Theater in der Westermühle
Dermatologie Klinik

NEW YORK

0 km 5
0 miles 3

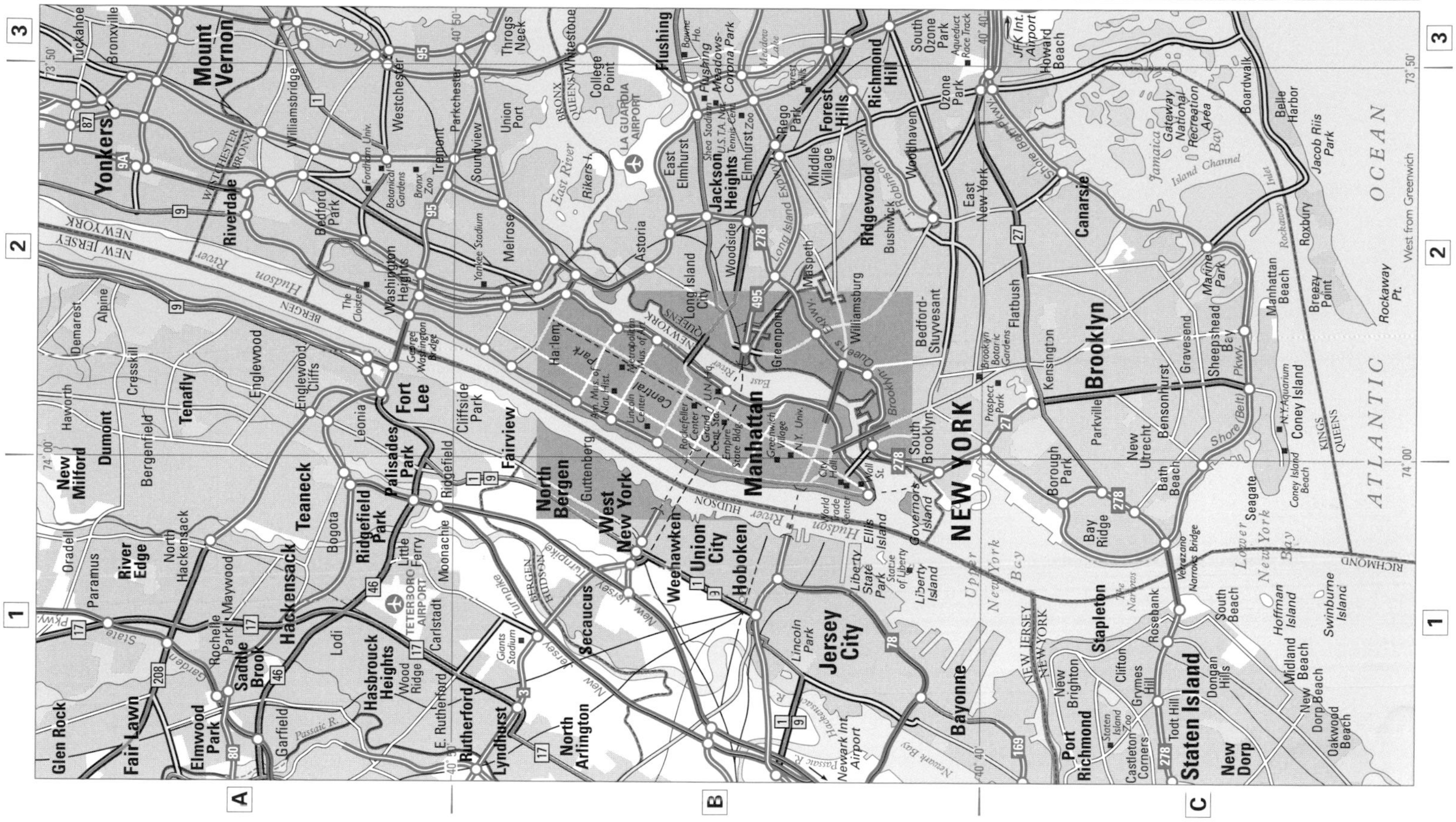
Yonkers
Mount Vernon
Riverdale
Bronxville
Tuckahoe
Flushing
Jackson Heights
Forest Hills
Richmond Hill
Ridgewood
Canarsie
Brooklyn
NEW YORK
Manhattan
Harlem
Long Island City
Fort Lee
Palisades Park
Teaneck
Hackensack
Fair Lawn
Glen Rock
Rutherford
Lyndhurst
North Arlington
Secaucus
Union City
Hoboken
Weehawken
West New York
North Bergen
Jersey City
Bayonne
Staten Island
Stapleton
Port Richmond
New Dorp
Coney Island
Rockaway Pt.
ATLANTIC OCEAN
Hudson River
East River
Upper New York Bay
Lower New York Bay
LA GUARDIA AIRPORT
JFK Int. Airport
TETERBORO AIRPORT
Newark Int. Airport
NEW JERSEY
NEW YORK

CENTRAL NEW YORK

0 km 2
0 miles 1

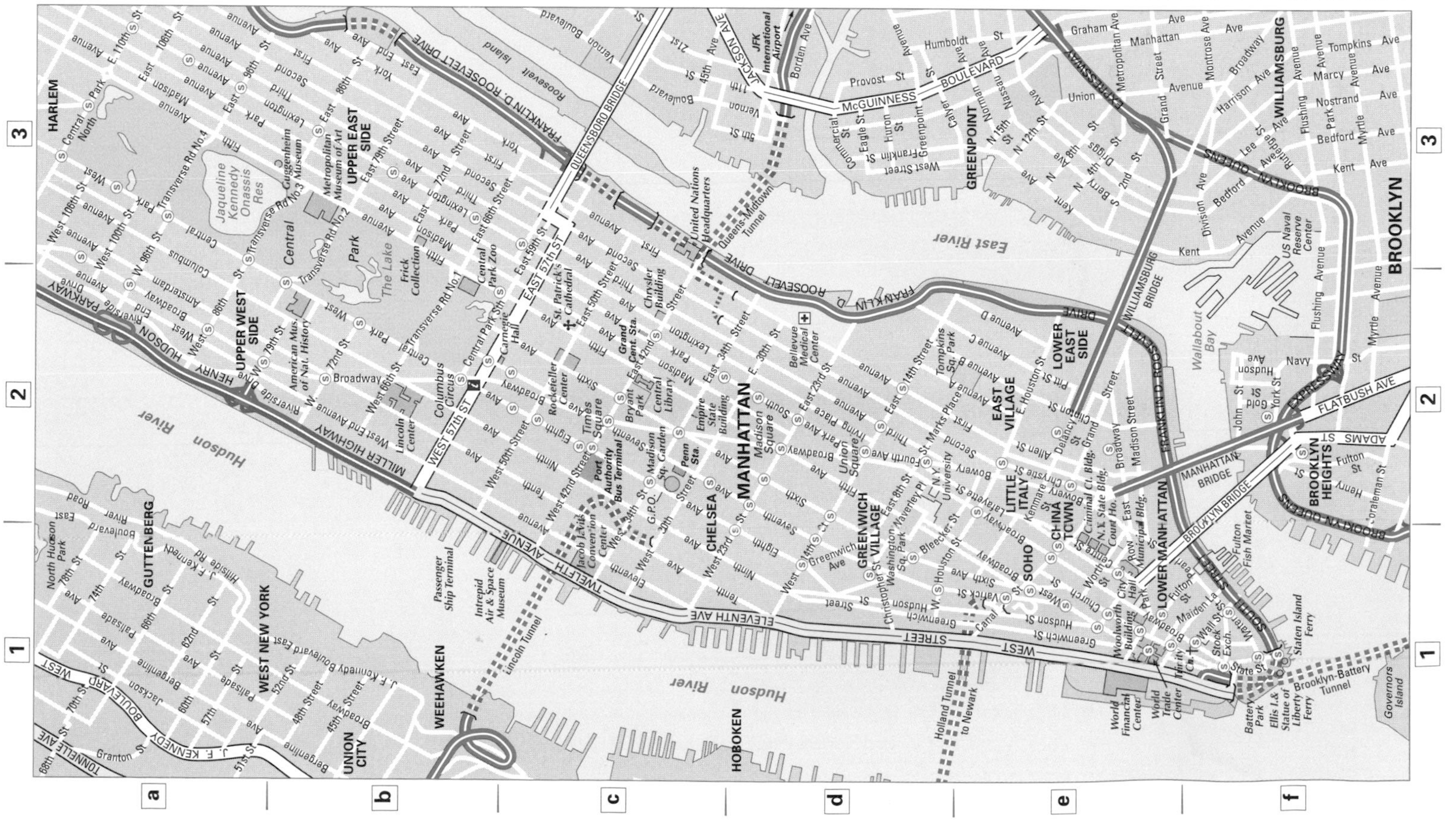
HARLEM
UPPER EAST SIDE
UPPER WEST SIDE
Central Park
MANHATTAN
CHELSEA
GREENWICH VILLAGE
EAST VILLAGE
LOWER EAST SIDE
SOHO
LITTLE ITALY
CHINA TOWN
LOWER MANHATTAN
GREENPOINT
WILLIAMSBURG
BROOKLYN
BROOKLYN HEIGHTS
GUTTENBERG
WEST NEW YORK
WEEHAWKEN
UNION CITY
HOBOKEN
Hudson River
East River
QUEENSBORO BRIDGE
WILLIAMSBURG BRIDGE
MANHATTAN BRIDGE
BROOKLYN BRIDGE
Lincoln Tunnel
Holland Tunnel to Newark
Governors Island

OSAKA

km 0 — 5
miles 0 — 3

135° 10' 135° 20' 135° 30'

▲509 Funasaka
Takarazuka Senriyama Yamada Hirakata
Karato Arima ▲462 Toyonaka Settsu Kori
▲598 ▲722 Rokkō-Zan Itami Suita Neyagawa
Tanigami ▲932 OSAKA INTERNATIONAL AIRPORT Higashiyodogawa Kadoma Shijonawate
▲428 Iwazono Hirota Asahi Moriguchi
Obu-tōge ▲365 Maya-Zan ▲699 Nishinomiya Jūsō Daitō
Õbu Kōbe University Ashiaya Naruo Amagasaki Oyodo Miyakojima 170
Okamoto 43 Umeda Kita Jōto Kōnoike
Nada Higashinada Nishiyodogawa Fukushima Higashi Minami Osaka Castle Higashinari Ishikiri
Fukiai Aji Nishi Ikuno 308
▲403 Ikuta Konohana Nawa Stadium Shitennoji Temple Higashiōsaka
Nagata KŌBE Rokkō Island Minato Taishō Tennoji ŌSAKA
Suma Port Island Kōbe Harbour Osaka Aquarium Suntory Museum Liberty Osaka Museum Zoo Abeno Kizuri Yamamoto
Osaka Harbour Nishinari Kyūhōji Yao
Higashisumiyoshi
Sumiyoshi Shrine Sumiyoshi Tainaka Onchi
Ikeuchi YAO AIRPORT Kashiwara
Matsubara Fujidera
Sakai

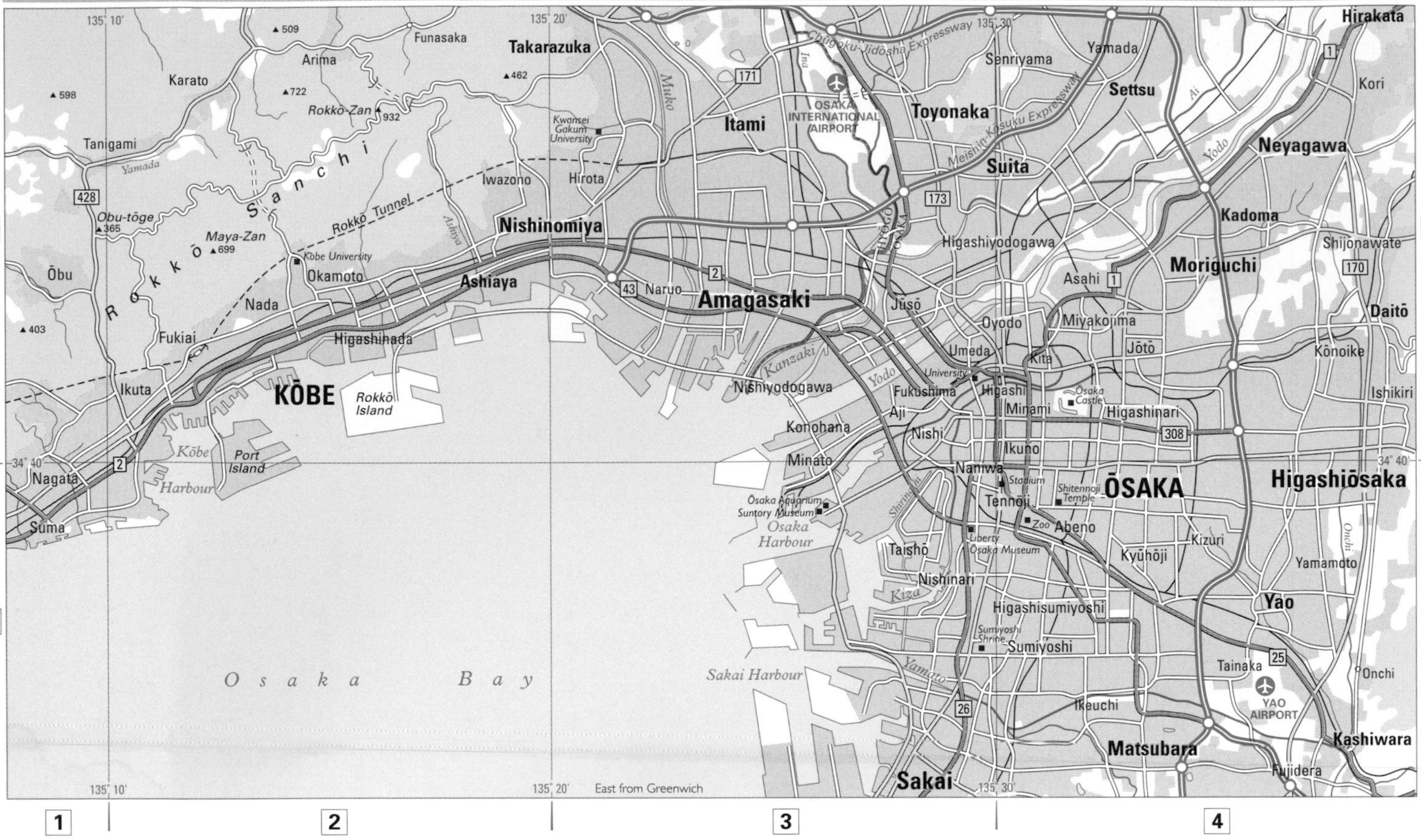

Osaka Bay
Sakai Harbour
East from Greenwich

1 2 3 4

OSLO

km 0 — 5
miles 0 — 3

60°00' 10°30' 10°40' 10°50'

By Tryvannshøgda ▲531 Maridalen
OSLO AKERSHUS Maridalsvatnet
Bogstadvatn ▲418 Alnsjøen
Burudvatn Sognsvatn Holmenkollen Kjelsås
Ila Røa Ris RING 3 Ullevål Gorud Rødtvet
Bærums Verk Lijordet 168 OSLO RING 2 Sinsen 163
Bryn 379 Haslum Ullern Skøyen Tøyen Alna
Kolsås 160 Stabekk Lysaker Universitet Vestbane Bryn
E16 Bærum 166 Norsk Folke Museum Ryen Oppsal Bøler
Tanum 164 Hovik Bygdøy Hovedøya Bekkelaget Østmark-kapellet
Skjependen Snarøya Fornebu Lindøya Lambertseter Nordstrand
Hvalstad Nesbru Nesøya Ostøya Frederikshavn Helsingborg København Hirtshals, Kiel Ormøya Oksval Malmøya Ljabru 155 Hauketo
Asker 165 Brønnøya Flaskebekk Skoklefall Klemetsrud
59°50' Konglungen Holmenfjorden Svestad Nesodden Torvvik Ingierstrand
Blakstad 157 ▲215 Kolbotn
167 Fjellstrand 156 Gjersjøen Myrvoll
Slemmestad Svestad Hasle Oppegård E18 ▲134
Nærsnes Garder Blylaget Oppegård

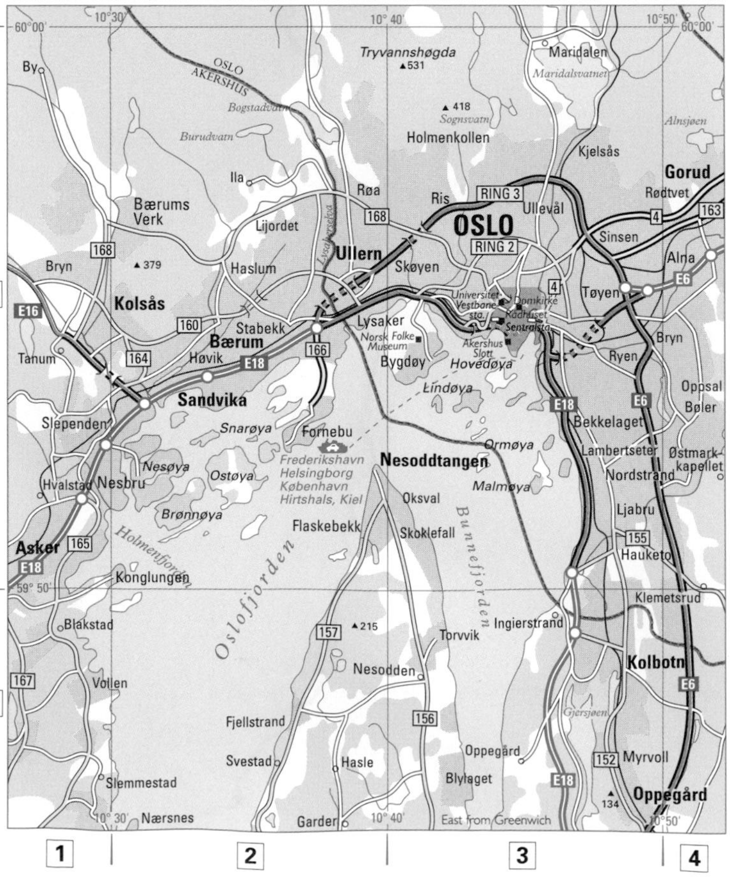

Oslofjorden *Bunnefjorden*
East from Greenwich

1 2 3 4

CENTRAL OSLO

km 0 — 0.5
miles 0 — 0.25

Rikshospitalet Vår Frelsers Gravlund Nordre gate
PARKVEIEN WERGELANDSVEIEN PILESTREDET Vor Frue hospitalet St. Olavs kirke MØLLERGATA
Slotts parken Kunstindustri-mus. Deichmanske bibliotek
Det Kongelige Slottet Historisk museum HAMMERSBORG TUNNELEN
ST. OLAVS GATE Nasjonal galleriet
KRISTIAN IV's GATE Universitet GRENSEN
Dronningparken National theatret Det Norske Teater Operaen STENERSGATA
DRAMMENSVEIEN Ibsen-museet Youngs Torget Oslo Spektrum
Stortinget VATERLAND TUNNELEN Grenland
MUNKEDAMSVEIEN Vestbane stasjonen Rådhus Domkirke Buss-terminalen
Rådhuset Sentralstasjon NYLANDSVEIEN
OSLO TUNNELEN Christiania torv Børsen BISPEGATA
Pipervika Museet for samtidskunst Arkitekt-museet
Hjemmefront-museet Astrup Fearnley-museet Bjørvika Bispevika
Akershus Slott og festning
Forsvars-museet
Frederikshavn, Helsingborg, København

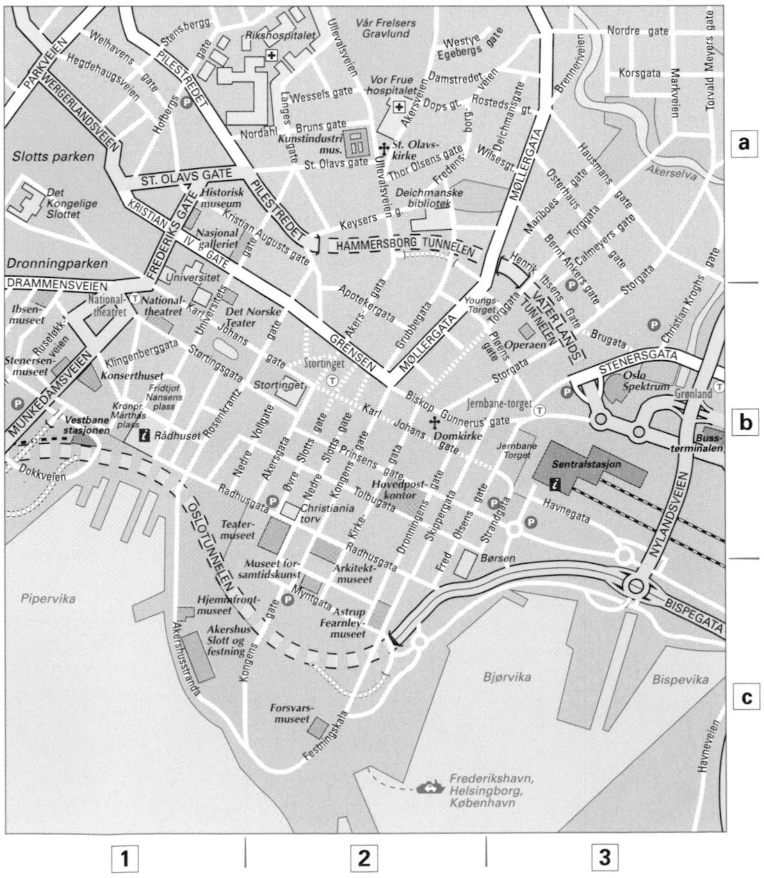

a b c

1 2 3

PARIS

0 — km — 5
0 — miles — 3

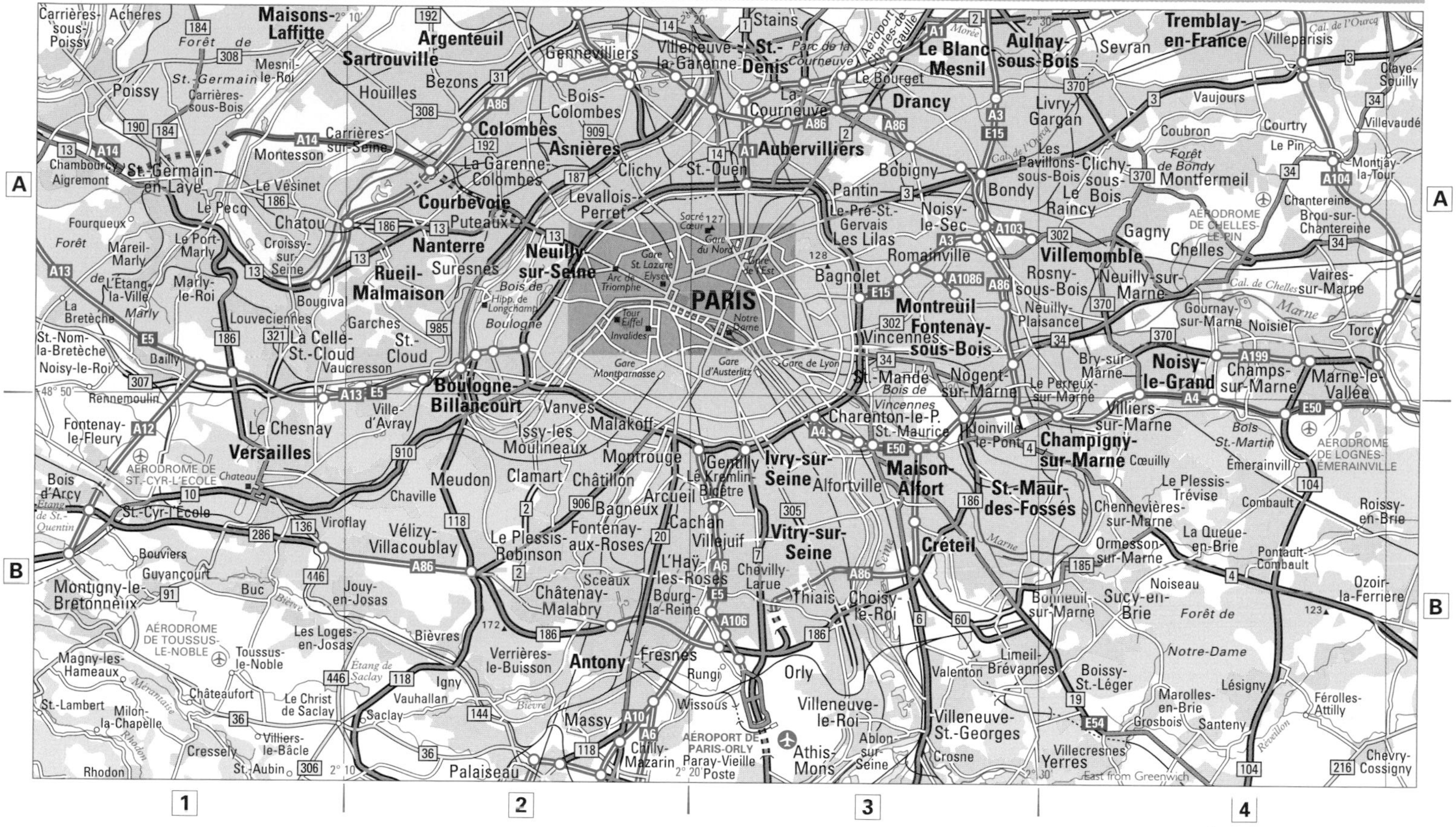

Carrières-sous-Poissy · Achères · Maisons-Laffitte · Argenteuil · Gennevilliers · Villeneuve-la-Garenne · St.-Denis · Stains · Le Blanc Mesnil · Aulnay-sous-Bois · Sevran · Tremblay-en-France · Villeparisis · Val de l'Ourcq

Poissy · Mesnil-le-Roi · Sartrouville · Bezons · Houilles · Bois-Colombes · La Courneuve · Le Bourget · Drancy · Livry-Gargan · Coubron · Courtry · Claye-Souilly

St.-Germain · Montesson · Colombes · Asnières · Clichy · St.-Ouen · Aubervilliers · Bobigny · Pantin · Clichy-sous-Bois · Montfermeil · Villevaudé

St.-Germain-en-Laye · Le Vésinet · La Garenne-Colombes · Levallois-Perret · Les Lilas · Le Pré-St.-Gervais · Noisy-le-Sec · Le Raincy · Gagny · Chelles · Brou-sur-Chantereine · AÉRODROME DE CHELLES-LE-PIN

Chatou · Courbevoie · Puteaux · Neuilly-sur-Seine · Gare St.-Lazare · Gare du Nord · Sacré Cœur · Romainville · Villemomble · Neuilly-sur-Marne · Vaires-sur-Marne

Nanterre · Suresnes · Arc de Triomphe · **PARIS** · Notre Dame · Bagnolet · Rosny-sous-Bois · Gournay-sur-Marne · Noisiel · Torcy

Rueil-Malmaison · Garches · Boulogne · Tour Eiffel · Invalides · Montreuil · Vincennes · Fontenay-sous-Bois · Bry-sur-Marne · Noisy-le-Grand · Marne-la-Vallée

Versailles · Le Chesnay · Boulogne-Billancourt · Vanves · Malakoff · Gare Montparnasse · Gare de Lyon · Gare d'Austerlitz · St.-Mandé · Charenton-le-P. · St.-Maurice · Nogent-sur-Marne · Le Perreux-sur-Marne · Villiers-sur-Marne · Champs-sur-Marne · AÉRODROME DE LOGNES-ÉMERAINVILLE

St.-Cyr-l'École · Issy-les-Moulineaux · Montrouge · Châtillon · Arcueil · Le Kremlin-Bicêtre · Ivry-sur-Seine · Gentilly · Alfortville · Maison-Alfort · Joinville-le-Pont · Champigny-sur-Marne · St.-Maur-des-Fossés · Chennevières-sur-Marne

Meudon · Clamart · Bagneux · Cachan · Villejuif · Vitry-sur-Seine · Créteil · Bonneuil-sur-Marne · Sucy-en-Brie · Ormesson-sur-Marne

Vélizy-Villacoublay · Le Plessis-Robinson · Fontenay-aux-Roses · Sceaux · L'Haÿ-les-Roses · Bourg-la-Reine · Chevilly-Larue · Thiais · Choisy-le-Roi · Limeil-Brévannes · Boissy-St.-Léger

Antony · Fresnes · Rungis · Orly · Valenton · Villeneuve-St.-Georges · Marolles-en-Brie · Santeny

AÉROPORT DE PARIS-ORLY · Athis-Mons · Ablon-sur-Seine · Crosne · Yerres · Villecresnes · Chevry-Cossigny

CENTRAL PARIS

0 — km — 1
0 — miles — 0.5

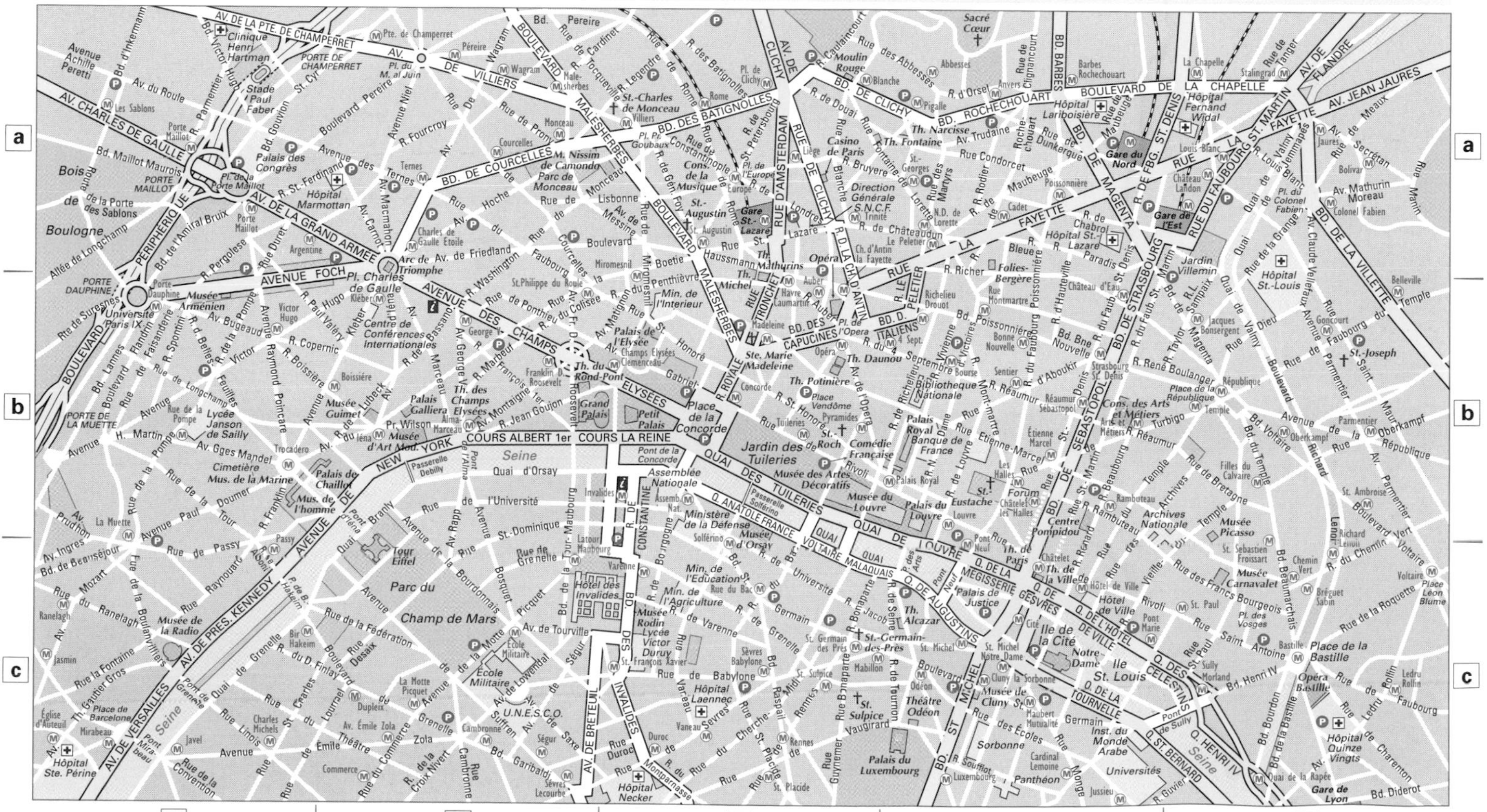

Bois de Boulogne · PORTE MAILLOT · Arc de Triomphe · AVENUE FOCH · PORTE DAUPHINE · Champs-Élysées · Place de la Concorde · Jardin des Tuileries · Musée du Louvre · Sacré Cœur · Moulin Rouge · Gare du Nord · Gare de l'Est · Opéra · Hôpital St.-Louis

Seine · Quai d'Orsay · Assemblée Nationale · Musée d'Orsay · Palais de Justice · Ile de la Cité · Notre Dame · Ile St.-Louis · Place de la Bastille · Opéra Bastille

Tour Eiffel · Champ de Mars · École Militaire · U.N.E.S.C.O. · Hôtel des Invalides · St.-Germain-des-Prés · St.-Sulpice · Jardin du Luxembourg · Panthéon · Sorbonne · Gare de Lyon

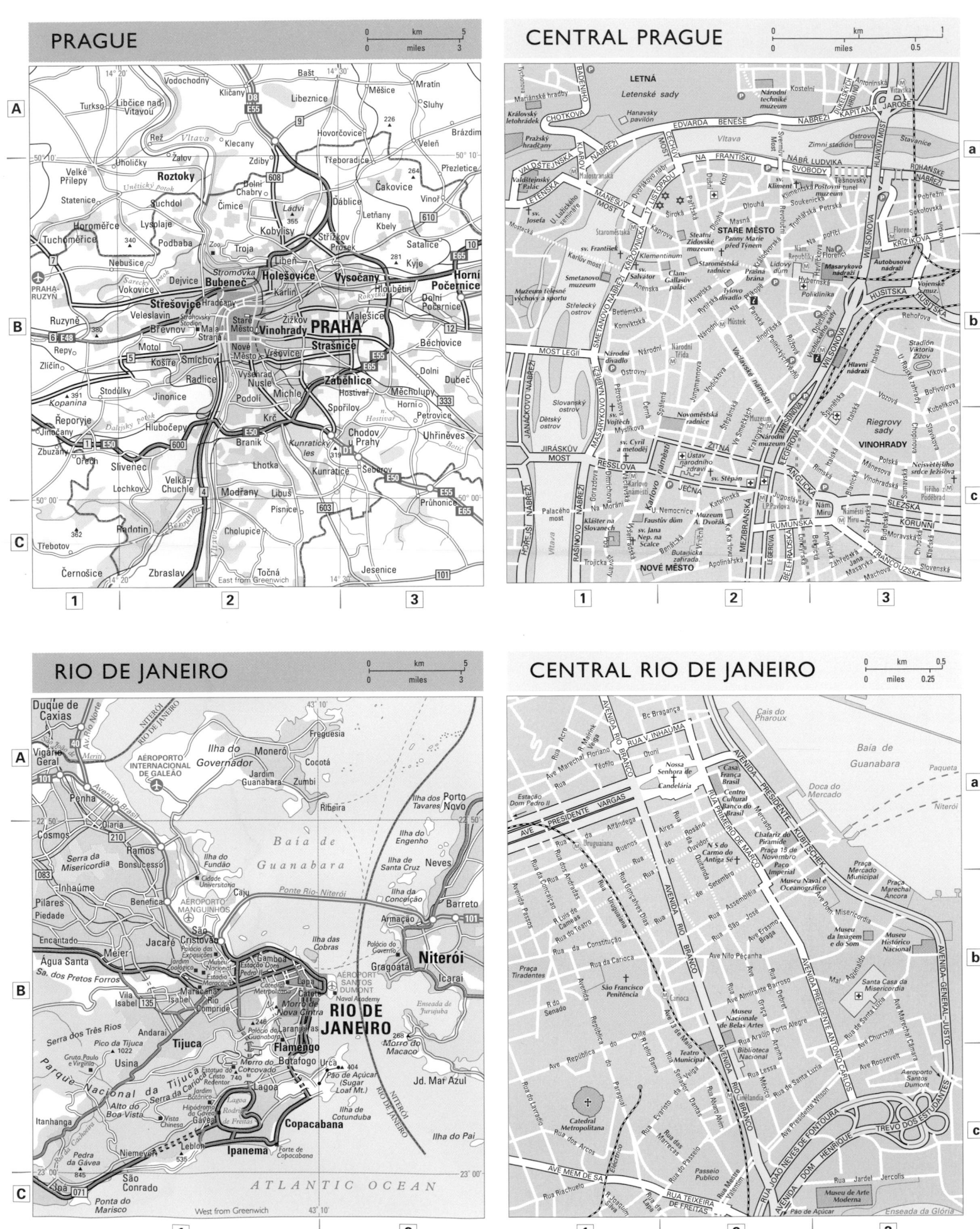
PRAGUE
0 km 5
0 miles 3
Vodochodny
Klíčany
Bašť
Měšice
Mratín
Libeznice
Sluhy
Turkso
Libčice nad Vltavou
Hovorčovice
Brázdim
Řež
Vltava
Klecany
Veleň
Úholičky
Žalov
Zdiby
Třeboradice
Přezletice
Velké Přílepy
Roztoky
Čakovice
Statenice
Dolní Chabry
Suchdol
Čimice
Ládví
Ďáblice
Vinoř
Letňany
Kbely
Horoměřice
Lysolaje
Kobylisy
Střížkov
Tuchoměřice
Podbaba
Prosek
Satalice
Troja
Kyje
Nebušice
Libeň
Horní Počernice
PRAHA-RUZYNĚ
Dejvice
Bubeneč
Holešovice
Vysočany
Vokovice
Stromovka
Hloubětín
Střešovice
Hradčany
Karlín
Dolní Počernice
Veleslavin
Strahovský Stadion
Ruzyně
Břevnov
Malá Strana
Staré Město
Vinohrady
PRAHA
Žižkov
Malešice
Repy
Motol
Nové Město
Vršovice
Strašnice
Běchovice
Zličín
Košíře
Smíchov
Radlice
Vyšehrad
Nusle
Záběhlice
Hostivař
Dolní
Dubeč
Stodůlky
Jinonice
Michle
Měcholupy
Kopanina
Podolí
Spořilov
Horní
Řeporyje
Hlubočepy
Krč
Petrovice
Jinočany
Braník
Chodov u Prahy
Uhříněves
Zbuzany
Kunratický les
Ořech
Slivenec
Lhotka
Kunratice
Šeberov
Velká Chuchle
Lochkov
Modřany
Libuš
Průhonice
Písnice
Radotín
Cholupice
Třebotov
Černošice
Zbraslav
Točná
Jesenice
East from Greenwich
CENTRAL PRAGUE
0 km 1
0 miles 0.5
LETNÁ
Letenské sady
Hanavský pavilón
Národní technické muzeum
Kostelní
Mariánské hradby
Královský letohrádek
CHOTKOVA
EDVARDA BENEŠE
NÁBŘEŽÍ KAPITÁNA JAROŠE
Pražský hradčany
Vltava
Zimní stadión
Štvanice
NA FRANTIŠKU
NÁBŘ. LUDVIKA SVOBODY
Valdštejnský palác
Malostranská
MÁNESŮV MOST
Široká
Pařížská
Dlouhá
Těšnovský tunel
Poštovní muzeum
Masná
STARÉ MĚSTO
Staroměstská
Starý Židovský hřbitov
Panny Marie před Týnem
sv. Františeke
Klementinum
Staroměstská radnice
Masarykovo nádraží
Autobusové nádraží
Prašná brána
Clam-Gallasův palác
Smetanovo muzeum
Muzeum tělesné výchovy a sportu
Střelecký ostrov
Tylovo divadlo
Hybernská
Poliklinika
HUSITSKÁ
Vojenské muz.
Betlémská
Konviktská
Můstek
MOST LEGIÍ
Národní divadlo
Národní třída
Ostrovní
Václavské náměstí
Hlavní nádraží
Stadión Viktoria Žižkov
Slovanský ostrov
Dětský ostrov
Novoměstská radnice
sv. Vojtěch
sv. Cyril a metoděj
Národní muzeum
Riegrovy sady
VINOHRADY
JIRÁSKŮV MOST
ŽITNÁ
RESSLOVA
Ústav národního zdraví
sv. Štěpán
JEČNÁ
Karlovo náměstí
Faustův dům
Muzeum A. Dvořák
Nám. Míru
SLEZSKÁ
KORUNNÍ
Palackého most
Klášter na Slovanech
sv. Jana Nep. na Skalce
RUMUNSKÁ
MEZIBRANSKÁ
Botanická zahrada
NOVÉ MĚSTO
FRANCOUZSKÁ
Slovenská
RIO DE JANEIRO
0 km 5
0 miles 3
Duque de Caxias
Vigário Geral
Freguesia
AEROPORTO INTERNACIONAL DE GALEÃO
Ilha do Governador
Moneró
Jardim Guanabara
Cocotá
Zumbi
Penha
Ribeira
Ilha dos Tavares
Porto Novo
Olaria
Cosmos
Ramos
Ilha do Engenho
Baía de Guanabara
Serra da Misericórdia
Bonsucesso
Ilha do Fundão
Cidade Universitária
Ilha de Santa Cruz
Neves
Inhaúma
Ponte Rio-Niterói
Pilares
Piedade
Caju
Ilha da Conceição
Barreto
Benefica
AEROPORTO MANGUINHOS
Armação
São Cristóvão
Encantado
Jacaré
Méier
Ilha das Cobras
Gamboa
Niterói
Gragoatá
Água Santa
AEROPORTO SANTOS DUMONT
Icaraí
Vila Isabel
Maracanã
Rio Comprido
Lapa
Catete
Naval Academy
Enseada de Jurujuba
RIO DE JANEIRO
Serra dos Três Rios
Andaraí
Tijuca
Flamengo
Morro do Macaco
Pico da Tijuca
Usina
Botafogo
Urca
Pão de Açúcar (Sugar Loaf Mt.)
Jd. Mar Azul
Parque Nacional da Tijuca
Corcovado
Lagoa
Alto do Boa Vista
Gávea
Itanhanga
Copacabana
Ilha de Cotunduba
Ilha do Pai
Ipanema
Leblon
Pedra da Gávea
São Conrado
ATLANTIC OCEAN
Ponta do Marisco
West from Greenwich
CENTRAL RIO DE JANEIRO
0 km 0.5
0 miles 0.25
Cais do Pharoux
Baía de Guanabara
AVENIDA RIO BRANCO
RUA V. INHAÚMA
Nossa Senhora da Candelária
Casa França Brasil
Centro Cultural Banco do Brasil
Doca do Mercado
Estação Dom Pedro II
AVE PRESIDENTE VARGAS
AVENIDA PRESIDENTE KUBITSCHEK
RUA PRIMEIRO DE MARÇO
Uruguaiana
N S do Carmo da Antiga Sé
Chafariz do Pirâmide
Praça 15 de Novembro
Paço Imperial
Museu Naval e Oceanográfico
Praça Mercado Municipal
Praça Marechal Âncora
Museu da Imagem e do Som
Museu Histórico Nacional
Praça Tiradentes
São Francisco Penitência
Carioca
Santa Casa da Misericórdia
Museu Nacionale de Belas Artes
Biblioteca Nacional
Teatro Municipal
Cinelândia
AVENIDA PRESIDENTE ANTÔNIO CARLOS
Aeroporto Santos Dumont
Catedral Metropolitana
Passeio Público
TREVO DOS ESTUDANTES
AVE MEM DE SÁ
RUA TEIXEIRA DE FREITAS
AVENIDA INFANTE DOM HENRIQUE
Museu de Arte Moderna
Pão de Açúcar
Enseada da Glória

ROME

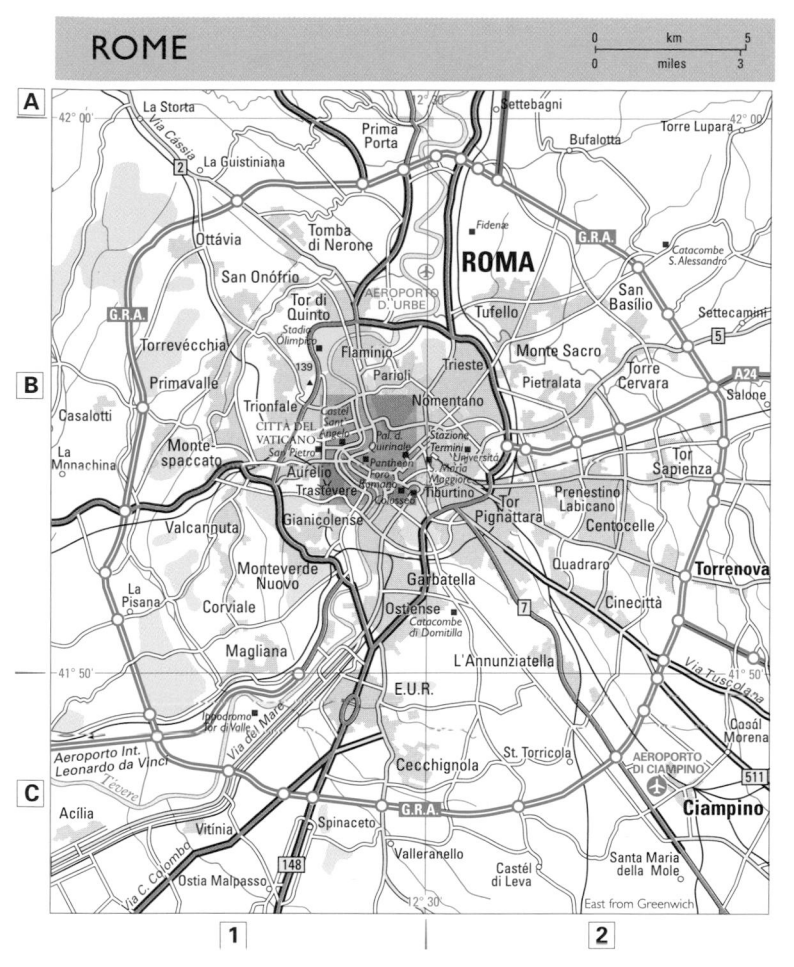

CENTRAL ROME

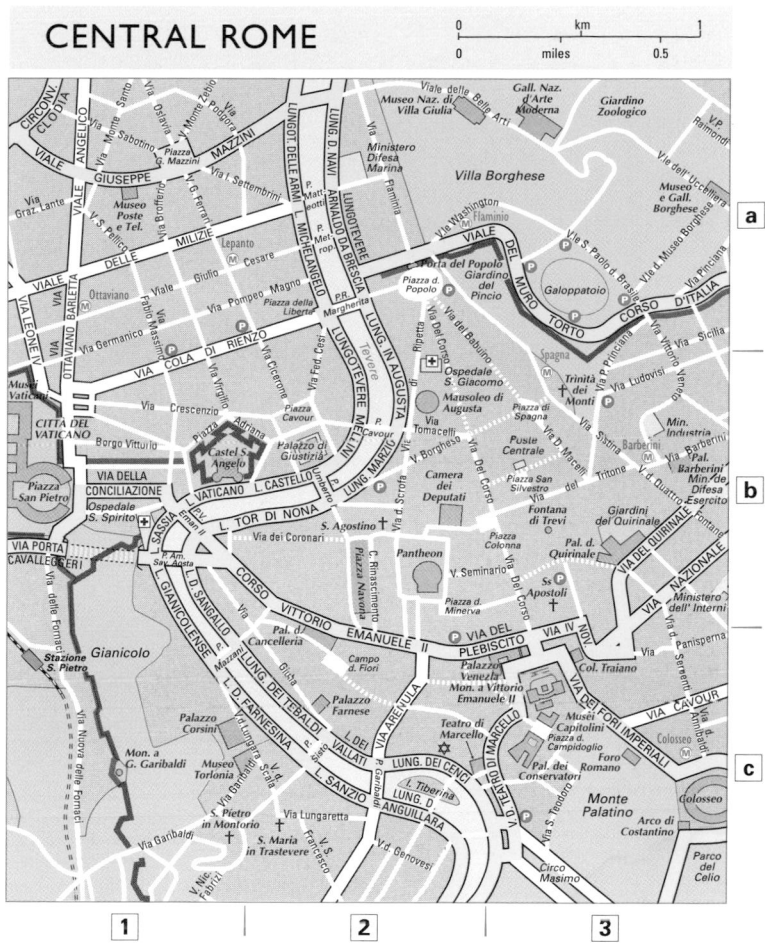

SAN FRANCISCO

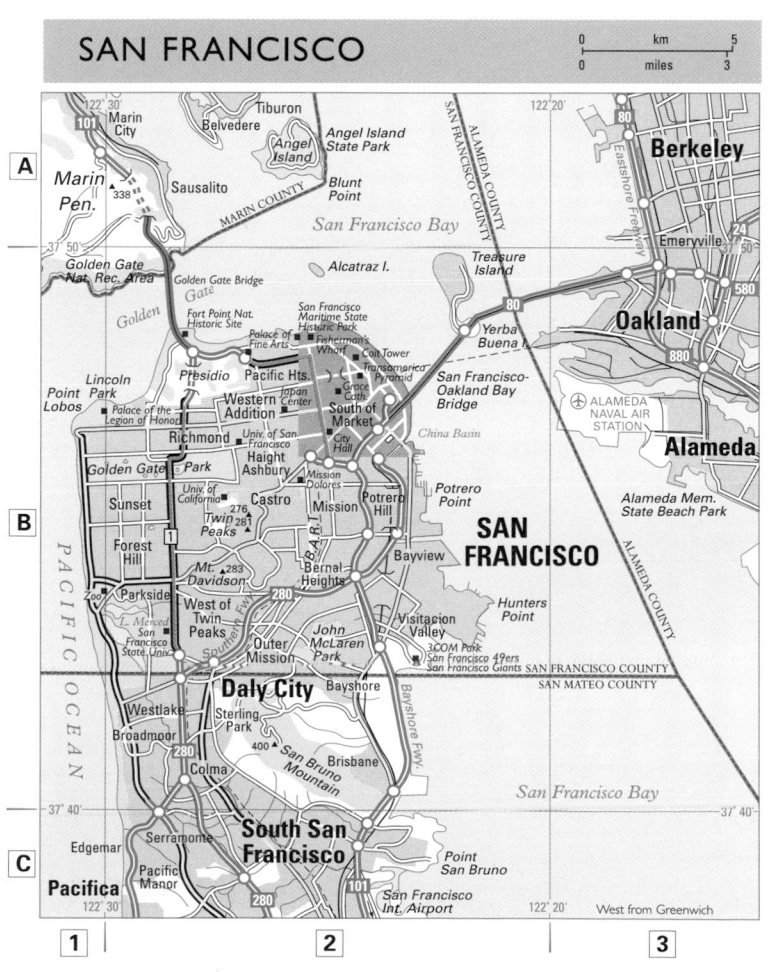

CENTRAL SAN FRANCISCO

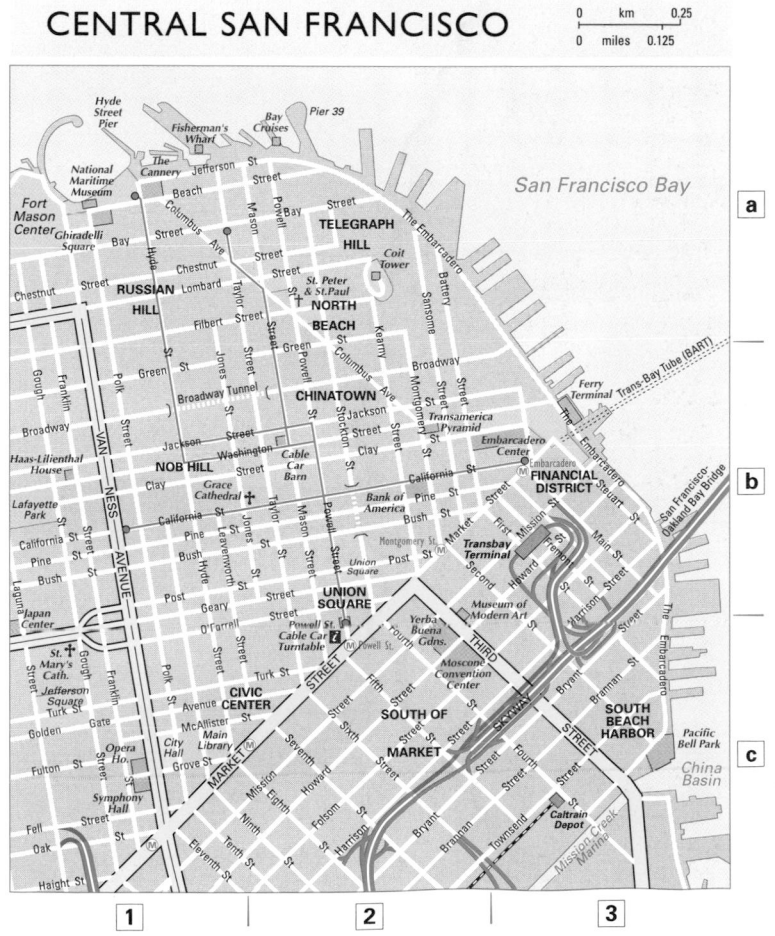

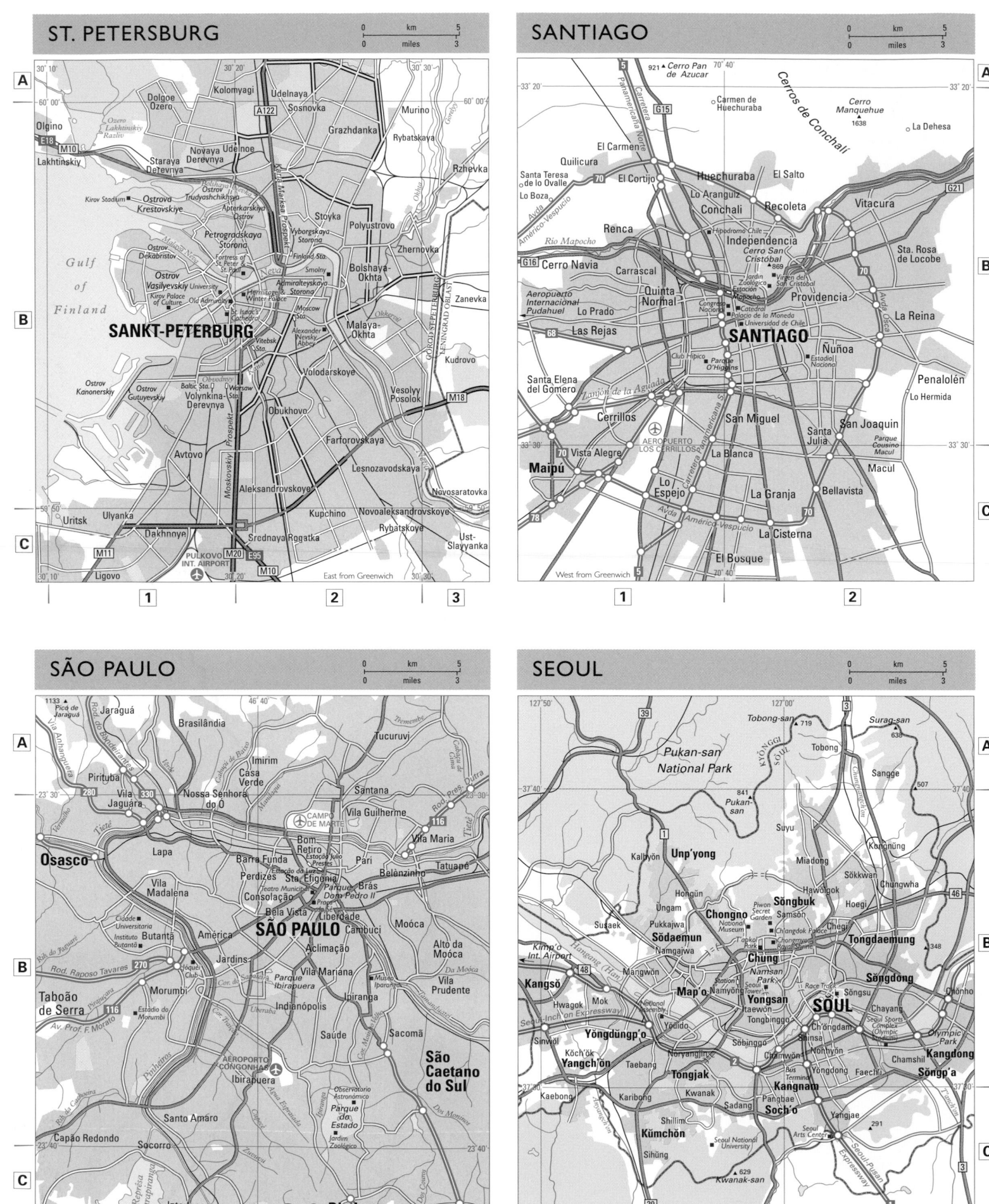

ST. PETERSBURG

0 — km — 5
0 — miles — 3

Olgino
Lakhtinskiy
Dolgoe Ozero
Kolomyagi
Udelnaya
Sosnovka
Murino
Ozero Lakhtinskiy Razliv
Novaya Udelnoe
Grazhdanka
Rybatskaya
Staraya Derevnya
Novaya Derevnya
Rzhevka
Kirov Stadium
Ostrova Krestovskiye
Ostrova Trudyashchikhsya
Apterkarskiy Ostrov
Vyborgskaya Storona
Stoyka
Polyustrovo
Zhernovka
Petrogradskaya Storona
Finland Sta.
Smolny
Bolshaya-Okhta
Ostrov Dekabristov
Ostrov Vasilyevskiy
University
Fortress of St. Peter & Paul
Admiralteyskaya Storona
Moscow Sta.
Okkervil
Zanevka
Gulf of Finland
Kirov Palace of Culture
St. Isaac's Cathedral
Old Admiralty
Hermitage & Winter Palace
Malaya-Okhta
Kudrovo
SANKT-PETERBURG
Vitebsk Sta.
Alexander Nevsky Abbey
Ostrov Kanonerskiy
Baltic Sta.
Obvodnyy
Volodarskoye
Ostrov Gutuyevskiy
Warsaw Sta.
Volynkina-Derevnya
Obukhovo
Vesolyy Posolok
Avtovo
Farforovskaya
Ulyanka
Lesnozavodskaya
Uritsk
Dakhnoye
Srednyaya Rogatka
Kupchino
Novoaleksandrovskoye
Rybatskoye
Novosaratovka
Ligovo
PULKOVO INT. AIRPORT
Aleksandrovskoye
Ust-Slavyanka
East from Greenwich

SANTIAGO

0 — km — 5
0 — miles — 3

Cerro Pan de Azucar
Carmen de Huechuraba
Cerro Manquehue 1638
La Dehesa
Cerros de Conchalí
El Carmen
Quilicura
Santa Teresa de lo Ovalle
Lo Boza
El Cortijo
Huechuraba
Lo Aranguiz
El Salto
Conchalí
Recoleta
Vitacura
Renca
Hipódromo Chile
Independencia
Cerro San Cristóbal 869
Sta. Rosa de Locobe
Cerro Navia
Carrascal
Jardin Zoológico
Virgen del San Cristóbal
Estación Mapocho
Providencia
La Reina
Aeropuerto Internacional Pudahuel
Quinta Normal
Congreso Nacional
Catedral
Palacio de la Moneda
Universidad de Chile
Las Rejas
SANTIAGO
Ñuñoa
Penalolén
Lo Hermida
Club Hípico
Parque O'Higgins
Estadio Nacional
Santa Elena del Gomero
Cerrillos
San Miguel
San Joaquin
Parque Cousino Macul
AEROPUERTO LOS CERRILLOS
Vista Alegre
Santa Julia
Macul
Maipú
La Blanca
Lo Espejo
La Granja
Bellavista
La Cisterna
La Pintana
El Bosque
West from Greenwich

SÃO PAULO

0 — km — 5
0 — miles — 3

Pico de Jaraguá 1133
Jaraguá
Brasilândia
Tucuruvi
Tremembé
Piritiba
Vila Jaguára
Nossa Senhora do Ó
Imirim
Casa Verde
Santana
Osasco
Lapa
Bom Retiro
Vila Guilherme
Vila Maria
Campo de Marte
Perdizes
Estação Júlio Prestes
Pari
Belenzinho
Tatuapé
Vila Madalena
Barra Funda
Sta. Efigênia
Estação da Luz
Brás
Teatro Municipal
Dom Pedro II
Cidade Universitária
Consolação
Butantã
Instituto Butantã
América
Bela Vista
Liberdade
Moóca
SÃO PAULO
Cambuci
Alto da Moóca
Jockey Club
Jardins
Aclimação
Da Moóca
Morumbi
Parque Ibirapuera
Vila Mariana
Vila Prudente
Taboão de Serra
Estádio do Morumbi
Indianópolis
Ipiranga
Saúde
Sacomã
AEROPORTO CONGONHAS
Ibirapuera
São Caetano do Sul
Observatório Astronômico
Parque do Estado
Jardim Zoológico
Santo Amaro
Capão Redondo
Socorro
Interlagos
Diadema
West from Greenwich

SEOUL

0 — km — 5
0 — miles — 3

Tobong-san 719
Surag-san 638
Pukan-san National Park
Tobong
Sanggé
Pukan-san 841
507
Suyu
Kanŭng
Kalhyŏn
Unp'yong
Miadong
Sökkwan
Chungwha
Hongŭn
Ungam
Hawŏlgok
Piwon Secret Garden
Songbuk
Samsŏn
Hoegi
Chongno
National Museum
Changdok Palace
Chongmyo Royal Shrine
Thegi
Södaemun
Tapkol Park
Tongdaemung
Namgajwa
348
Kimp'o Int. Airport
Chung
Station
Namsan Park
Namsan Tower
Songdong
Kangsŏ
Mangwŏn
National Assembly
Mok
Map'o
Yongsan
Itaewŏn
Race Track
Songsu
Chayang
Hwagok
Seoul Sports Complex
Olympic Park
Yŏŭido
Sŏbinggo
SŎUL
Ch'ŏngdam
Sinwŏl
Yŏngdŭngp'o
Noryangjin
Chamwŏn
Sinsa
Nonhyŏn
Ôhnho
Yangch'on
Taebang
Yongdong
Faechŏi
Kangdong
Tongjak
Bus Terminal
Kangnam
Songp'a
Kaebong
Karibong
Kwanak
Panghae
Sadang
Yangjae
Kümch'ŏn
Shillim
Seoul National University
Seoul Arts Center
291
Sihŭng
Kwanak-san 629
East from Greenwich

SHANGHAI

km 5 / miles 3

A
Liuhang
Yangjiazhuang
Wusong
Tangqiao
Baoshan
Gaoqiao
Yinhangzhen
31° 20'
Dachang Airfield
Jiangwan
Jiaodong University
Zhenru
Zhenru
Beijiao
Wujiaochang
Sun Lu
Yangpu Park
Donggou
Zhabei
Hongkou Stadium
Zhan
Heping Park
Yangpu
Fuxing Dao
Hongkou Park
Tomb of Lu Xun
Hongkou
Qingningsi
31°20'
B
312
Putuo
Jade Buddha Temple
Shangho
Shanghai
Zhabei
Tilangqiao
Yangshupu Lu
Yangpu Bridge
Zhoujiazhen
Changfeng Park
Zhongshan Park
Jingan
Huangpu
People's Park
People's Square
Shanghai Museum
Huangpu
Pudong Dadao
Yangjing
Beixing Jing Park
Changning
Xi Zhan
Yan'an Lu
Fuxing Park
Old City
Yuyuan Garden
Puxi
Huangpu
SHANGHAI
Shanghai Zoo
318
Xujiahui
Sun Yat Sen's Former Residence
Luwan
Nanshi
Pudong New Area
Hongqiao
Hongqiao Airport
Caoheijing
Gymnasium
Longhua Park
Fuxing Park
Nanshi
Nanpu Bridge
Beicai
31° 10'
Nanshi
Zhoujiadu
Chuanyang
31°10'
C
Longhua Pagoda
Sanlintang
LONGHUA AIRFIELD
320
Botanical Gardens
Gangkou
Huangpu Jiang
East from Greenwich 121°30'

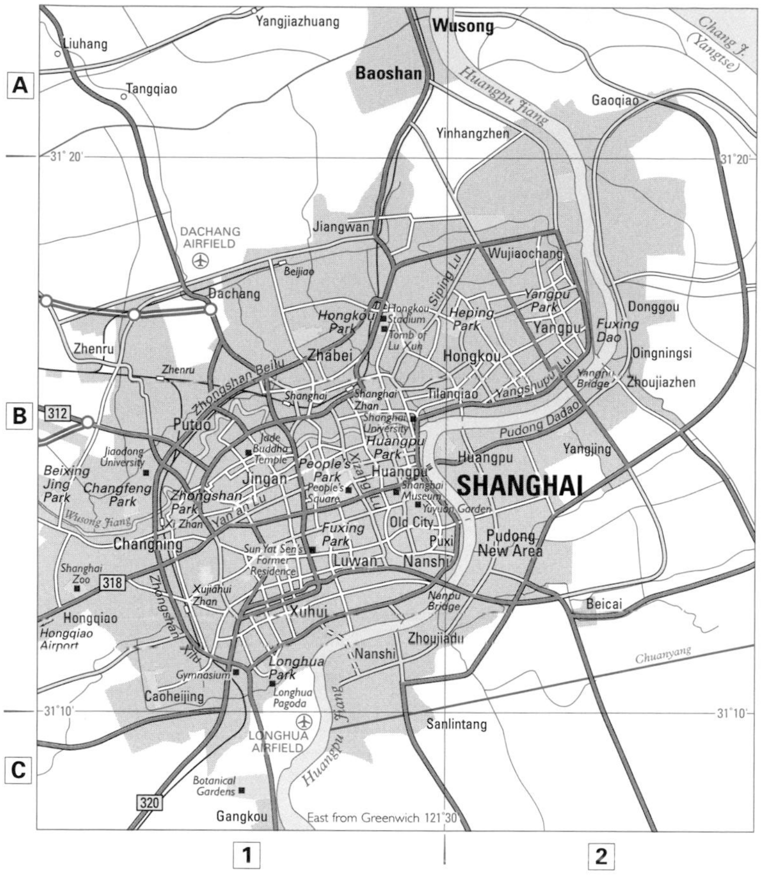

1   2

CENTRAL SINGAPORE

km 1 / miles 0.5

Temple
CAIRNHILL ROAD
RIDGECARD RD.
Istana (President's Residence)
Kandang Kerbau Hospital
Cuff Rd
CLEMENCEAU AVE
BUKIT TIMAH ROAD
Upper Weld Rd
Sim Lim Tower
Abdul Gaffoor Mosque
Central Park
Edinburgh
Sophia Road
MacKenzie
Zhujiao
SERANGOON ROAD
SHORT STREET
Dunlop St
JALAN BESAR
a
Thong Sia Bldg.
Emerald Hill
Mount Emily Park
Wilkie Road
Sim Lim Square
El Bujtin
Blanco Court
ORCHARD ROAD
Cuppage Centre
Faber House
Centrepoint
Orchard Plaza
Orchard Point
Sri Temasek
Sophia Road
Handy Road
Waterloo St
St. Joseph's Church
Bencoolen Mosque
MIDDLE ROAD
ROCHOR CANAL RD.
Bus Station
N2 Somerset
ORCHARD
ROAD
PENANG ROAD
N1 Dhoby Ghaut
Chesed El Synagogue
Sri Thandayuthapani Temple
Singapore Art Museum
VICTORIA
Raffles Hotel
b
RIVER VALLEY ROAD
KLANG LANE
Lloyd Rd
OXLEY
ORCHARD
BOULEVARD
AVENUE
Sacred Heart Church
Singapore Hist. Mus.
Battle Box
Fort Canning Park
CITY CENTRE
Asian Civ. Mus.
BRAS BASAH ROAD
Queen St
Resah St
ST ANDREW'S RD
Westin Plaza
Hong San See Temple
Van Kleef Aquarium
Canning Rise
Singapore Philatelic Mus.
Funan Centre
STAMFORD
HILL
City Hall
St. Andrew's Cathedral
War Memorial Park
CLEMENCEAU
TANK ROAD
Clarke Quay
North Boat Quay
Boat Quay
Supreme Court
Esplanade Park
Singapore Cricket Club
HAVELOCK ROAD
MERCHANT ROAD
Road
Road
Parliament Hse.
CONNAUGHT DR
c
Swee
Swee
Melaka Mosque
UPPER CROSS STREET
N CANAL RD
PICKERING STREET
SOUTH BRIDGE ROAD
Wak Hai Cheng Bio Temple
Raffles Landing Site
Empress Pl. Museum
Victoria Concert Hall & Theatre
Merlion Park
Marina Bay
Pearl's Hill City Park
Pearl's Hill Reservoir
Outram Park
People's Park Complex
NEW BRIDGE ROAD
Pagoda St
CHINATOWN
Jamae Mosque
Fuk Tak Ch'i Temple
C1 Raffles Place
Clifford Pier
SENTOSA
Smith St
Oriental Theatre
Temple St
Sri Mariamman Temple
QUAY

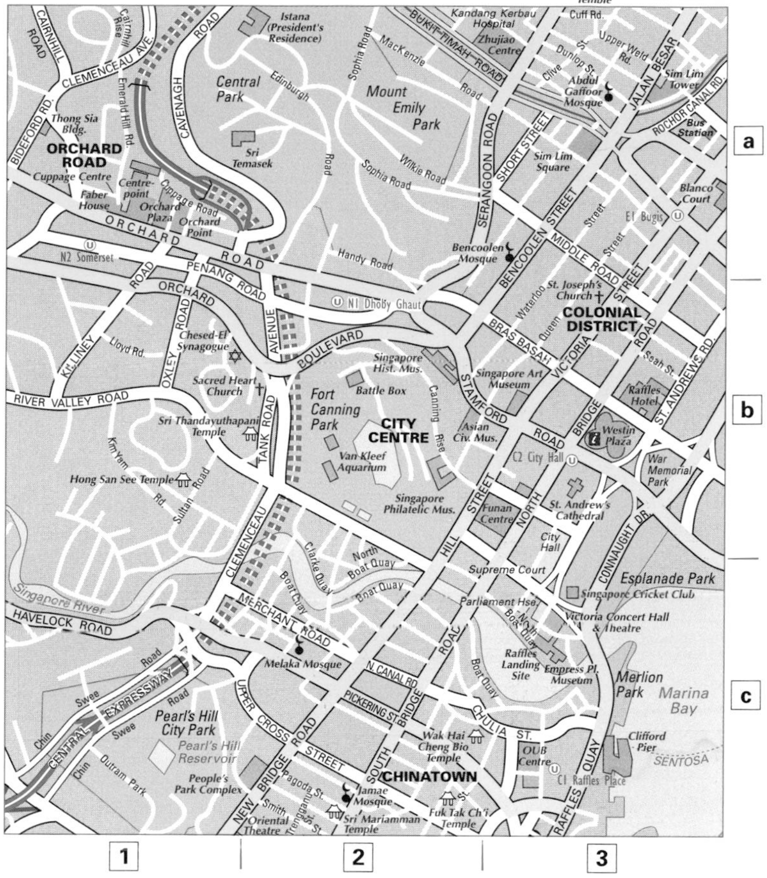

1   2   3

SINGAPORE

km 10 / miles 6

103°40'
Malaya
Johor Baharu
Sembawang
Selat Johor
103°50'
Kim
104°00'
MALAYSIA SINGAPORE
Kranji Ind. Est.
Woodlands New Town
Chong Pang
Pulau Seletar
Punggol Point
Pulau Ubin
Pulau Tekong Kechil
Pulau Tekong
A
Lim Chu Kang
Sungai Kadut Ind. Est.
Yishun New Town
Pulau Serangoon
Tg. Ladang
Sarimbun Res.
Sarimbun 85
Murai Res.
Ama Keng
Zoological Gardens
Seletar Reservoir
Nee Soon
SELETAR AIRPORT
Jalan Kayu
Punggol
Serangoon Harbour
Loyang Ind. Est.
Changi
CHANGI INTERNATIONAL AIRPORT
Choa Chu Kang
Bukit Panjang Nature Reserve
Seletar Hills
Pasir Ris
MALAYSIA SINGAPORE
Selat Johor
Causeway
P-yan Res.
Choa Chu Kang 88
Bulim
Bt. Panjang
Bukit Panjang
Upper Peirce Reservoir
Ang Mo Kio
Serangoon
Chia Keng
Yan Kit
Nanyang University
Bukit Timah Nature Reserve 106
162
MacRitchie Reservoir
Paya Lebar
PAYA LEBAR AIRPORT
Tampines
Simei
Tanah Merah Golf Course
Bukit Batok Nature Parks
Air View Park
Raffles Park
Pan-Island Expy.
Toa Payoh
Kg Landang
Bedok Reservoir
Jurong Town
Chinese & Japanese Gardens
Clementi
Maryland
Holland Village
Duneart
Geylang Serai
Chai Chee
Bedok
1°20'N
Tuas
Jurong
Bt. Peropok 62
Kg Tanjong Penjuru
Pandan Res.
Victoria Park
University of Singapore Botanic Gardens
Geylang
Katong
East Coast Park
1°20'N
Jurong Industrial Estate
Pasir Panjang
Queenstown
Telok Blangah
National Stadium
Kallang
East Coast Pkwy.
B
Pulau Pesek
Pulau Merlimau
Buona Vista Park
Mt. Faber 106
St Andrew's Cathedral
National Museum
City Hall
Thian Hock Keng
SINGAPORE
Straits of Singapore
B
Pulau Ayer Chawan
Pulau Seraya
Pulau Ayer Merbau
Cable Car
World Trade Centre
P. Brani
Keppel Harbour
Pulau Sakra
Selat Pandan
Sentosa
Pulau Bukum
Selat Sinki
103°40'
103°50'
East from Greenwich
104°00'

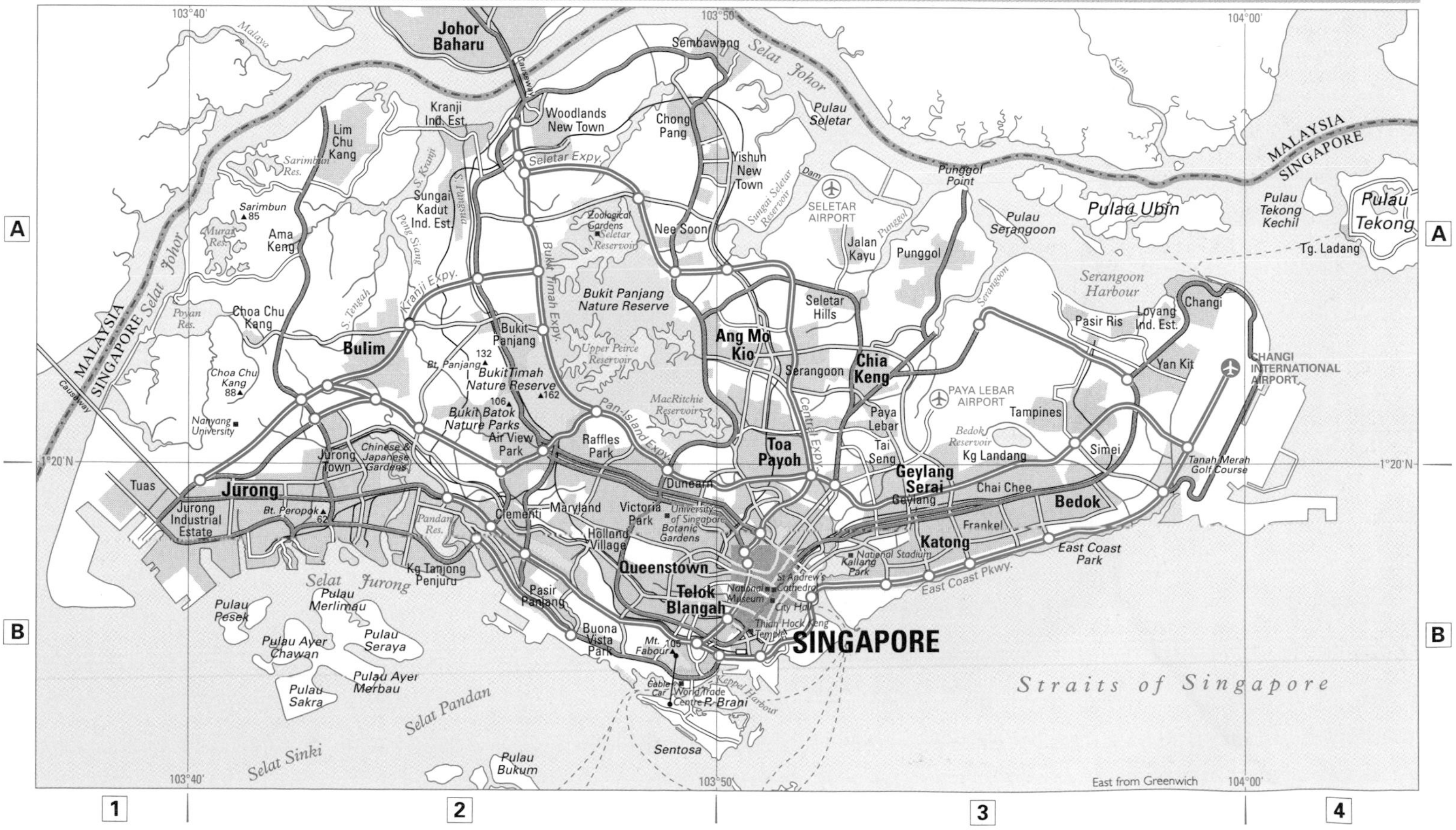

1   2   3   4

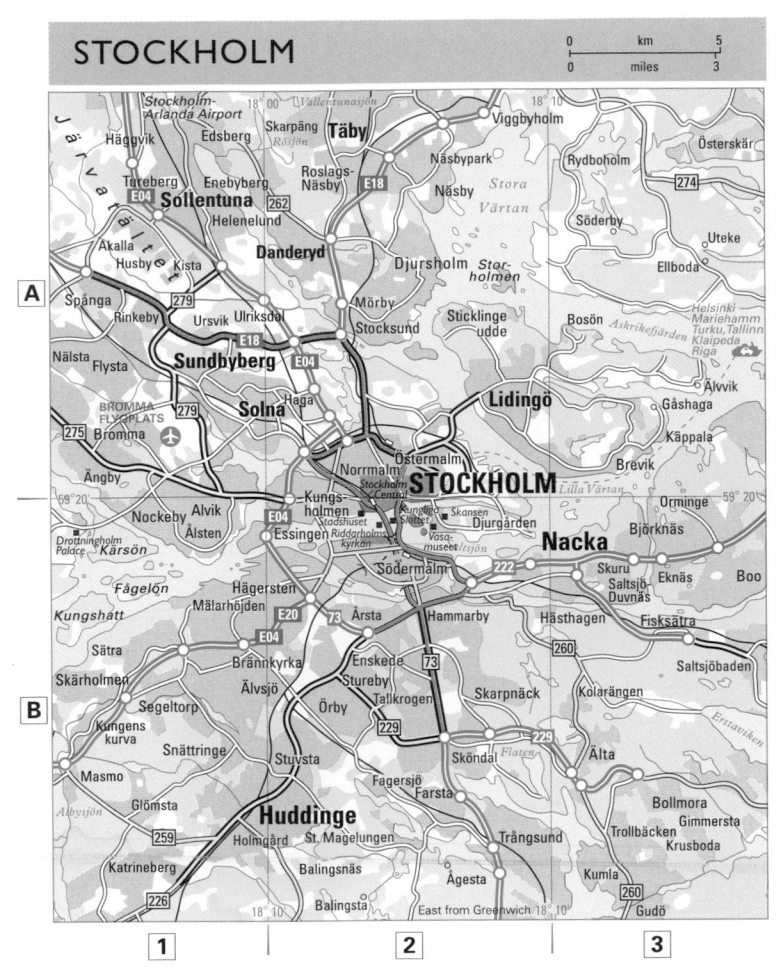
STOCKHOLM
0 km 5
0 miles 3
Stockholm-Arlanda Airport
Täby
Vallentunasjön
Viggbyholm
Häggvik
Edsberg
Skarpäng
Österskär
Näsbypark
Rydboholm
Sollentuna
Enebyberg
Roslags-Näsby
Näsby
Stora Värtan
Helenelund
Söderby
Uteke
Danderyd
Akalla
Husby
Kista
Djursholm
Ellboda
Spånga
Mörby
Rinkeby
Ursvik
Ulriksdal
Sticklinge udde
Bosön
Stocksund
Nälsta
Flysta
Sundbyberg
Älvvik
Lidingö
Gåshaga
Solna
Haga
Bromma
Käppala
Ängby
Norrmalm
Östermalm
Brevik
STOCKHOLM
Lilla Värtan
Kungsholmen
Orminge
Nockeby
Alvik
Ålsten
Djurgården
Björknäs
Nacka
Essingen
Södermalm
Drottningholm Palace
Kärsön
Eknäs
Boo
Fågelön
Hägersten
Saltsjö-Duvnäs
Mälarhöjden
Kungshatt
Årsta
Hammarby
Hästhagen
Fisksätra
Sätra
Brännkyrka
Enskede
Saltsjöbaden
Skärholmen
Stureby
Älvsjö
Tallkrogen
Skarpnäck
Kolarängen
Segeltorp
Örby
Kungens kurva
Snättringe
Stuvsta
Sköndal
Älta
Masmo
Fagersjö
Farsta
Glömsta
Huddinge
Bollmora
Gimmersta
Holmgård
St. Magelungen
Trångsund
Trollbäcken
Krusboda
Katrineberg
Balingsnäs
Ågesta
Kumla
Balingsta
East from Greenwich
Gudö
A
B
1
2
3

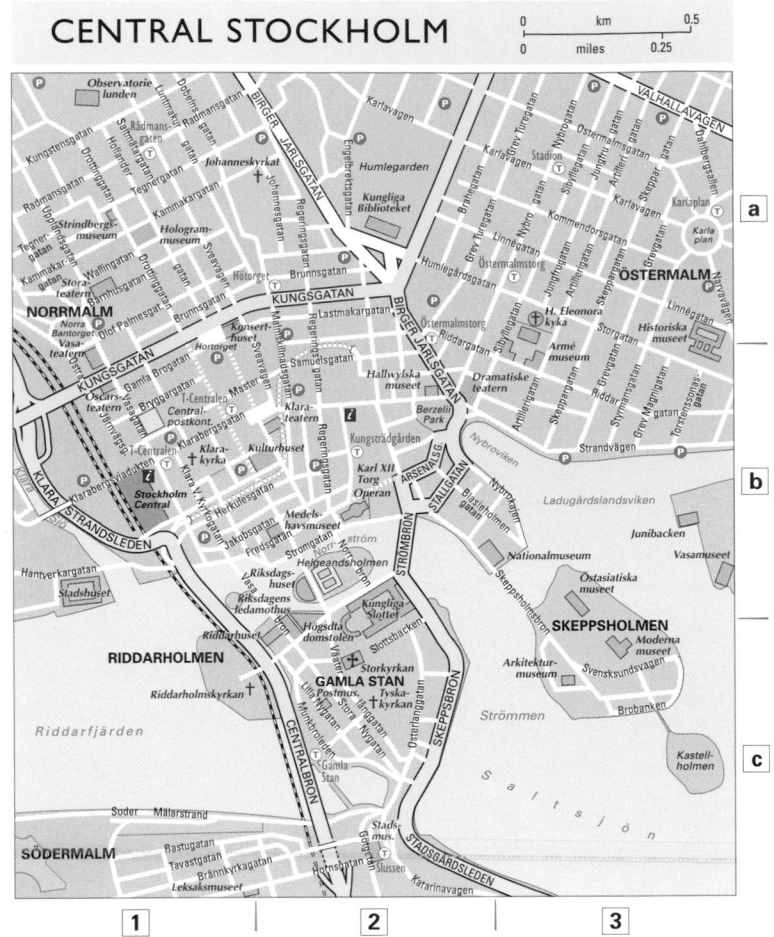
CENTRAL STOCKHOLM
0 km 0.5
0 miles 0.25
Observatorielunden
Karlavägen
VALHALLAVÄGEN
Humlegården
Kungliga Biblioteket
Johanneskyrkan
Strindbergsmuseum
Hologram-museum
ÖSTERMALM
NORRMALM
KUNGSGATAN
BIRGER JARLSGATAN
H. Eleonora kyrka
Armé museum
Historiska museet
Hallwylska museet
Dramatiska teatern
Berzelii Park
Strandvägen
Stockholm Central
Klara kyrka
Kulturhuset
Kungsträdgården
Karl XII Torg
Operan
Nybroviken
Ladugårdslandsviken
Junibacken
Vasamuseet
Nationalmuseum
Östasiatiska museet
SKEPPSHOLMEN
Moderna museet
Arkitektur-museum
Stadshuset
Riksdagshuset
Helgeandsholmen
Kungliga Slottet
Storkyrkan
RIDDARHOLMEN
Riddarholmskyrkan
GAMLA STAN
Tyska kyrkan
Riddarfjärden
Strömmen
Kastellholmen
Saltsjön
SÖDERMALM
Slussen
CENTRALBRON
SKEPPSBRON
STRÖMBRON
STADSGÅRDSLEDEN
a
b
c
1
2
3

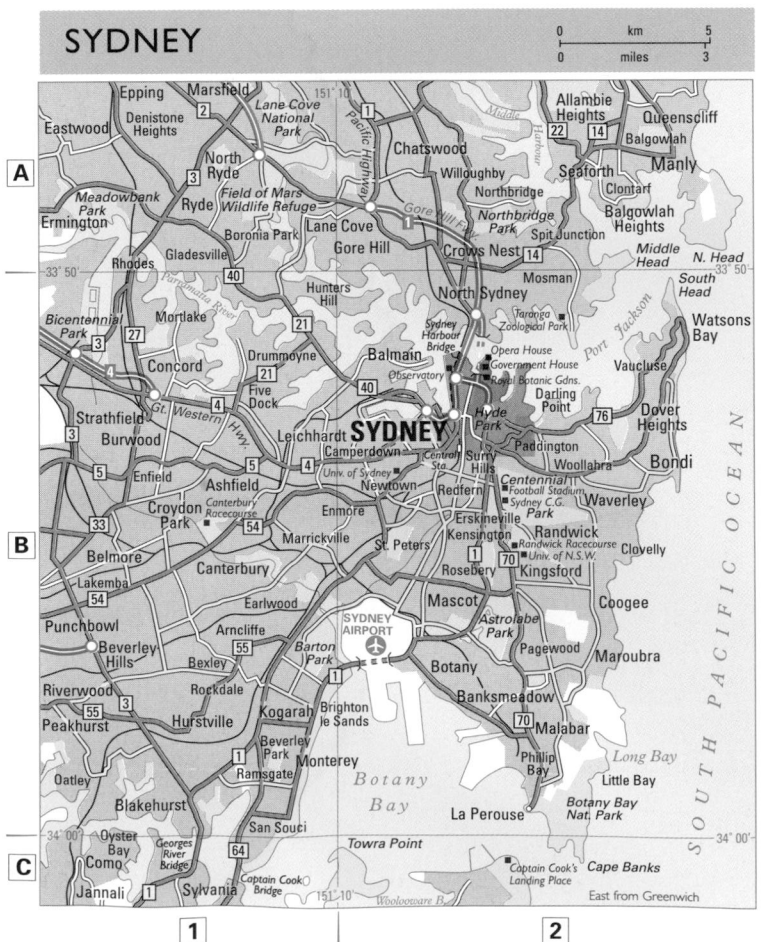
SYDNEY
0 km 5
0 miles 3
Epping
Marsfield
Lane Cove National Park
Allambie Heights
Queenscliff
Eastwood
Denistone Heights
Balgowlah
Chatswood
Manly
North Ryde
Willoughby
Seaforth
Meadowbank Park
Field of Mars Wildlife Refuge
Northbridge
Clontarf
Ermington
Ryde
Lane Cove
Balgowlah Heights
Boronia Park
Spit Junction
Gladesville
Gore Hill
Crows Nest
Middle Head
Rhodes
Mosman
N. Head
South Head
Hunters Hill
North Sydney
Bicentennial Park
Mortlake
Taronga Zoological Park
Watsons Bay
Port Jackson
Drummoyne
Balmain
Opera House
Concord
Vaucluse
Five Dock
Darling Point
Strathfield
Dover Heights
Burwood
Leichhardt
SYDNEY
Paddington
Camperdown
Woollahra
Bondi
Enfield
Ashfield
Newtown
Surry Hills
Redfern
Centennial Park
Croydon Park
Enmore
Waverley
Erskineville
Randwick
Clovelly
Marrickville
St. Peters
Kensington
Belmore
Canterbury
Rosebery
Kingsford
Lakemba
Earlwood
Mascot
Coogee
Punchbowl
Arncliffe
SYDNEY AIRPORT
Astrolabe Park
Beverley Hills
Bexley
Barton Park
Pagewood
Maroubra
Botany
Riverwood
Rockdale
Banksmeadow
Kogarah
Brighton le Sands
Peakhurst
Hurstville
Malabar
Long Bay
Beverley Park
Monterey
Phillip Bay
Little Bay
Oatley
Ramsgate
Botany Bay
Blakehurst
La Perouse
Botany Bay Nat. Park
San Souci
Oyster Bay
Como
Towra Point
Cape Banks
Jannali
Sylvania
Captain Cook's Landing Place
East from Greenwich
SOUTH PACIFIC OCEAN
A
B
C
1
2

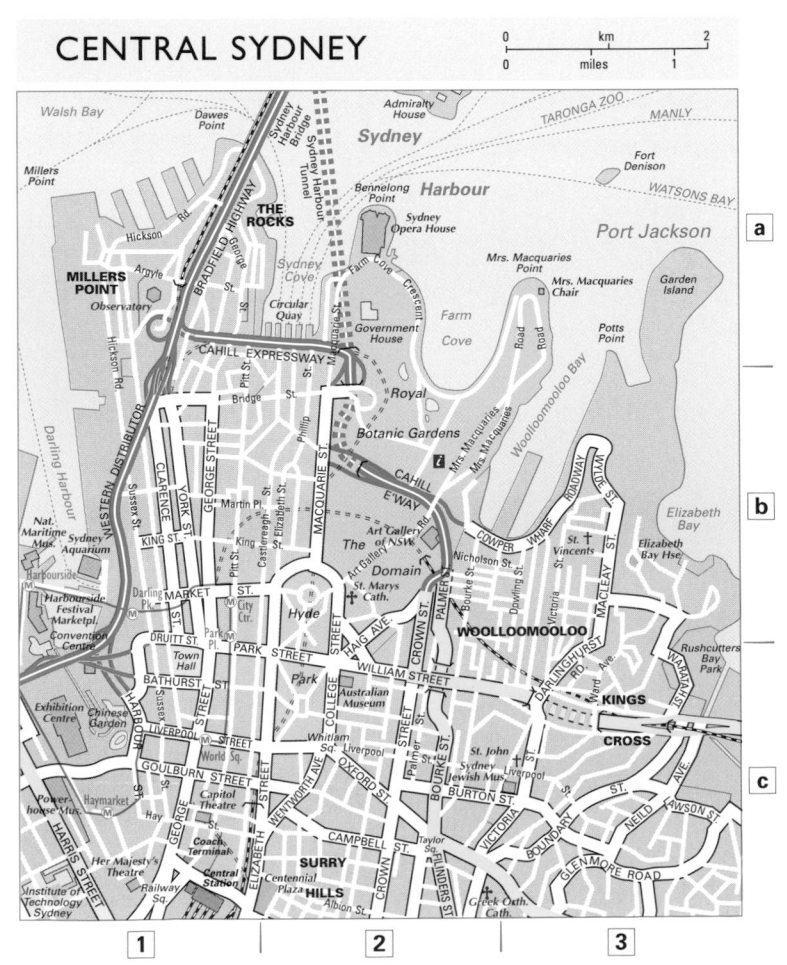
CENTRAL SYDNEY
0 km 2
0 miles 1
Walsh Bay
Dawes Point
Admiralty House
TARONGA ZOO
MANLY
Sydney Harbour Bridge
Sydney Harbour Tunnel
Sydney Harbour
Fort Denison
Millers Point
Bennelong Point
WATSONS BAY
THE ROCKS
Sydney Opera House
Port Jackson
MILLERS POINT
Observatory
Mrs. Macquaries Point
Mrs. Macquaries Chair
Garden Island
Sydney Cove
Circular Quay
Government House
Farm Cove
Potts Point
CAHILL EXPRESSWAY
Royal Botanic Gardens
Darling Harbour
WESTERN DISTRIBUTOR
GEORGE STREET
MACQUARIE ST.
CAHILL E'WAY
Woolloomooloo Bay
Elizabeth Bay
Nat. Maritime Mus.
Sydney Aquarium
KING ST.
Art Gallery of NSW
St. Vincents
Elizabeth Bay Hse.
The Domain
Harbourside Festival Marketpl.
MARKET ST.
Hyde Park
St. Marys Cath.
WOOLLOOMOOLOO
Rushcutters Bay Park
Convention Centre
Town Hall
PARK STREET
WILLIAM STREET
Australian Museum
KINGS CROSS
Exhibition Centre
Chinese Garden
LIVERPOOL
OXFORD ST.
Haymarket
Capitol Theatre
GOULBURN STREET
Powerhouse Mus.
Her Majesty's Theatre
Central Station
SURRY HILLS
CAMPBELL ST.
Institute of Technology Sydney
GLENMORE ROAD
Greek Orth. Cath.
a
b
c
1
2
3

TOKYO

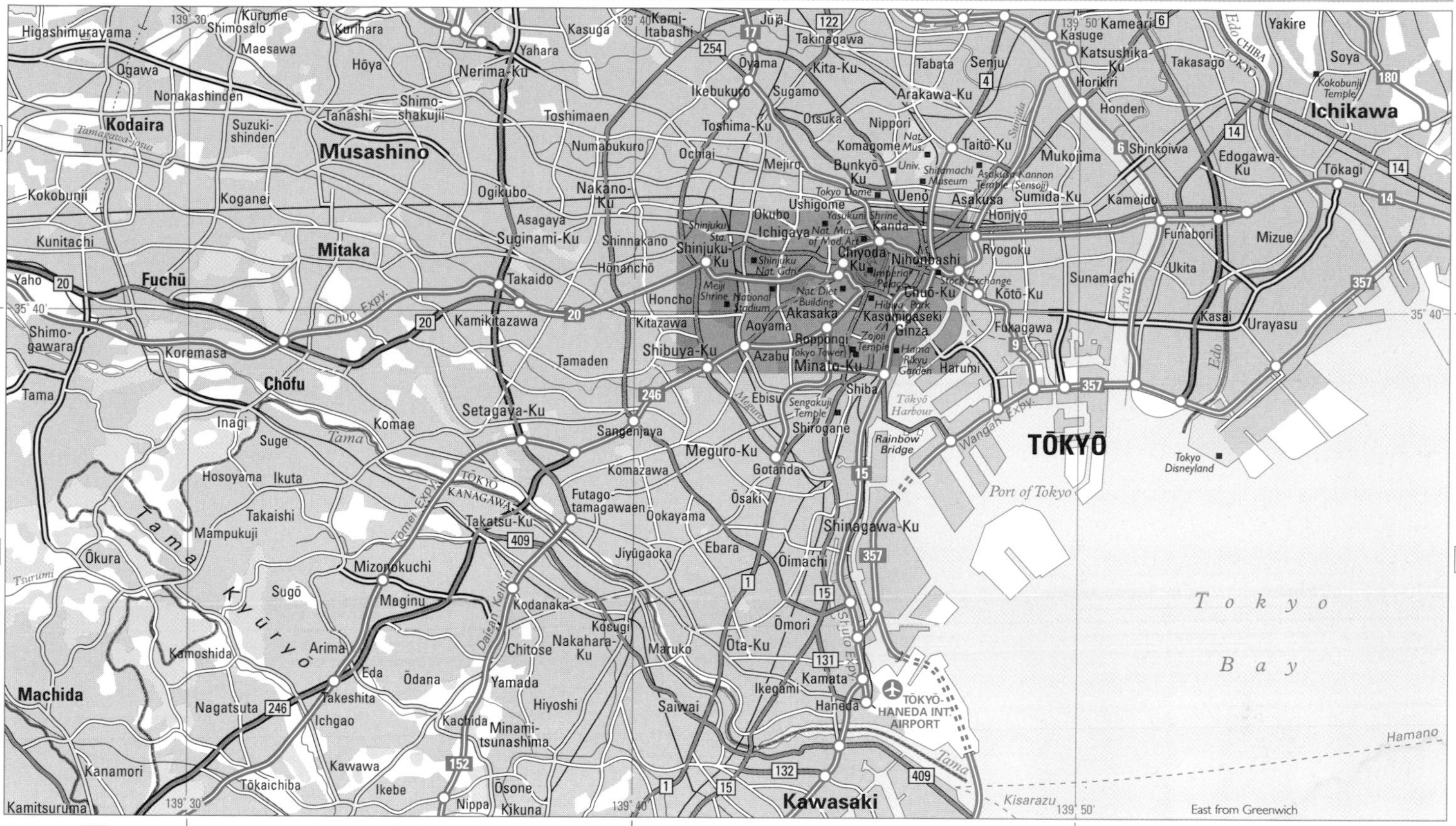

0 km 5
0 miles 3

Higashimurayama Shimosalo Kurume Kami- Jūjō Takinagawa 122 17 Kasuge Katsushika- Takasago 139 50 Kameari 6 Yakire Soya
Kodaira Ogawa Nonakashinden Shimo-shakujii Yahara Kasuga 139 40 Oyama Kita-Ku 254 Senju 4 Horikiri Honden Shinkoiwa 14 Edogawa- Tōkagi 14
A Musashino Hōya Nerima-Ku Ikebukuro Sugamo Arakawa-Ku Ushigome Mukojima Kameido 357 180 Ichikawa A
Mitaka Suzuki-shinden Tanashi Toshimaen Toshima-Ku Ōtsuka Nippori Asakusa Honjyo Funabori Mizue
Fuchū Koganei Asagaya Suginami-Ku Nakano-Ku Mejiro Bunkyō-Ku Ueno Sumida-Ku Kasai Urayasu
Kokubunji Kunitachi Takaido 20 Honancho Shinjuku-Ku Chiyoda Nihonbashi Chūō-Ku Kōtō-Ku
Yaho 20 Kamikitazawa Akasaka Roppongi Ginza Fukagawa 9 357
Shimo-gawara Koremasa Kitazawa Shibuya-Ku Minato-Ku Shiba Harumi
Chōfu Setagaya-Ku Tamaden Aoyama Ebisu Shirogane TŌKYŌ Tokyo Disneyland
Inagi Komae Sangenjaya Meguro-Ku Gotanda Rainbow Bridge Port of Tokyo
B Machida Tama Takatsu-Ku Komazawa Jiyūgaoka Ōsaki Shinagawa-Ku Tōkyō Harbour T o k y o B a y B
Nagatsuta 246 Mizonokuchi Ebara Ōimachi 357 15
Takeshita Ichgao Ōdana Yamada Hiyoshi Ōta-Ku Ōmori
Kanamori Kawawa Ikebe Saiwai Ikegami Kamata Haneda TŌKYŌ HANEDA INT AIRPORT Hamano
Kamitsuruma 139 30 Nippa Kikuna 1 15 132 Kawasaki 409 Kisarazu 139 50 East from Greenwich

1 2 3 4

CENTRAL TOKYO

0 km 1
0 miles 0.5

ŌKUBO-DŌRI AKIHABARA ASAKUSABASHI
SHINJUKU-KU ŌKUBO KUDANKITA
a ICHIGAYA JIMBŌCHO KANDA KODENMACHO a
YOTSUYA SANBANCHO MARUNOUCHI NIHONBASHI
b CHIYODA-KU CHŪŌ-KU b
AKASAKA KASUMIGASEKI GINZA
c SHIBUYA-KU AOYAMA TORANOMON SHIMBASHI TSUKIJI c
ROPPONGI MINATO-KU SHIBA HARUMI
AZABU

1 2 3 4 5

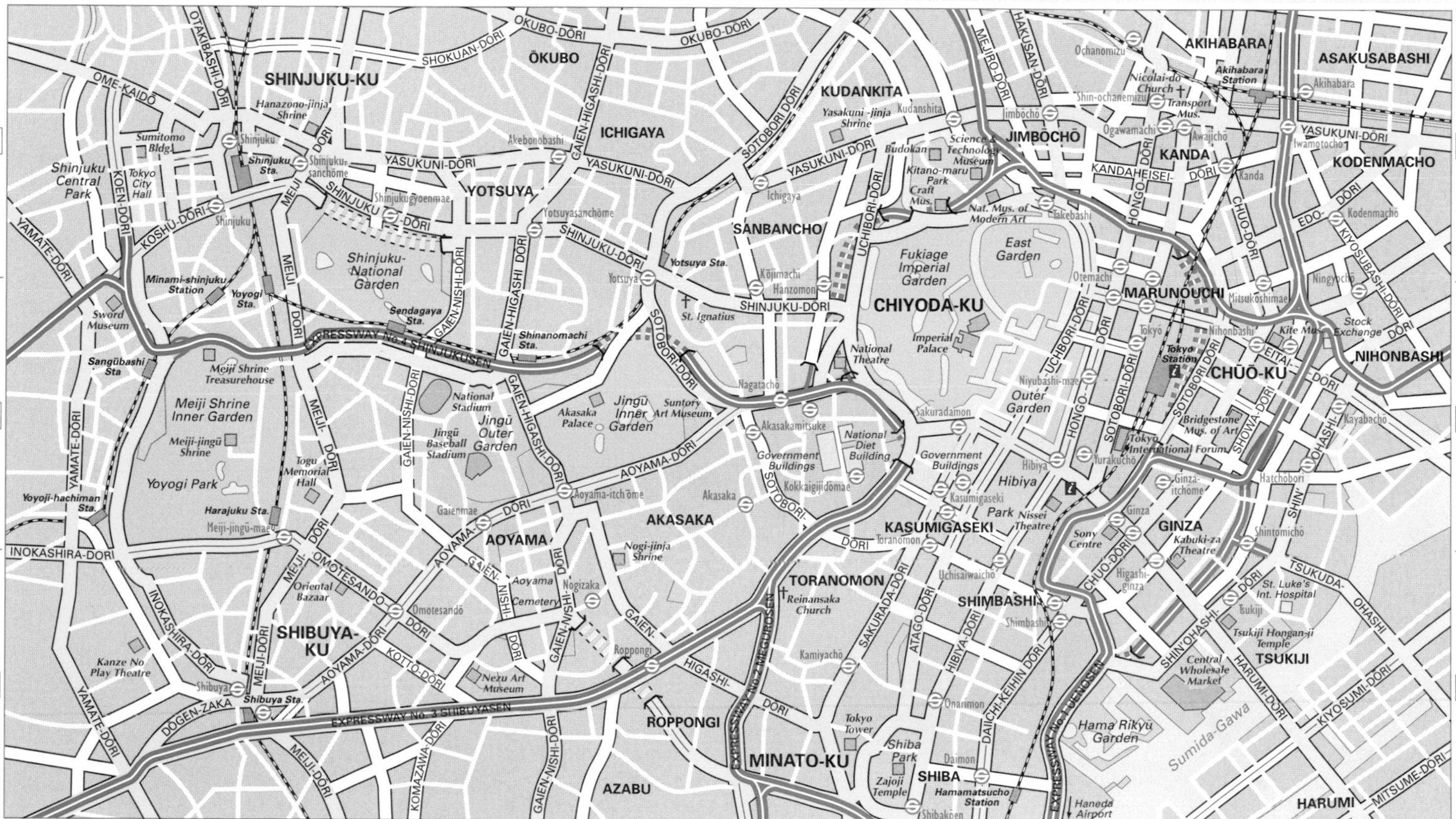

COPYRIGHT GEORGE PHILIP LTD

TEHRAN

km
miles

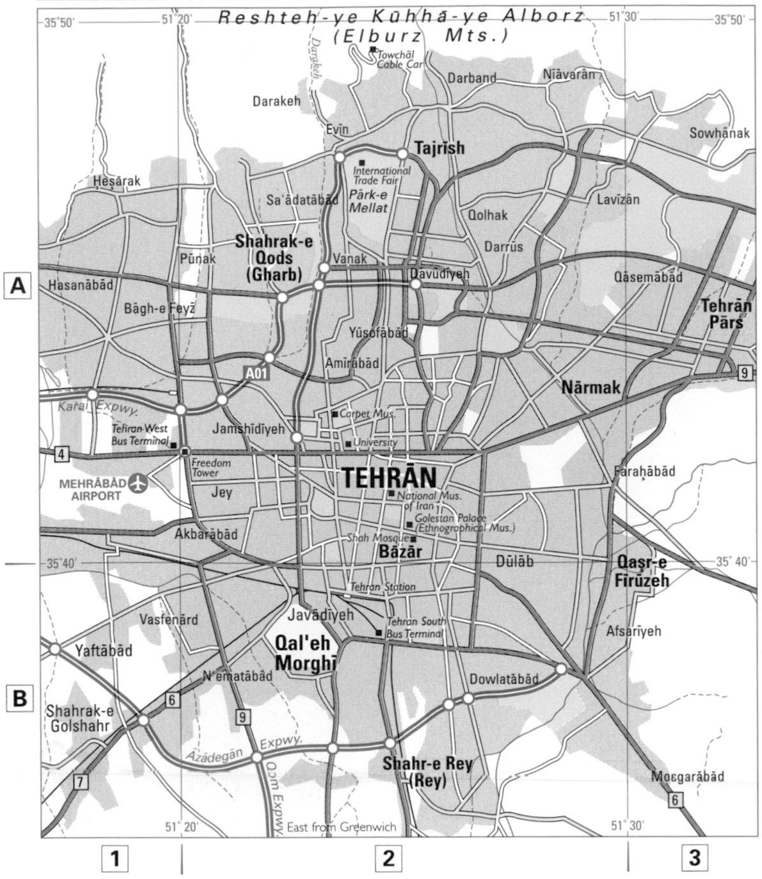

Reshteh-ye Kūhhā-ye Alborz
(Elburz Mts.)

Towchāl Cable Car
Darband Niāvarān
Darakeh
Evin
Tajrish
Sowhānak
Heşārak
Sa'ādatābād Park-e Mellat
International Trade Fair
Qolhak Lavizān
Shahrak-e Qods (Gharb)
Vanak Davūdīyeh Qāsemābād
Pūnak
Hasanābād
Bāgh-e Feyz Yūsefābād
Tehrān Pārs
Amīrābād
A01 Nārmak
9
Karaj Expwy.
Jamshīdīyeh
Carpet Mus.
Tehrān West Bus Terminal
University
4
Freedom Tower
TEHRĀN Farahābād
MEHRĀBĀD AIRPORT
Jey National Mus. of Iran
Golestan Palace (Ethnographical Mus.)
Akbarābād Shah Masque
Qaşr-e Firūzeh
Bāzār
Dūlāb
Tehrān Station
Vasfenārd
Javādīyeh
Afsarīyeh
Yaftābād Qal'eh Morghī Tehrān South Bus Terminal
N'ematābād
Dowlatābād
6
Shahrak-e Golshahr 9
7 Āzādegān Qom Expwy. Shahr-e Rey (Rey) Moşgarābād
6
East from Greenwich

TIANJIN

km
miles

205
Xiaodian
Da Yunhe Beicang
Dabizhuang
Yixingbu
Xinkai He
Hanjiashu Zhangguizhuang
Nandian
Dingzigu Xigu Park
Ziya He Tianjin Xi Zhan (Railway Station) Hebei Stadium
104 Xigu Jingang Qiao Zhangguizhuang
Honggiao The Grand Mosque Dabei (Grand Mercy) Temple
Da Yunhe (Grand Canal) Ximenwai Old Chinese District Dongmenwai
TIANJIN (TIENTSIN) Nanmenwai Hedong Tianjin Zhan (Railway Station)
Heping Jiefang Qiao Dongjuzi
Nankai University Antiques Market
Nankai Renmin Park
Shuishang Park Balitai Xinanlou
Tiaoyuan Pavilion Natural History Museum Jianshan Park Hexi
Aquatic Park Hai He
Liqizhuang Hexi Huidui
105 205
East from Greenwich 117°10' 39°00'

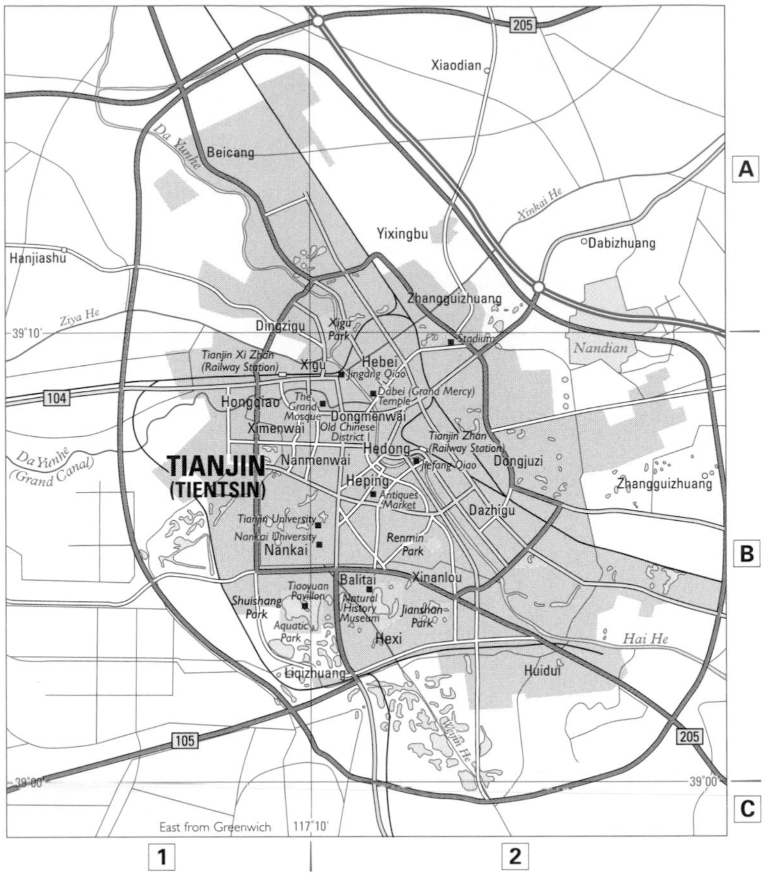

TORONTO

km
miles

27 YORK PEEL Humber 407 East Don Markham Metro Toronto Zoo Fairport
Thornhill Brown 48 Rouge West Rouge
Pine Grove Edgeley Concord YORK TORONTO Newtonbrook 401 2A Port Union Rouge Hill
Woodbridge Fisherville Willowdale Agincourt Malvern Highland Creek 2A
Humber Summit Black Creek Pioneer Village York University 11 Northmount 404 Woburn West Hill
Beaumonte Heights North York Lansing 401 Wexford Bendale
Thistletown 400 Armour Heights York Mills Scarborough
Kipling Heights DOWNSVIEW AIRPORT Don Mills Cliffside
Malton Downsview Lawrence Heights Wilket Creek Park Danforth 2
427 Rexdale Humberlea Ontario Science Centre
Woodbine Race Track 27 11 Leaside Thorncliffe Demonia Park
409 Weston Forest Hill East York 5 Birch Cliff
401 11 York Don Valley Pkwy. Kew Gardens
TORONTO INTERNATIONAL AIRPORT (LESTER B. PEARSON) Mount Dennis Casa Loma Riverdale Park
43°40' Humber Valley Village University of Toronto Parliament Buildings 42°20'
Hanlon Lambton Mills Swansea 5 CN Tower & SkyDome Union Sta.
Etobicoke Islington High Park Old Fort York TORONTO
427 Kingsway Parkdale TORONTO CITY CENTRE AIRPORT Toronto Harbour
Markland Wood Humber Bay Exhibition Place
Burnhamthorpe Summerville Humber Bay Ontario Place Island Park LAKE ONTARIO
Mimico Toronto Islands Gibraltar Point
Cooksville New Toronto West from Greenwich
Mississauga Long Branch
79°40' 79°30' 79°20' 79°10'

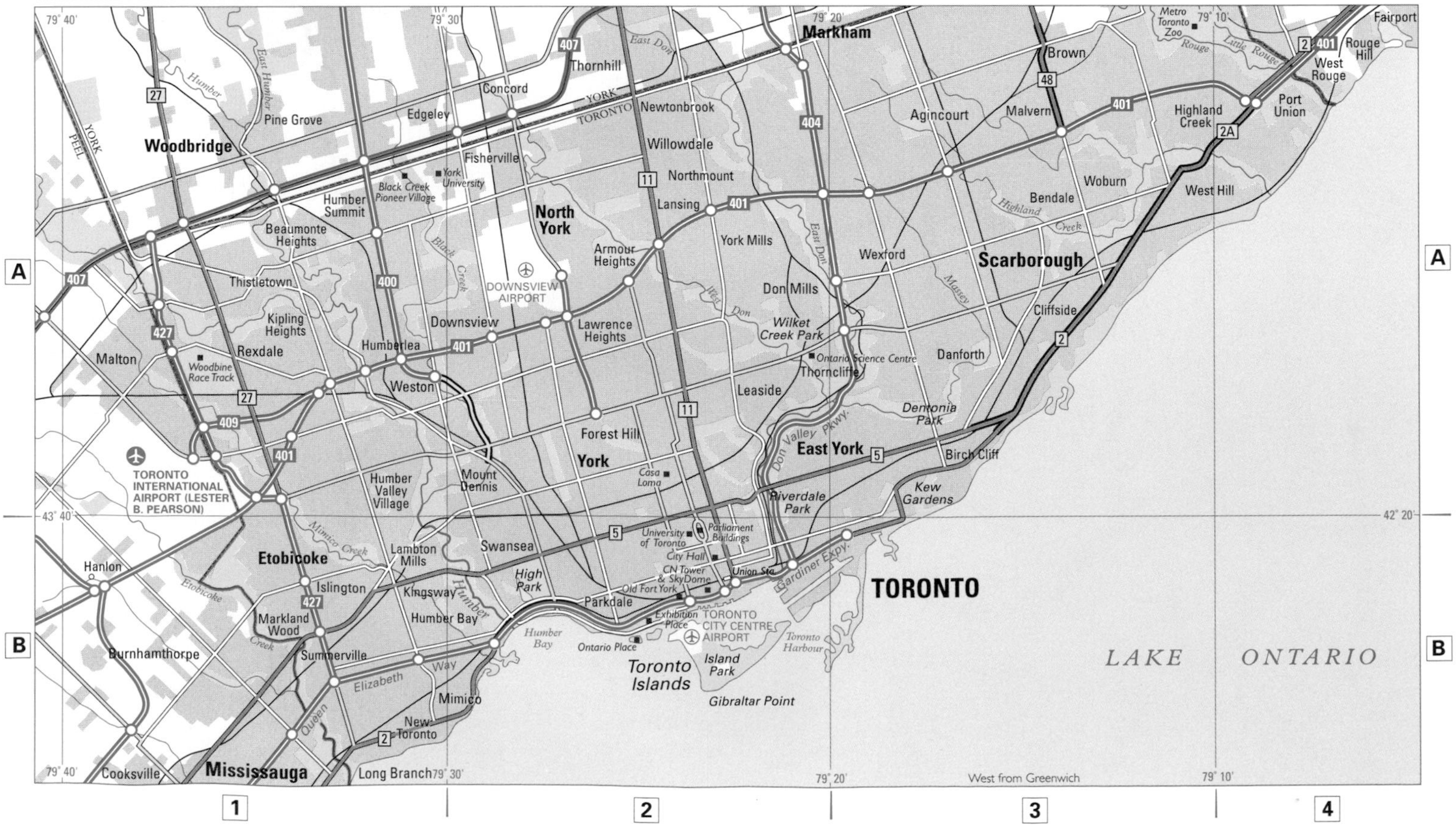

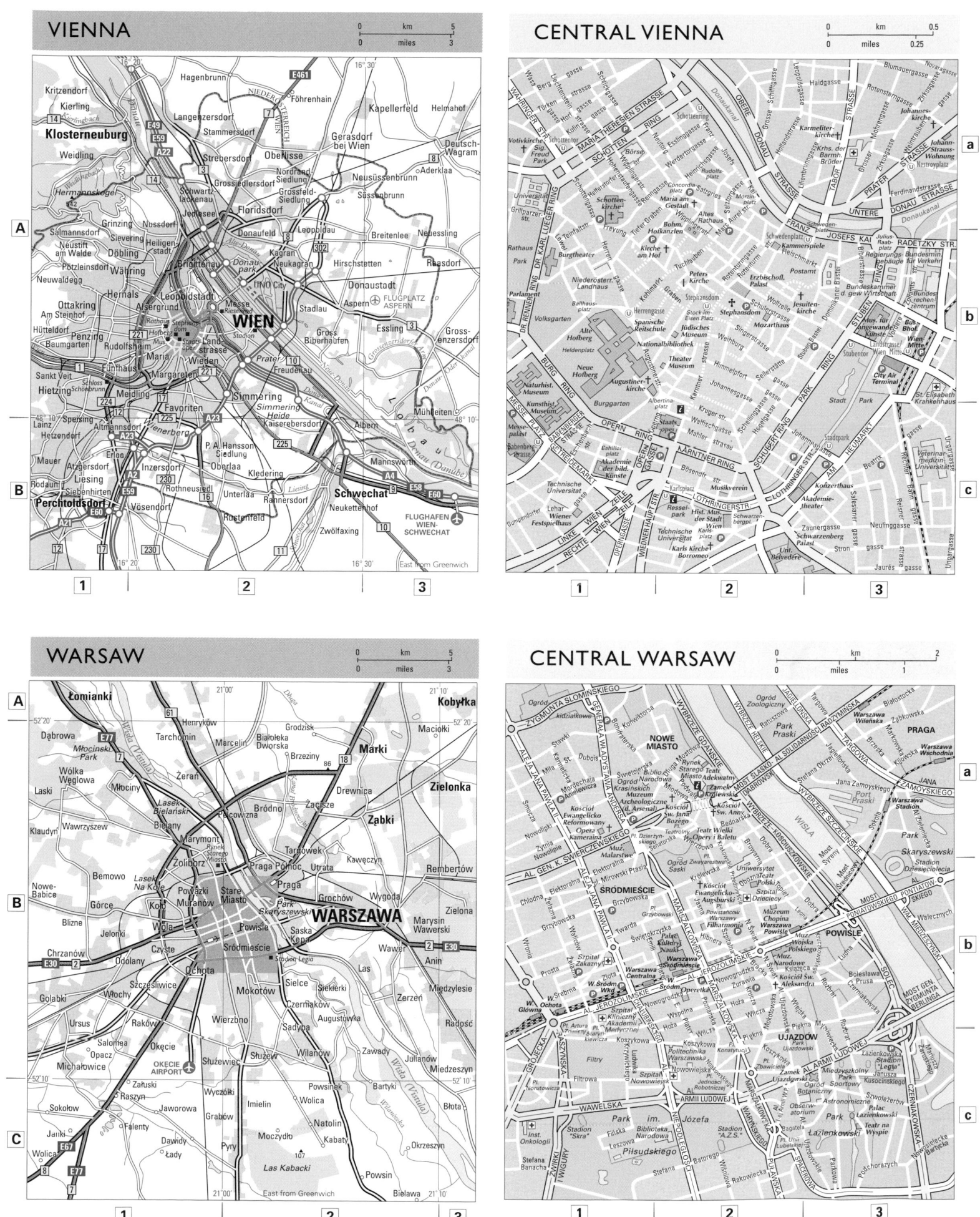
VIENNA
0 km 5
0 miles 3
CENTRAL VIENNA
0 km 0.5
0 miles 0.25
WARSAW
0 km 5
0 miles 3
CENTRAL WARSAW
0 km 2
0 miles 1
Klosterneuburg
WIEN
Floridsdorf
Leopoldstadt
Donaustadt
Simmering
Favoriten
Schwechat
FLUGHAFEN WIEN-SCHWECHAT
FLUGPLATZ ASPERN
Perchtoldsdorf
East from Greenwich
Stephansdom
Hofburg
Burgtheater
Parlament
Rathaus
Staatsoper
Stadtpark
Karlsplatz
Schwarzenberg Palast
WARSZAWA
Łomianki
Kobyłka
Marki
Zielonka
Ząbki
Praga
Śródmieście
Mokotów
Wilanów
Ochota
Wola
Żoliborz
Bielany
OKĘCIE AIRPORT
Las Kabacki
NOWE MIASTO
PRAGA
POWIŚLE
ŚRÓDMIEŚCIE
UJAZDÓW
Łazienkowski
Park Skaryszewski
Wisła

WASHINGTON

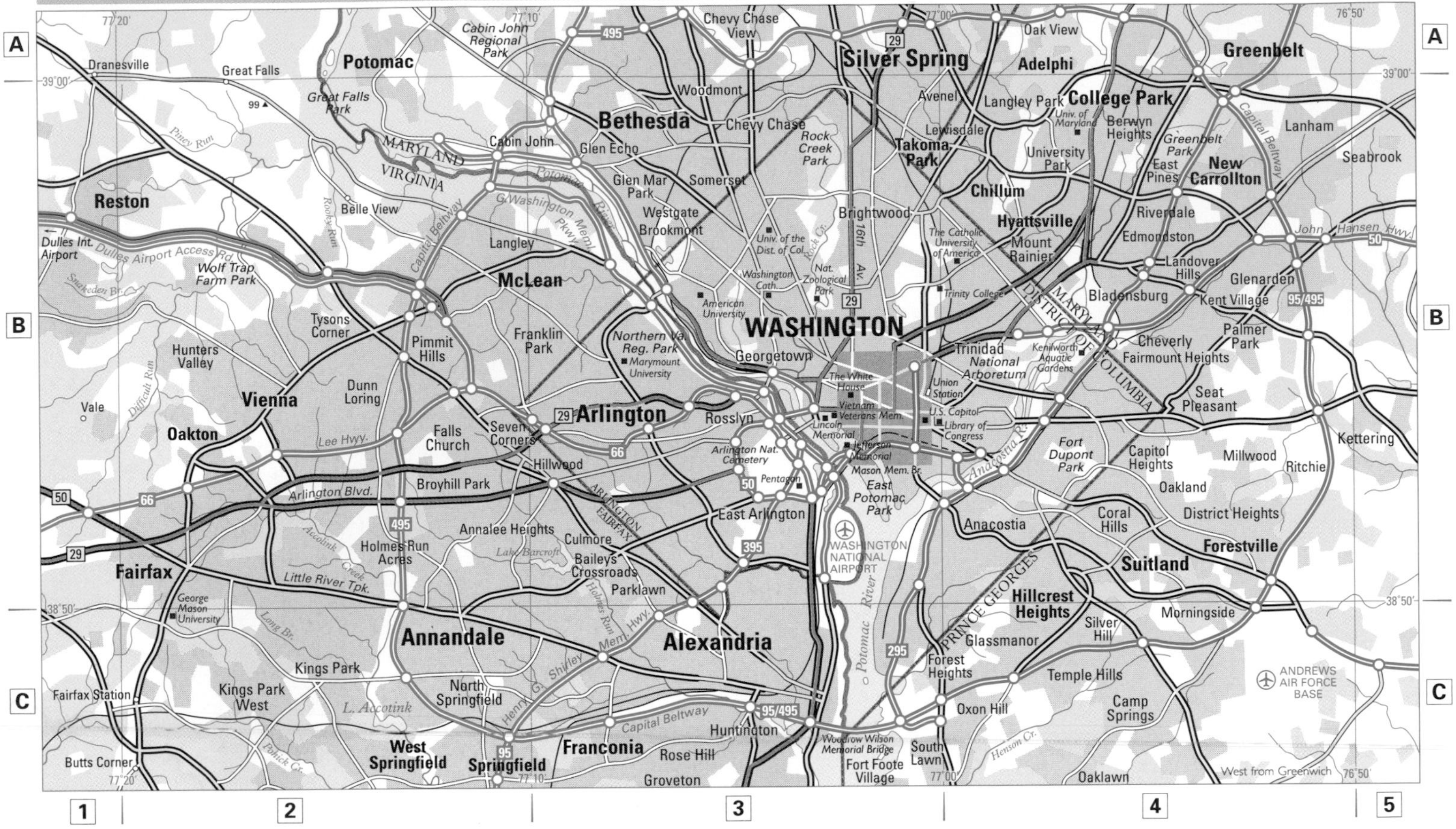

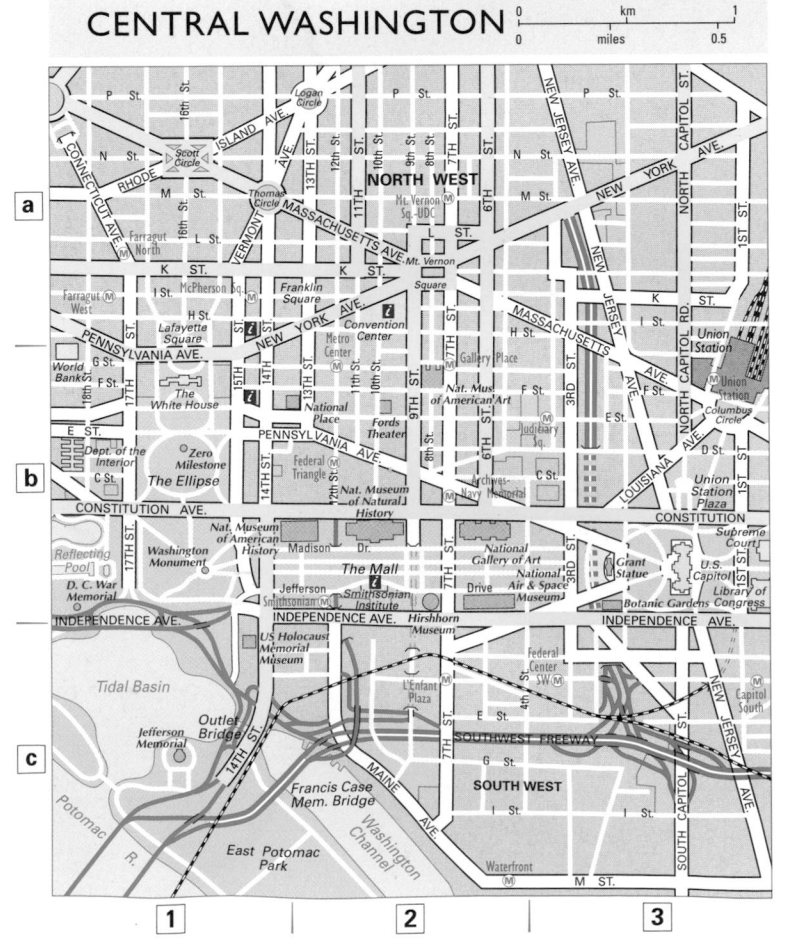

CENTRAL WASHINGTON

WELLINGTON

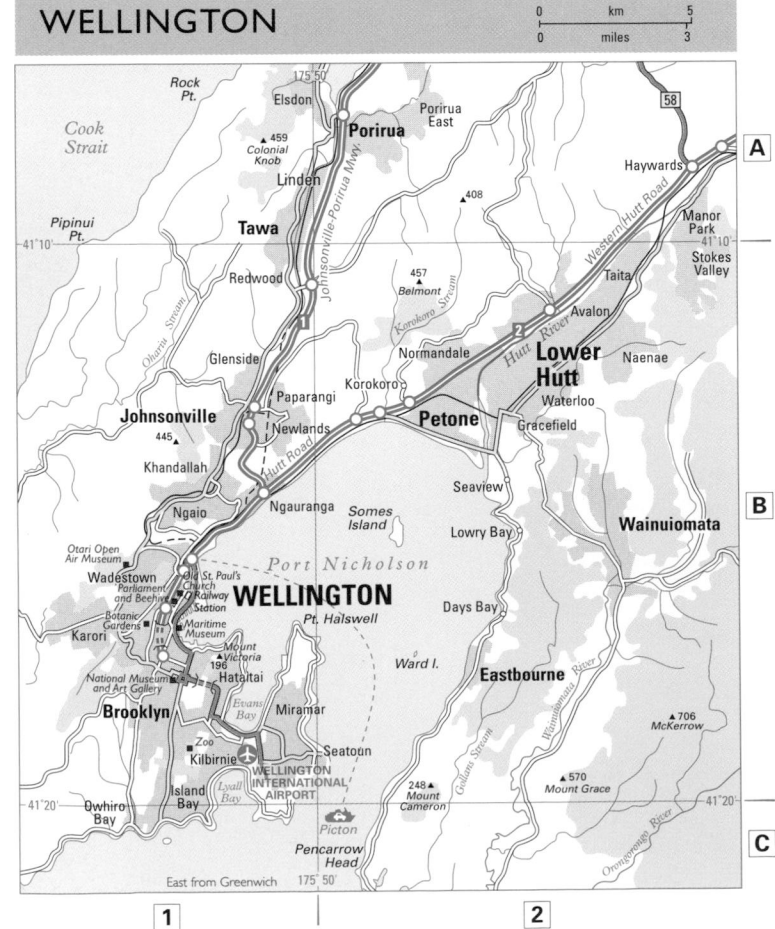

INDEX TO CITY MAPS

The index contains the names of all the principal places and features shown on the City Maps. Each name is followed by an additional entry in italics giving the name of the City Map within which it is located.

The number in bold type which follows each name refers to the number of the City Map page where that feature or place will be found.

The letter and figure which are immediately after the page number give the grid square on the map within which the feature or place is situated. The letter represents the latitude and the figure the longitude. Upper case letters refer to the City Maps, lower case letters to the Central Area Maps. The full geographic reference is provided in the border of the City Maps.

The location given is the centre of the city, suburb or feature and is not necessarily the name. Rivers, canals and roads are indexed to their name. Rivers carry the symbol → after their name.

An explanation of the alphabetical order rules and a list of the abbreviations used are to be found at the beginning of the World Map Index.

A

Aalām, Baghdad 3 B2
Aalsmeer, Amsterdam 2 B1
Abbey Wood, London 15 B4
Abcoude, Amsterdam 2 B2
Ābdin, Cairo 7 A2
Abeno, Osaka 22 B4
Aberdeen, Hong Kong 12 B2
Aberdour, Edinburgh 11 A2
Aberdour Castle, Edinburgh 11 A2
Abfanggraben →, Munich 20 A3
Ablon-sur-Seine, Paris 23 B3
Abord-à-Plouffe, Montreal 19 A1
Abramtsevo, Moscow 19 B4
Abu Dis, Jerusalem 13 B2
Abû en Numrus, Cairo 7 B2
Abu Ghosh, Jerusalem 13 B1
Acacias, Madrid 17 c2
Acassuso, Buenos Aires 7 A1
Accotink Cr. →, Washington 32 B2
Acheres, Paris 23 A1
Acilia, Rome 25 C1
Aclimação, São Paulo 26 B2
Acton, London 15 A2
Açúcar, Pão de, Rio de Janeiro 24 B2
Ada Beja, Lisbon 14 A1
Adams Park, Atlanta 3 B2
Adams Shore, Boston 6 B4
Addiscombe, London 15 B3
Adelphi, Washington 32 A4
Aderklaa, Vienna 31 A3
Admiralteyskaya Storona, St. Petersburg 26 B2
Affori, Milan 18 A2
Aflandshage, Copenhagen 10 B3
Afsariyeh, Tehran 30 B2
Agboyi Cr. →, Lagos 14 A2
Agerup, Copenhagen 10 A1
Agesta, Stockholm 28 B2
Agincourt, Toronto 30 A3
Agora, Athens 2 c1
Agra Canal, Delhi 10 B2
Agricola Oriental, Mexico City 18 B2
Agua Espraiada →, São Paulo 26 B2
Agualva-Cacem, Lisbon 14 A1
Agustino, Cerro El, Lima 16 B2
Ahrensfelde, Berlin 5 A4
Ahuntsic, Montreal 19 A1
Ai →, Osaka 22 A4
Aigremont, Paris 23 A1
Air View Park, Singapore 27 A2
Airport West, Melbourne 17 A1
Aiyaleo, Athens 2 B2
Aiyáleos, Óros, Athens 2 B1
Ajegunle, Lagos 14 B2
Aji, Osaka 22 A3
Ajuda, Lisbon 14 A1
Akalla, Stockholm 28 A1
Akasaka, Tokyo 29 b3
Akbarābād, Tehran 30 A2
Akershus Slott, Oslo 22 A3
Akihabara, Tokyo 29 a5
Akrópolis, Athens 2 c2
Al 'Azamiyah, Baghdad 3 A2
Al Quds = Jerusalem, Jerusalem 13 B2
Alaguntan, Lagos 14 B2
Alameda, San Francisco 25 B3
Alameda, Parque, Mexico City 18 b2
Alameda Memorial State Beach Park, San Francisco 25 B3
Albern, Vienna 31 B2
Albert Park, Melbourne 17 B1
Alberton, Johannesburg 13 B2
Albertslund, Copenhagen 10 B2
Albysjön, Stockholm 28 B1
Alcantara, Lisbon 14 A1
Alcatraz I., San Francisco 25 B2
Alcobendas, Madrid 17 A2
Alcorcón, Madrid 17 B1
Aldershof, Berlin 5 B4
Aldo Bonzi, Buenos Aires 7 C1
Aleksandrovskoye, St. Petersburg 26 B2
Alexander Nevsky Abbey, St. Petersburg 26 B2
Alexander Soutzos Moussío, Athens 2 b3
Alexandra, Johannesburg 13 A2
Alexandra, Singapore 27 B2
Alexandria, Washington 32 C3
Alfama, Lisbon 14 c3
Alfortville, Paris 23 B3
Algés, Lisbon 14 A1
Alhambra, Los Angeles 16 B4
Alibey →, Istanbul 12 B1
Alibey Barajı, Istanbul 12 B1
Alibeyköy, Istanbul 12 B1
Alimos, Athens 2 B2
Alipur, Calcutta 8 B1
Allach, Munich 20 A1
Allambie Heights, Sydney 28 A2
Allard Pierson Museum, Amsterdam 2 b2
Allermuir Hill, Edinburgh 11 B2
Allerton, Pt., Boston 6 B4
Allston, Boston 6 A3
Almada, Lisbon 14 A2
Almagro, Buenos Aires 7 B2
Almargem do Bispo, Lisbon 14 A1
Almazovo, Moscow 19 A6
Almirante G. Brown, Parque, Buenos Aires 7 C2
Almon, Jerusalem 13 B2
Almond →, Edinburgh 11 B2
Alnabru, Oslo 22 A4
Alnsjøen, Oslo 22 A4
Alperton, London 15 A2
Alpine, New York 21 A2
Alrode, Johannesburg 13 B2
Alsemerg, Brussels 6 B1
Alsergrund, Vienna 31 A2
Alsip, Chicago 9 C2
Älsten, Stockholm 28 B1
Älta, Stockholm 28 B3
Altadena, Los Angeles 16 A4
Alte-Donau →, Vienna 31 A2
Alte Hofburg, Vienna 31 b1
Alter Finkenkrug, Berlin 5 A1
Altes Rathaus, Munich 20 b3
Altglienicke, Berlin 5 B4
Altlandsberg, Berlin 5 A5
Altlandsberg Nord, Berlin 5 A5
Altmannsdorf, Vienna 31 B1
Alto da Moóca, São Paulo 26 B2
Alto do Pina, Lisbon 14 A2
Altona, Melbourne 17 B1
Alvaro Obregon, Mexico City 18 B1
Alvik, Stockholm 28 B1
Älvsjo, Stockholm 28 B2
Älvvik, Stockholm 28 A3
Am Hasenbergl, Munich 20 A2
Am Steinhof, Vienna 31 A1
Am Wald, Munich 20 B2
Ama Keng, Singapore 27 A2
Amadora, Lisbon 14 A1
Amagasaki, Osaka 22 A3
Amager, Copenhagen 10 B3
Amāl Qādisiya, Baghdad 3 B2
Amalienborg, Copenhagen 10 b3
Amata, Milan 18 A1
Ameixoeira, Lisbon 14 A2
América, São Paulo 26 B1
Amin, Baghdad 3 B2
Aminadov, Jerusalem 13 B1
Aminyevo, Moscow 19 B2
Amīrābād, Tehran 30 A2
Amora, Lisbon 14 B2
Amoreira, Lisbon 14 A1
Ampelokipi, Athens 2 B2
Amper →, Munich 20 A1
Amstel, Amsterdam 2 b2
Amstel →, Amsterdam 2 c2
Amstel-Drecht-Kanaal, Amsterdam 2 B2
Amstel Station, Amsterdam 2 c3
Amstelhof, Amsterdam 2 b2
Amstelveen, Amsterdam 2 B2
Amsterdam, Amsterdam 2 A2
Amsterdam-Rijnkanaal, Amsterdam 2 B3
Amsterdam Zoo, Amsterdam 2 b3
Amsterdam Zuidoost, Amsterdam 2 B2
Amsterdamse Bos, Amsterdam 2 B1
Anacostia, Washington 32 B4
Anadoluhisarı, Istanbul 12 B2
Anadolukavağı, Istanbul 12 A2
Anata, Jerusalem 13 B2
Ancol, Jakarta 13 A2
'Andalus, Baghdad 3 B1
Andarai, Rio de Janeiro 24 B1
Anderlecht, Brussels 6 A1
Anderson Park, Atlanta 3 B2
Andingmen, Beijing 4 B2
Andrews Air Force Base, Washington 32 C4
Ang Mo Kio, Singapore 27 A3
Ängby, Stockholm 28 A1
Angel I., San Francisco 25 A2
Angel Island State Park, San Francisco 25 A2
Angke, Kali →, Jakarta 13 A1
Angyalföld, Budapest 7 A2
Anik, Mumbai 20 A2
Anin, Warsaw 31 B2
Anjou, Montreal 19 A2
Annalee Heights, Washington 32 B2
Annandale, Washington 32 C2
Anne Frankhuis, Amsterdam 2 a1
Antony, Paris 23 B2
Anyangch'on, Seoul 26 C1
Aoyama, Tokyo 29 b2
Ap Lei Chau, Hong Kong 12 B1
Apapa, Lagos 14 B2
Apelação, Lisbon 14 A2
Apterkarskiy Ostrov, St. Petersburg 26 B2
Ar Kazimiyah, Baghdad 3 B1
Ara →, Tokyo 29 A4
Arakawa-Ku, Tokyo 29 A3
Arany-hegyi-patak →, Budapest 7 A2
Aravaca, Madrid 17 B1
Arbataash, Baghdad 3 A1
Arc de Triomphe, Paris 23 a2
Arcadia, Los Angeles 16 B4
Arceuil, Paris 23 B2
Arco Plaza, Los Angeles 16 b1
Arese, Milan 18 A1
Arganzuela, Madrid 17 B1
Argenteuil, Paris 23 A2
Argonne Forest, Chicago 9 C1
Argüelles, Madrid 17 a1
Arima, Osaka 22 A2
Arima, Tokyo 29 B2
Ários Págos, Athens 2 c1
Arkhangelskoye, Moscow 19 B1
Arlington, Boston 6 A2
Arlington, Washington 32 B3
Arlington Heights, Boston 6 A2
Arlington Nat. Cemetery, Washington 32 B3
Armação, Rio de Janeiro 24 B2
Armadale, Melbourne 17 B2
Armenian Quarter, Jerusalem 13 b3
Armour Heights, Toronto 30 A2
Arncliffe, Sydney 28 B1
Arnold Arboretum, Boston 6 B3
Árpádföld, Budapest 7 A3
Arrentela, Lisbon 14 B2
Årsta, Stockholm 28 B2
Art Institute, Chicago 9 c2
Artane, Dublin 11 A2
Artas, Jerusalem 13 B2
Arthur's Seat, Edinburgh 11 B3
Aryiróupolis, Athens 2 B2
Asagaya, Tokyo 29 A2
Asahi, Osaka 22 A4
Asakusa, Tokyo 29 A3
Asakusabashi, Tokyo 29 a5
Asati, Calcutta 8 C1
Aschheim, Munich 20 A3
Ascot Vale, Melbourne 17 A1
Ashburn, Chicago 9 C2
Ashburton, Melbourne 17 B2
Ashfield, Sydney 28 B1
Ashford, London 15 B1
Ashiya, Osaka 22 A2
Ashiya →, Osaka 22 A2
Ashtown, Dublin 11 A2
Askisto, Helsinki 12 B1
Askrikefjärden, Stockholm 28 A3
Asnières, Paris 23 A2
Aspern, Vienna 31 A3
Aspern, Flugplatz, Vienna 31 A3
Assago, Milan 18 B1
Assemblée Nationale, Paris 23 b3
Assendelft, Amsterdam 2 A1
Assiano, Milan 18 B1
Astoria, New York 21 B2
Astrolabe Park, Sydney 28 B2
Atarot Airport, Jerusalem 13 A2
Atghara, Calcutta 8 B2
Athens = Athínai, Athens 2 B2
Athínai, Athens 2 B2
Athínai-Ellinikón Airport, Athens 2 B2
Athis-Mons, Paris 23 B3
Athlone, Cape Town 8 A2
Atholl, Johannesburg 13 A2
Atifiya, Baghdad 3 A2
Atişalen, Istanbul 12 B1
Atlanta, Atlanta 3 B2
Atlanta History Center, Atlanta 3 B2
Atomium, Brussels 6 A2
Attiki, Athens 2 A2
Atzgersdorf, Vienna 31 B1
Aubervilliers, Paris 23 A3
Aubing, Munich 20 B1
Auburndale, Boston 6 A2
Auchendinny, Edinburgh 11 B2
Auckland Park, Johannesburg 13 B2
Auderghem, Brussels 6 B2
Augusta, Mausoleo di, Rome 25 b2
Augustówka, Warsaw 31 B2
Aulnay-sous-Bois, Paris 23 A3
Aurelio, Rome 25 B1
Ausīm, Cairo 7 A1
Austerlitz, Gare d', Paris 23 A3
Austin, Chicago 9 B2
Avalon, Wellington 32 B2
Avedøre, Copenhagen 10 B2
Avellaneda, Buenos Aires 7 C2
Avenel, Washington 32 A2
Avondale, Chicago 9 B2
Avondale Heights, Melbourne 17 A1
Avtovo, St. Petersburg 26 B1
Ayazağa, Istanbul 12 B1
Ayer Chawan, P., Singapore 27 B2
Ayer Merbau, P., Singapore 27 B2
Ayía Marina, Athens 2 C3
Ayía Paraskevi, Athens 2 A2
Áyios Dhimitrios, Athens 2 B2
Áyios Ioánnis Rendis, Athens 2 B1
Azabu, Tokyo 29 c3
Azcapotzalco, Mexico City 18 B1
Azteca, Estadia, Mexico City 18 C2
Azucar, Cerro Pan de, Santiago 26 A1

B

Baambrugge, Amsterdam 2 B2
Baba I., Karachi 14 B1
Babarpur, Delhi 10 A2
Babushkin, Moscow 19 A4
Back B., Mumbai 20 B1
Baclaran, Manila 17 B2
Bacoor, Manila 17 C1
Bacoor B., Manila 17 C1
Badalona, Barcelona 4 A2
Badhoevedorp, Amsterdam 2 A1
Badli, Delhi 10 A1
Bærum, Oslo 22 A2
Bağcılar, Istanbul 12 B1
Bäggio, Milan 18 B1
Bāgh-e-Feyz, Tehran 30 A1
Baghdād, Baghdad 3 A2
Bagmari, Calcutta 8 B2
Bagneux, Paris 23 B2
Bagnolet, Paris 23 A3
Bagsværd, Copenhagen 10 A2
Bagsværd Sø, Copenhagen 10 A2
Baguiati, Calcutta 8 B2
Bagumbayan, Manila 17 C2
Bahçeköy, Istanbul 12 A1
Bahtīm, Cairo 7 A2
Baileys Crossroads, Washington 32 B3
Bailly, Paris 23 A1
Bairro Alto, Lisbon 14 c1
Bairro Lopes, Lisbon 14 b3
Baisha, Canton 8 B2
Baisha →, Canton 8 B2
Baixa, Lisbon 14 c2
Baiyun Airport, Canton 8 A2
Baiyun Hill Scenic Spot, Canton 8 B2
Bakırköy, Istanbul 12 C1
Bakovka, Moscow 19 B2
Bal Harbor, Miami 18 A2
Balara, Manila 17 B2
Balashikha, Moscow 19 B5
Baldia, Karachi 14 A1
Baldoyle, Dublin 11 A3
Baldwin Hills, Los Angeles 16 B2
Baldwin Hills Res., Los Angeles 16 B2
Balgowlah, Sydney 28 A2
Balgowlah Heights, Sydney 28 A2
Balham, London 15 B3
Bali, Calcutta 8 B1
Baliganja, Calcutta 8 B2
Balingsnäs, Stockholm 28 B2
Balingsta, Stockholm 28 B2
Balintawak, Manila 17 B1
Balitai, Tianjin 30 B2
Ballerup, Copenhagen 10 A2
Ballinteer, Dublin 11 B2
Ballyboden, Dublin 11 B2
Ballybrack, Dublin 11 B3
Ballyfermot, Dublin 11 A1
Ballymorefinn Hill, Dublin 11 B1
Ballymun, Dublin 11 A2
Balmain, Sydney 28 B2
Baluhati, Calcutta 8 B1
Balvanera, Buenos Aires 7 B2
Balwyn, Melbourne 17 A2
Balwyn North, Melbourne 17 A2
Banática, Lisbon 14 A1
Banco do Brasil, Centro Cultural, Rio de Janeiro 24 a2
Bandra, Mumbai 20 A1
Bandra Pt., Mumbai 20 A1
Bang Kapi, Bangkok 3 B2
Bang Kholaem, Bangkok 3 A2
Bang Na, Bangkok 3 B2
Bang Phlad, Bangkok 3 a1
Bangkhen, Bangkok 3 A2
Bangkok = Krung Thep, Bangkok 3 B2
Bangkok Noi, Bangkok 3 B1
Bangkok Yai, Bangkok 3 B1
Banglamphoo, Bangkok 3 b2
Banglo, Calcutta 8 B1
Bangrak, Bangkok 3 B2
Bangsu, Bangkok 3 B2
Bank, London 15 b5
Bank of America, San Francisco 25 b2
Bank of China Tower, Hong Kong 12 c1
Banks, C., Sydney 28 C2
Banksmeadow, Sydney 28 B2
Banstala, Calcutta 8 B2
Bantra, Calcutta 8 B1
Baoshan, Shanghai 27 A1
Bar Giyora, Jerusalem 13 B1
Barahanagar, Calcutta 8 B2
Barajas, Madrid 17 B2
Barajas, Aeropuerto Transoceanico de, Madrid 17 B2
Barakpur, Calcutta 8 A2
Barberini, Palazzo, Rome 25 b3
Barbican, London 15 a4
Barcarena, Lisbon 14 A1
Barcarena, Rib. de →, Lisbon 14 A1
Barcelona, Barcelona 4 A2
Barcelona-Prat, Aeropuerta de, Barcelona 4 B1
Barceloneta, Barcelona 4 A2
Barking, London 15 A4
Barkingside, London 15 A4
Barnes, London 15 B2
Barnet, London 15 A2
Barra Andai, Karachi 14 B2
Barra Funda, São Paulo 26 B2
Barracas, Buenos Aires 7 B2
Barranco, Lima 16 B2
Barreiro, Lisbon 14 B2
Barreto, Rio de Janeiro 24 B2
Bartala, Calcutta 8 B1
Barton Park, Sydney 28 B1
Bartyki, Warsaw 31 C2
Barvikha, Moscow 19 B1
Bastille, Place de la, Paris 23 c5
Basus, Cairo 7 A2
Batanagar, Calcutta 8 B1
Bath Beach, New York 21 C1
Bath I., Karachi 14 B2
Batir, Jerusalem 13 B1
Batok, Bukit, Singapore 27 A2
Battersea, London 15 B3
Battery Park, New York 21 f1
Bauman, Moscow 19 B4
Baumgarten, Vienna 31 A1
Bay Harbour Islands, Miami 18 A2
Bay Ridge, New York 21 C1
Bayonne, New York 21 B1
Bayshore, San Francisco 25 B3
Bayswater, London 15 b2
Bayt Lahm = Bethlehem, Jerusalem 13 B2
Bayview, San Francisco 25 B2
Bāzār, Tehran 30 A2
Beachmont, Boston 6 A4
Beacon Hill, Hong Kong 12 A2
Beato, Lisbon 14 A2
Beaumont, Dublin 11 A2
Beaumonte Heights, Toronto 30 A1
Bebek, Istanbul 12 B2
Běchovice, Prague 24 B3
Beck L., Chicago 9 A1
Beckenham, London 15 B3
Beckton, London 15 A4
Becontree, London 15 A4
Beddington Corner, London 15 B3
Bedford, Boston 6 A2
Bedford Park, Chicago 9 C2
Bedford Park, New York 21 A2
Bedford Stuyvesant, New York 21 B2
Bedford View, Johannesburg 13 B2
Bedok, Singapore 27 B3
Bedok, Res., Singapore 27 A3
Beersel, Brussels 6 B1
Behala, Calcutta 8 B1
Bei Hai, Beijing 4 B2
Beicai, Shanghai 27 B2
Beicang, Tianjin 30 A1
Beihai Park, Beijing 4 b2
Beijing, Beijing 4 B1
Beit Ghur el-Fawqa, Jerusalem 13 A1
Beit Hanina, Jerusalem 13 B2
Beit Iksa, Jerusalem 13 B2
Beit I'nan, Jerusalem 13 A1
Beit Jala, Jerusalem 13 B2
Beit Lekhem = Bethlehem, Jerusalem 13 B2
Beit Nekofa, Jerusalem 13 B1
Beit Sahur, Jerusalem 13 B2
Beit Surik, Jerusalem 13 B1
Beit Zayit, Jerusalem 13 B1
Beitaipingzhuan, Beijing 4 B1
Beitar Illit, Jerusalem 13 B1
Beitsun, Canton 8 A1
Beitunya, Jerusalem 13 A2
Beixing Jing Park, Shanghai 27 B1
Békásmegyer, Budapest 7 A2
Bekkelaget, Oslo 22 A3
Bel Air, Los Angeles 16 B2
Bela Vista, São Paulo 26 B2
Bélanger, Montreal 19 A1
Belas, Lisbon 14 A1
Belas Artes, Museu Nacionale de, Rio de Janeiro 24 b2
Beleghata, Calcutta 8 B2
Belém, Lisbon 14 A1
Belém, Torre de, Lisbon 14 A1
Belénzinho, São Paulo 26 B2
Belgachiya, Calcutta 8 B2
Belgharia, Calcutta 8 B2
Belgrano, Buenos Aires 7 B2
Belgravia, London 15 c3
Bell, Los Angeles 16 C3
Bell Gardens, Los Angeles 16 C4
Bell Tower, Beijing 4 a2
Bellavista, Lima 16 B2
Bellavista, Santiago 26 C2
Belle Harbor, New York 21 C2
Belle View, Washington 32 B2
Bellevue, Schloss, Berlin 5 a2
Bellingham, London 15 B3
Bellwood, Chicago 9 B1
Belmont, Boston 6 A2
Belmont, London 15 A2
Belmont, Wellington 32 B2
Belmont Harbor, Chicago 9 B3
Belmore, Sydney 28 B1
Belur, Calcutta 8 B2
Belvedere, Atlanta 3 B3
Belvedere, London 15 B4
Belvedere, San Francisco 25 A2
Belyayevo Bogorodskoye, Moscow 19 C3
Bemowo, Warsaw 31 B1
Benaki, Moussío, Athens 2 b3
Bendale, Toronto 30 A3
Bendkhal, Mumbai 20 B2
Benefica, Rio de Janeiro 24 B1
Benfica, Lisbon 14 A1
Benito Juárez, Mexico City 18 B2
Benito Juárez, Aeropuerto Int., Mexico City 18 B2
Bensonhurst, New York 21 C2
Berchem-Sainte-Agathe, Brussels 6 A1
Berg am Laim, Munich 20 B2
Bergenfield, New York 21 A2
Bergham, Munich 20 B2
Bergvliet, Cape Town 8 B1
Beri, Barcelona 4 A1
Berkeley, San Francisco 25 A3
Berlin, Berlin 5 A3
Bermondsey, London 15 B3
Bernabeu, Estadio, Madrid 17 B1
Bernal Heights, San Francisco 25 B2
Berwyn, Chicago 9 B2
Berwyn Heights, Washington 32 B4
Besiktas, Istanbul 12 B2
Besòs →, Barcelona 4 A2
Bethesda, Washington 32 B3
Bethlehem, Jerusalem 13 B2
Bethnal Green, London 15 A3
Betor, Calcutta 8 B1
Beurs, Amsterdam 2 b2
Beverley Hills, Sydney 28 B1
Beverley Park, Sydney 28 B1
Beverly, Chicago 9 C3
Beverly Glen, Los Angeles 16 B2
Beverly Hills, Los Angeles 16 B2
Bexley, London 15 B4
Bexley, Sydney 28 B1
Bexleyheath, London 15 B4
Beykoz, Istanbul 12 B2
Beylerbeyi, Istanbul 12 B2
Beyoğlu, Istanbul 12 B1
Bezons, Paris 23 A2
Bezuidenhout Park, Johannesburg 13 B2
Bhadrakali, Calcutta 8 A2
Bhalswa, Delhi 10 A2
Bhambo Khan Qarmati, Karachi 14 B2
Bhatsala, Calcutta 8 B1
Bhawanipur, Calcutta 8 B2
Bhuleshwar, Mumbai 20 b2
Białołeka Dworska, Warsaw 31 B2
Biblioteca Nacional, Rio de Janeiro 24 c2
Bicentennial Park, Sydney 28 B1
Bickley, London 15 B4
Bidu, Jerusalem 13 B1
Bielany, Warsaw 31 B1
Bielawa, Warsaw 31 C2
Biesdorf, Berlin 5 A4
Bièvre →, Paris 23 B1
Bièvres, Paris 23 B2
Bilston, Edinburgh 11 B2
Binacayan, Manila 17 C1
Binondo, Manila 17 B1
Birak el Kiyam, Cairo 7 A1
Birch Cliff, Toronto 30 A3
Birkenstein, Berlin 5 A5
Birkholz, Berlin 5 A4
Birkholzaue, Berlin 5 A4
Birrarrung Park, Melbourne 17 A2
Biscayne Bay, Miami 18 B2
Biscayne Park, Miami 18 A2
Bishop Lavis, Cape Town 8 A2
Bishopscourt, Cape Town 8 A1
Bispebjerg, Copenhagen 10 A3
Biwon Secret Garden, Seoul 26 B1
Björknas, Stockholm 28 B3
Black Cr. →, Toronto 30 A2
Blackfen, London 15 B4
Blackheath, London 15 B4
Blackrock, Dublin 11 B2
Bladensburg, Washington 32 B4
Blair Village, Atlanta 3 C2
Blairgowrie, Johannesburg 13 A2
Blakehurst, Sydney 28 B1
Blakstad, Oslo 22 B1
Blankenburg, Berlin 5 A3
Blankenfelde, Berlin 5 A3
Blizne, Warsaw 31 B1
Bloomsbury, London 15 a3
Błota, Warsaw 31 C3
Blue Island, Chicago 9 C2
Bluebell, Dublin 11 B1
Bluff Hd., Hong Kong 12 B2
Blumberg, Berlin 5 A4
Blunt Pt., San Francisco 25 A2
Blutenburg, Munich 20 B1
Blylaget, Oslo 22 B3
Bo-Kaap Museum, Cape Town 8 c2
Boa Vista, Alto do, Rio de Janeiro 24 B1
Boardwalk, New York 21 C3
Boavista, Lisbon 14 A2
Bobigny, Paris 23 A3
Bocanegra, Lima 16 A2
Boedo, Buenos Aires 7 B2
Bogenhausen, Munich 20 B2
Bogorodskoye, Moscow 19 B4
Bogota, New York 21 A1
Bogstadvatnet, Oslo 22 A2
Bohnsdorf, Berlin 5 B4
Bois-Colombes, Paris 23 A2
Bois-d'Arcy, Paris 23 B1
Boissy-St.-Léger, Paris 23 B4
Boldinasco, Milan 18 B1
Bøler, Oslo 22 A4
Bollate, Milan 18 A1
Bollebeek, Brussels 6 A1
Bollensdorf, Berlin 5 A5
Bollmora, Stockholm 28 B3
Bolshaya-Okhta, St. Petersburg 26 B2
Bolton, Atlanta 3 B2
Bom Retiro, São Paulo 26 B2
Bombay = Mumbai, Mumbai 20 B2
Bondi, Sydney 28 B2
Bondy, Paris 23 A3
Bondy, Forêt de, Paris 23 A4
Bonifacio Monument, Manila 17 B1
Bonneuil-sur-Marne, Paris 23 B4
Bonnington, Edinburgh 11 B1
Bonnyrig and Lasswade, Edinburgh 11 B3
Bonsucesso, Rio de Janeiro 24 B1
Bonteheuwel, Cape Town 8 A2
Boo, Stockholm 28 A3
Booterstown, Dublin 11 B2
Borisovo, Moscow 19 C4
Borle, Mumbai 20 A2
Boronia Park, Sydney 28 A1
Borough Park, New York 21 C2
Bosmont, Johannesburg 13 B1
Bosön, Stockholm 28 A3
Bosporus = Istanbul Boğazi, Istanbul 12 B2
Bostancı, Istanbul 12 C2
Boston Harbor, Boston 6 A4
Botafogo, Rio de Janeiro 24 B1
Botanisk Have, Copenhagen 10 b2
Botany, Sydney 28 B2
Botany B., Sydney 28 B2
Botany Bay Nat. Park, Sydney 28 B2
Botič →, Prague 24 B3
Botica Sete, Lisbon 14 A1
Boucherville, Montreal 19 A3
Boucherville, Îs. de, Montreal 19 A3
Bougival, Paris 23 A1
Boulder Pt., Hong Kong 12 B1
Boulogne, Bois de, Paris 23 A2
Boulogne-Billancourt, Paris 23 A2
Bourg-la-Reine, Paris 23 B2
Bouviers, Paris 23 B1
Bovenkerk, Amsterdam 2 B2
Bovenkerker Polder, Amsterdam 2 B2
Bovisa, Milan 18 A2
Bow, London 15 A3
Bowery, New York 21 c2
Boyacıköy, Istanbul 12 B2
Boyle Heights, Los Angeles 16 B3
Bradbury Building, Los Angeles 16 b2
Braepark, Edinburgh 11 B2
Braid, Edinburgh 11 B2
Bramley, Johannesburg 13 A2
Brandenburger Tor, Berlin 5 A3
Brani, P., Singapore 27 B3
Branik, Prague 24 B2
Brännkyrka, Stockholm 28 B2
Brás, São Paulo 26 B2
Brasilândia, São Paulo 26 A1
Brateyevo, Moscow 19 C4
Bratsevo, Moscow 19 A2
Bray, Dublin 11 B3
Braybrook, Melbourne 17 A1
Brázdim, Prague 24 A3
Breach Candy, Mumbai 20 a1
Breakheart Reservation, Boston 6 A3
Brede, Copenhagen 10 A3
Breeds Pond, Boston 6 A4
Breezy Point, New York 21 C2
Breitenlee, Vienna 31 A3
Breña, Lima 16 B2
Brent, London 15 A2
Brent Res., London 15 A2
Brentford, London 15 B2
Brentwood Park, Los Angeles 16 B2
Brera, Milan 18 B2
Bresso, Milan 18 A2
Brevik, Stockholm 28 A3
Břevnov, Prague 24 B2
Bridgeport, Chicago 9 B3
Bridgetown, Cape Town 8 A2
Bridgeview, Chicago 9 C2
Brighton, Boston 6 A3
Brighton, Melbourne 17 B1
Brighton le Sands, Sydney 28 B1
Brighton Park, Chicago 9 C2
Brightwood, Washington 32 B3
Brigittenau, Vienna 31 A2
Brimbank Park, Melbourne 17 A1
Brisbane, San Francisco 25 B2
British Museum, London 15 a3
Britz, Berlin 5 B3
Brixton, London 15 B3
Broad Sd., Boston 6 A4
Broadmeadows, Melbourne 17 A1
Broadmoor, San Francisco 25 B2
Broadview, Chicago 9 B1
Broadway, New York 21 e1
Brockley, London 15 B3
Brödno, Warsaw 31 B2
Bródnowski, Kanal, Warsaw 31 B2
Broek in Waterland, Amsterdam 2 A2
Bromley, London 15 B4
Bromley Common, London 15 B4
Bromma, Stockholm 28 A1
Bromma flygplats, Stockholm 28 A1
Brompton, London 15 c2
Brøndby Strand, Copenhagen 10 B2
Brøndbyøster, Copenhagen 10 B2
Brøndbyvester, Copenhagen 10 B2
Brondesbury, London 15 A2
Brønnøya, Oslo 22 A2
Brønshøj, Copenhagen 10 A2

BRONXVILLE

Bronxville, *New York* 21 A3
Brookfield, *Chicago* 9 C1
Brookhaven, *Atlanta* 3 A2
Brookline, *Boston* 6 B3
Brooklyn, *Cape Town* 8 A1
Brooklyn, *New York* 21 C2
Brooklyn, *Wellington* 32 B1
Brooklyn Bridge, *New York* 21 f2
Brookmont, *Washington* 32 B3
Brossard, *Montreal* 19 B3
Brou-sur-Chantereine, *Paris* 23 A4
Brown, *Toronto* 30 A3
Broyhill Park, *Washington* 32 B2
Brughério, *Milan* 18 A2
Brunswick, *Melbourne* 17 A1
Brush Hill, *Boston* 6 B1
Brussegem, *Brussels* 6 A1
Brussel Nat. Luchthaven, *Brussels* 6 A2
Brussels = Bruxelles, *Brussels* 6 A2
Bruxelles, *Brussels* 6 A2
Bruzzano, *Milan* 18 A2
Bry-sur-Marne, *Paris* 23 A4
Bryanston, *Johannesburg* 13 A1
Bryn, *Oslo* 22 A1
Brzeziny, *Warsaw* 31 B2
Bubeneč, *Prague* 24 B2
Buc, *Paris* 23 B1
Buchenhain, *Munich* 20 B1
Buchholz, *Berlin* 5 A3
Buckhead, *Atlanta* 3 A2
Buckingham Palace, *London* 15 b3
Buckow, *Berlin* 5 B3
Buda, *Budapest* 7 A2
Budafok, *Budapest* 7 B2
Budaörs, *Budapest* 7 B1
Budapest, *Budapest* 7 B2
Budatétény, *Budapest* 7 B2
Budavaripalota, *Budapest* 7 b2
Buddinge, *Copenhagen* 10 A3
Budokan, *Tokyo* 29 a4
Buena Vista, *San Francisco* 25 B2
Buenos Aires, *Buenos Aires* 7 B2
Bufalotta, *Rome* 25 B2
Bugio, *Lisbon* 14 B1
Buiksloot, *Amsterdam* 2 A2
Buitenveldert, *Amsterdam* 2 B2
Buizingen, *Brussels* 6 B1
Bukit Panjang Nature Reserve, *Singapore* 27 A2
Bukit Timah Nature Reserve, *Singapore* 27 A2
Bukum, P., *Singapore* 27 B2
Bûlâq, *Cairo* 7 A2
Bule, *Manila* 17 C2
Bulim, *Singapore* 27 A2
Bullen Park, *Melbourne* 17 A2
Bundoora North, *Melbourne* 17 A2
Bundoora Park, *Melbourne* 17 A2
Bunker I., *Karachi* 14 B1
Bunkyo-Ku, *Tokyo* 29 A3
Bunnefjorden, *Oslo* 22 A3
Buona Vista Park, *Singapore* 27 B2
Burbank, *Chicago* 9 C2
Burbank, *Los Angeles* 16 A3
Burlington, *Boston* 6 A2
Burnham Park, *Chicago* 9 c2
Burnham Park Harbor, *Chicago* 9 B3
Burnhamthorpe, *Toronto* 30 B1
Burnt Oak, *London* 15 A2
Burntisland, *Edinburgh* 11 A2
Burnwynd, *Edinburgh* 11 B1
Burqa, *Jerusalem* 13 A2
Burtus, *Cairo* 7 A1
Burudvatn, *Oslo* 22 A2
Burwood, *Sydney* 28 B1
Bushwick, *New York* 21 B2
Bushy Park, *London* 15 B1
Butantã, *São Paulo* 26 B1
Butcher I., *Mumbai* 20 B2
Butts Corner, *Washington* 32 C2
Büyükdere, *Istanbul* 12 B2
Byculla, *Mumbai* 20 B2
Bygdøy, *Oslo* 22 A3

C

C.N. Tower, *Toronto* 30 B2
Cabaçu de Cima →, *São Paulo* 26 A2
Caballito, *Buenos Aires* 7 B2
Cabin John, *Washington* 32 B2
Cabin John Regional Park, *Washington* 32 A2
Cabinteely, *Dublin* 11 B3
Cabra, *Dublin* 11 A2
Cabuçú de Baixo →, *São Paulo* 26 A1
Cachan, *Paris* 23 B2
Cachenka →, *Moscow* 19 B1
Cachoeira, Rib. da →, *São Paulo* 26 B1
Cacilhas, *Lisbon* 14 A2
Cahuenga Pk., *Los Angeles* 16 B3
Cairo = El Qâhira, *Cairo* 7 A2
Caju, *Rio de Janeiro* 24 B1
Čakovice, *Prague* 24 B3
Calcutta = Kolkata, *Calcutta* 8 B2
California Inst. of Tech., *Los Angeles* 16 B4
California Plaza, *Los Angeles* 16 b1
California State Univ., *Los Angeles* 16 B3
Callao, *Lima* 16 B2
Caloocan, *Manila* 17 B1
Calumet Park, *Chicago* 9 C3
Calumet Sag Channel →, *Chicago* 9 C2
Calumpang, *Manila* 17 B2
Calvairate, *Milan* 18 B2
Camarate, *Lisbon* 14 A2
Camaroes, *Lisbon* 14 A1
Camberwell, *London* 15 B3
Camberwell, *Melbourne* 17 B2
Cambridge, *Boston* 6 A3
Cambridge Res., *Boston* 6 A2
Cambuci, *São Paulo* 26 B2
Camden, *London* 15 A3
Cameron, Mt., *Wellington* 32 B2
Çamlıca, *Istanbul* 12 B2
Camp Springs, *Washington* 32 C4
Campamento, *Madrid* 17 B1
Campbellfield, *Melbourne* 17 A1
Camperdown, *Sydney* 28 B2
Campidoglio, *Rome* 25 c3
Campo, Casa de, *Madrid* 17 B1
Campo F.C. Barcelona, *Barcelona* 4 A1
Campo Grando, *Lisbon* 14 A2
Campo Pequeño, *Lisbon* 14 A2
Campolide, *Lisbon* 14 A2
Camps Bay, *Cape Town* 8 A1
C'an San Joan, *Barcelona* 4 A2
Cañacao B., *Manila* 17 C1
Canarsie, *New York* 21 C2
Cancelleria, Palazzo dei, *Rome* 25 c2
Candiac, *Montreal* 19 B3
Caneças, *Lisbon* 14 A1
Canillas, *Madrid* 17 B2
Canillejas, *Madrid* 17 B2
Canning Town, *London* 15 A4
Canteras de Vallecas, *Madrid* 17 B2
Canterbury, *Melbourne* 17 A2
Canterbury, *Sydney* 28 B1
Canton = Guangzhou, *Canton* 8 B2
Caoheijing, *Shanghai* 27 B1
Capão Redondo, *São Paulo* 26 B1
Caparica, *Lisbon* 14 A2
Caparica, Costa da, *Lisbon* 14 B1
Cape Flats, *Cape Town* 8 B2
Cape Town, *Cape Town* 8 A1
Capitol Heights, *Washington* 32 B4
Capitol Hill, *Washington* 32 B4
Capitolini, Musei, *Rome* 25 c3
Captain Cook Bridge, *Sydney* 28 C1
Captain Cook Landing Place Park, *Sydney* 28 C2
Capuchos, *Lisbon* 14 B1
Carabanchel Alto, *Madrid* 17 B1
Carabanchel Bajo, *Madrid* 17 B1
Carapachay, *Buenos Aires* 7 B1
Caraza, *Buenos Aires* 7 C2
Caridad, *Manila* 17 C1
Carioca, Sa. da, *Rio de Janeiro* 24 B1
Carlstadt, *New York* 21 A1
Carlton, *Melbourne* 17 A1
Carmen de Huechuraba, *Santiago* 26 B1
Carmen de la Legua, *Lima* 16 B2
Carnaxide, *Lisbon* 14 A1
Carnegie, *Melbourne* 17 B2
Carnegie Hall, *New York* 21 c2
Carnide, *Lisbon* 14 A1
Carol City, *Miami* 18 A1
Carrascal, *Santiago* 26 B1
Carrickmines, *Dublin* 11 B3
Carrières-sous-Bois, *Paris* 23 A1
Carrières-sous-Poissy, *Paris* 23 A1
Carrières-sur-Seine, *Paris* 23 A2
Carrigeen Bay, *Dublin* 11 A3
Cartierville, *Montreal* 19 A1
Casa Verde, *São Paulo* 26 A1
Casál Morena, *Rome* 25 C2
Casalotti, *Rome* 25 B1
Cascade Heights, *Atlanta* 3 B2
Castél di Leva, *Rome* 25 C2
Castel Sant'Angelo, *Rome* 25 B1
Castle, *Dublin* 11 c2
Castle, *Edinburgh* 11 b2
Castle of Good Hope, *Cape Town* 8 c3
Castleknock, *Dublin* 11 A1
Castleton Corners, *New York* 21 C1
Catedral Metropolitana, *Mexico City* 18 b3
Catedral Metropolitana, *Rio de Janeiro* 24 c1
Catete, *Rio de Janeiro* 24 B1
Catford, *London* 15 B3
Caulfield, *Melbourne* 17 B2
Causeway Bay, *Hong Kong* 12 c3
Cavite, *Manila* 17 C1
Caxias, *Lisbon* 14 A1
Cebecci, *Istanbul* 12 B1
Cecchignola, *Rome* 25 C2
Cecilienhof, Schloss, *Berlin* 5 B1
Cedar Grove, *Atlanta* 3 C3
Cempaka Putih, *Jakarta* 13 B2
Çengelköy, *Istanbul* 12 B2
Cengkareng, *Jakarta* 13 A1
Centennial Park, *Sydney* 28 B2
Center Hill, *Atlanta* 3 B2
Centocelle, *Rome* 25 B2
Centraal Station, *Amsterdam* 2 a2
Central Park, *New York* 21 B2
Cerillos, *Santiago* 26 B1
Cerro de la Estrella, *Mexico City* 18 B2
Cerro de los Angeles, *Madrid* 17 C1
Cerro Navia, *Santiago* 26 B1
Certanovka →, *Moscow* 19 C3
Certanovo, *Moscow* 19 C3
Cesano Boscone, *Milan* 18 B1
Cesate, *Milan* 18 A1
Cha Kwo Ling, *Hong Kong* 12 B2
Chacarrita, *Buenos Aires* 7 B2
Chadwell Heath, *London* 15 A4
Chai Chee, *Singapore* 27 B3
Chai Wan, *Hong Kong* 12 B2
Chai Wan Kok, *Hong Kong* 12 A1
Chaillot, Palais de, *Paris* 23 b2
Chakdaha, *Calcutta* 8 C1
Chamartin, *Madrid* 17 B1
Chamberi, *Madrid* 17 B1
Chambourcy, *Paris* 23 A1
Champ de Mars, Parc du, *Paris* 23 c2
Champigny-sur-Marne, *Paris* 23 B4
Champlain, Pont, *Montreal* 19 B2
Champs Elysées, Avenue des, *Paris* 23 b2
Champs-sur-Marne, *Paris* 23 A4
Chamrail, *Calcutta* 8 B1
Chamshil, *Seoul* 26 B2
Chamwŏn, *Seoul* 26 B2
Chanakyapuri, *Delhi* 10 B2
Chanditala, *Calcutta* 8 A1
Changfeng Park, *Shanghai* 27 B1
Changi, *Singapore* 27 A3
Changi Int. Airport, *Singapore* 27 A3
Changning, *Shanghai* 27 B1
Chantereine, *Paris* 23 A4
Chantian, *Canton* 8 A2
Chao Phraya →, *Bangkok* 3 B2
Chaoyang, *Beijing* 4 B2
Chaoyangmen, *Beijing* 4 B2
Chapelizod, *Dublin* 11 A1
Chapultepec, Bosque de, *Mexico City* 18 B1
Chapultepec, Castillo de, *Mexico City* 18 B1
Charenton-le-Pont, *Paris* 23 B3
Charing Cross, *London* 15 b4
Charleroi, Kanal de →, *Brussels* 6 B1
Charles Bridge, *Prague* 24 b1
Charles Square, *Prague* 24 c1
Charlestown, *Boston* 6 A3
Charlottenburg, *Berlin* 5 A2
Charlottenburg, Schloss, *Berlin* 5 A2
Charlottenlund, *Copenhagen* 10 A3
Charlton, *London* 15 B4
Charneca, *Lisbon* 14 A2
Charneca, *Lisbon* 14 B1
Châteaufort, *Paris* 23 B1
Châtenay-Malabry, *Paris* 23 B2
Chatham, *Chicago* 9 C3
Châtillon, *Paris* 23 B2
Chatou, *Paris* 23 A1
Chatpur, *Calcutta* 8 B2
Chatswood, *Sydney* 28 A2
Chatuchak, *Bangkok* 3 B2
Chatuchak Park, *Bangkok* 3 B2
Chauki, *Karachi* 14 A1
Chavarria, *Lima* 16 B2
Chaville, *Paris* 23 B2
Chayang, *Seoul* 26 B2
Chegi, *Seoul* 26 B2
Chelles, *Paris* 23 A4
Chelles, Canal de, *Paris* 23 A4
Chells-le-Pin, Aérodrome, *Paris* 23 A4
Chelsea, *Boston* 6 A3
Chelsea, *London* 15 B2
Chelsea, *New York* 21 c1
Chembur, *Mumbai* 20 A2
Chennevières-sur-Marne, *Paris* 23 B4
Cheops, *Cairo* 7 B1
Cherepkovo, *Moscow* 19 B2
Chernyovo, *Moscow* 19 A1
Cheryomushki, *Moscow* 19 B3
Chestnut Hill, *Boston* 6 B2
Cheung Sha Wan, *Hong Kong* 12 A1
Cheverly, *Washington* 32 B4
Chevilly-Larue, *Paris* 23 B3
Chevry-Cossigny, *Paris* 23 B4
Chevy Chase, *Washington* 32 B3
Chevy Chase View, *Washington* 32 A3
Chia Keng, *Singapore* 27 A3
Chiaravalle Milanese, *Milan* 18 B2
Chicago, *Chicago* 9 B3
Chicago Harbor, *Chicago* 9 B3
Chicago Lawn, *Chicago* 9 C2
Chicago-Midway Airport, *Chicago* 9 C2
Chicago-O'Hare Int. Airport, *Chicago* 9 B1
Chicago Ridge, *Chicago* 9 C2
Chicago Sanitary and Ship Canal, *Chicago* 9 C2
Chienzui, *Canton* 8 A3
Chik Sha, *Hong Kong* 12 B2
Child's Hill, *London* 15 A2
Chilla Saroda, *Delhi* 10 B2
Chillum, *Washington* 32 B4
Chilly-Mazarin, *Paris* 23 B2
Chinatown, *Los Angeles* 16 a3
Chinatown, *New York* 21 e2
Chinatown, *San Francisco* 25 b2
Chinatown, *Singapore* 27 c2
Chingupota, *Calcutta* 8 C1
Chislehurst, *London* 15 B4
Chiswick, *London* 15 B2
Chiswick House, *London* 15 B2
Chitose, *Tokyo* 29 B2
Chitralada Palace, *Bangkok* 3 B2
Chiyoda-Ku, *Tokyo* 29 b4
Chkalova, *Moscow* 19 C5
Choa Chu Kang, *Singapore* 27 A2
Choboty, *Moscow* 19 C2
Chodov u Prahy, *Prague* 24 B3
Chōfu, *Tokyo* 29 B2
Choisy-le-Roi, *Paris* 23 B3
Cholupice, *Prague* 24 C2
Chom Thong, *Bangkok* 3 B1
Chong Pang, *Singapore* 27 A2
Ch'ŏngdam, *Seoul* 26 B2
Chongmyo Royal Shrine, *Seoul* 26 B1
Chongno, *Seoul* 26 B1
Chongwen, *Beijing* 4 B2
Chŏnho, *Seoul* 26 B2
Chopin, Muzeum, *Warsaw* 31 b2
Chornaya →, *Moscow* 19 B6
Chorrillos, *Lima* 16 C2
Chowpatty Beach, *Mumbai* 20 b1
Christian Quarter, *Jerusalem* 13 b3
Christiansborg, *Copenhagen* 10 c2
Christianshavn, *Copenhagen* 10 A3
Chrysler Building, *New York* 21 c2
Chrzanów, *Warsaw* 31 B1
Chuen Lung, *Hong Kong* 12 A1
Chuk Kok, *Hong Kong* 12 A2
Chulalongkom Univ., *Bangkok* 3 B2
Chung, *Seoul* 26 B1
Chunghwa, *Seoul* 26 B2
Chungnangch'on →, *Seoul* 26 B1
Chūō-Ku, *Tokyo* 29 b5
Church End, *London* 15 A2
Churchtown, *Dublin* 11 B2
Ciampino, *Rome* 25 C2
Ciampino, Aeroporto di, *Rome* 25 C2
Cicero, *Chicago* 9 B2
Cilandak, *Jakarta* 13 B1
Cilincing, *Jakarta* 13 A2
Ciliwung →, *Jakarta* 13 B2
Čimice, *Prague* 24 B2
Cinecittà, *Rome* 25 B2
Cinisello Bálsamo, *Milan* 18 A2
Cinkota, *Budapest* 7 A3
Cipete, *Jakarta* 13 B1
Citadella, *Budapest* 7 c2
Citta degli Studi, *Milan* 18 B2
Città del Vaticano, *Rome* 25 B1
City, *London* 15 A3
City Hall, *New York* 21 e1
Ciudad Deportiva, *Mexico City* 18 B2
Ciudad Fin de Semana, *Madrid* 17 B2
Ciudad General Belgrano, *Buenos Aires* 7 C1
Ciudad Lineál, *Madrid* 17 B2
Ciudad Satélite, *Mexico City* 18 A1
Ciudad Universitaria, *Buenos Aires* 7 B2
Ciudad Universitaria, *Mexico City* 18 C1
Ciutadella, Parc de la, *Barcelona* 4 b3
Civic Center, *Los Angeles* 16 b2
Clamart, *Paris* 23 B2
Clapham, *London* 15 B3
Clapton, *London* 15 A3
Claremont, *Cape Town* 8 A1
Clayhall, *London* 15 A4
Clerkenwell, *London* 15 a4
Clermiston, *Edinburgh* 11 B2
Clichy, *Paris* 23 A2
Clichy-sous-Bois, *Paris* 23 A4
Cliffside, *Toronto* 30 A3
Cliffside Park, *New York* 21 B2
Clifton, *Boston* 6 A4
Clifton, *Karachi* 14 B2
Clifton, *New York* 21 C1
Cliftondale, *Boston* 6 A3
Cloghran, *Dublin* 11 A2
Clonskeagh, *Dublin* 11 B2
Clontarf, *Dublin* 11 A2
Clontarf, *Sydney* 28 A2
Clovelly, *Sydney* 28 B2
Cobras, I. das, *Rio de Janeiro* 24 B2
Coburg, *Melbourne* 17 A1
Cochituate, *Boston* 6 A1
Cochituate, L., *Boston* 6 B1
Cocotá, *Rio de Janeiro* 24 A1
Cœuilly, *Paris* 23 B4
Coina, *Lisbon* 14 B2
Coit Tower, *San Francisco* 25 a2
Coker, *Lagos* 14 B2
Colaba, *Mumbai* 20 B1
Colaba Pt., *Mumbai* 20 B1
Colegiales, *Buenos Aires* 7 B2
Colindale, *London* 15 A2
Colinton, *Edinburgh* 11 B2
College Park, *Atlanta* 3 C2
College Park, *Washington* 32 B4
College Point, *New York* 21 B2
Collégien, *Paris* 23 A4
Collier Row, *London* 15 A4
Colliers Wood, *London* 15 B2
Colma, *San Francisco* 25 B2
Colney Hatch, *London* 15 A3
Cologno Monzese, *Milan* 18 A2
Colombes, *Paris* 23 A2
Colón, Monumente, *Barcelona* 4 c3
Colon, Plaza de, *Madrid* 17 a3
Colonia Güell, *Barcelona* 4 A1
Colonial Knob, *Wellington* 32 A1
Colosseo, *Rome* 25 c3
Columbus Circus, *New York* 21 b2
Combault, *Paris* 23 B4
Comércio, Praça do, *Lisbon* 14 A2
Commerce, *Los Angeles* 16 B4
Como, *Sydney* 28 C1
Company's Gardens, *Cape Town* 8 c2
Conceição, I. da, *Rio de Janeiro* 24 B2
Concertgebouw, *Amsterdam* 2 c1
Conchali, *Santiago* 26 B2
Concord, *Boston* 6 A1
Concord, *Sydney* 28 B1
Concord, *Toronto* 30 A2
Concorde, Place de la, *Paris* 23 b3
Concorezzo, *Milan* 18 A2
Coney Island, *New York* 21 C2
Congonhas, Aéroporto, *São Paulo* 26 B2
Connaught Place, *Delhi* 10 B2
Conservatori, Palazzo dei, *Rome* 25 c3
Consolação, *São Paulo* 26 B2
Constantia, *Cape Town* 8 B1
Constitución, *Buenos Aires* 7 B2
Constitution, *Atlanta* 3 B2
Convention and Exhibition Centre, *Hong Kong* 12 b2
Coogee, *Sydney* 28 B2
Cook Str., *Wellington* 32 A1
Cooksville, *Toronto* 30 B1
Coolock, *Dublin* 11 A2
Copacabana, *Rio de Janeiro* 24 B1
Copenhagen = København, *Copenhagen* 10 A2
Coral Gables, *Miami* 18 B2
Coral Hills, *Washington* 32 B4
Corcovado, Morro do, *Rio de Janeiro* 24 B1
Corduff, *Dublin* 11 A1
Cormano, *Milan* 18 A2
Cornaredo, *Milan* 18 A1
Córsico, *Milan* 18 B1
Corsini, Palazzo, *Rome* 25 c1
Corviale, *Rome* 25 B1
Coslada, *Madrid* 17 B2
Cossigny, *Paris* 23 B4
Cossipore, *Calcutta* 8 B2
Costantino, Arco di, *Rome* 25 c3
Costorphine, *Edinburgh* 11 B2
Cotao, *Lisbon* 14 A1
Côte St.-Luc, *Montreal* 19 B2
Cotunduba, I. de, *Rio de Janeiro* 24 B2
Coubron, *Paris* 23 A4
Countryside, *Chicago* 9 C1
Courbevoie, *Paris* 23 A2
Courtry, *Paris* 23 A4
Covent Garden, *London* 15 b4
Cowgate, *Edinburgh* 11 b3
Cowley, *London* 15 A1
Coyoacán, *Mexico City* 18 B2
Cragin, *Chicago* 9 B2
Craighall Park, *Johannesburg* 13 A2
Craiglockhart, *Edinburgh* 11 B2
Craigmillar, *Edinburgh* 11 B3
Cramond, *Edinburgh* 11 B2
Cramond Bridge, *Edinburgh* 11 B1
Cramond I., *Edinburgh* 11 B2
Cranford, *London* 15 B1
Crawford, *Cape Town* 8 A2
Crayford, *London* 15 B5
Creekmouth, *London* 15 A4
Crescenzago, *Milan* 18 A2
Cressely, *Paris* 23 B1
Cresskill, *New York* 21 A2
Creteil, *Paris* 23 B3
Cricklewood, *London* 15 A2
Cristo Redentor, Estatua do, *Rio de Janeiro* 24 B1
Crockenhill, *London* 15 B4
Croissy-Beaubourg, *Paris* 23 B4
Croissy-sur-Seine, *Paris* 23 A1
Crosby, *Johannesburg* 13 B1
Crosne, *Paris* 23 B3
Cross I., *Mumbai* 20 B2
Crouch End, *London* 15 A3
Crown Mine, *Johannesburg* 13 B1
Crows Nest, *Sydney* 28 A2
Croydon, *London* 15 B3
Croydon Park, *Sydney* 28 B1
Cruagh Mt., *Dublin* 11 B2
Crumlin, *Dublin* 11 B2
Cruz de Pau, *Lisbon* 14 B2
Crystal Palace, *London* 15 B3
Csepel, *Budapest* 7 B2
Csepelsziget, *Budapest* 7 B2
Csillaghegy, *Budapest* 7 A2
Csillagtelep, *Budapest* 7 B2
Csömör, *Budapest* 7 A3
Csömöri-patak →, *Budapest* 7 A3
Cuatro Vientos, *Madrid* 17 B1
Cuauhtémoc, *Mexico City* 18 B2
Cubao, *Manila* 17 B2
Çubuklu, *Istanbul* 12 B2
Cudahy, *Los Angeles* 16 C3
Cuicuilco, Pirámido de, *Mexico City* 18 C1
Culver City, *Los Angeles* 16 B2
Cumballa Hill, *Mumbai* 20 a1
Cumbres de Vallecas, *Madrid* 17 B2
Cupecé, *São Paulo* 26 B1
Currie, *Edinburgh* 11 B2
Cusago, *Milan* 18 B1
Cusano Milanino, *Milan* 18 A2
Custom House, *Dublin* 11 b3
Çuvuşabaşi →, *Istanbul* 12 B1
Czernriaków, *Warsaw* 31 B2
Czyste, *Warsaw* 31 B1

D

D.F. Malan Airport, *Cape Town* 8 A2
Da Moóca →, *São Paulo* 26 B2
Da Yunhe →, *Tianjin* 30 A1
Dabizhuang, *Tianjin* 30 A2
Ďablice, *Prague* 24 B2
Dąbrowa, *Warsaw* 31 B1
Dachang, *Shanghai* 27 B1
Dachang Airfield, *Shanghai* 27 B1
Dachau-Ost, *Munich* 20 A1
Dachauer Moos, *Munich* 20 A1
Dadar, *Mumbai* 20 A1
Dagenham, *London* 15 A4
Daglfing, *Munich* 20 B2
Daheisha, *Jerusalem* 13 B2
Dahlem, *Berlin* 5 B2
Dahlwitz-Hoppegarten, *Berlin* 5 A5
Dahongmen, *Beijing* 4 C2
Daitō, *Osaka* 22 A4
Dajiaoting, *Beijing* 4 B2
Dakhnoye, *St. Petersburg* 26 C1
Dalejsky potok →, *Prague* 24 B2
Dalgety Bay, *Edinburgh* 11 A1
Dalkeith, *Edinburgh* 11 B3
Dalkey, *Dublin* 11 B3
Dalkey Island, *Dublin* 11 B3
Dallgow, *Berlin* 5 A1
Dalmeny, *Edinburgh* 11 B1
Dalston, *London* 15 A3
Daly City, *San Francisco* 25 B2
Dam, *Amsterdam* 2 b2
Dam Rak, *Amsterdam* 2 a2
Damaia, *Lisbon* 14 A1
Dämeritzsee, *Berlin* 5 B5
Dan Ryan Woods, *Chicago* 9 C2
Danderhall, *Edinburgh* 11 B3
Danderyd, *Stockholm* 28 A2
Danforth, *Toronto* 30 A3
Darakeh, *Tehran* 30 A2
Darband, *Tehran* 30 A2
Darling Harbour, *Sydney* 28 b1
Darling Point, *Sydney* 28 B2
Darndale, *Dublin* 11 A2
Darrūs, *Tehran* 30 A2
Dartford, *London* 15 B5
Darya Ganj, *Delhi* 1 a3
Dashi, *Canton* 8 B2
Datansha, *Canton* 8 B2
Datun, *Beijing* 4 B2
Daulatpur, *Delhi* 10 A1
David's Citadel, *Jerusalem* 13 b3
David's Tomb, *Jerusalem* 13 b3
Davidson, Mt., *San Francisco* 25 B2
Davidson's Mains, *Edinburgh* 11 B2
Dāvūdiyeh, *Tehran* 30 A2
Davydkovo, *Moscow* 19 B2
Dawidy, *Warsaw* 31 C1
Days Bay, *Wellington* 32 B2
Dazhigu, *Tianjin* 30 B2
De Waag, *Amsterdam* 2 b2
Decatur, *Atlanta* 3 B3
Dedham, *Boston* 6 B2
Deer I., *Boston* 6 A4
Degunino, *Moscow* 19 A3
Deir Dibwan, *Jerusalem* 13 A2
Deir Ibzi'e, *Jerusalem* 13 A1
Dejvice, *Prague* 24 B2
Dekabristov, Ostrov, *St. Petersburg* 26 B1
Delhi, *Delhi* 10 B2
Delhi Gate, *Delhi* 1 b3
Demarest, *New York* 21 A2
Den Ilp, *Amsterdam* 2 A2
Denistone Heights, *Sydney* 28 A1
Dentonia Park, *Toronto* 30 A3
Deptford, *London* 15 B3
Deputati, Camera dei, *Rome* 25 b2
Des Plaines, *Chicago* 9 A1
Des Plaines →, *Chicago* 9 B1
Deshengmen, *Beijing* 4 B2
Deutsch-Wagram, *Vienna* 31 A3
Deutsche Oper, *Berlin* 5 A2
Deutscher Museum, *Munich* 20 B2
Devil's Peak, *Cape Town* 8 A1
Dháfni, *Athens* 2 B2
Dhakuria, *Calcutta* 8 B2
Dhamarakia, *Athens* 2 B1
Dharavi, *Mumbai* 20 A2
Dhrapersón, *Athens* 2 B1
Diadema, *São Paulo* 26 C2
Diegen, *Brussels* 6 A2
Diemen, *Amsterdam* 2 A2
Diepkloof, *Johannesburg* 13 B1
Dieprivier, *Cape Town* 8 B1
Difficult Run →, *Washington* 32 B2
Dilbeek, *Brussels* 6 A1
Dinzigu, *Tianjin* 30 A1
Dirnismaning, *Munich* 20 A2
District Heights, *Washington* 32 B4
Ditan Park, *Beijing* 4 a2
Diyāla →, *Baghdad* 3 B3
Djursholm, *Stockholm* 28 A2
Döberitz, *Berlin* 5 A1
Döbling, *Vienna* 31 A2
Docklands, *London* 15 A3
Dodder, R. →, *Dublin* 11 B1
Dodger Stadium, *Los Angeles* 16 B3
Dolgoe Ozero, *St. Petersburg* 26 A1
Doll Museum, *Delhi* 1 b3
Dollis Hill, *London* 15 A2
Dollymount, *Dublin* 11 A2
Dolni, *Prague* 24 B3
Dolni Chabry, *Prague* 24 B2
Dolni Počernice, *Prague* 24 B3
Dolphins Barn, *Dublin* 11 B2
Dom Pedro II, Parque, *São Paulo* 26 B2
Domain, The, *Sydney* 28 b2
Dome of the Rock, *Jerusalem* 13 b3
Don Mills, *Toronto* 30 A2
Don Muang Int. Airport, *Bangkok* 3 A2
Donaghmede, *Dublin* 11 A3
Donau-Oder Kanal, *Vienna* 31 A3
Donaufeld, *Vienna* 31 A2
Donaupark, *Vienna* 31 A2
Donaustadt, *Vienna* 31 A2
Dongan Hills, *New York* 21 C1
Dongcheng, *Beijing* 4 B2
Donggou, *Shanghai* 27 B2
Dongjiao, *Canton* 8 B2
Dongjuzi, *Tianjin* 30 B2
Dongmenwai, *Tianjin* 30 B2
Dongri, *Mumbai* 20 B2
Dongshanhu Park, *Canton* 8 B2
Dongzhimen, *Beijing* 4 B2
Donnybrook, *Dublin* 11 B2
Doornfontein, *Johannesburg* 13 B2
Dorchester, *Boston* 6 B3
Dorchester B., *Boston* 6 B3
Dornach, *Munich* 20 B3
Dorval, Aéroport de, *Montreal* 19 B1
Dos Couros →, *São Paulo* 26 C2
Dos Moninos →, *São Paulo* 26 C2
Douglas Park, *Chicago* 9 B2
Dover Heights, *Sydney* 28 B2
Dowlatābād, *Tehran* 30 B2
Downey, *Los Angeles* 16 C4
Downsview, *Toronto* 30 A1
Dragør, *Copenhagen* 10 B3
Drancy, *Paris* 23 A3
Dranesville, *Washington* 32 A1
Dreilinden, *Berlin* 5 B2
Drewnica, *Warsaw* 31 B2
Drigh Road, *Karachi* 14 A2
Drimnagh, *Dublin* 11 B2
Drogenbos, *Brussels* 6 B1
Druid Hills, *Atlanta* 3 B2
Drum Towwer, *Beijing* 4 a2
Drumcondra, *Dublin* 11 A2
Drummoyne, *Sydney* 28 B1
Drylaw, *Edinburgh* 11 B2
Dubeč, *Prague* 24 B3
Dublin, *Dublin* 11 A2
Dublin Airport, *Dublin* 11 A2
Dublin Bay, *Dublin* 11 B3
Dublin Harbour, *Dublin* 11 A2
Duddingston, *Edinburgh* 11 B3
Dugnano, *Milan* 18 A2
Dūlāb, *Tehran* 30 B2
Dulwich, *London* 15 B3
Dum Dum, *Calcutta* 8 B2
Dum Dum Int. Airport, *Calcutta* 8 B2
Dumont, *New York* 21 A2
Dún Laoghaire, *Dublin* 11 B3
Duna →, *Budapest* 7 A2
Duncan Dock, *Cape Town* 8 a3
Dundrum, *Dublin* 11 B2
Dunearn, *Singapore* 27 B2
Dunfermline, *Edinburgh* 11 A1
Dunn Loring, *Washington* 32 B2
Dunning, *Chicago* 9 B2
Dunvegan, *Johannesburg* 13 A2
Duomo, *Milan* 18 B2
Duque de Caxias, *Rio de Janeiro* 24 A1
Dusit, *Bangkok* 3 B2
Dusit Zoo, *Bangkok* 3 a2
Duvernay, *Montreal* 19 A1
Dworp, *Brussels* 6 B1
Dyakovo, *Moscow* 19 B3
Dzerzhinskiy, *Moscow* 19 C5
Dzerzhinskiy, *Moscow* 19 B3
Dzerzhinskiy Park, *Moscow* 19 B3

E

Eagle Rock, *Los Angeles* 16 B3
Ealing, *London* 15 A2
Earl's Court, *London* 15 c1
Earlsfield, *London* 15 B2
Earlwood, *Sydney* 28 B1
East Acton, *Boston* 6 A1
East Arlington, *Boston* 6 A3
East Arlington, *Washington* 32 B3
East Bedfont, *London* 15 B1
East Boston, *Boston* 6 A3
East Don →, *Toronto* 30 A2
East Elmhurst, *New York* 21 B2
East Finchley, *London* 15 A2
East Ham, *London* 15 A4
East Humber →, *Toronto* 30 A1
East Lamma Channel, *Hong Kong* 12 B1
East Lexington, *Boston* 6 A2
East Los Angeles, *Los Angeles* 16 B3
East Molesey, *London* 15 B1
East New York, *New York* 21 B2
East Pines, *Washington* 32 B4
East Point, *Atlanta* 3 B2
East Potomac Park, *Washington* 32 B3
East Pt., *Boston* 6 A4
East River →, *New York* 21 B2
East Rutherford, *New York* 21 A1
East Sheen, *London* 15 B2
East Village, *New York* 21 e2
East Wickham, *London* 15 B4
East York, *Toronto* 30 A2
Eastbourne, *Wellington* 32 B2
Eastcote, *London* 15 A1
Easter Howgate, *Edinburgh* 11 B2
Eastwood, *Sydney* 28 A1
Ebara, *Tokyo* 29 B3
Ebisu, *Tokyo* 29 B3
Ebute-Ikorodu, *Lagos* 14 A2
Ebute-Metta, *Lagos* 14 B2
Echo Park, *Los Angeles* 16 a1
Eda, *Tokyo* 29 B2
Edendale, *Johannesburg* 13 A2
Edenmore, *Dublin* 11 A2
Edgars Cr. →, *Melbourne* 17 A1
Edgeley, *Toronto* 30 A1
Edgemar, *San Francisco* 25 C2
Edinburgh, *Edinburgh* 11 B2
Edison Park, *Chicago* 9 A2
Edmondston, *Washington* 32 B4
Edmondstown, *Dublin* 11 B2
Edo →, *Tokyo* 29 B4
Edogawa-Ku, *Tokyo* 29 A4
Edsberg, *Stockholm* 28 A1
Edwards L., *Melbourne* 17 A1
Eiche, *Berlin* 5 A4
Eiche Sud, *Berlin* 5 A4
Eiffel, Tour, *Paris* 23 A2
Ein Arik, *Jerusalem* 13 A1
Ein Naquba, *Jerusalem* 13 B1
Ein Rafa, *Jerusalem* 13 B1
Eizariya, *Jerusalem* 13 B2
Ejby, *Copenhagen* 10 A2
Ejigbo, *Lagos* 14 A1
Ekeberg, *Oslo* 22 A3
Eknäs, *Stockholm* 28 B3
El 'Abbasiya, *Cairo* 7 A2
El Agustino, *Lima* 16 B2
El Baragil, *Cairo* 7 A1
El Basâlîn, *Cairo* 7 B2
El-Bira, *Jerusalem* 13 A2
El Bosque, *Santiago* 26 C2
El Carmen, *Santiago* 26 B1
El Cortijo, *Santiago* 26 B1
El Duqqi, *Cairo* 7 A2
El Encinar de los Reyes, *Madrid* 17 A2
El Ghurîya, *Cairo* 7 A2
El Gîza, *Cairo* 7 A2
El-Khadr, *Jerusalem* 13 B1
El Khalîfa, *Cairo* 7 A2
El Kôm el Ahmar, *Cairo* 7 A2
El Ma'âdi, *Cairo* 7 B2
El Matarîya, *Cairo* 7 A2
El Mohandessin, *Cairo* 7 A2
El Monte, *Los Angeles* 16 B4
El Mûskî, *Cairo* 7 A2
El Pardo, *Madrid* 17 A1
El Portal, *Miami* 18 A2
El Prat de Llobregat, *Barcelona* 4 B1
El Pueblo de L.A. Historic Park, *Los Angeles* 16 b2
El Qâhira, *Cairo* 7 A2
El Qubba, *Cairo* 7 A2
El Reloj, *Mexico City* 18 C2
El Retiro, *Madrid* 17 B1
El Salto, *Santiago* 26 B2
El Sereno, *Los Angeles* 16 B3
El Talibîya, *Cairo* 7 B2
El Vergel, *Mexico City* 18 C2
El Wâhli, *Cairo* 7 A2
El Zamâlik, *Cairo* 7 A2
El Zeitûn, *Cairo* 7 A2
Elephanta Caves, *Mumbai* 20 B2
Elephanta I., *Mumbai* 20 B2
Ellboda, *Stockholm* 28 A3
Ellinikón, *Athens* 2 B2
Ellis I., *New York* 21 B1
Elm Park, *London* 15 A5
Elmers End, *London* 15 B3
Elmhurst, *New York* 21 B2
Elmstead, *London* 15 B4
Elmwood Park, *Chicago* 9 B2
Elmwood Park, *New York* 21 A1
Elsdon, *Wellington* 32 A1
Elsiesrivier, *Cape Town* 8 A2
Elsternwick, *Melbourne* 17 B2
Eltham, *London* 15 B4
Elwood, *Melbourne* 17 B1
Élysée, *Paris* 23 A2
Elysian Park, *Los Angeles* 16 a3
Embajadores, *Madrid* 17 c2
Embarcadero Center, *San Francisco* 25 b3
Emek Refa'im, *Jerusalem* 13 c2
Émerainville, *Paris* 23 B4
Emeryville, *San Francisco* 25 A3
Eminönü, *Istanbul* 12 B1
Emmarentia, *Johannesburg* 13 A2
Empire State Building, *New York* 21 c2
Encantado, *Rio de Janeiro* 24 B1
Encino, *Los Angeles* 16 B2
Encino Res., *Los Angeles* 16 B1
Enebyberg, *Stockholm* 28 A1
Enfield, *Sydney* 28 B1
Engenho, I. do, *Rio de Janeiro* 24 B2
Englewood, *Chicago* 9 C3
Englewood, *New York* 21 A2
Englewood Cliffs, *New York* 21 A2
Enmore, *Sydney* 28 B2
Enskede, *Stockholm* 28 B2
Entrevias, *Madrid* 17 B1
Epping, *Sydney* 28 A1
Erawan Shrine, *Bangkok* 3 c3
Eregun, *Lagos* 14 A2
Erenköy, *Istanbul* 12 C2
Erith, *London* 15 B5
Erlaa, *Vienna* 31 B1
Ermington, *Sydney* 28 A1
Ermita, *Manila* 17 B1
Ershatou, *Canton* 8 B2
Erskineville, *Sydney* 28 B2
Erunkan, *Lagos* 14 A2
Erzsébet-Telep, *Budapest* 7 B3
Eschenried, *Munich* 20 A1
Esenler, *Istanbul* 12 B1
Esher, *London* 15 B1
Eskbank, *Edinburgh* 11 B3
Esperanza, *Mexico City* 18 c3
Esplanade Park, *Singapore* 27 c3
Esplugas, *Barcelona* 4 A1
Esposizione Univ. di Roma (E.U.R.), *Rome* 25 C1
Essendon, *Melbourne* 17 A1
Essendon Airport, *Melbourne* 17 A1
Essingen, *Stockholm* 28 B1
Essling, *Vienna* 31 A3
Est, Gare de l', *Paris* 23 a5
Estadio Maracanã, *Rio de Janeiro* 24 B1
Estado, Parque do, *São Paulo* 26 B2
Estefânia, *Lisbon* 14 a2
Estrela, Basilica da, *Lisbon* 14 A2
Ethnikó Arheologiko Moussío, *Athens* 2 a2
Etobicoke, *Toronto* 30 B1
Etobicoke Cr. →, *Toronto* 30 B1
Etterbeek, *Brussels* 6 B2
Euston, *London* 15 a3
Evanston, *Chicago* 9 A2
Even Sapir, *Jerusalem* 13 B1
Evere, *Brussels* 6 A2
Everett, *Boston* 6 A3
Evergreen Park, *Chicago* 9 C2
Evīn, *Tehran* 30 A2
Évzonos, *Athens* 2 B2
Ewu, *Lagos* 14 A1
Exchange Square, *Hong Kong* 12 c1
Exposições, Palácio das, *Rio de Janeiro* 24 B1
Eyüp, *Istanbul* 12 B1

F

Fabour, Mt., *Singapore* 27 B2
Faechi, *Seoul* 26 B2
Fælledparken, *Copenhagen* 10 A3
Fågelön, *Stockholm* 28 B1
Fagersjö, *Stockholm* 28 B2
Fair Lawn, *New York* 21 A1
Fairfax, *Washington* 32 B2
Fairfax Station, *Washington* 32 C2
Fairhaven Bay, *Boston* 6 A1
Fairhaven Hill, *Boston* 6 A1
Fairland, *Johannesburg* 13 A1
Fairmilehead, *Edinburgh* 11 B2
Fairmount Heights, *Washington* 32 B4
Fairport, *Toronto* 30 A4
Fairview, *New York* 21 B2
Falenty, *Warsaw* 31 C1
Fálirou, Órmos, *Athens* 2 B2
Falkenburg, *Berlin* 5 A4
Falkenhagen, *Berlin* 5 A1
Falkensee, *Berlin* 5 A1
Falls Church, *Washington* 32 B2
Falomo, *Lagos* 14 B2
False Bay, *Cape Town* 8 B2
Fangcun, *Canton* 8 B2
Faraḩābād, *Tehran* 30 A2
Farforovskaya, *St. Petersburg* 26 B2
Farningham, *London* 15 B5
Farrar Pond, *Boston* 6 A1
Farsta, *Stockholm* 28 B2
Fasanerie-Nord, *Munich* 20 A2
Fasangarten, *Munich* 20 B2
Fasting Palace, *Beijing* 4 c2
Fatih, *Istanbul* 12 B1
Favoriten, *Vienna* 31 B2
Fawkner, *Melbourne* 17 A1

KÁPOSZTÁSMEGYER

Káposztásmegyer, *Budapest* 7 A2
Kapotnya, *Moscow* 19 C4
Käppala, *Stockholm* 28 A3
Käpylä, *Helsinki* 12 B2
Karachi, *Karachi* 14 A2
Karachi Int. Airport, *Karachi* 14 A2
Karato, *Osaka* 22 A2
Karibong, *Seoul* 26 C1
Karkh, *Baghdad* 3 A2
Karlin, *Prague* 24 B2
Karlsfeld, *Munich* 20 A1
Karlshorst, *Berlin* 5 B4
Karlsplatz, *Munich* 20 b1
Karntner Strasse, *Vienna* 31 b2
Karol Bagh, *Delhi* 10 B2
Karolinenhof, *Berlin* 5 B4
Karori, *Wellington* 32 B1
Karow, *Berlin* 5 A3
Karrādah, *Baghdad* 3 B2
Kärsön, *Stockholm* 28 B1
Kasai, *Tokyo* 29 B4
Kashiwara, *Osaka* 22 B4
Kastellet, *Copenhagen* 10 a3
Kastrup, *Copenhagen* 10 B3
Kastrup Lufthavn, *Copenhagen* 10 B3
Kasuga, *Tokyo* 29 A2
Kasuge, *Tokyo* 29 A3
Kasumigaseki, *Tokyo* 29 b4
Katong, *Singapore* 27 B3
Katrineberg, *Stockholm* 28 B1
Katsushika-Ku, *Tokyo* 29 A4
Kau Pei Chau, *Hong Kong* 12 B2
Kau Yi Chau, *Hong Kong* 12 B1
Kaulsdorf, *Berlin* 5 B4
Kauniainen, *Helsinki* 12 B1
Kawasaki, *Tokyo* 29 B3
Kawawa, *Tokyo* 29 B2
Kawęczyn, *Warsaw* 31 B2
Kayu Putih, *Jakarta* 13 B2
Kbely, *Prague* 24 B3
Kebayoran Baru, *Jakarta* 13 B1
Kebayoran Lama, *Jakarta* 13 B1
Kebon Jeruk, *Jakarta* 13 B1
Kedar, *Jerusalem* 13 B2
Keilor, *Melbourne* 17 A1
Keilor North, *Melbourne* 17 A1
Keimola, *Helsinki* 12 A1
Kelenföld, *Budapest* 7 B2
Kelvin, *Johannesburg* 13 A2
Kemang, *Jakarta* 13 B1
Kemayoran, *Jakarta* 13 B2
Kemerburgaz, *Istanbul* 12 B1
Kempton Park Races, *London* 15 B1
Kendall Green, *Boston* 6 A2
Kenilworth, *Cape Town* 8 A1
Kennedy Town, *Hong Kong* 12 B1
Kennington, *London* 15 c4
Kensal Green, *London* 15 A2
Kensal Rise, *London* 15 a1
Kensington, *Johannesburg* 13 B2
Kensington, *London* 15 B2
Kensington, *New York* 21 C2
Kensington, *Sydney* 28 B2
Kensington Palace, *London* 15 A2
Kent Village, *Washington* 32 B4
Kentish Town, *London* 15 A3
Kenton, *London* 15 A2
Kenwood House, *London* 15 A3
Kepa, *Warsaw* 31 B2
Keppel Harbour, *Singapore* 27 B2
Keramíkos, *Athens* 2 b1
Kettering, *Washington* 32 B5
Kew, *London* 15 B2
Kew, *Melbourne* 17 A2
Kew Gardens, *London* 15 B2
Kew Gardens, *Toronto* 30 B3
Key Biscayne, *Miami* 18 B2
Khaidhárion, *Athens* 2 A1
Khalándrion, *Athens* 2 A2
Khalīj, *Baghdad* 3 B2
Khandallah, *Wellington* 32 B1
Khansā', *Baghdad* 3 A2
Kharavli, *Mumbai* 20 B2
Khefren, *Cairo* 7 B1
Khichripur, *Delhi* 10 B2
Khidirpur, *Calcutta* 8 B1
Khimki-Khovrino, *Moscow* 19 A3
Khirbet Jub e-Rum, *Jerusalem* 13 B2
Khlong San, *Bangkok* 3 B2
Khlong Toey, *Bangkok* 3 B2
Kholargós, *Athens* 2 B2
Khorel, *Calcutta* 8 A1
Khorosovo, *Moscow* 19 B2
Kiamari, *Karachi* 14 B1
Kierling, *Vienna* 31 A1
Kierlingbach →, *Vienna* 31 A1
Kifisós →, *Athens* 2 B2
Kikuna, *Tokyo* 29 B2
Kilbarrack, *Dublin* 11 A3
Kilbirnie, *Wellington* 32 B1
Kilburn, *London* 15 A2
Killakee, *Dublin* 11 B2
Killester, *Dublin* 11 A2
Killiney, *Dublin* 11 B3
Killiney Bay, *Dublin* 11 B3
Kilmacud, *Dublin* 11 B2
Kilmainham, *Dublin* 11 A2
Kilmashogue Mt., *Dublin* 11 B2
Kilmore, *Dublin* 11 A2
Kilnamanagh, *Dublin* 11 B1
Kilo, *Helsinki* 12 B1
Kilokri, *Delhi* 10 B2
Kiltiernan, *Dublin* 11 B2
Kimmage, *Dublin* 11 B2
Kindi, *Baghdad* 3 B2
Kinghorn, *Edinburgh* 11 A2
King's Cross, *London* 15 a4
Kings Cross, *Sydney* 28 c3
Kings Domain, *Melbourne* 17 A1
Kings Park, *Washington* 32 C2
Kings Park West, *Washington* 32 C2
Kingsbury, *London* 15 A2
Kingsbury, *Melbourne* 17 A2
Kingsford, *Sydney* 28 B2
Kingston upon Thames, *London* 15 B2
Kingston Vale, *London* 15 B2
Kingsway, *Toronto* 30 B1
Kinsaley, *Dublin* 11 A2
Kipling Heights, *Toronto* 30 A1
Kipséli, *Athens* 2 B2
Kirchstockbach, *Munich* 20 B3
Kirchtrudering, *Munich* 20 B3
Kirikiri, *Lagos* 14 B1
Kirke Værløse, *Copenhagen* 10 A1
Kirkhill, *Edinburgh* 11 B2
Kirkliston, *Edinburgh* 11 B1
Kirknewton, *Edinburgh* 11 B1
Kirov Palace of Culture, *St. Petersburg* 26 B1
Kısıklı, *Istanbul* 12 B2
Kispest, *Budapest* 7 B2
Kista, *Stockholm* 28 A1
Kita, *Osaka* 22 A4
Kita-Ku, *Tokyo* 29 A3
Kitazawa, *Tokyo* 29 B3
Kiu Tsiu, *Hong Kong* 12 A2
Kivistö, *Helsinki* 12 B2
Kızıltoprak, *Istanbul* 12 C2
Kizu →, *Osaka* 22 B3
Kizuri, *Osaka* 22 B4
Kjelsås, *Oslo* 22 A3
Kladow, *Berlin* 5 B1
Klampenborg, *Copenhagen* 10 A3
Klaudyń, *Warsaw* 31 B1
Klecany, *Prague* 24 A2
Kledering, *Vienna* 31 B2
Klein Jukskei →, *Johannesburg* 13 A1
Kleinmachnow, *Berlin* 5 B2
Kleinschönebeck, *Berlin* 5 B5
Klemetsrud, *Oslo* 22 A4
Kličany, *Prague* 24 A2
Klipriviersberg Nature Reserve, *Johannesburg* 13 B2
Klosterneuburg, *Vienna* 31 A1
Knesset, *Jerusalem* 13 b1
Knightsbridge, *London* 15 c2
Kőbánya, *Budapest* 7 B2
Kobbegem, *Brussels* 6 A1
Kōbe, *Osaka* 22 A2
Kōbe Harbour, *Osaka* 22 B2
København, *Copenhagen* 10 A2
Kobylisy, *Prague* 24 B2
Kobyłka, *Warsaw* 31 A3
Kŏch'ŏk, *Seoul* 26 B1
Kodaira, *Tokyo* 29 A1
Kodanaka, *Tokyo* 29 B2
Kodenmacho, *Tokyo* 29 a5
Koekelberg, *Brussels* 6 A1
Koganei, *Tokyo* 29 A2
Kogarah, *Sydney* 28 B1
Køge Bugt, *Copenhagen* 10 B2
Koivupää, *Helsinki* 12 B2
Koja, *Jakarta* 13 A2
Koja Utara, *Jakarta* 13 A2
Kokobunji, *Tokyo* 29 A1
Kokobunji-Temple, *Tokyo* 29 A4
Kolarängen, *Stockholm* 28 B3
Kolbotn, *Oslo* 22 B3
Kolkata, *Calcutta* 8 B2
Koło, *Warsaw* 31 B1
Kolokinthóu, *Athens* 2 B2
Kolomyagi, *St. Petersburg* 26 A1
Kolónos, *Athens* 2 B2
Kolsås, *Oslo* 22 A2
Komae, *Tokyo* 29 B2
Komagome, *Tokyo* 29 A3
Komazawa, *Tokyo* 29 B3
Kona, *Calcutta* 8 B1
Konala, *Helsinki* 12 B2
Kondli, *Delhi* 10 B2
Kongelige Slottet, *Oslo* 22 a1
Kongelunden, *Copenhagen* 10 B3
Kongens Lyngby, *Copenhagen* 10 A3
Kongnŭng, *Seoul* 26 B2
Kongo, *Helsinki* 12 A1
Koninklijk Paleis, *Amsterdam* 2 b2
Konnagar, *Calcutta* 8 A2
Konohana, *Osaka* 22 A3
Kōnoike, *Osaka* 22 A4
Konradshöhe, *Berlin* 5 A2
Kopanina, *Prague* 24 B1
Koparkhairna, *Mumbai* 20 A2
Köpenick, *Berlin* 5 B4
Korangi, *Karachi* 14 B2
Koremasa, *Tokyo* 29 B1
Korenevo, *Moscow* 19 B6
Kori, *Osaka* 22 A4
Koridhallós, *Athens* 2 B1
Korokoro, *Wellington* 32 B2
Korokoro Stream →, *Wellington* 32 B2
Kosino, *Moscow* 19 B5
Kosugi, *Tokyo* 29 B2
Kota, *Jakarta* 13 A1
Kotelyniki, *Moscow* 19 C5
Kōtō-Ku, *Tokyo* 29 A3
Kotrung, *Calcutta* 8 A2
Kouponia, *Athens* 2 B2
Kowloon, *Hong Kong* 12 B1
Kowloon Park, *Hong Kong* 12 a2
Kowloon Peak, *Hong Kong* 12 A2
Kowloon Res., *Hong Kong* 12 A1
Kowloon Tong, *Hong Kong* 12 A2
Kozhukhovo, *Moscow* 19 B5
Kraainem, *Brussels* 6 A2
Krailling, *Munich* 20 B1
Krampnitz, *Berlin* 5 B1
Krampnitzsee, *Berlin* 5 B1
Kranji, Sungei →, *Singapore* 27 A2
Kranji Industrial Estate, *Singapore* 27 A2
Kraskovo, *Moscow* 19 C5
Krasno-Presnenskaya, *Moscow* 19 B3
Krasnogorsk, *Moscow* 19 B1
Krč, *Prague* 24 B2
Krestovskiye, Ostrov, *St. Petersburg* 26 B1
Kreuzberg, *Berlin* 5 A3
Kritzendorf, *Vienna* 31 A1
Krumme Lanke, *Berlin* 5 B2
Krummensee, *Berlin* 5 A5
Krung Thep, *Bangkok* 3 B2
Krusboda, *Stockholm* 28 B3
Krylatskoye, *Moscow* 19 B2
Küçükköy, *Istanbul* 12 B1
Kudankita, *Tokyo* 29 a3
Kudrovo, *St. Petersburg* 26 B3
Kulosaari, *Helsinki* 12 B3
Kulturforum, *Berlin* 5 b3
Kultury i Nauki, Palac, *Warsaw* 31 b2
Kŭmch'ŏn, *Seoul* 26 C1
Kumla, *Stockholm* 28 B3
Kungens kurva, *Stockholm* 28 B1
Kungliga Slottet, *Stockholm* 28 b2
Kungshatt, *Stockholm* 28 B1
Kungsholmen, *Stockholm* 28 A2
Kuningan, *Jakarta* 13 B1
Kunitachi, *Tokyo* 29 A1
Kunming Hu, *Beijing* 4 B1
Kunratice, *Prague* 24 B2
Kunsthistorischesmuseum, *Vienna* 31 b1
Kuntsevo, *Moscow* 19 B2
Kupchino, *St. Petersburg* 26 B2
Kurbağalı →, *Istanbul* 12 C2
Kurihara, *Tokyo* 29 A2
Kurla, *Mumbai* 20 A2
Kurmuri, *Mumbai* 20 A2
Kurume, *Tokyo* 29 A2
Kuryanovo, *Moscow* 19 C4
Kuskovo, *Moscow* 19 B4
Kustia, *Calcutta* 8 B2
Kutsino, *Moscow* 19 B5
Kuzguncuk, *Istanbul* 12 B2
Kuzyminki, *Moscow* 19 B4
Kwai Chung, *Hong Kong* 12 A1
Kwanak, *Seoul* 26 C1
Kwanak-san, *Seoul* 26 C1
Kyje, *Prague* 24 B3
Kyūhōji, *Osaka* 22 B4

L

La Blanca, *Santiago* 26 C2
La Boca, *Buenos Aires* 7 B2
La Bretèche, *Paris* 23 A1
La Campiña, *Lima* 16 C2
La Celle-St.-Cloud, *Paris* 23 A1
La Ciudadela, *Mexico City* 18 c2
La Courneuve, *Paris* 23 A3
La Dehesa, *Santiago* 26 B2
La Encantada, *Lima* 16 C2
La Estación, *Madrid* 17 B1
La Floresta, *Barcelona* 4 A1
La Fortuna, *Madrid* 17 B1
La Fransa, *Barcelona* 4 A1
La Garenne-Colombes, *Paris* 23 A2
La Giustiniana, *Rome* 25 B1
La Grange, *Chicago* 9 C1
La Grange Park, *Chicago* 9 C1
La Granja, *Santiago* 26 C2
La Guardia Airport, *New York* 21 B2
La Hulpe, *Brussels* 6 B2
La Llacuna, *Barcelona* 4 A2
La Loma, *Mexico City* 18 A1
La Lucila, *Buenos Aires* 7 B2
La Maladrerie, *Paris* 23 A1
La Milla, Cerro, *Lima* 16 B2
La Monachina, *Rome* 25 B1
La Moraleja, *Madrid* 17 A2
La Nopalera, *Mexico City* 18 C2
La Paternal, *Buenos Aires* 7 B2
La Perla, *Lima* 16 B2
La Perouse, *Sydney* 28 B2
La Pineda, *Barcelona* 4 B1
La Pisana, *Rome* 25 B1
La Prairie, *Montreal* 19 B3
La Punta, *Lima* 16 B1
La Puntigala, *Barcelona* 4 A2
La Queue-en-Brie, *Paris* 23 B4
La Reina, *Santiago* 26 B2
La Ribera, *Barcelona* 4 A1
La Sagrera, *Barcelona* 4 A2
La Salada, *Buenos Aires* 7 C2
La Scala, *Milan* 18 B2
La Storta, *Rome* 25 A1
La Taxonera, *Barcelona* 4 A2
La Victoria, *Lima* 16 B2
Laajalahti, *Helsinki* 12 B1
Laajasalo, *Helsinki* 12 B3
Laaksolahti, *Helsinki* 12 B1
Lablâba, W. el →, *Cairo* 7 A2
Lac Cisterna, *Santiago* 26 C2
Lachine, *Montreal* 19 B1
Lad Phrao, *Bangkok* 3 B2
Ladera Heights, *Los Angeles* 16 C2
Ládví, *Prague* 24 B2
Łady, *Warsaw* 31 C1
Lafontaine, Parc, *Montreal* 19 A2
Lagoa, *Rio de Janeiro* 24 B1
Lagos, *Lagos* 14 B2
Lagos Harbour, *Lagos* 14 B2
Lagos-Ikeja Airport, *Lagos* 14 A1
Lagos Island, *Lagos* 14 B2
Lagos Lagoon, *Lagos* 14 B2
Laguna de B., *Manila* 17 C2
Laim, *Munich* 20 B2
Lainate, *Milan* 18 A1
Lainz, *Vienna* 31 B1
Lakemba, *Sydney* 28 B1
Lakeside, *Cape Town* 8 B1
Lakeside, *Johannesburg* 13 A2
Lakeview, *Chicago* 9 B3
Lakewood Park, *Atlanta* 3 B2
Lakhtinskiy, *St. Petersburg* 26 B1
Lakhtinskiy Razliv, Oz., *St. Petersburg* 26 B1
Lakshmanpur, *Calcutta* 8 B1
Lal Qila, *Delhi* 1 a3
Lam Tin, *Hong Kong* 12 B2
Lambert, *Oslo* 22 A3
Lambeth, *London* 15 B3
Lambrate, *Milan* 18 B2
Lambro, Parco, *Milan* 18 B2
Lambton Mills, *Toronto* 30 B1
Lamma I., *Hong Kong* 12 B1
Landover Hills, *Washington* 32 B4
Landsmeer, *Amsterdam* 2 A2
Landstrasse, *Vienna* 31 A2
Landwehr kanal, *Berlin* 5 B3
Lane Cove, *Sydney* 28 A1
Lane Cove National Park, *Sydney* 28 A1
Langa, *Cape Town* 8 A2
Langenzersdorf, *Vienna* 31 A2
Langer See, *Berlin* 5 B4
Langley, *Washington* 32 B2
Langley Park, *Washington* 32 B4
Langwald, *Munich* 20 A1
Lanham, *Washington* 32 B4
Lankwitz, *Berlin* 5 B3
L'Annunziatella, *Rome* 25 C2
Lansdowne, *Cape Town* 8 A2
Lansing, *Toronto* 30 A2
Lanús, *Buenos Aires* 7 C2
Lapa, *Rio de Janeiro* 24 B1
Laranjeiras, *Rio de Janeiro* 24 B1
Larísa Sta., *Athens* 2 a1
Las, *Warsaw* 31 B2
Las Corts, *Barcelona* 4 A1
Las Kabacki, *Warsaw* 31 C2
Las Pinas, *Manila* 17 C1
Las Rejas, *Santiago* 26 B1
Lasalle, *Montreal* 19 B2
Lasek Bielański, *Warsaw* 31 B1
Lasek Na Kole, *Warsaw* 31 B1
Laski, *Warsaw* 31 B1
Latina, *Madrid* 17 B1
Laurence G. Hanscom Field, *Boston* 6 A2
Lauttasaari, *Helsinki* 12 C2
Laval, *Montreal* 19 A1
Laval-des-Rapides, *Montreal* 19 A1
Lavīzān, *Tehran* 30 A2
Lavradio, *Lisbon* 14 A2
Lawndale, *Chicago* 9 B2
Lawrence Heights, *Toronto* 30 A2
Layari, *Karachi* 14 A2
Layari →, *Karachi* 14 A1
Lazare, Gare St., *Paris* 23 a3
Łazienkowski, Palac, *Warsaw* 31 c3
Łazienkowski Park, *Warsaw* 31 B2
Le Blanc-Mesnil, *Paris* 23 A3
Le Bourget, *Paris* 23 A3
Le Chenoi, *Brussels* 6 B2
Le Chesnay, *Paris* 23 B1
Le Christ de Saclay, *Paris* 23 B2
Le Kremlin-Bicêtre, *Paris* 23 B3
Le Mesnil-le-Roi, *Paris* 23 A1
Le Pecq, *Paris* 23 A1
Le Perreux, *Paris* 23 A3
Le Pin, *Paris* 23 A4
Le Plessis-Robinson, *Paris* 23 B2
Le Plessis-Trévise, *Paris* 23 B4
Le Port-Marly, *Paris* 23 A1
Le Pré-St.-Gervais, *Paris* 23 A3
Le Raincy, *Paris* 23 A4
Le Vésinet, *Paris* 23 A1
Lea Bridge, *London* 15 A3
Leaside, *Toronto* 30 A2
Leblon, *Rio de Janeiro* 24 B1
Lee, *London* 15 B4
Leganés, *Madrid* 17 C1
Legazpi, *Madrid* 17 B1
Lehtisaari, *Helsinki* 12 B2
Lei Yue Mun, *Hong Kong* 12 B2
Leião, *Lisbon* 14 A1
Leicester Square, *London* 15 b3
Leichhardt, *Sydney* 28 B1
Leith, *Edinburgh* 11 B3
Lemoyne, *Montreal* 19 B3
Lenin, *Moscow* 19 B3
Lenino, *Moscow* 19 C3
Leninskiye Gory, *Moscow* 19 B3
Lennox, *Los Angeles* 16 C2
Leonia, *New York* 21 A2
Leopardstown, *Dublin* 11 B2
Leopoldau, *Vienna* 31 A2
Leopoldstadt, *Vienna* 31 A2
Leportovo, *Moscow* 19 B4
Leppävaara, *Helsinki* 12 B1
Les Lilas, *Paris* 23 A3
Les Loges-en-Josas, *Paris* 23 B1
Les Pavillons-sous-Bois, *Paris* 23 A4
Lésigny, *Paris* 23 B4
Lesnozavodskaya, *St. Petersburg* 26 B2
L'Étang-la-Ville, *Paris* 23 A1
Letná, *Prague* 24 a1
Letňany, *Prague* 24 B3
Levallois-Perret, *Paris* 23 A2
Levent, *Istanbul* 12 B2
Lewisdale, *Washington* 32 B4
Lewisham, *London* 15 B3
Lexington, *Boston* 6 A2
Leyton, *London* 15 A3
Leytonstone, *London* 15 A4
L'Hay-les-Roses, *Paris* 23 B3
L'Hospitalet de Llobregat, *Barcelona* 4 A1
Lhotka, *Prague* 24 B2
Liangshui He →, *Beijing* 4 C2
Lianhua Chi, *Beijing* 4 B1
Lianhua He →, *Beijing* 4 B1
Libčice nad Vitavou, *Prague* 24 A2
Libeň, *Prague* 24 B2
Liberdade, *São Paulo* 26 B2
Liberdade, Ave da, *Lisbon* 14 b1
Liberton, *Edinburgh* 11 B3
Liberty I., *New York* 21 B1
Liberty State Park, *New York* 21 B1
Libeznice, *Prague* 24 A2
Library of Congress, *Washington* 32 c3
Libuš, *Prague* 24 B2
Lichiao, *Canton* 8 B2
Lichtenburg, *Berlin* 5 A4
Lichterfelde, *Berlin* 5 B2
Lidingö, *Stockholm* 28 A2
Licshi Lingyuan, *Canton* 8 B2
Liesing, *Vienna* 31 B1
Liesing →, *Vienna* 31 B2
Liffey, R. →, *Dublin* 11 A1
Ligovo, *St. Petersburg* 26 C1
Lijordet, *Oslo* 22 A2
Likavitos, *Athens* 2 b3
Likhoborka →, *Moscow* 19 A3
Lilla Värtan, *Stockholm* 28 A3
Lille Værløse, *Copenhagen* 10 A2
Liluah, *Calcutta* 8 B1
Lim Chu Kang, *Singapore* 27 A2
Lima, *Lima* 16 B2
Limbiate, *Milan* 18 A1
Limehouse, *London* 15 A3
Limeil-Brévannes, *Paris* 23 B3
Linate, Aeroporto Internazionale di, *Milan* 18 B2
Linbropark, *Johannesburg* 13 A2
Lincoln, *Boston* 6 A2
Lincoln Center, *New York* 21 b2
Lincoln Heights, *Los Angeles* 16 B3
Lincoln Park, *Chicago* 9 B3
Lincoln Park, *New York* 21 B1
Lincoln Park, *San Francisco* 25 B1
Lincolnwood, *Chicago* 9 A2
Linda-a-Pastora, *Lisbon* 14 A1
Linden, *Johannesburg* 13 A2
Linden, *Wellington* 32 A1
Lindenberg, *Berlin* 5 A4
Lindøya, *Oslo* 22 A3
Liniers, *Buenos Aires* 7 B1
Linkebeek, *Brussels* 6 B2
Linksfield, *Johannesburg* 13 A2
Linmeyer, *Johannesburg* 13 B2
Linna, *Helsinki* 12 A2
Lintuvaara, *Helsinki* 12 B1
Lion Rock Country Park, *Hong Kong* 12 A2
Lioúmi, *Athens* 2 B2
Liqizhuang, *Tianjin* 30 B2
Lisboa, *Lisbon* 14 A2
Lisbon = Lisboa, *Lisbon* 14 A2
Lishui, *Canton* 8 A1
Little B., *Sydney* 28 B2
Little Calumet →, *Chicago* 9 D3
Little Ferry, *New York* 21 A1
Little Italy, *New York* 21 e2
Little Mermaid, *Copenhagen* 10 a3
Little Rouge →, *Toronto* 30 A4
Little Tokyo, *Los Angeles* 16 c2
Liuhang, *Shanghai* 27 A1
Liurong Temple, *Canton* 8 B2
Liuxi →, *Canton* 8 B2
Liverpool Street, *London* 15 a5
Livry-Gargan, *Paris* 23 A4
Ljan, *Oslo* 22 A3
Llano de Can Gineu, *Barcelona* 4 A2
Llobregat →, *Barcelona* 4 A1
Lo Aranguiz, *Santiago* 26 B2
Lo Boza, *Santiago* 26 B1
Lo Chau, *Hong Kong* 12 B2
Lo Espejo, *Santiago* 26 C1
Lo Hermida, *Santiago* 26 B2
Lo Prado, *Santiago* 26 B1
Lo So Shing, *Hong Kong* 12 B1
Lo Wai, *Hong Kong* 12 A1
Loanhead, *Edinburgh* 11 B3
Lobau, *Vienna* 31 A3
Lobos, Pt., *San Francisco* 25 B1
Locham, *Munich* 20 B1
Lochino, *Moscow* 19 B1
Lochkov, *Prague* 24 B2
Lockhausen, *Munich* 20 A1
Lodi, *New York* 21 A1
Lodi Estate, *Delhi* 10 B2
Logan Int. Airport, *Boston* 6 A4
Logan Square, *Chicago* 9 B2
Lognes-Émerainville, Aérodrome de, *Paris* 23 B4
Löhme, *Berlin* 5 A5
Lolokhet, *Karachi* 14 A2
Lomas Chapultepec, *Mexico City* 18 B1
Lomas de San Angel Inn, *Mexico City* 18 B1
Lomas de Zamora, *Buenos Aires* 7 C2
Lombardy East, *Johannesburg* 13 A2
Łomianki, *Warsaw* 31 A1
Lomus Reforma, *Mexico City* 18 B1
London, *London* 15 A3
London Bridge, *London* 15 b5
London City Airport, *London* 15 A4
London Zoo, *London* 15 A3
Long B., *Sydney* 28 B2
Long Branch, *Toronto* 30 B1
Long Brook →, *Washington* 32 C2
Long Ditton, *London* 15 B2
Long I., *Boston* 6 B4
Long Island City, *New York* 21 B2
Long Street, *Cape Town* 8 c2
Longchamp, Hippodrôme de, *Paris* 23 A2
Longhua Pagoda, *Shanghai* 27 B1
Longhua Park, *Shanghai* 27 B1
Longjohn Slough, *Chicago* 9 C1
Longtan Hu →, *Beijing* 4 B2
Longue-Pointe, *Montreal* 19 A2
Longueuil, *Montreal* 19 A3
Loni, *Delhi* 10 A2
Loop, The, *Chicago* 9 c1
Lord's Cricket Ground, *London* 15 A2
Loreto, *Milan* 18 B2
Los Angeles Int. Airport, *Los Angeles* 16 C2
Los Cerrillos, Aeropuerto, *Santiago* 26 B1
Los Nietos, *Los Angeles* 16 C4
Los Olivos, *Lima* 16 A2
Los Reyes, *Mexico City* 18 B2
Lot, *Brussels* 6 B1
Loughlinstown, *Dublin* 11 B3
Loures, *Lisbon* 14 A1
Louveciennes, *Paris* 23 A1
Louvre, Musée du, *Paris* 23 b4
Louvre, Palais du, *Paris* 23 b4
Lower East Side, *New York* 21 e2
Lower Hutt, *Wellington* 32 B2
Lower Manhattan, *New York* 21 e1
Lower New York B., *New York* 21 C1
Lower Shing Mun Res., *Hong Kong* 12 A1
Lowry Bay, *Wellington* 32 B2
Lu Xun Museum, *Beijing* 4 b1
Lübars, *Berlin* 5 A3
Ludwigsfeld, *Munich* 20 A1
Luhu, *Canton* 8 B2
Lumiar, *Lisbon* 14 A2
Lumphini Park, *Bangkok* 3 B2
Lundtofte, *Copenhagen* 10 A3
Lung Mei, *Hong Kong* 12 A2
Luojiang, *Canton* 8 B2
Lustheim, *Munich* 20 A2
Luwan, *Shanghai* 27 B1
Luxembourg, Palais du, *Paris* 23 c4
Luzhniki Sports Centre, *Moscow* 19 B3
Lyndhurst, *New York* 21 B1
Lynn, *Boston* 6 A4
Lynn Harbor, *Boston* 6 A4
Lynn Woods Res., *Boston* 6 A3
Lyon, Gare de, *Paris* 23 c5
Lyons, *Chicago* 9 C2
Lysaker, *Oslo* 22 A2
Lysakerselva →, *Oslo* 22 A2
Lysolaje, *Prague* 24 B2
Lyubertsy, *Moscow* 19 B5
Lyublino, *Moscow* 19 B4

M

Ma Nam Wat, *Hong Kong* 12 A2
Ma On Shan Country Park, *Hong Kong* 12 A2
Ma'ale Adumim, *Jerusalem* 13 B2
Ma'ale Ha Khamisha, *Jerusalem* 13 B1
Ma'ale Mikhmas, *Jerusalem* 13 A2
Maantiekylä, *Helsinki* 12 A3
Maarifa, *Baghdad* 3 B2
Mabato Pt., *Manila* 17 C2
Macaco, Morro do, *Rio de Janeiro* 24 B2
McCook, *Chicago* 9 C2
Machelen, *Brussels* 6 A2
Machida, *Tokyo* 29 B1
Maciołki, *Warsaw* 31 B2
Mackayville, *Montreal* 19 A3
McKerrow, *Wellington* 32 B2
McKinley Park, *Chicago* 9 C2
Mclean, *Washington* 32 B2
Macopocho, R. →, *Santiago* 26 B1
MacRitchie Res., *Singapore* 27 A2
Macul, *Santiago* 26 C2
Madame Tussaud's, *London* 15 a3
Madhudaha, *Calcutta* 8 B2
Madhyamgram, *Calcutta* 8 A2
Madīnah Al Mansūr, *Baghdad* 3 B2
Mâdinet Nasr, *Cairo* 7 A2
Madison Avenue, *New York* 21 c2
Madison Square, *New York* 21 d2
Madrid, *Madrid* 17 B1
Madrona, *Barcelona* 4 A1
Maesawa, *Tokyo* 29 A2
Magdalena, *Lima* 16 B2
Magdalena Contreras, *Mexico City* 18 C1
Maghreb, *Baghdad* 3 A2
Maginu, *Tokyo* 29 B2
Magliana, *Rome* 25 B1
Magny-les-Hameaux, *Paris* 23 B1
Magonoy, *Manila* 17 B2
Mahalaxmi, *Mumbai* 20 a1
Maheshtala, *Calcutta* 8 C1
Mahim, *Mumbai* 20 A2
Mahim B., *Mumbai* 20 A1
Mahlsdorf, *Berlin* 5 A4
Mahmoodabad, *Karachi* 14 A2
Mahrauli, *Delhi* 10 B1
Mahul, *Mumbai* 20 A2
Maida Vale, *London* 15 a1
Maidstone, *Melbourne* 17 A1
Maipú, *Santiago* 26 C1
Maisonneuve, Parc, *Montreal* 19 A2
Maisons-Alfort, *Paris* 23 B3
Maisons-Laffitte, *Paris* 23 A1
Maissoneuve, *Montreal* 19 A2
Maitland, *Cape Town* 8 A1
Makati, *Manila* 17 B2
Mäkiniitty, *Helsinki* 12 A2
Mala Straná, *Prague* 24 B2
Malabar, *Mumbai* 20 B1
Malabar, *Sydney* 28 B2
Malabar Hill, *Mumbai* 20 B1
Malabar Pt., *Mumbai* 20 B1
Malabon, *Manila* 17 B1
Malacañang Palace, *Manila* 17 B1
Malahide, *Dublin* 11 A3
Malakhovka, *Moscow* 19 C6
Malakoff, *Paris* 23 B2
Mälarhöjaen, *Stockholm* 28 B1
Malate, *Manila* 17 B1
Malay Quarter, *Cape Town* 8 c2
Malaya Neva, *St. Petersburg* 26 B1
Malaya-Okhta, *St. Petersburg* 26 B2
Malchow, *Berlin* 5 A3
Malden, *Boston* 6 A3
Malden, *London* 15 B2
Maleizen, *Brussels* 6 B3
Malešice, *Prague* 24 B3
Malir →, *Karachi* 14 B2
Mall, The, *Washington* 32 b2
Malleny Mills, *Edinburgh* 11 B2
Malmi, *Helsinki* 12 B2
Malmøya, *Oslo* 22 A3
Måløv, *Copenhagen* 10 A2
Malpasso, Ost., *Rome* 25 C1
Malton, *Toronto* 30 A1
Malvern, *Johannesburg* 13 B2
Malvern, *Melbourne* 17 B2
Malvern, *Toronto* 30 A3
Mamonovo, *Moscow* 19 B2
Mampang Prapatan, *Jakarta* 13 B1
Mampukuji, *Tokyo* 29 B2
Man Budrukh, *Mumbai* 20 A2
Man Khurd, *Mumbai* 20 A2
Mandaluyong, *Manila* 17 B2
Mandaoli, *Delhi* 10 B2
Mandaqui →, *São Paulo* 26 A2
Mandoli, *Delhi* 10 A2
Mandvi, *Mumbai* 20 B2
Manenberg, *Cape Town* 8 A2
Mang Kung Uk, *Hong Kong* 12 B2
Mangolpuri, *Delhi* 10 A1
Manguinhos, Aéroporto, *Rio de Janeiro* 24 B1
Mangwŏn, *Seoul* 26 B1
Manhattan, *New York* 21 B2
Manhattan Beach, *New York* 21 C2
Manila, *Manila* 17 B1
Manila B., *Manila* 17 B1
Manila Int. Airport, *Manila* 17 B2
Mankkaa, *Helsinki* 12 B1
Manly, *Sydney* 28 A2
Mannswörth, *Vienna* 31 B3
Manor Park, *London* 15 A4
Manor Park, *Wellington* 32 A2
Manora, *Karachi* 14 B1
Manquehue, Cerro, *Santiago* 26 B2
Manzanares, Canal de, *Madrid* 17 C2
Mao Mausoleum, *Beijing* 4 c2
Map'o, *Seoul* 26 B1
Maracanã, *Rio de Janeiro* 24 B1
Maraoli, *Mumbai* 20 A2
Marblehead, *Boston* 6 A4
Marcelin, *Warsaw* 31 B1
Mareil-Marly, *Paris* 23 A1
Margareten, *Vienna* 31 A2
Maria, *Vienna* 31 A2
Maridalen, *Oslo* 22 A3
Maridalsvatnet, *Oslo* 22 A3
Mariendorf, *Berlin* 5 B3
Marienfelde, *Berlin* 5 B3
Marienplatz, *Munich* 20 b2
Marikina →, *Manila* 17 B2
Marin City, *San Francisco* 25 A1
Marin Headlands State Park, *San Francisco* 25 A2
Marin Pen., *San Francisco* 25 A1
Marina del Rey, *Los Angeles* 16 C2
Marine Drive, *Mumbai* 20 b1
Marino, *Dublin* 11 A2
Maritim, Museu, *Barcelona* 4 c2
Markham, *Toronto* 30 A2
Marki, *Warsaw* 31 B2
Markland Wood, *Toronto* 30 B1
Marly, Forêt de, *Paris* 23 A1
Marly-le-Roi, *Paris* 23 A1
Marne →, *Paris* 23 B3
Marne-la-Vallée, *Paris* 23 A4
Marolles-en-Brie, *Paris* 23 B4
Maroubra, *Sydney* 28 B2
Marquette Park, *Chicago* 9 C2
Marrickville, *Sydney* 28 B1
Marsfield, *Sydney* 28 A1
Marshall Field's, *Chicago* 9 c2
Marte, Campo de, *São Paulo* 26 B2
Martesana, Navíglio della, *Milan* 18 A2
Martin Luther King National Historic Site, *Atlanta* 3 B2
Martinez, *Buenos Aires* 7 A1
Martinkylä, *Helsinki* 12 B2
Martinsried, *Munich* 20 B1
Maruko, *Tokyo* 29 B3
Marunouchi, *Tokyo* 29 b4
Marusino, *Moscow* 19 B5
Maryino, *Moscow* 19 B4
Maryland, *Singapore* 27 B2
Marylebone, *London* 15 A2
Marymont, *Warsaw* 31 B1
Marysin Wawerski, *Warsaw* 31 B2
Marzahn, *Berlin* 5 A4
Mascot, *Sydney* 28 B2
Masmo, *Stockholm* 28 B1
Maspeth, *New York* 21 B2
Masr el Gedida, *Cairo* 7 A2
Masr el Qadîma, *Cairo* 7 A2
Massachusetts B., *Boston* 6 A4
Massachusett's Inst. of Tech., *Boston* 6 A3
Massamá, *Lisbon* 14 A1
Massey →, *Toronto* 30 A3
Massy, *Paris* 23 B2
Matihutong, *Beijing* 4 B1
Matinha, *Lisbon* 14 A2
Matramam, *Jakarta* 13 B2
Matsubara, *Osaka* 22 B4
Mattapan, *Boston* 6 B3
Mátyásföld, *Budapest* 7 A3
Mátyástemplom, *Budapest* 7 b1
Mau Tso Ngam, *Hong Kong* 12 A2
Mauer, *Vienna* 31 B1
Mauripur, *Karachi* 14 A1
Maxhof, *Munich* 20 B1
Maya-Zan, *Osaka* 22 A2
Mayfair, *Johannesburg* 13 B2
Mayfair, *London* 15 b3
Mayor, Plaza, *Madrid* 17 b2
Maywood, *Chicago* 9 B1
Maywood, *Los Angeles* 16 C3
Maywood, *New York* 21 A1
Mazagaon, *Mumbai* 20 a2
Me'a She' Arim, *Jerusalem* 13 a2
Meadowbank Park, *Sydney* 28 A1
Měcholupy, *Prague* 24 B3
Měčice, *Prague* 24 A3
Mecidiyeköy, *Istanbul* 12 B2
Medford, *Boston* 6 A3
Mediodia, *Madrid* 17 B2
Medvezhiy Ozyora, *Moscow* 19 A5
Meguro →, *Tokyo* 29 B3
Meguro-Ku, *Tokyo* 29 B3
Mehpalpur, *Delhi* 10 B1
Mehrābād Airport, *Tehran* 30 A1
Mehram Nagar, *Delhi* 10 B1
Mehrow, *Berlin* 5 A4
Mei Lanfang, *Beijing* 4 a2
Meidling, *Vienna* 31 A2
Méier, *Rio de Janeiro* 24 B1
Meiji Shrine, *Tokyo* 29 b1
Meise, *Brussels* 6 A1
Mejiro, *Tokyo* 29 A3
Melbourne, *Melbourne* 17 A1
Melbourne Airport, *Melbourne* 17 A1
Melkki, *Helsinki* 12 C2
Mellunkylä, *Helsinki* 12 B3
Mellunmäki, *Helsinki* 12 B3
Melrose, *Boston* 6 A3
Melrose, *New York* 21 B2
Melrose Park, *Chicago* 9 B1
Melsbroek, *Brussels* 6 A2
Menteng, *Jakarta* 13 B1
Mérantaise →, *Paris* 23 B1
Mercamadrid, *Madrid* 17 B2
Merced, L., *San Francisco* 25 B2
Meredale, *Johannesburg* 13 B1
Merlimau, P., *Singapore* 27 B2
Merri Cr. →, *Melbourne* 17 A1
Merrion, *Dublin* 11 B2
Merrionette Park, *Chicago* 9 C2
Merton, *London* 15 B2
Mesgarābād, *Tehran* 30 B3
Meshcherskiy, *Moscow* 19 B2
Messe, *Vienna* 31 A2
Messe-palast, *Vienna* 31 c1
Metanópoli, *Milan* 18 B2
Metropolitan Museum of Art, *New York* 21 b3
Meudon, *Paris* 23 B2
Mevaseret Tsiyon, *Jerusalem* 13 B1
Mevo Beitar, *Jerusalem* 13 B1
México, Ciudad de, *Mexico City* 18 B1
Meyersdal, *Johannesburg* 13 B2
Mezzano, *Milan* 18 B2
Mezzate, *Milan* 18 B2
Miadong, *Seoul* 26 B2
Miami, *Miami* 18 B2
Miami Beach, *Miami* 18 B2
Miami Canal →, *Miami* 18 A1
Miami Int. Airport, *Miami* 18 B1
Miami Shores, *Miami* 18 A2
Miami Springs, *Miami* 18 B1
Miasto, *Warsaw* 31 B2
Michałowice, *Warsaw* 31 B1
Michigan Avenue, *Chicago* 9 b2
Michle, *Prague* 24 B2
Middle Harbour, *Sydney* 28 A2
Middle Hd., *Sydney* 28 A2
Middle Park, *Melbourne* 17 B1
Middle Village, *New York* 21 B2
Middlesex Fells Reservation, *Boston* 6 A3
Midi, Gare du, *Brussels* 6 c1
Midland Beach, *New York* 21 C1
Miedzeszyn, *Warsaw* 31 B3
Międzylesie, *Warsaw* 31 B3
Miessaari, *Helsinki* 12 C1
Miguel Hidalgo, *Mexico City* 18 B1
Mikhelysona, *Moscow* 19 B5
Milano, *Milan* 18 B1
Milano Due, *Milan* 18 B2
Milano San Felice, *Milan* 18 B2
Milbertshofen, *Munich* 20 A2
Mill Hill, *London* 15 A2
Millennium Dome, *London* 15 A4
Miller Meadow, *Chicago* 9 B2
Millerhill, *Edinburgh* 11 B3
Millers Point, *Sydney* 28 a1
Milltown, *Dublin* 11 B2
Millwood, *Washington* 32 B4
Milnerton, *Cape Town* 8 A1
Milon-la-Chapelle, *Paris* 23 B1
Milton, *Boston* 6 B3
Milton Bridge, *Edinburgh* 11 B2
Mimico, *Toronto* 30 B2
Minami, *Osaka* 22 A4
Minamitsunashima, *Tokyo* 29 B2
Minato, *Osaka* 22 B3
Minato-Ku, *Tokyo* 29 c3
Minshât el Bekkarî, *Cairo* 7 A1
Minute Man Nat. Hist. Park, *Boston* 6 A2
Miraflores, *Lima* 16 B2
Miramar, *Wellington* 32 B1
Misericordia, Sa. da, *Rio de Janeiro* 24 B1
Mission, *San Francisco* 25 B2
Mississauga, *Toronto* 30 B1
Mitaka, *Tokyo* 29 A2
Mitcham, *London* 15 B2
Mitcham Common, *London* 15 B3
Mitchell's Plain, *Cape Town* 8 B2
Mitino, *Moscow* 19 A2
Mitte, *Berlin* 5 A3
Mittel Isarkanal →, *Munich* 20 A3
Mixcoac, *Mexico City* 18 B1
Mixcoac, Presa de, *Mexico City* 18 B1
Miyakojima, *Osaka* 22 A4
Mizonokuchi, *Tokyo* 29 B2
Mizue, *Tokyo* 29 A4
Młocinski Park, *Warsaw* 31 B1
Młociny, *Warsaw* 31 B1
Mnevniki, *Moscow* 19 B2
Moba, *Lagos* 14 B2
Moczydło, *Warsaw* 31 C2
Modderfontein, *Johannesburg* 13 A2
Modřany, *Prague* 24 B2
Mogyoród, *Budapest* 7 A3
Moinho Velho, Cor. →, *São Paulo* 26 B2
Mok, *Seoul* 26 B1
Mokotów, *Warsaw* 31 B2
Molenbeek-Saint-Jean, *Brussels* 6 A1
Molino de Rosas, *Mexico City* 18 B1
Mollem, *Brussels* 6 A1
Mollins de Rey, *Barcelona* 4 A1
Mondeor, *Johannesburg* 13 B2
Moneda, Palacio de la, *Santiago* 26 B2
Moneró, *Rio de Janeiro* 24 A1
Mong Kok, *Hong Kong* 12 B2
Monkstown, *Dublin* 11 B3
Monnickendam, *Amsterdam* 2 A3
Monrovia, *Los Angeles* 16 B4
Monsanto, *Lisbon* 14 A1
Monsanto, Parque Florestal de, *Lisbon* 14 A1
Mont Royal, *Montreal* 19 A2
Mont-Royal, Parc, *Montreal* 19 A2
Montana de Montjuich, *Barcelona* 4 A1
Monte Chingolo, *Buenos Aires* 7 C2

RAFFLES PARK

Monte Palatino, *Rome* 25 c3
Montebello, *Los Angeles* 16 B4
Montemor, *Lisbon* 14 A1
Monterey Park, *Los Angeles* 16 B4
Montespaccato, *Rome* 25 B1
Montesson, *Paris* 23 A1
Monteverde Nuovo, *Rome* 25 B1
Montfermeil, *Paris* 23 A4
Montigny-le-Bretonneux, *Paris* 23 B1
Montjay-la-Tour, *Paris* 23 A4
Montjuic, Parc de, *Barcelona* 4 c1
Montparnasse, Gare, *Paris* 23 A2
Montréal, *Montreal* 19 A2
Montréal, Î. de, *Montreal* 19 A2
Montréal, Univ. de, *Montreal* 19 B2
Montréal Est, *Montreal* 19 A2
Montréal Nord, *Montreal* 19 A2
Montréal Ouest, *Montreal* 19 B1
Montreuil, *Paris* 23 A3
Montrouge, *Paris* 23 B2
Montserrat, *Buenos Aires* 7 B2
Monza, *Milan* 18 A2
Monzoro, *Milan* 18 B1
Moóca, *São Paulo* 26 B2
Moonachie, *New York* 21 B1
Moonee Ponds, *Melbourne* 17 A1
Moonee Valley Racecourse, *Melbourne* 17 A1
Moosach, *Munich* 20 A2
Mora, *Mumbai* 20 B2
Moratalaz, *Madrid* 17 B2
Mörby, *Stockholm* 28 A2
Morden, *London* 15 B2
Morée →, *Paris* 23 A3
Morgan Park, *Chicago* 9 C3
Moriguchi, *Osaka* 22 A4
Morivione, *Milan* 18 B2
Morningside, *Edinburgh* 11 B2
Morningside, *Johannesburg* 13 A2
Morningside, *Washington* 32 C4
Morro Solar, Cerro, *Lima* 16 C2
Mortlake, *London* 15 B2
Mortlake, *Sydney* 28 B1
Morton Grove, *Chicago* 9 A2
Morumbi, *São Paulo* 26 B1
Moscavide, *Lisbon* 14 A2
Moscow = Moskva, *Moscow* 19 B3
Moskhaton, *Athens* 2 B2
Moskva, *Moscow* 19 B3
Moskva →, *Moscow* 19 B2
Moskvoretskiy, *Moscow* 19 B3
Mosman, *Sydney* 28 A2
Móstoles, *Madrid* 17 C1
Moti Bagh, *Delhi* 10 B2
Motol, *Prague* 24 B1
Motsa, *Jerusalem* 13 B2
Motsa Ilit, *Jerusalem* 13 B1
Motspur Park, *London* 15 B2
Mottingham, *London* 15 B4
Moulin Rouge, *Paris* 23 a3
Mount Dennis, *Toronto* 30 A2
Mount Greenwood, *Chicago* 9 C2
Mount Hood Memorial Park, *Boston* 6 A3
Mount Merrion, *Dublin* 11 B2
Mount Rainier, *Washington* 32 B4
Mount Vernon, *New York* 21 A3
Mount Vernon Square, *Washington* 32 a2
Mount Zion, *Jerusalem* 13 b3
Mozarthaus, *Vienna* 31 b2
Müggelberge, *Berlin* 5 B4
Müggelheim, *Berlin* 5 B5
Muggiò, *Milan* 18 A2
Mughal Gardens, *Delhi* 1 c1
Mühleiten, *Vienna* 31 A3
Mühlenfliess →, *Berlin* 5 A5
Muiden, *Amsterdam* 2 A3
Muiderpoort Station, *Amsterdam* 2 b3
Muizenberg, *Cape Town* 8 B1
Mujahidpur, *Delhi* 10 B2
Mukandpur, *Delhi* 10 A2
Mukhmas, *Jerusalem* 13 A2
Muko →, *Osaka* 22 A3
Mukojima, *Tokyo* 29 A3
Mulbarton, *Johannesburg* 13 B2
Mumbai, *Mumbai* 20 B2
Mumbai Harbour, *Mumbai* 20 B2
Münchehofe, *Berlin* 5 B5
München, *Munich* 20 B2
Munich = München, *Munich* 20 B2
Munkkiniemi, *Helsinki* 12 B2
Munro, *Buenos Aires* 7 B1
Murai Res., *Singapore* 27 A2
Muranów, *Warsaw* 31 B1
Murino, *St. Petersburg* 26 B2
Murrayfield, *Edinburgh* 11 B2
Musashino, *Tokyo* 29 A2
Museu Nacional, *Rio de Janeiro* 24 B1
Mushin, *Lagos* 14 A2
Musiektheater, *Amsterdam* 2 b2
Muslim Quarter, *Jerusalem* 13 a3
Musocco, *Milan* 18 B1
Mustansirīya, *Baghdad* 3 A2
Musturud, *Cairo* 7 A2
Muswell Hill, *London* 15 A3
Mutanabi, *Baghdad* 3 B2
Muthana, *Baghdad* 3 B2
Myakinino, *Moscow* 19 B2
Mykerinos, *Cairo* 7 B1
Myllypuro, *Helsinki* 12 B3

N

Nacka, *Stockholm* 28 B3
Nada, *Osaka* 22 A2
Naenae, *Wellington* 32 B2
Nærsnes, *Oslo* 22 B1
Nagata, *Osaka* 22 B1
Nagatsuta, *Tokyo* 29 B2
Nagytétény, *Budapest* 7 B1
Nahant, *Boston* 6 A4
Nahant B., *Boston* 6 A4
Nahant Harbor, *Boston* 6 A4
Nahr Dijlah →, *Baghdad* 3 B2
Najafgarh Drain →, *Delhi* 10 B1
Nakahara-Ku, *Tokyo* 29 B2
Nakano-Ku, *Tokyo* 29 A2
Namgajwa, *Seoul* 26 B1
Namsan Park, *Seoul* 26 B1
Namyŏng, *Seoul* 26 B1
Nanbiancun, *Canton* 8 B1
Nanchang He →, *Beijing* 4 B1
Nandang, *Canton* 8 B2
Nandian, *Tianjin* 30 A2
Nangal Dewat, *Delhi* 10 B1
Naniwa, *Osaka* 22 B3
Nankai, *Tianjin* 30 B1
Nanmenwai, *Tianjin* 30 B2
Nanole, *Mumbai* 20 A2
Nanpu Bridge, *Shanghai* 27 B2
Nanshi, *Shanghai* 27 B1
Nantasket Beach, *Boston* 6 B4
Nanterre, *Paris* 23 A2
Naoabad, *Calcutta* 8 C2
Napier Mole, *Karachi* 14 B1
Naraina, *Delhi* 10 B1
Nariman Point, *Mumbai* 20 c1
Nariman Pt., *Mumbai* 20 B1
Nārmak, *Tehran* 30 A2
Naruo, *Osaka* 22 A3
Näsby, *Stockholm* 28 A2
Näsbypark, *Stockholm* 28 A2
Nathan Road, *Hong Kong* 12 a2
Natick, *Boston* 6 B2
National Maritime Museum, *San Francisco* 25 a1
National Museum, *Bangkok* 3 b1
Nationalmuseum, *Stockholm* 28 b2
Natolin, *Warsaw* 31 C2
Naturhistorischesmuseum, *Vienna* 31 b1
Naucalpan de Juárez, *Mexico City* 18 B1
Naupada, *Mumbai* 20 A2
Navíglio di Pavia, *Milan* 18 B1
Navíglio Grande, *Milan* 18 B1
Navona, Piazza, *Rome* 25 b2
Navotas, *Manila* 17 B1
Navy Pier, *Chicago* 9 b3
Nazal Hikmat Beg, *Baghdad* 3 A2
Nazimabad, *Karachi* 14 A2
Nazlet el Simmân, *Cairo* 7 B1
Néa Alexandhria, *Athens* 2 B2
Néa Faliron, *Athens* 2 B1
Néa Ionía, *Athens* 2 A2
Néa Liósia, *Athens* 2 A2
Néa Smírni, *Athens* 2 B2
Neapolis, *Athens* 2 B2
Near North, *Chicago* 9 b2
Nebušice, *Prague* 24 B1
Nederhorst, *Amsterdam* 2 B3
Nedlitz, *Berlin* 5 B1
Nee Soon, *Singapore* 27 A2
Needham Heights, *Boston* 6 B2
Nekrasovka, *Moscow* 19 B5
N'ematābād, *Tehran* 30 B2
Nemchinovka, *Moscow* 19 B1
Nemzeti Muz, *Budapest* 7 c3
Neponsit, *New York* 21 C2
Nerima-Ku, *Tokyo* 29 A3
Nesodden, *Oslo* 22 B3
Nesoddtangen, *Oslo* 22 A3
Nesøya, *Oslo* 22 A2
Neu Aubing, *Munich* 20 B1
Neu Buch, *Berlin* 5 A4
Neu Buchhorst, *Berlin* 5 B5
Neu Fahrland, *Berlin* 5 B1
Neu Lindenberg, *Berlin* 5 A4
Neubiberg, *Munich* 20 B3
Neue Hofburg, *Vienna* 31 b1
Neuenhagen, *Berlin* 5 A4
Neuessling, *Vienna* 31 A3
Neuhausen, *Munich* 20 B2
Neuherberg, *Munich* 20 A2
Neuhönow, *Berlin* 5 A5
Neuilly-Plaisance, *Paris* 23 A4
Neuilly-sur-Marne, *Paris* 23 A4
Neuilly-sur-Seine, *Paris* 23 A2
Neukagran, *Vienna* 31 A2
Neukettenhof, *Vienna* 31 B2
Neukölln, *Berlin* 5 B3
Neuperlach, *Munich* 20 B2
Neuried, *Munich* 20 B1
Neustift am Walde, *Vienna* 31 A1
Neusüssenbrunn, *Vienna* 31 A2
Neuwaldegg, *Vienna* 31 A1
Neva →, *St. Petersburg* 26 B2
Neves, *Rio de Janeiro* 24 B2
New Baghdād, *Baghdad* 3 B2
New Barakpur, *Calcutta* 8 A2
New Brighton, *New York* 21 C1
New Canada, *Johannesburg* 13 B1
New Canada Dam, *Johannesburg* 13 B1
New Carrollton, *Washington* 32 B4
New Cross, *London* 15 B3
New Delhi, *Delhi* 10 B2
New Dorp, *New York* 21 C1
New Dorp Beach, *New York* 21 C1
New Malden, *London* 15 B2
New Milford, *New York* 21 A1
New Territories, *Hong Kong* 12 A1
New Toronto, *Toronto* 30 B1
New Town, *Edinburgh* 11 B2
New Utrecht, *New York* 21 C2
Newark B., *New York* 21 B1
Newbattle, *Edinburgh* 11 B3
Newbury Park, *London* 15 A4
Newcraighall, *Edinburgh* 11 B3
Newham, *London* 15 A4
Newhaven, *Edinburgh* 11 B2
Newington, *Edinburgh* 11 B2
Newington, *London* 15 c5
Newlands, *Johannesburg* 13 B1
Newlands, *Wellington* 32 B1
Newport, *Melbourne* 17 B1
Newton, *Boston* 6 B2
Newtonbrook, *Toronto* 30 A2
Newtongrange, *Edinburgh* 11 B3
Newtonville, *Boston* 6 A2
Newtown, *Sydney* 28 B2
Neyagawa, *Osaka* 22 A4
Ngaio, *Wellington* 32 B1
Ngau Chi Wan, *Hong Kong* 12 A2
Ngau Tau Kok, *Hong Kong* 12 B2
Ngauranga, *Wellington* 32 B1
Ngong Shuen Chau, *Hong Kong* 12 B1
Ngua Kok Wan, *Hong Kong* 12 A1
Nīāvarān, *Tehran* 30 A2
Nibra, *Calcutta* 8 B1
Nidāl, *Baghdad* 3 B2
Niddrie, *Edinburgh* 11 B3
Niddrie, *Melbourne* 17 A1
Nieder Neuendorf, *Berlin* 5 A2
Niederschöneweide, *Berlin* 5 B3
Niederschönhausen, *Berlin* 5 A3
Niemeyer, *Rio de Janeiro* 24 B1
Nieuw Zuid, *Amsterdam* 2 c2
Nieuwe Kerk, *Amsterdam* 2 b2
Nieuwendam, *Amsterdam* 2 A2
Nihonbashi, *Tokyo* 29 b5
Niipperi, *Helsinki* 12 B1
Níkaia, *Athens* 2 B1
Nikolassee, *Berlin* 5 B2
Nikolskiy, *Moscow* 19 B2
Nikolyskoye, *Moscow* 19 B5
Nikulino, *Moscow* 19 B2
Nil, Nahr en →, *Cairo* 7 B2
Nile = Nil, Nahr en →, *Cairo* 7 B2
Niles, *Chicago* 9 A2
Nimta, *Calcutta* 8 A2
Ningyuan, *Tianjin* 30 B2
Nippa, *Tokyo* 29 B2
Nippori, *Tokyo* 29 A3
Nishi, *Osaka* 22 A3
Nishinari, *Osaka* 22 B3
Nishiyodogawa, *Osaka* 22 A3
Niterói, *Rio de Janeiro* 24 B2
Nob Hill, *San Francisco* 25 b1
Nockeby, *Stockholm* 28 B1
Noel Park, *London* 15 A3
Nogatino, *Moscow* 19 B4
Nogent-sur-Marne, *Paris* 23 A3
Noida, *Delhi* 10 B2
Noiseau, *Paris* 23 B4
Noisiel, *Paris* 23 A4
Noisy-le-Grand, *Paris* 23 A4
Noisy-le-Roi, *Paris* 23 A1
Noisy-le-Sec, *Paris* 23 A3
Nokkala, *Helsinki* 12 C1
Nomentano, *Rome* 25 B2
Nonakashinden, *Tokyo* 29 A2
Nongminyundong Jiangxisuo, *Canton* 8 B2
Nonhyŏn, *Seoul* 26 B2
Nonthaburi, *Bangkok* 3 A1
Noon Gun, *Cape Town* 8 b1
Noorder Kerk, *Amsterdam* 2 a1
Noordgesig, *Johannesburg* 13 B1
Noordzeekanaal, *Amsterdam* 2 A1
Nord, Gare du, *Paris* 23 a4
Nordrand-Siedlung, *Vienna* 31 A2
Nordstrand, *Oslo* 22 A3
Normandale, *Wellington* 32 B2
Nørrebro, *Copenhagen* 10 a1
Norridge, *Chicago* 9 B2
Norrmalm, *Stockholm* 28 a1
North Arlington, *New York* 21 B1
North Bay Village, *Miami* 18 A2
North Bergen, *New York* 21 B1
North Branch Chicago River →, *Chicago* 9 B2
North Bull Island, *Dublin* 11 A3
North Cambridge, *Boston* 6 A3
North Cheam, *London* 15 B2
North Cohasset, *Boston* 6 B4
North Cray, *London* 15 B4
North Decatur, *Atlanta* 3 B3
North Druid Hills, *Atlanta* 3 B3
North Esk →, *Edinburgh* 11 B2
North Gyle, *Edinburgh* 11 B2
North Hackensack, *New York* 21 A1
North Harbor, *Manila* 17 B1
North Hd., *Sydney* 28 A2
North Hollywood, *Los Angeles* 16 B2
North Lexington, *Boston* 6 A2
North Miami, *Miami* 18 A2
North Miami Beach, *Miami* 18 A2
North Nazimabad, *Karachi* 14 A2
North Pt., *Hong Kong* 12 B2
North Queensferry, *Edinburgh* 11 A1
North Quincy, *Boston* 6 B3
North Res., *Boston* 6 A3
North Riverside, *Chicago* 9 B2
North Saugus, *Boston* 6 A3
North Shore Channel →, *Chicago* 9 B2
North Springfield, *Washington* 32 C2
North Sudbury, *Boston* 6 A1
North Sydney, *Sydney* 28 B2
North Woolwich, *London* 15 A4
North York, *Toronto* 30 A2
Northbridge, *Sydney* 28 A2
Northbridge Park, *Sydney* 28 A2
Northcliff, *Johannesburg* 13 A1
Northcote, *Melbourne* 17 A2
Northlake, *Chicago* 9 B1
Northmount, *Toronto* 30 A2
Northolt, *London* 15 A1
Northumberland Heath, *London* 15 B5
Northwood, *London* 15 A1
Norumbega Res., *Boston* 6 B2
Norwood, *Johannesburg* 13 A2
Norwood Park, *Chicago* 9 B2
Noryangjin, *Seoul* 26 B1
Nossa Senhora de Candelária, *Rio de Janeiro* 24 a2
Nossa Senhora do Ó, *São Paulo* 26 B1
Nossegem, *Brussels* 6 A3
Notre-Dame, *Montreal* 19 B3
Notre-Dame, *Paris* 23 c4
Notre-Dame, Bois, *Paris* 23 B4
Notre-Dame-de-Grace, *Montreal* 19 B2
Notting Hill, *London* 15 b1
Nova Milanese, *Milan* 18 A2
Novate Milanese, *Milan* 18 A1
Novaya Derevnya, *St. Petersburg* 26 A1
Nové Město, *Prague* 24 B2
Novoaleksandrovskoye, *St. Petersburg* 26 B2
Novogireyevo, *Moscow* 19 B4
Novoivanovskoye, *Moscow* 19 B1
Novonikolyskoye, *Moscow* 19 A1
Novosaratovka, *St. Petersburg* 26 B3
Nowe-Babice, *Warsaw* 31 B1
Nöykkiö, *Helsinki* 12 B1
Nueva Atzacoalco, *Mexico City* 18 B2
Nueva Pompeya, *Buenos Aires* 7 C2
Nueva Tenochtitlán, *Mexico City* 18 B2
Nuijala, *Helsinki* 12 B1
Numabukuro, *Tokyo* 29 A2
Nunez, *Buenos Aires* 7 B2
Nunhead, *London* 15 B3
Ñuñoa, *Santiago* 26 B2
Nusle, *Prague* 24 B2
Nussdorf, *Vienna* 31 A2
Nyanga, *Cape Town* 8 A2
Nymphenburg, *Munich* 20 B2
Nymphenburg, Schloss, *Munich* 20 B2

O

Oak Grove, *Atlanta* 3 A3
Oak Island, *Boston* 6 A4
Oak Lawn, *Chicago* 9 C2
Oak Park, *Chicago* 9 B2
Oak View, *Washington* 32 A4
Oakdale, *Atlanta* 3 A2
Oakland, *San Francisco* 25 B3
Oakland, *Washington* 32 B4
Oaklawn, *Washington* 32 C4
Oakleigh, *Melbourne* 17 B2
Oakton, *Washington* 32 B2
Oakwood Beach, *New York* 21 C1
Oatley, *Sydney* 28 B1
Obalende, *Lagos* 14 B2
Oba's Palace, *Lagos* 14 B2
Oberföhring, *Munich* 20 B2
Oberhaching, *Munich* 20 B2
Oberlaa, *Vienna* 31 B2
Oberlisse, *Vienna* 31 A2
Obermenzing, *Munich* 20 A1
Obermoos Schwaige, *Munich* 20 A1
Oberschleissheim, *Munich* 20 A2
Oberschöneweide, *Berlin* 5 B4
Observatory, *Johannesburg* 13 B2
Observatory, *Sydney* 28 a1
Ōbu, *Osaka* 22 A1
Obu-tōge, *Osaka* 22 A1
Óbuda, *Budapest* 7 A2
Obukhovo, *St. Petersburg* 26 B2
Obvodnyy Kanal, *St. Petersburg* 26 B1
Ocean Park, *Hong Kong* 12 B2
Ochakovo, *Moscow* 19 B2
Ochota, *Warsaw* 31 B1
O'Connell Street, *Dublin* 11 b2
Ōdana, *Tokyo* 29 B2
Öden-Stockach, *Munich* 20 B3
Odilampi, *Helsinki* 12 B1
Odintsovo, *Moscow* 19 B1
Odivelas, *Lisbon* 14 A1
Odolany, *Warsaw* 31 B1
Oeiras, *Lisbon* 14 A1
Ofin, *Lagos* 14 A3
Ogawa, *Tokyo* 29 A1
Ogden Park, *Chicago* 9 C2
Ogikubo, *Tokyo* 29 A2
Ogogoro, *Lagos* 14 B2
Ogoyo, *Lagos* 14 B2
Ogudu, *Lagos* 14 A2
Ohariu Stream →, *Wellington* 32 B1
O'Higgins, Parque, *Santiago* 26 B2
Ōimachi, *Tokyo* 29 B3
Ojota, *Lagos* 14 A2
Okamoto, *Osaka* 22 A2
Okęcie, *Warsaw* 31 B1
Okęcie Airport, *Warsaw* 31 B1
Okelra, *Lagos* 14 B2
Okeogbe, *Lagos* 14 B2
Okha, *Delhi* 10 B2
Okhta →, *St. Petersburg* 26 B2
Okkervil →, *St. Petersburg* 26 B2
Okrzeszyn, *Warsaw* 31 C2
Oksval, *Oslo* 22 A3
Oktyabrskiy, *Moscow* 19 B3
Ōkubo, *Tokyo* 29 a2
Ōkura, *Tokyo* 29 B1
Olari, *Helsinki* 12 B1
Olaria, *Rio de Janeiro* 24 B1
Old Admiralty, *St. Petersburg* 26 B1
Old City, *Delhi* 1 a3
Old City, *Jerusalem* 13 b3
Old City, *Shanghai* 27 B1
Old Fort = Purana Qila, *Delhi* 1 c3
Old Harbor, *Boston* 6 B3
Old Town, *Chicago* 9 B3
Old Town, *Edinburgh* 11 B2
Oldbawn, *Dublin* 11 B1
Olgino, *St. Petersburg* 26 A1
Olimpico, Estadio, *Mexico City* 18 C1
Olivais, *Lisbon* 14 A2
Olivar de los Padres, *Mexico City* 18 B1
Olivar del Conde, *Mexico City* 18 B1
Olivos, *Buenos Aires* 7 B2
Olona →, *Milan* 18 B1
Olympia, *London* 15 c1
Olympic Stadium, *Helsinki* 12 B2
Olympique, Stade, *Montreal* 19 A2
Omonias, Pl., *Athens* 2 b1
Ōmori, *Tokyo* 29 B3
Onchi, *Osaka* 22 B4
Onchi →, *Osaka* 22 B4
Onisigun, *Lagos* 14 A2
Ōokayama, *Tokyo* 29 B3
Oosterpark, *Amsterdam* 2 b3
Oostzaan, *Amsterdam* 2 A2
Opa-Locka, *Miami* 18 A1
Opa-Locka Airport, *Miami* 18 A1
Opacz, *Warsaw* 31 B1
Opera House, *Sydney* 28 a2
Ophirton, *Johannesburg* 13 B2
Oppegård, *Oslo* 22 B3
Oppem, *Brussels* 6 A1
Oppsal, *Oslo* 22 A4
Ora, *Jerusalem* 13 B1
Oradell, *New York* 21 A1
Orange Bowl Stadium, *Miami* 18 B2
Orangi, *Karachi* 14 A2
Orchard Road, *Singapore* 27 a1
Ordrup, *Copenhagen* 10 A3
Orech, *Prague* 24 B1
Øresund, *Copenhagen* 10 A3
Orient Heights, *Boston* 6 A4
Orlando Dam, *Johannesburg* 13 B1
Orlando East, *Johannesburg* 13 B1
Orlovo, *Moscow* 19 C2
Orly, *Paris* 23 B3
Ormesson-sur-Marne, *Paris* 23 B4
Ormond, *Melbourne* 17 B2
Ormøya, *Oslo* 22 A3
Orpington, *London* 15 B4
Orsay, Musée d', *Paris* 23 b3
Országház, *Budapest* 7 b2
Országos Levétár, *Budapest* 7 b1
Ortaköy, *Istanbul* 12 B2
Ortica, *Milan* 18 B2
Oruba, *Lagos* 14 A2
Orvostörteneti Múz., *Budapest* 7 c2
Ōsaka, *Osaka* 22 B4
Osaka B., *Osaka* 22 B2
Osaka Castle, *Osaka* 22 A4
Osaka Harbour, *Osaka* 22 B3
Osaka International Airport, *Osaka* 22 A3
Ōsaki, *Tokyo* 29 B3
Osasco, *São Paulo* 26 B1
Osdorf, *Berlin* 5 B3
Osdorp, *Amsterdam* 2 A1
Oshodi, *Lagos* 14 A2
Oslo, *Oslo* 22 A3
Oslofjorden, *Oslo* 22 B2
Ōsone, *Tokyo* 29 B2
Osorun, *Lagos* 14 A2
Ospiate, *Milan* 18 A1
Ostankino, *Moscow* 19 B3
Östasiatiskamuséet, *Stockholm* 28 b3
Österalm, *Stockholm* 28 a3
Østerbro, *Copenhagen* 10 a1
Osterley, *London* 15 B1
Osterley Park, *London* 15 B1
Östermalm, *Stockholm* 28 A2
Österskär, *Stockholm* 28 A3
Ostiense, *Rome* 25 B1
Østmarkkapellet, *Oslo* 22 A4
Ostøya, *Oslo* 22 A2
Østre Aker, *Oslo* 22 A3
Ōta-Ku, *Tokyo* 29 B3
Otaniemi, *Helsinki* 12 B1
Otari Open Air Museum, *Wellington* 32 B1
Otsuka, *Tokyo* 29 A3
Ottakring, *Vienna* 31 A1
Ottávia, *Rome* 25 B1
Ottery, *Cape Town* 8 B2
Ottobrunn, *Munich* 20 B3
Oud Zuid, *Amsterdam* 2 b1
Oude Kerk, *Amsterdam* 2 b2
Ouderkerk, *Amsterdam* 2 B2
Oulunkylä, *Helsinki* 12 B2
Ourcq, Canal de l', *Paris* 23 A3
Outer Mission, *San Francisco* 25 B2
Outremont, *Montreal* 19 A2
Overijse, *Brussels* 6 B3
Owhiro Bay, *Wellington* 32 C1
Oworonsoki, *Lagos* 14 A2
Oxford Street, *London* 15 b3
Oxgangs, *Edinburgh* 11 B2
Oxon Hill, *Washington* 32 C4
Oyodo, *Osaka* 22 A3
Oyster B., *Sydney* 28 C1
Oyster Rock, *Mumbai* 20 B1
Oyster Rocks, *Karachi* 14 B2
Ozoir-la-Ferrière, *Paris* 23 B4
Ozone Park, *New York* 21 B2

P

Pacific Heights, *San Francisco* 25 B2
Pacific Manor, *San Francisco* 25 C2
Pacific Palisades, *Los Angeles* 16 B1
Pacifica, *San Francisco* 25 C2
Paco, *Manila* 17 B1
Paco de Arcos, *Lisbon* 14 A1
Paco Imperial, *Rio de Janeiro* 24 a2
Paddington, *London* 15 b2
Paddington, *Sydney* 28 B2
Paderno, *Milan* 18 A1
Pagewood, *Sydney* 28 B2
Pagote, *Mumbai* 20 B2
Pai, I. do, *Rio de Janeiro* 24 B2
Pak Kong, *Hong Kong* 12 A2
Pakila, *Helsinki* 12 B2
Palacio de Bellas Artes, *Mexico City* 18 b2
Palacio de Communicaciones, *Madrid* 17 a3
Palacio Nacional, *Mexico City* 18 b3
Palacio Real, *Barcelona* 4 b3
Palacio Real, *Madrid* 17 b1
Palaión Fáliron, *Athens* 2 B2
Palais de Justice, *Brussels* 6 c2
Palais Royal, *Paris* 23 b4
Palais Royale, *Brussels* 6 b3
Palaiseau, *Paris* 23 B2
Palau Nacional Museu d'Art, *Barcelona* 4 c1
Palazzolo, *Milan* 18 A1
Palermo, *Buenos Aires* 7 B2
Palhais, *Lisbon* 14 B2
Palisades Park, *New York* 21 A1
Palmer Park, *Washington* 32 B4
Palmerston, *Dublin* 11 A1
Paloheinä, *Helsinki* 12 B2
Palomeras, *Madrid* 17 B2
Palos Heights, *Chicago* 9 D2
Palos Hills, *Chicago* 9 C2
Palos Hills Forest, *Chicago* 9 C1
Palos Park, *Chicago* 9 C1
Palpara, *Calcutta* 8 B2
Panchur, *Calcutta* 8 B1
Pandacan, *Manila* 17 B2
Pandan, Selat, *Singapore* 27 B2
Pandan Res., *Singapore* 27 B2
Panepistimio, *Athens* 2 b2
Pangbae, *Seoul* 26 C1
Pangrati, *Athens* 2 B2
Pangsua, Sungei →, *Singapore* 27 A2
Panihati, *Calcutta* 8 A2
Panjang, Bukit, *Singapore* 27 A2
Panje, *Mumbai* 20 B2
Panke →, *Berlin* 5 A3
Pankow, *Berlin* 5 A3
Panthéon, *Paris* 23 c4
Pantheon, *Rome* 25 b2
Pantin, *Paris* 23 A3
Pantitlán, *Mexico City* 18 B2
Panvel Cr. →, *Mumbai* 20 B2
Paparangi, *Wellington* 32 B1
Papiol, *Barcelona* 4 A1
Paramus, *New York* 21 A1
Paranaque, *Manila* 17 B1
Paray-Vieille-Poste, *Paris* 23 B3
Parco Regionale, *Milan* 18 A1
Parel, *Mumbai* 20 B1
Pari, *São Paulo* 26 B2
Parioli, *Rome* 25 B1
Paris, *Paris* 23 A3
Paris-Orly, Aéroport de, *Paris* 23 B3
Pārk-e Mellat, *Tehran* 30 A2
Park Ridge, *Chicago* 9 A1
Park Royal, *London* 15 A2
Parkchester, *New York* 21 B2
Parkdale, *Toronto* 30 B2
Parkhurst, *Johannesburg* 13 A2
Parklawn, *Washington* 32 B3
Parkmore, *Johannesburg* 13 A2
Parkside, *San Francisco* 25 B2
Parktown, *Johannesburg* 13 B2
Parktown North, *Johannesburg* 13 A2
Parkview, *Johannesburg* 13 A2
Parkville, *New York* 21 C2
Parkwood, *Cape Town* 8 B1
Parkwood, *Johannesburg* 13 A2
Parow, *Cape Town* 8 A2
Parque Chabuco, *Buenos Aires* 7 B2
Parque Patricios, *Buenos Aires* 7 B2
Parramatta →, *Sydney* 28 A1
Parthenon, *Athens* 2 c2
Paşabahçe, *Istanbul* 12 B2
Pasadena, *Los Angeles* 16 B4
Pasar Minggu, *Jakarta* 13 B1
Pasay, *Manila* 17 B1
Pascoe Vale, *Melbourne* 17 A1
Paseo de la Reforma, *Mexico City* 18 b2
Pasig, *Manila* 17 B2
Pasig →, *Manila* 17 B2
Pasila, *Helsinki* 12 B2
Pasing, *Munich* 20 B1
Pasir Panjang, *Singapore* 27 B2
Pasir Ris, *Singapore* 27 A3
Passaic →, *New York* 21 B1
Passirana, *Milan* 18 A1
Patel Nagar, *Delhi* 10 B1
Pateros, *Manila* 17 B2
Pathersville, *Atlanta* 3 B3
Pathumwan, *Bangkok* 3 B2
Patipukur, *Calcutta* 8 B2
Patisia, *Athens* 2 A2
Paulo E. Virginia, Gruta, *Rio de Janeiro* 24 B1
Paulshof, *Berlin* 5 A5
Pavshino, *Moscow* 19 B1
Paya Lebar, *Singapore* 27 A3
Peachtree →, *Atlanta* 3 B2
Peakhurst, *Sydney* 28 B1
Peania, *Athens* 2 B3
Peckham, *London* 15 B3
Peddocks I., *Boston* 6 B4
Pederstrup, *Copenhagen* 10 A2
Pedralbes, *Barcelona* 4 A1
Pedregal de San Angel, Jardines del, *Mexico City* 18 C1
Pekhorka →, *Moscow* 19 C6
Pekhra-Pokrovskoye, *Moscow* 19 A5
Pekhra-Yakovievskaya, *Moscow* 19 B5
Peking = Beijing, *Beijing* 4 B1
Pelcowizna, *Warsaw* 31 B2
Pelopónnisos Sta., *Athens* 2 a1
Penalolén, *Santiago* 26 B2
Pencarrow Hd., *Wellington* 32 C2
Peng Siang →, *Singapore* 27 A2
Penge, *London* 15 B3
Penha, *Rio de Janeiro* 24 A1
Penicuik, *Edinburgh* 11 B2
Penjaringan, *Jakarta* 13 A1
Penn Station, *New York* 21 c2
Pennsylvania Avenue, *Washington* 32 b1
Pentland Hills, *Edinburgh* 11 B1
Penyagino, *Moscow* 19 A2
Penzing, *Vienna* 31 A1
People's Park, *Shanghai* 27 B1
People's Square, *Shanghai* 27 B1
Perales del Rio, *Madrid* 17 C2
Peravillo, *Mexico City* 18 a3
Perchtoldsdorf, *Vienna* 31 B1
Perdizes, *São Paulo* 26 B2
Peredelkino, *Moscow* 19 C2
Pergamon Museum, *Berlin* 5 a4
Peristérion, *Athens* 2 A2
Perivale, *London* 15 A2
Perk, *Brussels* 6 A2
Perlach, *Munich* 20 B2
Perlacher Forst, *Munich* 20 B2
Pero, *Milan* 18 A1
Peropok, Bukit, *Singapore* 27 B2
Perovo, *Moscow* 19 B4
Pershing Square, *Los Angeles* 16 c1
Pertusella, *Milan* 18 A1
Pesagot, *Jerusalem* 13 A2
Pesanggrahag, Kali →, *Jakarta* 13 B1
Peschiera Borromeo, *Milan* 18 B2
Pesek, P., *Singapore* 27 B2
Pest, *Budapest* 7 B2
Pesterzsébet, *Budapest* 7 B2
Pesthidegkút, *Budapest* 7 A1
Pestimre, *Budapest* 7 B3
Pestlörinc, *Budapest* 7 B3
Pestújhely, *Budapest* 7 A2
Petas, *Helsinki* 12 B2
Petone, *Wellington* 32 B2
Petrogradskaya Storona, *St. Petersburg* 26 B2
Petroúpolis, *Athens* 2 A2
Petrovice, *Prague* 24 B3
Petrovskiy Park, *Moscow* 19 B3
Petrovsko-Razumovskoye, *Moscow* 19 B3
Pettycur, *Edinburgh* 11 A2
Peutie, *Brussels* 6 A2
Pfaueninsel, *Berlin* 5 B1
Phaya Thai, *Bangkok* 3 B2
Phihai, *Karachi* 14 A2
Phillip B., *Sydney* 28 B2
Phoenix Park, *Dublin* 11 A2
Phra Khanong, *Bangkok* 3 B2
Phra Pradaeng, *Bangkok* 3 C2
Phranakhon, *Bangkok* 3 B1
Picasso, Museu, *Barcelona* 4 c2
Piccadilly, *London* 15 b3
Pico Rivera, *Los Angeles* 16 C4
Piedade, *Lisbon* 14 A1
Piedade, *Rio de Janeiro* 24 B1
Piedade, Cova da, *Lisbon* 14 A2
Piedmont Park, *Atlanta* 3 B2
Pietralata, *Rome* 25 B2
Pihlajamäki, *Helsinki* 12 B2
Pihlajasaari, *Helsinki* 12 C2
Pilares, *Rio de Janeiro* 24 B1
Pilton, *Edinburgh* 11 B2
Pimlico, *London* 15 c3
Pimmit Hills, *Washington* 32 B2
Pine Grove, *Toronto* 30 A1
Pinewood, *Miami* 18 A2
Piney Run →, *Washington* 32 B2
Pinganli, *Beijing* 4 B2
Pingzhou, *Canton* 8 B2
Pinheiros →, *São Paulo* 26 B1
Pinjrapur, *Karachi* 14 A2
Pinner, *London* 15 A1
Pinner Green, *London* 15 A1
Pioltello, *Milan* 18 A2
Pipinui Pt., *Wellington* 32 A1
Piraévs, *Athens* 2 B1
Pirajuçara →, *São Paulo* 26 B1
Pirinççi, *Istanbul* 12 B1
Pirituba, *São Paulo* 26 A1
Pirkkola, *Helsinki* 12 B2
Písnice, *Prague* 24 C2
Pitampura, *Delhi* 10 A1
Pitkäjärvi, *Helsinki* 12 B1
Planegg, *Munich* 20 B1
Plumstead, *Cape Town* 8 B1
Plumstead, *London* 15 B4
Plyushchevo, *Moscow* 19 B4
Pníka, *Athens* 2 c1
Po Toi I., *Hong Kong* 12 B2
Po Toi O, *Hong Kong* 12 B2
Poasco, *Milan* 18 B2
Podbaba, *Prague* 24 B2
Podoli, *Prague* 24 B2
Poduskino, *Moscow* 19 B1
Pointe-Aux-Trembles, *Montreal* 19 A2
Poissy, *Paris* 23 A1
Pok Fu Lam, *Hong Kong* 12 B1
Pokrovsko-Sresnevo, *Moscow* 19 B2
Polton, *Edinburgh* 11 B3
Polyustrovo, *St. Petersburg* 26 B2
Pompidou, Centre, *Paris* 23 b4
Pomprap, *Bangkok* 3 B2
Pondok Indah, *Jakarta* 13 B1
Pont-Viau, *Montreal* 19 A1
Ponta do Marisco, *Rio de Janeiro* 24 C1
Pontault-Combault, *Paris* 23 B4
Pontinha, *Lisbon* 14 A1
Poplar, *London* 15 A3
Popolo, Porta del, *Rome* 25 a2
Poppintree, *Dublin* 11 A2
Porirua, *Wellington* 32 A2
Porirua East, *Wellington* 32 A2
Port I., *Osaka* 22 A2
Port Melbourne, *Melbourne* 17 B1
Port Nicholson, *Wellington* 32 B2
Port Philip Bay, *Melbourne* 17 B1
Port Richmond, *New York* 21 C1
Port Shelter, *Hong Kong* 12 A2
Port Union, *Toronto* 30 A4
Portage Park, *Chicago* 9 B2
Portal de la Pau, Pl., *Barcelona* 4 c2
Portela, Aeroporto da, *Lisbon* 14 A2
Portmarnock, *Dublin* 11 A3
Porto Brandão, *Lisbon* 14 A1
Porto Novo, *Rio de Janeiro* 24 A2
Porto Novo Cr. →, *Lagos* 14 B2
Portobello, *Edinburgh* 11 B3
Portrero, *San Francisco* 25 B3
Potomac, *Washington* 32 A2
Potomac →, *Washington* 32 B3
Potrero Pt., *San Francisco* 25 B2
Potsdam, *Berlin* 5 B1
Potsdamer Platz, *Berlin* 5 b3
Potzham, *Munich* 20 B2
Pötzleinsdorf, *Vienna* 31 A1
Povoa de Santo Adriao, *Lisbon* 14 A2
Powązki, *Warsaw* 31 B1
Powiśle, *Warsaw* 31 B2
Powsin, *Warsaw* 31 C2
Powsinek, *Warsaw* 31 C2
Poyan Res., *Singapore* 27 A2
Pozuelo de Alarcon, *Madrid* 17 B1
Prado, Museo del, *Madrid* 17 b3
Prado Churubusco, *Mexico City* 18 B2
Praga, *Warsaw* 31 B2
Prague = Praha, *Prague* 24 B2
Praha, *Prague* 24 B2
Praha-Ruzyně Airport, *Prague* 24 B1
Praires, R. des →, *Montreal* 19 A2
Prater, *Vienna* 31 A2
Precotto, *Milan* 18 A2
Prenestino Labicano, *Rome* 25 B2
Prenzlauerberg, *Berlin* 5 A3
Preston, *Melbourne* 17 A1
Pretos Forros, Sa. dos, *Rio de Janeiro* 24 B1
Préville, *Montreal* 19 B3
Přezletice, *Prague* 24 B3
Prima Porta, *Rome* 25 B1
Primavalle, *Rome* 25 B1
Primrose, *Johannesburg* 13 B2
Princes Street, *Edinburgh* 11 b2
Printer's Row, *Chicago* 9 d2
Progreso Nacional, *Mexico City* 18 A2
Prosek, *Prague* 24 B3
Prospect Hill Park, *Boston* 6 A2
Providencia, *Santiago* 26 B2
Prudential Building, *Chicago* 9 c2
Průhonice, *Prague* 24 C3
Psikhikón, *Athens* 2 A2
Pudong New Area, *Shanghai* 27 B2
Pueblo Libre, *Lima* 16 B2
Pueblo Nuevo, *Barcelona* 4 A2
Pueblo Nuevo, *Madrid* 17 B2
Puerta del Sol, Plaza, *Madrid* 17 b2
Puerto Madero, *Buenos Aires* 7 B2
Puerto Retiro, *Buenos Aires* 7 B2
Puhuangyu, *Beijing* 4 B2
Puistola, *Helsinki* 12 B3
Pukan-san, *Seoul* 26 B1
Pukinmäki, *Helsinki* 12 B2
Pukkajwa, *Seoul* 26 B1
Pulkovo Int. Airport, *St. Petersburg* 26 C1
Pullach, *Munich* 20 B1
Pulo Gadung, *Jakarta* 13 B2
Pūnak, *Tehran* 30 A2
Punchbowl, *Sydney* 28 B1
Punde, *Mumbai* 20 B2
Punggol, *Singapore* 27 A3
Punggol, Sungei →, *Singapore* 27 A3
Punggol Pt., *Singapore* 27 A3
Punjabi Bagh, *Delhi* 10 A1
Puotila, *Helsinki* 12 B3
Purana Qila, *Delhi* 1 c3
Puteaux, *Paris* 23 A2
Putilkovo, *Moscow* 19 A2
Putney, *London* 15 B2
Putuo, *Shanghai* 27 B1
Putxet, *Barcelona* 4 A1
Puxi, *Shanghai* 27 B1
Pydhuni, *Mumbai* 20 b2
Pyramids, *Cairo* 7 B1
Pyry, *Warsaw* 31 C1

Q

Qalandya, *Jerusalem* 13 A2
Qal'eh Morghī, *Tehran* 30 B2
Qanâ el Ismâ'ilîya, *Cairo* 7 A2
Qāsemābād, *Tehran* 30 A3
Qasr-e Firūzeh, *Tehran* 30 B3
Qatane, *Jerusalem* 13 B1
Qianmen, *Beijing* 4 B2
Qinghuayuan, *Beijing* 4 B1
Qingningsi, *Shanghai* 27 B2
Qolhak, *Tehran* 30 A2
Quadraro, *Rome* 25 B2
Quaid-i-Azam, *Karachi* 14 A1
Quartiere Zingone, *Milan* 18 B1
Quds, *Baghdad* 3 A2
Queen Mary Res., *London* 15 B1
Queen Street, *Edinburgh* 11 a1
Queensbury, *London* 15 A2
Queenscliffe, *Sydney* 28 A2
Queensferry, *Edinburgh* 11 B1
Queenstown, *Singapore* 27 B2
Quellerina, *Johannesburg* 13 A1
Queluz, *Lisbon* 14 A1
Quezon City, *Manila* 17 B2
Quezon Memorial Circle, *Manila* 17 B2
Quilicura, *Santiago* 26 B1
Quincy, *Boston* 6 B3
Quincy B., *Boston* 6 B4
Quinta Normal, *Santiago* 26 B1
Quinto de Stampi, *Milan* 18 B2
Quinto Romano, *Milan* 18 B1
Quirinale, *Rome* 25 B1
Quirinale, Palazzo dei, *Rome* 25 b3

R

Raasdorf, *Vienna* 31 A3
Rådhuset, *Oslo* 22 A3
Radlice, *Prague* 24 B2
Radość, *Warsaw* 31 B3
Radotin, *Prague* 24 C2
Rafat, *Jerusalem* 13 A2
Raffles Hotel, *Singapore* 27 b3
Raffles Park, *Singapore* 27 B2

Raheny, *Dublin* 11 A3
Rahnsdorf, *Berlin* 5 B5
Rainham, *London* 15 A5
Raj Ghat, *Delhi* 1 b3
Rajakylä, *Helsinki* 12 B3
Rajpath, *Delhi* 1 c2
Rajpura, *Delhi* 10 A2
Rákos-patak →, *Budapest* 7 B3
Rákoshegy, *Budapest* 7 B3
Rákoskeresztúr, *Budapest* 7 B3
Rákoskert, *Budapest* 7 B3
Rákosliget, *Budapest* 7 B3
Rákospalota, *Budapest* 7 A2
Rákosszentmihály, *Budapest* 7 A2
Raków, *Warsaw* 31 B1
Ram, *Jerusalem* 13 A2
Rām Allāh, *Jerusalem* 13 A2
Ramadān, *Baghdad* 3 B2
Ramakrishna Puram, *Delhi* 10 B1
Ramanathpur, *Calcutta* 8 A1
Rambla, La, *Barcelona* 4 b2
Rambler Channel, *Hong Kong* 12 A1
Ramenki, *Moscow* 19 B2
Ramersdorf, *Munich* 20 B2
Ramos, *Rio de Janeiro* 24 B1
Ramos Mejia, *Buenos Aires* 7 B1
Ramot, *Jerusalem* 13 B2
Rampur, *Delhi* 10 A2
Ramsgate, *Sydney* 28 B1
Rand Afrikaans Univ., *Johannesburg* 13 B2
Rand Airport, *Johannesburg* 13 B2
Randburg, *Johannesburg* 13 A1
Randhart, *Johannesburg* 13 B2
Randpark Ridge, *Johannesburg* 13 A1
Randwick, *Sydney* 28 B2
Ranelagh, *Dublin* 11 A2
Rannersdorf, *Vienna* 31 B2
Ransbèche, *Brussels* 6 B2
Ransdorp, *Amsterdam* 2 A2
Ranvad, *Mumbai* 20 B2
Raposo, *Lisbon* 14 A1
Rashtrapati Bhawan, *Delhi* 1 c1
Rasskazovka, *Moscow* 19 C2
Rastaala, *Helsinki* 12 B1
Rastila, *Helsinki* 12 B3
Raszyn, *Warsaw* 31 C1
Ratcha Thewi, *Bangkok* 3 b3
Rathfarnham, *Dublin* 11 B2
Ratho, *Edinburgh* 11 B1
Ratho Station, *Edinburgh* 11 B1
Rato, *Lisbon* 14 A2
Ravelston, *Edinburgh* 11 B2
Rawamangun, *Jakarta* 13 B2
Rayners Lane, *London* 15 A1
Raynes Park, *London* 15 B2
Raypur, *Calcutta* 8 C2
Razdory, *Moscow* 19 B1
Real Felipe, Fuerte, *Lima* 16 B2
Recoleta, *Buenos Aires* 7 B2
Recoleta, *Santiago* 26 B2
Red Fort = Lal Qila, *Delhi* 1 a3
Redbridge, *London* 15 A4
Redfern, *Sydney* 28 B2
Redwood, *Wellington* 32 B1
Reeves Hill, *Boston* 6 A1
Refshaleøen, *Copenhagen* 10 A3
Regents Park, *Johannesburg* 13 B2
Regent's Park, *London* 15 a2
Rego Park, *New York* 21 B2
Reichstag, *Berlin* 5 a3
Reina Sofia, Centro de Arte, *Madrid* 17 c3
Reinickendorf, *Berlin* 5 A3
Rekola, *Helsinki* 12 B3
Rembertów, *Warsaw* 31 B2
Rembrandthuis, *Amsterdam* 2 b2
Rembrandtpark, *Amsterdam* 2 A2
Rembrandtsplein, *Amsterdam* 2 b2
Remedios, Parque Nacional de los, *Mexico City* 18 B1
Remedios de Escalada, *Buenos Aires* 7 C2
Rémola, Laguna del, *Barcelona* 4 B1
Renca, *Santiago* 26 B1
Renmin Park, *Tianjin* 30 B2
Rennemoulin, *Paris* 23 A1
Řeporyje, *Prague* 24 B1
Republica, Plaza de la, *Mexico City* 18 b1
République, Place de la, *Paris* 23 b5
Repulse Bay, *Hong Kong* 12 B2
Repy, *Prague* 24 B1
Residenz, *Munich* 20 B2
Residenzmuseum, *Munich* 20 b3
Reston, *Washington* 32 B2
Retiro, *Buenos Aires* 7 B2
Retiro, *Madrid* 17 B1
Retreat, *Cape Town* 8 B1
Reutov, *Moscow* 19 B5
Réveillon →, *Paris* 23 B4
Revere, *Boston* 6 A3
Rexdale, *Toronto* 30 A1
Reynosa Tamaulipas, *Mexico City* 18 A1
Rho, *Milan* 18 A1
Rhodes, *Sydney* 28 A1
Rhodon, *Paris* 23 B1
Rhodon →, *Paris* 23 B1
Ribeira, *Rio de Janeiro* 24 A1
Ricarda, Laguna de la, *Barcelona* 4 B1
Richmond, *Melbourne* 17 A2
Richmond, *San Francisco* 25 B2
Richmond Hill, *New York* 21 B2
Richmond Park, *London* 15 B2
Richmond upon Thames, *London* 15 B2
Riddarholmen, *Stockholm* 28 c1
Riddarhuset, *Stockholm* 28 c2
Ridgefield, *New York* 21 B1
Ridgefield Park, *New York* 21 A1
Ridgewood, *New York* 21 B2
Riem, *Munich* 20 B3
Rijksmuseum, *Amsterdam* 2 b1
Rikers I., *New York* 21 B2
Riksdagensledamothus, *Stockholm* 28 b2
Riksdagshuset, *Stockholm* 28 b2
Rimac, *Lima* 16 B2
Ringsend, *Dublin* 11 A2
Rinkeby, *Stockholm* 28 A1
Rio Compride, *Rio de Janeiro* 24 B1
Rio de Janeiro, *Rio de Janeiro* 24 B1
Rio de la Plata, *Buenos Aires* 7 B2
Rio de Mouro, *Lisbon* 14 A1
Ripollet, *Barcelona* 4 A1
Ris, *Oslo* 22 A3
Risby, *Copenhagen* 10 A1
Rishra, *Calcutta* 8 A2
Ritchie, *Washington* 32 B4
Rithala, *Delhi* 10 A1
Rive Sud, Canal de la, *Montreal* 19 B2
River Edge, *New York* 21 A1
River Forest, *Chicago* 9 B2
River Grove, *Chicago* 9 B1
Riverdale, *New York* 21 A2
Riverdale, *Washington* 32 B4
Riverdale Park, *Toronto* 30 A2
Riverlea, *Johannesburg* 13 B1
Riverside, *Chicago* 9 C2
Riverwood, *Sydney* 28 B1
Rivière-des-Praires, *Montreal* 19 A2
Rixensart, *Brussels* 6 B3
Riyad, *Baghdad* 3 B2
Rizal Park, *Manila* 17 B1
Rizal Stadium, *Manila* 17 B1
Røa, *Oslo* 22 A2
Robbins, *Chicago* 9 D2
Robertsham, *Johannesburg* 13 B2
Rochelle Park, *New York* 21 A1
Rock Cr. →, *Washington* 32 B3
Rock Creek Park, *Washington* 32 B3
Rock Pt., *Wellington* 32 A1
Rockaway Pt., *New York* 21 C2
Rockdale, *Sydney* 28 B1
Rockefeller Center, *New York* 21 c2
Rodaon, *Vienna* 31 B1
Rødovre, *Copenhagen* 10 A2
Rodrigo de Freitas, L., *Rio de Janeiro* 24 B1
Roehampton, *London* 15 B2
Rogers Park, *Chicago* 9 A2
Roihuvuori, *Helsinki* 12 B3
Roissy-en-Brie, *Paris* 23 B4
Rokin, *Amsterdam* 2 b2
Rokkō I., *Osaka* 22 A2
Rokkō Sanchi, *Osaka* 22 A2
Rokkō-Zan, *Osaka* 22 A2
Rokytka →, *Prague* 24 B3
Roma, *Rome* 25 B1
Római-Fürdö, *Budapest* 7 A2
Romainville, *Paris* 23 A3
Romano Banco, *Milan* 18 B1
Romashkovo, *Moscow* 19 B1
Rome = Roma, *Rome* 25 B1
Romford, *London* 15 A5
Rondebosch, *Cape Town* 8 A1
Roppongi, *Tokyo* 29 c3
Rose Hill, *Washington* 32 C3
Rosebank, *New York* 21 C1
Rosebery, *Sydney* 28 B2
Rosedal La Candelaria, *Mexico City* 18 B2
Roseland, *Chicago* 9 C3
Rosemead, *Los Angeles* 16 B4
Rosemont, *Montreal* 19 A2
Rosenborg Have, *Copenhagen* 10 A3
Rosenthal, *Berlin* 5 A3
Rosettenville, *Johannesburg* 13 B2
Rosewell, *Edinburgh* 11 B3
Rosherville Dam, *Johannesburg* 13 B2
Rösjön, *Stockholm* 28 A2
Roslags-Näsby, *Stockholm* 28 A2
Roslin, *Edinburgh* 11 B3
Roslindale, *Boston* 6 B3
Rosny-sous-Bois, *Paris* 23 A4
Rosslyn, *Washington* 32 B3
Rosyth, *Edinburgh* 11 A1
Rotherhithe, *London* 15 B3
Rothneusiedl, *Vienna* 31 B2
Rothschmaige, *Munich* 20 A1
Rouge Hill, *Toronto* 30 A4
Round I., *Hong Kong* 12 B2
Roxbury, *Boston* 6 B3
Roxeth, *London* 15 A1
Royal Botanic Garden, *Edinburgh* 11 B2
Royal Botanic Gardens, *Sydney* 28 b2
Royal Grand Palace, *Bangkok* 3 b1
Royal Observatory, *Edinburgh* 11 B2
Royal Park, *Melbourne* 17 A1
Royal Turf Club, *Bangkok* 3 b2
Röylä, *Helsinki* 12 B1
Rozas, Portilleros de las, *Madrid* 17 B1
Roztoky, *Prague* 24 B2
Rozzano, *Milan* 18 B1
Rubi →, *Barcelona* 4 A1
Rublovo, *Moscow* 19 B2
Rudnevka →, *Moscow* 19 B5
Rudolfsheim, *Vienna* 31 A2
Rudolfshöhe, *Berlin* 5 A5
Rudow, *Berlin* 5 B3
Rueil-Malmaison, *Paris* 23 A2
Ruisbroek, *Brussels* 6 B1
Ruislip, *London* 15 A1
Rumelihisarı, *Istanbul* 12 B2
Rumyantsevo, *Moscow* 19 C2
Rungis, *Paris* 23 B3
Rusāfa, *Baghdad* 3 A2
Rush Green, *London* 15 A5
Russa, *Calcutta* 8 C2
Russian Hill, *San Francisco* 25 a1
Rustenfeld, *Vienna* 31 B2
Rutherford, *New York* 21 B1
Ruzyně, *Prague* 24 B1
Rybatskaya, *St. Petersburg* 26 B2
Rydboholm, *Stockholm* 28 A3
Ryde, *Sydney* 28 A1
Rynek, *Warsaw* 31 a2
Ryogoku, *Tokyo* 29 A3
Rzhevka, *St. Petersburg* 26 B3

S

Sa'ādatābād, *Tehran* 30 A2
Saadūn, *Baghdad* 3 B2
Saavedra, *Buenos Aires* 7 B2
Saboli, *Delhi* 10 A2
Sabugo, *Lisbon* 14 A1
Sabzi Mand, *Delhi* 10 A2
Sacavém, *Lisbon* 14 A2
Saclay, *Paris* 23 B2
Saclay, Étang de, *Paris* 23 B1
Sacomã, *São Paulo* 26 B2
Sacré Cœur, *Paris* 23 a4
Sacrow, *Berlin* 5 B1
Sacrower See, *Berlin* 5 B1
Sadang, *Seoul* 26 C1
Sadar Bazar, *Delhi* 1 a1
Saddām City, *Baghdad* 3 A2
Saddle Brook, *New York* 21 A1
Sadr, *Karachi* 14 A2
Sadyba, *Warsaw* 31 B2
Saft el Laban, *Cairo* 7 A2
Saganashkee Slough, *Chicago* 9 C1
Sagene, *Oslo* 22 A3
Sagrada Familia, Templo de, *Barcelona* 4 A2
Sagrado Familia, Templo de, *Barcelona* 4 a2
Sahar Int. Airport, *Mumbai* 20 A2
Sai Kung, *Hong Kong* 12 A2
Sai Wan Ho, *Hong Kong* 12 B2
Sai Ying Pun, *Hong Kong* 12 B1
St.-Aubin, *Paris* 23 B1
St.-Cloud, *Paris* 23 A2
St.-Cyr-l'École, *Paris* 23 B1
St.-Cyr-l'École, Aérodrome de, *Paris* 23 B1
St.-Denis, *Paris* 23 A3
St.-Germain, Forêt de, *Paris* 23 A1
St.-Germain-en-Laye, *Paris* 23 A1
St. Giles Cathedral, *Edinburgh* 11 b2
St. Helier, *London* 15 B2
St.-Hubert, *Montreal* 19 B3
St. Hubert, Galerie, *Brussels* 6 b2
St. Isaac's Cathedral, *St. Petersburg* 26 B1
St. Jacques →, *Montreal* 19 B3
St. James's, *London* 15 b3
St. John's Cathedral, *Hong Kong* 12 c1
St. Kilda, *Melbourne* 17 B1
St. Lambert, *Montreal* 19 A3
St.-Lambert, *Paris* 23 B1
St.-Laurent, *Montreal* 19 A1
St. Lawrence →, *Montreal* 19 B2
St.-Lazare, Gare, *Paris* 23 A2
St.-Léonard, *Montreal* 19 A2
St. Magelungen, *Stockholm* 28 B2
St.-Mandé, *Paris* 23 A3
St. Margaret's, *Dublin* 11 A2
St.-Martin, Bois, *Paris* 23 B4
St. Mary Cray, *London* 15 B4
St.-Maur-des-Fossés, *Paris* 23 B3
St.-Maurice, *Paris* 23 B3
St.-Michel, *Montreal* 19 A2
St. Nikolaus-Kirken, *Prague* 24 B2
St.-Ouen, *Paris* 23 A3
St. Patrick's Cathedral, *Dublin* 11 c1
St. Patrick's Cathedral, *New York* 21 c2
St. Paul's Cathedral, *London* 15 b4
St. Paul's Cray, *London* 15 B4
St. Peters, *Sydney* 28 B2
St. Petersburg = Sankt Peterburg, *St. Petersburg* 26 B1
St.-Pierre, *Montreal* 19 B2
St.-Quentin, Étang de, *Paris* 23 B1
St. Stephen's Green, *Dublin* 11 c3
St.-Vincent-de-Paul, *Montreal* 19 A2
Ste.-Catherine, *Montreal* 19 B2
Ste.-Hélène, Î., *Montreal* 19 A2
Saiwai, *Tokyo* 29 B3
Sakai, *Osaka* 22 B3
Sakai Harbour, *Osaka* 22 B3
Sakra, P., *Singapore* 27 B2
Salam, *Baghdad* 3 A2
Salamanca, *Madrid* 17 B1
Sâllynoggin, *Dublin* 11 B3
Salmannsdorf, *Vienna* 31 A1
Salmedina, *Madrid* 17 C2
Salomea, *Warsaw* 31 B1
Salsette I., *Mumbai* 20 A2
Salt Lake City, *Calcutta* 8 B2
Salt River, *Cape Town* 8 A1
Salt Water L., *Calcutta* 8 B2
Saltsjö-Duvnäs, *Stockholm* 28 B3
Saltykovka, *Moscow* 19 B5
Samatya, *Istanbul* 12 C1
Sampaloc, *Manila* 17 B1
Samphan Thawong, *Bangkok* 3 B2
Samsŏn, *Seoul* 26 B2
San Andrés, *Barcelona* 4 A2
San Angel, *Mexico City* 18 B1
San Angelo, Castel, *Rome* 25 b1
San Basilio, *Rome* 25 B2
San Borja, *Lima* 16 B3
San Bóvio, *Milan* 18 B2
San Bruno, Pt., *San Francisco* 25 C2
San Bruno Mt., *San Francisco* 25 B2
San Cristobal, *Buenos Aires* 7 B2
San Cristobal, *Madrid* 17 B2
San Cristóbal, Cerro, *Santiago* 26 B2
San Cristoforo, *Milan* 18 B1
San Donato Milanese, *Milan* 18 B2
San Francisco, *San Francisco* 25 B2
San Francisco B., *San Francisco* 25 B3
San Francisco Culhuacán, *Mexico City* 18 C2
San Fruttuoso, *Milan* 18 A2
San Gabriel, *Los Angeles* 16 B4
San Giuliano Milanese, *Milan* 18 B2
San Isidro, *Lima* 16 B2
San Jerónimo Lidice, *Mexico City* 18 C1
San Joaquin, *Santiago* 26 B2
San José Rio Hondo, *Mexico City* 18 B1
San Juan →, *Manila* 17 B2
San Juan de Aragón, *Mexico City* 18 B2
San Juan de Aragón, Parque, *Mexico City* 18 B2
San Juan de Lurigancho, *Lima* 16 A2
San Juan del Monte, *Manila* 17 B2
San Juan Ixtacala, *Mexico City* 18 A1
San Juan Toltotepec, *Mexico City* 18 B1
San Just Desvern, *Barcelona* 4 A1
San Justo, *Buenos Aires* 7 C1
San Lorenzo Tezonco, *Mexico City* 18 C2
San Luis, *Lima* 16 B2
San Marino, *Los Angeles* 16 B4
San Martin, *Barcelona* 4 A2
San Martin de Porras, *Lima* 16 B2
San Miguel, *Lima* 16 B2
San Miguel, *Santiago* 26 B2
San Nicolas, *Buenos Aires* 7 B2
San Onófrio, *Rome* 25 B1
San Pedro Martir, *Barcelona* 4 A1
San Pedro Zacatenco, *Mexico City* 18 A2
San Pietro, Piazza, *Rome* 25 b1
San Po Kong, *Hong Kong* 12 A2
San Rafael Chamapa, *Mexico City* 18 B1
San Rafael Hills, *Los Angeles* 16 A3
San Roque, *Manila* 17 B2
San Siro, *Milan* 18 B1
San Souci, *Sydney* 28 B1
San Telmo, *Buenos Aires* 7 B2
San Vicenc dels Horts, *Barcelona* 4 A1
Sanbancho, *Tokyo* 29 a3
Sandown, *Johannesburg* 13 A2
Sandown Park Races, *London* 15 B1
Sandton, *Johannesburg* 13 A2
Sandvika, *Oslo* 22 A2
Sandy Pond, *Boston* 6 A2
Sandyford, *Dublin* 11 B2
Sandymount, *Dublin* 11 B2
Sangenjaya, *Tokyo* 29 B2
Sangge, *Seoul* 26 B2
Sangley Pt., *Manila* 17 C1
Sankrail, *Calcutta* 8 B1
Sankt Peterburg, *St. Petersburg* 26 B1
Sankt Veit, *Vienna* 31 A1
Sanlihe, *Beijing* 4 B1
Sanlintang, *Shanghai* 27 C1
Sans, *Barcelona* 4 A1
Sant Agusti, *Barcelona* 4 c2
Sant Ambrogio, Basilica di, *Milan* 18 B2
Sant Boi de Llobregat, *Barcelona* 4 A1
Sant Cugat, *Barcelona* 4 A1
Sant Feliu de Llobregat, *Barcelona* 4 A1
Sant Joan Despi, *Barcelona* 4 A1
Sant Maria del Mar, *Barcelona* 4 b3
Sant Pau del Camp, *Barcelona* 4 c2
Santa Ana, *Manila* 17 B2
Santa Coloma de Gramanet, *Barcelona* 4 A2
Santa Cruz, *Manila* 17 B1
Santa Cruz, *Mumbai* 20 A1
Santa Cruz, I. de, *Rio de Janeiro* 24 B2
Santa Cruz de Olorde, *Barcelona* 4 A1
Santa Efigénia, *São Paulo* 26 B2
Santa Elena, *Manila* 17 B2
Santa Elena del Gomero, *Santiago* 26 B1
Santa Eulalia, *Barcelona* 4 A2
Santa Fe Springs, *Los Angeles* 16 C4
Santa Iria da Azóia, *Lisbon* 14 A2
Santa Julia, *Santiago* 26 C2
Santa Maria, *Mexico City* 18 a1
Santa Monica, *Los Angeles* 16 B2
Santa Monica Mts., *Los Angeles* 16 B2
Santa Rosa De Locobe, *Santiago* 26 B2
Santa Teresa de la Ovalle, *Santiago* 26 B1
Santahamina, *Helsinki* 12 C3
Santana, *São Paulo* 26 A2
Santeny, *Paris* 23 B4
Santiago, *Santiago* 26 B2
Santiago de Surco, *Lima* 16 B2
Santo Amaro, *Lisbon* 14 A1
Santo Amaro, *São Paulo* 26 B1
Santo Andre, *Lisbon* 14 B2
Santo Antão do Tojal, *Lisbon* 14 A2
Santo António, Qta. de, *Lisbon* 14 B1
Santo Tomas, Univ. of, *Manila* 17 B1
Santos Dumont, Aéroport, *Rio de Janeiro* 24 B2
Santoshpur, *Calcutta* 8 B1
Santragachi, *Calcutta* 8 B1
Santry, *Dublin* 11 A2
Sanyuanli, *Canton* 8 B2
São Caetano do Sul, *São Paulo* 26 B2
São Conrado, *Rio de Janeiro* 24 C1
São Cristovão, *Rio de Janeiro* 24 B1
São Francisco Penitência, *Rio de Janeiro* 24 b1
São Jorge, Castelo de, *Lisbon* 14 A2
São Juliao do Tojal, *Lisbon* 14 A2
São Paulo, *São Paulo* 26 B2
Sapa, *Calcutta* 8 B1
Sapateiro, Cor. do →, *São Paulo* 26 B1
Sarandi, *Buenos Aires* 7 C2
Saraswati →, *Calcutta* 8 A1
Sarecky potok →, *Prague* 24 B2
Sarimbun, *Singapore* 27 A2
Sarimbun Res., *Singapore* 27 A2
Sarıyer, *Istanbul* 12 A2
Saronikós Kólpos, *Athens* 2 B1
Sarriá, *Barcelona* 4 A1
Sarsuna, *Calcutta* 8 C1
Sartrouville, *Paris* 23 A2
Sasad, *Budapest* 7 B2
Sashalom, *Budapest* 7 A3
Saska, *Warsaw* 31 B2
Satalice, *Prague* 24 B3
Satgachi, *Calcutta* 8 B2
Sathorn, *Bangkok* 3 B2
Satpukur, *Calcutta* 8 B2
Sätra, *Stockholm* 28 B1
Sattru Pha, *Bangkok* 3 b2
Saúde, *São Paulo* 26 B2
Saugus, *Boston* 6 A3
Saugus →, *Boston* 6 A3
Sault-au-Récollet, *Montreal* 19 A2
Sausalito, *San Francisco* 25 A2
Sawah Besar, *Jakarta* 13 A1
Saxonville, *Boston* 6 B1
Scald Law, *Edinburgh* 11 B2
Scarborough, *Toronto* 30 A3
Sceaux, *Paris* 23 B2
Schaerbeek, *Brussels* 6 A2
Scharfenberg, *Berlin* 5 A2
Scheepvartmuseum, *Amsterdam* 2 b3
Schiller Park, *Chicago* 9 B1
Schiller Woods, *Chicago* 9 B1
Schiphol, Luchthaven, *Amsterdam* 2 B1
Schlachtensee, *Berlin* 5 B2
Schlossgarten, *Berlin* 5 A2
Schmargendorf, *Berlin* 5 B2
Schönblick, *Berlin* 5 B5
Schönbrunn, Schloss, *Vienna* 31 A1
Schöneberg, *Berlin* 5 B3
Schöneiche, *Berlin* 5 B5
Schönwalde, *Berlin* 5 A1
Schotschekloof, *Cape Town* 8 b1
Schulzendorf, *Berlin* 5 A2
Schwabing, *Munich* 20 B2
Schwanebeck, *Berlin* 5 A4
Schwanenwerder, *Berlin* 5 B2
Schwarzlackenau, *Vienna* 31 A2
Schwechat, *Vienna* 31 B2
Scitrek Museum, *Atlanta* 3 B2
Scott Monument, *Edinburgh* 11 b2
Scottdale, *Atlanta* 3 B3
Sea Point, *Cape Town* 8 A1
Seabrook, *Washington* 32 B5
Seacliff, *San Francisco* 25 B2
Seaforth, *Sydney* 28 A2
Seagate, *New York* 21 C1
Sears Tower, *Chicago* 9 c1
Seat Pleasant, *Washington* 32 B4
Seaview, *Wellington* 32 B2
Šeberov, *Prague* 24 B3
Secaucus, *New York* 21 B1
Seddinsee, *Berlin* 5 B5
Seeberg, *Berlin* 5 A5
Seeburg, *Berlin* 5 A1
Seefeld, *Berlin* 5 A5
Seegefeld, *Berlin* 5 A1
Seehof, *Berlin* 5 B2
Segeltorp, *Stockholm* 28 B1
Segrate, *Milan* 18 B2
Seguro, *Milan* 18 B1
Seine →, *Paris* 23 B3
Seixal, *Lisbon* 14 B2
Selby, *Johannesburg* 13 B2
Seletar, P., *Singapore* 27 A3
Seletar Hills, *Singapore* 27 A3
Seletar Res., *Singapore* 27 A2
Selhurst, *London* 15 B3
Sembawang, *Singapore* 27 A2
Senago, *Milan* 18 A1
Sendinger Tor Platz, *Munich* 20 c1
Sendling, *Munich* 20 B2
Senju, *Tokyo* 29 A3
Senriyama, *Osaka* 22 A4
Sentosa, P., *Singapore* 27 B2
Seoul = Sŏul, *Seoul* 26 B2
Seoul National Univ., *Seoul* 26 C1
Seoul Tower, *Seoul* 26 B1
Sepolia, *Athens* 2 A2
Sepulveda Flood Control Basin, *Los Angeles* 16 A2
Serangoon, *Singapore* 27 A3
Serangoon, P., *Singapore* 27 A3
Serangoon, Sungei →, *Singapore* 27 A3
Serangoon Harbour, *Singapore* 27 A3
Seraya, P., *Singapore* 27 B2
Serebryanka, *Moscow* 19 B5
Serebryanka →, *Moscow* 19 B4
Serramonte, *San Francisco* 25 C2
Sesto San Giovanni, *Milan* 18 A2
Sesto Ulteriano, *Milan* 18 B2
Setagaya-Ku, *Tokyo* 29 B2
Seter, *Oslo* 22 A3
Setia Budi, *Jakarta* 13 B1
Settebagni, *Rome* 25 A2
Settecamini, *Rome* 25 B2
Séttimo Milanese, *Milan* 18 B1
Settsu, *Osaka* 22 A4
Setuny →, *Moscow* 19 B2
Seutula, *Helsinki* 12 A2
Seven Corners, *Washington* 32 B3
Seven Kings, *London* 15 A4
Sévesco →, *Milan* 18 A1
Sevran, *Paris* 23 A4
Sewri, *Mumbai* 20 B2
Sforzesso, Castello, *Milan* 18 B2
Sha Kok Mei, *Hong Kong* 12 A2
Sha Tin, *Hong Kong* 12 A2
Sha Tin Wai, *Hong Kong* 12 A2
Shabrâmant, *Cairo* 7 B2
Shahdara, *Delhi* 10 A2
Shahe, *Canton* 8 B2
Shahr-e Rey, *Tehran* 30 B2
Shahrak-e Golshahr, *Tehran* 30 B1
Shahrak-e Qods, *Tehran* 30 A2
Shaikh Aomar, *Baghdad* 3 A2
Shakurbasti, *Delhi* 10 A1
Shalkiya, *Calcutta* 8 B2
Sham Shui Po, *Hong Kong* 12 B1
Shamapur, *Delhi* 10 A1
Shamian, *Canton* 8 B2
Shan Mei, *Hong Kong* 12 A2
Shanghai, *Shanghai* 27 B2
Shankill, *Dublin* 11 B3
Sharp I., *Hong Kong* 12 A2
Shastrinagar, *Delhi* 10 A2
Shau Kei Wan, *Hong Kong* 12 B2
Shawocun, *Beijing* 4 B1
Shayuan, *Canton* 8 B2
Sheepshead Bay, *New York* 21 C2
Shek O, *Hong Kong* 12 B2
Shelter I., *Hong Kong* 12 B2
Sheng Fa Shan, *Hong Kong* 12 A1
Shepherds Bush, *London* 15 A2
Shepperton, *London* 15 B1
Sherman Oaks, *Los Angeles* 16 B2
Sherman Park, *Chicago* 9 C2
Shet Bandar, *Mumbai* 20 B2
Sheung Lau Wan, *Hong Kong* 12 B2
Sheung Wan, *Hong Kong* 12 B1
Sheva, *Mumbai* 20 B2
Sheva Nhava, *Mumbai* 20 B2
Shiba, *Tokyo* 29 c4
Shibpur, *Calcutta* 8 B1
Shibuya-Ku, *Tokyo* 29 c1
Shijōnawate, *Osaka* 22 A4
Shillim, *Seoul* 26 C1
Shimogawara, *Tokyo* 29 B1
Shimosalo, *Tokyo* 29 A2
Shimoshakujii, *Tokyo* 29 A2
Shinagawa-Ku, *Tokyo* 29 B3
Shing Mun Res., *Hong Kong* 12 A1
Shinjuku-Ku, *Tokyo* 29 a1
Shinjuku National Garden, *Tokyo* 29 a2
Shinkoiwa, *Tokyo* 29 A4
Shinnakano, *Tokyo* 29 A3
Shinsa, *Seoul* 26 B2
Shipai, *Canton* 8 B3
Shirinashi →, *Osaka* 22 B3
Shirogane, *Tokyo* 29 B3
Shiweitang, *Canton* 8 B2
Shogunle, *Lagos* 14 A2
Shomolu, *Lagos* 14 A2
Shooters Hill, *London* 15 B4
Shoreditch, *London* 15 a5
Shortlands, *London* 15 B4
Shu' afat, *Jerusalem* 13 B2
Shubrâ, *Cairo* 7 A2
Shubrâ el Kheima, *Cairo* 7 A2
Shuikuo, *Canton* 8 A2
Shuishang Park, *Tianjin* 30 B1
Sidcup, *London* 15 B4
Siebenhirten, *Vienna* 31 B1
Siedlung, *Berlin* 5 A1
Siekierki, *Warsaw* 31 B2
Sielce, *Warsaw* 31 B2
Siemensstadt, *Berlin* 5 A2
Sierra Madre, *Los Angeles* 16 B4
Sievering, *Vienna* 31 A2
Sighthill, *Edinburgh* 11 B2
Signal Hill, *Cape Town* 8 A1
Sihŭng, *Seoul* 26 C1
Sikátorpuszta, *Budapest* 7 A3
Silampur, *Delhi* 10 B2
Silver Hill, *Boston* 6 A2
Silver Hill, *Washington* 32 C4
Silver Spring, *Washington* 32 A3
Silvermine Nature Reserve, *Cape Town* 8 B1
Silvolantekojärvi, *Helsinki* 12 B2
Simei, *Singapore* 27 A3
Simla, *Calcutta* 8 B2
Simmering, *Vienna* 31 A2
Simmering Heide, *Vienna* 31 A2
Simonkylä, *Helsinki* 12 B3
Singapore, *Singapore* 27 B3
Singapore, Univ. of, *Singapore* 27 B2
Sinicka →, *Moscow* 19 A1
Sinki, Selat, *Singapore* 27 B2
Sint-Genesius-Rode, *Brussels* 6 B2
Sinwŏl, *Seoul* 26 B1
Sion, *Mumbai* 20 A2
Sipson, *London* 15 B1
Siqeil, *Cairo* 7 A1
Şişli, *Istanbul* 12 B1
Skansen, *Stockholm* 28 B2
Skärholmen, *Stockholm* 28 B1
Skarpäng, *Stockholm* 28 A2
Skarpnäck, *Stockholm* 28 B2
Skaryszewski Park, *Warsaw* 31 B2
Skeppsholmen, *Stockholm* 28 c3
Skokie, *Chicago* 9 A2
Skokie →, *Chicago* 9 A2
Skoklefall, *Oslo* 22 A3
Sköndal, *Stockholm* 28 B2
Skovlunde, *Copenhagen* 10 A2
Skovshoved, *Copenhagen* 10 A3
Skuru, *Stockholm* 28 B3
Skyland, *Atlanta* 3 A3
Slade Green, *London* 15 B5
Slemmestad, *Oslo* 22 B1
Slependen, *Oslo* 22 A2
Slipi, *Jakarta* 13 B1
Slivenec, *Prague* 24 B2
Sloten, *Amsterdam* 2 A1
Sloterpark, *Amsterdam* 2 A1
Sluhy, *Prague* 24 A3
Służew, *Warsaw* 31 B2
Służewiec, *Warsaw* 31 B2
Smíchov, *Prague* 24 B2
Smith Forest Preserve, *Chicago* 9 B2
Smithsonian Institute, *Washington* 32 b2
Smolny, *St. Petersburg* 26 B2
Snake Creek Canal →, *Miami* 18 A2
Snarøya, *Oslo* 22 A2
Snättringe, *Stockholm* 28 B1
Sŏbinggo, *Seoul* 26 B1
Søborg, *Copenhagen* 10 A2
Sobreda, *Lisbon* 14 B1
Soch'o, *Seoul* 26 C1
Sŏdaemun, *Seoul* 26 B1
Söderby, *Stockholm* 28 A3
Södermalm, *Stockholm* 28 B2
Sodpur, *Calcutta* 8 A2
Soeurs, Î. des, *Montreal* 19 B2
Sognsvatn, *Oslo* 22 A3
Soho, *London* 15 b3
Soho, *New York* 21 e1
Soignes, Forêt de, *Brussels* 6 B2
Sok Kwu Wan, *Hong Kong* 12 B1
Sŏkkwan, *Seoul* 26 B2
Sokolniki, *Moscow* 19 B4
Sokolniki Park, *Moscow* 19 B4
Sokołów, *Warsaw* 31 C1
Solalinden, *Munich* 20 B3
Soldier Field, *Chicago* 9 e3
Sollentuna, *Stockholm* 28 A1
Solln, *Munich* 20 B2
Solna, *Stockholm* 28 A1
Solntsevo, *Moscow* 19 C2
Somerset, *Washington* 32 B3
Somerville, *Boston* 6 A3
Somes Is., *Wellington* 32 B2
Sonari, *Mumbai* 20 B2
Søndersø, *Copenhagen* 10 A2
Sŏngbuk, *Seoul* 26 B2
Sŏngdong, *Seoul* 26 B2
Sŏngp'a, *Seoul* 26 B2
Sŏngsu, *Seoul* 26 B2
Soong Qingling, Former Res. of, *Beijing* 4 a2
Soroksár, *Budapest* 7 B2
Soroksari Duna →, *Budapest* 7 B2
Sosenka →, *Moscow* 19 B4
Sosnovka, *St. Petersburg* 26 B2
Sŏul, *Seoul* 26 B2
Soundview, *New York* 21 B2
South Beach, *New York* 21 C1
South Beach Harbor, *San Francisco* 25 c3
South Bend Park, *Atlanta* 3 B2
South Boston, *Boston* 6 A3
South Brooklyn, *New York* 21 B2
South Decatur, *Atlanta* 3 B3
South Deering, *Chicago* 9 C3
South El Monte, *Los Angeles* 16 B4
South Gate, *Los Angeles* 16 C3
South Harbor, *Manila* 17 B1
South Harrow, *London* 15 A1
South Hd., *Sydney* 28 B2
South Hills, *Johannesburg* 13 B2
South Hornchurch, *London* 15 A5
South Kensington, *London* 15 c2
South Lawn, *Washington* 32 C3
South Lincoln, *Boston* 6 A2
South Miami, *Miami* 18 B1
South Norwood, *London* 15 B3
South of Market, *San Francisco* 25 B2
South Ozone Park, *New York* 21 B3
South Pasadena, *Los Angeles* 16 B4
South Res., *Boston* 6 A3
South Ruislip, *London* 15 A1
South San Francisco, *San Francisco* 25 C2
South San Gabriel, *Los Angeles* 16 B4
South Shore, *Chicago* 9 C3
South Sudbury, *Boston* 6 A1
Southall, *London* 15 A1
Southborough, *London* 15 B4
Southend, *London* 15 B3
Southfields, *London* 15 B2
Southwark, *London* 15 B3
Søvang, *Copenhagen* 10 B3
Soweto, *Johannesburg* 13 B1
Sowhānak, *Tehran* 30 A3
Soya, *Tokyo* 29 A4
Spandau, *Berlin* 5 A1
Spånga, *Stockholm* 28 A1
Spanische Reitschule, *Vienna* 31 b1
Spectacle I., *Boston* 6 A4
Speicher-See, *Munich* 20 A3
Speising, *Vienna* 31 B1
Sphinx, *Cairo* 7 B1
Spinaceto, *Rome* 25 C1
Spit Junction, *Sydney* 28 A2
Spořilov, *Prague* 24 B3
Spot Pond, *Boston* 6 A3
Spotswood, *Melbourne* 17 B1
Spree →, *Berlin* 5 A2
Spring Pond, *Boston* 6 A4
Springeberg, *Berlin* 5 B5
Springfield, *Washington* 32 C2
Squantum, *Boston* 6 B3
Srednaya Rogatka, *St. Petersburg* 26 C2
Sródmieście, *Warsaw* 31 B2
Saint-Gilles, *Brussels* 6 B2
Saint-Joose-Ten-Noode, *Brussels* 6 A2
Saint-Pieters-Leeuw, *Brussels* 6 B1
Saint-Stevens-Woluwe, *Brussels* 6 A2
Staaken, *Berlin* 5 A1
Stabekk, *Oslo* 22 A2
Stadhion, *Athens* 2 c3
Stadhuis, *Amsterdam* 2 b2
Stadlau, *Vienna* 31 A2
Stadshuset, *Stockholm* 28 b1
Stains, *Paris* 23 A3
Stamford Hill, *London* 15 A3
Stammersdorf, *Vienna* 31 A2
Stanley, *Hong Kong* 12 B2
Stanley Mound, *Hong Kong* 12 B2
Stanley Pen., *Hong Kong* 12 B2
Stanmore, *London* 15 A2
Stapleton, *New York* 21 C1
Star Ferry, *Hong Kong* 12 a2
Staraya Derevnya, *St. Petersburg* 26 B1
Stare, *Warsaw* 31 B2
Staré Město, *Prague* 24 B2
Starego Miasto, *Warsaw* 31 a2
Staten Island Zoo, *New York* 21 C1
Statenice, *Prague* 24 B1
Statue Square, *Hong Kong* 12 c1
Stedelijk Museum, *Amsterdam* 2 c1
Steele Creek, *Melbourne* 17 A1
Steenokkerzeel, *Brussels* 6 A2
Steglitz, *Berlin* 5 B2
Stepaside, *Dublin* 11 B2
Stephansdom, *Vienna* 31 b2
Stepney, *London* 15 A3
Sterling Park, *San Francisco* 25 B2
Sticklinge udde, *Stockholm* 28 A2
Stickney, *Chicago* 9 C2
Stillorgan, *Dublin* 11 B2
Stockholm, *Stockholm* 28 B2
Stocksund, *Stockholm* 28 A2
Stodůlky, *Prague* 24 B1
Stoke Newington, *London* 15 A3
Stokes Valley, *Wellington* 32 B2
Stone Canyon Res., *Los Angeles* 16 B2
Stone Park, *Chicago* 9 B1
Stonebridge, *London* 15 A2
Stoneham, *Boston* 6 A3
Stony Brook Res., *Boston* 6 B3
Stora Värtan, *Stockholm* 28 A2
Store Hareskov, *Copenhagen* 10 A2
Store Magleby, *Copenhagen* 10 B3
Storholmen, *Stockholm* 28 A2
Stoyka, *St. Petersburg* 26 B2
Straiton, *Edinburgh* 11 B3
Strand, *London* 15 b4
Strandfontein, *Cape Town* 8 B2
Strašnice, *Prague* 24 B2
Strasstrudering, *Munich* 20 B3
Stratford, *London* 15 A4
Strathfield, *Sydney* 28 B1
Streatham, *London* 15 B3
Streatham Vale, *London* 15 B3
Strebersdorf, *Vienna* 31 A2
Střešovice, *Prague* 24 B2
Střížkov, *Prague* 24 B2
Strogino, *Moscow* 19 B2
Strombeek-Bever, *Brussels* 6 A2
Stromovka, *Prague* 24 B2
Studio City, *Los Angeles* 16 B2
Stureby, *Stockholm* 28 B2
Stuvsta, *Stockholm* 28 B2
Subhepur, *Delhi* 10 A2
Sucat, *Manila* 17 C2
Suchdol, *Prague* 24 B2
Sucy-en-Brie, *Paris* 23 B4
Sudbury, *Boston* 6 A1
Sugamo, *Tokyo* 29 A3
Sugar Loaf Mt. = Açúcar, Pão de, *Rio de Janeiro* 24 B2
Suge, *Tokyo* 29 B2
Suginami-Ku, *Tokyo* 29 A2
Sugō, *Tokyo* 29 B2
Suita, *Osaka* 22 A4
Suitland, *Washington* 32 B4
Sukchar, *Calcutta* 8 A2
Suma, *Osaka* 22 B1
Sumida →, *Tokyo* 29 A3
Sumida-Ku, *Tokyo* 29 A3
Sumiyoshi, *Osaka* 22 B4
Summerville, *Toronto* 30 B1
Summit, *Chicago* 9 C2
Sunamachi, *Tokyo* 29 A4
Sunbury-on-Thames, *London* 15 B1
Sundbyberg, *Stockholm* 28 A1
Sundbyerne, *Copenhagen* 10 B3
Sung Kong, *Hong Kong* 12 B2
Sungei Kadut Industrial Estate, *Singapore* 27 A2
Sungei Selatar Res., *Singapore* 27 A3
Sunter, *Jakarta* 13 A2
Sunter, Kali →, *Jakarta* 13 B2
Suomenlinna, *Helsinki* 12 C2
Supreme Court, *Washington* 32 b3
Sura, *Calcutta* 8 B2
Surag-san, *Seoul* 26 A2
Surbiton, *London* 15 B2
Suresnes, *Paris* 23 A2
Surfside, *Miami* 18 A2
Surquillo, *Lima* 16 B2
Surrey Hills, *Sydney* 28 B2
Susaek, *Seoul* 26 B1
Süssenbrunn, *Vienna* 31 A2
Sutton, *Dublin* 11 A3
Sutton, *London* 15 B2
Suyu, *Seoul* 26 B2
Suzukishinden, *Tokyo* 29 A2
Svanemøllen, *Copenhagen* 10 A3
Sverdlov, *Moscow* 19 B3
Svestad, *Oslo* 22 B2
Svinö, *Helsinki* 12 C1
Swampscott, *Boston* 6 A4
Swanley, *London* 15 B4
Swansea, *Toronto* 30 B2
Swinburne I., *New York* 21 C1
Swords, *Dublin* 11 A2
Sydenham, *Johannesburg* 13 A2
Sydney, *Sydney* 28 B2
Sydney, Univ. of, *Sydney* 28 B2
Sydney Airport, *Sydney* 28 B2
Sydney Harbour Bridge, *Sydney* 28 B2
Sydstranden, *Copenhagen* 10 B3
Sylvania, *Sydney* 28 C1
Syntagma, Pl., *Athens* 2 b3
Syon Park, *London* 15 B2
Szczęśliwice, *Warsaw* 31 B1
Széchnenyi-hegy, *Budapest* 7 B1
Szent Istvánbaz, *Budapest* 7 b2
Széphalom, *Budapest* 7 A1

T

Tabata, *Tokyo* 29 A3
Tablada, *Buenos Aires* 7 C1
Table Bay, *Cape Town* 8 A1
Table Mountain, *Cape Town* 8 A1
Taboão da Serra, *São Paulo* 26 B1
Täby, *Stockholm* 28 A2

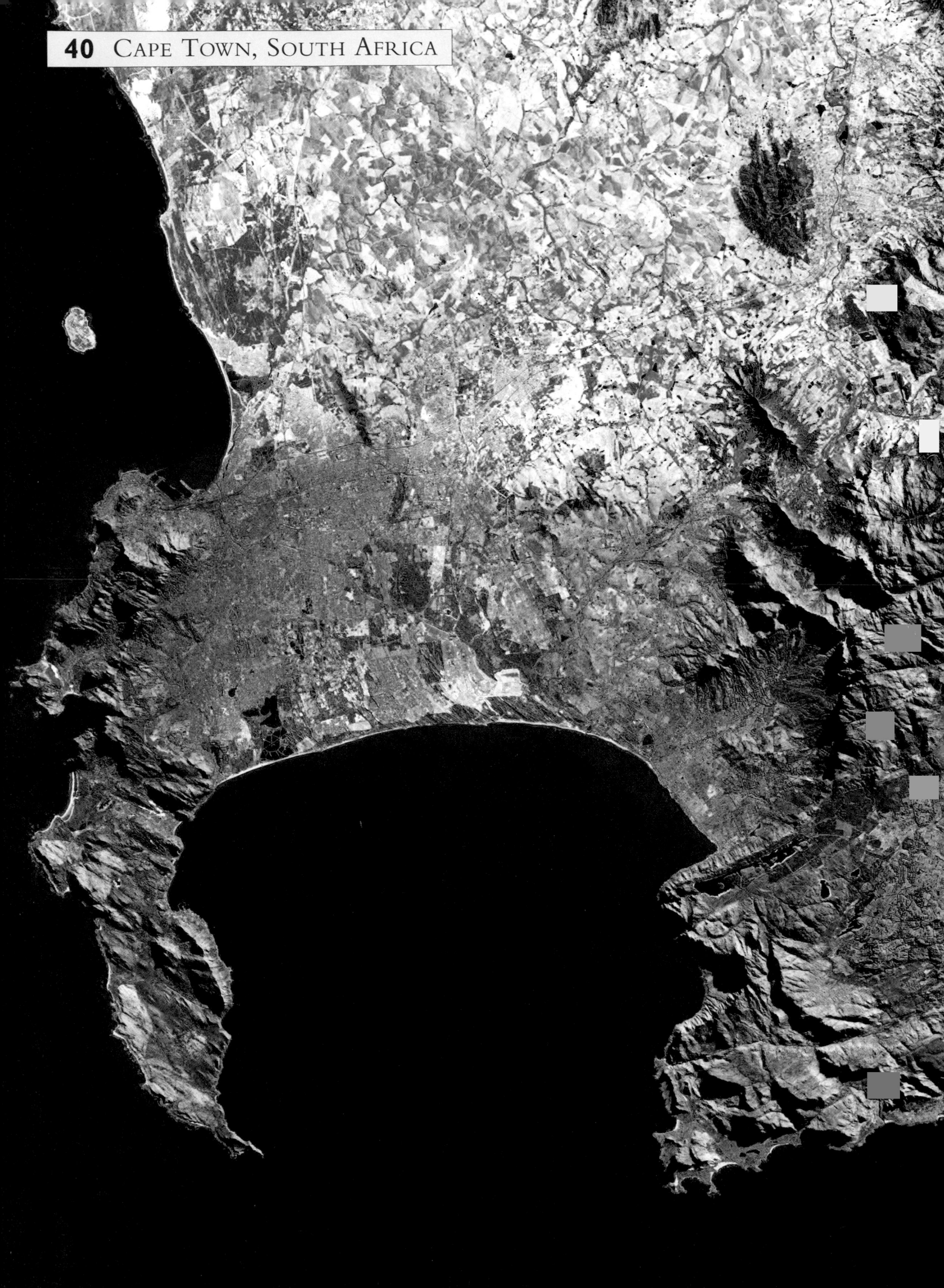

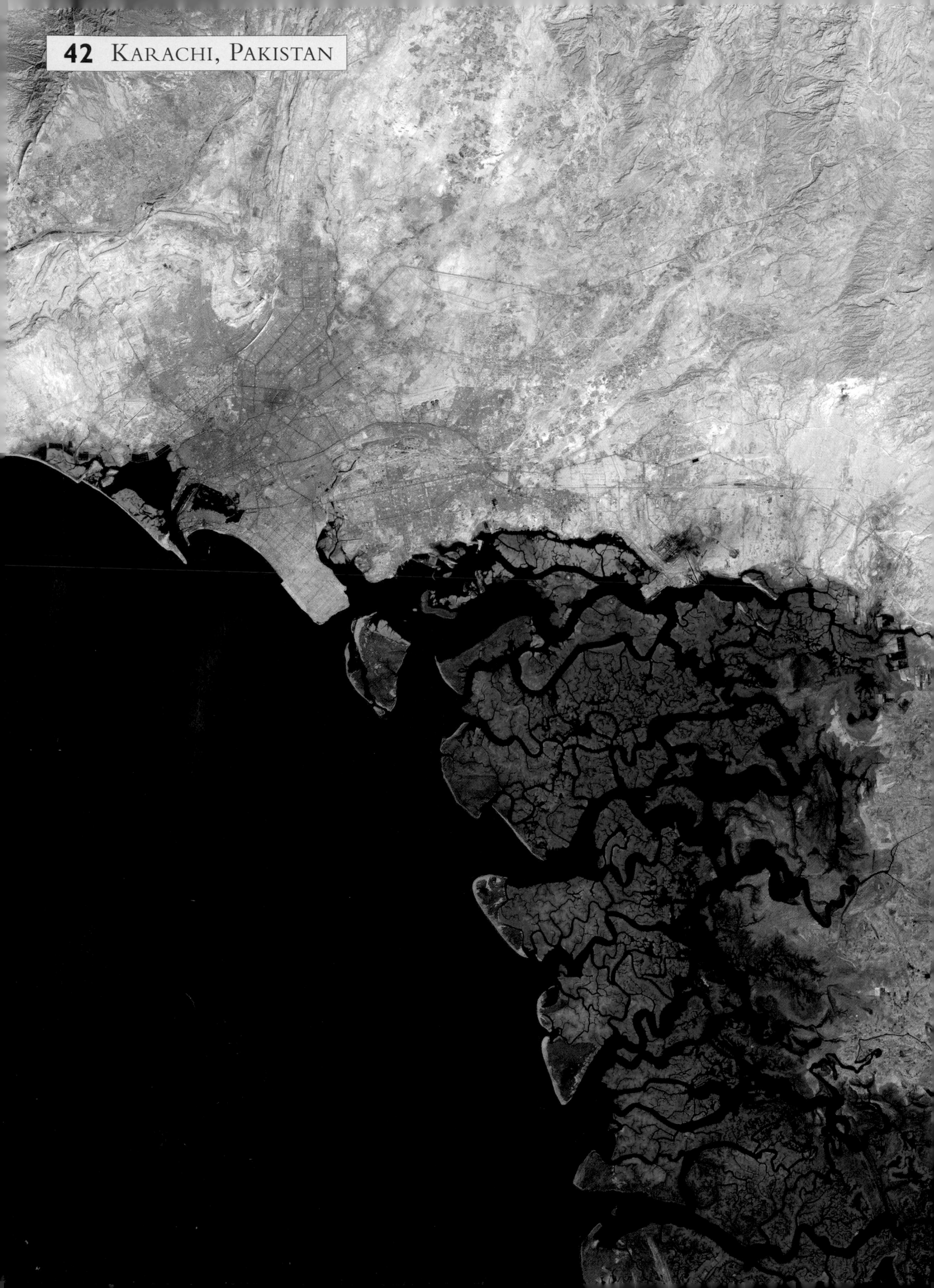

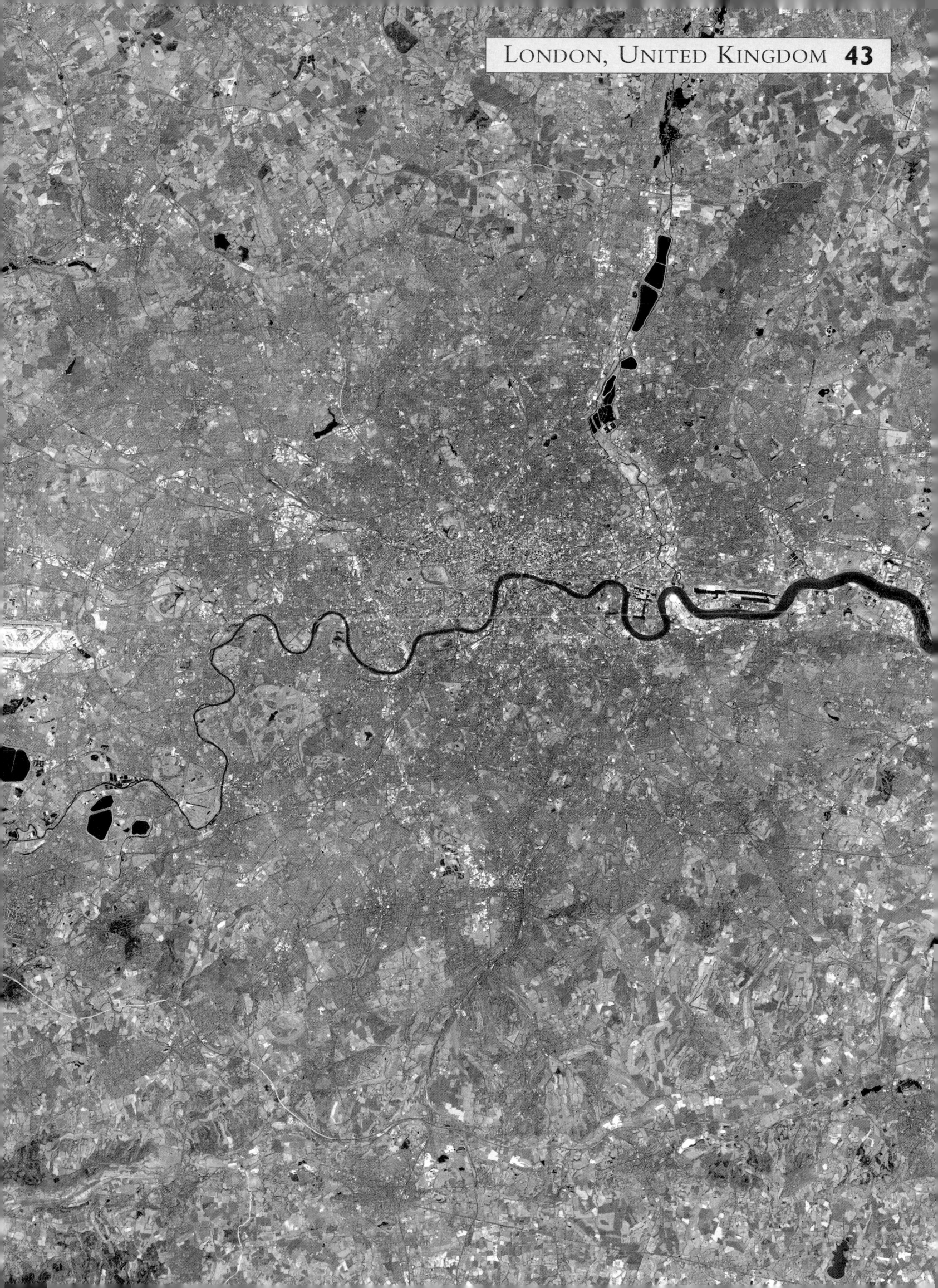

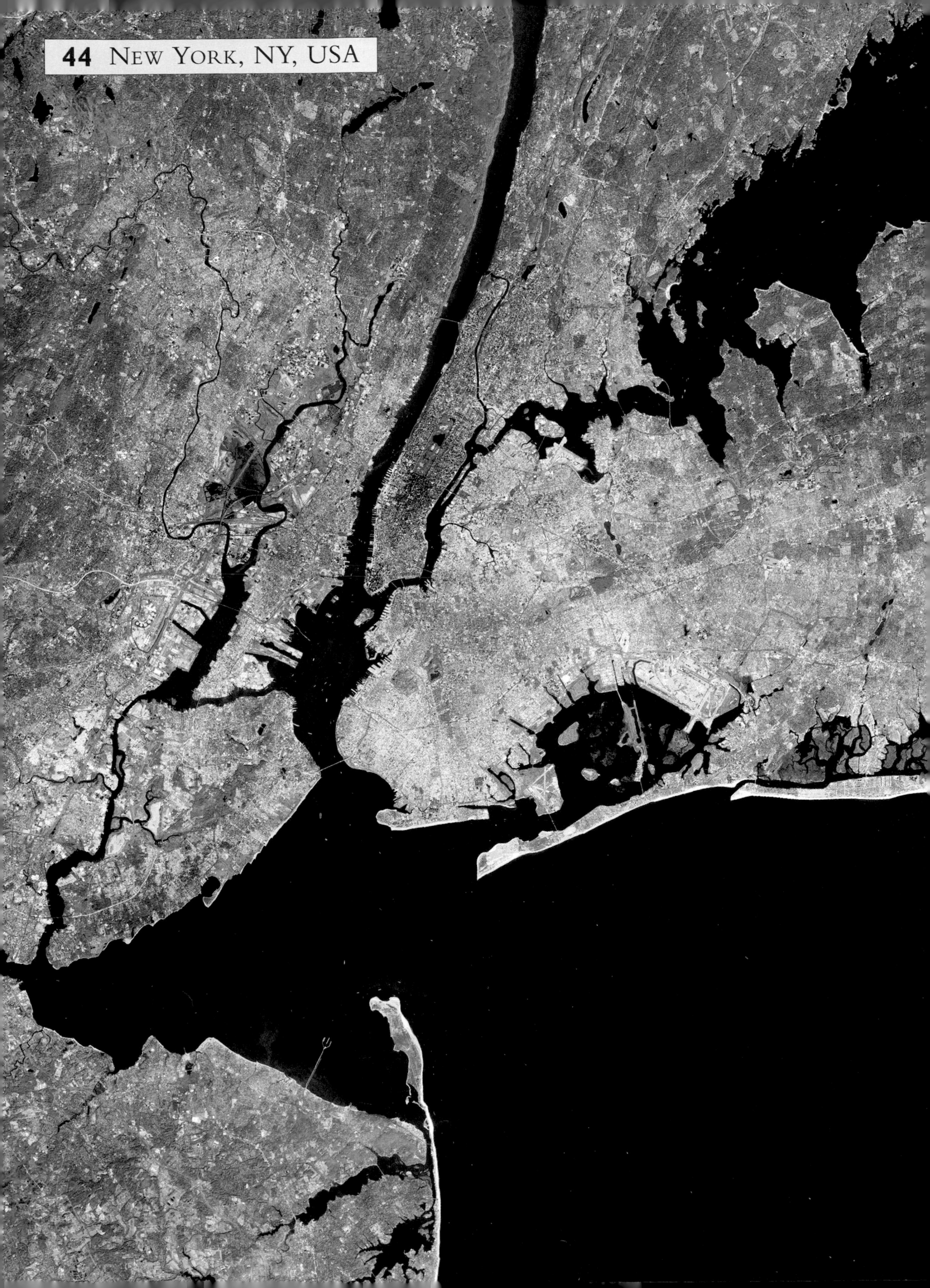

WORLD MAPS

SETTLEMENTS

■ PARIS   ▣ Berne   ◉ Livorno   ◉ Brugge   ◉ Algeciras   ○ Frejus   ○ Oberammergau   ○ Thira

Settlement symbols and type styles vary according to the scale of each map and indicate the importance
of towns on the map rather than specific population figures

∴ Ruins or Archæological Sites   ᴗ Wells in Desert

ADMINISTRATION

——— International Boundaries

− − − International Boundaries
(Undefined or Disputed)

·········· Internal Boundaries

National Parks

Country Names
NICARAGUA

Administrative
Area Names

KENT

CALABRIA

International boundaries show the *de facto* situation where there are rival claims to territory

COMMUNICATIONS

——— Principal Roads

——— Other Roads

⇥---⇤ Road Tunnels

≍ Passes

⊕ Airfields

——— Principal Railways

− − − Railways
Under Construction

——— Other Railways

⊣---⊢ Railway Tunnels

············ Principal Canals

PHYSICAL FEATURES

~~~ Perrenial Streams

- ~ - Intermittent Streams

⬭ Perennial Lakes

Intermittent Lakes

Swamps and Marshes

Permanent Ice
and Glaciers

▲ 8848   Elevations in metres

▼ 8500   Sea Depths in metres

1134   Height of Lake Surface
Above Sea Level in metres

ELEVATION AND DEPTH TINTS

Height of Land above Sea Level

in feet		6000	4000	3000	2000	1500	1000	400	200	0
in metres		18 000	12 000	9000	6000	4500	3000	1200	600	

Land Below Sea Level   Depth of Sea

	6000	12 000	15 000	18 000	24 000	in feet
0	200	2000	4000	5000	6000	8000	in metres

Some of the maps have different contours to highlight and clarify the principal relief features

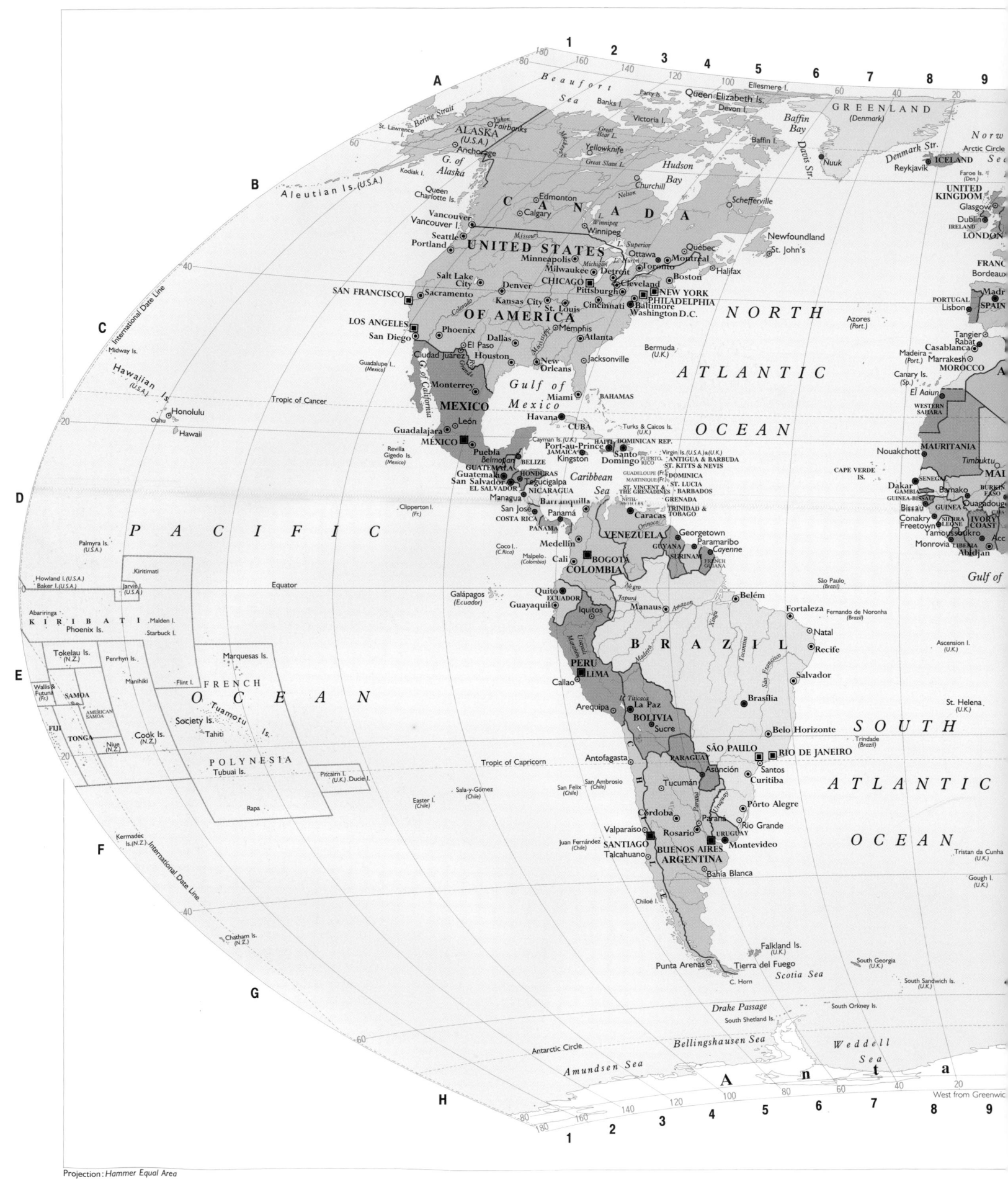

UNITED STATES OF AMERICA
CANADA
MEXICO
BRAZIL
ARGENTINA
NORTH ATLANTIC OCEAN
SOUTH ATLANTIC OCEAN
PACIFIC OCEAN
FRENCH POLYNESIA
GREENLAND (Denmark)
ALASKA (U.S.A.)
Hudson Bay
Gulf of Mexico
Caribbean Sea
Tropic of Cancer
Equator
Tropic of Capricorn
Antarctic Circle
International Date Line
Drake Passage
Bellingshausen Sea
Amundsen Sea
Weddell Sea
Scotia Sea
West from Greenwich

Projection: *Hammer Equal Area*

ARCTIC OCEAN

10 11 12 13 14 15 16 17 18

40 20 60 80 100 120 140 160 80 **A**

Svalbard
(Nor.)

Novaya
Zemlya
Severnaya
Zemlya

New Siberian Is.
Laptev Sea   East Siberian
Sea   Wrangel I.

an   Barents   Kara
Sea   Sea   Norilsk   Verkhoyansk   Arctic Circle

Murmansk   Yenisey   Lena   Magadan   Bering
Arkhangelsk   Salekhard   Yakutsk   Sea   60 **B**

NORWAY   FINLAND   R U S S I A   Okhotsk   Petropavlovsk-
SWEDEN   Helsinki   Sea of   Kamchatskiy
Oslo   ST. PETERSBURG   Perm   Yekaterinburg   Tomsk   Krasnoyarsk   Okhotsk   International
Stockholm   EST.   Kazan   Omsk   Novosibirsk   Irkutsk   Sakhalin   Date Line
Copenhagen   LATVIA   MOSCOW   Volga   Chelyabinsk   L. Baikal   Ulan Ude   Komsomolsk   Kuril
DENMARK   LITH.   Astana   Barnaul   Amur   Khabarovsk   Is.   40 **C**
mburg   Minsk   Saratov   KAZAKSTAN   Ulan Bator   Harbin   Vladivostok   Sapporo
Berlin   BELARUS   Qaraghandy   MONGOLIA   Changchun   NORTH   P A C I F I C
Brussels   POLAND   UKRAINE   Astrakhan   L. Balkhash   SHENYANG   KOREA   P'yongyang
Prague   Warsaw   Volgograd   Aral   Almaty   BEIJING   TIANJIN   Dalian   SEOUL   JAPAN
GERMANY   Kiev   Sea   Bishkek   KYRGYZSTAN   SOUTH   TŌKYŌ   OCEAN
PARIS   LUX.   Budapest   Caspian   UZBEKISTAN   Ürümqi   C H I N A   Lanzhou   Taiyuan   KOREA   Osaka
Vienna   AUSTRIA   ROMANIA   Tbilisi   GEORGIA   Samarqand   Ashgabat   TAJIKISTAN   Xi'an   Nanjing   Kitakyūshu
Milan   Bucharest   Baku   ARM.   AZER.   TURKMENISTAN   Dushanbe   Hwang-ho   SHANGHAI
Marseilles   BULGARIA   Black   Tabriz   Kābul   Chengdu   Wuhan   East China
Rome   ITALY   Sofia   Sea   Yerevan   Mashhad   AFGHANISTAN   Islamabad   TIBET   CHONGQING   Sea
Barcelona   Belgrade   Istanbul   Ankara   Baghdad   Eşfahān   Lahore   Lhasa   Fuzhou   **C**
Naples   YUG.   GREECE   TURKEY   Izmir   SYRIA   TEHRĀN   New Delhi   Kunming   GUANGZHOU   Taipei
Algiers   Sardinia   ALB.   Athens   CYPRUS   Beirut   Damascus   IRAQ   I R A N   Shīrāz   PAKISTAN   DELHI   NEPAL   Katmandu   BHU.   Tropic of Cancer
Tunis   MALTA   LEB.   ISR.   Amman   KUWAIT   The   Kanpur   Ganges   BANGLA.   Hanoi   HONG KONG
TUNISIA   Crete   Mediterranean   Jerusalem   JORDAN   Gulf   Abu Dhabi   I N D I A   DACCA   BURMA   Hainan   South
LIBYA   Sea   Benghazi   Alexandria   CAIRO   BAHRAIN   QATAR   Karachi   Ahmadabad   KOLKATA   MYANMAR   China   20 **D**
ERIA   CAIRO   Riyadh   Abu Dhabi   Arabian   (Calcutta)   Rangoon   Sea
EGYPT   Aswân   SAUDI   OMAN   Sea   Nagpur   MUMBAI   Bay of   THAILAND   VIET-   MANILA
NIGER   Mecca   ARABIA   Muscat   (Bombay)   Bengal   BANGKOK   NAM   PHILIPPINES
Niamey   Omdurmân   Amara   Red   YEMEN   Hyderabad   Phnom   Ho Chi Minh   FEDERATED STATES
CHAD   Khartoum   ERITREA   Sea   Aden   Socotra   Andaman Is.   CAMBODIA   Penh   City
NIGERIA   Kano   L. Chad   SUDAN   G. of Aden   (Yemen)   Bangalore   CHENNAI   (India)   MALAYSIA   PALAU   Caroline Is.   MARSHALL IS.   **D**
Abuja   Ndjamena   DJIBOUTI   (Madras)   SRI LANKA   Nicobar Is.   Kuala Lumpur   Yap   Truk   Pohnpei
Ibadan   CENTRAL   Addis Ababa   SOMALI   MALDIVES   Colombo   (India)   PEN. MALAYSIA   BRUNEI   OF MICRONESIA
Lagos   CAMEROON   AFRICAN   ETHIOPIA   REP.   Lakshadweep Is.   Medan   SABAH   SINGAPORE   Gilbert Is.
Douala   REP.   (India)   Sumatra   Borneo   NAURU   KIRIBATI
EQUATORIAL   Yaoundé   Bangui   UGANDA   Equator   I N D O N E S I A   IRIAN   **E**
GUINEA   Libreville   Kisangani   Kampala   KENYA   Palembang   Banjarmasin   JAYA   New
SÃO TOMÉ   GABON   Victoria   Nairobi   SEYCHELLES   Chagos Arch.   JAKARTA   Ujung Pandang   PAPUA   Ireland
& PRÍNCIPE   CONGO   CONGO   Kigali   RWANDA   (U.K.)   Bandung   Java   Surabaya   NEW   New   SOLOMON
Brazzaville   DEM. REP. OF THE   Zaïre   BURUNDI   Diego Garcia   Timor   GUINEA   Britain   IS.   TUVALU
CABINDA   Kinshasa   Bujumbura   L. Turkana   Amirante   Aldabra Is.   Agalega Is.   EAST   Port   C. York   Santa Cruz I.
(Angola)   Kananga   Dodoma   Is.   (Fr.)   TIMOR   Moresby
Luanda   Mombasa   Zanzibar   Cargados Carajos   Arafura Sea   **E**
TANZANIA   Dar es Salaam   COMOROS   Christmas I.   NEW   Darwin   VANUATU
ANGOLA   Lubumbashi   L. Tanganyika   Mayotte   Cocos Is.   (Austral.)   CALEDONIA   FIJI
Benguela   (Fr.)   (Austral.)   (Fr.)   Suva
Malawi   MADAGASCAR   Rodriguez   Cairns   20
ZAMBIA   Lilongwe   MAURITIUS   Port Hedland   Townsville   **F**
Lusaka   MALAWI   Antananarivo   RÉUNION (Fr.)   Alice Springs
NAMIBIA   Harare   Channel   Tropic of Capricorn   A U S T R A L I A   Rockhampton
ZIMBABWE   MOZAMBIQUE   Geraldton   Brisbane
Windhoek   Bulawayo   Mozambique   Amsterdam I.   Lord Howe I.   **F**
BOTSWANA   Pretoria   (Fr.)   Kalgoorlie-   (Austral.)
Gaborone   Johannesburg   St. Paul (Fr.)   Perth   Boulder   Newcastle   Norfolk I.
SOUTH   SWAZILAND   Fremantle   Great   Adelaide   Sydney   (Austral.)
Cape Town   AFRICA   LESOTHO   Durban   Australian   Darling   Canberra   Auckland
C. of Good Hope   Port Elizabeth   Bight   Melbourne   Tasman   North I.
Prince Edward Is.   Crozet Is.   Tasmania   Sea   NEW   40
(S. Africa)   (Fr.)   Kerguelen   ZEALAND   **G**
(Fr.)   Hobart   Wellington
McDonald Is.   Heard I.   South I.   Christchurch
Bouvet I.   (Austral.)   (Austral.)   Stewart I.   Dunedin
(Nor.)   S O U T H E R N   O C E A N   Campbell I.   Macquarie I.   Bounty Is.   (N.Z.)
(Austral.)   (Austral.)   Antipodes Is.   (N.Z.)
Auckland Is. (N.Z.)   **G**

c   t   i   c   a   Ross Sea   **H**
20   40   60   80   100   120   140   160   180   80
Antarctic Circle

East from Greenwich

10   11   12   13   14   15   16   17   18
60

Hanoi ● Capital Cities

100 0 200 400 600 800 1000 1200 1400 km
100 0 200 400 600 800 1000 miles

ft m
12 000 4000
6000 2000
4500 1500
3000 1000
1200 400
600 200
0 0
500 1500
1000 3000
2000 6000
3000 9000
4000 12 000
5000 15 000
m ft

Maximum extent of sea ice

Summer extent of sea ice

Ice caps and permanent ice shelf

PACIFIC OCEAN

ATLANTIC OCEAN

ARCTIC OCEAN

Bering Sea

Sea of Okhotsk

Beaufort Sea

Chukchi Sea

Laptev Sea

Kara Sea

Barents Sea

Greenland Sea

Norwegian Sea

North Sea

Baltic Sea

Black Sea

Hudson Bay

Baffin Bay

Davis Str.

Labrador

NORTH AMERICA

CANADA

GREENLAND (KALAALLIT NUNAAT) (Denmark)

ICELAND

UNITED KINGDOM

IRELAND

NORWAY

SWEDEN

FINLAND

DENMARK

GERMANY

POLAND

RUSSIA

ASIA

JAPAN

Hokkaidō

Sakhalin (Russia)

Kurilskiye Ostrova (Russia)

Svalbard (Norway)

Novaya Zemlya

Ellesmere I. (Canada)

Victoria Island

Banks I.

Mid-Atlantic Ridge

Lomonosov Ridge

Alpha Cordillera

Mendeleyev Ridge

Makarov Basin

Fram Basin

Nansen Basin

Canada Basin

Arctic Circle

NORTH POLE

North Magnetic Pole 1995

ANCHORAGE

MOSKVA

ST. PETERBURG

STOCKHOLM

HELSINKI

OSLO

LONDON

DUBLIN

KØBENHAVN

HAMBURG

BERLIN

WARSZAWA

AMSTERDAM

PRAHA

YEKATERINBURG

PERM

UFA

SAMARA

SARATOV

VOLGOGRAD

ROSTOV

ODESA

KYIV

VILNIUS

RIGA

TALLINN

MINSK

MURMANSK

ARKHANGELSK

KHABAROVSK

YAKUTSK

PETROPAVLOVSK-KAMCHATSKIY

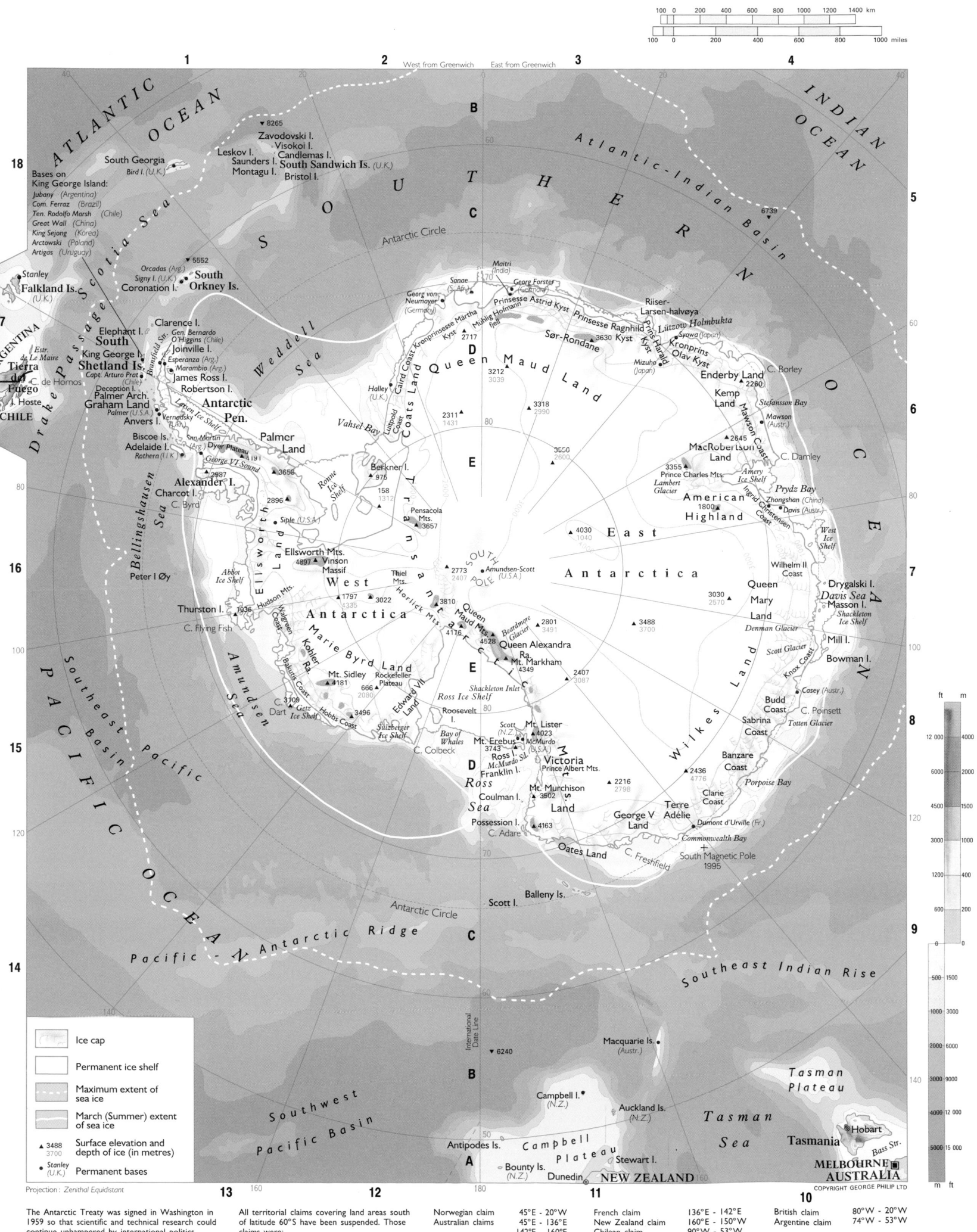

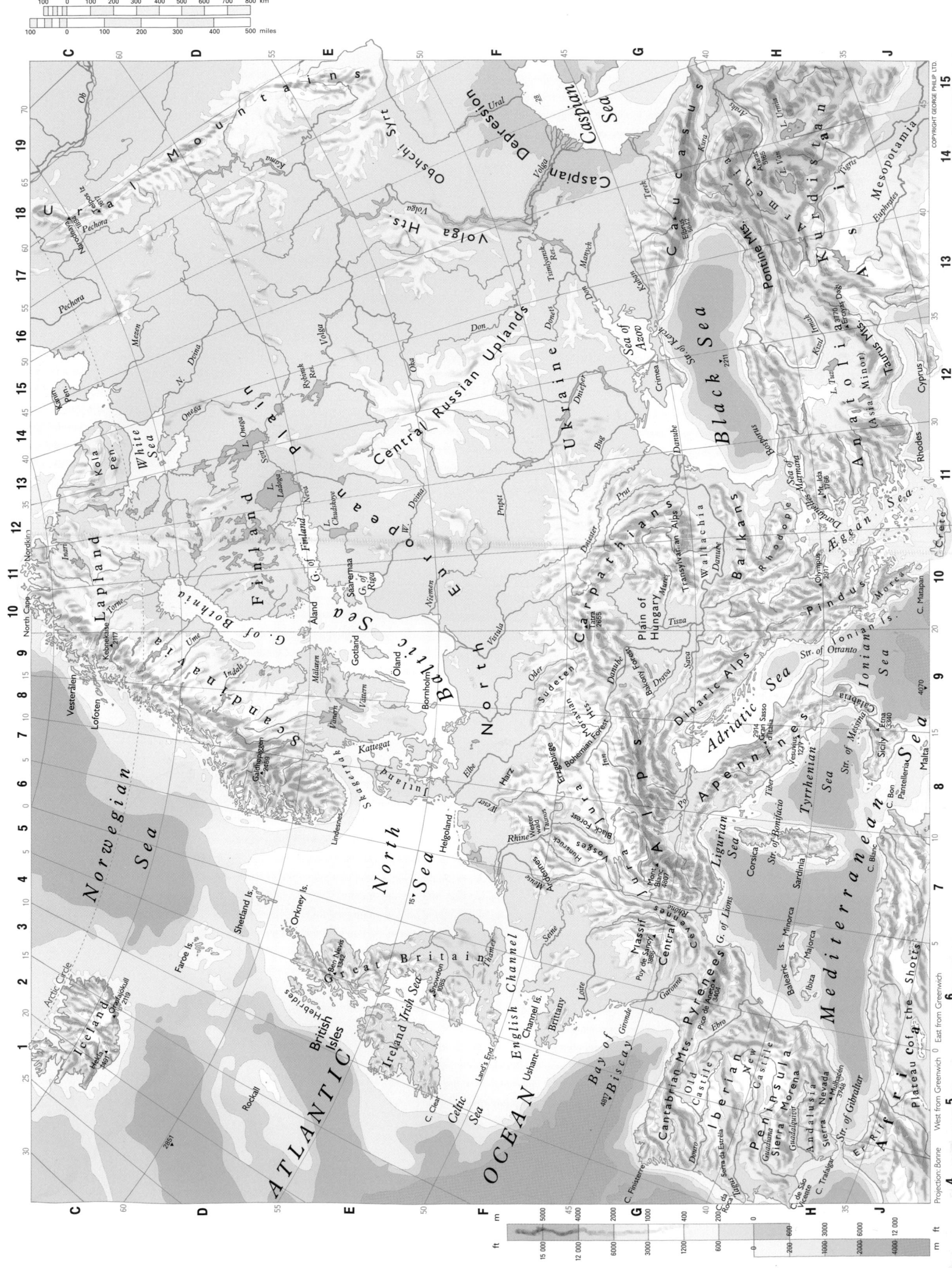

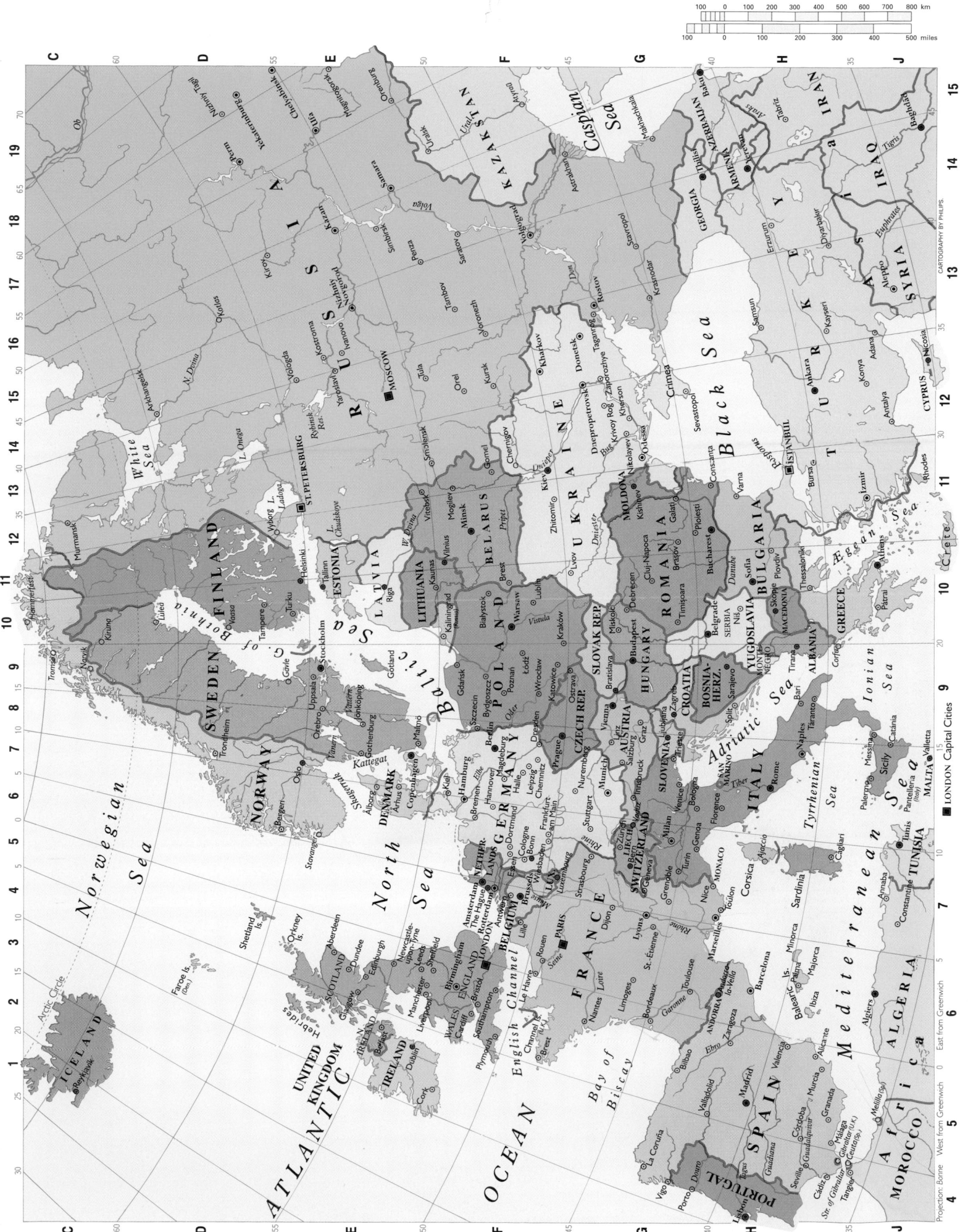

100 0 100 200 300 400 500 600 700 800 km

100 0 100 200 300 400 500 miles

CARTOGRAPHY BY PHILIP'S

■ LONDON Capital Cities

Projection: Bonne   West from Greenwich   0   East from Greenwich

SCANDINAVIA 1:5 000 000

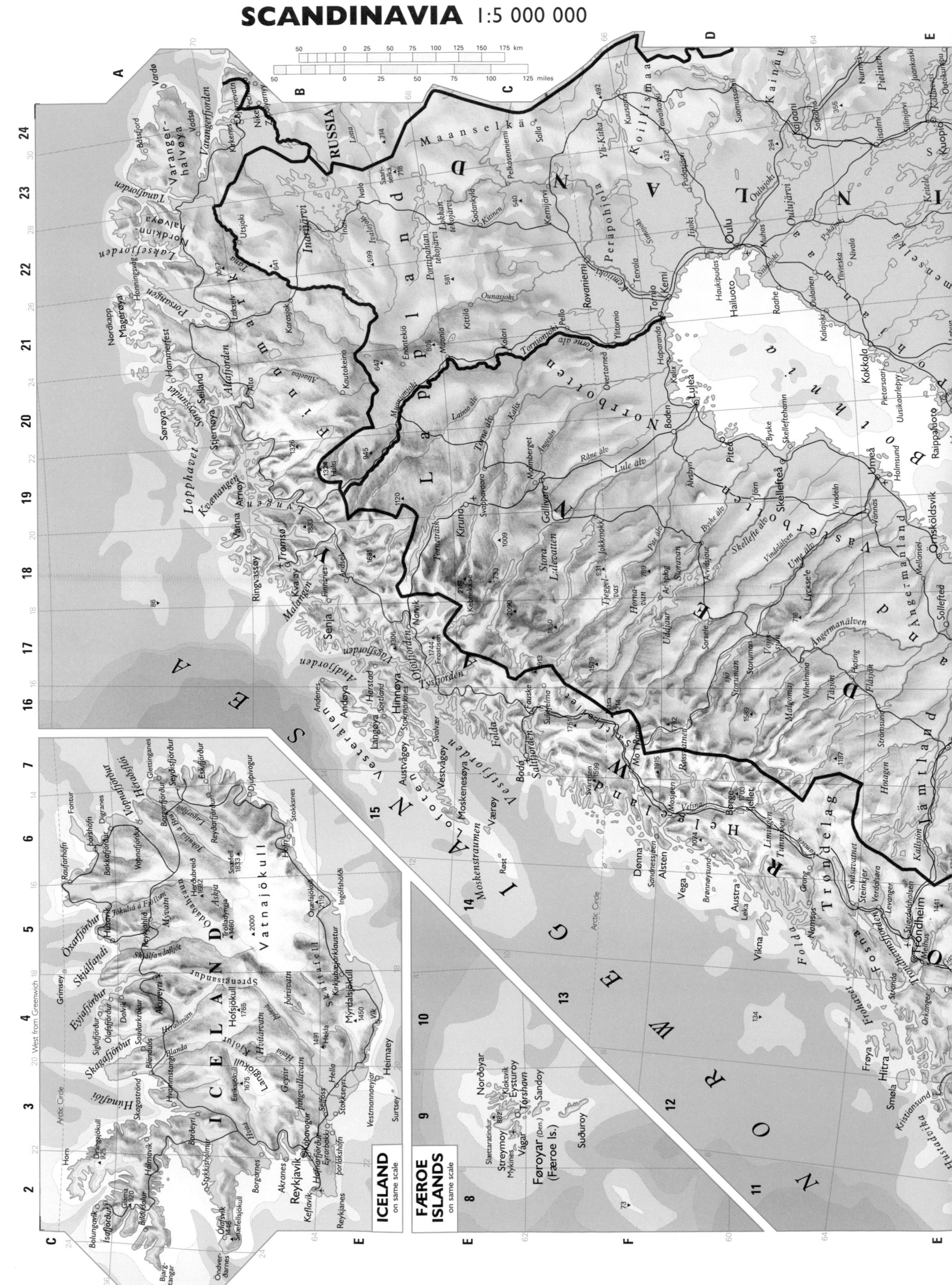

0 25 50 75 100 125 150 175 km
0 25 50 75 100 125 miles
RUSSIA
ICELAND
on same scale
FÆROE ISLANDS
on same scale
Færoyar (Den.)
(Færoe Is.)
Vatnajökull
Hofsjökull
Langjökull
Reykjavík
Akureyri
Heimaey
Surtsey
Tórshavn
Streymoy
Eysturoy
Vágar
Sandoy
Suðuroy
Norðoyar
Nordkapp
Magerøya
Hammerfest
Tromsø
Narvik
Bodø
Lofoten
Vesterålen
Senja
Finnmark
Varangerhalvøya
Trondheim
Trøndelag
Jämtland
Norrbotten
Lappland
Kiruna
Gällivare
Luleå
Umeå
Skellefteå
Piteå
Kemi
Tornio
Oulu
Rovaniemi
Kokkola
Hitra
Frøya
NORWEGIAN SEA
Arctic Circle
West from Greenwich

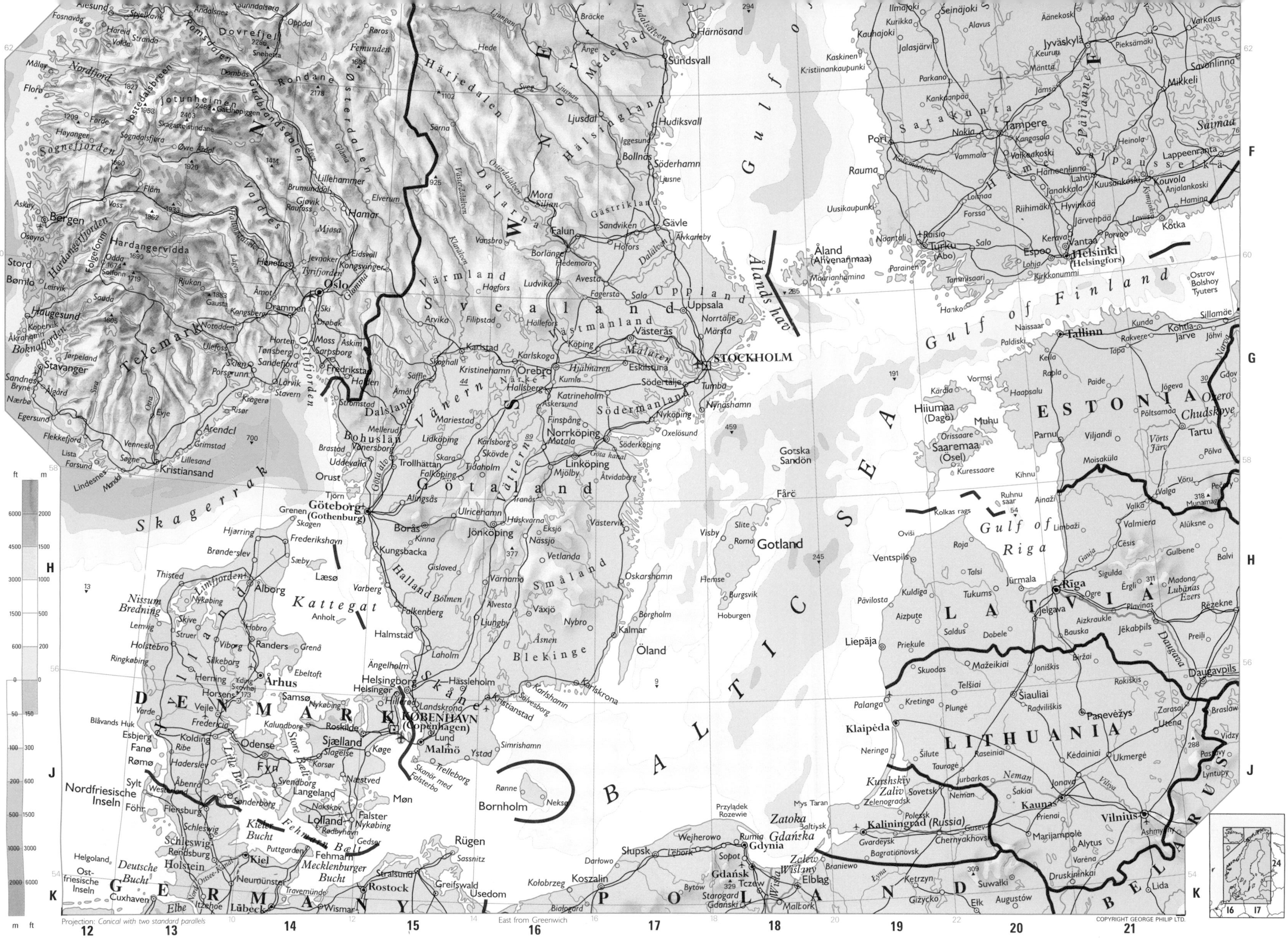

Scandinavia and the Baltic (map)

NORWAY

SWEDEN

FINLAND

ESTONIA

LATVIA

LITHUANIA

DENMARK

GERMANY

POLAND

BALTIC SEA

Gulf of Finland

Gulf of Bothnia

Gulf of Riga

Skagerrak

Kattegat

Ålands hav

STOCKHOLM

Helsinki (Helsingfors)

Tallinn

Riga

Vilnius

Oslo

KØBENHAVN (Copenhagen)

Göteborg (Gothenburg)

Malmö

Bergen

Stavanger

Gotland

Öland

Bornholm

Rügen

Åland (Ahvenanmaa)

Hiiumaa (Dagö)

Saaremaa (Ösel)

East from Greenwich

Projection: Conical with two standard parallels

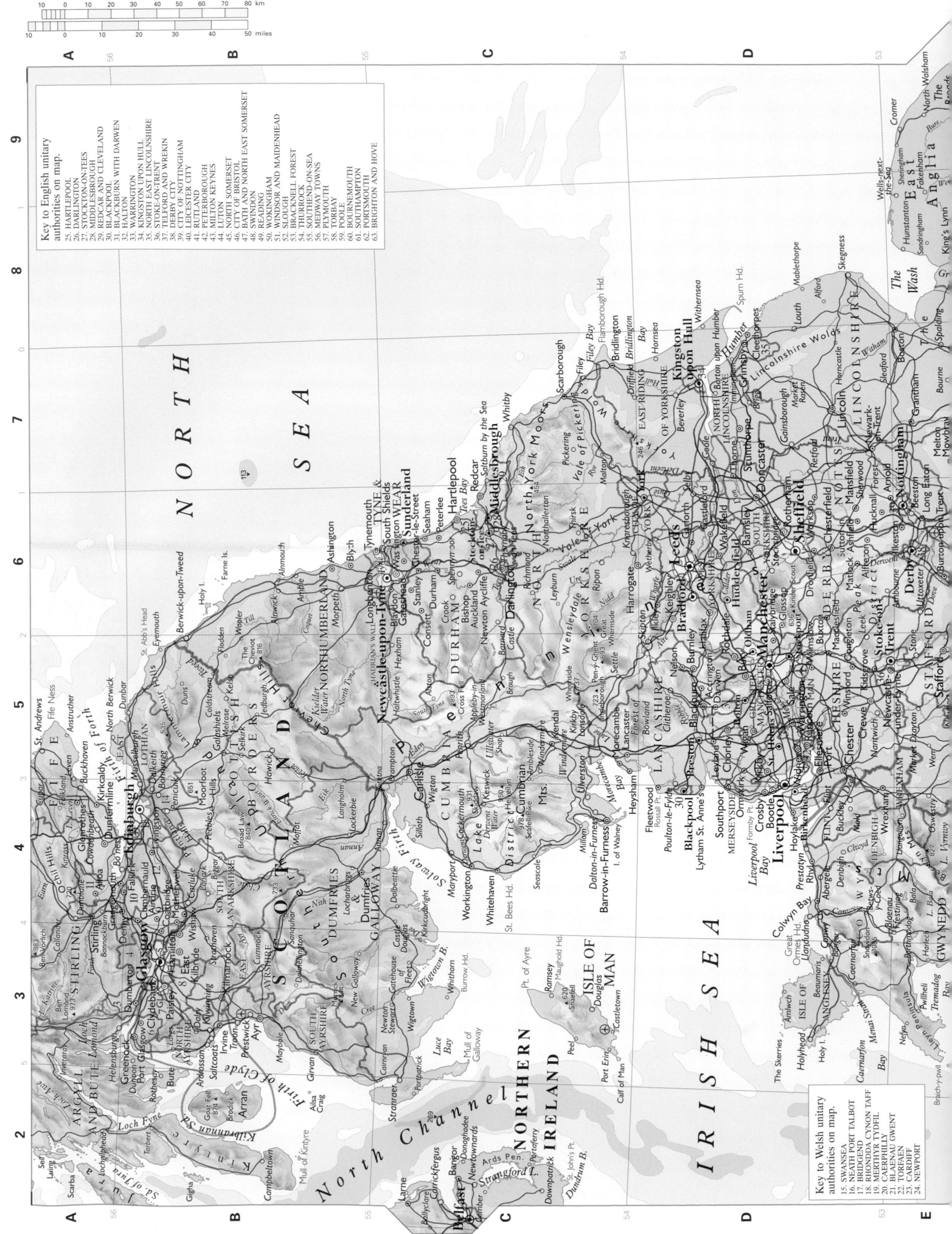

Key to English unitary authorities on map.

25. HARTLEPOOL
26. DARLINGTON
27. STOCKTON-ON-TEES
28. MIDDLESBROUGH
29. REDCAR AND CLEVELAND
30. BLACKPOOL
31. BLACKBURN WITH DARWEN
32. HALTON
33. WARRINGTON
34. KINGSTON UPON HULL
35. NORTH EAST LINCOLNSHIRE
36. NORTH LINCOLNSHIRE
37. STOKE-ON-TRENT
38. TELFORD AND WREKIN
39. DERBY CITY
40. CITY OF NOTTINGHAM
41. LEICESTER CITY
42. RUTLAND
43. PETERBOROUGH
44. MILTON KEYNES
45. LUTON
46. NORTH SOMERSET
47. CITY OF BRISTOL
48. BATH AND NORTH EAST SOMERSET
49. SWINDON
50. READING
51. WOKINGHAM
52. WINDSOR AND MAIDENHEAD
53. SLOUGH
54. BRACKNELL FOREST
55. THURROCK
56. SOUTHEND-ON-SEA
57. MEDWAY TOWNS
58. PLYMOUTH
59. TORBAY
60. POOLE
61. BOURNEMOUTH
62. SOUTHAMPTON
63. PORTSMOUTH
64. BRIGHTON AND HOVE

Key to Welsh unitary authorities on map.

15. SWANSEA
16. NEATH PORT TALBOT
17. BRIDGEND
18. RHONDDA CYNON TAFF
19. MERTHYR TYDFIL
20. CAERPHILLY
21. BLAENAU GWENT
22. TORFAEN
23. CARDIFF
24. NEWPORT

ENGLAND

WALES

FRANCE

NORMANDIE

HAUTE-NORMANDIE

MANCHE

CALVADOS

ENGLISH CHANNEL

Strait of Dover

Bristol Channel

Cardigan Bay

Baie de la Seine

Baie de la Somme

CHANNEL ISLANDS (UK)

ISLE OF WIGHT

Jersey   St. Helier

Guernsey   St. Peter Port

Alderney   Sark   Herm

London

Birmingham

Bristol

Cardiff   Swansea

Portsmouth   Southampton

Bournemouth   Brighton   Hove

Plymouth   Exeter

Le Havre   Rouen   Caen   Cherbourg

Isles of Scilly
On same scale

Projection: Lambert's Conformal Conic

COPYRIGHT GEORGE PHILIP LTD.

West from Greenwich   East from Greenwich

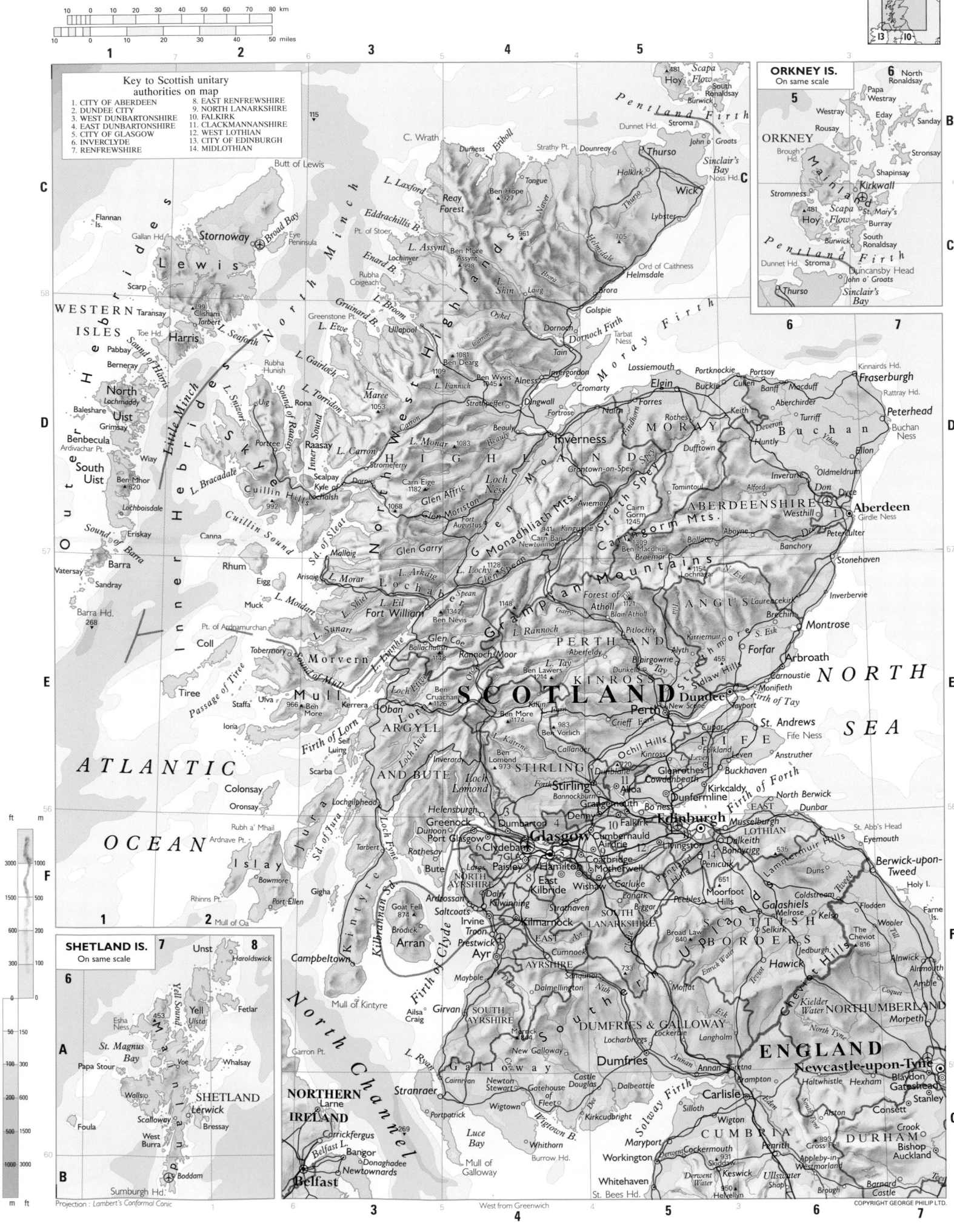

Key to Scottish unitary authorities on map
1. CITY OF ABERDEEN
2. DUNDEE CITY
3. WEST DUNBARTONSHIRE
4. EAST DUNBARTONSHIRE
5. CITY OF GLASGOW
6. INVERCLYDE
7. RENFREWSHIRE
8. EAST RENFREWSHIRE
9. NORTH LANARKSHIRE
10. FALKIRK
11. CLACKMANNANSHIRE
12. WEST LOTHIAN
13. CITY OF EDINBURGH
14. MIDLOTHIAN

ORKNEY IS.
On same scale

SHETLAND IS.
On same scale

SCOTLAND

ENGLAND

NORTH SEA

ATLANTIC OCEAN

Projection : Lambert's Conformal Conic

West from Greenwich

COPYRIGHT GEORGE PHILIP LTD.

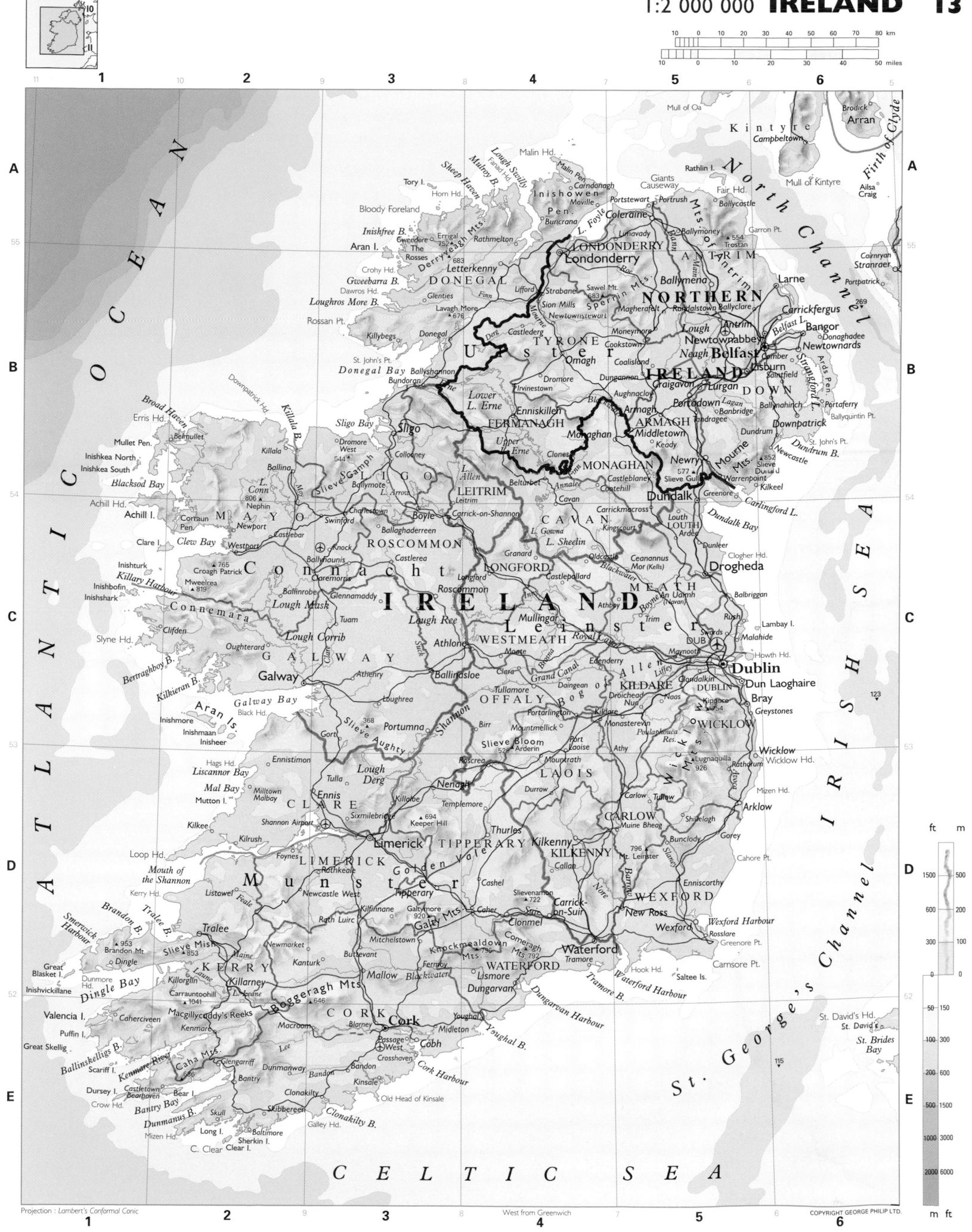

Projection : Lambert's Conformal Conic

West from Greenwich

ATLANTIC OCEAN
NORTH SEA
CELTIC SEA
IRISH SEA
English Channel
Shetland Is.
Orkney Is.
Outer Hebrides
Inner Hebrides
SCOTLAND
Grampian Mts.
North West Highlands
Southern Uplands
NORTHERN IRELAND
UNITED KINGDOM
IRELAND
ENGLAND
WALES
Pennines
Cambrian Mts.
Cardigan Bay
Bristol Channel
St. George's Channel
North Channel
Moray Firth
Pentland Firth
Str. of Dover
Channel Is. (U.K.)
NORWAY
NETHERLANDS
BELGIUM
FRANCE
Aberdeen
Dundee
Edinburgh
Glasgow
Belfast
Dublin
Cork
Limerick
Newcastle-upon-Tyne
Leeds
Manchester
Liverpool
Sheffield
BIRMINGHAM
LONDON
Bristol
Cardiff
Southampton
Plymouth
Kingston upon Hull
Middlesbrough
Sunderland
Bergen
Stavanger
Projection: Conical with two standard parallels
East from Greenwich
West from Greenwich
COPYRIGHT GEORGE PHILIP LTD.

10 0 10 20 30 40 50 60 70 80 90 km
10 0 10 20 30 40 50 60 miles

NORTH SEA

UNITED KINGDOM

Helgoland · Düne
Ostfriesische Inseln · Wangerooge · Spiekeroog · Langeoog · Baltrum · Norderney · Juist · Borkum
Scharhörn · Neuwerk · Alte Mellum · Minsen

Cromer · North Walsham · The Broads · Norwich · Great Yarmouth · Bungay · Beccles · Lowestoft · Southwold · Saxmundham · Aldeburgh · Woodbridge · Orford Ness · Felixstowe

Waddeneilanden · Schiermonnikoog · Ameland · Terschelling · West-Terschelling · Vlieland · Texel · Den Burg · Den Helder

Rottumeroog · Borkum · Norddeich · Norden · Esens · Aurich · Wittmund · Schortens · Wilhelmshaven · Emden · Ostfriesland · Leer · Weener · Papenburg · Aschendorf · Oldenburg · Hude · Varel · Rastede · Westerstede · Wiesmoor · Moormerland · Bad Zwischenahn

WESER-EMS · Cloppenburg · Garrel · Sögel · Löningen · Meppen · Haselünne · Quakenbrück · Vechta · Lohne · Bramsche · Osnabrück

Leeuwarden · Franeker · Harlingen · Bolsward · Sneek · Dokkum · Kollum · Zoutkamp · Bedum · Uithuizen · Groningen · Hoogezand-Sappemeer · Veendam · Stadskanaal · Ter Apel · Assen · Emmen · Hoogeveen · Meppel · Steenwijk

FRIESLAND · DRENTHE · NEDERLAND · NETHERLANDS

Schagen · Medemblik · Enkhuizen · Hoorn · Alkmaar · Heerhugowaard · Bergen · Castricum · IJmuiden · Zandvoort · Haarlem · Hillegom · Noordwijk · Katwijk · Leiden

HOLLAND · Amsterdam · Purmerend · Edam · Zaanstad · Bussum · Hilversum · Almere-Stad · Lelystad · FLEVOLAND · Dronten · Kampen · Zwolle · OVERIJSSEL · Raalte · Almelo · Nordhorn · Rheine

Utrecht · Zeist · Amersfoort · Barneveld · Apeldoorn · Deventer · Zutphen · Hengelo · Enschede · GELDERLAND

's-Gravenhage (Den Haag) · Delft · Zoetermeer · Gouda · Alphen a/d Rijn · Veenendaal · Ede · Arnhem · Doesburg · Winterswijk

Vlaardingen · Rotterdam · Schiedam · Gorinchem · Nijmegen · Kleve · NORDRHEIN

Europoort · Dordrecht · Waalwijk · 's-Hertogenbosch · Oss · Boxtel · Uden · Wesel

ZEELAND · Noord-beveland · Middelburg · Goes · Vlissingen · Oosterhout · Breda · Tilburg · Eindhoven · Helmond · Venray

Schouwen · Oosterschelde · Bergen op Zoom · Roosendaal · NOORD BRABANT · Venlo

Knokke-Heist · Zeebrugge · Blankenberge · De Haan · Oostende · Nieuwpoort · Brugge · Gent (Gand) · Eeklo · Sint-Niklaas · Antwerpen · ANTWERPEN

BELGIUM

Dunkerque · St-Pol-sur-Mer · Gravelines · Calais · Sangatte · Wissant · C. Gris Nez · Boulogne-sur-Mer · Étaples · Montreuil · Berck

Margate · North Foreland · Ramsgate · Deal · Dover

NORD · Lille · Roubaix · Tourcoing · Mouscron · Armentières · Béthune · Lens · Douai · Valenciennes · Maubeuge · PAS-DE-CALAIS · Arras · Cambrai

Mechelen · Leuven · Brussel Bruxelles · Aalst · Hasselt · Maastricht · Tongeren · LIMBURG · Aachen · Verviers · Liège · Namur · Charleroi · Mons · La Louvière

Roermond · Mönchengladbach · Krefeld · Duisburg · Essen · Oberhausen · Bochum · Dortmund · Düsseldorf · Wuppertal · Solingen · Remscheid · Köln · Bonn · WESTFALEN · NORDRHEIN · Münster · Hamm

FRANCE

Amiens · SOMME · Péronne · St-Quentin · Compiègne · Beauvais · OISE · Laon · AISNE · Soissons · Reims · MARNE · Châlons-en-Champagne · Épernay

PICARDIE · ARDENNES · Charleville-Mézières · Sedan · Bouillon · LUXEMBOURG · Bastogne · Arlon

Dinant · Marche-en-Famenne · La Roche-en-Ardenne · St-Hubert · Neufchâteau · RHEINLAND-PFALZ · Bitburg · Prüm · Wittlich · Bernkastel-Kues · Trier · Koblenz · Bad Ems · Wiesbaden · Mainz

LUXEMBOURG · Luxembourg · Mersch · Echternach · Grevenmacher · Ettelbruck

GERMANY · SAARLAND · Saarbrücken · Saarlouis · St. Wendel · Homburg · Neunkirchen · Kaiserslautern · Zweibrücken · Pirmasens · Landau

Metz · MOSELLE · Thionville · Verdun · MEUSE · Nancy · MEURTHE-ET-MOSELLE · LORRAINE · Toul · Commercy · St-Dizier · Bar-le-Duc

Strasbourg · BAS-RHIN · Haguenau · Wissembourg · Saverne · Sarrebourg

Paris · Versailles · YVELINES · SEINE-ET-MARNE · Meaux · Provins

Projection : Lambert's Conformal Conic

East from Greenwich

COPYRIGHT GEORGE PHILIP LTD.

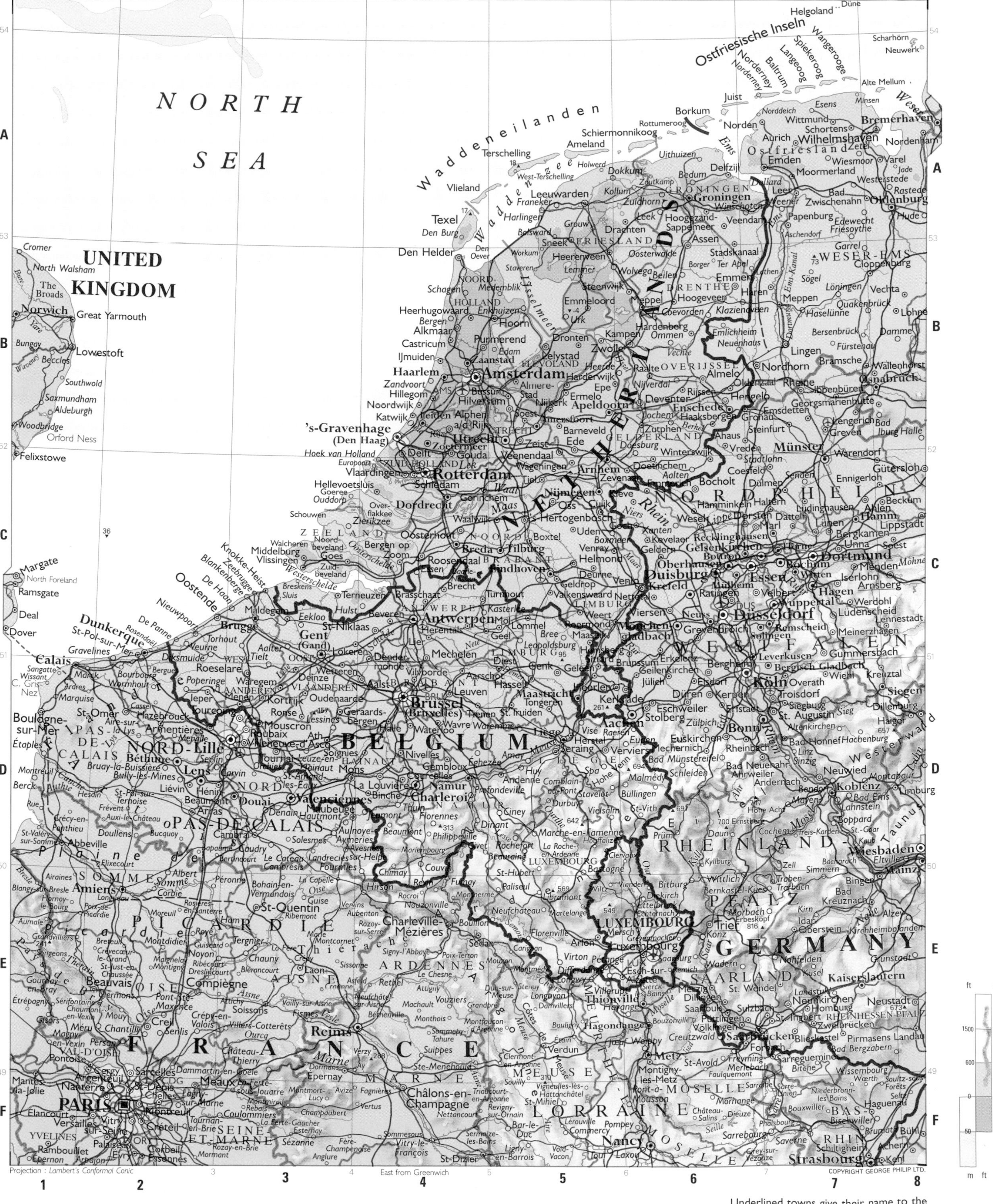

Underlined towns give their name to the administrative area in which they stand.

ft m
1500 · 500
600 · 200
0 · 0
50
m ft

NORTH SEA
BALTIC SEA
DENMARK
UNITED KINGDOM
NETHERLANDS
BELGIUM
LUXEMBOURG
GERMANY
FRANCE
SWITZERLAND
LIECHTENSTEIN
AUSTRIA
ITALY
SLOVENIA
CZECH
MONACO
SAN MARINO
ADRIATIC SEA
Golfo di Venézia
Golfo di Génova
AMSTERDAM
's-Gravenhage (Den Haag)
ROTTERDAM
BRUSSEL (Bruxelles)
LUXEMBOURG
PARIS
BERLIN
HAMBURG
MÜNCHEN (Munich)
PRAHA (Prague)
MILANO
TORINO (Turin)
LYON
MARSEILLE
Ljubljana
Zürich
Bern
Wien
Nordfriesische Inseln
Ostfriesische Inseln
Mecklenburger Bucht
Kieler Bucht
Fehmarn Bælt
Niedersachsen
Nordrhein-Westfalen
Brandenburg
Mecklenburg
Sachsen-Anhalt
Sachsen
Hessen
Thüringer Wald
Rheinland-Pfalz
Baden-Württemberg
Schwäbische Alb
Bayern
Erzgebirge
Böhmerwald
Tirol
Steiermark
Kärnten
Karnische Alpen
Dolomiti
Lombardia
Piemonte
Liguria
Riviera di Ponente
Riviera di Levante
Karawanken
Istra
Provence
Massif Central
Dauphiné
Lorraine
Alsace
Picardie
Ardennes
Île-de-France
Bourgogne
Franche-Comté
Champagne
Morvan
Nivernais
Lyonnais
Jura
Plateau de Langres
Vosges
Schwarzwald
Projection: Conical with two standard parallels

9 10 11 12 13 14 15 16

Zatoka Gdańska
Kaliningrad (Russia)
Vilnius
LITHUANIA
Wejherowo
Rumia
Gdynia
Sopot
Gdańsk
Tczew
Elbląg
Zalew Wiślany
Baltiysk
Gvardeysk
Chernyakhovsk
Gusev
Polessk
Bagrationovsk
Braniewo
Marijampolė
Prienai
Varėna
Druskininkai
Ashmyany
Vileyka
Smarhon
Maladzyechna
Barysaw
Krupki
Shklow
Mstsislaw
Zhodzina
MINSK
Cherven
Mahilyow
Krychaw
Cherykaw
Slawharad
Valozhyn
Dzyarzhynsk
Lida
Navahrudak
Hrodna
BELARUS
Bykhaw
Hrodzyanka
Asipovichy
Babruysk
Rahachow
Zhlobin
Homyel
Dobrush
Stowbtsy
Nyasvizh
Dzyatlava
Masty
Vawkavysk
Slonim
Baranavichy
Slutsk
Klyetsk
Salihorsk
Glusk
Aktsyabrski
Svyetlahorsk
Rechytsa
Lyakhavichy
Hantsavichy
Vasilevichi
Kalinkavichy
Svislach
Ivatsevichy
Pruzhany
Bereza
Tsyelyakhany
Yaselda
Luninyets
Pyetrikaw
Loyew
Khoyniki
Mazyr
Yelsk
Kobryn
Drogichyn
Zhabinka
Ivanava
Pinsk
Davyd Haradok
Brest
Pripet Marshes
Stolin
Malaryta
Ketrzyn
Giżycko
Suwałki
Augustów
Ełk
Olsztyn
Pojezierze Mazurskie
Malbork
Kwidzyn
Starogard Gdański
Bytów
Chojnice
Iława
Ostróda
Szczytno
Sokółka
Białystok
Łomża
Grudziądz
Świecie
Chełmno
Brodnica
Działdowo
Mława
Ostrołęka
Bydgoszcz
Toruń
Rypin
Ciechanów
Ostrów Mazowiecka
Hajnówka
Bielsk Podlaski
Inowrocław
Włocławek
Płock
Pułtusk
Sokołów Podlaski
Gniezno
Września
Legionowo
Mińsk Mazowiecki
WARSZAWA (Warsaw)
Pruszków
Otwock
Siedlce
Biała Podlaska
Kutno
Koło
Konin
Łęczyca
Łowicz
Żyrardów
Skierniewice
Międzyrzec Podlaski
Łuków
Kalisz
Zduńska Wola
Łódź
Pabianice
Grójec
Włodawa
Sieradz
Tomaszów Mazowiecki
Radom
Puławy
Lublin
Chełm
Piotrków Trybunalski
Końskie
Skarżysko-Kamienna
Starachowice
Świdnik
Kraśnik
Wieluń
Radomsko
Kielce
Ostrowiec-Świętokrzyski
Zamość
Wrocław
Kluczbork
Częstochowa
Sandomierz
Stalowa Wola
Opole
Myszków
Jędrzejów
Pińczów
Tarnobrzeg
Mielec
Zawiercie
Tarnowskie Góry
Zabrze
Bytom
Sosnowiec
Katowice
Gliwice
Chorzów
Tychy
Racibórz
Kraków
Oświęcim
Tarnów
Dębica
Rzeszów
Jarosław
Przemyśl
Bielsko-Biała
Bochnia
Jasło
Krosno
Sanok
Nowy Sącz
Żywiec
Nowy Targ
Zakopane
POLAND
Opava
Ostrava
Havířov
Karviná
Frýdek-Místek
Český Těšín
Přerov
Zlín
Brno
Považská Bystrica
Žilina
Martin
Ružomberok
Poprad
Prešov
Bardejov
Humenné
Michalovce
Košice
Trenčín
Prievidza
Banská Bystrica
Nízke Tatry
Vysoké Tatry
Zvolen
Topoľčany
Slovenské Rudohorie
Lučenec
Nitra
Trnava
Bratislava
Levice
Nové Zámky
Komárno
SLOVAK REP.
Vychodné Beskydy
Karpaty
Malé Karpaty
Biele Karpaty
Salgótarján
Miskolc
Ózd
Eger
Gyöngyös
Vác
Hatvan
Mezőkövesd
Nyíregyháza
Hajdúböszörmény
Debrecen
Esztergom
Dunakeszi
Jászberény
Győr
Tatabánya
Érd
BUDAPEST
Cegléd
Karcag
Pápa
Székesfehérvár
Veszprém
Szolnok
Mezőtúr
Szombathely
Ajka
Dunaújváros
Nagykőrös
Kecskemét
Balaton
Siófok
Kiskunfélegyháza
Csongrád
Békéscsaba
Szentes
Gyula
Orosháza
Hódmezővásárhely
Kiskőrös
Kalocsa
Nagykanizsa
Kaposvár
Szekszárd
Kiskunhalas
Szeged
Makó
Baja
Pécs
Mohács
HUNGARY
Sopron
Dunaj
Mosonmagyaróvár
Subotica
Senta
Sombor
Kikinda
Bečej
Vojvodina
Novi Sad
Zrenjanin
Vršac
Osijek
Vukovar
Vinkovci
Slavonski Brod
Petrovaradin
Sremska Mitrovica
Pančevo
Šabac
BEOGRAD (Belgrade)
Smederevo
Požarevac
Bosanska Gradiška
Banja Luka
Doboj
Brčko
Bijeljina
Tuzla
BOSNIA-HERZEGOVINA
Zenica
Travnik
Zepče
Srebrenica
Valjevo
Kragujevac
Jagodina
Čačak
Užice
Kraljevo
Sarajevo
Višegrad
Cincar
YUGOSLAVIA
CROATIA
Virovitica
Drava
Sava
Dunav
Tisa
Lviv (Lvov)
Yavoriv
Mostyska
Horodok
Sambir
Drohobych
Boryslav
Truskavets
Skole
Stryy
Kalush
Dolyna
Bolekhiv
Ivano-Frankivsk
Nadvirna
Kolomyya
Yaremcha
Pechenizhyn
Horodenka
Snyatyn
Chernivtsi
Novoselytsya
Hlyboka
Storozhynets
Khotyn
Uzhhorod
Chop
Mukacheve
Berehove
Khust
Tyachiv
Rakhiv
Yasinya
Vynohradiv
Sátoraljaújhely
Nesterov
Rava-Ruska
Sokal
Chervonohrad
Kamyanka-Buzka
Radekhiv
Brody
Berestechko
Kremenets
Dubno
Rivne
Zdolbuniv
Ostroh
Lutsk
Kivertsi
Olkesandriya
Kovel
Volodymyr-Volynskyy
Rozhyshche
Lyuboml
Novovolynsk
Horokhiv
Dubrovytsya
Kamin-Kashyrskyy
Staryy Chartoriysk
Kostopil
Korets
Olevsk
Belokorovichi
Korosten
Ovruch
Novohrad-Volynskyy
Malyn
Radomyshl
Zhytomyr
Korostyshev
KYYIV (Kiev)
Irpin
Fastiv
Vasylkiv
Shepetivka
Slavuta
Polonne
Izyaslav
Berdychiv
Bila Tserkva
Kozyatyn
Skvyra
Tarashcha
Zolochiv
Ternopil
Zbarazh
Starokonstyantyniv
Khmelnik
Khmelnytskyy
Vinnytsya
Berezhany
Rogatyn
Terebovlya
Hrymayliv
Kopychyntsi
Horodok
Skalat
Buchach
Chortkiv
Skala-Podilska
Kamyanets-Podilskyy
Zalishchyky
Dnister
Bar
Zhmerynka
Tulchyn
Mohyliv-Podilskyy
Vapnyarka
Bershad
Haysyn
Uman
Buh
Tetiyev
Lipovets
Zhashkiv
Haivoron
Balta
Ananyiv
Kotovsk
UKRAINE
Podilska Vysochyna
Chornobyl
Oster
Kyyivske Vdskh.
Desna
Dymer
Pripyat
Slutch
Teterev
Uzh
Dnipro
Ocnița
Lipcani
Yampil
Drochia
Soroca
Edineț
Florești
Rîbnița
Bălți
Fălești
Dubăsari Vdkhr.
Cornești
Orhei
Dubăsari
Ungheni
Chișinău
Tighina
Tiraspol
MOLDOVA
Cimișlia
Leova
Comrat
Basarabeasca
Bilhorod-Dnistrovskyy
Artsyz
Ciadîr-Lunga
Cahul
Tatarbunary
Bolhrad
Kiliya
Izmayil
Reni
Vylkove
Ozero Sasyk
Vulcănești
Sulina
Rozdilna
Nistru
Basarabia
Dorohoi
Rădăuți
Siret
Suceava
Botoșani
Fălticeni
Pașcani
Iași
Roman
Vaslui
Huși
Piatra Neamț
Bacău
Bârlad
Moinești
Onești
Tecuci
Focșani
Galați
Brăila
Tulcea
Babadag
Lacul Razelm
Rîmnicu Sărat
Buzău
Satu Mare
Carei
Baia Mare
Sighetu Marmației
Borșa
Vatra Dornei
Bistrița
Pietrosul
Dej
Zalău
Oradea
Salonta
Cluj-Napoca
Turda
Reghin
Târgu Mureș
Mureș
Odorheiu Secuiesc
Miercurea Ciuc
Munții Bihor
Aiud
Târnăveni
Sighișoara
Mediaș
Sfântu Gheorghe
Alba-Iulia
Brad
Arad
Sânnicolau Mare
Deva
Simeria
Hunedoara
Timișoara
Lugoj
Caransebeș
Reșița
Sibiu
Făgăraș
Brașov
Săcele
Petroșani
Vulcan
Vf. Peleaga
Parângul Mare
Moldoveanu
Vf. Omul
Câmpulung
Câmpina
Curtea de Argeș
Târgoviște
Ploiești
Râmnicu Vâlcea
Târgu-Jiu
Pitești
Bela Crkva
Orșova
Porțile de Fier
Drobeta-Turnu-Severin
Drăgășani
Slatina
Craiova
Roșiori-de-Vede
Alexandria
Giurgiu
Băilești
Caracal
Corabia
Turnu Măgurele
Zimnicea
BUCUREȘTI (Bucharest)
Oltenița
Slobozia
Fetești
Medgidia
Călărași
Cernavodă
Constanța
Mangalia
Năvodari
ROMANIA
Transilvania
Carpații Meridionali
Walachia
Dobruja
Dunărea (Danube)
Ialomița
Dâmbovița
Argeș
Olt
Jiu
Vedea
Timok
Morava
Negotin
Bor
Zaječar
Vidin
Lom
Oryakhova
Ruse
Razgrad
Tutrakan
Silistra
Dobrich
Balchik
Varna
Nos Kaliakra
BULGARIA

B
C
D
E
F
G

East from Greenwich

9 10 11 12 13 14 15

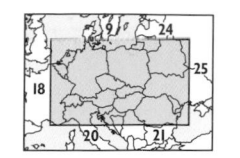

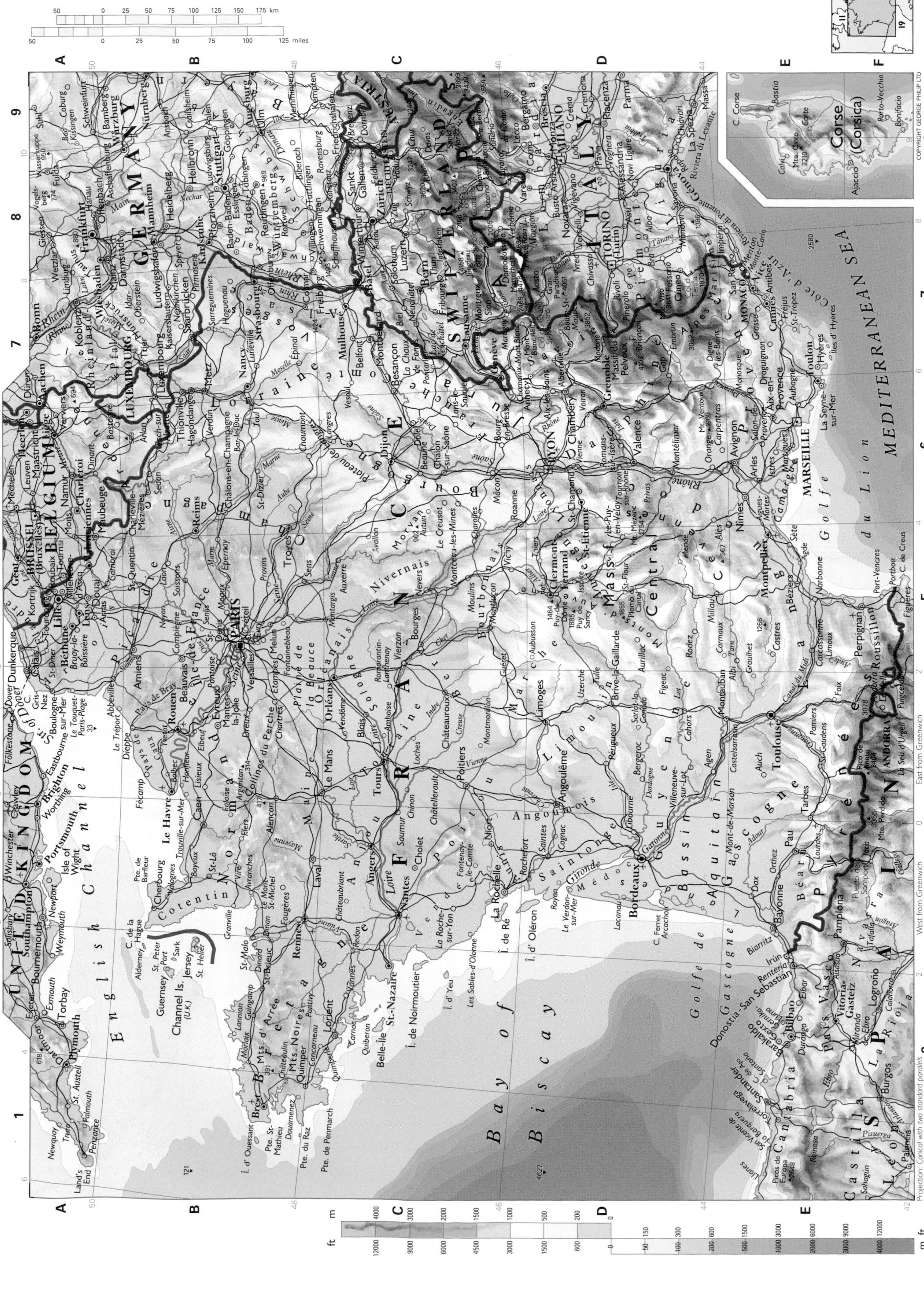

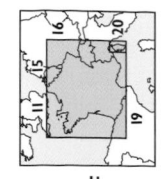

Corse (Corsica)

FRANCE 1:5 000 000
50 0 25 50 75 100 125 150 175 km
50 0 25 50 75 100 125 miles
11
15
16
19
20
m ft
4000 12000
3000 9000
2000 6000
1500 4500
1000 3000
500 1500
200 600
0 0
50 150
100 300
200 600
500 1500
1000 3000
2000 6000
3000 9000
4000 12000
Projection: Conical with two standard parallels
West from Greenwich 0 East from Greenwich

SPAIN

PORTUGAL

FRANCE

MOROCCO

ALGERIA

MEDITERRANEAN SEA

ATLANTIC OCEAN

Islas Baleares

MADRID · Barcelona · Valencia · Zaragoza · Sevilla · Málaga · Bilbao · Murcia · Córdoba · Granada · Alicante · Valladolid · Pamplona · Toledo · Salamanca · Oviedo · Gijón · Santander · Vitoria Gasteiz · Logroño · Huesca · Lleida · Tarragona · Castelló de la Plana · Albacete · Jaén · Almería · Cádiz · Huelva · Badajoz · Mérida · Cáceres · León · Burgos · Segovia · Guadalajara · A Coruña (La Coruña) · Santiago de Compostela · Lugo · Ourense (Orense) · Pontevedra · Vigo · Gibraltar (U.K.) · Ceuta (Sp.) · Melilla (Sp.) · Andorra

LISBOA · Porto · Coimbra · Braga · Faro · Évora · Setúbal · Portalegre · Beja

Mallorca · Menorca · Eivissa (Ibiza) · Formentera · Cabrera · Palma de Mallorca · Maó (Mahón)

Golfe du Lion · Golfe de Roses · Costa Brava · Costa Dorada · Costa Blanca · Costa del Sol · Golfo de Valencia · G. de Cádiz · Str. of Gibraltar · Cap de Creus · C. de la Nao · C. de Palos · C. de Gata · C. de São Vicente

Pyrénées · Cordillera Cantábrica · Sistema Ibérico · Sierra Morena · Sierra Nevada · Sierra de Gredos · Montes de Toledo · La Mancha · Serranía de Cuenca · Picos de Europa · Mulhacén 3478

Río Ebro · Río Duero · Río Tajo · Río Guadiana · Río Guadalquivir · Río Júcar · Río Segura · Río Miño · Río Douro

ALGER · Oran · Mostaganem · Tiaret · Tlemcen · Tétouan · Tanger · Ksar el Kebir · Larache

Projection: Conical with two standard parallels

COPYRIGHT GEORGE PHILIP LTD

km 50 0 25 50 75 100 125 150 175
miles 50 0 25 50 75 100 125

ft 6000 4500 3000 1500 600 0
m 2000 1500 1000 500 200 0 -150 -300 -600

SWITZERLAND
AUSTRIA
SLOVENIA
CROAT
FRANCE
ALGERIA
TUNISIA
MALTA
LIGURIAN SEA
TYRRHENIAN SEA
ADRIATIC SEA
MEDITER
Golfo di Génova
Golfo di Venézia
Golfe de Tunis
Golfe de Hammamet
Bouches de Bonifacio
Str. di Messina
Ísole Eólie
Ísole Égadi
Ísole Pelagie (Italy)
Ísole Ponziane
Corse
Sardegna
Elba
Dolomiti
Karnische Alpen
Alpes Maritimes
Riviera di Ponente
Riviera di Levante
Côte d'Azur
Ljubljana
Zagreb
Trieste
Rijeka
Venézia (Venice)
MILANO
TORINO (Turin)
Génova
Bologna
Firenze (Florence)
SAN MARINO
ROMA
VATICAN CITY
NÁPOLI
Bari
Palermo
Catánia
Messina
Cágliari
Sássari
Ajaccio
Bastia
Tunis
Valletta
LYON
Grenoble
MARSEILLE
Toulon
MONACO
Nice
Cannes
Avignon
Aix-en-Provence
Annaba
Constantine
Skikda
Bizerte
Sousse
Kairouan
Ancona
Pescara
Perúgia
Foggia
Taranto
Reggio di Calábria
Siracusa
Agrigento
Trápani
Split
Zadar
Banja Luka
Graz
Klagenfurt
Villach
Maribor
Verona
Pádova
Brescia
Bergamo
Parma
Módena
Ferrara
Ravenna
Rímini
Livorno
Pisa
Siena
Prato
Salerno
Potenza
Cosenza
Catanzaro
Projection: Conical with two standard parallels

HUNGARY
ROMANIA
Transilvania
Carpații Meridionali
UKRAINE
YUGOSLAVIA
Vojvodina
SERBIA
Kosovo
MONTENEGRO
BOSNIA-HERZEGOVINA
ALBANIA
MACEDONIA
BULGARIA
Stara Planina
Rhodopi Planina
Makedhonía
Thrace
GREECE
Pindhos Óros
Pelopónnisos
Kríti
TURKEY
Mysia
Lydia
Caria
Dobruja
Walachia
BLACK SEA
AEGEAN SEA
Marmara Denizi (Sea of Marmara)
IONIAN SEA
MEDITERRANEAN SEA
Str. of Otranto
Szeged
Timișoara
Arad
Sibiu
Brașov
Ploiești
BUCUREȘTI (Bucharest)
Constanța
Galați
Brăila
Craiova
Drobeta-Turnu-Severin
Novi Sad
BEOGRAD (Belgrade)
Sarajevo
Niš
Priština
Podgorica
Skopje
Tiranë
Durrës
Bitola
SOFIYA
Plovdiv
Varna
Burgas
Ruse
Pleven
Edirne
İSTANBUL
Bursa
Balıkesir
İZMIR (Smyrna)
Thessaloníki
Lárisa
Vólos
ATHÍNAI (Athens)
Pátrai
Kérkira (Corfu)
Lésvos
Khíos
Sámos
Ródhos (Rhodes)
Iráklion
Khaniá
Límnos
Thásos
Évvoia
Kíthira
Kárpathos
East from Greenwich

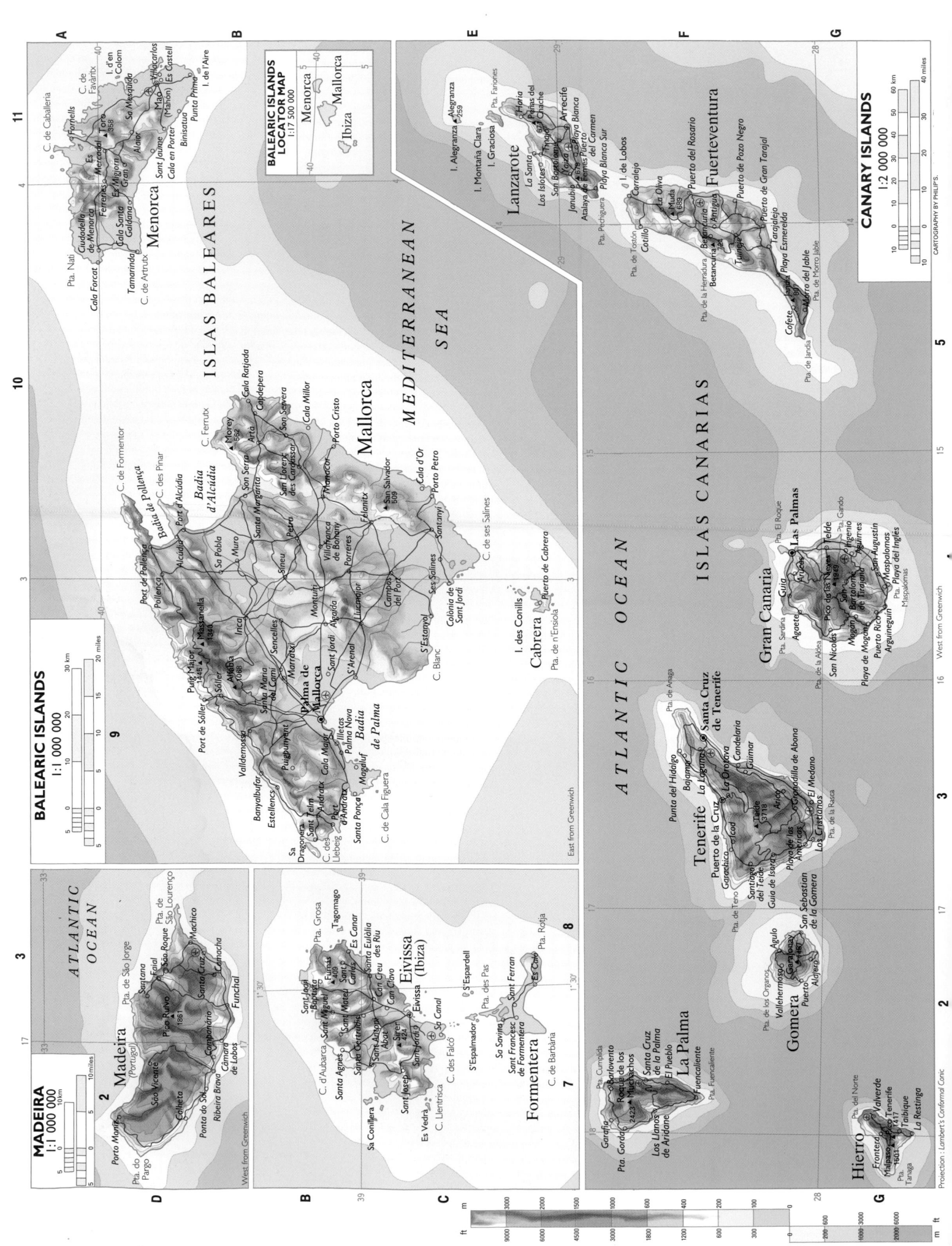

MEDITERRANEAN SEA

ISLAS BALEARES

ATLANTIC OCEAN

ISLAS CANARIAS

Menorca

C. de Caballería
Fornells
C. de Favàritx
I. d'en Colom
Sa Mesquida
Villacarlos
Es Castell
Maó (Mahón)
Punta Prima
I. de l'Aire
Pta. Nati
Toro 358
Sant Jaume
Cala en Porter
Binissafua
Ciudadella de Menorca
Es Mercadal
Ferreríes
Migjorn Gran
Alaior
Cala Santa Galdana
Cala Forcat
Tamarinda
C. de Arrutx

BALEARIC ISLANDS LOCATOR MAP 1:17 500 000
Menorca
Mallorca
Ibiza

Mallorca

C. de Formentor
C. des Pinar
Cala Rajada
Capdepera
Son Servera
Cala Millor
Porto Cristo
Cala d'Or
Porto Petro
Badia de Pollença
Badia d'Alcúdia
C. Ferrutx
Morey 562
Artà
Son Llorenç des Cardassar
Manacor
Felanitx
San Salvador 509
Santanyí
C. de ses Salines
Port de Pollença
Pollença
Alcúdia
Port d'Alcúdia
Sa Pobla
Muro
Santa Margarita
Petra
Vilafranca de Bonany
Porreres
Campos del Port
Ses Salines
Colònia de Sant Jordi
S'Estanyol
C. Blanc
Puig Major 1445
Massanella 1340
Alfàbia 1068
Inca
Sineu
Montuïri
Llucmajor
Sóller
Santa Maria del Camí
Marratxí
S'Arenal
Port de Sóller
Valldemossa
Banyalbufar
Estellencs
Puigpunyent
Andratx
Santa Ponça
Port d'Andratx
Sant Telm
C. des Llebeig
Sa Dragonera
C. de Cala Figuera
Palma de Mallorca
Illetas
Palma Nova
Cala Major
Magaluf
Badia de Palma
Sencelles
Sant Jordi
Agaida

C. des Salines
I. des Conills
Cabrera
Puerto de Cabrera
Pta. de n'Ensiola
I. des Conills

BALEARIC ISLANDS 1:1 000 000
0 5 10 15 20 30 km
0 5 10 15 20 miles

Madeira (Portugal)

ATLANTIC OCEAN
Porto Moniz
Pta. de São Lourenço
Machico
São Roque
Santana
Faial
Santo Cruz
Caniçal
Funchal
Câmara de Lobos
Pico Ruivo 1861
Campanário
Ribeira Brava
Ponta do Sol
Calheta
São Vicente
Pta. do Pargo

MADEIRA 1:1 000 000
0 5 10 km
0 5 10 miles

Eivissa (Ibiza)

Pta. Grosa
Tagomago
Es Canar
Santa Eulalia del Riu
Sant Carles
Pta. des Pas
S'Espardell
S'Espalmador
Es Canó
Pta. Rotja
Sant Joan Baptista
Portinatx
Santa Gertrudis
Sant Mateu
Can Clavo
Can Guell des Riu
Eivissa
Siren 424
Sant Josep
Sant Jordi
Sant Antoni Abat
Santa Agnès
Sant d'Aubarca
Sa Conillera
Es Vedrà
C. Llentrisca
Sa Savina
Es Caló
Sant Francesc de Formentera
Sant Ferran
Pta. de Barbària
C. des Falcó

Formentera

La Palma

Pta. Cumplida
Barlovento
Roque de los Muchachos 2423
Santa Cruz de la Palma
El Pueblo
Los Llanos de Aridane
Fuencaliente
Pta. Gorda
Garafía

Gomera

Pta. de los Órganos
Vallehermoso
Agulo
Garajonay 1487
Hermigua
San Sebastián de la Gomera
Alajeró
Puerto de...

Hierro

Pta. del Norte
Valverde
Frontera
Malpaso 1501
Pico de Tenerife 1417
Taíbique
La Restinga
Tanaga

Tenerife

Punta del Hidalgo
Bajamar
La Laguna
La Orotava
Santa Cruz de Tenerife
Candelaria
Güímar
Teide 3718
Icod
Garachico
Puerto de la Cruz
Santiago del Teide
Playa de las Américas
Granadilla de Abona
El Médano
Los Cristianos
Arona
Guía de Isora
Adeje
Pta. de Teno
Pta. de la Rasca

Gran Canaria

Las Palmas
Telde
Ingenio
Agüimes
Pico de las Nieves 1949
Arucas
Guía
Santa Lucía
San Bartolomé
Mogán
Puerto Rico
Playa del Inglés
Maspalomas
Agaete
San Nicolás
Arguineguín
San Agustín
Pta. Sardina
Pta. El Roque
Pta. de Maspalomas
Pta. de la Aldea

Lanzarote

I. Alegranza
Alegranza 259
I. Montaña Clara
I. Graciosa
Pta. Fariones
Haría
Peñas del Chache
Arrecife
Playa Blanca
Puerto del Carmen
La Santa
Los Isletes
Tinajo
Tías
San Bartolomé
Yaiza
Janubio
Atalaya de Femés
Playa Blanca Sur
Pta. Pechiguera
I. de Lobos

Fuerteventura

Corralejo
La Oliva
Puerto del Rosario
Puerto de Gran Tarajal
Puerto de Pozo Negro
Pta. de Tostón
Cotillo
Muda 689
Betancuria
Tarajalejo
Tuineje
Antigua
Pta. de la Herradura
Cofete
Jandía Playa Esmeralda
Morro del Jable
Pta. de Jandía
Pta. de Morro Jable

CANARY ISLANDS 1:2 000 000
0 10 20 30 40 50 60 km
0 10 20 30 40 miles
CARTOGRAPHY BY PHILIP'S

West from Greenwich
East from Greenwich

Projection: Lambert's Conformal Conic

ft m
9000 3000
6000 1800
4500 1500
3000 1200
1800 900
600 600
0 300
100
m ft
200 600
1000 3000
2000 6000

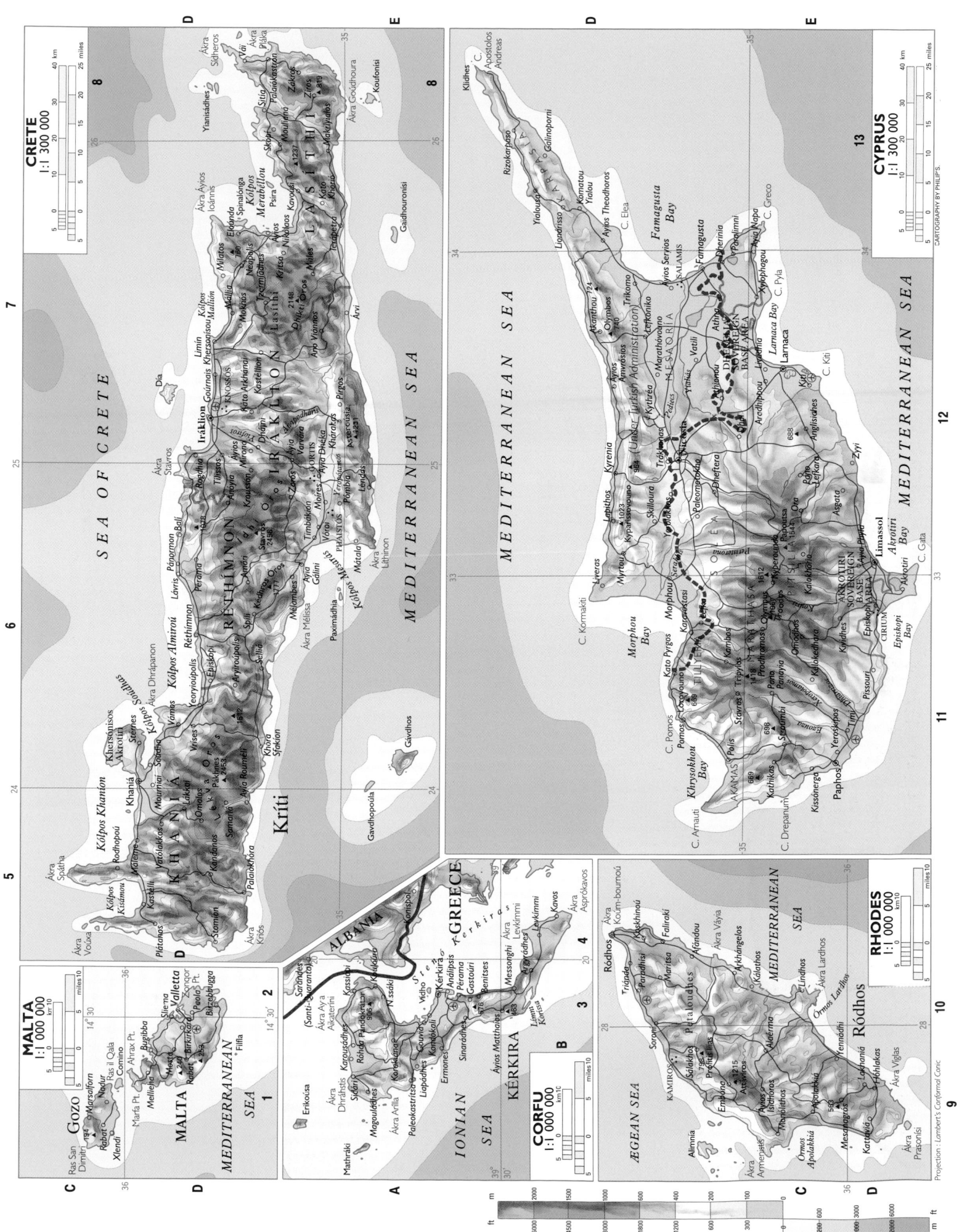

MALTA
1:1 000 000
Gozo
Marsalforn
Nadur
Rabat
Xlendi
Ras il Qala
Comino
Ahrax Pt.
Marfa Pt.
Bugibba
Mellieħa
MALTA
Mosta
Sliema
Valletta
Birkirkara
Rabat
Zonqor Pt.
Paola
Birżebbuġa
Filfla
MEDITERRANEAN SEA
CRETE
1:1 300 000
SEA OF CRETE
MEDITERRANEAN SEA
Kríti
KHANIÁ
RÉTHIMNON
IRÁKLION
LASÍTHI
Khaniá
Réthimnon
Iráklion
Áyios Nikólaos
Sitía
Ierápetra
Gávdhos
Gavdhopoúla
Día
Kólpos Khanion
Kólpos Soúdhas
Kólpos Almiroú
Kólpos Mirabéllou
Kólpos Mesarás
KNOSSOS
GORTIS
PHAISTOS
Lefka Óros
Ídhi Óros
Dhíkti Óros
CORFU
1:1 000 000
KÉRKIRA
Kérkira
IONIAN SEA
ALBANIA
GREECE
Sarandës (Santi-Quaranta)
Erikoúsa
Mathráki
Pandokrátor
RHODES
1:1 000 000
Ródhos
ÆGEAN SEA
MEDITERRANEAN SEA
Líndhos
KAMIROS
Petaloúdhes
Prasonísi
CYPRUS
1:1 300 000
MEDITERRANEAN SEA
Nicosia
Famagusta
Famagusta Bay
Larnaca
Larnaca Bay
Limassol
Akrotiri Bay
Paphos
Kyrenia
Morphou
Morphou Bay
Khrysokhou Bay
Episkopi Bay
KARPASIA
MESAORIA
TROODOS
Olympus
AKROTIRI SOVEREIGN BASE AREA
DHEKELIA SOVEREIGN BASE AREA
(Under Turkish Administration)
SALAMIS
CIRIUM
C. Apostolos Andreas
C. Greco
C. Gata
C. Kiti
C. Kormakiti
C. Arnauti
C. Drepanum
Projection : Lambert's Conformal Conic
CARTOGRAPHY BY PHILIP'S

24 EASTERN EUROPE AND TURKEY 1:10 000 000

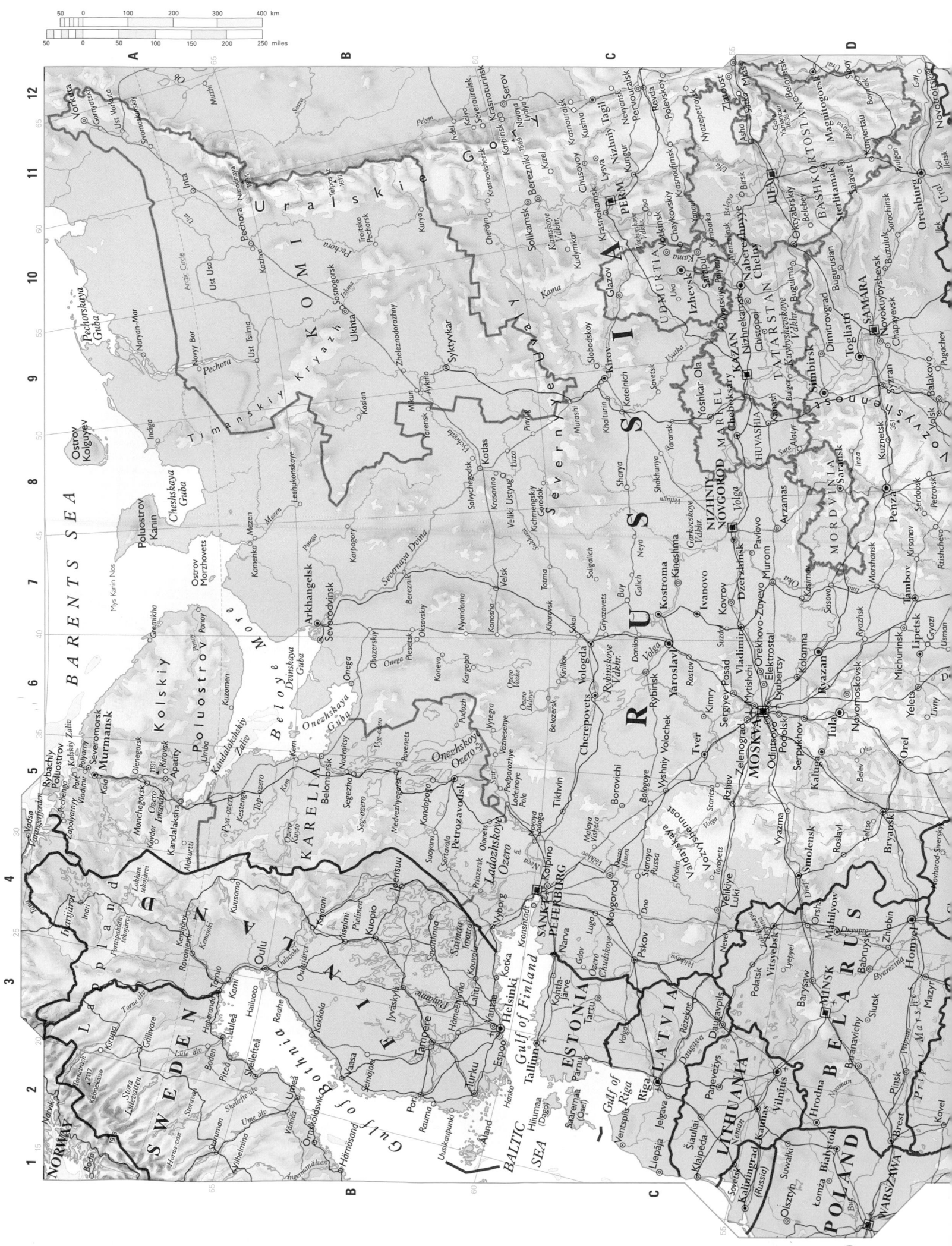
50 0 100 200 300 400 km
50 0 50 100 150 200 250 miles
BARENTS SEA
Beloye More
Gulf of Bothnia
Gulf of Finland
Gulf of Riga
BALTIC SEA
R U S S I A
F I N L A N D
S W E D E N
NORWAY
ESTONIA
LATVIA
LITHUANIA
BELARUS
POLAND
K O M I
KARELIA
UDMURTIA
TATARSTAN
BASHKORTOSTAN
CHUVASHIA
MARI EL
MORDVINIA
NIZHNIY NOVGOROD
Kolskiy Poluostrov
Lappland
Uralskie Gory
Timanskiy Kryazh
Severnyye Uvaly
MOSKVA
SANKT-PETERBURG
Helsinki
Tallinn
Riga
Vilnius
MINSK
WARSZAWA
Arkhangelsk
Murmansk
KAZAN
PERM
SAMARA
UFA
Nizhniy Novgorod
Yaroslavl
Vologda
Kirov
Syktyvkar
Petrozavodsk
Orenburg
Ladozhskoye Ozero
Onezhskoye Ozero
Ostrov Kolguyev
Kaliningrad (Russia)

26
44
17

BLACK SEA

CASPIAN SEA

MEDITERRANEAN SEA

Sea of Azov

UKRAINE

KAZAKSTAN

ROMANIA

MOLDOVA

BULGARIA

TURKEY

GEORGIA

ARMENIA

AZERBAIJAN

TURKMENISTAN

SYRIA

IRAQ

IRAN

CYPRUS

LEBANON

CRIMEA

m	ft
4000	12 000
3000	9000
2000	6000
1500	4500
1000	3000
500	1500
200	600
0	0
200	600
500	1500
1000	3000
2000	6000

Projection: Conical with two standard parallels

East from Greenwich

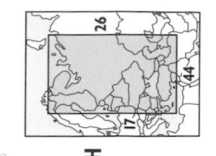

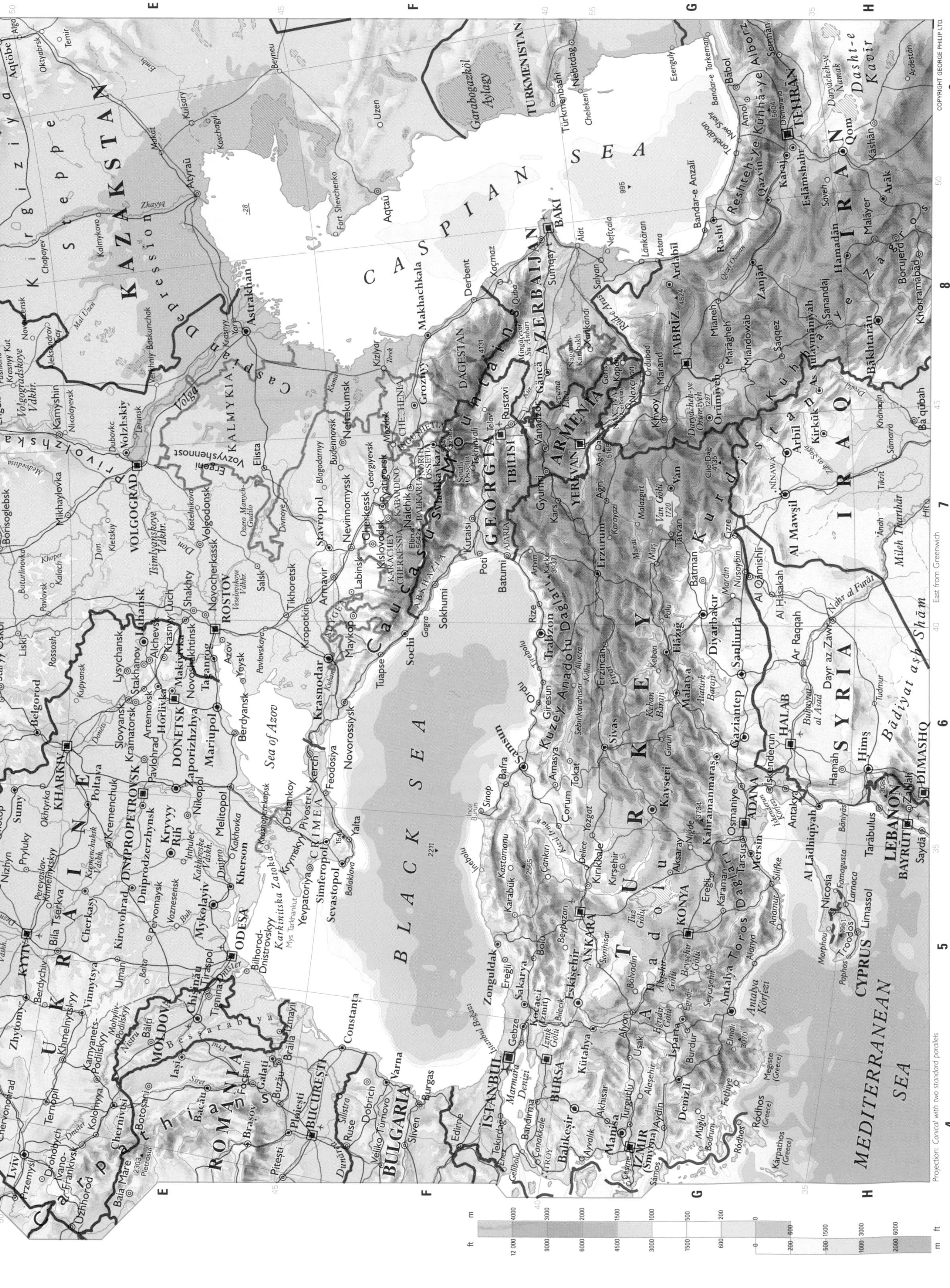

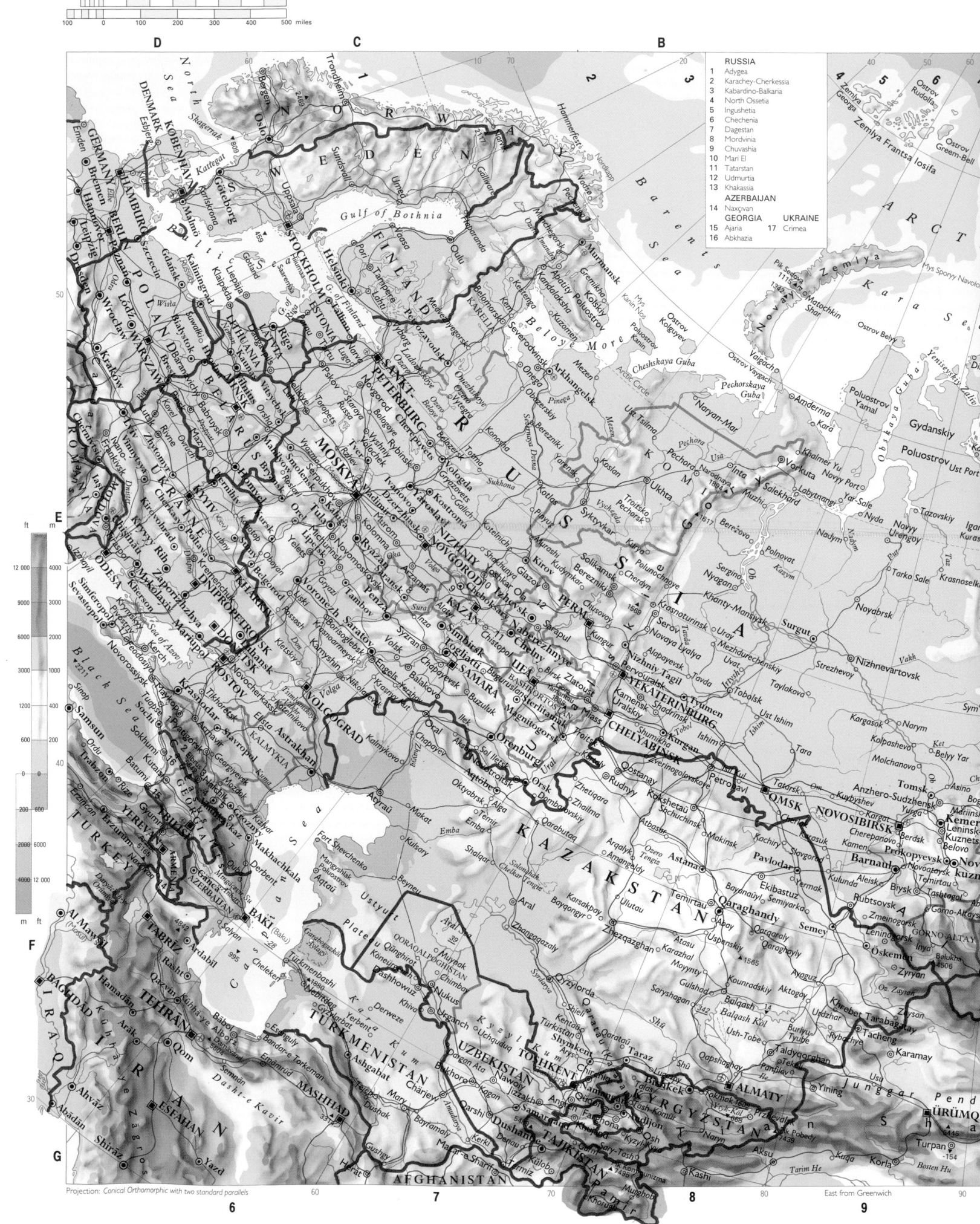

ASIA : Physical 1:50 000 000

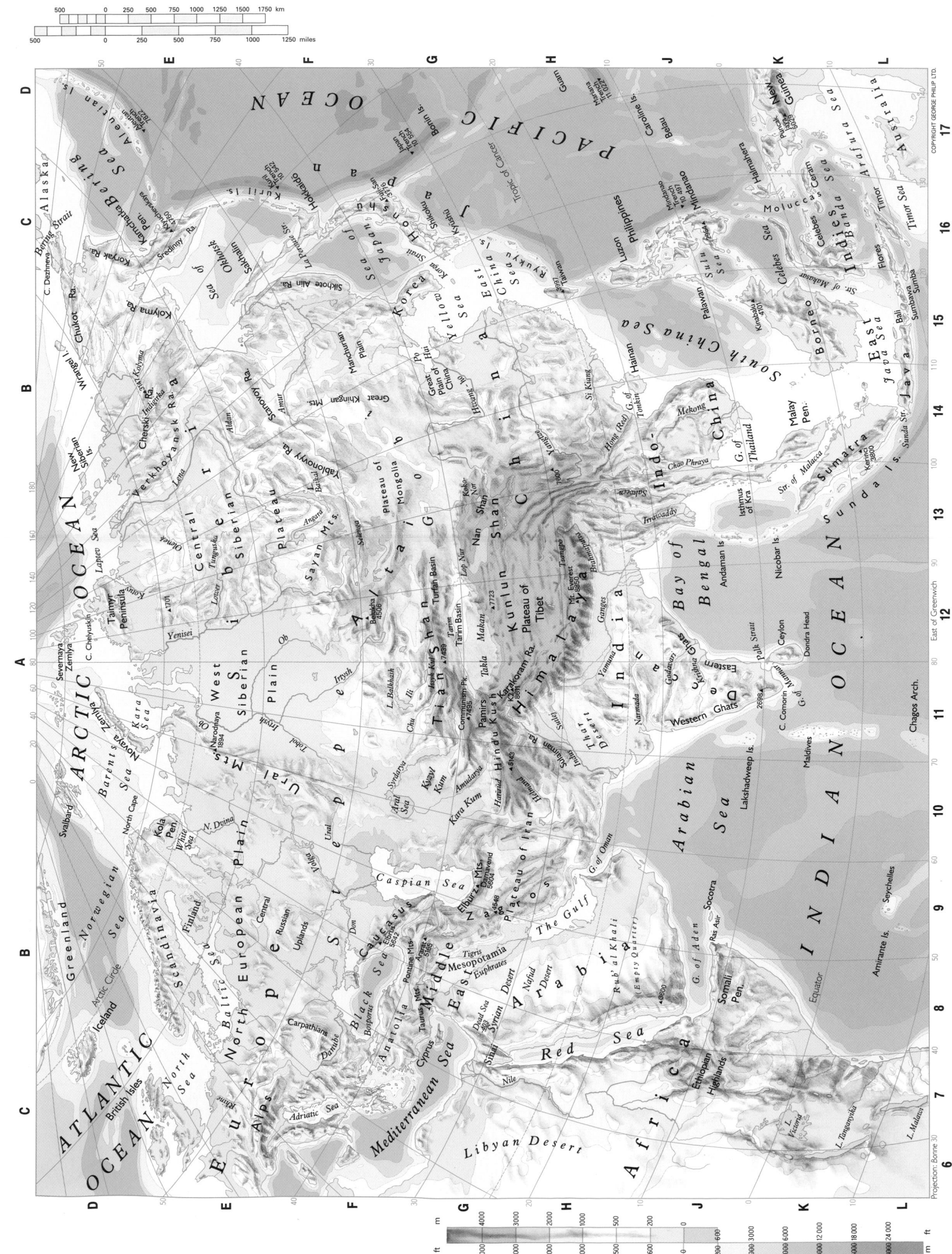

500 0 250 500 750 1000 1250 1500 1750 km
500 0 250 500 750 1000 1250 miles
ARCTIC OCEAN
ATLANTIC OCEAN
PACIFIC OCEAN
INDIAN OCEAN
Greenland
Svalbard
Iceland
British Isles
Arctic Circle
Norwegian Sea
North Sea
North Cape
Barents Sea
Novaya Zemlya
Kara Sea
Severnaya Zemlya
C. Chelyuskin
Taimyr Peninsula
Laptev Sea
New Siberian Is.
Wrangel I.
Chukot Ra.
C. Dezhneva
Bering Strait
Alaska
Bering Sea
Aleutian Is.
Aleutian Trench 7822
Kamchatka Pen.
Klyuchevskaya 4750
Sredinny Ra.
Koryak Ra.
Kolyma Ra.
Kolyma
Cherski Ra.
Indigirka
3147
Verkhoyansk Ra.
Lena
Olenek
Kotuy
Yenisei
1701
Central Siberian Plateau
Lower Tunguska
Aldan
Sea of Okhotsk
Sakhalin
Kuril Is.
Kuril Trench 10 542
Hokkaido
La Perouse Str.
Sikhote Alin Ra.
Stanovoy Ra.
Amur
Yablonovyy Ra.
L. Baikal
Angara
Sayan Mts.
Selenga
Scandinavia
Finland
Kola Pen.
White Sea
N. Dvina
Baltic Sea
North European Plain
Central Russian Uplands
Europe
Rhine
Alps
Adriatic Sea
Carpathians
Danube
Volga
Ural
Don
Steppe
Ural Mts.
Narodnaya 1894
West Siberian Plain
Siberia
Ob
Irtysh
Tobol
Black Sea
Bosporus
Caucasus
Elbrus 5642
Anatolia
Pontine Mts.
Taurus Mts.
Ararat 5165
Cyprus
Mediterranean Sea
Middle East
Mesopotamia
Tigris
Euphrates
Dead Sea 402
Syrian Desert
Sinai
Nile
Libyan Desert
Caspian Sea
Elburz Mts.
Damavand 5604
4548
Zagros
Plateau of Iran
Aral Sea
Syrdarya
Amudarya
Kyzyl Kum
Kara Kum
Harirud
Helmand
Hindu Kush
5143
Pamirs
Communism Pk. 7495
L. Balkhash
Ili
Chu
Issyk Kul
Tian Shan
7439
Altai
Belukha 4506
Turfan Basin
Tarim
Tarim Basin
Takla Makan
Lop Nur
Koko Nor
Nan Shan
Kunlun Shan
7723
Plateau of Tibet
Karakoram Ra.
K2 8611
Himalaya
Mt. Everest 8850
Tsangpo
Brahmaputra
Gobi
Plateau of Mongolia
Great Khingan Mts.
Manchurian Plain
Great Plain of China
Po Hai
Hwang-ho
China
Yangtze
7600
Si Kiang
Korea
Korea Strait
Yellow Sea
East China Sea
Ryukyu Is.
Taiwan
3997
Sea of Japan
Japan
Honshu
Fuji-San 3776
Shikoku
Kyushu
Japan Trench 10 554
Bonin Is.
Tropic of Cancer
Guam
Mariana Trench 11 022
Arabia
Nafud Desert
The Gulf
G. of Oman
Rub' al Khali (Empty Quarter)
3600
Red Sea
G. of Aden
Socotra
Ras Asir
Ethiopian Highlands
Somali Pen.
Africa
L. Victoria
L. Tanganyika
L. Malawi
Sulaiman Ra.
Indus
Sutlej
Thar Desert
Yamuna
Ganges
India
Narmada
Deccan
Godavari
Krishna
Western Ghats
Eastern Ghats
2698
C. Comorin
G. of Mannar
Palk Strait
Ceylon
Dondra Head
Arabian Sea
Lakshadweep Is.
Maldives
Bay of Bengal
Andaman Is.
Nicobar Is.
Equator
Amirante Is.
Seychelles
Chagos Arch.
Irrawaddy
Salween
Indo-China
Chao Phraya
Mekong
Hong (Red)
G. of Tonkin
Hainan
Isthmus of Kra
G. of Thailand
Malay Pen.
Str. of Malacca
Sumatra
Kerinci 3800
Sunda Is.
Sunda Str.
Java
Java Sea
East Indies
Bali
Sumbawa
Sumba
Flores
Timor
Timor Sea
Arafura Sea
Australia
South China Sea
Luzon
Philippines
Palawan
Sulu Sea
2954
Mindanao
Mindanao Trench 10 497
Caroline Is.
Belau
Borneo
Kinabalu 4101
Celebes Sea
Celebes
Str. of Makasar
Molucca Sea
Halmahera
Ceram
Banda Sea
Puncak Jaya 5029
New Guinea
Projection: Bonne
East of Greenwich
COPYRIGHT GEORGE PHILIP LTD.

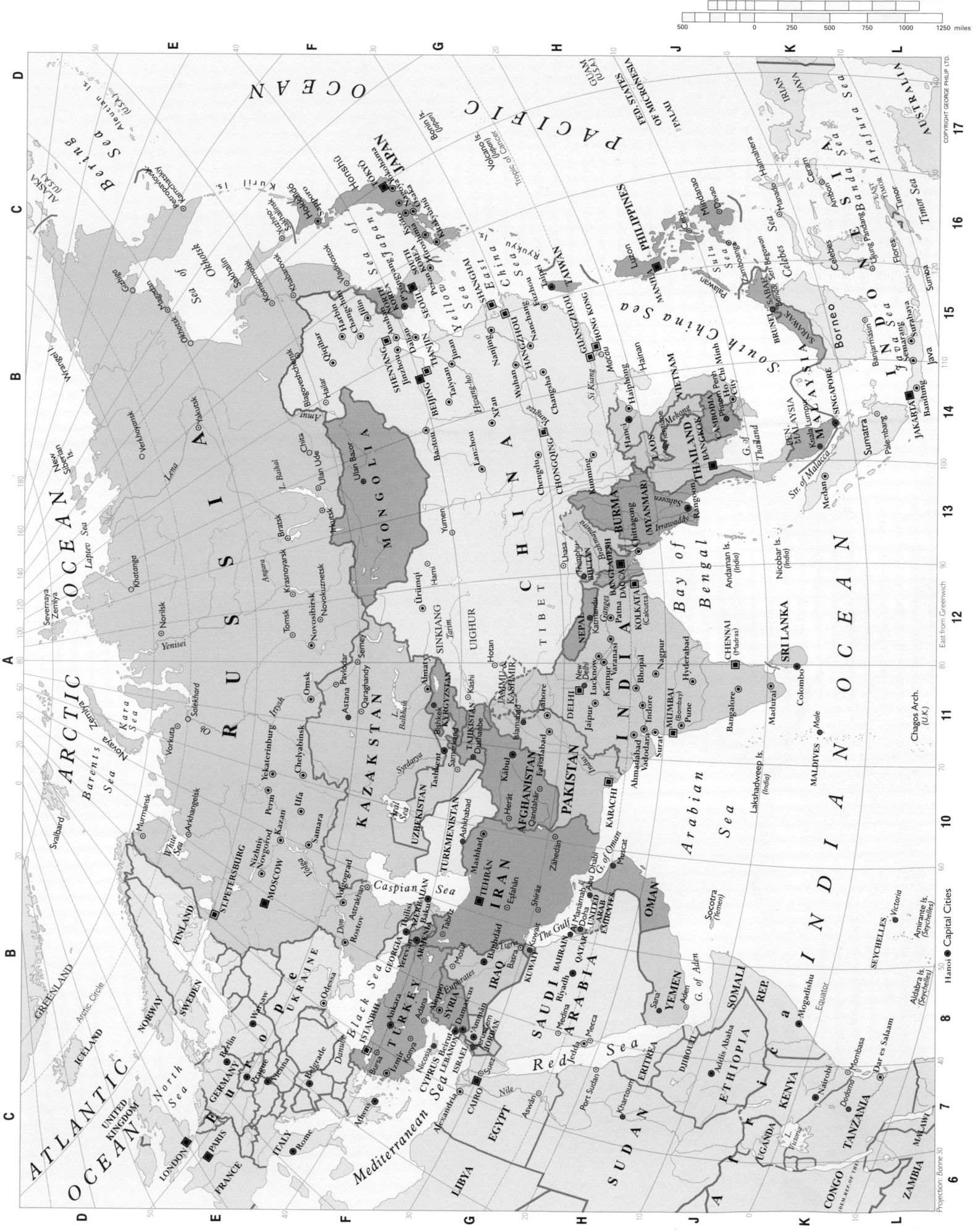

500 ├─ 0 ─┤ 250 500 750 1000 1250 1500 1750 km

500 0 250 500 750 1000 1250 miles

● Hanoi ● Capital Cities

East from Greenwich

Projection: Bonne 30

JAPAN 1:5 000 000

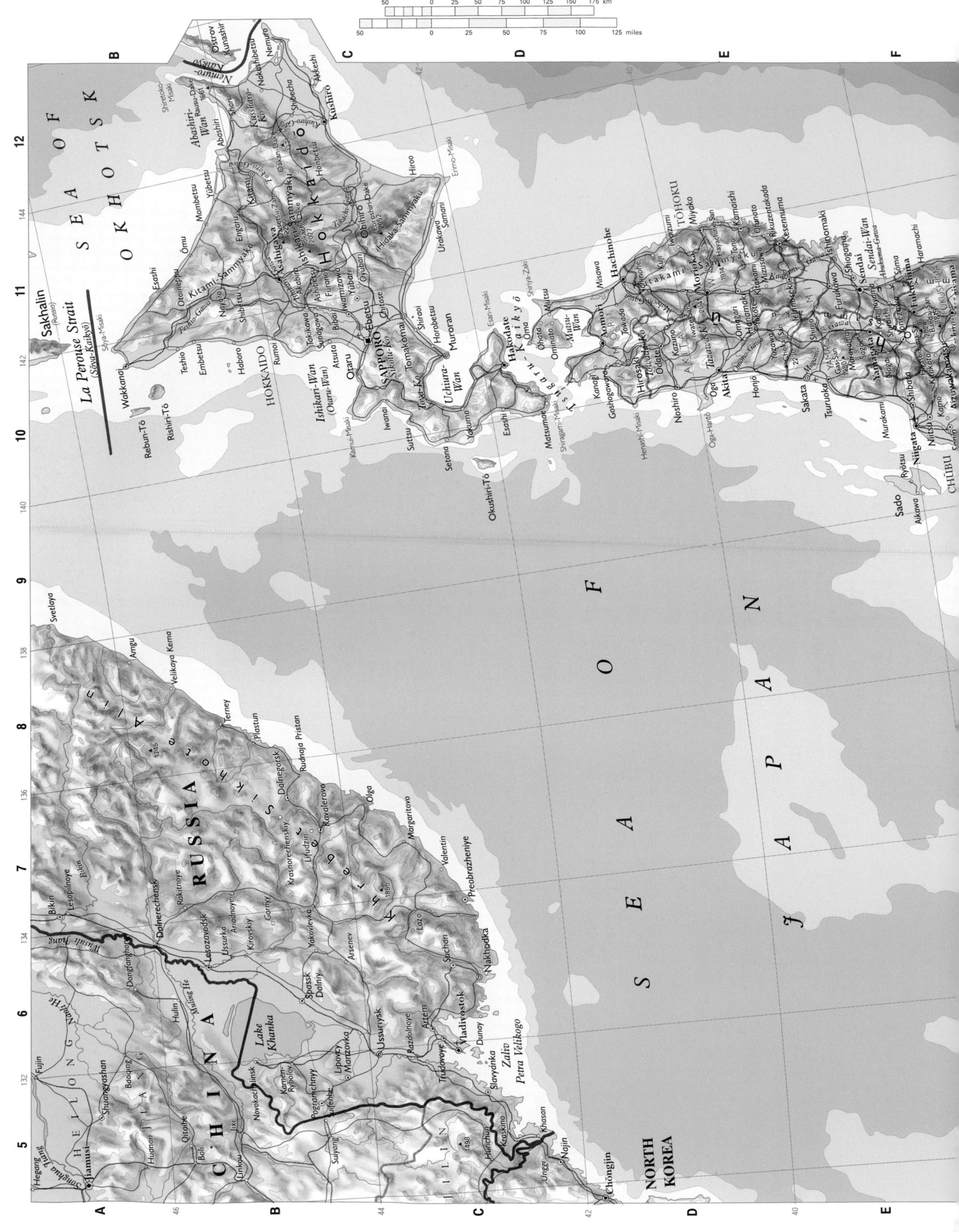

50 0 25 50 75 100 125 150 175 km

50 0 25 50 75 100 125 miles

B **C** **D** **E** **F**

SEA OF OKHOTSK

Ostrov Kunashir

Nemuro-Kaikyō

Nokkeushibetsu
Akkeshi

Shiretoko-Misaki

Abashiri
Abashiri-Wan
Rausu-Dake 1661
Shari
Kushiharo
Shibecha

Nemuro
Kushiro

12

Sōya-Misaki

Mombetsu
Yūbetsu

O-akan 1499
Teshikaga

Hiroo

Kitami-Sammyaku

Asahigawa
Asahi-Dake 2290
Ishikari-Sammyaku

Erimo-Misaki

HOKKAIDO

Sakhalin

La Perouse Strait
(Sōya-Kaikyō)

Otoineppu

Esashi

Teshio-Gawa
Nayoro
Shibetsu

Kamikawa
Ashibetsu
Furano

Obihiro

Tokachi-Dake 2077

Hidaka-Sammyaku

TŌHOKU

Miyako

Ichinohe

Hachinohe

Iwaizumi

Misawa

Towada

Aomori

Takamatsu

Morioka
Sammyaku

Kamaishi

Kuzumaki

Ōfunato

Rikuzentakada

Kesennuma

Ishinomaki

Sendai-Wan

Haramachi

11

Wakkanai

Rebun-Tō

Rishiri-Tō

Ōmu

Embetsu
Haboro

Teshio

Takikawa
Sungawa
Iwamizawa

Bibai

Yūbari

Ebetsu
SAPPORO

Chitose

Obihiro

Shiranuka

Esan-Misaki

Hakodate
Tsugaru-Kaikyō
Ōma

Ōhata

Mutsu

Shiriya-Zaki

Noheji

Towada-ko

Kazuno

Ōdate

Takanosu

Ō

HONSHŪ

Hirosaki

Tazawa-Ko

Kitakami

Furukawa

Shiogama
Sendai

Ishinomaki

Abukuma-Gawa

Sōma

Akita

Honjō

Yurihonjō

Kōriyama

Fukushima

10

HOKKAIDO

Ishikari-Wan
(Otaru-Wan)

Otaru

Iwanai

Suttsu

Setana

Okushiri-Tō

Toyako-Ko
Shiraoi

Horobetsu
Muroran

Uchiura-Wan

Yakumo

Esashi

Matsumae

Shiragami-Misaki

Henashi-Misaki

Oga-Hantō

Oga

Noshiro

AKITA

Yuzawa

Yamagata
Shinjo

Tsuruoka

Sakata

Murakami

Niitsu

Niigata

Shibata

CHŪBU

Sado

Aikawa

Ryōtsu

42

44

40

38

SEA OF JAPAN

SEA OF JAPAN

RUSSIA

Sikhote Alin

Svetlaya

Amgu

Velikaya Kema

Terney

Plastun

Rudnaja Pristan

Dalnegorsk

Kavalerovo

Olga

Margaritovo

Valentin

Preobrazheniye

Sikhote

Alin

1745

Bikin
Lesopilnoye

Bikin

Rakitnoye

Dalnerechensk

Krasnorechenskiy

Lifudzin

Ussurka

Ariadnoye

Kirovskiy

Gornly

Lozo

Arsenev

Yakovlevka

Stichan

Nakhodka

8

7

Ussuriysk

Spassk
Dalniy

Razdolnoye

Artem

Dunoy

Vladivostok

Zaliv
Petra Velikogo

6

Hulin

Muling He

Lake
Khanka

Novokachalinsk

Kamen-
Rybolov

Pogromnny

Jutichsk

Lipovcy

Martzovka

Slavyanka

Trudovoye

Zaliv

5

Fujin

Baoqing

CHINA

HEILONGJIANG

Qitaihe

Boli

Linkou

Suyang

JILIN

1498

Hunchun

Kraskino

Khasan

Unggi

Nojin

Chŏngjin

NORTH
KOREA

Hegang
Huanan

Shuangyashan

Songhua Jiang

Jiamusi

Wusuli Jiang

A **B** **C** **D** **E**

46

44

42

40

132

134

136

138

140

142

144

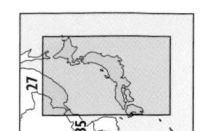

RYUKYU ISLANDS
on same scale

Projection: Conical with two standard parallels

East from Greenwich

100 0 100 200 300 400 500 600 km
100 0 100 200 300 400 miles

50
70
80
90
100

KAZAKSTAN

Karsakpay
Zhezqazghan
Qaraghandy
Moyynty
Qarqaraly
Rubtsovsk
Gorno-Altaysk
Semey
Öskemen
Leninogorsk
Zyryan
1565
Belukha
4506

RUSSIA
Munku-Sardyk 3491
Angarsk
Cheremkhovo
Irkutsk
455
Babush

Tannu Ola
Uvs Nuur
Hövsgöl Nuur
Hatgal
Selenge Mörön
Erdenet

B
342 Balqash Köl
Balqash
Taldyqorghan
Ayaguz
Tacheng
Ozero Alakol
Karamay
Fuhai
Uhungur He
Altay
Fuyun
Ulaangom
Hyargas Nuur
Nova
Har Us Nuur
4362
Döröö Nuur
Bayanhongor
Uliastay
Tsetserleg
Ulaanbaa

MONGO

Shū
Qapshaghay
Ile
Bole
Yining
Junggar Pendi
Manas
Shihezi
ÜRÜMQI
Qitai
5445
Barkol Kazak Zizhixian
4925
Hangayn Nuruu
Bugun
Altay
Dalandzadgad
Dzuuna

Bishkek
Maraz
ALMATY
Qapshaghay Bogeni
1609
Ysyk-Köl

KYRGYZSTAN
Naryn
Wensu
T i a n S h a n
Usu
Turpan
Hami
-154
Aydingkol Hu
Hami
Gaxun Nur

Namangan
Andijon
Pik Pobedy 7439
Aksu
Kuqa
Korla
Bosten Hu
Yanqi
Kuruktag
Ximiao

40
Kashi
Artux
Shule
XINJIANG
Tarim He
Tarim Pendi
Lop Nur
Dunhuang
Anxi
Yumen
Jiayuguan
Wuhai
25
Linh

Kongur Shan 7719
Muztagh-Ata 7546
Shache
Yecheng
Pishan
Hotan
UYGUR ZIZHIQU
(SINKIANG)
Qiemo
Qarqan He
Ruoqiang
Altun Shan
Mangnai
Har Hu
Qilian Shan
Zhangye
Shandan
Alka Zuoqi
Pingluo
NINGXIA
Wuzhong
HUIZU

Taxkorgan
Tajik Zizhixian
Taklamakan Shamo
Yutian
Ayakkum Hu
Tart
Da Qaidam
Qaidam Pendi
Tianjun
Golmud
Dulan
Qinghai Hu 3205
Gonghe
Minhe
Xining
ZIZHIQU
Baiyin
LANZHOU

Nanga Parbat
8126
K2 86
Karakoram
Aksai Chin
Hoh Xil Shan
Q I N G H A I
Linxia
Dingxi
Guyuan

C
JAMMU &
KASHMIR
Srinagar
Leh
Rutog
Kunlun Shan
Gyaring Hu
4237
Ngoring Hu
Maqen
6094
Bayan Har Shan
Min Xian
Tianshui
Baoji

Zaskar Mts.
Gar
XIZANG
ZIZHIQU
(TIBET)
Tanggula (Dangla) Shan
Yushu
Songpan
Wudu
3567
Qin

ft   m
18 000 6000
12 000 4000
9000   3000
6000   2000
4500   1500
3000   1000
1200   400
600   200
0   0
200   600
2000   6000
4000 12 000
6000 18 000
m   ft

Kamet 7756
Dehra Dun
Nanda Devi 7817
Mapam Yumco
Burang
Zhongba
UTTAR-ANCHAL
Amnapurna 8078
Dhaulagiri 8172
Siling Co
4495
Nam Co
4627
Nagqu
Amdo
Qamdo
S I C H
Gongga Shan 7556
Guangyuan
Mianyang
Deyang
Santai
Nanchong
Daxian

Meerut
Moradabad
DELHI
Bareli
New Delhi
Aligarh
Agra
N E P A L
Ghaghara
Manaslu 8156
Xainza
Nyainqentanglha Shan
Xigazê
Lhasa
Namcha Barwa 7756
Bomi
Markam
Zayu
Zhongdian
Xichang
CHENGDU
Ya'an
Leshan
Neijiang
CHONGQING
Hechuan

D
UTTAR PRADESH
KANPUR
LUCKNOW
Gwalior
Jhansi
Allahabad
Gorakhpur
Darbhanga
Biratnagar
Katmandu
Mt Everest 8850
Makalu 8481
Kanchenjunga
Thimbu
Punakha
BHUTAN
Yamzho Yumco
Yarlung Zangbo Jiang
Lhaze
H i m a l a y a
Dibrugarh
Sadiya
ARUNACHAL PRADESH
5881
Nu Jiang
Zhongdian
Lijiang
Panzhihua
Huili
Dali
Xiaguan
Zunyi
GUIZH
GUIYA

Sagar
I N D I A
PATNA
VARANASI
BIHAR
Gaya
Rajshahi
ASSAM
Gauhati
Tezpur
MEGHALAYA
Khasi Hills
Brahmaputra
NAGALAND
Imphal
3411
Silchar
Kachin
Myitkyina
3824
Tengchong
Boshan
Luxi
Chuxiong
Lupanshui
Zhanyi
Anshun
Duy

Tropic of Cancer
Jabalpur
MADHYA PRADESH
Ranchi
Jamshedpur
JHARKHAND
Asansol
Berhampore
Barddhaman
WEST
Haora
Bhatpara
Narayanganj
DHAKA
BANGLADESH
Khulna
Bhamo
Shwebo
BURMA
Lashio
Anning
Yuxi
Chengjiang
KUNMING
Kaiyuan
Xingyi
Mengzi
Hongshui He
Shiping
Jinghong
Gejiu
Wenshan
ZHU

Bilaspur
Raipur
CHHATTISGARH
Kharagpur
Baleshwar
KOLKATA
(CALCUTTA)
BENGAL
CHITTAGONG
Monywa
Mandalay
Myingyan
3053
Arakan Shan
Simao
Bose
Pingxiang
VIETNAM
ZI
Nanning
Hekou

E
NAGPUR
Chanda
ORISSA
Cuttack
Brahmapur
BAY OF
BENGAL
Akyab
(MYANMAR)
Pegu Yoma
Arakan Yoma
Irrawaddy
Yamethin
Taunggyi
Chiang Mai
Toungoo
THAILAND
(SIAM)
Mekong
Luang Prabang
LAOS
3143
Nam Dinh
HANOI
Hoa Binh
HAIPHO
G. of
Tonkin

Warangal
Vizianagaram
VISHAKHAPATNAM
80
Godavari

Projection: Bonne
3
90
4
100
East from Greenwich
5

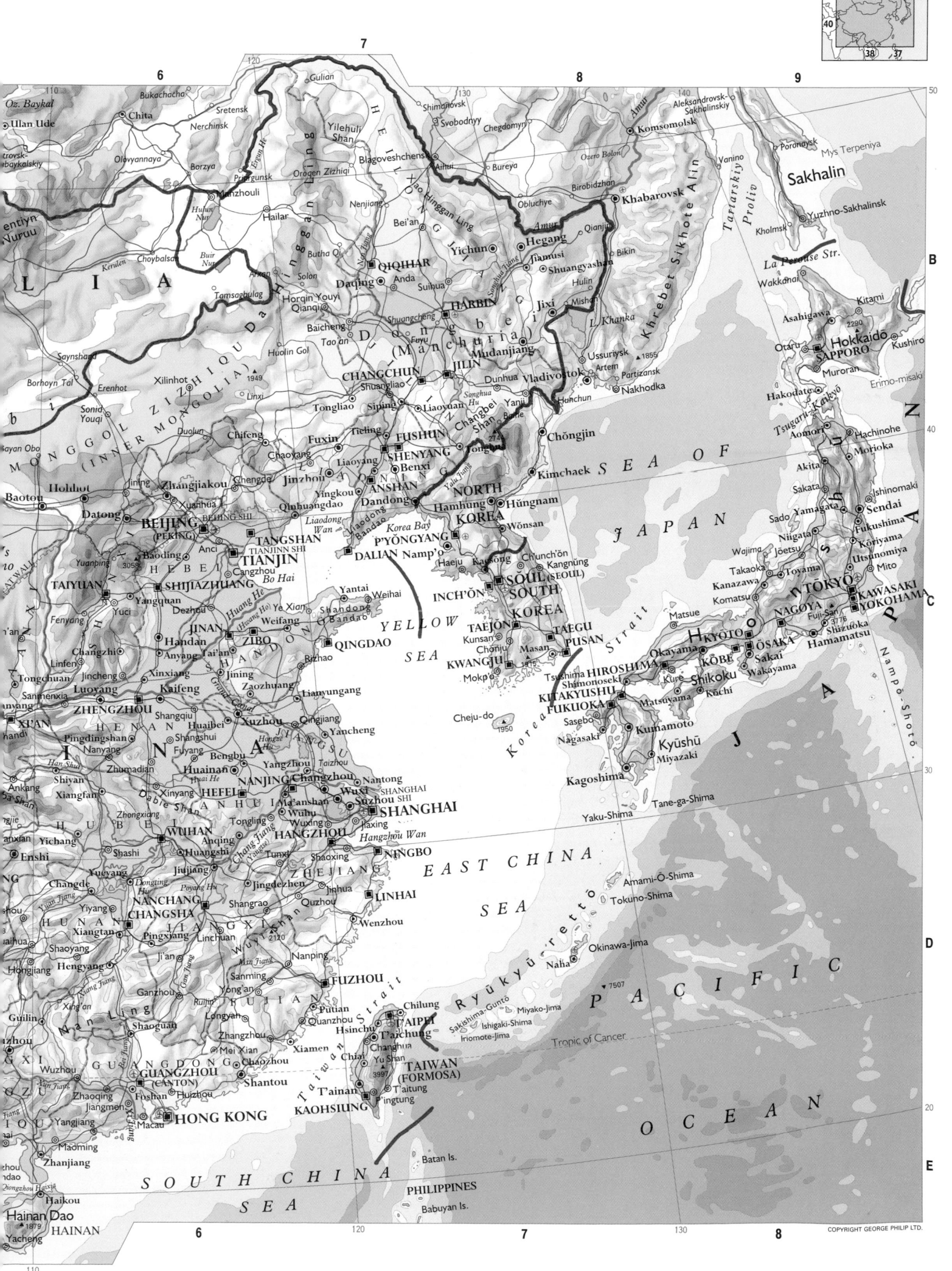

SEA OF JAPAN
YELLOW SEA
EAST CHINA SEA
SOUTH CHINA SEA
PACIFIC OCEAN
NORTH KOREA
SOUTH KOREA
TAIWAN (FORMOSA)
PHILIPPINES
HONG KONG
BEIJING (PEKING)
SHANGHAI
TIANJIN
P'YŎNGYANG
SOUL (SEOUL)
TŌKYŌ
Hokkaido
Sakhalin
Honshu
Kyūshū
Shikoku
Hainan Dao
Ryūkyū-rettō
Korea Strait
Taiwan Strait
Tropic of Cancer
Khabarovsk
Vladivostok
HARBIN
CHANGCHUN
SHENYANG
DALIAN
QINGDAO
NANJING
WUHAN
HANGZHOU
FUZHOU
GUANGZHOU (CANTON)
TAIPEI
KAOHSIUNG
PUSAN
TAEGU
OSAKA
KYŌTO
NAGOYA
YOKOHAMA
KAWASAKI
HIROSHIMA
FUKUOKA
KITAKYUSHU
SAPPORO
Sendai
COPYRIGHT GEORGE PHILIP LTD.

NORTHERN CHINA AND KOREA 1:6 000 000

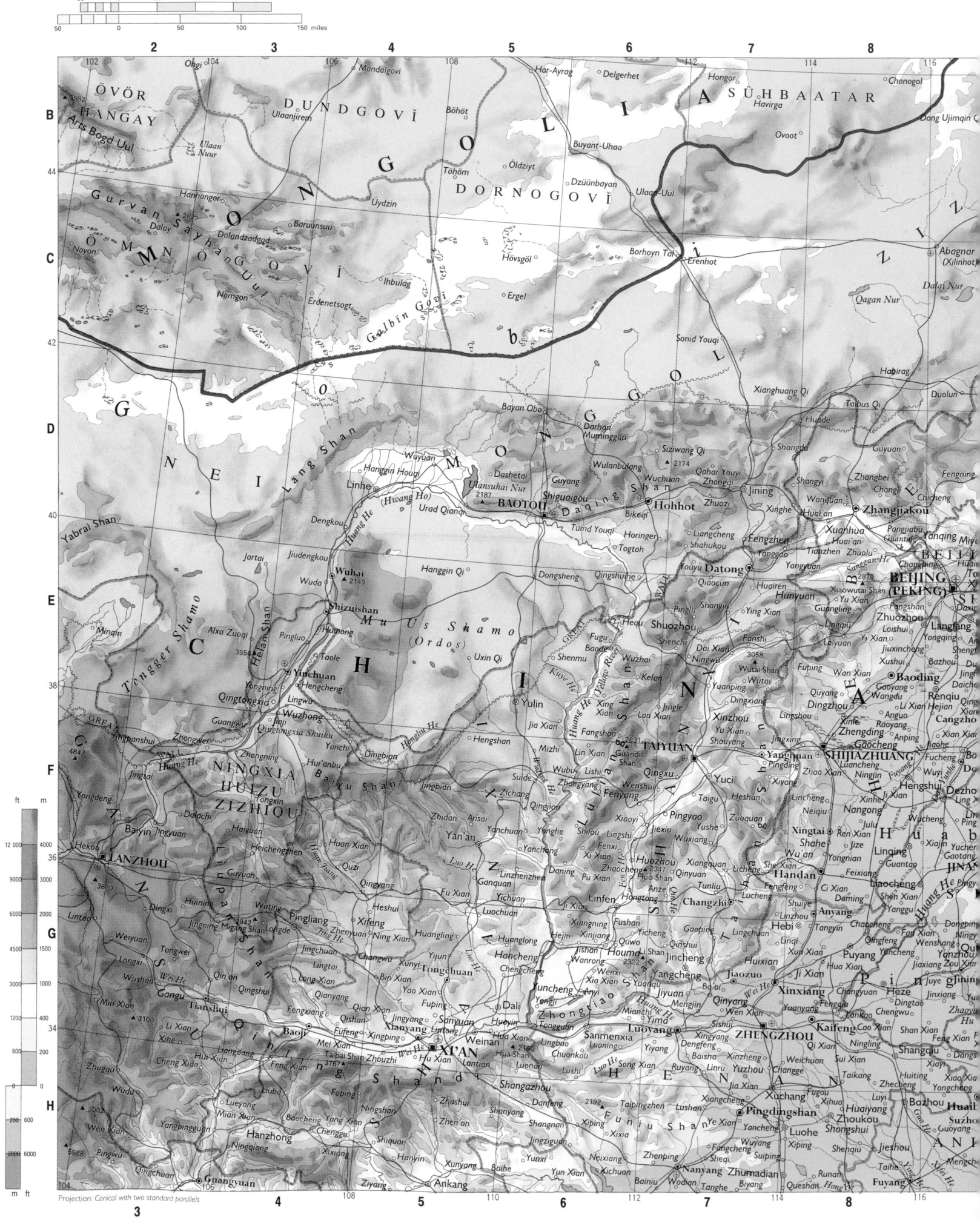

Projection: Conical with two standard parallels

27
31
32
33

9 10 11 12 13 14 15 16

HARBIN
CHANGCHUN
JILIN
SHENYANG
FUSHUN
ANSHAN
DALIAN
P'YŎNGYANG
SOUL
INCH'ŎN
TAEJŎN
TAEGU
KWANGJU
PUSAN
QINGDAO
TIANJIN

HEILONGJIANG
JILIN
LIAONING
NORTH KOREA
SOUTH KOREA
RUSSIA
JAPAN

Liaodong Wan
Korea Bay
Bo Hai
HUANG HAI
(Yellow Sea)
SEA OF JAPAN
Korea Strait
Laizhou Wan
Shandong Bandao
Liaodong Bandao
Changbai Shan
Zhangguangcai Ling

B C D E F G H

9 10 11 12 13 14 15

East from Greenwich

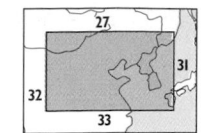

100 0 100 200 300 400 500 km
100 0 50 100 150 200 250 300 350 miles
BURMA (MYANMAR)
RANGOON (YANGON)
G. of Martaban
THAILAND
BANGKOK
LAOS
VIETNAM
CAMBODIA
Phnom Penh (Phnom Penh)
THANH PHO HO CHI MINH
Gulf of Thailand
ANDAMAN SEA
SOUTH CHINA SEA
Paracel Is.
Spratly Is.
MALAYSIA
PENINSULAR MALAYSIA
KUALA LUMPUR
SINGAPORE
Johor Baharu
BRUNEI
Bandar Seri Begawan
SARAWAK
SABAH
Kota Kinabalu
Borneo
KALIMANTAN
INDONESIA
Sumatera
MEDAN
Pekanbaru
Padang
Jambi
PALEMBANG
Bangka
Belitung
Pontianak
Banjarmasin
Balikpapan
Greater Sunda Islands
JAVA SEA
JAKARTA
BANDUNG
SEMARANG
SURABAYA
Jawa (Java)
Madura
Bali
Lombok
INDIAN OCEAN
Java Trench
Strait of Malacca
Selat Karimata
Kepulauan Mentawai
Nias
Siberut
Kepulauan Natuna
Kepulauan Anambas
Kepulauan Riau
Lingga
Projection: Mercator
East from Greenwich

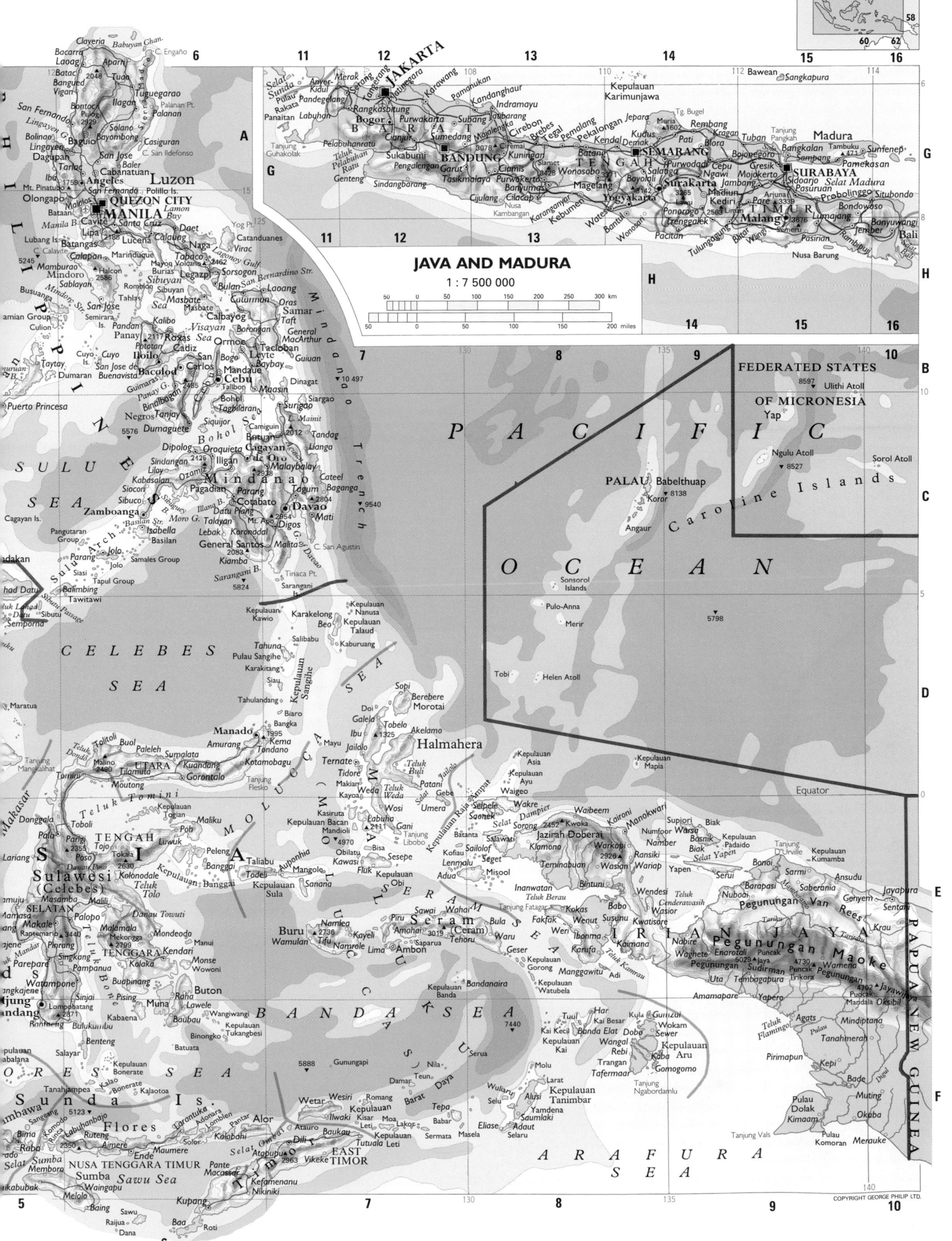
JAVA AND MADURA
1 : 7 500 000
JAKARTA
BANDUNG
SEMARANG
SURABAYA
Madura
Bali
PACIFIC OCEAN
FEDERATED STATES OF MICRONESIA
PALAU
Caroline Islands
Luzon
MANILA
QUEZON CITY
Mindanao
SULU SEA
CELEBES SEA
Sulawesi (Celebes)
Halmahera
MOLUCCA SEA
BANDA SEA
ARAFURA SEA
IRIAN JAYA
PAPUA NEW GUINEA
Mindanao Trench
Seram (Ceram)
Buru
Flores
Sumba
Sawu Sea
Timor
EAST TIMOR
NUSA TENGGARA TIMUR
Pegunungan Maoke
Equator

50 0 50 100 150 200 km
50 0 50 100 150 miles
BURMA (MYANMAR)
THAILAND
LAOS
VIETNAM
CAMBODIA
YUNNAN
GUANGXI ZHUANGZU ZIZHIQU
GUANGDONG
HAINAN
SHAN
KAYAH
MON
TENASSERIM
G. of Tonkin
Mekong
Salween
HANOI
Haiphong
Vientiane (Viangchan)
BANGKOK
RANGOON (YANGON)
Mandalay
Moulmein
Da Nang
Hue
Luang Prabang
Chiang Mai
Nakhon Ratchasima
Ubon Ratchathani
Khon Kaen
Udon Thani
Haikou
Zhanjiang
Nanning
Phnom Dangrek
Dawna Range
Bilauktaung
Khorat
Cao Nguyen Boloven
Tran Ninh
Qui Nhon
Buon Me Thuot
ANGKOR
Tonle Sap
Battambang

32
41
36
36

Gulf of Thailand

SOUTH CHINA SEA

MALAYSIA

PENINSULAR MALAYSIA

INDONESIA

Strait of Malacca

Myeik Kyunzu (Mergui Archipelago)

Malay Peninsula

Sumatera

Nam (Cochin China)

Phan

Chuor Phnum Damrei

Phnum Kravanh

Mekong

Tenasserim, Kui Buri, Prachuap Khiri Khan, Thap Sakae, Ban Ko Yai Chim, Bang Saphan, Kanmaw Kyun, Letsok-aw Kyun, Bokpyin, Lanbi Kyun, Pathiu, Ban Pak Chan, Chumphon, Kho Khot Kra, Kra Buri, Zadetkyi Kyun, Kawthaung, Sawi, Ko Tao, Ranong, Lang Suan, Ko Surin Nua, Ko Phangan, Ko Samui, Kapoe, Ban Bang Hin, Chaiya, Ban Don, Surat Thani, Ko Ra, Chieo Lan Res., Phun Phin, Si Chon, Ko Phra Thong, Ban Na San, Phonum, Tha Sala, Phangnga, Nakhon Si Thammarat, Thai Muang, Khok Kloi, Chawang, Pak Phanang, Ban Tha Nun, Krabi, Thung Song, Ban Ron Phibun, Phuket, Ko Phuket, Ko Yao Yai, Ban Khuan Mao, Ko Phi Phi, Huai Yot, Phatthalung, Ko Lanta Yai, Sikao, Trang, Thale Luang, Ban Sanam Chai, Kantang, Ko Talibong, Songkhla, Yong Sata, Rattaphum, Hat Yai, Langu, Ban Khlong Kua, Chana, Thepha, Laem Pho, Panare, Ko Tarutao, Satun, Khok Pho, Pattani, Sai Buri, Ko Batong, Sadao, Yala, Narathiwat, P. Langkawi, Kangar, Changlun, Raman, Rangae, Tumpat, Jitra, Kuala Nerang, Bannang Sata, Pasir Mas, Kota Baharu, Kampong To, Alor Setar, Sungai Kolok, Bacuk, Gurun, Betong, 1452, Pasir Putih, Baling, Kampung Raja, Sungai Petani, Butterworth, Kulim, Gerik, Keroh, Kuala Kerai, George Town, Pinang, Bukit Mertajam, Selama, Dabong, Kuala Terengganu, Bagan Serai, Lenggong, 2176, Marang, Kuala Berang, Taiping, Kuala Kangsar, Gua Musang, Kampung Jerangau, P. Tenggol, Port Weld, G. Korbu, 2182, Gunong Tahan, 2190, Dungun, Gunong, Bruas, Ipoh, Cameron Highlands, Batu Gajah, Kampar, Kemasik, Lumut, 2130, Kuala Lipis, Kampung Air Putih, Teluk Intan, Tapah, Bidor, Jerantut, Cukai, Bagan Datoh, Tanjong Malim, Raub, 2108, Sungai Lembing, Kuantan, Sabak Bernam, Kota Kubu Baharu, Bentung, Mentakab, Maran, Rawang, Karak, Pahang, Pekan, Kuala Selangor, Batu Caves, Jinjang, Kuala Lumpur, Ampang, Petaling Jaya, Kajang, Pelabuhan Kelang, Kelang, Kuala Kelawang, Kuala Rompin, Nenasi, Seremban, Kuala Pilah, Gemas, Padang Endau, Port Dickson, Tampin, Segamat, Mersing, Melaka, Jasin, Labis, Bekok, Kahang, Jemaluang, Muar, Yong Peng, Keluang, Batu Pahat, Air Hitam, Kulai, Kota Tinggi, Pontian Kecil, Johor Baharu, Kukup, SINGAPORE, Strait of Singapore, Batam, Bintan, Tanjungpinang

Pulau Tioman, P. Pemanggil, P. Aur, P. Babi Besar, Pulau Tinggi

Idi, Peureulak, Langsa, Kualasimpang, Pangkalanbrandan, Belawan, Medan, Binjai, 3012, Kutacane, Tebingtinggi, 2451, Kabanjahe, Pematangsiantar, Kisaran, Tanjungbalai, 2457, Danau Toba, Prapat, 2151, Samosir, 2157, Tarutung, 2300, Rantauprapat, Sibolga, 2009, Musala, Bagansiapiapi, Rupat, Dumai, Bengkalis

Laem Ngop, Ko Chang, Trat, Ko Kut, Khemarak Phouminville, 1172, Kachot, Koh Kong, Sre Ambel, Chaak Kampong Saom, Koh Rong, Kampong Saom, Ream, Koh Tang, Dao Phu Quoc, Koh Wai, Dao An Thoi, Hon Nam Du, Hon Panjang

Kompong Chhnang, 1813, Kompong Tralach, Phnom Penh, Kompong Speu, Tomnop Ta Suos, Angtassom, Chamkar Luong, Kampot, Chhuk, Kep, Takeo, Bathay, Kompong Luong, Prey Veng, Banam, Kompong Trach, Kompong Trabeck, Kompong Cham, Chhlong, Sre Khtum, Snoul, Tuy Duc, 1580, Bo Duc, Loc Ninh, Dong Xoai, Hoa Hiep, Chon Thanh, Tay Ninh, Moc Hoa, Tam Chau, Chau Doc, Cao Lanh, Tinh Bien, Ha Tien, Long Xuyen, Kien Tan, Duong Dong, Hon Chong, Rach Gia, Kien Binh, An Bien, Sa Dec, Vinh Long, Can Tho, Tra On, Mac Bac, Ba Dong, Vi Thanh, Soc Trang, Ca Mau, Bac Lieu, Dam Doi, Thuan Hoa, Cai Nuoc, Nam Can, Mui Ca Mau, Hon Khoai, Con Son

THANH PHO HO CHI MINH (SAIGON), Gia Dinh, Ben Luc, Tan An, Can Gio, Go Cong, My Tho, Ba Tri, Vung Tau, Bien Hoa, Xuan Loc, Long Thanh, Xuyen Moc, Cho Phuoc Hai, Ham Tan, Phan Thiet, Tuc Trung, Vo Dat, Ta Lai, Di Linh, Bao Loc, Cao Nguyen, Gia Nghia, Da Lat, 2287, Dong Ba Thin, Cam Ranh, Cam Lam, Phan Rang, Mui Dinh, Ca Na, Tuy Phong, Hoa Da, Nha Trang, Dien Khanh, Cu Lao Hon, Catwick Is.

Kepulauan Anambas (Indonesia), P. Mubur, P. Matak, P. Siantan, Jemaja, P. Midai, Laut, Telukbutun, Kepulauan Natuna Besar (Indonesia), Subi, Seraja, Serasan, Kepulauan Natuna Selatan (Indonesia), Tanjung Datu, Borneo, SARAWAK (Malaysia), Kucing

ft m: 9000 3000, 6000 2000, 4500 1500, 3000 1000, 1200 400, 600 200, 0 0, 200 600, 2000 6000 m ft

Projection: Conical with two standard parallels

East from Greenwich

98, 100, 102, 106, 108, 110

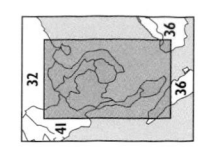

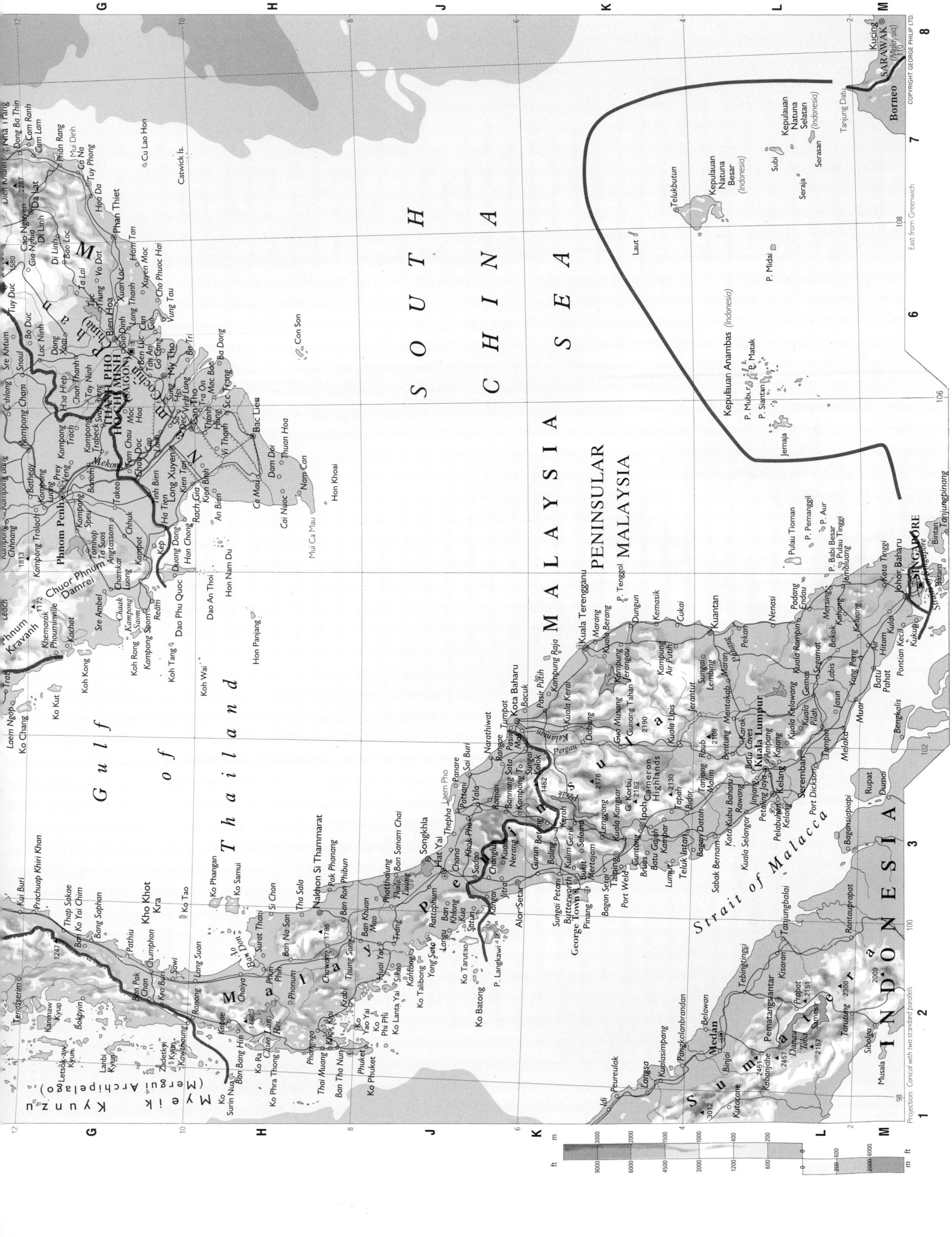

SOUTH ASIA 1:10 000 000

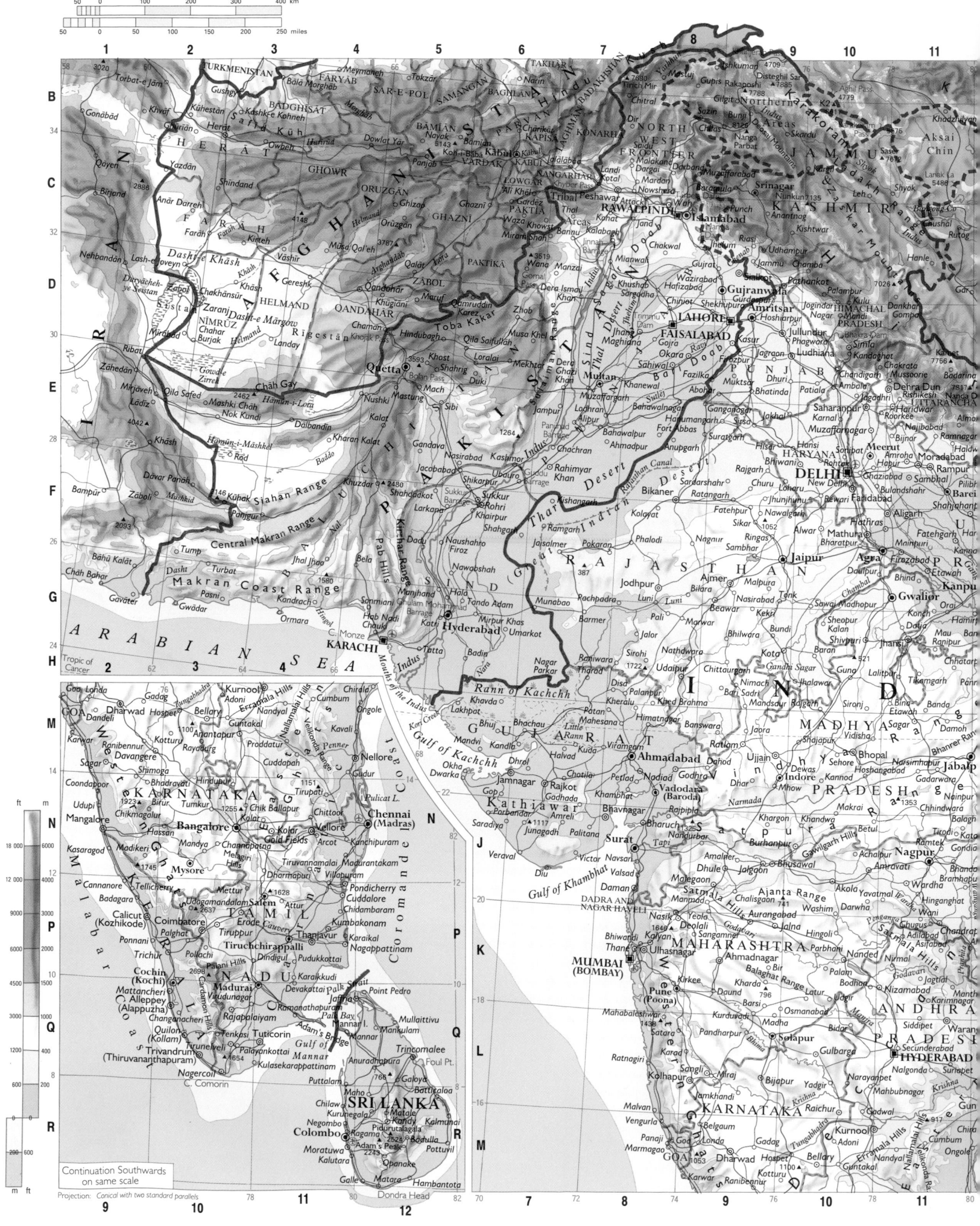

50 0 100 200 300 400 km
50 0 50 100 150 200 250 miles
ARABIAN SEA
AFGHANISTAN
PAKISTAN
INDIA
SRI LANKA
IRAN
TURKMENISTAN
KASHMIR
JAMMU
Northern Areas
Aksai Chin
Karakoram Range
Hindu Kush
BALUCHISTAN
SIND
PUNJAB
RAJASTHAN
GUJARAT
MADHYA PRADESH
MAHARASHTRA
KARNATAKA
KERALA
TAMIL NADU
ANDHRA PRADESH
HARYANA
HIMACHAL PRADESH
UTTARANCHAL
NORTH WEST FRONTIER
Thar Desert
Great Indian Desert
Makran Coast Range
Central Makran Range
Siahan Range
Toba Kakar
Sulaiman Range
Kirthar Range
Rann of Kachchh
Gulf of Kachchh
Gulf of Khambhat
Western Ghats
Eastern Ghats
Satpura Range
Vindhya Range
Malabar Coast
Coromandel Coast
Gulf of Mannar
Palk Strait
Adam's Bridge
Mouths of the Indus
Kabul
Islamabad
RAWALPINDI
LAHORE
FAISALABAD
Quetta
KARACHI
Hyderabad
Multan
Amritsar
Gujranwala
DELHI
New Delhi
Jaipur
Agra
Ahmadabad
Vadodara (Baroda)
Surat
MUMBAI (BOMBAY)
Pune (Poona)
Nagpur
Bhopal
Indore
HYDERABAD
Bangalore
Chennai (Madras)
Colombo
Tropic of Cancer
Continuation Southwards on same scale
Projection: Conical with two standard parallels

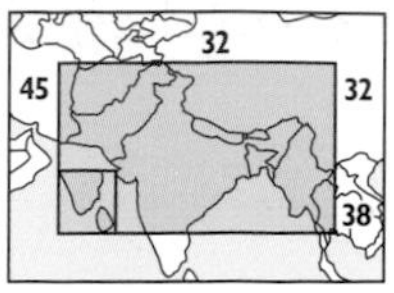

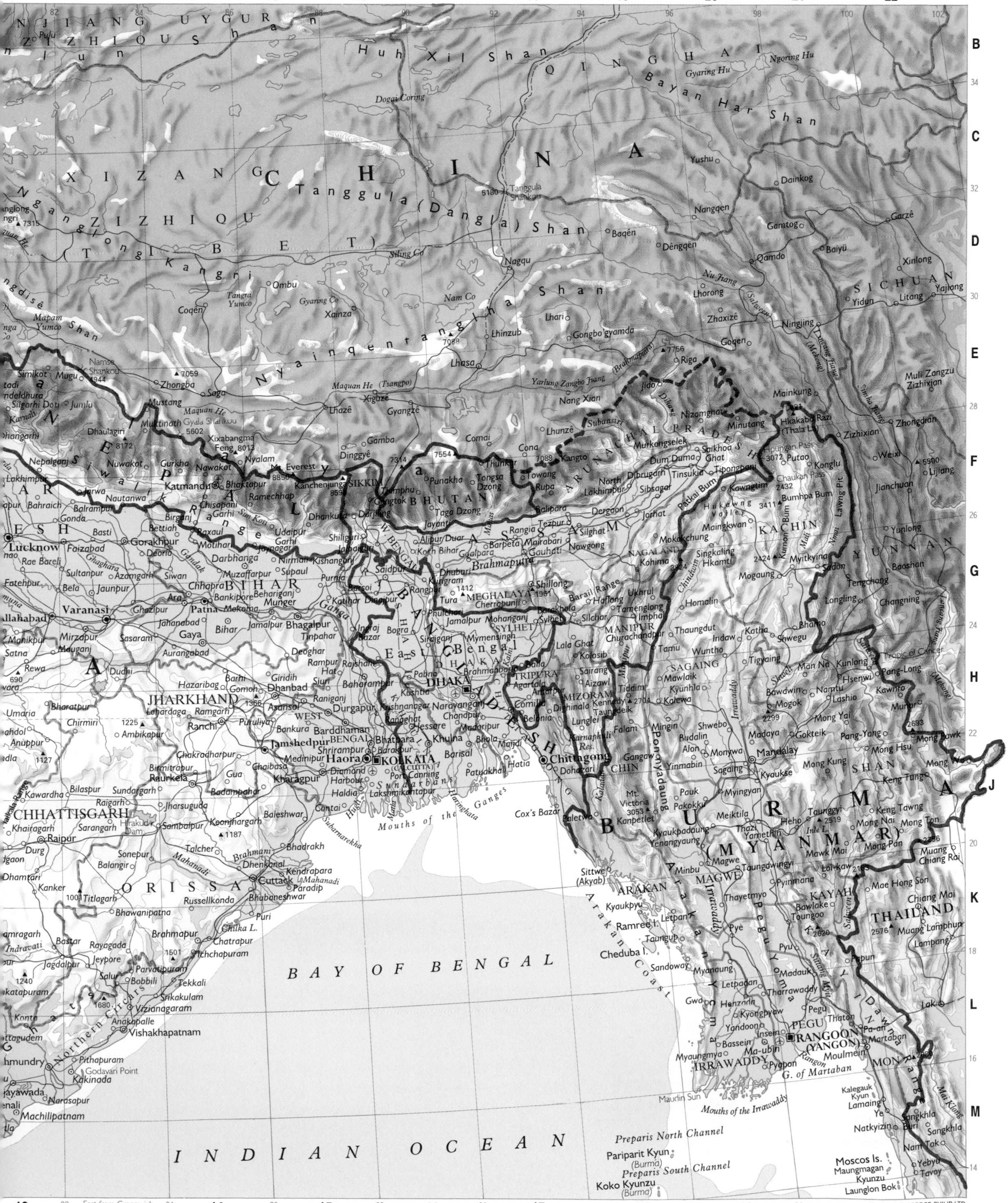

BAY OF BENGAL

INDIAN OCEAN

CHINA

XIZANG ZIZHIQU (TIBET)

QINGHAI

SICHUAN

YUNNAN

NEPAL

BHUTAN

BANGLADESH

BIHAR

JHARKHAND

WEST BENGAL

ORISSA

CHHATTISGARH

BURMA (MYANMAR)

THAILAND

ARUNACHAL PRADESH

ASSAM

MEGHALAYA

NAGALAND

MANIPUR

MIZORAM

TRIPURA

SIKKIM

KACHIN

SAGAING

SHAN

CHIN

ARAKAN

MAGWE

KAYAH

MON

IRRAWADDY

PEGU

Huh Xil Shan

Tanggula (Dangla) Shan

Bayan Har Shan

Nyainqentanglha Shan

Kunlun Shan

Ngangze Shan

Tangra Yumco

Nam Co

Mapam Yumco

Lhasa

Katmandu

Kanchenjunga 8598

Mt. Everest 8850

Dhaulagiri 8172

Xixabangma Feng 8013

DHAKA

KOLKATA (CALCUTTA)

Haora

Chittagong

Cox's Bazar

Brahmaputra

Ganga

Mouths of the Ganges

Sundarbans

Varanasi

Lucknow

Patna

Jamshedpur

Ranchi

Cuttack

Bhubaneswar

Puri

Chilka L.

Vishakhapatnam

Kakinada

Godavari Point

Tropic of Cancer

Northern Circar

Mandalay

RANGOON (YANGON)

Irrawaddy

Mouths of the Irrawaddy

G. of Martaban

Bassein

Pegu

Moulmein

Thaton

Sittwe (Akyab)

Ramree I.

Cheduba I.

Sandoway

Arakan Coast

Mt. Victoria 3053

Kanpetlet

Preparis North Channel

Preparis South Channel

Pariparit Kyun (Burma)

Koko Kyunzu (Burma)

Moscos Is.

Tavoy

East from Greenwich

COPYRIGHT GEORGE PHILIP LTD.

THE INDO-GANGETIC PLAIN 1:6 000 000

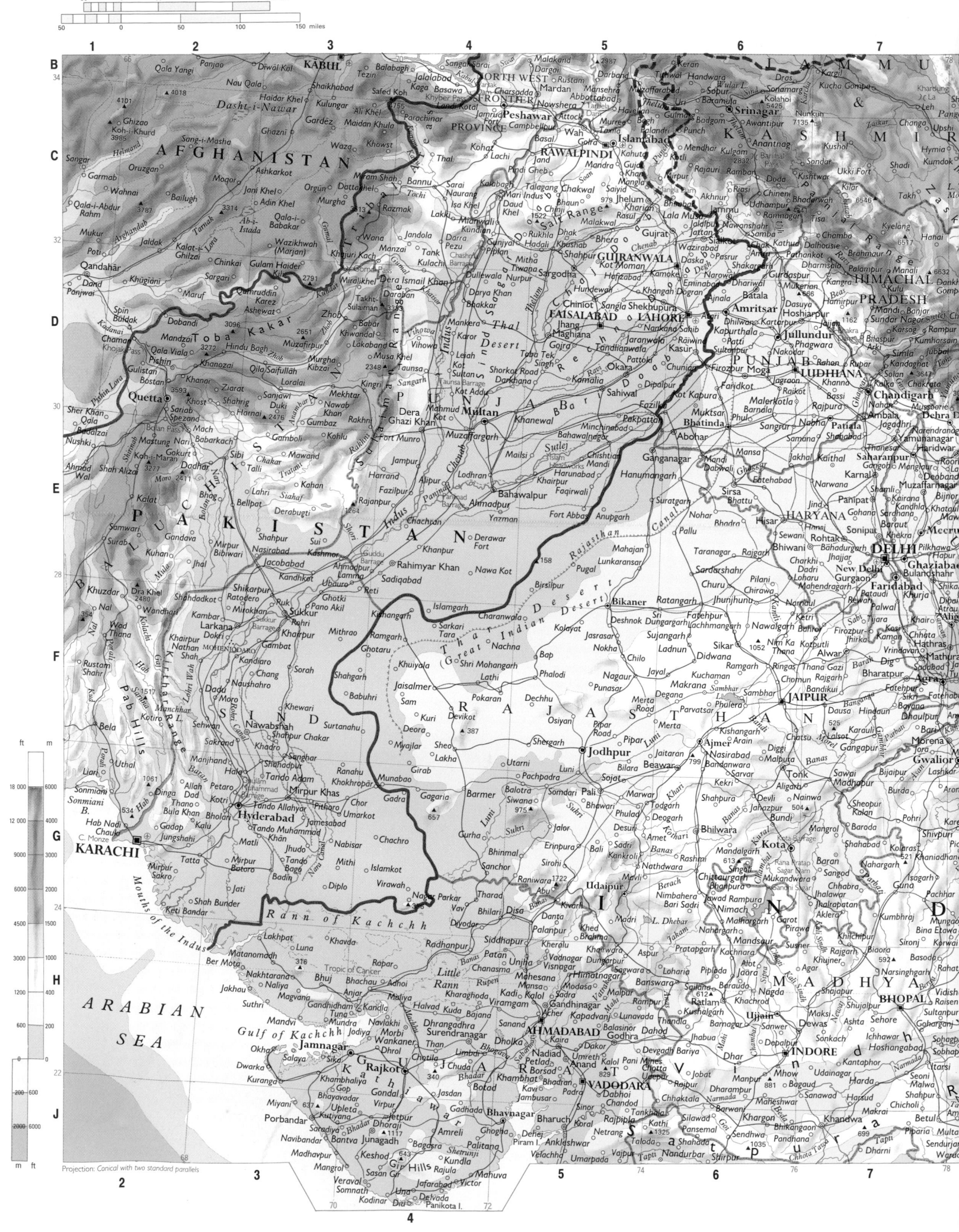
50 0 50 100 150 200 km
50 0 50 100 150 miles
AFGHANISTAN
PAKISTAN
BALUCHISTAN
SIND
PUNJAB
RAJASTHAN
JAMMU & KASHMIR
HIMACHAL PRADESH
HARYANA
MADHYA PRADESH
GUJARAT
NORTH WEST FRONTIER PROVINCE
INDIA
ARABIAN SEA
Gulf of Kachchh
Rann of Kachchh
Little Rann
Mouths of the Indus
Thar Desert (Great Indian Desert)
Thal Desert
Dasht-i-Nawar
Toba Kakar
Salt Range
Kirthar Range
Pab Hills
Gir Hills
Tropic of Cancer
KABUL
Kandahar
Quetta
Peshawar
ISLAMABAD
RAWALPINDI
Srinagar
GUJRANWALA
FAISALABAD
LAHORE
Amritsar
Jullundur
LUDHIANA
Chandigarh
Multan
Bahawalpur
Sukkur
Larkana
Hyderabad
KARACHI
Bikaner
Jodhpur
JAIPUR
Ajmer
DELHI
New Delhi
Agra
Gwalior
Kota
Udaipur
AHMADABAD
VADODARA
Rajkot
Jamnagar
Bhavnagar
Porbandar
Junagadh
INDORE
Ujjain
BHOPAL
Projection: Conical with two standard parallels
ft m
18 000 6000
12 000 4000
9000 3000
6000 2000
4500 1500
3000 1000
1200 400
600 200
0 0
200 600
2000 6000
m ft

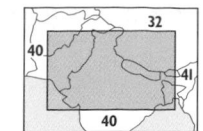

JAMMU AND KASHMIR
On same scale as Main Map

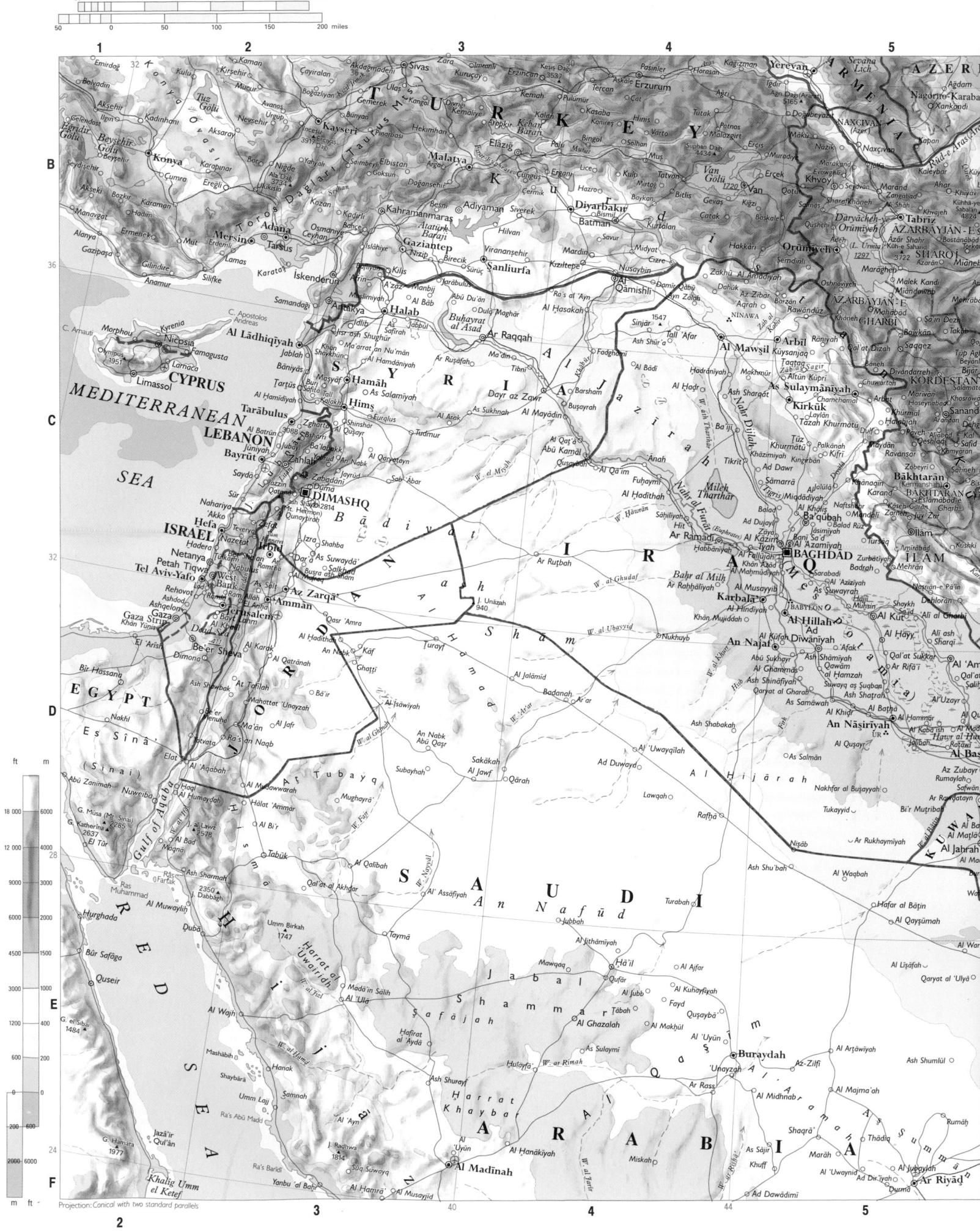

TURKEY
ARMENIA
AZERBAIJAN
SYRIA
CYPRUS
LEBANON
ISRAEL
JORDAN
IRAQ
EGYPT
SAUDI ARABIA
KUWAIT
MEDITERRANEAN SEA
RED SEA
Gulf of Aqaba
Es Sînâ' (Sinai)
Bādiyat ash Shām
Al Jazīrah
Mesopotamia
Al Ḥamād
An Nafūd
Jabal Shammar
Al Ḥijārah
Ḥarrat Khaybar
Al Qaṣīm
Ṣafājah
Toros Dağları
Tuz Gölü
Van Gölü
Daryācheh-ye Orūmīyeh
Buḥayrat al Asad
Milēḥ Tharthār
Baḥr al Milḥ
Dimona
Yerevan
Konya
Kayseri
Sivas
Malatya
Erzurum
Diyarbakır
Adana
Mersin
Gaziantep
Şanlıurfa
Nicosia
Limassol
Al Lādhiqīyah
Ḥalab
Ḥamāh
Ḥimṣ
Ṭarābulus
Bayrūt
DIMASHQ
Ḥefa
Tel Aviv-Yafo
Jerusalem
Amman
Az Zarqā'
Irbid
Al 'Aqabah
Elat
Gaza
Ar Raqqah
Dayr az Zawr
Al Mawṣil
Arbīl
Kirkūk
As Sulaymānīyah
BAGHDĀD
Karbalā'
An Najaf
Al Ḥillah
Ad Dīwānīyah
Al Kūt
An Nāṣirīyah
Ar Ramādī
Tabrīz
Orūmīyeh
Bākhtarān
Al Jahrah
Tabūk
Al Madīnah
Ar Riyāḍ
Buraydah
Ḥā'il
Al Jawf
Sakākah
Tayma
Al Wajh
Ḍubā
Hurghada
Quseir
Projection: Conical with two standard parallels

25
25
40
51
46

6 7 8 9 10

B C D E F

TURKMENISTAN
Kara Kum
Kopet Dagh
CASPIAN SEA
IRAN
Dasht-e Kavir
Dasht-e Lut
AFGHANISTAN
PAKISTAN
THE GULF
Gulf of Oman
UNITED ARAB EMIRATES
OMAN
QATAR
BAHRAIN
Reshteh-ye Kuhha-ye Alborz
Kuh-e Dinar
Zagros
Kuhha-ye Bashakerd
Safid Kuh
Dasht-e Margow
Gowd-e Zirreh
Daryacheh-ye Namak
Daryacheh-ye Namakzar
Namakzar-e Shahdad
Biaban-e Kerman
Hamun-e Jaz Murian
Hamun-i Mashkel
Makran
Al Jafurah

Baki
Türkmenbashi
Nebitdag
Ashgabat
Mary
Chärjew
Tejen
Sarakhs
Herat
Mashhad
Neyshabur
Sabzevar
Gorgan
Sari
Babol
Amol
Rasht
Ardabil
Qazvin
Karaj
Tehran
Rey
Qom
Kashan
Arak
Malayer
Borujerd
Khorramabad
Dezful
Ahvaz
Khorramshahr
Abadan
Masjed Soleyman
Esfahan
Najafabad
Shahr-e Kord
Yasuj
Yazd
Ardakan
Shiraz
Kazerun
Bushehr
Kerman
Rafsanjan
Sirjan
Bam
Zahedan
Zabol
Bandar Abbas
Qeshm
Jask
Chah Bahar
Birjand
Tabas
Qayen
Farah
Kuwayt
Ad Dammam
Al Manamah
Ad Dawhah
Dubayy
Abu Zaby
Al Ayn
Ras al Khaymah
Al Fujayrah
Ash Shariqah

Kuh-e Taftan 4042
Kuh-e Hazaran 4419
Kuh-e Jebal Barez 3962
Kuhbonan 2499

East from Greenwich
52 56 60
COPYRIGHT GEORGE PHILIP LTD.

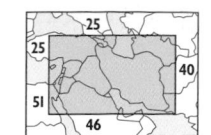

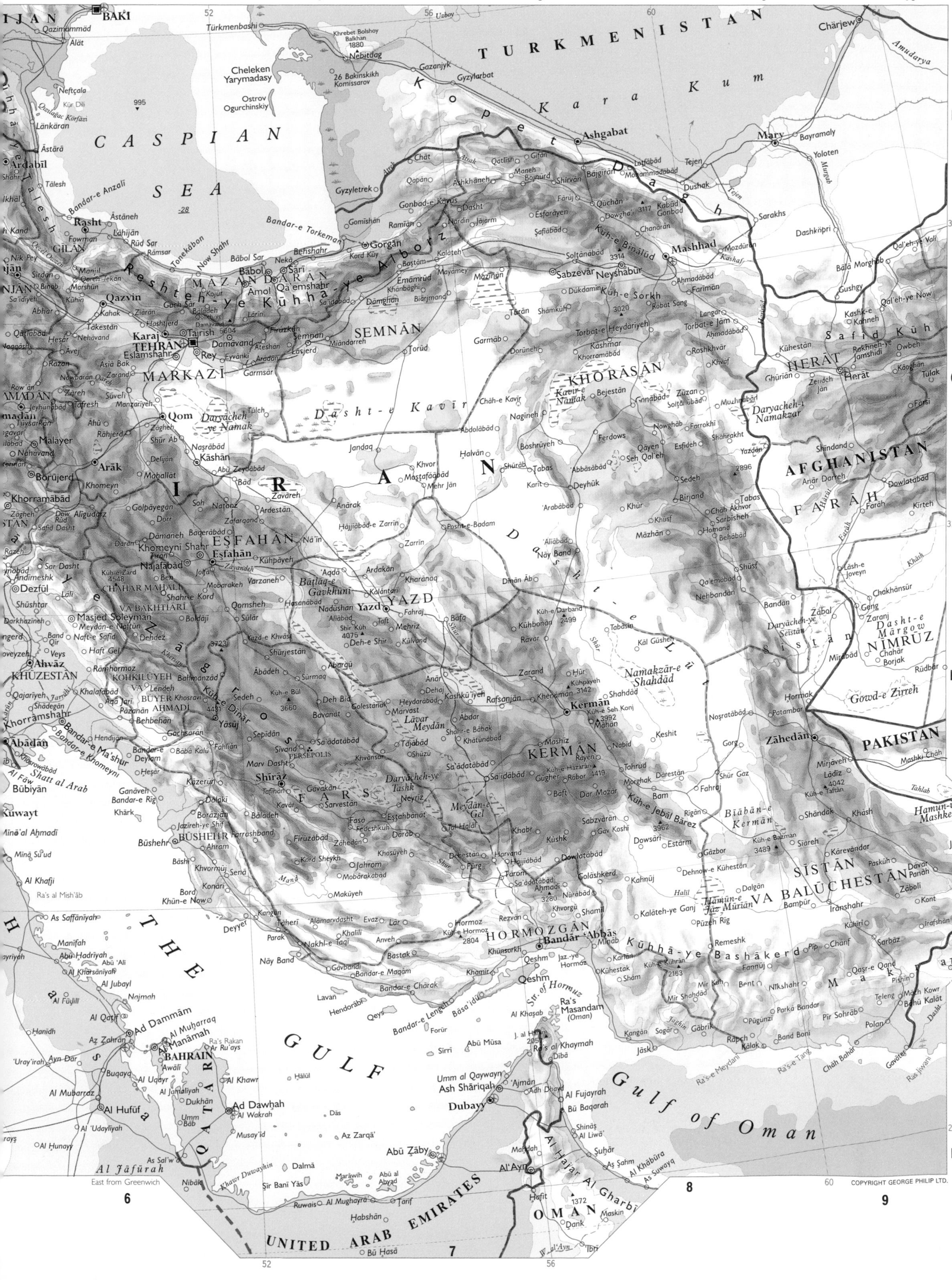

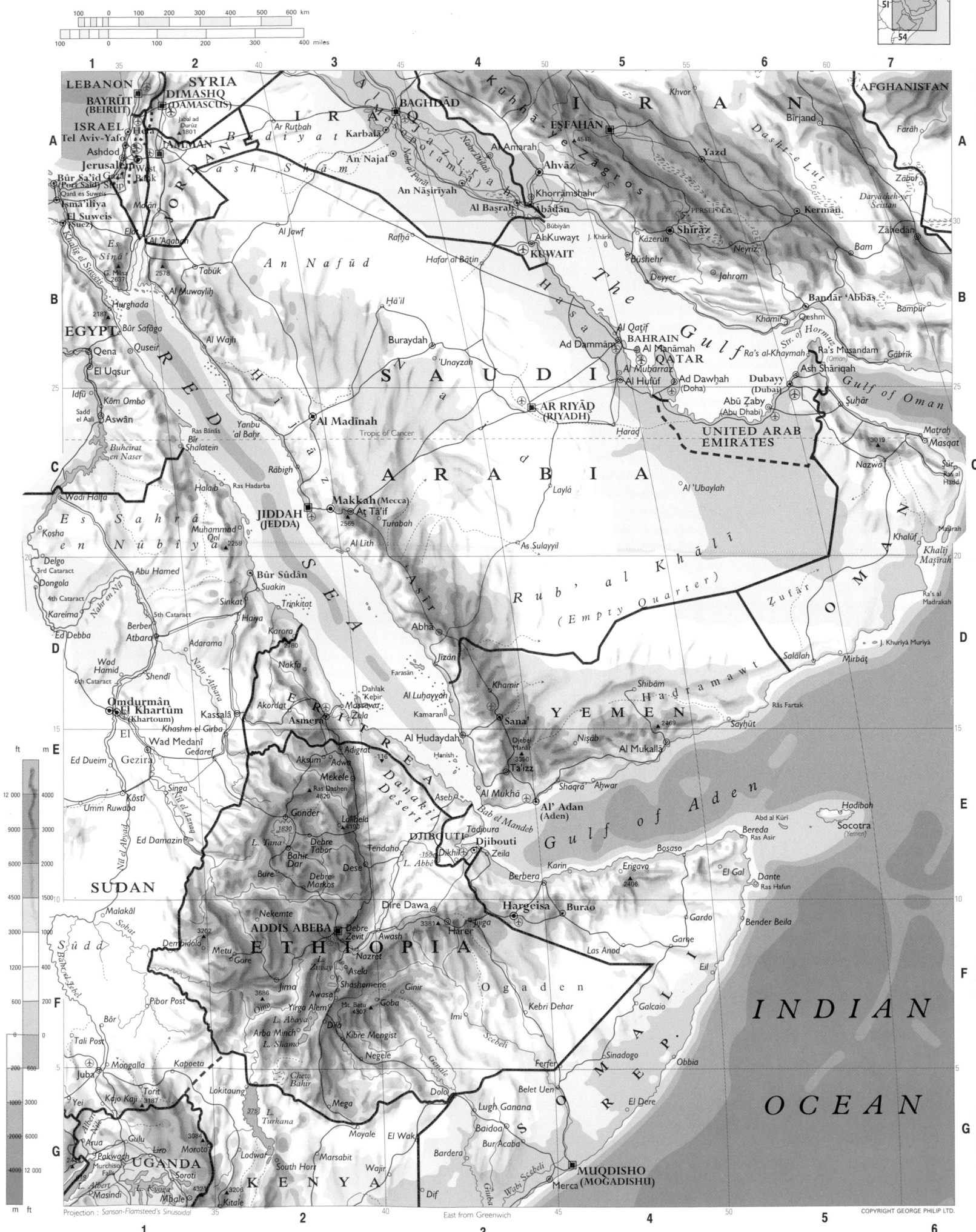

100 0 100 200 300 400 500 600 km
100 0 100 200 300 400 miles
LEBANON
SYRIA
BAYRŪT (BEIRUT)
DIMASHQ (DAMASCUS)
ISRAEL
Tel Aviv-Yafo
Ashdod
Jerusalem
West Bank
'AMMĀN
JORDAN
Bûr Sa'îd (Port Said)
Ismâ'ilîya
El Suweis (Suez)
Ma'ān
Elat
Al 'Aqabah
Es Sînâ'
G. Mûsa 2637
Tabūk
Al Muwaylih
Hurghada
EGYPT
Bûr Safâga
Quseir
Qena
El Uqsur
Idfû
Kôm Ombo
Aswân
Buheirat en Naser
Ras Bânâs
Bîr Shalatein
Halaib
Wadi Halfa
Es Sahrâ en Nûbîya
Kosha
Delgo
3rd Cataract
Dongola
4th Cataract
Kareima
Abu Hamed
Bûr Sûdân
Suakin
Sinkat
Berber
Atbara
5th Cataract
Ed Debba
Adarama
Wad Hamid
6th Cataract
Shendî
Omdurmân
El Khartûm (Khartoum)
Kassalâ
Khashm el Girba
Wad Medanî
Gedaref
Ed Dueim
Gezira
Kôstî
Umm Ruwaba
Singa
Ed Damazin
SUDAN
Malakâl
Sobat
Sûdd
Bahr el Jebel
Pibor Post
Bôr
Tali Post
Juba
Mongalla
Kapoeta
Torit
Yei
Kajo Kaji
Lokitaung
L. Turkana
Lodwar
UGANDA
Arua
Gulu
Moroto
Soroti
Masindi
Mbale
Kitale
KENYA
South Horr
Marsabit
Moyale
El Wak
Wajir
Dif
BAGHDĀD
IRAQ
Ar Rutbah
Karbalā
An Najaf
An Nāşirīyah
Al Başrah
Al 'Amārah
Bādiyat ash Shām
Al Jawf
Rafhā
An Nafūd
Hafar al Bāţin
Ḩā'il
Buraydah
'Unayzah
Al Wajh
Al Madīnah
Yanbu 'al Baḩr
Rābigh
Makkah (Mecca)
JIDDAH (JEDDA)
Aţ Ţā'if
Turabah
Al Līth
Abhā
Jīzān
Farasān
SAUDI ARABIA
AR RIYĀḐ (RIYADH)
Al Qaţīf
Ad Dammām
BAHRAIN
Al Manāmah
QATAR
Al Mubarraz
Al Hufūf
Ad Dawḩah (Doha)
Ḩaraḑ
Laylá
As Sulayyil
Rub' al Khālī (Empty Quarter)
Tropic of Cancer
KUWAIT
Al Kuwayt
ĀBĀDĀN
Khorramshahr
Ahvāz
IRAN
EŞFAHĀN
Kūhhā-ye Zāgros
Khvor
Bīrjand
Yazd
Dasht-e Lut
Kermān
Shīrāz
Kāzerūn
Būshehr
Deyyer
Jahrom
Neyrīz
Bam
Zāhedān
Zābol
Daryācheh-ye Seistan
Farāh
AFGHANISTAN
Bandār 'Abbās
Bampūr
Qeshm
Str. of Hormuz
Ra's Musandam
Ras al-Khaymah
Dubayy (Dubai)
Ash Shāriqah
Abū Zaby (Abu Dhabi)
UNITED ARAB EMIRATES
The Gulf
Gulf of Oman
Şuḩār
Maţraḩ
Masqat
Nazwá
Şūr
Ra's al Hadd
OMAN
Maşīrah
Khalīj Maşīrah
Ra's al Madrakah
Ẓufār
Şalālah
Mirbāţ
J. Khuriyā Muriyā
Al 'Ubaylah
Ḩaḑramawt
Shibām
YEMEN
Sana'
Al Ḩudaydah
Kamarān
Al Luhayyah
Ta'izz
Al Mukhā
Al 'Adan (Aden)
Al Mukallā
Sayhūt
Rās Fartak
Gulf of Aden
Socotra
Hadiboh
Abd al Kūrī
RED SEA
ERITREA
Asmera
Massawa
Akordat
Nakfa
Karora
Dahlak Kebir
Zula
Aksum
Adwa
Adigrat
Mekele
Danakil Desert
Aseb
Bab el Mandeb
DJIBOUTI
Djibouti
Tadjoura
Dikhil
Zeila
L. Abbe
Gonder
Ras Dashen 4620
L. Tana
Bahir Dar
Debre Tabor
Lalibela
Dese
Debre Markos
Bure
Tendaho
ETHIOPIA
ADDIS ABEBA
Debre Zeyit
Nekemte
Dembidolo
Metu
Gore
Awash
Dire Dawa
Harer
Jijiga
Nazret
Asela
Ziway
Shashemene
Jima
Awasa
Yirga Alem
Goba
Mt. Batu 4307
Ginir
Imi
L. Abaya
Arba Minch
L. Shamo
Dila
Kibre Mengist
Negele
Chew Bahir
Mega
Dolo
Ogaden
Kebri Dehar
Hargeisa
Burao
Berbera
Karin
Erigavo
Bosaso
Bereda
Ras Asir
El Gal
Dante
Ras Hafun
Gardo
Bender Beila
Garoe
Las Anod
Eil
Galcaio
Sinadogo
Obbia
Ferfer
Belet Uen
El Dere
Lugh Ganana
Baidoa
Bur Acaba
Bardera
SOMALI REP.
MUQDISHO (MOGADISHU)
Merca
INDIAN OCEAN
Projection : Sanson-Flamsteed's Sinusoidal
East from Greenwich
COPYRIGHT GEORGE PHILIP LTD.

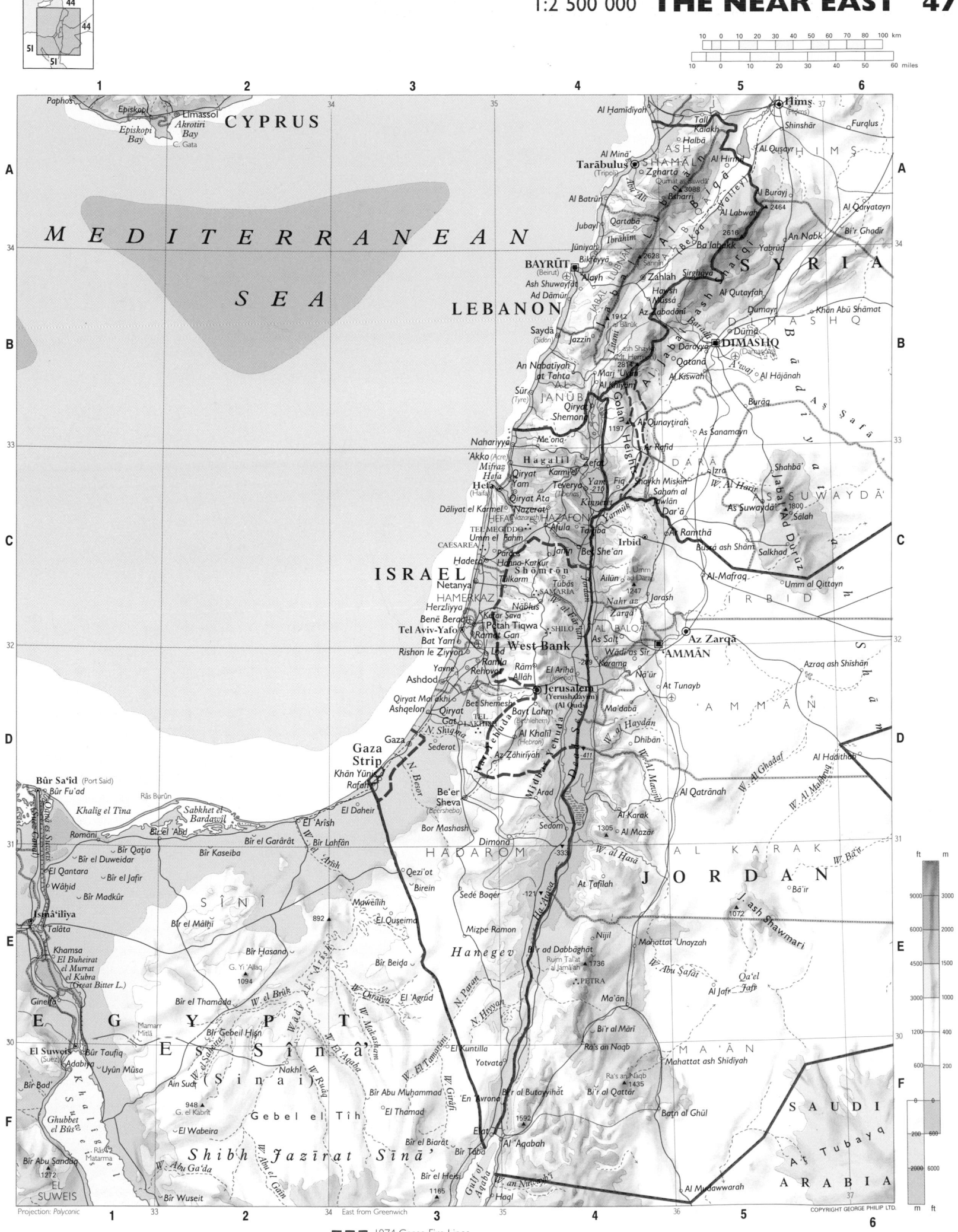

10 0 10 20 30 40 50 60 70 80 100 km

10 0 10 20 30 40 50 60 miles

Paphos°   Episkopi°   °Limassol   **C Y P R U S**
Akrotiri
Episkopi   Bay   C. Gata
Bay

M E D I T E R R A N E A N

S E A

Al Hamidiyah   °**Hims**
Tall   (Homs)
Kalakh
Halbā   Shinshār   Furqlus

ASH
Al Minā'°   SHAMĀL   Al Hirmil
Tarābulus ⊙   Zgharta   H I M S
(Tripoli)   Qurnat as Sawdā'
3088   Al Qusayr
Al Batrūn°   Bsharri   Al Buray
Jubayl°   Qartabā   Al Labwah   2464   Al Qaryatayn
Ibrāhim   2618
Jūniyah°   Bikfayyā   An Nabk   Bir Ghadir
BAYRŪT ⊙   2628   Ba'labakk   **S Y R I A**
(Beirut)   Sannin   Yabrūd
Ash Shuwayfāt°   °Alayh   Sirghāyā
Ad Dāmūr°   Zahlah   DIMASHQ
1942   Az Zabadāni   Dumā
LEBANON   Al Bārūk   Al Qutayfah
Saydā°   Jazzin   Dārayyā° ⊙ **DIMASHQ**   Khān Abū Shāmat
(Sidon)   (Damascus)
Mt Hermon   Qaṭanā°   A'waj   Al Hājānah
An Nabatiyah   2814
at Tahta°   Marj 'Uyūn   Burāq
Sūr°   Al Khiyam   Golan   Al Kiswah
(Tyre)   AL   Qiryat   Heights   DAR'A
JANŪB   Shemona   1197   Al Qunayṭirah   As Sanamayn   AS SUWAYDĀ'
Nahariyya°   Me'ona   Ar Rafid
Shahbā°   Jabal
°**Akko** (Acre)   Hagalil   Zefat   Izra°   W. Al Hārir
Mifraz   Qiryat   Karmi'el   Fiq   Shaykh Miskin   As Suwaydā'°   1800   Ad Durūz
Hefa   Yam   Yam -210   Saham al   Sālah
Hefa   Teverya   °Jawlān   Dar'ā
(Haifa)   Qiryat Ata   (Tiberias)   Dar'ā
Dāliyat el Karmel°   Nazerat   Kinneret
TEL MEGIDDO   HEFA   (Nazareth)   Yarmūk   Al Ramthā°
CAESAREA   Umm el Fahm°   HAZAFON   Buşrā ash Shām
Afula   Tubā   IRBID
°Hadera   Pardes   Jenin   Bet She'an   Ajlūn°   Umm al Qittayn
Hanna-Karkur   J. Umm   ad Dami
ISRAEL   Shomron   °Irbid   1247   °Al-Mafraq
Tulkarm°   SAMARIA   Ailūn°   °Jarash
Netanya   Tūbās°   Nahr az
HAMERKAZ   Nāblus°   Zarqā
Herzliyya°   Kefar Sava   J. al Fār
Benē Beraq°   °Petah Tiqwa   SHILO   As Salt°   **Az Zarqā**
Tel Aviv-Yafo   Ramat Gan   AL BALQĀ'   **AMMĀN** ⊡
Bat Yam   °Lod   **West Bank**   Wādi as Sir   Karama
Rishon le Ziyyon°   Ramla   Rām   El Arīhā   759
Yavne°   Allāh   (Jericho)   Na'ūr°   A M M Ā N
Ashdod°   Rehovot   At Tunayb°   Azraq ash Shishān
Qiryat Mal'akhi°   **Jerusalem**   Ma'dabā°
Ashqelon°   Bet Shemesh°   (Yerushalayim)
Qiryat   (Al Quds)
Gat°   TEL   Bayt Lahm
N. Shiqma   LAKHISH   (Bethlehem)   W. al Haydān
Gaza°   Al Khalil   Dhibān°   Al Hadithah°
Gaza   Sederot°   (Hebron)   W. al Mawjib
Strip   Az Zāhiriyāh°   -411
Khān Yūnis°   N. Besar   Arad°   'Al Karak°   W. Al Ghadaf   Al Qatrānah°
Rafah°   Be'er   Midbar Yehuda   W. al Mawjib
Būr Sa'id (Port Said)   Sheva   Sedom   1305   Al Mazar°
°Būr Fu'ad   (Beersheba)   'Al Karak
Khalig el Tina   Rās Burūn   El Daheir°   Bor Mashash°
Sabkhet el   **J O R D A N**
Romāni°   Bardawil   El 'Arish°   Dimona°   -333   W. al Hasa   AL KARAK
Bir el 'Abd°   HADAROM   At Tafilah°   W. Bā'ir
Bir Qatia°   Bir el Garārāt°   Bir Lahfān°   Bā'ir°
°Bir el Duweidar   Bir Kaseiba°   Sedé Boqer°   -121   J. ash Shawmari
El Qantara°   Bir el Jafir°   °Qezi'ot   Nijil°   Mahattat 'Unayzah   1072
°Wāhid   Bir Madkūr°   °Birein   Mahattat 'Unayzah
Ismā'iliya   892   Sedé Boqer°   Bi'r ad Dabbāghāt°   W. Abu Safāt
°Talāta   S Ī N Ī   El Quseima°   Rum Tal'at   1736
Khamsa°   Maweilih°   al Jamā'ah   Qa'el
El Buheirat   Hanegev   Mizpe Ramon°   °PETRA   Jafr°
el Murrat   G. Yi 'Allaq   El 'Ouseima°   Ma'ān°   Al Jafr°
el Kubra   1094   N. Paran   M A 'Ā N
(Great Bitter L.)   Bir Hasano°   Bi'r al Māri°
Ginelfa°   Bir el Thamāda°   W. el Brūk   N. Hiyyon   Ra's an Naqb°
W. el Agrūd   Ra's an Naqb°
E G Y P T   W. el Ouraiya   El 'Agrūd°   Mahattat ash Shidiyah
Mamarr   El Kuntilla°   Mahattat ash Shidiyah
El Suweis   Mitlā   Bir Gebeil Hisn°   'En Yahav°   1435
(Suez)   E   S Ī N Â'   Nakhl°   Yotvata°   **S A U D I**
°Būr Taufiq   (S i n a i)   W. El Tamāwn°   Bi'r al Butayyihāt°   Batn al Ghul°
Adabiya°   948   Bir Abu Muhammad°   Bi'r al Qattār°   **A R A B I A**
°Uyūn Mūsa   G. el Kabrit   El Thamad°   1592
Bir Bad'°   Gebel el Tih   **Elat**   At Tubayq
Ghubbet   El Wabeira°   Bir el Biarāt°   Al Mudawwarah°
el Bûs   Bir Abu Ga'da   Bir Tāba°   Al 'Aqabah
1272   **Shibh Jazirat Sina'**   Bir el Hersi°   Gulf of
EL   Bir Wuseit°   1165   Aqaba   an Nuşeib°
SUWEIS   Hagl°

Projection: Polyconic   East from Greenwich   COPYRIGHT GEORGE PHILIP LTD.

≡≡≡ 1974 Cease Fire Lines

See page 177 World: Regions in the News
for a map showing the areas under Palestinian control.

	ft	m
	9000	3000
	6000	2000
	4500	1500
	3000	1000
	1200	400
	600	200
	200	600
	2000	6000
	m	ft

AFRICA : Physical 1:42 000 000

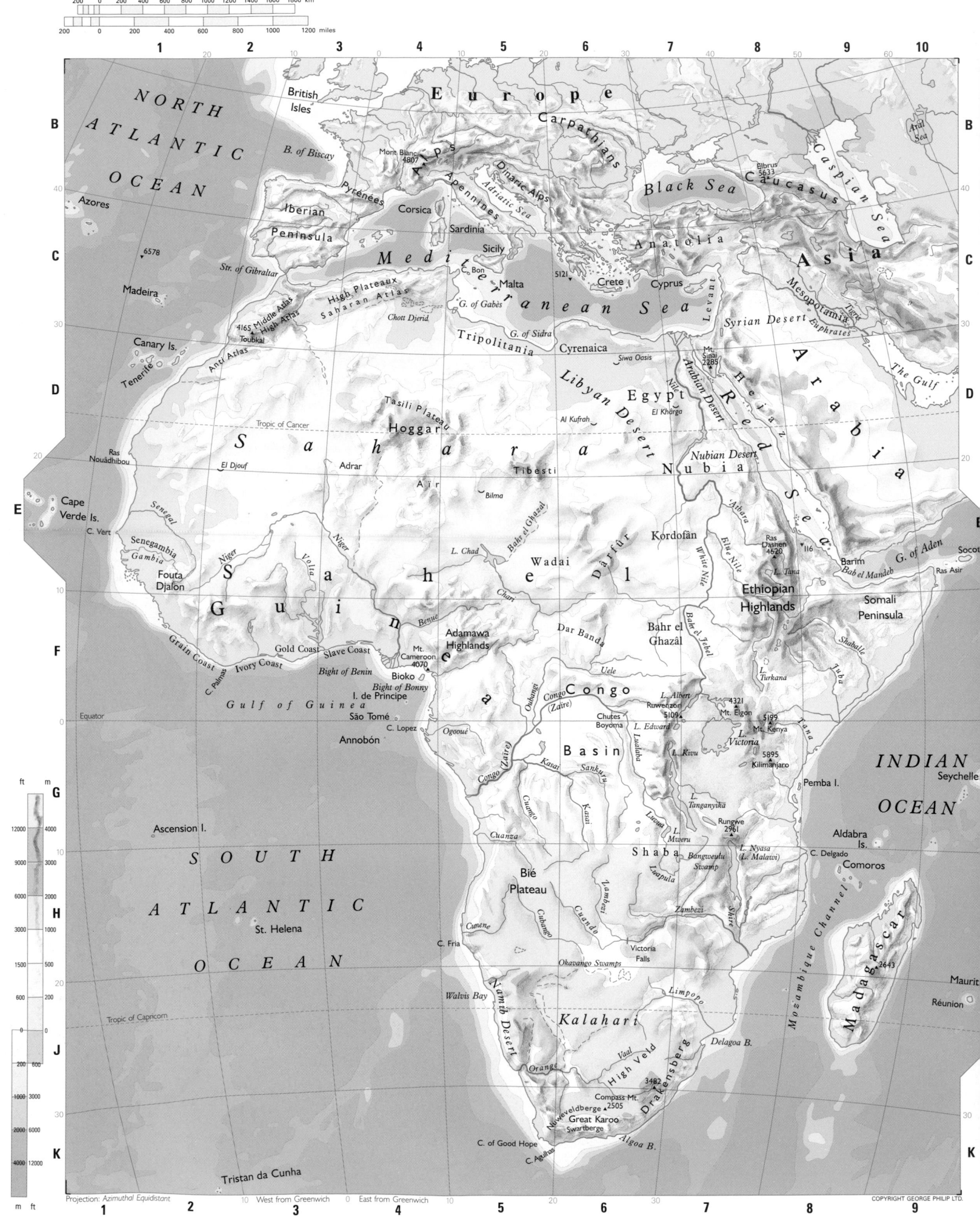
200 0 200 400 600 800 1000 1200 1400 1600 1800 km
200 0 200 400 600 800 1000 1200 miles
NORTH ATLANTIC OCEAN
British Isles
B. of Biscay
Europe
Carpathians
Mont Blanc 4807
Alps
Dinaric Alps
Apennines
Adriatic Sea
Black Sea
Elbrus 5633
Caucasus
Caspian Sea
Aral Sea
Azores
Pyrénées
Iberian Peninsula
Corsica
Sardinia
Sicily
Anatolia
Asia
6578
Str. of Gibraltar
Mediterranean Sea
C. Bon
Malta
5121
Crete
Cyprus
Levant
Mesopotamia
Tigris
Madeira
High Plateaux
Saharan Atlas
G. of Gabès
Chott Djerid
Syrian Desert
Euphrates
4165 Middle Atlas
High Atlas
Toubkal
Tripolitania
G. of Sidra
Cyrenaica
Canary Is.
Anti Atlas
Tenerife
Siwa Oasis
Mt. Sinai 2285
Arabia
The Gulf
Libyan Desert
Egypt
Nile
Arabian Desert
El Khârga
Hejaz
Red Sea
Tasili Plateau
Hoggar
Tropic of Cancer
Al Kufrah
Sahara
Ras Nouâdhibou
El Djouf
Adrar
Tibesti
Nubian Desert
Nubia
Aïr
Bilma
Cape Verde Is.
Senegal
C. Vert
Atbara
Bahr el Ghazal
Kordofân
Senegambia
Gambia
Niger
Volta
L. Chad
Wadai
Dârfûr
White Nile
Blue Nile
Ras Dashen 4620
116
Barim
G. of Aden
Bab el Mandeb
Socot
Ras Asir
Fouta Djalon
Sahel
L. Tana
Ethiopian Highlands
Chari
Somali Peninsula
Guinea
Benue
Dar Banda
Bahr el Ghazâl
Bahr el Jebel
Shaballe
Grain Coast
Gold Coast
Slave Coast
Adamawa Highlands
Mt. Cameroon 4070
Ivory Coast
C. Palmas
Bight of Benin
Bioko
Bight of Bonny
I. de Principe
Uele
L. Turkana
Juba
Gulf of Guinea
Oubangui
Congo (Zaïre)
Congo
L. Albert
Ruwenzori 5109
4321 Mt. Elgon
5199 Mt. Kenya
Tana
São Tomé
Equator
C. Lopez
Ogooué
Chutes Boyoma
L. Edward
L. Victoria
Annobón
Basin
Lualaba
L. Kivu
5895 Kilimanjaro
INDIAN OCEAN
Seychelle
Congo (Zaïre)
Kasai
Sankuru
Pemba I.
Cuango
L. Tanganyika
Rungwe 2961
Ascension I.
Cuanza
Lucuna
L. Mweru
Aldabra Is.
SOUTH ATLANTIC OCEAN
Shaba
Bangweulu Swamp
L. Nyasa (L. Malawi)
C. Delgado
Comoros
Bié Plateau
Luapula
Zambezi
Shire
Mozambique Channel
Madagascar
St. Helena
Cunene
Cubango
Cuando
C. Fria
Victoria Falls
Okavango Swamps
2643
Maurit
Walvis Bay
Namib Desert
Limpopo
Réunion
Tropic of Capricorn
Kalahari
Delagoa B.
Vaal
High Veld
Orange
Drakensberg
3482
Compass Mt. 2505
Nuweveldberge
Great Karoo
Swartberge
Algoa B.
C. of Good Hope
C. Agulhas
Tristan da Cunha
ft m
12000 4000
9000 3000
6000 2000
3000 1000
1500 500
600 200
0 0
200 600
1000 3000
2000 6000
4000 12000
m ft
Projection: Azimuthal Equidistant
10 West from Greenwich 0 East from Greenwich 10 20 30
1 2 3 4 5 6 7 8 9 10
B C D E F G H J K

200 0 200 400 600 800 1000 1200 1400 1600 1800 km
200 0 200 400 600 800 1000 1200 miles

NORTH
ATLANTIC
OCEAN

UNITED
KINGDOM
NETH.
LONDON
BELG.
PARIS
FRANCE
SWITZ.
B. of Biscay

GERMANY
CZECH REP.
Prague
Vienna
AUSTRIA
HUNGARY
CROATIA
BOS.-
HERZ.
YUG.
ALB.
MAC.

POLAND
Warsaw

UKRAINE
Kiev
Odessa
ROMANIA
BULGARIA
Black Sea

RUSSIA
Volgograd

KAZAKSTAN
Aral
Sea

Azores
(Port.)

Madeira
(Port.)

Lisbon
Madrid
PORTUGAL
SPAIN

Corsica
Rome
Sardinia
Sicily

ITALY
Adriatic Sea

Athens
GREECE

Crete

Mediterranean Sea

TURKEY
Ankara

GEORGIA
ARM.
AZER.
Baku
Caspian Sea

Tel Aviv
CYPRUS
LEB.
SYRIA
Aleppo
Damascus
Jaffa
ISRAEL
JORDAN
Jerusalem
Tigris
Euphrates
IRAQ
Baghdad
Basra
KUWAIT
Mosul

Esfahan
TEHRAN
IRAN

TURKMEN.

Canary Is.
(Sp.)

Algiers
Rabat
Casablanca
Tétouan
Fès
MOROCCO
Marrakesh

Annaba
Constantine
Tunis
TUNISIA
Sfax
MALTA
Tripoli
Misratah

Benghazi

Alexandria
Port Said
Suez
CAIRO
El Faiyûm

Port Sudan
Wadi Halfa
Aswan
Asyût
EGYPT

Suez

SAUDI
ARABIA
Medina
Jedda
Mecca
BAHRAIN
QATAR
The Gulf
Riyadh

El Aaiún
Fdérik
WESTERN SAHARA
Dakhla
Tropic of Cancer

ALGERIA
In Salah
Sahara

LIBYA
Marzûq
Al Jawf

Ras Nouârîhibou
Nouakchott
MAURITANIA

St-Louis
Senegal
Dakar
C. Vert
SENEGAL
GAMBIA
Banjul
GUINEA-BISSAU
Bissau

PE VERDE IS.
Praia

MALI
Bamako
Tombouctou
Agadès
Niger
Niamey
BURKINA
FASO
Ouagadougou
Bobo-
Dioulasso

NIGER

CHAD
L. Chad
Abéché
Ndjamena

SUDAN
El Fâsher
El Obeid
Omdurmân
Khartoum
Wâd Medani
Atbara
Atbara
Nile

ERITREA
Mesewa
Asmera

YEMEN
Socotra
(Yemen)

G. of Aden
DJIBOUTI
Djibouti
Berbera
Ras Asir

Conakry
Freetown
GUINEA
SIERRA
LEONE
LIBERIA
Monrovia

IVORY
COAST
Bouaké
Yamoussoukro
Abidjan

GHANA
Kumasi
Sekondi-
Takoradi
Accra
TOGO
Lomé
BENIN
Porto
Novo

NIGERIA
Kano
Maiduguri
Abuja
Ibadan
Lagos
Enugu
Port
Harcourt
Benue

CAMEROON
Douala
Yaoundé
Malabo
EQUATORIAL
GUINEA
SÃO TOMÉ & PRINCIPE
Bight of Benin

CENTRAL
AFRICAN REP.
Bangui

Wau
Malakâl
White Nile
Blue Nile
L. Tana

Addis Ababa
ETHIOPIA
Harer
Shabelle

SOMALI REP.
Mogadishu

Gulf of Guinea
Equator
Annobón
C. Lopez

GABON
Libreville

CONGO
Brazzaville
Pointe-Noire
CABINDA
(Angola)

Mbandaka
CONGO
(DEM. REP. OF THE)
Kisangani
Kinshasa
Matadi
Kasai
Kananga

L. Albert
L. Turkana
L. Edward
UGANDA
Kampala
L. Kivu
RWANDA
Kigali
BURUNDI
Bujumbura
L. Victoria
Kisumu
Lualaba

KENYA
Nairobi
Mombasa
Kismayu
Juba
Tana

INDIAN
OCEAN

SEYCHELLES

Ascension I.
(U.K.)

SOUTH
ATLANTIC
OCEAN

St. Helena
(U.K.)

Luanda
Lobito
Huambo
Namibe
ANGOLA
Cubango
Cuanza

C. Fria

Kananga
Cuango
L. Mweru
Likasi
Lubumbashi
Ndola
ZAMBIA
Lusaka
Zambezi
L. Tanganyika
Dodoma
TANZANIA
Zanzibar
Dar es Salaam

L. Malawi
MALAWI
Lilongwe
Blantyre
C. Delgado
Mocímboa
MOZAMBIQUE

COMOROS
Moroni
Mamoudzou
Mayotte
(Fr.)
Antsiranana
Mahajanga
Toamasina
Antananarivo
MADAGASCAR
Fianarantsoa

MAURITIUS
St-Denis
Port
Louis
Réunion
(Fr.)

Mozambique Channel
Aldabra
Is.

Livingstone
Harare
Bulawayo
ZIMBABWE
Beira
Limpopo

NAMIBIA
Windhoek

BOTSWANA
Gaborone

Orange
Kimberley
Vaal
Johannesburg
Pretoria
Mbabane
SWAZ.
Maputo
Maseru
LESOTHO
Durban

SOUTH AFRICA
Cape Town
C. of Good Hope
C. Agulhas
Port
Elizabeth
East
London

Tristan da Cunha
(U.K.)

NORTHERN AFRICA

1:15 000 000

Projection : Sanson-Flamsteed's Sinusoidal

46
52

MEDITERRANEAN SEA

LIBYA

EGYPT

SUDAN

CHAD

CENTRAL AFRICAN REPUBLIC

ETHIOPIA

SAUDI ARABIA

RED SEA

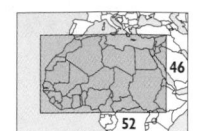

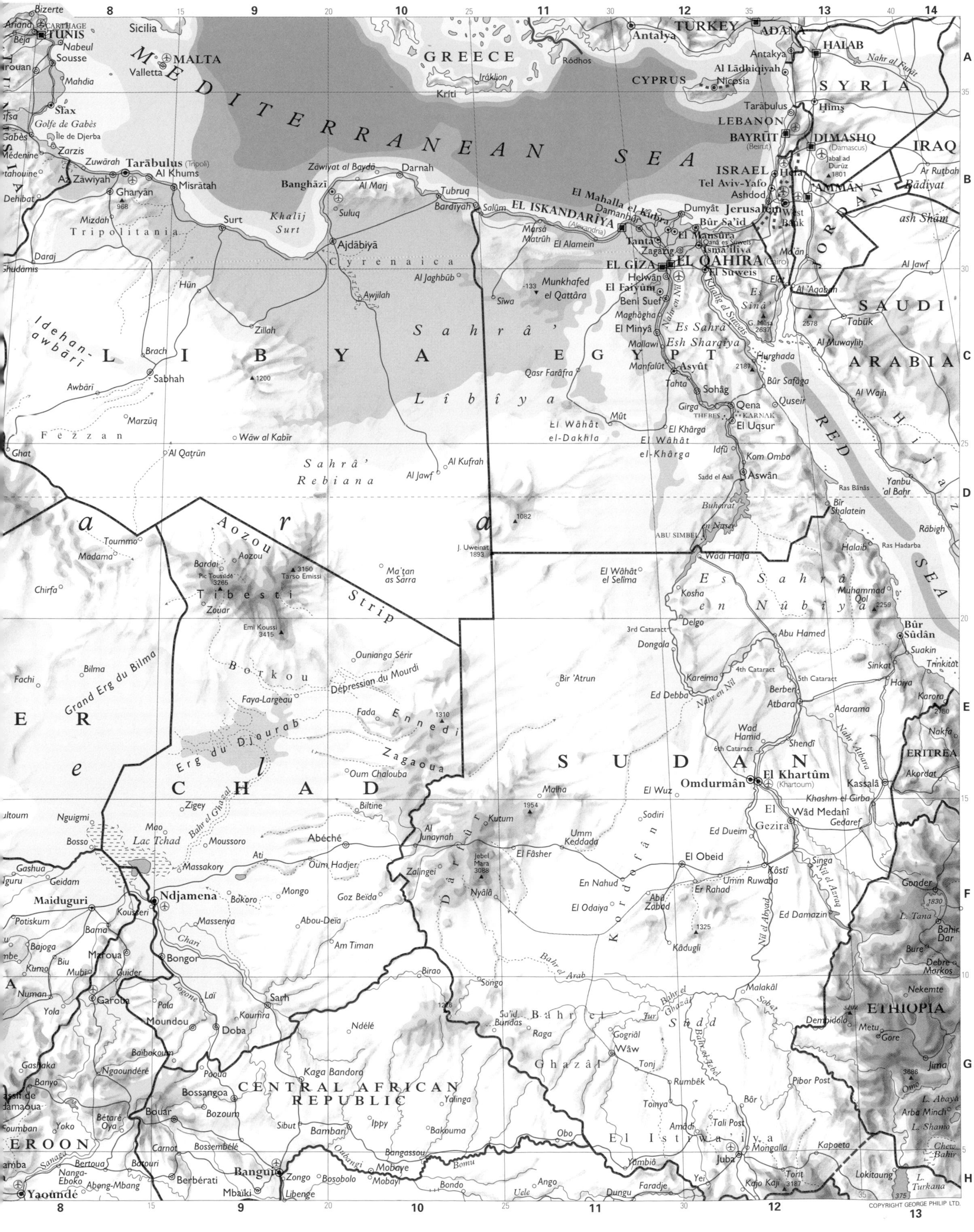

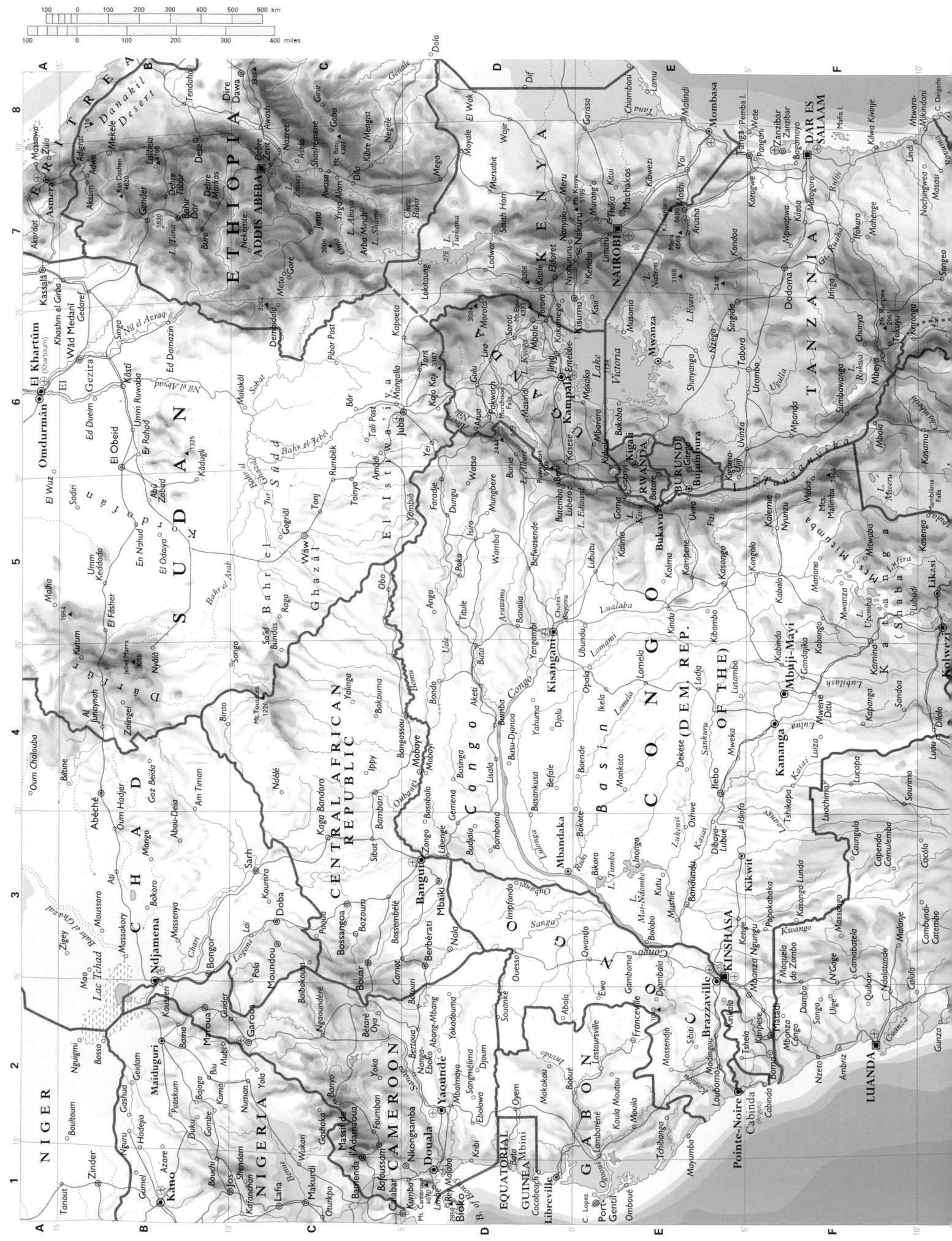
100 0 100 200 300 400 500 600 km
100 0 100 200 300 400 miles
NIGER
NIGERIA
CHAD
SUDAN
ETHIOPIA
ERITREA
KENYA
UGANDA
TANZANIA
RWANDA
BURUNDI
CENTRAL AFRICAN REPUBLIC
CAMEROON
EQUATORIAL GUINEA
GABON
CONGO
CONGO (DEM. REP. OF THE)
Danakil Desert
Omdurmân
El Khartûm
ADDIS ABEBA
Asmera
NAIROBI
Kampala
Kigali
Bujumbura
DAR ES SALAAM
Mombasa
Ndjamena
Bangui
Yaoundé
Douala
Libreville
Brazzaville
KINSHASA
LUANDA
Pointe-Noire
Kisangani
Mbandaka
Kananga
Mbuji-Mayi
Kano
Maiduguri
Juba
Lake Victoria
Lac Tchad
Congo Basin

50
51
46
57

ATLANTIC OCEAN

INDIAN OCEAN

NAMIBIA

BOTSWANA

ZIMBABWE

ZAMBIA

MALAWI

MOZAMBIQUE

SOUTH AFRICA

LESOTHO

SWAZILAND

Kalahari

Namib Desert

Skeleton Coast

Tropic of Capricorn

MADAGASCAR

On same scale as General Map

INDIAN OCEAN

ft	m
12 000	4000
9000	3000
6000	2000
4500	1500
3000	1000
1200	400
600	200
0	0
200	600
1000	3000
2000	6000
4000	12 000
m	ft

Projection : Sanson-Flamsteed's Sinusoidal

East from Greenwich

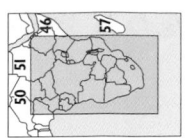

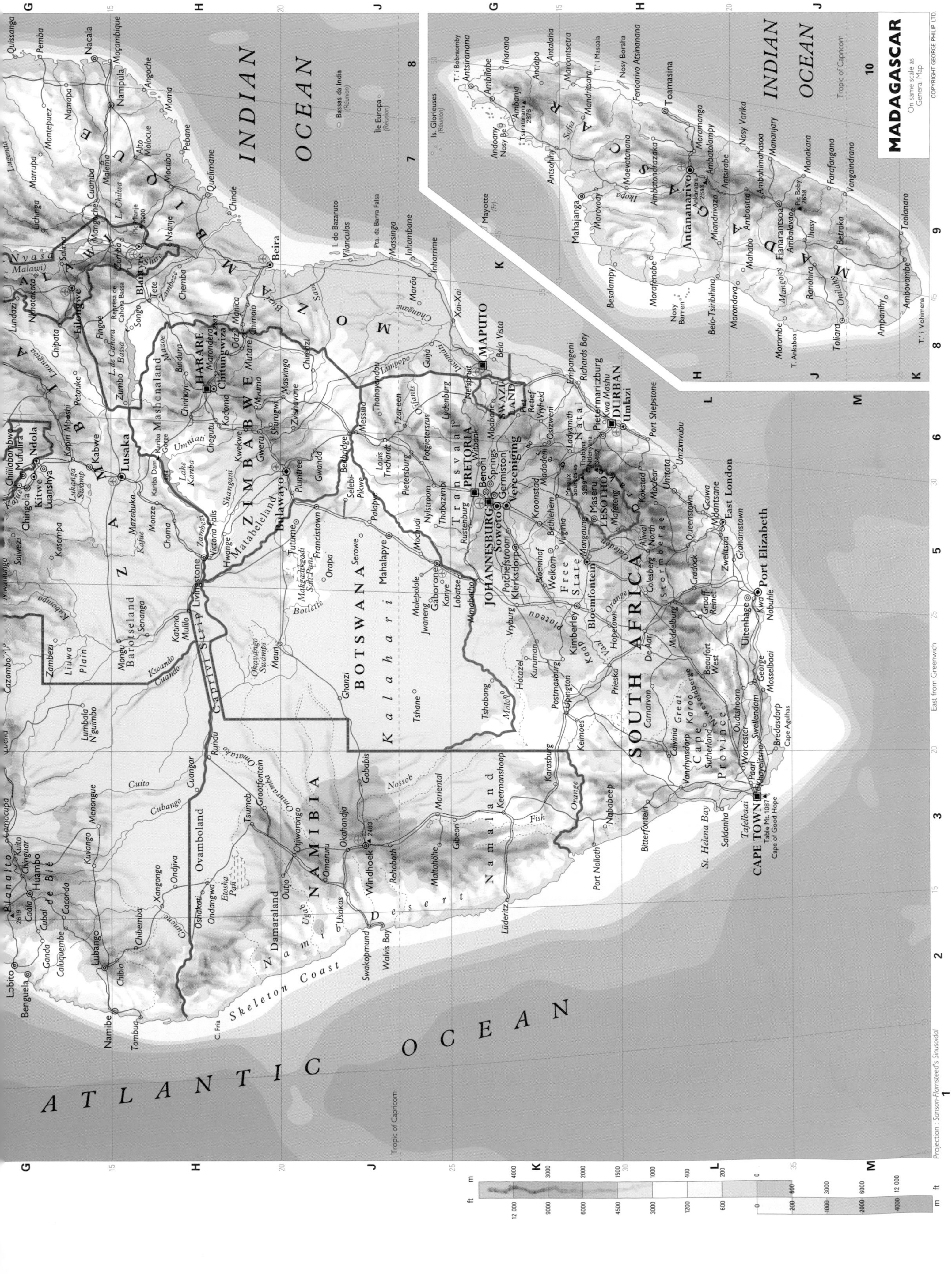

EAST AFRICA 1:8 000 000

50 0 50 100 150 200 250 300 km
50 0 50 100 150 200 miles
CENTRAL AFRICAN REPUBLIC
SUDAN
ETHIOPIA
SOMALI REP.
KENYA
UGANDA
TANZANIA
RWANDA
BURUNDI
L. Turkana (L. Rudolf)
Lake Victoria
L. Albert
L. Edward
L. Kivu
L. Tanganyika
L. Rukwa
NAIROBI
MOMBASA
Kilindini
DAR ES SALAAM
Zanzibar
Pemba I.
Kampala
Entebbe
Jinja
Kisumu
Mwanza
Tabora
Dodoma
Arusha
Moshi
Bujumbura
Bukavu
Kigoma-Ujiji
Kisangani
Juba
Tanga
Lamu
Malindi

51
46
52
53
57
57

ANGOLA
ZAMBIA
MALAWI
MOÇAMBIQUE
ZIMBABWE
BOTSWANA
SOUTH AFRICA
NAMIBIA
INDIAN OCEAN
L. Nyasa
L. Malawi
Lake Kariba
L. de Cahora Bassa
Zambezi
Lusaka
HARARE
Lilongwe
Blantyre
BULAWAYO
Beira
Lubumbashi

ft | m
18 000 | 6000
12 000 | 4000
9000 | 3000
6000 | 2000
4500 | 1500
3000 | 1000
1200 | 400
600 | 200
0 | 0
200 | 600
2000 | 6000

Projection: Lambert's Equivalent Azimuthal

East from Greenwich

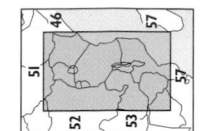

SOUTHERN AFRICA 1:8 000 000

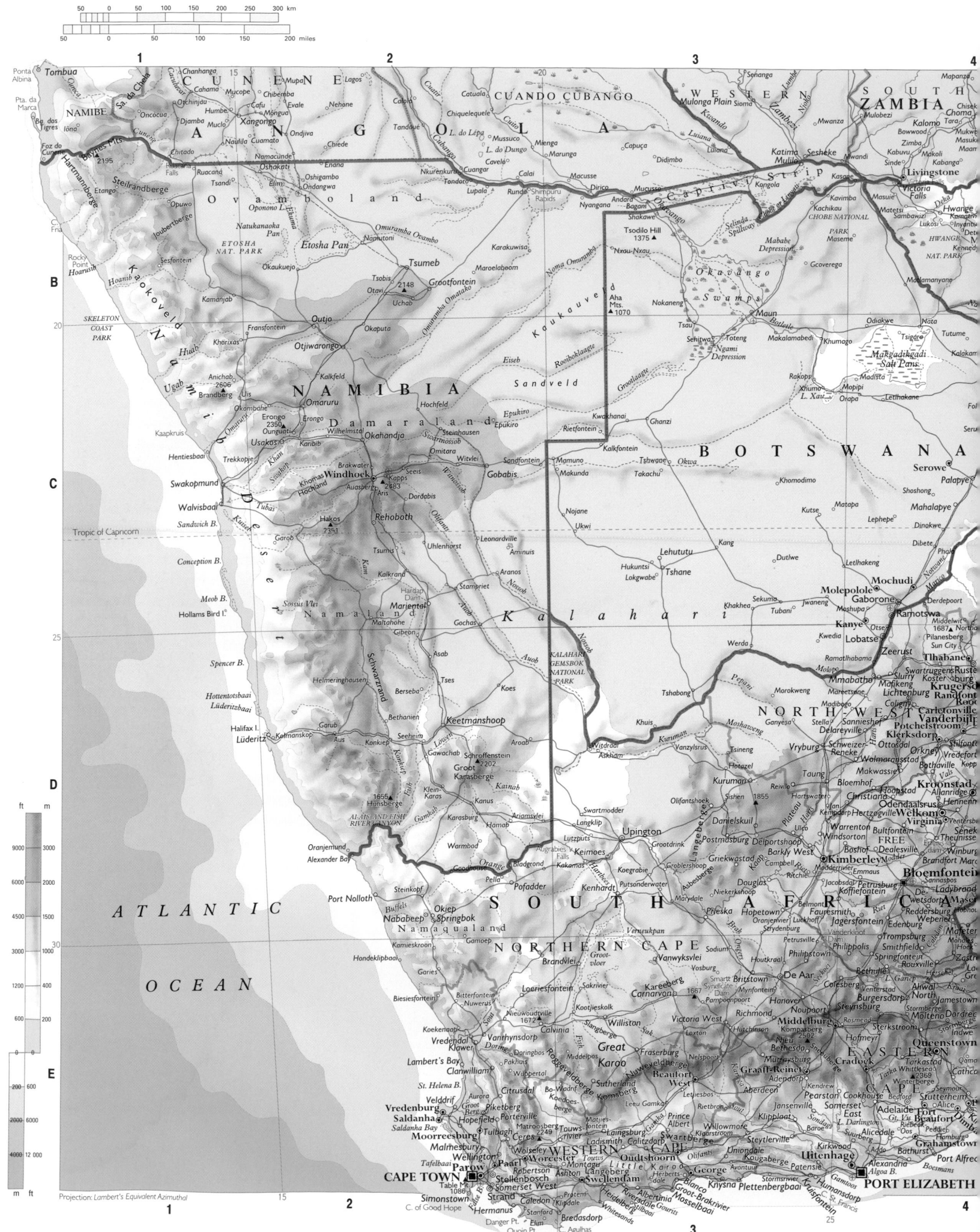

ANGOLA
CUNENE
CUANDO CUBANGO
NAMIBE
ZAMBIA
WESTERN
SOUTH
NAMIBIA
BOTSWANA
SOUTH AFRICA
NORTH-WEST
NORTHERN CAPE
WESTERN CAPE
EASTERN CAPE
FREE
ATLANTIC OCEAN
Ovamboland
Damaraland
Namaland
Namaqualand
Kaokoveld
Namib Desert
Kalahari
Sandveld
Kaukauveld
Great Karoo
Little Karoo
Okavango Swamps
Caprivi Strip
Etosha Pan
ETOSHA NAT. PARK
SKELETON COAST PARK
KALAHARI GEMSBOK NATIONAL PARK
CHOBE NATIONAL PARK
HWANGE NAT. PARK
Makgadikgadi Salt Pans
Ngami Depression
Tropic of Capricorn
Tombua
Windhoek
Swakopmund
Walvisbaai
Lüderitz
Keetmanshoop
Rehoboth
Tsumeb
Grootfontein
Outjo
Otjiwarongo
Okahandja
Gobabis
Mariental
Maun
Francistown
Serowe
Palapye
Mahalapye
Molepolole
Gaborone
Mochudi
Kanye
Lobatse
Ramotswa
Livingstone
Victoria Falls
Mafikeng
Mmabatho
Lichtenburg
Vryburg
Kuruman
Upington
Kimberley
Bloemfontein
Welkom
Kroonstad
Springbok
Port Nolloth
Calvinia
Vredendal
Saldanha
Vredenburg
Malmesbury
Paarl
Worcester
Stellenbosch
Swellendam
Oudtshoorn
George
Knysna
Plettenbergbaai
Mosselbaai
Beaufort West
Graaff-Reinet
Cradock
Middelburg
Colesberg
De Aar
Queenstown
Grahamstown
Uitenhage
CAPE TOWN
PORT ELIZABETH
C. of Good Hope
C. Agulhas
Hermanus
Simonstown
Projection: Lambert's Equivalent Azimuthal

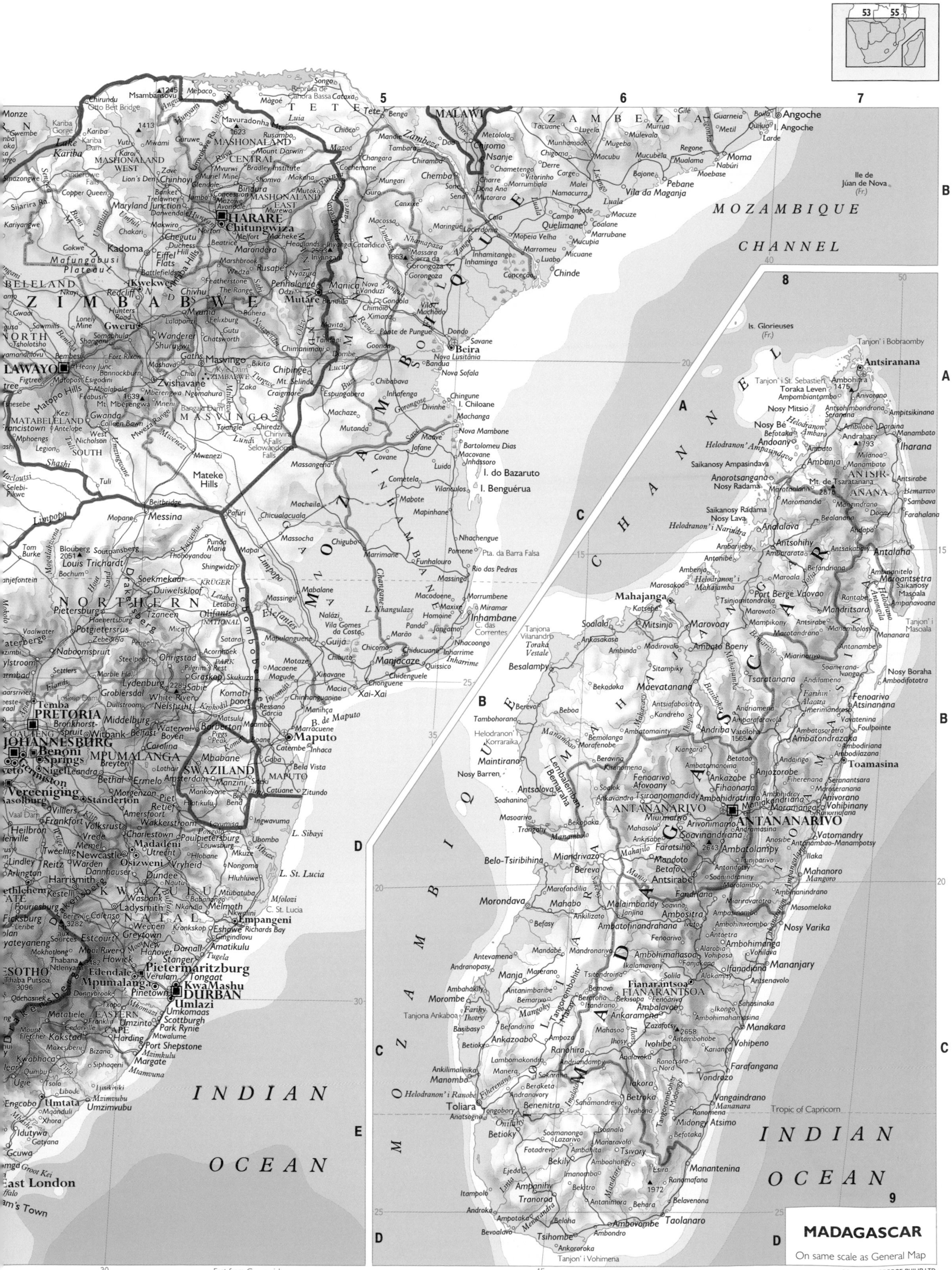

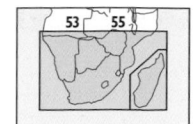

MADAGASCAR

On same scale as General Map

COPYRIGHT GEORGE PHILIP LTD.

East from Greenwich

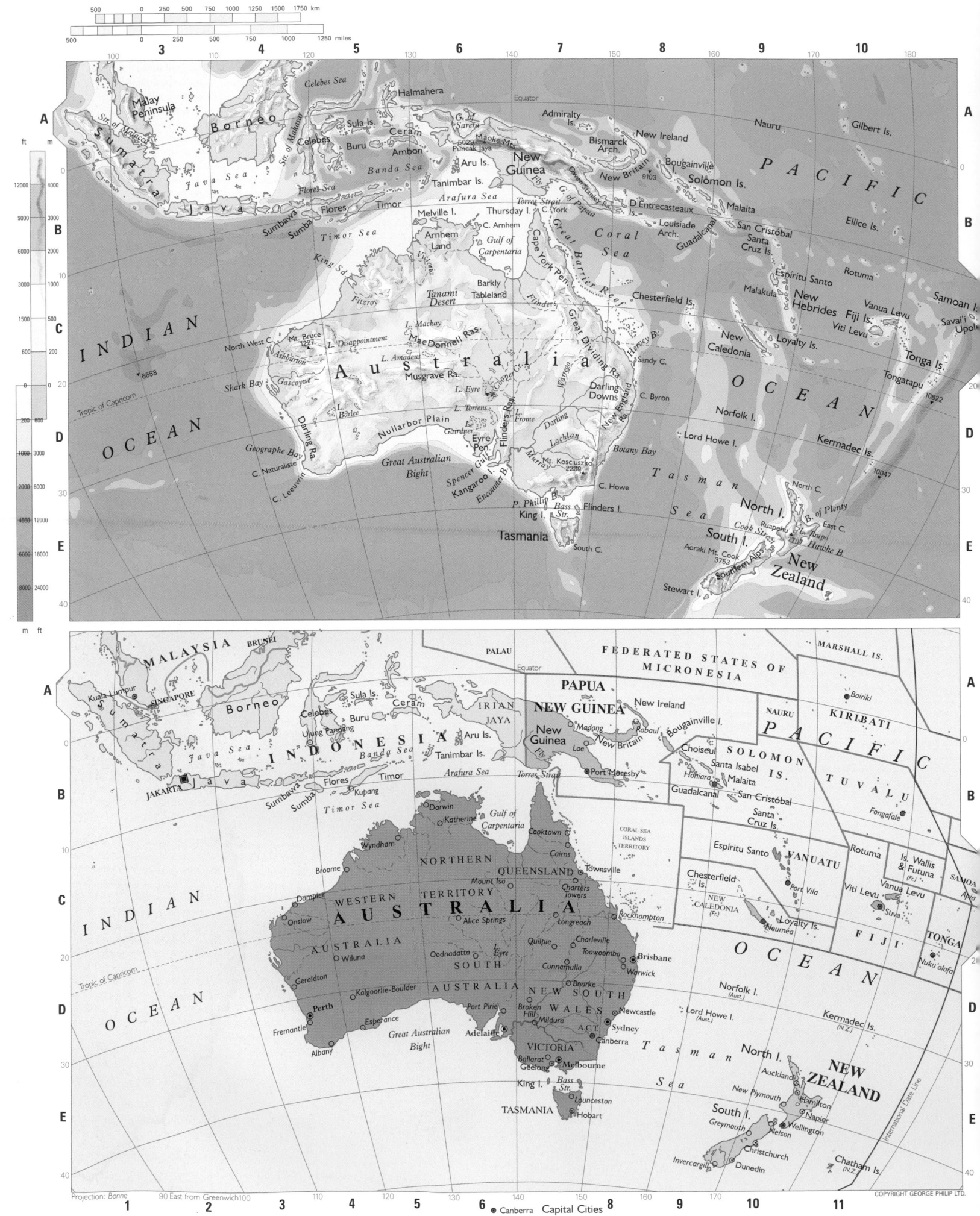

Physical map (top):

500 0 250 500 750 1000 1250 1500 1750 km
500 0 250 500 750 1000 1250 miles

3 4 5 6 7 8 9 10

ft m

12000 4000
9000 3000
6000 2000
3000 1000
1500 500
600 200
0 0
200 600
1000 3000
2000 6000
4000 12000
6000 18000
8000 24000
m ft

A
Malay Peninsula
Borneo
Celebes Sea
Halmahera
Admiralty Is.
Equator
Nauru
Gilbert Is.
Sula Is.
Ceram
G. of Sarera
New Ireland
Sumatra
Celebes
Buru
Ambon
5029 Maoke Mts. Puncak Jaya
Bismarck Arch.
New Britain
9103
Bougainville
Solomon Is.
PACIFIC
Java Sea
Banda Sea
New Guinea
Fly
Aru Is.

B
Java
Flores Sea
Tanimbar Is.
Arafura Sea
Torres Strait
G. of Papua
Great Stanley Ra.
D'Entrecasteaux
Malaita
Ellice Is.
Sumbawa
Sumba
Flores
Timor
Melville I.
Thursday I. C. York
Cape York Pen.
Great Barrier Reef
Coral Sea
Louisiade Arch.
Guadalcanal
San Cristóbal
Santa Cruz Is.
Timor Sea
C. Arnhem
Arnhem Land
Gulf of Carpentaria
Victoria
Espíritu Santo
Rotuma
Samoan Is.
King Sd.
Barkly Tableland
Flinders
New Hebrides
Fiji Is.
Vanua Levu
Savai'i
Upol

C
INDIAN
Fitzroy
Tanami Desert
L. Mackay
MacDonnell Ras.
Hervey B.
Malakula
Viti Levu
6658
Mt. Bruce 1227
L. Disappointment
Australia
Great Dividing Ra.
New Caledonia
Loyalty Is.
Tonga Is.
North West C.
Ashburton
L. Amadeus
Musgrave Ra.
Cooper Cr.
Sandy C.
OCEAN
Tropic of Capricorn
Shark Bay
Gascoyne
L. Eyre
Warrego
Darling Downs
C. Byron
Tongatapu
10822

D
OCEAN
L. Barlee
L. Torrens
L. Frome
Darling
New England Ra.
Norfolk I.
Kermadec Is.
Darling Ra.
Nullarbor Plain
Gairdner
Eyre Pen.
Lachlan
Murray
Botany Bay
Lord Howe I.
10047
Geographe Bay
C. Naturaliste
Great Australian Bight
Spencer Gulf
Kangaroo I.
Encounter B.
Mt. Kosciuszko 2230
C. Howe
Tasman Sea
North C.

E
C. Leeuwin
South C.
P. Phillip B. Bass Str.
King I. Flinders I.
Tasmania
B. of Plenty East C.
Ruapehu L. Taupo
Hawke B.
North I.
South I.
Aoraki Mt. Cook 3763 Southern Alps
Stewart I.
New Zealand

Political map (bottom):

A
MALAYSIA BRUNEI
PALAU
FEDERATED STATES OF MICRONESIA
MARSHALL IS.
Kuala Lumpur
SINGAPORE
Borneo
Sula Is.
Ceram
IRIAN JAYA
PAPUA NEW GUINEA
Bairiki
NAURU
KIRIBATI
Celebes
Buru
New Ireland
PACIFIC
Ujung Pandang
New Guinea
Madang
Rabaul
Bougainville I.
Aru Is.
Lae
New Britain
Choiseul
SOLOMON IS.
TUVALU
INDONESIA
Santa Isabel
Honiara
Malaita

B
JAKARTA
Java
Banda Sea
Tanimbar Is.
Port Moresby
Guadalcanal
San Cristóbal
Fongafale
Sumbawa
Sumba
Flores
Timor
Kupang
Arafura Sea
Torres Strait
Santa Cruz Is.
Timor Sea
Darwin
Katherine
Gulf of Carpentaria
CORAL SEA ISLANDS TERRITORY
Espíritu Santo
VANUATU
Rotuma
Is. Wallis & Futuna (Fr.)
SAMOA
Cooktown

C
Wyndham
Broome
NORTHERN TERRITORY
QUEENSLAND
Cairns
Townsville
Port Vila
Viti Levu
Vanua Levu
Apia
Dampier
WESTERN
Mount Isa
Charters Towers
Chesterfield Is.
NEW CALEDONIA (Fr.)
FIJI
Suva
Onslow
AUSTRALIA
TERRITORY
AUSTRALIA
Alice Springs
Longreach
Rockhampton
Nouméa
Loyalty Is.
TONGA

D
INDIAN
AUSTRALIA
SOUTH
Quilpie
Charleville
Toowoomba
Brisbane
Norfolk I. (Aust.)
Nuku'alofa
Geraldton
Oodnadatta
Wiluna
L. Eyre
Cunnamulla
Warwick
OCEAN
Tropic of Capricorn
Kalgoorlie-Boulder
AUSTRALIA
NEW SOUTH
Bourke
Lord Howe I. (Aust.)
Kermadec Is. (N.Z.)
Perth
Port Pirie
Broken Hill
WALES
Newcastle
Fremantle
Esperance
Mildura
A.C.T. Sydney
OCEAN
Albany
Adelaide
Great Australian Bight
VICTORIA
Canberra
Tasman Sea
North I.
NEW ZEALAND
Auckland

E
Ballarat
Geelong
Melbourne
King I.
Bass Str.
Sea
New Plymouth
Hamilton
Napier
TASMANIA
Launceston
Hobart
South I.
Wellington
Greymouth
Nelson
Invercargill
Dunedin
Christchurch
Chatham Is. (N.Z.)

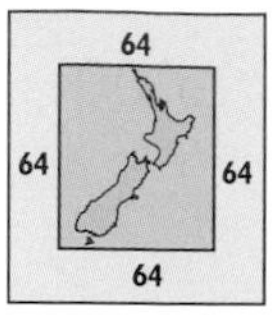

64
64 64
64
1

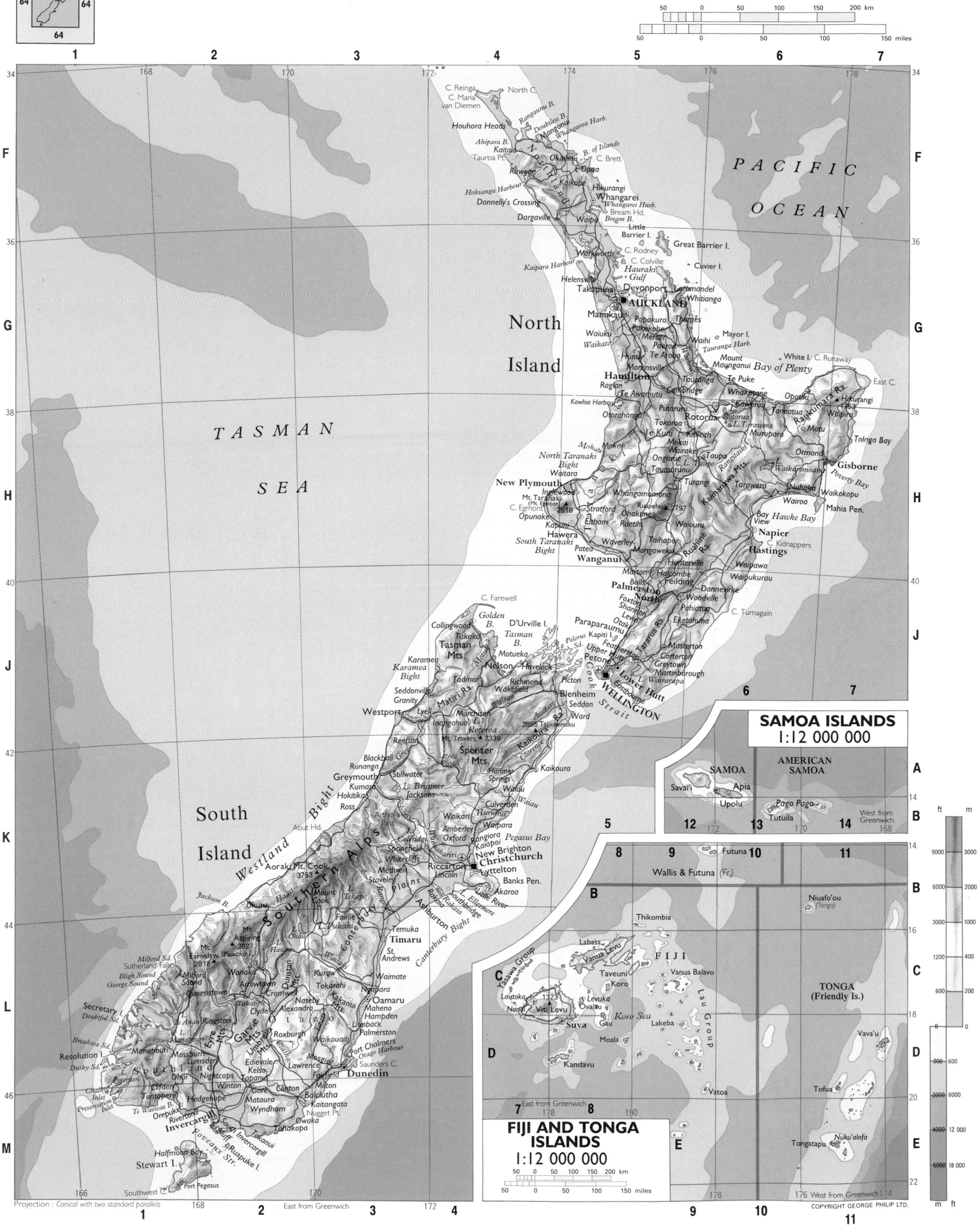

50   0   50   100   150   200 km
50   0   50   100   150 miles

34   34

PACIFIC

C. Reinga
C. Maria
van Diemen
North C.
Rangaunu B.
Houhora Heads
Doubtless B.
Mangonui
Ahipara B.
Kaitaia
Whangaroa Harb.
Tauroa Pt.
Rawene
Kaikohe
B. of Islands
Okaihau
Opua
C. Brett

OCEAN

F   F

Hokianga Harbour
Donnelly's Crossing
Hikurangi
Whangarei
Whangarei Harb.
Bream Hd.
Dargaville
Waipu
Bream B.
Little
Barrier I.
Great Barrier I.

36   36

Helensville
Kaipara Harbour
Warkworth
C. Rodney
C. Colville
Hauraki
Gulf
Cuvier I.
Takapuna
Devonport
Coromandel
Whitianga

North

G   **AUCKLAND**   G
Manukau
Papakura
Thames
Waiuku
Pukekohe
Mercer
Waihi
Mayor I.
Waikato
Paeroa
Te Aroha
Morrinsville
Tauranga Harb.
White I.   C. Runaway
Mount
Maunganui   Bay of Plenty
East C.
Huntly
Te Awamutu
Cambridge
Tauranga
Te Puke
Whakatane

Island

Hamilton
Raglan
Putaruru
Rotorua
Kawerau
Opotiki
Taneatua
Raukumara Ra.
Hikurangi
1753
Waipiro
Kawhia Harbour
Otorohanga
Tokoroa
L. Rotorua
L. Tarawera
Murupara
Motu
Kinleith
Kihikihi

38   38
Mokau
Mokai
Wairakei
Taupo
Rangitaiki
Talnga Bay
North Taranaki
Bight
Waitara
Ongarue
L. Taupo
Taumarunui
Waikaremoana
Gisborne
New Plymouth
Inglewood
Whangamomona
Turangi
Kaimanawa Mts.
Tarawera
Nuhaka
Waikokopu
Poverty Bay
Mt. Taranaki
(Mt. Egmont)
Ruapehu
2797
Ohakune
Waiouru
Wairoa
Mahia Pen.
C. Egmont
2518
Stratford
Bay
Hawke Bay
Opunake
Kapuni
Eltham
Raetihi
Waitomo
Napier
Hawera
Waverley
Mangaweka
C. Kidnappers
South Taranaki
Bight
Patea
Hastings
Marton
Hunterville
Waipawa
Wanganui
Halcombe
Feilding
Waipukurau
Bulls
Danneivirke
Palmerston
Foxton
Woodville
North
Shannon
Pahiatua
C. Turnagain

40   40
Levin
Eketahuna
Otaki
Paraparaumu
Masterton
Kapiti I.
Carterton
Greytown
Featherston
Martinborough
Upper
Hutt
Wairarapa
Petone
WELLINGTON
Lower Hutt

42   42

TASMAN

SEA

C. Farewell
Golden
B.
Collingwood
D'Urville I.
Takaka
Tasman
B.
Tasman Mts.
Motueka
Pelorus
Sd.
Karamea
Nelson
Havelock
Picton
Karamea
Bight
Richmond
Wakefield
Cook
Seddonville
Blenheim
Granity
Tadmor
Murchison
Seddon
Strait
Westport
Lyell
L. Rotoroa
Ward
Inangahua
Mt. Travers 2338
2885 Tapuaenuku
Reefton
Spenser
Mts.
Kaikoura
Blackball
Runanga
Clarence
Greymouth
Stillwater
Hanmer
Springs
Kumara
L. Brunner
Waiau
Hokitika
Jacksons
Culverden
Ross
Arthur's
Pass
Hurunui
Waikari
Waipara
Amberley
Rangiora
South
Colfridge
Oxford
Pegasus Bay
Kaiapoi
Whitecliffs
New Brighton
Springfield
Christchurch
Methven
Staveley
Riccarton
Lyttelton
Island
Lincoln
Akaroa
Aoraki/Mt. Cook
3753
Banks Pen.
Mount
Cook
L. Ellesmere
Rakaia
L. Tekapo
Ashburton
Southbridge
Fairlie
Methven
Jackson B.
Mt. Aspiring
3027
Okuru
Haast
L. Coleridge
Geraldine
Pleasant Pt.
Temuka
Ahaura
Timaru
Milford Sd.
Mt. Earnslaw 2818
St.
Andrews
Sutherland Falls
Wanaka
L. Wanaka
Bligh Sound
Milford Sound
Arrowtown
Hakataramea
Waimate
George Sound
Cromwell
Oamaru
Queenstown
Clyde
Naseby
Maheno
Secretary I.
Alexandra
Hampden
Doubtful Sd.
Roxburgh
Dunback
Palmerston
Resolution I.
Kingston
Lawrence
Port Chalmers
Otago Harbour
Dusky Sd.
Manapouri
Mossburn
Gore
Balclutha
Saunders C.
Breaksea Sd.
Lumsden
Edievale
Kelso
Tapanui
Dunedin
Preservation Inlet
Ohai
Nightcaps
Winton
Clinton
Milton
Chaslands
Riverton
Gore
Mataura
Kaitangata
Orepuki
Wyndham
Nugget Pt.
Tuatapere
Hedgehope
Owaka
Te Waewae B.
Invercargill
Bluff   Invercargill
Ruapuke I.
Tahakopa
Foveaux Str.
Halfmoon Bay
Stewart I.
Port Pegasus
Southwest C.

166   168   170   172   174   176   178

SAMOA ISLANDS
1:12 000 000
AMERICAN
SAMOA
SAMOA
Apia
Saval'i
Upolu
Pago Pago
Tutuila
West from
Greenwich

FIJI AND TONGA
ISLANDS
1:12 000 000
Futuna
Wallis & Futuna (Fr.)
Niuafo'ou
(Tonga)
Thikombia
Labasa
Ysawa Group
Vanua Levu
FIJI
Vanua Balavu
Lautoka
Taveuni
Kora
Nanti 1323
Levuka
TONGA
Viti Levu
Ovalau
(Friendly Is.)
Suva
Gau
Lakeba
Lau Group
Moala
Vava'u
Koro Sea
Moala
Kandavu
Vatoa
Tofua
Nuku'alofa
Tongatapu

50   0   50   100   150   200 km
50   0   50   100   150 miles

ft   m
9000   3000
6000   2000
3000   1000
1200   400
600   200
0
200   600
2000   6000
4000   12 000
6000   18 000
m   ft

INDONESIA

TIMOR SEA

Kupang
Timor
Roti
Sawu
Raijua
Dana
Semau

Sumba
Waingapu
Waikabubak
Melolo
Boing

Sumbawa
Bali
Lombok

C. Croker
C. McCluer
Croker I.
Grant I.
Coburg Pen.
P. Essington
C. Don
Dundas Str.
Van Diemen
C. Hotham
C. Gambier
Ngui
Port Darwin
Mandorah
Milikapiti
Melville I.
Bathurst I.
Pularumpi
C. Van Diemen
C. Fawcett
Darwin
Noogamati
Batchelor
Peron Is.
Anson B.
C. Scott
Pt. Blaze
Mt. Greenwood
152

Milingimbi
Oenpelli
Jabiru
480
KAKADU
NAT. PARK
Ram Jungle
Goinda
Pine Creek
Adelaide River
Daly River
Dali
Hayes Creek
Katherine
Gorge
Tindal
Fine Creek
Birdum
Creek
Larrimah
Beswick
Mataranka
Maranboy
Tanami Desert

NORTHERN TERRITORY

Top Springs
Hooker Creek
Mt. Singleton
808
Reynolds Ra.
Stuart Bluff Ra.
Yuendumu
Mt. Zeil
1524
Mt. Liebig
1510
Papunya
Haast Bluff
MacDonnell Ranges
Hermannsburg
James Ranges
George Gill
Ra.
Mt. Leister
901
Palmer

L. Bennett
L. White
L. Mackay
Lake Mackay
Stansmore Ra.
L. Wills
L. Hazlett
Gregory Lake
Billiluna
L. Hopkins
Bonython Ra.
Mt. Neale

Horden Hills
Lewis Ra.
Tanami
Nicholson

Dogurogu
Kakarindji
Waterloo
Victoria River
Victoria
Fitzmaurice
West Baines
Wingate Mts.
C. Hay
Wadeye
Pt. Keats
Dumbungurra
Oombulgurri
Lesser I.
Cambridge Gulf
Ord
Carr Boyd Ra.
Argyle
Turkey Creek
Kununurra
Pago
Albert Edward Ra.
Pentecost
McClintock Ra.
Swift Creek
Hells Creek
Chamberlain
Durack Range
Cockburn
Wyndham

Dussejour
C. Hay
Buckle Hd.
Queen's Ch.
Buckle Hd.
Quoin I.

Joseph Bonaparte Gulf

Talbot
Londonderry
C. Rulhieres
Berthier Is.
Eclipse Is.
Sir Graham Moore Is.
Long Reef
C. Bougainville
Admiralty Gulf
C. Voltaire
Montague Sd.
Bigge I.
York Sd.
Coronation Is.
Augustus I.
Adele I.
Hall Pt.
Camden Sd.
Brunswick B.
Prince Regent R.
Kalumburu
Drysdale
King Edward
Carson R.
Mt. Hann
776
Mt. Wells
970
Gibb River
Haun
Mt. Ord
937
Harding Ra.
Limon R.
King Leopold Ranges
Kimberley
Mueller Ra.
Gregory Ra.

Ashmore Reef
Cartier I.
Hibernia Reef

Browse I.
Seringapatam Reef
Scott Reef

Buccaneer Archipelago
Bonaparte Archipelago
C. Leveque
Cone Bay
Yampi
Kunmunya
Koolan
Cockatoo
King Sound
Derby
Meda
Mowanjum
Camballin
Liveringa
Fitzroy
Fitzroy Crossing
St. George Ra.
Margaret R.
Christmas Cr.
Gogo
Gt. Northern Hwy.

Lennard R.
Lanadi
Pender B.
Beagle Bay
Carnot B.
C. Boileau
Broome
Roebuck B.
Lacepede Is.
C. Latouche Treville
Lagrange B.
Lagrange
C. Bossut

Lynher Reef

Mermaid Reef
Clerke Reef
Rowley Shoals
Imperieuse Reef

Eighty Mile Beach
Sandfire Roadhouse
C. Keraudren
Poissonnier Pt.
Port Hedland
Goldsworthy
De Grey
Shay Gap
Shaw
Marble Bar
Yule
Nullagine
Shaw

Great Sandy Desert

Percival Lakes
L. Auld
L. Dora
Waukarlycarly
L. George
L. Tobin
Telfer Mine
Gregory Ra.
Isabella Ra.
Throssell Ra.
Poisonbush Ra.
Broadhurst
Blanche
L. Blanche
McKay Ra.
Mt. Robinson
Jigalong
L. Disappointment
Lake Disappointment
Oakover

Gibson Desert

Tropic of Capricorn
Paterson Ra.
Rudall
Patey
Tom Price
Mt. Bruce
1235
Mt. Meharry
1251
Ophthalmia Ra.
Newman
1050
Hamersley Range
Roy Hill
Fortescue
Weeli Wolli
Wittenoom
Paraburdoo
Duck Cr.
Ashburton

Dampier Archipelago
Monte Bello Is.
Barrow I.
Pasco I.
Legendre I.
Delambre I.
Depuch I.
Karratha
Dampier
Roebourne
Enderby
C. Preston
Cossack
Whim Creek
Pyramid
Peawah
Pamboong
Mt. Florance
Ashburton

Exmouth Gulf
Onslow
North West C.
Exmouth
Learmonth
Barradale Roadhouse
Nanutarra Roadhouse
P. Coates

INDIAN OCEAN

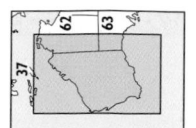

WESTERN AUSTRALIA

SOUTH AUSTRALIA

Great Victoria Desert

Gibson Desert

Nullarbor Plain

Hampton Tableland

Great Australian Bight

SOUTHERN OCEAN

INDIAN OCEAN

Petermann Ranges
ULURU NAT. PARK
Ayers Rock 868
Mt. Olga 1069
Everard Ranges
Musgrave Ranges
Mt. Musgrave 940
Morris 1387
Mann Ra.
Amata
L. Maurice
L. Dey-Dey
Wilkinson Lakes
L. Meramangye
Serpentine Lakes
Nurrari Lakes
The Officer
L. Ifould

Mt. Aloysius 1126
Blackstone Ra.
Rawlinson Ra.
Mt. Buchanan
Mt. Forrest
Cavenagh Ra.
Barrow Ra.
Warburton
Mt. Squires 705
Wanborn Ra.
Pt. Lillian 486
Macintosh Ra.
Saunders Pt. 466
Mt. Normanhurst
L. Burnside
L. Breaden
Baker L.
L. Gillen
L. Vee
L. Throssell
Ernest Giles Ra. 712
L. Carnegie
Carnarvon Ra.
L. Buchanan
Brassey Ra.
Mt. Essendon 906
L. Wells
L. Minigwal
L. Throssell
Coonana
L. Carey
Cosmo Newbery
Laverton
L. Rason
Rason L.
Raeside

Oldea
Watson
Fisher
Cook
Maralinga
Hughes
Forrest
Reid
Loongana
Naretha
Rawlinna
Cocklebiddy
Madura
Mundrabilla
Low Pt.
Eucla
Wilson Bluff
Head of Bight
Red Rocks Pt.
Pt. Culver
Pt. Dover

Kalgoorlie-Boulder
Kookynie
Leonora
Menzies
Broad Arrow
Mt. Burges 554
Coolgardie
Widgiemooltha
Norseman
L. Cowan
L. Lefroy
L. Dundas
Salmon Gums
Mt. Hope
L. Gilmore
L. Tay
Peak Eleanora 903
Mt. Ridley
Mt. Ragged 585
Balladonia
Zanthus
Balgair
Malcolm
Mt. Eureka 499
Mt. Redcliffe 576
L. Darlot
Bates Ra.
L. Way
L. Nabberu
Wiluna
Agnew
Barr Smith Ra.
Montague Ra.
Leinster
Mt. Alexander
Marmion
Bardoc
Mt. Elvire
Goongarrie

Esperance
Eastern Group
Middle I.
C. Pasley
C. Arid
Sandy Bight
South East Is.
Archipelago of the Recherche
Mondrain I.
Duke of Orleans B.

5632

Meekatharra
Cue
L. Austin
Mount Magnet
Sandstone
Nannine
Annean
Weemandoo 543
Tuckanarra
Wydgee
Robinson Ra.
Peak Hill
Mt. Fraser 799
Kumarina
Collier Ra.
Godfrey Ra.
Waldburg Ra.
Mt. Augustus 1105
Kennedy Ra.
Lyons
Carnarvon
Gascoyne Junction
Minnie Roadhouse
Mooloo Roadhouse

Payne's Find
Yalgoo
Mullewa
Three Springs
Morawa
Perenjori
Gutha
Mt. Singleton
L. Moore
Dalwallinu
Bencubbin
Mukinbudin
Southern Cross
Yellowdine
Koolyanobbing
Marvel Loch
Bullfinch
Merredin
Kellerberrin
Narembeen
Bruce Rock
Kondinin
Hyden
L. King
Lake Grace
L. Newdegate
Ravensthorpe
Hopetoun
L. Magenta

Geraldton
Northampton
Kalbarri
Dongara
Eneabba
Leeman
Cervantes
Jurien
North Hd.
Lancelin
Two Rocks
Yanchep
Wanneroo
Rockingham
Mandurah
PERTH
Fremantle
Kwinana
Armadale
Pinjarra
Dwellingup
Waroona
Harvey
Collie
Bunbury
Busselton
Margaret River
Augusta
C. Leeuwin
Nannup
Bridgetown
Manjimup
Pemberton
Northcliffe
Walpole
Denmark
Albany
Mt. Barker
Cranbrook
Tambellup
Gnowangerup
Jerramungup
Ongerup
Borden
Bremer Bay
Stirling Ra.
Bluff Knoll
King George Sd.
Bald Hd.

Moora
Dalwallinu
Wongan Hills
Dowerin
Northam
York
Beverley
Brookton
Corrigin
Narrogin
Wickepin
Wagin
Katanning
Wandering
Boddington

Shark Bay
Hamelin Pool
Denham
Peron
Monkey Mia
Dirk Hartog I.
Steep Pt.
Bernier I.
Dorre I.
C. St. Cricq
C. Ronsard
C. Cuvier
C. Farquhar
McLeod

Houtman Abrolhos
Geographe B.
Greenough
Bluff Pt.
Greenhead Chan.

Mt. Woodroffe 1440
1174

COPYRIGHT GEORGE PHILIP LTD.

Projection: Bonne

East from Greenwich

m ft

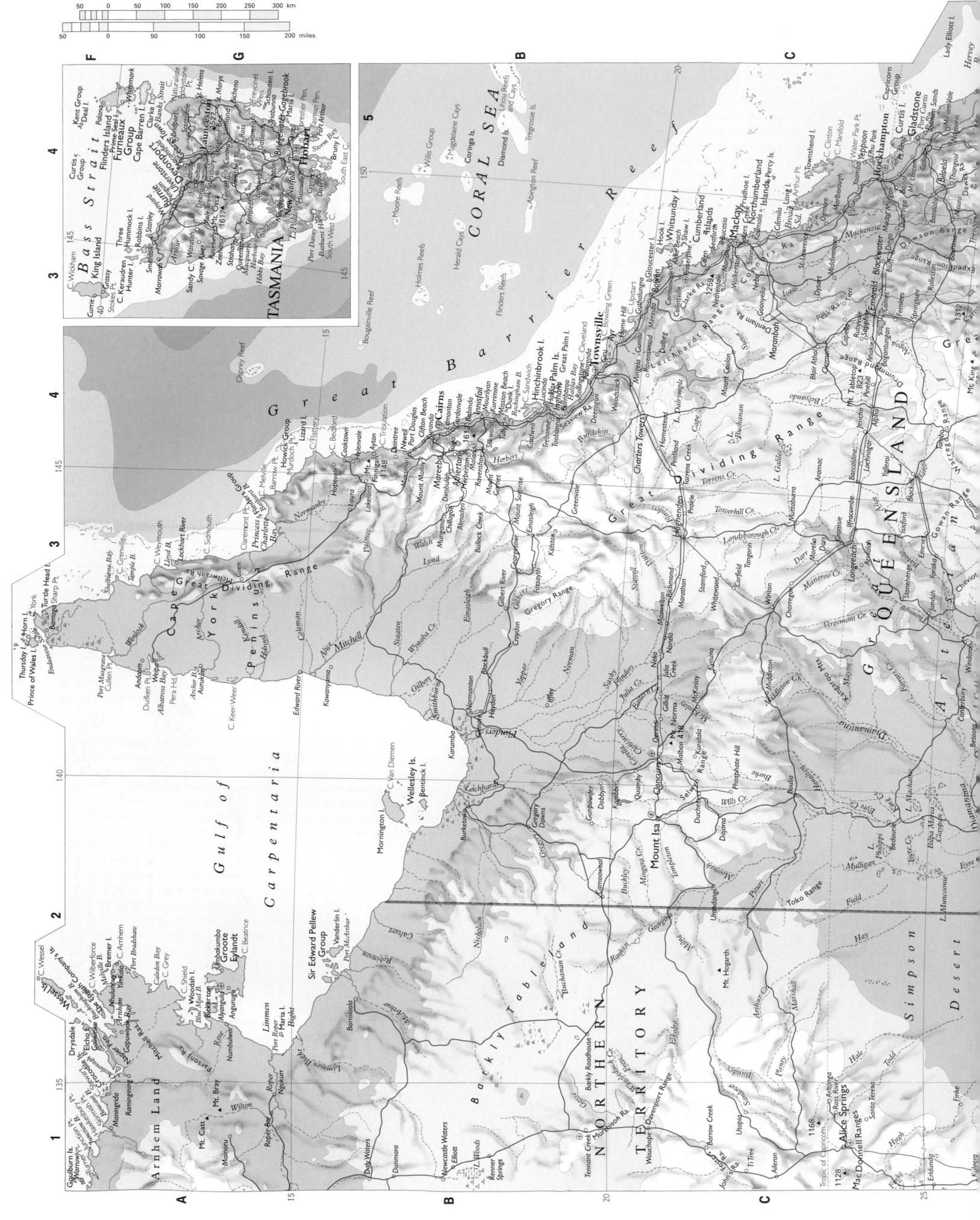

50 0 50 100 150 200 250 300 km
50 0 50 100 150 200 miles

TASMANIA

Bass Strait

CORAL SEA

Great Barrier Reef

Gulf of Carpentaria

Arnhem Land

Cape York Peninsula

Great Dividing Range

Barkly Tableland

NORTHERN TERRITORY

QUEENSLAND

Simpson Desert

Great Dividing Range

Great Artesian

Cairns

Townsville

Mackay

Rockhampton

Gladstone

Mount Isa

Alice Springs

Charters Towers

Tropic of Capricorn

SOUTH AUSTRALIA
NEW SOUTH WALES
VICTORIA
TASMAN SEA
SOUTHERN OCEAN
Bass Strait
ADELAIDE
MELBOURNE
SYDNEY
CANBERRA
BRISBANE
Gold Coast
Tweed Heads
Newcastle
Wollongong
Geelong
Ballarat
Bendigo
Broken Hill
Mildura
Port Augusta
Port Pirie
Whyalla
Port Lincoln
Mount Gambier
Warrnambool
Wagga Wagga
Albury
Dubbo
Tamworth
Armidale
Coffs Harbour
Toowoomba
Kangaroo I.
King Island
Flinders Island
Lake Eyre (North)
Lake Torrens
Lake Frome
Darling Downs
Projection: Bonne
East from Greenwich
COPYRIGHT, GEORGE PHILIP LTD.

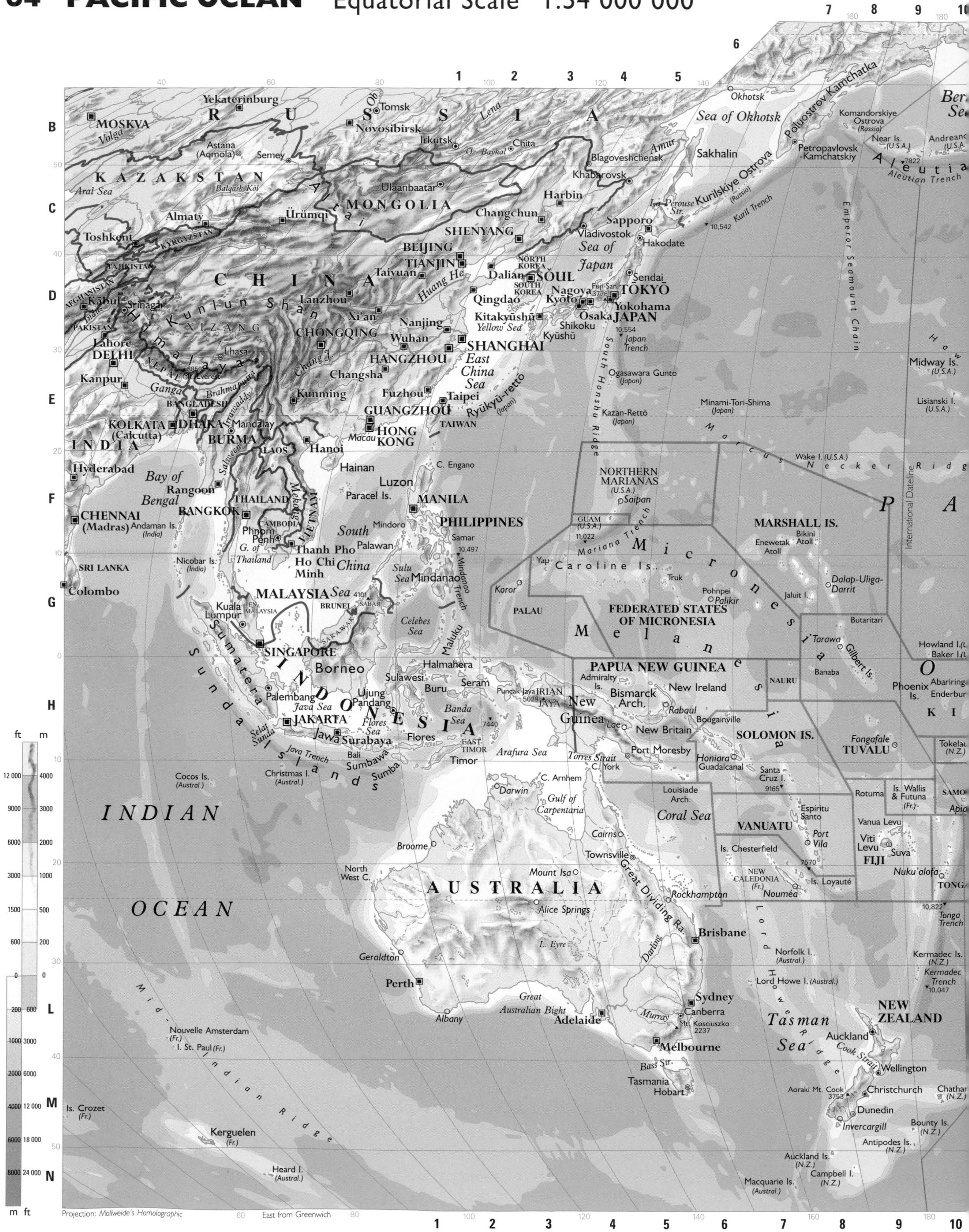

RUSSIA

Yekaterinburg
MOSKVA
Tomsk
Novosibirsk
Astana (Aqmola)
Semey
Irkutsk
Chita
Baykal
Blagoveshchensk
Okhotsk
Sea of Okhotsk
Poluostrov Kamchatka
Komandorskiye Ostrova (Russia)
Bering Sea
Near Is. (U.S.A.)
Andreano
Petropavlovsk-Kamchatskiy
KAZAKSTAN
Aral Sea
Balqash Köl
MONGOLIA
Ulaanbaatar
Ürümqi
Amur
Khabarovsk
Sakhalin
Kurilskiye Ostrova (Russia)
La Pérouse Str.
Kuril Trench
Aleutia
Aleutian Trench
Almaty
KYRGYZSTAN
Changchun
SHENYANG
Harbin
Vladivostok
Sapporo
Hakodate
10,542
Toshkent
TAJIKISTAN
BEIJING
TIANJIN
Taiyuan
NORTH KOREA
SŌUL
SOUTH KOREA
Sea of Japan
Sendai
Emperor Seamount Chain
AFGHANISTAN
Kabul
Srinagar
Lanzhou
Dalian
Qingdao
Nagoya
Kyōto
Fuji-San 3776
TOKYO
Yokohama
PAKISTAN
Lahore
C H I N A
Kunlun Shan
XIZANG
Xi'an
Huang He
Kitakyūshū
Osaka
JAPAN
Kyūshū
10,554
DELHI
NEPAL
Mt. Everest
Lhasa
CHONGQING
Wuhan
Yellow Sea
Shikoku
Japan Trench
Kanpur
Himalaya
Ganga
Chang J.
Nanjing
HANGZHOU
SHANGHAI
East China Sea
Ogasawara Gunto (Japan)
Midway Is. (U.S.A.)
Brahmaputra
Changsha
Lisianski I. (U.S.A.)
KOLKATA (Calcutta)
DHAKA
BANGLADESH
Mandalay
Kunming
Fuzhou
GUANGZHOU
Taipei
Ryūkyū-rettō (Japan)
Kazan-Rettō (Japan)
Minami-Tori-Shima (Japan)
I N D I A
BURMA
Irrawaddy
Salween
HONG KONG
Macau
TAIWAN
Marcus
Wake I. (U.S.A.)
Necker Ridge
Hyderabad
LAOS
Hanoi
Bay of Bengal
Rangoon
THAILAND
Hainan
Luzon
Paracel Is.
C. Engano
MANILA
NORTHERN MARIANAS (U.S.A.)
Saipan
P A
CHENNAI (Madras)
Andaman Is. (India)
BANGKOK
CAMBODIA
Phnom Penh
VIETNAM
Mekong
Mindoro
PHILIPPINES
Samar
GUAM (U.S.A.) 11,022
Mariana Trench
MARSHALL IS.
Enewetak Atoll
Bikini Atoll
Nicobar Is. (India)
South China Sea
Thanh Pho Ho Chi Minh
Palawan
10,497
Mindanao Trench
Yap
Caroline Is.
Micronesia
Dalap-Uliga-Darrit
SRI LANKA
Colombo
MALAYSIA
Sulu Sea
Mindanao
Koror
Truk
Pohnpei
Palikir
Jaluit I.
4101
PALAU
FEDERATED STATES OF MICRONESIA
Kuala Lumpur
BRUNEI
SABAH
Celebes Sea
Maluku
Butaritari
SINGAPORE
Borneo
SARAWAK
Halmahera
Melanesia
NAURU
Banaba
Tarawa
Gilbert Is.
Howland I.
Baker I.
Sumatera
Palembang
Java Sea
Ujung Pandang
Sulawesi
Buru
Seram
PAPUA NEW GUINEA
Admiralty Is.
New Ireland
Phoenix Is.
Abariringa
Enderbur
O
Sunda Islands
I N D O N E S I A
Puncak Jaya 5029
IRIAN JAYA
Bismarck Arch.
Rabaul
KI
JAKARTA
Flores Sea
Banda Sea
New Guinea
New Britain
Bougainville
Java Trench
Jawa
Surabaya
Bali
Flores
7440
Lae
Port Moresby
Honiara
SOLOMON IS.
Fongafale
TUVALU
Rotuma
Is. Wallis & Futuna (Fr.)
SAMO
Apia
Cocos Is. (Austral.)
Christmas I. (Austral.)
Sumbawa
Sumba
EAST TIMOR
Timor
Arafura Sea
Torres Strait
C. York
Guadalcanal
Santa Cruz I. 9165
Espíritu Santo
Vanua Levu
I N D I A N
C. Arnhem
Darwin
Gulf of Carpentaria
Louisiade Arch.
Coral Sea
VANUATU
Is. Chesterfield
Port Vila
Viti Levu
Suva
FIJI
Nuku'alofa
TONG
Broome
North West C.
Cairns
Mount Isa
Townsville
Great Dividing Ra.
NEW CALEDONIA (Fr.)
Nouméa
Is. Loyauté
7570
O C E A N
A U S T R A L I A
Alice Springs
Rockhampton
Norfolk I. (Austral.)
10,822
Tonga Trench
Geraldton
L. Eyre
Brisbane
Lord Howe I. (Austral.)
Kermadec Is. (N.Z.)
Kermadec Trench 10,047
Perth
Great Australian Bight
Sydney
Canberra
Mt. Kosciuszko 2237
Murray
Tasman Sea
NEW ZEALAND
Albany
Adelaide
Darling
Melbourne
Bass Str.
Tasmania
Hobart
Auckland
Cook Strait
Wellington
Aoraki Mt. Cook 3753
Christchurch
Chatham I. (N.Z.)
Nouvelle Amsterdam (Fr.)
I. St. Paul (Fr.)
Mid-Indian Ridge
Dunedin
Invercargill
Bounty Is. (N.Z.)
Is. Crozet (Fr.)
Antipodes Is. (N.Z.)
Auckland Is. (N.Z.)
Campbell I. (N.Z.)
Kerguelen (Fr.)
Macquarie Is. (Austral.)
Heard I. (Austral.)

Elevation scale (ft / m)

ft	m
12 000	4000
9000	3000
6000	2000
3000	1000
1500	500
600	200
0	0
200	600
1000	3000
2000	6000
4000	12 000
6000	18 000
8000	24 000

Projection: Mollweide's Homolographic
East from Greenwich

ALASKA
(U.S.A.)
Anchorage

Arctic Circle

Bristol Bay

Gulf of Alaska

Juneau

Prince of Wales I.
(U.S.A.) Prince Rupert
Queen Charlotte Is.
(Canada)

C A N A D A

Edmonton

Calgary

Winnipeg

L. Winnipeg

Vancouver
Vancouver I. Victoria
Seattle
Portland

Regina

L. Superior

Québec

St. Lawrence

Newfoundland

St. John's

N O R T H

Boise

Minneapolis

Missouri

L. Huron
Michigan
Montréal
Toronto Ottawa
Detroit L. Ontario
Buffalo
L. Erie

Boston

C. Mendocino

Salt Lake
City

Denver

Kansas City

Sacramento

4418

SAN FRANCISCO

UNITED STATES

St. Louis

CHICAGO

Pittsburgh

Cincinnati

NEW YORK CITY
PHILADELPHIA
Baltimore
Washington D.C.

A T L A N T I C

6741

LOS ANGELES
San Diego

Phoenix

Oklahoma City Memphis

Dallas

Atlanta

C. Hatteras

Bermuda
(U.K.)

Guadalupe
(Mex.)

Ciudad
Juárez

Houston

San Antonio

New
Orleans

Jacksonville

Sargasso Sea

O C E A N

Tropic of Cancer

Honolulu

Oahu
4205
Hawaii

HAWAIIAN IS.
(U.S.A.)

C. San Lucas

Gulf of Mexico

Monterrey

Miami

Florida

BAHAMAS

La Habana

CUBA

West Indies

Is. Revilla Gigedo
(Mex.)

Guadalajara

MEXICO

Mérida

Canal de Yucatán

JAMAICA

HAITI

9200
DOMINICAN REP.

Leeward
Is.

C I F I C

anston I.
(U.S.A.)

Palmyra I.
(U.S.A.)

I

F

I

C

7680
5700
Puebla

Acapulco

BELIZE

GUATEMALA
Guatemala
San Salvador
EL SALVADOR

HONDURAS

NICARAGUA

Managua

Kingston

Caribbean Sea

PUERTO
RICO
(U.S.A.)

BARBADOS

Windward Is.

North West Christmas Ridge

Teraina
Tabuaeran
Kiritimati

I. Clipperton
(Fr.)

Barranquilla

COSTA
RICA San José

Colón
PANAMÁ
Panamá

Maracaibo

Caracas

Orinoco

CARIBBEAN

Jarvis I.
(U.S.A.)

E

A

N

Equator

Galápagos
(Ecuador)

Medellín

I. del Coco
(Costa Rica)

I. de Malpelo
(Colombia)

Cali

Bogotá

COLOMBIA

VENEZUELA

B A T I

Malden I.

Starbuck I.

Quito
ECUADOR

Amazonas

Tongareva

Caroline I.

Guayaquil

Iquitos

Pukapuka
Manihiki

Vostok I.

C. Paliñas

BRAZIL

Flint I.

O A
A.)

Suwarrow Is.

Is. Marquises

Is. de la
Société

Trujillo

6369

PERU

Tuamotu

Ridge

Austral

Cook Is.
(N.Z.)

Papeete Tahiti

Is. Tuamotu

FRENCH POLYNESIA

East Pacific Ridge

LIMA

Cuzco

Nevada Ancohuma
6550

Rarotonga

Seamount Chain

Is. Tubuai

Mururoa

Rapa

Tropic of Capricorn

Arequipa

6866
Peru- Arica

L. Titicaca

La Paz
BOLIVIA

Ducie I.

Pitcairn I.
(U.K.)

Iquique
Chile

Sala-y-Gómez
(Chile)

San Felix
(Chile)

San Ambrosio
(Chile)

8050
Trench

Antofagasta

PARAGUAY

Asunción

I. de Pascua
(Chile)

San Miguel
de Tucumán

Porto
Alegre

Arch. de
Juan Fernández
(Chile)

Valparaíso

Córdoba
6960
Aconcagua

Rosario

URUGUAY

Pacific Antarctic Ridge

Chile Rise

SANTIAGO

Concepción

BUENOS
AIRES

Montevideo

Río de la Plata

ARGENTINA

Patagonia

SOUTH

ATLANTIC

6212

OCEAN

Punta Arenas

Est. de Magallanes

Tierra del Fuego

Falkland Is.
(U.K.)

South Georgia
(U.K.)

C. de Hornos

B
C
D
E
F
G
H
J
K
L
M
N

NORTH AMERICA : Physical 1:35 000 000

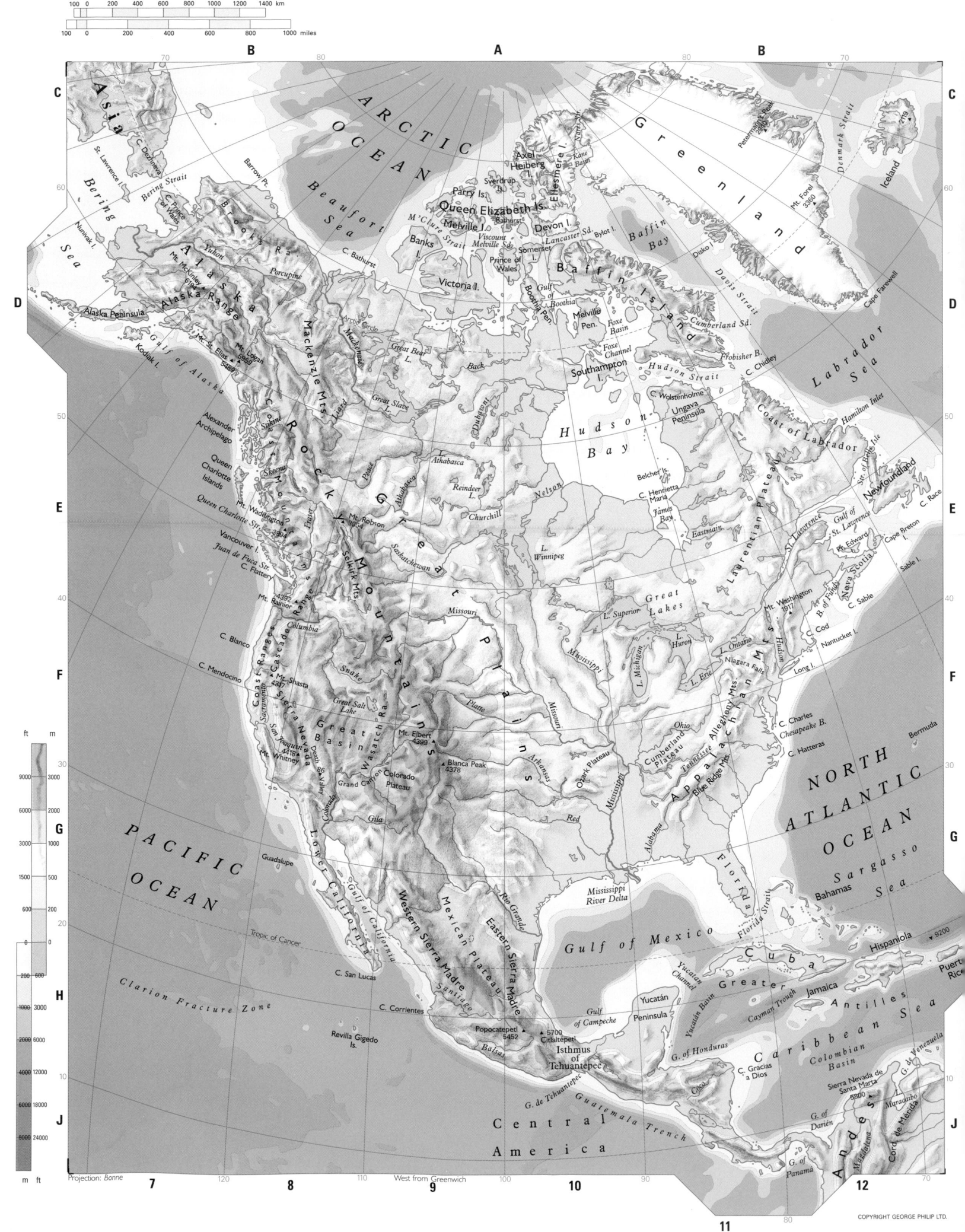
ARCTIC OCEAN
Beaufort Sea
Greenland
Baffin Bay
Baffin Island
Hudson Bay
Labrador Sea
Alaska Range
Rocky Mountains
Great Plains
Mackenzie Mts.
Coast Mountains
Great Lakes
Appalachian Mts.
Laurentian Plateau
Great Basin
Colorado Plateau
Mexican Plateau
Western Sierra Madre
Eastern Sierra Madre
Gulf of Mexico
NORTH ATLANTIC OCEAN
Sargasso Sea
PACIFIC OCEAN
Caribbean Sea
Greater Antilles
Central America
Andes
Bering Sea
Gulf of Alaska
Queen Elizabeth Is.
Mt. McKinley 6194
Mt. Logan 5959
Mt. St. Elias 5489
Mt. Robson 3954
Mt. Waddington 3994
Mt. Rainier 4392
Mt. Shasta 4317
Mt. Whitney 4418
Mt. Elbert 4399
Blanca Peak 4378
Popocatepetl 5452
Citlaltépetl 5700
Sierra Nevada de Santa Marta 5800
Mt. Forel 3360
Petermann Peak 2940
Mt. Washington 1917
Tropic of Cancer
Clarion Fracture Zone
Guatemala Trench
Projection: Bonne
West from Greenwich

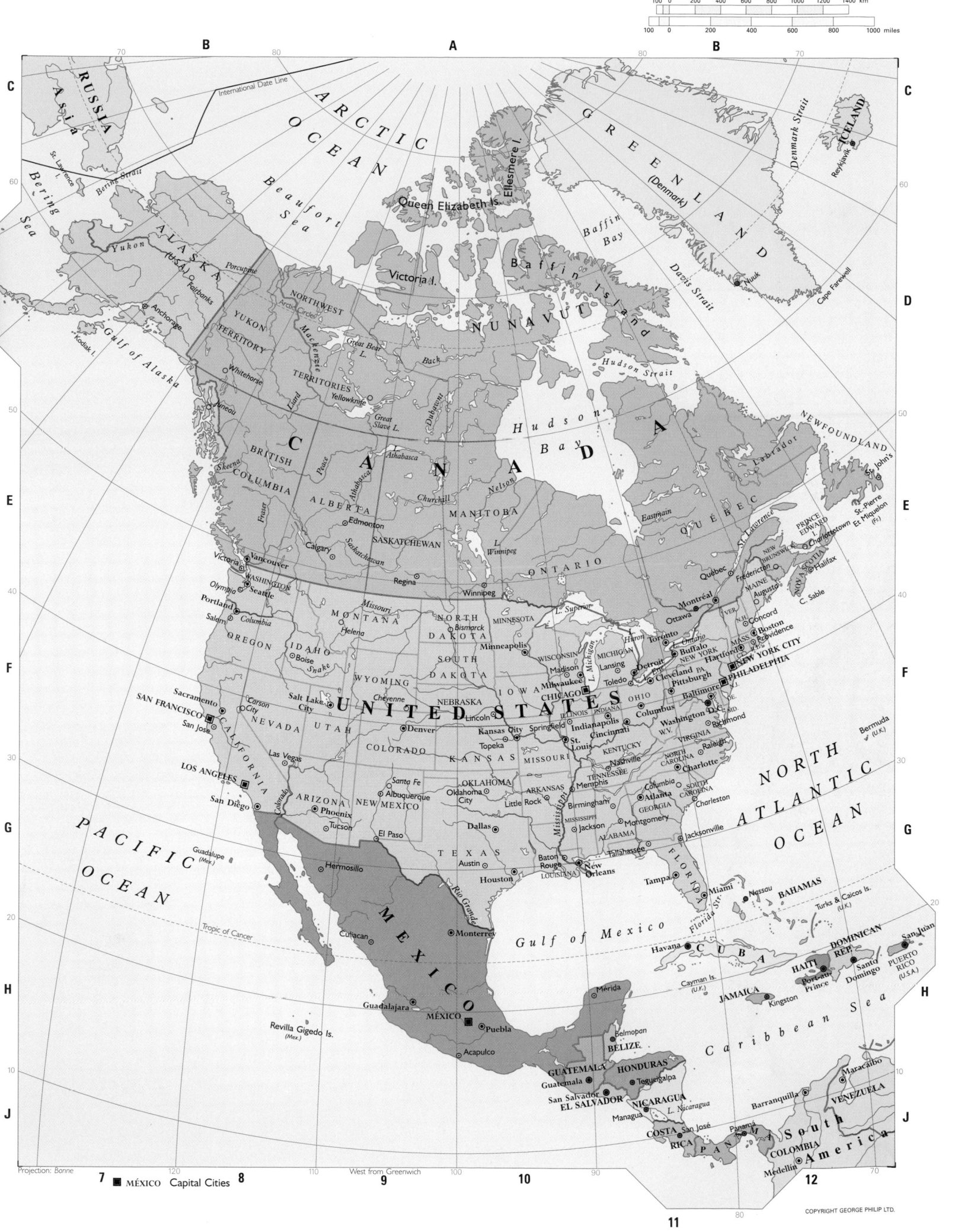
100 0 200 400 600 800 1000 1200 1400 km
100 0 200 400 600 800 1000 miles
RUSSIA
Asia
International Date Line
ARCTIC OCEAN
Bering Strait
Bering Sea
St. Lawrence I.
Beaufort Sea
Queen Elizabeth Is.
Ellesmere I.
GREENLAND (Denmark)
Denmark Strait
ICELAND
Reykjavik
Baffin Bay
Baffin Island
Davis Strait
Nuuk
Cape Farewell
Victoria I.
NUNAVUT
ALASKA (U.S.A.)
Yukon
Porcupine
Fairbanks
Anchorage
Kodiak I.
Gulf of Alaska
YUKON TERRITORY
Whitehorse
NORTHWEST TERRITORIES
Arctic Circle
Mackenzie
Great Bear L.
Back
Yellowknife
Great Slave L.
Liard
Dubawnt
Hudson Strait
Hudson Bay
CANADA
NEWFOUNDLAND
Labrador
St. John's
Juneau
BRITISH COLUMBIA
Skeena
Peace
Athabasca
L. Athabasca
ALBERTA
Churchill
Nelson
MANITOBA
Eastmain
QUÉBEC
St. Lawrence
PRINCE EDWARD I.
Charlottetown
St.-Pierre Et Miquelon (Fr.)
Fraser
Edmonton
SASKATCHEWAN
Saskatchewan
Calgary
L. Winnipeg
ONTARIO
NEW BRUNSWICK
NOVA SCOTIA
Halifax
Fredericton
Québec
Victoria
Vancouver
Regina
Winnipeg
Montréal
Ottawa
MAINE
Augusta
C. Sable
WASHINGTON
Olympia
Seattle
Portland
Salem
Columbia
OREGON
Missouri
MONTANA
Helena
NORTH DAKOTA
Bismarck
MINNESOTA
L. Superior
Toronto
VER.
N.H.
Concord
MASS.
Boston
Providence
IDAHO
Boise
Snake
Minneapolis
SOUTH DAKOTA
WISCONSIN
Madison
MICHIGAN
Lansing
L. Michigan
Huron
L. Ontario
Buffalo
NEW YORK
Hartford
NEW YORK CITY
PHILADELPHIA
WYOMING
Cheyenne
Milwaukee
Detroit
Toledo
Erie
Cleveland
PA.
Pittsburgh
N.J.
Sacramento
SAN FRANCISCO
San Jose
Carson City
NEVADA
Salt Lake City
UTAH
UNITED STATES
NEBRASKA
Lincoln
IOWA
CHICAGO
ILLINOIS
INDIANA
OHIO
Baltimore
DE.
MD.
Columbus
Washington D.C.
Richmond
Denver
Kansas City
Springfield
Indianapolis
Cincinnati
W.V.
VIRGINIA
Bermuda (U.K.)
CALIFORNIA
Las Vegas
COLORADO
KANSAS
Topeka
St. Louis
MISSOURI
KENTUCKY
Nashville
NORTH CAROLINA
Raleigh
Charlotte
NORTH ATLANTIC OCEAN
LOS ANGELES
San Diego
Colorado
ARIZONA
Phoenix
Tucson
Santa Fe
Albuquerque
NEW MEXICO
OKLAHOMA
Oklahoma City
ARKANSAS
Little Rock
TENNESSEE
Memphis
Mississippi
Birmingham
Columbia
Atlanta
SOUTH CAROLINA
Charleston
GEORGIA
PACIFIC OCEAN
Guadalupe (Mex.)
El Paso
Dallas
MISSISSIPPI
Jackson
ALABAMA
Montgomery
Jacksonville
TEXAS
Austin
Houston
Baton Rouge
LOUISIANA
New Orleans
Tallahassee
FLORIDA
Tampa
Miami
Nassau
BAHAMAS
Turks & Caicos Is. (U.K.)
Hermosillo
Rio Grande
MEXICO
Tropic of Cancer
Culiacan
Monterrey
Gulf of Mexico
Florida Str.
Havana
CUBA
DOMINICAN REP.
San Juan
PUERTO RICO (U.S.A.)
HAITI
Port-au-Prince
Santo Domingo
Cayman Is. (U.K.)
JAMAICA
Kingston
Mérida
Guadalajara
MÉXICO
Puebla
Revilla Gigedo Is. (Mex.)
Belmopan
BELIZE
Caribbean Sea
Acapulco
GUATEMALA
Guatemala
HONDURAS
Tegucigalpa
San Salvador
EL SALVADOR
NICARAGUA
Managua
L. Nicaragua
Barranquilla
Maracaibo
VENEZUELA
COSTA RICA
San José
Panamá
PANAMA
South America
COLOMBIA
Medellín
Projection: Bonne
West from Greenwich

■ MÉXICO Capital Cities

68 CANADA 1:15 000 000

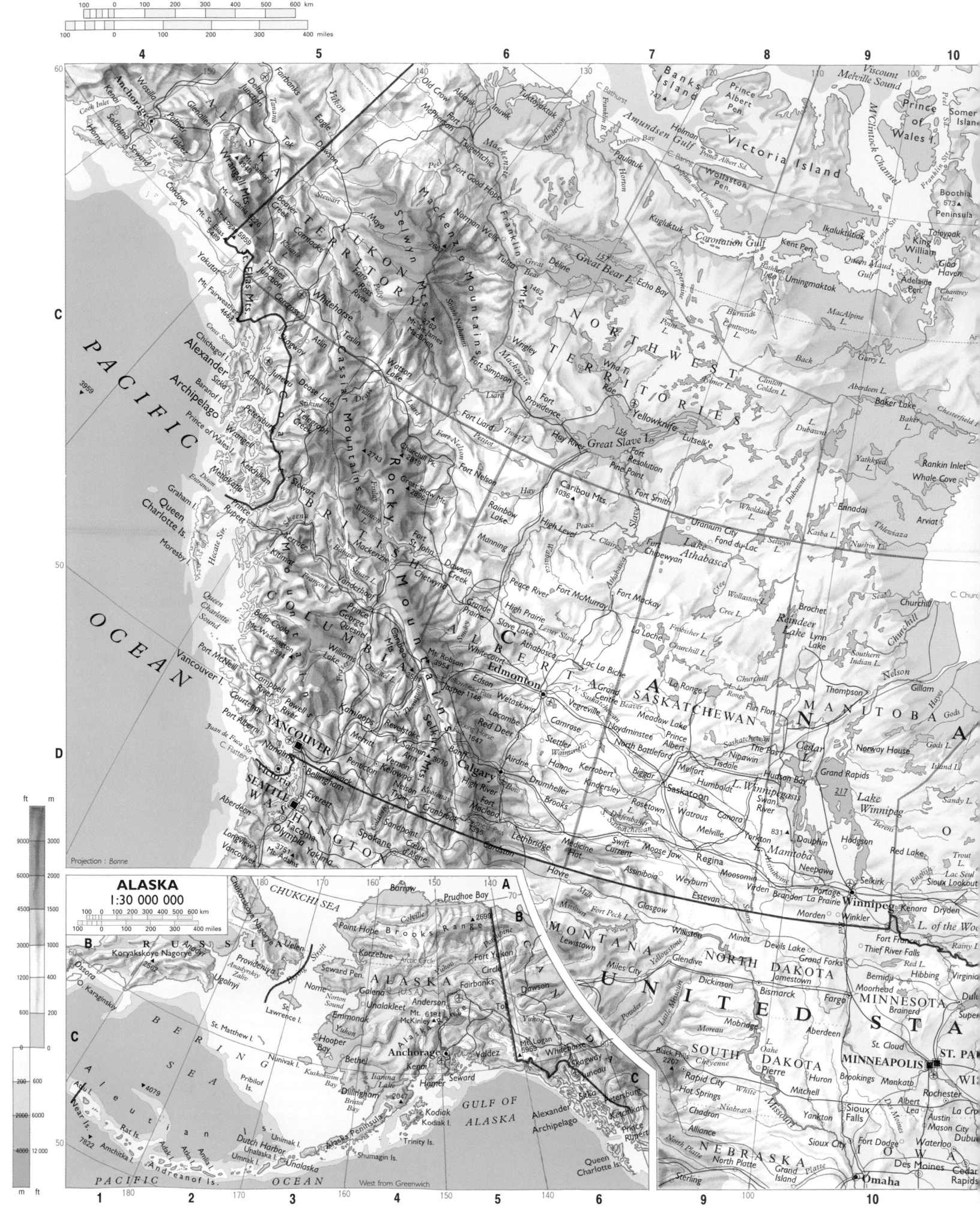

km
miles
PACIFIC
OCEAN
ALASKA
YUKON TERRITORY
NORTHWEST TERRITORIES
BRITISH COLUMBIA
ALBERTA
SASKATCHEWAN
MANITOBA
WASHINGTON
MONTANA
NORTH DAKOTA
SOUTH DAKOTA
NEBRASKA
MINNESOTA
IOWA
UNITED STATES
Anchorage
Fairbanks
Juneau
Whitehorse
Dawson
Inuvik
Yellowknife
Great Bear L.
Great Slave L.
Victoria Island
Banks Island
Lake Athabasca
Reindeer Lake
Lake Winnipeg
Edmonton
Calgary
VANCOUVER
Victoria
SEATTLE
Saskatoon
Regina
Winnipeg
MINNEAPOLIS
Omaha
Prince George
Prince Rupert
Kamloops
Rocky Mountains
Mackenzie Mountains
Selwyn Mts.
Coast Mountains
Cassiar Mountains
Vancouver I.
Queen Charlotte Is.
Alexander Archipelago
Amundsen Gulf
Coronation Gulf
Projection : Bonne
ALASKA
1:30 000 000
CHUKCHI SEA
BERING SEA
GULF OF ALASKA
Aleutian Is.
Brooks Range
Mt. McKinley 6194
Mt. Logan 5959
Kodiak I.
Alaska Peninsula
Nome
Barrow
Prudhoe Bay
West from Greenwich
ft
m

74
75

11 12 13 14 15 16

B C D E

Devon I.
Lancaster Sound
Baffin Bay
Nunavik
Uummannaq
GREENLAND
(KALAALLIT NUNAAT)
(Denmark)
Brodeur Peninsula
Arctic Bay
Nanisivik
Borden Pen.
Bylot I.
Pond Inlet
Clyde River
Qeqertarsuaq
Ilulissat
Qasigiannguit
Kangerlussuaq
Sisimiut
Maniitsoq
Nuuk
Kong Frederik VI's Kyst
Tasiilaq
Paamiut
Arsuk
Qaqortoq
Nanortalik
Baffin Island
Davis Strait
Fury and Hecla Str.
Igloolik
Simpson Pen.
Pelly Bay
Melville Peninsula
Sanirajak
Prince Charles I.
Air Force I.
Foxe Basin
Cumberland Peninsula
Pangnirtung
Cumberland Sd.
Rae Isthmus
Repulse Bay
NUNAVUT
Nettilling L.
Amadjuak L.
Foxe Pen.
Cape Dorset
Iqaluit
Hall Peninsula
Meta Incognita Peninsula
Kimmirut
Frobisher Bay
Resolution I.
Foxe Channel
Southampton I.
Salliq
Bell Pen.
Nottingham I.
Salisbury I.
Hudson Strait
Coats I.
Mansel I.
Ivujivik
Salluit
Kangiqsujuaq
Quaqtaq
Akpatok I.
C. Chidley
Labrador Sea
ATLANTIC OCEAN
Péninsule d'Ungava
Puvirnituq
Kangirsuk
Ungava Bay
Kangiqsualujjuaq
Hebron
Hudson Bay
Ottawa Is.
Kuujjuaq
Nain
NEWFOUNDLAND
Hopedale
Rigolet
Cartwright
Inukjuak
Sleeper Is.
King George Is.
Baker's Dozen Is.
Sanikiluaq
Belcher Is.
Kuujjuarapik
L. Minto
Schefferville
Smallwood Res.
Labrador
North West River
Happy Valley-Goose Bay
Churchill Falls
Port Hope Simpson
Belle Isle
C. Bauld
St. Anthony
L. Bienville
Rés. de Caniapiscau
Labrador City
Fermont
Esker
St-Augustin
Peawanuck
Winisk
C. Henrietta Maria
La Grande
Chisasibi
James Bay
Akimiski I.
Wemindji
Attawapiskat
Fort Albany
Charlton I.
Eastmain
Waskaganish
Moosonee
QUÉBEC
Rés. Manicouagan
Gagnon
Havre-St-Pierre
Natashquan
Î. d'Anticosti
Sept-Îles
Port-Cartier
Gulf of St. Lawrence
Deer Lake
Corner Brook
Grand Falls
Gander
Lewisporte
Bonavista
Carbonear
St. John's
Newfoundland
Stephenville
Channel-Port aux Basques
Marystown
Placentia
C. Race
Cabot Str.
ST.-PIERRE et MIQUELON (Fr.)
L. Mistassini
Chibougamau
Baie Comeau
Matane
Gaspé
Îs. de la Madeleine
Rimouski
Campbellton
Bathurst
PR. EDWARD I.
Summerside
Charlottetown
Cape Breton I.
Sydney
Glace Bay
Port Hawkesbury
Antigonish
New Glasgow
Truro
NOVA SCOTIA
Halifax
Dartmouth
Sable I. (Nova Scotia)
Bridgewater
Liverpool
Yarmouth
Digby
Kentville
Amherst
Moncton
NEW BRUNSWICK
Fredericton
Saint John
Miramichi
Edmundston
Rivière-du-Loup
Matagami
Chicoutimi
Jonquière
Dolbeau
Roberval
Hearst
Cochrane
Amos
Kapuskasing
Geraldton
Nipigon
Marathon
Timmins
Kirkland Lake
Rouyn-Noranda
Val-d'Or
La Tuque
Québec
Lévis
Thunder Bay
Lake Superior
Wawa
Chapleau
New Liskeard
Mont-Laurier
Shawinigan
Trois-Rivières
Thetford Mines
St-Hyacinthe
Sherbrooke
MAINE
Bangor
Augusta
Lewiston
Portland
Houghton
Marquette
Sault Ste. Marie
Elliot Lake
Sudbury
North Bay
MONTRÉAL
Hull
Ottawa
Pembroke
Cornwall
Burlington
Montpelier
VERMONT
NEW HAMPSHIRE
Concord
Manchester
BOSTON
Providence
Manitoulin I.
Parry Sound
Huntsville
Lake Huron
Georgian Bay
Owen Sound
Barrie
Peterborough
Belleville
Kingston
Oshawa
TORONTO
L. Ontario
Syracuse
Kitchener
Hamilton
London
Rochester
Albany
Springfield
MASS.
NEW YORK
HARTFORD
CONN.
R.I.
New Haven
Bridgeport
NEW YORK
Buffalo
Niagara Falls
Sarnia
Windsor
DETROIT
Toledo
CLEVELAND
L. Erie
Erie
Jamestown
Elmira
Binghamton
Scranton
Newark
N.J.
Allentown
Trenton
PENNSYLVANIA
MICHIGAN
Lake Michigan
Petoskey
Traverse City
Cadillac
Saginaw
Flint
Grand Rapids
Lansing
Manistique
Escanaba
Menominee
Green Bay
Sheboygan
MILWAUKEE
Racine
Kenosha
CHICAGO
Gary
South Bend
INDIANA
OHIO

West from Greenwich

11 12 13 14

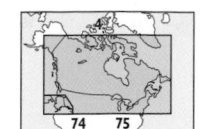

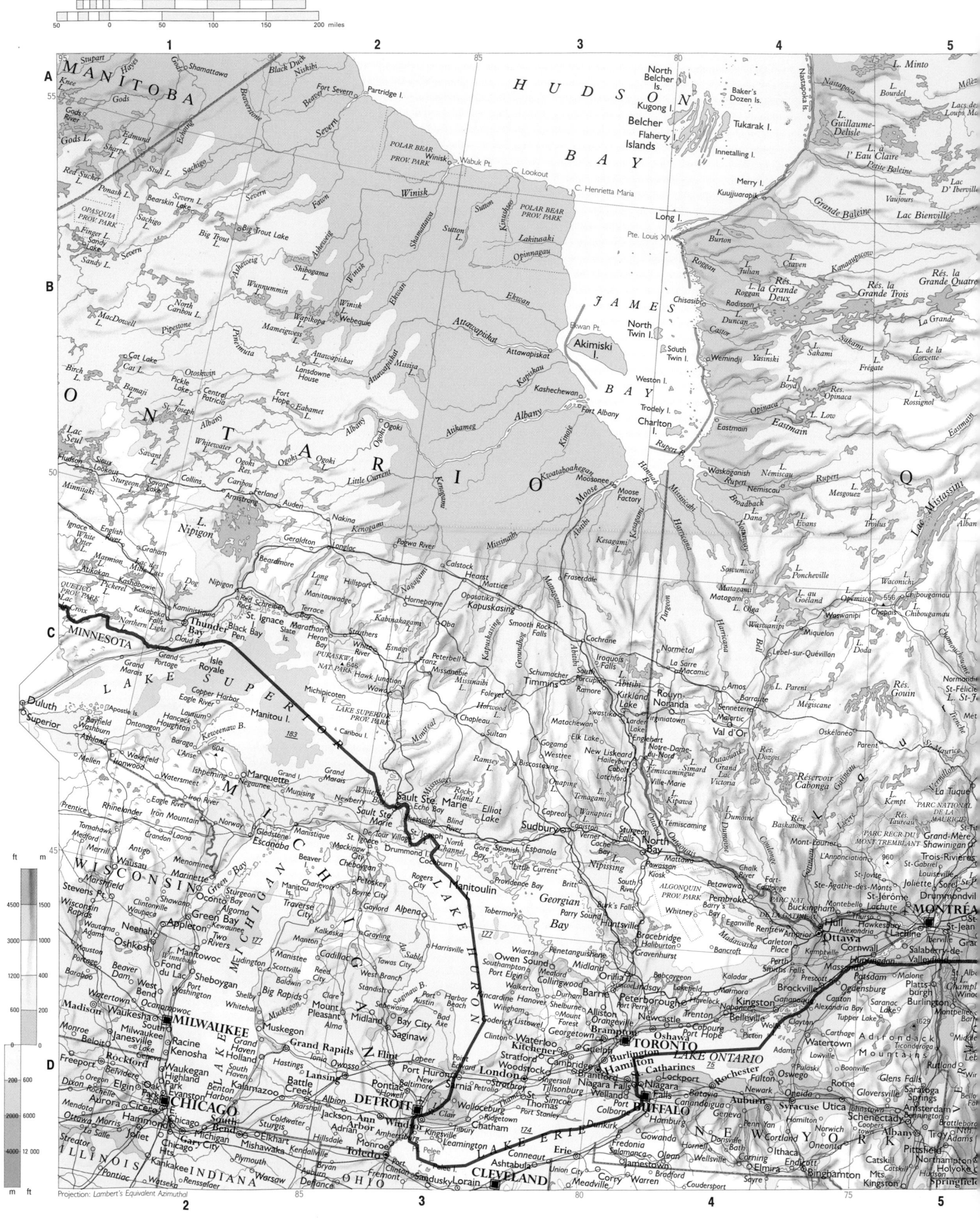
50 0 50 100 150 200 250 300 km
50 0 50 100 150 200 miles
1 2 3 4 5
A B C D
HUDSON BAY
JAMES BAY
MANITOBA
ONTARIO
MINNESOTA
WISCONSIN
MICHIGAN
ILLINOIS
INDIANA
OHIO
NEW YORK
LAKE SUPERIOR
LAKE MICHIGAN
LAKE HURON
LAKE ERIE
LAKE ONTARIO
Georgian Bay
Belcher Islands
Akimiski I.
North Twin I.
South Twin I.
Charlton I.
Baker's Dozen Is.
Tukarak I.
Flaherty I.
Kugong I.
North Belcher Is.
Long I.
C. Henrietta Maria
C. Lookout
Pte. Louis XIV
POLAR BEAR PROV. PARK
OPASQUIA PROV. PARK
QUETICO PROV. PARK
ALGONQUIN PROV. PARK
LAKE SUPERIOR PROV. PARK
PUKASKWA NAT. PARK
L. Nipigon
Lac Seul
L. Mistassini
Lac Bienville
L. Guillaume-Delisle
L. à l' Eau Claire
Rés. la Grande Deux
Rés. la Grande Trois
Rés. la Grande Quatre
Réservoir Cabonga
Rés. Gouin
Isle Royale
Manitoulin
Thunder Bay
Sault Ste. Marie
Sudbury
North Bay
Timmins
Kirkland Lake
Rouyn-Noranda
Val d'Or
Moosonee
Moose Factory
Fort Albany
Attawapiskat
Kashechewan
Eastmain
Waskaganish
Chisasibi
Hearst
Kapuskasing
Cochrane
Geraldton
Nipigon
Marathon
Wawa
Chapleau
Elliot Lake
Parry Sound
Huntsville
Owen Sound
Barrie
Orillia
Peterborough
Kingston
Belleville
Brockville
Ottawa
Hull
Pembroke
MONTREAL
Trois-Rivières
Shawinigan
La Tuque
Chibougamau
TORONTO
Hamilton
Oshawa
Kitchener
Waterloo
Guelph
Brampton
London
Windsor
Sarnia
St. Catharines
Niagara Falls
BUFFALO
Rochester
Syracuse
Utica
Albany
Schenectady
DETROIT
Toledo
CLEVELAND
Erie
Flint
Lansing
Grand Rapids
Saginaw
MILWAUKEE
CHICAGO
Green Bay
Duluth
Superior
Marquette
Adirondack Mountains
Projection: Lambert's Equivalent Azimuthal
ft m
4500 1500
3000 1000
1200 400
600 200
0 0
200 600
2000 6000
4000 12 000
m ft

69
73
80
76

6 7 8 9

A B C D

LABRADOR SEA

NEWFOUNDLAND

Labrador

QUÉBEC

Smallwood Reservoir

Rés. de Caniapiscau

Rés. Manicouagan

Mealy Mts.

Str. of Belle Isle

Long Range Mts.

Newfoundland

GROS MORNE NAT. PARK

TERRA NOVA NAT. PARK

Î. d'Anticosti

Dét. de Jacques-Cartier

Dét. d'Honguedo

GULF OF ST. LAWRENCE

St. Lawrence

Pén. de Gaspé

Mts. Chic-Chocs

PARC DE CONSERVATION DE LA GASPÉSIE

Îs. de la Madeleine (Québec)

Î. Brion

Cabot Strait

ST-PIERRE ET MIQUELON (France)

NEW BRUNSWICK

PRINCE EDWARD ISLAND

NOVA SCOTIA

CAPE BRETON HIGHLANDS NAT. PARK

KEJIMKUJIK NAT. PARK

Cape Breton Island

Bay of Fundy

Sable I. (Nova Scotia)

ATLANTIC OCEAN

MAINE

NEW HAMPSHIRE

MASS.

UNITED STATES

Nain, Davis Inlet, Hopedale, Postville, Makkovik, Rigolet, Cartwright, Black Tickle, Square Islands, Williams harbour, Port Hope Simpson, Battle Harbour, Mary's Harbour, St. Lewis, Red Bay, L'Anse au Loup, Forteau, Blanc-Sablon, Happy Valley-Goose Bay, North West River, Churchill Falls, Twin Falls, Esker, Schefferville, Labrador City, Wabush, Fermont, Sept-Îles, Port-Cartier, Baie Comeau, Havre-St-Pierre, Natashquan, Kegaska, Romaine, Harrington Harbour, St-Augustin, Gaspé, Matane, Rimouski, Rivière-du-Loup, Chicoutimi, Jonquière, Alma, Québec, Lévis, Sherbrooke, Campbellton, Bathurst, Edmundston, Fredericton, Saint John, Moncton, Charlottetown, Summerside, Truro, Halifax, Dartmouth, Yarmouth, Sydney, Glace Bay, Corner Brook, Stephenville, Grand Falls, Windsor, Gander, Channel-Port aux Basques, St. John's, Mt. Pearl, Bangor, Augusta, Portland, Manchester, Boston, Lowell, Quincy, Brockton

L'Anse aux Meadows, St. Anthony, Roddickton, Port au Choix, Deer Lake, Botwood, Lewisporte, Clarenville, Marystown, Burin, Placentia, Argentia, Trepassey, C. Race, C. Freels, C. Bonavista, C. St. George, C. Ray, C. North, C. Sable, C. Cod, C. de Gaspé, C. Harrison

1135, 1048, 1268, 1128, 1190, 814, 820, 532, 572, 610, 381

70 65 60 55 50 45

West from Greenwich

6 7 8

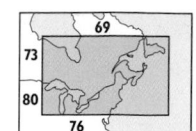

YUKON TERRITORY
NORTHWEST TERRITORIES
BRITISH COLUMBIA
ALBERTA
ALASKA (U.S.A.)
WASHINGTON
IDAHO
UNITED STATES
PACIFIC OCEAN
GREAT SLAVE LAKE
Queen Charlotte Islands
Queen Charlotte Sound
Vancouver Island
Whitehorse
Yellowknife
Edmonton
Calgary
Vancouver
Victoria
Seattle
Prince George
Prince Rupert
Kamloops
Kelowna
Red Deer
Lethbridge
Fort Nelson
Dawson Creek
Fort St. John
Grande Prairie
Juneau
Coast Mountains
Rocky Mountains
Skeena Mountains
Cassiar Mountains
Columbia Mts.
Cariboo Mts.
Monashee Mts.
Selkirk Mts.
Purcell Mts.
Caribou Mts.
Birch Mountains
Swan Hills
Buffalo Head Hills
Projection: Lambert's Equivalent Azimuthal
West from Greenwich

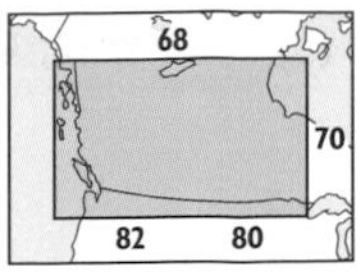
68
70
82
80

7
8
9
10
11
A
B
C
D
NUNAVUT
HUDSON
BAY
MANITOBA
SASKATCHEWAN
ONTARIO
MINNESOTA
NORTH DAKOTA
MONTANA
LAKE WINNIPEG
Lake Winnipegosis
Lake Manitoba
Cedar Lake
Lake Athabasca
Reindeer Lake
Wollaston L.
Southern Indian L.
Lake of the Woods
Lac La Ronge
Churchill
Nelson
Thompson
Flin Flon
The Pas
Lynn Lake
Uranium City
Fond-du-Lac
Prince Albert
North Battleford
Saskatoon
Regina
Moose Jaw
Swift Current
Yorkton
Lloydminster
Medicine Hat
Cypress Hills
Brandon
Dauphin
Portage la Prairie
Winnipeg
Selkirk
Kenora
Dryden
Fort Frances
International Falls
Grand Forks
Minot
Williston
Devils Lake
Bemidji
Duluth
Superior
Havre
Fort Peck Lake
Estevan
Weyburn
Arviat
Whale Cove
Gods L.
Island L.
Lac Seul
Nueltin L.
Kasba L.
Dubawnt L.
Lac la Croix

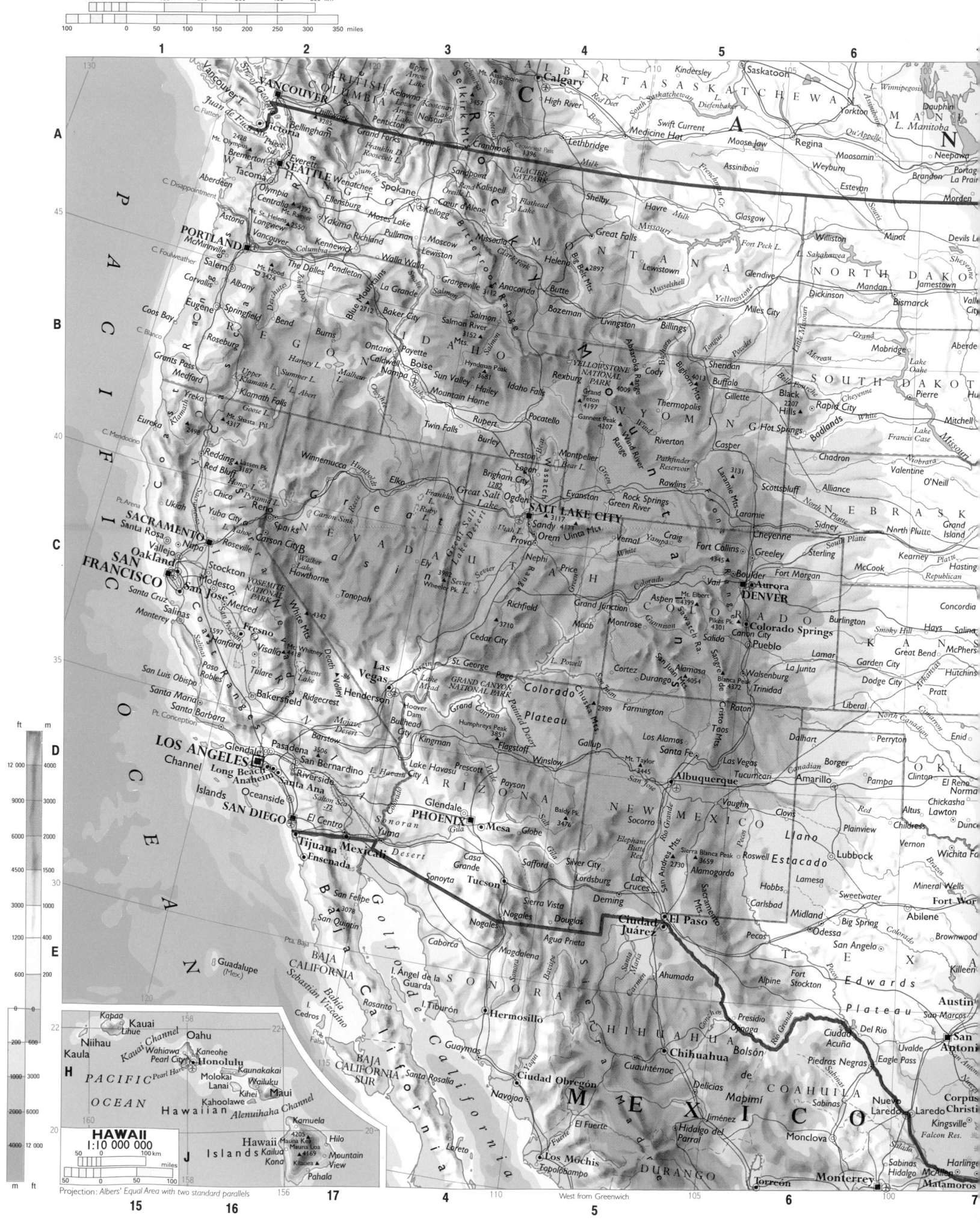

100 0 100 200 300 400 500 km
100 0 50 100 150 200 250 300 350 miles
BRITISH COLUMBIA
ALBERTA
SASKATCHEWAN
MANITOBA
CANADA
VANCOUVER
Victoria
Calgary
Saskatoon
Regina
Lethbridge
Medicine Hat
Moose Jaw
Swift Current
Kelowna
Penticton
Nelson
Cranbrook
Bellingham
Everett
SEATTLE
Tacoma
Olympia
Spokane
Wenatchee
Yakima
Ellensburg
Moses Lake
Kennewick
Richland
Walla Walla
Pullman
Moscow
Lewiston
Coeur d'Alene
Kalispell
Sandpoint
Missoula
Helena
Great Falls
Butte
Bozeman
Billings
Lewistown
Glasgow
Havre
Shelby
Miles City
Glendive
Williston
Minot
Bismarck
Dickinson
Mandan
Jamestown
NORTH DAKOTA
SOUTH DAKOTA
Pierre
Rapid City
Black Hills
Mobridge
MONTANA
WASHINGTON
PORTLAND
Salem
Corvallis
Albany
Eugene
Springfield
Coos Bay
Roseburg
Grants Pass
Medford
Klamath Falls
Bend
The Dalles
Pendleton
La Grande
Baker City
Burns
OREGON
IDAHO
Boise
Nampa
Caldwell
Ontario
Payette
Sun Valley
Hailey
Mountain Home
Twin Falls
Idaho Falls
Pocatello
Rexburg
Rupert
Burley
Salmon
YELLOWSTONE NATIONAL PARK
WYOMING
Cody
Sheridan
Buffalo
Gillette
Thermopolis
Riverton
Casper
Rawlins
Laramie
Cheyenne
Rock Springs
Green River
Evanston
Eureka
Redding
Red Bluff
Chico
Ukiah
Yuba City
SACRAMENTO
Santa Rosa
Napa
Vallejo
Oakland
SAN FRANCISCO
Stockton
Modesto
San Jose
Santa Cruz
Merced
Salinas
Monterey
Fresno
Hanford
Visalia
Tulare
Bakersfield
Paso Robles
San Luis Obispo
Santa Maria
Santa Barbara
LOS ANGELES
Glendale
Pasadena
Long Beach
Anaheim
Santa Ana
San Bernardino
Riverside
Oceanside
SAN DIEGO
El Centro
Tijuana
Mexicali
Ensenada
Reno
Sparks
Carson City
NEVADA
Winnemucca
Elko
Tonopah
Las Vegas
Henderson
Ely
Great Salt Lake
SALT LAKE CITY
Ogden
Logan
Provo
Orem
Sandy
UTAH
Richfield
Cedar City
St. George
Moab
Grand Junction
Montrose
COLORADO
Aspen
Vail
Boulder
DENVER
Aurora
Colorado Springs
Pueblo
Fort Collins
Greeley
Durango
Cortez
Alamosa
Trinidad
Walsenburg
La Junta
Lamar
ARIZONA
PHOENIX
Mesa
Glendale
Tucson
Yuma
Flagstaff
Prescott
Kingman
Lake Havasu City
Bullhead City
Payson
Globe
Safford
Sierra Vista
Nogales
Douglas
Winslow
Page
Colorado Plateau
GRAND CANYON NATIONAL PARK
NEW MEXICO
Albuquerque
Santa Fe
Los Alamos
Gallup
Farmington
Taos
Raton
Tucumcari
Las Vegas
Socorro
Silver City
Lordsburg
Deming
Las Cruces
Alamogordo
Roswell
Clovis
Hobbs
Carlsbad
Ciudad Juárez
El Paso
Llano Estacado
Amarillo
Lubbock
Midland
Odessa
Big Spring
Abilene
San Angelo
Pecos
Fort Stockton
Del Rio
TEXAS
OKLAHOMA
KANSAS
NEBRASKA
North Platte
Scottsbluff
Alliance
Sidney
Kearney
McCook
Garden City
Dodge City
Hutchinson
Great Bend
Liberal
Dalhart
Borger
Pampa
Lawton
Wichita Falls
MEXICO
SONORA
CHIHUAHUA
COAHUILA
DURANGO
BAJA CALIFORNIA
BAJA CALIFORNIA SUR
Hermosillo
Guaymas
Ciudad Obregón
Navojoa
Los Mochis
Topolobampo
El Fuerte
Chihuahua
Cuauhtémoc
Delicias
Jiménez
Hidalgo del Parral
Ojinaga
Ciudad Acuña
Piedras Negras
Monclova
Monterrey
Nuevo Laredo
Laredo
Torreón
Sabinas
Eagle Pass
Uvalde
Matamoros
McAllen
Santa Rosalía
Loreto
Golfo de California
Sonoran Desert
Mojave Desert
PACIFIC OCEAN
Rocky Mountains
Great Basin
Sierra Nevada
Cascade Range
Coast Ranges
Sierra Madre Occidental
Edwards Plateau
Guadalupe (Mex.)
HAWAII 1:10 000 000
Kauai
Niihau
Kaula
Oahu
Honolulu
Molokai
Lanai
Maui
Kahoolawe
Hawaii
Hilo
Kailua Kona
Mauna Kea
Mauna Loa
Hawaiian Islands
PACIFIC OCEAN
Projection: Albers' Equal Area with two standard parallels
West from Greenwich

68
69
86
87

8 9 10 11 12 13

A B C D E F

CANADA

Lake Winnipeg
Winnipeg
Lake of the Woods
Thunder Bay
Lake Superior
Sault Ste. Marie
Lake Michigan
Lake Huron
Lake Ontario
Lake Erie
MINNESOTA
WISCONSIN
MICHIGAN
IOWA
ILLINOIS
INDIANA
OHIO
PENNSYLVANIA
NEW YORK
VERMONT
NEW HAMPSHIRE
MAINE
MASS.
CONN.
NEW JERSEY
DEL.
MARYLAND
WEST VIRGINIA
VIRGINIA
KENTUCKY
TENNESSEE
NORTH CAROLINA
SOUTH CAROLINA
GEORGIA
ALABAMA
MISSISSIPPI
LOUISIANA
ARKANSAS
MISSOURI
FLORIDA
NEW BRUNSWICK
Québec
MONTREAL
Ottawa
TORONTO
Hamilton
MINNEAPOLIS
ST. PAUL
MILWAUKEE
CHICAGO
DETROIT
CLEVELAND
BUFFALO
PITTSBURGH
COLUMBUS
INDIANAPOLIS
CINCINNATI
ST. LOUIS
KANSAS CITY
BOSTON
HARTFORD
NEW YORK
PHILADELPHIA
BALTIMORE
WASHINGTON D.C.
Norfolk
Nashville
Memphis
CHARLOTTE
ATLANTA
Jacksonville
NEW ORLEANS
HOUSTON
DALLAS
TAMPA
MIAMI
Midwest
Appalachian Mountains
Ozark Plateau
Cumberland Plateau
ATLANTIC OCEAN
GULF OF MEXICO
Straits of Florida
BAHAMAS
Mississippi River Delta

95 90 85 80

8 9 10 11 12

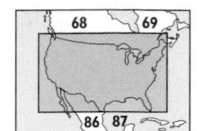

EASTERN UNITED STATES 1:6 000 000

50 0 50 100 150 200 km
50 0 50 100 150 miles
QUÉBEC
ONTARIO
MICHIGAN
WISCONSIN
ILLINOIS
INDIANA
OHIO
KENTUCKY
WEST VIRGINIA
VIRGINIA
PENNSYLVANIA
NEW YORK
NEW JERSEY
DELAWARE
MARYLAND
VERMONT
NEW HAMPSHIRE
MASS.
R.I.
LAKE SUPERIOR
LAKE MICHIGAN
LAKE HURON
LAKE ERIE
LAKE ONTARIO
Georgian Bay
Chesapeake Bay
Delaware Bay
MONTRÉAL
Québec
Ottawa
TORONTO
BUFFALO
BOSTON
HARTFORD
NEW YORK CITY
PHILADELPHIA
BALTIMORE
WASHINGTON D.C.
PITTSBURGH
CLEVELAND
COLUMBUS
CINCINNATI
DETROIT
CHICAGO
MILWAUKEE
INDIANAPOLIS
Sault Ste. Marie
Louisville
Lexington
Toledo
Dayton
Richmond

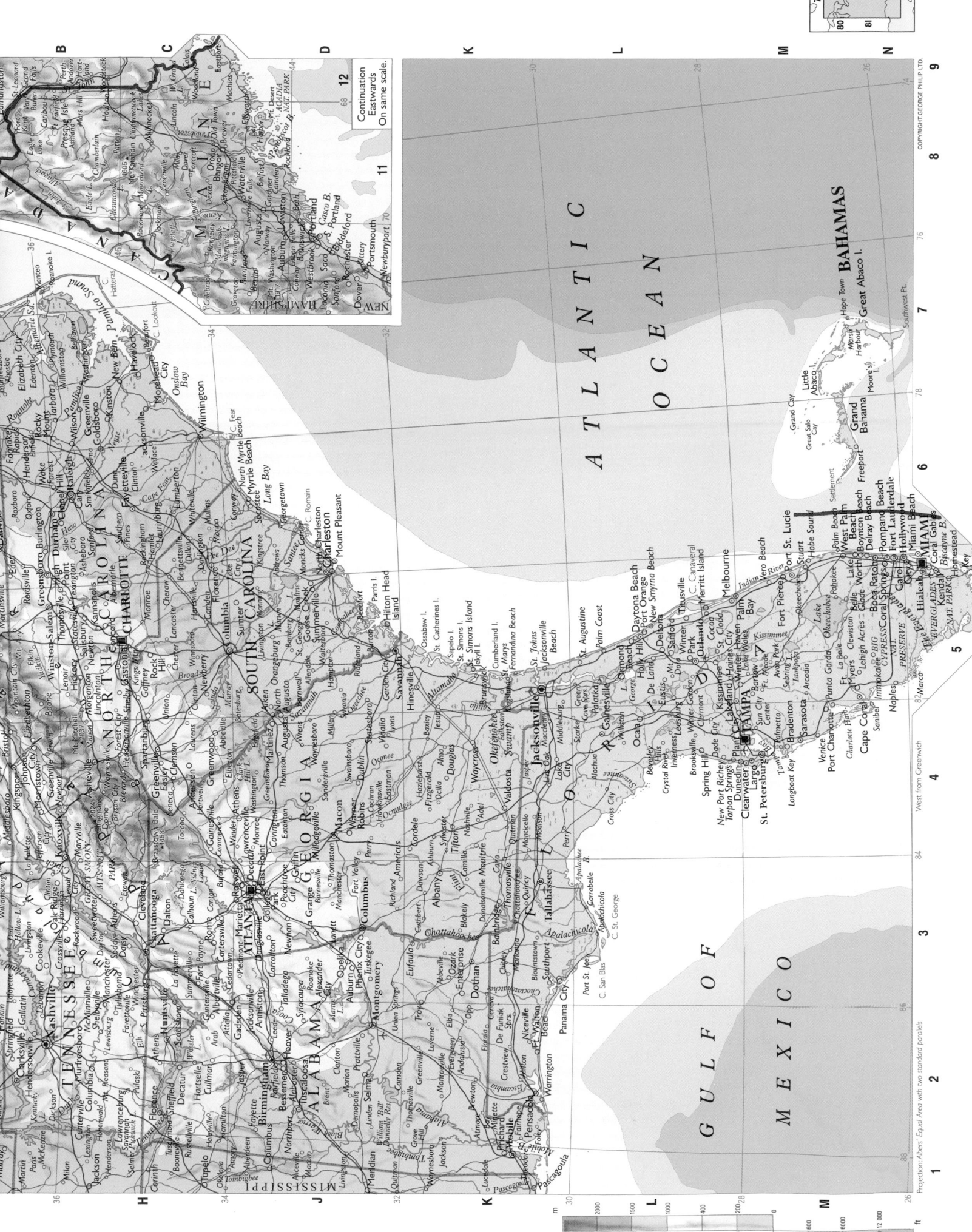

ATLANTIC

OCEAN

BAHAMAS

Hope Town
Great Abaco I.

Little
Abaco I.
Grand Cay
Great Sale
Cay
Grand
Bahama
Freeport

Southwest Pt.

CANADA

MAINE

Fort Kent
Van Buren
Caribou
Presque Isle
Houlton

12

Continuation
Eastwards
On same scale.

Mt. Desert I.
ACADIA
NAT. PARK
44

11

Lincoln
Orono
Old Town
Brewer
Bangor
Waterville
Augusta
Gardiner
Bath
Brunswick
Lewiston
Auburn
Portland
S. Portland
Biddeford
Saco

Belfast
Camden
Rockland

Casco B.

NEW
HAMPSHIRE

Dover
Rochester
Portsmouth
Portland
Newburyport

70

68

NORTH CAROLINA

Roanoke I.
Manteo
Nags Head
Hatteras
C. Hatteras

Pamlico Sound

New Bern
Havelock
Morehead
City
Beaufort
C. Lookout

Wilmington
C. Fear

Myrtle Beach
North Myrtle Beach
Long Bay

SOUTH CAROLINA

Charlotte
Gastonia
Concord

Columbia
Sumter
Florence

Charleston
North Charleston
Mount Pleasant

Hilton Head
Island

Parris I.

Savannah
Hinesville

GEORGIA

Atlanta
Marietta
Decatur
Griffin

Macon
Warner
Robins

Columbus

FLORIDA

Jacksonville
Jacksonville
Beach
St. Augustine

Palm Coast
Daytona Beach
Port Orange
New Smyrna Beach

Titusville
C. Canaveral
Merritt Island
Cocoa
Melbourne
Vero Beach

Indian River

Fort Pierce
Port St. Lucie
Stuart
Hobe Sound
West Palm
Beach
Palm Beach
Lake Worth
Boynton Beach
Delray Beach
Boca Raton
Pompano Beach
Fort Lauderdale
Hollywood
MIAMI
Hialeah
Miami Beach
Coral Gables
Biscayne B.
Kendall
Homestead

EVERGLADES
NAT. PARK

Florida Keys

BIG
CYPRESS
PRESERVE

Orlando
Winter
Park
Kissimmee
St. Cloud

TAMPA
St. Petersburg
Clearwater
Largo
Dunedin
Tarpon Springs
New Port Richey

Bradenton
Sarasota

Cape Coral
Fort
Myers
Naples
Marco

GULF OF

MEXICO

Tallahassee

Panama City

Apalachicola

TENNESSEE

Nashville

ALABAMA

Birmingham
Montgomery
Mobile

MISSISSIPPI

Pensacola

West from Greenwich

74

76

78

80

82

84

86

88

26

28

30

Projection: Albers' Equal Area with two standard parallels   COPYRIGHT GEORGE PHILIP LTD.

m
ft
6000
4500
3000
2000
1500
1000
600
400
200·600
0

ft m
12 000
6000
4000·600
2000
0

B
C
D
K
L
M
N

9
8
7
6
5
4
3
2
1

10 0 10 20 30 40 50 60 70 80 90 km
10 0 10 20 30 40 50 60 miles
Georgian Bay
Bruce Peninsula
LAKE HURON
ONTARIO
LAKE ONTARIO
LAKE ERIE
MICHIGAN
OHIO
PENNSYLVANIA
NEW
Allegheny Plateau
Allegheny Mountains
TORONTO
Mississauga
Hamilton
Burlington
Oakville
Kitchener
Waterloo
Guelph
Brampton
Cambridge
Brantford
London
Sarnia
Port Huron
DETROIT
Windsor
Chatham
St. Catharines
Niagara Falls
BUFFALO
Rochester
Oshawa
Peterborough
Barrie
Orillia
Owen Sound
L. Simcoe
Belleville
CLEVELAND
Lakewood
Akron
Canton
Youngstown
Warren
Erie
Jamestown
Olean
PITTSBURGH
Altoona
State College
Williamsport
Wheeling
Steubenville
Mansfield
Lorain
Elyria
Sandusky
Zanesville
Ft
m
6000
2000
4500
1500
3000
1000
1200
400
600
200
0
Projection: Bonne

70
76
76

8 9 10 11 12 13 14

A B C D E F G

CANADA
QUÉBEC
NEW YORK
VERMONT
NEW HAMPSHIRE
MAINE
MASSACHUSETTS
CONNECTICUT
RHODE ISLAND
NEW JERSEY
PENNSYLVANIA

ATLANTIC OCEAN

Long Island

Adirondack Mountains
Green Mountains
White Mountains
Catskill Mts.
Kittatinny Mts.
Blue Mts.

L. Champlain
L. Winnipesaukee

MONTREAL
Ottawa
Syracuse
Albany
BOSTON
HARTFORD
Providence
NEW YORK
PHILADELPHIA

West from Greenwich

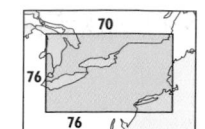

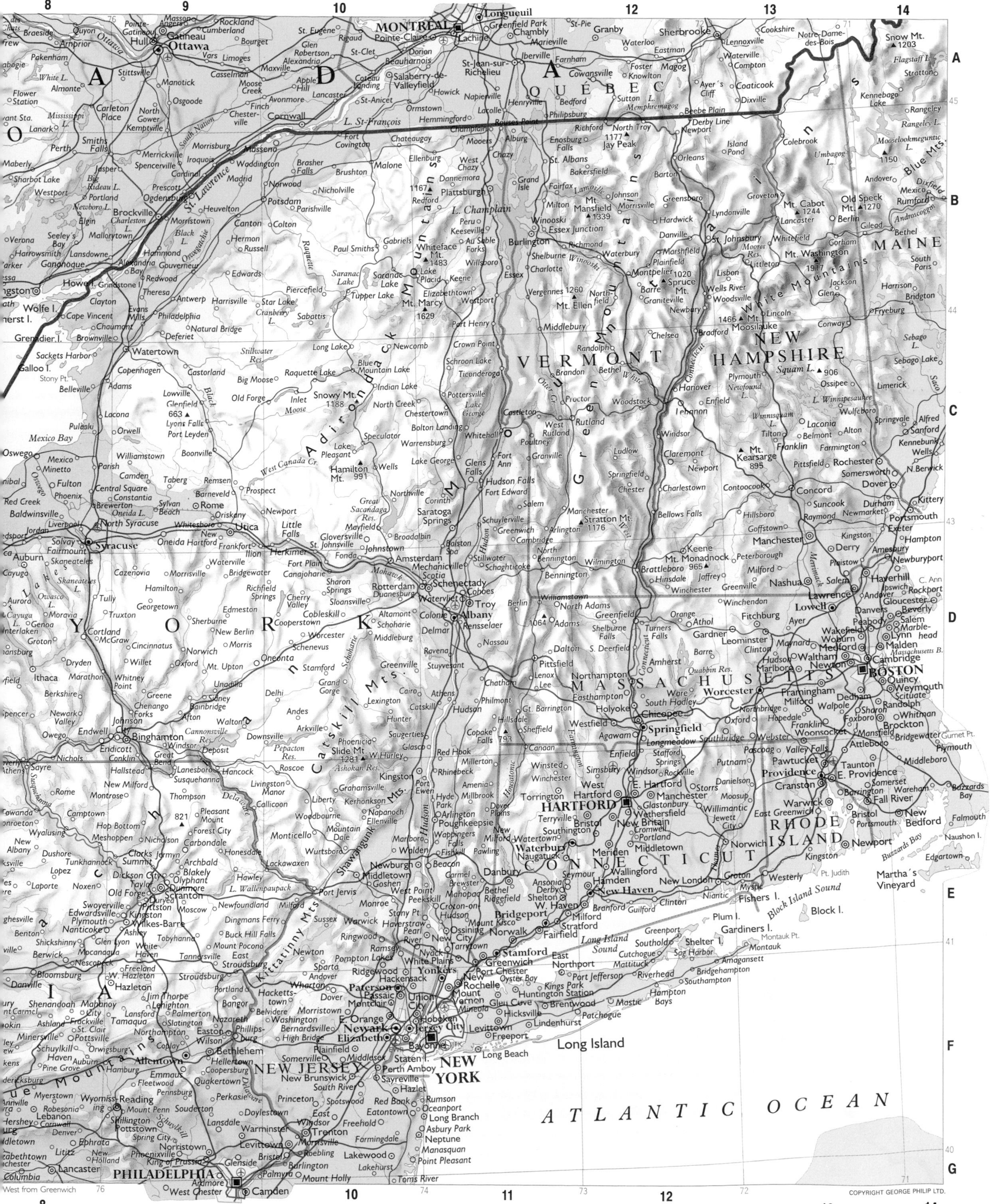

MIDDLE UNITED STATES 1:6 000 000

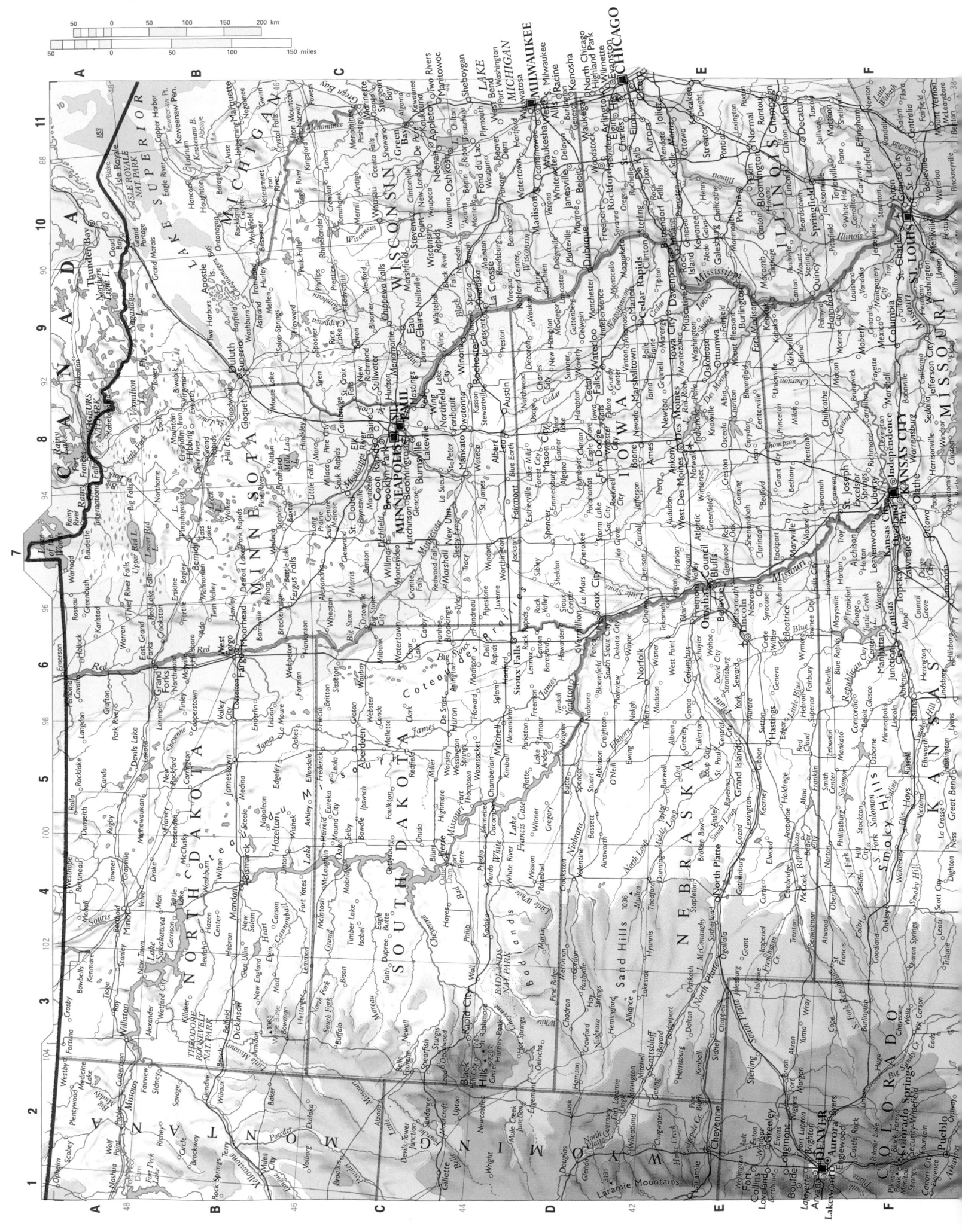
50 0 50 100 150 200 km
50 0 50 100 150 miles
CANADA
LAKE SUPERIOR
LAKE MICHIGAN
NORTH DAKOTA
SOUTH DAKOTA
MINNESOTA
WISCONSIN
IOWA
ILLINOIS
MISSOURI
NEBRASKA
KANSAS
COLORADO
WYOMING
MONTANA
MILWAUKEE
CHICAGO
MINNEAPOLIS
ST. PAUL
ST. LOUIS
KANSAS CITY
DENVER
Omaha
Des Moines
Duluth
Bismarck
Pierre
Lincoln
Sioux Falls
Fargo
Madison
Cheyenne
Colorado Springs
Pueblo
Rapid City
Sand Hills
Laramie Mountains
Smoky Hills
Black Hills
BADLANDS NAT. PARK
THEODORE ROOSEVELT NAT. PARK
ISLE ROYALE NAT. PARK
VOYAGEURS NAT. PARK
Mississippi
Missouri
Red
Lake of the Woods
A B C D E F
1 2 3 4 5 6 7 8 9 10 11

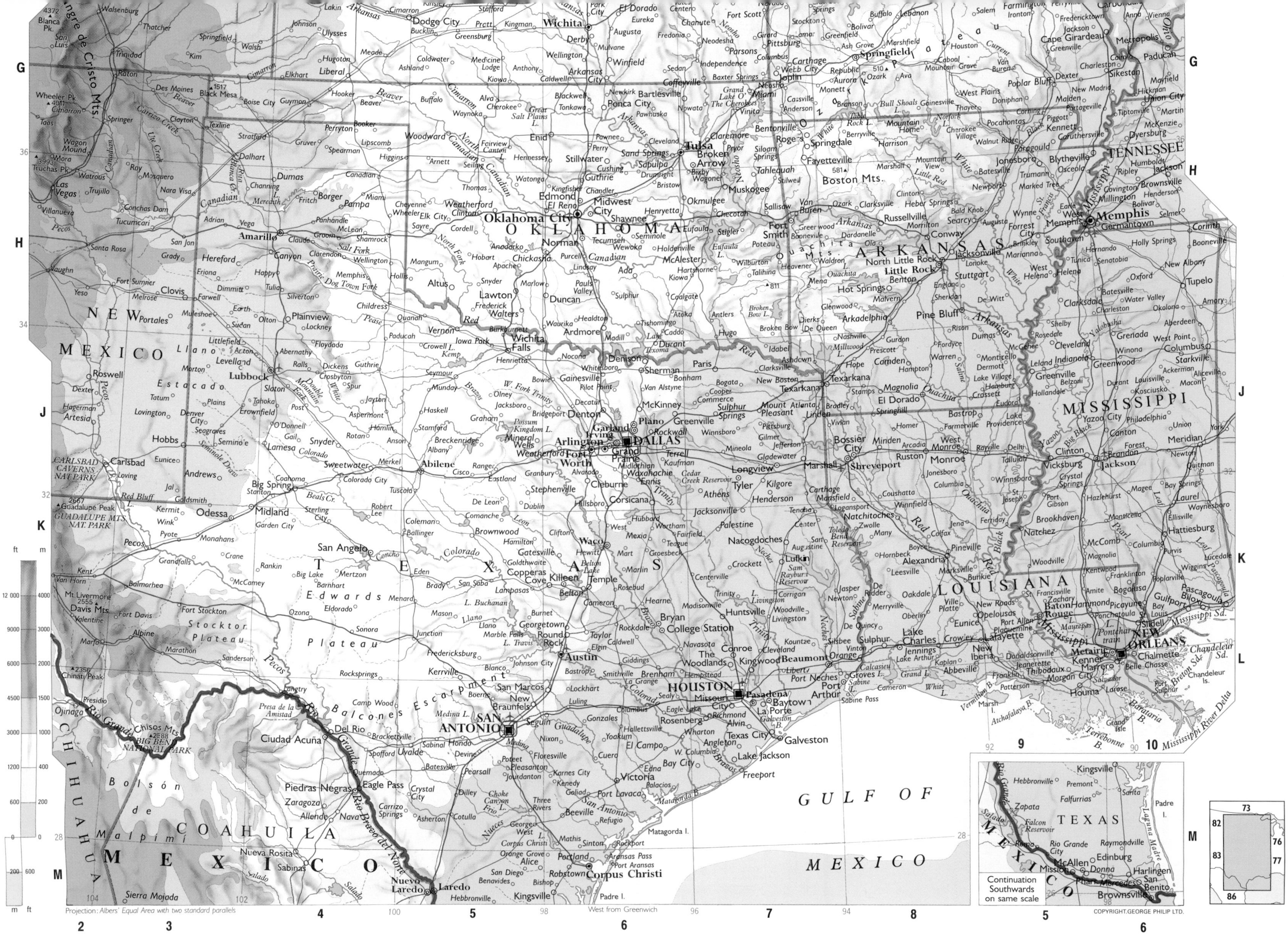

TENNESSEE

MISSISSIPPI

ARKANSAS

LOUISIANA

OKLAHOMA

TEXAS

NEW MEXICO

MEXICO

COAHUILA

CHIHUAHUA

GULF OF MEXICO

Sangre de Cristo Mts.

Edwards Plateau

Stockton Plateau

Llano Estacado

Projection: Albers' Equal Area with two standard parallels

COPYRIGHT GEORGE PHILIP LTD.

Continuation Southwards on same scale

WESTERN UNITED STATES 1:6 000 000

50 0 50 100 150 200 km
50 0 50 100 150 miles
BRITISH COLUMBIA
ALBERTA
SASKATCHEWAN
CANADA
WASHINGTON
OREGON
IDAHO
MONTANA
WYOMING
NEVADA
UTAH
ROCKY MOUNTAINS
Great Basin
Snake River Plain
Columbia Basin
Blue Mountains
Cascade Range
Klamath Mts.
Bighorn Mountains
Absaroka Range
Bitterroot Range
Salmon River Mountains
Sawtooth Range
Great Salt Lake
Great Salt Lake Desert
Uinta Mountains
VANCOUVER
SEATTLE
PORTLAND
SACRAMENTO
SALT LAKE CITY
Spokane
Boise
Great Falls
Billings
Missoula
Helena
Butte
Pocatello
Idaho Falls
Ogden
Provo
Reno
Eugene
Salem
Medford
Yakima
Tacoma
Olympia
Casper
Laramie

PACIFIC
OCEAN
LOS ANGELES
SAN DIEGO
Tijuana
Mexicali
PHOENIX
Tucson
Albuquerque
Santa Fe
El Paso
Ciudad Juárez
Chihuahua
Hermosillo
Las Vegas
Bakersfield
Fresno
San Jose
Santa Barbara
Flagstaff
Yuma
Ensenada
Nogales
Las Cruces
Gallup
Farmington
Durango
TEXAS
ARIZONA
NEW MEXICO
SONORA
CHIHUAHUA
BAJA CALIFORNIA
MEXICO
COLORADO
Golfo de California
Colorado Plateau
Mojave Desert
Sonoran Desert
Death Valley
Sierra Nevada
Coast Ranges
Sangre de Cristo Mts.
San Juan Mts.
Mogollon Rim
Painted Desert
Grand Canyon
Rio Grande
Colorado
Gila
Isla Guadalupe (Mexico)
Channel Is.
Desierto de Altar
Sierra de Juárez
Sierra de San Pedro Mártir
I. Tiburón
I. Ángel de la Guarda
Projection: Albers' Equal Area with two standard parallels
West from Greenwich
COPYRIGHT GEORGE PHILIP LTD.

WESTERN WASHINGTON REGION
On same scale

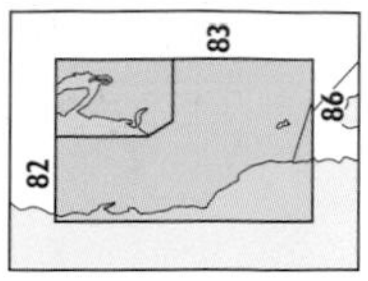

NEVADA
ARIZONA
CALIFORNIA
BAJA CALIFORNIA
MEXICO
SONORAN DESERT
MOJAVE DESERT

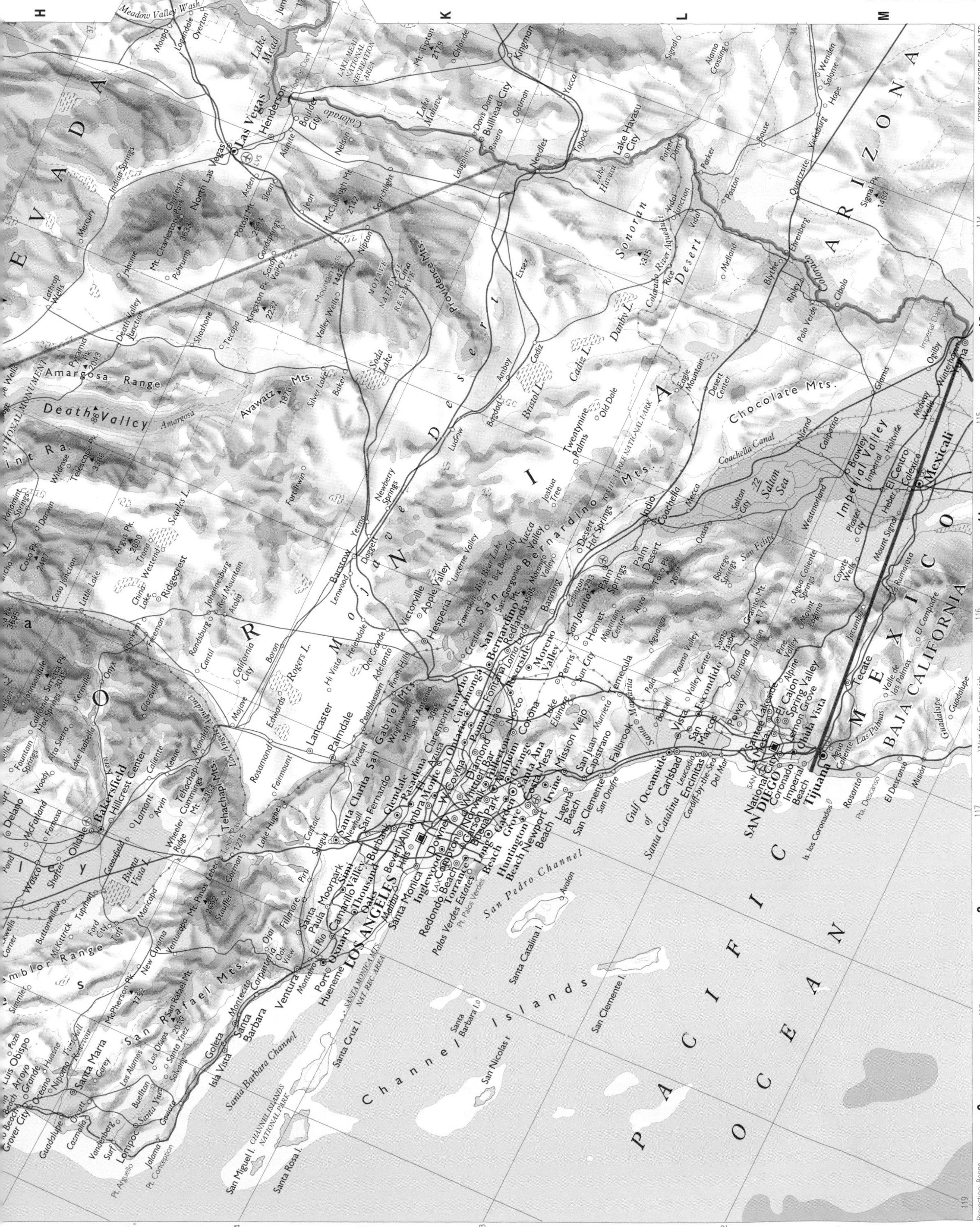

Meadow Valley Wash
Lake Mead
LAKE MEAD NATIONAL RECREATION AREA
Las Vegas
North Las Vegas
Henderson
Boulder City
Hoover Dam
Davis Dam
Bullhead City
Lake Havasu City
Kingman
Needles
Parker
Parker Dam
Blythe
Quartzsite
Wenden
Salome
Hope
Bouse

Mt Charleston 3633
Potosi Mt. 2594
McCullough Mt. 2142
Clark Mt. 2417
Providence Mts.
Mojave National Preserve
Soda Lake
Baker
Barstow
Daggett
Yermo
Newberry Springs
Ludlow
Amboy
Cadiz
Bristol L.
Danby L.
Essex
Chocolate Mts.
Coachella Canal

Death Valley
DEATH VALLEY NATIONAL MONUMENT
Amargosa Range
Telescope Pk. 3366
Shoshone
Tecopa
Pahrump

Ridgecrest
China Lake
Trona
Searles L.
Victorville
Apple Valley
Hesperia
Adelanto
Oro Grande
Helendale
Lucerne Valley
Big Bear City
Big Bear Lake
Yucca Valley
Twentynine Palms
JOSHUA TREE NATIONAL PARK
Joshua Tree

Bakersfield
Tehachapi
Mojave
California City
Rosamond
Lancaster
Palmdale
Edwards
Santa Clarita
San Fernando
San Gabriel Mts.
San Bernardino Mts.
San Bernardino
Redlands
Riverside
Moreno Valley
Hemet
San Jacinto 3505
Banning
Palm Springs
Desert Hot Springs
Palm Desert
Indio
Coachella
Mecca
Salton Sea
Salton City
Westmorland
Brawley
Imperial
El Centro
Calexico
Mexicali

LOS ANGELES
Pasadena
Glendale
Burbank
Santa Monica
Inglewood
Torrance
Long Beach
Redondo Beach
Palos Verdes Estates
Pt. Palos Verdes
Pomona
Ontario
Fontana
Rancho Cucamonga
Claremont
Chino
Corona
Norco
Anaheim
Santa Ana
Orange
Costa Mesa
Huntington Beach
Newport Beach
Irvine
Mission Viejo
San Juan Capistrano
San Clemente
Oceanside
Carlsbad
Encinitas
Escondido
Vista
San Marcos
Fallbrook
Temecula
Ramona
Poway
El Cajon
La Mesa
National City
Chula Vista
SAN DIEGO
Coronado
Imperial Beach
Tijuana
Rosarito

Santa Barbara
Goleta
Ventura
Oxnard
Santa Paula
Fillmore
Ojai
Simi Valley
Moorpark
Thousand Oaks
Camarillo
Port Hueneme
San Luis Obispo
Santa Maria
Lompoc
Vandenberg

PACIFIC OCEAN
Santa Barbara Channel
Channel Islands
CHANNEL ISLANDS NATIONAL PARK
San Miguel I.
Santa Rosa I.
Santa Cruz I.
Anacapa I.
Santa Barbara I.
Santa Catalina I.
San Clemente I.
San Nicolas I.
San Pedro Channel
Avalon
Gulf of Santa Catalina
Is. los Coronados

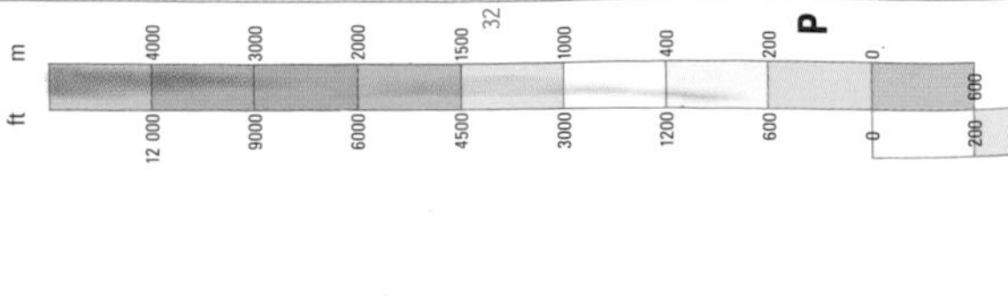

Colorado River
West from Greenwich
Projection Bonne
COPYRIGHT GEORGE PHILIP LTD.

Scale:
10 0 10 20 30 40 50 60 70 80 90 km
10 0 10 20 30 40 50 60 miles

m ft
4000 12 000
3000 9000
2000 6000
1500 4500
1000 3000
600 1200
200 600
0 0

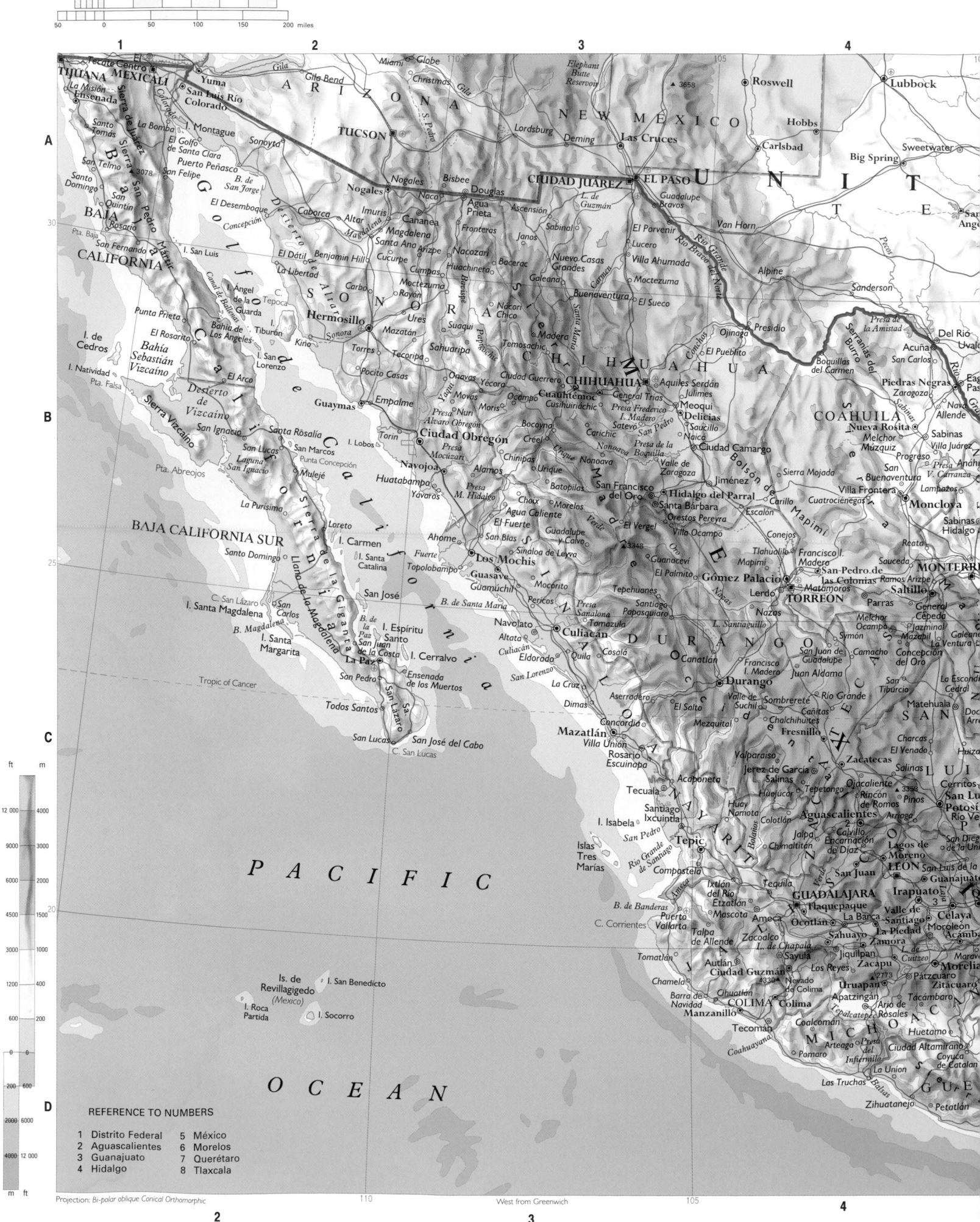

50 0 50 100 150 200 250 300 km
50 0 50 100 150 200 miles

REFERENCE TO NUMBERS

1 Distrito Federal
2 Aguascalientes
3 Guanajuato
4 Hidalgo
5 México
6 Morelos
7 Querétaro
8 Tlaxcala

ft   m
12 000 4000
9000   3000
6000   2000
4500   1500
3000   1000
1200   400
600   200
0   0
200   600
2000   6000
4000   12 000
m   ft

Projection: Bi-polar oblique Conical Orthomorphic

West from Greenwich

PACIFIC

OCEAN

Tropic of Cancer

Is. de Revillagigedo (Mexico)

I. San Benedicto
I. Roca Partida
I. Socorro

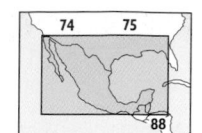

74 75
88

5 6 7 8

Wichita Falls · Denison · Sherman · Paris · Red · Hope · Camden · Greenville · Tuscaloosa · Opelika · Columbus · McRae · Ouachee
ARKANSAS · Texarkana · El Dorado · MISSISSIPPI · Greenwood · Meridian · ALABAMA · Phenix City · Americus · Cordele
FORT WORTH · Ranger · Denton · Greenville · Monroe · Vicksburg · Jackson · Selma · Montgomery · Troy · GEORGIA · Albany · Tifton · Waycross · Valdosta

A

Brownwood · Waco · Corsicana · Palestine · Nacogdoches · LOUISIANA · Natchez · Laurel · Hattiesburg · Dothan · Jim Woodruff Res. · Chattahoochee · Tallahassee · Lake City
Hillsboro · Tyler · Longview · Marshall · Shreveport · Tallulah
Temple · Jewett · Lufkin · Sam Rayburn Reservoir · Alexandria · McComb · Bogalusa · Baton Rouge · Hammond · Biloxi · Gulfport · MOBILE · Pensacola · Panama City · FLORIDA · Apalachee Bay · Suwannee
Huntsville · Bryan · Toledo Bend Res. · Sabine · Lake Charles · Lafayette · NEW ORLEANS · Mobile Bay · C. San Blas
Austin · HOUSTON · Beaumont · Port Arthur · Galveston · Atchafalaya Bay · Terrebonne Bay · Breton Sd. · Mississippi River Delta · Clearwater

B

SAN ANTONIO · Rosenberg · Victoria
Dilley · Alice · Corpus Christi
Laredo · Kingsville
Nuevo Laredo · Harlingen · Brownsville · Zapata

GULF · OF

McAllen · Camargo · Laguna Madre · Matamoros · Valle Hermoso · Santa Teresa
Reynosa · China · Mendez · San Fernando · Laguna Madre
Linares · Villagrán · Hidalgo · Santander Jiménez · MEXICO

C

Ciudad Victoria · La Pesca · Soto la Marina · Tropic of Cancer · La Esperanza · CUBA · Guane
Llera · Calles · Aldama · Pta. Jerez · Canal de Yucatán · C. San Antonio · C. Corrientes · La Fé
Ciudad Mante · I. Desterrada · I. Pérez (Mexico) · C. Catoche · Cancún
Altamira · C. Rojo · Pta. Yalkubul · Río Lagartos · El Cuyo · Puerto Juárez
Ciudad Madero · Tampico · Dzilam de Bravo · Tizimín · Puerto Morelos
Ciudad · Cárdenas de Valles · Pánuco · Ozuluama · L. de Tamiahua · Progreso · Motul · Temax · Espita
MAXCANÚ · Izamal · Valladolid · Cozumel · Isla Cozumel
GOLFO · Mérida · YUCATÁN · Sotuta · Chichén Itzá
Tempoal · Magozal · Tantoyuca · Ticul · Peto
Chicontepec · Tuxpan · Tenabo · Tekax · Bolonchenticul · Vigia Chico · B. de la Ascensión
Zimapán · Zacualtipán · Poza Rica · Papantla · Campeche · Hopelchén · Felipe Carrillo Puerto · B. del Espíritu Santo
Juan del Río · Huauchinango · Nautla · Golfo · Champotón · QUINTANA
Huichapan · Pachuca · Tulancingo · Misantla · de · Chenkán · ROO · Banco Chinchorro
Tulan · Zumpango · Teziutlán · Jalapa Enriquez · Campeche · Ciudad del Carmen · L. de Términos · Bacalar · B. de Chetumal
MÉXICO · Apizaco · Coatepec · Veracruz · Matamoros · Chetumal
Tlaxcala · Citlaltépetl · Alvarado · Tlacotalpan · CAMPECHE · Orange Walk · Ambergris Cay
PUEBLA · Córdoba · Orizaba · San Andrés · Frontera · Concepción · Hondo · BELIZE
Cuernavaca · Tehuacán · Coatzacoalcos · Paraíso · Palizada · Belize City · Turneffe Is.
Iguala · Chilac · Cosamaloapan · TABASCO · Villahermosa · Balancán · Belmopan · BELIZE · Is. de la Bahía
Chilapa · Acatlán · Tres Valles · Minatitlán · Cárdenas · Macuspana · Uaxactún · Benque Viejo · Dangriga · Roatán
Chilpancingo · Huajuapan de León · Asunción · San Juan Bautista · Acayucan · Teapa · Simojovel · L. Petén Itzá · Monkey River · Puerto Castilla · Iriona
Tierra Colorada · Silacayoapan · Nochixtlán · Jesús Carranza · Raudales de · Ocosingo · La Libertad · Flores · Golfo de Honduras · Trujillo
Ayutla · Tlaxiaco · Oaxaca · Tlacolula · Tehuantepec · Chiapa de · San Cristóbal de las Casas · Maya Mts. · San Ignacio · Tela · Balfate · Savá
Acapulco · Ometepec · Ocotlán · Ixtepec · Tuxtla Gutiérrez · La Independencia · San Luis · San Antonio · San Pedro Sula · El Progreso · HONDURAS · Olanchito
OAXACA · Ejutla · San Jerónimo Taviche · Matías Romero · Comitán · Punta Gorda · Puerto Barrios · Zacapa · Santa Bárbara · Yoro · Juticalpa · Catacamas
Pinotepa Nacional · Miahuatlán · Juchitán · Arriaga · Tonalá · Livingston · GUATEMALA · Chiquimula · Santa Rosa de Copán · L. de Yojoa
Tututepec · San Pedro Mixtepec · Pochutla · Salina Cruz · La Concordia · de Izabal · La Paz · Danlí
Puerto Escondido · Puerto Ángel · Golfo de · Pijijiapan · Motozintla · Cuilco · Huehuetenango · Cobán · GUATEMALA · Jalapa · TEGUCIGALPA · Yuscarán
Tehuantepec · Golfo de Mar Muerto · Mapastepec · Huixtla · Tapachula · San Marcos · Totonicapán · Sololá · Antigua · Amatitlán · La Esperanza
Coatepeque · Retalhuleu · Mazatenango · GUATEMALA

D

E

95 90 6 7

COPYRIGHT GEORGE PHILIP LTD.

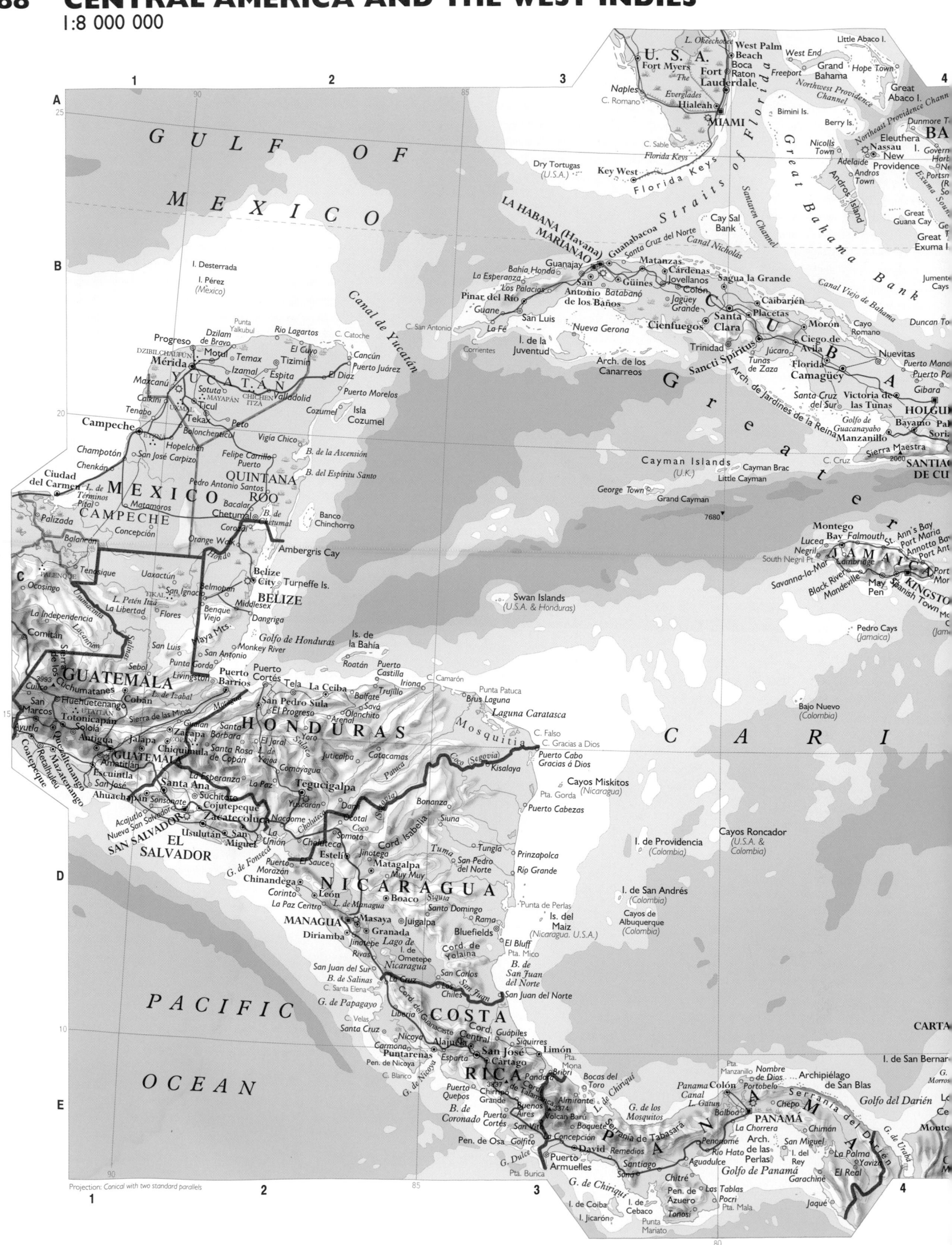

GULF OF MEXICO

PACIFIC OCEAN

U.S.A.

MEXICO

GUATEMALA

BELIZE

HONDURAS

EL SALVADOR

NICARAGUA

COSTA RICA

PANAMÁ

CUBA

JAMAICA

C A R I

Projection: Conical with two standard parallels

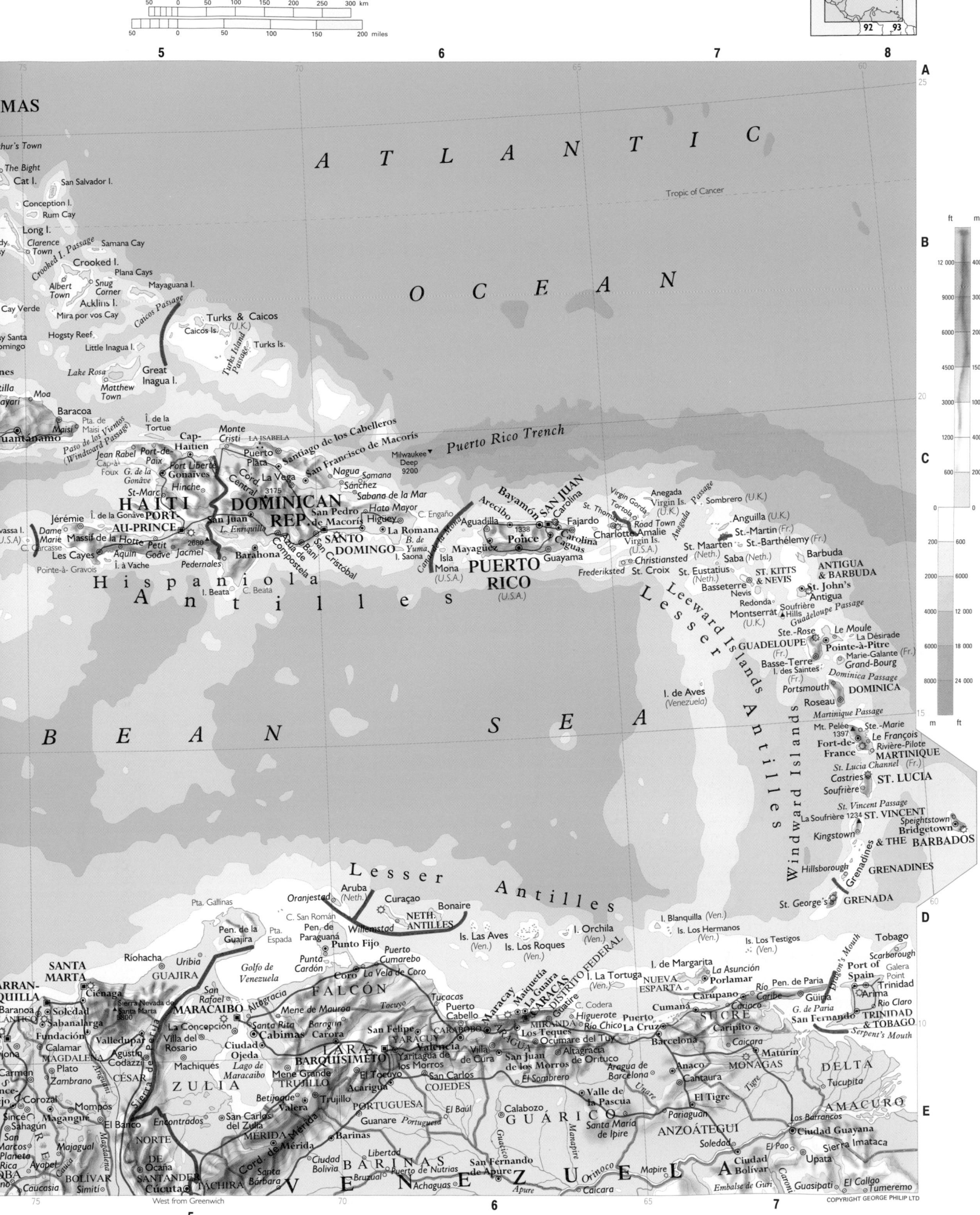

50 0 50 100 150 200 250 300 km

50 0 50 100 150 200 miles

5 **6** **7** **8**

ft m

12 000 4000

9000 3000

6000

4500 1500

3000 1000

1200 400

600 200

0 0

200 600

2000 6000

4000 12 000

6000 18 000

8000 24 000

m ft

BAMAS

Arthur's Town

The Bight
Cat I.

Conception I.
Rum Cay

Long I.

ndy
Cay

Clarence
Town
Samana Cay

Crooked I. Passage
Plana Cays

Albert
Town
Snug
Corner
Mayaguana I.

Acklins I.

Cay Verde
Mira por vos Cay

Hogsty Reef
Little Inagua I.

ay Santa
Domingo

Lake Rosa
Great
Inagua I.

anes

ntilla
Mayari

Moa

Matthew
Town

Caicos Passage

Turks & Caicos
(U.K.)

Caicos Is.
Turks Island
Turks Is.

Baracoa

Pta. de
Maisi

Î. de la
Tortue

Paso de los Vientos
(Windward Passage)

Monte
Cristi
LA ISABELA

Cap-
Haïtien

Jean Rabel Port-de-
Paix

Foux
Cap-à-
G. de la
Gonâve

Santiago de los Cabelleros

Puerto
Plata

San Francisco de Macorís

Milwaukee
Deep
9200

Puerto Rico Trench

Tropic of Cancer

Guantánamo

Maisi

St-Marc

Gonaïves
Hinche

Corail
Central
La Vega

Nagua
Samana

Sánchez

Sabana de la Mar

Bayamón SAN JUAN
Carolina

Virgin Gorda
Tortola

Anegada
Virgin Is.
(U.K.)

Sombrero (U.K.)

Anguilla (U.K.)

Jérémie
Î. de la Gonâve
HAITI
PORT-
AU-PRINCE

San Juan

2689

2890
3175

DOMINICAN
REP.

San Pedro
de Macorís

Hato Mayor

C. Engaño

Aguadilla
Arecibo
1338

Fajardo
Carolina

St. Thomas
Road Town

St.-Martin (Fr.)

avassa I.
(U.S.A.)

Dame
Massif de la Hotte
Petit

Les Cayes
Aquin
Godve

Jacmel

L. Enriquillo
SANTO
DOMINGO

San Cristóbal

La Romana

B. de
Yuma

Ponce
Caguas

Charlotte Amalie
Virgin Is.
(U.S.A.)

St. Maarten
(Neth.)

St.-Barthélemy (Fr.)

Barbuda

C. Carcasse

Pointe-à-Gravois

Î. à Vache

Pedernales

Barahona

Compostela

I. Saona

Isla
Mona
(U.S.A.)

PUERTO
RICO
(U.S.A.)

Guayama

Mayaguez

Christiansted
St. Croix
Frederiksted

St. Eustatius
(Neth.)

Saba (Neth.)

Basseterre

ST. KITTS
& NEVIS

ANTIGUA
& BARBUDA

St. John's
Antigua

H i s p a n i o l a

A n t i l l e s

I. Beata
C. Beata

Nevis
Redonda

Montserrat
(U.K.)

Soufrière
Hills

Guadeloupe Passage

Le Moule
La Désirade

A n t i l l e s

Ste.-Rose
Pointe-à-Pitre

Marie-Galante (Fr.)

Grand-Bourg

Basse-Terre
(Fr.)

GUADELOUPE
(Fr.)

I. des Saintes
(Fr.)

Dominica Passage

Portsmouth

Roseau

DOMINICA

B E A N

Martinique Passage

Mt. Pelée
1397

Ste.-Marie

Le François

A N

S E A

Fort-de-
France

Rivière-Pilote

MARTINIQUE

St. Lucia Channel (Fr.)

Castries
Soufrière

ST. LUCIA

I. de Aves
(Venezuela)

L e e w a r d   I s l a n d s

H i s p a n i o l a   I s l a n d

W i n d w a r d   I s l a n d s

L e s s e r   A n t i l l e s

St. Vincent Passage

La Soufrière 1234 ST. VINCENT

Speightstown

Bridgetown

Kingstown

Grenadines
& THE

BARBADOS

L e s s e r   A n t i l l e s

Aruba
(Neth.)

Oranjestad

Curaçao

Bonaire

NETH.
ANTILLES

Willemstad

Hillsborough

GRENADINES

St. George's GRENADA

I. Blanquilla (Ven.)

I. Orchila
(Ven.)

I. Los Hermanos
(Ven.)

Tobago

Pta. Gallinas

C. San Román

Pen. de
Paraguaná

Is. Las Aves
(Ven.)

Is. Los Roques
(Ven.)

Is. Los Testigos
(Ven.)

Scarborough

Port of
Spain

Galera
Point

Trinidad

Pen. de la
Guajira

Pta.
Espada

Punta
Cardón

Golfo de
Venezuela

Punto Fijo

Puerto
Cumarebo

Coro
La Vela de Coro

I. de Margarita

La Asunción

NUEVA
ESPARTA

Porlamar

I. La Tortuga
(Ven.)

C. Codera

Río
Caribe

Pen. de Paria

Carúpano

Güiria

Arima

Río Claro

ARRAN-
QUILLA

SANTA
MARTA

Ríohacha
Uribia

GUAJIRA

San
Rafael

FALCÓN

Tucacas

Maiquetía
La Guaira

Maracay

DISTRITO
FEDERAL

CARACAS

Cumaná

SUCRE

G. de Paria

San Fernando

TRINIDAD
& TOBAGO

Serpent's Mouth

Baranoa
Soledad
Fundación

Ciénaga

Sierra Nevada de
Santa Marta
5800

Altagracia
Mene de Mauroa

Tocuyo

Puerto
Cabello

Barcelona

Caicara

Maturín

MONAGAS

DELTA

Tucupita

ATLÁNTICO

Calamar

MAGDALENA

Plato
Zambrano

Agustín
Codazzi

Villa del
Rosario

MARACAIBO

Santa Rita

La Concepción

CABIMAS

Baragua
Carora

San Felipe

YARACUY

Valencia

Villa de
Cura

Higuerote
Ocumare del Tuy

Puerto
La Cruz

Anaco

El Tigre

AMACURO

Carmen
ince-
ejo

Mompos

El Banco

Machiques

Ciudad
Ojeda

Lago de
Maracaibo

Mene
Grande

LARA
BARQUISIMETO

CARABOBO

Yaritagua de
los Morros

MIRANDA

ARAGUA

San Juan
de los Morros

Altagracia
de Orituco

Aragua de
Barcelona

Valle de
la Pascua

El Sombrero

Ciudad Guayana

Soledad

Sierra Imataca

Ciudad
Bolívar

El Pao

Upata

Sincé
Majagual

Magangué

Entrecanos

San Carlos
del Zulia

TRUJILLO

ZULIA

COJEDES

Calabozo

Santa María
de Ipire

El Tigre

CÉSAR

Betijoque

PORTUGUESA

El Baúl

GUÁRICO

El Tigre

Los Barrancos

Sahagún

San
Planeta
Rica

Ayapel

NORTE

DE

Ocaña

MÉRIDA

Cord. de Mérida

Acarigua

Valera

Trujillo

Guanare
Portuguesa

Santa María
de Ipire

ANZOÁTEGUI

Ciudad Guayana

BA
Caucasia

Simití

SANTANDER

Cúcuta

TÁCHIRA

VENEZUELA

Ciudad
Bolivia

San Carlos

Barinas

LIBERTAD

BARINAS

San Fernando
de Apure

Guárico

Manapire

Uncare

Pariaguán

Ciudad
Bolívar

El Pao

El Callao

Tumeremo

Mompós
Magangué

El Banco

OBA

QBA

Bolívar

Ocaña

Santa
Bárbara

Bruzual

Achaguas

Puerto de Nutrias

Apure

Calcara

Orinoco

Mapire

Embalse de Guri

Caroní

Guasipati

West from Greenwich

COPYRIGHT GEORGE PHILIP LTD

5 **6** **7**

Tropic of Cancer

A

Yucatán Channel
Cuba
Greater Antilles
Turks & Caicos Is.
Gulf of Campeche
Yucatán Peninsula
Hispaniola
9200
Puerto Rico

NORTH

B

Isthmus of Tehuantepec
G. de Honduras
Jamaica
C. Gracias a Dios
Coco
L. Nicaragua
Caribbean Sea
Lesser Antilles
Guadeloupe
Dominica
Martinique
St. Lucia
St. Vincent
Barbados
Grenada
Tobago
Trinidad

ATLANTIC

OCEAN

Guatemala Trench
Panama Canal
Gulf of Darién
C. de la Aguja
Sierra Nevada de Santa Marta 5800
L. Maracaibo
I. Margarita
Orinoco
Cord. de Mérida

C

Cordillera Occidental
Cordillera Central
Cordillera Oriental
C. de San Francisco
Llanos
Meta
Guaviare
Guiana Highlands
Mt. Roraima 2810
Sierra Pacaraima
Caura
Caroní
Serra Tumucumaque
C. Orange

Gulf of Panamá
Caquetá
Negro
Branco
Equator
Marajó

0

Galapagos Is.
Cotopaxi 5897
Chimborazo 6267
Putumayo
Japurá
Napo
Amazon
Amazon
Tapajós
Tocantins
Marajó I.

D

G. of Guayaquil
Pta. Pariñas
Pta. Negra
Marañón
Ucayali
Juruá
Purus
S e l v a s
Madeira
Roosevelt
Aripuanã
Teles Pires
Arinos
Xingu
Araguaia
Araguaia
Paraíba
Plat. of Borborema
C. de São Roque
São Francisco

Huascarán 6768
Madre de Dios

Plateau of Mato Grosso

E

Chile
Chincha Alta
L. Titicaca
Nevada Ancohuma 6550
Bolivian Plateau
L. de Poopó
Guaporé
Mamoré
Brazilian Highlands
Abrolhos Bank

PACIFIC

Peru Trench
Paraguay
Paraná
Serra da Mantiqueira 2890
Pico da Bandeira

F

Tropic of Capricorn
San Félix
San Ambrosio
Atacama Desert
Cerro Ojos del Salado 6863
Gran Chaco
Pilcomayo
Iguaçu Falls
Uruguay
C. Frio
Serra do Mar

OCEAN

Arch. de Juan Fernández
Salinas Grandes
Salado
Entre Ríos

G

Mt. Aconcagua 6960
Sierra de Córdoba
L. Mar Chiquita
Paraná
Rio de la Plata
L. dos Patos

Chile Rise
Chiloé I.
Chubut
P a m p a s
Colorado
Bahía Blanca
G. San Matías
Valdés Peninsula

SOUTH

ATLANTIC

OCEAN

Argentine Basin

H

Chonos Archipelago
Taitao Peninsula
Gulf of Penas
Mte. San Valentín 4058
Negro
Gulf of San Jorge
6212

Wellington I.
Madre de Dios I.
Magellan's Str.
Patagonia
West Falkland
Falkland Is.
East Falkland

South Georgia

Santa Inés I.
Canal Cockburn
Tierra del Fuego
Staten I.
Canal Beagle
C. Horn

ft m
12000 4000
9000 3000
6000 2000
3000 1000
1500 500
600 200
0 0
200 600
1000 3000
2000 6000
4000 12000
6000 18000
8000 24000
m ft

100 0   200   400   600   800   1000 1200 1400 km

100 0   200   400   600   800   1000 miles

| | 1 | 2 | 3 | 4 | 5 | 6 | 7 |

Tropic of Cancer

A

Havana **CUBA** **BAHAMAS** Turks & Caicos Is. (U.K.)

N O R T H

20

A

HAITI **DOMINICAN REP.** Virgin Is. (U.K.) San Juan

A T L A N T I C

MEXICO JAMAICA Kingston Port-au-Prince PUERTO RICO (U.S.A.) ST. KITTS & NEVIS ANTIGUA & BARBUDA

BELIZE **GUADELOUPE** (Fr.) **DOMINICA** Basse-Terre

GUATEMALA **HONDURAS** *C a r i b b e a n   S e a* Fort-de-France **MARTINIQUE** (Fr.)

B Guatemala Tegucigalpa Castries **ST. LUCIA**

O C E A N

B

San Salvador **ST. VINCENT** **BARBADOS** Bridgetown

EL SALVADOR **NICARAGUA** Aruba Curaçao Kingstown St. George's **GRENADA**

Managua C. de la Aguja **TRINIDAD & TOBAGO**

COSTA San José Barranquilla Port of Spain

RICA Panamá Cartagena Maracaibo Caracas

G. of Darién Bárquisimeto Valencia

Cúcuta Orinoco

10 Medellín San Cristóbal Ciudad Guayana 10

Gulf of Panama Bucaramanga **VENEZUELA** Georgetown

C Cali **Bogotá** Georgetown Paramaribo **C**

COLOMBIA **GUYANA** Cayenne

RORAIMA **SURINAM** C. Orange

FRENCH GUIANA

Magdalena *Esequibo* AMAPÁ

Branco

0 Equator 0

Galapagos Is. (Ecuador) **Quito** Japurá Marajó I. Belém

ECUADOR Napo Putumayo Amazon

Guayaquil Amazon Santarém

G. of Guayaquil Iquitos Manaus São Luís Fortaleza

Marañón **AMAZONAS** **P A R Á** C. de São Roque

D Chiclayo Madeira MARANHÃO Teresina RIO G. DO NORTE Natal **D**

Trujillo Juruá Purus Tocantins PARAÍBA Campina Grande

Chimbote *Ucayali* ACRE Pôrto Velho Tapajós Xingu Araguaia PIAUÍ Recife

PERU RONDÔNIA PERNAMBUCO ALAGOAS Maceió

10 Madre de Dios **B R A Z I L** SERGIPE Aracaju 10

Callao **Lima** Mamoré **MATO GROSSO** B A H Í A Salvador

Cuzco Guaporé São Francisco

L. Titicaca Cuiabá GOIÁS

E Arequipa **BOLIVIA** DIS. FED. Brasília **E**

La Paz Cochabamba Goiânia **MINAS GERAIS**

Iquique Sucre Santa Cruz **MATO GROSSO** Belo ESPÍRITO SANTO

P A C I F I C **DO SUL** Horizonte Vitória

Paraguay Ribeirão Juiz Campos

20 Tropic of Capricorn Paraná Prêto de Fora 20

Antofagasta **PARAGUAY** Pilcomayo SÃO PAULO Campinas R. DE J.

San Félix (Chile) Asunción **PARANÁ** **SÃO** **RIO DE**

F San Ambrosio (Chile) Salta **A** Paraná **PAULO** **JANEIRO** **F**

O C E A N San Miguel de Tucumán **R** Curitiba Niterói

Resistencia Corrientes Uruguay SANTA CATARINA

G Salado **E** RIO GRANDE **G**

DO SUL Pôrto Alegre

Córdoba Santa Fe Pelotas

San Félix San Juan **N** Paraná

Arch. de Juan Fernández (Chile) Viña del Mar Rosario **URUGUAY**

Valparaíso Mendoza **T** Montevideo

30 **SANTIAGO** **BUENOS AIRES** 30

Talca **I** La Plata Río de la Plata

Concepción **N** Bahía Blanca Mar del Plata **SOUTH**

G Colorado **G**

Valdivia **A** Viedma **A T L A N T I C**

Puerto Montt Negro

Chubut **O C E A N**

40 Comodoro Rivadavia 40

Gulf of Penas Gulf of San Jorge

H **H**

FALKLAND IS. (U.K.)

West Falkland Stanley

Magellan's Str. East Falkland

Punta Arenas **Tierra del Fuego**

South Georgia (U.K.)

C. Horn

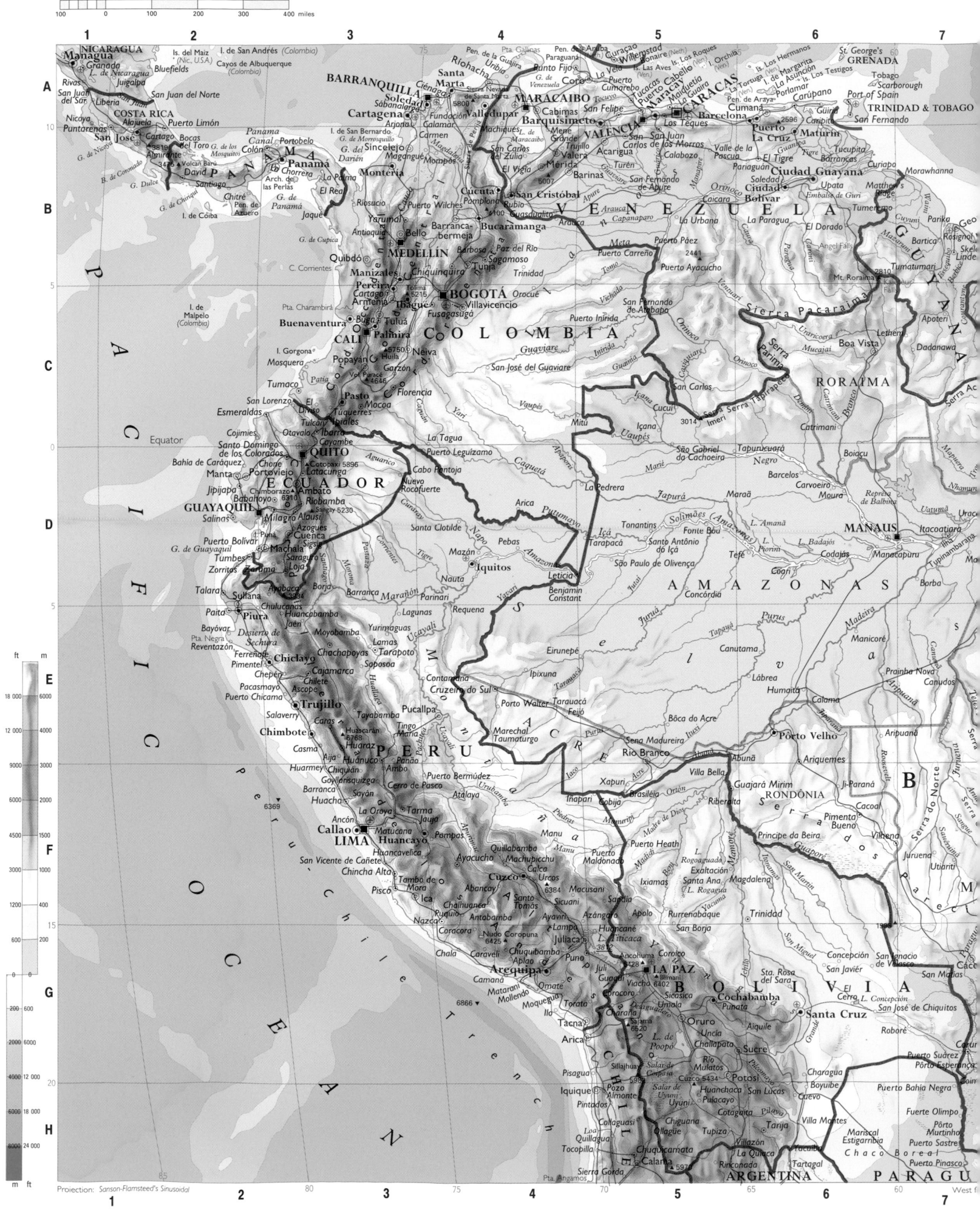

PACIFIC OCEAN
COLOMBIA
VENEZUELA
ECUADOR
PERU
BOLIVIA
AMAZONAS
RORAIMA
RONDÔNIA
GUYANA
PANAMA
COSTA RICA
NICARAGUA
TRINIDAD & TOBAGO
GRENADA
CHILE
ARGENTINA
PARAGU
BOGOTÁ
QUITO
LIMA
LA PAZ
CARACAS
MANAUS
Peru-Chile Trench
Equator
Projection: Sanson-Flamsteed's Sinusoidal

87
88
89
94
95

8 9 10 11 12 13

A B C D E F G H

ATLANTIC OCEAN

Equator

São Paulo (Braz.)
Rocas
Fernando de Noronha (Braz.)
Trindade (Braz.)
6059

Paramaribo
Nieuw Amsterdam
Nieuw Nickerie
Totness
Moengo
Kwakoegron
Albina
St-Laurent
Iracoubo
Sinnamary
Kourou
Cayenne
Kaw
Approuague
C. Orange
St-Georges
Oiapoque
Camopi
FRENCH GUIANA
SURINAM
Brof. Van Blommestein-meer
Serra Tumucumaque
Amapá
I. de Maracá
AMAPÁ
Araguari
Merirumã
Serra do Navio
Macapá
I. Caviana
I. Mexiana
Mazagão
C. Maguarinho
Chaves
Afuá
Soure
Curuçá
Salinópolis
Bragança
I. Grande de Gurupá
I. de Marajó
Vigia
Almeirim
Gurupá
Breves
BELÉM
Castanhal
Viseu
Óbidos
Monte Alegre
Prainha
Pôrto de Móz
Curralinho
Abaetetuba
Turiaçu
Cururupu
Alenquer
Amazonas (Amazon)
Cametá
Juruti
Santarém
Baião
Alcântara
B. de São Marcos
São Luís
Barreirinhas
Tutóia
Luis Correia
Camocim
Belterra
Aveiro
Brasília Legal
Altamira
PARÁ
Tucuruí
Pinheiro
Viana
Rosário
Itapecuru-Mirim
Santa Inês
Parnaíba
Granja
Itapipoca
Caucaia
FORTALEZA
Itaituba
Represa de Tucuruí
Bacabal
Brejo
Coroatá
Codó
Piracuruca
Piripiri
Sobral
Maranguape
Cascavel
Baturité
Russas
Aracati
Açailândia
Pedreiras
Caxias
Campo Maior
Ipu
Quixadá
Areia Branca
Macau
Ceará Mirim
C. de São Roque
Marabá
São João do Araguaia
MARANHÃO
Imperatriz
Teresina
Crateús
CEARÁ
Mossoró
RIO GRANDE DO NORTE
Natal
Carajás
Serra dos Carajás
Grajaú
Barra do Corda
Senador Pompeu
Caraúbas
Caicó
Currais Novos
Canguaretama
Mamanguape
Tocantinópolis
Pôrto Franco
Estreito
Carolina
Colinas
Amarante
Valença do Piauí
Iguatu
Cajàzeiras
Sousa
Patos
Alagoa Grande
Cabedelo
João Pessoa
Floriano
Oeiras
Picos
Crato
PARAÍBA
Campina Grande
Olinda
Araguaína
Riachão
Loreto
Nova Iorque
Uruçuí
PIAUÍ
Ouricuri
Chapada do Araripe
Juazeiro do Norte
Salgueiro
Caruaru
RECIFE
Jaboatão
Conceição do Araguaia
Paulistana
PERNAMBUCO
Pesqueira
Vitória de Santo Antão
Araguacema
Pedro Afonso
Serra do Penitente
Santa Filomena
São João do Piauí
Sa. Dois Irmãos
Petrolina
Garanhuns
Palmares
Caracol
Nôvo Remanso
Nova Cusa
Juazeiro
São Francisco
Paulo Afonso
Palmeira dos Índios
Rio Largo
Maceió
Arapiraca
Serra do Cachimbo
Palmas
Represa de Sobradinho
Senhor-do-Bonfim
Propriá
ALAGOAS
Penedo
SERGIPE
Capela
Parnaguá
Serra da Tabatinga
Chapada das Mangabeiras
Barra
Jacobina
Aracaju
Pôrto Nacional
TOCANTINS
Xique-Xique
Queimadas
São Cristóvão
Estância
Serrinha
BRAZIL
Mundo Novo
Santa Isabel do Morro
Gurupi
Peixe
Taguatinga
Barreiras
Ibotirama
Feira de Santana
Alagoinhas
BAHIA
Itaberaba
Cachoeira
Santo Amaro
SALVADOR
Serra Formosa
Serra do Roncador
Paraná
Campos Belos
São Domingos
Bom Jesus da Lapa
Serra do Sincorá
Castro Alves
Valença
B. de Todos os Santos
Nazaré
MATO GROSSO
Planalto do Mato Grosso
Santa Maria da Vitória
Serra Geral de Goiás
Serra Dourada
Jequié
Contas
Caetité
Carinhanha
Brumado
Ubaitaba
Posse
Niquelândia
Uruaçu
Aruanã
1678
Condeúba
Vitória da Conquista
Itabuna
Ilhéus
Canavieiras
Januária
Monte Azul
São Francisco
Cuiabá
Santo Antonio
Rondonópolis
Barra do Garças
Goiás
DIST. FED.
Formosa
Taguatinga
BRASÍLIA
Luziânia
Anápolis
Goiânia
Janaúba
Pedra Azul
Belmonte
Jequitinhonha
Pôrto Seguro
Montes Claros
Salinas
Serra do Espinhaço
Araçuaí
Itamaraju
GOIÁS
Vianópolis
Pirapora
Morrinhos
Paracatu
Teófilo Otoni
Prado
Caravelas
Nanuque
Alto Araguaia
Jataí
Rio Verde
Ipameri
Patos de Minas
Itumbiara
Catalão
Araguari
Diamantina
Mucuri
Governador Valadares
Conceição da Barra
São Mateus
Quirinópolis
Coxim
MATO GROSSO DO SUL
MINAS GERAIS
Uberlândia
Patrocínio
Curvelo
Ipatinga
Nova Venécia
Linhares
Itapeva
ESPÍRITO SANTO
Ituiutaba
Prata
Araxá
Ibiá
Sete Lagoas
Itabira
Colatina
Paranaíba
Uberaba
Frutal
Campo Grande
Miranda
Aquidauana
Santa Fé do Sul
Água Clara
São José do Rio Prêto
Barretos
BELO HORIZONTE
Sabará
Caratinga
Cariacica
Vitória
Vila Velha
Igarapava
Divinópolis
Nova Lima
Franca
Ponte Nova
2890
Ribas do Rio Pardo
Três Lagoas
Andradina
Araçatuba
Passos
Ribeirão Prêto
Conselheiro Lafaiete
Ouro Prêto
Ubá
Cachoeiro de Itapemirim
Panorama
Presidente Epitácio
Penápolis
Lins
Catanduva
Araraquara
Poços de Caldas
São João del Rei
Barbacena
Juiz de Fora
Itaperuna
Campos
Dourados
Presidente Prudente
Marília
Bauru
SÃO PAULO
Jaú
São Carlos
Moji-Mirim
Guaxupé
Três Rios
Nova Friburgo
Ponta Porã
Pedro Juan Caballero
Assis
Piracicaba
Limeira
Campinas
Volta Redonda
2787
Petrópolis
RIO DE JANEIRO
Niterói
Cabo Frio
Botucatu

55 50 45 40 35 30
10 5 0 5 10 15 20

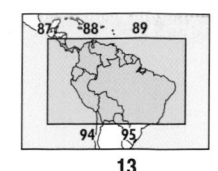

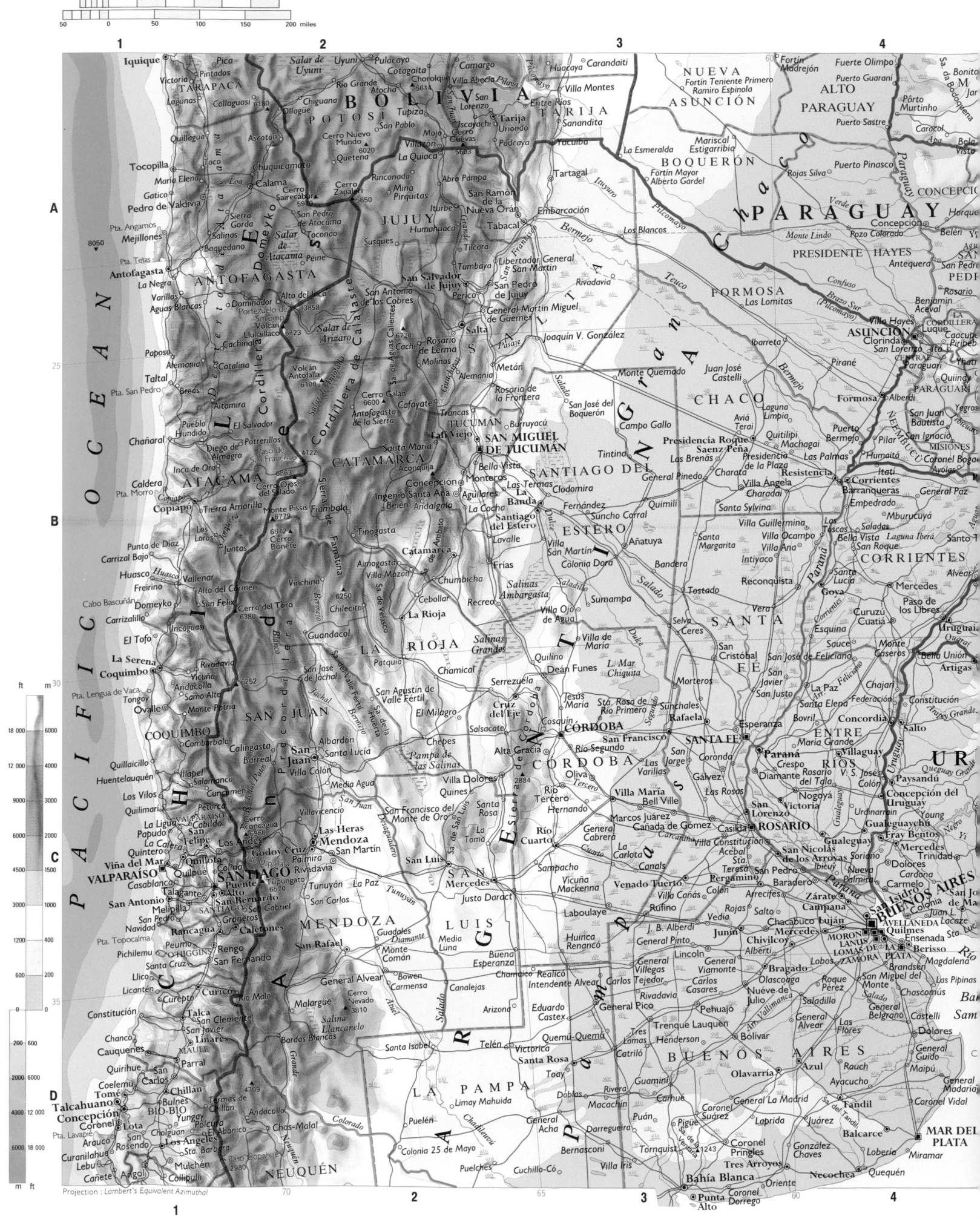

50 0 50 100 150 200 250 300 km
50 0 50 100 150 200 miles
PACIFIC OCEAN
BOLIVIA
PARAGUAY
CHILE
ARGENTINA
Andes
Gran Chaco
Pampa
POTOSÍ
TARIJA
TARAPACÁ
ANTOFAGASTA
ATACAMA
COQUIMBO
VALPARAÍSO
SANTIAGO
O'HIGGINS
MAULE
BÍO-BÍO
JUJUY
SALTA
TUCUMÁN
CATAMARCA
SANTIAGO DEL ESTERO
LA RIOJA
SAN JUAN
MENDOZA
SAN LUIS
CÓRDOBA
SANTA FÉ
CHACO
FORMOSA
CORRIENTES
ENTRE RÍOS
BUENOS AIRES
LA PAMPA
NEUQUÉN
NUEVA ASUNCIÓN
ALTO PARAGUAY
BOQUERÓN
PRESIDENTE HAYES
Iquique
Tocopilla
Antofagasta
Copiapó
La Serena
Coquimbo
Valparaíso
Santiago
Talcahuano
Concepción
San Salvador de Jujuy
Salta
San Miguel de Tucumán
Catamarca
La Rioja
San Juan
Mendoza
San Luis
Córdoba
Santa Fe
Rosario
Paraná
Corrientes
Resistencia
Asunción
Buenos Aires
Mar del Plata
Bahía Blanca
Tarija
Salar de Uyuni
Salar de Atacama
Cordillera de Domeyko
Cordillera de Calalaste
Salinas Grandes
Bermejo
Pilcomayo
Paraná
Uruguay
Salado
Colorado
Projection : Lambert's Equivalent Azimuthal

92 93
96

BELO
HORIZONTE
Nova Lima
Itabirito   Vitória
Congonhas   Ouro   Ponte Nova   Itaquari
Três Lagoas   Olímpia   Passos   Conselheiro   Prêto Pico da   Vila
Andradina   São José   Batatais   São Sebastião   Oliveira   Lafaiete   Bandeira   Velha
Xavantina   Mirassol   do Rio Prêto   Bebedouro   do Paraíso   Campo Belo   São João   Carangola   2880   Castelo   Guarapari
TO GROSSO   Mirandópolis   Araçatuba   Catanduva   Ribeirão   Represa de   del Rei   Ubá Muriaé
Nova Alvorada   Panorama   Taquaritinga   Prêto   Guaxupé   Pontas   Furnas   Lavras   Barbacena Cataguases   Cachoeiro
DO   SUL   do Sul   Adamantina   Penápolis   Jaboticabal   Mocóca   Alfenas   Varginha   Santos   Leopoldina   de Itapemirim
Dourados   Presidente   Lins   Bauru   Casa   Pocos de   Três   Dumont   Itaperuna
Santo   Epitácio   São   Branca   Caldas   Coracões   Juiz de Fora   Rios   Cambuci
Ivinhema   Anastácio   Araraquara   São   São João   Poço   Alegre   Lourenço   Além Paraíba   Guarus
Pôrto São José   Presidente   Garça   Carlos   da Boa Vista   Ouro Fino   Itajubá   2787   Volta   Barra do Pirai   Campos
Ponta Porã   Prudente   Marília   Jaú   Araras   Pinhal   Itajubá   Redonda   Petrópolis   Macaé   Cabo de
Pedro Juan Caballero   Rancharia   Rio Claro   Americana   Serrazul   Barra   RIO DE JANEIRO   São Tomé
Rosana   Assis   Cambará   Piracicaba   CAMPINAS   Bragança   NOVA IGUAÇU   DIQUE DE CAXIAS
Centenário do Sul   Santa Cruz   Mogi   Paulista   São José dos C.   Angra dos   SÃO GONÇALO
Paranavai   do Rio Pardo   CAMPINAS   Jundiai   Reis   NITERÓI
Londrina   Ourinhos   Botucatu   Itu   Taubaté   Ilha Grande   RIO DE JANEIRO
Maringá   Apucarana   Cornélio   Jacarèzinho   Avaré   Tatui   Sorocaba   Moji das Cruzes   Bahia da Ilha Grande   La. de Araruama
Cruzeiro   Procópio   SÃO PAULO   SANTO ANDRÉ   Tropic of Capricorn
Umuarama   Cianorte   Mandaguari   Itapetininga   São Bernardo   Cabo Frio
BRAZIL   Goio-Erê   Campo   Ibaiti   Itararé   do Campo   Santos
Guaíra   Mourão   Tibagi   Itapeva   Juquiá   Guarujá   Ilha de São Sebastião
Pôrto Mendes   Cândido de Abreu   Castro   Apiai   Registro   Itanhaém   Pta. de Boi
Toledo   Ubiratã   Pitanga   PARANÁ   Iguape
Cascavel   Sa. das Araras   Prudentópolis   Ponta   Palmeira   Ilha Comprida
Medianeira   Guarapuava   Grossa   CURITIBA   Ilha do Cardoso
Foz do Iguaçu   Irati   Antonina
Cat. do   Francisco   Laranjeiras   Paranaguá
Ciudad   Iguaçu   Beltrão   do Sul   Lapa   Matinhos
del Este   Bernardo   Pato Branco   Palmas   União da   Guaratuba
de Irigoyen   Vitória   Joinville
Eldorado   Clevelândia   Sa. da Fartura   Pôrto União   Rio Negro   São Francisco do Sul
San   Xanxerê   Caçador   1340   Mafra
PARANA   Pedro   São Miguel   Espigão   do Oeste
TAPUÁ   do Oeste   Canoinhas
Parana   Corpus   Uruguai   Chapecó   Joaçaba   Santa Cecília   Blumenau   Itajaí
MISIONES   Frederico   Curitibanos   Santa   Brusque
Oberá   Westphalen   Campos   Catarina   Rio do Sul
Leandro N. Alem   Enechim   Novos   SÃO JOSÉ
Candelaria   Palmeira   Lajes   Ilha de Santa Catarina
Apóstoles   das Missões   Florianópolis
São Javier   Carazinho   Passo   Lagoa   1808
San   Ijui   Fundo   Vermelha
Santo Angelo   Vacaria   Tubarão   Laguna
São Luis   Cruz Alta   Coxilha Grande   Cabo Santa Marta Grande
São Borja   Gonzaga   Guaporé   Bento Goncalves   Criciúma
Santiago   RIO GRANDE   Caxias do Sul   Araranguá
Santa Maria   Santa Cruz   Nôvo Hamburgo   Torres
Alegrete   do Sul   Montenegro   Taquara
sário do Sul   Canoas   São   Osório
Cachoeira do Sul   Rio Pardo   Leopoldo   ATLANTIC
DO SUL   Viamão   PÔRTO ALEGRE
Santana do   São   Caçapava   Sa. Encantadas
Livramento   Gabriel   do Sul   Tapes
Rivera   Dom Pedrito   Camaquã   OCEAN
Bagé   Sa. do Canguçu   Mostardas
Pinheiro   São Lourenço
Tacuarembó   Machado   Pelotas   do Sul
UAY   Fraile   Melo   Canguçu   Lagoa dos Patos
Muerto   São José do Norte
San Gregorio   Rio Branco   Jaguarão   Rio Grande
Blanquillo   Cerro   Mirim
Chato   Vergara   Lagoa Mangueira
Sarandí del Yi   Treinta   Tres
José Botile   Lascano   Santa Vitória do Palmar
y Ordóñez   Chuy
Aigua   Castillos
Tala   Minas   Rocha
elones   Piedras   San Carlos   5304
Pando   Maldonado
MONTEVIDEO
Plata
bón
Antonio

5   West from Greenwich   50   6   45   7   40   COPYRIGHT GEORGE PHILIP LTD

A
25
B
30
C
35
D

94 95

km
miles

PARAGUAY

BRASIL

SÃO PAULO

RIO DE JANEIRO
NOVA IGUAÇU

CURITIBA

SANTA CATARINA

RIO GRANDE DO SUL

PORTO ALEGRE

URUGUAY

MONTEVIDEO

BUENOS AIRES

La Plata
Avellaneda

CÓRDOBA

ROSARIO

Santa Fe
Paraná

SANTIAGO

Valparaíso
Viña del Mar

Mendoza

San Juan

San Miguel de Tucumán

Salta

Antofagasta

Bahía Blanca

Mar del Plata

Neuquén

A R G E N T I N A

C H I L E

P A T A G O N I A

Puerto Montt

Comodoro Rivadavia

Río Gallegos

Punta Arenas

Tierra del Fuego

Ushuaia

C. de Hornos (C. Horn)

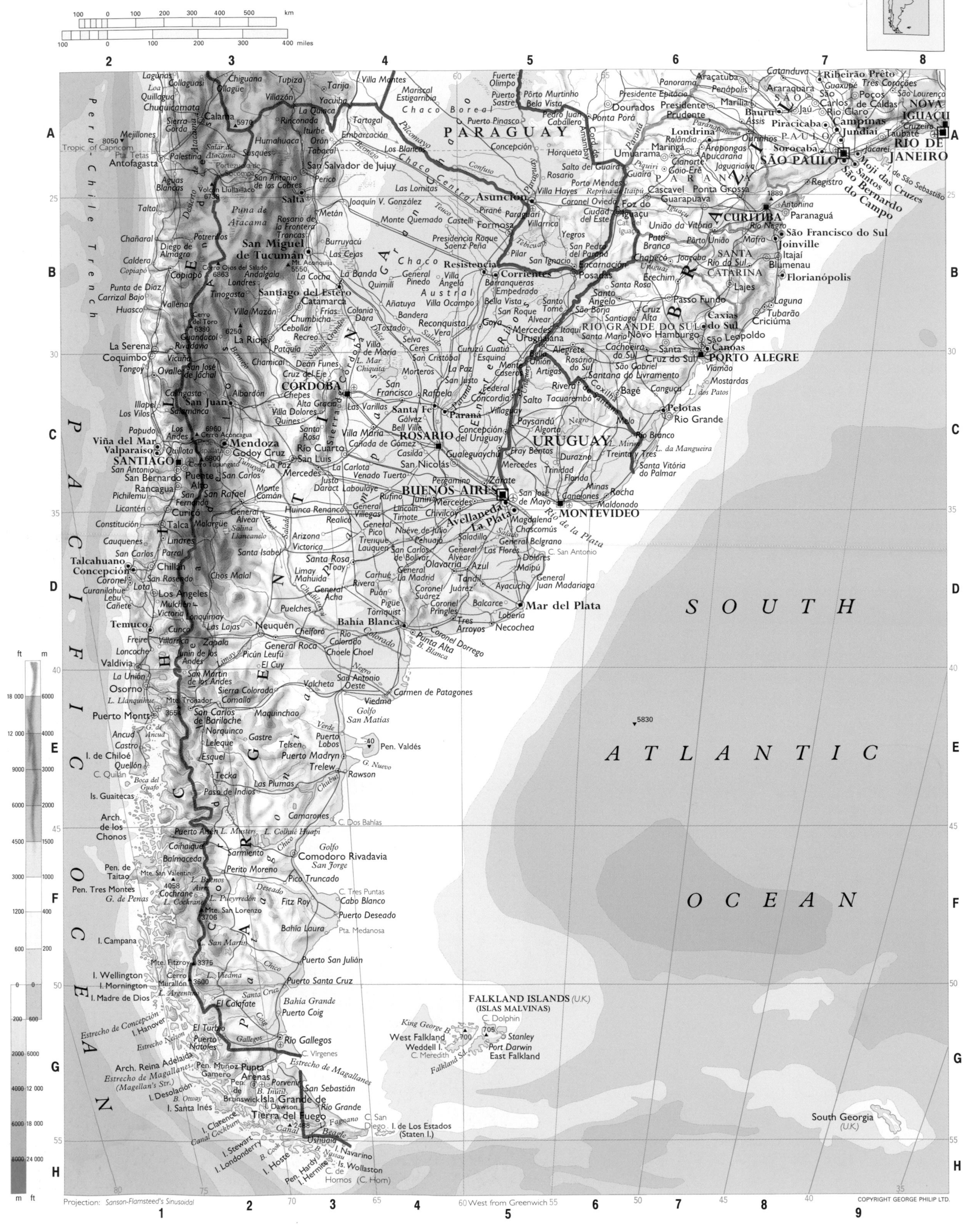

P A C I F I C   O C E A N

S O U T H   A T L A N T I C   O C E A N

FALKLAND ISLANDS (U.K.)
(ISLAS MALVINAS)
West Falkland   East Falkland
Stanley
Port Darwin

South Georgia (U.K.)

Estrecho de Magallanes (Magellan's Str.)

Tropic of Capricorn

Peru-Chile Trench

INDEX

The index contains the names of all the principal places and features shown on the World Maps. Each name is followed by an additional entry in italics giving the country or region within which it is located. The alphabetical order of names composed of two or more words is governed primarily by the first word and then by the second. This is an example of the rule:

Mīr Kūh, *Iran* . . . . **45 E8**   26 22N   58 55 E
Mīr Shahdād, *Iran* . . . . **45 E8**   26 15N   58 29 E
Mira, *Italy* . . . . **20 B5**   45 26N   12 8 E
Mira por vos Cay, *Bahamas* . **89 B5**   22 9N   74 30 W
Miraj, *India* . . . . **40 L9**   16 50N   74 45 E

Physical features composed of a proper name (Erie) and a description (Lake) are positioned alphabetically by the proper name. The description is positioned after the proper name and is usually abbreviated:

Erie, L., *N. Amer.* . . . . **78 D4**   42 15N   81 0 W

Where a description forms part of a settlement or administrative name however, it is always written in full and put in its true alphabetic position:

Mount Morris, *U.S.A.* . . . . . **78 D7**   42 44N   77 52 W

Names beginning with M' and Mc are indexed as if they were spelled Mac. Names beginning St. are alphabetised under Saint, but Sankt, Sint, Sant', Santa and San are all spelt in full and are alphabetised accordingly. If the same place name occurs two or more times in the index and all are in the same country, each is followed by the name of the administrative subdivision in which it is located. The names are placed in the alphabetical order of the subdivisions. For example:

Jackson, *Ky., U.S.A.* . . . . **76 G4**   37 33N   83 23 W
Jackson, *Mich., U.S.A.* . . . . . **76 D3**   42 15N   84 24 W
Jackson, *Minn., U.S.A.* . . . . . **80 D7**   43 37N   95 1 W

The number in bold type which follows each name in the index refers to the number of the map page where that feature or place will be found. This is usually the largest scale at which the place or feature appears.

The letter and figure which are in bold type immediately after the page number give the grid square on the map page, within which the feature is situated. The letter represents the latitude and the figure the longitude.

In some cases the feature itself may fall within the specified square, while the name is outside. This is usually the case only with features which are larger than a grid square.

For a more precise location the geographical coordinates which follow the letter/figure references give the latitude and the longitude of each place. The first set of figures represent the latitude which is the distance north or south of the Equator measured as an angle at the centre of the earth. The Equator is latitude 0°, the North Pole is 90°N, and the South Pole 90°S.

The second set of figures represent the longitude, which is the distance East or West of the prime meridian, which runs through Greenwich, England. Longitude is also measured as an angle at the centre of the earth and is given East or West of the prime meridian, from 0° to 180° in either direction.

The unit of measurement for latitude and longitude is the degree, which is subdivided into 60 minutes. Each index entry states the position of a place in degrees and minutes, a space being left between the degrees and the minutes.

The latitude is followed by N(orth) or S(outh) and the longitude by E(ast) or W(est).

Rivers are indexed to their mouths or confluences, and carry the symbol ➔ after their names. A solid square ■ follows the name of a country, while an open square □ refers to a first order administrative area.

Abbreviations used in the index

A.C.T. – Australian Capital Territory
Afghan. – Afghanistan
Ala. – Alabama
Alta. – Alberta
Amer. – America(n)
Arch. – Archipelago
Ariz. – Arizona
Ark. – Arkansas
Atl. Oc. – Atlantic Ocean
B. – Baie, Bahía, Bay, Bucht, Bugt
B.C. – British Columbia
Bangla. – Bangladesh
Barr. – Barrage
Bos.-H. – Bosnia-Herzegovina
C. – Cabo, Cap, Cape, Coast
C.A.R. – Central African Republic
C. Prov. – Cape Province
Calif. – California
Cent. – Central
Chan. – Channel
Colo. – Colorado
Conn. – Connecticut
Cord. – Cordillera
Cr. – Creek
Czech. – Czech Republic
D.C. – District of Columbia
Del. – Delaware
Dep. – Dependency
Des. – Desert
Dist. – District
Dj. – Djebel
Domin. – Dominica
Dom. Rep. – Dominican Republic
E. – East

E. Salv. – El Salvador
Eq. Guin. – Equatorial Guinea
Fla. – Florida
Falk. Is. – Falkland Is.
G. – Golfe, Golfo, Gulf, Guba, Gebel
Ga. – Georgia
Gt. – Great, Greater
Guinea-Biss. – Guinea-Bissau
H.K. – Hong Kong
H.P. – Himachal Pradesh
Hants. – Hampshire
Harb. – Harbor, Harbour
Hd. – Head
Hts. – Heights
I.(s). – Île, Ilha, Insel, Isla, Island, Isle
Ill. – Illinois
Ind. – Indiana
Ind. Oc. – Indian Ocean
Ivory C. – Ivory Coast
J. – Jabal, Jebel, Jazira
Junc. – Junction
K. – Kap, Kapp
Kans. – Kansas
Kep. – Kepulauan
Ky. – Kentucky
L. – Lac, Lacul, Lago, Lagoa, Lake, Limni, Loch, Lough
La. – Louisiana
Liech. – Liechtenstein
Lux. – Luxembourg
Mad. P. – Madhya Pradesh
Madag. – Madagascar
Man. – Manitoba
Mass. – Massachusetts

Md. – Maryland
Me. – Maine
Medit. S. – Mediterranean Sea
Mich. – Michigan
Minn. – Minnesota
Miss. – Mississippi
Mo. – Missouri
Mont. – Montana
Mozam. – Mozambique
Mt.(e) – Mont, Monte, Monti, Montaña, Mountain
N. – Nord, Norte, North, Northern, Nouveau
N.B. – New Brunswick
N.C. – North Carolina
N. Cal. – New Caledonia
N. Dak. – North Dakota
N.H. – New Hampshire
N.I. – North Island
N.J. – New Jersey
N. Mex. – New Mexico
N.S. – Nova Scotia
N.S.W. – New South Wales
N.W.T. – North West Territory
N.Y. – New York
N.Z. – New Zealand
Nebr. – Nebraska
Neths. – Netherlands
Nev. – Nevada
Nfld. – Newfoundland
Nic. – Nicaragua
O. – Oued, Ouadi
Occ. – Occidentale
Okla. – Oklahoma
Ont. – Ontario
Or. – Orientale

Oreg. – Oregon
Os. – Ostrov
Oz. – Ozero
P. – Pass, Passo, Pasul, Pulau
P.E.I. – Prince Edward Island
Pa. – Pennsylvania
Pac. Oc. – Pacific Ocean
Papua N.G. – Papua New Guinea
Pass. – Passage
Pen. – Peninsula, Péninsule
Phil. – Philippines
Pk. – Park, Peak
Plat. – Plateau
Prov. – Province, Provincial
Pt. – Point
Pta. – Ponta, Punta
Pte. – Pointe
Qué. – Québec
Queens. – Queensland
R. – Rio, River
R.I. – Rhode Island
Ra.(s). – Range(s)
Raj. – Rajasthan
Reg. – Region
Rep. – Republic
Res. – Reserve, Reservoir
S. – San, South, Sea
Si. Arabia – Saudi Arabia
S.C. – South Carolina
S. Dak. – South Dakota
S.I. – South Island
S. Leone – Sierra Leone
Sa. – Serra, Sierra
Sask. – Saskatchewan
Scot. – Scotland
Sd. – Sound

Sev. – Severnaya
Sib. – Siberia
Sprs. – Springs
St. – Saint
Sta. – Santa, Station
Ste. – Sainte
Sto. – Santo
Str. – Strait, Stretto
Switz. – Switzerland
Tas. – Tasmania
Tenn. – Tennessee
Tex. – Texas
Tg. – Tanjung
Trin. & Tob. – Trinidad & Tobago
U.A.E. – United Arab Emirates
U.K. – United Kingdom
U.S.A. – United States of America
Ut. P. – Uttar Pradesh
Va. – Virginia
Vdkhr. – Vodokhranilishche
Vf. – Vîrful
Vic. – Victoria
Vol. – Volcano
Vt. – Vermont
W. – Wadi, West
W. Va. – West Virginia
Wash. – Washington
Wis. – Wisconsin
Wlkp. – Wielkopolski
Wyo. – Wyoming
Yorks. – Yorkshire
Yug. – Yugoslavia

A Coruña

A

A Coruña, *Spain* **19 A1** 43 20N 8 25W
A Estrada, *Spain* **19 A1** 42 43N 8 27W
A Fonsagrada, *Spain* **19 A2** 43 8N 7 4W
Aachen, *Germany* **16 C4** 50 45N 6 6 E
Aalborg = Ålborg, *Denmark* **9 H13** 57 2N 9 54 E
Aalen, *Germany* **16 D6** 48 51N 10 6 E
Aalst, *Belgium* **15 D4** 50 56N 4 2 E
Aalten, *Neths.* **15 C6** 51 56N 6 35 E
Aalter, *Belgium* **15 C3** 51 5N 3 28 E
Äänekoski, *Finland* **9 E21** 62 36N 25 44 E
Aarau, *Switz.* **18 C8** 47 23N 8 4 E
Aare →, *Switz.* **18 C8** 47 33N 8 14 E
Aarhus = Århus, *Denmark* **9 H14** 56 8N 10 11 E
Aarschot, *Belgium* **15 D4** 50 59N 4 49 E
Aba, *Dem. Rep. of the Congo* **54 B3** 3 58N 30 17 E
Aba, *Nigeria* **50 G7** 5 10N 7 19 E
Ābādān, *Iran* **45 D6** 30 22N 48 20 E
Ābādeh, *Iran* **45 D7** 31 8N 52 40 E
Abadla, *Algeria* **50 B5** 31 2N 2 45W
Abaetetuba, *Brazil* **93 D9** 1 40S 48 50W
Abagnar Qi, *China* **34 C9** 43 52N 116 2 E
Abai, *Paraguay* **95 B4** 25 58S 55 54W
Abakan, *Russia* **27 D10** 53 40N 91 10 E
Abancay, *Peru* **92 F4** 13 35S 72 55W
Abariringa, *Kiribati* **64 H10** 2 50S 171 40W
Abarqū, *Iran* **45 D7** 31 10N 53 20 E
Abashiri, *Japan* **30 B12** 44 0N 144 15 E
Abashiri-Wan, *Japan* **30 C12** 44 0N 144 30 E
Ābay = Nîl el Azraq →, *Sudan* **51 E12** 15 38N 32 31 E
Abay, *Kazakstan* **26 E8** 49 38N 72 53 E
Abaya, L., *Ethiopia* **46 F2** 6 30N 37 50 E
Abaza, *Russia* **26 D9** 52 39N 90 6 E
'Abbāsābād, *Iran* **45 C8** 33 34N 58 23 E
Abbay = Nîl el Azraq →, *Sudan* **51 E12** 15 38N 32 31 E
Abbaye, Pt., *U.S.A.* **76 B1** 46 58N 88 8W
Abbé, L., *Ethiopia* **46 E3** 11 8N 41 47 E
Abbeville, *France* **18 A4** 50 6N 1 49 E
Abbeville, *Ala., U.S.A.* **77 K3** 31 34N 85 15W
Abbeville, *La., U.S.A.* **81 L8** 29 58N 92 8W
Abbeville, *S.C., U.S.A.* **77 H4** 34 11N 82 23W
Abbot Ice Shelf, *Antarctica* **5 D16** 73 0S 92 0W
Abbottabad, *Pakistan* **42 B5** 34 10N 73 15 E
Abd al Kūrī, *Ind. Oc.* **46 E5** 12 5N 52 20 E
Ābdar, *Iran* **45 D7** 30 16N 55 19 E
'Abdolābād, *Iran* **45 C8** 34 12N 56 30 E
Abdulpur, *Bangla.* **43 G13** 24 15N 88 59 E
Abéché, *Chad* **51 F10** 13 50N 20 35 E
Abengourou, *Ivory C.* **50 G5** 6 42N 3 27W
Åbenrå, *Denmark* **9 J13** 55 3N 9 25 E
Abeokuta, *Nigeria* **50 G6** 7 3N 3 19 E
Aber, *Uganda* **54 B3** 2 12N 32 25 E
Aberaeron, *U.K.* **11 E3** 52 15N 4 15W
Aberayron = Aberaeron, *U.K.* **11 E3** 52 15N 4 15W
Aberchirder, *U.K.* **12 D6** 57 34N 2 37W
Abercorn = Mbala, *Zambia* **55 D3** 8 46S 31 24 E
Abercorn, *Australia* **63 D5** 25 12S 151 5 E
Aberdare, *U.K.* **11 F4** 51 43N 3 27W
Aberdare Ra., *Kenya* **54 C4** 0 15S 36 50 E
Aberdeen, *Canada* **73 C7** 52 20N 106 8W
Aberdeen, *S. Africa* **56 E3** 32 28S 24 2 E
Aberdeen, *U.K.* **12 D6** 57 9N 2 5W
Aberdeen, *Ala., U.S.A.* **77 J1** 33 49N 88 33W
Aberdeen, *Idaho, U.S.A.* **82 E7** 42 57N 112 50W
Aberdeen, *Md., U.S.A.* **76 F7** 39 31N 76 10W
Aberdeen, *S. Dak., U.S.A.* **80 C5** 45 28N 98 29W
Aberdeen, *Wash., U.S.A.* **84 D3** 46 59N 123 50W
Aberdeen, City of □, *U.K.* **12 D6** 57 10N 2 10W
Aberdeenshire □, *U.K.* **12 D6** 57 17N 2 36W
Aberdovey = Aberdyfi, *U.K.* **11 E3** 52 33N 4 3W
Aberdyfi, *U.K.* **11 E3** 52 33N 4 3W
Aberfeldy, *U.K.* **12 E5** 56 37N 3 51W
Abergavenny, *U.K.* **11 F4** 51 49N 3 1W
Abergele, *U.K.* **10 D4** 53 17N 3 35W
Abernathy, *U.S.A.* **81 J4** 33 50N 101 51W
Abert, L., *U.S.A.* **82 E3** 42 38N 120 14W
Aberystwyth, *U.K.* **11 E3** 52 25N 4 5W
Abhā, *Si. Arabia* **46 D3** 18 0N 42 34 E
Abhar, *Iran* **45 B6** 36 9N 49 13 E
Abhayapuri, *India* **43 F14** 26 24N 90 38 E
Abidjan, *Ivory C.* **50 G5** 5 26N 3 58W
Abilene, *Kans., U.S.A.* **80 F6** 38 55N 97 13W
Abilene, *Tex., U.S.A.* **81 J5** 32 28N 99 43W
Abingdon, *U.K.* **11 F6** 51 40N 1 17W
Abingdon, *U.S.A.* **77 G5** 36 43N 81 59W
Abington Reef, *Australia* **62 B4** 18 0S 149 35 E
Abitau →, *Canada* **73 B7** 59 53N 109 3W
Abitibi →, *Canada* **70 B3** 51 3N 80 55W
Abitibi, L., *Canada* **70 C4** 48 40N 79 40W
Abkhaz Republic = Abkhazia □, *Georgia* **25 F7** 43 12N 41 5 E
Abkhazia □, *Georgia* **25 F7** 43 12N 41 5 E
Abminga, *Australia* **63 D1** 26 8S 134 51 E
Åbo = Turku, *Finland* **9 F20** 60 30N 22 19 E
Abohar, *India* **42 D6** 30 10N 74 10 E
Abomey, *Benin* **50 G6** 7 10N 2 5 E
Abong-Mbang, *Cameroon* **52 D2** 4 0N 13 8 E
Abou-Deïa, *Chad* **51 F9** 11 20N 19 20 E
Aboyne, *U.K.* **12 D6** 57 4N 2 47W
Abra Pampa, *Argentina* **94 A2** 22 43S 65 42W
Abraham L., *Canada* **72 C5** 52 15N 116 35W
Abreojos, Pta., *Mexico* **86 B2** 26 50N 113 40W
Abrud, *Romania* **17 E12** 46 19N 23 5 E
Absaroka Range, *U.S.A.* **82 D9** 44 45N 109 50W
Abu, *India* **42 G5** 24 41N 72 50 E
Abū al Abyad, *U.A.E.* **45 E7** 24 11N 53 50 E
Abū al Khaşīb, *Iraq* **45 D6** 30 25N 48 0 E
Abū 'Alī, *Si. Arabia* **45 E6** 27 20N 49 27 E
Abū 'Alī →, *Lebanon* **47 A4** 34 25N 35 50 E
Abu Dhabi = Abū Z̧āby, *U.A.E.* **46 C5** 24 28N 54 22 E
Abū Du'ān, *Syria* **44 B3** 36 25N 38 15 E
Abu el Gairi, W. →, *Egypt* **47 F2** 29 35N 33 30 E
Abu Ga'da, W. →, *Egypt* **47 F1** 29 15N 32 53 E
Abū Ḩadrīyah, *Si. Arabia* **45 E6** 27 20N 48 58 E
Abu Hamed, *Sudan* **51 E12** 19 32N 33 13 E
Abū Kamāl, *Syria* **44 C4** 34 30N 41 0 E
Abū Madd, Ra's, *Si. Arabia* **44 E3** 24 50N 37 7 E
Abū Mūsā, *U.A.E.* **45 E7** 25 52N 55 3 E
Abū Qaşr, *Si. Arabia* **44 D3** 30 21N 38 34 E
Abu Şafāt, W. →, *Jordan* **47 E5** 30 24N 36 7 E
Abu Simbel, *Egypt* **51 D12** 22 18N 31 40 E
Abū Şukhayr, *Iraq* **44 D5** 31 54N 44 30 E
Abu Zabad, *Sudan* **51 F11** 12 25N 29 10 E
Abū Z̧āby, *U.A.E.* **46 C5** 24 28N 54 22 E
Abū Zeydābād, *Iran* **45 C6** 33 54N 51 45 E
Abuja, *Nigeria* **50 G7** 9 16N 7 2 E
Abukuma-Gawa →, *Japan* **30 E10** 38 6N 140 52 E
Abukuma-Sammyaku, *Japan* **30 F10** 37 30N 140 45 E
Abunã, *Brazil* **92 E5** 9 40S 65 20W
Abunã →, *Brazil* **92 E5** 9 41S 65 20W
Aburo, *Dem. Rep. of the Congo* **54 B3** 2 4N 30 53 E
Abut Hd., *N.Z.* **59 K3** 43 7S 170 15 E
Acadia National Park, *U.S.A.* **77 C11** 44 20N 68 13W
Açailândia, *Brazil* **93 D9** 4 57S 47 0W
Acajutla, *El Salv.* **88 D2** 13 36N 89 50W
Acámbaro, *Mexico* **86 D4** 20 0N 100 40W
Acaponeta, *Mexico* **86 C3** 22 30N 105 20W
Acapulco, *Mexico* **87 D5** 16 51N 99 56W
Acarai, Serra, *Brazil* **92 C7** 1 50N 57 50W
Acarigua, *Venezuela* **92 B5** 9 33N 69 12W
Acatlán, *Mexico* **87 D5** 18 10N 98 3W
Acayucan, *Mexico* **87 D6** 17 59N 94 58W
Accomac, *U.S.A.* **76 G8** 37 43N 75 40W
Accra, *Ghana* **50 G5** 5 35N 0 6W
Accrington, *U.K.* **10 D5** 53 45N 2 22W
Acebal, *Argentina* **94 C3** 33 20S 60 50W
Aceh □, *Indonesia* **36 D1** 4 15N 97 30 E
Achalpur, *India* **40 J10** 21 22N 77 32 E
Acheng, *China* **35 B14** 45 30N 126 58 E
Acher, *India* **42 H5** 23 10N 72 32 E
Achill Hd., *Ireland* **13 C1** 53 58N 10 15W
Achill I., *Ireland* **13 C1** 53 58N 10 1W
Achinsk, *Russia* **27 D10** 56 20N 90 20 E
Acireale, *Italy* **20 F6** 37 37N 15 10 E
Ackerman, *U.S.A.* **81 J10** 33 19N 89 11W
Acklins I., *Bahamas* **89 B5** 22 30N 74 0W
Acme, *Canada* **72 C6** 51 33N 113 30W
Acme, *U.S.A.* **78 F5** 40 8N 79 26W
Aconcagua, Cerro, *Argentina* **94 C2** 32 39S 70 0W
Aconquija, Mt., *Argentina* **94 B2** 27 0S 66 0W
Açores, Is. dos = Azores, *Atl. Oc.* **50 A1** 38 44N 29 0W
Acornhoek, *S. Africa* **57 C5** 24 37S 31 2 E
Acraman, L., *Australia* **63 E2** 32 2S 135 23 E
Acre = 'Akko, *Israel* **47 C4** 32 55N 35 4 E
Acre □, *Brazil* **92 E4** 9 1S 71 0W
Acre →, *Brazil* **92 E5** 8 45S 67 22W
Acton, *Canada* **78 C4** 43 38N 80 3W
Acuña, *Mexico* **86 B4** 29 18N 100 55W
Ad Dammām, *Si. Arabia* **45 E6** 26 20N 50 5 E
Ad Dāmūr, *Lebanon* **47 B4** 33 44N 35 27 E
Ad Dawādimī, *Si. Arabia* **44 E5** 24 35N 44 15 E
Ad Dawḩah, *Qatar* **46 B5** 25 15N 51 35 E
Ad Dawr, *Iraq* **44 C4** 34 27N 43 47 E
Ad Dir'īyah, *Si. Arabia* **44 E5** 24 44N 46 35 E
Ad Dīwānīyah, *Iraq* **44 D5** 32 0N 45 0 E
Ad Dujayl, *Iraq* **44 C5** 33 51N 44 14 E
Ad Duwayd, *Si. Arabia* **44 D4** 30 15N 42 17 E
Ada, *Minn., U.S.A.* **80 B6** 47 18N 96 31W
Ada, *Okla., U.S.A.* **81 H6** 34 46N 96 41W
Adabiya, *Egypt* **47 F1** 29 53N 32 28 E
Adair, C., *Canada* **69 A12** 71 31N 71 24W
Adaja →, *Spain* **19 B3** 41 32N 4 52W
Adak I., *U.S.A.* **68 C2** 51 45N 176 45W
Adamaoua, Massif de l', *Cameroon* **51 G7** 7 20N 12 20 E
Adamawa Highlands = Adamaoua, Massif de l', *Cameroon* **51 G7** 7 20N 12 20 E
Adamello, Mte., *Italy* **18 C9** 46 9N 10 30 E
Adams, *Mass., U.S.A.* **79 D11** 42 38N 73 7W
Adams, *N.Y., U.S.A.* **79 C8** 43 49N 76 1W
Adams, *Wis., U.S.A.* **80 D10** 43 57N 89 49W
Adam's Bridge, *Sri Lanka* **40 Q11** 9 15N 79 40 E
Adams L., *Canada* **72 C5** 51 10N 119 40W
Adams Mt., *U.S.A.* **84 D5** 46 12N 121 30W
Adam's Peak, *Sri Lanka* **40 R12** 6 48N 80 30 E
Adana, *Turkey* **25 G6** 37 0N 35 16 E
Adapazarı = Sakarya, *Turkey* **25 F5** 40 48N 30 25 E
Adarama, *Sudan* **51 E12** 17 10N 34 52 E
Adare, C., *Antarctica* **5 D11** 71 0S 171 0 E
Adaut, *Indonesia* **37 F8** 8 8S 131 7 E
Adavale, *Australia* **63 D3** 25 52S 144 32 E
Adda →, *Italy* **18 D8** 45 8N 9 53 E
Addis Ababa = Addis Abeba, *Ethiopia* **46 F2** 9 2N 38 42 E
Addis Abeba, *Ethiopia* **46 F2** 9 2N 38 42 E
Addison, *U.S.A.* **78 D7** 42 1N 77 14W
Addo, *S. Africa* **56 E4** 33 32S 25 45 E
Ādeh, *Iran* **44 B5** 37 42N 45 11 E
Adel, *U.S.A.* **77 K4** 31 8N 83 25W
Adelaide, *Bahamas* **88 A4** 25 4N 77 31W
Adelaide, *S. Africa* **56 E4** 32 42S 26 20 E
Adelaide I., *Antarctica* **5 C17** 67 15S 68 30W
Adelaide Pen., *Canada* **68 B10** 68 15N 97 30W
Adelaide River, *Australia* **60 B5** 13 15S 131 7 E
Adelanto, *U.S.A.* **85 L9** 34 35N 117 22W
Adele I., *Australia* **60 C3** 15 32S 123 9 E
Adélie, Terre, *Antarctica* **5 C10** 68 0S 140 0 E
Adélie Land = Adélie, Terre, *Antarctica* **5 C10** 68 0S 140 0 E
Aden = Al 'Adan, *Yemen* **46 E4** 12 45N 45 0 E
Aden, G. of, *Asia* **46 E4** 12 30N 47 30 E
Adendorp, *S. Africa* **56 E3** 32 15S 24 30 E
Adh Dhayd, *U.A.E.* **45 E7** 25 17N 55 53 E
Adhoi, *India* **42 H4** 23 26N 70 32 E
Adi, *Indonesia* **37 E8** 4 15S 133 30 E
Adieu, C., *Australia* **61 F5** 32 0S 132 10 E
Adieu Pt., *Australia* **60 C3** 15 14S 124 35 E
Adige →, *Italy* **20 B5** 45 9N 12 20 E
Adigrat, *Ethiopia* **46 E2** 14 20N 39 26 E
Adilabad, *India* **40 K11** 19 33N 78 20 E
Adirondack Mts., *U.S.A.* **79 C10** 44 0N 74 0W
Adjumani, *Uganda* **54 B3** 3 20N 31 50 E
Adlavik Is., *Canada* **71 A8** 55 0N 58 40W
Admiralty G., *Australia* **60 B4** 14 20S 125 55 E
Admiralty I., *U.S.A.* **72 B2** 57 30N 134 30W
Admiralty Is., *Papua N. G.* **64 H6** 2 0S 147 0 E
Adonara, *Indonesia* **37 F6** 8 15S 123 5 E
Adoni, *India* **40 M10** 15 33N 77 18 E
Adour →, *France* **18 E3** 43 32N 1 32W
Adra, *India* **43 H12** 23 30N 86 42 E
Adra, *Spain* **19 D4** 36 43N 3 3W
Adrano, *Italy* **20 F6** 37 40N 14 50 E
Adrar, *Mauritania* **50 D3** 20 30N 7 30 E
Adrar des Iforas, *Algeria* **50 C5** 27 51N 0 11 E
Adrian, *Mich., U.S.A.* **76 E3** 41 54N 84 2W
Adrian, *Tex., U.S.A.* **81 H3** 35 16N 102 40W
Adriatic Sea, *Medit. S.* **20 C6** 43 0N 16 0 E
Adua, *Indonesia* **37 E7** 1 45S 129 50 E
Adwa, *Ethiopia* **46 E2** 14 15N 38 52 E
Adygea □, *Russia* **25 F7** 45 0N 40 0 E
Adzhar Republic = Ajaria □, *Georgia* **25 F7** 41 30N 42 0 E
Adzopé, *Ivory C.* **50 G5** 6 7N 3 49W
Ægean Sea, *Medit. S.* **21 E11** 38 30N 25 0 E
Aerhtai Shan, *Mongolia* **32 B4** 46 40N 92 45 E
'Afak, *Iraq* **44 C5** 32 4N 45 15 E
Afándou, *Greece* **23 C10** 36 18N 28 12 E
Afghanistan ■, *Asia* **40 C4** 33 0N 65 0 E
Aflou, *Algeria* **50 B6** 34 7N 2 3 E
Africa **48 E6** 10 0N 20 0 E
'Afrīn, *Syria* **44 B3** 36 32N 36 50 E
Afton, *N.Y., U.S.A.* **79 D9** 42 14N 75 32W
Afton, *Wyo., U.S.A.* **82 E8** 42 44N 110 56W
Afuá, *Brazil* **93 D8** 0 15S 50 20W
'Afula, *Israel* **47 C4** 32 37N 35 17 E
Afyon, *Turkey* **25 G5** 38 45N 30 33 E
Afyonkarahisar = Afyon, *Turkey* **25 G5** 38 45N 30 33 E
Agadès = Agadez, *Niger* **50 E7** 16 58N 7 59 E
Agadez, *Niger* **50 E7** 16 58N 7 59 E
Agadir, *Morocco* **50 B4** 30 28N 9 55W
Agaete, *Canary Is.* **22 F4** 28 6N 15 43W
Agar, *India* **42 H7** 23 40N 76 2 E
Agartala, *India* **41 H17** 23 50N 91 23 E
Agassiz, *Canada* **72 D4** 49 14N 121 46W
Agats, *Indonesia* **37 F9** 5 33S 138 0 E
Agawam, *U.S.A.* **79 D12** 42 5N 72 37W
Agboville, *Ivory C.* **50 G5** 5 55N 4 15W
Ağdam, *Azerbaijan* **44 B5** 40 0N 46 58 E
Agde, *France* **18 E5** 43 19N 3 28 E
Agen, *France* **18 D4** 44 12N 0 38 E
Āgh Kand, *Iran* **45 B6** 37 15N 48 4 E
Aginskoye, *Russia* **27 D12** 51 6N 114 32 E
Agnew, *Australia* **61 E3** 28 1S 120 31 E
Agori, *India* **43 G10** 24 33N 82 57 E
Agra, *India* **42 F7** 27 17N 77 58 E
Ağri, *Turkey* **25 G7** 39 44N 43 3 E
Agri →, *Italy* **20 D7** 40 13N 16 44 E
Ağrı Dağı, *Turkey* **25 G7** 39 50N 44 15 E
Ağri Karakose = Ağri, *Turkey* **25 G7** 39 44N 43 3 E
Agrigento, *Italy* **20 F5** 37 19N 13 34 E
Agrínion, *Greece* **21 E9** 38 37N 21 27 E
Agua Caliente, *Baja Calif., Mexico* **85 N10** 32 29N 116 59W
Agua Caliente, *Sinaloa, Mexico* **86 B3** 26 30N 108 20W
Agua Caliente Springs, *U.S.A.* **85 N10** 32 56N 116 19W
Água Clara, *Brazil* **93 H8** 20 25S 52 45W
Agua Hechicero, *Mexico* **85 N10** 32 26N 116 14W
Agua Prieta, *Mexico* **86 A3** 31 20N 109 32W
Aguadilla, *Puerto Rico* **89 C6** 18 26N 67 10W
Aguadulce, *Panama* **88 E3** 8 15N 80 32W
Aguanga, *U.S.A.* **85 M10** 33 27N 116 51W
Aguanish, *Canada* **71 B7** 50 14N 62 2W
Aguanus →, *Canada* **71 B7** 50 13N 62 5W
Aguapey →, *Argentina* **94 B4** 29 7S 56 36W
Aguaray Guazú →, *Paraguay* **94 A4** 24 47S 57 19W
Aguarico →, *Ecuador* **92 D3** 0 59S 75 11W
Aguas Blancas, *Chile* **94 A2** 24 15S 69 55W
Aguas Calientes, Sierra de, *Argentina* **94 B2** 25 26S 66 40W
Aguascalientes, *Mexico* **86 C4** 21 53N 102 12W
Aguascalientes □, *Mexico* **86 C4** 22 0N 102 20W
Aguilares, *Argentina* **94 B2** 27 26S 65 35W
Aguilas, *Spain* **19 D5** 37 23N 1 35W
Agüimes, *Canary Is.* **22 G4** 27 58N 15 27W
Aguja, C. de la, *Colombia* **90 B3** 11 18N 74 12W
Agulhas, C., *S. Africa* **56 E3** 34 52S 20 0 E
Agulo, *Canary Is.* **22 F2** 28 11N 17 12W
Agung, *Indonesia* **36 F5** 8 20S 115 28 E
Agur, *Uganda* **54 B3** 2 28N 32 55 E
Agusan →, *Phil.* **37 C7** 9 0N 125 30 E
Aha Mts., *Botswana* **56 B3** 19 45S 21 0 E
Ahaggar, *Algeria* **50 D7** 23 0N 6 30 E
Ahar, *Iran* **44 B5** 38 35N 47 0 E
Ahipara B., *N.Z.* **59 F4** 35 5S 173 5 E
Ahiri, *India* **40 K12** 19 30N 80 0 E
Ahmad Wal, *Pakistan* **42 E1** 29 18N 65 58 E
Ahmadabad, *India* **42 H5** 23 0N 72 40 E
Aḩmadābād, *Khorāsān, Iran* **45 C9** 35 3N 60 50 E
Aḩmadābād, *Khorāsān, Iran* **45 C8** 35 49N 59 42 E
Aḩmadī, *Iran* **45 E8** 27 56N 56 42 E
Ahmadnagar, *India* **40 K9** 19 7N 74 46 E
Ahmadpur, *Pakistan* **42 E4** 29 12N 71 10 E
Ahmadpur Lamma, *Pakistan* **42 E4** 28 19N 70 3 E
Ahmedabad = Ahmadabad, *India* **42 H5** 23 0N 72 40 E
Ahmednagar = Ahmadnagar, *India* **40 K9** 19 7N 74 46 E
Ahome, *Mexico* **86 B3** 25 55N 109 11W
Ahoskie, *U.S.A.* **77 G7** 36 17N 76 59W
Ahram, *Iran* **45 D6** 28 52N 51 16 E
Ahrax Pt., *Malta* **23 D1** 35 59N 14 22 E
Āhū, *Iran* **45 C6** 34 33N 50 2 E
Ahuachapán, *El Salv.* **88 D2** 13 54N 89 52W
Ahvāz, *Iran* **45 D6** 31 20N 48 40 E
Ahvenanmaa = Åland, *Finland* **9 F19** 60 15N 20 0 E
Aḩwar, *Yemen* **46 E4** 13 30N 46 40 E
Ai →, *India* **43 F14** 26 26N 90 44 E
Ai-Ais, *Namibia* **56 D2** 27 54S 17 59 E
Aichi □, *Japan* **31 G8** 35 0N 137 15 E
Aigua, *Uruguay* **95 C5** 34 13S 54 46W
Aigues-Mortes, *France* **18 E6** 43 35N 4 12 E
Aihui, *China* **33 A7** 50 10N 127 30 E
Aija, *Peru* **92 E3** 9 50S 77 45W
Aikawa, *Japan* **30 E9** 38 2N 138 15 E
Aiken, *U.S.A.* **77 J5** 33 34N 81 43W
Aileron, *Australia* **62 C1** 22 39S 133 20 E
Aillik, *Canada* **71 A8** 55 11N 59 18W
Ailsa Craig, *U.K.* **12 F3** 55 15N 5 6W
'Ailūn, *Jordan* **47 C4** 32 18N 35 47 E
Aim, *Russia* **27 D14** 59 0N 133 55 E
Aimere, *Indonesia* **37 F6** 8 45S 121 3 E
Aimogasta, *Argentina* **94 B2** 28 33S 66 50W
Aïn Ben Tili, *Mauritania* **50 C4** 25 59N 9 27W
Aïn Sefra, *Algeria* **50 B5** 32 47N 0 37W
Ain Sudr, *Egypt* **47 F2** 29 50N 33 6 E
Ainaži, *Latvia* **9 H21** 57 50N 24 24 E
Ainsworth, *U.S.A.* **80 D5** 42 33N 99 52W
Aiquile, *Bolivia* **92 G5** 18 10S 65 10W
Aïr, *Niger* **50 E7** 18 30N 8 0 E
Air Force I., *Canada* **69 B12** 67 58N 74 5W
Air Hitam, *Malaysia* **39 M4** 1 55N 103 11 E
Airdrie, *Canada* **72 C6** 51 18N 114 2W
Airdrie, *U.K.* **12 F5** 55 52N 3 57W
Aire →, *U.K.* **10 D7** 53 43N 0 55W
Aire, I. de l', *Spain* **22 B11** 39 48N 4 16 E
Airlie Beach, *Australia* **62 C4** 20 16S 148 43 E
Aisne →, *France* **18 B5** 49 26N 2 50 E
Ait, *India* **43 G8** 25 54N 79 14 E
Aitkin, *U.S.A.* **80 B8** 46 32N 93 42W
Aiud, *Romania* **17 E12** 46 19N 23 44 E
Aix-en-Provence, *France* **18 E6** 43 32N 5 27 E
Aix-la-Chapelle = Aachen, *Germany* **16 C4** 50 45N 6 6 E
Aix-les-Bains, *France* **18 D6** 45 41N 5 53 E
Aíyion, *Greece* **21 E10** 38 15N 22 5 E
Aizawl, *India* **41 H18** 23 40N 92 44 E
Aizkraukle, *Latvia* **9 H21** 56 36N 25 11 E
Aizpute, *Latvia* **9 H19** 56 43N 21 40 E
Aizuwakamatsu, *Japan* **30 F9** 37 30N 139 56 E
Ajaccio, *France* **18 F8** 41 55N 8 40 E
Ajaigarh, *India* **43 G9** 24 52N 80 16 E
Ajalpan, *Mexico* **87 D5** 18 22N 97 15W
Ajanta Ra., *India* **40 J9** 20 28N 75 50 E
Ajari Rep. = Ajaria □, *Georgia* **25 F7** 41 30N 42 0 E
Ajaria □, *Georgia* **25 F7** 41 30N 42 0 E
Ajax, *Canada* **78 C5** 43 50N 79 1W
Ajdābiyā, *Libya* **51 B10** 30 54N 20 4 E
Ajka, *Hungary* **17 E9** 47 4N 17 31 E
'Ajmān, *U.A.E.* **45 E7** 25 25N 55 30 E
Ajmer, *India* **42 F6** 26 28N 74 37 E
Ajnala, *India* **42 D6** 31 50N 74 48 E
Ajo, *U.S.A.* **83 K7** 32 22N 112 52W
Ajo, C. de, *Spain* **19 A4** 43 31N 3 35W
Akabira, *Japan* **30 C11** 43 33N 142 5 E
Akamas □, *Cyprus* **23 D11** 35 3N 32 18 E
Akanthou, *Cyprus* **23 D12** 35 22N 33 45 E
Akaroa, *N.Z.* **59 K4** 43 49S 172 59 E
Akashi, *Japan* **31 G7** 34 45N 134 58 E
Akbarpur, *Bihar, India* **43 G10** 24 39N 83 58 E
Akbarpur, *Ut. P., India* **43 F10** 26 25N 82 32 E
Akelamo, *Indonesia* **37 D7** 1 35N 129 40 E
Aketi, *Dem. Rep. of the Congo* **52 D4** 2 38N 23 47 E
Akharnaí, *Greece* **21 E10** 38 5N 23 44 E
Akhelóös →, *Greece* **21 E9** 38 19N 21 7 E
Akhisar, *Turkey* **21 E12** 38 56N 27 48 E
Akhnur, *India* **43 C6** 32 52N 74 45 E
Akhtyrka = Okhtyrka, *Ukraine* **25 D5** 50 25N 35 0 E
Aki, *Japan* **31 H6** 33 30N 133 54 E
Akimiski I., *Canada* **70 B3** 52 50N 81 30W
Akita, *Japan* **30 E10** 39 45N 140 7 E
Akita □, *Japan* **30 E10** 39 40N 140 30 E
Akjoujt, *Mauritania* **50 E3** 19 45N 14 15W
Akkeshi, *Japan* **30 C12** 43 2N 144 51 E
'Akko, *Israel* **47 C4** 32 55N 35 4 E
Aklavik, *Canada* **68 B6** 68 12N 135 0W
Aklera, *India* **42 G7** 24 26N 76 32 E
Akmolinsk = Astana, *Kazakstan* **26 D8** 51 10N 71 30 E
Akō, *Japan* **31 G7** 34 45N 134 24 E
Akola, *India* **40 J10** 20 42N 77 2 E
Akordat, *Eritrea* **46 D2** 15 30N 37 40 E
Akpatok I., *Canada* **69 B13** 60 25N 68 8W
Åkrahamn, *Norway* **9 G11** 59 15N 5 10 E
Akranes, *Iceland* **8 D2** 64 19N 22 5W
Akron, *Colo., U.S.A.* **80 E3** 40 10N 103 13W
Akron, *Ohio, U.S.A.* **78 E3** 41 5N 81 31W
Akrotiri, *Cyprus* **23 E11** 34 36N 32 57 E
Akrotiri Bay, *Cyprus* **23 E12** 34 35N 33 10 E
Aksai Chin, *India* **43 B8** 35 15N 79 55 E
Aksaray, *Turkey* **25 G5** 38 25N 34 2 E
Aksay, *Kazakstan* **25 D9** 51 11N 53 0 E
Akşehir, *Turkey* **44 B1** 38 18N 31 30 E
Akşehir Gölü, *Turkey* **25 G5** 38 30N 31 25 E
Aksu, *China* **32 B3** 41 5N 80 10 E
Aksum, *Ethiopia* **46 E2** 14 5N 38 40 E
Aktogay, *Kazakstan* **26 E8** 46 57N 79 40 E
Aktsyabrski, *Belarus* **17 B15** 52 38N 28 53 E
Aktyubinsk = Aqtöbe, *Kazakstan* **25 D10** 50 17N 57 10 E
Akure, *Nigeria* **50 G7** 7 15N 5 5 E
Akureyri, *Iceland* **8 D4** 65 40N 18 6W
Akuseki-Shima, *Japan* **31 K4** 29 27N 129 37 E
Akyab = Sittwe, *Burma* **41 J18** 20 18N 92 45 E
Al 'Adan, *Yemen* **46 E4** 12 45N 45 0 E
Al Aḩsā = Hasa □, *Si. Arabia* **45 E6** 25 50N 49 0 E
Al Ajfar, *Si. Arabia* **44 E4** 27 26N 43 0 E
Al Amādīyah, *Iraq* **44 B4** 37 5N 43 30 E
Al 'Amārah, *Iraq* **44 D5** 31 55N 47 15 E
Al 'Aqabah, *Jordan* **47 F4** 29 31N 35 0 E
Al Arak, *Syria* **44 C3** 34 38N 38 35 E
Al 'Aramah, *Si. Arabia* **44 E5** 25 30N 46 0 E
Al Arţāwīyah, *Si. Arabia* **44 E5** 26 31N 45 20 E
Al 'Āşimah = 'Ammān □, *Jordan* **47 D5** 31 40N 36 30 E
Al 'Assāfīyah, *Si. Arabia* **44 D3** 28 17N 38 59 E
Al 'Ayn, *Oman* **45 E7** 24 15N 55 45 E
Al 'Ayn, *Si. Arabia* **44 E3** 25 4N 38 6 E
Al 'Az̧amīyah, *Iraq* **44 C5** 33 22N 44 22 E
Al 'Azīzīyah, *Iraq* **44 C5** 32 54N 45 4 E
Al Bāb, *Syria* **44 B3** 36 23N 37 29 E
Al Bad', *Si. Arabia* **44 D2** 28 28N 35 1 E
Al Bādī, *Iraq* **44 C4** 35 56N 41 32 E
Al Baḩrah, *Kuwait* **44 D5** 29 40N 47 52 E
Al Baḩral Mayyit = Dead Sea, *Asia* **47 D4** 31 30N 35 30 E
Al Balqā' □, *Jordan* **47 C4** 32 5N 35 45 E
Al Bārūk, J., *Lebanon* **47 B4** 33 39N 35 40 E
Al Başrah, *Iraq* **44 D5** 30 30N 47 50 E
Al Baţḩā, *Iraq* **44 D5** 31 6N 45 53 E
Al Batrūn, *Lebanon* **47 A4** 34 15N 35 40 E
Al Bayḑā, *Libya* **51 B10** 32 50N 21 44 E
Al Biqā, *Lebanon* **47 A5** 34 10N 36 10 E

Amalner

Al Bi'r, Si. Arabia 44 D3 28 51N 36 16 E
Al Burayj, Syria 47 A5 34 15N 36 46 E
Al Faḍilī, Si. Arabia 45 E6 26 58N 49 10 E
Al Fallūjah, Iraq 44 C4 33 20N 43 55 E
Al Fāw, Iraq 45 D6 30 0N 48 30 E
Al Fujayrah, U.A.E. 45 E8 25 7N 56 18 E
Al Ghadaf, W. →, Jordan 47 D5 31 26N 36 43 E
Al Ghammās, Iraq 44 D5 31 45N 44 37 E
Al Ghazālah, Si. Arabia 44 E4 26 48N 41 19 E
Al Ḥadīthah, Iraq 44 C4 34 0N 41 13 E
Al Ḥadīthah, Si. Arabia 47 D6 31 28N 37 8 E
Al Ḥaḍr, Iraq 44 C4 35 35N 42 44 E
Al Hājānah, Syria 47 B5 33 20N 36 33 E
Al Hajar al Gharbī, Oman 45 E8 24 10N 56 15 E
Al Hāmad, Si. Arabia 44 D3 31 30N 39 30 E
Al Hamdānīyah, Syria 44 C3 35 25N 36 50 E
Al Ḥamīdīyah, Syria 47 A4 34 42N 35 57 E
Al Ḥammār, Iraq 44 D5 30 57N 46 51 E
Al Ḥamrā', Si. Arabia 44 E3 24 2N 38 55 E
Al Ḥanākīyah, Si. Arabia 44 E4 24 51N 40 31 E
Al Harīr, W. →, Syria 47 C4 32 44N 35 59 E
Al Ḥasā, W. →, Jordan 47 D4 31 4N 35 29 E
Al Ḥasakah, Syria 44 B4 36 35N 40 45 E
Al Haydān, W. →, Jordan 47 D4 31 29N 35 34 E
Al Ḥayy, Iraq 44 C5 32 5N 46 5 E
Al Ḥijarah, Asia 44 D4 30 0N 44 0 E
Al Ḥillah, Iraq 44 C5 32 30N 44 25 E
Al Ḥillah, Si. Arabia 46 B4 23 35N 46 50 E
Al Hindīyah, Iraq 44 C5 32 30N 44 10 E
Al Hirmil, Lebanon 47 A5 34 26N 36 24 E
Al Hoceïma, Morocco 50 A5 35 8N 3 58W
Al Ḥudaydah, Yemen 46 E3 14 50N 43 0 E
Al Hufūf, Si. Arabia 46 B4 25 25N 49 45 E
Al Ḥumayḍah, Si. Arabia 44 D2 29 14N 34 56 E
Al Ḥunayy, Si. Arabia 45 E6 25 58N 48 45 E
Al Īsāwīyah, Si. Arabia 44 D3 30 43N 37 59 E
Al Jafr, Jordan 47 E5 30 18N 36 14 E
Al Jāfūrah, Si. Arabia 45 E7 25 0N 50 15 E
Al Jaghbūb, Libya 51 C10 29 42N 24 38 E
Al Jahrah, Kuwait 44 D5 29 25N 47 40 E
Al Jalāmīd, Si. Arabia 44 D3 31 20N 40 6 E
Al Jamalīyah, Qatar 45 E6 25 37N 51 5 E
Al Janūb □, Lebanon 47 B4 33 20N 35 20 E
Al Jawf, Libya 51 D10 24 10N 23 24 E
Al Jawf, Si. Arabia 44 D3 29 55N 39 40 E
Al Jazirah, Iraq 44 C5 33 30N 44 0 E
Al Jithāmīyah, Si. Arabia 44 E4 27 41N 41 43 E
Al Jubayl, Si. Arabia 45 E6 27 0N 49 50 E
Al Jubaylah, Si. Arabia 44 E5 24 55N 46 25 E
Al Jubb, Si. Arabia 44 E4 27 11N 42 17 E
Al Junaynah, Sudan 51 F10 13 27N 22 45 E
Al Kabā'ish, Iraq 44 D5 30 58N 47 0 E
Al Karak, Jordan 47 D4 31 11N 35 42 E
Al Karak □, Jordan 47 E5 31 0N 36 0 E
Al Kāzim Tyah, Iraq 44 C5 33 22N 44 12 E
Al Khābūra, Oman 45 F8 23 57N 57 5 E
Al Khafji, Si. Arabia 45 E6 28 24N 48 29 E
Al Khalīl, West Bank 47 D4 31 32N 35 6 E
Al Khāliṣ, Iraq 44 C5 33 49N 44 32 E
Al Kharsānīyah, Si. Arabia 45 E6 27 13N 49 18 E
Al Khaṣab, Oman 45 E8 26 14N 56 15 E
Al Khawr, Qatar 45 E6 25 41N 51 30 E
Al Khiḍr, Iraq 44 D5 31 12N 45 33 E
Al Khiyām, Lebanon 47 B4 33 20N 35 36 E
Al Kiswah, Syria 47 B5 33 23N 36 14 E
Al Kūfah, Iraq 44 C5 32 2N 44 24 E
Al Kufrah, Libya 51 D10 24 17N 23 15 E
Al Kuhayfiyah, Si. Arabia 44 E4 27 12N 43 3 E
Al Kūt, Iraq 44 C5 32 30N 46 0 E
Al Kuwayt, Kuwait 46 B4 29 30N 48 0 E
Al Labwah, Lebanon 47 A5 34 11N 36 20 E
Al Lādhiqīyah, Syria 44 C2 35 30N 35 45 E
Al Līth, Si. Arabia 46 C3 20 9N 40 15 E
Al Liwā', Oman 45 E8 24 31N 56 36 E
Al Luḥayyah, Yemen 46 D3 15 45N 42 40 E
Al Madīnah, Iraq 44 D5 30 57N 47 16 E
Al Madīnah, Si. Arabia 46 C2 24 35N 39 52 E
Al Mafraq, Jordan 47 C5 32 17N 36 14 E
Al Maḥmūdīyah, Iraq 44 C5 33 3N 44 21 E
Al Majma'ah, Si. Arabia 44 E5 25 57N 45 22 E
Al Makhruq, W. →, Jordan 47 D6 31 28N 37 0 E
Al Makḥūl, Si. Arabia 44 E4 26 37N 42 39 E
Al Manāmah, Bahrain 46 B5 26 10N 50 30 E
Al Maqwa', Kuwait 44 D5 29 10N 47 59 E
Al Marj, Libya 51 B10 32 25N 20 30 E
Al Maṭlā, Kuwait 44 D5 29 24N 47 40 E
Al Mawjib, W. →, Jordan 47 D4 31 28N 35 36 E
Al Mawṣil, Iraq 44 B4 36 15N 43 5 E
Al Mayādin, Syria 44 C4 35 1N 40 27 E
Al Mazār, Jordan 47 D4 31 4N 35 41 E
Al Midhnab, Si. Arabia 44 E5 25 50N 44 18 E
Al Minā', Lebanon 47 A4 34 24N 35 49 E
Al Miqdādīyah, Iraq 44 C5 34 0N 45 0 E
Al Mubarraz, Si. Arabia 45 E6 25 30N 49 40 E
Al Mudawwarah, Jordan 47 F5 29 19N 36 0 E
Al Mughayrā', U.A.E. 45 E7 24 5N 53 32 E
Al Muḥarraq, Bahrain 45 E6 26 15N 50 40 E
Al Mukallā, Yemen 46 E4 14 33N 49 2 E
Al Mukhā, Yemen 46 E3 13 18N 43 15 E
Al Musayjīd, Si. Arabia 44 E3 24 5N 39 5 E
Al Musayyib, Iraq 44 C5 32 49N 44 20 E
Al Muwayliḥ, Si. Arabia 44 E2 27 40N 35 30 E
Al Qā'im, Iraq 44 C4 34 21N 41 7 E
Al Qalībah, Si. Arabia 44 D3 28 24N 37 42 E
Al Qāmishlī, Syria 44 B4 37 2N 41 14 E
Al Qaryatayn, Syria 47 A6 34 12N 37 13 E
Al Qaṣīm, Si. Arabia 44 E4 26 0N 43 0 E
Al Qaṭ'ā, Syria 44 C4 34 40N 40 48 E
Al Qaṭīf, Si. Arabia 45 E6 26 35N 50 0 E
Al Qatrānah, Jordan 47 D5 31 12N 36 6 E
Al Qaṭrūn, Libya 51 D9 24 56N 15 3 E
Al Qayṣūmah, Si. Arabia 44 D5 28 20N 46 7 E
Al Quds = Jerusalem, Israel 47 D4 31 47N 35 10 E
Al Qunayṭirah, Syria 47 C4 32 55N 35 45 E
Al Qurnah, Iraq 44 D5 31 1N 47 25 E
Al Quṣayr, Iraq 44 D5 30 39N 45 50 E
Al Quṣayr, Syria 47 A5 34 31N 36 34 E
Al Qutayfah, Syria 47 B5 33 44N 36 36 E
Al 'Ubaylah, Si. Arabia 46 C5 21 59N 50 57 E
Al 'Uḍaylīyah, Si. Arabia 45 E6 25 8N 49 18 E
Al 'Ulā, Si. Arabia 44 E3 26 35N 38 0 E
Al 'Uqayr, Si. Arabia 45 E6 25 40N 50 15 E
Al 'Uwaynid, Si. Arabia 44 E5 24 50N 46 0 E
Al 'Uwayqīlah, Si. Arabia 44 D4 30 30N 42 10 E
Al 'Uyūn, Ḥijāz, Si. Arabia 44 E3 24 33N 39 35 E
Al 'Uyūn, Najd, Si. Arabia 44 E4 26 30N 43 50 E
Al 'Uzayr, Iraq 44 D5 31 19N 47 25 E
Al Wajh, Si. Arabia 44 E3 26 10N 36 30 E
Al Wakrah, Qatar 45 E6 25 10N 51 40 E
Al Waqbah, Si. Arabia 44 D5 28 48N 45 33 E
Al Wari'āh, Si. Arabia 44 E5 27 51N 47 25 E
Ala Dağ, Turkey 44 B2 37 44N 35 9 E
Ala Tau Shankou = Dzungarian Gates, Asia 32 B3 45 0N 82 0 E
Alabama □, U.S.A. 77 J2 33 0N 87 0W
Alabama →, U.S.A. 77 K2 31 8N 87 57W
Alabaster, U.S.A. 77 J2 33 15N 86 49W
Alaçam Dağları, Turkey 21 E13 39 18N 28 49 E
Alachua, U.S.A. 77 L4 29 47N 82 30W
Alaérma, Greece 23 C9 36 9N 27 57 E
Alagoa Grande, Brazil 93 E11 7 3S 35 35W
Alagoas □, Brazil 93 E11 9 0S 36 0W
Alagoinhas, Brazil 93 F11 12 7S 38 20W
Alaior, Spain 22 B11 39 57N 4 8 E
Alajero, Canary Is. 22 F2 28 3N 17 13W
Alajuela, Costa Rica 88 D3 10 2N 84 8W
Alakamisy, Madag. 57 C8 21 19S 47 14 E
Alaknanda →, India 43 D8 30 8N 78 36 E
Alakurtti, Russia 24 A5 67 0N 30 30 E
Alamarvdasht, Iran 45 E7 27 37N 52 59 E
Alameda, Calif., U.S.A. 84 H4 37 46N 122 15W
Alameda, N. Mex., U.S.A. 83 J10 35 11N 106 37W
Alamo, U.S.A. 85 J11 37 22N 115 10W
Alamo Crossing, U.S.A. 85 L13 34 16N 113 33W
Alamogordo, U.S.A. 83 K11 32 54N 105 57W
Alamos, Mexico 86 B3 27 0N 109 0W
Alamosa, U.S.A. 83 H11 37 28N 105 52W
Åland, Finland 9 F19 60 15N 20 0 E
Ålands hav, Sweden 9 F18 60 0N 19 30 E
Alania = North Ossetia □, Russia 25 F7 43 30N 44 30 E
Alanya, Turkey 25 G5 36 38N 32 0 E
Alaotra, Farihin', Madag. 57 B8 17 30S 48 30 E
Alapayevsk, Russia 26 D7 57 52N 61 42 E
Alappuzha = Alleppey, India 40 Q10 9 30N 76 28 E
Alarobia-Vohiposa, Madag. 57 C8 20 59S 47 9 E
Alaşehir, Turkey 21 E13 38 23N 28 30 E
Alaska □, U.S.A. 68 B5 64 0N 154 0W
Alaska, G. of, Pac. Oc. 68 C5 58 0N 145 0W
Alaska Peninsula, U.S.A. 68 C4 56 0N 159 0W
Alaska Range, U.S.A. 68 B4 62 50N 151 0W
Älät, Azerbaijan 25 G8 39 58N 49 25 E
Alatyr, Russia 24 D8 54 55N 46 35 E
Alausi, Ecuador 92 D3 2 0S 78 50W
Alava, C., U.S.A. 82 B1 48 10N 124 44W
Alavus, Finland 9 E20 62 35N 23 36 E
'Alayh, Lebanon 47 B4 33 46N 35 33 E
Alba, Italy 18 D8 44 42N 8 2 E
Alba-Iulia, Romania 17 E12 46 8N 23 39 E
Albacete, Spain 19 C5 39 0N 1 50W
Albanel, L., Canada 70 B5 50 55N 73 12W
Albania ■, Europe 21 D9 41 0N 20 0 E
Albany, Australia 61 G2 35 1S 117 58 E
Albany, Ga., U.S.A. 77 K3 31 35N 84 10W
Albany, N.Y., U.S.A. 79 D11 42 39N 73 45W
Albany, Oreg., U.S.A. 82 D2 44 38N 123 6W
Albany, Tex., U.S.A. 81 J5 32 44N 99 18W
Albany →, Canada 70 B3 52 17N 81 31W
Albardón, Argentina 94 C2 31 20S 68 30W
Albatross B., Australia 62 A3 12 45S 141 30 E
Albemarle, U.S.A. 77 H5 35 21N 80 11W
Albemarle Sd., U.S.A. 77 H7 36 5N 76 0W
Alberche →, Spain 19 C3 39 58N 4 46W
Alberdi, Paraguay 94 B4 26 14S 58 20W
Albert, L., Africa 54 B3 1 30N 31 0 E
Albert Edward Ra., Australia 60 C4 18 17S 127 57 E
Albert Lea, U.S.A. 80 D8 43 39N 93 22W
Albert Nile →, Uganda 54 B3 3 36N 32 2 E
Albert Town, Bahamas 89 B5 22 37N 74 33W
Alberta □, Canada 72 C6 54 40N 115 0W
Alberti, Argentina 94 D3 35 1S 60 16W
Albertinia, S. Africa 56 E3 34 11S 21 34 E
Alberton, Canada 71 C7 46 50N 64 0W
Albertville = Kalemie, Dem. Rep. of the Congo 54 D2 5 55S 29 9 E
Albertville, France 18 D7 45 40N 6 22 E
Albertville, U.S.A. 77 H2 34 16N 86 13W
Albi, France 18 E5 43 56N 2 9 E
Albia, U.S.A. 80 E8 41 2N 92 48W
Albina, Surinam 93 B8 5 37N 54 15W
Albina, Ponta, Angola 56 B1 15 52S 11 44 E
Albion, Mich., U.S.A. 76 D3 42 15N 84 45W
Albion, Nebr., U.S.A. 80 E6 41 42N 98 0W
Albion, Pa., U.S.A. 78 E4 41 53N 80 22W
Alborán, Medit. S. 19 E4 35 57N 3 0W
Ålborg, Denmark 9 H13 57 2N 9 54 E
Alborz, Reshteh-ye Kūhhā-ye, Iran 45 C7 36 0N 52 0 E
Albuquerque, U.S.A. 83 J10 35 5N 106 39W
Albuquerque, Cayos de, Caribbean 88 D3 12 10N 81 50W
Alburg, U.S.A. 79 B11 44 59N 73 18W
Alcalá de Henares, Spain 19 B4 40 28N 3 22W
Alcalá la Real, Spain 19 D4 37 27N 3 57W
Álcamo, Italy 20 F5 37 59N 12 55 E
Alcañiz, Spain 19 B5 41 2N 0 8W
Alcântara, Brazil 93 D10 2 20S 44 30W
Alcántara, Embalse de, Spain 19 C2 39 44N 6 50W
Alcantarilla, Spain 19 D5 37 59N 1 12W
Alcaraz, Sierra de, Spain 19 C4 38 40N 2 20W
Alcaudete, Spain 19 D3 37 35N 4 5W
Alcázar de San Juan, Spain 19 C4 39 24N 3 12W
Alchevsk, Ukraine 25 E6 48 30N 38 45 E
Alcira = Alzira, Spain 19 C5 39 9N 0 30W
Alcova, U.S.A. 82 E10 42 34N 106 43W
Alcoy, Spain 19 C5 38 43N 0 30W
Alcúdia, Spain 22 B10 39 51N 3 7 E
Alcúdia, B. d', Spain 22 B10 39 47N 3 15 E
Aldabra Is., Seychelles 49 G8 9 22S 46 28 E
Aldama, Mexico 87 C5 23 0N 98 4W
Aldan, Russia 27 D13 58 40N 125 30 E
Aldan →, Russia 27 C13 63 28N 129 35 E
Aldea, Pta. de la, Canary Is. 22 G4 28 0N 15 50W
Aldeburgh, U.K. 11 E9 52 10N 1 37 E
Alder Pk., U.S.A. 84 K5 35 53N 121 22W
Alderney, U.K. 11 H5 49 42N 2 11W
Aldershot, U.K. 11 F7 51 15N 0 44W
Aledo, U.S.A. 80 E9 41 12N 90 45W
Aleg, Mauritania 50 E3 17 3N 13 55W
Alegranza, Canary Is. 22 E6 29 23N 13 32W
Alegranza, I., Canary Is. 22 E6 29 23N 13 32W
Alegre, Brazil 95 A7 20 50S 41 30W
Alegrete, Brazil 95 B4 29 40S 56 0W
Aleisk, Russia 26 D9 52 40N 83 0 E
Aleksandriya = Oleksandriya, Ukraine 17 C14 50 37N 26 19 E
Aleksandrov Gay, Russia 25 D8 50 9N 48 34 E
Aleksandrovsk-Sakhalinskiy, Russia 27 D15 50 50N 142 20 E
Além Paraíba, Brazil 95 A7 21 52S 42 41W
Alemania, Argentina 94 B2 25 40S 65 30W
Alemania, Chile 94 B2 25 10S 69 55W
Alençon, France 18 B4 48 27N 0 4 E
Alenquer, Brazil 93 D8 1 56S 54 46W
Alenuihaha Channel, U.S.A. 74 H17 20 30N 156 0W
Aleppo = Ḥalab, Syria 44 B3 36 10N 37 15 E
Alès, France 18 D6 44 9N 4 5 E
Alessándria, Italy 18 D8 44 54N 8 37 E
Ålesund, Norway 9 E12 62 28N 6 12 E
Aleutian Is., Pac. Oc. 68 C2 52 0N 175 0W
Aleutian Trench, Pac. Oc. 64 C10 48 0N 180 0 E
Alexander, U.S.A. 80 B3 47 51N 103 39W
Alexander, Mt., Australia 61 E3 28 58S 120 16 E
Alexander Arch., U.S.A. 68 C6 56 0N 136 0W
Alexander Bay, S. Africa 56 D2 28 40S 16 30 E
Alexander City, U.S.A. 77 J3 32 56N 85 58W
Alexander I., Antarctica 5 C17 69 0S 70 0W
Alexandra, N.Z. 59 L2 45 14S 169 25 E
Alexandra Falls, Canada 72 A5 60 29N 116 18W
Alexandria = El Iskandarîya, Egypt 51 B11 31 13N 29 58 E
Alexandria, B.C., Canada 72 C4 52 35N 122 27W
Alexandria, Ont., Canada 79 A10 45 19N 74 38W
Alexandria, Romania 17 G13 43 57N 25 24 E
Alexandria, S. Africa 56 E4 33 38S 26 28 E
Alexandria, U.K. 12 F4 55 59N 4 35W
Alexandria, La., U.S.A. 81 K8 31 18N 92 27W
Alexandria, Minn., U.S.A. 80 C7 45 53N 95 22W
Alexandria, S. Dak., U.S.A. 80 D6 43 39N 97 47W
Alexandria, Va., U.S.A. 76 F7 38 48N 77 3W
Alexandria Bay, U.S.A. 79 B9 44 20N 75 55W
Alexandroúpolis, Greece 21 D11 40 50N 25 54 E
Alexis →, Canada 71 B8 52 33N 56 8W
Alexis Creek, Canada 72 C4 52 10N 123 20W
Alfabia, Spain 22 B9 39 44N 2 44 E
Alfenas, Brazil 95 A6 21 20S 46 10W
Alford, Aberds., U.K. 12 D6 57 14N 2 41W
Alford, Lincs., U.K. 10 D8 53 15N 0 10 E
Alfred, Maine, U.S.A. 79 C14 43 29N 70 43W
Alfred, N.Y., U.S.A. 78 D7 42 16N 77 48W
Alfreton, U.K. 10 D6 53 6N 1 24W
Alga, Kazakstan 25 E10 49 53N 57 20 E
Algaida, Spain 22 B9 39 33N 2 53 E
Ålgård, Norway 9 G11 58 46N 5 53 E
Algarve, Portugal 19 D1 36 58N 8 20W
Algeciras, Spain 19 D3 36 9N 5 28W
Algemesí, Spain 19 C5 39 11N 0 27W
Alger, Algeria 50 A6 36 42N 3 8 E
Algeria ■, Africa 50 C6 28 30N 2 0 E
Alghero, Italy 20 D3 40 33N 8 19 E
Algiers = Alger, Algeria 50 A6 36 42N 3 8 E
Algoa B., S. Africa 56 E4 33 50S 25 45 E
Algoma, U.S.A. 76 C2 44 36N 87 26W
Algona, U.S.A. 80 D7 43 4N 94 14W
Algonac, U.S.A. 78 D2 42 37N 82 32W
Algonquin Prov. Park, Canada 70 C4 45 50N 78 30W
Algorta, Uruguay 96 C5 32 25S 57 23W
Alhambra, U.S.A. 85 L8 34 8N 118 6W
Alhucemas = Al Hoceïma, Morocco 50 A5 35 8N 3 58W
'Alī al Gharbī, Iraq 44 C5 32 30N 46 45 E
'Alī ash Sharqī, Iraq 44 C5 32 7N 46 44 E
'Alī Khēl, Afghan. 42 C3 33 57N 69 43 E
Alī Shāh, Iran 44 B5 38 9N 45 50 E
'Alīābād, Khorāsān, Iran 45 C8 32 30N 57 30 E
'Alīābād, Kordestān, Iran 44 C5 35 4N 46 58 E
'Alīābād, Yazd, Iran 45 D7 31 41N 53 49 E
Aliağa, Turkey 21 E12 38 47N 26 59 E
Aliákmon →, Greece 21 D10 40 30N 22 36 E
Alicante, Spain 19 C5 38 23N 0 30W
Alice, S. Africa 56 E4 32 48S 26 55 E
Alice, U.S.A. 81 M5 27 45N 98 5W
Alice →, Queens., Australia 62 C3 24 2S 144 50 E
Alice →, Queens., Australia 62 B3 15 35S 142 20 E
Alice Arm, Canada 72 B3 55 29N 129 31W
Alice Springs, Australia 62 C1 23 40S 133 50 E
Alicedale, S. Africa 56 E4 33 15S 26 4 E
Aliceville, U.S.A. 77 J1 33 8N 88 9W
Aliganj, India 43 F8 27 30N 79 10 E
Aligarh, Raj., India 42 G7 25 55N 76 15 E
Aligarh, Ut. P., India 42 F8 27 55N 78 10 E
Alīgūdarz, Iran 45 C6 33 25N 49 45 E
Alimnía, Greece 23 C9 36 16N 27 43 E
Alingsås, Sweden 9 H15 57 56N 12 31 E
Alipur, Pakistan 42 E4 29 25N 70 55 E
Alipur Duar, India 41 F16 26 30N 89 35 E
Aliquippa, U.S.A. 78 F4 40 37N 80 15W
Alitus = Alytus, Lithuania 9 J21 54 24N 24 3 E
Aliwal North, S. Africa 56 E4 30 45S 26 45 E
Alix, Canada 72 C6 52 24N 113 11W
Aljustrel, Portugal 19 D1 37 55N 8 10W
Alkmaar, Neths. 15 B4 52 37N 4 45 E
All American Canal, U.S.A. 83 K6 32 45N 115 15W
Allagash →, U.S.A. 77 B11 47 5N 69 3W
Allah Dad, Pakistan 42 G2 25 38N 67 34 E
Allahabad, India 43 G9 25 25N 81 58 E
Allan, Canada 73 C7 51 53N 106 4W
Allanridge, S. Africa 56 D4 27 45S 26 40 E
Allegany, U.S.A. 78 D6 42 6N 78 30W
Allegheny →, U.S.A. 78 F5 40 27N 80 1W
Allegheny Mts., U.S.A. 76 G6 38 15N 80 10W
Allegheny Reservoir, U.S.A. 78 E6 41 50N 79 0W
Allen, Bog of, Ireland 13 C5 53 15N 7 0W
Allen, L., Ireland 13 B3 54 8N 8 4W
Allendale, U.S.A. 77 J5 33 1N 81 18W
Allende, Mexico 86 B4 28 20N 100 50W
Allentown, U.S.A. 79 F9 40 37N 75 29W
Alleppey, India 40 Q10 9 30N 76 28 E
Aller →, Germany 16 B5 52 56N 9 12 E
Alliance, Nebr., U.S.A. 80 D3 42 6N 102 52W
Alliance, Ohio, U.S.A. 78 F3 40 55N 81 6W
Allier →, France 18 C5 46 57N 3 4 E
Alliford Bay, Canada 72 C2 53 12N 131 58W
Alliston, Canada 78 B5 44 9N 79 52W
Alloa, U.K. 12 E5 56 7N 3 47W
Allora, Australia 63 D5 28 2S 152 0 E
Alluitsup Paa, Greenland 4 C5 60 30N 45 35W
Alma, Canada 71 C5 48 35N 71 40W
Alma, Ga., U.S.A. 77 K4 31 33N 82 28W
Alma, Kans., U.S.A. 80 F6 39 1N 96 17W
Alma, Mich., U.S.A. 76 D3 43 23N 84 39W
Alma, Nebr., U.S.A. 80 E5 40 6N 99 22W
Alma Ata = Almaty, Kazakstan 26 E8 43 15N 76 57 E
Almada, Portugal 19 C1 38 40N 9 9W
Almaden, Australia 62 B3 17 22S 144 40 E
Almadén, Spain 19 C3 38 49N 4 52W
Almanor, L., U.S.A. 82 F3 40 14N 121 9W
Almansa, Spain 19 C5 38 51N 1 5W
Almanzor, Pico, Spain 19 B3 40 15N 5 18W
Almanzora →, Spain 19 D5 37 14N 1 46W
Almaty, Kazakstan 26 E8 43 15N 76 57 E
Almazán, Spain 19 B4 41 30N 2 30W
Almeirim, Brazil 93 D8 1 30S 52 34W
Almelo, Neths. 15 B6 52 22N 6 42 E
Almendralejo, Spain 19 C2 38 41N 6 26W
Almere-Stad, Neths. 15 B5 52 20N 5 15 E
Almería, Spain 19 D4 36 52N 2 27W
Almirante, Panama 88 E3 9 10N 82 30W
Almiroú, Kólpos, Greece 23 D6 35 23N 24 20 E
Almond, U.S.A. 78 D7 42 19N 77 44W
Almont, U.S.A. 78 D1 42 55N 83 3W
Almonte, Canada 79 A8 45 14N 76 12W
Almora, India 43 E8 29 38N 79 40 E
Alness, U.K. 12 D4 57 41N 4 16W
Alnmouth, U.K. 10 B6 55 24N 1 37W
Alnwick, U.K. 10 B6 55 24N 1 42W
Aloi, Uganda 54 B3 2 16N 33 10 E
Alon, Burma 41 H19 22 12N 95 5 E
Alor, Indonesia 37 F6 8 15S 124 30 E
Alor Setar, Malaysia 39 J3 6 7N 100 22 E
Alot, India 42 H6 23 56N 75 40 E
Aloysius, Mt., Australia 61 E4 26 0S 128 38 E
Alpaugh, U.S.A. 84 K7 35 53N 119 29W
Alpena, U.S.A. 76 C4 45 4N 83 27W
Alpha, Australia 62 C4 23 39S 146 37 E
Alphen aan den Rijn, Neths. 15 B4 52 7N 4 40 E
Alpine, Ariz., U.S.A. 83 K9 33 51N 109 9W
Alpine, Calif., U.S.A. 85 N10 32 50N 116 46W
Alpine, Tex., U.S.A. 81 K3 30 22N 103 40W
Alps, Europe 18 C8 46 30N 9 30 E
Alsace, France 18 B7 48 15N 7 25 E
Alsask, Canada 73 C7 51 21N 109 59W
Alsasua, Spain 19 A4 42 54N 2 10W
Alsek →, U.S.A. 72 B1 59 10N 138 12W
Alsten, Norway 8 D15 65 58N 12 40 E
Alston, U.K. 10 C5 54 49N 2 25W
Alta, Norway 8 B20 69 57N 23 10 E
Alta Gracia, Argentina 94 C3 31 40S 64 30W
Alta Sierra, U.S.A. 85 K8 35 42N 118 33W
Altaelva →, Norway 8 B20 69 54N 23 17 E
Altafjorden, Norway 8 A20 70 5N 23 5 E
Altai = Aerhtai Shan, Mongolia 32 B4 46 40N 92 45 E
Altamaha →, U.S.A. 77 K5 31 20N 81 20W
Altamira, Brazil 93 D8 3 12S 52 10W
Altamira, Chile 94 B2 25 47S 69 51W
Altamira, Mexico 87 C5 22 24N 97 55W
Altamont, U.S.A. 79 D10 42 43N 74 3W
Altamura, Italy 20 D7 40 49N 16 33 E
Altanbulag, Mongolia 32 A5 50 16N 106 30 E
Altar, Mexico 86 A2 30 40N 111 50W
Altar, Desierto de, Mexico 86 B2 30 10N 112 0W
Altata, Mexico 86 C3 24 30N 108 0W
Altavista, U.S.A. 76 G6 37 6N 79 17W
Altay, China 32 B3 47 48N 88 10 E
Altea, Spain 19 C5 38 38N 0 2W
Altiplano = Bolivian Plateau, S. Amer. 90 E4 20 0S 67 30W
Alto Araguaia, Brazil 93 G8 17 15S 53 20W
Alto Cuchumatanes = Cuchumatanes, Sierra de los, Guatemala 88 C1 15 35N 91 25W
Alto del Carmen, Chile 94 B1 28 46S 70 30W
Alto del Inca, Chile 94 A2 24 10S 68 10W
Alto Ligonha, Mozam. 55 F4 15 30S 38 11 E
Alto Molocue, Mozam. 55 F4 15 50S 37 35 E
Alto Paraguay □, Paraguay 94 A4 21 0S 58 30W
Alto Paraná □, Paraguay 95 B5 25 30S 54 50W
Alton, Canada 78 C4 43 54N 80 5W
Alton, U.K. 11 F7 51 9N 0 59W
Alton, Ill., U.S.A. 80 F9 38 53N 90 11W
Alton, N.H., U.S.A. 79 C13 43 27N 71 13W
Altoona, U.S.A. 78 F6 40 31N 78 24W
Altūn Kūprī, Iraq 44 C5 35 45N 44 9 E
Altun Shan, China 32 C3 38 30N 88 0 E
Alturas, U.S.A. 82 F3 41 29N 120 32W
Altus, U.S.A. 81 H5 34 38N 99 20W
Alucra, Turkey 25 F6 40 22N 38 47 E
Alūksne, Latvia 9 H22 57 24N 27 3 E
Alunite, U.S.A. 85 K12 35 59N 114 55W
Alusi, Indonesia 37 F8 7 35S 131 40 E
Alva, U.S.A. 81 G5 36 48N 98 40W
Alvarado, Mexico 87 D5 18 40N 95 50W
Alvarado, U.S.A. 81 J6 32 24N 97 13W
Alvaro Obregón, Presa, Mexico 86 B3 27 55N 109 52W
Alvear, Argentina 94 B4 29 5S 56 30W
Alvesta, Sweden 9 H16 56 54N 14 35 E
Alvin, U.S.A. 81 L7 29 26N 95 15W
Alvinston, Canada 78 D3 42 49N 81 52W
Älvkarleby, Sweden 9 F17 60 34N 17 26 E
Alvord Desert, U.S.A. 82 E4 42 30N 118 25W
Älvsbyn, Sweden 8 D19 65 40N 21 0 E
Alwar, India 42 F7 27 38N 76 34 E
Alxa Zuoqi, China 34 E3 38 50N 105 40 E
Alyangula, Australia 62 A2 13 55S 136 30 E
Alyata = Älät, Azerbaijan 25 G8 39 58N 49 25 E
Alyth, U.K. 12 E5 56 38N 3 13W
Alytus, Lithuania 9 J21 54 24N 24 3 E
Alzada, U.S.A. 80 C2 45 2N 104 25W
Alzira, Spain 19 C5 39 9N 0 30W
Am Timan, Chad 51 F10 11 0N 20 10 E
Amadeus, L., Australia 61 D5 24 54S 131 0 E
Amadi, Dem. Rep. of the Congo 54 B2 3 40N 26 40 E
Amâdi, Sudan 51 G12 5 29N 30 25 E
Amadjuak L., Canada 69 B12 65 0N 71 8W
Amagansett, U.S.A. 79 F12 40 59N 72 9W
Amagasaki, Japan 31 G7 34 42N 135 20 E
Amahai, Indonesia 37 E7 3 20S 128 55 E
Amakusa-Shotō, Japan 31 H5 32 15N 130 10 E
Åmål, Sweden 9 G15 59 3N 12 42 E
Amaliás, Greece 21 F9 37 47N 21 22 E
Amalner, India 40 J9 21 5N 75 5 E

Amamapare

Amamapare, *Indonesia* **37 E9** 4 53S 136 38 E
Amambaí, *Brazil* **95 A4** 23 5S 55 13W
Amambaí →, *Brazil* **95 A5** 23 22S 53 56W
Amambay □, *Paraguay* **95 A4** 23 0S 56 0W
Amambay, Cordillera de, *S. Amer.* **95 A4** 23 0S 55 45W
Amami-Guntō, *Japan* **31 L4** 27 16N 129 21 E
Amami-Ō-Shima, *Japan* **31 L4** 28 0N 129 0 E
Amaná, L., *Brazil* **92 D6** 2 35S 64 40W
Amanat →, *India* **43 G11** 24 7N 84 4 E
Amanda Park, *U.S.A.* **84 C3** 47 28N 123 55W
Amangeldy, *Kazakstan* **26 D7** 50 10N 65 10 E
Amapá, *Brazil* **93 C8** 2 5N 50 50W
Amapá □, *Brazil* **93 C8** 1 40N 52 0W
Amarante, *Brazil* **93 E10** 6 14S 42 50W
Amaranth, *Canada* **73 C9** 50 36N 98 43W
Amargosa →, *U.S.A.* **85 J10** 36 14N 116 51W
Amargosa Range, *U.S.A.* **85 J10** 36 20N 116 45W
Amári, *Greece* **23 D6** 35 13N 24 40 E
Amarillo, *U.S.A.* **81 H4** 35 13N 101 50W
Amarkantak, *India* **43 H9** 22 40N 81 45 E
Amaro, Mte., *Italy* **20 C6** 42 5N 14 5 E
Amarpur, *India* **43 G12** 25 5N 87 0 E
Amarwara, *India* **43 H8** 22 18N 79 10 E
Amasya □, *Turkey* **25 F6** 40 40N 35 50 E
Amata, *Australia* **61 E5** 26 9S 131 9 E
Amatikulu, *S. Africa* **57 D5** 29 3S 31 33 E
Amatitlán, *Guatemala* **88 D1** 14 29N 90 38W
Amay, *Belgium* **15 D5** 50 33N 5 19 E
Amazon = Amazonas →, *S. Amer.* **93 D9** 0 5S 50 0W
Amazonas □, *Brazil* **92 E6** 5 0S 65 0W
Amazonas →, *S. Amer.* **93 D9** 0 5S 50 0W
Ambah, *India* **42 F8** 26 43N 78 13 E
Ambahakily, *Madag.* **57 C7** 21 36S 43 41 E
Ambahita, *Madag.* **57 C8** 24 1S 45 16 E
Ambala, *India* **42 D7** 30 23N 76 56 E
Ambalavao, *Madag.* **57 C8** 21 50S 46 56 E
Ambanja, *Madag.* **57 A8** 13 40S 48 27 E
Ambararata, *Madag.* **57 B8** 15 3S 48 33 E
Ambarchik, *Russia* **27 C17** 69 40N 162 20 E
Ambarijeby, *Madag.* **57 A8** 14 56S 47 41 E
Ambaro, Helodranon', *Madag.* **57 A8** 13 23S 48 38 E
Ambato, *Ecuador* **92 D3** 1 5S 78 42W
Ambato, *Madag.* **57 A8** 13 24S 48 29 E
Ambato, Sierra de, *Argentina* **94 B2** 28 25S 66 10W
Ambato Boeny, *Madag.* **57 B8** 16 28S 46 43 E
Ambatofinandrahana, *Madag.* **57 C8** 20 33S 46 48 E
Ambatolampy, *Madag.* **57 B8** 19 20S 47 35 E
Ambatomainty, *Madag.* **57 B8** 17 41S 45 40 E
Ambatomanoina, *Madag.* **57 B8** 18 18S 47 37 E
Ambatondrazaka, *Madag.* **57 B8** 17 55S 48 28 E
Ambatosoratra, *Madag.* **57 B8** 17 37S 48 31 E
Ambenja, *Madag.* **57 B8** 15 17S 46 58 E
Amberg, *Germany* **16 D6** 49 26N 11 52 E
Ambergris Cay, *Belize* **87 D7** 18 0N 88 0W
Amberley, *N.Z.* **59 K4** 43 9S 172 44 E
Ambikapur, *India* **43 H10** 23 15N 83 15 E
Ambilobé, *Madag.* **57 A8** 13 10S 49 3 E
Ambinanindrano, *Madag.* **57 C8** 20 5S 48 23 E
Ambinanitelo, *Madag.* **57 B8** 15 21S 49 35 E
Ambinda, *Madag.* **57 B8** 16 25S 45 52 E
Amble, *U.K.* **10 B6** 55 20N 1 36W
Ambleside, *U.K.* **10 C5** 54 26N 2 58W
Ambo, *Peru* **92 F3** 10 5S 76 10W
Amboahangy, *Madag.* **57 C8** 24 15S 46 22 E
Ambodifototra, *Madag.* **57 B8** 16 59S 49 52 E
Ambodilazana, *Madag.* **57 B8** 18 6S 49 10 E
Ambodiriana, *Madag.* **57 B8** 17 55S 49 18 E
Ambohidratrimo, *Madag.* **57 B8** 18 50S 47 26 E
Ambohidray, *Madag.* **57 B8** 18 36S 48 18 E
Ambohimahamasina, *Madag.* **57 C8** 21 56S 47 11 E
Ambohimahasoa, *Madag.* **57 C8** 21 7S 47 13 E
Ambohimanga, *Madag.* **57 C8** 20 52S 47 36 E
Ambohimitombo, *Madag.* **57 C8** 20 43S 47 26 E
Ambohitra, *Madag.* **57 A8** 12 30S 49 10 E
Amboise, *France* **18 C4** 47 24N 1 2 E
Ambon, *Indonesia* **37 E7** 3 43S 128 12 E
Ambondro, *Madag.* **57 D8** 25 13S 45 44 E
Amboseli, L., *Kenya* **54 C4** 2 40S 37 10 E
Ambositra, *Madag.* **57 C8** 20 31S 47 25 E
Ambovombe, *Madag.* **57 D8** 25 11S 46 5 E
Amboy, *U.S.A.* **85 L11** 34 33N 115 45W
Amboyna Cay, *S. China Sea* **36 C4** 7 50N 112 50 E
Ambridge, *U.S.A.* **78 F4** 40 36N 80 14W
Ambriz, *Angola* **52 F2** 7 48S 13 8 E
Amchitka I., *U.S.A.* **68 C1** 51 32N 179 0 E
Amderma, *Russia* **26 C7** 69 45N 61 30 E
Amdhi, *India* **43 H9** 23 51N 81 27 E
Ameca, *Mexico* **86 C4** 20 30N 104 0W
Ameca →, *Mexico* **86 C3** 20 40N 105 15W
Amecameca, *Mexico* **87 D5** 19 7N 98 46W
Ameland, *Neths.* **15 A5** 53 27N 5 45 E
Amenia, *U.S.A.* **79 E11** 41 51N 73 33W
American Falls, *U.S.A.* **82 E7** 42 47N 112 51W
American Falls Reservoir, *U.S.A.* **82 E7** 42 47N 112 52W
American Fork, *U.S.A.* **82 F8** 40 23N 111 48W
American Highland, *Antarctica* **5 D6** 73 0S 75 0 E
American Samoa ■, *Pac. Oc.* **59 B13** 14 20S 170 40W
Americana, *Brazil* **95 A6** 22 45S 47 20W
Americus, *U.S.A.* **77 K3** 32 4N 84 14W
Amersfoort, *Neths.* **15 B5** 52 9N 5 23 E
Amersfoort, *S. Africa* **57 D4** 26 59S 29 53 E
Amery Ice Shelf, *Antarctica* **5 C6** 69 30S 72 0 E
Ames, *U.S.A.* **80 E8** 42 2N 93 37W
Amesbury, *U.S.A.* **79 D14** 42 51N 70 56W
Amet, *India* **42 G5** 25 18N 73 56 E
Amga, *Russia* **27 C14** 60 50N 132 0 E
Amga →, *Russia* **27 C14** 62 38N 134 32 E
Amgu, *Russia* **27 E14** 45 45N 137 15 E
Amgun →, *Russia* **27 D14** 52 56N 139 38 E
Amherst, *Canada* **71 C7** 45 48N 64 8W
Amherst, *Mass., U.S.A.* **79 D12** 42 23N 72 31W
Amherst, *N.Y., U.S.A.* **78 D6** 42 59N 78 48W
Amherst, *Ohio, U.S.A.* **78 E2** 41 24N 82 14W
Amherst I., *Canada* **79 B8** 44 8N 76 43W
Amherstburg, *Canada* **70 D3** 42 6N 83 6W
Amiata, Mte., *Italy* **20 C4** 42 53N 11 37 E
Amidon, *U.S.A.* **80 B3** 46 29N 103 19W
Amiens, *France* **18 B5** 49 54N 2 16 E
Aminuis, *Namibia* **56 C2** 23 43S 19 21 E
Amīrābād, *Iran* **44 C5** 33 20N 46 16 E
Amirante Is., *Seychelles* **28 K9** 6 0S 53 0 E
Amisk L., *Canada* **73 C8** 54 35N 102 15W
Amistad, Presa de la, *Mexico* **86 B4** 29 24N 101 0W
Amite, *U.S.A.* **81 K9** 30 44N 90 30W
Amla, *India* **42 J8** 21 56N 78 7 E
Amlia I., *U.S.A.* **68 C2** 52 4N 173 30W
Amlwch, *U.K.* **10 D3** 53 24N 4 20W
'Ammān, *Jordan* **47 D4** 31 57N 35 52 E
'Ammān □, *Jordan* **47 D5** 31 40N 36 30 E
Ammanford, *U.K.* **11 F4** 51 48N 3 59W
Ammassalik = Tasiilaq, *Greenland* **4 C6** 65 40N 37 20W
Ammon, *U.S.A.* **82 E8** 43 28N 111 58W
Amnat Charoen, *Thailand* **38 E5** 15 51N 104 38 E
Amnura, *Bangla.* **43 G13** 24 37N 88 25 E
Āmol, *Iran* **45 B7** 36 23N 52 20 E
Amorgós, *Greece* **21 F11** 36 50N 25 57 E
Amory, *U.S.A.* **77 J1** 33 59N 88 29W
Amos, *Canada* **70 C4** 48 35N 78 5W
Åmot, *Norway* **9 G13** 59 57N 9 54 E
Amoy = Xiamen, *China* **33 D6** 24 25N 118 4 E
Ampanavoana, *Madag.* **57 B9** 15 41S 50 22 E
Ampang, *Malaysia* **39 L3** 3 8N 101 45 E
Ampangalana, Lakandranon', *Madag.* **57 C8** 22 48S 47 50 E
Ampanihy, *Madag.* **57 C7** 24 40S 44 45 E
Amparafaravola, *Madag.* **57 B8** 17 35S 48 13 E
Ampasinambo, *Madag.* **57 C8** 20 31S 48 0 E
Ampasindava, Helodranon', *Madag.* **57 A8** 13 40S 48 15 E
Ampasindava, Saikanosy, *Madag.* **57 A8** 13 42S 47 55 E
Ampenan, *Indonesia* **36 F5** 8 35S 116 13 E
Amper →, *Germany* **16 D6** 48 29N 11 55 E
Ampitsikinana, *Réunion* **57 A8** 12 57S 49 49 E
Ampombiantambo, *Madag.* **57 A8** 12 42S 48 57 E
Ampotaka, *Madag.* **57 D7** 25 3S 44 41 E
Ampoza, *Madag.* **57 C7** 22 20S 44 44 E
Amqui, *Canada* **71 C6** 48 28N 67 27W
Amravati, *India* **40 J10** 20 55N 77 45 E
Amreli, *India* **42 J4** 21 35N 71 17 E
Amritsar, *India* **42 D6** 31 35N 74 57 E
Amroha, *India* **43 E8** 28 53N 78 30 E
Amsterdam, *Neths.* **15 B4** 52 23N 4 54 E
Amsterdam, *U.S.A.* **79 D10** 42 56N 74 11W
Amsterdam, I. = Nouvelle-Amsterdam, I., *Ind. Oc.* **3 F13** 38 30S 77 30 E
Amstetten, *Austria* **16 D8** 48 7N 14 51 E
Amudarya →, *Uzbekistan* **26 E6** 43 58N 59 34 E
Amundsen Gulf, *Canada* **68 A7** 71 0N 124 0W
Amundsen Sea, *Antarctica* **5 D15** 72 0S 115 0W
Amuntai, *Indonesia* **36 E5** 2 28S 115 25 E
Amur →, *Russia* **27 D15** 52 56N 141 10 E
Amurang, *Indonesia* **37 D6** 1 5N 124 40 E
Amursk, *Russia* **27 D14** 50 14N 136 54 E
Amyderya = Amudarya →, *Uzbekistan* **26 E6** 43 58N 59 34 E
An Bien, *Vietnam* **39 H5** 9 45N 105 0 E
An Hoa, *Vietnam* **38 E7** 15 40N 108 5 E
An Nabatīyah at Tahta, *Lebanon* **47 B4** 33 23N 35 27 E
An Nabk, *Si. Arabia* **44 D3** 31 20N 37 20 E
An Nabk, *Syria* **47 A5** 34 2N 36 44 E
An Nafūd, *Si. Arabia* **44 D4** 28 15N 41 0 E
An Najaf, *Iraq* **44 C5** 32 3N 44 15 E
An Nāşirīyah, *Iraq* **44 D5** 31 0N 46 15 E
An Nhon, *Vietnam* **38 F7** 13 55N 109 7 E
An Nu'ayrīyah, *Si. Arabia* **45 E6** 27 30N 48 30 E
An Nuwayb'ī, W. →, *Si. Arabia* **47 F3** 29 18N 34 57 E
An Thoi, Dao, *Vietnam* **39 H4** 9 58N 104 0 E
An Uaimh, *Ireland* **13 C5** 53 39N 6 41W
Anabar →, *Russia* **27 B12** 73 8N 113 36 E
'Anabtā, *West Bank* **47 C4** 32 19N 35 7 E
Anaconda, *U.S.A.* **82 C7** 46 8N 112 57W
Anacortes, *U.S.A.* **84 B4** 48 30N 122 37W
Anadarko, *U.S.A.* **81 H5** 35 4N 98 15W
Anadolu, *Turkey* **25 G5** 39 0N 30 0 E
Anadyr, *Russia* **27 C18** 64 35N 177 20 E
Anadyr →, *Russia* **27 C18** 64 55N 176 5 E
Anadyrskiy Zaliv, *Russia* **27 C19** 64 0N 180 0 E
Anaga, Pta. de, *Canary Is.* **22 F3** 28 34N 16 9W
'Ānah, *Iraq* **44 C4** 34 25N 42 0 E
Anaheim, *U.S.A.* **85 M9** 33 50N 117 55W
Anahim Lake, *Canada* **72 C3** 52 28N 125 18W
Anáhuac, *Mexico* **86 B4** 27 14N 100 9W
Anakapalle, *India* **41 L13** 17 42N 83 6 E
Anakie, *Australia* **62 C4** 23 32S 147 45 E
Analalava, *Madag.* **57 A8** 14 35S 48 0 E
Analavoka, *Madag.* **57 C8** 22 23S 46 30 E
Análipsis, *Greece* **23 A3** 39 36N 19 55 E
Anambar →, *Pakistan* **42 D3** 30 15N 68 50 E
Anambas, Kepulauan, *Indonesia* **39 L6** 3 20N 106 30 E
Anambas Is. = Anambas, Kepulauan, *Indonesia* **39 L6** 3 20N 106 30 E
Anamosa, *U.S.A.* **80 D9** 42 7N 91 17W
Anamur, *Turkey* **25 G5** 36 8N 32 58 E
Anan, *Japan* **31 H7** 33 54N 134 40 E
Anand, *India* **42 H5** 22 32N 72 59 E
Anantnag, *India* **43 C6** 33 45N 75 10 E
Ananyiv, *Ukraine* **17 E15** 47 44N 29 58 E
Anapodháris →, *Greece* **23 E7** 34 59N 25 20 E
Anápolis, *Brazil* **93 G9** 16 15S 48 50W
Anapu →, *Brazil* **93 D8** 1 53S 50 53W
Anār, *Iran* **45 D7** 30 55N 55 13 E
Anārak, *Iran* **45 C7** 33 25N 53 40 E
Anas →, *India* **42 H5** 23 26N 74 0 E
Anatolia = Anadolu, *Turkey* **25 G5** 39 0N 30 0 E
Anatsogno, *Madag.* **57 C7** 23 33S 43 46 E
Añatuya, *Argentina* **94 B3** 28 20S 62 50W
Anaunethad L., *Canada* **73 A8** 60 55N 104 25W
Anbyŏn, *N. Korea* **35 E14** 39 1N 127 35 E
Ancaster, *Canada* **78 C5** 43 13N 79 59W
Anchor Bay, *U.S.A.* **84 G3** 38 48N 123 34W
Anchorage, *U.S.A.* **68 B5** 61 13N 149 54W
Anci, *China* **34 E9** 39 20N 116 40 E
Ancohuma, Nevada, *Bolivia* **92 G5** 16 0S 68 50W
Ancón, *Peru* **92 F3** 11 50S 77 10W
Ancona, *Italy* **20 C5** 43 38N 13 30 E
Ancud, *Chile* **96 E2** 42 0S 73 50W
Ancud, G. de, *Chile* **96 E2** 42 0S 73 0W
Anda, *China* **33 B7** 46 24N 125 19 E
Andacollo, *Argentina* **94 D1** 37 10S 70 42W
Andacollo, *Chile* **94 C1** 30 14S 71 6W
Andaingo, *Madag.* **57 B8** 18 12S 48 17 E
Andalgalá, *Argentina* **94 B2** 27 40S 66 30W
Åndalsnes, *Norway* **9 E12** 62 35N 7 43 E
Andalucía □, *Spain* **19 D3** 37 35N 5 0W
Andalusia = Andalucía □, *Spain* **19 D3** 37 35N 5 0W
Andalusia, *U.S.A.* **77 K2** 31 18N 86 29W
Andaman Is., *Ind. Oc.* **29 H13** 12 30N 92 30 E
Andaman Sea, *Ind. Oc.* **36 B1** 13 0N 96 0 E
Andamooka Opal Fields, *Australia* **63 E2** 30 27S 137 9 E
Andapa, *Madag.* **57 A8** 14 39S 49 39 E
Andara, *Namibia* **56 B3** 18 2S 21 9 E
Andenes, *Norway* **8 B17** 69 19N 16 18 E
Andenne, *Belgium* **15 D5** 50 28N 5 5 E
Anderson, *Alaska, U.S.A.* **68 B5** 64 25N 149 15W
Anderson, *Calif., U.S.A.* **82 F2** 40 27N 122 18W
Anderson, *Ind., U.S.A.* **76 E3** 40 10N 85 41W
Anderson, *Mo., U.S.A.* **81 G7** 36 39N 94 27W
Anderson, *S.C., U.S.A.* **77 H4** 34 31N 82 39W
Anderson →, *Canada* **68 B7** 69 42N 129 0W
Andes, *U.S.A.* **79 D10** 42 12N 74 47W
Andes, Cord. de los, *S. Amer.* **92 H5** 20 0S 68 0W
Andfjorden, *Norway* **8 B17** 69 10N 16 20 E
Andhra Pradesh □, *India* **40 L11** 18 0N 79 0 E
Andijon, *Uzbekistan* **26 E8** 41 10N 72 15 E
Andikíthira, *Greece* **21 G10** 35 52N 23 15 E
Andilamena, *Madag.* **57 B8** 17 1S 48 35 E
Andīmeshk, *Iran* **45 C6** 32 27N 48 21 E
Andizhan = Andijon, *Uzbekistan* **26 E8** 41 10N 72 15 E
Andoany, *Madag.* **57 A8** 13 25S 48 16 E
Andong, *S. Korea* **35 F15** 36 40N 128 43 E
Andongwei, *China* **35 G10** 35 6N 119 20 E
Andoom, *Australia* **62 A3** 12 25S 141 53 E
Andorra ■, *Europe* **18 E4** 42 30N 1 30 E
Andorra La Vella, *Andorra* **18 E4** 42 31N 1 32 E
Andover, *U.K.* **11 F6** 51 12N 1 29W
Andover, *Maine, U.S.A.* **79 B14** 44 38N 70 45W
Andover, *Mass., U.S.A.* **79 D13** 42 40N 71 8W
Andover, *N.J., U.S.A.* **79 F10** 40 59N 74 45W
Andover, *N.Y., U.S.A.* **78 D7** 42 10N 77 48W
Andover, *Ohio, U.S.A.* **78 E4** 41 36N 80 34W
Andøya, *Norway* **8 B16** 69 10N 15 50 E
Andradina, *Brazil* **93 H8** 20 54S 51 23W
Andrahary, Mt., *Madag.* **57 A8** 13 37S 49 17 E
Andramasina, *Madag.* **57 B8** 19 11S 47 35 E
Andranopasy, *Madag.* **57 C7** 21 17S 43 44 E
Andranovory, *Madag.* **57 C7** 23 8S 44 10 E
Andratx, *Spain* **22 B9** 39 39N 2 25 E
Andreanof Is., *U.S.A.* **68 C2** 51 30N 176 0W
Andrews, *S.C., U.S.A.* **77 J6** 33 27N 79 34W
Andrews, *Tex., U.S.A.* **81 J3** 32 19N 102 33W
Ándria, *Italy* **20 D7** 41 13N 16 17 E
Andriamena, *Madag.* **57 B8** 17 26S 47 30 E
Andriandampy, *Madag.* **57 C8** 22 45S 45 41 E
Andriba, *Madag.* **57 B8** 17 30S 46 58 E
Androka, *Madag.* **57 C7** 24 58S 44 2 E
Andropov = Rybinsk, *Russia* **24 C6** 58 5N 38 50 E
Ándros, *Greece* **21 F11** 37 50N 24 57 E
Andros I., *Bahamas* **88 B4** 24 30N 78 0W
Andros Town, *Bahamas* **88 B4** 24 43N 77 47W
Androscoggin →, *U.S.A.* **79 C14** 43 58N 70 0W
Andselv, *Norway* **8 B18** 69 4N 18 34 E
Andújar, *Spain* **19 C3** 38 3N 4 5W
Andulo, *Angola* **52 G3** 11 25S 16 45 E
Anegada I., *U.S. Virgin Is.* **89 C7** 18 45N 64 20W
Anegada Passage, *W. Indies* **89 C7** 18 15N 63 45W
Aneto, Pico de, *Spain* **19 A6** 42 37N 0 40 E
Ang Thong, *Thailand* **38 E3** 14 35N 100 31 E
Angamos, Punta, *Chile* **94 A1** 23 1S 70 32W
Angara →, *Russia* **27 D10** 58 5N 94 20 E
Angarsk, *Russia* **27 D11** 52 30N 104 0 E
Angas Hills, *Australia* **60 D4** 23 0S 127 50 E
Angaur I., *Pac. Oc.* **37 C8** 6 54N 134 9 E
Ånge, *Sweden* **9 E16** 62 31N 15 35 E
Ángel, Salto = Angel Falls, *Venezuela* **92 B6** 5 57N 62 30W
Ángel de la Guarda, I., *Mexico* **86 B2** 29 30N 113 30W
Angel Falls, *Venezuela* **92 B6** 5 57N 62 30W
Angeles, *Phil.* **37 A6** 15 9N 120 33 E
Ängelholm, *Sweden* **9 H15** 56 15N 12 58 E
Angels Camp, *U.S.A.* **84 G6** 38 4N 120 32W
Ångermanälven →, *Sweden* **8 E17** 62 40N 18 0 E
Ångermanland, *Sweden* **8 E18** 63 36N 17 45 E
Angers, *Canada* **79 A9** 45 31N 75 29W
Angers, *France* **18 C3** 47 30N 0 35W
Ängesån →, *Sweden* **8 C20** 66 16N 22 47 E
Angikuni L., *Canada* **73 A9** 62 0N 100 0W
Angkor, *Cambodia* **38 F4** 13 22N 103 50 E
Anglesey, Isle of □, *U.K.* **10 D3** 53 16N 4 18W
Angleton, *U.S.A.* **81 L7** 29 10N 95 26W
Anglisidhes, *Cyprus* **23 E12** 34 51N 33 27 E
Angmagssalik = Tasiilaq, *Greenland* **4 C6** 65 40N 37 20W
Ango, *Dem. Rep. of the Congo* **54 B2** 4 10N 26 5 E
Angoche, *Mozam.* **55 F4** 16 8S 39 55 E
Angoche, I., *Mozam.* **55 F4** 16 20S 39 50 E
Angol, *Chile* **94 D1** 37 56S 72 45W
Angola, *Ind., U.S.A.* **76 E3** 41 38N 85 0W
Angola, *N.Y., U.S.A.* **78 D5** 42 38N 79 2W
Angola ■, *Africa* **53 G3** 12 0S 18 0 E
Angoulême, *France* **18 D4** 45 39N 0 10 E
Angoumois, *France* **18 D3** 45 50N 0 25 E
Angra dos Reis, *Brazil* **95 A7** 23 0S 44 10W
Angren, *Uzbekistan* **26 E8** 41 1N 70 12 E
Angtassom, *Cambodia* **39 G5** 11 1N 104 41 E
Angu, *Dem. Rep. of the Congo* **54 B1** 3 23N 24 30 E
Anguang, *China* **35 B12** 45 15N 123 45 E
Anguilla ■, *W. Indies* **89 C7** 18 14N 63 5W
Anguo, *China* **34 E8** 38 28N 115 15 E
Angurugu, *Australia* **62 A2** 14 0S 136 25 E
Angus □, *U.K.* **12 E6** 56 46N 2 56W
Angwa →, *Zimbabwe* **57 B5** 16 0S 30 23 E
Anhanduí →, *Brazil* **95 A5** 21 46S 52 9W
Anholt, *Denmark* **9 H14** 56 42N 11 33 E
Anhui □, *China* **33 C6** 32 0N 117 0 E
Anhwei = Anhui □, *China* **33 C6** 32 0N 117 0 E
Anichab, *Namibia* **56 C1** 21 0S 14 46 E
Animas →, *U.S.A.* **83 H9** 36 43N 108 13W
Anivorano, *Madag.* **57 B8** 18 44S 48 58 E
Anjalankoski, *Finland* **9 F22** 60 45N 26 51 E
Anjar, *India* **42 H4** 23 6N 70 10 E
Anjou, *France* **18 C3** 47 20N 0 15W
Anjozorobe, *Madag.* **57 B8** 18 22S 47 52 E
Anju, *N. Korea* **35 E13** 39 36N 125 40 E
Ankaboa, Tanjona, *Madag.* **57 C7** 21 58S 43 20 E
Ankang, *China* **34 H5** 32 40N 109 1 E
Ankara, *Turkey* **25 G5** 39 57N 32 54 E
Ankaramena, *Madag.* **57 C8** 21 57S 46 39 E
Ankaratra, *Madag.* **53 H9** 19 25S 47 12 E
Ankasakasa, *Madag.* **57 B7** 16 21S 44 52 E
Ankavandra, *Madag.* **57 B8** 18 46S 45 18 E
Ankazoabo, *Madag.* **57 C7** 22 18S 44 31 E
Ankazobe, *Madag.* **57 B8** 18 20S 47 10 E
Ankeny, *U.S.A.* **80 E8** 41 44N 93 36W
Ankilimalinika, *Madag.* **57 C7** 22 58S 43 45 E
Ankilizato, *Madag.* **57 C8** 20 25S 45 1 E
Ankisabe, *Madag.* **57 B8** 19 17S 46 29 E
Ankoro, *Dem. Rep. of the Congo* **54 D2** 6 45S 26 55 E
Ankororoka, *Madag.* **57 D8** 25 30S 45 11 E
Anmyŏn-do, *S. Korea* **35 F14** 36 25N 126 25 E
Ann, C., *U.S.A.* **79 D14** 42 38N 70 35W
Ann Arbor, *U.S.A.* **76 D4** 42 17N 83 45W
Anna, *U.S.A.* **81 G10** 37 28N 89 15W
Annaba, *Algeria* **50 A7** 36 50N 7 46 E
Annalee →, *Ireland* **13 B4** 54 2N 7 24W
Annam, *Vietnam* **38 E7** 16 0N 108 0 E
Annamitique, Chaîne, *Asia* **38 D6** 17 0N 106 0 E
Annan, *U.K.* **12 G5** 54 59N 3 16W
Annan →, *U.K.* **12 G5** 54 58N 3 16W
Annapolis, *U.S.A.* **76 F7** 38 59N 76 30W
Annapolis Royal, *Canada* **71 D6** 44 44N 65 32W
Annapurna, *Nepal* **43 E10** 28 34N 83 50 E
Annean, L., *Australia* **61 E2** 26 54S 118 14 E
Annecy, *France* **18 D7** 45 55N 6 8 E
Anning, *China* **32 D5** 24 55N 102 26 E
Anniston, *U.S.A.* **77 J3** 33 39N 85 50W
Annobón, *Atl. Oc.* **49 G4** 1 25S 5 36 E
Annotto Bay, *Jamaica* **88 C4** 18 17N 76 45W
Annville, *U.S.A.* **79 F8** 40 20N 76 31W
Áno Viánnos, *Greece* **23 D7** 35 2N 25 21 E
Anorotsangana, *Madag.* **57 A8** 13 56S 47 55 E
Anosibe, *Madag.* **57 B8** 19 26S 48 13 E
Anóyia, *Greece* **23 D6** 35 16N 24 52 E
Anping, *Hebei, China* **34 E8** 38 15N 115 30 E
Anping, *Liaoning, China* **35 D12** 41 5N 123 30 E
Anqing, *China* **33 C6** 30 30N 117 3 E
Anqiu, *China* **35 F10** 36 25N 119 10 E
Ansai, *China* **34 F5** 36 50N 109 20 E
Ansbach, *Germany* **16 D6** 49 28N 10 34 E
Anshan, *China* **35 D12** 41 5N 122 58 E
Anshun, *China* **32 D5** 26 18N 105 57 E
Ansley, *U.S.A.* **80 E5** 41 18N 99 23W
Anson, *U.S.A.* **81 J5** 32 45N 99 54W
Anson B., *Australia* **60 B5** 13 20S 130 6 E
Ansongo, *Mali* **50 E6** 15 25N 0 35 E
Ansonia, *U.S.A.* **79 E11** 41 21N 73 5W
Anstruther, *U.K.* **12 E6** 56 14N 2 41W
Ansudu, *Indonesia* **37 E9** 2 11S 139 22 E
Antabamba, *Peru* **92 F4** 14 40S 73 0W
Antakya, *Turkey* **25 G6** 36 14N 36 10 E
Antalaha, *Madag.* **57 A9** 14 57S 50 20 E
Antalya, *Turkey* **25 G5** 36 52N 30 45 E
Antalya Körfezi, *Turkey* **25 G5** 36 15N 31 30 E
Antambohobe, *Madag.* **57 C8** 22 20S 46 47 E
Antanambao-Manampotsy, *Madag.* **57 B8** 19 29S 48 34 E
Antanambe, *Madag.* **57 B8** 16 26S 49 52 E
Antananarivo, *Madag.* **57 B8** 18 55S 47 31 E
Antananarivo □, *Madag.* **57 B8** 19 0S 47 0 E
Antanifotsy, *Madag.* **57 B8** 19 39S 47 19 E
Antanimbaribe, *Madag.* **57 C7** 21 30S 44 48 E
Antanimora, *Madag.* **57 C8** 24 49S 45 40 E
Antarctic Pen., *Antarctica* **5 C18** 67 0S 60 0W
Antarctica **5 E3** 90 0S 0 0W
Antelope, *Zimbabwe* **55 G2** 21 2S 28 31 E
Antequera, *Paraguay* **94 A4** 24 8S 57 7W
Antequera, *Spain* **19 D3** 37 5N 4 33W
Antero, Mt., *U.S.A.* **83 G10** 38 41N 106 15W
Antevamena, *Madag.* **57 C7** 21 2S 44 8 E
Anthony, *Kans., U.S.A.* **81 G5** 37 9N 98 2W
Anthony, *N. Mex., U.S.A.* **83 K10** 32 0N 106 36W
Anti Atlas, *Morocco* **50 C4** 30 0N 8 30W
Anti-Lebanon = Ash Sharqi, Al Jabal, *Lebanon* **47 B5** 33 40N 36 10 E
Antibes, *France* **18 E7** 43 34N 7 6 E
Anticosti, Î. d', *Canada* **71 C7** 49 30N 63 0W
Antigo, *U.S.A.* **80 C10** 45 9N 89 9W
Antigonish, *Canada* **71 C7** 45 38N 61 58W
Antigua, *Canary Is.* **22 F5** 28 24N 14 1W
Antigua, *W. Indies* **89 C7** 17 0N 61 50W
Antigua & Barbuda ■, *W. Indies* **89 C7** 17 20N 61 48W
Antigua Guatemala, *Guatemala* **88 D1** 14 34N 90 41W
Antilla, *Cuba* **88 B4** 20 40N 75 50W
Antilles = West Indies, *Cent. Amer.* **89 D7** 15 0N 65 0W
Antioch, *U.S.A.* **84 G5** 38 1N 121 48W
Antioquia, *Colombia* **92 B3** 6 40N 75 55W
Antipodes Is., *Pac. Oc.* **64 M9** 49 45S 178 40 E
Antlers, *U.S.A.* **81 H7** 34 14N 95 37W
Antoetra, *Madag.* **57 C8** 20 46S 47 20 E
Antofagasta, *Chile* **94 A1** 23 50S 70 30W
Antofagasta □, *Chile* **94 A2** 24 0S 69 0W
Antofagasta de la Sierra, *Argentina* **94 B2** 26 5S 67 20W
Antofalla, *Argentina* **94 B2** 25 30S 68 5W
Antofalla, Salar de, *Argentina* **94 B2** 25 40S 67 45W
Anton, *U.S.A.* **81 J3** 33 49N 102 10W
Antongila, Helodrano, *Madag.* **57 B8** 15 30S 49 50 E
Antonibé, *Madag.* **57 B8** 15 7S 47 24 E
Antonibé, Presqu'île d', *Madag.* **57 A8** 14 55S 47 20 E
Antonina, *Brazil* **95 B6** 25 26S 48 42W
Antrim, *U.K.* **13 B5** 54 43N 6 14W
Antrim, *U.S.A.* **78 F3** 40 7N 81 21W
Antrim □, *U.K.* **13 B5** 54 56N 6 25W
Antrim, Mts. of, *U.K.* **13 A5** 55 3N 6 14W
Antrim Plateau, *Australia* **60 C4** 18 8S 128 20 E
Antsakabary, *Madag.* **57 B8** 15 3S 48 56 E
Antsalova, *Madag.* **57 B7** 18 40S 44 37 E

Ashland

Antsenavolo, Madag. 57 C8 21 24S 48 3 E
Antsiafabositra, Madag. 57 B8 17 18S 46 57 E
Antsirabe, Antananarivo, Madag. 57 B8 19 55S 47 2 E
Antsirabe, Antsiranana, Madag. 57 A8 14 0S 49 59 E
Antsirabe, Mahajanga, Madag. 57 B8 15 57S 48 58 E
Antsiranana, Madag. 57 A8 12 25S 49 20 E
Antsiranana □, Madag. 57 A8 12 16S 49 17 E
Antsohihy, Madag. 57 A8 14 50S 47 59 E
Antsohimbondrona Seranana, Madag. 57 A8 13 7S 48 48 E
Antu, China 35 C15 42 30N 128 20 E
Antwerp = Antwerpen, Belgium 15 C4 51 13N 4 25 E
Antwerp, U.S.A. 79 B9 44 12N 75 37W
Antwerpen, Belgium 15 C4 51 13N 4 25 E
Antwerpen □, Belgium 15 C4 51 15N 4 40 E
Anupgarh, India 42 E5 29 10N 73 10 E
Anuppur, India 43 H9 23 6N 81 41 E
Anuradhapura, Sri Lanka 40 Q12 8 22N 80 28 E
Anveh, Iran 45 E7 27 23N 54 11 E
Anvers = Antwerpen, Belgium 15 C4 51 13N 4 25 E
Anvers I., Antarctica 5 C17 64 30S 63 40W
Anxi, China 32 B4 40 30N 95 43 E
Anxious B., Australia 63 E1 33 24S 134 45 E
Anyang, China 34 F8 36 5N 114 21 E
Anyer-Kidul, Indonesia 37 G11 6 4S 105 53 E
Anyi, China 34 G6 35 2N 111 2 E
Anza, U.S.A. 85 M10 33 35N 116 39W
Anze, China 34 F7 36 10N 112 12 E
Anzhero-Sudzhensk, Russia 26 D9 56 10N 86 0 E
Ánzio, Italy 20 D5 41 27N 12 37 E
Aoga-Shima, Japan 31 H9 32 28N 139 46 E
Aomen = Macau □, China 33 D6 22 16N 113 35 E
Aomori, Japan 30 D10 40 45N 140 45 E
Aomori □, Japan 30 D10 40 45N 140 40 E
Aonla, India 43 E8 28 16N 79 11 E
Aoraki Mount Cook, N.Z. 59 K3 43 36S 170 9 E
Aosta, Italy 18 D7 45 45N 7 20 E
Aoukâr, Mauritania 50 E4 17 40N 10 0W
Apa →, S. Amer. 94 A4 22 6S 58 2W
Apache, U.S.A. 81 H5 34 54N 98 22W
Apache Junction, U.S.A. 83 K8 33 25N 111 33W
Apalachee B., U.S.A. 77 L4 30 0N 84 0W
Apalachicola, U.S.A. 77 L3 29 43N 84 59W
Apalachicola →, U.S.A. 77 L3 29 43N 84 58W
Apaporis →, Colombia 92 D5 1 23S 69 25W
Aparri, Phil. 37 A6 18 22N 121 38 E
Apatity, Russia 24 A5 67 34N 33 22 E
Apatzingán, Mexico 86 D4 19 0N 102 20W
Apeldoorn, Neths. 15 B5 52 13N 5 57 E
Apennines = Appennini, Italy 20 B4 44 0N 10 0 E
Apia, Samoa 59 A13 13 50S 171 50W
Apiacás, Serra dos, Brazil 92 E7 9 50S 57 0W
Apies →, S. Africa 57 D4 25 15S 28 8 E
Apizaco, Mexico 87 D5 19 26N 98 9W
Aplao, Peru 92 G4 16 0S 72 40W
Apo, Mt., Phil. 37 C7 6 53N 125 14 E
Apolakkiá, Greece 23 C9 36 5N 27 48 E
Apolakkiá, Órmos, Greece 23 C9 36 5N 27 45 E
Apolo, Bolivia 92 F5 14 30S 68 30W
Aporé →, Brazil 93 G8 19 27S 50 57W
Apostle Is., U.S.A. 80 B9 47 0N 90 40W
Apóstoles, Argentina 95 B4 28 0S 56 0W
Apostolos Andreas, C., Cyprus 23 D13 35 42N 34 35 E
Apoteri, Guyana 92 C7 4 2N 58 32W
Appalachian Mts., U.S.A. 76 G6 38 0N 80 0W
Appennini, Italy 20 B4 44 0N 10 0 E
Apple Hill, Canada 79 A10 45 13N 74 46W
Apple Valley, U.S.A. 85 L9 34 32N 117 14W
Appleby-in-Westmorland, U.K. 10 C5 54 35N 2 29W
Appleton, U.S.A. 76 C1 44 16N 88 25W
Approuague →, Fr. Guiana 93 C8 4 30N 51 57W
Aprília, Italy 20 D5 41 36N 12 39 E
Apsley, Canada 78 B6 44 45N 78 6W
Apucarana, Brazil 95 A5 23 55S 51 33W
Apure →, Venezuela 92 B5 7 37N 66 25W
Apurimac →, Peru 92 F4 12 17S 73 56W
Āqā Jari, Iran 45 D6 30 42N 49 50 E
Aqaba = Al 'Aqabah, Jordan 47 F4 29 31N 35 0 E
Aqaba, G. of, Red Sea 44 D2 28 15N 33 20 E
'Aqabah, Khalīj al = Aqaba, G. of, Red Sea 44 D2 28 15N 33 20 E
'Aqdā, Iran 45 C7 32 26N 53 37 E
Aqmola = Astana, Kazakstan 26 D8 51 10N 71 30 E
'Aqrah, Iraq 44 B4 36 46N 43 45 E
Aqtaū, Kazakstan 26 E6 43 39N 51 12 E
Aqtöbe, Kazakstan 25 D10 50 17N 57 10 E
Aquidauana, Brazil 93 H7 20 30S 55 50W
Aquiles Serdán, Mexico 86 B3 28 37N 105 54W
Aquin, Haiti 89 C5 18 16N 73 24W
Aquitain, Bassin, France 18 D3 44 0N 0 30W
Aqviligjuaq = Pelly Bay, Canada 69 B11 68 38N 89 50W
Ar Rachidiya = Er Rachidia, Morocco 50 B5 31 58N 4 20W
Ar Rafid, Syria 47 C4 32 57N 35 52 E
Ar Rahhālīyah, Iraq 44 C4 32 44N 43 23 E
Ar Ramādī, Iraq 44 C4 33 25N 43 20 E
Ar Ramthā, Jordan 47 C5 32 34N 36 0 E
Ar Raqqah, Syria 44 C3 35 59N 39 8 E
Ar Rass, Si. Arabia 44 E4 25 50N 43 40 E
Ar Rifā'ī, Iraq 44 D5 31 50N 46 10 E
Ar Riyāḍ, Si. Arabia 46 C4 24 41N 46 42 E
Ar Ru'ays, Qatar 45 E6 26 8N 51 12 E
Ar Rukhaymīyah, Iraq 44 D5 29 22N 45 38 E
Ar Ruṣāfah, Syria 44 C3 35 45N 38 49 E
Ar Ruṭbah, Iraq 44 C4 33 0N 40 15 E
Ara, India 43 G11 25 35N 84 32 E
Arab, U.S.A. 77 H2 34 19N 86 30W
'Arab, Bahr el →, Sudan 51 G11 9 0N 29 30 E
Arab, Shatt al →, Asia 45 D6 30 0N 48 31 E
'Arabābād, Iran 45 C8 33 2N 57 41 E
Arabia, Asia 28 G8 25 0N 45 0 E
Arabian Desert = Es Sahrâ' Esh Sharqîya, Egypt 51 C12 27 30N 32 30 E
Arabian Gulf = Gulf, The, Asia 45 E6 27 0N 50 0 E
Arabian Sea, Ind. Oc. 29 H10 16 0N 65 0 E
Aracaju, Brazil 93 F11 10 55S 37 4W
Aracati, Brazil 93 D11 4 30S 37 44W
Araçatuba, Brazil 95 A5 21 10S 50 30W
Aracena, Spain 19 D2 37 53N 6 38W
Araçuaí, Brazil 93 G10 16 52S 42 4W
'Arad, Israel 47 D4 31 15N 35 12 E
Arad, Romania 17 E11 46 10N 21 20 E
Arādān, Iran 45 C7 35 21N 52 30 E
Aradhippou, Cyprus 23 E12 34 57N 33 36 E
Arafura Sea, E. Indies 28 K17 9 0S 135 0 E
Aragón □, Spain 19 B5 41 25N 0 40W
Aragón →, Spain 19 A5 42 13N 1 44W
Araguacema, Brazil 93 E9 8 50S 49 20W
Araguaia →, Brazil 93 E9 5 21S 48 41W
Araguaína, Brazil 93 E9 7 12S 48 12W
Araguari, Brazil 93 G9 18 38S 48 11W
Araguari →, Brazil 93 C9 1 15N 49 55W
Arain, India 42 F6 26 27N 75 2 E
Arak, Algeria 50 C6 25 20N 3 45 E
Arāk, Iran 45 C6 34 0N 49 40 E
Arakan Coast, Burma 41 K19 19 0N 94 0 E
Arakan Yoma, Burma 41 K19 20 0N 94 40 E
Araks = Aras, Rūd-e →, Asia 44 B5 40 5N 48 29 E
Aral, Kazakstan 26 E7 46 41N 61 45 E
Aral Sea, Asia 26 E7 44 30N 60 0 E
Aral Tengizi = Aral Sea, Asia 26 E7 44 30N 60 0 E
Aralsk = Aral, Kazakstan 26 E7 46 41N 61 45 E
Aralskoye More = Aral Sea, Asia 26 E7 44 30N 60 0 E
Aramac, Australia 62 C4 22 58S 145 14 E
Aran I., Ireland 13 A3 55 0N 8 30W
Aran Is., Ireland 13 C2 53 6N 9 38W
Aranda de Duero, Spain 19 B4 41 39N 3 42W
Arandān, Iran 44 C5 35 23N 46 55 E
Aranjuez, Spain 19 B4 40 1N 3 40W
Aranos, Namibia 56 C2 24 9S 19 7 E
Aransas Pass, U.S.A. 81 M6 27 55N 97 9W
Aranyaprathet, Thailand 38 F4 13 41N 102 30 E
Arapahoe, U.S.A. 80 E5 40 18N 99 54W
Arapey Grande →, Uruguay 94 C4 30 55S 57 49W
Arapgir, Turkey 44 B3 39 5N 38 30 E
Arapiraca, Brazil 93 E11 9 45S 36 39W
Arapongas, Brazil 95 A5 23 29S 51 28W
Ar'ar, Si. Arabia 44 D4 30 59N 41 2 E
Araranguá, Brazil 95 B6 29 0S 49 30W
Araraquara, Brazil 93 H9 21 50S 48 0W
Ararás, Serra das, Brazil 95 B5 25 0S 53 10W
Ararat, Mt. = Ağrı Dağı, Turkey 25 G7 39 50N 44 15 E
Araria, India 43 F12 26 9N 87 33 E
Araripe, Chapada do, Brazil 93 E11 7 20S 40 0W
Araruama, L. de, Brazil 95 A7 22 53S 42 12W
Aras, Rūd-e →, Asia 44 B5 40 5N 48 29 E
Arauca, Colombia 92 B4 7 0N 70 40W
Arauca →, Venezuela 92 B5 7 24N 66 35W
Arauco, Chile 94 D1 37 16S 73 25W
Araxá, Brazil 93 G9 19 35S 46 55W
Araya, Pen. de, Venezuela 92 A6 10 40N 64 0W
Arba Minch, Ethiopia 46 F2 6 0N 37 30 E
Arbat, Iraq 44 C5 35 25N 45 35 E
Árbatax, Italy 20 E3 39 56N 9 42 E
Arbīl, Iraq 44 B5 36 15N 44 5 E
Arborfield, Canada 73 C8 53 6N 103 39W
Arborg, Canada 73 C9 50 54N 97 13W
Arbroath, U.K. 12 E6 56 34N 2 35W
Arbuckle, U.S.A. 84 F4 39 1N 122 3W
Arcachon, France 18 D3 44 40N 1 10W
Arcade, Calif., U.S.A. 85 L8 34 2N 118 15W
Arcade, N.Y., U.S.A. 78 D6 42 32N 78 25W
Arcadia, Fla., U.S.A. 77 M5 27 13N 81 52W
Arcadia, La., U.S.A. 81 J8 32 33N 92 55W
Arcadia, Pa., U.S.A. 78 F6 40 47N 78 51W
Arcata, U.S.A. 82 F1 40 52N 124 5W
Archangel = Arkhangelsk, Russia 24 B7 64 38N 40 36 E
Archbald, U.S.A. 79 E9 41 30N 75 32W
Archer →, Australia 62 A3 13 28S 141 41 E
Archer B., Australia 62 A3 13 20S 141 30 E
Archers Post, Kenya 54 B4 0 35N 37 35 E
Arches National Park, U.S.A. 83 G9 38 45N 109 25W
Arckaringa Cr. →, Australia 63 D2 28 10S 135 22 E
Arco, U.S.A. 82 E7 43 38N 113 18W
Arcos de la Frontera, Spain 19 D3 36 45N 5 49W
Arcot, India 40 N11 12 53N 79 20 E
Arctic Bay, Canada 69 A11 73 1N 85 7W
Arctic Ocean, Arctic 4 B18 78 0N 160 0W
Arctic Red River = Tsiigehtchic, Canada 68 B6 67 15N 134 0W
Arda →, Bulgaria 21 D12 41 40N 26 30 E
Ardabīl, Iran 45 B6 38 15N 48 18 E
Ardakān = Sepīdān, Iran 45 D7 30 20N 52 5 E
Ardakān, Iran 45 C7 32 19N 53 59 E
Ardee, Ireland 13 C5 53 52N 6 33W
Arden, Canada 78 B8 44 43N 76 56W
Arden, Calif., U.S.A. 84 G5 38 36N 121 33W
Arden, Nev., U.S.A. 85 J11 36 1N 115 14W
Ardenne, Belgium 16 D3 49 50N 5 5 E
Ardennes = Ardenne, Belgium 16 D3 49 50N 5 5 E
Arderin, Ireland 13 C4 53 2N 7 39W
Ardestān, Iran 45 C7 33 20N 52 25 E
Ardivachar Pt., U.K. 12 D1 57 23N 7 26W
Ardmore, Okla., U.S.A. 81 H6 34 10N 97 8W
Ardmore, Pa., U.S.A. 79 G9 39 58N 75 18W
Ardnamurchan, Pt. of, U.K. 12 E2 56 43N 6 14W
Ardnave Pt., U.K. 12 F2 55 53N 6 20W
Ardrossan, U.K. 12 F4 55 39N 4 49W
Ards Pen., U.K. 13 B6 54 33N 5 34W
Arecibo, Puerto Rico 89 C6 18 29N 66 43W
Areia Branca, Brazil 93 E11 5 0S 37 0W
Arena, Pt., U.S.A. 84 G3 38 57N 123 44W
Arenal, Honduras 88 C2 15 21N 86 50W
Arendal, Norway 9 G13 58 28N 8 46 E
Arequipa, Peru 92 G4 16 20S 71 30W
Arévalo, Spain 19 B3 41 3N 4 43W
Arezzo, Italy 20 C4 43 25N 11 53 E
Arga, Turkey 44 B3 38 21N 37 59 E
Arganda, Spain 19 B4 40 19N 3 26W
Argenta, Canada 72 C5 50 11N 116 56W
Argentan, France 18 B4 48 45N 0 1W
Argentário, Mte., Italy 20 C4 42 24N 11 9 E
Argentia, Canada 71 C9 47 18N 53 58W
Argentina ■, S. Amer. 96 D3 35 0S 66 0W
Argentina Is., Antarctica 5 C17 66 0S 64 0W
Argentino, L., Argentina 96 G2 50 10S 73 0W
Argeş →, Romania 17 F14 44 5N 26 38 E
Arghandab →, Afghan. 42 D1 31 30N 64 15 E
Argolikós Kólpos, Greece 21 F10 37 20N 22 52 E
Árgos, Greece 21 F10 37 40N 22 43 E
Argostólion, Greece 21 E9 38 12N 20 33 E
Arguello, Pt., U.S.A. 85 L6 34 35N 120 39W
Arguineguín, Canary Is. 22 G4 27 46N 15 41W
Argun →, Russia 27 D13 53 20N 121 28 E
Argus Pk., U.S.A. 85 K9 35 52N 117 26W
Argyle, L., Australia 60 C4 16 20S 128 40 E
Argyll & Bute □, U.K. 12 E3 56 13N 5 28W
Århus, Denmark 9 H14 56 8N 10 11 E
Ariadnoye, Russia 30 B7 45 8N 134 25 E
Ariamsvlei, Namibia 56 D2 28 9S 19 51 E
Arica, Chile 92 G4 18 32S 70 20W
Arica, Colombia 92 D4 2 0S 71 50W
Arico, Canary Is. 22 F3 28 9N 16 29W
Arid, C., Australia 61 F3 34 1S 123 10 E
Arida, Japan 31 G7 34 5N 135 8 E
Arilla, Ákra, Greece 23 A3 39 43N 19 39 E
Arima, Trin. & Tob. 89 D7 10 38N 61 17W
Arinos →, Brazil 92 F7 10 25S 58 20W
Ario de Rosales, Mexico 86 D4 19 12N 102 0W
Aripuanã, Brazil 92 E6 9 25S 60 30W
Aripuanã →, Brazil 92 E6 5 7S 60 25W
Ariquemes, Brazil 92 E6 9 55S 63 6W
Arisaig, U.K. 12 E3 56 55N 5 51W
Aristazabal I., Canada 72 C3 52 40N 129 10W
Arivonimamo, Madag. 57 B8 19 1S 47 11 E
Arizaro, Salar de, Argentina 94 A2 24 40S 67 50W
Arizona, Argentina 94 D2 35 45S 65 25W
Arizona □, U.S.A. 83 J8 34 0N 112 0W
Arizpe, Mexico 86 A2 30 20N 110 11W
Arjeplog, Sweden 8 D18 66 3N 18 2 E
Arjona, Colombia 92 A3 10 14N 75 22W
Arjuna, Indonesia 37 G15 7 49S 112 34 E
Arka, Russia 27 C15 60 15N 142 0 E
Arkadelphia, U.S.A. 81 H8 34 7N 93 4W
Arkaig, L., U.K. 12 E3 56 59N 5 10W
Arkalyk = Arqalyk, Kazakstan 26 D7 50 13N 66 50 E
Arkansas □, U.S.A. 81 H8 35 0N 92 30W
Arkansas →, U.S.A. 81 J9 33 47N 91 4W
Arkansas City, U.S.A. 81 G6 37 4N 97 2W
Arkaroola, Australia 63 E2 30 20S 139 22 E
Arkhángelos, Greece 23 C10 36 13N 28 7 E
Arkhangelsk, Russia 24 B7 64 38N 40 36 E
Arki, India 42 D7 31 9N 76 58 E
Arklow, Ireland 13 D5 52 48N 6 10W
Arkport, U.S.A. 78 D7 42 24N 77 42W
Arkticheskiy, Mys, Russia 27 A10 81 10N 95 0 E
Arkville, U.S.A. 79 D10 42 9N 74 37W
Arlanzón →, Spain 19 A3 42 3N 4 17W
Arlbergpass, Austria 16 E6 47 9N 10 12 E
Arles, France 18 E6 43 41N 4 40 E
Arlington, S. Africa 57 D4 28 1S 27 53 E
Arlington, N.Y., U.S.A. 79 E11 41 42N 73 54W
Arlington, Oreg., U.S.A. 82 D3 45 43N 120 12W
Arlington, S. Dak., U.S.A. 80 C6 44 22N 97 8W
Arlington, Tex., U.S.A. 81 J6 32 44N 97 7W
Arlington, Va., U.S.A. 76 F7 38 53N 77 7W
Arlington, Vt., U.S.A. 79 C11 43 5N 73 9W
Arlington, Wash., U.S.A. 84 B4 48 12N 122 8W
Arlington Heights, U.S.A. 76 D2 42 5N 87 59W
Arlit, Niger 50 E7 19 0N 7 38 E
Arlon, Belgium 15 E5 49 42N 5 49 E
Arltunga, Australia 62 C1 23 26S 134 41 E
Armagh, U.K. 13 B5 54 21N 6 39W
Armagh □, U.K. 13 B5 54 18N 6 37W
Armavir, Russia 25 E7 45 2N 41 7 E
Armenia, Colombia 92 C3 4 35N 75 45W
Armenia ■, Asia 25 F7 40 20N 45 0 E
Armenistís, Ákra, Greece 23 C9 36 8N 27 42 E
Armour, U.S.A. 80 D5 43 19N 98 21W
Armstrong, B.C., Canada 72 C5 50 25N 119 10W
Armstrong, Ont., Canada 70 B2 50 18N 89 4W
Arnarfjörður, Iceland 8 D2 65 48N 23 40W
Arnaud →, Canada 69 B12 60 0N 70 0W
Arnauti, C., Cyprus 23 D11 35 6N 32 17 E
Arnett, U.S.A. 81 G5 36 8N 99 46W
Arnhem, Neths. 15 C5 51 58N 5 55 E
Arnhem, C., Australia 62 A2 12 20S 137 30 E
Arnhem B., Australia 62 A2 12 20S 136 10 E
Arnhem Land, Australia 62 A1 13 10S 134 30 E
Arno →, Italy 20 C4 43 41N 10 17 E
Arnold, U.K. 10 D6 53 1N 1 7W
Arnold, U.S.A. 84 G6 38 15N 120 20W
Arnot, Canada 73 B9 55 56N 96 41W
Arnøy, Norway 8 A19 70 9N 20 40 E
Arnprior, Canada 79 A8 45 26N 76 21W
Arnsberg, Germany 16 C5 51 24N 8 5 E
Aroab, Namibia 56 D2 26 41S 19 39 E
Aron, India 42 G6 25 57N 77 56 E
Arqalyk, Kazakstan 26 D7 50 13N 66 50 E
Arrah = Ara, India 43 G11 25 35N 84 32 E
Arran, U.K. 12 F3 55 34N 5 12W
Arras, France 18 A5 50 17N 2 46 E
Arrecife, Canary Is. 22 F6 28 57N 13 37W
Arrecifes, Argentina 94 C3 34 6S 60 9W
Arrée, Mts. d', France 18 B2 48 26N 3 55W
Arriaga, Chiapas, Mexico 87 D6 16 15N 93 52W
Arriaga, San Luis Potosí, Mexico 86 C4 21 55N 101 23W
Arrilalah, Australia 62 C3 23 43S 143 54 E
Arrino, Australia 61 E2 29 30S 115 40 E
Arrow, L., Ireland 13 B3 54 3N 8 19W
Arrowhead, L., U.S.A. 85 L9 34 16N 117 10W
Arrowtown, N.Z. 59 L2 44 57S 168 50 E
Arroyo Grande, U.S.A. 85 K6 35 7N 120 35W
Ars, Iran 44 B5 37 9N 47 46 E
Arsenault L., Canada 73 B7 55 6N 108 32W
Arsenev, Russia 30 B6 44 10N 133 15 E
Árta, Greece 21 E9 39 8N 21 2 E
Artà, Spain 22 B10 39 41N 3 21 E
Arteaga, Mexico 86 D4 18 50N 102 20W
Artem, Russia 30 C6 43 22N 132 13 E
Artemovsk, Russia 27 D10 54 45N 93 35 E
Artemovsk, Ukraine 25 E6 48 35N 38 0 E
Artesia = Mosomane, Botswana 56 C4 24 2S 26 19 E
Artesia, U.S.A. 81 J2 32 51N 104 24W
Arthur, Canada 78 C4 43 50N 80 32W
Arthur →, Australia 62 G3 41 2S 144 40 E
Arthur Cr. →, Australia 62 C2 22 30S 136 25 E
Arthur Pt., Australia 62 C5 22 7S 150 3 E
Arthur River, Australia 61 F2 33 20S 117 2 E
Arthur's Pass, N.Z. 59 K3 42 54S 171 35 E
Arthur's Town, Bahamas 89 B4 24 38N 75 42W
Artigas, Uruguay 94 C4 30 20S 56 30W
Artillery L., Canada 73 A7 63 9N 107 52W
Artois, France 18 A5 50 20N 2 30 E
Artrutx, C. de, Spain 22 B10 39 55N 3 49 E
Artsyz, Ukraine 17 E15 46 4N 29 26 E
Artvin, Turkey 25 F7 41 14N 41 44 E
Aru, Kepulauan, Indonesia 37 F8 6 0S 134 30 E
Aru Is. = Aru, Kepulauan, Indonesia 37 F8 6 0S 134 30 E
Arua, Uganda 54 B3 3 1N 30 58 E
Aruanã, Brazil 93 F8 14 54S 51 10W
Aruba ■, W. Indies 89 D6 12 30N 70 0W
Arucas, Canary Is. 22 F4 28 7N 15 32W
Arun →, Nepal 43 F12 26 55N 87 10 E
Arun →, U.K. 11 G7 50 49N 0 33W
Arunachal Pradesh □, India 41 F19 28 0N 95 0 E
Arusha, Tanzania 54 C4 3 20S 36 40 E
Arusha □, Tanzania 54 C4 4 0S 36 30 E
Arusha Chini, Tanzania 54 C4 3 32S 37 20 E
Aruwimi →, Dem. Rep. of the Congo 54 B1 1 13N 23 36 E
Arvada, Colo., U.S.A. 80 F2 39 48N 105 5W
Arvada, Wyo., U.S.A. 82 D10 44 39N 106 8W
Árvi, Greece 23 E7 34 59N 25 28 E
Arviat, Canada 73 A10 61 6N 93 59W
Arvidsjaur, Sweden 8 D18 65 35N 19 10 E
Arvika, Sweden 9 G15 59 40N 12 36 E
Arvin, U.S.A. 85 K8 35 12N 118 50W
Arwal, India 43 G11 25 15N 84 41 E
Arxan, China 33 B6 47 11N 119 57 E
Aryirádhes, Greece 23 B3 39 27N 19 58 E
Aryiroúpolis, Greece 23 D6 35 17N 24 20 E
Arys, Kazakstan 26 E7 42 26N 68 48 E
Arzamas, Russia 24 C7 55 27N 43 55 E
Aş Şafā, Syria 47 B6 33 10N 37 0 E
As Saffānīyah, Si. Arabia 45 E6 27 55N 48 50 E
As Safīrah, Syria 44 B3 36 5N 37 21 E
Aş Şahm, Oman 45 E8 24 10N 56 53 E
As Sājir, Si. Arabia 44 E5 25 11N 44 36 E
As Salamīyah, Syria 44 C3 35 1N 37 2 E
As Salmān, Iraq 44 D5 30 30N 44 32 E
As Salṭ, Jordan 47 C4 32 2N 35 43 E
As Sal'w'a, Qatar 45 E6 24 23N 50 50 E
As Samāwah, Iraq 44 D5 31 15N 45 15 E
As Sanamayn, Syria 47 B5 33 3N 36 10 E
As Sohar = Şuḩār, Oman 46 C6 24 20N 56 40 E
As Sukhnah, Syria 44 C3 34 52N 38 52 E
As Sulaymānīyah, Iraq 44 C5 35 35N 45 29 E
As Sulaymī, Si. Arabia 44 E4 26 17N 41 21 E
As Sulayyil, Si. Arabia 46 C4 20 27N 45 34 E
As Summān, Si. Arabia 44 E5 25 0N 47 0 E
As Suwaydā', Syria 47 C5 32 40N 36 30 E
As Suwaydā' □, Syria 47 C5 32 45N 36 45 E
As Suwayq, Oman 45 F8 23 51N 57 26 E
As Şuwayrah, Iraq 44 C5 32 55N 45 0 E
Asab, Namibia 56 D2 25 30S 18 0 E
Asad, Buḩayrat al, Syria 44 C3 36 0N 38 15 E
Asahi-Gawa →, Japan 31 G6 34 36N 133 58 E
Asahigawa, Japan 30 C11 43 46N 142 22 E
Asamankese, Ghana 50 G5 5 50N 0 40W
Asan →, India 43 F8 26 37N 78 24 E
Asansol, India 43 H12 23 40N 87 1 E
Asbesberge, S. Africa 56 D3 29 0S 23 0 E
Asbestos, Canada 71 C5 45 47N 71 58W
Asbury Park, U.S.A. 79 F10 40 13N 74 1W
Ascensión, Mexico 86 A3 31 6N 107 59W
Ascensión, B. de la, Mexico 87 D7 19 50N 87 20W
Ascension I., Atl. Oc. 49 G2 8 0S 14 15W
Aschaffenburg, Germany 16 D5 49 58N 9 6 E
Aschersleben, Germany 16 C6 51 45N 11 29 E
Áscoli Piceno, Italy 20 C5 42 51N 13 34 E
Ascope, Peru 92 E3 7 46S 79 8W
Ascotán, Chile 94 A2 21 45S 68 17W
Aseb, Eritrea 46 E3 13 0N 42 40 E
Asela, Ethiopia 46 F2 8 0N 39 0 E
Asenovgrad, Bulgaria 21 C11 42 1N 24 51 E
Aserradero, Mexico 86 C3 23 40N 105 43W
Asgata, Cyprus 23 E12 34 46N 33 15 E
Ash Fork, U.S.A. 83 J7 35 13N 112 29W
Ash Grove, U.S.A. 81 G8 37 19N 93 35W
Ash Shabakah, Iraq 44 D4 30 49N 43 39 E
Ash Shamāl □, Lebanon 47 A5 34 25N 36 0 E
Ash Shāmīyah, Iraq 44 D5 31 55N 44 35 E
Ash Shāriqah, U.A.E. 46 B6 25 23N 55 26 E
Ash Sharmah, Si. Arabia 44 D2 28 1N 35 16 E
Ash Sharqāt, Iraq 44 C4 35 27N 43 16 E
Ash Sharqi, Al Jabal, Lebanon 47 B5 33 40N 36 10 E
Ash Shaṭrah, Iraq 44 D5 31 30N 46 10 E
Ash Shawbak, Jordan 44 D2 30 32N 35 34 E
Ash Shawmari, J., Jordan 47 E5 30 35N 36 35 E
Ash Shināfīyah, Iraq 44 D5 31 35N 44 39 E
Ash Shu'bah, Si. Arabia 44 D5 28 54N 44 44 E
Ash Shumlūl, Si. Arabia 44 E5 26 31N 47 20 E
Ash Shūr'a, Iraq 44 C4 35 58N 43 13 E
Ash Shurayf, Si. Arabia 44 E3 25 43N 39 14 E
Ash Shuwayfāt, Lebanon 47 B4 33 45N 35 30 E
Asha, Russia 24 D10 55 0N 57 16 E
Ashau, Vietnam 38 D6 16 6N 107 22 E
Ashbourne, U.K. 10 D6 53 2N 1 43W
Ashburn, U.S.A. 77 K4 31 43N 83 39W
Ashburton, N.Z. 59 K3 43 53S 171 48 E
Ashburton →, Australia 60 D1 21 40S 114 56 E
Ashcroft, Canada 72 C4 50 40N 121 20W
Ashdod, Israel 47 D3 31 49N 34 35 E
Ashdown, U.S.A. 81 J7 33 40N 94 8W
Asheboro, U.S.A. 77 H6 35 43N 79 49W
Ashern, Canada 73 C9 51 11N 98 21W
Asherton, U.S.A. 81 L5 28 27N 99 46W
Asheville, U.S.A. 77 H4 35 36N 82 33W
Ashewat, Pakistan 42 D3 31 22N 68 32 E
Asheweig →, Canada 70 B2 54 17N 87 12W
Ashford, Australia 63 D5 29 15S 151 3 E
Ashford, U.K. 11 F8 51 8N 0 53 E
Ashgabat, Turkmenistan 26 F6 38 0N 57 50 E
Ashibetsu, Japan 30 C11 43 31N 142 11 E
Ashikaga, Japan 31 F9 36 28N 139 29 E
Ashington, U.K. 10 B6 55 11N 1 33W
Ashizuri-Zaki, Japan 31 H6 32 44N 133 0 E
Ashkarkot, Afghan. 42 C2 33 3N 67 58 E
Ashkhabad = Ashgabat, Turkmenistan 26 F6 38 0N 57 50 E
Āshkhāneh, Iran 45 B8 37 26N 56 55 E
Ashland, Kans., U.S.A. 81 G5 37 11N 99 46W

Ashland

Ashland, Ky., U.S.A. 76 F4 38 28N 82 38W
Ashland, Mont., U.S.A. 82 D10 45 36N 106 16W
Ashland, Ohio, U.S.A. 78 F2 40 52N 82 19W
Ashland, Oreg., U.S.A. 82 E2 42 12N 122 43W
Ashland, Pa., U.S.A. 79 F8 40 45N 76 22W
Ashland, Va., U.S.A. 76 G7 37 46N 77 29W
Ashland, Wis., U.S.A. 80 B9 46 35N 90 53W
Ashley, N. Dak., U.S.A. 80 B5 46 2N 99 22W
Ashley, Pa., U.S.A. 79 E9 41 12N 75 55W
Ashmore Reef, Australia 60 B3 12 14S 123 5 E
Ashmyany, Belarus 9 J21 54 26N 25 52 E
Ashokan Reservoir, U.S.A. 79 E10 41 56N 74 13W
Ashqelon, Israel 47 D3 31 42N 34 35 E
Ashta, India 42 H7 23 1N 76 43 E
Ashtabula, U.S.A. 78 E4 41 52N 80 47W
Ashton, S. Africa 56 E3 33 50S 20 5 E
Ashton, U.S.A. 82 D8 44 4N 111 27W
Ashuanipi, L., Canada 71 B6 52 45N 66 15W
Ashville, U.S.A. 78 F6 40 34N 78 33W
Asia 28 E11 45 0N 75 0 E
Asia, Kepulauan, Indonesia 37 D8 1 0N 131 13 E
Asīā Bak, Iran 45 C6 35 19N 50 30 E
Asifabad, India 40 K11 19 20N 79 24 E
Asinara, Italy 20 D3 41 4N 8 16 E
Asinara, G. dell', Italy 20 D3 41 0N 8 30 E
Asino, Russia 26 D9 57 0N 86 0 E
Asipovichy, Belarus 17 B15 53 19N 28 33 E
'Asīr □, Si. Arabia 46 D3 18 40N 42 30 E
Asir, Ras, Somali Rep. 46 E5 11 55N 51 10 E
Askersund, Sweden 9 G16 58 53N 14 55 E
Askham, S. Africa 56 D3 26 59S 20 47 E
Askim, Norway 9 G14 59 35N 11 10 E
Askja, Iceland 8 D5 65 3N 16 48W
Askøy, Norway 9 F11 60 29N 5 10 E
Asmara = Asmera, Eritrea 46 D2 15 19N 38 55 E
Asmera, Eritrea 46 D2 15 19N 38 55 E
Åsnen, Sweden 9 H16 56 37N 14 45 E
Aspen, U.S.A. 83 G10 39 11N 106 49W
Aspermont, U.S.A. 81 J4 33 8N 100 14W
Aspiring, Mt., N.Z. 59 L2 44 23S 168 46 E
Asprókavos, Ákra, Greece 23 B4 39 21N 20 6 E
Aspur, India 42 H6 23 58N 74 7 E
Asquith, Canada 73 C7 52 8N 107 13W
Assam □, India 41 G18 26 0N 93 0 E
Asse, Belgium 15 D4 50 24N 4 10 E
Assen, Neths. 15 A6 53 0N 6 35 E
Assiniboia, Canada 73 D7 49 40N 105 59W
Assiniboine →, Canada 73 D9 49 53N 97 8W
Assiniboine, Mt., Canada 72 C5 50 52N 115 39W
Assis, Brazil 95 A5 22 40S 50 20W
Assisi, Italy 20 C5 43 4N 12 37 E
Assynt, L., U.K. 12 C3 58 10N 5 3W
Astana, Kazakstan 26 D8 51 10N 71 30 E
Āstāneh, Iran 45 B6 37 17N 49 59 E
Astara, Azerbaijan 25 G8 38 30N 48 50 E
Asteroúsia, Greece 23 E7 34 59N 25 3 E
Asti, Italy 18 D8 44 54N 8 12 E
Astipálaia, Greece 21 F12 36 32N 26 22 E
Astorga, Spain 19 A2 42 29N 6 8W
Astoria, U.S.A. 84 D3 46 11N 123 50W
Astrakhan, Russia 25 E8 46 25N 48 5 E
Asturias □, Spain 19 A3 43 15N 6 0W
Asunción, Paraguay 94 B4 25 10S 57 30W
Asunción Nochixtlán, Mexico 87 D5 17 28N 97 14W
Aswa →, Uganda 54 B3 3 43N 31 55 E
Aswân, Egypt 51 D12 24 4N 32 57 E
Aswân High Dam = Sadd el Aali, Egypt 51 D12 23 54N 32 54 E
Asyût, Egypt 51 C12 27 11N 31 4 E
At Ţafīlah, Jordan 47 E4 30 45N 35 30 E
Aţ Ţā'if, Si. Arabia 46 C3 21 5N 40 27 E
Aţ Ţirāq, Si. Arabia 44 E5 27 19N 44 33 E
Aţ Tubayq, Si. Arabia 44 D3 29 30N 37 0 E
Atacama □, Chile 94 B2 27 30S 70 0W
Atacama, Desierto de, Chile 94 A2 24 0S 69 20W
Atacama, Salar de, Chile 94 A2 23 30S 68 20W
Atalaya, Peru 92 F4 10 45S 73 50W
Atalaya de Femes, Canary Is. 22 F6 28 56N 13 47W
Atami, Japan 31 G9 35 5N 139 4 E
Atapupu, Indonesia 37 F6 9 0S 124 51 E
Atâr, Mauritania 50 D3 20 30N 13 5W
Atari, Pakistan 42 D6 30 56N 74 2 E
Atascadero, U.S.A. 84 K6 35 29N 120 40W
Atasu, Kazakstan 26 E8 48 30N 71 0 E
Atatürk Barajı, Turkey 25 G6 37 28N 38 30 E
Atauro, Indonesia 37 F7 8 10S 125 30 E
'Atbara, Sudan 51 E12 17 42N 33 59 E
'Atbara, Nahr →, Sudan 51 E12 17 40N 33 56 E
Atbasar, Kazakstan 26 D7 51 48N 68 20 E
Atchafalaya B., U.S.A. 81 L9 29 25N 91 25W
Atchison, U.S.A. 80 F7 39 34N 95 7W
Āteshān, Iran 45 C7 35 35N 52 37 E
Ath, Belgium 15 D3 50 38N 3 47 E
Athabasca, Canada 72 C6 54 45N 113 20W
Athabasca →, Canada 73 B6 58 40N 110 50W
Athabasca, L., Canada 73 B7 59 15N 109 15W
Athboy, Ireland 13 C5 53 37N 6 56W
Athenry, Ireland 13 C3 53 18N 8 44W
Athens = Athínai, Greece 21 F10 37 58N 23 46 E
Athens, Ala., U.S.A. 77 H2 34 48N 86 58W
Athens, Ga., U.S.A. 77 J4 33 57N 83 23W
Athens, N.Y., U.S.A. 79 D11 42 16N 73 49W
Athens, Ohio, U.S.A. 76 F4 39 20N 82 6W
Athens, Pa., U.S.A. 79 E8 41 57N 76 31W
Athens, Tenn., U.S.A. 77 H3 35 27N 84 36W
Athens, Tex., U.S.A. 81 J7 32 12N 95 51W
Atherley, Canada 78 B5 44 37N 79 20W
Atherton, Australia 62 B4 17 17S 145 30 E
Athienou, Cyprus 23 D12 35 3N 33 32 E
Athínai, Greece 21 F10 37 58N 23 46 E
Athlone, Ireland 13 C4 53 25N 7 56W
Athna, Cyprus 23 D12 35 3N 33 47 E
Athol, U.S.A. 79 D12 42 36N 72 14W
Atholl, Forest of, U.K. 12 E5 56 51N 3 50W
Atholville, Canada 71 C6 47 59N 66 43W
Áthos, Greece 21 D11 40 9N 24 22 E
Athy, Ireland 13 C5 53 0N 7 0W
Ati, Chad 51 F9 13 13N 18 20 E
Atiak, Uganda 54 B3 3 12N 32 2 E
Atik L., Canada 73 B9 55 15N 96 0W
Atikameg →, Canada 70 B3 52 30N 82 46W
Atikokan, Canada 70 C1 48 45N 91 37W
Atikonak L., Canada 71 B7 52 40N 64 32W
Atka, Russia 27 C16 60 50N 151 48 E
Atka I., U.S.A. 68 C2 52 7N 174 30W
Atkinson, U.S.A. 80 D5 42 32N 98 59W
Atlanta, Ga., U.S.A. 77 J3 33 45N 84 23W
Atlanta, Tex., U.S.A. 81 J7 33 7N 94 10W
Atlantic, U.S.A. 80 E7 41 24N 95 1W
Atlantic City, U.S.A. 76 F8 39 21N 74 27W
Atlantic Ocean 2 E9 0 0 20 0W
Atlas Mts. = Haut Atlas, Morocco 50 B4 32 30N 5 0W
Atlin, Canada 72 B2 59 31N 133 41W
Atlin, L., Canada 72 B2 59 26N 133 45W
Atlin Prov. Park, Canada 72 B2 59 10N 134 30W
Atmore, U.S.A. 77 K2 31 2N 87 29W
Atoka, U.S.A. 81 H6 34 23N 96 8W
Atolia, U.S.A. 85 K9 35 19N 117 37W
Atrai →, Bangla. 43 G13 24 7N 89 22 E
Atrak = Atrek →, Turkmenistan 45 B8 37 35N 53 58 E
Atrauli, India 42 E8 28 2N 78 20 E
Atrek →, Turkmenistan 45 B8 37 35N 53 58 E
Atsuta, Japan 30 C10 43 24N 141 26 E
Attalla, U.S.A. 77 H2 34 1N 86 6W
Attapu, Laos 38 E6 14 48N 106 50 E
Attáviros, Greece 23 C9 36 12N 27 50 E
Attawapiskat, Canada 70 B3 52 56N 82 24W
Attawapiskat →, Canada 70 B3 52 57N 82 18W
Attawapiskat L., Canada 70 B2 52 18N 87 54W
Attica, Ind., U.S.A. 76 E2 40 18N 87 15W
Attica, Ohio, U.S.A. 78 E2 41 4N 82 53W
Attikamagen L., Canada 71 B6 55 0N 66 30W
Attleboro, U.S.A. 79 E13 41 57N 71 17W
Attock, Pakistan 42 C5 33 52N 72 20 E
Attopeu = Attapu, Laos 38 E6 14 48N 106 50 E
Attu I., U.S.A. 68 C1 52 55N 172 55 E
Attur, India 40 P11 11 35N 78 30 E
Atuel →, Argentina 94 D2 36 17S 66 50W
Åtvidaberg, Sweden 9 G17 58 12N 16 0 E
Atwater, U.S.A. 84 H6 37 21N 120 37W
Atwood, Canada 78 C3 43 40N 81 1W
Atwood, U.S.A. 80 F4 39 48N 101 3W
Atyraū, Kazakstan 25 E9 47 5N 52 0 E
Au Sable, U.S.A. 78 B1 44 25N 83 20W
Au Sable →, U.S.A. 76 C4 44 25N 83 20W
Au Sable Forks, U.S.A. 79 B11 44 27N 73 41W
Au Sable Pt., U.S.A. 78 B1 44 20N 83 20W
Aubagne, France 18 E6 43 17N 5 37 E
Aubarca, C. d', Spain 22 B7 39 4N 1 22 E
Aube →, France 18 B5 48 34N 3 43 E
Auberry, U.S.A. 84 H7 37 7N 119 29W
Auburn, Ala., U.S.A. 77 J3 32 36N 85 29W
Auburn, Calif., U.S.A. 84 G5 38 54N 121 4W
Auburn, Ind., U.S.A. 76 E3 41 22N 85 4W
Auburn, Maine, U.S.A. 77 C10 44 6N 70 14W
Auburn, N.Y., U.S.A. 79 D8 42 56N 76 34W
Auburn, Nebr., U.S.A. 80 E7 40 23N 95 51W
Auburn, Pa., U.S.A. 79 F8 40 36N 76 6W
Auburn, Wash., U.S.A. 84 C4 47 18N 122 14W
Auburn Ra., Australia 63 D5 25 15S 150 30 E
Auburndale, U.S.A. 77 L5 28 4N 81 48W
Aubusson, France 18 D5 45 57N 2 11 E
Auch, France 18 E4 43 39N 0 36 E
Auckland, N.Z. 59 G5 36 52S 174 46 E
Auckland Is., Pac. Oc. 64 N8 50 40S 166 5 E
Aude →, France 18 E5 43 13N 3 14 E
Auden, Canada 70 B2 50 14N 87 53W
Audubon, U.S.A. 80 E7 41 43N 94 56W
Augathella, Australia 63 D4 25 48S 146 35 E
Aughnacloy, U.K. 13 B5 54 25N 6 59W
Augrabies Falls, S. Africa 56 D3 28 35S 20 20 E
Augsburg, Germany 16 D6 48 25N 10 52 E
Augusta, Australia 61 F2 34 19S 115 9 E
Augusta, Italy 20 F6 37 13N 15 13 E
Augusta, Ark., U.S.A. 81 H9 35 17N 91 22W
Augusta, Ga., U.S.A. 77 J5 33 28N 81 58W
Augusta, Kans., U.S.A. 81 G6 37 41N 96 59W
Augusta, Maine, U.S.A. 69 D13 44 19N 69 47W
Augusta, Mont., U.S.A. 82 C7 47 30N 112 24W
Augustów, Poland 17 B12 53 51N 23 0 E
Augustus, Mt., Australia 61 D2 24 20S 116 50 E
Augustus I., Australia 60 C3 15 20S 124 30 E
Aukum, U.S.A. 84 G6 38 34N 120 43W
Auld, L., Australia 60 D3 22 25S 123 50 E
Ault, U.S.A. 80 E2 40 35N 104 44W
Aunis, France 18 C3 46 5N 0 50W
Auponhia, Indonesia 37 E7 1 58S 125 27 E
Aur, Pulau, Malaysia 39 L5 2 35N 104 10 E
Auraiya, India 43 F8 26 28N 79 33 E
Aurangabad, Bihar, India 43 G11 24 45N 84 18 E
Aurangabad, Maharashtra, India 40 K9 19 50N 75 23 E
Aurich, Germany 16 B4 53 28N 7 28 E
Aurillac, France 18 D5 44 55N 2 26 E
Aurora, Canada 78 C5 44 0N 79 28W
Aurora, S. Africa 56 E2 32 40S 18 29 E
Aurora, Colo., U.S.A. 80 F2 39 44N 104 52W
Aurora, Ill., U.S.A. 76 E1 41 45N 88 19W
Aurora, Mo., U.S.A. 81 G8 36 58N 93 43W
Aurora, N.Y., U.S.A. 79 D8 42 45N 76 42W
Aurora, Nebr., U.S.A. 80 E6 40 52N 98 0W
Aurora, Ohio, U.S.A. 78 E3 41 21N 81 20W
Aurukun, Australia 62 A3 13 20S 141 45 E
Aus, Namibia 56 D2 26 35S 16 12 E
Ausable →, Canada 78 C3 43 19N 81 46W
Auschwitz = Oświęcim, Poland 17 C10 50 2N 19 11 E
Austin, Minn., U.S.A. 80 D8 43 40N 92 58W
Austin, Nev., U.S.A. 82 G5 39 30N 117 4W
Austin, Pa., U.S.A. 78 E6 41 38N 78 6W
Austin, Tex., U.S.A. 81 K6 30 17N 97 45W
Austin, L., Australia 61 E2 27 40S 118 0 E
Austin I., Canada 73 A10 61 10N 94 0W
Austra, Norway 8 D14 65 8N 11 55 E
Austral Is. = Tubuai Is., Pac. Oc. 65 K13 25 0S 150 0W
Austral Seamount Chain, Pac. Oc. 65 K13 24 0S 150 0W
Australia ■, Oceania 64 K5 23 0S 135 0 E
Australind, Australia 61 F2 33 17S 115 42 E
Austria ■, Europe 16 E8 47 0N 14 0 E
Austvågøy, Norway 8 B16 68 20N 14 40 E
Autlán, Mexico 86 D4 19 40N 104 30W
Autun, France 18 C6 46 58N 4 17 E
Auvergne, France 18 D5 45 20N 3 15 E
Auvergne, Mts. d', France 18 D5 45 20N 2 55 E
Auxerre, France 18 C5 47 48N 3 32 E
Ava, U.S.A. 81 G8 36 57N 92 40W
Avallon, France 18 C5 47 30N 3 53 E
Avalon, U.S.A. 85 M8 33 21N 118 20W
Avalon Pen., Canada 71 C9 47 30N 53 20W
Avanos, Turkey 44 B2 38 43N 34 51 E
Avaré, Brazil 95 A6 23 4S 48 58W
Avawatz Mts., U.S.A. 85 K10 35 40N 116 30W
Aveiro, Brazil 93 D7 3 10S 55 5W
Aveiro, Portugal 19 B1 40 37N 8 38W
Āvej, Iran 45 C6 35 40N 49 15 E
Avellaneda, Argentina 94 C4 34 50S 58 10W
Avellino, Italy 20 D6 40 54N 14 47 E
Avenal, U.S.A. 84 K6 36 0N 120 8W
Aversa, Italy 20 D6 40 58N 14 12 E
Avery, U.S.A. 82 C6 47 15N 115 49W
Aves, Is. las, Venezuela 89 D6 12 0N 67 30W
Avesta, Sweden 9 F17 60 9N 16 10 E
Avezzano, Italy 20 C5 42 2N 13 25 E
Aviá Terai, Argentina 94 B3 26 45S 60 50W
Aviemore, U.K. 12 D5 57 12N 3 50W
Avignon, France 18 E6 43 57N 4 50 E
Ávila, Spain 19 B3 40 39N 4 43W
Avila Beach, U.S.A. 85 K6 35 11N 120 44W
Avilés, Spain 19 A3 43 35N 5 57W
Avis, U.S.A. 78 E7 41 11N 77 19W
Avoca, U.S.A. 78 D7 42 25N 77 25W
Avoca →, Ireland 13 D5 52 48N 6 10W
Avola, Canada 72 C5 51 45N 119 19W
Avola, Italy 20 F6 36 56N 15 7 E
Avon, U.S.A. 78 D7 42 55N 77 45W
Avon →, Australia 61 F2 31 40S 116 7 E
Avon →, Bristol, U.K. 11 F5 51 29N 2 41W
Avon →, Dorset, U.K. 11 G6 50 44N 1 46W
Avon →, Warks., U.K. 11 E5 52 0N 2 8W
Avon Park, U.S.A. 77 M5 27 36N 81 31W
Avondale, Zimbabwe 55 F3 17 43S 30 58 E
Avonlea, Canada 73 D8 50 0N 105 0W
Avonmore, Canada 79 A10 45 10N 74 58W
Avranches, France 18 B3 48 40N 1 20W
A'waj →, Syria 47 B5 33 23N 36 20 E
Awaji-Shima, Japan 31 G7 34 30N 134 50 E
'Awālī, Bahrain 45 E6 26 0N 50 30 E
Awantipur, India 43 C6 33 55N 75 3 E
Awasa, Ethiopia 46 F2 7 2N 38 28 E
Awash, Ethiopia 46 F3 9 1N 40 10 E
Awatere →, N.Z. 59 J5 41 37S 174 10 E
Awbārī, Libya 51 C8 26 46N 12 57 E
Awe, L., U.K. 12 E3 56 17N 5 16W
Awjilah, Libya 51 C10 29 8N 21 7 E
Axe →, U.K. 11 F5 50 42N 3 4W
Axel Heiberg I., Canada 4 B3 80 0N 90 0W
Axim, Ghana 50 H5 4 51N 2 15W
Axiós →, Greece 21 D10 40 57N 22 35 E
Axminster, U.K. 11 G4 50 46N 3 0W
Ayabaca, Peru 92 D3 4 40S 79 53W
Ayabe, Japan 31 G7 35 20N 135 20 E
Ayacucho, Argentina 94 D4 37 5S 58 20W
Ayacucho, Peru 92 F4 13 0S 74 0W
Ayaguz, Kazakstan 26 E9 48 10N 80 10 E
Ayamonte, Spain 19 D2 37 12N 7 24W
Ayan, Russia 27 D14 56 30N 138 16 E
Ayaviri, Peru 92 F4 14 50S 70 35W
Aydın, Turkey 21 F12 37 51N 27 51 E
Aydin □, Turkey 25 G4 37 50N 28 0 E
Ayer, U.S.A. 79 D13 42 34N 71 35W
Ayer's Cliff, Canada 79 A12 45 10N 72 3W
Ayers Rock, Australia 61 E5 25 23S 131 5 E
Ayia Aikaterini, Ákra, Greece 23 A3 39 50N 19 50 E
Ayia Dhéka, Greece 23 D6 35 3N 24 58 E
Ayia Gálini, Greece 23 D6 35 6N 24 41 E
Ayia Napa, Cyprus 23 E13 34 59N 34 0 E
Ayia Phyla, Cyprus 23 E12 34 43N 33 1 E
Ayia Varvára, Greece 23 D7 35 8N 25 1 E
Áyios Amvrósios, Cyprus 23 D12 35 20N 33 35 E
Áyios Evstrátios, Greece 21 E11 39 34N 24 58 E
Áyios Ioánnis, Ákra, Greece 23 D7 35 20N 25 40 E
Áyios Isidhoros, Greece 23 C9 36 9N 27 51 E
Áyios Matthaíos, Greece 23 B3 39 30N 19 47 E
Áyios Nikólaos, Greece 23 D7 35 11N 25 41 E
Áyios Seryios, Cyprus 23 D12 35 12N 33 53 E
Áyios Theodhoros, Cyprus 23 D13 35 22N 34 1 E
Aykino, Russia 24 B8 62 15N 49 56 E
Aylesbury, U.K. 11 F7 51 49N 0 49W
Aylmer, Canada 78 D4 42 46N 80 59W
Aylmer, L., Canada 68 B8 64 0N 110 8W
'Ayn, Wādī al, Oman 45 F7 22 15N 55 28 E
Ayn Dār, Si. Arabia 45 E7 25 55N 49 10 E
Ayn Zālah, Iraq 44 B4 36 45N 42 35 E
Ayolas, Paraguay 94 B4 27 10S 56 59W
Ayon, Ostrov, Russia 27 C17 69 50N 169 0 E
'Ayoûn el 'Atroûs, Mauritania 50 E4 16 38N 9 37W
Ayr, Australia 62 B4 19 35S 147 25 E
Ayr, Canada 78 C4 43 17N 80 27W
Ayr, U.K. 12 F4 55 28N 4 38W
Ayr →, U.K. 12 F4 55 28N 4 38W
Ayre, Pt. of, U.K. 10 C3 54 25N 4 21W
Ayton, Australia 62 B4 15 56S 145 22 E
Aytos, Bulgaria 21 C12 42 42N 27 16 E
Ayu, Kepulauan, Indonesia 37 D8 0 35N 131 5 E
Ayutla, Guatemala 88 D1 14 40N 92 10W
Ayutla, Mexico 87 D5 16 58N 99 17W
Ayvacık, Turkey 21 E12 39 36N 26 24 E
Ayvalık, Turkey 21 E12 39 20N 26 46 E
Az Zabadānī, Syria 47 B5 33 43N 36 5 E
Az Ẓāhirīyah, West Bank 47 D3 31 25N 34 58 E
Az Ẓahrān, Si. Arabia 45 E6 26 10N 50 7 E
Az Zarqā, Jordan 47 C5 32 5N 36 4 E
Az Zarqā', U.A.E. 45 E7 24 53N 53 4 E
Az Zībār, Iraq 44 B5 36 52N 44 4 E
Az Zilfī, Si. Arabia 44 E5 26 12N 44 52 E
Az Zubayr, Iraq 44 D5 30 26N 47 40 E
Azamgarh, India 43 F10 26 5N 83 13 E
Azangaro, Peru 92 F4 14 55S 70 13W
Āzār Shahr, Iran 44 B5 37 45N 45 59 E
Azarān, Iran 44 B5 37 25N 47 16 E
Azärbayjan = Azerbaijan ■, Asia 25 F8 40 20N 48 0 E
Āzarbāyjān-e Gharbī □, Iran 44 B5 37 0N 44 30 E
Āzarbāyjān-e Sharqī □, Iran 44 B5 37 20N 47 0 E
Azare, Nigeria 50 F8 11 55N 10 10 E
A'zāz, Syria 44 B3 36 36N 37 4 E
Azbine = Aïr, Niger 50 E7 18 30N 8 0 E
Azerbaijan ■, Asia 25 F8 40 20N 48 0 E
Azerbaijchan = Azerbaijan ■, Asia 25 F8 40 20N 48 0 E
Azimganj, India 43 G13 24 14N 88 16 E
Azogues, Ecuador 92 D3 2 35S 78 0W
Azores, Atl. Oc. 50 A1 38 44N 29 0W
Azov, Russia 25 E6 47 3N 39 25 E
Azov, Sea of, Europe 25 E6 46 0N 36 30 E
Azovskoye More = Azov, Sea of, Europe 25 E6 46 0N 36 30 E
Azraq ash Shīshān, Jordan 47 D5 31 50N 36 49 E
Aztec, U.S.A. 83 H10 36 49N 107 59W
Azúa de Compostela, Dom. Rep. 89 C5 18 25N 70 44W
Azuaga, Spain 19 C3 38 16N 5 39W
Azuero, Pen. de, Panama 88 E3 7 30N 80 30W
Azul, Argentina 94 D4 36 42S 59 43W
Azusa, U.S.A. 85 L9 34 8N 117 52W

B

Ba Don, Vietnam 38 D6 17 45N 106 26 E
Ba Dong, Vietnam 39 H6 9 40N 106 33 E
Ba Ngoi = Cam Lam, Vietnam 39 G7 11 54N 109 10 E
Ba Tri, Vietnam 39 G6 10 2N 106 36 E
Ba Xian = Bazhou, China 34 E9 39 8N 116 22 E
Baa, Indonesia 37 F6 10 50S 123 0 E
Baarle-Nassau, Belgium 15 C4 51 27N 4 56 E
Bab el Mandeb, Red Sea 46 E3 12 35N 43 25 E
Bābā, Koh-i-, Afghan. 40 B5 34 30N 67 0 E
Baba Burnu, Turkey 21 E12 39 29N 26 2 E
Bābā Kalū, Iran 45 D6 30 7N 50 49 E
Babadag, Romania 17 F15 44 53N 28 44 E
Babadayhan, Turkmenistan 26 F7 37 42N 60 23 E
Babaeski, Turkey 21 D12 41 26N 27 6 E
Babahoyo, Ecuador 92 D3 1 40S 79 30W
Babai = Sarju →, India 43 F9 27 21N 81 23 E
Babar, Indonesia 37 F7 8 0S 129 30 E
Babar, Pakistan 42 D3 31 7N 69 32 E
Babarkach, Pakistan 42 E3 29 45N 68 0 E
Babb, U.S.A. 82 B7 48 51N 113 27W
Babelthuap, Pac. Oc. 37 C8 7 30N 134 30 E
Baberu, India 43 G9 25 33N 80 43 E
Babi Besar, Pulau, Malaysia 39 L4 2 25N 103 59 E
Babinda, Australia 62 B4 17 20S 145 56 E
Babine, Canada 72 B3 55 22N 126 37W
Babine →, Canada 72 B3 55 45N 127 44W
Babine L., Canada 72 C3 54 48N 126 0W
Babo, Indonesia 37 E8 2 30S 133 30 E
Bābol, Iran 45 B7 36 40N 52 50 E
Bābol Sar, Iran 45 B7 36 45N 52 45 E
Babruysk, Belarus 17 B15 53 10N 29 15 E
Babuhri, India 42 F3 26 49N 69 43 E
Babusar Pass, Pakistan 43 B5 35 12N 73 59 E
Babuyan Chan., Phil. 37 A6 18 40N 121 30 E
Babylon, Iraq 44 C5 32 34N 44 22 E
Bac Can, Vietnam 38 A5 22 8N 105 49 E
Bac Giang, Vietnam 38 B6 21 16N 106 11 E
Bac Lieu, Vietnam 39 H5 9 17N 105 43 E
Bac Ninh, Vietnam 38 B6 21 13N 106 4 E
Bac Phan, Vietnam 38 B5 22 0N 105 0 E
Bac Quang, Vietnam 38 A5 22 30N 104 48 E
Bacabal, Brazil 93 D10 4 15S 44 45W
Bacalar, Mexico 87 D7 18 50N 87 27W
Bacan, Kepulauan, Indonesia 37 E7 0 35S 127 30 E
Bacarra, Phil. 37 A6 18 15N 120 37 E
Bacău, Romania 17 E14 46 35N 26 55 E
Bacerac, Mexico 86 A3 30 18N 108 50W
Bach Long Vi, Dao, Vietnam 38 B6 20 10N 107 40 E
Bachelina, Russia 26 D7 57 45N 67 20 E
Bachhwara, India 43 G11 25 35N 85 54 E
Back →, Canada 68 B9 65 10N 104 0W
Bacolod, Phil. 37 B6 10 40N 122 57 E
Bacuk, Malaysia 39 J4 6 4N 102 25 E
Bād, Iran 45 C7 33 41N 52 1 E
Bad →, U.S.A. 80 C4 44 21N 100 22W
Bad Axe, U.S.A. 78 C2 43 48N 83 0W
Bad Ischl, Austria 16 E7 47 44N 13 38 E
Bad Kissingen, Germany 16 C6 50 11N 10 4 E
Bad Lands, U.S.A. 80 D3 43 40N 102 10W
Bada Barabil, India 43 H11 22 7N 85 24 E
Badagara, India 40 P9 11 35N 75 40 E
Badajós, L., Brazil 92 D6 3 15S 62 50W
Badajoz, Spain 19 C2 38 50N 6 59W
Badalona, Spain 19 B7 41 26N 2 15 E
Badalzai, Afghan. 42 E1 29 50N 65 35 E
Badampahar, India 41 H15 22 10N 86 10 E
Badanah, Si. Arabia 44 D4 30 58N 41 30 E
Badarinath, India 43 D8 30 45N 79 30 E
Badas, Kepulauan, Indonesia 36 D3 0 45N 107 5 E
Baddo →, Pakistan 40 F4 28 0N 64 20 E
Bade, Indonesia 37 F9 7 10S 139 35 E
Baden, Austria 16 D9 48 1N 16 13 E
Baden, U.S.A. 78 F4 40 38N 80 14W
Baden-Baden, Germany 16 D5 48 44N 8 13 E
Baden-Württemberg □, Germany 16 D5 48 20N 8 40 E
Badgastein, Austria 16 E7 47 7N 13 9 E
Badger, Canada 71 C8 49 0N 56 4W
Badger, U.S.A. 84 J7 36 38N 119 1W
Bādghīsāt □, Afghan. 40 B3 35 0N 63 0 E
Badgom, India 43 B6 34 1N 74 45 E
Badin, Pakistan 42 G3 24 38N 68 54 E
Badlands National Park, U.S.A. 80 D3 43 38N 102 56W
Badrah, Iraq 44 C5 33 6N 45 58 E
Badrinath, India 43 D8 30 44N 79 29 E
Badulla, Sri Lanka 40 R12 7 1N 81 7 E
Baena, Spain 19 D3 37 37N 4 20W
Baeza, Spain 19 D4 37 57N 3 25W
Baffin B., Canada 69 A13 72 0N 64 0W
Baffin I., Canada 69 B12 68 0N 75 0W
Bafing →, Mali 50 F3 13 49N 10 50W
Bafliyūn, Syria 44 B3 36 37N 36 59 E
Bafoulabé, Mali 50 F3 13 50N 10 55W
Bāfq, Iran 45 D7 31 40N 55 25 E
Bafra, Turkey 25 F6 41 34N 35 54 E
Bāft, Iran 45 D8 29 15N 56 38 E
Bafwasende, Dem. Rep. of the Congo 54 B2 1 3N 27 5 E
Bagamoyo, Tanzania 54 D4 6 28S 38 55 E
Bagan Datoh, Malaysia 39 L3 3 59N 100 47 E
Bagan Serai, Malaysia 39 K3 5 1N 100 32 E
Baganga, Phil. 37 C7 7 34N 126 33 E
Bagani, Namibia 56 B3 18 7S 21 41 E
Bagansiapiapi, Indonesia 36 D2 2 12N 100 50 E
Bagasra, India 42 J4 21 30N 71 0 E

Baranof I.

Baranof I., U.S.A. 68 C6 57 0N 135 0W
Barapasi, Indonesia 37 E9 2 15S 137 5 E
Barasat, India 43 H13 22 46N 88 31 E
Barat Daya, Kepulauan, Indonesia 37 F7 7 30S 128 0 E
Barataria B., U.S.A. 81 L10 29 20N 89 55W
Barauda, India 42 H6 23 33N 75 15 E
Baraut, India 42 E7 29 13N 77 7 E
Barbacena, Brazil 95 A7 21 15S 43 56W
Barbados ■, W. Indies 89 D8 13 10N 59 30W
Barbària, C. de, Spain 22 C7 38 39N 1 24 E
Barbastro, Spain 19 A6 42 2N 0 5 E
Barberton, S. Africa 57 D5 25 42S 31 2 E
Barberton, U.S.A. 78 E3 41 0N 81 39W
Barbosa, Colombia 92 B4 5 57N 73 37W
Barbourville, U.S.A. 77 G4 36 52N 83 53W
Barbuda, W. Indies 89 C7 17 30N 61 40W
Barcaldine, Australia 62 C4 23 43S 145 6 E
Barcellona Pozzo di Gotto, Italy 20 E6 38 9N 15 13 E
Barcelona, Spain 19 B7 41 21N 2 10 E
Barcelona, Venezuela 92 A6 10 10N 64 40W
Barcelos, Brazil 92 D6 1 0S 63 0W
Barcoo →, Australia 62 D3 25 30S 142 50 E
Bardaï, Chad 51 D9 21 25N 17 0 E
Bardas Blancas, Argentina 94 D2 35 49S 69 45W
Barddhaman, India 43 H12 23 14N 87 39 E
Bardejov, Slovak Rep. 17 D11 49 18N 21 15 E
Bardera, Somali Rep. 46 G3 2 20N 42 27 E
Bardīyah, Libya 51 B10 31 45N 25 5 E
Bardsey I., U.K. 10 E3 52 45N 4 47W
Bardstown, U.S.A. 76 G3 37 49N 85 28W
Bareilly, India 43 E8 28 22N 79 27 E
Barela, India 43 H9 23 6N 80 3 E
Barents Sea, Arctic 4 B9 73 0N 39 0 E
Barfleur, Pte. de, France 18 B3 49 42N 1 16W
Bargara, Australia 62 C5 24 50S 152 25 E
Barguzin, Russia 27 D11 53 37N 109 37 E
Barh, India 43 G11 25 29N 85 46 E
Barhaj, India 43 F10 26 18N 83 44 E
Barharwa, India 43 G12 24 52N 87 47 E
Barhi, India 43 G11 24 15N 85 25 E
Bari, India 42 F7 26 39N 77 39 E
Bari, Italy 20 D7 41 8N 16 51 E
Bari Doab, Pakistan 42 D5 30 20N 73 0 E
Bari Sadri, India 42 G6 24 28N 74 30 E
Barīdī, Ra's, Si. Arabia 44 E3 24 17N 37 31 E
Barīm, Yemen 48 E8 12 39N 43 25 E
Barinas, Venezuela 92 B4 8 36N 70 15W
Baring, C., Canada 68 B8 70 0N 117 30W
Baringo, Kenya 54 B4 0 47N 36 16 E
Baringo, L., Kenya 54 B4 0 47N 36 16 E
Barisal, Bangla. 41 H17 22 45N 90 20 E
Barisan, Bukit, Indonesia 36 E2 3 30S 102 15 E
Barito →, Indonesia 36 E4 4 0S 114 50 E
Bark L., Canada 78 A7 45 27N 77 51W
Barkakana, India 43 H11 23 37N 85 29 E
Barker, U.S.A. 78 C6 43 20N 78 33W
Barkley, L., U.S.A. 77 G2 37 1N 88 14W
Barkley Sound, Canada 72 D3 48 50N 125 10W
Barkly East, S. Africa 56 E4 30 58S 27 33 E
Barkly Roadhouse, Australia 62 B2 19 52S 135 50 E
Barkly Tableland, Australia 62 B2 17 50S 136 40 E
Barkly West, S. Africa 56 D3 28 5S 24 31 E
Barkol Kazak Zizhixian, China 32 B4 43 37N 93 2 E
Bârlad, Romania 17 E14 46 15N 27 38 E
Bârlad →, Romania 17 F14 45 38N 27 32 E
Barlee, L., Australia 61 E2 29 15S 119 30 E
Barlee, Mt., Australia 61 D4 24 38S 128 13 E
Barletta, Italy 20 D7 41 19N 16 17 E
Barlovento, Canary Is. 22 F2 28 48N 17 48W
Barlow L., Canada 73 A8 62 0N 103 0W
Barmer, India 42 G4 25 45N 71 20 E
Barmouth, U.K. 10 E3 52 44N 4 4W
Barna →, India 43 G10 25 21N 83 3 E
Barnagar, India 42 H6 23 7N 75 19 E
Barnala, India 42 D6 30 23N 75 33 E
Barnard Castle, U.K. 10 C6 54 33N 1 55W
Barnaul, Russia 26 D9 53 20N 83 40 E
Barnesville, U.S.A. 77 J3 33 3N 84 9W
Barnet □, U.K. 11 F7 51 38N 0 9W
Barneveld, Neths. 15 B5 52 7N 5 36 E
Barneveld, U.S.A. 79 C9 43 16N 75 14W
Barnhart, U.S.A. 81 K4 31 8N 101 10W
Barnsley, U.K. 10 D6 53 34N 1 27W
Barnstaple, U.K. 11 F3 51 5N 4 4W
Barnstaple Bay = Bideford Bay, U.K. 11 F3 51 5N 4 20W
Barnsville, U.S.A. 80 B6 46 43N 96 28W
Barnwell, U.S.A. 77 J5 33 15N 81 23W
Baro, Nigeria 50 G7 8 35N 6 18 E
Baroda = Vadodara, India 42 H5 22 20N 73 10 E
Baroda, India 42 G7 25 29N 76 35 E
Baroe, S. Africa 56 E3 33 13S 24 33 E
Baron Ra., Australia 60 D4 23 30S 127 45 E
Barotseland, Zambia 53 H4 15 0S 24 0 E
Barpeta, India 41 F17 26 20N 91 10 E
Barques, Pt. Aux, U.S.A. 78 B2 44 4N 82 58W
Barquísimeto, Venezuela 92 A5 10 4N 69 19W
Barr Smith Range, Australia 61 E3 27 4S 120 20 E
Barra, Brazil 93 F10 11 5S 43 10W
Barra, U.K. 12 E1 57 0N 7 29W
Barra, Sd. of, U.K. 12 D1 57 4N 7 25W
Barra de Navidad, Mexico 86 D4 19 12N 104 41W
Barra do Corda, Brazil 93 E9 5 30S 45 10W
Barra do Piraí, Brazil 95 A7 22 30S 43 50W
Barra Falsa, Pta. da, Mozam. 57 C6 22 58S 35 37 E
Barra Hd., U.K. 12 E1 56 47N 7 40W
Barra Mansa, Brazil 95 A7 22 35S 44 12W
Barrackpur = Barakpur, India 43 H13 22 44N 88 30 E
Barradale Roadhouse, Australia 60 D1 22 42S 114 58 E
Barraigh = Barra, U.K. 12 E1 57 0N 7 29W
Barranca, Lima, Peru 92 F3 10 45S 77 50W
Barranca, Loreto, Peru 92 D3 4 50S 76 50W
Barrancabermeja, Colombia 92 B4 7 0N 73 50W
Barrancas, Venezuela 92 B6 8 55N 62 5W
Barrancos, Portugal 19 C2 38 10N 6 58W
Barranqueras, Argentina 94 B4 27 30S 59 0W
Barranquilla, Colombia 92 A4 11 0N 74 50W
Barraute, Canada 70 C4 48 26N 77 38W
Barre, Mass., U.S.A. 79 D12 42 25N 72 6W
Barre, Vt., U.S.A. 79 B12 44 12N 72 30W
Barreal, Argentina 94 C2 31 33S 69 28W
Barreiras, Brazil 93 F10 12 8S 45 0W
Barreirinhas, Brazil 93 D10 2 30S 42 50W
Barreiro, Portugal 19 C1 38 40N 9 6W
Barren, Nosy, Madag. 57 B7 18 25S 43 40 E
Barretos, Brazil 93 H9 20 30S 48 35W
Barrhead, Canada 72 C6 54 10N 114 24W
Barrie, Canada 78 B5 44 24N 79 40W
Barrière, Canada 72 C4 51 12N 120 7W
Barrington, U.S.A. 79 E13 41 44N 71 18W
Barrington L., Canada 73 B8 56 55N 100 15W
Barringun, Australia 63 D4 29 1S 145 41 E
Barro do Garças, Brazil 93 G8 15 54S 52 16W
Barron, U.S.A. 80 C9 45 24N 91 51W
Barrow, U.S.A. 68 A4 71 18N 156 47W
Barrow →, Ireland 13 D5 52 25N 6 58W
Barrow, Pt., U.S.A. 66 B4 71 10N 156 20W
Barrow Creek, Australia 62 C1 21 30S 133 55 E
Barrow I., Australia 60 D2 20 45S 115 20 E
Barrow-in-Furness, U.K. 10 C4 54 7N 3 14W
Barrow Pt., Australia 62 A3 14 20S 144 40 E
Barrow Ra., Australia 61 E4 26 0S 127 40 E
Barrow Str., Canada 4 B3 74 20N 95 0W
Barry, U.K. 11 F4 51 24N 3 16W
Barry's Bay, Canada 78 A7 45 29N 77 41W
Barsat, Pakistan 43 A5 36 10N 72 45 E
Barsham, Syria 44 C4 35 21N 40 33 E
Barsi, India 40 K9 18 10N 75 50 E
Barsoi, India 41 G15 25 48N 87 57 E
Barstow, U.S.A. 85 L9 34 54N 117 1W
Barthélemy, Col, Vietnam 38 C5 19 26N 104 6 E
Bartica, Guyana 92 B7 6 25N 58 40W
Bartlesville, U.S.A. 81 G7 36 45N 95 59W
Bartlett, U.S.A. 84 J8 36 29N 118 2W
Bartlett, L., Canada 72 A5 63 5N 118 20W
Bartolomeu Dias, Mozam. 55 G4 21 10S 35 8 E
Barton, U.S.A. 79 B12 44 45N 72 11W
Barton upon Humber, U.K. 10 D7 53 41N 0 25W
Bartow, U.S.A. 77 M5 27 54N 81 50W
Barú, Volcan, Panama 88 E3 8 55N 82 35W
Barumba, Dem. Rep. of the Congo 54 B1 1 3N 23 37 E
Baruunsuu, Mongolia 34 C3 43 43N 105 35 E
Barwani, India 42 H6 22 2N 74 57 E
Barysaw, Belarus 17 A15 54 17N 28 28 E
Barzān, Iraq 44 B5 36 55N 44 3 E
Bāsa'idū, Iran 45 E7 26 35N 55 20 E
Basal, Pakistan 42 C5 33 33N 72 13 E
Basankusa, Dem. Rep. of the Congo 52 D3 1 5N 19 50 E
Basarabeasca, Moldova 17 E15 46 21N 28 58 E
Basawa, Afghan. 42 B4 34 15N 70 50 E
Bascuñán, C., Chile 94 B1 28 52S 71 35W
Basel, Switz. 18 C7 47 35N 7 35 E
Bashākerd, Kūhhā-ye, Iran 45 E8 26 42N 58 35 E
Bashaw, Canada 72 C6 52 35N 112 58W
Bāshī, Iran 45 D6 28 41N 51 4 E
Bashkir Republic = Bashkortostan □, Russia 24 D10 54 0N 57 0 E
Bashkortostan □, Russia 24 D10 54 0N 57 0 E
Basibasy, Madag. 57 C7 22 10S 43 40 E
Basilan I., Phil. 37 C6 6 35N 122 0 E
Basilan Str., Phil. 37 C6 6 50N 122 0 E
Basildon, U.K. 11 F8 51 34N 0 28 E
Basim = Washim, India 40 J10 20 3N 77 0 E
Basin, U.S.A. 82 D9 44 23N 108 2W
Basingstoke, U.K. 11 F6 51 15N 1 5W
Baskatong, Rés., Canada 70 C4 46 46N 75 50W
Basle = Basel, Switz. 18 C7 47 35N 7 35 E
Basoda, India 42 H7 23 52N 77 54 E
Basoka, Dem. Rep. of the Congo 54 B1 1 16N 23 40 E
Basque Provinces = País Vasco □, Spain 19 A4 42 50N 2 45W
Basra = Al Başrah, Iraq 44 D5 30 30N 47 50 E
Bass Str., Australia 62 F4 39 15S 146 30 E
Bassano, Canada 72 C6 50 48N 112 20W
Bassano del Grappa, Italy 20 B4 45 46N 11 44 E
Bassas da India, Ind. Oc. 53 J7 22 0S 39 0 E
Basse-Terre, Guadeloupe 89 C7 16 0N 61 44W
Bassein, Burma 41 L19 16 45N 94 30 E
Basseterre, St. Kitts & Nevis 89 C7 17 17N 62 43W
Bassett, U.S.A. 80 D5 42 35N 99 32W
Bassi, India 42 D7 30 44N 76 21 E
Bastak, Iran 45 E7 27 15N 54 25 E
Baştām, Iran 45 B7 36 29N 55 4 E
Bastar, India 41 K12 19 15N 81 40 E
Basti, India 43 F10 26 52N 82 55 E
Bastia, France 18 E8 42 40N 9 30 E
Bastogne, Belgium 15 D5 50 1N 5 43 E
Bastrop, La., U.S.A. 81 J9 32 47N 91 55W
Bastrop, Tex., U.S.A. 81 K6 30 7N 97 19W
Bat Yam, Israel 47 C3 32 2N 34 44 E
Bata, Eq. Guin. 52 D1 1 57N 9 50 E
Bataan □, Phil. 37 B6 14 40N 120 25 E
Batabanó, Cuba 88 B3 22 40N 82 20W
Batabanó, G. de, Cuba 88 B3 22 30N 82 30W
Batac, Phil. 37 A6 18 3N 120 34 E
Batagai, Russia 27 C14 67 38N 134 38 E
Batala, India 42 D6 31 48N 75 12 E
Batama, Dem. Rep. of the Congo 54 B2 0 58N 26 33 E
Batamay, Russia 27 C13 63 30N 129 15 E
Batang, Indonesia 37 G13 6 55S 109 45 E
Batangas, Phil. 37 B6 13 35N 121 10 E
Batanta, Indonesia 37 E8 0 55S 130 40 E
Batatais, Brazil 95 A6 20 54S 47 37W
Batavia, U.S.A. 78 D6 43 0N 78 11W
Batchelor, Australia 60 B5 13 4S 131 1 E
Batdambang, Cambodia 38 F4 13 7N 103 12 E
Bates Ra., Australia 61 E3 27 27S 121 5 E
Batesburg-Leesville, U.S.A. 77 J5 33 54N 81 33W
Batesville, Ark., U.S.A. 81 H9 35 46N 91 39W
Batesville, Miss., U.S.A. 81 H10 34 19N 89 57W
Batesville, Tex., U.S.A. 81 L5 28 58N 99 37W
Bath, Canada 79 B8 44 11N 76 47W
Bath, U.K. 11 F5 51 23N 2 22W
Bath, Maine, U.S.A. 77 D11 43 55N 69 49W
Bath, N.Y., U.S.A. 78 D7 42 20N 77 19W
Bath & North East Somerset □, U.K. 11 F5 51 21N 2 27W
Batheay, Cambodia 39 G5 11 59N 104 57 E
Bathurst = Banjul, Gambia 50 F2 13 28N 16 40W
Bathurst, Canada 71 C6 47 37N 65 43W
Bathurst, S. Africa 56 E4 33 30S 26 50 E
Bathurst, C., Canada 68 A7 70 34N 128 0W
Bathurst B., Australia 62 A3 14 16S 144 25 E
Bathurst Harb., Australia 62 G4 43 15S 146 10 E
Bathurst I., Australia 60 B5 11 30S 130 10 E
Bathurst I., Canada 4 B2 76 0N 100 30W
Bathurst Inlet, Canada 68 B9 66 50N 108 1W
Batman, Turkey 25 G7 37 55N 41 5 E
Baţn al Ghūl, Jordan 47 F4 29 36N 35 56 E
Batna, Algeria 50 A7 35 34N 6 15 E
Batoka, Zambia 55 F2 16 45S 27 15 E
Baton Rouge, U.S.A. 81 K9 30 27N 91 11W
Batong, Ko, Thailand 39 J2 6 32N 99 12 E
Batopilas, Mexico 86 B3 27 0N 107 45W
Batouri, Cameroon 52 D2 4 30N 14 25 E
Båtsfjord, Norway 8 A23 70 38N 29 39 E
Battambang = Batdambang, Cambodia 38 F4 13 7N 103 12 E
Batticaloa, Sri Lanka 40 R12 7 43N 81 45 E
Battipáglia, Italy 20 D6 40 37N 14 58 E
Battle, U.K. 11 G8 50 55N 0 30 E
Battle →, Canada 73 C7 52 43N 108 15W
Battle Creek, U.S.A. 76 D3 42 19N 85 11W
Battle Ground, U.S.A. 84 E4 45 47N 122 32W
Battle Harbour, Canada 71 B8 52 16N 55 35W
Battle Lake, U.S.A. 80 B7 46 17N 95 43W
Battle Mountain, U.S.A. 82 F5 40 38N 116 56W
Battlefields, Zimbabwe 55 F2 18 37S 29 47 E
Battleford, Canada 73 C7 52 45N 108 15W
Batu, Ethiopia 46 F2 6 55N 39 45 E
Batu, Kepulauan, Indonesia 36 E1 0 30S 98 25 E
Batu Caves, Malaysia 39 L3 3 15N 101 40 E
Batu Gajah, Malaysia 39 K3 4 28N 101 3 E
Batu Is. = Batu, Kepulauan, Indonesia 36 E1 0 30S 98 25 E
Batu Pahat, Malaysia 39 M4 1 50N 102 56 E
Batuata, Indonesia 37 F6 6 12S 122 42 E
Batumi, Georgia 25 F7 41 39N 41 44 E
Baturaja, Indonesia 36 E2 4 11S 104 15 E
Baturité, Brazil 93 D11 4 28S 38 45W
Bau, Malaysia 36 D4 1 25N 110 9 E
Baubau, Indonesia 37 F6 5 25S 122 38 E
Bauchi, Nigeria 50 F7 10 22N 9 48 E
Baudette, U.S.A. 80 A7 48 43N 94 36W
Bauer, C., Australia 63 E1 32 44S 134 4 E
Bauhinia, Australia 62 C4 24 35S 149 18 E
Baukau, E. Timor 37 F7 8 27S 126 27 E
Bauld, C., Canada 69 C14 51 38N 55 26W
Bauru, Brazil 95 A6 22 10S 49 0W
Bausi, India 43 G12 24 48N 87 1 E
Bauska, Latvia 9 H21 56 24N 24 15 E
Bautzen, Germany 16 C8 51 10N 14 26 E
Bavānāt, Iran 45 D7 30 28N 53 27 E
Bavaria = Bayern □, Germany 16 D6 48 50N 12 0 E
Bavispe →, Mexico 86 B3 29 30N 109 11W
Bawdwin, Burma 41 H20 23 5N 97 20 E
Bawean, Indonesia 36 F4 5 46S 112 35 E
Bawku, Ghana 50 F5 11 3N 0 19W
Bawlake, Burma 41 K20 19 11N 97 21 E
Baxley, U.S.A. 77 K4 31 47N 82 21W
Baxter, U.S.A. 80 B7 46 21N 94 17W
Baxter Springs, U.S.A. 81 G7 37 2N 94 44W
Bay City, Mich., U.S.A. 76 D4 43 36N 83 54W
Bay City, Tex., U.S.A. 81 L7 28 59N 95 58W
Bay Minette, U.S.A. 77 K2 30 53N 87 46W
Bay Roberts, Canada 71 C9 47 36N 53 16W
Bay St. Louis, U.S.A. 81 K10 30 19N 89 20W
Bay Springs, U.S.A. 81 K10 31 59N 89 17W
Bay View, N.Z. 59 H6 39 25S 176 50 E
Baya, Dem. Rep. of the Congo 55 E2 11 53S 27 25 E
Bayamo, Cuba 88 B4 20 20N 76 40W
Bayamón, Puerto Rico 89 C6 18 24N 66 10W
Bayan Har Shan, China 32 C4 34 0N 98 0 E
Bayan Hot = Alxa Zuoqi, China 34 E3 38 50N 105 40 E
Bayan Obo, China 34 D5 41 52N 109 59 E
Bayan-Ovoo = Erdenetsogt, Mongolia 34 C4 42 55N 106 5 E
Bayana, India 42 F7 26 55N 77 18 E
Bayanaūyl, Kazakstan 26 D8 50 45N 75 45 E
Bayandalay, Mongolia 34 C2 43 30N 103 29 E
Bayanhongor, Mongolia 32 B5 46 8N 102 43 E
Bayard, N. Mex., U.S.A. 83 K9 32 46N 108 8W
Bayard, Nebr., U.S.A. 80 E3 41 45N 103 20W
Baybay, Phil. 37 B6 10 40N 124 55 E
Bayern □, Germany 16 D6 48 50N 12 0 E
Bayeux, France 18 B3 49 17N 0 42W
Bayfield, Canada 78 C3 43 34N 81 42W
Bayfield, U.S.A. 80 B9 46 49N 90 49W
Bayındır, Turkey 21 E12 38 13N 27 39 E
Baykal, Oz., Russia 27 D11 53 0N 108 0 E
Baykan, Turkey 44 B4 38 7N 41 44 E
Baykonur = Bayqongyr, Kazakstan 26 E7 47 48N 65 50 E
Baymak, Russia 24 D10 52 36N 58 19 E
Baynes Mts., Namibia 56 B1 17 15S 13 0 E
Bayombong, Phil. 37 A6 16 30N 121 10 E
Bayonne, France 18 E3 43 30N 1 28W
Bayonne, U.S.A. 79 F10 40 40N 74 7W
Bayovar, Peru 92 E2 5 50S 81 0W
Bayqongyr, Kazakstan 26 E7 47 48N 65 50 E
Bayram-Ali = Bayramaly, Turkmenistan 26 F7 37 37N 62 10 E
Bayramaly, Turkmenistan 26 F7 37 37N 62 10 E
Bayramiç, Turkey 21 E12 39 48N 26 36 E
Bayreuth, Germany 16 D6 49 56N 11 35 E
Bayrūt, Lebanon 47 B4 33 53N 35 31 E
Bays, L. of, Canada 78 A5 45 15N 79 4W
Baysville, Canada 78 A5 45 9N 79 7W
Bayt Lahm, West Bank 47 D4 31 43N 35 12 E
Baytown, U.S.A. 81 L7 29 43N 94 59W
Baza, Spain 19 D4 37 30N 2 47W
Bazaruto, I. do, Mozam. 57 C6 21 40S 35 28 E
Bazhou, China 34 E9 39 8N 116 22 E
Bazmān, Kūh-e, Iran 45 D9 28 4N 60 1 E
Beach, U.S.A. 80 B3 46 58N 104 0W
Beach City, U.S.A. 78 F3 40 39N 81 35W
Beachy Hd., U.K. 11 G8 50 44N 0 15 E
Beacon, Australia 61 F2 30 26S 117 52 E
Beacon, U.S.A. 79 E11 41 30N 73 58W
Beaconsfield, Australia 62 G4 41 11S 146 48 E
Beagle, Canal, S. Amer. 96 H3 55 0S 68 30W
Beagle Bay, Australia 60 C3 16 58S 122 40 E
Bealanana, Madag. 57 A8 14 33S 48 44 E
Beals Cr. →, U.S.A. 81 J4 32 10N 100 51W
Beamsville, Canada 78 C5 43 12N 79 28W
Bear →, Calif., U.S.A. 84 G5 38 56N 121 36W
Bear →, Utah, U.S.A. 74 B4 41 30N 112 8W
Bear I., Ireland 13 E2 51 38N 9 50W
Bear L., Canada 73 B9 55 8N 96 0W
Bear L., U.S.A. 82 F8 41 59N 111 21W
Beardmore, Canada 70 C2 49 36N 87 57W
Beardmore Glacier, Antarctica 5 E11 84 30S 170 0 E
Beardstown, U.S.A. 80 F9 40 1N 90 26W
Bearma →, India 43 G8 24 20N 79 51 E
Béarn, France 18 E3 43 20N 0 30W
Bearpaw Mts., U.S.A. 82 B9 48 12N 109 30W
Bearskin Lake, Canada 70 B1 53 58N 91 2W
Beas →, India 42 D6 31 10N 74 59 E
Beata, C., Dom. Rep. 89 C5 17 40N 71 30W
Beata, I., Dom. Rep. 89 C5 17 34N 71 31W
Beatrice, U.S.A. 80 E6 40 16N 96 45W
Beatrice, Zimbabwe 55 F3 18 15S 30 55 E
Beatrice, C., Australia 62 A2 14 20S 136 55 E
Beatton →, Canada 72 B4 56 15N 120 45W
Beatton River, Canada 72 B4 57 26N 121 20W
Beatty, U.S.A. 84 J10 36 54N 116 46W
Beauce, Plaine de la, France 18 B4 48 10N 1 45 E
Beauceville, Canada 71 C5 46 13N 70 46W
Beaudesert, Australia 63 D5 27 59S 153 0 E
Beaufort, Malaysia 36 C5 5 30N 115 40 E
Beaufort, N.C., U.S.A. 77 H7 34 43N 76 40W
Beaufort, S.C., U.S.A. 77 J5 32 26N 80 40W
Beaufort Sea, Arctic 4 B1 72 0N 140 0W
Beaufort West, S. Africa 56 E3 32 18S 22 36 E
Beauharnois, Canada 79 A11 45 20N 73 52W
Beaulieu →, Canada 72 A6 62 3N 113 11W
Beauly, U.K. 12 D4 57 30N 4 28W
Beauly →, U.K. 12 D4 57 29N 4 27W
Beaumaris, U.K. 10 D3 53 16N 4 6W
Beaumont, Belgium 15 D4 50 15N 4 14 E
Beaumont, U.S.A. 81 K7 30 5N 94 6W
Beaune, France 18 C6 47 2N 4 50 E
Beaupré, Canada 71 C5 47 3N 70 54W
Beauraing, Belgium 15 D4 50 7N 4 57 E
Beauséjour, Canada 73 C9 50 5N 96 35W
Beauvais, France 18 B5 49 25N 2 8 E
Beauval, Canada 73 B7 55 9N 107 37W
Beaver, Okla., U.S.A. 81 G4 36 49N 100 31W
Beaver, Pa., U.S.A. 78 F4 40 42N 80 19W
Beaver, Utah, U.S.A. 83 G7 38 17N 112 38W
Beaver →, B.C., Canada 72 B4 59 52N 124 20W
Beaver →, Ont., Canada 70 A2 55 55N 87 48W
Beaver →, Sask., Canada 73 B7 55 26N 107 45W
Beaver →, U.S.A. 81 G5 36 35N 99 30W
Beaver City, U.S.A. 80 E5 40 8N 99 50W
Beaver Creek, Canada 68 B5 63 0N 141 0W
Beaver Dam, U.S.A. 80 D10 43 28N 88 50W
Beaver Falls, U.S.A. 78 F4 40 46N 80 20W
Beaver Hill L., Canada 73 C10 54 5N 94 50W
Beaver I., U.S.A. 76 C3 45 40N 85 33W
Beaverhill L., Canada 72 C6 53 27N 112 32W
Beaverlodge, Canada 72 B5 55 11N 119 29W
Beaverstone →, Canada 70 B2 54 59N 89 25W
Beaverton, Canada 78 B5 44 26N 79 9W
Beaverton, U.S.A. 84 E4 45 29N 122 48W
Beawar, India 42 F6 26 3N 74 18 E
Bebedouro, Brazil 95 A6 21 0S 48 25W
Beboa, Madag. 57 B7 17 22S 44 33 E
Beccles, U.K. 11 E9 52 27N 1 35 E
Bečej, Serbia, Yug. 21 B9 45 36N 20 3 E
Béchar, Algeria 50 B5 31 38N 2 18W
Beckley, U.S.A. 76 G5 37 47N 81 11W
Beddouza, Ras, Morocco 50 B4 32 33N 9 9W
Bedford, Canada 79 A12 45 7N 72 59W
Bedford, S. Africa 56 E4 32 40S 26 10 E
Bedford, U.K. 11 E7 52 8N 0 28W
Bedford, Ind., U.S.A. 76 F2 38 52N 86 29W
Bedford, Iowa, U.S.A. 80 E7 40 40N 94 44W
Bedford, Ohio, U.S.A. 78 E3 41 23N 81 32W
Bedford, Pa., U.S.A. 78 F6 40 1N 78 30W
Bedford, Va., U.S.A. 76 G6 37 20N 79 31W
Bedford, C., Australia 62 B4 15 14S 145 21 E
Bedfordshire □, U.K. 11 E7 52 4N 0 28W
Bedourie, Australia 62 C2 24 30S 139 30 E
Bedum, Neths. 15 A6 53 18N 6 36 E
Beebe Plain, Canada 79 A12 45 1N 72 9W
Beech Creek, U.S.A. 78 E7 41 5N 77 36W
Beenleigh, Australia 63 D5 27 43S 153 10 E
Be'er Menuha, Israel 44 D2 30 19N 35 8 E
Be'er Sheva, Israel 47 D3 31 15N 34 48 E
Beersheba = Be'er Sheva, Israel 47 D3 31 15N 34 48 E
Beestekraal, S. Africa 57 D4 25 23S 27 38 E
Beeston, U.K. 10 E6 52 56N 1 14W
Beeville, U.S.A. 81 L6 28 24N 97 45W
Befale, Dem. Rep. of the Congo 52 D4 0 25N 20 45 E
Befandriana, Mahajanga, Madag. 57 B8 15 16S 48 32 E
Befandriana, Toliara, Madag. 57 C7 21 55S 44 0 E
Befasy, Madag. 57 C7 20 33S 44 23 E
Befotaka, Antsiranana, Madag. 57 A8 13 15S 48 16 E
Befotaka, Fianarantsoa, Madag. 57 C8 23 49S 47 0 E
Begusarai, India 43 G12 25 24N 86 9 E
Behābād, Iran 45 C8 32 24N 59 47 E
Behala, India 43 H13 22 30N 88 20 E
Behara, Madag. 57 C8 24 55S 46 20 E
Behbehān, Iran 45 D6 30 30N 50 15 E
Behm Canal, U.S.A. 72 B2 55 10N 131 0W
Behshahr, Iran 45 B7 36 45N 53 35 E
Bei Jiang →, China 33 D6 23 2N 112 58 E
Bei'an, China 33 B7 48 10N 126 20 E
Beihai, China 33 D5 21 28N 109 6 E
Beijing, China 34 E9 39 55N 116 20 E
Beijing □, China 34 E9 39 55N 116 20 E
Beilen, Neths. 15 B6 52 52N 6 27 E
Beinn na Faoghla = Benbecula, U.K. 12 D1 57 26N 7 21W
Beipiao, China 35 D11 41 52N 120 32 E
Beira, Mozam. 55 F3 19 50S 34 52 E
Beirut = Bayrūt, Lebanon 47 B4 33 53N 35 31 E
Beiseker, Canada 72 C6 51 23N 113 32W
Beitaolaizhao, China 35 B13 44 58N 125 58 E
Beitbridge, Zimbabwe 55 G3 22 12S 30 0 E
Beizhen = Binzhou, China 35 F10 37 20N 118 2 E
Beizhen, China 35 D11 41 38N 121 54 E
Beizhengzhen, China 35 B13 44 31N 123 30 E
Beja, Portugal 19 C2 38 2N 7 53W
Béja, Tunisia 51 A7 36 43N 9 12 E
Bejaïa, Algeria 50 A7 36 42N 5 2 E

Big Bend

Béjar, *Spain* **19 B3** 40 23N 5 46W
Bejestān, *Iran* **45 C8** 34 30N 58 5 E
Békéscsaba, *Hungary* **17 E11** 46 40N 21 5 E
Bekily, *Madag.* **57 C8** 24 13S 45 19 E
Bekisopa, *Madag.* **57 C8** 21 40S 45 54 E
Bekitro, *Madag.* **57 C8** 24 33S 45 18 E
Bekodoka, *Madag.* **57 B8** 16 58S 45 7 E
Bekok, *Malaysia* **39 L4** 2 20N 103 7 E
Bekopaka, *Madag.* **57 B7** 19 9S 44 48 E
Bela, *India* **43 G10** 25 50N 82 0 E
Bela, *Pakistan* **42 F2** 26 12N 66 20 E
Bela Crkva, *Serbia, Yug.* **21 B9** 44 55N 21 27 E
Bela Vista, *Brazil* **94 A4** 22 12S 56 20W
Bela Vista, *Mozam.* **57 D5** 26 10S 32 44 E
Belan →, *India* **43 G9** 24 2N 81 45 E
Belarus ■, *Europe* **17 B14** 53 30N 27 0 E
Belau = Palau ■, *Pac. Oc.* **28 J17** 7 30N 134 30 E
Belavenona, *Madag.* **57 C8** 24 50S 47 4 E
Belawan, *Indonesia* **36 D1** 3 33N 98 32 E
Belaya →, *Russia* **24 C9** 54 40N 56 0 E
Belaya Tserkov = Bila Tserkva, *Ukraine* **17 D16** 49 45N 30 10 E
Belcher Is., *Canada* **70 A3** 56 15N 78 45W
Belden, *U.S.A.* **84 E5** 40 2N 121 17W
Belebey, *Russia* **24 D9** 54 7N 54 7 E
Belém, *Brazil* **93 D9** 1 20S 48 30W
Belén, *Argentina* **94 B2** 27 40S 67 5W
Belén, *Paraguay* **94 A4** 23 30S 57 6W
Belen, *U.S.A.* **83 J10** 34 40N 106 46W
Belet Uen, *Somali Rep.* **46 G4** 4 30N 45 5 E
Belev, *Russia* **24 D6** 53 50N 36 5 E
Belfair, *U.S.A.* **84 C4** 47 27N 122 50W
Belfast, *S. Africa* **57 D5** 25 42S 30 2 E
Belfast, *U.K.* **13 B6** 54 37N 5 56W
Belfast, *Maine, U.S.A.* **77 C11** 44 26N 69 1W
Belfast, *N.Y., U.S.A.* **78 D6** 42 21N 78 7W
Belfast L., *U.K.* **13 B6** 54 40N 5 50W
Belfield, *U.S.A.* **80 B3** 46 53N 103 12W
Belfort, *France* **18 C7** 47 38N 6 50 E
Belfry, *U.S.A.* **82 D9** 45 9N 109 1W
Belgaum, *India* **40 M9** 15 55N 74 35 E
Belgium ■, *Europe* **15 D4** 50 30N 5 0 E
Belgorod, *Russia* **25 D6** 50 35N 36 35 E
Belgorod-Dnestrovskiy = Bilhorod-Dnistrovskyy, *Ukraine* **25 E6** 46 11N 30 23 E
Belgrade = Beograd, *Serbia, Yug.* **21 B9** 44 50N 20 37 E
Belgrade, *U.S.A.* **82 D8** 45 47N 111 11W
Belhaven, *U.S.A.* **77 H7** 35 33N 76 37W
Beli Drim →, *Europe* **21 C9** 42 6N 20 25 E
Belinyu, *Indonesia* **36 E3** 1 35S 105 50 E
Beliton Is. = Belitung, *Indonesia* **36 E3** 3 10S 107 50 E
Belitung, *Indonesia* **36 E3** 3 10S 107 50 E
Belize ■, *Cent. Amer.* **87 D7** 17 0N 88 30W
Belize City, *Belize* **87 D7** 17 25N 88 0W
Belkovskiy, Ostrov, *Russia* **27 B14** 75 32N 135 44 E
Bell →, *Canada* **70 C4** 49 48N 77 38W
Bell I., *Canada* **71 B8** 50 46N 55 35W
Bell-Irving →, *Canada* **72 B3** 56 12N 129 5W
Bell Peninsula, *Canada* **69 B11** 63 50N 82 0W
Bell Ville, *Argentina* **94 C3** 32 40S 62 40W
Bella Bella, *Canada* **72 C3** 52 10N 128 10W
Bella Coola, *Canada* **72 C3** 52 25N 126 40W
Bella Unión, *Uruguay* **94 C4** 30 15S 57 40W
Bella Vista, *Corrientes, Argentina* **94 B4** 28 33S 59 0W
Bella Vista, *Tucuman, Argentina* **94 B2** 27 10S 65 25W
Bellaire, *U.S.A.* **78 F4** 40 1N 80 45W
Bellary, *India* **40 M10** 15 10N 76 56 E
Bellata, *Australia* **63 D4** 29 53S 149 46 E
Belle-Chasse, *U.S.A.* **81 L10** 29 51N 89 59W
Belle Fourche, *U.S.A.* **80 C3** 44 40N 103 51W
Belle Fourche →, *U.S.A.* **80 C3** 44 26N 102 18W
Belle Glade, *U.S.A.* **77 M5** 26 41N 80 40W
Belle-Île, *France* **18 C2** 47 20N 3 10W
Belle Isle, *Canada* **71 B8** 51 57N 55 25W
Belle Isle, Str. of, *Canada* **71 B8** 51 30N 56 30W
Belle Plaine, *U.S.A.* **80 E8** 41 54N 92 17W
Bellefontaine, *U.S.A.* **76 E4** 40 22N 83 46W
Bellefonte, *U.S.A.* **78 F7** 40 55N 77 47W
Belleoram, *Canada* **71 C8** 47 31N 55 25W
Belleville, *Canada* **78 B7** 44 10N 77 23W
Belleville, *Ill., U.S.A.* **80 F10** 38 31N 89 59W
Belleville, *Kans., U.S.A.* **80 F6** 39 50N 97 38W
Belleville, *N.Y., U.S.A.* **79 C8** 43 46N 76 10W
Bellevue, *Canada* **72 D6** 49 35N 114 22W
Bellevue, *Idaho, U.S.A.* **82 E6** 43 28N 114 16W
Bellevue, *Nebr., U.S.A.* **80 E7** 41 8N 95 53W
Bellevue, *Ohio, U.S.A.* **78 E2** 41 17N 82 51W
Bellevue, *Wash., U.S.A.* **84 C4** 47 37N 122 12W
Bellin = Kangirsuk, *Canada* **69 B13** 60 0N 70 0W
Bellingham, *U.S.A.* **68 D7** 48 46N 122 29W
Bellingshausen Sea, *Antarctica* **5 C17** 66 0S 80 0W
Bellinzona, *Switz.* **18 C8** 46 11N 9 1 E
Bello, *Colombia* **92 B3** 6 20N 75 33W
Bellows Falls, *U.S.A.* **79 C12** 43 8N 72 27W
Bellpat, *Pakistan* **42 E3** 29 0N 68 5 E
Belluno, *Italy* **20 A5** 46 9N 12 13 E
Bellwood, *U.S.A.* **78 F6** 40 36N 78 20W
Belmont, *Canada* **78 D3** 42 53N 81 5W
Belmont, *S. Africa* **56 D3** 29 28S 24 22 E
Belmont, *U.S.A.* **78 D6** 42 14N 78 2W
Belmonte, *Brazil* **93 G11** 16 0S 39 0W
Belmopan, *Belize* **87 D7** 17 18N 88 30W
Belmullet, *Ireland* **13 B2** 54 14N 9 58W
Belo Horizonte, *Brazil* **93 G10** 19 55S 43 56W
Belo-sur-Mer, *Madag.* **57 C7** 20 42S 44 0 E
Belo-Tsiribihina, *Madag.* **57 B7** 19 40S 44 30 E
Belogorsk, *Russia* **27 D13** 51 0N 128 20 E
Beloha, *Madag.* **57 D8** 25 10S 45 3 E
Beloit, *Kans., U.S.A.* **80 F5** 39 28N 98 6W
Beloit, *Wis., U.S.A.* **80 D10** 42 31N 89 2W
Belokorovichi, *Ukraine* **17 C15** 51 7N 28 2 E
Belomorsk, *Russia* **24 B5** 64 35N 34 54 E
Belonia, *India* **41 H17** 23 15N 91 30 E
Beloretsk, *Russia* **24 D10** 53 58N 58 24 E
Belorussia = Belarus ■, *Europe* **17 B14** 53 30N 27 0 E
Belovo, *Russia* **26 D9** 54 30N 86 0 E
Beloye, Ozero, *Russia* **24 B6** 60 10N 37 35 E
Beloye More, *Russia* **24 A6** 66 30N 38 0 E
Belozersk, *Russia* **24 B6** 60 1N 37 45 E
Belpre, *U.S.A.* **76 F5** 39 17N 81 34W
Belrain, *India* **43 E9** 28 23N 80 55 E
Belt, *U.S.A.* **82 C8** 47 23N 110 55W
Belterra, *Brazil* **93 D8** 2 45S 55 0W
Belton, *U.S.A.* **81 K6** 31 3N 97 28W
Belton L., *U.S.A.* **81 K6** 31 8N 97 32W
Beltsy = Bălţi, *Moldova* **17 E14** 47 48N 27 58 E
Belturbet, *Ireland* **13 B4** 54 6N 7 26W
Belukha, *Russia* **26 E9** 49 50N 86 50 E
Beluran, *Malaysia* **36 C5** 5 48N 117 35 E
Belvidere, *Ill., U.S.A.* **80 D10** 42 15N 88 50W
Belvidere, *N.J., U.S.A.* **79 F9** 40 50N 75 5W
Belyando →, *Australia* **62 C4** 21 38S 146 50 E
Belyy, Ostrov, *Russia* **26 B8** 73 30N 71 0 E
Belyy Yar, *Russia* **26 D9** 58 26N 84 39 E
Belzoni, *U.S.A.* **81 J9** 33 11N 90 29W
Bemaraha, Lembalemban' i, *Madag.* **57 B7** 18 40S 44 45 E
Bemarivo, *Madag.* **57 C7** 21 45S 44 45 E
Bemarivo →, *Antsiranana, Madag.* **57 A9** 14 9S 50 9 E
Bemarivo →, *Mahajanga, Madag.* **57 B8** 15 27S 47 40 E
Bemavo, *Madag.* **57 C8** 21 33S 45 25 E
Bembéréke, *Benin* **50 F6** 10 11N 2 43 E
Bembesi, *Zimbabwe* **55 G2** 20 0S 28 58 E
Bembesi →, *Zimbabwe* **55 F2** 18 57S 27 47 E
Bemetara, *India* **43 J9** 21 42N 81 32 E
Bemidji, *U.S.A.* **80 B7** 47 28N 94 53W
Bemolanga, *Madag.* **57 B8** 17 44S 45 6 E
Ben, *Iran* **45 C6** 32 32N 50 45 E
Ben Cruachan, *U.K.* **12 E3** 56 26N 5 8W
Ben Dearg, *U.K.* **12 D4** 57 47N 4 56W
Ben Hope, *U.K.* **12 C4** 58 25N 4 36W
Ben Lawers, *U.K.* **12 E4** 56 32N 4 14W
Ben Lomond, *N.S.W., Australia* **63 E5** 30 1S 151 43 E
Ben Lomond, *Tas., Australia* **62 G4** 41 38S 147 42 E
Ben Lomond, *U.K.* **12 E4** 56 11N 4 38W
Ben Luc, *Vietnam* **39 G6** 10 39N 106 29 E
Ben Macdhui, *U.K.* **12 D5** 57 4N 3 40W
Ben Mhor, *U.K.* **12 D1** 57 15N 7 18W
Ben Moro, *Arg. & Buto, U.K.* **12 E2** 56 26N 6 1W
Ben More, *Stirl., U.K.* **12 E4** 56 23N 4 32W
Ben More Assynt, *U.K.* **12 C4** 50 0N 4 52W
Ben Nevis, *U.K.* **12 E3** 56 48N 5 1W
Ben Quang, *Vietnam* **38 D6** 17 3N 106 55 E
Ben Vorlich, *U.K.* **12 E4** 56 21N 4 14W
Ben Wyvis, *U.K.* **12 D4** 57 40N 4 35W
Bena, *Nigeria* **50 F7** 11 20N 5 50 E
Benares = Varanasi, *India* **43 G10** 25 22N 83 0 E
Benavente, *Spain* **19 A3** 42 2N 5 43W
Benavides, *U.S.A.* **81 M5** 27 36N 98 25W
Benbecula, *U.K.* **12 D1** 57 26N 7 21W
Bend, *U.S.A.* **82 D3** 44 4N 121 19W
Bender Beila, *Somali Rep.* **46 F5** 9 30N 50 48 E
Bendery = Tighina, *Moldova* **17 E15** 46 50N 29 30 E
Benē Beraq, *Israel* **47 C3** 32 6N 34 51 E
Benenitra, *Madag.* **57 C8** 23 27S 45 5 E
Benevento, *Italy* **20 D6** 41 8N 14 45 E
Benga, *Mozam.* **55 F3** 16 11S 33 40 E
Bengal, Bay of, *Ind. Oc.* **41 M17** 15 0N 90 0 E
Bengbu, *China* **35 H9** 32 58N 117 20 E
Benghazi = Banghāzī, *Libya* **51 B10** 32 11N 20 3 E
Bengkalis, *Indonesia* **36 D2** 1 30N 102 10 E
Bengkulu, *Indonesia* **36 E2** 3 50S 102 12 E
Bengkulu □, *Indonesia* **36 E2** 3 48S 102 16 E
Bengough, *Canada* **73 D7** 49 25N 105 10W
Benguela, *Angola* **53 G2** 12 37S 13 25 E
Benguérua, I., *Mozam.* **57 C6** 21 58S 35 28 E
Beni, *Dem. Rep. of the Congo* **54 B2** 0 30N 29 27 E
Beni →, *Bolivia* **92 F5** 10 23S 65 24W
Beni Mellal, *Morocco* **50 B4** 32 21N 6 21W
Beni Suef, *Egypt* **51 C12** 29 5N 31 6 E
Beniah L., *Canada* **72 A6** 63 23N 112 17W
Benicia, *U.S.A.* **84 G4** 38 3N 122 9W
Benidorm, *Spain* **19 C5** 38 33N 0 9W
Benin ■, *Africa* **50 G6** 10 0N 2 0 E
Benin, Bight of, *W. Afr.* **50 H6** 5 0N 3 0 E
Benin City, *Nigeria* **50 G7** 6 20N 5 31 E
Benitses, *Greece* **23 A3** 39 32N 19 55 E
Benjamin Aceval, *Paraguay* **94 A4** 24 58S 57 34W
Benjamin Constant, *Brazil* **92 D4** 4 40S 70 15W
Benjamin Hill, *Mexico* **86 A2** 30 10N 111 10W
Benkelman, *U.S.A.* **80 E4** 40 3N 101 32W
Bennett, *Canada* **72 B2** 59 56N 134 53W
Bennett, L., *Australia* **60 D5** 22 50S 131 2 E
Bennetta, Ostrov, *Russia* **27 B15** 76 21N 148 56 E
Bennettsville, *U.S.A.* **77 H6** 34 37N 79 41W
Bennington, *N.H., U.S.A.* **79 D11** 43 0N 71 55W
Bennington, *Vt., U.S.A.* **79 D11** 42 53N 73 12W
Benoni, *S. Africa* **57 D4** 26 11S 28 18 E
Benque Viejo, *Belize* **87 D7** 17 5N 89 8W
Benson, *Ariz., U.S.A.* **83 L8** 31 58N 110 18W
Benson, *Minn., U.S.A.* **80 C7** 45 19N 95 36W
Bent, *Iran* **45 E8** 26 20N 59 31 E
Benteng, *Indonesia* **37 F6** 6 10S 120 30 E
Bentinck I., *Australia* **62 B2** 17 3S 139 35 E
Bento Gonçalves, *Brazil* **95 B5** 29 10S 51 31W
Benton, *Ark., U.S.A.* **81 H8** 34 34N 92 35W
Benton, *Calif., U.S.A.* **84 H8** 37 48N 118 32W
Benton, *Ill., U.S.A.* **80 G10** 38 0N 88 55W
Benton, *Pa., U.S.A.* **79 E8** 41 12N 76 23W
Benton Harbor, *U.S.A.* **76 D2** 42 6N 86 27W
Bentonville, *U.S.A.* **81 G7** 36 22N 94 13W
Bentung, *Malaysia* **39 L3** 3 31N 101 55 E
Benue →, *Nigeria* **50 G7** 7 48N 6 46 E
Benxi, *China* **35 D12** 41 20N 123 48 E
Beo, *Indonesia* **37 D7** 4 25N 126 50 E
Beograd, *Serbia, Yug.* **21 B9** 44 50N 20 37 E
Beppu, *Japan* **31 H5** 33 15N 131 30 E
Beqaa Valley = Al Biqā, *Lebanon* **47 A5** 34 10N 36 10 E
Ber Mota, *India* **42 H3** 23 27N 68 34 E
Berach →, *India* **42 G6** 25 15N 75 2 E
Beraketa, *Madag.* **57 C7** 23 7S 44 25 E
Berat, *Albania* **21 D8** 40 43N 19 59 E
Berau, Teluk, *Indonesia* **37 E8** 2 30S 132 30 E
Beravina, *Madag.* **57 B8** 18 10S 45 14 E
Berber, *Sudan* **51 E12** 18 0N 34 0 E
Berbera, *Somali Rep.* **46 E4** 10 30N 45 2 E
Berbérati, *C.A.R.* **52 D3** 4 15N 15 40 E
Berbice →, *Guyana* **92 B7** 6 20N 57 32W
Berdichev = Berdychiv, *Ukraine* **17 D15** 49 57N 28 30 E
Berdsk, *Russia* **26 D9** 54 47N 83 2 E
Berdyansk, *Ukraine* **25 E6** 46 45N 36 50 E
Berdychiv, *Ukraine* **17 D15** 49 57N 28 30 E
Berea, *U.S.A.* **76 G3** 37 34N 84 17W
Berebere, *Indonesia* **37 D7** 2 25N 128 45 E
Bereda, *Somali Rep.* **46 E5** 11 45N 51 0 E
Berehove, *Ukraine* **17 D12** 48 15N 22 35 E
Berekum, *Ghana* **50 G5** 7 29N 2 34W
Berens →, *Canada* **73 C9** 52 25N 97 2W
Berens I., *Canada* **73 C9** 52 18N 97 18W
Berens River, *Canada* **73 C9** 52 25N 97 0W
Beresford, *U.S.A.* **80 D6** 43 5N 96 47W
Berestechko, *Ukraine* **17 C13** 50 22N 25 5 E
Berevo, *Mahajanga, Madag.* **57 B7** 17 14S 44 17 E
Berevo, *Toliara, Madag.* **57 B7** 19 44S 44 58 E
Bereza = Byaroza, *Belarus* **17 B13** 52 31N 24 51 E
Berezhany, *Ukraine* **17 D13** 49 26N 24 58 E
Berezina = Byarezina →, *Belarus* **17 B16** 52 33N 30 14 E
Berezniki, *Russia* **24 B7** 62 51N 42 40 E
Berezniki, *Russia* **24 C10** 59 24N 56 46 E
Berezovo, *Russia* **26 C7** 64 0N 65 0 E
Berga, *Spain* **19 A6** 42 6N 1 48 E
Bergama, *Turkey* **21 E12** 39 8N 27 11 E
Bérgamo, *Italy* **18 D8** 45 41N 9 43 E
Bergen, *Neths.* **15 B4** 52 40N 4 43 E
Bergen, *Norway* **9 F11** 60 20N 5 20 E
Bergen, *U.S.A.* **78 C7** 43 5N 77 57W
Bergen op Zoom, *Neths.* **15 C4** 51 28N 4 18 E
Bergerac, *France* **18 D4** 44 51N 0 30 E
Bergholz, *U.S.A.* **78 F4** 40 31N 80 53W
Bergisch Gladbach, *Germany* **15 D7** 50 59N 7 8 E
Bergville, *S. Africa* **57 D4** 28 52S 29 18 E
Berhala, Selat, *Indonesia* **36 E2** 1 0S 104 15 E
Berhampore = Baharampur, *India* **43 G13** 24 2N 88 27 E
Berhampur = Brahmapur, *India* **41 K14** 19 15N 84 54 E
Bering Sea, *Pac. Oc.* **68 C1** 58 0N 171 0 E
Bering Strait, *Pac. Oc.* **68 B3** 65 30N 169 0W
Beringovskiy, *Russia* **27 C18** 63 3N 179 19 E
Berisso, *Argentina* **94 C4** 34 56S 57 50W
Berja, *Spain* **19 D4** 36 50N 2 56W
Berkeley, *U.S.A.* **84 H4** 37 52N 122 16W
Berkner I., *Antarctica* **5 D18** 79 30S 50 0W
Berkshire, *U.S.A.* **79 D8** 42 19N 76 11W
Berkshire Downs, *U.K.* **11 F6** 51 33N 1 29W
Berlin, *Germany* **16 B7** 52 30N 13 25 E
Berlin, *Md., U.S.A.* **76 F8** 38 20N 75 13W
Berlin, *N.H., U.S.A.* **79 B13** 44 28N 71 11W
Berlin, *N.Y., U.S.A.* **79 D11** 42 42N 73 23W
Berlin, *Wis., U.S.A.* **76 D1** 43 58N 88 57W
Berlin L., *U.S.A.* **78 E4** 41 3N 81 0W
Bermejo →, *Formosa, Argentina* **94 B4** 26 51S 58 23W
Bermejo →, *San Juan, Argentina* **94 C2** 32 30S 67 30W
Bermen, L., *Canada* **71 B6** 53 35N 68 55W
Bermuda ■, *Atl. Oc.* **66 F13** 32 45N 65 0W
Bern, *Switz.* **18 C7** 46 57N 7 28 E
Bernalillo, *U.S.A.* **83 J10** 35 18N 106 33W
Bernardo de Irigoyen, *Argentina* **95 B5** 26 15S 53 40W
Bernardo O'Higgins □, *Chile* **94 C1** 34 15S 70 45W
Bernardsville, *U.S.A.* **79 F10** 40 43N 74 34W
Bernasconi, *Argentina* **94 D3** 37 55S 63 44W
Bernburg, *Germany* **16 C6** 51 47N 11 44 E
Berne = Bern, *Switz.* **18 C7** 46 57N 7 28 E
Berneray, *U.K.* **12 D1** 57 43N 7 11W
Bernier I., *Australia* **61 D1** 24 50S 113 12 E
Bernina, Piz, *Switz.* **18 C8** 46 20N 9 54 E
Beroroha, *Madag.* **57 C8** 21 40S 45 10 E
Beroun, *Czech Rep.* **16 D8** 49 57N 14 5 E
Berriane, *Algeria* **50 B6** 32 50N 3 46 E
Berry, *France* **18 C5** 46 50N 2 0 E
Berry Is., *Bahamas* **88 A4** 25 40N 77 50W
Berryessa L., *U.S.A.* **84 G4** 38 31N 122 6W
Berryville, *U.S.A.* **81 G8** 36 22N 93 34W
Berseba, *Namibia* **56 D2** 26 0S 17 46 E
Bershad, *Ukraine* **17 D15** 48 22N 29 31 E
Berthold, *U.S.A.* **80 A4** 48 19N 101 44W
Berthoud, *U.S.A.* **80 E2** 40 19N 105 5W
Bertoua, *Cameroon* **52 D2** 4 30N 13 45 E
Bertraghboy B., *Ireland* **13 C2** 53 22N 9 54W
Berwick, *U.S.A.* **79 E8** 41 3N 76 14W
Berwick-upon-Tweed, *U.K.* **10 B6** 55 46N 2 0W
Berwyn Mts., *U.K.* **10 E4** 52 54N 3 26W
Besal, *Pakistan* **43 B5** 35 4N 73 56 E
Besalampy, *Madag.* **57 B7** 16 43S 44 29 E
Besançon, *France* **18 C7** 47 15N 6 2 E
Besar, *Indonesia* **36 E5** 2 40S 116 0 E
Besnard L., *Canada* **73 B7** 55 25N 106 0W
Besni, *Turkey* **44 B3** 37 41N 37 52 E
Besor, N. →, *Egypt* **47 D3** 31 28N 34 22 E
Bessarabiya, *Moldova* **17 E15** 47 0N 28 10 E
Bessarabka = Basarabeasca, *Moldova* **17 E15** 46 21N 28 58 E
Bessemer, *Ala., U.S.A.* **77 J2** 33 24N 86 58W
Bessemer, *Mich., U.S.A.* **80 B9** 46 29N 90 3W
Bessemer, *Pa., U.S.A.* **78 F4** 40 59N 80 30W
Beswick, *Australia* **60 B5** 14 34S 132 53 E
Bet She'an, *Israel* **47 C4** 32 30N 35 30 E
Bet Shemesh, *Israel* **47 D4** 31 44N 35 0 E
Betafo, *Madag.* **57 B8** 19 50S 46 51 E
Betancuria, *Canary Is.* **22 F5** 28 25N 14 3W
Betanzos, *Spain* **19 A1** 43 15N 8 12W
Bétaré Oya, *Cameroon* **52 C2** 5 40N 14 5 E
Betatao, *Madag.* **57 B8** 18 11S 47 52 E
Bethal, *S. Africa* **57 D4** 26 27S 29 28 E
Bethanien, *Namibia* **56 D2** 26 31S 17 8 E
Bethany, *Canada* **78 B6** 44 11N 78 34W
Bethany, *U.S.A.* **80 E7** 40 16N 94 2W
Bethel, *Alaska, U.S.A.* **68 B3** 60 48N 161 45W
Bethel, *Conn., U.S.A.* **79 E11** 41 22N 73 25W
Bethel, *Maine, U.S.A.* **79 B14** 44 25N 70 47W
Bethel, *Vt., U.S.A.* **79 C12** 43 50N 72 38W
Bethel Park, *U.S.A.* **78 F4** 40 20N 80 1W
Bethlehem = Bayt Lahm, *West Bank* **47 D4** 31 43N 35 12 E
Bethlehem, *S. Africa* **57 D4** 28 14S 28 18 E
Bethlehem, *U.S.A.* **79 F9** 40 37N 75 23W
Bethulie, *S. Africa* **56 E4** 30 30S 25 59 E
Béthune, *France* **18 A5** 50 30N 2 38 E
Betioky, *Madag.* **57 C7** 23 48S 44 20 E
Betong, *Thailand* **39 K3** 5 45N 101 5 E
Betoota, *Australia* **62 D3** 25 45S 140 42 E
Betroka, *Madag.* **57 C8** 23 16S 46 0 E
Betsiamites, *Canada* **71 C6** 48 56N 68 40W
Betsiamites →, *Canada* **71 C6** 48 56N 68 38W
Betsiboka →, *Madag.* **57 B8** 16 3S 46 36 E
Bettendorf, *U.S.A.* **80 E9** 41 32N 90 30W
Bettiah, *India* **43 F11** 26 48N 84 33 E
Betul, *India* **40 J10** 21 58N 77 59 E
Betung, *Malaysia* **36 D4** 1 24N 111 31 E
Betws-y-Coed, *U.K.* **10 D4** 53 5N 3 48W
Beulah, *Mich., U.S.A.* **76 C2** 44 38N 86 6W
Beulah, *N. Dak., U.S.A.* **80 B4** 47 16N 101 47W
Beveren, *Belgium* **15 C4** 51 12N 4 16 E
Beverley, *Australia* **61 F2** 32 9S 116 56 E
Beverley, *U.K.* **10 D7** 53 51N 0 26W
Beverley Hills, *U.S.A.* **77 L4** 28 56N 82 28W
Beverly, *U.S.A.* **79 D14** 42 33N 70 53W
Beverly Hills, *U.S.A.* **85 L8** 34 4N 118 25W
Bevoalavo, *Madag.* **57 D7** 25 13S 45 26 E
Bewas →, *India* **43 H8** 23 59N 79 21 E
Bexhill, *U.K.* **11 G8** 50 51N 0 29 E
Beyānlū, *Iran* **44 C5** 36 0N 47 51 E
Beyneu, *Kazakstan* **25 E10** 45 18N 55 9 E
Beypazarı, *Turkey* **25 F5** 40 10N 31 56 E
Beyşehir Gölü, *Turkey* **25 G5** 37 41N 31 33 E
Béziers, *France* **18 E5** 43 20N 3 12 E
Bezwada = Vijayawada, *India* **41 L12** 16 31N 80 39 E
Bhabua, *India* **43 G10** 25 3N 83 37 E
Bhachau, *India* **40 H7** 23 20N 70 16 E
Bhadar →, *Gujarat, India* **42 H5** 22 17N 72 20 E
Bhadar →, *Gujarat, India* **42 J3** 21 27N 69 47 E
Bhadarwah, *India* **43 C6** 32 58N 75 46 E
Bhadohi, *India* **43 G10** 25 25N 82 34 E
Bhadra, *India* **42 E6** 29 8N 75 14 E
Bhadrakh, *India* **41 J15** 21 10N 86 30 E
Bhadran, *India* **42 H5** 22 19N 72 6 E
Bhadravati, *India* **40 N9** 13 49N 75 40 E
Bhag, *Pakistan* **42 E2** 29 2N 67 49 E
Bhagalpur, *India* **43 G12** 25 10N 87 0 E
Bhagirathi →, *Ut. P., India* **43 D8** 30 8N 78 35 E
Bhagirathi →, *W. Bengal, India* **43 H13** 23 25N 88 23 E
Bhakkar, *Pakistan* **42 D4** 31 40N 71 5 E
Bhakra Dam, *India* **42 D7** 31 30N 76 45 E
Bhamo, *Burma* **41 G20** 24 15N 97 15 E
Bhandara, *India* **40 J11** 21 5N 79 42 E
Bhanpura, *India* **42 G6** 24 31N 75 44 E
Bhanrer Ra., *India* **43 H8** 23 40N 79 45 E
Bhaptiahi, *India* **43 F12** 26 19N 86 44 E
Bharat = India ■, *Asia* **40 K11** 20 0N 78 0 E
Bharatpur, *Mad. P., India* **43 H9** 23 44N 81 46 E
Bharatpur, *Raj., India* **42 F7** 27 15N 77 30 E
Bharno, *India* **43 H11** 23 14N 84 53 E
Bhatinda, *India* **42 D6** 30 15N 74 57 E
Bhatpara, *India* **43 H13** 22 50N 88 25 E
Bhattu, *India* **42 E6** 29 36N 75 19 E
Bhaun, *Pakistan* **42 C5** 32 55N 72 40 E
Bhaunagar = Bhavnagar, *India* **40 J8** 21 45N 72 10 E
Bhavnagar, *India* **40 J8** 21 45N 72 10 E
Bhawari, *India* **42 G5** 25 42N 73 4 E
Bhayavadar, *India* **42 J4** 21 51N 70 15 E
Bhera, *Pakistan* **42 C5** 32 29N 72 57 E
Bhikangaon, *India* **42 J6** 21 52N 75 57 E
Bhilsa = Vidisha, *India* **42 H7** 23 28N 77 53 E
Bhilwara, *India* **42 G6** 25 25N 74 38 E
Bhima →, *India* **40 L10** 16 25N 77 17 E
Bhimbar, *Pakistan* **43 C6** 32 59N 74 3 E
Bhind, *India* **43 F8** 26 30N 78 46 E
Bhinga, *India* **43 F9** 27 43N 81 56 E
Bhinmal, *India* **42 G5** 25 0N 72 15 E
Bhiwandi, *India* **40 K8** 19 20N 73 0 E
Bhiwani, *India* **42 E7** 28 50N 76 9 E
Bhogava →, *India* **42 H5** 22 26N 72 20 E
Bhola, *Bangla.* **41 H17** 22 45N 90 35 E
Bholari, *Pakistan* **42 G3** 25 19N 68 13 E
Bhopal, *India* **42 H7** 23 20N 77 30 E
Bhubaneshwar, *India* **41 J14** 20 15N 85 50 E
Bhuj, *India* **42 H3** 23 15N 69 49 E
Bhusaval, *India* **40 J9** 21 3N 75 46 E
Bhutan ■, *Asia* **41 F17** 27 25N 90 30 E
Biafra, B. of = Bonny, Bight of, *Africa* **52 D1** 3 30N 9 20 E
Biak, *Indonesia* **37 E9** 1 10S 136 6 E
Biała Podlaska, *Poland* **17 B12** 52 4N 23 6 E
Białogard, *Poland* **16 A8** 54 2N 15 58 E
Białystok, *Poland* **17 B12** 53 10N 23 10 E
Biaora, *India* **42 H7** 23 56N 76 56 E
Bīārjmand, *Iran* **45 B7** 36 6N 55 53 E
Biaro, *Indonesia* **37 D7** 2 5N 125 26 E
Biarritz, *France* **18 E3** 43 29N 1 33W
Bibai, *Japan* **30 C10** 43 19N 141 52 E
Bibby I., *Canada* **73 A10** 61 55N 93 0W
Biberach, *Germany* **16 D5** 48 5N 9 47 E
Bibungwa, *Dem. Rep. of the Congo* **54 C2** 2 40S 28 15 E
Bic, *Canada* **71 C6** 48 20N 68 41W
Bicester, *U.K.* **11 F6** 51 54N 1 9W
Bicheno, *Australia* **62 G4** 41 52S 148 18 E
Bichia, *India* **43 H9** 22 27N 80 42 E
Bickerton I., *Australia* **62 A2** 13 45S 136 10 E
Bida, *Nigeria* **50 G7** 9 3N 5 58 E
Bidar, *India* **40 L10** 17 55N 77 35 E
Biddeford, *U.S.A.* **77 D10** 43 30N 70 28W
Bideford, *U.K.* **11 F3** 51 1N 4 13W
Bideford Bay, *U.K.* **11 F3** 51 5N 4 20W
Bidhuna, *India* **43 F8** 26 49N 79 31 E
Bidor, *Malaysia* **39 K3** 4 6N 101 15 E
Bié, Planalto de, *Angola* **53 G3** 12 0S 16 0 E
Bieber, *U.S.A.* **82 F3** 41 7N 121 8W
Biel, *Switz.* **18 C7** 47 8N 7 14 E
Bielefeld, *Germany* **16 B5** 52 1N 8 33 E
Biella, *Italy* **18 D8** 45 34N 8 3 E
Bielsk Podlaski, *Poland* **17 B12** 52 47N 23 12 E
Bielsko-Biała, *Poland* **17 D10** 49 50N 19 2 E
Bien Hoa, *Vietnam* **39 G6** 10 57N 106 49 E
Bienne = Biel, *Switz.* **18 C7** 47 8N 7 14 E
Bienville, L., *Canada* **70 A5** 55 5N 72 40W
Biesiesfontein, *S. Africa* **56 E2** 30 57S 17 58 E
Big →, *Canada* **71 B8** 54 50N 58 55W
Big B., *Canada* **71 A7** 55 43N 60 35W
Big Bear City, *U.S.A.* **85 L10** 34 16N 116 51W
Big Bear Lake, *U.S.A.* **85 L10** 34 15N 116 56W
Big Belt Mts., *U.S.A.* **82 C8** 46 30N 111 25W
Big Bend, *Swaziland* **57 D5** 26 50S 31 58 E

Big Bend National Park

Big Bend National Park, U.S.A. 81 L3 29 20N 103 5W
Big Black →, U.S.A. 81 K9 32 3N 91 4W
Big Blue →, U.S.A. 80 F6 39 35N 96 34W
Big Creek, U.S.A. 84 H7 37 11N 119 14W
Big Cypress National Preserve, U.S.A. 77 M5 26 0N 81 10W
Big Cypress Swamp, U.S.A. 77 M5 26 12N 81 10W
Big Falls, U.S.A. 80 A8 48 12N 93 48W
Big Fork →, U.S.A. 80 A8 48 31N 93 43W
Big Horn Mts. = Bighorn Mts., U.S.A. 82 D10 44 30N 107 30W
Big I., Canada 72 A5 61 7N 116 45W
Big Lake, U.S.A. 81 K4 31 12N 101 28W
Big Moose, U.S.A. 79 C10 43 49N 74 58W
Big Muddy Cr. →, U.S.A. 80 A2 48 8N 104 36W
Big Pine, U.S.A. 84 H8 37 10N 118 17W
Big Piney, U.S.A. 82 E8 42 32N 110 7W
Big Rapids, U.S.A. 76 D3 43 42N 85 29W
Big Rideau L., Canada 79 B8 44 40N 76 15W
Big River, Canada 73 C7 53 50N 107 0W
Big Run, U.S.A. 78 F6 40 57N 78 55W
Big Sable Pt., U.S.A. 76 C2 44 3N 86 1W
Big Salmon →, Canada 72 A2 61 52N 134 55W
Big Sand L., Canada 73 B9 57 45N 99 45W
Big Sandy, U.S.A. 82 B8 48 11N 110 7W
Big Sandy →, U.S.A. 76 F4 38 25N 82 36W
Big Sandy Cr. →, U.S.A. 80 F3 38 7N 102 29W
Big Sioux →, U.S.A. 80 D6 42 29N 96 27W
Big Spring, U.S.A. 81 J4 32 15N 101 28W
Big Stone City, U.S.A. 80 C6 45 18N 96 28W
Big Stone Gap, U.S.A. 77 G4 36 52N 82 47W
Big Stone L., U.S.A. 80 C6 45 30N 96 35W
Big Sur, U.S.A. 84 J5 36 15N 121 48W
Big Timber, U.S.A. 82 D9 45 50N 109 57W
Big Trout L., Canada 70 B2 53 40N 90 0W
Big Trout Lake, Canada 70 B2 53 45N 90 0W
Biğa, Turkey 21 D12 40 13N 27 14 E
Bigadiç, Turkey 21 E13 39 22N 28 7 E
Biggar, Canada 73 C7 52 4N 108 0W
Biggar, U.K. 12 F5 55 38N 3 32W
Bigge I., Australia 60 B4 14 35S 125 10 E
Biggenden, Australia 63 D5 25 31S 152 4 E
Biggleswade, U.K. 11 E7 52 5N 0 14W
Biggs, U.S.A. 84 F5 39 25N 121 43W
Bighorn, U.S.A. 82 C10 46 10N 107 27W
Bighorn →, U.S.A. 82 C10 46 10N 107 28W
Bighorn L., U.S.A. 82 D9 44 55N 108 15W
Bighorn Mts., U.S.A. 82 D10 44 30N 107 30W
Bigstone L., Canada 73 C9 53 42N 95 44W
Bigwa, Tanzania 54 D4 7 10S 39 10 E
Bihać, Bos.-H. 16 F8 44 49N 15 57 E
Bihar, India 43 G11 25 5N 85 40 E
Bihar □, India 43 G12 25 0N 86 0 E
Biharamulo, Tanzania 54 C3 2 25S 31 25 E
Bihariganj, India 43 G12 25 44N 86 59 E
Bihor, Munţii, Romania 17 E12 46 29N 22 47 E
Bijagós, Arquipélago dos, Guinea-Biss. 50 F2 11 15N 16 10W
Bijaipur, India 42 F7 26 2N 77 20 E
Bijapur, Karnataka, India 40 L9 16 50N 75 55 E
Bijapur, Mad. P., India 41 K12 18 50N 80 50 E
Bījār, Iran 44 C5 35 52N 47 35 E
Bijawar, India 43 G8 24 38N 79 30 E
Bijeljina, Bos.-H. 21 B8 44 46N 19 14 E
Bijnor, India 42 E8 29 27N 78 11 E
Bikaner, India 42 E5 28 2N 73 18 E
Bikapur, India 43 F10 26 30N 82 7 E
Bikeqi, China 34 D6 40 43N 111 20 E
Bikfayyā, Lebanon 47 B4 33 55N 35 41 E
Bikin, Russia 27 E14 46 50N 134 20 E
Bikin →, Russia 30 A7 46 51N 134 2 E
Bikini Atoll, Marshall Is. 64 F8 12 0N 167 30 E
Bikita, Zimbabwe 57 C5 20 6S 31 41 E
Bila Tserkva, Ukraine 17 D16 49 45N 30 10 E
Bilara, India 42 F5 26 14N 73 53 E
Bilaspur, Mad. P., India 43 H10 22 2N 82 15 E
Bilaspur, Punjab, India 42 D7 31 19N 76 50 E
Bilauk Taungdan, Thailand 38 F2 13 0N 99 0 E
Bilbao, Spain 19 A4 43 16N 2 56W
Bilbo = Bilbao, Spain 19 A4 43 16N 2 56W
Bíldudalur, Iceland 8 D2 65 41N 23 36W
Bílé Karpaty, Europe 17 D9 49 5N 18 0 E
Bilecik, Turkey 25 F5 40 5N 30 5 E
Bilgram, India 43 F9 27 11N 80 2 E
Bilhaur, India 43 F9 26 51N 80 5 E
Bilhorod-Dnistrovskyy, Ukraine 25 E5 46 11N 30 23 E
Bilibino, Russia 27 C17 68 3N 166 20 E
Bilibiza, Mozam. 55 E5 12 30S 40 20 E
Billabalong Roadhouse, Australia 61 E2 27 25S 115 49 E
Billiluna, Australia 60 C4 19 37S 127 41 E
Billings, U.S.A. 82 D9 45 47N 108 30W
Billiton Is. = Belitung, Indonesia 36 E3 3 10S 107 50 E
Bilma, Niger 51 E8 18 50N 13 30 E
Biloela, Australia 62 C5 24 24S 150 31 E
Biloxi, U.S.A. 81 K10 30 24N 88 53W
Bilpa Morea Claypan, Australia 62 D3 25 0S 140 0 E
Biltine, Chad 51 F10 14 40N 20 50 E
Bima, Indonesia 37 F5 8 22S 118 49 E
Bimini Is., Bahamas 88 A4 25 42N 79 25W
Bin Xian, Heilongjiang, China 35 B14 45 42N 127 32 E
Bin Xian, Shaanxi, China 34 G5 35 2N 108 4 E
Bina-Etawah, India 42 G8 24 13N 78 14 E
Bīnāb, Iran 45 B6 36 35N 48 41 E
Binalbagan, Phil. 37 B6 10 12N 122 50 E
Bīnālūd, Kūh-e, Iran 45 B8 36 30N 58 30 E
Binatang = Bintangor, Malaysia 36 D4 2 10N 111 40 E
Binche, Belgium 15 D4 50 26N 4 10 E
Bindki, India 43 F9 26 2N 80 36 E
Bindura, Zimbabwe 55 F3 17 18S 31 18 E
Bingara, Australia 63 D5 29 52S 150 36 E
Bingham, U.S.A. 77 C11 45 3N 69 53W
Binghamton, U.S.A. 79 D9 42 6N 75 55W
Bingöl, Turkey 44 B4 38 53N 40 29 E
Binh Dinh = An Nhon, Vietnam 38 F7 13 55N 109 7 E
Binh Khe, Vietnam 38 F7 13 57N 108 51 E
Binh Son, Vietnam 38 E7 15 20N 108 40 E
Binhai, China 35 G10 34 2N 119 49 E
Binisatua, Spain 22 B11 39 50N 4 11 E
Binjai, Indonesia 36 D3 3 20N 98 30 E
Binongko, Indonesia 37 F6 5 57S 124 2 E
Binscarth, Canada 73 C8 50 37N 101 17W
Bintan, Indonesia 36 D2 1 0N 104 0 E
Bintangor, Malaysia 36 D4 2 10N 111 40 E
Bintulu, Malaysia 36 D4 3 10N 113 0 E
Bintuni, Indonesia 37 E8 2 7S 133 32 E
Binzert = Bizerte, Tunisia 51 A7 37 15N 9 50 E
Binzhou, China 35 F10 37 20N 118 2 E
Bío Bío □, Chile 94 D1 37 35S 72 0W
Bioko, Eq. Guin. 52 D1 3 30N 8 40 E
Bir, India 40 K9 19 4N 75 46 E
Bîr Abu Muḥammad, Egypt 47 F3 29 44N 34 14 E
Bi'r ad Dabbāghāt, Jordan 47 E4 30 26N 35 32 E
Bi'r al Butayyihāt, Jordan 47 F4 29 47N 35 20 E
Bi'r al Mārī, Jordan 47 E4 30 4N 35 33 E
Bi'r al Qattār, Jordan 47 F4 29 47N 35 32 E
Bir Atrun, Sudan 51 E11 18 15N 26 40 E
Bîr Beiḍa, Egypt 47 E3 30 25N 34 29 E
Bîr el 'Abd, Egypt 47 D2 31 2N 33 0 E
Bîr el Biarât, Egypt 47 F3 29 30N 34 43 E
Bîr el Duweidar, Egypt 47 E1 30 56N 32 32 E
Bîr el Garârât, Egypt 47 D2 31 3N 33 34 E
Bîr el Heisi, Egypt 47 F3 29 22N 34 36 E
Bîr el Jafir, Egypt 47 E1 30 50N 32 41 E
Bîr el Mâlḥi, Egypt 47 E2 30 38N 33 19 E
Bîr el Thamâda, Egypt 47 E2 30 12N 33 27 E
Bîr Gebeil Ḥiṣn, Egypt 47 E2 30 2N 33 18 E
Bi'r Ghadīr, Syria 47 A6 34 6N 37 3 E
Bîr Ḥasana, Egypt 47 E2 30 29N 33 46 E
Bîr Kaseiba, Egypt 47 E2 31 0N 33 17 E
Bîr Lahfân, Egypt 47 E2 31 0N 33 51 E
Bîr Madkûr, Egypt 47 E1 30 44N 32 33 E
Bîr Mogreïn, Mauritania 50 C3 25 10N 11 25W
Bi'r Muṭribah, Kuwait 44 D5 29 54N 47 17 E
Bîr Qaṭia, Egypt 47 E1 30 58N 32 45 E
Bîr Shalatein, Egypt 51 D13 23 5N 35 25 E
Biratnagar, Nepal 43 F12 26 27N 87 17 E
Birawa, Dem. Rep. of the Congo 54 C2 2 20S 28 48 E
Birch →, Canada 72 B6 58 28N 112 17W
Birch Hills, Canada 73 C7 52 59N 105 25W
Birch I., Canada 73 C9 52 26N 99 54W
Birch L., N.W.T., Canada 72 A5 62 4N 116 33W
Birch L., Ont., Canada 70 B1 51 23N 92 18W
Birch Mts., Canada 72 B6 57 30N 113 10W
Birch River, Canada 73 C8 52 24N 101 6W
Bird, Canada 73 B10 56 30N 94 13W
Bird I. = Las Aves, Is., W. Indies 89 C7 15 45N 63 55W
Birdsville, Australia 62 D2 25 51S 139 20 E
Birdum Cr. →, Australia 60 C5 15 14S 133 0 E
Birecik, Turkey 44 B3 37 2N 38 0 E
Birein, Israel 47 E3 30 50N 34 28 E
Bireuen, Indonesia 36 C1 5 14N 96 39 E
Birigui, Brazil 95 A5 21 18S 50 16W
Birjand, Iran 45 C8 32 53N 59 13 E
Birkenhead, U.K. 10 D4 53 23N 3 2W
Bîrlad = Bârlad, Romania 17 E14 46 15N 27 38 E
Birmingham, U.K. 11 E6 52 29N 1 52W
Birmingham, U.S.A. 77 J2 33 31N 86 48W
Birmitrapur, India 41 H14 22 24N 84 46 E
Birni Nkonni, Niger 50 F7 13 55N 5 15 E
Birnin Kebbi, Nigeria 50 F6 12 32N 4 12 E
Birobidzhan, Russia 27 E14 48 50N 132 50 E
Birr, Ireland 13 C4 53 6N 7 54W
Birrie →, Australia 63 D4 29 43S 146 37 E
Birsilpur, India 42 E5 28 11N 72 15 E
Birsk, Russia 24 C10 55 25N 55 30 E
Birtle, Canada 73 C8 50 30N 101 5W
Birur, India 40 N9 13 30N 75 55 E
Biržai, Lithuania 9 H21 56 11N 24 45 E
Birzebbugga, Malta 23 D2 35 49N 14 32 E
Bisa, Indonesia 37 E7 1 15S 127 28 E
Bisalpur, India 43 E8 28 14N 79 48 E
Bisbee, U.S.A. 83 L9 31 27N 109 55W
Biscay, B. of, Atl. Oc. 18 D1 45 0N 2 0W
Biscayne B., U.S.A. 77 N5 25 40N 80 12W
Biscoe Bay, Antarctica 5 D13 77 0S 152 0W
Biscoe Is., Antarctica 5 C17 66 0S 67 0W
Biscostasing, Canada 70 C3 47 18N 82 9W
Bishkek, Kyrgyzstan 26 E8 42 54N 74 46 E
Bishnupur, India 43 H12 23 8N 87 20 E
Bisho, S. Africa 57 E4 32 50S 27 23 E
Bishop, Calif., U.S.A. 84 H8 37 22N 118 24W
Bishop, Tex., U.S.A. 81 M6 27 35N 97 48W
Bishop Auckland, U.K. 10 C6 54 39N 1 40W
Bishop's Falls, Canada 71 C8 49 2N 55 30W
Bishop's Stortford, U.K. 11 F8 51 52N 0 10 E
Bisina, L., Uganda 54 B3 1 38N 33 56 E
Biskra, Algeria 50 B7 34 50N 5 44 E
Bismarck, U.S.A. 80 B4 46 48N 100 47W
Bismarck Arch., Papua N. G. 64 H7 2 30S 150 0 E
Biso, Uganda 54 B3 1 44N 31 26 E
Bison, U.S.A. 80 C3 45 31N 102 28W
Bīsotūn, Iran 44 C5 34 23N 47 26 E
Bissagos = Bijagós, Arquipélago dos, Guinea-Biss. 50 F2 11 15N 16 10W
Bissau, Guinea-Biss. 50 F2 11 45N 15 45W
Bistcho L., Canada 72 B5 59 45N 118 50W
Bistriţa, Romania 17 E13 47 9N 24 35 E
Bistriţa →, Romania 17 E14 46 30N 26 57 E
Biswan, India 43 F9 27 29N 81 2 E
Bitlis, Turkey 44 B4 38 20N 42 3 E
Bitola, Macedonia 21 D9 41 1N 21 20 E
Bitolj = Bitola, Macedonia 21 D9 41 1N 21 20 E
Bitter Creek, U.S.A. 82 F9 41 33N 108 33W
Bitterfontein, S. Africa 56 E2 31 1S 18 32 E
Bitterroot →, U.S.A. 82 C6 46 52N 114 7W
Bitterroot Range, U.S.A. 82 D6 46 0N 114 20W
Bitterwater, U.S.A. 84 J6 36 23N 121 0W
Biu, Nigeria 51 F8 10 40N 12 3 E
Biwa-Ko, Japan 31 G8 35 15N 136 10 E
Biwabik, U.S.A. 80 B8 47 32N 92 21W
Bixby, U.S.A. 81 H7 35 57N 95 53W
Biyang, China 34 H7 32 38N 113 21 E
Biysk, Russia 26 D9 52 40N 85 0 E
Bizana, S. Africa 57 E4 30 50S 29 52 E
Bizen, Japan 31 G7 34 43N 134 8 E
Bizerte, Tunisia 51 A7 37 15N 9 50 E
Bjargtangar, Iceland 8 D1 65 30N 24 30W
Bjelovar, Croatia 20 B7 45 56N 16 49 E
Bjørnevatn, Norway 8 B23 69 40N 30 0 E
Bjørnøya, Arctic 4 B8 74 30N 19 0 E
Black = Da →, Vietnam 38 B5 21 15N 105 20 E
Black →, Canada 78 B5 44 42N 79 19W
Black →, Ariz., U.S.A. 83 K8 33 44N 110 13W
Black →, Ark., U.S.A. 81 H9 35 38N 91 20W
Black →, Mich., U.S.A. 78 D2 42 59N 82 27W
Black →, N.Y., U.S.A. 79 C8 43 59N 76 4W
Black →, Wis., U.S.A. 80 D9 43 57N 91 22W
Black Bay Pen., Canada 70 C2 48 38N 88 21W
Black Birch L., Canada 73 B7 56 53N 107 45W
Black Diamond, Canada 72 C6 50 45N 114 14W
Black Duck →, Canada 70 A2 56 51N 89 2W
Black Forest = Schwarzwald, Germany 16 D5 48 30N 8 20 E
Black Forest, U.S.A. 80 F2 39 0N 104 43W
Black Hd., Ireland 13 C2 53 9N 9 16W
Black Hills, U.S.A. 80 D3 44 0N 103 45W
Black I., Canada 73 C9 51 12N 96 30W
Black L., Canada 73 B7 59 12N 105 15W
Black L., Mich., U.S.A. 76 C3 45 28N 84 16W
Black L., N.Y., U.S.A. 79 B9 44 31N 75 36W
Black Lake, Canada 73 B7 59 11N 105 20W
Black Mesa, U.S.A. 81 G3 36 58N 102 58W
Black Mt. = Mynydd Du, U.K. 11 F4 51 52N 3 50W
Black Mts., U.K. 11 F4 51 55N 3 7W
Black Range, U.S.A. 83 K10 33 15N 107 50W
Black River, Jamaica 88 C4 18 0N 77 50W
Black River Falls, U.S.A. 80 C9 44 18N 90 51W
Black Sea, Eurasia 25 F6 43 30N 35 0 E
Black Tickle, Canada 71 B8 53 28N 55 45W
Black Volta →, Africa 50 G5 8 41N 1 33W
Black Warrior →, U.S.A. 77 J2 32 32N 87 51W
Blackall, Australia 62 C4 24 25S 145 45 E
Blackball, N.Z. 59 K3 42 22S 171 26 E
Blackbull, Australia 62 B3 17 55S 141 45 E
Blackburn, U.K. 10 D5 53 45N 2 29W
Blackburn with Darwen □, U.K. 10 D5 53 45N 2 29W
Blackfoot, U.S.A. 82 E7 43 11N 112 21W
Blackfoot →, U.S.A. 82 C7 46 52N 113 53W
Blackfoot River Reservoir, U.S.A. 82 E8 43 0N 111 43W
Blackpool, U.K. 10 D4 53 49N 3 3W
Blackpool □, U.K. 10 D4 53 49N 3 3W
Blackriver, U.S.A. 78 B1 44 46N 83 17W
Blacks Harbour, Canada 71 C6 45 3N 66 49W
Blacksburg, U.S.A. 76 G5 37 14N 80 25W
Blacksod B., Ireland 13 B1 54 6N 10 0W
Blackstone, U.S.A. 76 G7 37 4N 78 0W
Blackstone Ra., Australia 61 E4 26 0S 128 30 E
Blackwater, Australia 62 C4 23 35S 148 53 E
Blackwater →, Meath, Ireland 13 C4 53 39N 6 41W
Blackwater →, Waterford, Ireland 13 D4 52 4N 7 52W
Blackwater →, U.K. 13 B5 54 31N 6 35W
Blackwell, U.S.A. 81 G6 36 48N 97 17W
Blackwells Corner, U.S.A. 85 K7 35 37N 119 47W
Blaenau Ffestiniog, U.K. 10 E4 53 0N 3 56W
Blaenau Gwent □, U.K. 11 F4 51 48N 3 12W
Blagodarnoye = Blagodarnyy, Russia 25 E7 45 7N 43 37 E
Blagodarnyy, Russia 25 E7 45 7N 43 37 E
Blagoevgrad, Bulgaria 21 C10 42 2N 23 5 E
Blagoveshchensk, Russia 27 D13 50 20N 127 30 E
Blain, U.S.A. 78 F7 40 20N 77 31W
Blaine, Minn., U.S.A. 80 C8 45 10N 93 13W
Blaine, Wash., U.S.A. 84 B4 48 59N 122 45W
Blaine Lake, Canada 73 C7 52 51N 106 52W
Blair, U.S.A. 80 E6 41 33N 96 8W
Blair Athol, Australia 62 C4 22 42S 147 31 E
Blair Atholl, U.K. 12 E5 56 46N 3 50W
Blairgowrie, U.K. 12 E5 56 35N 3 21W
Blairsden, U.S.A. 84 F6 39 47N 120 37W
Blairsville, U.S.A. 78 F5 40 26N 79 16W
Blake Pt., U.S.A. 80 A10 48 11N 88 25W
Blakely, Ga., U.S.A. 77 K3 31 23N 84 56W
Blakely, Pa., U.S.A. 79 E9 41 28N 75 37W
Blanc, C., Spain 22 B9 39 21N 2 51 E
Blanc, Mont, Alps 18 D7 45 48N 6 50 E
Blanc-Sablon, Canada 71 B8 51 24N 57 12W
Blanca, B., Argentina 96 D4 39 10S 61 30W
Blanca Peak, U.S.A. 83 H11 37 35N 105 29W
Blanche, C., Australia 63 E1 33 1S 134 9 E
Blanche, L., S. Austral., Australia 63 D2 29 15S 139 40 E
Blanche, L., W. Austral., Australia 60 D3 22 25S 123 17 E
Blanco, S. Africa 56 E3 33 55S 22 23 E
Blanco, U.S.A. 81 K5 30 6N 98 25W
Blanco →, Argentina 94 C2 30 20S 68 42W
Blanco, C., Costa Rica 88 E2 9 34N 85 8W
Blanco, C., U.S.A. 82 E1 42 51N 124 34W
Blanda →, Iceland 8 D3 65 37N 20 9W
Blandford Forum, U.K. 11 G5 50 51N 2 9W
Blanding, U.S.A. 83 H9 37 37N 109 29W
Blanes, Spain 19 B7 41 40N 2 48 E
Blankenberge, Belgium 15 C3 51 20N 3 9 E
Blanquilla, I., Venezuela 89 D7 11 51N 64 37W
Blanquillo, Uruguay 95 C4 32 53S 55 37W
Blantyre, Malawi 55 F4 15 45S 35 0 E
Blarney, Ireland 13 E3 51 56N 8 33W
Blasdell, U.S.A. 78 D6 42 48N 78 50W
Blåvands Huk, Denmark 9 J13 55 33N 8 4 E
Blaydon, U.K. 10 C6 54 58N 1 42W
Blaze, Pt., Australia 60 B5 12 56S 130 11 E
Blekinge, Sweden 9 H16 56 25N 15 20 E
Blenheim, Canada 78 D3 42 20N 82 0W
Blenheim, N.Z. 59 J4 41 38S 173 57 E
Bletchley, U.K. 11 F7 51 59N 0 44W
Blida, Algeria 50 A6 36 30N 2 49 E
Bligh Sound, N.Z. 59 L1 44 47S 167 32 E
Blind River, Canada 70 C3 46 10N 82 58W
Bliss, Idaho, U.S.A. 82 E6 42 56N 114 57W
Bliss, N.Y., U.S.A. 78 D6 42 34N 78 15W
Blissfield, U.S.A. 78 F3 40 24N 81 58W
Blitar, Indonesia 37 H15 8 5S 112 11 E
Block I., U.S.A. 79 E13 41 11N 71 35W
Block Island Sd., U.S.A. 79 E13 41 15N 71 40W
Blodgett Iceberg Tongue, Antarctica 5 C9 66 8S 130 35 E
Bloemfontein, S. Africa 56 D4 29 6S 26 7 E
Bloemhof, S. Africa 56 D4 27 38S 25 32 E
Blois, France 18 C4 47 35N 1 20 E
Blönduós, Iceland 8 D3 65 40N 20 12W
Bloodvein →, Canada 73 C9 51 47N 96 43W
Bloody Foreland, Ireland 13 A3 55 10N 8 17W
Bloomer, U.S.A. 80 C9 45 6N 91 29W
Bloomfield, Canada 78 C7 43 59N 77 14W
Bloomfield, Iowa, U.S.A. 80 E8 40 45N 92 25W
Bloomfield, N. Mex., U.S.A. 83 H10 36 43N 107 59W
Bloomfield, Nebr., U.S.A. 80 D6 42 36N 97 39W
Bloomington, Ill., U.S.A. 80 E10 40 28N 89 0W
Bloomington, Ind., U.S.A. 76 F2 39 10N 86 32W
Bloomington, Minn., U.S.A. 80 C8 44 50N 93 17W
Bloomsburg, U.S.A. 79 F8 41 0N 76 27W
Blora, Indonesia 37 G14 6 57S 111 25 E
Blossburg, U.S.A. 78 E7 41 41N 77 4W
Blouberg, S. Africa 57 C4 23 8S 28 59 E
Blountstown, U.S.A. 77 K3 30 27N 85 3W
Blue Earth, U.S.A. 80 D8 43 38N 94 6W
Blue Mesa Reservoir, U.S.A. 83 G10 38 28N 107 20W
Blue Mountain Lake, U.S.A. 79 C10 43 52N 74 30W
Blue Mts., Maine, U.S.A. 79 B14 44 50N 70 35W
Blue Mts., Oreg., U.S.A. 82 D4 45 15N 119 0W
Blue Mts., Pa., U.S.A. 79 F8 41 0N 76 27W
Blue Mud B., Australia 62 A2 13 30S 136 0 E
Blue Nile = Nîl el Azraq →, Sudan 51 E12 15 38N 32 31 E
Blue Rapids, U.S.A. 80 F6 39 41N 96 39W
Blue Ridge Mts., U.S.A. 77 G5 36 30N 80 15W
Blue River, Canada 72 C5 52 6N 119 18W
Bluefield, U.S.A. 76 G5 37 15N 81 17W
Bluefields, Nic. 88 D3 12 20N 83 50W
Bluff, Australia 62 C4 23 35S 149 4 E
Bluff, N.Z. 59 M2 46 37S 168 20 E
Bluff, U.S.A. 83 H9 37 17N 109 33W
Bluff Knoll, Australia 61 F2 34 24S 118 15 E
Bluff Pt., Australia 61 E1 27 50S 114 5 E
Bluffton, U.S.A. 76 E3 40 44N 85 11W
Blumenau, Brazil 95 B6 27 0S 49 0W
Blunt, U.S.A. 80 C5 44 31N 99 59W
Bly, U.S.A. 82 E3 42 24N 121 3W
Blyth, Canada 78 C3 43 44N 81 26W
Blyth, U.K. 10 B6 55 8N 1 31W
Blythe, U.S.A. 85 M12 33 37N 114 36W
Blytheville, U.S.A. 81 H10 35 56N 89 55W
Bo, S. Leone 50 G3 7 55N 11 50W
Bo Duc, Vietnam 39 G6 11 58N 106 50 E
Bo Hai, China 35 E10 39 0N 119 0 E
Bo Xian = Bozhou, China 34 H8 33 55N 115 41 E
Boa Vista, Brazil 92 C6 2 48N 60 30W
Boaco, Nic. 88 D2 12 29N 85 35W
Bo'ai, China 34 G7 35 10N 113 3 E
Boalsburg, U.S.A. 78 F7 40 46N 77 47W
Boane, Mozam. 57 D5 26 6S 32 19 E
Boardman, U.S.A. 78 E4 41 2N 80 40W
Bobbili, India 41 K13 18 35N 83 30 E
Bobcaygeon, Canada 78 B6 44 33N 78 33W
Bobo-Dioulasso, Burkina Faso 50 F5 11 8N 4 13W
Bóbr →, Poland 16 B8 52 4N 15 4 E
Bobraomby, Tanjon' i, Madag. 57 A8 12 40S 49 10 E
Bobruysk = Babruysk, Belarus 17 B15 53 10N 29 15 E
Boby, Pic, Madag. 53 J9 22 12S 46 55 E
Bôca do Acre, Brazil 92 E5 8 50S 67 27W
Boca Raton, U.S.A. 77 M5 26 21N 80 5W
Bocas del Toro, Panama 88 E3 9 15N 82 20W
Bochnia, Poland 17 D11 49 58N 20 27 E
Bochum, Germany 16 C4 51 28N 7 13 E
Bocoyna, Mexico 86 B3 27 52N 107 35W
Bodaybo, Russia 27 D12 57 50N 114 0 E
Boddam, U.K. 12 B7 59 56N 1 17W
Boddington, Australia 61 F2 32 50S 116 30 E
Bodega Bay, U.S.A. 84 G3 38 20N 123 3W
Boden, Sweden 8 D19 65 50N 21 42 E
Bodensee, Europe 18 C8 47 35N 9 25 E
Bodhan, India 40 K10 18 40N 77 44 E
Bodmin, U.K. 11 G3 50 28N 4 43W
Bodmin Moor, U.K. 11 G3 50 33N 4 36W
Bodø, Norway 8 C16 67 17N 14 24 E
Bodrog →, Hungary 17 D11 48 11N 21 22 E
Bodrum, Turkey 21 F12 37 3N 27 30 E
Boende, Dem. Rep. of the Congo 52 E4 0 24S 21 12 E
Boerne, U.S.A. 81 L5 29 47N 98 44W
Boesmans →, S. Africa 56 E4 33 42S 26 39 E
Bogalusa, U.S.A. 81 K10 30 47N 89 52W
Bogan →, Australia 63 D4 29 59S 146 17 E
Bogantungan, Australia 62 C4 23 41S 147 17 E
Bogata, U.S.A. 81 J7 33 28N 95 13W
Boggabilla, Australia 63 D5 28 36S 150 24 E
Boggeragh Mts., Ireland 13 D3 52 2N 8 55W
Boglan = Solhan, Turkey 44 B4 38 57N 41 3 E
Bognor Regis, U.K. 11 G7 50 47N 0 40W
Bogo, Phil. 37 B6 11 3N 124 0 E
Bogor, Indonesia 36 F3 6 36S 106 48 E
Bogotá, Colombia 92 C4 4 34N 74 0W
Bogotol, Russia 26 D9 56 15N 89 50 E
Bogra, Bangla. 41 G16 24 51N 89 22 E
Boguchany, Russia 27 D10 58 40N 97 30 E
Bohemian Forest = Böhmerwald, Germany 16 D7 49 8N 13 14 E
Böhmerwald, Germany 16 D7 49 8N 13 14 E
Bohol □, Phil. 37 C6 9 50N 124 10 E
Bohol Sea, Phil. 37 C6 9 0N 124 0 E
Bohuslän, Sweden 9 G14 58 25N 12 0 E
Boi, Pta. de, Brazil 95 A6 23 55S 45 15W
Boiaçu, Brazil 92 D6 0 27S 61 46W
Boileau, C., Australia 60 C3 17 40S 122 7 E
Boise, U.S.A. 82 E5 43 37N 116 13W
Boise City, U.S.A. 81 G3 36 44N 102 31W
Boissevain, Canada 73 D8 49 15N 100 5W
Bojador C., W. Sahara 50 C3 26 0N 14 30W
Bojana →, Albania 21 D8 41 52N 19 22 E
Bojnūrd, Iran 45 B8 37 30N 57 20 E
Bojonegoro, Indonesia 37 G14 7 11S 111 54 E
Bokaro, India 43 H11 23 46N 85 55 E
Bokhara →, Australia 63 D4 29 55S 146 42 E
Boknafjorden, Norway 9 G11 59 14N 5 40 E
Bokoro, Chad 51 F9 12 25N 17 14 E
Bokpyin, Burma 39 G2 11 18N 98 42 E
Bolan →, Pakistan 42 E2 28 38N 67 42 E
Bolan Pass, Pakistan 40 E5 29 50N 67 20 E
Bolaños →, Mexico 86 C4 21 14N 104 8W
Bolbec, France 18 B4 49 30N 0 30 E
Boldājī, Iran 45 D6 31 56N 51 3 E
Bole, China 32 B3 45 11N 81 37 E
Bolekhiv, Ukraine 17 D12 49 0N 23 57 E
Bolesławiec, Poland 16 C8 51 17N 15 37 E
Bolgrad = Bolhrad, Ukraine 17 F15 45 40N 28 32 E
Bolhrad, Ukraine 17 F15 45 40N 28 32 E
Bolívar, Argentina 94 D3 36 15S 60 53W

C

Carbó

Caazapá □, Paraguay 95 B4 26 10S 56 0W
Cabanatuan, Phil. 37 A6 15 30N 120 58 E
Cabano, Canada 71 C6 47 40N 68 56W
Cabazon, U.S.A. 85 M10 33 55N 116 47W
Cabedelo, Brazil 93 E12 7 0S 34 50W
Cabildo, Chile 94 C1 32 30S 71 5W
Cabimas, Venezuela 92 A4 10 23N 71 25W
Cabinda, Angola 52 F2 5 33S 12 11 E
Cabinda □, Angola 52 F2 5 0S 12 30 E
Cabinet Mts., U.S.A. 82 C6 48 0N 115 30W
Cabo Blanco, Argentina 96 F3 47 15S 65 47W
Cabo Frio, Brazil 95 A7 22 51S 42 3W
Cabo Pantoja, Peru 92 D3 1 0S 75 10W
Cabonga, Réservoir, Canada 70 C4 47 20N 76 40W
Cabool, U.S.A. 81 G8 37 7N 92 6W
Caboolture, Australia 63 D5 27 5S 152 58 E
Cabora Bassa Dam = Cahora Bassa, Reprêsa de, Mozam. 55 F3 15 20S 32 50 E
Caborca, Mexico 86 A2 30 40N 112 10W
Cabot, Mt., U.S.A. 79 B13 44 30N 71 25W
Cabot Hd., Canada 78 A3 45 14N 81 17W
Cabot Str., Canada 71 C8 47 15N 59 40W
Cabra, Spain 19 D3 37 30N 4 28W
Cabrera, Spain 22 B9 39 8N 2 57 E
Cabri, Canada 73 C7 50 35N 108 25W
Cabriel →, Spain 19 C5 39 14N 1 3W
Caçador, Brazil 95 B5 26 47S 51 0W
Čačak, Serbia, Yug. 21 C9 43 54N 20 20 E
Caçapava do Sul, Brazil 95 C5 30 30S 53 30W
Cáceres, Brazil 92 G7 16 5S 57 40W
Cáceres, Spain 19 C2 39 26N 6 23W
Cache Bay, Canada 70 C4 46 22N 80 0W
Cache Cr. →, U.S.A. 84 G5 38 42N 121 42W
Cache Creek, Canada 72 C4 50 48N 121 19W
Cachi, Argentina 94 B2 25 5S 66 10W
Cachimbo, Serra do, Brazil 93 E7 9 30S 55 30W
Cachinal de la Sierra, Chile 94 A2 24 58S 69 32W
Cachoeira, Brazil 93 F11 12 30S 39 0W
Cachoeira do Sul, Brazil 95 C5 30 3S 52 53W
Cachoeiro de Itapemirim, Brazil 95 A7 20 51S 41 7W
Cacoal, Brazil 92 F6 11 32S 61 18W
Cacólo, Angola 52 G3 10 9S 19 21 E
Caconda, Angola 53 G3 13 48S 15 8 E
Caddo, U.S.A. 81 H6 34 7N 96 16W
Cader Idris, U.K. 11 E4 52 42N 3 53W
Cadereyta, Mexico 86 B5 25 36N 100 0W
Cadibarrawirracanna, L., Australia 63 D2 28 52S 135 27 E
Cadillac, U.S.A. 76 C3 44 15N 85 24W
Cadiz, Phil. 37 B6 10 57N 123 15 E
Cádiz, Spain 19 D2 36 30N 6 20W
Cadiz, Calif., U.S.A. 85 L11 34 30N 115 28W
Cadiz, Ohio, U.S.A. 78 F4 40 22N 81 0W
Cádiz, G. de, Spain 19 D2 36 40N 7 0W
Cadiz L., U.S.A. 83 J6 34 18N 115 24W
Cadney Park, Australia 63 D1 27 55S 134 3 E
Cadomin, Canada 72 C5 53 2N 117 20W
Cadotte Lake, Canada 72 B5 56 26N 116 23W
Cadoux, Australia 61 F2 30 46S 117 7 E
Caen, France 18 B3 49 10N 0 22W
Caernarfon, U.K. 10 D3 53 8N 4 16W
Caernarfon B., U.K. 10 D3 53 4N 4 40W
Caernarvon = Caernarfon, U.K. 10 D3 53 8N 4 16W
Caerphilly, U.K. 11 F4 51 35N 3 13W
Caerphilly □, U.K. 11 F4 51 37N 3 12W
Caesarea, Israel 47 C3 32 30N 34 53 E
Caetité, Brazil 93 F10 13 50S 42 32W
Cafayate, Argentina 94 B2 26 2S 66 0W
Cafu, Angola 56 B2 16 30S 15 8 E
Cagayan de Oro, Phil. 37 C6 8 30N 124 40 E
Cagayan Is., Phil. 37 C5 9 40N 121 16 E
Cágliari, Italy 20 E3 39 13N 9 7 E
Cágliari, G. di, Italy 20 E3 39 8N 9 11 E
Caguán →, Colombia 92 D4 0 8S 74 18W
Caguas, Puerto Rico 89 C6 18 14N 66 2W
Caha Mts., Ireland 13 E2 51 45N 9 40W
Cahama, Angola 56 B1 16 17S 14 19 E
Caher, Ireland 13 D4 52 22N 7 56W
Cahersiveen, Ireland 13 E1 51 56N 10 14W
Cahora Bassa, Reprêsa de, Mozam. 55 F3 15 20S 32 50 E
Cahore Pt., Ireland 13 D5 52 33N 6 12W
Cahors, France 18 D4 44 27N 1 27 E
Cahul, Moldova 17 F15 45 50N 28 15 E
Cai Bau, Dao, Vietnam 38 B6 21 10N 107 27 E
Cai Nuoc, Vietnam 39 H5 8 56N 105 1 E
Caia, Mozam. 55 F4 17 51S 35 24 E
Caianda, Angola 55 E1 11 2S 23 31 E
Caibarién, Cuba 88 B4 22 30N 79 30W
Caicara, Venezuela 92 B5 7 38N 66 10W
Caicó, Brazil 93 E11 6 20S 37 0W
Caicos Is., Turks & Caicos 89 B5 21 40N 71 40W
Caicos Passage, W. Indies 89 B5 22 45N 72 45W
Caird Coast, Antarctica 5 D1 75 0S 25 0W
Cairn Gorm, U.K. 12 D5 57 7N 3 39W
Cairngorm Mts., U.K. 12 D5 57 6N 3 42W
Cairnryan, U.K. 12 G3 54 59N 5 1W
Cairns, Australia 62 B4 16 57S 145 45 E
Cairns L., Canada 73 C10 51 42N 94 30W
Cairo = El Qâhira, Egypt 51 B12 30 1N 31 14 E
Cairo, Ga., U.S.A. 77 K3 30 52N 84 13W
Cairo, Ill., U.S.A. 81 G10 37 0N 89 11W
Cairo, N.Y., U.S.A. 79 D11 42 18N 74 0W
Caithness, Ord of, U.K. 12 C5 58 8N 3 36W
Cajamarca, Peru 92 E3 7 5S 78 28W
Cajàzeiras, Brazil 93 E11 6 52S 38 30W
Cala d'Or, Spain 22 B10 39 23N 3 14 E
Cala en Porter, Spain 22 B11 39 52N 4 8 E
Cala Figuera, C. de, Spain 22 B9 39 27N 2 31 E
Cala Forcat, Spain 22 B10 40 0N 3 47 E
Cala Major, Spain 22 B9 39 33N 2 37 E
Cala Mezquida = Sa Mesquida, Spain 22 B11 39 55N 4 16 E
Cala Millor, Spain 22 B10 39 35N 3 22 E
Cala Ratjada, Spain 22 B10 39 43N 3 27 E
Cala Santa Galdana, Spain 22 B10 39 56N 3 58 E
Calabar, Nigeria 50 H7 4 57N 8 20 E
Calabogie, Canada 79 A8 45 18N 76 43W
Calabozo, Venezuela 92 B5 9 0N 67 28W
Calábria □, Italy 20 E7 39 0N 16 30 E
Calafate, Argentina 96 G2 50 19S 72 15W
Calahorra, Spain 19 A5 42 18N 1 59W
Calais, France 18 A4 50 57N 1 56 E
Calais, U.S.A. 77 C12 45 11N 67 17W
Calalaste, Cord. de, Argentina 94 B2 25 0S 67 0W
Calama, Brazil 92 E6 8 0S 62 50W
Calama, Chile 94 A2 22 30S 68 55W
Calamar, Colombia 92 A4 10 15N 74 55W
Calamian Group, Phil. 37 B5 11 50N 119 55 E
Calamocha, Spain 19 B5 40 50N 1 17W
Calang, Indonesia 36 D1 4 37N 95 37 E
Calapan, Phil. 37 B6 13 25N 121 7 E
Călărași, Romania 17 F14 44 12N 27 20 E
Calatayud, Spain 19 B5 41 20N 1 40W
Calauag, Phil. 37 B6 13 55N 122 15 E
Calavite, C., Phil. 37 B6 13 26N 120 20 E
Calbayog, Phil. 37 B6 12 4N 124 38 E
Calca, Peru 92 F4 13 22S 72 0W
Calcasieu L., U.S.A. 81 L8 29 55N 93 18W
Calcutta = Kolkata, India 43 H13 22 36N 88 24 E
Calcutta, U.S.A. 78 F4 40 40N 80 34W
Caldas da Rainha, Portugal 19 C1 39 24N 9 8W
Calder →, U.K. 10 D6 53 44N 1 22W
Caldera, Chile 94 B1 27 5S 70 55W
Caldwell, Idaho, U.S.A. 82 E5 43 40N 116 41W
Caldwell, Kans., U.S.A. 81 G6 37 2N 97 37W
Caldwell, Tex., U.S.A. 81 K6 30 32N 96 42W
Caledon, S. Africa 56 E2 34 14S 19 26 E
Caledon →, S. Africa 56 E4 30 31S 26 5 E
Caledon B., Australia 62 A2 12 45S 137 0 E
Caledonia, Canada 78 C5 43 7N 79 58W
Caledonia, U.S.A. 78 D7 42 58N 77 51W
Calemba, Angola 56 B2 16 0S 15 44 E
Calen, Australia 62 C4 20 56S 148 48 E
Caletones, Chile 94 C1 34 6S 70 27W
Calexico, U.S.A. 85 N11 32 40N 115 30W
Calf of Man, U.K. 10 C3 54 3N 4 48W
Calgary, Canada 72 C6 51 0N 114 10W
Calheta, Madeira 22 D2 32 44N 17 11W
Calhoun, U.S.A. 77 H3 34 30N 84 57W
Cali, Colombia 92 C3 3 25N 76 35W
Calicut, India 40 P9 11 15N 75 43 E
Caliente, U.S.A. 83 H6 37 37N 114 31W
California, Mo., U.S.A. 80 F8 38 38N 92 34W
California, Pa., U.S.A. 78 F5 40 4N 79 54W
California □, U.S.A. 84 H7 37 30N 119 30W
California, Baja, Mexico 86 A1 32 10N 115 12W
California, Baja, T.N. = Baja California □, Mexico 86 B2 30 0N 115 0W
California, Baja, T.S. = Baja California Sur □, Mexico 86 B2 25 50N 111 50W
California, G. de, Mexico 86 B2 27 0N 111 0W
California City, U.S.A. 85 K9 35 10N 117 55W
California Hot Springs, U.S.A. 85 K8 35 51N 118 41W
Calingasta, Argentina 94 C2 31 15S 69 30W
Calipatria, U.S.A. 85 M11 33 8N 115 31W
Calistoga, U.S.A. 84 G4 38 35N 122 35W
Calitzdorp, S. Africa 56 E3 33 33S 21 42 E
Callabonna, L., Australia 63 D3 29 40S 140 5 E
Callan, Ireland 13 D4 52 32N 7 24W
Callander, U.K. 12 E4 56 15N 4 13W
Callao, Peru 92 F3 12 0S 77 0W
Calles, Mexico 87 C5 23 2N 98 42W
Callicoon, U.S.A. 79 E9 41 46N 75 3W
Calling Lake, Canada 72 B6 55 15N 113 12W
Calliope, Australia 62 C5 24 0S 151 16 E
Calne, U.K. 11 F6 51 26N 2 0W
Calola, Angola 56 B2 16 25S 17 48 E
Caloundra, Australia 63 D5 26 45S 153 10 E
Calpella, U.S.A. 84 F3 39 14N 123 12W
Calpine, U.S.A. 84 F6 39 40N 120 27W
Calstock, Canada 70 C3 49 47N 84 9W
Caltagirone, Italy 20 F6 37 14N 14 31 E
Caltanissetta, Italy 20 F6 37 29N 14 4 E
Calulo, Angola 52 G2 10 1S 14 56 E
Calvert →, Australia 62 B2 16 17S 137 44 E
Calvert I., Canada 72 C3 51 30N 128 0W
Calvert Ra., Australia 60 D3 24 0S 122 30 E
Calvi, France 18 E8 42 34N 8 45 E
Calviá, Spain 19 C7 39 34N 2 31 E
Calvillo, Mexico 86 C4 21 51N 102 43W
Calvinia, S. Africa 56 E2 31 28S 19 45 E
Calwa, U.S.A. 84 J7 36 42N 119 46W
Cam →, U.K. 11 E8 52 21N 0 16 E
Cam Lam, Vietnam 39 G7 11 54N 109 10 E
Cam Pha, Vietnam 38 B6 21 7N 107 18 E
Cam Ranh, Vietnam 39 G7 11 54N 109 12 E
Cam Xuyen, Vietnam 38 C6 18 15N 106 0 E
Camabatela, Angola 52 F3 8 20S 15 26 E
Camacha, Madeira 22 D3 32 41N 16 49W
Camacho, Mexico 86 C4 24 25N 102 18W
Camacupa, Angola 53 G3 11 58S 17 22 E
Camagüey, Cuba 88 B4 21 20N 78 0W
Camaná, Peru 92 G4 16 30S 72 50W
Camanche Reservoir, U.S.A. 84 G6 38 14N 121 1W
Camaquã, Brazil 95 C5 30 51S 51 49W
Camaquã →, Brazil 95 C5 31 17S 51 47W
Câmara de Lobos, Madeira 22 D3 32 39N 16 59W
Camargo, Mexico 87 B5 26 19N 98 50W
Camargue, France 18 E6 43 34N 4 34 E
Camarillo, U.S.A. 85 L7 34 13N 119 2W
Camarón, C., Honduras 88 C2 16 0N 85 5W
Camarones, Argentina 96 E3 44 50S 65 40W
Camas, U.S.A. 84 E4 45 35N 122 24W
Camas Valley, U.S.A. 82 E2 43 2N 123 40W
Camballin, Australia 60 C3 17 59S 124 12 E
Cambará, Brazil 95 A5 23 2S 50 5W
Cambay = Khambhat, India 42 H5 22 23N 72 33 E
Cambay, G. of = Khambhat, G. of, India 40 J8 20 45N 72 30 E
Cambodia ■, Asia 38 F5 12 15N 105 0 E
Camborne, U.K. 11 G2 50 12N 5 19W
Cambrai, France 18 A5 50 11N 3 14 E
Cambria, U.S.A. 84 K5 35 34N 121 5W
Cambrian Mts., U.K. 11 E4 52 3N 3 57W
Cambridge, Canada 78 C4 43 23N 80 15W
Cambridge, Jamaica 88 C4 18 18N 77 54W
Cambridge, N.Z. 59 G5 37 54S 175 29 E
Cambridge, U.K. 11 E8 52 12N 0 8 E
Cambridge, Mass., U.S.A. 79 D13 42 22N 71 6W
Cambridge, Minn., U.S.A. 80 C8 45 34N 93 13W
Cambridge, N.Y., U.S.A. 79 C11 43 2N 73 22W
Cambridge, Nebr., U.S.A. 80 E4 40 17N 100 10W
Cambridge, Ohio, U.S.A. 78 F3 40 2N 81 35W
Cambridge Bay = Ikaluktutiak, Canada 68 B9 69 10N 105 0W
Cambridge G., Australia 60 B4 14 55S 128 15 E
Cambridge Springs, U.S.A. 78 E4 41 48N 80 4W
Cambridgeshire □, U.K. 11 E7 52 25N 0 7W
Cambuci, Brazil 95 A7 21 35S 41 55W
Cambundi-Catembo, Angola 52 G3 10 10S 17 35 E
Camden, Ala., U.S.A. 77 K2 31 59N 87 17W
Camden, Ark., U.S.A. 81 J8 33 35N 92 50W
Camden, Maine, U.S.A. 77 C11 44 13N 69 4W
Camden, N.J., U.S.A. 79 G9 39 56N 75 7W
Camden, N.Y., U.S.A. 79 C9 43 20N 75 45W
Camden, S.C., U.S.A. 77 H5 34 16N 80 36W
Camden Sd., Australia 60 C3 15 27S 124 25 E
Camdenton, U.S.A. 81 F8 38 1N 92 45W
Cameron, Ariz., U.S.A. 83 J8 35 53N 111 25W
Cameron, La., U.S.A. 81 L8 29 48N 93 20W
Cameron, Mo., U.S.A. 80 F7 39 44N 94 14W
Cameron, Tex., U.S.A. 81 K6 30 51N 96 59W
Cameron Highlands, Malaysia 39 K3 4 27N 101 22 E
Cameron Hills, Canada 72 B5 59 48N 118 0W
Cameroon ■, Africa 52 C2 6 0N 12 30 E
Cameroun, Mt., Cameroon 52 D1 4 13N 9 10 E
Cametá, Brazil 93 D9 2 12S 49 30W
Camiguin I., Phil. 37 C6 18 56N 121 55 E
Camilla, U.S.A. 77 K3 31 14N 84 12W
Caminha, Portugal 19 B1 41 50N 8 50W
Camino, U.S.A. 84 G6 38 44N 120 41W
Camira Creek, Australia 63 D5 29 15S 152 58 E
Cammal, U.S.A. 78 E7 41 24N 77 28W
Camocim, Brazil 93 D10 2 55S 40 50W
Camooweal, Australia 62 B2 19 56S 138 7 E
Camopi, Fr. Guiana 93 C8 3 12N 52 17W
Camp Borden, Canada 78 B5 44 18N 79 56W
Camp Hill, U.S.A. 78 F8 40 14N 76 55W
Camp Nelson, U.S.A. 85 J8 36 8N 118 39W
Camp Pendleton, U.S.A. 85 M9 33 16N 117 23W
Camp Verde, U.S.A. 83 J8 34 34N 111 51W
Camp Wood, U.S.A. 81 L5 29 40N 100 1W
Campana, Argentina 94 C4 34 10S 58 55W
Campana, I., Chile 96 F1 48 20S 75 20W
Campanário, Madeira 22 D2 32 39N 17 2W
Campània □, Italy 20 D6 41 0N 14 30 E
Campbell, S. Africa 56 D3 28 48S 23 44 E
Campbell, Calif., U.S.A. 84 H5 37 17N 121 57W
Campbell, Ohio, U.S.A. 78 E4 41 5N 80 37W
Campbell I., Pac. Oc. 64 N8 52 30S 169 0 E
Campbell L., Canada 73 A7 63 14N 106 55W
Campbell River, Canada 72 C3 50 5N 125 20W
Campbell Town, Australia 62 G4 41 52S 147 30 E
Campbellford, Canada 78 B7 44 18N 77 48W
Campbellpur, Pakistan 42 C5 33 46N 72 26 E
Campbellsville, U.S.A. 76 G3 37 21N 85 20W
Campbellton, Canada 71 C6 47 57N 66 43W
Campbeltown, U.K. 12 F3 55 26N 5 36W
Campeche, Mexico 87 D6 19 50N 90 32W
Campeche □, Mexico 87 D6 19 50N 90 32W
Campeche, Golfo de, Mexico 87 D6 19 30N 93 0W
Camperville, Canada 73 C8 51 59N 100 9W
Câmpina, Romania 17 F13 45 10N 25 45 E
Campina Grande, Brazil 93 E11 7 20S 35 47W
Campinas, Brazil 95 A6 22 50S 47 0W
Campo Grande, Brazil 93 H8 20 25S 54 40W
Campo Maior, Brazil 93 D10 4 50S 42 12W
Campo Mourão, Brazil 95 A5 24 3S 52 22W
Campobasso, Italy 20 D6 41 34N 14 39 E
Campos, Brazil 95 A7 21 50S 41 20W
Campos Belos, Brazil 93 F9 13 10S 47 3W
Campos del Puerto, Spain 22 B10 39 26N 3 1 E
Campos Novos, Brazil 95 B5 27 21S 51 50W
Camptonville, U.S.A. 84 F5 39 27N 121 3W
Camptown, U.S.A. 79 E8 41 44N 76 14W
Câmpulung, Romania 17 F13 45 17N 25 3 E
Camrose, Canada 72 C6 53 0N 112 50W
Camsell Portage, Canada 73 B7 59 37N 109 15W
Çan, Turkey 21 D12 40 2N 27 3 E
Can Clavo, Spain 22 C7 38 57N 1 27 E
Can Creu, Spain 22 C7 38 58N 1 28 E
Can Gio, Vietnam 39 G6 10 25N 106 58 E
Can Tho, Vietnam 39 G5 10 2N 105 46 E
Canaan, U.S.A. 79 D11 42 2N 73 20W
Canada ■, N. Amer. 68 C10 60 0N 100 0W
Cañada de Gómez, Argentina 94 C3 32 40S 61 30W
Canadian, U.S.A. 81 H4 35 55N 100 23W
Canadian →, U.S.A. 81 H7 35 28N 95 3W
Canajoharie, U.S.A. 79 D10 42 54N 74 35W
Çanakkale, Turkey 21 D12 40 8N 26 24 E
Çanakkale Boğazı, Turkey 21 D12 40 17N 26 32 E
Canal Flats, Canada 72 C5 50 10N 115 48W
Canalejas, Argentina 94 D2 35 15S 66 34W
Canals, Argentina 94 C3 33 35S 62 53W
Canandaigua, U.S.A. 78 D7 42 54N 77 17W
Canandaigua L., U.S.A. 78 D7 42 47N 77 19W
Cananea, Mexico 86 A2 31 0N 110 20W
Canarias, Is., Atl. Oc. 22 F4 28 30N 16 0W
Canarreos, Arch. de los, Cuba 88 B3 21 35N 81 40W
Canary Is. = Canarias, Is., Atl. Oc. 22 F4 28 30N 16 0W
Canaseraga, U.S.A. 78 D7 42 27N 77 45W
Canatlán, Mexico 86 C4 24 31N 104 47W
Canaveral, C., U.S.A. 77 L5 28 27N 80 32W
Canavieiras, Brazil 93 G11 15 39S 39 0W
Canby, Calif., U.S.A. 82 F3 41 27N 120 52W
Canby, Minn., U.S.A. 80 C6 44 43N 96 16W
Canby, Oreg., U.S.A. 84 E4 45 16N 122 42W
Cancún, Mexico 87 C7 21 8N 86 44W
Candelaria, Argentina 95 B4 27 29S 55 44W
Candelaria, Canary Is. 22 F3 28 22N 16 22W
Candia = Iráklion, Greece 23 D7 35 20N 25 12 E
Candle L., Canada 73 C7 53 50N 105 18W
Candlemas I., Antarctica 5 B1 57 3S 26 40W
Cando, U.S.A. 80 A5 48 32N 99 12W
Canea = Khaniá, Greece 23 D6 35 30N 24 4 E
Canelones, Uruguay 95 C4 34 32S 56 17W
Cañete, Chile 94 D1 37 50S 73 30W
Cañete, Peru 92 F3 13 8S 76 30W
Cangas de Narcea, Spain 19 A2 43 10N 6 32W
Canguaretama, Brazil 93 E11 6 20S 35 5W
Canguçu, Brazil 95 C5 31 22S 52 43W
Canguçu, Serra do, Brazil 95 C5 31 20S 52 40W
Cangzhou, China 34 E9 38 19N 116 52 E
Caniapiscau →, Canada 71 A6 56 40N 69 30W
Caniapiscau, Rés. de, Canada 71 B6 54 10N 69 55W
Canicattì, Italy 20 F5 37 21N 13 51 E
Canim Lake, Canada 72 C4 51 47N 120 54W
Canindeyu □, Paraguay 95 A5 24 10S 55 0W
Canisteo, U.S.A. 78 D7 42 16N 77 36W
Canisteo →, U.S.A. 78 D7 42 7N 77 8W
Cañitas, Mexico 86 C4 23 36N 102 43W
Çankırı, Turkey 25 F5 40 40N 33 37 E
Cankuzo, Burundi 54 C3 3 10S 30 31 E
Canmore, Canada 72 C5 51 7N 115 18W
Canna, U.K. 12 D2 57 3N 6 33W
Cannanore, India 40 P9 11 53N 75 27 E
Cannes, France 18 E7 43 32N 7 1 E
Canning Town = Port Canning, India 43 H13 22 23N 88 40 E
Cannington, Canada 78 B5 44 20N 79 2W
Cannock, U.K. 11 E5 52 41N 2 1W
Cannon Ball →, U.S.A. 80 B4 46 20N 100 38W
Cannondale Mt., Australia 62 D4 25 13S 148 57 E
Cannonsville Reservoir, U.S.A. 79 D9 42 4N 75 22W
Cannonvale, Australia 62 C4 20 17S 148 43 E
Canoas, Brazil 95 B5 29 56S 51 11W
Canoe L., Canada 73 B7 55 10N 108 15W
Canon City, U.S.A. 80 F2 38 27N 105 14W
Canora, Canada 73 C8 51 40N 102 30W
Canso, Canada 71 C7 45 20N 61 0W
Cantabria □, Spain 19 A4 43 10N 4 0W
Cantabrian Mts. = Cantábrica, Cordillera, Spain 19 A3 43 0N 5 10W
Cantábrica, Cordillera, Spain 19 A3 43 0N 5 10W
Cantal, Plomb du, France 18 D5 45 3N 2 45 E
Canterbury, Australia 62 D3 25 23S 141 53 E
Canterbury, U.K. 11 F9 51 16N 1 6 E
Canterbury Bight, N.Z. 59 L3 44 16S 171 55 E
Canterbury Plains, N.Z. 59 K3 43 55S 171 22 E
Cantil, U.S.A. 85 K9 35 18N 117 58W
Canton = Guangzhou, China 33 D6 23 5N 113 10 E
Canton, Ga., U.S.A. 77 H3 34 14N 84 29W
Canton, Ill., U.S.A. 80 E9 40 33N 90 2W
Canton, Miss., U.S.A. 81 J9 32 37N 90 2W
Canton, Mo., U.S.A. 80 E9 40 8N 91 32W
Canton, N.Y., U.S.A. 79 B9 44 36N 75 10W
Canton, Ohio, U.S.A. 78 F3 40 48N 81 23W
Canton, Pa., U.S.A. 78 E8 41 39N 76 51W
Canton, S. Dak., U.S.A. 80 D6 43 18N 96 35W
Canton L., U.S.A. 81 G5 36 6N 98 35W
Canudos, Brazil 92 E7 7 13S 58 5W
Canumã →, Brazil 92 D7 3 55S 59 10W
Canutama, Brazil 92 E6 6 30S 64 20W
Canutillo, U.S.A. 83 L10 31 55N 106 36W
Canvey, U.K. 11 F8 51 31N 0 37 E
Canyon, U.S.A. 81 H4 34 59N 101 55W
Canyonlands National Park, U.S.A. 83 G9 38 15N 110 0W
Canyonville, U.S.A. 82 E2 42 56N 123 17W
Cao Bang, Vietnam 38 A6 22 40N 106 15 E
Cao He →, China 35 D13 40 10N 124 32 E
Cao Lanh, Vietnam 39 G5 10 27N 105 38 E
Cao Xian, China 34 G8 34 50N 115 35 E
Cap-aux-Meules, Canada 71 C7 47 23N 61 52W
Cap-Chat, Canada 71 C6 49 6N 66 40W
Cap-de-la-Madeleine, Canada 70 C5 46 22N 72 31W
Cap-Haïtien, Haiti 89 C5 19 40N 72 20W
Capac, U.S.A. 78 C2 43 1N 82 56W
Capanaparo →, Venezuela 92 B5 7 1N 67 7W
Cape →, Australia 62 C4 20 59S 146 51 E
Cape Barren I., Australia 62 G4 40 25S 148 15 E
Cape Breton Highlands Nat. Park, Canada 71 C7 46 50N 60 40W
Cape Breton I., Canada 71 C7 46 0N 60 30W
Cape Charles, U.S.A. 76 G8 37 16N 76 1W
Cape Coast, Ghana 50 G5 5 5N 1 15W
Cape Coral, U.S.A. 77 M5 26 33N 81 57W
Cape Dorset, Canada 69 B12 64 14N 76 32W
Cape Fear →, U.S.A. 77 H6 33 53N 78 1W
Cape Girardeau, U.S.A. 81 G10 37 19N 89 32W
Cape May, U.S.A. 76 F8 38 56N 74 56W
Cape May Point, U.S.A. 76 F8 38 56N 74 58W
Cape Province, S. Africa 53 L3 32 0S 23 0 E
Cape Tormentine, Canada 71 C7 46 8N 63 47W
Cape Town, S. Africa 56 E2 33 55S 18 22 E
Cape Verde Is. ■, Atl. Oc. 49 E1 17 10N 25 20W
Cape Vincent, U.S.A. 79 B8 44 8N 76 20W
Cape York Peninsula, Australia 62 A3 12 0S 142 30 E
Capela, Brazil 93 F11 10 30S 37 0W
Capella, Australia 62 C4 23 2S 148 1 E
Capim →, Brazil 93 D9 1 40S 47 47W
Capitan, U.S.A. 83 K11 33 35N 105 35W
Capitol Reef National Park, U.S.A. 83 G8 38 15N 111 10W
Capitola, U.S.A. 84 J5 36 59N 121 57W
Capoche →, Mozam. 55 F3 15 35S 33 0 E
Capraia, Italy 18 E8 43 2N 9 50 E
Capreol, Canada 70 C3 46 43N 80 56W
Capri, Italy 20 D6 40 33N 14 14 E
Capricorn Group, Australia 62 C5 23 30S 151 55 E
Capricorn Ra., Australia 60 D2 23 20S 116 50 E
Caprivi Strip, Namibia 56 B3 18 0S 23 0 E
Caquetá →, Colombia 92 D5 1 15S 69 15W
Caracal, Romania 17 F13 44 8N 24 22 E
Caracas, Venezuela 92 A5 10 30N 66 55W
Caracol, Mato Grosso do Sul, Brazil 94 A4 22 18S 57 1W
Caracol, Piauí, Brazil 93 E10 9 15S 43 22W
Carajas, Brazil 93 E8 6 5S 50 23W
Carajás, Serra dos, Brazil 93 E8 6 0S 51 30W
Carangola, Brazil 95 A7 20 44S 42 5W
Caransebeș, Romania 17 F12 45 28N 22 18 E
Caraquet, Canada 71 C6 47 48N 64 57W
Caras, Peru 92 E3 9 3S 77 47W
Caratasca, L., Honduras 88 C3 15 20N 83 40W
Caratinga, Brazil 93 G10 19 50S 42 10W
Caraúbas, Brazil 93 E11 5 43S 37 33W
Caravaca = Caravaca de la Cruz, Spain 19 C5 38 8N 1 52W
Caravaca de la Cruz, Spain 19 C5 38 8N 1 52W
Caravelas, Brazil 93 G11 17 45S 39 15W
Caraveli, Peru 92 G4 15 45S 73 25W
Caràzinho, Brazil 95 B5 28 16S 52 46W
Carballo, Spain 19 A1 43 13N 8 41W
Carberry, Canada 73 D9 49 50N 99 25W
Carbó, Mexico 86 B2 29 42N 110 58W

Carbonara, C.

Carbonara, C., *Italy* **20 E3** 39 6N 9 31 E
Carbondale, *Colo., U.S.A.* **82 G10** 39 24N 107 13W
Carbondale, *Ill., U.S.A.* **81 G10** 37 44N 89 13W
Carbondale, *Pa., U.S.A.* **79 E9** 41 35N 75 30W
Carbonear, *Canada* **71 C9** 47 42N 53 13W
Carbónia, *Italy* **20 E3** 39 10N 8 30 E
Carcajou, *Canada* **72 B5** 57 47N 117 6W
Carcarana →, *Argentina* **94 C3** 32 27S 60 48W
Carcasse, C., *Haiti* **89 C5** 18 30N 74 28W
Carcassonne, *France* **18 E5** 43 13N 2 20 E
Carcross, *Canada* **72 A2** 60 13N 134 45W
Cardamon Hills, *India* **40 Q10** 9 30N 77 15 E
Cárdenas, *Cuba* **88 B3** 23 0N 81 30W
Cárdenas, *San Luis Potosí, Mexico* **87 C5** 22 0N 99 41W
Cárdenas, *Tabasco, Mexico* **87 D6** 17 59N 93 21W
Cardiff, *U.K.* **11 F4** 51 29N 3 10W
Cardiff □, *U.K.* **11 F4** 51 31N 3 12W
Cardiff-by-the-Sea, *U.S.A.* **85 M9** 33 1N 117 17W
Cardigan, *U.K.* **11 E3** 52 5N 4 40W
Cardigan B., *U.K.* **11 E3** 52 30N 4 30W
Cardinal, *Canada* **79 B9** 44 47N 75 23W
Cardona, *Uruguay* **94 C4** 33 53S 57 18W
Cardoso, Ilha do, *Brazil* **95 B5** 25 8S 47 58W
Cardston, *Canada* **72 D6** 49 15N 113 20W
Cardwell, *Australia* **62 B4** 18 14S 146 2 E
Careen L., *Canada* **73 B7** 57 0N 108 11W
Carei, *Romania* **17 E12** 47 40N 22 29 E
Careme = Ciremai, *Indonesia* **37 G13** 6 55S 108 27 E
Carey, *U.S.A.* **82 E7** 43 19N 113 57W
Carey, L., *Australia* **61 E3** 29 0S 122 15 E
Carey L., *Canada* **73 A8** 62 12N 102 55W
Carhué, *Argentina* **94 D3** 37 10S 62 50W
Caria, *Turkey* **21 F13** 37 20N 28 10 E
Cariacica, *Brazil* **93 H10** 20 16S 40 25W
Caribbean Sea, *W. Indies* **89 D5** 15 0N 75 0W
Cariboo Mts., *Canada* **72 C4** 53 0N 121 0W
Caribou, *U.S.A.* **77 B12** 46 52N 68 1W
Caribou →, *Man., Canada* **73 B10** 59 20N 94 44W
Caribou →, *N.W.T., Canada* **72 A3** 61 27N 125 45W
Caribou I., *Canada* **70 C2** 47 22N 85 49W
Caribou Is., *Canada* **72 A6** 61 55N 113 15W
Caribou L., *Man., Canada* **73 B9** 59 21N 96 10W
Caribou L., *Ont., Canada* **70 B2** 50 25N 89 5W
Caribou Mts., *Canada* **72 B5** 59 12N 115 40W
Carichic, *Mexico* **86 B3** 27 56N 107 3W
Carillo, *Mexico* **86 B4** 26 50N 103 55W
Carinhanha, *Brazil* **93 F10** 14 15S 44 46W
Carinhanha →, *Brazil* **93 F10** 14 20S 43 47W
Carinthia = Kärnten □, *Austria* **16 E8** 46 52N 13 30 E
Caripito, *Venezuela* **92 A6** 10 8N 63 6W
Carleton, Mt., *Canada* **71 C6** 47 23N 66 53W
Carleton Place, *Canada* **79 A8** 45 8N 76 9W
Carletonville, *S. Africa* **56 D4** 26 23S 27 22 E
Carlin, *U.S.A.* **82 F5** 40 43N 116 7W
Carlingford L., *U.K.* **13 B5** 54 3N 6 9W
Carlinville, *U.S.A.* **80 F10** 39 17N 89 53W
Carlisle, *U.K.* **10 C5** 54 54N 2 56W
Carlisle, *U.S.A.* **78 F7** 40 12N 77 12W
Carlos Casares, *Argentina* **94 D3** 35 32S 61 20W
Carlos Tejedor, *Argentina* **94 D3** 35 25S 62 25W
Carlow, *Ireland* **13 D5** 52 50N 6 56W
Carlow □, *Ireland* **13 D5** 52 43N 6 50W
Carlsbad, *Calif., U.S.A.* **85 M9** 33 10N 117 21W
Carlsbad, *N. Mex., U.S.A.* **81 J2** 32 25N 104 14W
Carlsbad Caverns National Park, *U.S.A.* **81 J2** 32 10N 104 35W
Carluke, *U.K.* **12 F5** 55 45N 3 50W
Carlyle, *Canada* **73 D8** 49 40N 102 20W
Carmacks, *Canada* **68 B6** 62 5N 136 16W
Carman, *Canada* **73 D9** 49 30N 98 0W
Carmarthen, *U.K.* **11 F3** 51 52N 4 19W
Carmarthen B., *U.K.* **11 F3** 51 40N 4 30W
Carmarthenshire □, *U.K.* **11 F3** 51 55N 4 13W
Carmaux, *France* **18 D5** 44 3N 2 10 E
Carmel, *U.S.A.* **79 E11** 41 26N 73 41W
Carmel-by-the-Sea, *U.S.A.* **84 J5** 36 33N 121 55W
Carmel Valley, *U.S.A.* **84 J5** 36 29N 121 43W
Carmelo, *Uruguay* **94 C4** 34 0S 58 20W
Carmen, *Colombia* **92 B3** 9 43N 75 8W
Carmen, *Paraguay* **95 B4** 27 13S 56 12W
Carmen →, *Mexico* **86 A3** 30 42N 106 29W
Carmen, I., *Mexico* **86 B2** 26 0N 111 20W
Carmen de Patagones, *Argentina* **96 E4** 40 50S 63 0W
Carmensa, *Argentina* **94 D2** 35 15S 67 40W
Carmi, *Canada* **72 D5** 49 36N 119 8W
Carmi, *U.S.A.* **76 F1** 38 5N 88 10W
Carmichael, *U.S.A.* **84 G5** 38 38N 121 19W
Carmila, *Australia* **62 C4** 21 55S 149 24 E
Carmona, *Costa Rica* **88 E2** 10 0N 85 15W
Carmona, *Spain* **19 D3** 37 28N 5 42W
Carn Ban, *U.K.* **12 D4** 57 7N 4 15W
Carn Eige, *U.K.* **12 D3** 57 17N 5 8W
Carnac, *France* **18 C2** 47 35N 3 6W
Carnamah, *Australia* **61 E2** 29 41S 115 53 E
Carnarvon, *Australia* **61 D1** 24 51S 113 42 E
Carnarvon, *S. Africa* **56 E3** 30 56S 22 8 E
Carnarvon Ra., *Queens., Australia* **62 D4** 25 15S 148 30 E
Carnarvon Ra., *W. Austral., Australia* **61 E3** 25 20S 120 45 E
Carnation, *U.S.A.* **84 C5** 47 39N 121 55W
Carndonagh, *Ireland* **13 A4** 55 16N 7 15W
Carnduff, *Canada* **73 D8** 49 10N 101 50W
Carnegie, *U.S.A.* **78 F4** 40 24N 80 5W
Carnegie, L., *Australia* **61 E3** 26 5S 122 30 E
Carnic Alps = Karnische Alpen, *Europe* **16 E7** 46 36N 13 0 E
Carniche Alpi = Karnische Alpen, *Europe* **16 E7** 46 36N 13 0 E
Carnot, *C.A.R.* **52 D3** 4 59N 15 56 E
Carnot, C., *Australia* **63 E2** 34 57S 135 38 E
Carnot B., *Australia* **60 C3** 17 20S 122 15 E
Carnoustie, *U.K.* **12 E6** 56 30N 2 42W
Carnsore Pt., *Ireland* **13 D5** 52 10N 6 22W
Caro, *U.S.A.* **76 D4** 43 29N 83 24W
Carol City, *U.S.A.* **77 N5** 25 56N 80 16W
Carolina, *Brazil* **93 E9** 7 10S 47 30W
Carolina, *Puerto Rico* **89 C6** 18 23N 65 58W
Carolina, *S. Africa* **57 D5** 26 5S 30 6 E
Caroline I., *Kiribati* **65 H12** 9 15S 150 3W
Caroline Is., *Micronesia* **28 J17** 8 0N 150 0 E
Caroni →, *Venezuela* **92 B6** 8 21N 62 43W
Caronie = Nébrodi, Monti, *Italy* **20 F6** 37 54N 14 35 E
Carpathians, *Europe* **17 D11** 49 30N 21 0 E
Carpaţii Meridionali, *Romania* **17 F13** 45 30N 25 0 E
Carpentaria, G. of, *Australia* **62 A2** 14 0S 139 0 E
Carpentras, *France* **18 D6** 44 3N 5 2 E
Carpi, *Italy* **20 B4** 44 47N 10 53 E
Carpinteria, *U.S.A.* **85 L7** 34 24N 119 31W
Carr Boyd Ra., *Australia* **60 C4** 16 15S 128 35 E
Carrabelle, *U.S.A.* **77 L3** 29 51N 84 40W
Carranza, Presa V., *Mexico* **86 B4** 27 20N 100 50W
Carrara, *Italy* **18 D9** 44 5N 10 6 E
Carrauntoohill, *Ireland* **13 D2** 52 0N 9 45W
Carrick-on-Shannon, *Ireland* **13 C3** 53 57N 8 5W
Carrick-on-Suir, *Ireland* **13 D4** 52 21N 7 24W
Carrickfergus, *U.K.* **13 B6** 54 43N 5 49W
Carrickmacross, *Ireland* **13 C5** 53 59N 6 43W
Carrington, *U.S.A.* **80 B5** 47 27N 99 8W
Carrizal Bajo, *Chile* **94 B1** 28 5S 71 20W
Carrizalillo, *Chile* **94 B1** 29 5S 71 30W
Carrizo Cr. →, *U.S.A.* **81 G3** 36 55N 103 55W
Carrizo Springs, *U.S.A.* **81 L5** 28 31N 99 52W
Carrizozo, *U.S.A.* **83 K11** 33 38N 105 53W
Carroll, *U.S.A.* **80 D7** 42 4N 94 52W
Carrollton, *Ga., U.S.A.* **77 J3** 33 35N 85 5W
Carrollton, *Ill., U.S.A.* **80 F9** 39 18N 90 24W
Carrollton, *Ky., U.S.A.* **76 F3** 38 41N 85 11W
Carrollton, *Mo., U.S.A.* **80 F8** 39 22N 93 30W
Carrollton, *Ohio, U.S.A.* **78 F3** 40 34N 81 5W
Carron →, *U.K.* **12 D4** 57 53N 4 22W
Carron, L., *U.K.* **12 D3** 57 22N 5 35W
Carrot →, *Canada* **73 C8** 53 50N 101 17W
Carrot River, *Canada* **73 C8** 53 17N 103 35W
Carruthers, *Canada* **73 C7** 52 52N 109 16W
Carson, *Calif., U.S.A.* **85 M8** 33 48N 118 17W
Carson, *N. Dak., U.S.A.* **80 B4** 46 25N 101 34W
Carson →, *U.S.A.* **84 F8** 39 45N 118 40W
Carson City, *U.S.A.* **84 F7** 39 10N 119 46W
Carson Sink, *U.S.A.* **82 G4** 39 50N 118 25W
Cartagena, *Colombia* **92 A3** 10 25N 75 33W
Cartagena, *Spain* **19 D5** 37 38N 0 59W
Cartago, *Colombia* **92 C3** 4 45N 75 55W
Cartago, *Costa Rica* **88 E3** 9 50N 83 55W
Cartersville, *U.S.A.* **77 H3** 34 10N 84 48W
Carterton, *N.Z.* **59 J5** 41 2S 175 31 E
Carthage, *Tunisia* **51 A8** 36 50N 10 21 E
Carthage, *Ill., U.S.A.* **80 E9** 40 25N 91 8W
Carthage, *Mo., U.S.A.* **81 G7** 37 11N 94 19W
Carthage, *N.Y., U.S.A.* **76 D8** 43 59N 75 37W
Carthage, *Tex., U.S.A.* **81 J7** 32 9N 94 20W
Cartier I., *Australia* **60 B3** 12 31S 123 29 E
Cartwright, *Canada* **71 B8** 53 41N 56 58W
Caruaru, *Brazil* **93 E11** 8 15S 35 55W
Carúpano, *Venezuela* **92 A6** 10 39N 63 15W
Caruthersville, *U.S.A.* **81 G10** 36 11N 89 39W
Carvoeiro, *Brazil* **92 D6** 1 30S 61 59W
Carvoeiro, C., *Portugal* **19 C1** 39 21N 9 24W
Cary, *U.S.A.* **77 H6** 35 47N 78 46W
Casa Grande, *U.S.A.* **83 K8** 32 53N 111 45W
Casablanca, *Chile* **94 C1** 33 20S 71 25W
Casablanca, *Morocco* **50 B4** 33 36N 7 36W
Cascade, *Idaho, U.S.A.* **82 D5** 44 31N 116 2W
Cascade, *Mont., U.S.A.* **82 C8** 47 16N 111 42W
Cascade Locks, *U.S.A.* **84 E5** 45 40N 121 54W
Cascade Ra., *U.S.A.* **84 D5** 47 0N 121 30W
Cascade Reservoir, *U.S.A.* **82 D5** 44 32N 116 3W
Cascais, *Portugal* **19 C1** 38 41N 9 25W
Cascavel, *Brazil* **95 A5** 24 57S 53 28W
Cáscina, *Italy* **20 C4** 43 41N 10 33 E
Casco B., *U.S.A.* **77 D10** 43 45N 70 0W
Caserta, *Italy* **20 D6** 41 4N 14 20 E
Cashel, *Ireland* **13 D4** 52 30N 7 53W
Casiguran, *Phil.* **37 A6** 16 22N 122 7 E
Casilda, *Argentina* **94 C3** 33 10S 61 10W
Casino, *Australia* **63 D5** 28 52S 153 3 E
Casiquiare →, *Venezuela* **92 C5** 2 1N 67 7W
Casma, *Peru* **92 E3** 9 30S 78 20W
Casmalia, *U.S.A.* **85 L6** 34 50N 120 32W
Caspe, *Spain* **19 B5** 41 14N 0 1W
Casper, *U.S.A.* **82 E10** 42 51N 106 19W
Caspian Depression, *Eurasia* **25 E8** 47 0N 48 0 E
Caspian Sea, *Eurasia* **25 F9** 43 0N 50 0 E
Cass Lake, *U.S.A.* **80 B7** 47 23N 94 37W
Cassadaga, *U.S.A.* **78 D5** 42 20N 79 19W
Casselman, *Canada* **79 A9** 45 19N 75 5W
Casselton, *U.S.A.* **80 B6** 46 54N 97 13W
Cassiar, *Canada* **72 B3** 59 16N 129 40W
Cassiar Mts., *Canada* **72 B2** 59 30N 130 30W
Cassino, *Italy* **20 D5** 41 30N 13 49 E
Cassville, *U.S.A.* **81 G8** 36 41N 93 52W
Castaic, *U.S.A.* **85 L8** 34 30N 118 38W
Castalia, *U.S.A.* **78 E2** 41 24N 82 49W
Castanhal, *Brazil* **93 D9** 1 18S 47 55W
Castellammare di Stábia, *Italy* **20 D6** 40 42N 14 29 E
Castelli, *Argentina* **94 D4** 36 7S 57 47W
Castelló de la Plana, *Spain* **19 C5** 39 58N 0 3W
Castelo, *Brazil* **95 A7** 20 33S 41 14W
Castelo Branco, *Portugal* **19 C2** 39 50N 7 31W
Castelsarrasin, *France* **18 E4** 44 2N 1 7 E
Castelvetrano, *Italy* **20 F5** 37 41N 12 47 E
Casterton, *Australia* **63 F3** 37 30S 141 30 E
Castile, *U.S.A.* **78 D6** 42 38N 78 3W
Castilla-La Mancha □, *Spain* **19 C4** 39 30N 3 30W
Castilla y Leon □, *Spain* **19 B3** 42 0N 5 0W
Castillos, *Uruguay* **95 C5** 34 12S 53 52W
Castle Dale, *U.S.A.* **82 G8** 39 13N 111 1W
Castle Douglas, *U.K.* **12 G5** 54 56N 3 56W
Castle Rock, *Colo., U.S.A.* **80 F2** 39 22N 104 51W
Castle Rock, *Wash., U.S.A.* **84 D4** 46 17N 122 54W
Castlebar, *Ireland* **13 C2** 53 52N 9 18W
Castleblaney, *Ireland* **13 B5** 54 7N 6 44W
Castlederg, *U.K.* **13 B4** 54 42N 7 35W
Castleford, *U.K.* **10 D6** 53 43N 1 21W
Castlegar, *Canada* **72 D5** 49 20N 117 40W
Castlepollard, *Ireland* **13 C4** 53 41N 7 19W
Castlerea, *Ireland* **13 C3** 53 46N 8 29W
Castlereagh →, *Australia* **63 E4** 30 12S 147 32 E
Castlereagh B., *Australia* **62 A2** 12 10S 135 10 E
Castleton, *U.S.A.* **79 C11** 43 37N 73 11W
Castletown, *U.K.* **10 C3** 54 5N 4 38W
Castletown Bearhaven, *Ireland* **13 E2** 51 39N 9 55W
Castor, *Canada* **72 C6** 52 15N 111 50W
Castor →, *Canada* **70 B4** 53 24N 78 58W
Castorland, *U.S.A.* **79 C9** 43 53N 75 31W
Castres, *France* **18 E5** 43 37N 2 13 E
Castricum, *Neths.* **15 B4** 52 33N 4 40 E
Castries, *St. Lucia* **89 D7** 14 2N 60 58W
Castro, *Brazil* **95 A6** 24 45S 50 0W
Castro, *Chile* **96 E2** 42 30S 73 50W
Castro Alves, *Brazil* **93 F11** 12 46S 39 33W
Castroville, *U.S.A.* **84 J5** 36 46N 121 45W
Castuera, *Spain* **19 C3** 38 43N 5 37W
Cat Ba, Dao, *Vietnam* **38 B6** 20 50N 107 0 E
Cat I., *Bahamas* **89 B4** 24 30N 75 30W
Cat L., *Canada* **70 B1** 51 40N 91 50W
Cat Lake, *Canada* **70 B1** 51 40N 91 50W
Catacamas, *Honduras* **88 D2** 14 54N 85 56W
Cataguases, *Brazil* **95 A7** 21 23S 42 39W
Catalão, *Brazil* **93 G9** 18 10S 47 57W
Çatalca, *Turkey* **21 D13** 41 8N 28 27 E
Catalina, *Canada* **71 C9** 48 31N 53 4W
Catalina, *Chile* **94 B2** 25 13S 69 43W
Catalina, *U.S.A.* **83 K8** 32 30N 110 50W
Catalonia = Cataluña □, *Spain* **19 B6** 41 40N 1 15 E
Cataluña □, *Spain* **19 B6** 41 40N 1 15 E
Catamarca, *Argentina* **94 B2** 28 30S 65 50W
Catamarca □, *Argentina* **94 B2** 27 0S 65 50W
Catanduanes □, *Phil.* **37 B6** 13 50N 124 20 E
Catanduva, *Brazil* **95 A6** 21 5S 48 58W
Catánia, *Italy* **20 F6** 37 30N 15 6 E
Catanzaro, *Italy* **20 E7** 38 54N 16 35 E
Catarman, *Phil.* **37 B6** 12 28N 124 35 E
Cateel, *Phil.* **37 C7** 7 47N 126 24 E
Catembe, *Mozam.* **57 D5** 26 0S 32 33 E
Caterham, *U.K.* **11 F7** 51 15N 0 4W
Cathcart, *S. Africa* **56 E4** 32 18S 27 10 E
Cathlamet, *U.S.A.* **84 D3** 46 12N 123 23W
Catlettsburg, *U.S.A.* **76 F4** 38 25N 82 36W
Catoche, C., *Mexico* **87 C7** 21 40N 87 8W
Catriló, *Argentina* **94 D3** 36 26S 63 24W
Catrimani, *Brazil* **92 C6** 0 27N 61 41W
Catrimani →, *Brazil* **92 C6** 0 28N 61 44W
Catskill, *U.S.A.* **79 D11** 42 14N 73 52W
Catskill Mts., *U.S.A.* **79 D10** 42 10N 74 25W
Catt, Mt., *Australia* **62 A1** 13 49S 134 23 E
Cattaraugus, *U.S.A.* **78 D6** 42 22N 78 52W
Catuala, *Angola* **56 B2** 16 25S 19 2 E
Catuane, *Mozam.* **57 D5** 26 48S 32 18 E
Catur, *Mozam.* **55 E4** 13 45S 35 30 E
Catwick Is., *Vietnam* **39 G7** 10 0N 109 0 E
Cauca →, *Colombia* **92 B4** 8 54N 74 28W
Caucaia, *Brazil* **93 D11** 3 40S 38 35W
Caucasus Mountains, *Eurasia* **25 F7** 42 50N 44 0 E
Caungula, *Angola* **52 F3** 8 26S 18 38 E
Cauquenes, *Chile* **94 D1** 36 0S 72 22W
Caura →, *Venezuela* **92 B6** 7 38N 64 53W
Cauresi →, *Mozam.* **55 F3** 17 8S 33 0 E
Causapscal, *Canada* **71 C6** 48 19N 67 12W
Cauvery →, *India* **40 P11** 11 9N 78 52 E
Caux, Pays de, *France* **18 B4** 49 38N 0 35 E
Cavalier, *U.S.A.* **80 A6** 48 48N 97 37W
Cavalleria, C. de, *Spain* **22 A11** 40 5N 4 5 E
Cavan, *Ireland* **13 B4** 54 0N 7 22W
Cavan □, *Ireland* **13 C4** 54 1N 7 16W
Cave Creek, *U.S.A.* **83 K7** 33 50N 111 57W
Cavenagh Ra., *Australia* **61 E4** 26 12S 127 55 E
Caviana, I., *Brazil* **93 C8** 0 10N 50 10W
Cavite, *Phil.* **37 B6** 14 29N 120 55 E
Cawnpore = Kanpur, *India* **43 F9** 26 28N 80 20 E
Caxias, *Brazil* **93 D10** 4 55S 43 20W
Caxias do Sul, *Brazil* **95 B5** 29 10S 51 10W
Cay Sal Bank, *Bahamas* **88 B4** 23 45N 80 0W
Cayambe, *Ecuador* **92 C3** 0 3N 78 8W
Cayenne, *Fr. Guiana* **93 B8** 5 5N 52 18W
Cayman Brac, *Cayman Is.* **88 C4** 19 43N 79 49W
Cayman Is. ■, *W. Indies* **88 C3** 19 40N 80 30W
Cayo Romano, *Cuba* **88 B4** 22 0N 78 0W
Cayuga, *Canada* **78 D5** 42 59N 79 50W
Cayuga, *U.S.A.* **79 D8** 42 54N 76 44W
Cayuga L., *U.S.A.* **79 D8** 42 41N 76 41W
Cazenovia, *U.S.A.* **79 D9** 42 56N 75 51W
Cazombo, *Angola* **53 G4** 11 54S 22 56 E
Ceanannus Mor, *Ireland* **13 C5** 53 44N 6 53W
Ceará = Fortaleza, *Brazil* **93 D11** 3 45S 38 35W
Ceará □, *Brazil* **93 E11** 5 0S 40 0W
Ceará Mirim, *Brazil* **93 E11** 5 38S 35 25W
Cebaco, I. de, *Panama* **88 E3** 7 33N 81 9W
Cebollar, *Argentina* **94 B2** 29 10S 66 35W
Cebu, *Phil.* **37 B6** 10 18N 123 54 E
Cecil Plains, *Australia* **63 D5** 27 30S 151 11 E
Cedar →, *U.S.A.* **80 E9** 41 17N 91 21W
Cedar City, *U.S.A.* **83 H7** 37 41N 113 4W
Cedar Creek Reservoir, *U.S.A.* **81 J6** 32 11N 96 4W
Cedar Falls, *Iowa, U.S.A.* **80 D8** 42 32N 92 27W
Cedar Falls, *Wash., U.S.A.* **84 C5** 47 25N 121 45W
Cedar Key, *U.S.A.* **77 L4** 29 8N 83 2W
Cedar L., *Canada* **73 C9** 53 10N 100 0W
Cedar Rapids, *U.S.A.* **80 E9** 41 59N 91 40W
Cedartown, *U.S.A.* **77 H3** 34 1N 85 15W
Cedarvale, *Canada* **72 B3** 55 1N 128 22W
Cedarville, *S. Africa* **57 E4** 30 23S 29 3 E
Cedral, *Mexico* **86 C4** 23 50N 100 42W
Cedro, *Brazil* **93 E11** 6 34S 39 3W
Cedros, I. de, *Mexico* **86 B1** 28 10N 115 20W
Ceduna, *Australia* **63 E1** 32 7S 133 46 E
Cefalù, *Italy* **20 E6** 38 2N 14 1 E
Cegléd, *Hungary* **17 E10** 47 11N 19 47 E
Celaya, *Mexico* **86 C4** 20 31N 100 37W
Celebes Sea, *Indonesia* **37 D6** 3 0N 123 0 E
Celina, *U.S.A.* **76 E3** 40 33N 84 35W
Celje, *Slovenia* **16 E8** 46 16N 15 18 E
Celle, *Germany* **16 B6** 52 37N 10 4 E
Cenderwasih, Teluk, *Indonesia* **37 E9** 3 0S 135 20 E
Center, *N. Dak., U.S.A.* **80 B4** 47 7N 101 18W
Center, *Tex., U.S.A.* **81 K7** 31 48N 94 11W
Centerburg, *U.S.A.* **78 F2** 40 18N 82 42W
Centerville, *Calif., U.S.A.* **84 J7** 36 44N 119 30W
Centerville, *Iowa, U.S.A.* **80 E8** 40 44N 92 52W
Centerville, *Pa., U.S.A.* **78 F5** 40 3N 79 59W
Centerville, *Tenn., U.S.A.* **77 H2** 35 47N 87 28W
Centerville, *Tex., U.S.A.* **81 K7** 31 16N 95 59W
Central □, *Kenya* **54 C4** 0 30S 37 30 E
Central □, *Malawi* **55 E3** 13 30S 33 30 E
Central □, *Zambia* **55 E2** 14 25S 28 50 E
Central, Cordillera, *Colombia* **92 C4** 5 0N 75 0W
Central, Cordillera, *Costa Rica* **88 D3** 10 10N 84 5W
Central, Cordillera, *Dom. Rep.* **89 C5** 19 15N 71 0W
Central African Rep. ■, *Africa* **52 C4** 7 0N 20 0 E
Central America, *America* **66 H11** 12 0N 85 0W
Central Butte, *Canada* **73 C7** 50 48N 106 31W
Central City, *Colo., U.S.A.* **82 G11** 39 48N 105 31W
Central City, *Ky., U.S.A.* **76 G2** 37 18N 87 7W
Central City, *Nebr., U.S.A.* **80 E6** 41 7N 98 0W
Central I., *Kenya* **54 B4** 3 30N 36 0 E
Central Makran Range, *Pakistan* **40 F4** 26 30N 64 15 E
Central Patricia, *Canada* **70 B1** 51 30N 90 9W
Central Point, *U.S.A.* **82 E2** 42 23N 122 55W
Central Russian Uplands, *Europe* **6 E13** 54 0N 36 0 E
Central Siberian Plateau, *Russia* **28 C14** 65 0N 105 0 E
Central Square, *U.S.A.* **79 C8** 43 17N 76 9W
Centralia, *Ill., U.S.A.* **80 F10** 38 32N 89 8W
Centralia, *Mo., U.S.A.* **80 F8** 39 13N 92 8W
Centralia, *Wash., U.S.A.* **84 D4** 46 43N 122 58W
Cephalonia = Kefallinía, *Greece* **21 E9** 38 20N 20 30 E
Cepu, *Indonesia* **37 G14** 7 9S 111 35 E
Ceram = Seram, *Indonesia* **37 E7** 3 10S 129 0 E
Ceram Sea = Seram Sea, *Indonesia* **37 E7** 2 30S 128 30 E
Ceredigion □, *U.K.* **11 E3** 52 16N 4 15W
Ceres, *Argentina* **94 B3** 29 55S 61 55W
Ceres, *S. Africa* **56 E2** 33 21S 19 18 E
Ceres, *U.S.A.* **84 H6** 37 35N 120 57W
Cerignola, *Italy* **20 D6** 41 17N 15 53 E
Cerigo = Kíthira, *Greece* **21 F10** 36 8N 23 0 E
Çerkezköy, *Turkey* **21 D12** 41 17N 28 0 E
Cerralvo, I., *Mexico* **86 C3** 24 20N 109 45W
Cerritos, *Mexico* **86 C4** 22 27N 100 20W
Cerro Chato, *Uruguay* **95 C4** 33 6S 55 8W
Cerventes, *Australia* **61 F2** 30 31S 115 3 E
Cervera, *Spain* **19 B6** 41 40N 1 16 E
Cesena, *Italy* **20 B5** 44 8N 12 15 E
Cēsis, *Latvia* **9 H21** 57 18N 25 15 E
České Budějovice, *Czech Rep.* **16 D8** 48 55N 14 25 E
Českomoravská Vrchovina, *Czech Rep.* **16 D8** 49 30N 15 40 E
Çeşme, *Turkey* **21 E12** 38 20N 26 23 E
Cetinje, *Montenegro, Yug.* **21 C8** 42 23N 18 59 E
Cetraro, *Italy* **20 E6** 39 31N 15 55 E
Ceuta, *N. Afr.* **19 E3** 35 52N 5 18W
Cévennes, *France* **18 D5** 44 10N 3 50 E
Ceyhan, *Turkey* **44 B2** 37 4N 35 47 E
Ceylon = Sri Lanka ■, *Asia* **40 R12** 7 30N 80 50 E
Cha-am, *Thailand* **38 F2** 12 48N 99 58 E
Cha Pa, *Vietnam* **38 A4** 22 20N 103 47 E
Chacabuco, *Argentina* **94 C3** 34 40S 60 27W
Chachapoyas, *Peru* **92 E3** 6 15S 77 50W
Chachoengsao, *Thailand* **38 F3** 13 42N 101 5 E
Chachran, *Pakistan* **40 E7** 28 55N 70 30 E
Chachro, *Pakistan* **42 G4** 25 5N 70 15 E
Chaco □, *Argentina* **94 B3** 26 30S 61 0W
Chaco □, *Paraguay* **94 B4** 26 0S 60 0W
Chaco →, *U.S.A.* **83 H9** 36 46N 108 39W
Chaco Austral, *S. Amer.* **96 B4** 27 0S 61 30W
Chaco Boreal, *S. Amer.* **92 H6** 22 0S 60 0W
Chaco Central, *S. Amer.* **96 A4** 24 0S 61 0W
Chacon, C., *U.S.A.* **72 C2** 54 42N 132 0W
Chad ■, *Africa* **51 F8** 15 0N 17 15 E
Chad, L. = Tchad, L., *Chad* **51 F8** 13 30N 14 30 E
Chadan, *Russia* **27 D10** 51 17N 91 35 E
Chadileuvú →, *Argentina* **94 D2** 37 46S 66 0W
Chadiza, *Zambia* **55 E3** 14 45S 32 27 E
Chadron, *U.S.A.* **80 D3** 42 50N 103 0W
Chadyr-Lunga = Ciadâr-Lunga, *Moldova* **17 E15** 46 3N 28 51 E
Chae Hom, *Thailand* **38 C2** 18 43N 99 35 E
Chaem →, *Thailand* **38 C2** 18 11N 98 38 E
Chaeryŏng, *N. Korea* **35 E13** 38 24N 125 36 E
Chagai Hills = Chāh Gay, *Afghan.* **40 E3** 29 30N 64 0 E
Chagda, *Russia* **27 D14** 58 45N 130 38 E
Chagos Arch., *Ind. Oc.* **29 K11** 6 0S 72 0 E
Chagrin Falls, *U.S.A.* **78 E3** 41 26N 81 24W
Chāh Ākhvor, *Iran* **45 C8** 32 41N 59 40 E
Chāh Bahar, *Iran* **45 E9** 25 20N 60 40 E
Chāh-e Kavīr, *Iran* **45 C8** 34 29N 56 52 E
Chāh Gay, *Afghan.* **40 E3** 29 30N 64 0 E
Chahar Burjak, *Afghan.* **40 D3** 30 15N 62 0 E
Chahār Mahāll va Bakhtīarī □, *Iran* **45 C6** 32 0N 49 0 E
Chaibasa, *India* **41 H14** 22 42N 85 49 E
Chainat, *Thailand* **38 E3** 15 11N 100 8 E
Chaiya, *Thailand* **39 H2** 9 23N 99 14 E
Chaj Doab, *Pakistan* **42 C5** 32 15N 73 0 E
Chajari, *Argentina* **94 C4** 30 42S 58 0W
Chak Amru, *Pakistan* **42 C6** 32 22N 75 11 E
Chakar →, *Pakistan* **42 E3** 29 29N 68 2 E
Chakari, *Zimbabwe* **57 B4** 18 5S 29 51 E
Chake Chake, *Tanzania* **54 D4** 5 15S 39 45 E
Chakhānsūr, *Afghan.* **40 D3** 31 10N 62 0 E
Chakonipau, L., *Canada* **71 A6** 56 18N 68 30W
Chakradharpur, *India* **43 H11** 22 45N 85 40 E
Chakrata, *India* **42 D7** 30 42N 77 51 E
Chakwal, *Pakistan* **42 C5** 32 56N 72 53 E
Chala, *Peru* **92 G4** 15 48S 74 20W
Chalchihuites, *Mexico* **86 C4** 23 29N 103 53W
Chalcis = Khalkís, *Greece* **21 E10** 38 27N 23 42 E
Chaleur B., *Canada* **71 C6** 47 55N 65 30W
Chalfant, *U.S.A.* **84 H8** 37 32N 118 21W
Chalhuanca, *Peru* **92 F4** 14 15S 73 15W
Chalisgaon, *India* **40 J9** 20 30N 75 10 E
Chalk River, *Canada* **70 C4** 46 1N 77 27W
Chalky Inlet, *N.Z.* **59 M1** 46 3S 166 31 E
Challapata, *Bolivia* **92 G5** 18 53S 66 50W
Challis, *U.S.A.* **82 D6** 44 30N 114 14W
Chalmette, *U.S.A.* **81 L10** 29 56N 89 58W
Chalon-sur-Saône, *France* **18 C6** 46 48N 4 50 E
Châlons-en-Champagne, *France* **18 B6** 48 58N 4 20 E
Chalyaphum, *Thailand* **38 E4** 15 48N 102 2 E
Cham, Cu Lao, *Vietnam* **38 E7** 15 57N 108 30 E
Chama, *U.S.A.* **83 H10** 36 54N 106 35W
Chamaicó, *Argentina* **94 D3** 35 3S 64 58W

Chimán

Chimán, *Panama* 88 E4 8 45N 78 40W
Chimanimani, *Zimbabwe* 57 B5 19 48S 32 52 E
Chimay, *Belgium* 15 D4 50 3N 4 20 E
Chimayo, *U.S.A.* 83 H11 36 0N 105 56W
Chimbay, *Uzbekistan* 26 E6 42 57N 59 47 E
Chimborazo, *Ecuador* 92 D3 1 29S 78 55W
Chimbote, *Peru* 92 E3 9 0S 78 35W
Chimkent = Shymkent, *Kazakstan* 26 E7 42 18N 69 36 E
Chimoio, *Mozam.* 55 F3 19 4S 33 30 E
Chimpembe, *Zambia* 55 D2 9 31S 29 33 E
Chin □, *Burma* 41 J18 22 0N 93 0 E
Chin Ling Shan = Qinling Shandi, *China* 34 H5 33 50N 108 10 E
China, *Mexico* 87 B5 25 40N 99 20W
China ■, *Asia* 33 C6 30 0N 110 0 E
China Lake, *U.S.A.* 85 K9 35 44N 117 37W
Chinan = Jinan, *China* 34 F9 36 38N 117 1 E
Chinandega, *Nic.* 88 D2 12 35N 87 12W
Chinati Peak, *U.S.A.* 81 L2 29 57N 104 29W
Chincha Alta, *Peru* 92 F3 13 25S 76 7W
Chinchaga →, *Canada* 72 B5 58 53N 118 20W
Chinchilla, *Australia* 63 D5 26 45S 150 38 E
Chinchorro, Banco, *Mexico* 87 D7 18 35N 87 20W
Chinchou = Jinzhou, *China* 35 D11 41 5N 121 3 E
Chincoteague, *U.S.A.* 76 G8 37 56N 75 23W
Chinde, *Mozam.* 55 F4 18 35S 36 30 E
Chindo, *S. Korea* 35 G14 34 28N 126 15 E
Chindwin →, *Burma* 41 J19 21 26N 95 15 E
Chineni, *India* 43 C6 33 2N 75 15 E
Chinga, *Mozam.* 55 F4 15 13S 38 35 E
Chingola, *Zambia* 55 E2 12 31S 27 53 E
Chingole, *Malawi* 55 E3 13 4S 34 17 E
Ch'ingtao = Qingdao, *China* 35 F11 36 5N 120 20 E
Chinguetti, *Mauritania* 50 D3 20 25N 12 24W
Chingune, *Mozam.* 57 C5 20 33S 34 58 E
Chinhae, *S. Korea* 35 G15 35 9N 128 47 E
Chinhanguanine, *Mozam.* 57 D5 25 21S 32 30 E
Chinhoyi, *Zimbabwe* 55 F3 17 20S 30 8 E
Chini, *India* 42 D8 31 32N 78 15 E
Chiniot, *Pakistan* 42 D5 31 45N 73 0 E
Chínipas, *Mexico* 86 B3 27 22N 108 32W
Chinji, *Pakistan* 42 C5 32 42N 72 22 E
Chinju, *S. Korea* 35 G15 35 12N 128 2 E
Chinle, *U.S.A.* 83 H9 36 9N 109 33W
Chinnampo = Namp'o, *N. Korea* 35 E13 38 52N 125 10 E
Chino, *Japan* 31 G9 35 59N 138 9 E
Chino, *U.S.A.* 85 L9 34 1N 117 41W
Chino Valley, *U.S.A.* 83 J7 34 45N 112 27W
Chinon, *France* 18 C4 47 10N 0 15 E
Chinook, *U.S.A.* 82 B9 48 35N 109 14W
Chinsali, *Zambia* 55 E3 10 30S 32 2 E
Chióggia, *Italy* 20 B5 45 13N 12 17 E
Chios = Khíos, *Greece* 21 E12 38 27N 26 9 E
Chipata, *Zambia* 55 E3 13 38S 32 28 E
Chipinge, *Zimbabwe* 55 G3 20 13S 32 28 E
Chipley, *U.S.A.* 77 K3 30 47N 85 32W
Chipman, *Canada* 71 C6 46 6N 65 53W
Chipoka, *Malawi* 55 E3 13 57S 34 28 E
Chippenham, *U.K.* 11 F5 51 27N 2 6W
Chippewa →, *U.S.A.* 80 C8 44 25N 92 5W
Chippewa Falls, *U.S.A.* 80 C9 44 56N 91 24W
Chipping Norton, *U.K.* 11 F6 51 56N 1 32W
Chiputneticook Lakes, *U.S.A.* 77 C11 45 35N 67 35W
Chiquián, *Peru* 92 F3 10 10S 77 0W
Chiquimula, *Guatemala* 88 D2 14 51N 89 37W
Chiquinquira, *Colombia* 92 B4 5 37N 73 50W
Chirala, *India* 40 M12 15 50N 80 26 E
Chiramba, *Mozam.* 55 F3 16 55S 34 39 E
Chirawa, *India* 42 E6 28 14N 75 42 E
Chirchiq, *Uzbekistan* 26 E7 41 29N 69 35 E
Chiredzi, *Zimbabwe* 57 C5 21 0S 31 38 E
Chiricahua Peak, *U.S.A.* 83 L9 31 51N 109 18W
Chiriquí, G. de, *Panama* 88 E3 8 0N 82 10W
Chiriquí, L. de, *Panama* 88 E3 9 10N 82 0W
Chirivira Falls, *Zimbabwe* 55 G3 21 10S 32 12 E
Chirmiri, *India* 41 H13 23 15N 82 20 E
Chirripó Grande, Cerro, *Costa Rica* 88 E3 9 29N 83 29W
Chirundu, *Zimbabwe* 57 B4 16 3S 28 50 E
Chisamba, *Zambia* 55 E2 14 55S 28 20 E
Chisapani Garhi, *Nepal* 41 F14 27 30N 84 2 E
Chisasibi, *Canada* 70 B4 53 50N 79 0W
Chisholm, *Canada* 72 C6 54 55N 114 10W
Chisholm, *U.S.A.* 80 B8 47 29N 92 53W
Chishtian Mandi, *Pakistan* 42 E5 29 50N 72 55 E
Chisimaio, *Somali Rep.* 49 G8 0 22S 42 32 E
Chisimba Falls, *Zambia* 55 E3 10 12S 30 56 E
Chişinău, *Moldova* 17 E15 47 2N 28 50 E
Chisos Mts., *U.S.A.* 81 L3 29 5N 103 15W
Chistopol, *Russia* 24 C9 55 25N 50 38 E
Chita, *Russia* 27 D12 52 0N 113 35 E
Chitipa, *Malawi* 55 D3 9 41S 33 19 E
Chitose, *Japan* 30 C10 42 49N 141 39 E
Chitral, *Pakistan* 40 B7 35 50N 71 56 E
Chitré, *Panama* 88 E3 7 59N 80 27W
Chittagong, *Bangla.* 41 H17 22 19N 91 48 E
Chittagong □, *Bangla.* 41 G17 24 5N 91 0 E
Chittaurgarh, *India* 42 G6 24 52N 74 38 E
Chittoor, *India* 40 N11 13 15N 79 5 E
Chitungwiza, *Zimbabwe* 55 F3 18 0S 31 6 E
Chiusi, *Italy* 20 C4 43 1N 11 57 E
Chivasso, *Italy* 18 D7 45 11N 7 53 E
Chivhu, *Zimbabwe* 55 F3 19 2S 30 52 E
Chivilcoy, *Argentina* 94 C4 34 55S 60 0W
Chiwanda, *Tanzania* 55 E3 11 23S 34 55 E
Chizera, *Zambia* 55 E2 13 10S 25 0 E
Chkalov = Orenburg, *Russia* 24 D10 51 45N 55 6 E
Chloride, *U.S.A.* 85 K12 35 25N 114 12W
Cho Bo, *Vietnam* 38 B5 20 46N 105 10 E
Cho-do, *N. Korea* 35 E13 38 30N 124 40 E
Cho Phuoc Hai, *Vietnam* 39 G6 10 26N 107 18 E
Choba, *Kenya* 54 B4 2 30N 38 5 E
Chobe National Park, *Botswana* 56 B4 18 0S 25 0 E
Choch'iwŏn, *S. Korea* 35 F14 36 37N 127 18 E
Chocolate Mts., *U.S.A.* 85 M11 33 15N 115 15W
Choctawhatchee →, *U.S.A.* 77 K3 30 25N 86 8W
Choele Choel, *Argentina* 96 D3 39 11S 65 40W
Choix, *Mexico* 86 B3 26 40N 108 23W
Chojnice, *Poland* 17 B9 53 42N 17 32 E
Chōkai-San, *Japan* 30 E10 39 6N 140 3 E
Choke Canyon L., *U.S.A.* 81 L5 28 30N 98 20W
Chokurdakh, *Russia* 27 B15 70 38N 147 55 E
Cholame, *U.S.A.* 84 K6 35 44N 120 18W
Cholet, *France* 18 C3 47 4N 0 52W
Cholguan, *Chile* 94 D1 37 10S 72 3W
Choluteca, *Honduras* 88 D2 13 20N 87 14W
Choluteca →, *Honduras* 88 D2 13 0N 87 20W
Chom Bung, *Thailand* 38 F2 13 37N 99 36 E
Chom Thong, *Thailand* 38 C2 18 25N 98 41 E
Choma, *Zambia* 55 F2 16 48S 26 59 E
Chomun, *India* 42 F6 27 15N 75 40 E
Chomutov, *Czech Rep.* 16 C7 50 28N 13 23 E
Chon Buri, *Thailand* 38 F3 13 21N 101 1 E
Chon Thanh, *Vietnam* 39 G6 11 24N 106 36 E
Ch'onan, *S. Korea* 35 F14 36 48N 127 9 E
Chone, *Ecuador* 92 D3 0 40S 80 0W
Chong Kai, *Cambodia* 38 F4 13 57N 103 35 E
Chong Mek, *Thailand* 38 E5 15 10N 105 27 E
Chŏngdo, *S. Korea* 35 G15 35 38N 128 42 E
Chŏngha, *S. Korea* 35 F15 36 12N 129 21 E
Chŏngjin, *N. Korea* 35 D15 41 47N 129 50 E
Chŏngjiu, *S. Korea* 35 F14 36 39N 127 27 E
Chŏngju, *N. Korea* 35 E13 39 40N 125 5 E
Chongli, *China* 34 D8 40 58N 115 15 E
Chongqing, *China* 32 D5 29 35N 106 25 E
Chongqing Shi □, *China* 32 C5 30 0N 108 0 E
Chonguene, *Mozam.* 57 C5 25 3S 33 49 E
Chŏngŭp, *S. Korea* 35 G14 35 35N 126 50 E
Chŏnju, *S. Korea* 35 G14 35 50N 127 4 E
Chonos, Arch. de los, *Chile* 96 F2 45 0S 75 0W
Chop, *Ukraine* 17 D12 48 26N 22 12 E
Chopim →, *Brazil* 95 B5 25 35S 53 5W
Chor, *Pakistan* 42 G3 25 31N 69 46 E
Chorbat La, *India* 43 B7 34 42N 76 37 E
Chorley, *U.K.* 10 D5 53 39N 2 38W
Chornobyl, *Ukraine* 17 C16 51 20N 30 15 E
Chorolque, Cerro, *Bolivia* 94 A2 20 59S 66 5W
Chorregon, *Australia* 62 C3 22 40S 143 32 E
Chortkiv, *Ukraine* 17 D13 49 2N 25 46 E
Ch'ŏrwon, *S. Korea* 35 E14 38 15N 127 10 E
Chorzów, *Poland* 17 C10 50 18N 18 57 E
Chos-Malal, *Argentina* 94 D1 37 20S 70 15W
Ch'osan, *N. Korea* 35 D13 40 50N 125 47 E
Choszczno, *Poland* 16 B8 53 7N 15 25 E
Choteau, *U.S.A.* 82 C7 47 49N 112 11W
Chotila, *India* 42 H4 22 23N 71 15 E
Chotta Udepur, *India* 42 H6 22 19N 74 1 E
Chowchilla, *U.S.A.* 84 H6 37 7N 120 16W
Choybalsan, *Mongolia* 33 B6 48 4N 114 30 E
Christchurch, *N.Z.* 59 K4 43 33S 172 47 E
Christchurch, *U.K.* 11 G6 50 44N 1 47W
Christian I., *Canada* 78 B4 44 50N 80 12W
Christiana, *S. Africa* 56 D4 27 52S 25 8 E
Christiansted, *U.S. Virgin Is.* 89 C7 17 45N 64 42W
Christie B., *Canada* 73 A6 62 32N 111 10W
Christina →, *Canada* 73 B6 56 40N 111 3W
Christmas Cr. →, *Australia* 60 C4 18 29S 125 23 E
Christmas I. = Kiritimati, *Kiribati* 65 G12 1 58N 157 27W
Christmas I., *Ind. Oc.* 64 J2 10 30S 105 40 E
Christopher L., *Australia* 61 D4 24 49S 127 42 E
Chtimba, *Malawi* 55 E3 10 35S 34 13 E
Chu = Shū, *Kazakstan* 26 E8 43 36N 73 42 E
Chu →, *Vietnam* 38 C5 19 53N 105 45 E
Chu Lai, *Vietnam* 38 E7 15 28N 108 45 E
Ch'uanchou = Quanzhou, *China* 33 D6 24 55N 118 34 E
Chuankou, *China* 34 G6 34 20N 110 59 E
Chubbuck, *U.S.A.* 82 E7 42 55N 112 28W
Chūbu □, *Japan* 31 F8 36 45N 137 30 E
Chubut →, *Argentina* 96 E3 43 20S 65 5W
Chuchi L., *Canada* 72 B4 55 12N 124 30W
Chuda, *India* 42 H4 22 29N 71 41 E
Chudskoye, Ozero, *Russia* 9 G22 58 13N 27 30 E
Chūgoku □, *Japan* 31 G6 35 0N 133 0 E
Chūgoku-Sanchi, *Japan* 31 G6 35 0N 133 0 E
Chugwater, *U.S.A.* 80 E2 41 46N 104 50W
Chukchi Sea, *Russia* 27 C19 68 0N 175 0W
Chukotskoye Nagorye, *Russia* 27 C18 68 0N 175 0 E
Chula Vista, *U.S.A.* 85 N9 32 39N 117 5W
Chulucanas, *Peru* 92 E2 5 8S 80 10W
Chulym →, *Russia* 26 D9 57 43N 83 51 E
Chum Phae, *Thailand* 38 D4 16 40N 102 6 E
Chum Saeng, *Thailand* 38 E3 15 55N 100 15 E
Chumar, *India* 43 C8 32 40N 78 35 E
Chumbicha, *Argentina* 94 B2 29 0S 66 10W
Chumikan, *Russia* 27 D14 54 40N 135 10 E
Chumphon, *Thailand* 39 G2 10 35N 99 14 E
Chumuare, *Mozam.* 55 E3 14 31S 31 50 E
Chumunjin, *S. Korea* 35 F15 37 55N 128 54 E
Chuna →, *Russia* 27 D10 57 47N 94 37 E
Ch'unch'ŏn, *S. Korea* 35 F14 37 58N 127 44 E
Chunchura, *India* 43 H13 22 53N 88 27 E
Chunga, *Zambia* 55 F2 15 0S 26 2 E
Chunggang-ŭp, *N. Korea* 35 D14 41 48N 126 48 E
Chunghwa, *N. Korea* 35 E13 38 52N 125 47 E
Ch'ungju, *S. Korea* 35 F14 36 58N 127 58 E
Chungking = Chongqing, *China* 32 D5 29 35N 106 25 E
Ch'ungmu, *S. Korea* 35 G15 34 50N 128 20 E
Chungt'iaoshan = Zhongtiao Shan, *China* 34 G6 35 0N 111 10 E
Chunian, *Pakistan* 42 D6 30 57N 74 0 E
Chunya, *Tanzania* 55 D3 8 30S 33 27 E
Chunyang, *China* 35 C15 43 38N 129 23 E
Chuquibamba, *Peru* 92 G4 15 47S 72 44W
Chuquicamata, *Chile* 94 A2 22 15S 69 0W
Chur, *Switz.* 18 C8 46 52N 9 32 E
Churachandpur, *India* 41 G18 24 20N 93 40 E
Churchill, *Canada* 73 B10 58 47N 94 11W
Churchill →, *Man., Canada* 73 B10 58 47N 94 12W
Churchill →, *Nfld., Canada* 71 B7 53 19N 60 10W
Churchill, C., *Canada* 73 B10 58 46N 93 12W
Churchill Falls, *Canada* 71 B7 53 36N 64 19W
Churchill L., *Canada* 73 B7 55 55N 108 20W
Churchill Pk., *Canada* 72 B3 58 10N 125 10W
Churki, *India* 43 H10 23 50N 83 12 E
Churu, *India* 42 E6 28 20N 74 50 E
Churún Merú = Angel Falls, *Venezuela* 92 B6 5 57N 62 30W
Chushal, *India* 43 C8 33 40N 78 40 E
Chuska Mts., *U.S.A.* 83 H9 36 15N 108 50W
Chusovoy, *Russia* 24 C10 58 22N 57 50 E
Chute-aux-Outardes, *Canada* 71 C6 49 7N 68 24W
Chuuronjang, *N. Korea* 35 D15 41 35N 129 40 E
Chuvash Republic = Chuvashia □, *Russia* 24 C8 55 30N 47 0 E
Chuvashia □, *Russia* 24 C8 55 30N 47 0 E
Chuwārtah, *Iraq* 44 C5 35 43N 45 34 E
Chūy = Shū →, *Kazakstan* 28 E10 45 0N 67 44 E
Chuy, *Uruguay* 95 C5 33 41S 53 27W
Ci Xian, *China* 34 F8 36 20N 114 25 E
Ciadâr-Lunga, *Moldova* 17 E15 46 3N 28 51 E
Ciamis, *Indonesia* 37 G13 7 20S 108 21 E
Cianjur, *Indonesia* 37 G12 6 49S 107 8 E
Cianorte, *Brazil* 95 A5 23 37S 52 37W
Cibola, *U.S.A.* 85 M12 33 17N 114 42W
Cicero, *U.S.A.* 76 E2 41 48N 87 48W
Ciechanów, *Poland* 17 B11 52 52N 20 38 E
Ciego de Avila, *Cuba* 88 B4 21 50N 78 50W
Ciénaga, *Colombia* 92 A4 11 1N 74 15W
Cienfuegos, *Cuba* 88 B3 22 10N 80 30W
Cieszyn, *Poland* 17 D10 49 45N 18 35 E
Cieza, *Spain* 19 C5 38 17N 1 23W
Cihuatlán, *Mexico* 86 D4 19 14N 104 35W
Cijara, Embalse de, *Spain* 19 C3 39 18N 4 52W
Cijulang, *Indonesia* 37 G13 7 42S 108 27 E
Cilacap, *Indonesia* 37 G13 7 43S 109 0 E
Cill Chainnigh = Kilkenny, *Ireland* 13 D4 52 39N 7 15W
Cilo Dağı, *Turkey* 25 G7 37 28N 43 55 E
Cima, *U.S.A.* 85 K11 35 14N 115 30W
Cimarron, *Kans., U.S.A.* 81 G4 37 48N 100 21W
Cimarron, *N. Mex., U.S.A.* 81 G2 36 31N 104 55W
Cimarron →, *U.S.A.* 81 G6 36 10N 96 17W
Cimişlia, *Moldova* 17 E15 46 34N 28 44 E
Cimone, Mte., *Italy* 20 B4 44 12N 10 42 E
Cinca →, *Spain* 19 B6 41 26N 0 21 E
Cincar, *Bos.-H.* 20 C7 43 55N 17 5 E
Cincinnati, *U.S.A.* 76 F3 39 6N 84 31W
Cincinnatus, *U.S.A.* 79 D9 42 33N 75 54W
Çine, *Turkey* 21 F13 37 37N 28 2 E
Ciney, *Belgium* 15 D5 50 18N 5 5 E
Cinto, Mte., *France* 18 E8 42 24N 8 54 E
Circle, *Alaska, U.S.A.* 68 B5 65 50N 144 4W
Circle, *Mont., U.S.A.* 80 B2 47 25N 105 35W
Circleville, *U.S.A.* 76 F4 39 36N 82 57W
Cirebon, *Indonesia* 36 F3 6 45S 108 32 E
Ciremai, *Indonesia* 37 G13 6 55S 108 27 E
Cirencester, *U.K.* 11 F6 51 43N 1 57W
Cirium, *Cyprus* 23 E11 34 40N 32 53 E
Cisco, *U.S.A.* 81 J5 32 23N 98 59W
Citlaltépetl, *Mexico* 87 D5 19 0N 97 20W
Citrus Heights, *U.S.A.* 84 G5 38 42N 121 17W
Citrusdal, *S. Africa* 56 E2 32 35S 19 0 E
Città di Castello, *Italy* 20 C5 43 27N 12 14 E
Ciudad Altamirano, *Mexico* 86 D4 18 20N 100 40W
Ciudad Bolívar, *Venezuela* 92 B6 8 5N 63 36W
Ciudad Camargo, *Mexico* 86 B3 27 41N 105 10W
Ciudad de Valles, *Mexico* 87 C5 22 0N 99 0W
Ciudad del Carmen, *Mexico* 87 D6 18 38N 91 50W
Ciudad del Este, *Paraguay* 95 B5 25 30S 54 50W
Ciudad Delicias = Delicias, *Mexico* 86 B3 28 10N 105 30W
Ciudad Guayana, *Venezuela* 92 B6 8 0N 62 30W
Ciudad Guerrero, *Mexico* 86 B3 28 33N 107 28W
Ciudad Guzmán, *Mexico* 86 D4 19 40N 103 30W
Ciudad Juárez, *Mexico* 86 A3 31 40N 106 28W
Ciudad Madero, *Mexico* 87 C5 22 19N 97 50W
Ciudad Mante, *Mexico* 87 C5 22 50N 99 0W
Ciudad Obregón, *Mexico* 86 B3 27 28N 109 59W
Ciudad Real, *Spain* 19 C4 38 59N 3 55W
Ciudad Rodrigo, *Spain* 19 B2 40 35N 6 32W
Ciudad Trujillo = Santo Domingo, *Dom. Rep.* 89 C6 18 30N 69 59W
Ciudad Victoria, *Mexico* 87 C5 23 41N 99 9W
Ciudadela, *Spain* 22 B10 40 0N 3 50 E
Civitanova Marche, *Italy* 20 C5 43 18N 13 44 E
Civitavécchia, *Italy* 20 C4 42 6N 11 48 E
Cizre, *Turkey* 25 G7 37 19N 42 10 E
Clackmannanshire □, *U.K.* 12 E5 56 10N 3 43W
Clacton-on-Sea, *U.K.* 11 F9 51 47N 1 11 E
Claire, L., *Canada* 72 B6 58 35N 112 5W
Clairton, *U.S.A.* 78 F5 40 18N 79 53W
Clallam Bay, *U.S.A.* 84 B2 48 15N 124 16W
Clanton, *U.S.A.* 77 J2 32 51N 86 38W
Clanwilliam, *S. Africa* 56 E2 32 11S 18 52 E
Clara, *Ireland* 13 C4 53 21N 7 37W
Claraville, *U.S.A.* 85 K8 35 24N 118 20W
Clare, *U.S.A.* 76 D3 43 49N 84 46W
Clare □, *Ireland* 13 D3 52 45N 9 0W
Clare →, *Ireland* 13 C2 53 20N 9 2W
Clare I., *Ireland* 13 C1 53 49N 10 0W
Claremont, *Calif., U.S.A.* 85 L9 34 6N 117 43W
Claremont, *N.H., U.S.A.* 79 C12 43 23N 72 20W
Claremont Pt., *Australia* 62 A3 14 1S 143 41 E
Claremore, *U.S.A.* 81 G7 36 19N 95 36W
Claremorris, *Ireland* 13 C3 53 45N 9 0W
Clarence →, *Australia* 63 D5 29 25S 153 22 E
Clarence →, *N.Z.* 59 K4 42 10S 173 56 E
Clarence, I., *Chile* 96 G2 54 0S 72 0W
Clarence I., *Antarctica* 5 C18 61 10S 54 0W
Clarence Str., *Australia* 60 B5 12 0S 131 0 E
Clarence Town, *Bahamas* 89 B5 23 6N 74 59W
Clarendon, *Pa., U.S.A.* 78 E5 41 47N 79 6W
Clarendon, *Tex., U.S.A.* 81 H4 34 56N 100 53W
Clarenville, *Canada* 71 C9 48 10N 54 1W
Claresholm, *Canada* 72 D6 50 0N 113 33W
Clarie Coast, *Antarctica* 5 C9 68 0S 135 0 E
Clarinda, *U.S.A.* 80 E7 40 44N 95 2W
Clarion, *Iowa, U.S.A.* 80 D8 42 44N 93 44W
Clarion, *Pa., U.S.A.* 78 E5 41 13N 79 23W
Clarion →, *U.S.A.* 78 E5 41 7N 79 41W
Clark, *U.S.A.* 80 C6 44 53N 97 44W
Clark, Pt., *Canada* 78 B3 44 4N 81 45W
Clark Fork, *U.S.A.* 82 B5 48 9N 116 11W
Clark Fork →, *U.S.A.* 82 B5 48 9N 116 15W
Clarkdale, *U.S.A.* 83 J7 34 46N 112 3W
Clarke City, *Canada* 71 B6 50 12N 66 38W
Clarke I., *Australia* 62 G4 40 32S 148 10 E
Clarke Ra., *Australia* 62 C4 20 40S 148 30 E
Clark's Fork →, *U.S.A.* 82 D9 45 39N 108 43W
Clark's Harbour, *Canada* 71 D6 43 25N 65 38W
Clarks Hill L., *U.S.A.* 77 J4 33 40N 82 12W
Clarks Summit, *U.S.A.* 79 E9 41 30N 75 42W
Clarksburg, *U.S.A.* 76 F5 39 17N 80 30W
Clarksdale, *U.S.A.* 81 H9 34 12N 90 35W
Clarksville, *Ark., U.S.A.* 81 H8 35 28N 93 28W
Clarksville, *Tenn., U.S.A.* 77 G2 36 32N 87 21W
Clarksville, *Tex., U.S.A.* 81 J7 33 37N 95 3W
Clatskanie, *U.S.A.* 84 D3 46 6N 123 12W
Claude, *U.S.A.* 81 H4 35 7N 101 22W
Claveria, *Phil.* 37 A6 18 37N 121 4 E
Clay, *U.S.A.* 84 G5 38 17N 121 10W
Clay Center, *U.S.A.* 80 F6 39 23N 97 8W
Claypool, *U.S.A.* 83 K8 33 25N 110 51W
Claysburg, *U.S.A.* 78 F6 40 17N 78 27W
Claysville, *U.S.A.* 78 F4 40 7N 80 25W
Clayton, *N. Mex., U.S.A.* 81 G3 36 27N 103 11W
Clayton, *N.Y., U.S.A.* 79 B8 44 14N 76 5W
Clear, C., *Ireland* 13 E2 51 25N 9 32W
Clear, L., *Canada* 78 A7 45 26N 77 12W
Clear Hills, *Canada* 72 B5 56 40N 119 30W
Clear I., *Ireland* 13 E2 51 26N 9 30W
Clear L., *U.S.A.* 84 F4 39 2N 122 47W
Clear Lake, *Iowa, U.S.A.* 80 D8 43 8N 93 23W
Clear Lake, *S. Dak., U.S.A.* 80 C6 44 45N 96 41W
Clear Lake Reservoir, *U.S.A.* 82 F3 41 56N 121 5W
Clearfield, *Pa., U.S.A.* 78 E6 41 2N 78 27W
Clearfield, *Utah, U.S.A.* 82 F8 41 7N 112 2W
Clearlake, *U.S.A.* 82 G2 38 57N 122 38W
Clearlake Highlands, *U.S.A.* 84 G4 38 57N 122 38W
Clearwater, *Canada* 72 C4 51 38N 120 2W
Clearwater, *U.S.A.* 77 M4 27 58N 82 48W
Clearwater →, *Alta., Canada* 72 C6 52 22N 114 57W
Clearwater →, *Alta., Canada* 73 B6 56 44N 111 23W
Clearwater L., *Canada* 73 C9 53 34N 99 49W
Clearwater Mts., *U.S.A.* 82 C6 46 5N 115 20W
Clearwater Prov. Park, *Canada* 73 C8 54 0N 101 0W
Clearwater River Prov. Park, *Canada* 73 B7 56 55N 109 10W
Cleburne, *U.S.A.* 81 J6 32 21N 97 23W
Clee Hills, *U.K.* 11 E5 52 26N 2 35W
Cleethorpes, *U.K.* 10 D7 53 33N 0 3W
Cleeve Cloud, *U.K.* 11 F6 51 56N 2 0W
Clemson, *U.S.A.* 77 H4 34 41N 82 50W
Clerke Reef, *Australia* 60 C2 17 22S 119 20 E
Clermont, *Australia* 62 C4 22 49S 147 39 E
Clermont, *U.S.A.* 77 L5 28 33N 81 46W
Clermont-Ferrand, *France* 18 D5 45 46N 3 4 E
Clervaux, *Lux.* 15 D6 50 4N 6 2 E
Clevedon, *U.K.* 11 F5 51 26N 2 52W
Cleveland, *Miss., U.S.A.* 81 J9 33 45N 90 43W
Cleveland, *Ohio, U.S.A.* 78 E3 41 30N 81 42W
Cleveland, *Okla., U.S.A.* 81 G6 36 19N 96 28W
Cleveland, *Tenn., U.S.A.* 77 H3 35 10N 84 53W
Cleveland, *Tex., U.S.A.* 81 K7 30 21N 95 5W
Cleveland, C., *Australia* 62 B4 19 11S 147 1 E
Cleveland, Mt., *U.S.A.* 82 B7 48 56N 113 51W
Cleveland Heights, *U.S.A.* 78 E3 41 30N 81 34W
Clevelândia, *Brazil* 95 B5 26 24S 52 23W
Clew B., *Ireland* 13 C2 53 50N 9 49W
Clewiston, *U.S.A.* 77 M5 26 45N 80 56W
Clifden, *Ireland* 13 C1 53 29N 10 1W
Clifden, *N.Z.* 59 M1 46 1S 167 42 E
Cliffdell, *U.S.A.* 84 D5 46 56N 121 5W
Cliffy Hd., *Australia* 61 G2 35 1S 116 29 E
Clifton, *Australia* 63 D5 27 59S 151 53 E
Clifton, *Ariz., U.S.A.* 83 K9 33 3N 109 18W
Clifton, *Colo., U.S.A.* 83 G9 39 7N 108 25W
Clifton, *Tex., U.S.A.* 81 K6 31 47N 97 35W
Clifton Beach, *Australia* 62 B4 16 46S 145 39 E
Climax, *Canada* 73 D7 49 10N 108 20W
Clinch →, *U.S.A.* 77 H3 35 53N 84 29W
Clingmans Dome, *U.S.A.* 77 H4 35 34N 83 30W
Clint, *U.S.A.* 83 L10 31 35N 106 14W
Clinton, *B.C., Canada* 72 C4 51 6N 121 35W
Clinton, *Ont., Canada* 78 C3 43 37N 81 32W
Clinton, *N.Z.* 59 M2 46 12S 169 23 E
Clinton, *Ark., U.S.A.* 81 H8 35 36N 92 28W
Clinton, *Conn., U.S.A.* 79 E12 41 17N 72 32W
Clinton, *Ill., U.S.A.* 80 E10 40 9N 88 57W
Clinton, *Ind., U.S.A.* 76 F2 39 40N 87 24W
Clinton, *Iowa, U.S.A.* 80 E9 41 51N 90 12W
Clinton, *Mass., U.S.A.* 79 D13 42 25N 71 41W
Clinton, *Miss., U.S.A.* 81 J9 32 20N 90 20W
Clinton, *Mo., U.S.A.* 80 F8 38 22N 93 46W
Clinton, *N.C., U.S.A.* 77 H6 35 0N 78 22W
Clinton, *Okla., U.S.A.* 81 H5 35 31N 98 58W
Clinton, *S.C., U.S.A.* 77 H5 34 29N 81 53W
Clinton, *Tenn., U.S.A.* 77 G3 36 6N 84 8W
Clinton, *Wash., U.S.A.* 84 C4 47 59N 122 21W
Clinton C., *Australia* 62 C5 22 30S 150 45 E
Clinton Colden L., *Canada* 68 B9 63 58N 107 27W
Clintonville, *U.S.A.* 80 C10 44 37N 88 46W
Clipperton, I., *Pac. Oc.* 65 F17 10 18N 109 13W
Clisham, *U.K.* 12 D2 57 57N 6 49W
Clitheroe, *U.K.* 10 D5 53 53N 2 22W
Clo-oose, *Canada* 84 B2 48 39N 124 49W
Cloates, Pt., *Australia* 60 D1 22 43S 113 40 E
Clocolan, *S. Africa* 57 D4 28 55S 27 34 E
Clodomira, *Argentina* 94 B3 27 35S 64 14W
Clogher Hd., *Ireland* 13 C5 53 48N 6 14W
Clonakilty, *Ireland* 13 E3 51 37N 8 53W
Clonakilty B., *Ireland* 13 E3 51 35N 8 51W
Cloncurry, *Australia* 62 C3 20 40S 140 28 E
Cloncurry →, *Australia* 62 B3 18 37S 140 40 E
Clondalkin, *Ireland* 13 C5 53 19N 6 25W
Clones, *Ireland* 13 B4 54 11N 7 15W
Clonmel, *Ireland* 13 D4 52 21N 7 42W
Cloquet, *U.S.A.* 80 B8 46 43N 92 28W
Clorinda, *Argentina* 94 B4 25 16S 57 45W
Cloud Bay, *Canada* 70 C2 48 5N 89 26W
Cloud Peak, *U.S.A.* 82 D10 44 23N 107 11W
Cloudcroft, *U.S.A.* 83 K11 32 58N 105 45W
Cloverdale, *U.S.A.* 84 G4 38 48N 123 1W
Clovis, *Calif., U.S.A.* 84 J7 36 49N 119 42W
Clovis, *N. Mex., U.S.A.* 81 H3 34 24N 103 12W
Cloyne, *Canada* 78 B7 44 49N 77 11W
Cluj-Napoca, *Romania* 17 E12 46 47N 23 38 E
Clutha →, *N.Z.* 59 M2 46 20S 169 49 E
Clwyd →, *U.K.* 10 D4 53 19N 3 31W
Clyde, *Canada* 72 C6 54 9N 113 39W
Clyde, *N.Z.* 59 L2 45 12S 169 20 E
Clyde, *U.S.A.* 78 C8 43 5N 76 52W
Clyde →, *U.K.* 12 F4 55 55N 4 30W
Clyde, Firth of, *U.K.* 12 F3 55 22N 5 1W
Clyde River, *Canada* 69 A13 70 30N 68 30W
Clydebank, *U.K.* 12 F4 55 54N 4 23W
Clymer, *N.Y., U.S.A.* 78 D5 42 1N 79 37W
Clymer, *Pa., U.S.A.* 78 D5 40 40N 79 1W
Coachella, *U.S.A.* 85 M10 33 41N 116 10W
Coachella Canal, *U.S.A.* 85 N12 32 43N 114 57W
Coahoma, *U.S.A.* 81 J4 32 18N 101 18W
Coahuayana →, *Mexico* 86 D4 18 41N 103 45W
Coahuila □, *Mexico* 86 B4 27 0N 103 0W
Coal →, *Canada* 72 B3 59 39N 126 57W
Coalane, *Mozam.* 55 F4 17 48S 37 2 E
Coalcomán, *Mexico* 86 D4 18 40N 103 10W

Corrientes

Coaldale, Canada 72 D6 49 45N 112 35W
Coalgate, U.S.A. 81 H6 34 32N 96 13W
Coalinga, U.S.A. 84 J6 36 9N 120 21W
Coalisland, U.K. 13 B5 54 33N 6 42W
Coalville, U.K. 10 E6 52 44N 1 23W
Coalville, U.S.A. 82 F8 40 55N 111 24W
Coari, Brazil 92 D6 4 8S 63 7W
Coast □, Kenya 54 C4 2 40S 39 45 E
Coast Mts., Canada 72 C3 55 0N 129 20W
Coast Ranges, U.S.A. 84 G4 39 0N 123 0W
Coatbridge, U.K. 12 F4 55 52N 4 6W
Coatepec, Mexico 87 D5 19 27N 96 58W
Coatepeque, Guatemala 88 D1 14 46N 91 55W
Coatesville, U.S.A. 76 F8 39 59N 75 50W
Coaticook, Canada 79 A13 45 10N 71 46W
Coats I., Canada 69 B11 62 30N 83 0W
Coats Land, Antarctica 5 D1 77 0S 25 0W
Coatzacoalcos, Mexico 87 D6 18 7N 94 25W
Cobalt, Canada 70 C4 47 25N 79 42W
Cobán, Guatemala 88 C1 15 30N 90 21W
Cóbh, Ireland 13 E3 51 51N 8 17W
Cobija, Bolivia 92 F5 11 0S 68 50W
Cobleskill, U.S.A. 79 D10 42 41N 74 29W
Coboconk, Canada 78 B6 44 39N 78 48W
Cobourg, Canada 78 C6 43 58N 78 10W
Cobourg Pen., Australia 60 B5 11 20S 132 15 E
Cóbuè, Mozam. 55 E3 12 0S 34 58 E
Coburg, Germany 16 C6 50 15N 10 58 E
Cocanada = Kakinada, India 41 L13 16 57N 82 11 E
Cochabamba, Bolivia 92 G5 17 26S 66 10W
Cochemane, Mozam. 55 F3 17 0S 32 54 E
Cochin, India 40 Q10 9 59N 76 22 E
Cochin China = Nam-Phan, Vietnam 39 G6 10 30N 106 0 E
Cochran, U.S.A. 77 J4 32 23N 83 21W
Cochrane, Alta., Canada 72 C6 51 11N 114 30W
Cochrane, Ont., Canada 70 C3 49 0N 81 0W
Cochrane, Chile 96 F2 47 15S 72 33W
Cochrane →, Canada 73 B8 59 0N 103 40W
Cochrane, L., Chile 96 F2 47 10S 72 0W
Cochranton, U.S.A. 78 E4 41 31N 80 3W
Cockburn, Canal, Chile 96 G2 54 30S 72 0W
Cockburn I., Canada 70 C3 45 55N 83 22W
Cockburn Ra., Australia 60 C4 15 46S 128 0 E
Cockermouth, U.K. 10 C4 54 40N 3 22W
Cocklebiddy, Australia 61 F4 32 0S 126 3 E
Coco →, Cent. Amer. 88 D3 15 0N 83 8W
Coco, I. del, Pac. Oc. 65 G19 5 25N 87 55W
Cocoa, U.S.A. 77 L5 28 21N 80 44W
Cocobeach, Gabon 52 D1 0 59N 9 34 E
Cocos Is., Ind. Oc. 64 J1 12 10S 96 55 E
Cod, C., U.S.A. 76 D10 42 5N 70 10W
Codajás, Brazil 92 D6 3 55S 62 0W
Codó, Brazil 93 D10 4 30S 43 55W
Cody, U.S.A. 82 D9 44 32N 109 3W
Coe Hill, Canada 78 B7 44 52N 77 50W
Coelemu, Chile 94 D1 36 30S 72 48W
Coen, Australia 62 A3 13 52S 143 12 E
Cœur d'Alene, U.S.A. 82 C5 47 45N 116 51W
Cœur d'Alene L., U.S.A. 82 C5 47 32N 116 48W
Coevorden, Neths. 15 B6 52 40N 6 44 E
Cofete, Canary Is. 22 F5 28 6N 14 23W
Coffeyville, U.S.A. 81 G7 37 2N 95 37W
Coffin B., Australia 63 E2 34 38S 135 28 E
Coffin Bay, Australia 63 E2 34 37S 135 29 E
Coffin Bay Peninsula, Australia 63 E2 34 32S 135 15 E
Cognac, France 18 D3 45 41N 0 20W
Cohocton, U.S.A. 78 D7 42 30N 77 30W
Cohocton →, U.S.A. 78 D7 42 9N 77 6W
Cohoes, U.S.A. 79 D11 42 46N 73 42W
Coiba, I., Panama 88 E3 7 30N 81 40W
Coig →, Argentina 96 G3 51 0S 69 10W
Coigeach, Rubha, U.K. 12 C3 58 6N 5 26W
Coihaique, Chile 96 F2 45 30S 71 45W
Coimbatore, India 40 P10 11 2N 76 59 E
Coimbra, Brazil 92 G7 19 55S 57 48W
Coimbra, Portugal 19 B1 40 15N 8 27W
Coín, Spain 19 D3 36 40N 4 48W
Coipasa, Salar de, Bolivia 92 G5 19 26S 68 9W
Cojimies, Ecuador 92 C3 0 20N 80 0W
Cojutepequé, El Salv. 88 D2 13 41N 88 54W
Cokeville, U.S.A. 82 E8 42 5N 110 57W
Colatina, Brazil 93 G10 19 32S 40 37W
Colbeck, C., Antarctica 5 D13 77 6S 157 48W
Colborne, Canada 78 C7 44 0N 77 53W
Colby, U.S.A. 80 F4 39 24N 101 3W
Colchester, U.K. 11 F8 51 54N 0 55 E
Cold L., Canada 73 C7 54 33N 110 5W
Coldstream, Canada 72 C5 50 13N 119 11W
Coldstream, U.K. 12 F6 55 39N 2 15W
Coldwater, Canada 78 B5 44 42N 79 40W
Coldwater, Kans., U.S.A. 81 G5 37 16N 99 20W
Coldwater, Mich., U.S.A. 76 E3 41 57N 85 0W
Colebrook, U.S.A. 79 B13 44 54N 71 30W
Coleman, U.S.A. 81 K5 31 50N 99 26W
Coleman →, Australia 62 B3 15 6S 141 38 E
Colenso, S. Africa 57 D4 28 44S 29 50 E
Coleraine, U.K. 13 A5 55 8N 6 41W
Coleridge, L., N.Z. 59 K3 43 17S 171 30 E
Colesberg, S. Africa 56 E4 30 45S 25 5 E
Coleville, U.S.A. 84 G7 38 34N 119 30W
Colfax, Calif., U.S.A. 84 F6 39 6N 120 57W
Colfax, La., U.S.A. 81 K8 31 31N 92 42W
Colfax, Wash., U.S.A. 82 C5 46 53N 117 22W
Colhué Huapi, L., Argentina 96 F3 45 30S 69 0W
Coligny, S. Africa 57 D4 26 17S 26 15 E
Colima, Mexico 86 D4 19 14N 103 43W
Colima □, Mexico 86 D4 19 10N 103 40W
Colima, Nevado de, Mexico 86 D4 19 35N 103 45W
Colina, Chile 94 C1 33 13S 70 45W
Colinas, Brazil 93 E10 6 0S 44 10W
Coll, U.K. 12 E2 56 39N 6 34W
Collaguasi, Chile 94 A2 21 5S 68 45W
Collarenebri, Australia 63 D4 29 33S 148 34 E
Colleen Bawn, Zimbabwe 55 G2 21 0S 29 12 E
College Park, U.S.A. 77 J3 33 40N 84 27W
College Station, U.S.A. 81 K6 30 37N 96 21W
Collie, Australia 61 F2 33 22S 116 8 E
Collier B., Australia 60 C3 16 10S 124 15 E
Collier Ra., Australia 61 D2 24 45S 119 10 E
Collina, Passo di, Italy 20 B4 44 2N 10 56 E
Collingwood, Canada 78 B4 44 29N 80 13W
Collingwood, N.Z. 59 J4 40 41S 172 40 E
Collins, Canada 70 B2 50 17N 89 27W
Collinsville, Australia 62 C4 20 30S 147 56 E
Collipulli, Chile 94 D1 37 55S 72 30W
Collooney, Ireland 13 B3 54 11N 8 29W
Colmar, France 18 B7 48 5N 7 20 E
Cologne = Köln, Germany 16 C4 50 56N 6 57 E
Colom, I. d'en, Spain 22 B11 39 58N 4 16 E
Coloma, U.S.A. 84 G6 38 48N 120 53W
Colomb-Béchar = Béchar, Algeria 50 B5 31 38N 2 18W
Colombia ■, S. Amer. 92 C4 3 45N 73 0W
Colombian Basin, S. Amer. 66 H12 14 0N 76 0W
Colombo, Sri Lanka 40 R11 6 56N 79 58 E
Colón, Buenos Aires, Argentina 94 C3 33 53S 61 7W
Colón, Entre Ríos, Argentina 94 C4 32 12S 58 10W
Colón, Cuba 88 B3 22 42N 80 54W
Colón, Panama 88 E4 9 20N 79 54W
Colonia de Sant Jordi, Spain 22 B9 39 19N 2 59 E
Colonia del Sacramento, Uruguay 94 C4 34 25S 57 50W
Colonia Dora, Argentina 94 B3 28 34S 62 59W
Colonial Beach, U.S.A. 76 F7 38 15N 76 58W
Colonie, U.S.A. 79 D11 42 43N 73 50W
Colonsay, Canada 73 C7 51 59N 105 52W
Colonsay, U.K. 12 E2 56 5N 6 12W
Colorado □, U.S.A. 83 G10 39 30N 105 30W
Colorado →, Argentina 96 D4 39 50S 62 8W
Colorado →, N. Amer. 83 L6 31 45N 114 40W
Colorado →, U.S.A. 81 L7 28 36N 95 59W
Colorado City, U.S.A. 81 J4 32 24N 100 52W
Colorado Plateau, U.S.A. 83 H8 37 0N 111 0W
Colorado River Aqueduct, U.S.A. 85 L12 34 17N 114 10W
Colorado Springs, U.S.A. 80 F2 38 50N 104 49W
Colotlán, Mexico 86 C4 22 6N 103 16W
Colstrip, U.S.A. 82 D10 45 53N 106 38W
Colton, U.S.A. 79 B10 44 33N 74 56W
Columbia, Ky., U.S.A. 76 G3 37 6N 85 18W
Columbia, La., U.S.A. 81 J8 32 6N 92 5W
Columbia, Miss., U.S.A. 81 K10 31 15N 89 50W
Columbia, Mo., U.S.A. 80 F8 38 57N 92 20W
Columbia, Pa., U.S.A. 79 F8 40 2N 76 30W
Columbia, S.C., U.S.A. 77 J5 34 0N 81 2W
Columbia, Tenn., U.S.A. 77 H2 35 37N 87 2W
Columbia →, N. Amer. 84 D2 46 15N 124 5W
Columbia, C., Canada 4 A4 83 0N 70 0W
Columbia, District of □, U.S.A. 76 F7 38 55N 77 0W
Columbia, Mt., Canada 72 C5 52 8N 117 20W
Columbia Basin, U.S.A. 82 C4 46 45N 119 5W
Columbia Falls, U.S.A. 82 B6 48 23N 114 11W
Columbia Mts., Canada 72 C5 52 0N 119 0W
Columbia Plateau, U.S.A. 82 D5 44 0N 117 30W
Columbiana, U.S.A. 78 F4 40 53N 80 42W
Columbretes, Is., Spain 19 C6 39 50N 0 50 E
Columbus, Ga., U.S.A. 77 J3 32 28N 84 59W
Columbus, Ind., U.S.A. 76 F3 39 13N 85 55W
Columbus, Kans., U.S.A. 81 G7 37 10N 94 50W
Columbus, Miss., U.S.A. 77 J1 33 30N 88 25W
Columbus, Mont., U.S.A. 82 D9 45 38N 109 15W
Columbus, N. Mex., U.S.A. 83 L10 31 50N 107 38W
Columbus, Nebr., U.S.A. 80 E6 41 26N 97 22W
Columbus, Ohio, U.S.A. 76 F4 39 58N 83 0W
Columbus, Tex., U.S.A. 81 L6 29 42N 96 33W
Colusa, U.S.A. 84 F4 39 13N 122 1W
Colville, U.S.A. 82 B5 48 33N 117 54W
Colville →, U.S.A. 68 A4 70 25N 150 30W
Colville, C., N.Z. 59 G5 36 29S 175 21 E
Colwood, Canada 84 B3 48 26N 123 29W
Colwyn Bay, U.K. 10 D4 53 18N 3 44W
Comácchio, Italy 20 B5 44 42N 12 11 E
Comalcalco, Mexico 87 D6 18 16N 93 13W
Comallo, Argentina 96 E2 41 0S 70 5W
Comanche, U.S.A. 81 K5 31 54N 98 36W
Comayagua, Honduras 88 D2 14 25N 87 37W
Combahee →, U.S.A. 77 J5 32 30N 80 31W
Combarbalá, Chile 94 C1 31 11S 71 2W
Comber, Canada 78 D2 42 14N 82 33W
Comber, U.K. 13 B6 54 33N 5 45W
Combermere, Canada 78 A7 45 22N 77 37W
Comblain-au-Pont, Belgium 15 D5 50 29N 5 35 E
Comeragh Mts., Ireland 13 D4 52 18N 7 34W
Comet, Australia 62 C4 23 36S 148 38 E
Comilla, Bangla. 41 H17 23 28N 91 10 E
Comino, Malta 23 C1 36 2N 14 20 E
Comino, C., Italy 20 D3 40 32N 9 49 E
Comitán, Mexico 87 D6 16 18N 92 9W
Commerce, Ga., U.S.A. 77 H4 34 12N 83 28W
Commerce, Tex., U.S.A. 81 J7 33 15N 95 54W
Committee B., Canada 69 B11 68 30N 86 30W
Commonwealth B., Antarctica 5 C10 67 0S 144 0 E
Commoron Cr. →, Australia 63 D5 28 22S 150 8 E
Communism Pk. = Kommunizma, Pik, Tajikistan 26 F8 39 0N 72 2 E
Como, Italy 18 D8 45 47N 9 5 E
Como, Lago di, Italy 18 D8 46 0N 9 11 E
Comodoro Rivadavia, Argentina 96 F3 45 50S 67 40W
Comorin, C., India 40 Q10 8 3N 77 40 E
Comoro Is. = Comoros ■, Ind. Oc. 49 H8 12 10S 44 15 E
Comoros ■, Ind. Oc. 49 H8 12 10S 44 15 E
Comox, Canada 72 D4 49 42N 124 55W
Compiègne, France 18 B5 49 24N 2 50 E
Compostela, Mexico 86 C4 21 15N 104 53W
Comprida, I., Brazil 95 A6 24 50S 47 42W
Compton, Canada 79 A13 45 14N 71 49W
Compton, U.S.A. 85 M8 33 54N 118 13W
Comrat, Moldova 17 E15 46 18N 28 40 E
Con Cuong, Vietnam 38 C5 19 2N 104 54 E
Con Son, Vietnam 39 H6 8 41N 106 37 E
Conakry, Guinea 50 G3 9 29N 13 49W
Conara, Australia 62 G4 41 50S 147 26 E
Concarneau, France 18 C2 47 52N 3 56W
Conceição, Mozam. 55 F4 18 47S 36 7 E
Conceição da Barra, Brazil 93 G11 18 35S 39 45W
Conceição do Araguaia, Brazil 93 E9 8 0S 49 2W
Concepción, Argentina 94 B2 27 20S 65 35W
Concepción, Bolivia 92 G6 16 15S 62 8W
Concepción, Chile 94 D1 36 50S 73 0W
Concepción, Mexico 87 D6 18 15N 90 5W
Concepción, Paraguay 94 A4 23 22S 57 26W
Concepción □, Chile 94 D1 37 0S 72 30W
Concepción →, Mexico 86 A2 30 32N 113 2W
Concepción, Est. de, Chile 96 G2 50 30S 74 55W
Concepción, L., Bolivia 92 G6 17 20S 61 20W
Concepción, Punta, Mexico 86 B2 26 55N 111 59W
Concepción del Oro, Mexico 86 C4 24 40N 101 30W
Concepción del Uruguay, Argentina 94 C4 32 35S 58 20W
Conception, Pt., U.S.A. 85 L6 34 27N 120 28W
Conception B., Canada 71 C9 47 45N 53 0W
Conception B., Namibia 56 C1 23 55S 14 22 E
Conception I., Bahamas 89 B4 23 52N 75 9W
Concession, Zimbabwe 55 F3 17 27S 30 56 E
Conchas Dam, U.S.A. 81 H2 35 22N 104 11W
Concho, U.S.A. 83 J9 34 28N 109 36W
Concho →, U.S.A. 81 K5 31 34N 99 43W
Conchos →, Chihuahua, Mexico 86 B4 29 32N 105 0W
Conchos →, Tamaulipas, Mexico 87 B5 25 9N 98 35W
Concord, Calif., U.S.A. 84 H4 37 59N 122 2W
Concord, N.C., U.S.A. 77 H5 35 25N 80 35W
Concord, N.H., U.S.A. 79 C13 43 12N 71 32W
Concordia, Argentina 94 C4 31 20S 58 2W
Concórdia, Brazil 92 D5 4 36S 66 36W
Concordia, Mexico 86 C3 23 18N 106 2W
Concordia, U.S.A. 80 F6 39 34N 97 40W
Concrete, U.S.A. 82 B3 48 32N 121 45W
Condamine, Australia 63 D5 26 56S 150 9 E
Conde, U.S.A. 80 C5 45 9N 98 6W
Condeúba, Brazil 93 F10 14 52S 42 0W
Condon, U.S.A. 82 D3 45 14N 120 11W
Conegliano, Italy 20 B5 45 53N 12 18 E
Conejera, I. = Conills, I. des, Spain 22 B9 39 11N 2 58 E
Conejos, Mexico 86 B4 26 14N 103 53W
Confuso →, Paraguay 94 B4 25 9S 57 34W
Congleton, U.K. 10 D5 53 10N 2 13W
Congo (Kinshasa) = Congo, Dem. Rep. of the ■, Africa 52 E4 3 0S 23 0 E
Congo ■, Africa 52 E3 1 0S 16 0 E
Congo →, Africa 52 F2 6 4S 12 24 E
Congo, Dem. Rep. of the ■, Africa 52 E4 3 0S 23 0 E
Congo Basin, Africa 52 E4 0 10S 24 30 E
Congonhas, Brazil 95 A7 20 30S 43 52W
Congress, U.S.A. 83 J7 34 9N 112 51W
Conills, I. des, Spain 22 B9 39 11N 2 58 E
Coniston, Canada 70 C3 46 29N 80 51W
Conjeeveram = Kanchipuram, India 40 N11 12 52N 79 45 E
Conklin, Canada 73 B6 55 38N 111 5W
Conklin, U.S.A. 79 D9 42 2N 75 49W
Conn, L., Ireland 13 B2 54 3N 9 15W
Connacht □, Ireland 13 C2 53 43N 9 12W
Conneaut, U.S.A. 78 E4 41 57N 80 34W
Connecticut □, U.S.A. 79 E12 41 30N 72 45W
Connecticut →, U.S.A. 79 E12 41 16N 72 20W
Connell, U.S.A. 82 C4 46 40N 118 52W
Connellsville, U.S.A. 78 F5 40 1N 79 35W
Connemara, Ireland 13 C2 53 29N 9 45W
Connemaugh →, U.S.A. 78 F5 40 28N 79 19W
Connersville, U.S.A. 76 F3 39 39N 85 8W
Connors Ra., Australia 62 C4 21 40S 149 10 E
Conquest, Canada 73 C7 51 32N 107 14W
Conrad, U.S.A. 82 B8 48 10N 111 57W
Conroe, U.S.A. 81 K7 30 19N 95 27W
Consecon, Canada 78 C7 44 0N 77 31W
Conselheiro Lafaiete, Brazil 95 A7 20 40S 43 48W
Consett, U.K. 10 C6 54 51N 1 50W
Consort, Canada 73 C6 52 1N 110 46W
Constance = Konstanz, Germany 16 E5 47 40N 9 10 E
Constance, L. = Bodensee, Europe 18 C8 47 35N 9 25 E
Constanța, Romania 17 F15 44 14N 28 38 E
Constantia, U.S.A. 79 C8 43 15N 76 1W
Constantine, Algeria 50 A7 36 25N 6 42 E
Constitución, Chile 94 D1 35 20S 72 30W
Constitución, Uruguay 94 C4 31 0S 57 50W
Consul, Canada 73 D7 49 20N 109 30W
Contact, U.S.A. 82 F6 41 46N 114 45W
Contai, India 43 J12 21 54N 87 46 E
Contamana, Peru 92 E4 7 19S 74 55W
Contas →, Brazil 93 F11 14 17S 39 1W
Contoocook, U.S.A. 79 C13 43 13N 71 45W
Contra Costa, Mozam. 57 D5 25 9S 33 30 E
Contwoyto L., Canada 68 B8 65 42N 110 50W
Conway = Conwy, U.K. 10 D4 53 17N 3 50W
Conway = Conwy →, U.K. 10 D4 53 17N 3 50W
Conway, Ark., U.S.A. 81 H8 35 5N 92 26W
Conway, N.H., U.S.A. 79 C13 43 59N 71 7W
Conway, S.C., U.S.A. 77 J6 33 51N 79 3W
Conway, L., Australia 63 D2 28 17S 135 35 E
Conwy, U.K. 10 D4 53 17N 3 50W
Conwy □, U.K. 10 D4 53 10N 3 44W
Conwy →, U.K. 10 D4 53 17N 3 50W
Coober Pedy, Australia 63 D1 29 1S 134 43 E
Cooch Behar = Koch Bihar, India 41 F16 26 22N 89 29 E
Cooinda, Australia 60 B5 13 15S 130 5 E
Cook, Australia 61 F5 30 37S 130 25 E
Cook, U.S.A. 80 B8 47 49N 92 39W
Cook, B., Chile 96 H3 55 10S 70 0W
Cook, C., Canada 72 C3 50 8N 127 55W
Cook, Mt. = Aoraki Mount Cook, N.Z. 59 K3 43 36S 170 9 E
Cook Inlet, U.S.A. 68 C4 60 0N 152 0W
Cook Is., Pac. Oc. 65 J12 17 0S 160 0W
Cook Strait, N.Z. 59 J5 41 15S 174 29 E
Cookeville, U.S.A. 77 G3 36 10N 85 30W
Cookhouse, S. Africa 56 E4 32 44S 25 47 E
Cookshire, Canada 79 A13 45 25N 71 38W
Cookstown, U.K. 13 B5 54 39N 6 45W
Cooksville, Canada 78 C5 43 36N 79 35W
Cooktown, Australia 62 B4 15 30S 145 16 E
Cooladdi, Australia 63 D4 26 37S 145 23 E
Coolgardie, Australia 61 F3 30 55S 121 8 E
Coolidge, U.S.A. 83 K8 32 59N 111 31W
Coolidge Dam, U.S.A. 83 K8 33 0N 110 20W
Coon Rapids, U.S.A. 80 C8 45 9N 93 19W
Coonana, Australia 61 F3 31 0S 123 0 E
Coondapoor, India 40 N9 13 42N 74 40 E
Cooninie, L., Australia 63 D2 26 4S 139 59 E
Cooper, U.S.A. 81 J7 33 23N 95 42W
Cooper Cr. →, Australia 63 D2 28 29S 137 46 E
Cooperstown, N. Dak., U.S.A. 80 B5 47 27N 98 8W
Cooperstown, N.Y., U.S.A. 79 D10 42 42N 74 56W
Coorabie, Australia 61 F5 31 54S 132 18 E
Coorow, Australia 61 E2 29 53S 116 2 E
Cooroy, Australia 63 D5 26 22S 152 54 E
Coos Bay, U.S.A. 82 E1 43 22N 124 13W
Coosa →, U.S.A. 77 J2 32 30N 86 16W
Cootehill, Ireland 13 B4 54 4N 7 5W
Copahue Paso, Argentina 94 D1 37 49S 71 8W
Copainalá, Mexico 87 D6 17 8N 93 11W
Copake Falls, U.S.A. 79 D11 42 7N 73 31W
Copán, Honduras 88 D2 14 50N 89 9W
Cope, U.S.A. 80 F3 39 40N 102 51W
Copenhagen = København, Denmark 9 J15 55 41N 12 34 E
Copenhagen, U.S.A. 79 C9 43 54N 75 41W
Copiapó, Chile 94 B1 27 30S 70 20W
Copiapó →, Chile 94 B1 27 19S 70 56W
Coplay, U.S.A. 79 F9 40 44N 75 29W
Copp L., Canada 72 A6 60 14N 114 40W
Coppename →, Surinam 93 B7 5 48N 55 55W
Copper Harbor, U.S.A. 76 B2 47 28N 87 53W
Copper Queen, Zimbabwe 55 F2 17 29S 29 18 E
Copperas Cove, U.S.A. 81 K6 31 8N 97 54W
Copperbelt □, Zambia 55 E2 13 15S 27 30 E
Coppermine = Kugluktuk, Canada 68 B8 67 50N 115 5W
Coppermine →, Canada 68 B8 67 49N 116 4W
Copperopolis, U.S.A. 84 H6 37 58N 120 38W
Coquet →, U.K. 10 B6 55 20N 1 32W
Coquille, U.S.A. 82 E1 43 11N 124 11W
Coquimbo, Chile 94 C1 30 0S 71 20W
Coquimbo □, Chile 94 C1 31 0S 71 0W
Corabia, Romania 17 G13 43 48N 24 30 E
Coracora, Peru 92 G4 15 5S 73 45W
Coraki, Australia 63 D5 28 59S 153 17 E
Coral, U.S.A. 78 F5 40 29N 79 10W
Coral Gables, U.S.A. 77 N5 25 45N 80 16W
Coral Harbour = Salliq, Canada 69 B11 64 8N 83 10W
Coral Sea, Pac. Oc. 64 J7 15 0S 150 0 E
Coral Springs, U.S.A. 77 M5 26 16N 80 13W
Coraopolis, U.S.A. 78 F4 40 31N 80 10W
Corato, Italy 20 D7 41 9N 16 25 E
Corbin, U.S.A. 76 G3 36 57N 84 6W
Corby, U.K. 11 E7 52 30N 0 41W
Corcaigh = Cork, Ireland 13 E3 51 54N 8 29W
Corcoran, U.S.A. 84 J7 36 6N 119 33W
Corcubión, Spain 19 A1 42 56N 9 12W
Cordele, U.S.A. 77 K4 31 58N 83 47W
Cordell, U.S.A. 81 H5 35 17N 98 59W
Córdoba, Argentina 94 C3 31 20S 64 10W
Córdoba, Mexico 87 D5 18 50N 97 0W
Córdoba, Spain 19 D3 37 50N 4 50W
Córdoba □, Argentina 94 C3 31 22S 64 15W
Córdoba, Sierra de, Argentina 94 C3 31 10S 64 25W
Cordova, U.S.A. 68 B5 60 33N 145 45W
Corella →, Australia 62 B3 19 34S 140 47 E
Corfield, Australia 62 C3 21 40S 143 21 E
Corfu = Kérkira, Greece 23 A3 39 38N 19 50 E
Corfu, Str. of, Greece 23 A4 39 34N 20 0 E
Coria, Spain 19 C2 39 58N 6 33W
Corigliano Cálabro, Italy 20 E7 39 36N 16 31 E
Coringa Is., Australia 62 B4 16 58S 149 58 E
Corinth = Kórinthos, Greece 21 F10 37 56N 22 55 E
Corinth, Miss., U.S.A. 77 H1 34 56N 88 31W
Corinth, N.Y., U.S.A. 79 C11 43 15N 73 49W
Corinth, G. of = Korinthiakós Kólpos, Greece 21 E10 38 16N 22 30 E
Corinto, Brazil 93 G10 18 20S 44 30W
Corinto, Nic. 88 D2 12 30N 87 10W
Cork, Ireland 13 E3 51 54N 8 29W
Cork □, Ireland 13 E3 51 57N 8 40W
Cork Harbour, Ireland 13 E3 51 47N 8 16W
Çorlu, Turkey 21 D12 41 11N 27 49 E
Cormack L., Canada 72 A4 60 56N 121 37W
Cormorant, Canada 73 C8 54 14N 100 35W
Cormorant L., Canada 73 C8 54 15N 100 50W
Corn Is. = Maíz, Is. del, Nic. 88 D3 12 15N 83 4W
Cornélio Procópio, Brazil 95 A5 23 7S 50 40W
Corner Brook, Canada 71 C8 48 57N 57 58W
Cornești, Moldova 17 E15 47 21N 28 1 E
Corning, Ark., U.S.A. 81 G9 36 25N 90 35W
Corning, Calif., U.S.A. 82 G2 39 56N 122 11W
Corning, Iowa, U.S.A. 80 E7 40 59N 94 44W
Corning, N.Y., U.S.A. 78 D7 42 9N 77 3W
Cornwall, Canada 79 A10 45 2N 74 44W
Cornwall, U.S.A. 79 F8 40 17N 76 25W
Cornwall □, U.K. 11 G3 50 26N 4 40W
Coro, Venezuela 92 A5 11 25N 69 41W
Coroatá, Brazil 93 D10 4 8S 44 0W
Corocoro, Bolivia 92 G5 17 15S 68 28W
Coroico, Bolivia 92 G5 16 0S 67 50W
Coromandel, N.Z. 59 G5 36 45S 175 31 E
Coromandel Coast, India 40 N12 12 30N 81 0 E
Corona, Calif., U.S.A. 85 M9 33 53N 117 34W
Corona, N. Mex., U.S.A. 83 J11 34 15N 105 36W
Coronach, Canada 73 D7 49 7N 105 31W
Coronado, U.S.A. 85 N9 32 41N 117 11W
Coronado, B. de, Costa Rica 88 E3 9 0N 83 40W
Coronados, Is. los, U.S.A. 85 N9 32 25N 117 15W
Coronation, Canada 72 C6 52 5N 111 27W
Coronation Gulf, Canada 68 B8 68 25N 110 0W
Coronation I., Antarctica 5 C18 60 45S 46 0W
Coronation Is., Australia 60 B3 14 57S 124 55 E
Coronda, Argentina 94 C3 31 58S 60 56W
Coronel, Chile 94 D1 37 0S 73 10W
Coronel Bogado, Paraguay 94 B4 27 11S 56 18W
Coronel Dorrego, Argentina 94 D3 38 40S 61 10W
Coronel Oviedo, Paraguay 94 B4 25 24S 56 30W
Coronel Pringles, Argentina 94 D3 38 0S 61 30W
Coronel Suárez, Argentina 94 D3 37 30S 61 52W
Coronel Vidal, Argentina 94 D4 37 28S 57 45W
Coropuna, Nevado, Peru 92 G4 15 30S 72 41W
Corozal, Belize 87 D7 18 23N 88 23W
Corpus, Argentina 95 B4 27 10S 55 30W
Corpus Christi, U.S.A. 81 M6 27 47N 97 24W
Corpus Christi, L., U.S.A. 81 L6 28 2N 97 52W
Corralejo, Canary Is. 22 F6 28 43N 13 53W
Corraun Pen., Ireland 13 C2 53 54N 9 54W
Correntes, C. das, Mozam. 57 C6 24 6S 35 34 E
Corrib, L., Ireland 13 C2 53 27N 9 16W
Corrientes, Argentina 94 B4 27 30S 58 45W
Corrientes □, Argentina 94 B4 28 0S 57 0W

Detour, Pt.

Daly City, *U.S.A.* **84 H4** 37 42N 122 28W
Daly L., *Canada* **73 B7** 56 32N 105 39W
Daly River, *Australia* **60 B5** 13 46S 130 42 E
Daly Waters, *Australia* **62 B1** 16 15S 133 24 E
Dam Doi, *Vietnam* **39 H5** 8 50N 105 12 E
Dam Ha, *Vietnam* **38 B6** 21 21N 107 36 E
Daman, *India* **40 J8** 20 25N 72 57 E
Dāmaneh, *Iran* **45 C6** 33 1N 50 29 E
Damanhûr, *Egypt* **51 B12** 31 0N 30 30 E
Damant L., *Canada* **73 A7** 61 45N 105 5W
Damanzhuang, *China* **34 E9** 38 5N 116 35 E
Damar, *Indonesia* **37 F7** 7 7S 128 40 E
Damaraland, *Namibia* **56 C2** 20 0S 15 0 E
Damascus = Dimashq, *Syria* **47 B5** 33 30N 36 18 E
Damāvand, *Iran* **45 C7** 35 47N 52 0 E
Damāvand, Qolleh-ye, *Iran* **45 C7** 35 56N 52 10 E
Damba, *Angola* **52 F3** 6 44S 15 20 E
Dâmboviţa →, *Romania* **17 F14** 44 12N 26 26 E
Dame Marie, *Haiti* **89 C5** 18 36N 74 26W
Dāmghān, *Iran* **45 B7** 36 10N 54 17 E
Damiel, *Spain* **19 C4** 39 4N 3 37W
Damietta = Dumyât, *Egypt* **51 B12** 31 24N 31 48 E
Daming, *China* **34 F8** 36 15N 115 6 E
Damīr Qābū, *Syria* **44 B4** 36 58N 41 51 E
Dammam = Ad Dammām, *Si. Arabia* **45 E6** 26 20N 50 5 E
Damodar →, *India* **43 H12** 23 17N 87 35 E
Damoh, *India* **43 H8** 23 50N 79 28 E
Dampier, *Australia* **60 D2** 20 41S 116 42 E
Dampier, Selat, *Indonesia* **37 E8** 0 40S 131 0 E
Dampier Arch., *Australia* **60 D2** 20 38S 116 32 E
Damrei, Chuor Phnum, *Cambodia* **39 G4** 11 30N 103 0 E
Dan Xian, *China* **38 C7** 19 31N 109 33 E
Dana, *Indonesia* **37 F6** 11 0S 122 52 E
Dana, L., *Canada* **70 B4** 50 53N 77 20W
Dana, Mt., *U.S.A.* **84 H7** 37 54N 119 12W
Danakil Desert, *Ethiopia* **46 E3** 12 45N 41 0 E
Danané, *Ivory C.* **50 G4** 7 16N 8 9W
Danau Poso, *Indonesia* **37 E6** 1 52S 120 35 E
Danbury, *U.S.A.* **79 E11** 41 24N 73 28W
Danby L., *U.S.A.* **83 J6** 34 13N 115 5W
Dand, *Afghan.* **42 D1** 31 28N 65 32 E
Dandeldhura, *Nepal* **43 E9** 29 20N 80 35 E
Dandeli, *India* **40 M9** 15 5N 74 30 E
Dandong, *China* **35 D13** 40 10N 124 20 E
Danfeng, *China* **34 H6** 33 45N 110 25 E
Danger Is. = Pukapuka, *Cook Is.* **65 J11** 10 53S 165 49W
Danger Pt., *S. Africa* **56 E2** 34 40S 19 17 E
Dangla Shan = Tanggula Shan, *China* **32 C4** 32 40N 92 10 E
Dangrek, Phnom, *Thailand* **38 E5** 14 15N 105 0 E
Dangriga, *Belize* **87 D7** 17 0N 88 13W
Dangshan, *China* **34 G9** 34 27N 116 22 E
Daniel, *U.S.A.* **82 E8** 42 52N 110 4W
Daniel's Harbour, *Canada* **71 B8** 50 13N 57 35W
Danielskuil, *S. Africa* **56 D3** 28 11S 23 33 E
Danielson, *U.S.A.* **79 E13** 41 48N 71 53W
Danilov, *Russia* **24 C7** 58 16N 40 13 E
Daning, *China* **34 F6** 36 28N 110 45 E
Danissa, *Kenya* **54 B5** 3 15N 40 58 E
Ḍank, *Oman* **45 F8** 23 33N 56 16 E
Dankhar Gompa, *India* **40 C11** 32 10N 78 10 E
Danlí, *Honduras* **88 D2** 14 4N 86 35W
Dannemora, *U.S.A.* **79 B11** 44 43N 73 44W
Dannevirke, *N.Z.* **59 J6** 40 12S 176 8 E
Dannhauser, *S. Africa* **57 D5** 28 0S 30 3 E
Dansville, *U.S.A.* **78 D7** 42 34N 77 42W
Danta, *India* **42 G5** 24 11N 72 46 E
Dantan, *India* **43 J12** 21 57N 87 20 E
Dante, *Somali Rep.* **46 E5** 10 25N 51 16 E
Danube = Dunărea →, *Europe* **17 F15** 45 20N 29 40 E
Danvers, *U.S.A.* **79 D14** 42 34N 70 56W
Danville, *Ill., U.S.A.* **76 E2** 40 8N 87 37W
Danville, *Ky., U.S.A.* **76 G3** 37 39N 84 46W
Danville, *Pa., U.S.A.* **79 F8** 40 58N 76 37W
Danville, *Va., U.S.A.* **77 G6** 36 36N 79 23W
Danville, *Vt., U.S.A.* **79 B12** 44 25N 72 9W
Danzig = Gdańsk, *Poland* **17 A10** 54 22N 18 40 E
Dapaong, *Togo* **50 F6** 10 55N 0 16 E
Daqing Shan, *China* **34 D6** 40 40N 111 0 E
Dar Banda, *Africa* **48 F6** 8 0N 23 0 E
Dar el Beida = Casablanca, *Morocco* **50 B4** 33 36N 7 36W
Dar es Salaam, *Tanzania* **54 D4** 6 50S 39 12 E
Dar Mazār, *Iran* **45 D8** 29 14N 57 20 E
Dar'ā, *Syria* **47 C5** 32 36N 36 7 E
Dar'ā □, *Syria* **47 C5** 32 55N 36 10 E
Dārāb, *Iran* **45 D7** 28 50N 54 30 E
Daraban, *Pakistan* **42 D4** 31 44N 70 20 E
Daraina, *Madag.* **57 A8** 13 12S 49 40 E
Daraj, *Libya* **51 B8** 30 10N 10 28 E
Dārān, *Iran* **45 C6** 32 59N 50 24 E
Dārayyā, *Syria* **47 B5** 33 28N 36 15 E
Darband, *Pakistan* **42 B5** 34 20N 72 50 E
Darband, Kūh-e, *Iran* **45 D8** 31 34N 57 8 E
Darbhanga, *India* **43 F11** 26 15N 85 55 E
D'Arcy, *Canada* **72 C4** 50 27N 122 35W
Dardanelle, *Ark., U.S.A.* **81 H8** 35 13N 93 9W
Dardanelle, *Calif., U.S.A.* **84 G7** 38 20N 119 50W
Dardanelles = Çanakkale Boğazı, *Turkey* **21 D12** 40 17N 26 32 E
Dārestān, *Iran* **45 D8** 29 9N 58 42 E
Dârfûr, *Sudan* **51 F10** 13 40N 24 0 E
Dargai, *Pakistan* **42 B4** 34 25N 71 55 E
Dargan Ata, *Turkmenistan* **26 E7** 40 29N 62 10 E
Dargaville, *N.Z.* **59 F4** 35 57S 173 52 E
Darhan, *Mongolia* **32 B5** 49 37N 106 21 E
Darhan Muminggan Lianheqi, *China* **34 D6** 41 40N 110 28 E
Darıca, *Turkey* **21 D13** 40 45N 29 23 E
Darién, G. del, *Colombia* **92 B3** 9 0N 77 0W
Dariganga = Ovoot, *Mongolia* **34 B7** 45 21N 113 45 E
Darjeeling = Darjiling, *India* **43 F13** 27 3N 88 18 E
Darjiling, *India* **43 F13** 27 3N 88 18 E
Darkan, *Australia* **61 F2** 33 20S 116 43 E
Darkhana, *Pakistan* **42 D5** 30 39N 72 11 E
Darkhazineh, *Iran* **45 D6** 31 54N 48 39 E
Darkot Pass, *Pakistan* **43 A5** 36 45N 73 26 E
Darling Downs, *Australia* **63 D5** 27 30S 150 30 E
Darling Ra., *Australia* **61 F2** 32 30S 116 0 E
Darlington, *U.K.* **10 C6** 54 32N 1 33W
Darlington, *U.S.A.* **77 H6** 34 18N 79 52W
Darlington □, *U.K.* **10 C6** 54 32N 1 33W
Darlington, L., *S. Africa* **56 E4** 33 10S 25 9 E
Darlot, L., *Australia* **61 E3** 27 48S 121 35 E
Darłowo, *Poland* **16 A9** 54 25N 16 25 E
Darmstadt, *Germany* **16 D5** 49 51N 8 39 E
Darnah, *Libya* **51 B10** 32 45N 22 45 E
Darnall, *S. Africa* **57 D5** 29 23S 31 18 E
Darnley, C., *Antarctica* **5 C6** 68 0S 69 0 E
Darnley B., *Canada* **68 B7** 69 30N 123 30W
Darr →, *Australia* **62 C3** 23 39S 143 50 E
Darra Pezu, *Pakistan* **42 C4** 32 19N 70 44 E
Darrequeira, *Argentina* **94 D3** 37 42S 63 10W
Darrington, *U.S.A.* **82 B3** 48 15N 121 36W
Dart →, *U.K.* **11 G4** 50 24N 3 39W
Dart, C., *Antarctica* **5 D14** 73 6S 126 20W
Dartford, *U.K.* **11 F8** 51 26N 0 13 E
Dartmoor, *U.K.* **11 G4** 50 38N 3 57W
Dartmouth, *Canada* **71 D7** 44 40N 63 30W
Dartmouth, *U.K.* **11 G4** 50 21N 3 36W
Dartmouth, L., *Australia* **63 D4** 26 4S 145 18 E
Dartuch, C. = Artrutx, C. de, *Spain* **22 B10** 39 55N 3 49 E
Darvaza, *Turkmenistan* **26 E6** 40 11N 58 24 E
Darvel, Teluk = Lahad Datu, Teluk, *Malaysia* **37 D5** 4 50N 118 20 E
Darwen, *U.K.* **10 D5** 53 42N 2 29W
Darwendale, *Zimbabwe* **57 B5** 17 41S 30 33 E
Darwha, *India* **40 J10** 20 15N 77 45 E
Darwin, *Australia* **60 B5** 12 25S 130 51 E
Darwin, *U.S.A.* **85 J9** 36 15N 117 35W
Darya Khan, *Pakistan* **42 D4** 31 48N 71 6 E
Daryoi Amu = Amudarya →, *Uzbekistan* **26 E6** 43 58N 59 34 E
Dās, *U.A.E.* **45 E7** 25 20N 53 30 E
Dashen, Ras, *Ethiopia* **46 E2** 13 8N 38 26 E
Dashetai, *China* **34 D5** 41 0N 109 5 E
Dashhowuz, *Turkmenistan* **26 E6** 41 49N 59 58 E
Dashköpri, *Turkmenistan* **45 B9** 36 16N 62 8 E
Dasht, *Iran* **45 B8** 37 17N 56 7 E
Dasht →, *Pakistan* **40 G2** 25 10N 61 40 E
Daska, *Pakistan* **42 C6** 32 20N 74 20 E
Dasuya, *India* **42 D6** 31 49N 75 38 E
Datça, *Turkey* **21 F12** 36 46N 27 40 E
Datia, *India* **43 G8** 25 39N 78 27 E
Datong, *China* **34 D7** 40 6N 113 18 E
Dattakhel, *Pakistan* **42 C3** 32 54N 69 46 E
Datu, Tanjung, *Indonesia* **36 D3** 2 5N 109 39 E
Datu Piang, *Phil.* **37 C6** 7 2N 124 30 E
Datuk, Tanjong = Datu, Tanjung, *Indonesia* **36 D3** 2 5N 109 39 E
Daud Khel, *Pakistan* **42 C4** 32 53N 71 34 E
Daudnagar, *India* **43 G11** 25 2N 84 24 E
Daugava →, *Latvia* **9 H21** 57 4N 24 3 E
Daugavpils, *Latvia* **9 J22** 55 53N 26 32 E
Daulpur, *India* **42 F7** 26 45N 77 59 E
Dauphin, *Canada* **73 C8** 51 9N 100 5W
Dauphin, *U.S.A.* **78 F8** 40 22N 76 56W
Dauphin L., *Canada* **73 C9** 51 20N 99 45W
Dauphiné, *France* **18 D6** 45 15N 5 25 E
Dausa, *India* **42 F7** 26 52N 76 20 E
Davangere, *India* **40 M9** 14 25N 75 55 E
Davao, *Phil.* **37 C7** 7 0N 125 40 E
Davao G., *Phil.* **37 C7** 6 30N 125 48 E
Dāvar Panāh, *Iran* **45 E9** 27 25N 62 15 E
Davenport, *Calif., U.S.A.* **84 H4** 37 1N 122 12W
Davenport, *Iowa, U.S.A.* **80 E9** 41 32N 90 35W
Davenport, *Wash., U.S.A.* **82 C4** 47 39N 118 9W
Davenport Ra., *Australia* **62 C1** 20 28S 134 0 E
Daventry, *U.K.* **11 E6** 52 16N 1 10W
David, *Panama* **88 E3** 8 30N 82 30W
David City, *U.S.A.* **80 E6** 41 15N 97 8W
David Gorodok = Davyd Haradok, *Belarus* **17 B14** 52 4N 27 8 E
Davidson, *Canada* **73 C7** 51 16N 105 59W
Davis, *U.S.A.* **84 G5** 38 33N 121 44W
Davis Dam, *U.S.A.* **85 K12** 35 11N 114 34W
Davis Inlet, *Canada* **71 A7** 55 50N 60 59W
Davis Mts., *U.S.A.* **81 K2** 30 50N 103 55W
Davis Sea, *Antarctica* **5 C7** 66 0S 92 0 E
Davis Str., *N. Amer.* **69 B14** 65 0N 58 0W
Davos, *Switz.* **18 C8** 46 48N 9 49 E
Davy L., *Canada* **73 B7** 58 53N 108 18W
Davyd Haradok, *Belarus* **17 B14** 52 4N 27 8 E
Dawei, *Burma* **38 E2** 14 2N 98 12 E
Dawes Ra., *Australia* **62 C5** 24 40S 150 40 E
Dawlish, *U.K.* **11 G4** 50 35N 3 28W
Dawna Ra., *Burma* **38 D2** 16 30N 98 30 E
Dawros Hd., *Ireland* **13 B3** 54 50N 8 33W
Dawson, *Canada* **68 B6** 64 10N 139 30W
Dawson, *U.S.A.* **77 K3** 31 46N 84 27W
Dawson, I., *Chile* **96 G2** 53 50S 70 50W
Dawson B., *Canada* **73 C8** 52 53N 100 49W
Dawson Creek, *Canada* **72 B4** 55 45N 120 15W
Dawson Inlet, *Canada* **73 A10** 61 50N 93 25W
Dawson Ra., *Australia* **62 C4** 24 30S 149 48 E
Dax, *France* **18 E3** 43 44N 1 3W
Daxian, *China* **32 C5** 31 15N 107 23 E
Daxindian, *China* **35 F11** 37 30N 120 50 E
Daxinggou, *China* **35 C15** 43 25N 129 40 E
Daxue Shan, *China* **32 C5** 30 30N 101 30 E
Dayr az Zawr, *Syria* **44 C4** 35 20N 40 5 E
Daysland, *Canada* **72 C6** 52 50N 112 20W
Dayton, *Nev., U.S.A.* **84 F7** 39 14N 119 36W
Dayton, *Ohio, U.S.A.* **76 F3** 39 45N 84 12W
Dayton, *Pa., U.S.A.* **78 F5** 40 53N 79 15W
Dayton, *Tenn., U.S.A.* **77 H3** 35 30N 85 1W
Dayton, *Wash., U.S.A.* **82 C4** 46 19N 117 59W
Dayton, *Wyo., U.S.A.* **82 D10** 44 53N 107 16W
Daytona Beach, *U.S.A.* **77 L5** 29 13N 81 1W
Dayville, *U.S.A.* **82 D4** 44 28N 119 32W
De Aar, *S. Africa* **56 E3** 30 39S 24 0 E
De Funiak Springs, *U.S.A.* **77 K2** 30 43N 86 7W
De Grey →, *Australia* **60 D2** 20 12S 119 13 E
De Haan, *Belgium* **15 C3** 51 16N 3 2 E
De Kalb, *U.S.A.* **80 E10** 41 56N 88 46W
De Land, *U.S.A.* **77 L5** 29 2N 81 18W
De Leon, *U.S.A.* **81 J5** 32 7N 98 32W
De Panne, *Belgium* **15 C2** 51 6N 2 34 E
De Pere, *U.S.A.* **76 C1** 44 27N 88 4W
De Queen, *U.S.A.* **81 H7** 34 2N 94 21W
De Quincy, *U.S.A.* **81 K8** 30 27N 93 26W
De Ridder, *U.S.A.* **81 K8** 30 51N 93 17W
De Smet, *U.S.A.* **80 C6** 44 23N 97 33W
De Soto, *U.S.A.* **80 F9** 38 8N 90 34W
De Tour Village, *U.S.A.* **76 C4** 46 0N 83 56W
De Witt, *U.S.A.* **81 H9** 34 18N 91 20W
Dead Sea, *Asia* **47 D4** 31 30N 35 30 E
Deadwood, *U.S.A.* **80 C3** 44 23N 103 44W
Deadwood L., *Canada* **72 B3** 59 10N 128 30W
Deal, *U.K.* **11 F9** 51 13N 1 25 E
Deal I., *Australia* **62 F4** 39 30S 147 20 E
Dealesville, *S. Africa* **56 D4** 28 41S 25 44 E
Dean →, *Canada* **72 C3** 52 49N 126 58W
Dean, Forest of, *U.K.* **11 F5** 51 45N 2 33W
Dean Chan., *Canada* **72 C3** 52 30N 127 15W
Deán Funes, *Argentina* **94 C3** 30 20S 64 20W
Dease →, *Canada* **72 B3** 59 56N 128 32W
Dease L., *Canada* **72 B2** 58 40N 130 5W
Dease Lake, *Canada* **72 B2** 58 25N 130 6W
Death Valley, *U.S.A.* **85 J10** 36 15N 116 50W
Death Valley Junction, *U.S.A.* **85 J10** 36 20N 116 25W
Death Valley National Park, *U.S.A.* **85 J10** 36 45N 117 15W
Debar, *Macedonia* **21 D9** 41 31N 20 30 E
Debden, *Canada* **73 C7** 53 30N 106 50W
Dębica, *Poland* **17 C11** 50 2N 21 25 E
Debolt, *Canada* **72 B5** 55 12N 118 1W
Deborah East, L., *Australia* **61 F2** 30 45S 119 0 E
Deborah West, L., *Australia* **61 F2** 30 45S 118 50 E
Debre Markos, *Ethiopia* **46 E2** 10 20N 37 40 E
Debre Tabor, *Ethiopia* **46 E2** 11 50N 38 26 E
Debre Zeyit, *Ethiopia* **46 F2** 11 48N 38 30 E
Debrecen, *Hungary* **17 E11** 47 33N 21 42 E
Decatur, *Ala., U.S.A.* **77 H2** 34 36N 86 59W
Decatur, *Ga., U.S.A.* **77 J3** 33 47N 84 18W
Decatur, *Ill., U.S.A.* **80 F10** 39 51N 88 57W
Decatur, *Ind., U.S.A.* **76 E3** 40 50N 84 56W
Decatur, *Tex., U.S.A.* **81 J6** 33 14N 97 35W
Deccan, *India* **40 L11** 18 0N 79 0 E
Deception Bay, *Australia* **63 D5** 27 10S 153 5 E
Deception L., *Canada* **73 B8** 56 33N 104 13W
Dechhu, *India* **42 F5** 26 46N 72 20 E
Děčín, *Czech Rep.* **16 C8** 50 47N 14 12 E
Deckerville, *U.S.A.* **78 C2** 43 32N 82 44W
Decorah, *U.S.A.* **80 D9** 43 18N 91 48W
Dedéagach = Alexandroúpolis, *Greece* **21 D11** 40 50N 25 54 E
Dedham, *U.S.A.* **79 D13** 42 15N 71 10W
Dedza, *Malawi* **55 E3** 14 20S 34 20 E
Dee →, *Aberds., U.K.* **12 D6** 57 9N 2 5W
Dee →, *Dumf. & Gall., U.K.* **12 G4** 54 51N 4 3W
Dee →, *Wales, U.K.* **10 D4** 53 22N 3 17W
Deep B., *Canada* **72 A5** 61 15N 116 35W
Deepwater, *Australia* **63 D5** 29 25S 151 51 E
Deer →, *Canada* **73 B10** 58 23N 94 13W
Deer L., *Canada* **73 C10** 52 40N 94 20W
Deer Lake, *Nfld., Canada* **71 C8** 49 11N 57 27W
Deer Lake, *Ont., Canada* **73 C10** 52 36N 94 20W
Deer Lodge, *U.S.A.* **82 C7** 46 24N 112 44W
Deer Park, *U.S.A.* **82 C5** 47 57N 117 28W
Deer River, *U.S.A.* **80 B8** 47 20N 93 48W
Deeragun, *Australia* **62 B4** 19 16S 146 33 E
Deerdepoort, *S. Africa* **56 C4** 24 37S 26 27 E
Deferiet, *U.S.A.* **79 B9** 44 2N 75 41W
Defiance, *U.S.A.* **76 E3** 41 17N 84 22W
Degana, *India* **42 F6** 26 50N 74 20 E
Dégelis, *Canada* **71 C6** 47 30N 68 35W
Deggendorf, *Germany* **16 D7** 48 50N 12 57 E
Degh →, *Pakistan* **42 D5** 31 3N 73 21 E
Deh Bīd, *Iran* **45 D7** 30 39N 53 11 E
Deh-e Shīr, *Iran* **45 D7** 31 29N 53 45 E
Dehaj, *Iran* **45 D7** 30 42N 54 53 E
Dehak, *Iran* **45 E9** 27 11N 62 37 E
Dehdez, *Iran* **45 D6** 31 43N 50 17 E
Dehej, *India* **42 J5** 21 44N 72 40 E
Dehestān, *Iran* **45 D7** 28 30N 55 35 E
Dehgolān, *Iran* **44 C5** 35 17N 47 25 E
Dehibat, *Tunisia* **51 B8** 32 0N 10 47 E
Dehlorān, *Iran* **44 C5** 32 41N 47 16 E
Dehnow-e Kūhestān, *Iran* **45 E8** 27 58N 58 32 E
Dehra Dun, *India* **42 D8** 30 20N 78 4 E
Dehri, *India* **43 G11** 24 50N 84 15 E
Dehui, *China* **35 B13** 44 30N 125 40 E
Deinze, *Belgium* **15 D3** 50 59N 3 32 E
Dej, *Romania* **17 E12** 47 10N 23 52 E
Deka →, *Zimbabwe* **56 B4** 18 4S 26 42 E
Dekese, *Dem. Rep. of the Congo* **52 E4** 3 24S 21 24 E
Del Mar, *U.S.A.* **85 N9** 32 58N 117 16W
Del Norte, *U.S.A.* **83 H10** 37 41N 106 21W
Del Rio, *U.S.A.* **81 L4** 29 22N 100 54W
Delambre I., *Australia* **60 D2** 20 26S 117 5 E
Delano, *U.S.A.* **85 K7** 35 46N 119 15W
Delano Peak, *U.S.A.* **83 G7** 38 22N 112 22W
Delareyville, *S. Africa* **56 D4** 26 41S 25 26 E
Delaronde L., *Canada* **73 C7** 54 3N 107 3W
Delavan, *U.S.A.* **80 D10** 42 38N 88 39W
Delaware, *U.S.A.* **76 E4** 40 18N 83 4W
Delaware □, *U.S.A.* **76 F8** 39 0N 75 20W
Delaware →, *U.S.A.* **79 G9** 39 15N 75 20W
Delaware B., *U.S.A.* **76 F8** 39 0N 75 10W
Delay →, *Canada* **71 A5** 56 56N 71 28W
Delevan, *U.S.A.* **78 D6** 42 29N 78 29W
Delft, *Neths.* **15 B4** 52 1N 4 22 E
Delfzijl, *Neths.* **15 A6** 53 20N 6 55 E
Delgado, C., *Mozam.* **55 E5** 10 45S 40 40 E
Delgerhet, *Mongolia* **34 B6** 45 50N 110 30 E
Delgo, *Sudan* **51 D12** 20 6N 30 40 E
Delhi, *Canada* **78 D4** 42 51N 80 30W
Delhi, *India* **42 E7** 28 38N 77 17 E
Delhi, *La., U.S.A.* **81 J9** 32 28N 91 30W
Delhi, *N.Y., U.S.A.* **79 D10** 42 17N 74 55W
Delia, *Canada* **72 C6** 51 38N 112 23W
Delice, *Turkey* **25 G5** 39 54N 34 2 E
Delicias, *Mexico* **86 B3** 28 10N 105 30W
Delījān, *Iran* **45 C6** 33 59N 50 40 E
Déline, *Canada* **68 B7** 65 10N 123 30W
Delisle, *Canada* **73 C7** 51 55N 107 8W
Dell City, *U.S.A.* **83 L11** 31 56N 105 12W
Dell Rapids, *U.S.A.* **80 D6** 43 50N 96 43W
Delmar, *U.S.A.* **79 D11** 42 37N 73 47W
Delmenhorst, *Germany* **16 B5** 53 3N 8 37 E
Delonga, Ostrova, *Russia* **27 B15** 76 40N 149 20 E
Deloraine, *Australia* **62 G4** 41 30S 146 40 E
Deloraine, *Canada* **73 D8** 49 15N 100 29W
Delphi, *U.S.A.* **76 E2** 40 36N 86 41W
Delphos, *U.S.A.* **76 E3** 40 51N 84 21W
Delportshoop, *S. Africa* **56 D3** 28 22S 24 20 E
Delray Beach, *U.S.A.* **77 M5** 26 28N 80 4W
Delta, *Colo., U.S.A.* **83 G9** 38 44N 108 4W
Delta, *Utah, U.S.A.* **82 G7** 39 21N 112 35W
Delta Junction, *U.S.A.* **68 B5** 64 2N 145 44W
Deltona, *U.S.A.* **77 L5** 28 54N 81 16W
Delungra, *Australia* **63 D5** 29 39S 150 51 E
Delvada, *India* **42 J4** 20 46N 71 2 E
Delvinë, *Albania* **21 E9** 39 59N 20 6 E
Demak, *Indonesia* **37 G14** 6 53S 110 38 E
Demanda, Sierra de la, *Spain* **19 A4** 42 15N 3 0W
Demavand = Damāvand, *Iran* **45 C7** 35 47N 52 0 E
Dembia, *Dem. Rep. of the Congo* **54 B2** 3 33N 25 48 E
Dembidolo, *Ethiopia* **46 F1** 8 34N 34 50 E
Demchok, *India* **43 C8** 32 42N 79 29 E
Demer →, *Belgium* **15 D4** 50 57N 4 42 E
Deming, *N. Mex., U.S.A.* **83 K10** 32 16N 107 46W
Deming, *Wash., U.S.A.* **84 B4** 48 50N 122 13W
Demini →, *Brazil* **92 D6** 0 46S 62 56W
Demirci, *Turkey* **21 E13** 39 2N 28 38 E
Demirköy, *Turkey* **21 D12** 41 49N 27 45 E
Demopolis, *U.S.A.* **77 J2** 32 31N 87 50W
Dempo, *Indonesia* **36 E2** 4 2S 103 15 E
Den Burg, *Neths.* **15 A4** 53 3N 4 47 E
Den Chai, *Thailand* **38 D3** 17 59N 100 4 E
Den Haag = 's-Gravenhage, *Neths.* **15 B4** 52 7N 4 17 E
Den Helder, *Neths.* **15 B4** 52 57N 4 45 E
Den Oever, *Neths.* **15 B5** 52 56N 5 2 E
Denair, *U.S.A.* **84 H6** 37 32N 120 48W
Denau, *Uzbekistan* **26 F7** 38 16N 67 54 E
Denbigh, *Canada* **78 A7** 45 8N 77 15W
Denbigh, *U.K.* **10 D4** 53 12N 3 25W
Denbighshire □, *U.K.* **10 D4** 53 8N 3 22W
Dendang, *Indonesia* **36 E3** 3 7S 107 56 E
Dendermonde, *Belgium* **15 C4** 51 2N 4 5 E
Dengfeng, *China* **34 G7** 34 25N 113 2 E
Dengkou, *China* **34 D4** 40 18N 106 55 E
Denham, *Australia* **61 E1** 25 56S 113 31 E
Denham Ra., *Australia* **62 C4** 21 55S 147 46 E
Denham Sd., *Australia* **61 E1** 25 45S 113 15 E
Denholm, *Canada* **73 C7** 52 39N 108 1W
Denia, *Spain* **19 C6** 38 49N 0 8 E
Denial B., *Australia* **63 E1** 32 14S 133 32 E
Denison, *Iowa, U.S.A.* **80 E7** 42 1N 95 21W
Denison, *Tex., U.S.A.* **81 J6** 33 45N 96 33W
Denison Plains, *Australia* **60 C4** 18 35S 128 0 E
Denizli, *Turkey* **25 G4** 37 42N 29 2 E
Denman Glacier, *Antarctica* **5 C7** 66 45S 99 25 E
Denmark, *Australia* **61 F2** 34 59S 117 25 E
Denmark ■, *Europe* **9 J13** 55 45N 10 0 E
Denmark Str., *Atl. Oc.* **4 C6** 66 0N 30 0W
Dennison, *U.S.A.* **78 F3** 40 24N 81 19W
Denny, *U.K.* **12 E5** 56 1N 3 55W
Denpasar, *Indonesia* **36 F5** 8 45S 115 14 E
Denton, *Mont., U.S.A.* **82 C9** 47 19N 109 57W
Denton, *Tex., U.S.A.* **81 J6** 33 13N 97 8W
D'Entrecasteaux, Pt., *Australia* **61 F2** 34 50S 115 57 E
Denver, *Colo., U.S.A.* **80 F2** 39 44N 104 59W
Denver, *Pa., U.S.A.* **79 F8** 40 14N 76 8W
Denver City, *U.S.A.* **81 J3** 32 58N 102 50W
Deoband, *India* **42 E7** 29 42N 77 43 E
Deogarh, *India* **42 G5** 25 32N 73 54 E
Deoghar, *India* **43 G12** 24 30N 86 42 E
Deolali, *India* **40 K8** 19 58N 73 50 E
Deoli = Devli, *India* **42 G6** 25 50N 75 20 E
Deora, *India* **42 F4** 26 22N 70 55 E
Deori, *India* **43 H8** 23 24N 79 1 E
Deoria, *India* **43 F10** 26 31N 83 48 E
Deosai Mts., *Pakistan* **43 B6** 35 40N 75 0 E
Deosri, *India* **43 F14** 26 46N 90 29 E
Depalpur, *India* **42 H6** 22 51N 75 33 E
Deping, *China* **35 F9** 37 25N 116 58 E
Deposit, *U.S.A.* **79 D9** 42 4N 75 25W
Depuch I., *Australia* **60 D2** 20 37S 117 44 E
Deputatskiy, *Russia* **27 C14** 69 18N 139 54 E
Dera Ghazi Khan, *Pakistan* **42 D4** 30 5N 70 43 E
Dera Ismail Khan, *Pakistan* **42 D4** 31 50N 70 50 E
Derabugti, *Pakistan* **42 E3** 29 2N 69 9 E
Derawar Fort, *Pakistan* **42 E4** 28 46N 71 20 E
Derbent, *Russia* **25 F8** 42 5N 48 15 E
Derby, *Australia* **60 C3** 17 18S 123 38 E
Derby, *U.K.* **10 E6** 52 56N 1 28W
Derby, *Conn., U.S.A.* **79 E11** 41 19N 73 5W
Derby, *Kans., U.S.A.* **81 G6** 37 33N 97 16W
Derby, *N.Y., U.S.A.* **78 D6** 42 41N 78 58W
Derby City □, *U.K.* **10 E6** 52 56N 1 28W
Derby Line, *U.S.A.* **79 B12** 45 0N 72 6W
Derbyshire □, *U.K.* **10 D6** 53 11N 1 38W
Derg →, *U.K.* **13 B4** 54 44N 7 26W
Derg, L., *Ireland* **13 D3** 53 0N 8 20W
Dergaon, *India* **41 F19** 26 45N 94 0 E
Dermott, *U.S.A.* **81 J9** 33 32N 91 26W
Derry = Londonderry, *U.K.* **13 B4** 55 0N 7 20W
Derry = Londonderry □, *U.K.* **13 B4** 55 0N 7 20W
Derry, *N.H., U.S.A.* **79 D13** 42 53N 71 19W
Derry, *Pa., U.S.A.* **78 F5** 40 20N 79 18W
Derryveagh Mts., *Ireland* **13 B3** 54 56N 8 11W
Derwent →, *Cumb., U.K.* **10 C4** 54 39N 3 33W
Derwent →, *Derby, U.K.* **10 E6** 52 57N 1 28W
Derwent →, *N. Yorks., U.K.* **10 D7** 53 45N 0 58W
Derwent Water, *U.K.* **10 C4** 54 35N 3 9W
Des Moines, *Iowa, U.S.A.* **80 E8** 41 35N 93 37W
Des Moines, *N. Mex., U.S.A.* **81 G3** 36 46N 103 50W
Des Moines →, *U.S.A.* **80 E9** 40 23N 91 25W
Desaguadero →, *Argentina* **94 C2** 34 30S 66 46W
Desaguadero →, *Bolivia* **92 G5** 16 35S 69 5W
Descanso, Pta., *Mexico* **85 N9** 32 21N 117 3W
Deschaillons, *Canada* **71 C5** 46 32N 72 7W
Deschambault L., *Canada* **73 C8** 54 50N 103 30W
Deschutes →, *U.S.A.* **82 D3** 45 38N 120 55W
Dese, *Ethiopia* **46 E2** 11 5N 39 40 E
Deseado →, *Argentina* **96 F3** 47 45S 65 54W
Desert Center, *U.S.A.* **85 M11** 33 43N 115 24W
Desert Hot Springs, *U.S.A.* **85 M10** 33 58N 116 30W
Deshnok, *India* **42 F5** 27 48N 73 21 E
Desna →, *Ukraine* **17 C16** 50 33N 30 32 E
Desolación, I., *Chile* **96 G2** 53 0S 74 0W
Despeñaperros, Paso, *Spain* **19 C4** 38 24N 3 30W
Dessau, *Germany* **16 C7** 51 51N 12 14 E
Dessye = Dese, *Ethiopia* **46 E2** 11 5N 39 40 E
Desuri, *India* **42 G5** 25 18N 73 35 E
Det Udom, *Thailand* **38 E5** 14 54N 105 5 E
Dete, *Zimbabwe* **56 B4** 18 38S 26 50 E
Detmold, *Germany* **16 C5** 51 56N 8 52 E
Detour, Pt., *U.S.A.* **76 C2** 45 40N 86 40W

Detroit

Gaula

Franklinton, U.S.A. **81 K9** 30 51N 90 9W
Franklinville, U.S.A. **78 D6** 42 20N 78 27W
Franks Pk., U.S.A. **82 E9** 43 58N 109 18W
Fransfontein, Namibia **56 C2** 20 12S 15 1 E
Frantsa Iosifa, Zemlya, Russia **26 A6** 82 0N 55 0 E
Franz, Canada **70 C3** 48 25N 84 30W
Franz Josef Land = Frantsa Iosifa, Zemlya, Russia **26 A6** 82 0N 55 0 E
Fraser, U.S.A. **78 D2** 42 32N 82 57W
Fraser →, B.C., Canada **72 D4** 49 7N 123 11W
Fraser →, Nfld., Canada **71 A7** 56 39N 62 10W
Fraser, Mt., Australia **61 E2** 25 35S 118 20 E
Fraser I., Australia **63 D5** 25 15S 153 10 E
Fraser Lake, Canada **72 C4** 54 0N 124 50W
Fraserburg, S. Africa **56 E3** 31 55S 21 30 E
Fraserburgh, U.K. **12 D6** 57 42N 2 1W
Fraserdale, Canada **70 C3** 49 55N 81 37W
Fray Bentos, Uruguay **94 C4** 33 10S 58 15W
Fredericia, Denmark **9 J13** 55 34N 9 45 E
Frederick, Md., U.S.A. **76 F7** 39 25N 77 25W
Frederick, Okla., U.S.A. **81 H5** 34 23N 99 1W
Frederick, S. Dak., U.S.A. **80 C5** 45 50N 98 31W
Fredericksburg, Pa., U.S.A. **79 F8** 40 27N 76 26W
Fredericksburg, Tex., U.S.A. **81 K5** 30 16N 98 52W
Fredericksburg, Va., U.S.A. **76 F7** 38 18N 77 28W
Fredericktown, Mo., U.S.A. **81 G9** 37 34N 90 18W
Fredericktown, Ohio, U.S.A. **78 F2** 40 29N 82 33W
Frederico I. Madero, Presa, Mexico **86 B3** 28 7N 105 40W
Frederico Westphalen, Brazil **95 B5** 27 22S 53 24W
Fredericton, Canada **71 C6** 45 57N 66 40W
Fredericton Junction, Canada **71 C6** 45 41N 66 40W
Frederikshåb = Paamiut, Greenland **4 C5** 62 0N 49 43W
Frederikshavn, Denmark **9 H14** 57 28N 10 31 E
Frederiksted, U.S. Virgin Is. **89 C7** 17 43N 64 53W
Fredonia, Ariz., U.S.A. **83 H7** 36 57N 112 32W
Fredonia, Kans., U.S.A. **81 G7** 37 32N 95 49W
Fredonia, N.Y., U.S.A. **78 D5** 42 26N 79 20W
Fredrikstad, Norway **9 G14** 59 13N 10 57 E
Free State □, S. Africa **56 D4** 28 30S 27 0 E
Freehold, U.S.A. **79 F10** 40 16N 74 17W
Freel Peak, U.S.A. **84 G7** 38 52N 119 54W
Freeland, U.S.A. **79 E9** 41 1N 75 54W
Freels, C., Canada **71 C9** 49 15N 53 30W
Freeman, Calif., U.S.A. **85 K9** 35 35N 117 53W
Freeman, S. Dak., U.S.A. **80 D6** 43 21N 97 26W
Freeport, Bahamas **88 A4** 26 30N 78 47W
Freeport, Ill., U.S.A. **80 D10** 42 17N 89 36W
Freeport, N.Y., U.S.A. **79 F11** 40 39N 73 35W
Freeport, Ohio, U.S.A. **78 F3** 40 12N 81 15W
Freeport, Pa., U.S.A. **78 F5** 40 41N 79 41W
Freeport, Tex., U.S.A. **81 L7** 28 57N 95 21W
Freetown, S. Leone **50 G3** 8 30N 13 17W
Frégate, L., Canada **70 B5** 53 15N 74 45W
Fregenal de la Sierra, Spain **19 C2** 38 10N 6 39W
Freibourg = Fribourg, Switz. **18 C7** 46 49N 7 9 E
Freiburg, Germany **16 E4** 47 59N 7 51 E
Freire, Chile **96 D2** 38 54S 72 38W
Freirina, Chile **94 B1** 28 30S 71 10W
Freising, Germany **16 D6** 48 24N 11 45 E
Freistadt, Austria **16 D8** 48 30N 14 30 E
Fréjus, France **18 E7** 43 25N 6 44 E
Fremantle, Australia **61 F2** 32 7S 115 47 E
Fremont, Calif., U.S.A. **84 H4** 37 32N 121 57W
Fremont, Mich., U.S.A. **76 D3** 43 28N 85 57W
Fremont, Nebr., U.S.A. **80 E6** 41 26N 96 30W
Fremont, Ohio, U.S.A. **76 E4** 41 21N 83 7W
Fremont →, U.S.A. **83 G8** 38 24N 110 42W
French Camp, U.S.A. **84 H5** 37 53N 121 16W
French Creek →, U.S.A. **78 E5** 41 24N 79 50W
French Guiana ■, S. Amer. **93 C8** 4 0N 53 0W
French Polynesia ■, Pac. Oc. **65 K13** 20 0S 145 0W
Frenchman Cr. →, N. Amer. **82 B10** 48 31N 107 10W
Frenchman Cr. →, U.S.A. **80 E4** 40 14N 100 50W
Fresco →, Brazil **93 E8** 7 15S 51 30W
Freshfield, C., Antarctica **5 C10** 68 25S 151 10 E
Fresnillo, Mexico **86 C4** 23 10N 103 0W
Fresno, U.S.A. **84 J7** 36 44N 119 47W
Fresno Reservoir, U.S.A. **82 B9** 48 36N 109 57W
Frew →, Australia **62 C2** 20 0S 135 38 E
Frewsburg, U.S.A. **78 D5** 42 3N 79 10W
Freycinet Pen., Australia **62 G4** 42 10S 148 25 E
Fria, C., Namibia **56 B1** 18 0S 12 0 E
Friant, U.S.A. **84 J7** 36 59N 119 43W
Frías, Argentina **94 B2** 28 40S 65 5W
Fribourg, Switz. **18 C7** 46 49N 7 9 E
Friday Harbor, U.S.A. **84 B3** 48 32N 123 1W
Friedens, U.S.A. **78 F6** 40 3N 78 59W
Friedrichshafen, Germany **16 E5** 47 39N 9 30 E
Friendly Is. = Tonga ■, Pac. Oc. **59 D11** 19 50S 174 30W
Friendship, U.S.A. **78 D6** 42 12N 78 8W
Friesland □, Neths. **15 A5** 53 5N 5 50 E
Frio →, U.S.A. **81 L5** 28 26N 98 11W
Frio, C., Brazil **90 F6** 22 50S 41 50W
Friona, U.S.A. **81 H3** 34 38N 102 43W
Fritch, U.S.A. **81 H4** 35 38N 101 36W
Frobisher B., Canada **69 B13** 62 30N 66 0W
Frobisher Bay = Iqaluit, Canada **69 B13** 63 44N 68 31W
Frobisher L., Canada **73 B7** 56 20N 108 16W
Frohavet, Norway **8 E13** 64 0N 9 30 E
Frome, U.K. **11 F5** 51 14N 2 19W
Frome →, U.K. **11 G5** 50 41N 2 6W
Front Range, U.S.A. **74 C5** 40 25N 105 45W
Front Royal, U.S.A. **76 F6** 38 55N 78 12W
Frontera, Canary Is. **22 G2** 27 47N 17 59W
Frontera, Mexico **87 D6** 18 30N 92 40W
Fronteras, Mexico **86 A3** 30 56N 109 31W
Frosinone, Italy **20 D5** 41 38N 13 19 E
Frostburg, U.S.A. **76 F6** 39 39N 78 56W
Frostisen, Norway **8 B17** 68 14N 17 10 E
Frøya, Norway **8 E13** 63 43N 8 40 E
Frunze = Bishkek, Kyrgyzstan **26 E8** 42 54N 74 46 E
Frutal, Brazil **93 H9** 20 0S 49 0W
Frýdek-Místek, Czech Rep. **17 D10** 49 40N 18 20 E
Fryeburg, U.S.A. **79 B14** 44 1N 70 59W
Fu Xian = Wafangdian, China **35 E11** 39 38N 121 58 E
Fu Xian, China **34 G5** 36 0N 109 20 E
Fucheng, China **34 F9** 37 50N 116 10 E
Fuchou = Fuzhou, China **33 D6** 26 5N 119 16 E
Fuchū, Japan **31 G6** 34 34N 133 14 E
Fuencaliente, Canary Is. **22 F2** 28 28N 17 50W
Fuencaliente, Pta., Canary Is. **22 F2** 28 27N 17 51W
Fuengirola, Spain **19 D3** 36 32N 4 41W
Fuentes de Oñoro, Spain **19 B2** 40 33N 6 52W
Fuerte →, Mexico **86 B3** 25 50N 109 25W
Fuerte Olimpo, Paraguay **94 A4** 21 0S 57 51W
Fuerteventura, Canary Is. **22 F6** 28 30N 14 0W
Fufeng, China **34 G5** 34 22N 108 0 E
Fugou, China **34 G8** 34 3N 114 25 E
Fugu, China **34 E6** 39 2N 111 3 E
Fuhai, China **32 B3** 47 2N 87 25 E
Fuḩaymī, Iraq **44 C4** 34 16N 42 10 E
Fuji, Japan **31 G9** 35 9N 138 39 E
Fuji-San, Japan **31 G9** 35 22N 138 44 E
Fuji-Yoshida, Japan **31 G9** 35 30N 138 46 E
Fujian □, China **33 D6** 26 0N 118 0 E
Fujinomiya, Japan **31 G9** 35 10N 138 40 E
Fujisawa, Japan **31 G9** 35 22N 139 29 E
Fujiyama, Mt. = Fuji-San, Japan **31 G9** 35 22N 138 44 E
Fukien = Fujian □, China **33 D6** 26 0N 118 0 E
Fukuchiyama, Japan **31 G7** 35 19N 135 9 E
Fukue-Shima, Japan **31 H4** 32 40N 128 45 E
Fukui, Japan **31 F8** 36 5N 136 10 E
Fukui □, Japan **31 G8** 36 0N 136 12 E
Fukuoka, Japan **31 H5** 33 39N 130 21 E
Fukuoka □, Japan **31 H5** 33 30N 131 0 E
Fukushima, Japan **30 F10** 37 44N 140 28 E
Fukushima □, Japan **30 F10** 37 30N 140 15 E
Fukuyama, Japan **31 G6** 34 35N 133 20 E
Fulda, Germany **16 C5** 50 32N 9 40 E
Fulda →, Germany **16 C5** 51 25N 9 39 E
Fulford Harbour, Canada **84 B3** 48 47N 123 27W
Fullerton, Calif., U.S.A. **85 M9** 33 53N 117 56W
Fullerton, Nebr., U.S.A. **80 E6** 41 22N 97 58W
Fulongquan, China **35 B13** 44 20N 124 42 E
Fulton, Mo., U.S.A. **80 F9** 38 52N 91 57W
Fulton, N.Y., U.S.A. **79 C8** 43 19N 76 25W
Funabashi, Japan **31 G10** 35 45N 140 0 E
Funafuti = Fongafale, Tuvalu **64 H9** 8 31S 179 13 E
Funchal, Madeira **22 D3** 32 38N 16 54W
Fundación, Colombia **92 A4** 10 31N 74 11W
Fundão, Portugal **19 B2** 40 8N 7 30W
Fundy, B. of, Canada **71 D6** 45 0N 66 0W
Funhalouro, Mozam. **57 C5** 23 3S 34 25 E
Funing, Hebei, China **35 E10** 39 53N 119 12 E
Funing, Jiangsu, China **35 H10** 33 45N 119 50 E
Funiu Shan, China **34 H7** 33 30N 112 20 E
Funtua, Nigeria **50 F7** 11 30N 7 18 E
Fuping, Hebei, China **34 E8** 38 48N 114 12 E
Fuping, Shaanxi, China **34 G5** 34 42N 109 10 E
Furano, Japan **30 C11** 43 21N 142 23 E
Furāt, Nahr al →, Asia **44 D5** 31 0N 47 25 E
Fürg, Iran **45 D7** 28 18N 55 13 E
Furnás, Spain **22 B8** 39 3N 1 32 E
Furnas, Reprêsa de, Brazil **95 A6** 20 50S 45 30W
Furneaux Group, Australia **62 G4** 40 10S 147 50 E
Furqlus, Syria **47 A6** 34 36N 37 8 E
Fürstenwalde, Germany **16 B8** 52 22N 14 3 E
Fürth, Germany **16 D6** 49 28N 10 59 E
Furukawa, Japan **30 E10** 38 34N 140 58 E
Fury and Hecla Str., Canada **69 B11** 69 56N 84 0W
Fusagasuga, Colombia **92 C4** 4 21N 74 22W
Fushan, Shandong, China **35 F11** 37 30N 121 15 E
Fushan, Shanxi, China **34 G6** 35 58N 111 51 E
Fushun, China **35 D12** 41 50N 123 56 E
Fusong, China **35 C14** 42 20N 127 15 E
Futuna, Wall. & F. Is. **59 B8** 14 25S 178 20W
Fuxin, China **35 C11** 42 5N 121 48 E
Fuyang, China **34 H8** 33 0N 115 48 E
Fuyang He →, China **34 E9** 38 12N 117 0 E
Fuyu, China **35 B13** 45 12N 124 43 E
Fuzhou, China **33 D6** 26 5N 119 16 E
Fylde, U.K. **10 D5** 53 50N 2 58W
Fyn, Denmark **9 J14** 55 20N 10 30 E
Fyne, L., U.K. **12 F3** 55 59N 5 23W

G

Gabela, Angola **52 G2** 11 0S 14 24 E
Gabès, Tunisia **51 B8** 33 53N 10 2 E
Gabès, G. de, Tunisia **51 B8** 34 0N 10 30 E
Gabon ■, Africa **52 E2** 0 10S 10 0 E
Gaborone, Botswana **56 C4** 24 45S 25 57 E
Gabriels, U.S.A. **79 B10** 44 26N 74 12W
Gābrīk, Iran **45 E8** 25 44N 58 28 E
Gabrovo, Bulgaria **21 C11** 42 52N 25 19 E
Gāch Sār, Iran **45 B6** 36 7N 51 19 E
Gachsārān, Iran **45 D6** 30 15N 50 45 E
Gadag, India **40 M9** 15 30N 75 45 E
Gadap, Pakistan **42 G2** 25 5N 67 28 E
Gadarwara, India **43 H8** 22 50N 78 50 E
Gadhada, India **42 J4** 22 0N 71 35 E
Gadra, Pakistan **42 G4** 25 40N 70 38 E
Gadsden, U.S.A. **77 H3** 34 1N 86 1W
Gadwal, India **40 L10** 16 10N 77 50 E
Gaffney, U.S.A. **77 H5** 35 5N 81 39W
Gafsa, Tunisia **50 B7** 34 24N 8 43 E
Gagaria, India **42 G4** 25 43N 70 46 E
Gagnoa, Ivory C. **50 G4** 6 56N 5 16W
Gagnon, Canada **71 B6** 51 50N 68 5W
Gagnon, L., Canada **73 A6** 62 3N 110 27W
Gahini, Rwanda **54 C3** 1 50S 30 30 E
Gahmar, India **43 G10** 25 27N 83 49 E
Gai Xian = Gaizhou, China **35 D12** 40 22N 122 20 E
Gaïdhouronísi, Greece **23 E7** 34 53N 25 41 E
Gail, U.S.A. **81 J4** 32 46N 101 27W
Gaillimh = Galway, Ireland **13 C2** 53 17N 9 3W
Gaines, U.S.A. **78 E7** 41 46N 77 35W
Gainesville, Fla., U.S.A. **77 L4** 29 40N 82 20W
Gainesville, Ga., U.S.A. **77 H4** 34 18N 83 50W
Gainesville, Mo., U.S.A. **81 G8** 36 36N 92 26W
Gainesville, Tex., U.S.A. **81 J6** 33 38N 97 8W
Gainsborough, U.K. **10 D7** 53 24N 0 46W
Gairloch, L., U.K. **12 D3** 57 43N 5 45W
Gaizhou, China **35 D12** 40 22N 122 20 E
Gaj →, Pakistan **42 F2** 26 26N 67 21 E
Gakuch, Pakistan **43 A5** 36 7N 73 45 E
Galán, Cerro, Argentina **94 B2** 25 55S 66 52W
Galana →, Kenya **54 C5** 3 9S 40 8 E
Galápagos, Pac. Oc. **90 D1** 0 0 91 0W
Galashiels, U.K. **12 F6** 55 37N 2 49W
Galaţi, Romania **17 F15** 45 27N 28 2 E
Galatina, Italy **21 D8** 40 10N 18 10 E
Galax, U.S.A. **77 G5** 36 40N 80 56W
Galcaio, Somali Rep. **46 F4** 6 30N 47 30 E
Galdhøpiggen, Norway **9 F12** 61 38N 8 18 E
Galeana, Chihuahua, Mexico **86 A3** 30 7N 107 38W
Galeana, Nuevo León, Mexico **86 A3** 24 50N 100 4W
Galela, Indonesia **37 D7** 1 50N 127 49 E
Galena, U.S.A. **68 B4** 64 44N 156 56W
Galera Pt., Trin. & Tob. **89 D7** 10 49N 60 54W
Galesburg, U.S.A. **80 E9** 40 57N 90 22W
Galeton, U.S.A. **78 E7** 41 44N 77 39W
Galich, Russia **24 C7** 58 22N 42 24 E
Galicia □, Spain **19 A2** 42 43N 7 45W
Galilee = Hagalil, Israel **47 C4** 32 53N 35 18 E
Galilee, L., Australia **62 C4** 22 20S 145 50 E
Galilee, Sea of = Yam Kinneret, Israel **47 C4** 32 45N 35 35 E
Galinoporni, Cyprus **23 D13** 35 31N 34 18 E
Galion, U.S.A. **78 F2** 40 44N 82 47W
Galiuro Mts., U.S.A. **83 K8** 32 30N 110 20W
Galiwinku, Australia **62 A2** 12 2S 135 34 E
Gallan Hd., U.K. **12 C1** 58 15N 7 2W
Gallatin, U.S.A. **77 G2** 36 24N 86 27W
Galle, Sri Lanka **40 R12** 6 5N 80 10 E
Gállego →, Spain **19 B5** 41 39N 0 51W
Gallegos →, Argentina **96 G3** 51 35S 69 0W
Galley Hd., Ireland **13 E3** 51 32N 8 55W
Gallinas, Pta., Colombia **92 A4** 12 28N 71 40W
Gallipoli = Gelibolu, Turkey **21 D12** 40 28N 26 43 E
Gallipoli, Italy **21 D8** 40 3N 17 58 E
Gallipolis, U.S.A. **76 F4** 38 49N 82 12W
Gällivare, Sweden **8 C19** 67 9N 20 40 E
Galloo I., U.S.A. **79 C8** 43 55N 76 25W
Galloway, U.K. **12 F4** 55 1N 4 29W
Galloway, Mull of, U.K. **12 G4** 54 39N 4 52W
Gallup, U.S.A. **83 J9** 35 32N 108 45W
Galoya, Sri Lanka **40 Q12** 8 10N 80 55 E
Galt, U.S.A. **84 G5** 38 15N 121 18W
Galty Mts., Ireland **13 D3** 52 22N 8 10W
Galtymore, Ireland **13 D3** 52 21N 8 11W
Galva, U.S.A. **80 E9** 41 10N 90 3W
Galveston, U.S.A. **81 L7** 29 18N 94 48W
Galveston B., U.S.A. **81 L7** 29 36N 94 50W
Gálvez, Argentina **94 C3** 32 0S 61 14W
Galway, Ireland **13 C2** 53 17N 9 3W
Galway □, Ireland **13 C2** 53 22N 9 1W
Galway B., Ireland **13 C2** 53 13N 9 10W
Gam →, Vietnam **38 B5** 21 55N 105 12 E
Gamagōri, Japan **31 G8** 34 50N 137 14 E
Gambat, Pakistan **42 F3** 27 17N 68 26 E
Gambhir →, India **42 F6** 26 58N 77 27 E
Gambia ■, W. Afr. **50 F2** 13 25N 16 0W
Gambia →, W. Afr. **50 F2** 13 28N 16 34W
Gambier, U.S.A. **78 F2** 40 22N 82 23W
Gambier, C., Australia **60 B5** 11 56S 130 57 E
Gambo, Canada **71 C9** 48 47N 54 13W
Gamboli, Pakistan **42 E3** 29 53N 68 24 E
Gamboma, Congo **52 E3** 1 55S 15 52 E
Gamka →, S. Africa **56 E3** 33 18S 21 39 E
Gamkab →, Namibia **56 D2** 28 4S 17 54 E
Gamlakarleby = Kokkola, Finland **8 E20** 63 50N 23 8 E
Gammon →, Canada **73 C9** 51 24N 95 44W
Gamtoos →, S. Africa **56 E4** 33 58S 25 1 E
Gan Jiang →, China **33 D6** 29 15N 116 0 E
Ganado, U.S.A. **83 J9** 35 43N 109 33W
Gananoque, Canada **79 B8** 44 20N 76 10W
Ganāveh, Iran **45 D6** 29 35N 50 35 E
Gäncä, Azerbaijan **25 F8** 40 45N 46 20 E
Gancheng, China **38 C7** 18 51N 108 37 E
Gand = Gent, Belgium **15 C3** 51 2N 3 42 E
Ganda, Angola **53 G2** 13 3S 14 35 E
Gandajika, Dem. Rep. of the Congo **52 F4** 6 45S 23 57 E
Gandak →, India **43 G11** 25 39N 85 13 E
Gandava, Pakistan **42 E2** 28 32N 67 32 E
Gander, Canada **71 C9** 48 58N 54 35W
Gander L., Canada **71 C9** 48 58N 54 35W
Ganderowe Falls, Zimbabwe **55 F2** 17 20S 29 10 E
Gandhi Sagar, India **42 G6** 24 40N 75 40 E
Gandhinagar, India **42 H5** 23 15N 72 45 E
Gandía, Spain **19 C5** 38 58N 0 9W
Gando, Pta., Canary Is. **22 G4** 27 55N 15 22W
Ganedidalem = Gani, Indonesia **37 E7** 0 48S 128 14 E
Ganga →, India **43 H14** 23 20N 90 30 E
Ganga Sagar, India **43 J13** 21 38N 88 5 E
Gangan →, India **43 E8** 28 38N 78 58 E
Ganganagar, India **42 E5** 29 56N 73 56 E
Gangapur, India **42 F7** 26 32N 76 49 E
Gangaw, Burma **41 H19** 22 5N 94 5 E
Gangdisê Shan, China **41 D12** 31 20N 81 0 E
Ganges = Ganga →, India **43 H14** 23 20N 90 30 E
Ganges, Canada **72 D4** 48 51N 123 31W
Ganges, Mouths of the, India **43 J14** 21 30N 90 0 E
Gangoh, India **42 E7** 29 46N 77 18 E
Gangroti, India **43 D8** 30 50N 79 10 E
Gangtok, India **41 F16** 27 20N 88 37 E
Gangu, China **34 G3** 34 40N 105 15 E
Gangyao, China **35 B14** 44 12N 126 37 E
Gani, Indonesia **37 E7** 0 48S 128 14 E
Ganj, India **43 F8** 27 45N 78 57 E
Gannett Peak, U.S.A. **82 E9** 43 11N 109 39W
Ganquan, China **34 F5** 36 20N 109 20 E
Gansu □, China **34 G3** 36 0N 104 0 E
Ganta, Liberia **50 G4** 7 15N 8 59W
Gantheaume B., Australia **61 E1** 27 40S 114 10 E
Gantsevichi = Hantsavichy, Belarus **17 B14** 52 49N 26 30 E
Ganyem = Genyem, Indonesia **37 E10** 2 46S 140 12 E
Ganyu, China **35 G10** 34 50N 119 8 E
Ganzhou, China **33 D6** 25 51N 114 56 E
Gao, Mali **50 E5** 16 15N 0 5W
Gaomi, China **35 F10** 36 20N 119 42 E
Gaoping, China **34 G7** 35 45N 112 55 E
Gaotang, China **34 F9** 36 50N 116 15 E
Gaoua, Burkina Faso **50 F5** 10 20N 3 8W
Gaoual, Guinea **50 F3** 11 45N 13 25W
Gaoxiong = Kaohsiung, Taiwan **33 D7** 22 35N 120 16 E
Gaoyang, China **34 E8** 38 40N 115 45 E
Gaoyou Hu, China **35 H10** 32 45N 119 20 E
Gaoyuan, China **35 F9** 37 8N 117 58 E
Gap, France **18 D7** 44 33N 6 5 E
Gapat →, India **43 G10** 24 30N 82 28 E
Gapuwiyak, Australia **62 A2** 12 25S 135 43 E
Gar, China **32 C2** 32 10N 79 58 E
Garabogazköl Aylagy, Turkmenistan **25 F9** 41 0N 53 30 E
Garachico, Canary Is. **22 F3** 28 22N 16 46W
Garachiné, Panama **88 E4** 8 0N 78 12W
Garafia, Canary Is. **22 F2** 28 48N 17 57W
Garah, Australia **63 D4** 29 5S 149 38 E
Garajonay, Canary Is. **22 F2** 28 7N 17 14W
Garanhuns, Brazil **93 E11** 8 50S 36 30W
Garautha, India **43 G8** 25 34N 79 18 E
Garba Tula, Kenya **54 B4** 0 30N 38 32 E
Garberville, U.S.A. **82 F2** 40 6N 123 48W
Garbiyang, India **43 D9** 30 8N 80 54 E
Garda, L. di, Italy **20 B4** 45 40N 10 41 E
Garde L., Canada **73 A7** 62 50N 106 13W
Garden City, Ga., U.S.A. **77 J5** 32 6N 81 9W
Garden City, Kans., U.S.A. **81 G4** 37 58N 100 53W
Garden City, Tex., U.S.A. **81 K4** 31 52N 101 29W
Garden Grove, U.S.A. **85 M9** 33 47N 117 55W
Gardēz, Afghan. **42 C3** 33 37N 69 9 E
Gardiner, Maine, U.S.A. **77 C11** 44 14N 69 47W
Gardiner, Mont., U.S.A. **82 D8** 45 2N 110 22W
Gardiners I., U.S.A. **79 E12** 41 6N 72 6W
Gardner, U.S.A. **79 D13** 42 34N 71 59W
Gardner Canal, Canada **72 C3** 53 27N 128 8W
Gardnerville, U.S.A. **84 G7** 38 56N 119 45W
Gardo, Somali Rep. **46 F4** 9 30N 49 6 E
Garey, U.S.A. **85 L6** 34 53N 120 19W
Garfield, U.S.A. **82 C5** 47 1N 117 9W
Garforth, U.K. **10 D6** 53 47N 1 24W
Gargano, Mte., Italy **20 D6** 41 43N 15 43 E
Garibaldi Prov. Park, Canada **72 D4** 49 50N 122 40W
Gariep, L., S. Africa **56 E4** 30 40S 25 40 E
Garies, S. Africa **56 E2** 30 32S 17 59 E
Garigliano →, Italy **20 D5** 41 13N 13 45 E
Garissa, Kenya **54 C4** 0 25S 39 40 E
Garland, Tex., U.S.A. **81 J6** 32 55N 96 38W
Garland, Utah, U.S.A. **82 F7** 41 47N 112 10W
Garm, Tajikistan **26 F8** 39 0N 70 20 E
Garmāb, Iran **45 C8** 35 25N 56 45 E
Garmisch-Partenkirchen, Germany **16 E6** 47 30N 11 6 E
Garmo, Qullai = Kommunizma, Pik, Tajikistan **26 F8** 39 0N 72 2 E
Garmsār, Iran **45 C7** 35 20N 52 25 E
Garner, U.S.A. **80 D8** 43 6N 93 36W
Garnett, U.S.A. **80 F7** 38 17N 95 14W
Garo Hills, India **43 G14** 25 30N 90 30 E
Garoe, Somali Rep. **46 F4** 8 25N 48 33 E
Garonne →, France **18 D3** 45 2N 0 36W
Garot, India **42 G6** 24 19N 75 41 E
Garoua, Cameroon **51 G8** 9 19N 13 21 E
Garrauli, India **43 G8** 25 5N 79 22 E
Garrison, Mont., U.S.A. **82 C7** 46 31N 112 49W
Garrison, N. Dak., U.S.A. **80 B4** 47 40N 101 25W
Garrison Res. = Sakakawea, L., U.S.A. **80 B4** 47 30N 101 25W
Garron Pt., U.K. **13 A6** 55 3N 5 59W
Garry →, U.K. **12 E5** 56 44N 3 47W
Garry, L., Canada **68 B9** 65 58N 100 18W
Garsen, Kenya **54 C5** 2 20S 40 5 E
Garson L., Canada **73 B6** 56 19N 110 2W
Garu, India **43 H11** 23 40N 84 14 E
Garub, Namibia **56 D2** 26 37S 16 0 E
Garut, Indonesia **37 G12** 7 14S 107 53 E
Garvie Mts., N.Z. **59 L2** 45 30S 168 50 E
Garwa = Garoua, Cameroon **51 G8** 9 19N 13 21 E
Garwa, India **43 G10** 24 11N 83 47 E
Gary, U.S.A. **76 E2** 41 36N 87 20W
Garzê, China **32 C5** 31 38N 100 1 E
Garzón, Colombia **92 C3** 2 10N 75 40W
Gas-San, Japan **30 E10** 38 32N 140 1 E
Gasan Kuli = Esenguly, Turkmenistan **26 F6** 37 37N 53 59 E
Gascogne, France **18 E4** 43 45N 0 20 E
Gascogne, G. de, Europe **18 D2** 44 0N 2 0W
Gascony = Gascogne, France **18 E4** 43 45N 0 20 E
Gascoyne →, Australia **61 D1** 24 52S 113 37 E
Gascoyne Junction, Australia **61 E2** 25 2S 115 17 E
Gashaka, Nigeria **51 G8** 7 20N 11 29 E
Gasherbrum, Pakistan **43 B7** 35 40N 76 40 E
Gashua, Nigeria **51 F8** 12 54N 11 0 E
Gaspé, Canada **71 C7** 48 52N 64 30W
Gaspé, C. de, Canada **71 C7** 48 48N 64 7W
Gaspé, Pén. de, Canada **71 C6** 48 45N 65 40W
Gaspésie, Parc de Conservation de la, Canada **71 C6** 48 55N 65 50W
Gasteiz = Vitoria-Gasteiz, Spain **19 A4** 42 50N 2 41W
Gastonia, U.S.A. **77 H5** 35 16N 81 11W
Gastre, Argentina **96 E3** 42 20S 69 15W
Gata, C., Cyprus **23 E12** 34 34N 33 2 E
Gata, C. de, Spain **19 D4** 36 41N 2 13W
Gata, Sierra de, Spain **19 B2** 40 20N 6 45W
Gataga →, Canada **72 B3** 58 35N 126 59W
Gatehouse of Fleet, U.K. **12 G4** 54 53N 4 12W
Gates, U.S.A. **78 C7** 43 9N 77 42W
Gateshead, U.K. **10 C6** 54 57N 1 35W
Gatesville, U.S.A. **81 K6** 31 26N 97 45W
Gaths, Zimbabwe **55 G3** 20 2S 30 32 E
Gatico, Chile **94 A1** 22 29S 70 20W
Gatineau, Canada **79 A9** 45 29N 75 38W
Gatineau →, Canada **70 C4** 45 27N 75 42W
Gatineau, Parc Nat. de la, Canada **70 C4** 45 40N 76 0W
Gatton, Australia **63 D5** 27 32S 152 17 E
Gatun, L., Panama **88 E4** 9 7N 79 56W
Gatyana, S. Africa **57 E4** 32 16S 28 31 E
Gau, Fiji **59 D8** 18 2S 179 18 E
Gauer L., Canada **73 B9** 57 0N 97 50W
Gauhati, India **41 F17** 26 10N 91 45 E
Gauja →, Latvia **9 H21** 57 10N 24 16 E
Gaula →, Norway **8 E14** 63 21N 10 14 E

Gauri Phanta

Gauri Phanta, *India* 43 E9 28 41N 80 36 E
Gausta, *Norway* 9 G13 59 48N 8 40 E
Gauteng □, *S. Africa* 57 D4 26 0S 28 0 E
Gāv Koshī, *Iran* 45 D8 28 38N 57 12 E
Gāvakān, *Iran* 45 D7 29 37N 53 10 E
Gavāter, *Iran* 45 E9 25 10N 61 31 E
Gāvbandī, *Iran* 45 E7 27 12N 53 4 E
Gavdhopoúla, *Greece* 23 E6 34 56N 24 0 E
Gávdhos, *Greece* 23 E6 34 50N 24 5 E
Gaviota, *U.S.A.* 85 L6 34 29N 120 13W
Gāvkhūnī, Bāţlāq-e, *Iran* 45 C7 32 6N 52 52 E
Gävle, *Sweden* 9 F17 60 40N 17 9 E
Gawachab, *Namibia* 56 D2 27 4S 17 55 E
Gawilgarh Hills, *India* 40 J10 21 15N 76 45 E
Gaxun Nur, *China* 32 B5 42 22N 100 30 E
Gay, *Russia* 24 D10 51 27N 58 27 E
Gaya, *India* 43 G11 24 47N 85 4 E
Gaya, *Niger* 50 F6 11 52N 3 28 E
Gaylord, *U.S.A.* 76 C3 45 2N 84 41W
Gayndah, *Australia* 63 D5 25 35S 151 32 E
Gaysin = Haysyn, *Ukraine* 17 D15 48 57N 29 25 E
Gayvoron = Hayvoron, *Ukraine* 17 D15 48 22N 29 52 E
Gaza, *Gaza Strip* 47 D3 31 30N 34 28 E
Gaza □, *Mozam.* 57 C5 23 10S 32 45 E
Gaza Strip □, *Asia* 47 D3 31 29N 34 25 E
Gazanjyk, *Turkmenistan* 45 B7 39 16N 55 32 E
Gāzbor, *Iran* 45 D8 28 5N 58 51 E
Gazi, *Dem. Rep. of the Congo* 54 B1 1 3N 24 30 E
Gaziantep, *Turkey* 25 G6 37 6N 37 23 E
Gcoverega, *Botswana* 56 B3 19 8S 24 18 E
Gcuwa, *S. Africa* 57 E4 32 20S 28 11 E
Gdańsk, *Poland* 17 A10 54 22N 18 40 E
Gdańska, Zatoka, *Poland* 17 A10 54 30N 19 20 E
Gdov, *Russia* 9 G22 58 48N 27 55 E
Gdynia, *Poland* 17 A10 54 35N 18 33 E
Gebe, *Indonesia* 37 D7 0 5N 129 25 E
Gebze, *Turkey* 21 D13 40 47N 29 25 E
Gedaref, *Sudan* 51 F13 14 2N 35 28 E
Gediz →, *Turkey* 21 E12 38 35N 26 48 E
Gedser, *Denmark* 9 J14 54 35N 11 55 E
Geegully Cr. →, *Australia* 60 C3 18 32S 123 41 E
Geel, *Belgium* 15 C4 51 10N 4 59 E
Geelvink B. = Cenderwasih, Teluk, *Indonesia* 37 E9 3 0S 135 20 E
Geelvink Chan., *Australia* 61 E1 28 30S 114 0 E
Geesthacht, *Germany* 16 B6 53 26N 10 22 E
Geidam, *Nigeria* 51 F8 12 57N 11 57 E
Geikie →, *Canada* 73 B8 57 45N 103 52W
Geistown, *U.S.A.* 78 F6 40 18N 78 52W
Geita, *Tanzania* 54 C3 2 48S 32 12 E
Gejiu, *China* 32 D5 23 20N 103 10 E
Gel, Meydān-e, *Iran* 45 D7 29 4N 54 50 E
Gela, *Italy* 20 F6 37 4N 14 15 E
Gelderland □, *Neths.* 15 B6 52 5N 6 10 E
Geldrop, *Neths.* 15 C5 51 25N 5 32 E
Geleen, *Neths.* 15 D5 50 57N 5 49 E
Gelibolu, *Turkey* 21 D12 40 28N 26 43 E
Gelsenkirchen, *Germany* 16 C4 51 32N 7 6 E
Gemas, *Malaysia* 39 L4 2 37N 102 36 E
Gembloux, *Belgium* 15 D4 50 34N 4 43 E
Gemena, *Dem. Rep. of the Congo* 52 D3 3 13N 19 48 E
Gemerek, *Turkey* 44 B3 39 15N 36 10 E
Gemlik, *Turkey* 21 D13 40 26N 29 9 E
Genale →, *Ethiopia* 46 F2 6 2N 39 1 E
General Acha, *Argentina* 94 D3 37 20S 64 38W
General Alvear, *Buenos Aires, Argentina* 94 D4 36 0S 60 0W
General Alvear, *Mendoza, Argentina* 94 D2 35 0S 67 40W
General Artigas, *Paraguay* 94 B4 26 52S 56 16W
General Belgrano, *Argentina* 94 D4 36 35S 58 47W
General Cabrera, *Argentina* 94 C3 32 53S 63 52W
General Cepeda, *Mexico* 86 B4 25 23N 101 27W
General Guido, *Argentina* 94 D4 36 40S 57 50W
General Juan Madariaga, *Argentina* 94 D4 37 0S 57 0W
General La Madrid, *Argentina* 94 D3 37 17S 61 20W
General MacArthur, *Phil.* 37 B7 11 18N 125 28 E
General Martin Miguel de Güemes, *Argentina* 94 A3 24 50S 65 0W
General Paz, *Argentina* 94 B4 27 45S 57 36W
General Pico, *Argentina* 94 D3 35 45S 63 50W
General Pinedo, *Argentina* 94 B3 27 15S 61 20W
General Pinto, *Argentina* 94 C3 34 45S 61 50W
General Roca, *Argentina* 96 D3 39 2S 67 35W
General Santos, *Phil.* 37 C7 6 5N 125 14 E
General Trevino, *Mexico* 87 B5 26 14N 99 29W
General Trías, *Mexico* 86 B3 28 21N 106 22W
General Viamonte, *Argentina* 94 D3 35 1S 61 3W
General Villegas, *Argentina* 94 D3 35 5S 63 0W
Genesee, *Idaho, U.S.A.* 82 C5 46 33N 116 56W
Genesee, *Pa., U.S.A.* 78 E7 41 59N 77 54W
Genesee →, *U.S.A.* 78 C7 43 16N 77 36W
Geneseo, *Ill., U.S.A.* 80 E9 41 27N 90 9W
Geneseo, *N.Y., U.S.A.* 78 D7 42 48N 77 49W
Geneva = Genève, *Switz.* 18 C7 46 12N 6 9 E
Geneva, *Ala., U.S.A.* 77 K3 31 2N 85 52W
Geneva, *N.Y., U.S.A.* 78 D8 42 52N 76 59W
Geneva, *Nebr., U.S.A.* 80 E6 40 32N 97 36W
Geneva, *Ohio, U.S.A.* 78 E4 41 48N 80 57W
Geneva, L. = Léman, L., *Europe* 18 C7 46 26N 6 30 E
Geneva, L., *U.S.A.* 76 D1 42 38N 88 30W
Genève, *Switz.* 18 C7 46 12N 6 9 E
Genil →, *Spain* 19 D3 37 42N 5 19W
Genk, *Belgium* 15 D5 50 58N 5 32 E
Gennargentu, Mti. del, *Italy* 20 D3 40 1N 9 19 E
Genoa = Génova, *Italy* 18 D8 44 25N 8 57 E
Genoa, *N.Y., U.S.A.* 79 D8 42 40N 76 32W
Genoa, *Nebr., U.S.A.* 80 E6 41 27N 97 44W
Genoa, *Nev., U.S.A.* 84 F7 39 2N 119 50W
Génova, *Italy* 18 D8 44 25N 8 57 E
Génova, G. di, *Italy* 20 C3 44 0N 9 0 E
Genriyetty, Ostrov, *Russia* 27 B16 77 6N 156 30 E
Gent, *Belgium* 15 C3 51 2N 3 42 E
Genteng, *Indonesia* 37 G12 7 22S 106 24 E
Genyem, *Indonesia* 37 E10 2 46S 140 12 E
Geographe B., *Australia* 61 F2 33 30S 115 15 E
Geographe Chan., *Australia* 61 D1 24 30S 113 0 E
Georga, Zemlya, *Russia* 26 A5 80 30N 49 0 E
George, *S. Africa* 56 E3 33 58S 22 29 E
George →, *Canada* 71 A6 58 49N 66 10W
George, L., *Australia* 60 D3 22 45S 123 40 E
George, L., *Uganda* 54 B3 0 5N 30 10 E
George, L., *Fla., U.S.A.* 77 L5 29 17N 81 36W
George, L., *N.Y., U.S.A.* 79 C11 43 37N 73 33W
George Gill Ra., *Australia* 60 D5 24 22S 131 45 E
George River = Kangiqsualujjuaq, *Canada* 69 C13 58 30N 65 59W
George Sound, *N.Z.* 59 L1 44 52S 167 25 E
George Town, *Australia* 62 G4 41 6S 146 49 E
George Town, *Bahamas* 88 B4 23 33N 75 47W
George Town, *Cayman Is.* 88 C3 19 20N 81 24W
George Town, *Malaysia* 39 K3 5 25N 100 15 E
George V Land, *Antarctica* 5 C10 69 0S 148 0 E
George VI Sound, *Antarctica* 5 D17 71 0S 68 0W
George West, *U.S.A.* 81 L5 28 20N 98 7W
Georgetown, *Australia* 62 B3 18 17S 143 33 E
Georgetown, *Ont., Canada* 78 C5 43 40N 79 56W
Georgetown, *P.E.I., Canada* 71 C7 46 13N 62 24W
Georgetown, *Gambia* 50 F3 13 30N 14 47W
Georgetown, *Guyana* 92 B7 6 50N 58 12W
Georgetown, *Calif., U.S.A.* 84 G6 38 54N 120 50W
Georgetown, *Colo., U.S.A.* 82 G11 39 42N 105 42W
Georgetown, *Ky., U.S.A.* 76 F3 38 13N 84 33W
Georgetown, *N.Y., U.S.A.* 79 D9 42 46N 75 44W
Georgetown, *Ohio, U.S.A.* 76 F4 38 52N 83 54W
Georgetown, *S.C., U.S.A.* 77 J6 33 23N 79 17W
Georgetown, *Tex., U.S.A.* 81 K6 30 38N 97 41W
Georgia □, *U.S.A.* 77 K5 32 50N 83 15W
Georgia ■, *Asia* 25 F7 42 0N 43 0 E
Georgia, Str. of, *Canada* 72 D4 49 25N 124 0W
Georgian B., *Canada* 78 A4 45 15N 81 0W
Georgina →, *Australia* 62 C2 23 30S 139 47 E
Georgina I., *Canada* 78 B5 44 22N 79 17W
Georgiu-Dezh = Liski, *Russia* 25 D6 51 3N 39 30 E
Georgiyevsk, *Russia* 25 F7 44 12N 43 28 E
Gera, *Germany* 16 C7 50 53N 12 4 E
Geraardsbergen, *Belgium* 15 D3 50 45N 3 53 E
Geral, Serra, *Brazil* 95 B6 26 25S 50 0W
Geral de Goiás, Serra, *Brazil* 93 F9 12 0S 46 0W
Geraldine, *U.S.A.* 82 C8 47 36N 110 16W
Geraldton, *Australia* 61 E1 28 48S 114 32 E
Geraldton, *Canada* 70 C2 49 44N 86 59W
Gereshk, *Afghan.* 40 D4 31 47N 64 35 E
Gerik, *Malaysia* 39 K3 5 50N 101 15 E
Gering, *U.S.A.* 80 E3 41 50N 103 40W
Gerlach, *U.S.A.* 82 F4 40 39N 119 21W
Germansen Landing, *Canada* 72 B4 55 43N 124 40W
Germantown, *U.S.A.* 81 M10 35 5N 89 49W
Germany ■, *Europe* 16 C6 51 0N 10 0 E
Germī, *Iran* 45 B6 39 1N 48 3 E
Germiston, *S. Africa* 57 D4 26 15S 28 10 E
Gernika-Lumo, *Spain* 19 A4 43 19N 2 40W
Gero, *Japan* 31 G8 35 48N 137 14 E
Gerona = Girona, *Spain* 19 B7 41 58N 2 46 E
Gerrard, *Canada* 72 C5 50 30N 117 17W
Geser, *Indonesia* 37 E8 3 50S 130 54 E
Getafe, *Spain* 19 B4 40 18N 3 44W
Gettysburg, *Pa., U.S.A.* 76 F7 39 50N 77 14W
Gettysburg, *S. Dak., U.S.A.* 80 C5 45 1N 99 57W
Getxo, *Spain* 19 A4 43 21N 2 59W
Getz Ice Shelf, *Antarctica* 5 D14 75 0S 130 0W
Geyser, *U.S.A.* 82 C8 47 16N 110 30W
Geyserville, *U.S.A.* 84 G4 38 42N 122 54W
Ghaggar →, *India* 42 E6 29 30N 74 53 E
Ghaghara →, *India* 43 G11 25 45N 84 40 E
Ghaghat →, *Bangla.* 43 G13 25 19N 89 38 E
Ghagra, *India* 43 H11 23 17N 84 33 E
Ghagra →, *India* 43 F9 27 29N 81 9 E
Ghana ■, *W. Afr.* 50 G5 8 0N 1 0W
Ghansor, *India* 43 H9 22 39N 80 1 E
Ghanzi, *Botswana* 56 C3 21 50S 21 34 E
Ghardaïa, *Algeria* 50 B6 32 20N 3 37 E
Gharyān, *Libya* 51 B8 32 10N 13 0 E
Ghat, *Libya* 51 D8 24 59N 10 11 E
Ghatal, *India* 43 H12 22 40N 87 46 E
Ghatampur, *India* 43 F9 26 8N 80 13 E
Ghatsila, *India* 43 H12 22 36N 86 29 E
Ghaţţī, *Si. Arabia* 44 D3 31 16N 37 31 E
Ghawdex = Gozo, *Malta* 23 C1 36 3N 14 13 E
Ghazal, Bahr el →, *Chad* 51 F9 13 0N 15 47 E
Ghazâl, Bahr el →, *Sudan* 51 G12 9 31N 30 25 E
Ghaziabad, *India* 42 E7 28 42N 77 26 E
Ghazipur, *India* 43 G10 25 38N 83 35 E
Ghaznī, *Afghan.* 42 C3 33 30N 68 28 E
Ghaznī □, *Afghan.* 40 C6 32 10N 68 20 E
Ghent = Gent, *Belgium* 15 C3 51 2N 3 42 E
Gheorghe Gheorghiu-Dej = Oneşti, *Romania* 17 E14 46 17N 26 47 E
Ghīnah, Wādī al →, *Si. Arabia* 44 D3 30 27N 38 14 E
Ghizao, *Afghan.* 42 C1 33 20N 65 44 E
Ghizar →, *Pakistan* 43 A5 36 15N 73 43 E
Ghotaru, *India* 42 F4 27 20N 70 1 E
Ghotki, *Pakistan* 42 E3 28 5N 69 21 E
Ghowr □, *Afghan.* 40 C4 34 0N 64 20 E
Ghudaf, W. al →, *Iraq* 44 C4 32 56N 43 30 E
Ghudāmis, *Libya* 49 C4 30 11N 9 29 E
Ghughri, *India* 43 H9 22 39N 80 41 E
Ghugus, *India* 40 K11 19 58N 79 12 E
Ghulam Mohammad Barrage, *Pakistan* 42 G3 25 30N 68 20 E
Ghūrīān, *Afghan.* 40 B2 34 17N 61 25 E
Gia Dinh, *Vietnam* 39 G6 10 49N 106 42 E
Gia Lai = Plei Ku, *Vietnam* 38 F7 13 57N 108 0 E
Gia Nghia, *Vietnam* 39 G6 11 58N 107 42 E
Gia Ngoc, *Vietnam* 38 E7 14 50N 108 58 E
Gia Vuc, *Vietnam* 38 E7 14 42N 108 34 E
Giant Forest, *U.S.A.* 84 J8 36 36N 118 43W
Giants Causeway, *U.K.* 13 A5 55 16N 6 29W
Giarabub = Al Jaghbūb, *Libya* 51 C10 29 42N 24 38 E
Giarre, *Italy* 20 F6 37 43N 15 11 E
Gibara, *Cuba* 88 B4 21 9N 76 11W
Gibb River, *Australia* 60 C4 16 26S 126 26 E
Gibbon, *U.S.A.* 80 E5 40 45N 98 51W
Gibeon, *Namibia* 56 D2 25 9S 17 43 E
Gibraltar ■, *Europe* 19 D3 36 7N 5 22W
Gibraltar, Str. of, *Medit. S.* 19 E3 35 55N 5 40W
Gibson Desert, *Australia* 60 D4 24 0S 126 0 E
Gibsons, *Canada* 72 D4 49 24N 123 32W
Gibsonville, *U.S.A.* 84 F6 39 46N 120 54W
Giddings, *U.S.A.* 81 K6 30 11N 96 56W
Giebnegáisi = Kebnekaise, *Sweden* 8 C18 67 53N 18 33 E
Giessen, *Germany* 16 C5 50 34N 8 41 E
Gīfān, *Iran* 45 B8 37 54N 57 28 E
Gift Lake, *Canada* 72 B5 55 53N 115 49W
Gifu, *Japan* 31 G8 35 30N 136 45 E
Gifu □, *Japan* 31 G8 35 40N 137 0 E
Giganta, Sa. de la, *Mexico* 86 B2 25 30N 111 30W
Gigha, *U.K.* 12 F3 55 42N 5 44W
Gíglio, *Italy* 20 C4 42 20N 10 52 E
Gijón, *Spain* 19 A3 43 32N 5 42W
Gil I., *Canada* 72 C3 53 12N 129 15W
Gila →, *U.S.A.* 83 K6 32 43N 114 33W
Gila Bend, *U.S.A.* 83 K7 32 57N 112 43W
Gila Bend Mts., *U.S.A.* 83 K7 33 10N 113 0W
Gīlān □, *Iran* 45 B6 37 0N 50 0 E
Gilbert →, *Australia* 62 B3 16 35S 141 15 E
Gilbert Is., *Kiribati* 64 G9 1 0N 172 0 E
Gilbert River, *Australia* 62 B3 18 9S 142 52 E
Gilead, *U.S.A.* 79 B14 44 24N 70 59W
Gilford I., *Canada* 72 C3 50 40N 126 30W
Gilgil, *Kenya* 54 C4 0 30S 36 20 E
Gilgit, *India* 43 B6 35 50N 74 15 E
Gilgit →, *Pakistan* 43 B6 35 44N 74 37 E
Gillam, *Canada* 73 B10 56 20N 94 40W
Gillen, L., *Australia* 61 E3 26 11S 124 38 E
Gillette, *U.S.A.* 80 C2 44 18N 105 30W
Gilliat, *Australia* 62 C3 20 40S 141 28 E
Gillingham, *U.K.* 11 F8 51 23N 0 33 E
Gilmer, *U.S.A.* 81 J7 32 44N 94 57W
Gilmore, L., *Australia* 61 F3 32 29S 121 37 E
Gilroy, *U.S.A.* 84 H5 37 1N 121 34W
Gimli, *Canada* 73 C9 50 40N 97 0W
Gin Gin, *Australia* 63 D5 25 0S 151 58 E
Gingin, *Australia* 61 F2 31 22S 115 54 E
Gingindlovu, *S. Africa* 57 D5 29 2S 31 30 E
Ginir, *Ethiopia* 46 F3 7 6N 40 40 E
Gióna, Óros, *Greece* 21 E10 38 38N 22 14 E
Gir Hills, *India* 42 J4 21 0N 71 0 E
Girab, *India* 42 F4 26 2N 70 38 E
Girâfi, W. →, *Egypt* 47 F3 29 58N 34 39 E
Girard, *Kans., U.S.A.* 81 G7 37 31N 94 51W
Girard, *Ohio, U.S.A.* 78 E4 41 9N 80 42W
Girard, *Pa., U.S.A.* 78 E4 42 0N 80 19W
Girdle Ness, *U.K.* 12 D6 57 9N 2 3W
Giresun, *Turkey* 25 F6 40 55N 38 30 E
Girga, *Egypt* 51 C12 26 17N 31 55 E
Giri →, *India* 42 D7 30 28N 77 41 E
Giridih, *India* 43 G12 24 10N 86 21 E
Girne = Kyrenia, *Cyprus* 23 D12 35 20N 33 20 E
Girona, *Spain* 19 B7 41 58N 2 46 E
Gironde →, *France* 18 D3 45 32N 1 7W
Giru, *Australia* 62 B4 19 30S 147 5 E
Girvan, *U.K.* 12 F4 55 14N 4 51W
Gisborne, *N.Z.* 59 H7 38 39S 178 5 E
Gisenyi, *Rwanda* 54 C2 1 41S 29 15 E
Gislaved, *Sweden* 9 H15 57 19N 13 32 E
Gitega, *Burundi* 54 C2 3 26S 29 56 E
Giuba →, *Somali Rep.* 46 G3 1 30N 42 35 E
Giurgiu, *Romania* 17 G13 43 52N 25 57 E
Giza = El Gîza, *Egypt* 51 C12 30 0N 31 10 E
Gizhiga, *Russia* 27 C17 62 3N 160 30 E
Gizhiginskaya Guba, *Russia* 27 C16 61 0N 158 0 E
Giżycko, *Poland* 17 A11 54 2N 21 48 E
Gjirokastër, *Albania* 21 D9 40 7N 20 10 E
Gjoa Haven, *Canada* 68 B10 68 20N 96 8W
Gjøvik, *Norway* 9 F14 60 47N 10 43 E
Glace Bay, *Canada* 71 C8 46 11N 59 58W
Glacier Bay National Park and Preserve, *U.S.A.* 72 B1 58 45N 136 30W
Glacier National Park, *Canada* 72 C5 51 15N 117 30W
Glacier National Park, *U.S.A.* 82 B7 48 30N 113 18W
Glacier Peak, *U.S.A.* 82 B3 48 7N 121 7W
Gladewater, *U.S.A.* 81 J7 32 33N 94 56W
Gladstone, *Australia* 62 C5 23 52S 151 16 E
Gladstone, *Canada* 73 C9 50 13N 98 57W
Gladstone, *U.S.A.* 76 C2 45 51N 87 1W
Gladwin, *U.S.A.* 76 D3 43 59N 84 29W
Glåma = Glomma →, *Norway* 9 G14 59 12N 10 57 E
Gláma, *Iceland* 8 D2 65 48N 23 0W
Glamis, *U.S.A.* 85 N11 32 55N 115 5W
Glasco, *Kans., U.S.A.* 80 F6 39 22N 97 50W
Glasco, *N.Y., U.S.A.* 79 D11 42 3N 73 57W
Glasgow, *U.K.* 12 F4 55 51N 4 15W
Glasgow, *Ky., U.S.A.* 76 G3 37 0N 85 55W
Glasgow, *Mont., U.S.A.* 82 B10 48 12N 106 38W
Glasgow, City of □, *U.K.* 12 F4 55 51N 4 12W
Glaslyn, *Canada* 73 C7 53 22N 108 21W
Glastonbury, *U.K.* 11 F5 51 9N 2 43W
Glastonbury, *U.S.A.* 79 E12 41 43N 72 37W
Glazov, *Russia* 24 C9 58 9N 52 40 E
Gleichen, *Canada* 72 C6 50 52N 113 3W
Gleiwitz = Gliwice, *Poland* 17 C10 50 22N 18 41 E
Glen, *U.S.A.* 79 B13 44 7N 71 11W
Glen Affric, *U.K.* 12 D3 57 17N 5 1W
Glen Canyon, *U.S.A.* 83 H8 37 30N 110 40W
Glen Canyon Dam, *U.S.A.* 83 H8 36 57N 111 29W
Glen Canyon National Recreation Area, *U.S.A.* 83 H8 37 15N 111 0W
Glen Coe, *U.K.* 12 E3 56 40N 5 0W
Glen Cove, *U.S.A.* 79 F11 40 52N 73 38W
Glen Garry, *U.K.* 12 D3 57 3N 5 7W
Glen Innes, *Australia* 63 D5 29 44S 151 44 E
Glen Lyon, *U.S.A.* 79 E8 41 10N 76 5W
Glen Mor, *U.K.* 12 D4 57 9N 4 37W
Glen Moriston, *U.K.* 12 D4 57 11N 4 52W
Glen Robertson, *Canada* 79 A10 45 22N 74 30W
Glen Spean, *U.K.* 12 E4 56 53N 4 40W
Glen Ullin, *U.S.A.* 80 B4 46 49N 101 50W
Glencoe, *Canada* 78 D3 42 45N 81 43W
Glencoe, *S. Africa* 57 D5 28 11S 30 11 E
Glencoe, *U.S.A.* 80 C7 44 46N 94 9W
Glendale, *Ariz., U.S.A.* 83 K7 33 32N 112 11W
Glendale, *Calif., U.S.A.* 85 L8 34 9N 118 15W
Glendale, *Zimbabwe* 55 F3 17 22S 31 5 E
Glendive, *U.S.A.* 80 B2 47 7N 104 43W
Glendo, *U.S.A.* 80 D2 42 30N 105 2W
Glenfield, *U.S.A.* 79 C9 43 43N 75 24W
Glengarriff, *Ireland* 13 E2 51 45N 9 34W
Glenmont, *U.S.A.* 78 F2 40 31N 82 6W
Glenmorgan, *Australia* 63 D4 27 14S 149 42 E
Glenn, *U.S.A.* 84 F4 39 31N 122 1W
Glennallen, *U.S.A.* 68 B5 62 7N 145 33W
Glennamaddy, *Ireland* 13 C3 53 37N 8 33W
Glenns Ferry, *U.S.A.* 82 E6 42 57N 115 18W
Glenore, *Australia* 62 B3 17 50S 141 12 E
Glenreagh, *Australia* 63 E5 30 2S 153 1 E
Glenrock, *U.S.A.* 82 E11 42 52N 105 52W
Glenrothes, *U.K.* 12 E5 56 12N 3 10W
Glens Falls, *U.S.A.* 79 C11 43 19N 73 39W
Glenside, *U.S.A.* 79 F9 40 6N 75 9W
Glenties, *Ireland* 13 B3 54 49N 8 16W
Glenville, *U.S.A.* 76 F5 38 56N 80 50W
Glenwood, *Canada* 71 C9 49 0N 54 58W
Glenwood, *Ark., U.S.A.* 81 H8 34 20N 93 33W
Glenwood, *Iowa, U.S.A.* 80 E7 41 3N 95 45W
Glenwood, *Minn., U.S.A.* 80 C7 45 39N 95 23W
Glenwood, *Wash., U.S.A.* 84 D5 46 1N 121 17W
Glenwood Springs, *U.S.A.* 82 G10 39 33N 107 19W
Glettinganes, *Iceland* 8 D7 65 30N 13 37W
Gliwice, *Poland* 17 C10 50 22N 18 41 E
Globe, *U.S.A.* 83 K8 33 24N 110 47W
Głogów, *Poland* 16 C9 51 37N 16 5 E
Glomma →, *Norway* 9 G14 59 12N 10 57 E
Glorieuses, Is., *Ind. Oc.* 57 A8 11 30S 47 20 E
Glossop, *U.K.* 10 D6 53 27N 1 56W
Gloucester, *U.K.* 11 F5 51 53N 2 15W
Gloucester, *U.S.A.* 79 D14 42 37N 70 40W
Gloucester I., *Australia* 62 C4 20 0S 148 30 E
Gloucester Point, *U.S.A.* 76 G7 37 15N 76 29W
Gloucestershire □, *U.K.* 11 F5 51 46N 2 15W
Gloversville, *U.S.A.* 79 C10 43 3N 74 21W
Glovertown, *Canada* 71 C9 48 40N 54 3W
Glusk, *Belarus* 17 B15 52 53N 28 41 E
Gmünd, *Austria* 16 D8 48 45N 15 0 E
Gmunden, *Austria* 16 E7 47 55N 13 48 E
Gniezno, *Poland* 17 B9 52 30N 17 35 E
Gnowangerup, *Australia* 61 F2 33 58S 117 59 E
Go Cong, *Vietnam* 39 G6 10 22N 106 40 E
Gō-no-ura, *Japan* 31 H4 33 44N 129 40 E
Goa, *India* 40 M8 15 33N 73 59 E
Goa □, *India* 40 M8 15 33N 73 59 E
Goalpara, *India* 41 F17 26 10N 90 40 E
Goaltor, *India* 43 H12 22 43N 87 10 E
Goalundo Ghat, *Bangla.* 43 H13 23 50N 89 47 E
Goat Fell, *U.K.* 12 F3 55 38N 5 11W
Goba, *Ethiopia* 46 F2 7 1N 39 59 E
Goba, *Mozam.* 57 D5 26 15S 32 13 E
Gobabis, *Namibia* 56 C2 22 30S 19 0 E
Gobi, *Asia* 34 C6 44 0N 110 0 E
Gobō, *Japan* 31 H7 33 53N 135 10 E
Gochas, *Namibia* 56 C2 24 59S 18 55 E
Godavari →, *India* 41 L13 16 25N 82 18 E
Godavari Pt., *India* 41 L13 17 0N 82 20 E
Godbout, *Canada* 71 C6 49 20N 67 38W
Godda, *India* 43 G12 24 50N 87 13 E
Goderich, *Canada* 78 C3 43 45N 81 41W
Godfrey Ra., *Australia* 61 D2 24 0S 117 0 E
Godhavn = Qeqertarsuaq, *Greenland* 4 C5 69 15N 53 38W
Godhra, *India* 42 H5 22 49N 73 40 E
Godoy Cruz, *Argentina* 94 C2 32 56S 68 52W
Gods →, *Canada* 70 A1 56 22N 92 51W
Gods L., *Canada* 70 B1 54 40N 94 15W
Gods River, *Canada* 73 C10 54 50N 94 5W
Godthåb = Nuuk, *Greenland* 69 B14 64 10N 51 35W
Godwin Austen = K2, *Pakistan* 43 B7 35 58N 76 32 E
Goeie Hoop, Kaap die = Good Hope, C. of, *S. Africa* 56 E2 34 24S 18 30 E
Goéland, L. au, *Canada* 70 C4 49 50N 76 48W
Goeree, *Neths.* 15 C3 51 50N 4 0 E
Goes, *Neths.* 15 C3 51 30N 3 55 E
Goffstown, *U.S.A.* 79 C13 43 1N 71 36W
Gogama, *Canada* 70 C3 47 35N 81 43W
Gogebic, L., *U.S.A.* 80 B10 46 30N 89 35W
Gogra = Ghaghara →, *India* 43 G11 25 45N 84 40 E
Gogriâl, *Sudan* 51 G11 8 30N 28 8 E
Gohana, *India* 42 E7 29 8N 76 42 E
Goharganj, *India* 42 H7 23 1N 77 41 E
Goi →, *India* 42 H6 22 4N 74 46 E
Goiânia, *Brazil* 93 G9 16 43S 49 20W
Goiás, *Brazil* 93 G8 15 55S 50 10W
Goiás □, *Brazil* 93 F9 12 10S 48 0W
Goio-Erê, *Brazil* 95 A5 24 12S 53 1W
Gojō, *Japan* 31 G7 34 21N 135 42 E
Gojra, *Pakistan* 42 D5 31 10N 72 40 E
Gökçeada, *Turkey* 21 D11 40 10N 25 50 E
Gökova Körfezi, *Turkey* 21 F12 36 55N 27 50 E
Gokteik, *Burma* 41 H20 22 26N 97 0 E
Gokurt, *Pakistan* 42 E2 29 40N 67 26 E
Gokwe, *Zimbabwe* 57 B4 18 7S 28 58 E
Gola, *India* 43 E9 28 3N 80 32 E
Golakganj, *India* 43 F13 26 8N 89 52 E
Golan Heights = Hagolan, *Syria* 47 C4 33 0N 35 45 E
Goläshkerd, *Iran* 45 E8 27 59N 57 16 E
Golchikha, *Russia* 4 B12 71 45N 83 30 E
Golconda, *U.S.A.* 82 F5 40 58N 117 30W
Gold, *U.S.A.* 78 E7 41 52N 77 50W
Gold Beach, *U.S.A.* 82 E1 42 25N 124 25W
Gold Coast, *W. Afr.* 50 H5 4 0N 1 40W
Gold Hill, *U.S.A.* 82 E2 42 26N 123 3W
Gold River, *Canada* 72 D3 49 46N 126 3W
Golden, *Canada* 72 C5 51 20N 116 59W
Golden B., *N.Z.* 59 J4 40 40S 172 50 E
Golden Gate, *U.S.A.* 82 H2 37 54N 122 30W
Golden Hinde, *Canada* 72 D3 49 40N 125 44W
Golden Lake, *Canada* 78 A7 45 34N 77 21W
Golden Vale, *Ireland* 13 D3 52 33N 8 17W
Goldendale, *U.S.A.* 82 D3 45 49N 120 50W
Goldfield, *U.S.A.* 83 H5 37 42N 117 14W
Goldsand L., *Canada* 73 B8 57 2N 101 8W
Goldsboro, *U.S.A.* 77 H7 35 23N 77 59W
Goldsmith, *U.S.A.* 81 K3 31 59N 102 37W
Goldsworthy, *Australia* 60 D2 20 21S 119 30 E
Goldthwaite, *U.S.A.* 81 K5 31 27N 98 34W
Goleniów, *Poland* 16 B8 53 35N 14 50 E
Golestānak, *Iran* 45 D7 30 36N 54 14 E
Goleta, *U.S.A.* 85 L7 34 27N 119 50W
Golfito, *Costa Rica* 88 E3 8 41N 83 5W
Golfo Aranci, *Italy* 20 D3 40 59N 9 38 E
Goliad, *U.S.A.* 81 L6 28 40N 97 23W
Golpāyegān, *Iran* 45 C6 33 27N 50 18 E
Golra, *Pakistan* 42 C5 33 37N 72 56 E
Golspie, *U.K.* 12 D5 57 58N 3 59W
Goma, *Dem. Rep. of the Congo* 54 C2 1 37S 29 10 E

Greymouth

Gomal Pass, *Pakistan* 42 D3 31 56N 69 20 E
Gomati →, *India* 43 G10 25 32N 83 11 E
Gombari, *Dem. Rep. of the Congo* 54 B2 2 45N 29 3 E
Gombe, *Nigeria* 51 F8 10 19N 11 2 E
Gombe →, *Tanzania* 54 C3 4 38S 31 40 E
Gomel = Homyel, *Belarus* 17 B16 52 28N 31 0 E
Gomera, *Canary Is.* 22 F2 28 7N 17 14W
Gómez Palacio, *Mexico* 86 B4 25 40N 104 0W
Gomīshān, *Iran* 45 B7 37 4N 54 6 E
Gomogomo, *Indonesia* 37 F8 6 39S 134 43 E
Gomoh, *India* 41 H15 23 52N 86 10 E
Gompa = Ganta, *Liberia* 50 G4 7 15N 8 59W
Gonābād, *Iran* 45 C8 34 15N 58 45 E
Gonaïves, *Haiti* 89 C5 19 20N 72 42W
Gonâve, G. de la, *Haiti* 89 C5 19 29N 72 42W
Gonâve, I. de la, *Haiti* 89 C5 18 45N 73 0W
Gonbad-e Kāvūs, *Iran* 45 B7 37 20N 55 25 E
Gonda, *India* 43 F9 27 9N 81 58 E
Gondal, *India* 42 J4 21 58N 70 52 E
Gonder, *Ethiopia* 46 E2 12 39N 37 30 E
Gondia, *India* 40 J12 21 23N 80 10 E
Gondola, *Mozam.* 55 F3 19 10S 33 37 E
Gönen, *Turkey* 21 D12 40 6N 27 39 E
Gonghe, *China* 32 C5 36 18N 100 32 E
Gongolgon, *Australia* 63 E4 30 21S 146 54 E
Gongzhuling, *China* 35 C13 43 30N 124 40 E
Gonzales, *Calif., U.S.A.* 84 J5 36 30N 121 26W
Gonzales, *Tex., U.S.A.* 81 L6 29 30N 97 27W
González Chaves, *Argentina* 94 D3 38 2S 60 5W
Good Hope, C. of, *S. Africa* 56 E2 34 24S 18 30 E
Gooderham, *Canada* 78 B6 44 54N 78 21W
Goodhouse, *S. Africa* 56 D2 28 57S 18 13 E
Gooding, *U.S.A.* 82 E6 42 56N 114 43W
Goodland, *U.S.A.* 80 F4 39 21N 101 43W
Goodlow, *Canada* 72 B4 56 20N 120 8W
Goodooga, *Australia* 63 D4 29 3S 147 28 E
Goodsprings, *U.S.A.* 85 K11 35 49N 115 27W
Goole, *U.K.* 10 D7 53 42N 0 53W
Goomalling, *Australia* 61 F2 31 15S 116 49 E
Goomeri, *Australia* 63 D5 26 12S 152 6 E
Goonda, *Mozam.* 55 F3 19 48S 33 57 E
Goondiwindi, *Australia* 63 D5 28 30S 150 21 E
Goongarrie, L., *Australia* 61 F3 30 3S 121 9 E
Goonyella, *Australia* 62 C4 21 47S 147 58 E
Goose →, *Canada* 71 B7 53 20N 60 35W
Goose Creek, *U.S.A.* 77 J5 32 59N 80 2W
Goose L., *U.S.A.* 82 F3 41 56N 120 26W
Gop, *India* 40 H6 22 5N 69 50 E
Gopalganj, *India* 43 F11 26 28N 84 30 E
Göppingen, *Germany* 16 D5 48 42N 9 39 E
Gorakhpur, *India* 43 F10 26 47N 83 23 E
Goražde, *Bos.-H.* 21 C8 43 38N 18 58 E
Gorda, *U.S.A.* 84 K5 35 53N 121 26W
Gorda, Pta., *Canary Is.* 22 F2 28 45N 18 0W
Gorda, Pta., *Nic.* 88 D3 14 20N 83 10W
Gordan B., *Australia* 60 B5 11 35S 130 10 E
Gordon, *U.S.A.* 80 D3 42 48N 102 12W
Gordon →, *Australia* 62 G4 42 27S 145 30 E
Gordon L., *Alta., Canada* 73 B6 56 30N 110 25W
Gordon L., *N.W.T., Canada* 72 A6 63 5N 113 11W
Gordonvale, *Australia* 62 B4 17 5S 145 50 E
Gore, *Ethiopia* 46 F2 8 12N 35 32 E
Gore, *N.Z.* 59 M2 46 5S 168 58 E
Gore Bay, *Canada* 70 C3 45 57N 82 28W
Gorey, *Ireland* 13 D5 52 41N 6 18W
Gorg, *Iran* 45 D8 29 29N 59 43 E
Gorgān, *Iran* 45 B7 36 50N 54 29 E
Gorgona, I., *Colombia* 92 C3 3 0N 78 10W
Gorham, *U.S.A.* 79 B13 44 23N 71 10W
Goriganga →, *India* 43 E9 29 45N 80 23 E
Gorinchem, *Neths.* 15 C4 51 50N 4 59 E
Goris, *Armenia* 25 G8 39 31N 46 22 E
Gorízia, *Italy* 20 B5 45 56N 13 37 E
Gorki = Nizhniy Novgorod, *Russia* 24 C7 56 20N 44 0 E
Gorkiy = Nizhniy Novgorod, *Russia* 24 C7 56 20N 44 0 E
Gorkovskoye Vdkhr., *Russia* 24 C7 57 2N 43 4 E
Görlitz, *Germany* 16 C8 51 9N 14 58 E
Gorlovka = Horlivka, *Ukraine* 25 E6 48 19N 38 5 E
Gorman, *U.S.A.* 85 L8 34 47N 118 51W
Gorna Dzhumayo = Blagoevgrad, *Bulgaria* 21 C10 42 2N 23 5 E
Gorna Oryakhovitsa, *Bulgaria* 21 C11 43 7N 25 40 E
Gorno-Altay □, *Russia* 26 D9 51 0N 86 0 E
Gorno-Altaysk, *Russia* 26 D9 51 50N 86 5 E
Gornyatski, *Russia* 24 A11 67 32N 64 3 E
Gornyy, *Russia* 30 B6 44 57N 133 59 E
Gorodenka = Horodenka, *Ukraine* 17 D13 48 41N 25 29 E
Gorodok = Horodok, *Ukraine* 17 D12 49 46N 23 32 E
Gorokhov = Horokhiv, *Ukraine* 17 C13 50 30N 24 45 E
Goromonzi, *Zimbabwe* 55 F3 17 52S 31 22 E
Gorong, Kepulauan, *Indonesia* 37 E8 3 59S 131 25 E
Gorongose →, *Mozam.* 57 C5 20 30S 34 40 E
Gorongoza, *Mozam.* 55 F3 18 44S 34 2 E
Gorongoza, Sa. da, *Mozam.* 55 F3 18 27S 34 2 E
Gorontalo, *Indonesia* 37 D6 0 35N 123 5 E
Gort, *Ireland* 13 C3 53 3N 8 49W
Gortis, *Greece* 23 D6 35 4N 24 58 E
Gorzów Wielkopolski, *Poland* 16 B8 52 43N 15 15 E
Goshen, *Calif., U.S.A.* 84 J7 36 21N 119 25W
Goshen, *Ind., U.S.A.* 76 E3 41 35N 85 50W
Goshen, *N.Y., U.S.A.* 79 E10 41 24N 74 20W
Goshogawara, *Japan* 30 D10 40 48N 140 27 E
Goslar, *Germany* 16 C6 51 54N 10 25 E
Gospič, *Croatia* 16 F8 44 35N 15 23 E
Gosport, *U.K.* 11 G6 50 48N 1 9W
Gosse →, *Australia* 62 B1 19 32S 134 37 E
Göta älv →, *Sweden* 9 H14 57 42N 11 54 E
Göta kanal, *Sweden* 9 G16 58 30N 15 58 E
Götaland, *Sweden* 9 G15 57 30N 14 30 E
Göteborg, *Sweden* 9 H14 57 43N 11 59 E
Gotha, *Germany* 16 C6 50 56N 10 42 E
Gothenburg = Göteborg, *Sweden* 9 H14 57 43N 11 59 E
Gothenburg, *U.S.A.* 80 E4 40 56N 100 10W
Gotland, *Sweden* 9 H18 57 30N 18 33 E
Gotō-Rettō, *Japan* 31 H4 32 55N 129 5 E
Gotska Sandön, *Sweden* 9 G18 58 24N 19 15 E
Gōtsu, *Japan* 31 G6 35 0N 132 14 E
Gott Pk., *Canada* 72 C4 50 18N 122 16W
Göttingen, *Germany* 16 C5 51 31N 9 55 E
Gottwaldov = Zlín, *Czech Rep.* 17 D9 49 14N 17 40 E
Goubangzi, *China* 35 D11 41 20N 121 52 E
Gouda, *Neths.* 15 B4 52 1N 4 42 E
Goúdhoura, Ákra, *Greece* 23 E8 34 59N 26 6 E
Gough I., *Atl. Oc.* 2 G9 40 10S 9 45W
Gouin, Rés., *Canada* 70 C5 48 35N 74 40W
Goulburn Is., *Australia* 62 A1 11 40S 133 20 E
Goulimine, *Morocco* 50 C3 28 56N 10 0W
Gourits →, *S. Africa* 56 E3 34 21S 21 52 E
Goúrnais, *Greece* 23 D7 35 19N 25 16 E
Gouverneur, *U.S.A.* 79 B9 44 20N 75 28W
Gouviá, *Greece* 23 A3 39 39N 19 50 E
Governador Valadares, *Brazil* 93 G10 18 15S 41 57W
Governor's Harbour, *Bahamas* 88 A4 25 10N 76 14W
Govindgarh, *India* 43 G9 24 23N 81 18 E
Gowan Ra., *Australia* 62 D4 25 0S 145 0 E
Gowanda, *U.S.A.* 78 D6 42 28N 78 56W
Gower, *U.K.* 11 F3 51 35N 4 10W
Gowna, L., *Ireland* 13 C4 53 51N 7 34W
Goya, *Argentina* 94 B4 29 10S 59 10W
Goyder Lagoon, *Australia* 63 D2 27 3S 138 58 E
Goyllarisquisga, *Peru* 92 F3 10 31S 76 24W
Goz Beïda, *Chad* 51 F10 12 10N 21 20 E
Gozo, *Malta* 23 C1 36 3N 14 13 E
Graaff-Reinet, *S. Africa* 56 E3 32 13S 24 32 E
Gračac, *Croatia* 16 F8 44 18N 15 57 E
Gracias a Dios, C., *Honduras* 88 D3 15 0N 83 10W
Graciosa, I., *Canary Is.* 22 E6 29 15N 13 32W
Grado, *Spain* 19 A2 43 23N 6 4W
Grady, *U.S.A.* 81 H3 34 49N 103 19W
Grafham Water, *U.K.* 11 E7 52 19N 0 18W
Grafton, *Australia* 63 D5 29 38S 152 58 E
Grafton, *N. Dak., U.S.A.* 80 A6 48 25N 97 25W
Grafton, *W. Va., U.S.A.* 76 F5 39 21N 80 2W
Graham, *Canada* 70 C1 49 20N 90 30W
Graham, *U.S.A.* 81 J5 33 6N 98 35W
Graham, Mt., *U.S.A.* 83 K9 32 42N 109 52W
Graham Bell, Ostrov = Greem-Bell, Ostrov, *Russia* 26 A7 81 0N 62 0 E
Graham I., *Canada* 72 C2 53 40N 132 30W
Graham Land, *Antarctica* 5 C17 65 0S 64 0W
Grahamstown, *S. Africa* 56 E4 33 19S 26 31 E
Grahamsville, *U.S.A.* 79 E10 41 51N 74 33W
Grain Coast, *W. Afr.* 50 H3 4 20N 10 0W
Grajaú, *Brazil* 93 E9 5 50S 46 4W
Grajaú →, *Brazil* 93 D10 3 41S 44 48W
Grampian, *U.S.A.* 78 F6 40 58N 78 37W
Grampian Highlands = Grampian Mts., *U.K.* 12 E5 56 50N 4 0W
Grampian Mts., *U.K.* 12 E5 56 50N 4 0W
Gran Canaria, *Canary Is.* 22 G4 27 55N 15 35W
Gran Chaco, *S. Amer.* 94 B3 25 0S 61 0W
Gran Paradiso, *Italy* 18 D7 45 33N 7 17 E
Gran Sasso d'Itália, *Italy* 20 C5 42 27N 13 42 E
Granada, *Nic.* 88 D2 11 58N 86 0W
Granada, *Spain* 19 D4 37 10N 3 35W
Granada, *U.S.A.* 81 F3 38 4N 102 19W
Granadilla de Abona, *Canary Is.* 22 F3 28 7N 16 33W
Granard, *Ireland* 13 C4 53 47N 7 30W
Granbury, *U.S.A.* 81 J6 32 27N 97 47W
Granby, *Canada* 79 A12 45 25N 72 45W
Granby, *U.S.A.* 82 F11 40 5N 105 56W
Grand →, *Canada* 78 D5 42 51N 79 34W
Grand →, *Mo., U.S.A.* 80 F8 39 23N 93 7W
Grand →, *S. Dak., U.S.A.* 80 C4 45 40N 100 45W
Grand Bahama, *Bahamas* 88 A4 26 40N 78 30W
Grand Bank, *Canada* 71 C8 47 6N 55 48W
Grand Bassam, *Ivory C.* 50 G5 5 10N 3 49W
Grand-Bourg, *Guadeloupe* 89 C7 15 53N 61 19W
Grand Canal = Yun Ho →, *China* 35 E9 39 10N 117 10 E
Grand Canyon, *U.S.A.* 83 H7 36 3N 112 9W
Grand Canyon National Park, *U.S.A.* 83 H7 36 15N 112 30W
Grand Cayman, *Cayman Is.* 88 C3 19 20N 81 20W
Grand Centre, *Canada* 73 C6 54 25N 110 13W
Grand Coulee, *U.S.A.* 82 C4 47 57N 119 0W
Grand Coulee Dam, *U.S.A.* 82 C4 47 57N 118 59W
Grand Erg Occidental, *Algeria* 50 B6 30 20N 1 0 E
Grand Erg Oriental, *Algeria* 50 B7 30 0N 6 30 E
Grand Falls, *Canada* 71 C6 47 3N 67 44W
Grand Falls-Windsor, *Canada* 71 C8 48 56N 55 40W
Grand Forks, *Canada* 72 D5 49 0N 118 30W
Grand Forks, *U.S.A.* 80 B6 47 55N 97 3W
Grand Gorge, *U.S.A.* 79 D10 42 21N 74 29W
Grand Haven, *U.S.A.* 76 D2 43 4N 86 13W
Grand I., *Mich., U.S.A.* 76 B2 46 31N 86 40W
Grand I., *N.Y., U.S.A.* 78 D6 43 0N 78 58W
Grand Island, *U.S.A.* 80 E5 40 55N 98 21W
Grand Isle, *La., U.S.A.* 81 L9 29 14N 90 0W
Grand Isle, *Vt., U.S.A.* 79 B11 44 43N 73 18W
Grand Junction, *U.S.A.* 83 G9 39 4N 108 33W
Grand L., *N.B., Canada* 71 C6 45 57N 66 7W
Grand L., *Nfld., Canada* 71 C8 49 0N 57 30W
Grand L., *Nfld., Canada* 71 B7 53 40N 60 30W
Grand L., *U.S.A.* 81 L8 29 55N 92 47W
Grand Lake, *U.S.A.* 82 F11 40 15N 105 49W
Grand Manan I., *Canada* 71 D6 44 45N 66 52W
Grand Marais, *Canada* 80 B9 47 45N 90 25W
Grand Marais, *U.S.A.* 76 B3 46 40N 85 59W
Grand-Mère, *Canada* 70 C5 46 36N 72 40W
Grand Portage, *U.S.A.* 80 B10 47 58N 89 41W
Grand Prairie, *U.S.A.* 81 J6 32 47N 97 0W
Grand Rapids, *Canada* 73 C9 53 12N 99 19W
Grand Rapids, *Mich., U.S.A.* 76 D2 42 58N 85 40W
Grand Rapids, *Minn., U.S.A.* 80 B8 47 14N 93 31W
Grand St-Bernard, Col du, *Europe* 18 D7 45 50N 7 10 E
Grand Teton, *U.S.A.* 82 E8 43 54N 111 50W
Grand Teton National Park, *U.S.A.* 82 D8 43 50N 110 50W
Grand Union Canal, *U.K.* 11 E7 52 7N 0 53W
Grand View, *Canada* 73 C8 51 10N 100 42W
Grande →, *Jujuy, Argentina* 94 A2 24 20S 65 2W
Grande →, *Mendoza, Argentina* 94 D2 36 52S 69 45W
Grande →, *Bolivia* 92 G6 15 51S 64 39W
Grande →, *Bahia, Brazil* 93 F10 11 30S 44 30W
Grande →, *Minas Gerais, Brazil* 93 H8 20 6S 51 4W
Grande, B., *Argentina* 96 G3 50 30S 68 20W
Grande, Rio →, *U.S.A.* 81 N6 25 58N 97 9W
Grande Baleine, R. de la →, *Canada* 70 A4 55 16N 77 47W
Grande Cache, *Canada* 72 C5 53 53N 119 8W
Grande-Entrée, *Canada* 71 C7 47 30N 61 40W
Grande Prairie, *Canada* 72 B5 55 10N 118 50W
Grande-Rivière, *Canada* 71 C7 48 26N 64 30W
Grande-Vallée, *Canada* 71 C6 49 14N 65 8W
Grandfalls, *U.S.A.* 81 K3 31 20N 102 51W
Grandview, *U.S.A.* 82 C4 46 15N 119 54W
Graneros, *Chile* 94 C1 34 5S 70 45W
Grangemouth, *U.K.* 12 E5 56 1N 3 42W
Granger, *U.S.A.* 82 F9 41 35N 109 58W
Grangeville, *U.S.A.* 82 D5 45 56N 116 7W
Granisle, *Canada* 72 C3 54 53N 126 13W
Granite City, *U.S.A.* 80 F9 38 42N 90 9W
Granite Falls, *U.S.A.* 80 C7 44 49N 95 33W
Granite L., *Canada* 71 C8 48 8N 57 5W
Granite Mt., *U.S.A.* 85 M10 33 5N 116 28W
Granite Pk., *U.S.A.* 82 D9 45 10N 109 48W
Graniteville, *U.S.A.* 79 B12 44 8N 72 29W
Granity, *N.Z.* 59 J3 41 39S 171 51 E
Granja, *Brazil* 93 D10 3 7S 40 50W
Granollers, *Spain* 19 B7 41 39N 2 18 E
Grant, *U.S.A.* 80 E4 40 53N 101 42W
Grant, Mt., *U.S.A.* 82 G4 38 34N 118 48W
Grant City, *U.S.A.* 80 E7 40 29N 94 25W
Grant I., *Australia* 60 B5 11 10S 132 52 E
Grant Range, *U.S.A.* 83 G6 38 30N 115 25W
Grantham, *U.K.* 10 E7 52 55N 0 38W
Grantown-on-Spey, *U.K.* 12 D5 57 20N 3 36W
Grants, *U.S.A.* 83 J10 35 9N 107 52W
Grants Pass, *U.S.A.* 82 E2 42 26N 123 19W
Grantsville, *U.S.A.* 82 F7 40 36N 112 28W
Granville, *France* 18 B3 48 50N 1 35W
Granville, *N. Dak., U.S.A.* 80 A4 48 16N 100 47W
Granville, *N.Y., U.S.A.* 79 C11 43 24N 73 16W
Granville, *Ohio, U.S.A.* 78 F2 40 4N 82 31W
Granville L., *Canada* 73 B8 56 18N 100 30W
Graskop, *S. Africa* 57 C5 24 56S 30 49 E
Grass →, *Canada* 73 B9 56 3N 96 33W
Grass Range, *U.S.A.* 82 C9 47 0N 109 0W
Grass River Prov. Park, *Canada* 73 C8 54 40N 100 50W
Grass Valley, *Calif., U.S.A.* 84 F6 39 13N 121 4W
Grass Valley, *Oreg., U.S.A.* 82 D3 45 22N 120 47W
Grasse, *France* 18 E7 43 38N 6 56 E
Grassflat, *U.S.A.* 78 F6 41 0N 78 6W
Grasslands Nat. Park, *Canada* 73 D7 49 11N 107 38W
Grassy, *Australia* 62 G3 40 3S 144 5 E
Graulhet, *France* 18 E4 43 45N 1 59 E
Gravelbourg, *Canada* 73 D7 49 50N 106 35W
's-Gravenhage, *Neths.* 15 B4 52 7N 4 17 E
Gravenhurst, *Canada* 78 B5 44 52N 79 20W
Gravesend, *Australia* 63 D5 29 35S 150 20 E
Gravesend, *U.K.* 11 F8 51 26N 0 22 E
Gravois, Pointe-à-, *Haiti* 89 C5 18 15N 73 56W
Grayling, *U.S.A.* 76 C3 44 40N 84 43W
Grays Harbor, *U.S.A.* 82 C1 46 59N 124 1W
Grays L., *U.S.A.* 82 E8 43 4N 111 26W
Grays River, *U.S.A.* 84 D3 46 21N 123 37W
Graz, *Austria* 16 E8 47 4N 15 27 E
Greasy L., *Canada* 72 A4 62 55N 122 12W
Great Abaco I., *Bahamas* 88 A4 26 25N 77 10W
Great Artesian Basin, *Australia* 62 C3 23 0S 144 0 E
Great Australian Bight, *Australia* 61 F5 33 30S 130 0 E
Great Bahama Bank, *Bahamas* 88 B4 23 15N 78 0W
Great Barrier I., *N.Z.* 59 G5 36 11S 175 25 E
Great Barrier Reef, *Australia* 62 B4 18 0S 146 50 E
Great Barrington, *U.S.A.* 79 D11 42 12N 73 22W
Great Basin, *U.S.A.* 82 G5 40 0N 117 0W
Great Basin Nat. Park, *U.S.A.* 82 G6 38 55N 114 14W
Great Bear →, *Canada* 68 B7 65 0N 124 0W
Great Bear L., *Canada* 68 B7 65 30N 120 0W
Great Belt = Store Bælt, *Denmark* 9 J14 55 20N 11 0 E
Great Bend, *Kans., U.S.A.* 80 F5 38 22N 98 46W
Great Bend, *Pa., U.S.A.* 79 E9 41 58N 75 45W
Great Blasket I., *Ireland* 13 D1 52 6N 10 32W
Great Britain, *Europe* 6 E5 54 0N 2 15W
Great Codroy, *Canada* 71 C8 47 51N 59 16W
Great Dividing Ra., *Australia* 62 C4 23 0S 146 0 E
Great Driffield = Driffield, *U.K.* 10 C7 54 0N 0 26W
Great Exuma I., *Bahamas* 88 B4 23 30N 75 50W
Great Falls, *U.S.A.* 82 C8 47 30N 111 17W
Great Fish = Groot Vis →, *S. Africa* 56 E4 33 28S 27 5 E
Great Guana Cay, *Bahamas* 88 B4 24 0N 76 20W
Great Inagua I., *Bahamas* 89 B5 21 0N 73 20W
Great Indian Desert = Thar Desert, *India* 42 F5 28 0N 72 0 E
Great Karoo, *S. Africa* 56 E3 31 55S 21 0 E
Great Lake, *Australia* 62 G4 41 50S 146 40 E
Great Lakes, *N. Amer.* 66 E11 46 0N 84 0W
Great Malvern, *U.K.* 11 E5 52 7N 2 18W
Great Miami →, *U.S.A.* 76 F3 39 20N 84 40W
Great Ormes Head, *U.K.* 10 D4 53 20N 3 52W
Great Ouse →, *U.K.* 10 E8 52 48N 0 21 E
Great Palm I., *Australia* 62 B4 18 45S 146 40 E
Great Plains, *N. Amer.* 74 A6 47 0N 105 0W
Great Ruaha →, *Tanzania* 54 D4 7 56S 37 52 E
Great Sacandaga Res., *U.S.A.* 79 C10 43 6N 74 16W
Great Saint Bernard Pass = Grand St-Bernard, Col du, *Europe* 18 D7 45 50N 7 10 E
Great Salt L., *U.S.A.* 82 F7 41 15N 112 40W
Great Salt Lake Desert, *U.S.A.* 82 F7 40 50N 113 30W
Great Salt Plains L., *U.S.A.* 81 G5 36 45N 98 8W
Great Sandy Desert, *Australia* 60 D3 21 0S 124 0 E
Great Sangi = Sangihe, Pulau, *Indonesia* 37 D7 3 35N 125 30 E
Great Skellig, *Ireland* 13 E1 51 47N 10 33W
Great Slave L., *Canada* 72 A5 61 23N 115 38W
Great Smoky Mts. Nat. Park, *U.S.A.* 77 H4 35 40N 83 40W
Great Snow Mt., *Canada* 72 B4 57 26N 124 0W
Great Stour = Stour →, *U.K.* 11 F9 51 18N 1 22 E
Great Victoria Desert, *Australia* 61 E4 29 30S 126 30 E
Great Wall, *China* 34 E5 38 30N 109 30 E
Great Whernside, *U.K.* 10 C6 54 10N 1 58W
Great Yarmouth, *U.K.* 11 E9 52 37N 1 44 E
Greater Antilles, *W. Indies* 89 C5 17 40N 74 0W
Greater London □, *U.K.* 11 F7 51 31N 0 6W
Greater Manchester □, *U.K.* 10 D5 53 30N 2 15W
Greater Sunda Is., *Indonesia* 36 F4 7 0S 112 0 E
Greco, C., *Cyprus* 23 E13 34 57N 34 5 E
Gredos, Sierra de, *Spain* 19 B3 40 20N 5 0W
Greece, *U.S.A.* 78 C7 43 13N 77 41W
Greece ■, *Europe* 21 E9 40 0N 23 0 E
Greeley, *Colo., U.S.A.* 80 E2 40 25N 104 42W
Greeley, *Nebr., U.S.A.* 80 E5 41 33N 98 32W
Greem-Bell, Ostrov, *Russia* 26 A7 81 0N 62 0 E
Green, *U.S.A.* 82 E2 43 9N 123 22W
Green →, *Ky., U.S.A.* 76 G2 37 54N 87 30W
Green →, *Utah, U.S.A.* 83 G9 38 11N 109 53W
Green B., *U.S.A.* 76 C2 45 0N 87 30W
Green Bay, *U.S.A.* 76 C2 44 31N 88 0W
Green Cove Springs, *U.S.A.* 77 L5 29 59N 81 42W
Green Lake, *Canada* 73 C7 54 17N 107 47W
Green Mts., *U.S.A.* 79 C12 43 45N 72 45W
Green River, *Utah, U.S.A.* 83 G8 38 59N 110 10W
Green River, *Wyo., U.S.A.* 82 F9 41 32N 109 28W
Green Valley, *U.S.A.* 83 L8 31 52N 110 56W
Greenbank, *U.S.A.* 84 B4 48 6N 122 34W
Greenbush, *Mich., U.S.A.* 78 B1 44 35N 83 19W
Greenbush, *Minn., U.S.A.* 80 A6 48 42N 96 11W
Greencastle, *U.S.A.* 76 F2 39 38N 86 52W
Greene, *U.S.A.* 79 D9 42 20N 75 46W
Greenfield, *Calif., U.S.A.* 84 J5 36 19N 121 15W
Greenfield, *Calif., U.S.A.* 85 K8 35 15N 119 0W
Greenfield, *Ind., U.S.A.* 76 F3 39 47N 85 46W
Greenfield, *Iowa, U.S.A.* 80 E7 41 18N 94 28W
Greenfield, *Mass., U.S.A.* 79 D12 42 35N 72 36W
Greenfield, *Mo., U.S.A.* 81 G8 37 25N 93 51W
Greenfield Park, *Canada* 79 A11 45 29N 73 29W
Greenland ■, *N. Amer.* 4 C5 66 0N 45 0W
Greenland Sea, *Arctic* 4 B7 73 0N 10 0W
Greenock, *U.K.* 12 F4 55 57N 4 46W
Greenore, *Ireland* 13 B5 54 2N 6 8W
Greenore Pt., *Ireland* 13 D5 52 14N 6 19W
Greenough, *Australia* 61 E1 28 58S 114 43 E
Greenough →, *Australia* 61 E1 28 51S 114 38 E
Greenough Pt., *Canada* 78 B3 44 58N 81 26W
Greenport, *U.S.A.* 79 E12 41 6N 72 22W
Greensboro, *Ga., U.S.A.* 77 J4 33 35N 83 11W
Greensboro, *N.C., U.S.A.* 77 G6 36 4N 79 48W
Greensboro, *Vt., U.S.A.* 79 B12 44 36N 72 18W
Greensburg, *Ind., U.S.A.* 76 F3 39 20N 85 29W
Greensburg, *Kans., U.S.A.* 81 G5 37 36N 99 18W
Greensburg, *Pa., U.S.A.* 78 F5 40 18N 79 33W
Greenstone Pt., *U.K.* 12 D3 57 55N 5 37W
Greenvale, *Australia* 62 B4 18 59S 145 7 E
Greenville, *Ala., U.S.A.* 77 K2 31 50N 86 38W
Greenville, *Calif., U.S.A.* 84 E6 40 8N 120 57W
Greenville, *Maine, U.S.A.* 77 C11 45 28N 69 35W
Greenville, *Mich., U.S.A.* 76 D3 43 11N 85 15W
Greenville, *Miss., U.S.A.* 81 J9 33 24N 91 4W
Greenville, *Mo., U.S.A.* 81 G9 37 8N 90 27W
Greenville, *N.C., U.S.A.* 77 H7 35 37N 77 23W
Greenville, *N.H., U.S.A.* 79 D13 42 46N 71 49W
Greenville, *N.Y., U.S.A.* 79 D10 42 25N 74 1W
Greenville, *Ohio, U.S.A.* 76 E3 40 6N 84 38W
Greenville, *Pa., U.S.A.* 78 E4 41 24N 80 23W
Greenville, *S.C., U.S.A.* 77 H4 34 51N 82 24W
Greenville, *Tenn., U.S.A.* 77 G4 36 13N 82 51W
Greenville, *Tex., U.S.A.* 81 J6 33 8N 96 7W
Greenwater Lake Prov. Park, *Canada* 73 C8 52 32N 103 30W
Greenwich, *Conn., U.S.A.* 79 E11 41 2N 73 38W
Greenwich, *N.Y., U.S.A.* 79 C11 43 5N 73 30W
Greenwich, *Ohio, U.S.A.* 78 E2 41 2N 82 31W
Greenwich □, *U.K.* 11 F8 51 29N 0 1 E
Greenwood, *Canada* 72 D5 49 10N 118 40W
Greenwood, *Ark., U.S.A.* 81 H7 35 13N 94 16W
Greenwood, *Ind., U.S.A.* 76 F2 39 37N 86 7W
Greenwood, *Miss., U.S.A.* 81 J9 33 31N 90 11W
Greenwood, *S.C., U.S.A.* 77 H4 34 12N 82 10W
Greenwood, Mt., *Australia* 60 B5 13 48S 130 4 E
Gregory, *U.S.A.* 80 D5 43 14N 99 20W
Gregory →, *Australia* 62 B2 17 53S 139 17 E
Gregory, L., *S. Austral., Australia* 63 D2 28 55S 139 0 E
Gregory, L., *W. Austral., Australia* 61 E2 25 38S 119 58 E
Gregory Downs, *Australia* 62 B2 18 35S 138 45 E
Gregory L., *Australia* 60 D4 20 0S 127 40 E
Gregory Ra., *Queens., Australia* 62 B3 19 30S 143 40 E
Gregory Ra., *W. Austral., Australia* 60 D3 21 20S 121 12 E
Greifswald, *Germany* 16 A7 54 5N 13 23 E
Greiz, *Germany* 16 C7 50 39N 12 10 E
Gremikha, *Russia* 24 A6 67 59N 39 47 E
Grenå, *Denmark* 9 H14 56 25N 10 53 E
Grenada, *U.S.A.* 81 J10 33 47N 89 49W
Grenada ■, *W. Indies* 89 D7 12 10N 61 40W
Grenadier I., *U.S.A.* 79 B8 44 3N 76 22W
Grenadines, *St. Vincent* 89 D7 12 40N 61 20W
Grenen, *Denmark* 9 H14 57 44N 10 40 E
Grenfell, *Canada* 73 C8 50 30N 102 56W
Grenoble, *France* 18 D6 45 12N 5 42 E
Grenville, C., *Australia* 62 A3 12 0S 143 13 E
Grenville Chan., *Canada* 72 C3 53 40N 129 46W
Gresham, *U.S.A.* 84 E4 45 30N 122 26W
Gresik, *Indonesia* 37 G15 7 13S 112 38 E
Gretna, *U.K.* 12 F5 55 0N 3 3W
Grevenmacher, *Lux.* 15 E6 49 41N 6 26 E
Grey →, *Canada* 71 C8 47 34N 57 6W
Grey →, *N.Z.* 59 K3 42 27S 171 12 E
Grey, C., *Australia* 62 A2 13 0S 136 35 E
Grey Ra., *Australia* 63 D3 27 0S 143 30 E
Greybull, *U.S.A.* 82 D9 44 30N 108 3W
Greymouth, *N.Z.* 59 K3 42 29S 171 13 E

H

Herbertsdale

Häme, *Finland* **9 F20** 61 38N 25 10 E
Hämeenlinna, *Finland* **9 F21** 61 0N 24 28 E
Hamelin Pool, *Australia* **61 E1** 26 22S 114 20 E
Hameln, *Germany* **16 B5** 52 6N 9 21 E
Hamerkaz □, *Israel* **47 C3** 32 15N 34 55 E
Hamersley Ra., *Australia* **60 D2** 22 0S 117 45 E
Hamhung, *N. Korea* **35 E14** 39 54N 127 30 E
Hami, *China* **32 B4** 42 55N 93 25 E
Hamilton, *Canada* **78 C5** 43 15N 79 50W
Hamilton, *N.Z.* **59 G5** 37 47S 175 19 E
Hamilton, *U.K.* **12 F4** 55 46N 4 2W
Hamilton, *Ala., U.S.A.* **77 H1** 34 9N 87 59W
Hamilton, *Mont., U.S.A.* **82 C6** 46 15N 114 10W
Hamilton, *N.Y., U.S.A.* **79 D9** 42 50N 75 33W
Hamilton, *Ohio, U.S.A.* **76 F3** 39 24N 84 34W
Hamilton, *Tex., U.S.A.* **81 K5** 31 42N 98 7W
Hamilton →, *Australia* **62 C2** 23 30S 139 47 E
Hamilton City, *U.S.A.* **84 F4** 39 45N 122 1W
Hamilton Inlet, *Canada* **71 B8** 54 0N 57 30W
Hamilton Mt., *U.S.A.* **79 C10** 43 25N 74 22W
Hamina, *Finland* **9 F22** 60 34N 27 12 E
Hamirpur, *H.P., India* **42 D7** 31 41N 76 31 E
Hamirpur, *Ut. P., India* **43 G9** 25 57N 80 9 E
Hamlet, *U.S.A.* **77 H6** 34 53N 79 42W
Hamlin = Hameln, *Germany* **16 B5** 52 6N 9 21 E
Hamlin, *N.Y., U.S.A.* **78 C7** 43 17N 77 55W
Hamlin, *Tex., U.S.A.* **81 J4** 32 53N 100 8W
Hamm, *Germany* **16 C4** 51 40N 7 50 E
Ḩammār, Hawr al, *Iraq* **44 D5** 30 50N 47 10 E
Hammerfest, *Norway* **8 A20** 70 39N 23 41 E
Hammond, *Ind., U.S.A.* **76 E2** 41 38N 87 30W
Hammond, *La., U.S.A.* **81 K9** 30 30N 90 28W
Hammond, *N.Y., U.S.A.* **79 B9** 44 27N 75 42W
Hammondsport, *U.S.A.* **78 D7** 42 25N 77 13W
Hammonton, *U.S.A.* **76 F8** 39 39N 74 48W
Hampden, *N.Z.* **59 L3** 45 18S 170 50 E
Hampshire □, *U.K.* **11 F6** 51 7N 1 23W
Hampshire Downs, *U.K.* **11 F6** 51 15N 1 10W
Hampton, *N.B., Canada* **71 C6** 45 32N 65 51W
Hampton, *Ont., Canada* **78 C6** 43 58N 78 45W
Hampton, *Ark., U.S.A.* **81 J8** 33 32N 92 28W
Hampton, *Iowa, U.S.A.* **80 D8** 42 45N 93 13W
Hampton, *N.H., U.S.A.* **79 D14** 42 57N 70 50W
Hampton, *S.C., U.S.A.* **77 J5** 32 52N 81 7W
Hampton, *Va., U.S.A.* **76 G7** 37 2N 76 21W
Hampton Bays, *U.S.A.* **79 F12** 40 53N 72 30W
Hampton Tableland, *Australia* **61 F4** 32 0S 127 0 E
Hamyang, *S. Korea* **35 G14** 35 32N 127 42 E
Han Pijesak, *Bos.-H.* **21 B8** 44 5N 18 57 E
Hanak, *Si. Arabia* **44 E3** 25 32N 37 0 E
Hanamaki, *Japan* **30 E10** 39 23N 141 7 E
Hanang, *Tanzania* **54 C4** 4 30S 35 25 E
Hanau, *Germany* **16 C5** 50 7N 8 56 E
Hanbogd = Ihbulag, *Mongolia* **34 C4** 43 11N 107 10 E
Hancheng, *China* **34 G6** 35 31N 110 25 E
Hancock, *Mich., U.S.A.* **80 B10** 47 8N 88 35W
Hancock, *N.Y., U.S.A.* **79 E9** 41 57N 75 17W
Handa, *Japan* **31 G8** 34 53N 136 55 E
Handan, *China* **34 F8** 36 35N 114 28 E
Handeni, *Tanzania* **54 D4** 5 25S 38 2 E
Handwara, *India* **43 B6** 34 21N 74 20 E
Hanegev, *Israel* **47 E4** 30 50N 35 0 E
Hanford, *U.S.A.* **84 J7** 36 20N 119 39W
Hang Chat, *Thailand* **38 C2** 18 20N 99 21 E
Hang Dong, *Thailand* **38 C2** 18 41N 98 55 E
Hangang →, *S. Korea* **35 F14** 37 50N 126 30 E
Hangayn Nuruu, *Mongolia* **32 B4** 47 30N 99 0 E
Hangchou = Hangzhou, *China* **33 C7** 30 18N 120 11 E
Hanggin Houqi, *China* **34 D4** 40 58N 107 4 E
Hanggin Qi, *China* **34 E5** 39 52N 108 50 E
Hangu, *China* **35 E9** 39 18N 117 53 E
Hangzhou, *China* **33 C7** 30 18N 120 11 E
Hangzhou Wan, *China* **33 C7** 30 15N 120 45 E
Hanhongor, *Mongolia* **34 C3** 43 55N 104 28 E
Ḩanīdh, *Si. Arabia* **45 E6** 26 35N 48 38 E
Ḩanīsh, *Yemen* **46 E3** 13 45N 42 46 E
Hankinson, *U.S.A.* **80 B6** 46 4N 96 54W
Hanko, *Finland* **9 G20** 59 50N 22 57 E
Hanksville, *U.S.A.* **83 G8** 38 22N 110 43W
Hanle, *India* **43 C8** 32 42N 79 4 E
Hanmer Springs, *N.Z.* **59 K4** 42 32S 172 50 E
Hann →, *Australia* **60 C4** 17 26S 126 17 E
Hann, Mt., *Australia* **60 C4** 15 45S 126 0 E
Hanna, *Canada* **72 C6** 51 40N 111 54W
Hanna, *U.S.A.* **82 F10** 41 52N 106 34W
Hannah B., *Canada* **70 B4** 51 40N 80 0W
Hannibal, *Mo., U.S.A.* **80 F9** 39 42N 91 22W
Hannibal, *N.Y., U.S.A.* **79 C8** 43 19N 76 35W
Hannover, *Germany* **16 B5** 52 22N 9 46 E
Hanoi, *Vietnam* **32 D5** 21 5N 105 55 E
Hanover = Hannover, *Germany* **16 B5** 52 22N 9 46 E
Hanover, *Canada* **78 B3** 44 9N 81 2W
Hanover, *S. Africa* **56 E3** 31 4S 24 29 E
Hanover, *N.H., U.S.A.* **79 C12** 43 42N 72 17W
Hanover, *Ohio, U.S.A.* **78 F2** 40 4N 82 16W
Hanover, *Pa., U.S.A.* **76 F7** 39 48N 76 59W
Hanover, I., *Chile* **96 G2** 51 0S 74 50W
Hansdiha, *India* **43 G12** 24 36N 87 5 E
Hansi, *India* **42 E6** 29 10N 75 57 E
Hantsavichy, *Belarus* **17 B14** 52 49N 26 30 E
Hanumangarh, *India* **42 E6** 29 35N 74 19 E
Hanzhong, *China* **34 H4** 33 10N 107 1 E
Hanzhuang, *China* **35 G9** 34 33N 117 23 E
Haora, *India* **43 H13** 22 37N 88 20 E
Haparanda, *Sweden* **8 D21** 65 52N 24 8 E
Happy, *U.S.A.* **81 H4** 34 45N 101 52W
Happy Camp, *U.S.A.* **82 F2** 41 48N 123 23W
Happy Valley-Goose Bay, *Canada* **71 B7** 53 15N 60 20W
Hapsu, *N. Korea* **35 D15** 41 13N 128 51 E
Hapur, *India* **42 E7** 28 45N 77 45 E
Ḩaql, *Si. Arabia* **47 F3** 29 10N 34 58 E
Har, *Indonesia* **37 F8** 5 16S 133 14 E
Har-Ayrag, *Mongolia* **34 B5** 45 47N 109 16 E
Har Hu, *China* **32 C4** 38 20N 97 38 E
Har Us Nuur, *Mongolia* **32 B4** 48 0N 92 0 E
Har Yehuda, *Israel* **47 D3** 31 35N 34 57 E
Ḩaraḑ, *Si. Arabia* **46 C4** 24 22N 49 0 E
Haranomachi, *Japan* **30 F10** 37 38N 140 58 E
Harare, *Zimbabwe* **55 F3** 17 43S 31 2 E
Harbin, *China* **35 B14** 45 48N 126 40 E
Harbor Beach, *U.S.A.* **78 C2** 43 51N 82 39W
Harbour Breton, *Canada* **71 C8** 47 29N 55 50W
Harbour Deep, *Canada* **71 B8** 50 25N 56 32W
Harda, *India* **42 H7** 22 27N 77 5 E
Hardangerfjorden, *Norway* **9 F12** 60 5N 6 0 E
Hardangervidda, *Norway* **9 F12** 60 7N 7 20 E
Hardap Dam, *Namibia* **56 C2** 24 32S 17 50 E
Hardenberg, *Neths.* **15 B6** 52 34N 6 37 E
Harderwijk, *Neths.* **15 B5** 52 21N 5 38 E
Hardey →, *Australia* **60 D2** 22 45S 116 8 E
Hardin, *U.S.A.* **82 D10** 45 44N 107 37W
Harding, *S. Africa* **57 E4** 30 35S 29 55 E
Harding Ra., *Australia* **60 C3** 16 17S 124 55 E
Hardisty, *Canada* **72 C6** 52 40N 111 18W
Hardoi, *India* **43 F9** 27 26N 80 6 E
Hardwar = Haridwar, *India* **42 E8** 29 58N 78 9 E
Hardwick, *U.S.A.* **79 B12** 44 30N 72 22W
Hardy, Pen., *Chile* **96 H3** 55 30S 68 20W
Hare B., *Canada* **71 B8** 51 15N 55 45W
Hareid, *Norway* **9 E12** 62 22N 6 1 E
Harer, *Ethiopia* **46 F3** 9 20N 42 8 E
Hargeisa, *Somali Rep.* **46 F3** 9 30N 44 2 E
Hari →, *Indonesia* **36 E2** 1 16S 104 5 E
Haria, *Canary Is.* **22 E6** 29 8N 13 32W
Haridwar, *India* **42 E8** 29 58N 78 9 E
Harim, Jabal al, *Oman* **45 E8** 25 58N 56 14 E
Haringhata →, *Bangla.* **41 J16** 22 0N 89 58 E
Harīrūd →, *Asia* **40 A2** 37 24N 60 38 E
Härjedalen, *Sweden* **9 E15** 62 22N 13 5 E
Harlan, *Iowa, U.S.A.* **80 E7** 41 39N 95 19W
Harlan, *Ky., U.S.A.* **77 G4** 36 51N 83 19W
Harlech, *U.K.* **10 E3** 52 52N 4 6W
Harlem, *U.S.A.* **82 B9** 48 32N 108 47W
Harlingen, *Neths.* **15 A5** 53 11N 5 25 E
Harlingen, *U.S.A.* **81 M6** 26 12N 97 42W
Harlow, *U.K.* **11 F8** 51 46N 0 8 E
Harlowton, *U.S.A.* **82 C9** 46 26N 109 50W
Harnai, *Pakistan* **42 D2** 30 6N 67 56 E
Harney Basin, *U.S.A.* **82 E4** 43 30N 119 0W
Harney L., *U.S.A.* **82 E4** 43 14N 119 8W
Harney Peak, *U.S.A.* **80 D3** 43 52N 103 32W
Härnösand, *Sweden* **9 E17** 62 38N 17 55 E
Haroldswick, *U.K.* **12 A8** 60 48N 0 50W
Harp L., *Canada* **71 A7** 55 5N 61 50W
Harper, *Liberia* **50 H4** 4 25N 7 43W
Harrai, *India* **43 H8** 22 37N 79 13 E
Harrand, *Pakistan* **42 E4** 29 28N 70 3 E
Harricana →, *Canada* **70 B4** 50 56N 79 32W
Harriman, *U.S.A.* **77 H3** 35 56N 84 33W
Harrington Harbour, *Canada* **71 B8** 50 31N 59 30W
Harris, *U.K.* **12 D2** 57 50N 6 55W
Harris, Sd. of, *U.K.* **12 D1** 57 44N 7 6W
Harris L., *Australia* **63 E2** 31 10S 135 10 E
Harris Pt., *Canada* **78 C2** 43 6N 82 9W
Harrisburg, *Ill., U.S.A.* **81 G10** 37 44N 88 32W
Harrisburg, *Nebr., U.S.A.* **80 E3** 41 33N 103 44W
Harrisburg, *Pa., U.S.A.* **78 F8** 40 16N 76 53W
Harrismith, *S. Africa* **57 D4** 28 15S 29 8 E
Harrison, *Ark., U.S.A.* **81 G8** 36 14N 93 7W
Harrison, *Maine, U.S.A.* **79 B14** 44 7N 70 39W
Harrison, *Nebr., U.S.A.* **80 D3** 42 41N 103 53W
Harrison, C., *Canada* **71 B8** 54 55N 57 55W
Harrison L., *Canada* **72 D4** 49 33N 121 50W
Harrisonburg, *U.S.A.* **76 F6** 38 27N 78 52W
Harrisonville, *U.S.A.* **80 F7** 38 39N 94 21W
Harriston, *Canada* **78 C4** 43 57N 80 53W
Harrisville, *Mich., U.S.A.* **78 B1** 44 39N 83 17W
Harrisville, *N.Y., U.S.A.* **79 B9** 44 9N 75 19W
Harrisville, *Pa., U.S.A.* **78 E5** 41 8N 80 0W
Harrodsburg, *U.S.A.* **76 G3** 37 46N 84 51W
Harrogate, *U.K.* **10 C6** 54 0N 1 33W
Harrow □, *U.K.* **11 F7** 51 35N 0 21W
Harrowsmith, *Canada* **79 B8** 44 24N 76 40W
Harry S. Truman Reservoir, *U.S.A.* **80 F7** 38 16N 93 24W
Harsin, *Iran* **44 C5** 34 18N 47 33 E
Harstad, *Norway* **8 B17** 68 48N 16 30 E
Harsud, *India* **42 H7** 22 6N 76 44 E
Hart, *U.S.A.* **76 D2** 43 42N 86 22W
Hartbees →, *S. Africa* **56 D3** 28 45S 20 32 E
Hartford, *Conn., U.S.A.* **79 E12** 41 46N 72 41W
Hartford, *Ky., U.S.A.* **76 G2** 37 27N 86 55W
Hartford, *S. Dak., U.S.A.* **80 D6** 43 38N 96 57W
Hartford, *Wis., U.S.A.* **80 D10** 43 19N 88 22W
Hartford City, *U.S.A.* **76 E3** 40 27N 85 22W
Hartland, *Canada* **71 C6** 46 20N 67 32W
Hartland Pt., *U.K.* **11 F3** 51 1N 4 32W
Hartlepool, *U.K.* **10 C6** 54 42N 1 13W
Hartlepool □, *U.K.* **10 C6** 54 42N 1 17W
Hartley Bay, *Canada* **72 C3** 53 25N 129 15W
Hartmannberge, *Namibia* **56 B1** 17 0S 13 0 E
Hartney, *Canada* **73 D8** 49 30N 100 35W
Harts →, *S. Africa* **56 D3** 28 24S 24 17 E
Hartselle, *U.S.A.* **77 H2** 34 27N 86 56W
Hartshorne, *U.S.A.* **81 H7** 34 51N 95 34W
Hartstown, *U.S.A.* **78 E4** 41 33N 80 23W
Hartsville, *U.S.A.* **77 H5** 34 23N 80 4W
Hartswater, *S. Africa* **56 D3** 27 34S 24 43 E
Hartwell, *U.S.A.* **77 H4** 34 21N 82 56W
Harunabad, *Pakistan* **42 E5** 29 35N 73 8 E
Harvand, *Iran* **45 D7** 28 25N 55 43 E
Harvey, *Australia* **61 F2** 33 5S 115 54 E
Harvey, *Ill., U.S.A.* **76 E2** 41 36N 87 50W
Harvey, *N. Dak., U.S.A.* **80 B5** 47 47N 99 56W
Harwich, *U.K.* **11 F9** 51 56N 1 17 E
Haryana □, *India* **42 E7** 29 0N 76 10 E
Haryn →, *Belarus* **17 B14** 52 7N 27 17 E
Harz, *Germany* **16 C6** 51 38N 10 44 E
Hasa □, *Si. Arabia* **45 E6** 25 50N 49 0 E
Ḩasanābād, *Iran* **45 C7** 32 8N 52 44 E
Hasdo →, *India* **43 J10** 21 44N 82 44 E
Hashimoto, *Japan* **31 G7** 34 19N 135 37 E
Hashtjerd, *Iran* **45 C6** 35 52N 50 40 E
Haskell, *U.S.A.* **81 J5** 33 10N 99 44W
Haslemere, *U.K.* **11 F7** 51 5N 0 43W
Hasselt, *Belgium* **15 D5** 50 56N 5 21 E
Hassi Messaoud, *Algeria* **50 B7** 31 51N 6 1 E
Hässleholm, *Sweden* **9 H15** 56 10N 13 46 E
Hastings, *N.Z.* **59 H6** 39 39S 176 52 E
Hastings, *U.K.* **11 G8** 50 51N 0 35 E
Hastings, *Mich., U.S.A.* **76 D3** 42 39N 85 17W
Hastings, *Minn., U.S.A.* **80 C8** 44 44N 92 51W
Hastings, *Nebr., U.S.A.* **80 E5** 40 35N 98 23W
Hat Yai, *Thailand* **39 J3** 7 1N 100 27 E
Hatanbulag = Ergel, *Mongolia* **34 C5** 43 8N 109 5 E
Hatay = Antalya, *Turkey* **25 G5** 36 52N 30 45 E
Hatch, *U.S.A.* **83 K10** 32 40N 107 9W
Hatchet L., *Canada* **73 B8** 58 36N 103 40W
Hateruma-Shima, *Japan* **31 M1** 24 3N 123 47 E
Hatgal, *Mongolia* **32 A5** 50 26N 100 9 E
Hathras, *India* **42 F8** 27 36N 78 6 E
Hatia, *Bangla.* **41 H17** 22 30N 91 5 E
Hato Mayor, *Dom. Rep.* **89 C6** 18 46N 69 15W
Hatta, *India* **43 G8** 24 7N 79 36 E
Hatteras, C., *U.S.A.* **77 H8** 35 14N 75 32W
Hattiesburg, *U.S.A.* **81 K10** 31 20N 89 17W
Hatvan, *Hungary* **17 E10** 47 40N 19 45 E
Hau Bon = Cheo Reo, *Vietnam* **36 B3** 13 25N 108 28 E
Hau Duc, *Vietnam* **38 E7** 15 20N 108 13 E
Haugesund, *Norway* **9 G11** 59 23N 5 13 E
Haukipudas, *Finland* **8 D21** 65 12N 25 20 E
Haultain →, *Canada* **73 B7** 55 51N 106 46W
Hauraki G., *N.Z.* **59 G5** 36 35S 175 5 E
Haut Atlas, *Morocco* **50 B4** 32 30N 5 0W
Haut-Zaïre = Orientale □, *Dem. Rep. of the Congo* **54 B2** 2 20N 26 0 E
Hautes Fagnes = Hohe Venn, *Belgium* **15 D6** 50 30N 6 5 E
Hauts Plateaux, *Algeria* **48 C4** 35 0N 1 0 E
Havana = La Habana, *Cuba* **88 B3** 23 8N 82 22W
Havana, *U.S.A.* **80 E9** 40 18N 90 4W
Havant, *U.K.* **11 G7** 50 51N 0 58W
Havasu, L., *U.S.A.* **85 L12** 34 18N 114 28W
Havel →, *Germany* **16 B7** 52 50N 12 3 E
Havelian, *Pakistan* **42 B5** 34 2N 73 10 E
Havelock, *Canada* **78 B7** 44 26N 77 53W
Havelock, *N.Z.* **59 J4** 41 17S 173 48 E
Havelock, *U.S.A.* **77 H7** 34 53N 76 54W
Haverfordwest, *U.K.* **11 F3** 51 48N 4 58W
Haverhill, *U.S.A.* **79 D13** 42 47N 71 5W
Haverstraw, *U.S.A.* **79 E11** 41 12N 73 58W
Havîrga, *Mongolia* **34 B7** 45 41N 113 5 E
Havířov, *Czech Rep.* **17 D10** 49 46N 18 20 E
Havlíčkův Brod, *Czech Rep.* **16 D8** 49 36N 15 33 E
Havre, *U.S.A.* **82 B9** 48 33N 109 41W
Havre-Aubert, *Canada* **71 C7** 47 12N 61 56W
Havre-St.-Pierre, *Canada* **71 B7** 50 18N 63 33W
Haw →, *U.S.A.* **77 H6** 35 36N 79 3W
Hawaii □, *U.S.A.* **74 H16** 19 30N 156 30W
Hawaii I., *Pac. Oc.* **74 J17** 20 0N 155 0W
Hawaiian Is., *Pac. Oc.* **74 H17** 20 30N 156 0W
Hawaiian Ridge, *Pac. Oc.* **65 E11** 24 0N 165 0W
Hawarden, *U.S.A.* **80 D6** 43 0N 96 29W
Hawea, L., *N.Z.* **59 L2** 44 28S 169 19 E
Hawera, *N.Z.* **59 H5** 39 35S 174 19 E
Hawick, *U.K.* **12 F6** 55 26N 2 47W
Hawk Junction, *Canada* **70 C3** 48 5N 84 38W
Hawke B., *N.Z.* **59 H6** 39 25S 177 20 E
Hawkesbury, *Canada* **70 C5** 45 37N 74 37W
Hawkesbury I., *Canada* **72 C3** 53 37N 129 3W
Hawkesbury Pt., *Australia* **62 A1** 11 55S 134 5 E
Hawkinsville, *U.S.A.* **77 J4** 32 17N 83 28W
Hawley, *Minn., U.S.A.* **80 B6** 46 53N 96 19W
Hawley, *Pa., U.S.A.* **79 E9** 41 28N 75 11W
Ḩawrān, W. →, *Iraq* **44 C4** 33 58N 42 34 E
Hawsh Müssá, *Lebanon* **47 B4** 33 45N 35 55 E
Hawthorne, *U.S.A.* **82 G4** 38 32N 118 38W
Hay →, *Australia* **62 C2** 24 50S 138 0 E
Hay →, *Canada* **72 A5** 60 50N 116 26W
Hay, C., *Australia* **60 B4** 14 5S 129 29 E
Hay I., *Canada* **78 B4** 44 53N 80 58W
Hay L., *Canada* **72 B5** 58 50N 118 50W
Hay-on-Wye, *U.K.* **11 E4** 52 5N 3 8W
Hay River, *Canada* **72 A5** 60 51N 115 44W
Hay Springs, *U.S.A.* **80 D3** 42 41N 102 41W
Haya = Tehoru, *Indonesia* **37 E7** 3 23S 129 30 E
Hayachine-San, *Japan* **30 E10** 39 34N 141 29 E
Hayden, *U.S.A.* **82 F10** 40 30N 107 16W
Haydon, *Australia* **62 B3** 18 0S 141 30 E
Hayes, *U.S.A.* **80 C4** 44 23N 101 1W
Hayes →, *Canada* **70 A1** 57 3N 92 12W
Hayes Creek, *Australia* **60 B5** 13 43S 131 22 E
Hayle, *U.K.* **11 G2** 50 11N 5 26W
Hayling I., *U.K.* **11 G7** 50 48N 0 59W
Hayrabolu, *Turkey* **21 D12** 41 12N 27 5 E
Hays, *Canada* **72 C6** 50 6N 111 48W
Hays, *U.S.A.* **80 F5** 38 53N 99 20W
Haysyn, *Ukraine* **17 D15** 48 57N 29 25 E
Hayvoron, *Ukraine* **17 D15** 48 22N 29 52 E
Hayward, *Calif., U.S.A.* **84 H4** 37 40N 122 5W
Hayward, *Wis., U.S.A.* **80 B9** 46 1N 91 29W
Haywards Heath, *U.K.* **11 G7** 51 0N 0 5W
Hazafon □, *Israel* **47 C4** 32 40N 35 20 E
Hazārān, Kūh-e, *Iran* **45 D8** 29 35N 57 20 E
Hazard, *U.S.A.* **76 G4** 37 15N 83 12W
Hazaribag, *India* **43 H11** 23 58N 85 26 E
Hazaribag Road, *India* **43 G11** 24 12N 85 57 E
Hazelton, *Canada* **72 B3** 55 20N 127 42W
Hazelton, *U.S.A.* **80 B4** 46 29N 100 17W
Hazen, *U.S.A.* **80 B4** 47 18N 101 38W
Hazlehurst, *Ga., U.S.A.* **77 K4** 31 52N 82 36W
Hazlehurst, *Miss., U.S.A.* **81 K9** 31 52N 90 24W
Hazlet, *U.S.A.* **79 F10** 40 25N 74 12W
Hazleton, *U.S.A.* **79 F9** 40 57N 75 59W
Hazlett, L., *Australia* **60 D4** 21 30S 128 48 E
Hazro, *Turkey* **44 B4** 38 15N 40 47 E
Head of Bight, *Australia* **61 F5** 31 30S 131 25 E
Headlands, *Zimbabwe* **55 F3** 18 15S 32 2 E
Healdsburg, *U.S.A.* **84 G4** 38 37N 122 52W
Healdton, *U.S.A.* **81 H6** 34 14N 97 29W
Heany Junction, *Zimbabwe* **57 C4** 20 0S 28 54 E
Heard I., *Ind. Oc.* **3 G13** 53 0S 74 0 E
Hearne, *U.S.A.* **81 K6** 30 53N 96 36W
Hearst, *Canada* **70 C3** 49 40N 83 41W
Heart →, *U.S.A.* **80 B4** 46 46N 100 50W
Heart's Content, *Canada* **71 C9** 47 54N 53 27W
Heath Pt., *Canada* **71 C7** 49 8N 61 40W
Heavener, *U.S.A.* **81 H7** 34 53N 94 36W
Hebbronville, *U.S.A.* **81 M5** 27 18N 98 41W
Hebei □, *China* **34 E9** 39 0N 116 0 E
Hebel, *Australia* **63 D4** 28 58S 147 47 E
Heber, *U.S.A.* **85 N11** 32 44N 115 32W
Heber City, *U.S.A.* **82 F8** 40 31N 111 25W
Heber Springs, *U.S.A.* **81 H9** 35 30N 92 2W
Hebert, *Canada* **73 C7** 50 30N 107 10W
Hebgen L., *U.S.A.* **82 D8** 44 52N 111 20W
Hebi, *China* **34 G8** 35 57N 114 7 E
Hebrides, *U.K.* **6 D4** 57 30N 7 0W
Hebrides, Sea of the, *U.K.* **12 D2** 57 5N 7 0W
Hebron = Al Khalīl, *West Bank* **47 D4** 31 32N 35 6 E
Hebron, *Canada* **69 C13** 58 5N 62 30W
Hebron, *N. Dak., U.S.A.* **80 B3** 46 54N 102 3W
Hebron, *Nebr., U.S.A.* **80 E6** 40 10N 97 35W
Hecate Str., *Canada* **72 C2** 53 10N 130 30W
Heceta I., *U.S.A.* **72 B2** 55 46N 133 40W
Hechi, *China* **32 D5** 24 40N 108 2 E
Hechuan, *China* **32 C5** 30 2N 106 12 E
Hecla, *U.S.A.* **80 C5** 45 53N 98 9W
Hecla I., *Canada* **73 C9** 51 10N 96 43W
Hede, *Sweden* **9 E15** 62 23N 13 30 E
Hedemora, *Sweden* **9 F16** 60 18N 15 58 E
Heerde, *Neths.* **15 B6** 52 24N 6 2 E
Heerenveen, *Neths.* **15 B5** 52 57N 5 55 E
Heerhugowaard, *Neths.* **15 B4** 52 40N 4 51 E
Heerlen, *Neths.* **18 A6** 50 55N 5 58 E
Ḩefa, *Israel* **47 C4** 32 46N 35 0 E
Ḩefa □, *Israel* **47 C4** 32 40N 35 0 E
Hefei, *China* **33 C6** 31 52N 117 18 E
Hegang, *China* **33 B8** 47 20N 130 19 E
Heichengzhen, *China* **34 F4** 36 24N 106 3 E
Heidelberg, *Germany* **16 D5** 49 24N 8 42 E
Heidelberg, *S. Africa* **56 E3** 34 6S 20 59 E
Heilbron, *S. Africa* **57 D4** 27 16S 27 59 E
Heilbronn, *Germany* **16 D5** 49 9N 9 13 E
Heilongjiang □, *China* **33 B7** 48 0N 126 0 E
Heilunkiang = Heilongjiang □, *China* **33 B7** 48 0N 126 0 E
Heimaey, *Iceland* **8 E3** 63 26N 20 17W
Heinola, *Finland* **9 F22** 61 13N 26 2 E
Heinze Kyun, *Burma* **38 E1** 14 25N 97 45 E
Heishan, *China* **35 D12** 41 40N 122 5 E
Heishui, *China* **35 C10** 42 8N 119 30 E
Hejaz = Ḩijāz □, *Si. Arabia* **46 C2** 24 0N 40 0 E
Hejian, *China* **34 E9** 38 25N 116 5 E
Hejin, *China* **34 G6** 35 35N 110 42 E
Hekımhan, *Turkey* **44 B3** 38 50N 37 55 E
Hekla, *Iceland* **8 E4** 63 56N 19 35W
Hekou, *China* **32 D5** 22 30N 103 59 E
Helan Shan, *China* **34 E3** 38 30N 105 55 E
Helen Atoll, *Pac. Oc.* **37 D8** 2 40N 132 0 E
Helena, *Ark., U.S.A.* **81 H9** 34 32N 90 36W
Helena, *Mont., U.S.A.* **82 C7** 46 36N 112 2W
Helendale, *U.S.A.* **85 L9** 34 44N 117 19W
Helensburgh, *U.K.* **12 E4** 56 1N 4 43W
Helensville, *N.Z.* **59 G5** 36 41S 174 29 E
Helenvale, *Australia* **62 B4** 15 43S 145 14 E
Helgeland, *Norway* **8 C15** 66 7N 13 29 E
Helgoland, *Germany* **16 A4** 54 10N 7 53 E
Heligoland = Helgoland, *Germany* **16 A4** 54 10N 7 53 E
Heligoland B. = Deutsche Bucht, *Germany* **16 A5** 54 15N 8 0 E
Hella, *Iceland* **8 E3** 63 50N 20 24W
Hellertown, *U.S.A.* **79 F9** 40 35N 75 21W
Hellespont = Çanakkale Boğazı, *Turkey* **21 D12** 40 17N 26 32 E
Hellevoetsluis, *Neths.* **15 C4** 51 50N 4 8 E
Hellín, *Spain* **19 C5** 38 31N 1 40W
Helmand □, *Afghan.* **40 D4** 31 20N 64 0 E
Helmand →, *Afghan.* **40 D2** 31 12N 61 34 E
Helmeringhausen, *Namibia* **56 D2** 25 54S 16 57 E
Helmond, *Neths.* **15 C5** 51 29N 5 41 E
Helmsdale, *U.K.* **12 C5** 58 7N 3 39W
Helmsdale →, *U.K.* **12 C5** 58 7N 3 40W
Helong, *China* **35 C15** 42 40N 129 0 E
Helper, *U.S.A.* **82 G8** 39 41N 110 51W
Helsingborg, *Sweden* **9 H15** 56 3N 12 42 E
Helsingfors = Helsinki, *Finland* **9 F21** 60 15N 25 3 E
Helsingør, *Denmark* **9 H15** 56 2N 12 35 E
Helsinki, *Finland* **9 F21** 60 15N 25 3 E
Helston, *U.K.* **11 G2** 50 6N 5 17W
Helvellyn, *U.K.* **10 C4** 54 32N 3 1W
Helwân, *Egypt* **51 C12** 29 50N 31 20 E
Hemel Hempstead, *U.K.* **11 F7** 51 44N 0 28W
Hemet, *U.S.A.* **85 M10** 33 45N 116 58W
Hemingford, *U.S.A.* **80 D3** 42 19N 103 4W
Hemmingford, *Canada* **79 A11** 45 3N 73 35W
Hempstead, *U.S.A.* **81 K6** 30 6N 96 5W
Hemse, *Sweden* **9 H18** 57 15N 18 22 E
Henan □, *China* **34 H8** 34 0N 114 0 E
Henares →, *Spain* **19 B4** 40 24N 3 30W
Henashi-Misaki, *Japan* **30 D9** 40 37N 139 51 E
Henderson, *Argentina* **94 D3** 36 18S 61 43W
Henderson, *Ky., U.S.A.* **76 G2** 37 50N 87 35W
Henderson, *N.C., U.S.A.* **77 G6** 36 20N 78 25W
Henderson, *Nev., U.S.A.* **85 J12** 36 2N 114 59W
Henderson, *Tenn., U.S.A.* **77 H1** 35 26N 88 38W
Henderson, *Tex., U.S.A.* **81 J7** 32 9N 94 48W
Hendersonville, *N.C., U.S.A.* **77 H4** 35 19N 82 28W
Hendersonville, *Tenn., U.S.A.* **77 G2** 36 18N 86 37W
Hendījān, *Iran* **45 D6** 30 14N 49 43 E
Hendorābī, *Iran* **45 E7** 26 40N 53 37 E
Hengcheng, *China* **34 E4** 38 18N 106 28 E
Hengdaohezi, *China* **35 B15** 44 52N 129 0 E
Hengelo, *Neths.* **15 B6** 52 16N 6 48 E
Hengshan, *China* **34 F5** 37 58N 109 5 E
Hengshui, *China* **34 F8** 37 41N 115 40 E
Hengyang, *China* **33 D6** 26 59N 112 22 E
Henlopen, C., *U.S.A.* **76 F8** 38 48N 75 6W
Hennenman, *S. Africa* **56 D4** 27 59S 27 1 E
Hennessey, *U.S.A.* **81 G6** 36 6N 97 54W
Henrietta, *U.S.A.* **81 J5** 33 49N 98 12W
Henrietta, Ostrov = Genriyetty, Ostrov, *Russia* **27 B16** 77 6N 156 30 E
Henrietta Maria, C., *Canada* **70 A3** 55 9N 82 20W
Henry, *U.S.A.* **80 E10** 41 7N 89 22W
Henryetta, *U.S.A.* **81 H7** 35 27N 95 59W
Henryville, *Canada* **79 A11** 45 8N 73 11W
Hensall, *Canada* **78 C3** 43 26N 81 30W
Hentiesbaai, *Namibia* **56 C1** 22 8S 14 18 E
Hentiyn Nuruu, *Mongolia* **33 B5** 48 30N 108 30 E
Henzada, *Burma* **41 L19** 17 38N 95 26 E
Heppner, *U.S.A.* **82 D4** 45 21N 119 33W
Hepworth, *Canada* **78 B3** 44 37N 81 9W
Hequ, *China* **34 E6** 39 20N 111 15 E
Héraðsflói, *Iceland* **8 D6** 65 42N 14 12W
Héraðsvötn →, *Iceland* **8 D4** 65 45N 19 25W
Herald Cays, *Australia* **62 B4** 16 58S 149 9 E
Herāt, *Afghan.* **40 B3** 34 20N 62 7 E
Herāt □, *Afghan.* **40 B3** 35 0N 62 0 E
Herbert →, *Australia* **62 B4** 18 31S 146 17 E
Herberton, *Australia* **62 B4** 17 20S 145 25 E
Herbertsdale, *S. Africa* **56 E3** 34 1S 21 46 E

Herceg-Novi

Herceg-Novi, Montenegro, Yug. 21 C8 42 30N 18 33 E
Herchmer, Canada 73 B10 57 22N 94 10W
Herðubreið, Iceland 8 D5 65 11N 16 21W
Hereford, U.K. 11 E5 52 4N 2 43W
Hereford, U.S.A. 81 H3 34 49N 102 24W
Herefordshire □, U.K. 11 E5 52 8N 2 40W
Herentals, Belgium 15 C4 51 12N 4 51 E
Herford, Germany 16 B5 52 7N 8 39 E
Herington, U.S.A. 80 F6 38 40N 96 57W
Herkimer, U.S.A. 79 D10 43 0N 74 59W
Herlong, U.S.A. 84 E6 40 8N 120 8W
Herm, U.K. 11 H5 49 30N 2 28W
Hermann, U.S.A. 80 F9 38 42N 91 27W
Hermannsburg, Australia 60 D5 23 57S 132 45 E
Hermanus, S. Africa 56 E2 34 27S 19 12 E
Hermiston, U.S.A. 82 D4 45 51N 119 17W
Hermite, I., Chile 96 H3 55 50S 68 0W
Hermon, U.S.A. 79 B9 44 28N 75 14W
Hermon, Mt. = Shaykh, J. ash, Lebanon 47 B4 33 25N 35 50 E
Hermosillo, Mexico 86 B2 29 10N 111 0W
Hernád →, Hungary 17 D11 47 56N 21 8 E
Hernandarias, Paraguay 95 B5 25 20S 54 40W
Hernandez, U.S.A. 84 J6 36 24N 120 46W
Hernando, Argentina 94 C3 32 28S 63 40W
Hernando, U.S.A. 81 H10 34 50N 90 0W
Herndon, U.S.A. 78 F8 40 43N 76 51W
Herne, Germany 15 C7 51 32N 7 14 E
Herne Bay, U.K. 11 F9 51 21N 1 8 E
Herning, Denmark 9 H13 56 8N 8 58 E
Heroica = Caborca, Mexico 86 A2 30 40N 112 10W
Heroica Nogales = Nogales, Mexico 86 A2 31 20N 110 56W
Heron Bay, Canada 70 C2 48 40N 86 25W
Herradura, Pta. de la, Canary Is. 22 F5 28 26N 14 8W
Herreid, U.S.A. 80 C4 45 50N 100 4W
Herrin, U.S.A. 81 G10 37 48N 89 2W
Herriot, Canada 73 B8 56 22N 101 16W
Hershey, U.S.A. 79 F8 40 17N 76 39W
Hersonissos, Greece 23 D7 35 18N 25 22 E
Herstal, Belgium 15 D5 50 40N 5 38 E
Hertford, U.K. 11 F7 51 48N 0 4W
Hertfordshire □, U.K. 11 F7 51 51N 0 5W
's-Hertogenbosch, Neths. 15 C5 51 42N 5 17 E
Hertzogville, S. Africa 56 D4 28 9S 25 30 E
Hervey B., Australia 62 C5 25 0S 152 52 E
Herzliyya, Israel 47 C3 32 10N 34 50 E
Ḩeşār, Fārs, Iran 45 D6 29 52N 50 16 E
Ḩeşār, Markazī, Iran 45 C6 35 50N 49 12 E
Heshui, China 34 G5 35 48N 108 0 E
Heshun, China 34 F7 37 22N 113 32 E
Hesperia, U.S.A. 85 L9 34 25N 117 18W
Hesse = Hessen □, Germany 16 C5 50 30N 9 0 E
Hessen □, Germany 16 C5 50 30N 9 0 E
Hetch Hetchy Aqueduct, U.S.A. 84 H5 37 29N 122 19W
Hettinger, U.S.A. 80 C3 46 0N 102 42W
Heuvelton, U.S.A. 79 B9 44 37N 75 25W
Hewitt, U.S.A. 81 K6 31 27N 97 11W
Hexham, U.K. 10 C5 54 58N 2 4W
Hexigten Qi, China 35 C9 43 18N 117 30 E
Ḩeydarābād, Iran 45 D7 30 33N 55 38 E
Heysham, U.K. 10 C5 54 3N 2 53W
Heze, China 34 G8 35 14N 115 20 E
Hi Vista, U.S.A. 85 L9 34 45N 117 46W
Hialeah, U.S.A. 77 N5 25 50N 80 17W
Hiawatha, U.S.A. 80 F7 39 51N 95 32W
Hibbing, U.S.A. 80 B8 47 25N 92 56W
Hibbs B., Australia 62 G4 42 35S 145 15 E
Hibernia Reef, Australia 60 B3 12 0S 123 23 E
Hickman, U.S.A. 81 G10 36 34N 89 11W
Hickory, U.S.A. 77 H5 35 44N 81 21W
Hicks L., Canada 73 A9 61 25N 100 0W
Hicksville, U.S.A. 79 F11 40 46N 73 32W
Hida-Gawa →, Japan 31 G8 35 26N 137 3 E
Hida-Sammyaku, Japan 31 F8 36 30N 137 40 E
Hidaka-Sammyaku, Japan 30 C11 42 35N 142 45 E
Hidalgo, Mexico 87 C5 24 15N 99 26W
Hidalgo □, Mexico 87 C5 20 30N 99 10W
Hidalgo, Presa M., Mexico 86 B3 26 30N 108 35W
Hidalgo, Pta. del, Canary Is. 22 F3 28 33N 16 19W
Hidalgo del Parral, Mexico 86 B3 26 58N 105 40W
Hierro, Canary Is. 22 G1 27 44N 18 0W
Higashiajima-San, Japan 30 F10 37 40N 140 10 E
Higashiōsaka, Japan 31 G7 34 40N 135 37 E
Higgins, U.S.A. 81 G4 36 7N 100 2W
Higgins Corner, U.S.A. 84 F5 39 2N 121 5W
High Atlas = Haut Atlas, Morocco 50 B4 32 30N 5 0W
High Bridge, U.S.A. 79 F10 40 40N 74 54W
High Level, Canada 72 B5 58 31N 117 8W
High Point, U.S.A. 77 H6 35 57N 80 0W
High Prairie, Canada 72 B5 55 30N 116 30W
High River, Canada 72 C6 50 30N 113 50W
High Tatra = Tatry, Slovak Rep. 17 D11 49 20N 20 0 E
High Veld, Africa 48 J6 27 0S 27 0 E
High Wycombe, U.K. 11 F7 51 37N 0 45W
Highland □, U.K. 12 D4 57 17N 4 21W
Highland Park, U.S.A. 76 D2 42 11N 87 48W
Highmore, U.S.A. 80 C5 44 31N 99 27W
Highrock L., Man., Canada 73 B8 55 45N 100 30W
Highrock L., Sask., Canada 73 B7 57 5N 105 32W
Higüey, Dom. Rep. 89 C6 18 37N 68 42W
Hiiumaa, Estonia 9 G20 58 50N 22 45 E
Ḩijāz □, Si. Arabia 46 C2 24 0N 40 0 E
Hijo = Tagum, Phil. 37 C7 7 33N 125 53 E
Hikari, Japan 31 H5 33 58N 131 58 E
Hiko, U.S.A. 84 H11 37 32N 115 14W
Hikone, Japan 31 G8 35 15N 136 10 E
Hikurangi, N.Z. 59 F5 35 36S 174 17 E
Hikurangi, Mt., N.Z. 59 H6 37 55S 178 4 E
Hildesheim, Germany 16 B5 52 9N 9 56 E
Hill →, Australia 61 F2 30 23S 115 3 E
Hill City, Idaho, U.S.A. 82 E6 43 18N 115 3W
Hill City, Kans., U.S.A. 80 F5 39 22N 99 51W
Hill City, S. Dak., U.S.A. 80 D3 43 56N 103 35W
Hill Island L., Canada 73 A7 60 30N 109 50W
Hillcrest Center, U.S.A. 85 K8 35 23N 118 57W
Hillegom, Neths. 15 B4 52 18N 4 35 E
Hillerød, Denmark 9 J15 55 56N 12 19 E
Hillsboro, Kans., U.S.A. 80 F6 38 21N 97 12W
Hillsboro, N. Dak., U.S.A. 80 B6 47 26N 97 3W
Hillsboro, N.H., U.S.A. 79 C13 43 7N 71 54W
Hillsboro, Ohio, U.S.A. 76 F4 39 12N 83 37W
Hillsboro, Oreg., U.S.A. 84 E4 45 31N 122 59W
Hillsboro, Tex., U.S.A. 81 J6 32 1N 97 8W
Hillsborough, Grenada 89 D7 12 28N 61 28W
Hillsdale, Mich., U.S.A. 76 E3 41 56N 84 38W
Hillsdale, N.Y., U.S.A. 79 D11 42 11N 73 30W
Hillsport, Canada 70 C2 49 27N 85 34W
Hilo, U.S.A. 74 J17 19 44N 155 5W
Hilton, U.S.A. 78 C7 43 17N 77 48W
Hilton Head Island, U.S.A. 77 J5 32 13N 80 45W
Hilversum, Neths. 15 B5 52 14N 5 10 E
Himachal Pradesh □, India 42 D7 31 30N 77 0 E
Himalaya, Asia 43 E11 29 0N 84 0 E
Himatnagar, India 40 H8 23 37N 72 57 E
Himeji, Japan 31 G7 34 50N 134 40 E
Himi, Japan 31 F8 36 50N 136 55 E
Ḩimş, Syria 47 A5 34 40N 36 45 E
Ḩimş □, Syria 47 A6 34 30N 37 0 E
Hinche, Haiti 89 C5 19 9N 72 1W
Hinchinbrook I., Australia 62 B4 18 20S 146 15 E
Hinckley, U.K. 11 E6 52 33N 1 22W
Hinckley, U.S.A. 80 B8 46 1N 92 56W
Hindaun, India 42 F7 26 44N 77 5 E
Hindu Bagh, Pakistan 42 D2 30 56N 67 50 E
Hindu Kush, Asia 40 B7 36 0N 71 0 E
Hindubagh, Pakistan 40 D5 30 56N 67 57 E
Hindupur, India 40 N10 13 49N 77 32 E
Hines Creek, Canada 72 B5 56 20N 118 40W
Hinesville, U.S.A. 77 K5 31 51N 81 36W
Hinganghat, India 40 J11 20 30N 78 52 E
Hingham, U.S.A. 82 B8 48 33N 110 25W
Hingir, India 43 J10 21 57N 83 41 E
Hingoli, India 40 K10 19 41N 77 15 E
Hinna = Imi, Ethiopia 46 F3 6 28N 42 10 E
Hinnøya, Norway 8 B16 68 35N 15 50 E
Hinojosa del Duque, Spain 19 C3 38 30N 5 9W
Hinsdale, U.S.A. 79 D12 42 47N 72 29W
Hinton, Canada 72 C5 53 26N 117 34W
Hinton, U.S.A. 76 G5 37 40N 80 54W
Hirado, Japan 31 H4 33 22N 129 33 E
Hirakud Dam, India 41 J13 21 32N 83 45 E
Hiran →, India 43 H8 23 6N 79 21 E
Hirapur, India 43 G8 24 22N 79 13 E
Hiratsuka, Japan 31 G9 35 19N 139 21 E
Hiroo, Japan 30 C11 42 17N 143 19 E
Hirosaki, Japan 30 D10 40 34N 140 28 E
Hiroshima, Japan 31 G6 34 24N 132 30 E
Hiroshima □, Japan 31 G6 34 50N 133 0 E
Hisar, India 42 E6 29 12N 75 45 E
Hisb →, Iraq 44 D5 31 45N 44 17 E
Ḩismá, Si. Arabia 44 D3 28 30N 36 0 E
Hispaniola, W. Indies 89 C5 19 0N 71 0W
Hīt, Iraq 44 C4 33 38N 42 49 E
Hita, Japan 31 H5 33 20N 130 58 E
Hitachi, Japan 31 F10 36 36N 140 39 E
Hitchin, U.K. 11 F7 51 58N 0 16W
Hitoyoshi, Japan 31 H5 32 13N 130 45 E
Hitra, Norway 8 E13 63 30N 8 45 E
Hixon, Canada 72 C4 53 25N 122 35W
Ḩiyyon, N. →, Israel 47 E4 30 25N 35 10 E
Hjalmar L., Canada 73 A7 61 33N 109 25W
Hjälmaren, Sweden 9 G16 59 18N 15 40 E
Hjørring, Denmark 9 H13 57 29N 9 59 E
Hkakabo Razi, Burma 41 E20 28 25N 97 23 E
Hlobane, S. Africa 57 D5 27 42S 31 0 E
Hluhluwe, S. Africa 57 D5 28 1S 32 15 E
Hlyboka, Ukraine 17 D13 48 5N 25 56 E
Ho Chi Minh City = Thanh Pho Ho Chi Minh, Vietnam 39 G6 10 58N 106 40 E
Ho Thuong, Vietnam 38 C5 19 32N 105 48 E
Hoa Binh, Vietnam 38 B5 20 50N 105 20 E
Hoa Da, Vietnam 39 G7 11 16N 108 40 E
Hoa Hiep, Vietnam 39 G5 11 34N 105 51 E
Hoai Nhon, Vietnam 38 E7 14 28N 109 1 E
Hoang Lien Son, Vietnam 38 A4 22 0N 104 0 E
Hoanib →, Namibia 56 B2 19 27S 12 46 E
Hoare B., Canada 69 B13 65 17N 62 30W
Hoarusib →, Namibia 56 B2 19 3S 12 36 E
Hobart, Australia 62 G4 42 50S 147 21 E
Hobart, U.S.A. 81 H5 35 1N 99 6W
Hobbs, U.S.A. 81 J3 32 42N 103 8W
Hobbs Coast, Antarctica 5 D14 74 50S 131 0W
Hobe Sound, U.S.A. 77 M5 27 4N 80 8W
Hoboken, U.S.A. 79 F10 40 45N 74 4W
Hobro, Denmark 9 H13 56 39N 9 46 E
Hoburgen, Sweden 9 H18 56 55N 18 7 E
Hochfeld, Namibia 56 C2 21 28S 17 58 E
Hodaka-Dake, Japan 31 F8 36 17N 137 39 E
Hodgeville, Canada 73 C7 50 7N 106 58W
Hodgson, Canada 73 C9 51 13N 97 36W
Hódmezővásárhely, Hungary 17 E11 46 28N 20 22 E
Hodna, Chott el, Algeria 50 A6 35 26N 4 43 E
Hodonín, Czech Rep. 17 D9 48 50N 17 10 E
Hoeamdong, N. Korea 35 C16 42 30N 130 16 E
Hoek van Holland, Neths. 15 C4 52 0N 4 7 E
Hoengsŏng, S. Korea 35 F14 37 29N 127 59 E
Hoeryong, N. Korea 35 C15 42 30N 129 45 E
Hoeyang, N. Korea 35 E14 38 43N 127 36 E
Hof, Germany 16 C6 50 19N 11 55 E
Hofmeyr, S. Africa 56 E4 31 39S 25 50 E
Höfn, Iceland 8 D6 64 15N 15 13W
Hofors, Sweden 9 F17 60 31N 16 15 E
Hofsjökull, Iceland 8 D4 64 49N 18 48W
Hōfu, Japan 31 G5 34 3N 131 34 E
Hogan Group, Australia 63 F4 39 13S 147 1 E
Hogarth, Mt., Australia 62 C2 21 48S 136 58 E
Hoggar = Ahaggar, Algeria 50 D7 23 0N 6 30 E
Hogsty Reef, Bahamas 89 B5 21 41N 73 48W
Hoh →, U.S.A. 84 C2 47 45N 124 29W
Hohe Venn, Belgium 15 D6 50 30N 6 5 E
Hohenwald, U.S.A. 77 H2 35 33N 87 33W
Hoher Rhön = Rhön, Germany 16 C5 50 24N 9 58 E
Hohhot, China 34 D6 40 52N 111 40 E
Hóhlakas, Greece 23 D9 35 57N 27 53 E
Hoi An, Vietnam 38 E7 15 30N 108 19 E
Hoi Xuan, Vietnam 38 B5 20 25N 105 9 E
Hoisington, U.S.A. 80 F5 38 31N 98 47W
Hōjō, Japan 31 H6 33 58N 132 46 E
Hokianga Harbour, N.Z. 59 F4 35 31S 173 22 E
Hokitika, N.Z. 59 K3 42 42S 171 0 E
Hokkaidō □, Japan 30 C11 43 30N 143 0 E
Holbrook, U.S.A. 83 J8 34 54N 110 10W
Holden, U.S.A. 82 G7 39 6N 112 16W
Holdenville, U.S.A. 81 H6 35 5N 96 24W
Holdrege, U.S.A. 80 E5 40 26N 99 23W
Holguín, Cuba 88 B4 20 50N 76 20W
Hollams Bird I., Namibia 56 C1 24 40S 14 30 E
Holland, Mich., U.S.A. 76 D2 42 47N 86 7W
Holland, N.Y., U.S.A. 78 D6 42 38N 78 32W
Hollandale, U.S.A. 81 J9 33 10N 90 51W
Hollandia = Jayapura, Indonesia 37 E10 2 28S 140 38 E
Holley, U.S.A. 78 C6 43 14N 78 2W
Hollidaysburg, U.S.A. 78 F6 40 26N 78 24W
Hollis, U.S.A. 81 H5 34 41N 99 55W
Hollister, Calif., U.S.A. 84 J5 36 51N 121 24W
Hollister, Idaho, U.S.A. 82 E6 42 21N 114 35W
Holly Hill, U.S.A. 77 L5 29 16N 81 3W
Holly Springs, U.S.A. 81 H10 34 46N 89 27W
Hollywood, U.S.A. 77 N5 26 1N 80 9W
Holman, Canada 68 A8 70 44N 117 44W
Hólmavík, Iceland 8 D3 65 42N 21 40W
Holmen, U.S.A. 80 D9 43 58N 91 15W
Holmes Reefs, Australia 62 B4 16 27S 148 0 E
Holmsund, Sweden 8 E19 63 41N 20 20 E
Holroyd →, Australia 62 A3 14 10S 141 36 E
Holstebro, Denmark 9 H13 56 22N 8 37 E
Holsworthy, U.K. 11 G3 50 48N 4 22W
Holton, Canada 71 B8 54 31N 57 12W
Holton, U.S.A. 80 F7 39 28N 95 44W
Holtville, U.S.A. 85 N11 32 49N 115 23W
Holwerd, Neths. 15 A5 53 22N 5 54 E
Holy I., Angl., U.K. 10 D3 53 17N 4 37W
Holy I., Northumb., U.K. 10 B6 55 40N 1 47W
Holyhead, U.K. 10 D3 53 18N 4 38W
Holyoke, Colo., U.S.A. 80 E3 40 35N 102 18W
Holyoke, Mass., U.S.A. 79 D12 42 12N 72 37W
Holyrood, Canada 71 C9 47 27N 53 8W
Homa Bay, Kenya 54 C3 0 36S 34 30 E
Homalin, Burma 41 G19 24 55N 95 0 E
Homand, Iran 45 C8 32 28N 59 37 E
Homathko →, Canada 72 C4 51 0N 124 56W
Hombori, Mali 50 E5 15 20N 1 38W
Home B., Canada 69 B13 68 40N 67 10W
Home Hill, Australia 62 B4 19 43S 147 25 E
Homedale, U.S.A. 82 E5 43 37N 116 56W
Homer, Alaska, U.S.A. 68 C4 59 39N 151 33W
Homer, La., U.S.A. 81 J8 32 48N 93 4W
Homer City, U.S.A. 78 F5 40 32N 79 10W
Homestead, Australia 62 C4 20 20S 145 40 E
Homestead, U.S.A. 77 N5 25 28N 80 29W
Homewood, U.S.A. 84 F6 39 4N 120 8W
Homoine, Mozam. 57 C6 23 55S 35 8 E
Homs = Ḩimş, Syria 47 A5 34 40N 36 45 E
Homyel, Belarus 17 B16 52 28N 31 0 E
Hon Chong, Vietnam 39 G5 10 25N 104 30 E
Hon Me, Vietnam 38 C5 19 23N 105 56 E
Honan = Henan □, China 34 H8 34 0N 114 0 E
Honbetsu, Japan 30 C11 43 7N 143 37 E
Honcut, U.S.A. 84 F5 39 20N 121 32W
Hondeklipbaai, S. Africa 56 E2 30 19S 17 17 E
Hondo, Japan 31 H5 32 27N 130 12 E
Hondo, U.S.A. 81 L5 29 21N 99 9W
Hondo →, Belize 87 D7 18 25N 88 21W
Honduras ■, Cent. Amer. 88 D2 14 40N 86 30W
Honduras, G. de, Caribbean 88 C2 16 50N 87 0W
Hønefoss, Norway 9 F14 60 10N 10 18 E
Honesdale, U.S.A. 79 E9 41 34N 75 16W
Honey L., U.S.A. 84 E6 40 15N 120 19W
Honfleur, France 18 B4 49 25N 0 13 E
Hong →, Vietnam 32 D5 22 0N 104 0 E
Hong Gai, Vietnam 38 B6 20 57N 107 5 E
Hong He →, China 34 H8 32 25N 115 35 E
Hong Kong □, China 33 D6 22 11N 114 14 E
Hongch'ŏn, S. Korea 35 F14 37 44N 127 53 E
Hongjiang, China 33 D5 27 7N 109 59 E
Hongliu He →, China 34 F5 38 0N 109 50 E
Hongor, Mongolia 34 B7 45 45N 112 50 E
Hongsa, Laos 38 C3 19 43N 101 20 E
Hongshui He →, China 33 D5 23 48N 109 30 E
Hongsŏng, S. Korea 35 F14 36 37N 126 38 E
Hongtong, China 34 F6 36 16N 111 40 E
Honguedo, Détroit d', Canada 71 C7 49 15N 64 0W
Hongwon, N. Korea 35 E14 40 0N 127 56 E
Hongze Hu, China 35 H10 33 15N 118 35 E
Honiara, Solomon Is. 64 H7 9 27S 159 57 E
Honiton, U.K. 11 G4 50 47N 3 11W
Honjō, Japan 30 E10 39 23N 140 3 E
Honningsvåg, Norway 8 A21 70 59N 25 59 E
Honolulu, U.S.A. 74 H16 21 19N 157 52W
Honshū, Japan 33 C8 36 0N 138 0 E
Hood, Mt., U.S.A. 82 D3 45 23N 121 42W
Hood, Pt., Australia 61 F2 34 23S 119 34 E
Hood River, U.S.A. 82 D3 45 43N 121 31W
Hoodsport, U.S.A. 84 C3 47 24N 123 9W
Hoogeveen, Neths. 15 B6 52 44N 6 28 E
Hoogezand-Sappemeer, Neths. 15 A6 53 9N 6 45 E
Hooghly = Hugli →, India 43 J13 21 56N 88 4 E
Hooghly-Chinsura = Chunchura, India 43 H13 22 53N 88 27 E
Hook Hd., Ireland 13 D5 52 7N 6 56W
Hook I., Australia 62 C4 20 4S 149 0 E
Hook of Holland = Hoek van Holland, Neths. 15 C4 52 0N 4 7 E
Hooker, U.S.A. 81 G4 36 52N 101 13W
Hooker Creek, Australia 60 C5 18 23S 130 38 E
Hoonah, U.S.A. 72 B1 58 7N 135 27W
Hooper Bay, U.S.A. 68 B3 61 32N 166 6W
Hoopeston, U.S.A. 76 E2 40 28N 87 40W
Hoopstad, S. Africa 56 D4 27 50S 25 55 E
Hoorn, Neths. 15 B5 52 38N 5 4 E
Hoover, U.S.A. 77 J2 33 20N 86 11W
Hoover Dam, U.S.A. 85 K12 36 1N 114 44W
Hooversville, U.S.A. 78 F6 40 9N 78 55W
Hop Bottom, U.S.A. 79 E9 41 42N 75 46W
Hope, Canada 72 D4 49 25N 121 25W
Hope, Ariz., U.S.A. 85 M13 33 43N 113 42W
Hope, Ark., U.S.A. 81 J8 33 40N 93 36W
Hope, L., S. Austral., Australia 63 D2 28 24S 139 18 E
Hope, L., W. Austral., Australia 61 F3 32 35S 120 15 E
Hope I., Canada 78 B4 44 55N 80 11W
Hope Town, Bahamas 88 A4 26 35N 76 57W
Hopedale, Canada 71 A7 55 28N 60 13W
Hopedale, U.S.A. 79 D13 42 8N 71 33W
Hopefield, S. Africa 56 E2 33 3S 18 22 E
Hopei = Hebei □, China 34 E9 39 0N 116 0 E
Hopelchén, Mexico 87 D7 19 46N 89 50W
Hopetoun, Australia 61 F3 33 57S 120 7 E
Hopetown, S. Africa 56 D3 29 34S 24 3 E
Hopevale, Australia 62 B4 15 16S 145 20 E
Hopewell, U.S.A. 76 G7 37 18N 77 17W
Hopkins, L., Australia 60 D4 24 15S 128 35 E
Hopkinsville, U.S.A. 77 G2 36 52N 87 29W
Hopland, U.S.A. 84 G3 38 58N 123 7W
Hoquiam, U.S.A. 84 D3 46 59N 123 53W
Horden Hills, Australia 60 D5 20 15S 130 0 E
Horinger, China 34 D6 40 28N 111 48 E
Horlick Mts., Antarctica 5 E15 84 0S 102 0W
Horlivka, Ukraine 25 E6 48 19N 38 5 E
Hormak, Iran 45 D9 29 58N 60 51 E
Hormoz, Iran 45 E7 27 35N 55 0 E
Hormoz, Jaz.-ye, Iran 45 E8 27 8N 56 28 E
Hormozgān □, Iran 45 E8 27 30N 56 0 E
Hormuz, Kūh-e, Iran 45 E7 27 27N 55 10 E
Hormuz, Str. of, The Gulf 45 E8 26 30N 56 30 E
Horn, Austria 16 D8 48 39N 15 40 E
Horn, Iceland 8 C2 66 28N 22 28W
Horn →, Canada 72 A5 61 30N 118 1W
Horn, Cape = Hornos, C. de, Chile 96 H3 55 50S 67 30W
Horn Head, Ireland 13 A3 55 14N 8 0W
Horn I., Australia 62 A3 10 37S 142 17 E
Horn Mts., Canada 72 A5 62 15N 119 15W
Hornavan, Sweden 8 C17 66 15N 17 30 E
Hornbeck, U.S.A. 81 K8 31 20N 93 24W
Hornbrook, U.S.A. 82 F2 41 55N 122 33W
Horncastle, U.K. 10 D7 53 13N 0 7W
Hornell, U.S.A. 78 D7 42 20N 77 40W
Hornell L., Canada 72 A5 62 20N 119 25W
Hornepayne, Canada 70 C3 49 14N 84 48W
Hornings Mills, Canada 78 B4 44 9N 80 12W
Hornitos, U.S.A. 84 H6 37 30N 120 14W
Hornos, C. de, Chile 96 H3 55 50S 67 30W
Hornsea, U.K. 10 D7 53 55N 0 11W
Horobetsu, Japan 30 C10 42 24N 141 6 E
Horodenka, Ukraine 17 D13 48 41N 25 29 E
Horodok, Khmelnytskyy, Ukraine 17 D14 49 10N 26 34 E
Horodok, Lviv, Ukraine 17 D12 49 46N 23 32 E
Horokhiv, Ukraine 17 C13 50 30N 24 45 E
Horqin Youyi Qianqi, China 35 A12 46 5N 122 3 E
Horqueta, Paraguay 94 A4 23 15S 56 55W
Horse Creek, U.S.A. 80 E3 41 57N 105 10W
Horse Is., Canada 71 B8 50 15N 55 50W
Horsefly L., Canada 72 C4 52 25N 121 0W
Horseheads, U.S.A. 78 D8 42 10N 76 49W
Horsens, Denmark 9 J13 55 52N 9 51 E
Horsham, U.K. 11 F7 51 4N 0 20W
Horten, Norway 9 G14 59 25N 10 32 E
Horton, U.S.A. 80 F7 39 40N 95 32W
Horton →, Canada 68 B7 69 56N 126 52W
Horwood L., Canada 70 C3 48 5N 82 20W
Hose, Gunung-Gunung, Malaysia 36 D4 2 5N 114 6 E
Ḩoseynābād, Khuzestān, Iran 45 C6 32 45N 48 20 E
Ḩoseynābād, Kordestān, Iran 44 C5 35 33N 47 8 E
Hoshangabad, India 42 H7 22 45N 77 45 E
Hoshiarpur, India 42 D6 31 30N 75 58 E
Hospet, India 40 M10 15 15N 76 20 E
Hoste, I., Chile 96 H3 55 0S 69 0W
Hot, Thailand 38 C2 18 8N 98 29 E
Hot Creek Range, U.S.A. 82 G6 38 40N 116 20W
Hot Springs, Ark., U.S.A. 81 H8 34 31N 93 3W
Hot Springs, S. Dak., U.S.A. 80 D3 43 26N 103 29W
Hotagen, Sweden 8 E16 63 50N 14 30 E
Hotan, China 32 C2 37 25N 79 55 E
Hotazel, S. Africa 56 D3 27 17S 22 58 E
Hotchkiss, U.S.A. 83 G10 38 48N 107 43W
Hotham, C., Australia 60 B5 12 2S 131 18 E
Hoting, Sweden 8 D17 64 8N 16 15 E
Hotte, Massif de la, Haiti 89 C5 18 30N 73 45W
Hottentotsbaai, Namibia 56 D1 26 8S 14 59 E
Houei Sai, Laos 38 B3 20 18N 100 26 E
Houffalize, Belgium 15 D5 50 8N 5 48 E
Houghton, Mich., U.S.A. 80 B10 47 7N 88 34W
Houghton, N.Y., U.S.A. 78 D6 42 25N 78 10W
Houghton L., U.S.A. 76 C3 44 21N 84 44W
Houhora Heads, N.Z. 59 F4 34 49S 173 9 E
Houlton, U.S.A. 77 B12 46 8N 67 51W
Houma, U.S.A. 81 L9 29 36N 90 43W
Housatonic →, U.S.A. 79 E11 41 10N 73 7W
Houston, Canada 72 C3 54 25N 126 39W
Houston, Mo., U.S.A. 81 G9 37 22N 91 58W
Houston, Tex., U.S.A. 81 L7 29 46N 95 22W
Hout →, S. Africa 57 C4 23 4S 29 36 E
Houtkraal, S. Africa 56 E3 30 23S 24 5 E
Houtman Abrolhos, Australia 61 E1 28 43S 113 48 E
Hovd, Mongolia 32 B4 48 2N 91 37 E
Hove, U.K. 11 G7 50 50N 0 10W
Hoveyzeh, Iran 45 D6 31 27N 48 4 E
Hövsgöl, Mongolia 34 C5 43 37N 109 39 E
Hövsgöl Nuur, Mongolia 32 A5 51 0N 100 30 E
Howard, Australia 63 D5 25 16S 152 32 E
Howard, Pa., U.S.A. 78 F7 41 1N 77 40W
Howard, S. Dak., U.S.A. 80 C6 44 1N 97 32W
Howe, U.S.A. 82 E7 43 48N 113 0W
Howe I., Canada 79 B8 44 16N 76 17W
Howell, U.S.A. 76 D4 42 36N 83 56W
Howick, Canada 79 A11 45 11N 73 51W
Howick, S. Africa 57 D5 29 28S 30 14 E
Howick Group, Australia 62 A4 14 20S 145 30 E
Howitt, L., Australia 63 D2 27 40S 138 40 E
Howland I., Pac. Oc. 64 G10 0 48N 176 38W
Howrah = Haora, India 43 H13 22 37N 88 20 E
Howth Hd., Ireland 13 C5 53 22N 6 3W
Höxter, Germany 16 C5 51 46N 9 22 E
Hoy, U.K. 12 C5 58 50N 3 15W
Høyanger, Norway 9 F12 61 13N 6 4 E
Hoyerswerda, Germany 16 C8 51 26N 14 14 E
Hoylake, U.K. 10 D4 53 24N 3 10W
Hpa-an = Pa-an, Burma 41 L20 16 51N 97 40 E
Hpungan Pass, Burma 41 F20 27 30N 96 55 E
Hradec Králové, Czech Rep. 16 C8 50 15N 15 50 E
Hrodna, Belarus 17 B12 53 42N 23 52 E
Hrodzyanka, Belarus 17 B15 53 31N 28 42 E
Hron →, Slovak Rep. 17 E10 47 49N 18 45 E
Hrvatska = Croatia ■, Europe 16 F9 45 20N 16 0 E

Indramayu

Hrymayliv, *Ukraine* .... **17 D14** 49 20N 26 5 E
Hsenwi, *Burma* .... **41 H20** 23 22N 97 55 E
Hsiamen = Xiamen, *China* **33 D6** 24 25N 118 4 E
Hsian = Xi'an, *China* ...... **34 G5** 34 15N 109 0 E
Hsinchu, *Taiwan* .... **33 D7** 24 48N 120 58 E
Hsinhailien = Lianyungang, *China* .... **35 G10** 34 40N 119 11 E
Hsüchou = Xuzhou, *China* . **35 G9** 34 18N 117 10 E
Hu Xian, *China* .... **34 G5** 34 8N 108 42 E
Hua Hin, *Thailand* .... **38 F2** 12 34N 99 58 E
Hua Xian, *Henan, China* ... **34 G8** 35 30N 114 30 E
Hua Xian, *Shaanxi, China* . **34 G5** 34 30N 109 48 E
Huab →, *Namibia* .... **56 B2** 20 52S 13 25 E
Huachinera, *Mexico* **86 A3** 30 9N 108 55W
Huacho, *Peru* **92 F3** 11 10S 77 35W
Huade, *China* .... **34 D7** 41 55N 113 59 E
Huadian, *China* .... **35 C14** 43 0N 126 40 E
Huai He →, *China* .... **33 C6** 33 0N 118 30 E
Huai Yot, *Thailand* .... **39 J2** 7 45N 99 37 E
Huai'an, *Hebei, China* ..... **34 D8** 40 30N 114 20 E
Huai'an, *Jiangsu, China* ... **35 H10** 33 30N 119 10 E
Huaibei, *China* .... **34 G9** 34 0N 116 48 E
Huaide = Gongzhuling, *China* .... **35 C13** 43 30N 124 40 E
Huaidezhen, *China* .... **35 C13** 43 48N 124 50 E
Huainan, *China* .... **33 C6** 32 38N 116 58 E
Huairen, *China* .... **34 E7** 39 48N 113 20 E
Huairou, *China* .... **34 D9** 40 20N 116 35 E
Huaiyang, *China* .... **34 H8** 33 40N 114 52 E
Huaiyin, *China* .... **35 H10** 33 30N 119 2 E
Huaiyuan, *China* .... **35 H9** 32 55N 117 10 E
Huajianzi, *China* .... **35 D13** 41 23N 125 20 E
Huajuapan de Leon, *Mexico* **87 D5** 17 50N 97 48W
Hualapai Peak, *U.S.A.* **83 J7** 35 5N 113 54W
Huallaga →, *Peru* **92 E3** 5 15S 75 30W
Huambo, *Angola* .... **53 G3** 12 42S 15 54 E
Huan Jiang →, *China* ..... **34 G5** 34 28N 109 0 E
Huan Xian, *China* .... **34 F4** 36 33N 107 7 E
Huancabamba, *Peru* **92 E3** 5 10S 79 15W
Huancane, *Peru* **92 G5** 15 10S 69 44W
Huancavelica, *Peru* **92 F3** 12 50S 75 5W
Huancayo, *Peru* **92 F3** 12 5S 75 12W
Huanchaca, *Bolivia* **92 H5** 20 15S 66 40W
Huang Hai = Yellow Sea, *China* .... **35 G12** 35 0N 123 0 E
Huang He →, *China* ...... **35 F10** 37 55N 118 50 E
Huang Xian, *China* .... **35 F11** 37 38N 120 30 E
Huangling, *China* .... **34 G5** 35 34N 109 15 E
Huanglong, *China* .... **34 G5** 35 30N 109 59 E
Huangshan, *China* .... **33 D6** 29 42N 118 25 E
Huangshi, *China* .... **33 C6** 30 10N 115 3 E
Huangsongdian, *China* ... **35 C14** 43 45N 127 25 E
Huantai, *China* .... **35 F9** 36 58N 117 56 E
Huánuco, *Peru* **92 E3** 9 55S 76 15W
Huaraz, *Peru* **92 E3** 9 30S 77 32W
Huarmey, *Peru* **92 F3** 10 5S 78 5W
Huascarán, *Peru* **92 E3** 9 8S 77 36W
Huasco, *Chile* **94 B1** 28 30S 71 15W
Huasco →, *Chile* **94 B1** 28 27S 71 13W
Huasna, *U.S.A.* **85 K6** 35 6N 120 24W
Huatabampo, *Mexico* **86 B3** 26 50N 109 50W
Huauchinango, *Mexico* ... **87 C5** 20 11N 98 3W
Huautla de Jiménez, *Mexico* **87 D5** 18 8N 96 51W
Huay Namota, *Mexico* **86 C4** 21 56N 104 30W
Huayin, *China* .... **34 G6** 34 35N 110 5 E
Hubbard, *Ohio, U.S.A.* **78 E4** 41 9N 80 34W
Hubbard, *Tex., U.S.A.* **81 K6** 31 51N 96 48W
Hubbart Pt., *Canada* **73 B10** 59 21N 94 41W
Hubei □, *China* .... **33 C6** 31 0N 112 0 E
Huch'ang, *N. Korea* .... **35 D14** 41 25N 127 2 E
Hucknall, *U.K.* **10 D6** 53 3N 1 13W
Huddersfield, *U.K.* **10 D6** 53 39N 1 47W
Hudiksvall, *Sweden* ...... **9 F17** 61 43N 17 10 E
Hudson, *Canada* **70 B1** 50 6N 92 9W
Hudson, *Mass., U.S.A.* **79 D13** 42 23N 71 34W
Hudson, *N.Y., U.S.A.* **79 D11** 42 15N 73 46W
Hudson, *Wis., U.S.A.* **80 C8** 44 58N 92 45W
Hudson, *Wyo., U.S.A.* **82 E9** 42 54N 108 35W
Hudson →, *U.S.A.* **79 F10** 40 42N 74 2W
Hudson Bay, *Nunavut, Canada* **69 C11** 60 0N 86 0W
Hudson Bay, *Sask., Canada* **73 C8** 52 51N 102 23W
Hudson Falls, *U.S.A.* **79 C11** 43 18N 73 35W
Hudson Mts., *Antarctica* .. **5 D16** 74 32S 99 20W
Hudson Str., *Canada* **69 B13** 62 0N 70 0W
Hudson's Hope, *Canada* .. **72 B4** 56 0N 121 54W
Hue, *Vietnam* .... **38 D6** 16 30N 107 35 E
Huehuetenango, *Guatemala* **88 C1** 15 20N 91 28W
Huejúcar, *Mexico* **86 C4** 22 21N 103 13W
Huelva, *Spain* **19 D2** 37 18N 6 57W
Huentelauquén, *Chile* **94 C1** 31 38S 71 33W
Huerta, Sa. de la, *Argentina* **94 C2** 31 10S 67 30W
Huesca, *Spain* **19 A5** 42 8N 0 25W
Huetamo, *Mexico* **86 D4** 18 36N 100 54W
Hugh →, *Australia* .... **62 D1** 25 1S 134 1 E
Hughenden, *Australia* .... **62 C3** 20 52S 144 10 E
Hughes, *Australia* .... **61 F4** 30 42S 129 31 E
Hughesville, *U.S.A.* **79 E8** 41 14N 76 44W
Hugli →, *India* .... **43 J13** 21 56N 88 4 E
Hugo, *Colo., U.S.A.* **80 F3** 39 8N 103 28W
Hugo, *Okla., U.S.A.* **81 H7** 34 1N 95 31W
Hugoton, *U.S.A.* **81 G4** 37 11N 101 21W
Hui Xian = Huixian, *China* . **34 G7** 35 27N 113 12 E
Hui Xian, *China* .... **34 H4** 33 50N 106 4 E
Hui'anbu, *China* .... **34 F4** 37 28N 106 38 E
Huichapán, *Mexico* **87 C5** 20 24N 99 40W
Huifa He →, *China* ...... **35 C14** 43 0N 127 50 E
Huila, Nevado del, *Colombia* **92 C3** 3 0N 76 0W
Huimin, *China* .... **35 F9** 37 27N 117 28 E
Huinan, *China* .... **35 C14** 42 40N 126 2 E
Huinca Renancó, *Argentina* **94 C3** 34 51S 64 22W
Huining, *China* .... **34 G3** 35 38N 105 0 E
Huinong, *China* .... **34 E4** 39 5N 106 35 E
Huisache, *Mexico* **86 C4** 22 55N 100 25W
Huiting, *China* .... **34 G9** 34 5N 116 5 E
Huixian, *China* .... **34 G7** 35 27N 113 12 E
Huixtla, *Mexico* **87 D6** 15 9N 92 28W
Huize, *China* .... **32 D5** 26 24N 103 15 E
Hukawng Valley, *Burma* .. **41 F20** 26 30N 96 30 E
Hukuntsi, *Botswana* ...... **56 C3** 23 58S 21 45 E
Ḥulayfā', *Si. Arabia* ...... **44 E4** 25 58N 40 45 E
Huld = Ulaanjirem, *Mongolia* .... **34 B3** 45 5N 105 30 E
Hulin He →, *China* .... **35 B12** 45 0N 122 10 E
Hull = Kingston upon Hull, *U.K.* **10 D7** 53 45N 0 21W
Hull, *Canada* **79 A9** 45 25N 75 44W
Hull →, *U.K.* **10 D7** 53 44N 0 20W
Hulst, *Neths.* .... **15 C4** 51 17N 4 2 E
Hulun Nur, *China* .... **33 B6** 49 0N 117 30 E
Humahuaca, *Argentina* ... **94 A2** 23 10S 65 25W
Humaitá, *Brazil* **92 E6** 7 35S 63 1W
Humaitá, *Paraguay* **94 B4** 27 2S 58 31W
Humansdorp, *S. Africa* ... **56 E3** 34 2S 24 46 E
Humbe, *Angola* .... **56 B1** 16 40S 14 55 E
Humber →, *U.K.* **10 D7** 53 42N 0 27W
Humboldt, *Canada* **73 C7** 52 15N 105 9W
Humboldt, *Iowa, U.S.A.* ... **80 D7** 42 44N 94 13W
Humboldt, *Tenn., U.S.A.* .. **81 H10** 35 50N 88 55W
Humboldt →, *U.S.A.* **82 F4** 39 59N 118 36W
Humboldt Gletscher, *Greenland* **4 B4** 79 30N 62 0W
Hume, *U.S.A.* **84 J8** 36 48N 118 54W
Humenné, *Slovak Rep.* .... **17 D11** 48 55N 21 50 E
Humphreys, Mt., *U.S.A.* ... **84 H8** 37 17N 118 40W
Humphreys Peak, *U.S.A.* .. **83 J8** 35 21N 111 41W
Humptulips, *U.S.A.* **84 C3** 47 14N 123 57W
Hūn, *Libya* .... **51 C9** 29 2N 16 0 E
Hun Jiang →, *China* ...... **35 D13** 40 50N 125 38 E
Húnaflói, *Iceland* **8 D3** 65 50N 20 50W
Hunan □, *China* .... **33 D6** 27 30N 112 0 E
Hunchun, *China* .... **35 C16** 42 52N 130 28 E
Hundewali, *Pakistan* ..... **42 D5** 31 55N 72 38 E
Hundred Mile House, *Canada* **72 C4** 51 38N 121 18W
Hunedoara, *Romania* ..... **17 F12** 45 40N 22 50 E
Hung Yen, *Vietnam* .... **38 B6** 20 39N 106 4 E
Hungary ■, *Europe* ...... **17 E10** 47 20N 19 20 E
Hungary, Plain of, *Europe* . **6 F10** 47 0N 20 0 E
Hungerford, *Australia* ..... **63 D3** 28 58S 144 24 E
Hŭngnam, *N. Korea* ...... **35 E14** 39 49N 127 45 E
Hunsberge, *Namibia* ...... **56 D2** 27 45S 17 12 E
Hunsrück, *Germany* ...... **16 D4** 49 56N 7 27 E
Hunstanton, *U.K.* .... **10 E8** 52 56N 0 29 E
Hunter, *U.S.A.* **79 D10** 42 13N 74 13W
Hunter I., *Australia* .... **62 G3** 40 30S 144 45 E
Hunter I., *Canada* **72 C3** 51 55N 128 0W
Hunters Road, *Zimbabwe* . **55 F2** 19 9S 29 49 E
Hunterville, *N.Z.* .... **59 H5** 39 56S 175 35 E
Huntingburg, *U.S.A.* **76 F2** 38 18N 86 57W
Huntingdon, *Canada* **70 C5** 45 6N 74 10W
Huntingdon, *U.K.* **11 E7** 52 20N 0 11W
Huntingdon, *U.S.A.* **78 F6** 40 30N 78 1W
Huntington, *Ind., U.S.A.* ... **76 E3** 40 53N 85 30W
Huntington, *Oreg., U.S.A.* . **82 D5** 44 21N 117 16W
Huntington, *Utah, U.S.A.* .. **82 G8** 39 20N 110 58W
Huntington, *W. Va., U.S.A.* **76 F4** 38 25N 82 27W
Huntington Beach, *U.S.A.* . **85 M9** 33 40N 118 5W
Huntington Station, *U.S.A.* **79 F11** 40 52N 73 26W
Huntly, *N.Z.* .... **59 G5** 37 34S 175 11 E
Huntly, *U.K.* **12 D6** 57 27N 2 47W
Huntsville, *Canada* **78 A5** 45 20N 79 14W
Huntsville, *Ala., U.S.A.* ... **77 H2** 34 44N 86 35W
Huntsville, *Tex., U.S.A.* ... **81 K7** 30 43N 95 33W
Hunyani →, *Zimbabwe* ... **55 F3** 15 57S 30 39 E
Hunyuan, *China* .... **34 E7** 39 42N 113 42 E
Hunza →, *India* .... **43 B6** 35 54N 74 20 E
Huo Xian = Huozhou, *China* **34 F6** 36 36N 111 42 E
Huong Hoa, *Vietnam* ..... **38 D6** 16 37N 106 45 E
Huong Khe, *Vietnam* ..... **38 C5** 18 13N 105 41 E
Huonville, *Australia* ...... **62 G4** 43 0S 147 5 E
Huozhou, *China* .... **34 F6** 36 36N 111 42 E
Hupeh = Hubei □, *China* . **33 C6** 31 0N 112 0 E
Ḥūr, *Iran* .... **45 D8** 30 50N 57 7 E
Hurd, C., *Canada* **78 A3** 45 13N 81 44W
Hure Qi, *China* .... **35 C11** 42 45N 121 45 E
Hurghada, *Egypt* .... **51 C12** 27 15N 33 50 E
Hurley, *N. Mex., U.S.A.* ... **83 K9** 32 42N 108 8W
Hurley, *Wis., U.S.A.* **80 B9** 46 27N 90 11W
Huron, *Calif., U.S.A.* **84 J6** 36 12N 120 6W
Huron, *Ohio, U.S.A.* **78 E2** 41 24N 82 33W
Huron, *S. Dak., U.S.A.* **80 C5** 44 22N 98 13W
Huron, L., *U.S.A.* **78 B2** 44 30N 82 40W
Hurricane, *U.S.A.* **83 H7** 37 11N 113 17W
Hurunui →, *N.Z.* .... **59 K4** 42 54S 173 18 E
Húsavík, *Iceland* **8 C5** 66 3N 17 21W
Huşi, *Romania* .... **17 E15** 46 41N 28 7 E
Huskvarna, *Sweden* ...... **9 H16** 57 47N 14 15 E
Hustadvika, *Norway* ...... **8 E12** 63 0N 7 0 E
Hustontown, *U.S.A.* **78 F6** 40 3N 78 2W
Hutchinson, *Kans., U.S.A.* . **81 F6** 38 5N 97 56W
Hutchinson, *Minn., U.S.A.* . **80 C7** 44 54N 94 22W
Hutte Sauvage, L. de la, *Canada* **71 A7** 56 15N 64 45W
Hutton, Mt., *Australia* .... **63 D4** 25 51S 148 20 E
Huy, *Belgium* .... **15 D5** 50 31N 5 15 E
Huzhou, *China* .... **33 C7** 30 51N 120 8 E
Hvammstangi, *Iceland* **8 D3** 65 24N 20 57W
Hvar, *Croatia* .... **20 C7** 43 11N 16 28 E
Hvítá →, *Iceland* **8 D3** 64 30N 21 58W
Hwachŏn-chŏsuji, *S. Korea* **35 E14** 38 5N 127 50 E
Hwang Ho = Huang He →, *China* .... **35 F10** 37 55N 118 50 E
Hwange, *Zimbabwe* ...... **55 F2** 18 18S 26 30 E
Hwange Nat. Park, *Zimbabwe* .... **56 B4** 19 0S 26 30 E
Hyannis, *Mass., U.S.A.* ... **76 E10** 41 39N 70 17W
Hyannis, *Nebr., U.S.A.* ... **80 E4** 42 0N 101 46W
Hyargas Nuur, *Mongolia* .. **32 B4** 49 0N 93 0 E
Hydaburg, *U.S.A.* **72 B2** 55 15N 132 50W
Hyde Park, *U.S.A.* **79 E11** 41 47N 73 56W
Hyden, *Australia* .... **61 F2** 32 24S 118 53 E
Hyder, *U.S.A.* **72 B2** 55 55N 130 5W
Hyderabad, *India* .... **40 L11** 17 22N 78 29 E
Hyderabad, *Pakistan* ..... **42 G3** 25 23N 68 24 E
Hyères, *France* .... **18 E7** 43 8N 6 9 E
Hyères, Îs. d', *France* .... **18 E7** 43 0N 6 20 E
Hyesan, *N. Korea* .... **35 D15** 41 20N 128 10 E
Hyland →, *Canada* **72 B3** 59 52N 128 12W
Hymia, *India* .... **43 C8** 33 40N 78 2 E
Hyndman Peak, *U.S.A.* ... **82 E6** 43 45N 114 8W
Hyōgo □, *Japan* .... **31 G7** 35 15N 134 50 E
Hyrum, *U.S.A.* **82 F8** 41 38N 111 51W
Hysham, *U.S.A.* **82 C10** 46 18N 107 14W
Hythe, *U.K.* .... **11 F9** 51 4N 1 5 E
Hyūga, *Japan* .... **31 H5** 32 25N 131 35 E
Hyvinge = Hyvinkää, *Finland* .... **9 F21** 60 38N 24 50 E
Hyvinkää, *Finland* .... **9 F21** 60 38N 24 50 E

I

I-n-Gall, *Niger* .... **50 E7** 16 51N 7 1 E
Iaco →, *Brazil* **92 E5** 9 3S 68 34W
Iakora, *Madag.* .... **57 C8** 23 6S 46 40 E
Ialomiţa →, *Romania* ..... **17 F14** 44 42N 27 51 E
Iaşi, *Romania* .... **17 E14** 47 10N 27 40 E
Ib →, *India* .... **43 J10** 21 34N 83 48 E
Iba, *Phil.* .... **37 A6** 15 22N 120 0 E
Ibadan, *Nigeria* .... **50 G6** 7 22N 3 58 E
Ibagué, *Colombia* **92 C3** 4 20N 75 20W
Ibar →, *Serbia, Yug.* ...... **21 C9** 43 43N 20 45 E
Ibaraki □, *Japan* .... **31 F10** 36 10N 140 10 E
Ibarra, *Ecuador* **92 C3** 0 21N 78 7W
Ibembo, *Dem. Rep. of the Congo* .... **54 B1** 2 35N 23 35 E
Ibera, L., *Argentina* **94 B4** 28 30S 57 9W
Iberian Peninsula, *Europe* . **6 H5** 40 0N 5 0W
Iberville, *Canada* **79 A11** 45 19N 73 17W
Iberville, Lac d', *Canada* ... **70 A5** 55 55N 73 15W
Ibiá, *Brazil* **93 G9** 19 30S 46 30W
Ibiapaba, Sa. da, *Brazil* **93 D10** 4 0S 41 30W
Ibicuí →, *Brazil* **95 B4** 29 25S 56 47W
Ibicuy, *Argentina* **94 C4** 33 55S 59 10W
Ibiza = Eivissa, *Spain* ..... **22 C7** 38 54N 1 26 E
Ibo, *Mozam.* .... **55 E5** 12 22S 40 40 E
Ibonma, *Indonesia* .... **37 E8** 3 29S 133 31 E
Ibotirama, *Brazil* **93 F10** 12 13S 43 12W
Ibrāhīm →, *Lebanon* ..... **47 A4** 34 4N 35 38 E
'Ibrī, *Oman* .... **45 F8** 23 14N 56 30 E
Ibu, *Indonesia* .... **37 D7** 1 35N 127 33 E
Ibusuki, *Japan* .... **31 J5** 31 12N 130 40 E
Ica, *Peru* **92 F3** 14 0S 75 48W
Iça →, *Brazil* **92 D5** 2 55S 67 58W
Içana, *Brazil* **92 C5** 0 21N 67 19W
Içana →, *Brazil* **92 C5** 0 26N 67 19W
Içel = Mersin, *Turkey* ..... **25 G5** 36 51N 34 36 E
Iceland ■, *Europe* **8 D4** 64 45N 19 0W
Ich'ang = Yichang, *China* .. **33 C6** 30 40N 111 20 E
Ichchapuram, *India* .... **41 K14** 19 10N 84 40 E
Ichhawar, *India* .... **42 H7** 23 1N 77 1 E
Ichihara, *Japan* .... **31 G10** 35 28N 140 5 E
Ichikawa, *Japan* .... **31 G9** 35 44N 139 55 E
Ichilo →, *Bolivia* **92 G6** 15 57S 64 50W
Ichinohe, *Japan* .... **30 D10** 40 13N 141 17 E
Ichinomiya, *Japan* .... **31 G8** 35 18N 136 48 E
Ichinoseki, *Japan* .... **30 E10** 38 55N 141 8 E
Icod, *Canary Is.* **22 F3** 28 22N 16 43W
Ida Grove, *U.S.A.* **80 D7** 42 21N 95 28W
Idabel, *U.S.A.* **81 J7** 33 54N 94 50W
Idaho □, *U.S.A.* **82 D7** 45 0N 115 0W
Idaho City, *U.S.A.* **82 E6** 43 50N 115 50W
Idaho Falls, *U.S.A.* **82 E7** 43 30N 112 2W
Idar-Oberstein, *Germany* .. **16 D4** 49 43N 7 16 E
Idfû, *Egypt* .... **51 D12** 24 55N 32 49 E
Ídhi Óros, *Greece* .... **23 D6** 35 15N 24 45 E
Ídhra, *Greece* .... **21 F10** 37 20N 23 28 E
Idi, *Indonesia* .... **36 C1** 5 2N 97 37 E
Idiofa, *Dem. Rep. of the Congo* .... **52 E3** 4 55S 19 42 E
Idlib, *Syria* .... **44 C3** 35 55N 36 36 E
Idria, *U.S.A.* **84 J6** 36 25N 120 41W
Idutywa, *S. Africa* .... **57 E4** 32 8S 28 18 E
Ieper, *Belgium* .... **15 D2** 50 51N 2 53 E
Ierápetra, *Greece* .... **23 E7** 35 1N 25 44 E
Iesi, *Italy* .... **20 C5** 43 31N 13 14 E
Ifakara, *Tanzania* .... **52 F7** 8 8S 36 41 E
'Ifāl, W. al →, *Si. Arabia* .. **44 D2** 28 7N 35 3 E
Ifanadiana, *Madag.* .... **57 C8** 21 19S 47 39 E
Ife, *Nigeria* .... **50 G6** 7 30N 4 31 E
Iffley, *Australia* .... **62 B3** 18 53S 141 12 E
Iforas, Adrar des, *Africa* ... **50 E6** 19 40N 1 40 E
Ifould, L., *Australia* .... **61 F5** 30 52S 132 6 E
Iganga, *Uganda* .... **54 B3** 0 37N 33 28 E
Igarapava, *Brazil* **93 H9** 20 3S 47 47W
Igarka, *Russia* .... **26 C9** 67 30N 86 33 E
Igatimi, *Paraguay* **95 A4** 24 5S 55 40W
Iggesund, *Sweden* .... **9 F17** 61 39N 17 10 E
Iglésias, *Italy* .... **20 E3** 39 19N 8 32 E
Igloolik, *Canada* **69 B11** 69 20N 81 49W
Igluligaarjuk, *Canada* **69 B10** 63 21N 90 42W
Iglulik = Igloolik, *Canada* .. **69 B11** 69 20N 81 49W
Ignace, *Canada* **70 C1** 49 30N 91 40W
İğneada Burnu, *Turkey* .... **21 D13** 41 53N 28 2 E
Igoumenítsa, *Greece* ...... **21 E9** 39 32N 20 18 E
Iguaçu →, *Brazil* **95 B5** 25 36S 54 36W
Iguaçu, Cat. del, *Brazil* **95 B5** 25 41S 54 26W
Iguaçu Falls = Iguaçu, Cat. del, *Brazil* **95 B5** 25 41S 54 26W
Iguala, *Mexico* **87 D5** 18 20N 99 40W
Igualada, *Spain* .... **19 B6** 41 37N 1 37 E
Iguassu = Iguaçu →, *Brazil* **95 B5** 25 36S 54 36W
Iguatu, *Brazil* **93 E11** 6 20S 39 18W
Iharana, *Madag.* .... **57 A9** 13 25S 50 0 E
Ihbulag, *Mongolia* .... **34 C4** 43 11N 107 10 E
Iheya-Shima, *Japan* ...... **31 L3** 27 4N 127 58 E
Ihosy, *Madag.* .... **57 C8** 22 24S 46 8 E
Ihotry, Farihy, *Madag.* .... **57 C7** 21 56S 43 41 E
Ii, *Finland* .... **8 D21** 65 19N 25 22 E
Ii-Shima, *Japan* .... **31 L3** 26 43N 127 47 E
Iida, *Japan* .... **31 G8** 35 35N 137 50 E
Iijoki →, *Finland* .... **8 D21** 65 20N 25 20 E
Iisalmi, *Finland* .... **8 E22** 63 32N 27 10 E
Iiyama, *Japan* .... **31 F9** 36 51N 138 22 E
Iizuka, *Japan* .... **31 H5** 33 38N 130 42 E
Ijebu-Ode, *Nigeria* .... **50 G6** 6 47N 3 58 E
IJmuiden, *Neths.* .... **15 B4** 52 28N 4 35 E
IJssel →, *Neths.* .... **15 B5** 52 35N 5 50 E
IJsselmeer, *Neths.* .... **15 B5** 52 45N 5 20 E
Ijuí, *Brazil* **95 B5** 28 23S 53 55W
Ijuí →, *Brazil* **95 B4** 27 58S 55 20W
Ikalamavony, *Madag.* ..... **57 C8** 21 9S 46 35 E
Ikaluktutiak, *Canada* **68 B9** 69 10N 105 0W
Ikare, *Nigeria* .... **50 G7** 7 32N 5 40 E
Ikaría, *Greece* .... **21 F12** 37 35N 26 10 E
Ikeda, *Japan* .... **31 G6** 34 1N 133 48 E
Ikela, *Dem. Rep. of the Congo* .... **52 E4** 1 6S 23 6 E
Iki, *Japan* .... **31 H4** 33 45N 129 42 E
Ikimba L., *Tanzania* .... **54 C3** 1 30S 31 20 E
Ikongo, *Madag.* .... **57 C8** 21 52S 47 27 E
Ikopa →, *Madag.* .... **57 B8** 16 45S 46 40 E
Ikungu, *Tanzania* .... **54 C3** 1 33S 33 42 E
Ilagan, *Phil.* .... **37 A6** 17 7N 121 53 E
Ilaka, *Madag.* .... **57 B8** 19 33S 48 52 E
Īlām, *Iran* .... **44 C5** 33 36N 46 36 E
Ilam, *Nepal* .... **43 F12** 26 58N 87 58 E
Ilam □, *Iran* .... **44 C5** 33 0N 47 0 E
Ilanskiy, *Russia* .... **27 D10** 56 14N 96 3 E
Iława, *Poland* .... **17 B10** 53 36N 19 34 E
Ile →, *Kazakstan* .... **26 E8** 45 53N 77 10 E
Ile-à-la-Crosse, *Canada* ... **73 B7** 55 27N 107 53W
Ile-à-la-Crosse, Lac, *Canada* **73 B7** 55 40N 107 45W
Île-de-France □, *France* ... **18 B5** 49 0N 2 20 E
Ilebo, *Dem. Rep. of the Congo* .... **52 E4** 4 17S 20 55 E
Ilek, *Russia* .... **26 D6** 51 32N 53 21 E
Ilek →, *Russia* .... **24 D9** 51 30N 53 22 E
Ilesha, *Nigeria* .... **50 G6** 7 37N 4 40 E
Ilford, *Canada* **73 B9** 56 4N 95 35W
Ilfracombe, *Australia* ..... **62 C3** 23 30S 144 30 E
Ilfracombe, *U.K.* **11 F3** 51 12N 4 8W
Ilhéus, *Brazil* **93 F11** 14 49S 39 2W
Ili = Ile →, *Kazakstan* .... **26 E8** 45 53N 77 10 E
Iliamna L., *U.S.A.* **68 C4** 59 30N 155 0W
Iligan, *Phil.* .... **37 C6** 8 12N 124 13 E
Ilion, *U.S.A.* **79 D9** 43 1N 75 2W
Ilkeston, *U.K.* **10 E6** 52 58N 1 19W
Ilkley, *U.K.* **10 D6** 53 56N 1 48W
Illampu = Ancohuma, Nevada, *Bolivia* **92 G5** 16 0S 68 50W
Illana B., *Phil.* .... **37 C6** 7 35N 123 45 E
Illapel, *Chile* **94 C1** 32 0S 71 10W
Iller →, *Germany* .... **16 D6** 48 23N 9 58 E
Illetas, *Spain* .... **22 B9** 39 32N 2 35 E
Illimani, Nevado, *Bolivia* .. **92 G5** 16 30S 67 50W
Illinois □, *U.S.A.* **80 E10** 40 15N 89 30W
Illinois →, *U.S.A.* **75 C8** 38 58N 90 28W
Illium = Troy, *Turkey* ...... **21 E12** 39 57N 26 12 E
Illizi, *Algeria* .... **50 C7** 26 31N 8 32 E
Ilmajoki, *Finland* .... **9 E20** 62 44N 22 34 E
Ilmen, Ozero, *Russia* ...... **24 C5** 58 15N 31 10 E
Ilo, *Peru* **92 G4** 17 40S 71 20W
Iloilo, *Phil.* .... **37 B6** 10 45N 122 33 E
Ilorin, *Nigeria* .... **50 G6** 8 30N 4 35 E
Ilwaco, *U.S.A.* **84 D2** 46 19N 124 3W
Ilwaki, *Indonesia* .... **37 F7** 7 55S 126 30 E
Imabari, *Japan* .... **31 G6** 34 4N 133 0 E
Imaloto →, *Madag.* .... **57 C8** 23 27S 45 13 E
Imandra, Ozero, *Russia* .... **24 A5** 67 30N 33 0 E
Imanombo, *Madag.* .... **57 C8** 24 26S 45 49 E
Imari, *Japan* .... **31 H4** 33 15N 129 52 E
Imatra, *Finland* .... **24 B4** 61 12N 28 48 E
Imbil, *Australia* .... **63 D5** 26 22S 152 32 E
imeni 26 Bakinskikh Komissarov = Neftçala, *Azerbaijan* .... **25 G8** 39 19N 49 12 E
imeni 26 Bakinskikh Komissarov, *Turkmenistan* .... **45 B7** 39 22N 54 10 E
Imeri, Serra, *Brazil* **92 C5** 0 50N 65 25W
Imerimandroso, *Madag.* ... **57 B8** 17 26S 48 35 E
Imi, *Ethiopia* .... **46 F3** 6 28N 42 10 E
Imlay, *U.S.A.* **82 F4** 40 40N 118 9W
Imlay City, *U.S.A.* **78 D1** 43 2N 83 5W
Immingham, *U.K.* **10 D7** 53 37N 0 13W
Immokalee, *U.S.A.* **77 M5** 26 25N 81 25W
Ímola, *Italy* .... **20 B4** 44 20N 11 42 E
Imperatriz, *Brazil* **93 E9** 5 30S 47 29W
Impéria, *Italy* .... **18 E8** 43 53N 8 3 E
Imperial, *Canada* **73 C7** 51 21N 105 28W
Imperial, *Calif., U.S.A.* **85 N11** 32 51N 115 34W
Imperial, *Nebr., U.S.A.* **80 E4** 40 31N 101 39W
Imperial Beach, *U.S.A.* **85 N9** 32 35N 117 8W
Imperial Dam, *U.S.A.* **85 N12** 32 55N 114 25W
Imperial Reservoir, *U.S.A.* . **85 N12** 32 53N 114 28W
Imperial Valley, *U.S.A.* **85 N11** 33 0N 115 30W
Imperieuse Reef, *Australia* **60 C2** 17 36S 118 50 E
Impfondo, *Congo* .... **52 D3** 1 40N 18 0 E
Imphal, *India* .... **41 G18** 24 48N 93 56 E
İmroz = Gökçeada, *Turkey* **21 D11** 40 10N 25 50 E
Imuris, *Mexico* **86 A2** 30 47N 110 52W
Imuruan B., *Phil.* .... **37 B5** 10 40N 119 10 E
In Salah, *Algeria* .... **50 C6** 27 10N 2 32 E
Ina, *Japan* .... **31 G8** 35 50N 137 55 E
Inangahua, *N.Z.* .... **59 J3** 41 52S 171 59 E
Inanwatan, *Indonesia* ..... **37 E8** 2 8S 132 10 E
Iñapari, *Peru* **92 F5** 11 0S 69 40W
Inari, *Finland* .... **8 B22** 68 54N 27 5 E
Inarijärvi, *Finland* .... **8 B22** 69 0N 28 0 E
Inawashiro-Ko, *Japan* ..... **30 F10** 37 29N 140 6 E
Inca, *Spain* .... **22 B9** 39 43N 2 54 E
Inca de Oro, *Chile* **94 B2** 26 45S 69 54W
Incaguasi, *Chile* **94 B1** 29 12S 71 5W
İnce Burun, *Turkey* .... **25 F5** 42 7N 34 56 E
İncesu, *Turkey* .... **44 B2** 38 38N 35 11 E
Inch'ŏn, *S. Korea* .... **35 F14** 37 27N 126 40 E
İncirliova, *Turkey* .... **21 F12** 37 50N 27 41 E
Incline Village, *U.S.A.* **82 G4** 39 10N 119 58W
Incomáti →, *Mozam.* ...... **57 D5** 25 46S 32 43 E
Indalsälven →, *Sweden* .. **9 E17** 62 36N 17 30 E
Indaw, *Burma* .... **41 G20** 24 15N 96 5 E
Independence, *Calif., U.S.A.* **84 J8** 36 48N 118 12W
Independence, *Iowa, U.S.A.* **80 D9** 42 28N 91 54W
Independence, *Kans., U.S.A.* **81 G7** 37 14N 95 42W
Independence, *Ky., U.S.A.* **76 F3** 38 57N 84 33W
Independence, *Mo., U.S.A.* **80 F7** 39 6N 94 25W
Independence Fjord, *Greenland* **4 A6** 82 10N 29 0W
Independence Mts., *U.S.A.* **82 F5** 41 20N 116 0W
Index, *U.S.A.* **84 C5** 47 50N 121 33W
India ■, *Asia* .... **40 K11** 20 0N 78 0 E
Indian →, *U.S.A.* **77 M5** 27 59N 80 34W
Indian Cabins, *Canada* **72 B5** 59 52N 117 40W
Indian Harbour, *Canada* ... **71 B8** 54 27N 57 13W
Indian Head, *Canada* **73 C8** 50 30N 103 41W
Indian Lake, *U.S.A.* **79 C10** 43 47N 74 16W
Indian Ocean .... **28 K11** 5 0S 75 0 E
Indian Springs, *U.S.A.* **85 J11** 36 35N 115 40W
Indiana, *U.S.A.* **78 F5** 40 37N 79 9W
Indiana □, *U.S.A.* **76 F3** 40 0N 86 0W
Indianapolis, *U.S.A.* **76 F2** 39 46N 86 9W
Indianola, *Iowa, U.S.A.* **80 E8** 41 22N 93 34W
Indianola, *Miss., U.S.A.* ... **81 J9** 33 27N 90 39W
Indiga, *Russia* .... **24 A8** 67 38N 49 9 E
Indigirka →, *Russia* ...... **27 B15** 70 48N 148 54 E
Indio, *U.S.A.* **85 M10** 33 43N 116 13W
Indo-China, *Asia* .... **28 H14** 15 0N 102 0 E
Indonesia ■, *Asia* .... **36 F5** 5 0S 115 0 E
Indore, *India* .... **42 H6** 22 42N 75 53 E
Indramayu, *Indonesia* ..... **37 G13** 6 20S 108 19 E

Jūrmala

Jamanxim →, Brazil 93 D7 4 43S 56 18W
Jambi, Indonesia 36 E2 1 38S 103 30 E
Jambi □, Indonesia 36 E2 1 30S 102 30 E
Jambusar, India 42 H5 22 3N 72 51 E
James →, S. Dak., U.S.A. 80 D6 42 52N 97 18W
James →, Va., U.S.A. 76 G7 36 56N 76 27W
James B., Canada 70 B3 54 0N 80 0W
James Ranges, Australia 60 D5 24 10S 132 30 E
James Ross I., Antarctica 5 C18 63 58S 57 50W
Jamesabad, Pakistan 42 G3 25 17N 69 15 E
Jamestown, S. Africa 56 E4 31 6S 26 45 E
Jamestown, N. Dak., U.S.A. 80 B5 46 54N 98 42W
Jamestown, N.Y., U.S.A. 78 D5 42 6N 79 14W
Jamestown, Pa., U.S.A. 78 E4 41 29N 80 27W
Jamīlābād, Iran 45 C6 34 24N 48 28 E
Jamiltepec, Mexico 87 D5 16 17N 97 49W
Jamira →, India 43 J13 21 35N 88 28 E
Jamkhandi, India 40 L9 16 30N 75 15 E
Jammu, India 42 C6 32 43N 74 54 E
Jammu & Kashmir □, India 43 B7 34 25N 77 0 E
Jamnagar, India 42 H4 22 30N 70 6 E
Jamni →, India 43 G8 25 13N 78 35 E
Jampur, Pakistan 42 E4 29 39N 70 40 E
Jamrud, Pakistan 42 C4 33 59N 71 24 E
Jämsä, Finland 9 F21 61 53N 25 10 E
Jamshedpur, India 43 H12 22 44N 86 12 E
Jamtara, India 43 H12 23 59N 86 49 E
Jämtland, Sweden 8 E15 63 31N 14 0 E
Jan L., Canada 73 C8 54 56N 102 55W
Jan Mayen, Arctic 4 B7 71 0N 9 0W
Janakkala, Finland 9 F21 60 54N 24 36 E
Janaúba, Brazil 93 G10 15 48S 43 19W
Jand, Pakistan 42 C5 33 30N 72 6 E
Jandaq, Iran 45 C7 34 3N 54 22 E
Jandia, Canary Is. 22 F5 28 6N 14 21W
Jandia, Pta. de, Canary Is. 22 F5 28 3N 14 31W
Jandola, Pakistan 42 C4 32 20N 70 9 E
Jandowae, Australia 63 D5 26 45S 151 7 E
Janesville, U.S.A. 80 D10 42 41N 89 1W
Jangamo, Mozam. 57 C6 24 6S 35 21 E
Janghai, India 43 G10 25 33N 82 19 E
Janīn, West Bank 47 C4 32 28N 35 18 E
Janjgir, India 43 J10 22 1N 82 34 E
Janjina, Madag. 57 C8 20 30S 45 50 E
Janos, Mexico 86 A3 30 45N 108 10W
Januária, Brazil 93 G10 15 25S 44 25W
Janubio, Canary Is. 22 F6 28 56N 13 50W
Jaora, India 42 H6 23 40N 75 10 E
Japan ■, Asia 31 G8 36 0N 136 0 E
Japan, Sea of, Asia 30 E7 40 0N 135 0 E
Japan Trench, Pac. Oc. 28 F18 32 0N 142 0 E
Japen = Yapen, Indonesia 37 E9 1 50S 136 0 E
Japla, India 43 G11 24 33N 84 1 E
Japurá →, Brazil 92 D5 3 8S 65 46W
Jaquarão, Brazil 95 C5 32 34S 53 23W
Jaqué, Panama 88 E4 7 27N 78 8W
Jarābulus, Syria 44 B3 36 49N 38 1 E
Jarama →, Spain 19 B4 40 24N 3 32W
Jaranwala, Pakistan 42 D5 31 15N 73 26 E
Jarash, Jordan 47 C4 32 17N 35 54 E
Jardim, Brazil 94 A4 21 28S 56 2W
Jardines de la Reina, Arch. de los, Cuba 88 B4 20 50N 78 50W
Jargalang, China 35 C12 43 5N 122 55 E
Jargalant = Hovd, Mongolia 32 B4 48 2N 91 37 E
Jari →, Brazil 93 D8 1 9S 51 54W
Jarīr, W. al →, Si. Arabia 44 E4 25 38N 42 30 E
Jarosław, Poland 17 C12 50 2N 22 42 E
Jarrahdale, Australia 61 F2 32 24S 116 5 E
Jarrahi →, Iran 45 D6 30 49N 48 48 E
Jarres, Plaine des, Laos 38 C4 19 27N 103 10 E
Jartai, China 34 E3 39 45N 105 48 E
Jarud Qi, China 35 B11 44 28N 120 50 E
Järvenpää, Finland 9 F21 60 29N 25 5 E
Jarvis, Canada 78 D4 42 53N 80 6W
Jarvis I., Pac. Oc. 65 H12 0 15S 160 5W
Jarwa, India 43 F10 27 38N 82 30 E
Jasdan, India 42 H4 22 2N 71 12 E
Jashpurnagar, India 43 H11 22 54N 84 9 E
Jasidih, India 43 G12 24 31N 86 39 E
Jäsimīyah, Iraq 44 C5 33 45N 44 41 E
Jasin, Malaysia 39 L4 2 20N 102 26 E
Jäsk, Iran 45 E8 25 38N 57 45 E
Jasło, Poland 17 D11 49 45N 21 30 E
Jaso, India 43 G9 24 30N 80 29 E
Jasper, Alta., Canada 72 C5 52 55N 118 5W
Jasper, Ont., Canada 79 B9 44 52N 75 57W
Jasper, Ala., U.S.A. 77 J2 33 50N 87 17W
Jasper, Fla., U.S.A. 77 K4 30 31N 82 57W
Jasper, Ind., U.S.A. 76 F2 38 24N 86 56W
Jasper, Tex., U.S.A. 81 K8 30 56N 94 1W
Jasper Nat. Park, Canada 72 C5 52 50N 118 8W
Jasrasar, India 42 F5 27 43N 73 49 E
Jászberény, Hungary 17 E10 47 30N 19 55 E
Jataí, Brazil 93 G8 17 58S 51 48W
Jati, Pakistan 42 G3 24 20N 68 19 E
Jatibarang, Indonesia 37 G13 6 28S 108 18 E
Jatinegara, Indonesia 37 G12 6 13S 106 52 E
Játiva = Xátiva, Spain 19 C5 38 59N 0 32W
Jaú, Brazil 95 A6 22 10S 48 30W
Jauja, Peru 92 F3 11 45S 75 15W
Jaunpur, India 43 G10 25 46N 82 44 E
Java = Jawa, Indonesia 36 F3 7 0S 110 0 E
Java Barat □, Indonesia 37 G12 7 0S 107 0 E
Java Sea, Indonesia 36 E3 4 35S 107 15 E
Java Tengah □, Indonesia 37 G14 7 0S 110 0 E
Java Timur □, Indonesia 37 G15 8 0S 113 0 E
Java Trench, Ind. Oc. 36 F3 9 0S 105 0 E
Javhlant = Ulyasutay, Mongolia 32 B4 47 56N 97 28 E
Jawa, Indonesia 36 F3 7 0S 110 0 E
Jawad, India 42 G6 24 36N 74 51 E
Jay Peak, U.S.A. 79 B12 44 55N 72 32W
Jaya, Puncak, Indonesia 37 E9 3 57S 137 17 E
Jayanti, India 41 F16 26 45N 89 40 E
Jayapura, Indonesia 37 E10 2 28S 140 38 E
Jayawijaya, Pegunungan, Indonesia 37 E9 5 0S 139 0 E
Jaynagar, India 41 F15 26 43N 86 9 E
Jayrūd, Syria 44 C3 33 49N 36 44 E
Jayton, U.S.A. 81 J4 33 15N 100 34W
Jāz Mūrīān, Hāmūn-e, Iran 45 E8 27 20N 58 55 E
Jazīreh-ye Shīf, Iran 45 D6 29 4N 50 54 E
Jazminal, Mexico 86 C4 24 56N 101 25W
Jazzīn, Lebanon 47 B4 33 31N 35 35 E
Jean, U.S.A. 85 K11 35 47N 115 20W
Jean Marie River, Canada 72 A4 61 32N 120 38W
Jean Rabel, Haiti 89 C5 19 50N 73 5W
Jeanerette, U.S.A. 81 L9 29 55N 91 40W
Jeanette, Ostrov = Zhannetty, Ostrov, Russia 27 B16 76 43N 158 0 E
Jeannette, U.S.A. 78 F5 40 20N 79 36W
Jebāl Bārez, Kūh-e, Iran 45 D8 28 30N 58 20 E
Jebel, Bahr el →, Sudan 51 G12 9 30N 30 25 E
Jedburgh, U.K. 12 F6 55 29N 2 33W
Jedda = Jiddah, Si. Arabia 46 C2 21 29N 39 10 E
Jeddore L., Canada 71 C8 48 3N 55 55W
Jędrzejów, Poland 17 C11 50 35N 20 15 E
Jefferson, Iowa, U.S.A. 80 D7 42 1N 94 23W
Jefferson, Ohio, U.S.A. 78 E4 41 44N 80 46W
Jefferson, Tex., U.S.A. 81 J7 32 46N 94 21W
Jefferson, Mt., Nev., U.S.A. 82 G5 38 51N 117 0W
Jefferson, Mt., Oreg., U.S.A. 82 D3 44 41N 121 48W
Jefferson City, Mo., U.S.A. 80 F8 38 34N 92 10W
Jefferson City, Tenn., U.S.A. 77 G4 36 7N 83 30W
Jeffersontown, U.S.A. 76 F3 38 12N 85 35W
Jeffersonville, U.S.A. 76 F3 38 17N 85 44W
Jeffrey City, U.S.A. 82 E10 42 30N 107 49W
Jega, Nigeria 50 F6 12 15N 4 23 E
Jēkabpils, Latvia 9 H21 56 29N 25 57 E
Jekyll I., U.S.A. 77 K5 31 4N 81 25W
Jelenia Góra, Poland 16 C8 50 50N 15 45 E
Jelgava, Latvia 9 H20 56 41N 23 49 E
Jemaja, Indonesia 39 L5 3 5N 105 45 E
Jemaluang, Malaysia 39 L4 2 16N 103 52 E
Jember, Indonesia 37 H15 8 11S 113 41 E
Jembongan, Malaysia 36 C5 6 45N 117 20 E
Jena, Germany 16 C6 50 54N 11 35 E
Jena, U.S.A. 81 K8 31 41N 92 8W
Jenkins, U.S.A. 76 G4 37 10N 82 38W
Jenner, U.S.A. 84 G3 38 27N 123 7W
Jennings, U.S.A. 81 K8 30 13N 92 40W
Jepara, Indonesia 37 G14 7 40S 109 14 E
Jequié, Brazil 93 F10 13 51S 40 5W
Jequitinhonha, Brazil 93 G10 16 30S 41 0W
Jequitinhonha →, Brazil 93 G11 15 51S 38 53W
Jerantut, Malaysia 39 L4 3 56N 102 22 E
Jérémie, Haiti 89 C5 18 40N 74 10W
Jerez, Punta, Mexico 87 C5 22 58N 97 40W
Jerez de García Salinas, Mexico 86 C4 22 39N 103 0W
Jerez de la Frontera, Spain 19 D2 36 41N 6 7W
Jerez de los Caballeros, Spain 19 C2 38 20N 6 45W
Jericho = El Arīḥā, West Bank 47 D4 31 52N 35 27 E
Jericho, Australia 62 C4 23 38S 146 6 E
Jerid, Chott = Djerid, Chott, Tunisia 50 B7 33 42N 8 30 E
Jermyn, U.S.A. 79 E9 41 31N 75 31W
Jerome, U.S.A. 82 E6 42 44N 114 31W
Jerramungup, Australia 61 F2 33 55S 118 55 E
Jersey, U.K. 11 H5 49 11N 2 7W
Jersey City, U.S.A. 79 F10 40 44N 74 4W
Jersey Shore, U.S.A. 78 E7 41 12N 77 15W
Jerseyville, U.S.A. 80 F9 39 7N 90 20W
Jerusalem, Israel 47 D4 31 47N 35 10 E
Jervis Inlet, Canada 72 C4 50 0N 123 57W
Jesi = Iesi, Italy 20 C5 43 31N 13 14 E
Jesselton = Kota Kinabalu, Malaysia 36 C5 6 0N 116 4 E
Jessore, Bangla. 41 H16 23 10N 89 10 E
Jesup, U.S.A. 77 K5 31 36N 81 53W
Jesús Carranza, Mexico 87 D5 17 28N 95 1W
Jesús María, Argentina 94 C3 30 59S 64 5W
Jetmore, U.S.A. 81 F5 38 4N 99 54W
Jetpur, India 42 J4 21 45N 70 10 E
Jevnaker, Norway 9 F14 60 15N 10 26 E
Jewett, U.S.A. 78 F3 40 22N 81 2W
Jewett City, U.S.A. 79 E13 41 36N 72 0W
Jeyḥūnābād, Iran 45 C6 34 58N 48 59 E
Jeypore, India 41 K13 18 50N 82 38 E
Jha Jha, India 43 G12 24 46N 86 22 E
Jhaarkand = Jharkhand □, India 43 H11 24 0N 85 50 E
Jhabua, India 42 H6 22 46N 74 36 E
Jhajjar, India 42 E7 28 37N 76 42 E
Jhal, Pakistan 42 E2 28 17N 67 27 E
Jhal Jhao, Pakistan 40 F4 26 20N 65 35 E
Jhalawar, India 42 G7 24 40N 76 10 E
Jhalida, India 43 H11 23 22N 85 58 E
Jhalrapatan, India 42 G7 24 33N 76 10 E
Jhang Maghiana, Pakistan 42 D5 31 15N 72 22 E
Jhansi, India 43 G8 25 30N 78 36 E
Jhargram, India 43 H12 22 27N 86 59 E
Jharia, India 43 H12 23 45N 86 26 E
Jharkhand □, India 43 H11 24 0N 85 50 E
Jharsuguda, India 41 J14 21 56N 84 5 E
Jhelum, Pakistan 42 C5 33 0N 73 45 E
Jhelum →, Pakistan 42 D5 31 20N 72 10 E
Jhilmilli, India 43 H10 23 24N 82 51 E
Jhudo, Pakistan 42 G3 24 58N 69 18 E
Jhunjhunu, India 42 E6 28 10N 75 30 E
Ji-Paraná, Brazil 92 F6 10 52S 62 57W
Ji Xian, Hebei, China 34 F8 37 35N 115 30 E
Ji Xian, Henan, China 34 G8 35 22N 114 5 E
Ji Xian, Shanxi, China 34 F6 36 7N 110 40 E
Jia Xian, Henan, China 34 H7 33 59N 113 12 E
Jia Xian, Shaanxi, China 34 E6 38 12N 110 28 E
Jiamusi, China 33 B8 46 40N 130 26 E
Ji'an, Jiangxi, China 33 D6 27 6N 114 59 E
Ji'an, Jilin, China 35 D14 41 5N 126 10 E
Jianchang, China 35 D11 40 55N 120 35 E
Jianchangying, China 35 D10 40 10N 118 50 E
Jiangcheng, China 32 D5 22 36N 101 52 E
Jiangmen, China 33 D6 22 32N 113 0 E
Jiangsu □, China 35 H11 33 0N 120 0 E
Jiangxi □, China 33 D6 27 30N 116 0 E
Jiao Xian = Jiaozhou, China 35 F11 36 18N 120 1 E
Jiaohe, Hebei, China 34 E9 38 2N 116 20 E
Jiaohe, Jilin, China 35 C14 43 40N 127 22 E
Jiaozhou, China 35 F11 36 18N 120 1 E
Jiaozhou Wan, China 35 F11 36 5N 120 10 E
Jiaozuo, China 34 G7 35 16N 113 12 E
Jiawang, China 35 G9 34 28N 117 26 E
Jiaxiang, China 34 G9 35 25N 116 20 E
Jiaxing, China 33 C7 30 49N 120 45 E
Jiayi = Chiai, Taiwan 33 D7 23 29N 120 25 E
Jibuti = Djibouti ■, Africa 46 E3 12 0N 43 0 E
Jicarón, I., Panama 88 E3 7 10N 81 50W
Jiddah, Si. Arabia 46 C2 21 29N 39 10 E
Jido, India 41 E19 29 2N 94 58 E
Jieshou, China 34 H8 33 18N 115 22 E
Jiexiu, China 34 F6 37 2N 111 55 E
Jiggalong, Australia 60 D3 23 21S 120 47 E
Jigni, India 43 G8 25 45N 79 25 E
Jihlava, Czech Rep. 16 D8 49 28N 15 35 E
Jihlava →, Czech Rep. 17 D9 48 55N 16 36 E
Jijiga, Ethiopia 46 F3 9 20N 42 50 E
Jilin, China 35 C14 43 44N 126 30 E
Jilin □, China 35 C14 44 0N 127 0 E
Jilong = Chilung, Taiwan 33 D7 25 3N 121 45 E
Jim Thorpe, U.S.A. 79 F9 40 52N 75 44W
Jima, Ethiopia 46 F2 7 40N 36 47 E
Jiménez, Mexico 86 B4 27 10N 104 54W
Jimo, China 35 F11 36 23N 120 30 E
Jin Xian = Jinzhou, China 34 E8 38 2N 115 2 E
Jin Xian, China 35 E11 38 55N 121 42 E
Jinan, China 34 F9 36 38N 117 1 E
Jincheng, China 34 G7 35 29N 112 50 E
Jind, India 42 E7 29 19N 76 22 E
Jindřichův Hradec, Czech Rep. 16 D8 49 10N 15 2 E
Jing He →, China 34 G5 34 27N 109 4 E
Jingbian, China 34 F5 37 20N 108 30 E
Jingchuan, China 34 G4 35 20N 107 20 E
Jingdezhen, China 33 D6 29 20N 117 11 E
Jinggu, China 32 D5 23 35N 100 41 E
Jinghai, China 34 E9 38 55N 116 55 E
Jingle, China 34 E6 38 20N 111 55 E
Jingning, China 34 G3 35 30N 105 43 E
Jingpo Hu, China 35 C15 43 55N 128 55 E
Jingtai, China 34 F3 37 10N 104 6 E
Jingxing, China 34 E8 38 2N 114 8 E
Jingyang, China 34 G5 34 30N 108 50 E
Jingyu, China 35 C14 42 25N 126 45 E
Jingyuan, China 34 F3 36 30N 104 40 E
Jingziguan, China 34 H6 33 15N 111 0 E
Jinhua, China 33 D6 29 8N 119 38 E
Jining, Nei Monggol Zizhiqu, China 34 D7 41 5N 113 0 E
Jining, Shandong, China 34 G9 35 22N 116 34 E
Jinja, Uganda 54 B3 0 25N 33 12 E
Jinjang, Malaysia 39 L3 3 13N 101 39 E
Jinji, China 34 F4 37 58N 106 8 E
Jinnah Barrage, Pakistan 40 C7 32 58N 71 33 E
Jinotega, Nic. 88 D2 13 6N 85 59W
Jinotepe, Nic. 88 D2 11 50N 86 10W
Jinsha Jiang →, China 32 D5 28 50N 104 36 E
Jinxi, China 35 D11 40 52N 120 50 E
Jinxiang, China 34 G9 35 5N 116 22 E
Jinzhou, Hebei, China 34 E8 38 2N 115 2 E
Jinzhou, Liaoning, China 35 D11 41 5N 121 3 E
Jiparaná →, Brazil 92 E6 8 3S 62 52W
Jipijapa, Ecuador 92 D2 1 0S 80 40W
Jiquilpan, Mexico 86 D4 19 57N 102 42W
Jishan, China 34 G6 35 34N 110 58 E
Jisr ash Shughūr, Syria 44 C3 35 49N 36 18 E
Jitarning, Australia 61 F2 32 48S 117 57 E
Jitra, Malaysia 39 J3 6 16N 100 25 E
Jiu →, Romania 17 F12 43 47N 23 48 E
Jiudengkou, China 34 E4 39 56N 106 40 E
Jiujiang, China 33 D6 29 42N 115 58 E
Jiutai, China 35 B13 44 10N 125 50 E
Jiuxincheng, China 34 E8 39 17N 115 59 E
Jixi, China 35 B16 45 20N 130 50 E
Jiyang, China 35 F9 37 0N 117 12 E
Jiyuan, China 34 G7 35 7N 112 57 E
Jīzān, Si. Arabia 46 D3 17 0N 42 20 E
Jize, China 34 F8 36 54N 114 56 E
Jīzl, Wādī al, Si. Arabia 44 E3 25 39N 38 25 E
Jizō-Zaki, Japan 31 G6 35 34N 133 20 E
Jizzakh, Uzbekistan 26 E7 40 6N 67 50 E
Joaçaba, Brazil 95 B5 27 5S 51 31W
João Pessoa, Brazil 93 E12 7 10S 34 52W
Joaquín V. González, Argentina 94 B3 25 10S 64 0W
Jobat, India 42 H6 22 25N 74 34 E
Jodhpur, India 42 F5 26 23N 73 8 E
Jodiya, India 42 H4 22 42N 70 18 E
Joensuu, Finland 24 B4 62 37N 29 49 E
Jōetsu, Japan 31 F9 37 12N 138 10 E
Jofane, Mozam. 57 C5 21 15S 34 18 E
Jogbani, India 43 F12 26 25N 87 15 E
Jõgeva, Estonia 9 G22 58 45N 26 24 E
Jogjakarta = Yogyakarta, Indonesia 36 F4 7 49S 110 22 E
Johannesburg, S. Africa 57 D4 26 10S 28 2 E
Johannesburg, U.S.A. 85 K9 35 22N 117 38W
Johilla →, India 43 H9 23 37N 81 14 E
John Day, U.S.A. 82 D4 44 25N 118 57W
John Day →, U.S.A. 82 D3 45 44N 120 39W
John D'Or Prairie, Canada 72 B5 58 30N 115 8W
John H. Kerr Reservoir, U.S.A. 77 G6 36 36N 78 18W
John o' Groats, U.K. 12 C5 58 38N 3 4W
Johnnie, U.S.A. 85 J10 36 25N 116 5W
John's Ra., Australia 62 C1 21 55S 133 23 E
Johnson, Kans., U.S.A. 81 G4 37 34N 101 45W
Johnson, Vt., U.S.A. 79 B12 44 38N 72 41W
Johnson City, N.Y., U.S.A. 79 D9 42 7N 75 58W
Johnson City, Tenn., U.S.A. 77 G4 36 19N 82 21W
Johnson City, Tex., U.S.A. 81 K5 30 17N 98 25W
Johnsonburg, U.S.A. 78 E6 41 29N 78 41W
Johnsondale, U.S.A. 85 K8 35 58N 118 32W
Johnson's Crossing, Canada 72 A2 60 29N 133 18W
Johnston, L., Australia 61 F3 32 25S 120 30 E
Johnston Falls = Mambilima Falls, Zambia 55 E2 10 31S 28 45 E
Johnston I., Pac. Oc. 65 F11 17 10N 169 8W
Johnstone Str., Canada 72 C3 50 28N 126 0W
Johnstown, N.Y., U.S.A. 79 C10 43 0N 74 22W
Johnstown, Ohio, U.S.A. 78 F2 40 9N 82 41W
Johnstown, Pa., U.S.A. 78 F6 40 20N 78 55W
Johor Baharu, Malaysia 39 M4 1 28N 103 46 E
Jõhvi, Estonia 9 G22 59 22N 27 27 E
Joinville, Brazil 95 B6 26 15S 48 55W
Joinville I., Antarctica 5 C18 65 0S 55 30W
Jojutla, Mexico 87 D5 18 37N 99 11W
Jokkmokk, Sweden 8 C18 66 35N 19 50 E
Jökulsá á Bru →, Iceland 8 D6 65 40N 14 16W
Jökulsá á Fjöllum →, Iceland 8 C5 66 10N 16 30W
Jolfā, Āzarbājān-e Sharqī, Iran 44 B5 38 57N 45 38 E
Jolfā, Eşfahan, Iran 45 C6 32 58N 51 37 E
Joliet, U.S.A. 76 E1 41 32N 88 5W
Joliette, Canada 70 C5 46 3N 73 24W
Jolo, Phil. 37 C6 6 0N 121 0 E
Jolon, U.S.A. 84 K5 35 58N 121 9W
Jombang, Indonesia 37 G15 7 33S 112 14 E
Jonava, Lithuania 9 J21 55 8N 24 12 E
Jones Sound, Canada 4 B3 76 0N 85 0W
Jonesboro, Ark., U.S.A. 81 H9 35 50N 90 42W
Jonesboro, La., U.S.A. 81 J8 32 15N 92 43W
Joniškis, Lithuania 9 H20 56 13N 23 35 E
Jönköping, Sweden 9 H16 57 45N 14 8 E
Jonquière, Canada 71 C5 48 27N 71 14W
Joplin, U.S.A. 81 G7 37 6N 94 31W
Jora, India 42 F6 26 20N 77 49 E
Jordan, Mont., U.S.A. 82 C10 47 19N 106 55W
Jordan, N.Y., U.S.A. 79 C8 43 4N 76 29W
Jordan ■, Asia 47 E5 31 0N 36 0 E
Jordan →, Asia 47 D4 31 48N 35 32 E
Jordan Valley, U.S.A. 82 E5 42 59N 117 3W
Jorhat, India 41 F19 26 45N 94 12 E
Jörn, Sweden 8 D19 65 4N 20 1 E
Jorong, Indonesia 36 E4 3 58S 114 56 E
Jørpeland, Norway 9 G11 59 3N 6 1 E
Jorquera →, Chile 94 B2 28 3S 69 58W
Jos, Nigeria 50 G7 9 53N 8 51 E
José Batlle y Ordóñez, Uruguay 95 C4 33 20S 55 10W
Joseph, L., Nfld., Canada 71 B6 52 45N 65 18W
Joseph, L., Ont., Canada 78 A5 45 10N 79 44W
Joseph Bonaparte G., Australia 60 B4 14 35S 128 50 E
Joshinath, India 43 D8 30 34N 79 34 E
Joshua Tree, U.S.A. 85 L10 34 8N 116 19W
Joshua Tree National Park, U.S.A. 85 M10 33 55N 116 0W
Jostedalsbreen, Norway 9 F12 61 40N 6 59 E
Jotunheimen, Norway 9 F13 61 35N 8 25 E
Joubertberge, Namibia 56 B1 18 30S 14 0 E
Jourdanton, U.S.A. 81 L5 28 55N 98 33W
Jovellanos, Cuba 88 B3 22 40N 81 10W
Ju Xian, China 35 F10 36 35N 118 20 E
Juan Aldama, Mexico 86 C4 24 20N 103 23W
Juan Bautista Alberdi, Argentina 94 C3 34 26S 61 48W
Juan de Fuca Str., Canada 84 B3 48 15N 124 0W
Juan de Nova, Ind. Oc. 57 B7 17 3S 43 45 E
Juan Fernández, Arch. de, Pac. Oc. 90 G2 33 50S 80 0W
Juan José Castelli, Argentina 94 B3 25 27S 60 57W
Juan L. Lacaze, Uruguay 94 C4 34 26S 57 25W
Juankoski, Finland 8 E23 63 3N 28 19 E
Juárez, Argentina 94 D4 37 40S 59 43W
Juárez, Mexico 85 N11 32 20N 115 57W
Juárez, Sierra de, Mexico 86 A1 32 0N 116 0W
Juàzeiro, Brazil 93 E10 9 30S 40 30W
Juàzeiro do Norte, Brazil 93 E11 7 10S 39 18W
Juba, Sudan 51 H12 4 50N 31 35 E
Jubayl, Lebanon 47 A4 34 5N 35 39 E
Jubbah, Si. Arabia 44 D4 28 2N 40 56 E
Jubbal, India 42 D7 31 5N 77 40 E
Jubbulpore = Jabalpur, India 43 H8 23 9N 79 58 E
Jubilee L., Australia 61 E4 29 0S 126 50 E
Juby, C., Morocco 50 C3 28 0N 12 59W
Júcar = Xúquer →, Spain 19 C5 39 5N 0 10W
Júcaro, Cuba 88 B4 21 37N 78 51W
Juchitán, Mexico 87 D5 16 27N 95 5W
Judaea = Har Yehuda, Israel 47 D3 31 35N 34 57 E
Judith →, U.S.A. 82 C9 47 44N 109 39W
Judith, Pt., U.S.A. 79 E13 41 22N 71 29W
Judith Gap, U.S.A. 82 C9 46 41N 109 45W
Jugoslavia = Yugoslavia ■, Europe 21 B9 43 20N 20 0 E
Juigalpa, Nic. 88 D2 12 6N 85 26W
Juiz de Fora, Brazil 95 A7 21 43S 43 19W
Jujuy □, Argentina 94 A2 23 20S 65 40W
Julesburg, U.S.A. 80 E3 40 59N 102 16W
Juli, Peru 92 G5 16 10S 69 25W
Julia Cr. →, Australia 62 C3 20 0S 141 11 E
Julia Creek, Australia 62 C3 20 39S 141 44 E
Juliaca, Peru 92 G4 15 25S 70 10W
Julian, U.S.A. 85 M10 33 4N 116 38W
Julian L., Canada 70 B4 54 25N 77 57W
Julianatop, Surinam 93 C7 3 40N 56 30W
Julianehåb = Qaqortoq, Greenland 69 B6 60 43N 46 0W
Julimes, Mexico 86 B3 28 25N 105 27W
Jullundur, India 42 D6 31 20N 75 40 E
Julu, China 34 F8 37 15N 115 2 E
Jumbo, Zimbabwe 55 F3 17 30S 30 58 E
Jumbo Pk., U.S.A. 85 J12 36 12N 114 11W
Jumentos Cays, Bahamas 88 B4 23 0N 75 40W
Jumilla, Spain 19 C5 38 28N 1 19W
Jumla, Nepal 43 E10 29 15N 82 13 E
Jumna = Yamuna →, India 43 G9 25 30N 81 53 E
Junagadh, India 42 J4 21 30N 70 30 E
Junction, Tex., U.S.A. 81 K5 30 29N 99 46W
Junction, Utah, U.S.A. 83 G7 38 14N 112 13W
Junction B., Australia 62 A1 11 52S 133 55 E
Junction City, Kans., U.S.A. 80 F6 39 2N 96 50W
Junction City, Oreg., U.S.A. 82 D2 44 13N 123 12W
Junction Pt., Australia 62 A1 11 45S 133 50 E
Jundah, Australia 62 C3 24 46S 143 2 E
Jundiaí, Brazil 95 A6 24 30S 47 0W
Juneau, U.S.A. 72 B2 58 18N 134 25W
Jungfrau, Switz. 18 C7 46 32N 7 58 E
Junggar Pendi, China 32 B3 44 30N 86 0 E
Jungshahi, Pakistan 42 G2 24 52N 67 44 E
Juniata →, U.S.A. 78 F7 40 30N 77 40W
Junín, Argentina 94 C3 34 33S 60 57W
Junín de los Andes, Argentina 96 D2 39 45S 71 0W
Jūniyah, Lebanon 47 B4 33 59N 35 38 E
Juntas, Chile 94 B2 28 24S 69 58W
Juntura, U.S.A. 82 E4 43 45N 118 5W
Jur, Nahr el →, Sudan 51 G11 8 45N 29 15 E
Jura = Jura, Mts. du, Europe 18 C7 46 40N 6 5 E
Jura = Schwäbische Alb, Germany 16 D5 48 20N 9 30 E
Jura, U.K. 12 F3 56 0N 5 50W
Jura, Mts. du, Europe 18 C7 46 40N 6 5 E
Jura, Sd. of, U.K. 12 F3 55 57N 5 45W
Jurbarkas, Lithuania 9 J20 55 4N 22 46 E
Jurien, Australia 61 F2 30 18S 115 2 E
Jūrmala, Latvia 9 H20 56 58N 23 34 E

Kentucky

Kaposvár, Hungary 17 E9 46 25N 17 47 E
Kapowsin, U.S.A. 84 D4 46 59N 122 13W
Kapps, Namibia 56 C2 22 32S 17 18 E
Kapsan, N. Korea 35 D15 41 4N 128 19 E
Kapsukas = Marijampolė, Lithuania 9 J20 54 33N 23 19 E
Kapuas →, Indonesia 36 E3 0 25S 109 20 E
Kapuas Hulu, Pegunungan, Malaysia 36 D4 1 30N 113 30 E
Kapuas Hulu Ra. = Kapuas Hulu, Pegunungan, Malaysia 36 D4 1 30N 113 30 E
Kapulo, Dem. Rep. of the Congo 55 D2 8 18S 29 15 E
Kapuni, N.Z. 59 H5 39 29S 174 8 E
Kapurthala, India 42 D6 31 23N 75 25 E
Kapuskasing, Canada 70 C3 49 25N 82 30W
Kapuskasing →, Canada 70 C3 49 49N 82 0W
Kaputar, Australia 63 E5 30 15S 150 10 E
Kaputir, Kenya 54 B4 2 5N 35 28 E
Kara, Russia 26 C7 69 10N 65 0 E
Kara Bogaz Gol, Zaliv = Garabogazköl Aylagy, Turkmenistan 25 F9 41 0N 53 30 E
Kara Kalpak Republic = Qoraqalpoghistan □, Uzbekistan 26 E6 43 0N 58 0 E
Kara Kum, Turkmenistan 26 F6 39 30N 60 0 E
Kara Sea, Russia 26 B7 75 0N 70 0 E
Karabiğa, Turkey 21 D12 40 23N 27 17 E
Karabük, Turkey 25 F5 41 12N 32 37 E
Karaburun, Turkey 21 E12 38 41N 26 28 E
Karabutak = Qarabutaq, Kazakstan 26 E7 49 59N 60 14 E
Karacabey, Turkey 21 D13 40 12N 28 21 E
Karacasu, Turkey 21 F13 37 43N 28 35 E
Karachey-Cherkessia □, Russia 25 F7 43 40N 41 30 E
Karachi, Pakistan 42 G2 24 53N 67 0 E
Karad, India 40 L9 17 15N 74 10 E
Karaganda = Qaraghandy, Kazakstan 26 E8 49 50N 73 10 E
Karagayly, Kazakstan 26 E8 49 26N 76 0 E
Karaginskiy, Ostrov, Russia 27 D17 58 45N 164 0 E
Karagiye, Vpadina, Kazakstan 25 F9 43 27N 51 45 E
Karagiye Depression = Karagiye, Vpadina, Kazakstan 25 F9 43 27N 51 45 E
Karagola Road, India 43 G12 25 29N 87 23 E
Karaikal, India 40 P11 10 59N 79 50 E
Karaikkudi, India 40 P11 10 5N 78 45 E
Karaj, Iran 45 C6 35 48N 51 0 E
Karak, Malaysia 39 L4 3 25N 102 2 E
Karakalpakstan = Qoraqalpoghistan □, Uzbekistan 26 E6 43 0N 58 0 E
Karakelong, Indonesia 37 D7 4 35N 126 50 E
Karakitang, Indonesia 37 D7 3 14N 125 28 E
Karaklis = Vanadzor, Armenia 25 F7 40 48N 44 30 E
Karakol, Kyrgyzstan 26 E8 42 30N 78 20 E
Karakoram Pass, Pakistan 43 B7 35 33N 77 50 E
Karakoram Ra., Pakistan 43 B7 35 30N 77 0 E
Karakuwisa, Namibia 56 B2 18 56S 19 40 E
Karalon, Russia 27 D12 57 5N 115 50 E
Karama, Jordan 47 D4 31 57N 35 35 E
Karaman, Turkey 25 G5 37 14N 33 13 E
Karamay, China 32 B3 45 30N 84 58 E
Karambu, Indonesia 36 E5 3 53S 116 6 E
Karamea Bight, N.Z. 59 J3 41 22S 171 40 E
Karamnasa →, India 43 G10 25 31N 83 52 E
Karand, Iran 44 C5 34 16N 46 15 E
Karanganyar, Indonesia 37 G13 7 38S 109 37 E
Karanjia, India 43 J11 21 47N 85 58 E
Karasburg, Namibia 56 D2 28 0S 18 44 E
Karasino, Russia 26 C9 66 50N 86 50 E
Karasjok, Norway 8 B21 69 27N 25 30 E
Karasuk, Russia 26 D8 53 44N 78 2 E
Karasuyama, Japan 31 F10 36 39N 140 9 E
Karatau, Khrebet = Qarataū, Kazakstan 26 E7 43 30N 69 30 E
Karatsu, Japan 31 H5 33 26N 129 58 E
Karaul, Russia 26 B9 70 6N 82 15 E
Karauli, India 42 F7 26 30N 77 4 E
Karavostasi, Cyprus 23 D11 35 8N 32 50 E
Karawang, Indonesia 37 G12 6 30S 107 15 E
Karawanken, Europe 16 E8 46 30N 14 40 E
Karayazı, Turkey 25 G7 39 41N 42 9 E
Karazhal, Kazakstan 26 E8 48 2N 70 49 E
Karbalā', Iraq 44 C5 32 36N 44 3 E
Karcag, Hungary 17 E11 47 19N 20 57 E
Karcha →, Pakistan 43 B7 34 45N 76 10 E
Karchana, India 43 G9 25 17N 81 56 E
Kardhítsa, Greece 21 E9 39 23N 21 54 E
Kärdla, Estonia 9 G20 58 50N 22 40 E
Kareeberge, S. Africa 56 E3 30 59S 21 50 E
Kareha →, India 43 G12 25 44N 86 21 E
Kareima, Sudan 51 E12 18 30N 31 49 E
Karelia □, Russia 24 A5 65 30N 32 30 E
Karelian Republic = Karelia □, Russia 24 A5 65 30N 32 30 E
Karera, India 42 G8 25 32N 78 9 E
Kārevāndar, Iran 45 E9 27 53N 60 44 E
Kargasok, Russia 26 D9 59 3N 80 53 E
Kargat, Russia 26 D9 55 10N 80 15 E
Kargil, India 43 B7 34 32N 76 12 E
Kargopol, Russia 24 B6 61 30N 38 58 E
Karhal, India 43 F8 27 1N 78 57 E
Karīān, Iran 45 E8 26 57N 57 14 E
Karianga, Madag. 57 C8 22 25S 47 22 E
Kariba, Zimbabwe 55 F2 16 28S 28 50 E
Kariba, L., Zimbabwe 55 F2 16 40S 28 25 E
Kariba Dam, Zimbabwe 55 F2 16 30S 28 35 E
Kariba Gorge, Zambia 55 F2 16 30S 28 50 E
Karibib, Namibia 56 C2 22 0S 15 56 E
Karimata, Kepulauan, Indonesia 36 E3 1 25S 109 0 E
Karimata, Selat, Indonesia 36 E3 2 0S 108 40 E
Karimata Is. = Karimata, Kepulauan, Indonesia 36 E3 1 25S 109 0 E
Karimnagar, India 40 K11 18 26N 79 10 E
Karimunjawa, Kepulauan, Indonesia 36 F4 5 50S 110 30 E
Karin, Somali Rep. 46 E4 10 50N 45 52 E
Karit, Iran 45 C8 33 29N 56 55 E
Kariya, Japan 31 G8 34 58N 137 1 E
Kariyangwe, Zimbabwe 57 B4 18 0S 27 38 E
Karkaralinsk = Qarqaraly, Kazakstan 26 E8 49 26N 75 30 E
Karkheh →, Iran 44 D5 31 2N 47 29 E
Karkinitska Zatoka, Ukraine 25 E5 45 56N 33 0 E
Karkinitskiy Zaliv = Karkinitska Zatoka, Ukraine 25 E5 45 56N 33 0 E
Karl-Marx-Stadt = Chemnitz, Germany 16 C7 50 51N 12 54 E
Karlovac, Croatia 16 F8 45 31N 15 36 E
Karlovo, Bulgaria 21 C11 42 38N 24 47 E
Karlovy Vary, Czech Rep. 16 C7 50 13N 12 51 E
Karlsbad = Karlovy Vary, Czech Rep. 16 C7 50 13N 12 51 E
Karlsborg, Sweden 9 G16 58 33N 14 33 E
Karlshamn, Sweden 9 H16 56 10N 14 51 E
Karlskoga, Sweden 9 G16 59 28N 14 33 E
Karlskrona, Sweden 9 H16 56 10N 15 35 E
Karlsruhe, Germany 16 D5 49 0N 8 23 E
Karlstad, Sweden 9 G15 59 23N 13 30 E
Karlstad, U.S.A. 80 A6 48 35N 96 31W
Karmi'el, Israel 47 C4 32 55N 35 18 E
Karnak, Egypt 51 C12 25 43N 32 39 E
Karnal, India 42 E7 29 42N 77 2 E
Karnali →, Nepal 43 E9 28 45N 81 16 E
Karnaphuli Res., Bangla. 41 H18 22 40N 92 20 E
Karnaprayag, India 43 D8 30 16N 79 15 E
Karnataka □, India 40 N10 13 15N 77 0 E
Karnes City, U.S.A. 81 L6 28 53N 97 54W
Karnische Alpen, Europe 16 E7 46 36N 13 0 E
Kärnten □, Austria 16 E8 46 52N 13 30 E
Karoi, Zimbabwe 55 F2 16 48S 29 45 E
Karonga, Malawi 55 D3 9 57S 33 55 E
Karor, Pakistan 42 D4 31 15N 70 59 E
Karora, Sudan 51 E13 17 44N 38 15 E
Karpasia □, Cyprus 23 D13 35 32N 34 15 E
Kárpathos, Greece 21 G12 35 37N 27 10 E
Karpinsk, Russia 24 C11 59 45N 60 1 E
Karpogory, Russia 24 B7 64 0N 44 27 E
Karpuz Burnu = Apostolos Andreas, C., Cyprus 23 D13 35 42N 34 35 E
Karratha, Australia 60 D2 20 53S 116 40 E
Kars, Turkey 25 F7 40 40N 43 5 E
Karsakpay, Kazakstan 26 E7 47 55N 66 40 E
Karshi = Qarshi, Uzbekistan 26 F7 38 53N 65 48 E
Karsiyang, India 43 F13 26 56N 88 18 E
Karsog, India 42 D7 31 23N 77 12 E
Kartaly, Russia 26 D7 53 3N 60 40 E
Kartapur, India 42 D6 31 27N 75 32 E
Karthaus, U.S.A. 78 E6 41 8N 78 9W
Karufa, Indonesia 37 E8 3 50S 133 20 E
Karumba, Australia 62 B3 17 31S 140 50 E
Karumo, Tanzania 54 C3 2 25S 32 50 E
Karumwa, Tanzania 54 C3 3 12S 32 38 E
Kārūn →, Iran 45 D6 30 26N 48 10 E
Karungu, Kenya 54 C3 0 50S 34 10 E
Karviná, Czech Rep. 17 D10 49 53N 18 31 E
Karwan →, India 42 F8 27 26N 78 4 E
Karwar, India 40 M9 14 55N 74 13 E
Karwi, India 43 G9 25 12N 80 57 E
Kasache, Malawi 55 E3 13 25S 34 20 E
Kasai →, Dem. Rep. of the Congo 52 E3 3 30S 16 10 E
Kasaï-Oriental □, Dem. Rep. of the Congo 54 D1 5 0S 24 30 E
Kasaji, Dem. Rep. of the Congo 55 E1 10 25S 23 27 E
Kasama, Zambia 55 E3 10 16S 31 9 E
Kasan-dong, N. Korea 35 D14 41 18N 126 55 E
Kasane, Namibia 56 B3 17 34S 24 50 E
Kasanga, Tanzania 55 D3 8 30S 31 10 E
Kasaragod, India 40 N9 12 30N 74 58 E
Kasba L., Canada 73 A8 60 20N 102 10W
Kāseh Garān, Iran 44 C5 34 5N 46 2 E
Kasempa, Zambia 55 E2 13 30S 25 44 E
Kasenga, Dem. Rep. of the Congo 55 E2 10 20S 28 45 E
Kasese, Uganda 54 B3 0 13N 30 3 E
Kasewa, Zambia 55 E2 14 28S 28 53 E
Kasganj, India 43 F8 27 48N 78 42 E
Kashabowie, Canada 70 C1 48 40N 90 26W
Kashaf, Iran 45 C9 35 58N 61 7 E
Kāshān, Iran 45 C6 34 5N 51 30 E
Kashechewan, Canada 70 B3 52 18N 81 37W
Kashgar = Kashi, China 32 C2 39 30N 76 2 E
Kashi, China 32 C2 39 30N 76 2 E
Kashimbo, Dem. Rep. of the Congo 55 E2 11 12S 26 19 E
Kashipur, India 43 E8 29 15N 79 0 E
Kashiwazaki, Japan 31 F9 37 22N 138 33 E
Kashk-e Kohneh, Afghan. 40 B3 34 55N 62 30 E
Kashkū'īyeh, Iran 45 D7 30 31N 55 40 E
Kāshmar, Iran 45 C8 35 16N 58 26 E
Kashmir, Asia 43 C7 34 0N 76 0 E
Kashmor, Pakistan 42 E3 28 28N 69 32 E
Kashun Noerh = Gaxun Nur, China 32 B5 42 22N 100 30 E
Kasiari, India 43 H12 22 8N 87 14 E
Kasimov, Russia 24 D7 54 55N 41 20 E
Kasinge, Dem. Rep. of the Congo 54 D2 6 15S 26 58 E
Kasiruta, Indonesia 37 E7 0 25S 127 12 E
Kaskaskia →, U.S.A. 80 G10 37 58N 89 57W
Kaskattama →, Canada 73 B10 57 3N 90 4W
Kaskinen, Finland 9 E19 62 22N 21 15 E
Kaslo, Canada 72 D5 49 55N 116 55W
Kasmere L., Canada 73 B8 59 34N 101 10W
Kasongo, Dem. Rep. of the Congo 54 C2 4 30S 26 33 E
Kasongo Lunda, Dem. Rep. of the Congo 52 F3 6 35S 16 49 E
Kásos, Greece 21 G12 35 20N 26 55 E
Kassalâ, Sudan 51 E13 15 30N 36 0 E
Kassel, Germany 16 C5 51 18N 9 26 E
Kassiópi, Greece 23 A3 39 48N 19 53 E
Kasson, U.S.A. 80 C8 44 2N 92 45W
Kastamonu, Turkey 25 F5 41 25N 33 43 E
Kastélli, Greece 23 D5 35 29N 23 38 E
Kastéllion, Greece 23 D7 35 12N 25 20 E
Kasterlee, Belgium 15 C4 51 15N 4 59 E
Kastoría, Greece 21 D9 40 30N 21 19 E
Kasulu, Tanzania 54 C3 4 37S 30 5 E
Kasumi, Japan 31 G7 35 38N 134 38 E
Kasungu, Malawi 55 E3 13 0S 33 29 E
Kasur, Pakistan 42 D6 31 5N 74 25 E
Kataba, Zambia 55 F2 16 5S 25 10 E
Katahdin, Mt., U.S.A. 77 C11 45 54N 68 56W
Katako Kombe, Dem. Rep. of the Congo 54 C1 3 25S 24 20 E
Katale, Tanzania 54 C3 4 52S 31 7 E
Katanda, Katanga, Dem. Rep. of the Congo 54 D1 7 52S 24 13 E
Katanda, Nord-Kivu, Dem. Rep. of the Congo 54 C2 0 55S 29 21 E
Katanga □, Dem. Rep. of the Congo 54 D2 8 0S 25 0 E
Katangi, India 40 J11 21 56N 79 50 E
Katanning, Australia 61 F2 33 40S 117 33 E
Katavi Swamp, Tanzania 54 D3 6 50S 31 10 E
Kateríni, Greece 21 D10 40 18N 22 37 E
Katghora, India 43 H10 22 30N 82 33 E
Katha, Burma 41 G20 24 10N 96 30 E
Katherîna, Gebel, Egypt 44 D2 28 30N 33 57 E
Katherine, Australia 60 B5 14 27S 132 20 E
Katherine Gorge, Australia 60 B5 14 18S 132 28 E
Kathi, India 42 J6 21 47N 74 3 E
Kathiawar, India 42 H4 22 20N 71 0 E
Kathikas, Cyprus 23 E11 34 55N 32 25 E
Kathua, India 42 C6 32 23N 75 34 E
Katihar, India 43 G12 25 34N 87 36 E
Katima Mulilo, Zambia 56 B3 17 28S 24 13 E
Katimbira, Malawi 55 E3 12 40S 34 0 E
Katingan = Mendawai →, Indonesia 36 E4 3 30S 113 0 E
Katiola, Ivory C. 50 G4 8 10N 5 10W
Katmandu, Nepal 43 F11 27 45N 85 20 E
Katni, India 43 H9 23 51N 80 24 E
Káto Arkhánai, Greece 23 D7 35 15N 25 10 E
Káto Khorió, Greece 23 D7 35 3N 25 47 E
Káto Pyrgos, Cyprus 23 D11 35 11N 32 41 E
Katompe, Dem. Rep. of the Congo 54 D2 6 2S 26 23 E
Katonga →, Uganda 54 B3 0 34N 31 50 E
Katowice, Poland 17 C10 50 17N 19 5 E
Katrine, L., U.K. 12 E4 56 15N 4 30W
Katrineholm, Sweden 9 G17 59 9N 16 12 E
Katsepe, Madag. 57 B8 15 45S 46 15 E
Katsina, Nigeria 50 F7 13 0N 7 32 E
Katsumoto, Japan 31 H4 33 51N 129 42 E
Katsuura, Japan 31 G10 35 10N 140 20 E
Katsuyama, Japan 31 F8 36 3N 136 30 E
Kattaviá, Greece 23 D9 35 57N 27 46 E
Kattegat, Denmark 9 H14 56 40N 11 20 E
Katumba, Dem. Rep. of the Congo 54 D2 7 40S 25 17 E
Katungu, Kenya 54 C5 2 55S 40 3 E
Katwa, India 43 H13 23 30N 88 5 E
Katwijk, Neths. 15 B4 52 12N 4 24 E
Kauai, U.S.A. 74 H15 22 3N 159 30W
Kauai Channel, U.S.A. 74 H15 21 45N 158 50W
Kaufman, U.S.A. 81 J6 32 35N 96 19W
Kauhajoki, Finland 9 E20 62 25N 22 10 E
Kaukauna, U.S.A. 76 C1 44 17N 88 17W
Kaukauveld, Namibia 56 C3 20 0S 20 15 E
Kaunakakai, U.S.A. 74 H16 21 6N 157 1W
Kaunas, Lithuania 9 J20 54 54N 23 54 E
Kaunia, Bangla. 43 G13 25 46N 89 26 E
Kautokeino, Norway 8 B20 69 0N 23 4 E
Kauwapur, India 43 F10 27 31N 82 18 E
Kavacha, Russia 27 C17 60 16N 169 51 E
Kavalerovo, Russia 30 B7 44 15N 135 4 E
Kavali, India 40 M12 14 55N 80 1 E
Kaválla, Greece 21 D11 40 57N 24 28 E
Kavār, Iran 45 D7 29 11N 52 44 E
Kavi, India 42 H5 22 12N 72 38 E
Kavimba, Botswana 56 B3 18 2S 24 38 E
Kavīr, Dasht-e, Iran 45 C7 34 30N 55 0 E
Kavos, Greece 23 B4 39 23N 20 3 E
Kaw, Fr. Guiana 93 C8 4 30N 52 15W
Kawagama L., Canada 78 A6 45 18N 78 45W
Kawagoe, Japan 31 G9 35 55N 139 29 E
Kawaguchi, Japan 31 G9 35 52N 139 45 E
Kawambwa, Zambia 55 D2 9 48S 29 3 E
Kawanoe, Japan 31 G6 34 1N 133 34 E
Kawardha, India 43 J9 22 0N 81 17 E
Kawasaki, Japan 31 G9 35 35N 139 42 E
Kawasi, Indonesia 37 E7 1 38S 127 28 E
Kawerau, N.Z. 59 H6 38 7S 176 42 E
Kawhia Harbour, N.Z. 59 H5 38 5S 174 51 E
Kawio, Kepulauan, Indonesia 37 D7 4 30N 125 30 E
Kawnro, Burma 41 H21 22 48N 99 8 E
Kawthaung, Burma 39 H2 10 5N 98 36 E
Kawthoolei = Kayin □, Burma 41 L20 18 0N 97 30 E
Kawthule = Kayin □, Burma 41 L20 18 0N 97 30 E
Kaya, Burkina Faso 50 F5 13 4N 1 10W
Kayah □, Burma 41 K20 19 15N 97 15 E
Kayan →, Indonesia 36 D5 2 55N 117 35 E
Kaycee, U.S.A. 82 E10 43 43N 106 38W
Kayeli, Indonesia 37 E7 3 20S 127 10 E
Kayenta, U.S.A. 83 H8 36 44N 110 15W
Kayes, Mali 50 F3 14 25N 11 30W
Kayin □, Burma 41 L20 18 0N 97 30 E
Kayoa, Indonesia 37 D7 0 1N 127 28 E
Kayomba, Zambia 55 E1 13 11S 24 2 E
Kayseri, Turkey 25 G6 38 45N 35 30 E
Kaysville, U.S.A. 82 F8 41 2N 111 56W
Kazachye, Russia 27 B14 70 52N 135 58 E
Kazakstan ■, Asia 26 E7 50 0N 70 0 E
Kazan, Russia 24 C8 55 50N 49 10 E
Kazan →, Canada 73 A9 64 3N 95 35W
Kazan-Rettō, Pac. Oc. 64 E6 25 0N 141 0 E
Kazanlŭk, Bulgaria 21 C11 42 38N 25 20 E
Kazatin = Kozyatyn, Ukraine 17 D15 49 45N 28 50 E
Kāzerūn, Iran 45 D6 29 38N 51 40 E
Kazi Magomed = Qazimämmäd, Azerbaijan 45 A6 40 3N 49 0 E
Kazuno, Japan 30 D10 40 10N 140 45 E
Kazym →, Russia 26 C7 63 54N 65 50 E
Kéa, Greece 21 F11 37 35N 24 22 E
Keady, U.K. 13 B5 54 15N 6 42W
Kearney, U.S.A. 80 E5 40 42N 99 5W
Kearny, U.S.A. 83 K8 33 3N 110 55W
Kearsarge, Mt., U.S.A. 79 C13 43 22N 71 50W
Keban, Turkey 25 G6 38 50N 38 50 E
Keban Barajı, Turkey 25 G6 38 41N 38 33 E
Kebnekaise, Sweden 8 C18 67 53N 18 33 E
Kebri Dehar, Ethiopia 46 F3 6 45N 44 17 E
Kebumen, Indonesia 37 G13 7 42S 109 40 E
Kechika →, Canada 72 B3 59 41N 127 12W
Kecskemét, Hungary 17 E10 46 57N 19 42 E
Kėdainiai, Lithuania 9 J21 55 15N 24 2 E
Kedarnath, India 43 D8 30 44N 79 4 E
Kedgwick, Canada 71 C6 47 40N 67 20W
Kédhros Óros, Greece 23 D6 35 11N 24 37 E
Kediri, Indonesia 36 F4 7 51S 112 1 E
Keeler, U.S.A. 84 J9 36 29N 117 52W
Keeley L., Canada 73 C7 54 54N 108 8W
Keeling Is. = Cocos Is., Ind. Oc. 64 J1 12 10S 96 55 E
Keelung = Chilung, Taiwan 33 D7 25 3N 121 45 E
Keene, Canada 78 B6 44 15N 78 10W
Keene, Calif., U.S.A. 85 K8 35 13N 118 33W
Keene, N.H., U.S.A. 79 D12 42 56N 72 17W
Keene, N.Y., U.S.A. 79 B11 44 16N 73 46W
Keeper Hill, Ireland 13 D3 52 45N 8 16W
Keer-Weer, C., Australia 62 A3 14 0S 141 32 E
Keeseville, U.S.A. 79 B11 44 29N 73 30W
Keetmanshoop, Namibia 56 D2 26 35S 18 8 E
Keewatin, Canada 73 D10 49 46N 94 34W
Keewatin →, Canada 73 B8 56 29N 100 46W
Kefallinía, Greece 21 E9 38 20N 20 30 E
Kefamenanu, Indonesia 37 F6 9 28S 124 29 E
Kefar Sava, Israel 47 C3 32 11N 34 54 E
Keffi, Nigeria 50 G7 8 55N 7 43 E
Keflavík, Iceland 8 D2 64 2N 22 35W
Keg River, Canada 72 B5 57 54N 117 55W
Kegaska, Canada 71 B7 50 9N 61 18W
Keighley, U.K. 10 D6 53 52N 1 54W
Keila, Estonia 9 G21 59 18N 24 25 E
Keimoes, S. Africa 56 D3 28 41S 20 59 E
Keitele, Finland 8 E22 63 10N 26 20 E
Keith, U.K. 12 D6 57 32N 2 57W
Keizer, U.S.A. 82 D2 44 57N 123 1W
Kejimkujik Nat. Park, Canada 71 D6 44 25N 65 25W
Kejserr Franz Joseph Fd., Greenland 4 B6 73 30N 24 30W
Kekri, India 42 G6 26 0N 75 10 E
Kelan, China 34 E6 38 43N 111 31 E
Kelang, Malaysia 39 L3 3 2N 101 26 E
Kelantan →, Malaysia 39 J4 6 13N 102 14 E
Kelkit →, Turkey 25 F6 40 45N 36 32 E
Kellerberrin, Australia 61 F2 31 36S 117 38 E
Kellett, C., Canada 4 B1 72 0N 126 0W
Kelleys I., U.S.A. 78 E2 41 36N 82 42W
Kellogg, U.S.A. 82 C5 47 32N 116 7W
Kells = Ceanannus Mor, Ireland 13 C5 53 44N 6 53W
Kelokedhara, Cyprus 23 E11 34 48N 32 39 E
Kelowna, Canada 72 D5 49 50N 119 25W
Kelseyville, U.S.A. 84 G4 38 59N 122 50W
Kelso, N.Z. 59 L2 45 54S 169 15 E
Kelso, U.K. 12 F6 55 36N 2 26W
Kelso, U.S.A. 84 D4 46 9N 122 54W
Keluang, Malaysia 39 L4 2 3N 103 18 E
Kelvington, Canada 73 C8 52 10N 103 30W
Kem, Russia 24 B5 65 0N 34 38 E
Kem →, Russia 24 B5 64 57N 34 41 E
Kema, Indonesia 37 D7 1 22N 125 8 E
Kemah, Turkey 44 B3 39 32N 39 5 E
Kemaman, Malaysia 36 D2 4 12N 103 18 E
Kemano, Canada 72 C3 53 35N 128 0W
Kemasik, Malaysia 39 K4 4 25N 103 27 E
Kemerovo, Russia 26 D9 55 20N 86 5 E
Kemi, Finland 8 D21 65 44N 24 34 E
Kemi älv = Kemijoki →, Finland 8 D21 65 47N 24 32 E
Kemijärvi, Finland 8 C22 66 43N 27 22 E
Kemijoki →, Finland 8 D21 65 47N 24 32 E
Kemmerer, U.S.A. 82 F8 41 48N 110 32W
Kemmuna = Comino, Malta 23 C1 36 2N 14 20 E
Kemp, L., U.S.A. 81 J5 33 46N 99 9W
Kemp Land, Antarctica 5 C5 69 0S 55 0 E
Kempt, L., Canada 70 C5 47 25N 74 22W
Kempten, Germany 16 E6 47 45N 10 17 E
Kempton, Australia 62 G4 42 31S 147 12 E
Kemptville, Canada 79 B9 45 0N 75 38W
Ken →, India 43 G9 25 13N 80 27 E
Kenai, U.S.A. 68 B4 60 33N 151 16W
Kendai, India 43 H10 22 45N 82 37 E
Kendal, Indonesia 37 G14 6 56S 110 14 E
Kendal, U.K. 10 C5 54 20N 2 44W
Kendall, U.S.A. 77 N5 25 41N 80 19W
Kendall →, Australia 62 A3 14 4S 141 35 E
Kendallville, U.S.A. 76 E3 41 27N 85 16W
Kendari, Indonesia 37 E6 3 50S 122 30 E
Kendawangan, Indonesia 36 E4 2 32S 110 17 E
Kendrapara, India 41 J15 20 35N 86 30 E
Kendrew, S. Africa 56 E3 32 32S 24 30 E
Kene Thao, Laos 38 D3 17 44N 101 10 E
Kenedy, U.S.A. 81 L6 28 49N 97 51W
Kenema, S. Leone 50 G3 7 50N 11 14W
Keng Kok, Laos 38 D5 16 26N 105 12 E
Keng Tawng, Burma 41 J21 20 45N 98 18 E
Keng Tung, Burma 41 J21 21 0N 99 30 E
Kengeja, Tanzania 54 D4 5 26S 39 45 E
Kenhardt, S. Africa 56 D3 29 19S 21 12 E
Kenitra, Morocco 50 B4 34 15N 6 40W
Kenli, China 35 F10 37 30N 118 20 E
Kenmare, Ireland 13 E2 51 53N 9 36W
Kenmare, U.S.A. 80 A3 48 41N 102 5W
Kenmare River, Ireland 13 E2 51 48N 9 51W
Kennebago Lake, U.S.A. 79 A14 45 4N 70 40W
Kennebec, U.S.A. 80 D5 43 54N 99 52W
Kennebec →, U.S.A. 77 D11 43 45N 69 46W
Kennebunk, U.S.A. 79 C14 43 23N 70 33W
Kennedy, Zimbabwe 56 B4 18 52S 27 10 E
Kennedy Ra., Australia 61 D2 24 45S 115 10 E
Kennedy Taungdeik, Burma 41 H18 23 15N 93 45 E
Kenner, U.S.A. 81 L9 29 59N 90 15W
Kennet →, U.K. 11 F7 51 27N 0 57W
Kenneth Ra., Australia 61 D2 23 50S 117 8 E
Kennett, U.S.A. 81 G9 36 14N 90 3W
Kennewick, U.S.A. 82 C4 46 12N 119 7W
Kenogami →, Canada 70 B3 51 6N 84 28W
Kenora, Canada 73 D10 49 47N 94 29W
Kenosha, U.S.A. 76 D2 42 35N 87 49W
Kensington, Canada 71 C7 46 28N 63 34W
Kent, Ohio, U.S.A. 78 E3 41 9N 81 22W
Kent, Tex., U.S.A. 81 K2 31 4N 104 13W
Kent, Wash., U.S.A. 84 C4 47 23N 122 14W
Kent □, U.K. 11 F8 51 12N 0 40 E
Kent Group, Australia 62 F4 39 30S 147 20 E
Kent Pen., Canada 68 B9 68 30N 107 0W
Kentaū, Kazakstan 26 E7 43 32N 68 36 E
Kentland, U.S.A. 76 E2 40 46N 87 27W
Kenton, U.S.A. 76 E4 40 39N 83 37W
Kentucky □, U.S.A. 76 G3 37 0N 84 0W

Korshunovo

Korshunovo, Russia 27 D12 58 37N 110 10 E
Korsør, Denmark 9 J14 55 20N 11 9 E
Kortrijk, Belgium 15 D3 50 50N 3 17 E
Korwai, India 42 G8 24 7N 78 5 E
Koryakskoye Nagorye, Russia 27 C18 61 0N 171 0 E
Koryŏng, S. Korea 35 G15 35 44N 128 15 E
Kos, Greece 21 F12 36 50N 27 15 E
Koschagyl, Kazakstan 25 E9 46 40N 54 0 E
Kościan, Poland 17 B9 52 5N 16 40 E
Kosciusko, U.S.A. 81 J10 33 4N 89 35W
Kosha, Sudan 51 D12 20 50N 30 30 E
K'oshih = Kashi, China 32 C2 39 30N 76 2 E
Koshiki-Rettō, Japan 31 J4 31 45N 129 49 E
Kosi, India 42 F7 27 48N 77 29 E
Kosi →, India 43 E8 28 41N 78 57 E
Košice, Slovak Rep. 17 D11 48 42N 21 15 E
Koskhinoú, Greece 23 C10 36 23N 28 13 E
Koslan, Russia 24 B8 63 34N 49 14 E
Kosŏng, N. Korea 35 E15 38 40N 128 22 E
Kosovo □, Yugoslavia 21 C9 42 30N 21 0 E
Kosovska Mitrovica, Kosovo, Yug. 21 C9 42 54N 20 52 E
Kossou, L. de, Ivory C. 50 G4 6 59N 5 31W
Koster, S. Africa 56 D4 25 52S 26 54 E
Kôstî, Sudan 51 F12 13 8N 32 43 E
Kostopil, Ukraine 17 C14 50 51N 26 22 E
Kostroma, Russia 24 C7 57 50N 40 58 E
Kostrzyn, Poland 16 B8 52 35N 14 39 E
Koszalin, Poland 16 A9 54 11N 16 8 E
Kot Addu, Pakistan 42 D4 30 30N 71 0 E
Kot Kapura, India 42 D6 30 35N 74 50 E
Kot Moman, Pakistan 42 C5 32 13N 73 0 E
Kot Sultan, Pakistan 42 D4 30 46N 70 56 E
Kota, India 42 G6 25 14N 75 49 E
Kota Baharu, Malaysia 39 J4 6 7N 102 14 E
Kota Barrage, India 42 G6 25 6N 75 51 E
Kota Belud, Malaysia 36 C5 6 21N 116 26 E
Kota Kinabalu, Malaysia 36 C5 6 0N 116 4 E
Kota Kubu Baharu, Malaysia 39 L3 3 34N 101 39 E
Kota Tinggi, Malaysia 39 M4 1 44N 103 53 E
Kotaagung, Indonesia 36 F2 5 38S 104 29 E
Kotabaru, Indonesia 36 E5 3 20S 116 20 E
Kotabumi, Indonesia 36 E2 4 49S 104 54 E
Kotamobagu, Indonesia 37 D6 0 57N 124 31 E
Kotcho L., Canada 72 B4 59 7N 121 12W
Kotdwara, India 43 E8 29 45N 78 32 E
Kotelnich, Russia 24 C8 58 22N 48 24 E
Kotelnikovo, Russia 25 E7 47 38N 43 8 E
Kotelnyy, Ostrov, Russia 27 B14 75 10N 139 0 E
Kothari →, India 42 G6 25 20N 75 4 E
Kothi, Mad. P., India 43 H10 23 21N 82 3 E
Kothi, Mad. P., India 43 G9 24 45N 80 40 E
Kotiro, Pakistan 42 F2 26 17N 67 13 E
Kotka, Finland 9 F22 60 28N 26 58 E
Kotlas, Russia 24 B8 61 17N 46 43 E
Kotli, Pakistan 42 C5 33 30N 73 55 E
Kotma, India 43 H9 23 12N 81 58 E
Kotmul, Pakistan 43 B6 35 32N 75 10 E
Kotor, Montenegro, Yug. 21 C8 42 25N 18 47 E
Kotovsk, Ukraine 17 E15 47 45N 29 35 E
Kotputli, India 42 F7 27 43N 76 12 E
Kotri, Pakistan 42 G3 25 22N 68 22 E
Kotturu, India 40 M10 14 45N 76 10 E
Kotuy →, Russia 27 B11 71 54N 102 6 E
Kotzebue, U.S.A. 68 B3 66 53N 162 39W
Koudougou, Burkina Faso 50 F5 12 10N 2 20W
Koufonísi, Greece 23 E8 34 56N 26 8 E
Kougaberge, S. Africa 56 E3 33 48S 23 50 E
Kouilou →, Congo 52 E2 4 10S 12 5 E
Koula Moutou, Gabon 52 E2 1 15S 12 25 E
Koulen = Kulen, Cambodia 38 F5 13 50N 104 40 E
Kouloúra, Greece 23 A3 39 42N 19 54 E
Koúm-bournoú, Ákra, Greece 23 C10 36 15N 28 11 E
Koumala, Australia 62 C4 21 38S 149 15 E
Koumra, Chad 51 G9 8 50N 17 35 E
Kounradskiy, Kazakstan 26 E8 46 59N 75 0 E
Kountze, U.S.A. 81 K7 30 22N 94 19W
Kouris →, Cyprus 23 E11 34 38N 32 54 E
Kourou, Fr. Guiana 93 B8 5 9N 52 39W
Kousseri, Cameroon 51 F8 12 0N 14 55 E
Kouvola, Finland 9 F22 60 52N 26 43 E
Kovdor, Russia 24 A5 67 34N 30 24 E
Kovel, Ukraine 17 C13 51 11N 24 38 E
Kovrov, Russia 24 C7 56 25N 41 25 E
Kowanyama, Australia 62 B3 15 29S 141 44 E
Kowŏn, N. Korea 35 E14 39 26N 127 14 E
Köyceğiz, Turkey 21 F13 36 57N 28 40 E
Koza, Japan 31 L3 26 19N 127 46 E
Kozan, Turkey 44 B2 37 26N 35 50 E
Kozáni, Greece 21 D9 40 19N 21 47 E
Kozhikode = Calicut, India 40 P9 11 15N 75 43 E
Kozhva, Russia 24 A10 65 10N 57 0 E
Kozyatyn, Ukraine 17 D15 49 45N 28 50 E
Kra, Isthmus of = Kra, Kho Khot, Thailand 39 G2 10 15N 99 30 E
Kra, Kho Khot, Thailand 39 G2 10 15N 99 30 E
Kra Buri, Thailand 39 G2 10 22N 98 46 E
Kraai →, S. Africa 56 E4 30 40S 26 45 E
Krabi, Thailand 39 H2 8 4N 98 55 E
Kracheh, Cambodia 38 F6 12 32N 106 10 E
Kragan, Indonesia 37 G14 6 43S 111 38 E
Kragerø, Norway 9 G13 58 52N 9 25 E
Kragujevac, Serbia, Yug. 21 B9 44 2N 20 56 E
Krajina, Bos.-H. 20 B7 44 45N 16 35 E
Krakatau = Rakata, Pulau, Indonesia 36 F3 6 10S 105 20 E
Krakatoa = Rakata, Pulau, Indonesia 36 F3 6 10S 105 20 E
Krakor, Cambodia 38 F5 12 32N 104 12 E
Kraków, Poland 17 C10 50 4N 19 57 E
Kralanh, Cambodia 38 F4 13 35N 103 25 E
Kraljevo, Serbia, Yug. 21 C9 43 44N 20 41 E
Kramatorsk, Ukraine 25 E6 48 50N 37 30 E
Kramfors, Sweden 9 E17 62 55N 17 48 E
Kranj, Slovenia 16 E8 46 16N 14 22 E
Krankskop, S. Africa 57 D5 28 0S 30 47 E
Krasavino, Russia 24 B8 60 58N 46 29 E
Kraskino, Russia 27 E14 42 44N 130 48 E
Kraśnik, Poland 17 C12 50 55N 22 15 E
Krasnoarmeysk, Russia 26 D5 51 0N 45 42 E
Krasnodar, Russia 25 E6 45 5N 39 0 E
Krasnokamsk, Russia 24 C10 58 4N 55 48 E
Krasnoperekopsk, Ukraine 25 E5 46 0N 33 54 E
Krasnorechenskiy, Russia 30 B7 44 41N 135 14 E
Krasnoselkup, Russia 26 C9 65 20N 82 10 E
Krasnoturinsk, Russia 24 C11 59 46N 60 12 E
Krasnoufimsk, Russia 24 C10 56 36N 57 38 E
Krasnouralsk, Russia 24 C11 58 21N 60 3 E
Krasnovishersk, Russia 24 B10 60 23N 57 3 E
Krasnovodsk = Türkmenbashi, Turkmenistan 25 G9 40 5N 53 5 E
Krasnoyarsk, Russia 27 D10 56 8N 93 0 E
Krasnyy Kut, Russia 25 D8 50 50N 47 0 E
Krasnyy Luch, Ukraine 25 E6 48 13N 39 0 E
Krasnyy Yar, Russia 25 E8 46 43N 48 23 E
Kratie = Kracheh, Cambodia 38 F6 12 32N 106 10 E
Krau, Indonesia 37 E10 3 19S 140 5 E
Kravanh, Chuor Phnum, Cambodia 39 G4 12 0N 103 32 E
Krefeld, Germany 16 C4 51 20N 6 33 E
Kremen, Croatia 16 F8 44 28N 15 53 E
Kremenchug = Kremenchuk, Ukraine 25 E5 49 5N 33 25 E
Kremenchuk, Ukraine 25 E5 49 5N 33 25 E
Kremenchuksk Vdskh., Ukraine 25 E5 49 20N 32 30 E
Kremenets, Ukraine 17 C13 50 8N 25 43 E
Kremmling, U.S.A. 82 F10 40 4N 106 24W
Krems, Austria 16 D8 48 25N 15 36 E
Kretinga, Lithuania 9 J19 55 53N 21 15 E
Kribi, Cameroon 52 D1 2 57N 9 56 E
Krichev = Krychaw, Belarus 17 B16 53 40N 31 41 E
Kriós, Ákra, Greece 23 D5 35 13N 23 34 E
Krishna →, India 41 M12 15 57N 80 59 E
Krishnanagar, India 43 H13 23 24N 88 33 E
Kristiansand, Norway 9 G13 58 8N 8 1 E
Kristianstad, Sweden 9 H16 56 2N 14 9 E
Kristiansund, Norway 8 E12 63 7N 7 45 E
Kristiinankaupunki, Finland 9 E19 62 16N 21 21 E
Kristinehamn, Sweden 9 G16 59 18N 14 7 E
Kristinestad = Kristiinankaupunki, Finland 9 E19 62 16N 21 21 E
Kríti, Greece 23 D7 35 15N 25 0 E
Kritsá, Greece 23 D7 35 10N 25 41 E
Krivoy Rog = Kryvyy Rih, Ukraine 25 E5 47 51N 33 20 E
Krk, Croatia 16 F8 45 8N 14 40 E
Krokodil →, Mozam. 57 D5 25 14S 32 18 E
Krong Kaoh Kong, Cambodia 36 B2 11 35N 103 0 E
Kronprins Olav Kyst, Antarctica 5 C5 69 0S 42 0 E
Kronshtadt, Russia 24 B4 59 57N 29 51 E
Kroonstad, S. Africa 56 D4 27 43S 27 19 E
Kropotkin, Russia 25 E7 45 28N 40 28 E
Krosno, Poland 17 D11 49 42N 21 46 E
Krotoszyn, Poland 17 C9 51 42N 17 23 E
Kroussón, Greece 23 D6 35 13N 24 59 E
Kruger Nat. Park, S. Africa 57 C5 23 30S 31 40 E
Krugersdorp, S. Africa 57 D4 26 5S 27 46 E
Kruisfontein, S. Africa 56 E3 33 59S 24 43 E
Krung Thep = Bangkok, Thailand 38 F3 13 45N 100 35 E
Krupki, Belarus 17 A15 54 19N 29 8 E
Kruševac, Serbia, Yug. 21 C9 43 35N 21 28 E
Krychaw, Belarus 17 B16 53 40N 31 41 E
Krymskiy Poluostrov = Krymskyy Pivostriv, Ukraine 25 F5 45 0N 34 0 E
Krymskyy Pivostriv, Ukraine 25 F5 45 0N 34 0 E
Kryvyy Rih, Ukraine 25 E5 47 51N 33 20 E
Ksar el Kebir, Morocco 50 B4 35 0N 6 0W
Ksar es Souk = Er Rachidia, Morocco 50 B5 31 58N 4 20W
Kuala Belait, Malaysia 36 D4 4 35N 114 11 E
Kuala Berang, Malaysia 39 K4 5 5N 103 1 E
Kuala Dungun = Dungun, Malaysia 39 K4 4 45N 103 25 E
Kuala Kangsar, Malaysia 39 K3 4 46N 100 56 E
Kuala Kelawang, Malaysia 39 L4 2 56N 102 5 E
Kuala Kerai, Malaysia 39 K4 5 30N 102 12 E
Kuala Lipis, Malaysia 39 K4 4 10N 102 3 E
Kuala Lumpur, Malaysia 39 L3 3 9N 101 41 E
Kuala Nerang, Malaysia 39 J3 6 16N 100 37 E
Kuala Pilah, Malaysia 39 L4 2 45N 102 15 E
Kuala Rompin, Malaysia 39 L4 2 49N 103 29 E
Kuala Selangor, Malaysia 39 L3 3 20N 101 15 E
Kuala Sepetang, Malaysia 39 K3 4 49N 100 28 E
Kuala Terengganu, Malaysia 39 K4 5 20N 103 8 E
Kualajelai, Indonesia 36 E4 2 58S 110 46 E
Kualakapuas, Indonesia 36 E4 2 55S 114 20 E
Kualakurun, Indonesia 36 E4 1 10S 113 50 E
Kualapembuang, Indonesia 36 E4 3 14S 112 38 E
Kualasimpang, Indonesia 36 D1 4 17N 98 3 E
Kuancheng, China 35 D10 40 37N 118 30 E
Kuandang, Indonesia 37 D6 0 56N 123 1 E
Kuandian, China 35 D13 40 45N 124 45 E
Kuangchou = Guangzhou, China 33 D6 23 5N 113 10 E
Kuantan, Malaysia 39 L4 3 49N 103 20 E
Kuba = Quba, Azerbaijan 25 F8 41 21N 48 32 E
Kuban →, Russia 25 E6 45 20N 37 30 E
Kubokawa, Japan 31 H6 33 12N 133 8 E
Kucha Gompa, India 43 B7 34 25N 76 56 E
Kuchaman, India 42 F6 27 13N 74 47 E
Kuchinda, India 43 J11 21 44N 84 21 E
Kuching, Malaysia 36 D4 1 33N 110 25 E
Kuchino-eruba-Jima, Japan 31 J5 30 28N 130 12 E
Kuchino-Shima, Japan 31 K4 29 57N 129 55 E
Kuchinotsu, Japan 31 H5 32 36N 130 11 E
Kucing = Kuching, Malaysia 36 D4 1 33N 110 25 E
Kud →, Pakistan 42 F2 26 5N 66 20 E
Kuda, India 40 H7 23 10N 71 15 E
Kudat, Malaysia 36 C5 6 55N 116 55 E
Kudus, Indonesia 37 G14 6 48S 110 51 E
Kudymkar, Russia 24 C9 59 1N 54 39 E
Kueiyang = Guiyang, China 32 D5 26 32N 106 40 E
Kufra Oasis = Al Kufrah, Libya 51 D10 24 17N 23 15 E
Kufstein, Austria 16 E7 47 35N 12 11 E
Kugluktuk, Canada 68 B8 67 50N 115 5W
Kugong I., Canada 70 A4 56 18N 79 50W
Kūhak, Iran 40 F3 27 12N 63 10 E
Kuhan, Pakistan 42 E2 28 19N 67 14 E
Kūhbonān, Iran 45 D8 31 23N 56 19 E
Kūhestak, Iran 45 E8 26 47N 57 2 E
Kuhin, Iran 45 B6 36 22N 49 40 E
Kūhīrī, Iran 45 E9 26 55N 61 2 E
Kūhpāyeh, Eşfahan, Iran 45 C7 32 44N 52 20 E
Kūhpāyeh, Kermān, Iran 45 D8 30 35N 57 15 E
Kūhrān, Kūh-e, Iran 45 E8 26 46N 58 12 E
Kui Buri, Thailand 39 F2 12 3N 99 52 E
Kuiseb →, Namibia 56 B2 22 59S 14 31 E
Kuito, Angola 53 G3 12 22S 16 55 E
Kuiu I., U.S.A. 72 B2 57 45N 134 10W
Kujang, N. Korea 35 E14 39 57N 126 1 E
Kuji, Japan 30 D10 40 11N 141 46 E
Kujū-San, Japan 31 H5 33 5N 131 15 E
Kukës, Albania 21 C9 42 5N 20 27 E
Kukup, Malaysia 39 M4 1 20N 103 27 E
Kula, Turkey 21 E13 38 32N 28 40 E
Kulachi, Pakistan 42 D4 31 56N 70 27 E
Kulai, Malaysia 39 M4 1 44N 103 35 E
Kulal, Mt., Kenya 54 B4 2 42N 36 57 E
Kulasekarappattinam, India 40 Q11 8 20N 78 5 E
Kuldīga, Latvia 9 H19 56 58N 21 59 E
Kuldja = Yining, China 26 E9 43 58N 81 10 E
Kulen, Cambodia 38 F5 13 50N 104 40 E
Kulgam, India 43 C6 33 36N 75 2 E
Kulgera, Australia 62 D1 25 50S 133 18 E
Kulim, Malaysia 39 K3 5 22N 100 34 E
Kulin, Australia 61 F2 32 40S 118 2 E
Kŭlob, Tajikistan 26 F7 37 55N 69 50 E
Kulsary, Kazakstan 25 E9 46 59N 54 1 E
Kulti, India 43 H12 23 43N 86 50 E
Kulu, India 42 D7 31 58N 77 6 E
Kulumbura, Australia 60 B4 13 55S 126 35 E
Kulunda, Russia 26 D8 52 35N 78 57 E
Kulungar, Afghan. 42 C3 34 0N 69 2 E
Kūlvand, Iran 45 D7 31 21N 54 35 E
Kulyab = Kŭlob, Tajikistan 26 F7 37 55N 69 50 E
Kuma →, Russia 25 F8 44 55N 47 0 E
Kumagaya, Japan 31 F9 36 9N 139 22 E
Kumai, Indonesia 36 E4 2 44S 111 43 E
Kumamba, Kepulauan, Indonesia 37 E9 1 36S 138 45 E
Kumamoto, Japan 31 H5 32 45N 130 45 E
Kumamoto □, Japan 31 H5 32 55N 130 55 E
Kumanovo, Macedonia 21 C9 42 9N 21 42 E
Kumara, N.Z. 59 K3 42 37S 171 12 E
Kumarina, Australia 61 D2 24 41S 119 32 E
Kumasi, Ghana 50 G5 6 41N 1 38W
Kumayri = Gyumri, Armenia 25 F7 40 47N 43 50 E
Kumba, Cameroon 52 D1 4 36N 9 24 E
Kumbakonam, India 40 P11 10 58N 79 25 E
Kumbarilla, Australia 63 D5 27 15S 150 55 E
Kumbhraj, India 42 G7 24 22N 77 3 E
Kumbia, Australia 63 D5 26 41S 151 39 E
Kŭmch'ŏn, N. Korea 35 E14 38 10N 126 29 E
Kumdok, India 43 C8 33 32N 78 10 E
Kume-Shima, Japan 31 L3 26 20N 126 47 E
Kumertau, Russia 24 D10 52 45N 55 57 E
Kumharsain, India 42 D7 31 19N 77 27 E
Kŭmhwa, S. Korea 35 E14 38 17N 127 28 E
Kumi, Uganda 54 B3 1 30N 33 58 E
Kumla, Sweden 9 G16 59 8N 15 10 E
Kumo, Nigeria 51 F8 10 1N 11 12 E
Kumon Bum, Burma 41 F20 26 30N 97 15 E
Kunashir, Ostrov, Russia 27 E15 44 0N 146 0 E
Kunda, Estonia 9 G22 59 30N 26 34 E
Kunda, India 43 G9 25 43N 81 31 E
Kundar →, Pakistan 42 D3 31 56N 69 19 E
Kundian, Pakistan 42 C4 32 27N 71 28 E
Kundla, India 42 J4 21 21N 71 25 E
Kunga →, Bangla. 43 J13 21 46N 89 30 E
Kunghit I., Canada 72 C2 52 6N 131 3W
Kungrad = Qŭnghirot, Uzbekistan 26 E6 43 6N 58 54 E
Kungsbacka, Sweden 9 H15 57 30N 12 5 E
Kungur, Russia 24 C10 57 25N 56 57 E
Kunhar →, Pakistan 43 B5 34 20N 73 30 E
Kuningan, Indonesia 37 G13 6 59S 108 29 E
Kunlong, Burma 41 H21 23 20N 98 50 E
Kunlun Shan, Asia 32 C3 36 0N 86 30 E
Kunming, China 32 D5 25 1N 102 41 E
Kunsan, S. Korea 35 G14 35 59N 126 45 E
Kununurra, Australia 60 C4 15 40S 128 50 E
Kunwari →, India 43 F8 26 26N 79 11 E
Kunya-Urgench = Köneürgench, Turkmenistan 26 E6 42 19N 59 10 E
Kuopio, Finland 8 E22 62 53N 27 35 E
Kupa →, Croatia 16 F9 45 28N 16 24 E
Kupang, Indonesia 37 F6 10 19S 123 39 E
Kupreanof I., U.S.A. 72 B2 56 50N 133 30W
Kupyansk-Uzlovoi, Ukraine 25 E6 49 40N 37 43 E
Kuqa, China 32 B3 41 35N 82 30 E
Kür →, Azerbaijan 25 G8 39 29N 49 15 E
Kür Dili, Azerbaijan 45 B6 39 3N 49 13 E
Kura = Kür →, Azerbaijan 25 G8 39 29N 49 15 E
Kuranda, Australia 62 B4 16 48S 145 35 E
Kuranga, India 42 H3 22 4N 69 10 E
Kurashiki, Japan 31 G6 34 40N 133 50 E
Kurayoshi, Japan 31 G6 35 26N 133 50 E
Kŭrdzhali, Bulgaria 21 D11 41 38N 25 21 E
Kure, Japan 31 G6 34 14N 132 32 E
Kuressaare, Estonia 9 G20 58 15N 22 30 E
Kurgan, Russia 26 D7 55 26N 65 18 E
Kuri, India 42 F4 26 37N 70 43 E
Kuria Maria Is. = Khurīyā Murīyā, Jazā'ir, Oman 46 D6 17 30N 55 58 E
Kuridala, Australia 62 C3 21 16S 140 29 E
Kurigram, Bangla. 41 G16 25 49N 89 39 E
Kurikka, Finland 9 E20 62 36N 22 24 E
Kuril Is. = Kurilskiye Ostrova, Russia 27 E15 45 0N 150 0 E
Kuril Trench, Pac. Oc. 28 E19 44 0N 153 0 E
Kurilsk, Russia 27 E15 45 14N 147 53 E
Kurilskiye Ostrova, Russia 27 E15 45 0N 150 0 E
Kurino, Japan 31 J5 31 57N 130 43 E
Kurinskaya Kosa = Kür Dili, Azerbaijan 45 B6 39 3N 49 13 E
Kurnool, India 40 M11 15 45N 78 0 E
Kuro-Shima, Kagoshima, Japan 31 J4 30 50N 129 57 E
Kuro-Shima, Okinawa, Japan 31 M2 24 14N 124 1 E
Kurow, N.Z. 59 L3 44 44S 170 29 E
Kurram →, Pakistan 42 C4 32 36N 71 20 E
Kurrimine, Australia 62 B4 17 47S 146 6 E
Kurshskiy Zaliv, Russia 9 J19 55 9N 21 6 E
Kursk, Russia 24 D6 51 42N 36 11 E
Kuruçay, Turkey 44 B3 39 39N 38 29 E
Kuruktag, China 32 B3 41 0N 89 0 E
Kuruman, S. Africa 56 D3 27 28S 23 28 E
Kuruman →, S. Africa 56 D3 26 56S 20 39 E
Kurume, Japan 31 H5 33 15N 130 30 E
Kurunegala, Sri Lanka 40 R12 7 30N 80 23 E
Kurya, Russia 24 B10 61 42N 57 9 E
Kus Gölü, Turkey 21 D12 40 10N 27 55 E
Kuşadası, Turkey 21 F12 37 52N 27 15 E
Kusatsu, Japan 31 F9 36 37N 138 36 E
Kusawa L., Canada 72 A1 60 20N 136 13W
Kushalgarh, India 42 H6 23 10N 74 27 E
Kushikino, Japan 31 J5 31 44N 130 16 E
Kushima, Japan 31 J5 31 29N 131 14 E
Kushimoto, Japan 31 H7 33 28N 135 47 E
Kushiro, Japan 30 C12 43 0N 144 25 E
Kushiro-Gawa →, Japan 30 C12 42 59N 144 23 E
Kūshk, Iran 45 D8 28 46N 56 51 E
Kushka = Gushgy, Turkmenistan 26 F7 35 20N 62 18 E
Kūshkī, Iran 44 C5 33 31N 47 13 E
Kushol, India 43 C7 33 40N 76 36 E
Kushtia, Bangla. 41 H16 23 55N 89 5 E
Kushva, Russia 24 C10 58 18N 59 45 E
Kuskokwim B., U.S.A. 68 C3 59 45N 162 25W
Kusmi, India 43 H10 23 17N 83 55 E
Kussharo-Ko, Japan 30 C12 43 38N 144 21 E
Kustanay = Qostanay, Kazakstan 26 D7 53 10N 63 35 E
Kut, Ko, Thailand 39 G4 11 40N 102 35 E
Kütahya, Turkey 25 G5 39 30N 30 2 E
Kutaisi, Georgia 25 F7 42 19N 42 40 E
Kutaraja = Banda Aceh, Indonesia 36 C1 5 35N 95 20 E
Kutch, Gulf of = Kachchh, Gulf of, India 42 H3 22 50N 69 15 E
Kutch, Rann of = Kachchh, Rann of, India 42 H4 24 0N 70 0 E
Kutiyana, India 42 J4 21 36N 70 2 E
Kutno, Poland 17 B10 52 15N 19 23 E
Kutse, Botswana 56 C3 21 7S 22 16 E
Kutu, Dem. Rep. of the Congo 52 E3 2 40S 18 11 E
Kutum, Sudan 51 F10 14 10N 24 40 E
Kuujjuaq, Canada 69 C13 58 6N 68 15W
Kuujjuarapik, Canada 70 A4 55 20N 77 35W
Kuŭp-tong, N. Korea 35 D14 40 45N 126 1 E
Kuusamo, Finland 8 D23 65 57N 29 8 E
Kuusankoski, Finland 9 F22 60 55N 26 38 E
Kuwait = Al Kuwayt, Kuwait 46 B4 29 30N 48 0 E
Kuwait ■, Asia 46 B4 29 30N 47 30 E
Kuwana, Japan 31 G8 35 5N 136 43 E
Kuwana →, India 43 F10 26 25N 83 15 E
Kuybyshev = Samara, Russia 24 D9 53 8N 50 6 E
Kuybyshev, Russia 26 D8 55 27N 78 19 E
Kuybyshevskoye Vdkhr., Russia 24 C8 55 2N 49 30 E
Kuye He →, China 34 E6 38 23N 110 46 E
Kūyeh, Iran 44 B5 38 45N 47 57 E
Kūysanjaq, Iraq 44 B5 36 5N 44 38 E
Kuyto, Ozero, Russia 24 B5 65 6N 31 20 E
Kuyumba, Russia 27 C10 60 58N 96 59 E
Kuzey Anadolu Dağları, Turkey 25 F6 41 30N 35 0 E
Kuznetsk, Russia 24 D8 53 12N 46 40 E
Kuzomen, Russia 24 A6 66 22N 36 50 E
Kvænangen, Norway 8 A19 70 5N 21 15 E
Kvaløy, Norway 8 B18 69 40N 18 30 E
Kvarner, Croatia 16 F8 44 50N 14 10 E
Kvarnerič, Croatia 16 F8 44 43N 14 37 E
Kwa-Nobuhle, S. Africa 53 L5 33 50S 25 22 E
Kwabhaca, S. Africa 57 E4 30 51S 29 0 E
Kwakhanai, Botswana 56 C3 21 39S 21 16 E
Kwakoegron, Surinam 93 B7 5 12N 55 25W
Kwale, Kenya 54 C4 4 15S 39 31 E
KwaMashu, S. Africa 57 D5 29 45S 30 58 E
Kwando →, Africa 56 B3 18 27S 23 32 E
Kwangdaeri, N. Korea 35 D14 40 31N 127 32 E
Kwangju, S. Korea 35 G14 35 9N 126 54 E
Kwango →, Dem. Rep. of the Congo 52 E3 3 14S 17 22 E
Kwangsi-Chuang = Guangxi Zhuangzu Zizhiqu □, China 33 D5 24 0N 109 0 E
Kwangtung = Guangdong □, China 33 D6 23 0N 113 0 E
Kwataboahegan →, Canada 70 B3 51 9N 80 50W
Kwatisore, Indonesia 37 E8 3 18S 134 50 E
KwaZulu Natal □, S. Africa 57 D5 29 0S 30 0 E
Kweichow = Guizhou □, China 32 D5 27 0N 107 0 E
Kwekwe, Zimbabwe 55 F2 18 58S 29 48 E
Kwidzyn, Poland 17 B10 53 44N 18 55 E
Kwinana New Town, Australia 61 F2 32 15S 115 47 E
Kwoka, Indonesia 37 E8 0 31S 132 27 E
Kyabra Cr. →, Australia 63 D3 25 36S 142 55 E
Kyaikto, Burma 38 D1 17 20N 97 3 E
Kyakhta, Russia 27 D11 50 30N 106 25 E
Kyancutta, Australia 63 E2 33 8S 135 33 E
Kyaukpadaung, Burma 41 J19 20 52N 95 8 E
Kyaukpyu, Burma 41 K18 19 28N 93 30 E
Kyaukse, Burma 41 J20 21 36N 96 10 E
Kyburz, U.S.A. 84 G6 38 47N 120 18W
Kyelang, India 42 C7 32 35N 77 2 E
Kyenjojo, Uganda 54 B3 0 40N 30 37 E
Kyle, Canada 73 C7 50 50N 108 2W
Kyle Dam, Zimbabwe 55 G3 20 15S 31 0 E
Kyle of Lochalsh, U.K. 12 D3 57 17N 5 44W
Kymijoki →, Finland 9 F22 60 30N 26 55 E
Kynuna, Australia 62 C3 21 37S 141 55 E
Kyō-ga-Saki, Japan 31 G7 35 45N 135 15 E
Kyoga, L., Uganda 54 B3 1 35N 33 0 E
Kyogle, Australia 63 D5 28 40S 153 0 E
Kyongju, S. Korea 35 G15 35 51N 129 14 E
Kyongpyaw, Burma 41 L19 17 12N 95 10 E
Kyŏngsŏng, N. Korea 35 D15 41 35N 129 36 E
Kyōto, Japan 31 G7 35 0N 135 45 E
Kyōto □, Japan 31 G7 35 15N 135 45 E
Kyparissovouno, Cyprus 23 D12 35 19N 33 10 E
Kyperounda, Cyprus 23 E11 34 56N 32 58 E
Kyrenia, Cyprus 23 D12 35 20N 33 20 E
Kyrgyzstan ■, Asia 26 E8 42 0N 75 0 E
Kyrönjoki →, Finland 8 E19 63 14N 21 45 E
Kystatyam, Russia 27 C13 67 20N 123 10 E
Kythréa, Cyprus 23 D12 35 15N 33 29 E

Lapseki

Kyunhla, *Burma* **41 H19** 23 25N 95 15 E
Kyuquot Sound, *Canada* **72 D3** 50 2N 127 22W
Kyūshū, *Japan* **31 H5** 33 0N 131 0 E
Kyūshū □, *Japan* **31 H5** 33 0N 131 0 E
Kyūshū-Sanchi, *Japan* **31 H5** 32 35N 131 17 E
Kyustendil, *Bulgaria* **21 C10** 42 16N 22 41 E
Kyusyur, *Russia* **27 B13** 70 19N 127 30 E
Kyyiv, *Ukraine* **17 C16** 50 30N 30 28 E
Kyyivske Vdskh., *Ukraine* **17 C16** 51 0N 30 25 E
Kyzyl, *Russia* **27 D10** 51 50N 94 30 E
Kyzyl Kum, *Uzbekistan* **26 E7** 42 30N 65 0 E
Kyzyl-Kyya, *Kyrgyzstan* **26 E8** 40 16N 72 8 E
Kzyl-Orda = Qyzylorda, *Kazakstan* **26 E7** 44 48N 65 28 E

L

La Alcarria, *Spain* **19 B4** 40 31N 2 45W
La Asunción, *Venezuela* **92 A6** 11 2N 63 53W
La Baie, *Canada* **71 C5** 48 19N 70 53W
La Banda, *Argentina* **94 B3** 27 45S 64 10W
La Barca, *Mexico* **86 C4** 20 20N 102 40W
La Barge, *U.S.A.* **82 E8** 42 16N 110 12W
La Belle, *U.S.A.* **77 M5** 26 46N 81 26W
La Biche →, *Canada* **72 B4** 59 57N 123 50W
La Biche, L., *Canada* **72 C6** 54 50N 112 5W
La Bomba, *Mexico* **86 A1** 31 53N 115 2W
La Calera, *Chile* **94 C1** 32 50S 71 10W
La Canal = Sa Canal, *Spain* **22 C7** 38 51N 1 23 E
La Carlota, *Argentina* **94 C3** 33 30S 63 20W
La Ceiba, *Honduras* **88 C2** 15 40N 86 50W
La Chaux-de-Fonds, *Switz.* **18 C7** 47 7N 6 50 E
La Chorrera, *Panama* **88 E4** 8 53N 79 47W
La Cocha, *Argentina* **94 B2** 27 50S 65 40W
La Concepción, *Panama* **88 E3** 8 31N 82 37W
La Concordia, *Mexico* **87 D6** 16 8N 92 38W
La Coruña = A Coruña, *Spain* **19 A1** 43 20N 8 25W
La Crescent, *U.S.A.* **80 D9** 43 50N 91 18W
La Crete, *Canada* **72 B5** 58 11N 116 24W
La Crosse, *Kans., U.S.A.* **80 F5** 38 32N 99 18W
La Crosse, *Wis., U.S.A.* **80 D9** 43 48N 91 15W
La Cruz, *Costa Rica* **88 D2** 11 4N 85 39W
La Cruz, *Mexico* **86 C3** 23 55N 106 54W
La Désirade, *Guadeloupe* **89 C7** 16 18N 61 3W
La Escondida, *Mexico* **86 C5** 24 6N 99 55W
La Esmeralda, *Paraguay* **94 A3** 22 16S 62 33W
La Esperanza, *Cuba* **88 B3** 22 46N 83 44W
La Esperanza, *Honduras* **88 D2** 14 15N 88 10W
La Estrada = A Estrada, *Spain* **19 A1** 42 43N 8 27W
La Fayette, *U.S.A.* **77 H3** 34 42N 85 17W
La Fé, *Cuba* **88 B3** 22 2N 84 15W
La Follette, *U.S.A.* **77 G3** 36 23N 84 7W
La Grande, *U.S.A.* **82 D4** 45 20N 118 5W
La Grande →, *Canada* **70 B5** 53 50N 79 0W
La Grande Deux, Rés., *Canada* **70 B4** 53 40N 76 55W
La Grande Quatre, Rés., *Canada* **70 B5** 54 0N 73 15W
La Grande Trois, Rés., *Canada* **70 B4** 53 40N 75 10W
La Grange, *Calif., U.S.A.* **84 H6** 37 42N 120 27W
La Grange, *Ga., U.S.A.* **77 J3** 33 2N 85 2W
La Grange, *Ky., U.S.A.* **76 F3** 38 25N 85 23W
La Grange, *Tex., U.S.A.* **81 L6** 29 54N 96 52W
La Guaira, *Venezuela* **92 A5** 10 36N 66 56W
La Habana, *Cuba* **88 B3** 23 8N 82 22W
La Independencia, *Mexico* **87 D6** 16 31N 91 47W
La Isabela, *Dom. Rep.* **89 C5** 19 58N 71 2W
La Junta, *U.S.A.* **81 F3** 37 59N 103 33W
La Laguna, *Canary Is.* **22 F3** 28 28N 16 18W
La Libertad, *Guatemala* **88 C1** 16 47N 90 7W
La Libertad, *Mexico* **86 B2** 29 55N 112 41W
La Ligua, *Chile* **94 C1** 32 30S 71 16W
La Línea de la Concepción, *Spain* **19 D3** 36 15N 5 23W
La Loche, *Canada* **73 B7** 56 29N 109 26W
La Louvière, *Belgium* **15 D4** 50 27N 4 10 E
La Malbaie, *Canada* **71 C5** 47 40N 70 10W
La Mancha, *Spain* **19 C4** 39 10N 2 54W
La Martre, L., *Canada* **72 A5** 63 15N 117 55W
La Mesa, *U.S.A.* **85 N9** 32 46N 117 3W
La Misión, *Mexico* **86 A1** 32 5N 116 50W
La Moure, *U.S.A.* **80 B5** 46 21N 98 18W
La Negra, *Chile* **94 A1** 23 46S 70 18W
La Oliva, *Canary Is.* **22 F6** 28 36N 13 57W
La Orotava, *Canary Is.* **22 F3** 28 22N 16 31W
La Oroya, *Peru* **92 F3** 11 32S 75 54W
La Palma, *Canary Is.* **22 F2** 28 40N 17 50W
La Palma, *Panama* **88 E4** 8 15N 78 0W
La Palma del Condado, *Spain* **19 D2** 37 21N 6 38W
La Paloma, *Chile* **94 C1** 30 35S 71 0W
La Pampa □, *Argentina* **94 D2** 36 50S 66 0W
La Paragua, *Venezuela* **92 B6** 6 50N 63 20W
La Paz, *Entre Ríos, Argentina* **94 C4** 30 50S 59 45W
La Paz, *San Luis, Argentina* **94 C2** 33 30S 67 20W
La Paz, *Bolivia* **92 G5** 16 20S 68 10W
La Paz, *Honduras* **88 D2** 14 20N 87 47W
La Paz, *Mexico* **86 C2** 24 10N 110 20W
La Paz Centro, *Nic.* **88 D2** 12 20N 86 41W
La Pedrera, *Colombia* **92 D5** 1 18S 69 43W
La Pérade, *Canada* **71 C5** 46 35N 72 12W
La Perouse Str., *Asia* **30 B11** 45 40N 142 0 E
La Pesca, *Mexico* **87 C5** 23 46N 97 47W
La Piedad, *Mexico* **86 C4** 20 20N 102 1W
La Pine, *U.S.A.* **82 E3** 43 40N 121 30W
La Plata, *Argentina* **94 D4** 35 0S 57 55W
La Pocatière, *Canada* **71 C5** 47 22N 70 2W
La Porte, *Ind., U.S.A.* **76 E2** 41 36N 86 43W
La Porte, *Tex., U.S.A.* **81 L7** 29 39N 95 1W
La Purísima, *Mexico* **86 B2** 26 10N 112 4W
La Push, *U.S.A.* **84 C2** 47 55N 124 38W
La Quiaca, *Argentina* **94 A2** 22 5S 65 35W
La Restinga, *Canary Is.* **22 G2** 27 38N 17 59W
La Rioja, *Argentina* **94 B2** 29 20S 67 0W
La Rioja □, *Argentina* **94 B2** 29 30S 67 0W
La Rioja □, *Spain* **19 A4** 42 20N 2 20W
La Robla, *Spain* **19 A3** 42 50N 5 41W
La Roche-en-Ardenne, *Belgium* **15 D5** 50 11N 5 35 E
La Roche-sur-Yon, *France* **18 C3** 46 40N 1 25W
La Rochelle, *France* **18 C3** 46 10N 1 9W
La Roda, *Spain* **19 C4** 39 13N 2 15W
La Romana, *Dom. Rep.* **89 C6** 18 27N 68 57W
La Ronge, *Canada* **73 B7** 55 5N 105 20W
La Rumorosa, *Mexico* **85 N10** 32 33N 116 4W
La Sabina = Sa Savina, *Spain* **22 C7** 38 44N 1 25 E
La Salle, *U.S.A.* **80 E10** 41 20N 89 6W
La Santa, *Canary Is.* **22 E6** 29 5N 13 40W
La Sarre, *Canada* **70 C4** 48 45N 79 15W
La Scie, *Canada* **71 C8** 49 57N 55 36W
La Selva Beach, *U.S.A.* **84 J5** 36 56N 121 51W
La Serena, *Chile* **94 B1** 29 55S 71 10W
La Seu d'Urgell, *Spain* **19 A6** 42 22N 1 23 E
La Seyne-sur-Mer, *France* **18 E6** 43 7N 5 52 E
La Soufrière, *St. Vincent* **89 D7** 13 20N 61 11W
La Spézia, *Italy* **18 D8** 44 7N 9 50 E
La Tagua, *Colombia* **92 C4** 0 3N 74 40W
La Tortuga, *Venezuela* **89 D6** 11 0N 65 22W
La Tuque, *Canada* **70 C5** 47 30N 72 50W
La Unión, *Chile* **96 E2** 40 10S 73 0W
La Unión, *El Salv.* **88 D2** 13 20N 87 50W
La Unión, *Mexico* **86 D4** 17 58N 101 49W
La Urbana, *Venezuela* **92 B5** 7 8N 66 56W
La Vall d'Uixó, *Spain* **19 C5** 39 49N 0 15W
La Vega, *Dom. Rep.* **89 C5** 19 20N 70 30W
La Vela de Coro, *Venezuela* **92 A5** 11 27N 69 34W
La Venta, *Mexico* **87 D6** 18 8N 94 3W
La Ventura, *Mexico* **86 C4** 24 38N 100 54W
Labasa, *Fiji* **59 C8** 16 30S 179 10 E
Labe = Elbe →, *Europe* **16 B5** 53 50N 9 0 E
Labé, *Guinea* **50 F3** 11 24N 12 16W
Laberge, L., *Canada* **72 A1** 61 11N 135 12W
Labinsk, *Russia* **25 F7** 44 40N 40 48 E
Labis, *Malaysia* **39 L4** 2 22N 103 2 E
Laboulaye, *Argentina* **94 C3** 34 10S 63 30W
Labrador, *Canada* **71 B7** 53 20N 61 0W
Labrador City, *Canada* **71 B6** 52 57N 66 55W
Labrador Sea, *Atl. Oc.* **69 C14** 57 0N 54 0W
Lábrea, *Brazil* **92 E6** 7 15S 64 51W
Labuan, *Malaysia* **36 C5** 5 20N 115 14 E
Labuan, Pulau, *Malaysia* **36 C5** 5 21N 115 13 E
Labuha, *Indonesia* **37 E7** 0 30S 127 30 E
Labuhan, *Indonesia* **37 G11** 6 22S 105 50 E
Labuhanbajo, *Indonesia* **37 F6** 8 28S 119 54 E
Labuk, Telok, *Malaysia* **36 C5** 6 10N 117 50 E
Labyrinth, L., *Australia* **63 E2** 30 40S 135 11 E
Labytnangi, *Russia* **26 C7** 66 39N 66 21 E
Lac Bouchette, *Canada* **71 C5** 48 16N 72 11W
Lac Édouard, *Canada* **70 C5** 47 40N 72 16W
Lac La Biche, *Canada* **72 C6** 54 45N 111 58W
Lac la Martre = Wha Ti, *Canada* **68 B8** 63 8N 117 16W
Lac La Ronge Prov. Park, *Canada* **73 B7** 55 9N 104 41W
Lac-Mégantic, *Canada* **71 C5** 45 35N 70 53W
Lac Thien, *Vietnam* **38 F7** 12 25N 108 11 E
Lacanau, *France* **18 D3** 44 58N 1 5W
Lacantúm →, *Mexico* **87 D6** 16 36N 90 40W
Laccadive Is. = Lakshadweep Is., *India* **29 H11** 10 0N 72 30 E
Lacepede Is., *Australia* **60 C3** 16 55S 122 0 E
Lacerdónia, *Mozam.* **55 F4** 18 3S 35 35 E
Lacey, *U.S.A.* **84 C4** 47 7N 122 49W
Lachhmangarh, *India* **42 F6** 27 50N 75 4 E
Lachi, *Pakistan* **42 C4** 33 25N 71 20 E
Lachine, *Canada* **79 A11** 45 30N 73 40W
Lachute, *Canada* **70 C5** 45 39N 74 21W
Lackawanna, *U.S.A.* **78 D6** 42 50N 78 50W
Lackawaxen, *U.S.A.* **79 E10** 41 29N 74 59W
Lacolle, *Canada* **79 A11** 45 5N 73 22W
Lacombe, *Canada* **72 C6** 52 30N 113 44W
Lacona, *U.S.A.* **79 C8** 43 39N 76 10W
Laconia, *U.S.A.* **79 C13** 43 32N 71 28W
Ladakh Ra., *India* **43 C8** 34 0N 78 0 E
Ladismith, *S. Africa* **56 E3** 33 28S 21 15 E
Lādīz, *Iran* **45 D9** 28 55N 61 15 E
Ladnun, *India* **42 F6** 27 38N 74 25 E
Ladoga, L. = Ladozhskoye Ozero, *Russia* **24 B5** 61 15N 30 30 E
Ladozhskoye Ozero, *Russia* **24 B5** 61 15N 30 30 E
Lady Elliott I., *Australia* **62 C5** 24 7S 152 42 E
Lady Grey, *S. Africa* **56 E4** 30 43S 27 13 E
Ladybrand, *S. Africa* **56 D4** 29 9S 27 29 E
Ladysmith, *Canada* **72 D4** 49 0N 123 49W
Ladysmith, *S. Africa* **57 D4** 28 32S 29 46 E
Ladysmith, *U.S.A.* **80 C9** 45 28N 91 12W
Lae, *Papua N. G.* **64 H6** 6 40S 147 2 E
Laem Ngop, *Thailand* **39 F4** 12 10N 102 26 E
Laem Pho, *Thailand* **39 J3** 6 55N 101 19 E
Læsø, *Denmark* **9 H14** 57 15N 11 5 E
Lafayette, *Colo., U.S.A.* **80 F2** 39 58N 105 12W
Lafayette, *Ind., U.S.A.* **76 E2** 40 25N 86 54W
Lafayette, *La., U.S.A.* **81 K9** 30 14N 92 1W
Lafayette, *Tenn., U.S.A.* **77 G2** 36 31N 86 2W
Laferte →, *Canada* **72 A5** 61 53N 117 44W
Lafia, *Nigeria* **50 G7** 8 30N 8 34 E
Lafleche, *Canada* **73 D7** 49 45N 106 40W
Lagan →, *U.K.* **13 B6** 54 36N 5 55W
Lagarfljót →, *Iceland* **8 D6** 65 40N 14 18W
Lågen →, *Oppland, Norway* **9 F14** 61 8N 10 25 E
Lågen →, *Vestfold, Norway* **9 G14** 59 3N 10 3 E
Laghouat, *Algeria* **50 B6** 33 50N 2 59 E
Lagoa Vermelha, *Brazil* **95 B5** 28 13S 51 32W
Lagonoy G., *Phil.* **37 B6** 13 35N 123 50 E
Lagos, *Nigeria* **50 G6** 6 25N 3 27 E
Lagos, *Portugal* **19 D1** 37 5N 8 41W
Lagos de Moreno, *Mexico* **86 C4** 21 21N 101 55W
Lagrange, *Australia* **60 C3** 18 45S 121 43 E
Lagrange B., *Australia* **60 C3** 18 38S 121 42 E
Laguna, *Brazil* **95 B6** 28 30S 48 50W
Laguna, *U.S.A.* **83 J10** 35 2N 107 25W
Laguna Beach, *U.S.A.* **85 M9** 33 33N 117 47W
Laguna Limpia, *Argentina* **94 B4** 26 32S 59 45W
Lagunas, *Chile* **94 A2** 21 0S 69 45W
Lagunas, *Peru* **92 E3** 5 10S 75 35W
Lahad Datu, *Malaysia* **37 C5** 5 0N 118 20 E
Lahad Datu, Teluk, *Malaysia* **37 D5** 4 50N 118 20 E
Lahan Sai, *Thailand* **38 E4** 14 25N 102 52 E
Lahanam, *Laos* **38 D5** 16 16N 105 16 E
Lahar, *India* **43 F8** 26 12N 78 57 E
Laharpur, *India* **43 F9** 27 43N 80 56 E
Lahat, *Indonesia* **36 E2** 3 45S 103 30 E
Lahewa, *Indonesia* **36 D1** 1 22N 97 12 E
Lāhījān, *Iran* **45 B6** 37 10N 50 6 E
Lahn →, *Germany* **16 C4** 50 19N 7 37 E
Laholm, *Sweden* **9 H15** 56 30N 13 2 E
Lahore, *Pakistan* **42 D6** 31 32N 74 22 E
Lahri, *Pakistan* **42 E3** 29 11N 68 13 E
Lahti, *Finland* **9 F21** 60 58N 25 40 E
Lahtis = Lahti, *Finland* **9 F21** 60 58N 25 40 E
Laï, *Chad* **51 G9** 9 25N 16 18 E
Lai Chau, *Vietnam* **38 A4** 22 5N 103 3 E
Laila = Laylá, *Si. Arabia* **46 C4** 22 10N 46 40 E
Laingsburg, *S. Africa* **56 E3** 33 9S 20 52 E
Lainio älv →, *Sweden* **8 C20** 67 35N 22 40 E
Lairg, *U.K.* **12 C4** 58 2N 4 24W
Laishui, *China* **34 E8** 39 23N 115 45 E
Laiwu, *China* **35 F9** 36 15N 117 40 E
Laixi, *China* **35 F11** 36 50N 120 31 E
Laiyang, *China* **35 F11** 36 59N 120 45 E
Laiyuan, *China* **34 E8** 39 20N 114 40 E
Laizhou, *China* **35 F10** 37 8N 119 57 E
Laizhou Wan, *China* **35 F10** 37 30N 119 30 E
Laja →, *Mexico* **86 C4** 20 55N 100 46W
Lajes, *Brazil* **95 B5** 27 48S 50 20W
Lak Sao, *Laos* **38 C5** 18 11N 104 59 E
Lakaband, *Pakistan* **42 D3** 31 2N 69 15 E
Lake Alpine, *U.S.A.* **84 G7** 38 29N 120 0W
Lake Andes, *U.S.A.* **80 D5** 43 9N 98 32W
Lake Arthur, *U.S.A.* **81 K8** 30 5N 92 41W
Lake Charles, *U.S.A.* **81 K8** 30 14N 93 13W
Lake City, *Colo., U.S.A.* **83 G10** 38 2N 107 19W
Lake City, *Fla., U.S.A.* **77 K4** 30 11N 82 38W
Lake City, *Mich., U.S.A.* **76 C3** 44 20N 85 13W
Lake City, *Minn., U.S.A.* **80 C8** 44 27N 92 16W
Lake City, *Pa., U.S.A.* **78 D4** 42 1N 80 21W
Lake City, *S.C., U.S.A.* **77 J6** 33 52N 79 45W
Lake Cowichan, *Canada* **72 D4** 48 49N 124 3W
Lake District, *U.K.* **10 C4** 54 35N 3 20 E
Lake Elsinore, *U.S.A.* **85 M9** 33 38N 117 20W
Lake George, *U.S.A.* **79 C11** 43 26N 73 43W
Lake Grace, *Australia* **61 F2** 33 7S 118 28 E
Lake Harbour = Kimmirut, *Canada* **69 B13** 62 50N 69 50W
Lake Havasu City, *U.S.A.* **85 L12** 34 27N 114 22W
Lake Hughes, *U.S.A.* **85 L8** 34 41N 118 26W
Lake Isabella, *U.S.A.* **85 K8** 35 38N 118 28W
Lake Jackson, *U.S.A.* **81 L7** 29 3N 95 27W
Lake Junction, *U.S.A.* **82 D8** 44 35N 110 28W
Lake King, *Australia* **61 F2** 33 5S 119 45 E
Lake Lenore, *Canada* **73 C8** 52 24N 104 59W
Lake Louise, *Canada* **72 C5** 51 30N 116 10W
Lake Mead National Recreation Area, *U.S.A.* **85 K12** 36 15N 114 30W
Lake Mills, *U.S.A.* **80 D8** 43 25N 93 32W
Lake Placid, *U.S.A.* **79 B11** 44 17N 73 59W
Lake Pleasant, *U.S.A.* **79 C10** 43 28N 74 25W
Lake Providence, *U.S.A.* **81 J9** 32 48N 91 10W
Lake St. Peter, *Canada* **78 A6** 45 18N 78 2W
Lake Superior Prov. Park, *Canada* **70 C3** 47 45N 84 45W
Lake Village, *U.S.A.* **81 J9** 33 20N 91 17W
Lake Wales, *U.S.A.* **77 M5** 27 54N 81 35W
Lake Worth, *U.S.A.* **77 M5** 26 37N 80 3W
Lakeba, *Fiji* **59 D9** 18 13S 178 47W
Lakefield, *Canada* **78 B6** 44 25N 78 16W
Lakehurst, *U.S.A.* **79 F10** 40 1N 74 19W
Lakeland, *Australia* **62 B3** 15 49S 144 57 E
Lakeland, *U.S.A.* **77 M5** 28 3N 81 57W
Lakeport, *Calif., U.S.A.* **84 F4** 39 3N 122 55W
Lakeport, *Mich., U.S.A.* **78 C2** 43 7N 82 30W
Lakeside, *Ariz., U.S.A.* **83 J9** 34 9N 109 58W
Lakeside, *Calif., U.S.A.* **85 N10** 32 52N 116 55W
Lakeside, *Nebr., U.S.A.* **80 D3** 42 3N 102 26W
Lakeside, *Ohio, U.S.A.* **78 E2** 41 32N 82 46W
Lakeview, *U.S.A.* **82 E3** 42 11N 120 21W
Lakeville, *U.S.A.* **80 C8** 44 39N 93 14W
Lakewood, *Colo., U.S.A.* **80 F2** 39 44N 105 5W
Lakewood, *N.J., U.S.A.* **79 F10** 40 6N 74 13W
Lakewood, *N.Y., U.S.A.* **78 D5** 42 6N 79 19W
Lakewood, *Ohio, U.S.A.* **78 E3** 41 29N 81 48W
Lakewood, *Wash., U.S.A.* **84 C4** 47 11N 122 32W
Lakha, *India* **42 F4** 26 9N 70 54 E
Lakhaniá, *Greece* **23 D9** 35 58N 27 54 E
Lakhimpur, *India* **43 F9** 27 57N 80 46 E
Lakhnadon, *India* **43 H8** 22 36N 79 36 E
Lakhonpheng, *Laos* **38 E5** 15 54N 105 34 E
Lakhpat, *India* **42 H3** 23 48N 68 47 E
Lakin, *U.S.A.* **81 G4** 37 57N 101 15W
Lakitusaki →, *Canada* **70 B3** 54 21N 82 25W
Lakki, *Pakistan* **42 C4** 32 36N 70 55 E
Lákkoi, *Greece* **23 D5** 35 24N 23 57 E
Lakonikós Kólpos, *Greece* **21 F10** 36 40N 22 40 E
Lakor, *Indonesia* **37 F7** 8 15S 128 17 E
Lakota, *Ivory C.* **50 G4** 5 50N 5 30W
Lakota, *U.S.A.* **80 A5** 48 2N 98 21W
Laksar, *India* **42 E8** 29 46N 78 3 E
Laksefjorden, *Norway* **8 A22** 70 45N 26 50 E
Lakselv, *Norway* **8 A21** 70 2N 25 0 E
Lakshadweep Is., *India* **29 H11** 10 0N 72 30 E
Lakshmanpur, *India* **43 H10** 22 58N 83 3 E
Lakshmikantapur, *India* **43 H13** 22 5N 88 20 E
Lala Ghat, *India* **41 G18** 24 30N 92 40 E
Lala Musa, *Pakistan* **42 C5** 32 40N 73 57 E
Lalago, *Tanzania* **54 C3** 3 28S 33 58 E
Lalapanzi, *Zimbabwe* **55 F3** 19 20S 30 15 E
L'Albufera, *Spain* **19 C5** 39 20N 0 27W
Lalganj, *India* **43 G11** 25 52N 85 13 E
Lalgola, *India* **43 G13** 24 25N 88 15 E
Lālī, *Iran* **45 C6** 32 21N 49 6 E
Lalibela, *Ethiopia* **46 E2** 12 2N 39 2 E
Lalin, *China* **35 B14** 45 12N 127 0 E
Lalín, *Spain* **19 A1** 42 40N 8 5W
Lalin He →, *China* **35 B13** 45 32N 125 40 E
Lalitpur, *India* **43 G8** 24 42N 78 28 E
Lalkua, *India* **43 E8** 29 5N 79 31 E
Lalsot, *India* **42 F7** 26 34N 76 20 E
Lam, *Vietnam* **38 B6** 21 21N 106 31 E
Lam Pao Res., *Thailand* **38 D4** 16 50N 103 15 E
Lamaing, *Burma* **41 M20** 15 25N 97 53 E
Lamar, *Colo., U.S.A.* **80 F3** 38 5N 102 37W
Lamar, *Mo., U.S.A.* **81 G7** 37 30N 94 16W
Lamas, *Peru* **92 E3** 6 28S 76 31W
Lambaréné, *Gabon* **52 E2** 0 41S 10 12 E
Lambay I., *Ireland* **13 C5** 53 29N 6 1W
Lambert Glacier, *Antarctica* **5 D6** 71 0S 70 0 E
Lambert's Bay, *S. Africa* **56 E2** 32 5S 18 17 E
Lambeth, *Canada* **78 D3** 42 54N 81 18W
Lambomakondro, *Madag.* **57 C7** 22 41S 44 44 E
Lame Deer, *U.S.A.* **82 D10** 45 37N 106 40W
Lamego, *Portugal* **19 B2** 41 5N 7 52W
Lamèque, *Canada* **71 C7** 47 45N 64 38W
Lamesa, *U.S.A.* **81 J4** 32 44N 101 58W
Lamía, *Greece* **21 E10** 38 55N 22 26 E
Lammermuir Hills, *U.K.* **12 F6** 55 50N 2 40W
Lamoille →, *U.S.A.* **79 B11** 44 38N 73 13W
Lamon B., *Phil.* **37 B6** 14 30N 122 20 E
Lamont, *Canada* **72 C6** 53 46N 112 50W
Lamont, *Calif., U.S.A.* **85 K8** 35 15N 118 55W
Lamont, *Wyo., U.S.A.* **82 E10** 42 13N 107 29W
Lampa, *Peru* **92 G4** 15 22S 70 22W
Lampang, *Thailand* **38 C2** 18 16N 99 32 E
Lampasas, *U.S.A.* **81 K5** 31 4N 98 11W
Lampazos de Naranjo, *Mexico* **86 B4** 27 2N 100 32W
Lampedusa, *Medit. S.* **20 G5** 35 36N 12 40 E
Lampeter, *U.K.* **11 E3** 52 7N 4 4W
Lampione, *Medit. S.* **20 G5** 35 33N 12 20 E
Lampman, *Canada* **73 D8** 49 25N 102 50W
Lampung □, *Indonesia* **36 F2** 5 30S 104 30 E
Lamta, *India* **43 H9** 22 8N 80 7 E
Lamu, *Kenya* **54 C5** 2 16S 40 55 E
Lamy, *U.S.A.* **83 J11** 35 29N 105 53W
Lan Xian, *China* **34 E6** 38 15N 111 35 E
Lanak La, *India* **43 B8** 34 27N 79 32 E
Lanak'o Shank'ou = Lanak La, *India* **43 B8** 34 27N 79 32 E
Lanark, *Canada* **79 A8** 45 1N 76 22W
Lanark, *U.K.* **12 F5** 55 40N 3 47W
Lanbi Kyun, *Burma* **39 G2** 10 50N 98 20 E
Lancang Jiang →, *China* **32 D5** 21 40N 101 10 E
Lancashire □, *U.K.* **10 D5** 53 50N 2 48W
Lancaster, *Canada* **79 A10** 45 10N 74 30W
Lancaster, *U.K.* **10 C5** 54 3N 2 48W
Lancaster, *Calif., U.S.A.* **85 L8** 34 42N 118 8W
Lancaster, *Ky., U.S.A.* **76 G3** 37 37N 84 35W
Lancaster, *N.H., U.S.A.* **79 B13** 44 29N 71 34W
Lancaster, *N.Y., U.S.A.* **78 D6** 42 54N 78 40W
Lancaster, *Ohio, U.S.A.* **76 F4** 39 43N 82 36W
Lancaster, *Pa., U.S.A.* **79 F8** 40 2N 76 19W
Lancaster, *S.C., U.S.A.* **77 H5** 34 43N 80 46W
Lancaster, *Wis., U.S.A.* **80 D9** 42 51N 90 43W
Lancaster Sd., *Canada* **69 A11** 74 13N 84 0W
Lancelin, *Australia* **61 F2** 31 0S 115 18 E
Lanchow = Lanzhou, *China* **34 F2** 36 1N 103 52 E
Lanciano, *Italy* **20 C6** 42 14N 14 23 E
Lancun, *China* **35 F11** 36 25N 120 10 E
Landeck, *Austria* **16 E6** 47 9N 10 34 E
Lander, *U.S.A.* **82 E9** 42 50N 108 44W
Lander →, *Australia* **60 D5** 22 0S 132 0 E
Landes, *France* **18 D3** 44 0N 1 0W
Landi Kotal, *Pakistan* **42 B4** 34 7N 71 6 E
Landisburg, *U.S.A.* **78 F7** 40 21N 77 19W
Land's End, *U.K.* **11 G2** 50 4N 5 44W
Landsborough Cr. →, *Australia* **62 C3** 22 28S 144 35 E
Landshut, *Germany* **16 D7** 48 34N 12 8 E
Landskrona, *Sweden* **9 J15** 55 53N 12 50 E
Lanesboro, *U.S.A.* **79 E9** 41 57N 75 34W
Lanett, *U.S.A.* **77 J3** 32 52N 85 12W
Lang Qua, *Vietnam* **38 A5** 22 16N 104 27 E
Lang Shan, *China* **34 D4** 41 0N 106 30 E
Lang Son, *Vietnam* **38 B6** 21 52N 106 42 E
Lang Suan, *Thailand* **39 H2** 9 57N 99 4 E
La'nga Co, *China* **41 D12** 30 45N 81 15 E
Langar, *Iran* **45 C9** 35 23N 60 25 E
Langara I., *Canada* **72 C2** 54 14N 133 1W
Langdon, *U.S.A.* **80 A5** 48 45N 98 22W
Langeberg, *S. Africa* **56 E3** 33 55S 21 0 E
Langeberge, *S. Africa* **56 D3** 28 15S 22 33 E
Langeland, *Denmark* **9 J14** 54 56N 10 48 E
Langenburg, *Canada* **73 C8** 50 51N 101 43W
Langholm, *U.K.* **12 F5** 55 9N 3 0W
Langjökull, *Iceland* **8 D3** 64 39N 20 12W
Langkawi, Pulau, *Malaysia* **39 J2** 6 25N 99 45 E
Langklip, *S. Africa* **56 D3** 28 12S 20 20 E
Langkon, *Malaysia* **36 C5** 6 30N 116 40 E
Langlade, *St- P. & M.* **71 C8** 46 50N 56 20W
Langley, *Canada* **84 A4** 49 7N 122 39W
Langøya, *Norway* **8 B16** 68 45N 14 50 E
Langreo, *Spain* **19 A3** 43 18N 5 40W
Langres, *France* **18 C6** 47 52N 5 20 E
Langres, Plateau de, *France* **18 C6** 47 45N 5 3 E
Langsa, *Indonesia* **36 D1** 4 30N 97 57 E
Langtry, *U.S.A.* **81 L4** 29 49N 101 34W
Langu, *Thailand* **39 J2** 6 53N 99 47 E
Languedoc, *France* **18 E5** 43 58N 3 55 E
Langxiangzhen, *China* **34 E9** 39 43N 116 8 E
Lanigan, *Canada* **73 C7** 51 51N 105 2W
Lankao, *China* **34 G8** 34 48N 114 50 E
Länkäran, *Azerbaijan* **25 G8** 38 48N 48 52 E
Lannion, *France* **18 B2** 48 46N 3 29W
L'Annonciation, *Canada* **70 C5** 46 25N 74 55W
Lansdale, *U.S.A.* **79 F9** 40 14N 75 17W
Lansdowne, *Canada* **79 B8** 44 24N 76 1W
Lansdowne, *India* **43 E8** 29 50N 78 41 E
Lansdowne House, *Canada* **70 B2** 52 14N 87 53W
L'Anse, *U.S.A.* **76 B1** 46 45N 88 27W
L'Anse au Loup, *Canada* **71 B8** 51 32N 56 50W
L'Anse aux Meadows, *Canada* **71 B8** 51 36N 55 32W
Lansford, *U.S.A.* **79 F9** 40 50N 75 53W
Lansing, *U.S.A.* **76 D3** 42 44N 84 33W
Lanta Yai, Ko, *Thailand* **39 J2** 7 35N 99 3 E
Lantian, *China* **34 G5** 34 11N 109 20 E
Lanus, *Argentina* **94 C4** 34 44S 58 27W
Lanusei, *Italy* **20 E3** 39 52N 9 34 E
Lanzarote, *Canary Is.* **22 F6** 29 0N 13 40W
Lanzhou, *China* **34 F2** 36 1N 103 52 E
Lao Bao, *Laos* **38 D6** 16 35N 106 30 E
Lao Cai, *Vietnam* **38 A4** 22 30N 103 57 E
Laoag, *Phil.* **37 A6** 18 7N 120 34 E
Laoang, *Phil.* **37 B7** 12 32N 125 8 E
Laoha He →, *China* **35 C11** 43 25N 120 35 E
Laois □, *Ireland* **13 D4** 52 57N 7 36W
Laon, *France* **18 B5** 49 33N 3 35 E
Laona, *U.S.A.* **76 C1** 45 34N 88 40W
Laos ■, *Asia* **38 D5** 17 45N 105 0 E
Lapa, *Brazil* **95 B6** 25 46S 49 44W
Lapeer, *U.S.A.* **76 D4** 43 3N 83 19W
Lapithos, *Cyprus* **23 D12** 35 21N 33 11 E
Lapland = Lappland, *Europe* **8 B21** 68 7N 24 0 E
Laporte, *U.S.A.* **79 E8** 41 25N 76 30W
Lappeenranta, *Finland* **9 F23** 61 3N 28 12 E
Lappland, *Europe* **8 B21** 68 7N 24 0 E
Laprida, *Argentina* **94 D3** 37 34S 60 45W
Lapseki, *Turkey* **21 D12** 40 20N 26 41 E

Mallorytown

McCusker →, *Canada* **73 B7** 55 32N 108 39W
McDame, *Canada* **72 B3** 59 44N 128 59W
McDermitt, *U.S.A.* **82 F5** 41 59N 117 43W
McDonald, *U.S.A.* **78 F4** 40 22N 80 14W
Macdonald, L., *Australia* **60 D4** 23 30S 129 0 E
McDonald Is., *Ind. Oc.* **3 G13** 53 0S 73 0 E
MacDonnell Ranges, *Australia* **60 D5** 23 40S 133 0 E
MacDowell L., *Canada* **70 B1** 52 15N 92 45W
Macduff, *U.K.* **12 D6** 57 40N 2 31W
Macedonia = Makedhonía □, *Greece* **21 D10** 40 39N 22 0 E
Macedonia, *U.S.A.* **78 E3** 41 19N 81 31W
Macedonia ■, *Europe* **21 D9** 41 53N 21 40 E
Maceió, *Brazil* **93 E11** 9 40S 35 41W
Macerata, *Italy* **20 C5** 43 18N 13 27 E
McFarland, *U.S.A.* **85 K7** 35 41N 119 14W
McFarlane →, *Canada* **73 B7** 59 12N 107 58W
McGehee, *U.S.A.* **81 J9** 33 38N 91 24W
McGill, *U.S.A.* **82 G6** 39 23N 114 47W
Macgillycuddy's Reeks, *Ireland* **13 E2** 51 58N 9 45W
McGraw, *U.S.A.* **79 D8** 42 36N 76 8W
McGregor, *U.S.A.* **80 D9** 43 1N 91 11W
McGregor Ra., *Australia* **63 D3** 27 0S 142 45 E
Mach, *Pakistan* **40 E5** 29 50N 67 20 E
Māch Kowr, *Iran* **45 E9** 25 48N 61 28 E
Machado = Jiparaná →, *Brazil* **92 E6** 8 3S 62 52W
Machagai, *Argentina* **94 B3** 26 56S 60 2W
Machakos, *Kenya* **54 C4** 1 30S 37 15 E
Machala, *Ecuador* **92 D3** 3 20S 79 57W
Machanga, *Mozam.* **57 C6** 20 59S 35 0 E
Machattie, L., *Australia* **62 C2** 24 50S 139 48 E
Machava, *Mozam.* **57 D5** 25 54S 32 28 E
Machece, *Mozam.* **55 F4** 19 15S 35 32 E
Macheke, *Zimbabwe* **57 B5** 18 5S 31 51 E
Machhu →, *India* **42 H4** 23 6N 70 46 E
Machias, *Maine, U.S.A.* **77 C12** 44 43N 67 28W
Machias, *N.Y., U.S.A.* **78 D6** 42 25N 78 30W
Machichi →, *Canada* **73 B10** 57 3N 92 6W
Machico, *Madeira* **22 D3** 32 43N 16 44W
Machilipatnam, *India* **41 L12** 16 12N 81 8 E
Machiques, *Venezuela* **92 A4** 10 4N 72 34W
Machupicchu, *Peru* **92 F4** 13 8S 72 30W
Machynlleth, *U.K.* **11 E4** 52 35N 3 50W
Macia, *Mozam.* **57 D5** 25 2S 33 8 E
McIlwraith Ra., *Australia* **62 A3** 13 50S 143 20 E
McInnes L., *Canada* **73 C10** 52 13N 93 45W
McIntosh, *U.S.A.* **80 C4** 45 55N 101 21W
McIntosh L., *Canada* **73 B8** 55 45N 105 0W
Macintosh Ra., *Australia* **61 E4** 27 39S 125 32 E
Macintyre →, *Australia* **63 D5** 28 37S 150 47 E
Mackay, *Australia* **62 C4** 21 8S 149 11 E
Mackay, *U.S.A.* **82 E7** 43 55N 113 37W
MacKay →, *Canada* **72 B6** 57 10N 111 38W
Mackay, L., *Australia* **60 D4** 22 30S 129 0 E
McKay Ra., *Australia* **60 D3** 23 0S 122 30 E
McKeesport, *U.S.A.* **78 F5** 40 21N 79 52W
McKellar, *Canada* **78 A5** 45 30N 79 55W
McKenna, *U.S.A.* **84 D4** 46 56N 122 33W
Mackenzie, *Canada* **72 B4** 55 20N 123 5W
McKenzie, *U.S.A.* **77 G1** 36 8N 88 31W
Mackenzie →, *Australia* **62 C4** 23 38S 149 46 E
Mackenzie →, *Canada* **68 B6** 69 10N 134 20W
McKenzie →, *U.S.A.* **82 D2** 44 7N 123 6W
Mackenzie Bay, *Canada* **4 B1** 69 0N 137 30W
Mackenzie City = Linden, *Guyana* **92 B7** 6 0N 58 10W
Mackenzie Mts., *Canada* **68 B6** 64 0N 130 0W
Mackinaw City, *U.S.A.* **76 C3** 45 47N 84 44W
McKinlay, *Australia* **62 C3** 21 16S 141 18 E
McKinlay →, *Australia* **62 C3** 20 50S 141 28 E
McKinley, Mt., *U.S.A.* **68 B4** 63 4N 151 0W
McKinley Sea, *Arctic* **4 A7** 82 0N 0 0W
McKinney, *U.S.A.* **81 J6** 33 12N 96 37W
Mackinnon Road, *Kenya* **54 C4** 3 40S 39 1 E
McKittrick, *U.S.A.* **85 K7** 35 18N 119 37W
Macklin, *Canada* **73 C7** 52 20N 109 56W
McLaughlin, *U.S.A.* **80 C4** 45 49N 100 49W
Maclean, *Australia* **63 D5** 29 26S 153 16 E
McLean, *U.S.A.* **81 H4** 35 14N 100 36W
McLeansboro, *U.S.A.* **80 F10** 38 6N 88 32W
Maclear, *S. Africa* **57 E4** 31 2S 28 23 E
McLennan, *Canada* **72 B5** 55 42N 116 50W
McLeod →, *Canada* **72 C5** 54 9N 115 44W
MacLeod, B., *Canada* **73 A7** 62 53N 110 0W
McLeod, L., *Australia* **61 D1** 24 9S 113 47 E
MacLeod Lake, *Canada* **72 C4** 54 58N 123 0W
McLoughlin, Mt., *U.S.A.* **82 E2** 42 27N 122 19W
McMechen, *U.S.A.* **78 G4** 39 57N 80 44W
McMinnville, *Oreg., U.S.A.* **82 D2** 45 13N 123 12W
McMinnville, *Tenn., U.S.A.* **77 H3** 35 41N 85 46W
McMurdo Sd., *Antarctica* **5 D11** 77 0S 170 0 E
McMurray = Fort McMurray, *Canada* **72 B6** 56 44N 111 7W
McMurray, *U.S.A.* **84 B4** 48 19N 122 14W
Macodoene, *Mozam.* **57 C6** 23 32S 35 5 E
Macomb, *U.S.A.* **80 E9** 40 27N 90 40W
Mâcon, *France* **18 C6** 46 19N 4 50 E
Macon, *Ga., U.S.A.* **77 J4** 32 51N 83 38W
Macon, *Miss., U.S.A.* **77 J1** 33 7N 88 34W
Macon, *Mo., U.S.A.* **80 F8** 39 44N 92 28W
Macossa, *Mozam.* **55 F3** 17 55S 33 56 E
Macoun L., *Canada* **73 B8** 56 32N 103 40W
Macovane, *Mozam.* **57 C6** 21 30S 35 2 E
McPherson, *U.S.A.* **80 F6** 38 22N 97 40W
McPherson Pk., *U.S.A.* **85 L7** 34 53N 119 53W
McPherson Ra., *Australia* **63 D5** 28 15S 153 15 E
Macquarie →, *Australia* **63 E4** 30 5S 147 30 E
Macquarie Harbour, *Australia* **62 G4** 42 15S 145 23 E
Macquarie Is., *Pac. Oc.* **64 N7** 54 36S 158 55 E
MacRobertson Land, *Antarctica* **5 D6** 71 0S 64 0 E
Macroom, *Ireland* **13 E3** 51 54N 8 57W
MacTier, *Canada* **78 A5** 45 9N 79 46W
Macubela, *Mozam.* **55 F4** 16 53S 37 49 E
Macuiza, *Mozam.* **55 F3** 18 7S 34 29 E
Macusani, *Peru* **92 F4** 14 4S 70 29W
Macuse, *Mozam.* **55 F4** 17 45S 37 10 E
Macuspana, *Mexico* **87 D6** 17 46N 92 36W
Macusse, *Angola* **56 B3** 17 48S 20 23 E
Madadeni, *S. Africa* **57 D5** 27 43S 30 3 E
Madagascar ■, *Africa* **57 C8** 20 0S 47 0 E
Madā'in Sālih, *Si. Arabia* **44 E3** 26 46N 37 57 E
Madama, *Niger* **51 D8** 22 0N 13 40 E
Madame I., *Canada* **71 C7** 45 30N 60 58W
Madaripur, *Bangla.* **41 H17** 23 19N 90 15 E
Madauk, *Burma* **41 L20** 17 56N 96 52 E
Madawaska, *Canada* **78 A7** 45 30N 78 0W
Madawaska →, *Canada* **78 A8** 45 27N 76 21W
Madaya, *Burma* **41 H20** 22 12N 96 10 E
Maddalena, *Italy* **20 D3** 41 16N 9 23 E
Madeira, *Atl. Oc.* **22 D3** 32 50N 17 0W
Madeira →, *Brazil* **92 D7** 3 22S 58 45W
Madeleine, Îs. de la, *Canada* **71 C7** 47 30N 61 40W
Madera, *Mexico* **86 B3** 29 12N 108 7W
Madera, *Calif., U.S.A.* **84 J6** 36 57N 120 3W
Madera, *Pa., U.S.A.* **78 F6** 40 49N 78 26W
Madha, *India* **40 L9** 18 0N 75 30 E
Madhavpur, *India* **42 J3** 21 15N 69 58 E
Madhepura, *India* **43 F12** 26 11N 86 23 E
Madhubani, *India* **43 F12** 26 21N 86 7 E
Madhupur, *India* **43 G12** 24 16N 86 39 E
Madhya Pradesh □, *India* **42 J8** 22 50N 78 0 E
Madidi →, *Bolivia* **92 F5** 12 32S 66 52W
Madikeri, *India* **40 N9** 12 30N 75 45 E
Madill, *U.S.A.* **81 H6** 34 6N 96 46W
Madimba, *Dem. Rep. of the Congo* **52 E3** 4 58S 15 5 E
Ma'din, *Syria* **44 C3** 35 45N 39 36 E
Madingou, *Congo* **52 E2** 4 10S 13 33 E
Madirovalo, *Madag.* **57 B8** 16 26S 46 32 E
Madison, *Calif., U.S.A.* **84 G5** 38 41N 121 59W
Madison, *Fla., U.S.A.* **77 K4** 30 28N 83 25W
Madison, *Ind., U.S.A.* **76 F3** 38 44N 85 23W
Madison, *Nebr., U.S.A.* **80 E6** 41 50N 97 27W
Madison, *Ohio, U.S.A.* **78 E3** 41 46N 81 3W
Madison, *S. Dak., U.S.A.* **80 D6** 44 0N 97 7W
Madison, *Wis., U.S.A.* **80 D10** 43 4N 89 24W
Madison →, *U.S.A.* **82 D8** 45 56N 111 31W
Madison Heights, *U.S.A.* **76 G6** 37 25N 79 8W
Madisonville, *Ky., U.S.A.* **76 G2** 37 20N 87 30W
Madisonville, *Tex., U.S.A.* **81 K7** 30 57N 95 55W
Madista, *Botswana* **56 C4** 21 15S 25 6 E
Madiun, *Indonesia* **36 F4** 7 38S 111 32 E
Madoc, *Canada* **78 B7** 44 30N 77 28W
Madona, *Latvia* **9 H22** 56 53N 26 5 E
Madrakah, Ra's al, *Oman* **46 D6** 19 0N 57 50 E
Madras = Chennai, *India* **40 N12** 13 8N 80 19 E
Madras = Tamil Nadu □, *India* **40 P10** 11 0N 77 0 E
Madras, *U.S.A.* **82 D3** 44 38N 121 8W
Madre, Laguna, *U.S.A.* **81 M6** 27 0N 97 30W
Madre, Sierra, *Phil.* **37 A6** 17 0N 122 0 E
Madre de Dios →, *Bolivia* **92 F5** 10 59S 66 8W
Madre de Dios, I., *Chile* **96 G1** 50 20S 75 10W
Madre del Sur, Sierra, *Mexico* **87 D5** 17 30N 100 0W
Madre Occidental, Sierra, *Mexico* **86 B3** 27 0N 107 0W
Madre Oriental, Sierra, *Mexico* **86 C5** 25 0N 100 0W
Madri, *India* **42 G5** 24 16N 73 32 E
Madrid, *Spain* **19 B4** 40 25N 3 45W
Madrid, *U.S.A.* **79 B9** 44 45N 75 8W
Madura, *Australia* **61 F4** 31 55S 127 0 E
Madura, *Indonesia* **37 G15** 7 30S 114 0 E
Madura, Selat, *Indonesia* **37 G15** 7 30S 113 20 E
Madurai, *India* **40 Q11** 9 55N 78 10 E
Madurantakam, *India* **40 N11** 12 30N 79 50 E
Mae Chan, *Thailand* **38 B2** 20 9N 99 52 E
Mae Hong Son, *Thailand* **38 C2** 19 16N 97 56 E
Mae Khlong →, *Thailand* **38 F3** 13 24N 100 0 E
Mae Phrik, *Thailand* **38 D2** 17 27N 99 7 E
Mae Ramat, *Thailand* **38 D2** 16 58N 98 31 E
Mae Rim, *Thailand* **38 C2** 18 54N 98 57 E
Mae Sot, *Thailand* **38 D2** 16 43N 98 34 E
Mae Suai, *Thailand* **38 C2** 19 39N 99 33 E
Mae Tha, *Thailand* **38 C2** 18 28N 99 8 E
Maebashi, *Japan* **31 F9** 36 24N 139 4 E
Maesteg, *U.K.* **11 F4** 51 36N 3 40W
Maestra, Sierra, *Cuba* **88 B4** 20 15N 77 0W
Maevatanana, *Madag.* **57 B8** 16 56S 46 49 E
Mafeking = Mafikeng, *S. Africa* **56 D4** 25 50S 25 38 E
Mafeking, *Canada* **73 C8** 52 40N 101 10W
Mafeteng, *Lesotho* **56 D4** 29 51S 27 15 E
Mafia I., *Tanzania* **54 D4** 7 45S 39 50 E
Mafikeng, *S. Africa* **56 D4** 25 50S 25 38 E
Mafra, *Brazil* **95 B6** 26 10S 49 55W
Mafra, *Portugal* **19 C1** 38 55N 9 20W
Mafungabusi Plateau, *Zimbabwe* **55 F2** 18 30S 29 8 E
Magadan, *Russia* **27 D16** 59 38N 150 50 E
Magadi, *Kenya* **54 C4** 1 54S 36 19 E
Magadi, L., *Kenya* **54 C4** 1 54S 36 19 E
Magaliesburg, *S. Africa* **57 D4** 26 0S 27 32 E
Magallanes, Estrecho de, *Chile* **96 G2** 52 30S 75 0W
Magangué, *Colombia* **92 B4** 9 14N 74 45W
Magdalen Is. = Madeleine, Îs. de la, *Canada* **71 C7** 47 30N 61 40W
Magdalena, *Argentina* **94 D4** 35 5S 57 30W
Magdalena, *Bolivia* **92 F6** 13 13S 63 57W
Magdalena, *Mexico* **86 A2** 30 50N 112 0W
Magdalena, *U.S.A.* **83 J10** 34 7N 107 15W
Magdalena →, *Colombia* **92 A4** 11 6N 74 51W
Magdalena →, *Mexico* **86 A2** 30 40N 112 25W
Magdalena, B., *Mexico* **86 C2** 24 30N 112 10W
Magdalena, Llano de la, *Mexico* **86 C2** 25 0N 111 30W
Magdeburg, *Germany* **16 B6** 52 7N 11 38 E
Magdelaine Cays, *Australia* **62 B5** 16 33S 150 18 E
Magee, *U.S.A.* **81 K10** 31 52N 89 44W
Magelang, *Indonesia* **36 F4** 7 29S 110 13 E
Magellan's Str. = Magallanes, Estrecho de, *Chile* **96 G2** 52 30S 75 0W
Magenta, L., *Australia* **61 F2** 33 30S 119 2 E
Magerøya, *Norway* **8 A21** 71 3N 25 40 E
Maggiore, Lago, *Italy* **18 D8** 45 57N 8 39 E
Maghâgha, *Egypt* **51 C12** 28 38N 30 50 E
Magherafelt, *U.K.* **13 B5** 54 45N 6 37W
Maghreb, *N. Afr.* **50 B5** 32 0N 4 0W
Magistralnyy, *Russia* **27 D11** 56 16N 107 36 E
Magnetic Pole (North) = North Magnetic Pole, *Canada* **4 B2** 77 58N 102 8W
Magnetic Pole (South) = South Magnetic Pole, *Antarctica* **5 C9** 64 8S 138 8 E
Magnitogorsk, *Russia* **24 D10** 53 27N 59 4 E
Magnolia, *Ark., U.S.A.* **81 J8** 33 16N 93 14W
Magnolia, *Miss., U.S.A.* **81 K9** 31 9N 90 28W
Magog, *Canada* **79 A12** 45 18N 72 9W
Magoro, *Uganda* **54 B3** 1 45N 34 12 E
Magosa = Famagusta, *Cyprus* **23 D12** 35 8N 33 55 E
Magouládhes, *Greece* **23 A3** 39 45N 19 42 E
Magoye, *Zambia* **55 F2** 16 1S 27 30 E
Magozal, *Mexico* **87 C5** 21 34N 97 59W
Magpie, L., *Canada* **71 B7** 51 0N 64 41W
Magrath, *Canada* **72 D6** 49 25N 112 50W
Maguarinho, C., *Brazil* **93 D9** 0 15S 48 30W
Magude, *Mozam.* **57 D5** 25 2S 32 40 E
Mağusa = Famagusta, *Cyprus* **23 D12** 35 8N 33 55 E
Maguse L., *Canada* **73 A9** 61 40N 95 10W
Maguse Pt., *Canada* **73 A10** 61 20N 93 50W
Magvana, *India* **42 H3** 23 13N 69 22 E
Magwe, *Burma* **41 J19** 20 10N 95 0 E
Maha Sarakham, *Thailand* **38 D4** 16 12N 103 16 E
Mahābād, *Iran* **44 B5** 36 50N 45 45 E
Mahabharat Lekh, *Nepal* **43 E10** 28 30N 82 0 E
Mahabo, *Madag.* **57 C7** 20 23S 44 40 E
Mahadeo Hills, *India* **43 H8** 22 20N 78 30 E
Mahaffey, *U.S.A.* **78 F6** 40 53N 78 44W
Mahagi, *Dem. Rep. of the Congo* **54 B3** 2 20N 31 0 E
Mahajamba →, *Madag.* **57 B8** 15 33S 47 8 E
Mahajamba, Helodranon' i, *Madag.* **57 B8** 15 24S 47 5 E
Mahajan, *India* **42 E5** 28 48N 73 56 E
Mahajanga, *Madag.* **57 B8** 15 40S 46 25 E
Mahajanga □, *Madag.* **57 B8** 17 0S 47 0 E
Mahajilo →, *Madag.* **57 B8** 19 42S 45 22 E
Mahakam →, *Indonesia* **36 E5** 0 35S 117 17 E
Mahalapye, *Botswana* **56 C4** 23 1S 26 51 E
Maḩallāt, *Iran* **45 C6** 33 55N 50 30 E
Māhān, *Iran* **45 D8** 30 5N 57 18 E
Mahan →, *India* **43 H10** 23 30N 82 50 E
Mahanadi →, *India* **41 J15** 20 20N 86 25 E
Mahananda →, *India* **43 G12** 25 12N 87 52 E
Mahanoro, *Madag.* **57 B8** 19 54S 48 48 E
Mahanoy City, *U.S.A.* **79 F8** 40 49N 76 9W
Maharashtra □, *India* **40 J9** 20 30N 75 30 E
Mahari Mts., *Tanzania* **54 D3** 6 20S 30 0 E
Mahasham, W. →, *Egypt* **47 E3** 30 15N 34 10 E
Mahasoa, *Madag.* **57 C8** 22 12S 46 6 E
Mahasolo, *Madag.* **57 B8** 19 7S 46 22 E
Mahattat ash Shīdīyah, *Jordan* **47 F4** 29 55N 35 55 E
Mahattat 'Unayzah, *Jordan* **47 E4** 30 30N 35 47 E
Mahavavy →, *Madag.* **57 B8** 15 57S 45 54 E
Mahaxay, *Laos* **38 D5** 17 22N 105 12 E
Mahbubnagar, *India* **40 L10** 16 45N 77 59 E
Maḩḑah, *Oman* **45 E7** 24 24N 55 59 E
Mahdia, *Tunisia* **51 A8** 35 28N 11 0 E
Mahe, *India* **43 C8** 33 10N 78 32 E
Mahendragarh, *India* **42 E7** 28 17N 76 14 E
Mahenge, *Tanzania* **55 D4** 8 45S 36 41 E
Maheno, *N.Z.* **59 L3** 45 10S 170 50 E
Mahesana, *India* **42 H5** 23 39N 72 26 E
Maheshwar, *India* **42 H6** 22 11N 75 35 E
Mahgawan, *India* **43 F8** 26 29N 78 37 E
Mahi →, *India* **42 H5** 22 15N 72 55 E
Mahia Pen., *N.Z.* **59 H6** 39 9S 177 55 E
Mahilyow, *Belarus* **17 B16** 53 55N 30 18 E
Mahmud Kot, *Pakistan* **42 D4** 30 16N 71 0 E
Mahnomen, *U.S.A.* **80 B7** 47 19N 95 58W
Mahoba, *India* **43 G8** 25 15N 79 55 E
Mahón = Maó, *Spain* **22 B11** 39 53N 4 16 E
Mahone Bay, *Canada* **71 D7** 44 30N 64 20W
Mahopac, *U.S.A.* **79 E11** 41 22N 73 45W
Mahuva, *India* **42 J4** 21 5N 71 48 E
Mai-Ndombe, L., *Dem. Rep. of the Congo* **52 E3** 2 0S 18 20 E
Mai-Sai, *Thailand* **38 B2** 20 20N 99 55 E
Maicurú →, *Brazil* **93 D8** 2 14S 54 17W
Maidan Khula, *Afghan.* **42 C3** 33 36N 69 50 E
Maidenhead, *U.K.* **11 F7** 51 31N 0 42W
Maidstone, *Canada* **73 C7** 53 5N 109 20W
Maidstone, *U.K.* **11 F8** 51 16N 0 32 E
Maiduguri, *Nigeria* **51 F8** 12 0N 13 20 E
Maihar, *India* **43 G9** 24 16N 80 45 E
Maijdi, *Bangla.* **41 H17** 22 48N 91 10 E
Maikala Ra., *India* **41 J12** 22 0N 81 0 E
Mailani, *India* **43 E9** 28 17N 80 21 E
Mailsi, *Pakistan* **42 E5** 29 48N 72 15 E
Main →, *Germany* **16 C5** 50 0N 8 18 E
Main →, *U.K.* **13 B5** 54 48N 6 18W
Maine, *France* **18 C3** 48 20N 0 15W
Maine □, *U.S.A.* **77 C11** 45 20N 69 0W
Maine →, *Ireland* **13 D2** 52 9N 9 45W
Maingkwan, *Burma* **41 F20** 26 15N 96 37 E
Mainit, L., *Phil.* **37 C7** 9 31N 125 30 E
Mainland, *Orkney, U.K.* **12 C5** 58 59N 3 8W
Mainland, *Shet., U.K.* **12 A7** 60 15N 1 22W
Mainoru, *Australia* **62 A1** 14 0S 134 6 E
Mainpuri, *India* **43 F8** 27 18N 79 4 E
Maintirano, *Madag.* **57 B7** 18 3S 44 1 E
Mainz, *Germany* **16 C5** 50 1N 8 14 E
Maipú, *Argentina* **94 D4** 36 52S 57 50W
Maiquetía, *Venezuela* **92 A5** 10 36N 66 57W
Mairabari, *India* **41 F18** 26 30N 92 22 E
Maisí, *Cuba* **89 B5** 20 17N 74 9W
Maisí, Pta. de, *Cuba* **89 B5** 20 10N 74 10W
Maitland →, *Canada* **78 C3** 43 45N 81 43W
Maiz, Is. del, *Nic.* **88 D3** 12 15N 83 4W
Maizuru, *Japan* **31 G7** 35 25N 135 22 E
Majalengka, *Indonesia* **37 G13** 6 50S 108 13 E
Majene, *Indonesia* **37 E5** 3 38S 118 57 E
Majorca = Mallorca, *Spain* **22 B10** 39 30N 3 0 E
Makaha, *Zimbabwe* **57 B5** 17 20S 32 39 E
Makalamabedi, *Botswana* **56 C3** 20 19S 23 51 E
Makale, *Indonesia* **37 E5** 3 6S 119 51 E
Makamba, *Burundi* **54 C2** 4 8S 29 49 E
Makarikari = Makgadikgadi Salt Pans, *Botswana* **56 C4** 20 40S 25 45 E
Makarovo, *Russia* **27 D11** 57 40N 107 45 E
Makasar = Ujung Pandang, *Indonesia* **37 F5** 5 10S 119 20 E
Makasar, Selat, *Indonesia* **37 E5** 1 0S 118 20 E
Makasar, Str. of = Makasar, Selat, *Indonesia* **37 E5** 1 0S 118 20 E
Makat, *Kazakstan* **25 E9** 47 39N 53 19 E
Makedhonía □, *Greece* **21 D10** 40 39N 22 0 E
Makedonija = Macedonia ■, *Europe* **21 D9** 41 53N 21 40 E
Makeyevka = Makiyivka, *Ukraine* **25 E6** 48 0N 38 0 E
Makgadikgadi Salt Pans, *Botswana* **56 C4** 20 40S 25 45 E
Makhachkala, *Russia* **25 F8** 43 0N 47 30 E
Makhmūr, *Iraq* **44 C4** 35 46N 43 35 E
Makian, *Indonesia* **37 D7** 0 20N 127 20 E
Makindu, *Kenya* **54 C4** 2 18S 37 50 E
Makinsk, *Kazakstan* **26 D8** 52 37N 70 26 E
Makiyivka, *Ukraine* **25 E6** 48 0N 38 0 E
Makkah, *Si. Arabia* **46 C2** 21 30N 39 54 E
Makkovik, *Canada* **71 A8** 55 10N 59 10W
Makó, *Hungary* **17 E11** 46 14N 20 33 E
Makokou, *Gabon* **52 D2** 0 40N 12 50 E
Makongo, *Dem. Rep. of the Congo* **54 B2** 3 25N 26 17 E
Makoro, *Dem. Rep. of the Congo* **54 B2** 3 10N 29 59 E
Makrai, *India* **40 H10** 22 2N 77 0 E
Makran Coast Range, *Pakistan* **40 G4** 25 40N 64 0 E
Makrana, *India* **42 F6** 27 2N 74 46 E
Makriyialos, *Greece* **23 D7** 35 2N 25 59 E
Mākū, *Iran* **44 B5** 39 15N 44 31 E
Makunda, *Botswana* **56 C3** 22 30S 20 7 E
Makurazaki, *Japan* **31 J5** 31 15N 130 20 E
Makurdi, *Nigeria* **50 G7** 7 43N 8 35 E
Makūyeh, *Iran* **45 D7** 28 7N 53 9 E
Makwassie, *S. Africa* **56 D4** 27 17S 26 0 E
Makwiro, *Zimbabwe* **57 B5** 17 58S 30 25 E
Mal B., *Ireland* **13 D2** 52 50N 9 30W
Mala, Pta., *Panama* **88 E3** 7 28N 80 2W
Malabar Coast, *India* **40 P9** 11 0N 75 0 E
Malabo = Rey Malabo, *Eq. Guin.* **52 D1** 3 45N 8 50 E
Malacca, Str. of, *Indonesia* **39 L3** 3 0N 101 0 E
Malad City, *U.S.A.* **82 E7** 42 12N 112 15W
Maladzyechna, *Belarus* **17 A14** 54 20N 26 50 E
Málaga, *Spain* **19 D3** 36 43N 4 23W
Malagarasi, *Tanzania* **54 D3** 5 5S 30 50 E
Malagarasi →, *Tanzania* **54 D2** 5 12S 29 47 E
Malagasy Rep. = Madagascar ■, *Africa* **57 C8** 20 0S 47 0 E
Malahide, *Ireland* **13 C5** 53 26N 6 9W
Malaimbandy, *Madag.* **57 C8** 20 20S 45 36 E
Malakâl, *Sudan* **51 G12** 9 33N 31 40 E
Malakand, *Pakistan* **42 B4** 34 40N 71 55 E
Malakwal, *Pakistan* **42 C5** 32 34N 73 13 E
Malamala, *Indonesia* **37 E6** 3 21S 120 55 E
Malanda, *Australia* **62 B4** 17 22S 145 35 E
Malang, *Indonesia* **36 F4** 7 59S 112 45 E
Malangen, *Norway* **8 B18** 69 24N 18 37 E
Malanje, *Angola* **52 F3** 9 36S 16 17 E
Mälaren, *Sweden* **9 G17** 59 30N 17 10 E
Malargüe, *Argentina* **94 D2** 35 32S 69 30W
Malartic, *Canada* **70 C4** 48 9N 78 9W
Malaryta, *Belarus* **17 C13** 51 50N 24 3 E
Malatya, *Turkey* **25 G6** 38 25N 38 20 E
Malawi ■, *Africa* **55 E3** 11 55S 34 0 E
Malawi, L. = Nyasa, L., *Africa* **55 E3** 12 30S 34 30 E
Malay Pen., *Asia* **39 J3** 7 25N 100 0 E
Malaya Vishera, *Russia* **24 C5** 58 55N 32 25 E
Malaybalay, *Phil.* **37 C7** 8 5N 125 7 E
Malāyer, *Iran* **45 C6** 34 19N 48 51 E
Malaysia ■, *Asia* **39 K4** 5 0N 110 0 E
Malazgirt, *Turkey* **25 G7** 39 10N 42 33 E
Malbon, *Australia* **62 C3** 21 5S 140 17 E
Malbooma, *Australia* **63 E1** 30 41S 134 11 E
Malbork, *Poland* **17 B10** 54 3N 19 1 E
Malcolm, *Australia* **61 E3** 28 51S 121 25 E
Malcolm, Pt., *Australia* **61 F3** 33 48S 123 45 E
Maldah, *India* **43 G13** 25 2N 88 9 E
Maldegem, *Belgium* **15 C3** 51 14N 3 26 E
Malden, *Mass., U.S.A.* **79 D13** 42 26N 71 4W
Malden, *Mo., U.S.A.* **81 G10** 36 34N 89 57W
Malden I., *Kiribati* **65 H12** 4 3S 155 1W
Maldives ■, *Ind. Oc.* **29 J11** 5 0N 73 0 E
Maldonado, *Uruguay* **95 C5** 34 59S 55 0W
Maldonado, Punta, *Mexico* **87 D5** 16 19N 98 35W
Malé, *Maldives* **29 J11** 4 0N 73 28 E
Malé Karpaty, *Slovak Rep.* **17 D9** 48 30N 17 20 E
Maléa, Ákra, *Greece* **21 F10** 36 28N 23 7 E
Malegaon, *India* **40 J9** 20 30N 74 38 E
Malei, *Mozam.* **55 F4** 17 12S 36 58 E
Malek Kandī, *Iran* **44 B5** 37 9N 46 6 E
Malela, *Dem. Rep. of the Congo* **54 C2** 4 22S 26 8 E
Malema, *Mozam.* **55 E4** 14 57S 37 20 E
Máleme, *Greece* **23 D5** 35 31N 23 49 E
Maleny, *Australia* **63 D5** 26 45S 152 52 E
Malerkotla, *India* **42 D6** 30 32N 75 58 E
Máles, *Greece* **23 D7** 35 6N 25 35 E
Malgomaj, *Sweden* **8 D17** 64 40N 16 30 E
Malha, *Sudan* **51 E11** 15 8N 25 10 E
Malhargarh, *India* **42 G6** 24 17N 74 59 E
Malheur →, *U.S.A.* **82 D5** 44 4N 116 59W
Malheur L., *U.S.A.* **82 E4** 43 20N 118 48W
Mali ■, *Africa* **50 E5** 17 0N 3 0W
Mali →, *Burma* **41 G20** 25 40N 97 40 E
Mali Kyun, *Burma* **38 F2** 13 0N 98 20 E
Malibu, *U.S.A.* **85 L8** 34 2N 118 41W
Maliku, *Indonesia* **37 E6** 0 39S 123 16 E
Malili, *Indonesia* **37 E6** 2 42S 121 6 E
Malimba, Mts., *Dem. Rep. of the Congo* **54 D2** 7 30S 29 30 E
Malin Hd., *Ireland* **13 A4** 55 23N 7 23W
Malin Pen., *Ireland* **13 A4** 55 20N 7 17W
Malindi, *Kenya* **54 C5** 3 12S 40 5 E
Malines = Mechelen, *Belgium* **15 C4** 51 2N 4 29 E
Malino, *Indonesia* **37 D6** 1 0N 121 0 E
Malinyi, *Tanzania* **55 D4** 8 56S 36 0 E
Malita, *Phil.* **37 C7** 6 19N 125 39 E
Maliwun, *Burma* **36 B1** 10 17N 98 40 E
Maliya, *India* **42 H4** 23 5N 70 46 E
Malkara, *Turkey* **21 D12** 40 53N 26 53 E
Mallaig, *U.K.* **12 D3** 57 0N 5 50W
Mallawan, *India* **43 F9** 27 4N 80 12 E
Mallawi, *Egypt* **51 C12** 27 44N 30 44 E
Mállia, *Greece* **23 D7** 35 17N 25 32 E
Mallión, Kólpos, *Greece* **23 D7** 35 19N 25 27 E
Mallorca, *Spain* **22 B10** 39 30N 3 0 E
Mallorytown, *Canada* **79 B9** 44 29N 75 53W

Mallow, *Ireland* **13 D3** 52 8N 8 39W
Malmberget, *Sweden* **8 C19** 67 11N 20 40 E
Malmédy, *Belgium* **15 D6** 50 25N 6 2 E
Malmesbury, *S. Africa* **56 E2** 33 28S 18 41 E
Malmö, *Sweden* **9 J15** 55 36N 12 59 E
Malolos, *Phil.* **37 B6** 14 50N 120 49 E
Malombe L., *Malawi* **55 E4** 14 40S 35 15 E
Malone, *U.S.A.* **79 B10** 44 51N 74 18W
Måløy, *Norway* **9 F11** 61 57N 5 6 E
Malpaso, *Canary Is.* **22 G1** 27 43N 18 3W
Malpelo, I. de, *Colombia* **92 C2** 4 3N 81 35W
Malpur, *India* **42 H5** 23 21N 73 27 E
Malpura, *India* **42 F6** 26 17N 75 23 E
Malta, *Idaho, U.S.A.* **82 E7** 42 18N 113 22W
Malta, *Mont., U.S.A.* **82 B10** 48 21N 107 52W
Malta ■, *Europe* **23 D2** 35 50N 14 30 E
Maltahöhe, *Namibia* **56 C2** 24 55S 17 0 E
Malton, *Canada* **78 C5** 43 42N 79 38W
Malton, *U.K.* **10 C7** 54 8N 0 49W
Maluku, *Indonesia* **37 E7** 1 0S 127 0 E
Maluku □, *Indonesia* **37 E7** 3 0S 128 0 E
Maluku Sea = Molucca Sea, *Indonesia* **37 E6** 0 0 125 0 E
Malvan, *India* **40 L8** 16 2N 73 30 E
Malvern, *U.S.A.* **81 H8** 34 22N 92 49W
Malvern Hills, *U.K.* **11 E5** 52 0N 2 19W
Malvinas, Is. = Falkland Is. □, *Atl. Oc.* **96 G5** 51 30S 59 0W
Malya, *Tanzania* **54 C3** 3 5S 33 38 E
Malyn, *Ukraine* **17 C15** 50 46N 29 3 E
Malyy Lyakhovskiy, Ostrov, *Russia* **27 B15** 74 7N 140 36 E
Mama, *Russia* **27 D12** 58 18N 112 54 E
Mamanguape, *Brazil* **93 E11** 6 50S 35 4W
Mamarr Mitlā, *Egypt* **47 E1** 30 2N 32 54 E
Mamasa, *Indonesia* **37 E5** 2 55S 119 20 E
Mambasa, *Dem. Rep. of the Congo* **54 B2** 1 22N 29 3 E
Mamberamo →, *Indonesia* **37 E9** 2 0S 137 50 E
Mambilima Falls, *Zambia* **55 E2** 10 31S 28 45 E
Mambirima, *Dem. Rep. of the Congo* **55 E2** 11 25S 27 33 E
Mambo, *Tanzania* **54 C4** 4 52S 38 22 E
Mambrui, *Kenya* **54 C5** 3 5S 40 5 E
Mamburao, *Phil.* **37 B6** 13 13N 120 39 E
Mameigwess L., *Canada* **70 B2** 52 35N 87 50W
Mammoth, *U.S.A.* **83 K8** 32 43N 110 39W
Mammoth Cave National Park, *U.S.A.* **76 G3** 37 8N 86 13W
Mamoré →, *Bolivia* **92 F5** 10 23S 65 53W
Mamou, *Guinea* **50 F3** 10 15N 12 0W
Mampikony, *Madag.* **57 B8** 16 6S 47 38 E
Mamuju, *Indonesia* **37 E5** 2 41S 118 50 E
Mamuno, *Botswana* **56 C3** 22 16S 20 1 E
Man, *Ivory C.* **50 G4** 7 30N 7 40W
Man, I. of, *U.K.* **10 C3** 54 15N 4 30W
Man-Bazar, *India* **43 H12** 23 4N 86 39 E
Man Na, *Burma* **41 H20** 23 27N 97 19 E
Mana →, *Fr. Guiana* **93 B8** 5 45N 53 55W
Manaar, G. of = Mannar, G. of, *Asia* **40 Q11** 8 30N 79 0 E
Manacapuru, *Brazil* **92 D6** 3 16S 60 37W
Manacor, *Spain* **22 B10** 39 34N 3 13 E
Manado, *Indonesia* **37 D6** 1 29N 124 51 E
Managua, *Nic.* **88 D2** 12 6N 86 20W
Managua, L. de, *Nic.* **88 D2** 12 20N 86 30W
Manakara, *Madag.* **57 C8** 22 8S 48 1 E
Manali, *India* **42 C7** 32 16N 77 10 E
Manama = Al Manāmah, *Bahrain* **46 B5** 26 10N 50 30 E
Manambao →, *Madag.* **57 B7** 17 35S 44 0 E
Manambato, *Madag.* **57 A8** 13 43S 49 7 E
Manambolo →, *Madag.* **57 B7** 19 18S 44 22 E
Manambolosy, *Madag.* **57 B8** 16 2S 49 40 E
Mananara, *Madag.* **57 B8** 16 10S 49 46 E
Mananara →, *Madag.* **57 C8** 23 21S 47 42 E
Mananjary, *Madag.* **57 C8** 21 13S 48 20 E
Manantenina, *Madag.* **57 C8** 24 17S 47 19 E
Manaos = Manaus, *Brazil* **92 D7** 3 0S 60 0W
Manapire →, *Venezuela* **92 B5** 7 42N 66 7W
Manapouri, *N.Z.* **59 L1** 45 34S 167 39 E
Manapouri, L., *N.Z.* **59 L1** 45 32S 167 32 E
Manār, Jabal, *Yemen* **46 E3** 14 2N 44 17 E
Manaravolo, *Madag.* **57 C8** 23 59S 45 39 E
Manas, *China* **32 B3** 44 17N 85 56 E
Manas →, *India* **41 F17** 26 12N 90 40 E
Manaslu, *Nepal* **43 E11** 28 33N 84 33 E
Manasquan, *U.S.A.* **79 F10** 40 8N 74 3W
Manassa, *U.S.A.* **83 H11** 37 11N 105 56W
Manaung, *Burma* **41 K18** 18 45N 93 40 E
Manaus, *Brazil* **92 D7** 3 0S 60 0W
Manawan L., *Canada* **73 B8** 55 24N 103 14W
Manbij, *Syria* **44 B3** 36 31N 37 57 E
Manchegorsk, *Russia* **26 C4** 67 54N 32 58 E
Manchester, *U.K.* **10 D5** 53 29N 2 12W
Manchester, *Calif., U.S.A.* **84 G3** 38 58N 123 41W
Manchester, *Conn., U.S.A.* **79 E12** 41 47N 72 31W
Manchester, *Ga., U.S.A.* **77 J3** 32 51N 84 37W
Manchester, *Iowa, U.S.A.* **80 D9** 42 29N 91 27W
Manchester, *Ky., U.S.A.* **76 G4** 37 9N 83 46W
Manchester, *N.H., U.S.A.* **79 D13** 42 59N 71 28W
Manchester, *N.Y., U.S.A.* **78 D7** 42 56N 77 16W
Manchester, *Pa., U.S.A.* **79 F8** 40 4N 76 43W
Manchester, *Tenn., U.S.A.* **77 H2** 35 29N 86 5W
Manchester, *Vt., U.S.A.* **79 C11** 43 10N 73 5W
Manchester L., *Canada* **73 A7** 61 28N 107 29W
Manchhar L., *Pakistan* **42 F2** 26 25N 67 39 E
Manchuria = Dongbei, *China* **35 D13** 45 0N 125 0 E
Manchurian Plain, *China* **28 E16** 47 0N 124 0 E
Mand →, *India* **43 J10** 21 42N 83 15 E
Mand →, *Iran* **45 D7** 28 20N 52 30 E
Manda, *Ludewe, Tanzania* **55 E3** 10 30S 34 40 E
Manda, *Mbeya, Tanzania* **54 D3** 7 58S 32 29 E
Manda, *Mbeya, Tanzania* **55 D3** 8 30S 32 49 E
Mandabé, *Madag.* **57 C7** 21 0S 44 55 E
Mandaguari, *Brazil* **95 A5** 23 32S 51 42W
Mandah = Töhöm, *Mongolia* **34 B5** 44 27N 108 2 E
Mandal, *Norway* **9 G12** 58 2N 7 25 E
Mandala, Puncak, *Indonesia* **37 E10** 4 44S 140 20 E
Mandalay, *Burma* **41 J20** 22 0N 96 4 E
Mandale = Mandalay, *Burma* **41 J20** 22 0N 96 4 E
Mandalgarh, *India* **42 G6** 25 12N 75 6 E
Mandalgovi, *Mongolia* **34 B4** 45 45N 106 10 E
Mandalī, *Iraq* **44 C5** 33 43N 45 28 E
Mandan, *U.S.A.* **80 B4** 46 50N 100 54W
Mandar, Teluk, *Indonesia* **37 E5** 3 35S 119 15 E
Mandaue, *Phil.* **37 B6** 10 20N 123 56 E
Mandera, *Kenya* **54 B5** 3 55N 41 53 E
Mandi, *India* **42 D7** 31 39N 76 58 E
Mandi Dabwali, *India* **42 E6** 29 58N 74 42 E
Mandimba, *Mozam.* **55 E4** 14 20S 35 40 E
Mandioli, *Indonesia* **37 E7** 0 40S 127 20 E
Mandla, *India* **43 H9** 22 39N 80 30 E
Mandorah, *Australia* **60 B5** 12 32S 130 42 E
Mandoto, *Madag.* **57 B8** 19 34S 46 17 E
Mandra, *Pakistan* **42 C5** 33 23N 73 12 E
Mandrare →, *Madag.* **57 D8** 25 10S 46 30 E
Mandritsara, *Madag.* **57 B8** 15 50S 48 49 E
Mandronarivo, *Madag.* **57 C8** 21 7S 45 38 E
Mandsaur, *India* **42 G6** 24 3N 75 8 E
Mandurah, *Australia* **61 F2** 32 36S 115 48 E
Mandvi, *India* **42 H3** 22 51N 69 22 E
Mandya, *India* **40 N10** 12 30N 77 0 E
Mandzai, *Pakistan* **42 D2** 30 55N 67 6 E
Maneh, *Iran* **45 B8** 37 39N 57 7 E
Manera, *Madag.* **57 C7** 22 55S 44 20 E
Maneroo Cr. →, *Australia* **62 C3** 23 21S 143 53 E
Manfalût, *Egypt* **51 C12** 27 20N 30 52 E
Manfredónia, *Italy* **20 D6** 41 38N 15 55 E
Mangabeiras, Chapada das, *Brazil* **93 F9** 10 0S 46 30W
Mangalia, *Romania* **17 G15** 43 50N 28 35 E
Mangalore, *India* **40 N9** 12 55N 74 47 E
Mangan, *India* **43 F13** 27 31N 88 32 E
Mangaung, *S. Africa* **53 K5** 29 10S 26 25 E
Mangawan, *India* **43 G9** 24 41N 81 33 E
Mangaweka, *N.Z.* **59 H5** 39 48S 175 47 E
Manggar, *Indonesia* **36 E3** 2 50S 108 10 E
Manggawitu, *Indonesia* **37 E8** 4 8S 133 32 E
Mangindrano, *Madag.* **57 A8** 14 17S 48 58 E
Mangkalihat, Tanjung, *Indonesia* **37 D5** 1 2N 118 59 E
Mangla, *Pakistan* **42 C5** 33 7N 73 39 E
Mangla Dam, *Pakistan* **43 C5** 33 9N 73 44 E
Manglaur, *India* **42 E7** 29 44N 77 49 E
Mangnai, *China* **32 C4** 37 52N 91 43 E
Mango, *Togo* **50 F6** 10 20N 0 30 E
Mangoche, *Malawi* **55 E4** 14 25S 35 16 E
Mangoky →, *Madag.* **57 C7** 21 29S 43 41 E
Mangole, *Indonesia* **37 E6** 1 50S 125 55 E
Mangombe, *Dem. Rep. of the Congo* **54 C2** 1 20S 26 48 E
Mangonui, *N.Z.* **59 F4** 35 1S 173 32 E
Mangoro →, *Madag.* **57 B8** 20 0S 48 45 E
Mangrol, *Mad. P., India* **42 J4** 21 7N 70 7 E
Mangrol, *Raj., India* **42 G6** 25 20N 76 31 E
Mangueira, L. da, *Brazil* **95 C5** 33 0S 52 50W
Mangum, *U.S.A.* **81 H5** 34 53N 99 30W
Mangyshlak Poluostrov, *Kazakstan* **26 E6** 44 30N 52 30 E
Manhattan, *U.S.A.* **80 F6** 39 11N 96 35W
Manhiça, *Mozam.* **57 D5** 25 23S 32 49 E
Mania →, *Madag.* **57 B8** 19 42S 45 22 E
Manica, *Mozam.* **57 B5** 18 58S 32 59 E
Manica □, *Mozam.* **57 B5** 19 10S 33 45 E
Manicaland □, *Zimbabwe* **55 F3** 19 0S 32 30 E
Manicoré, *Brazil* **92 E6** 5 48S 61 16W
Manicouagan →, *Canada* **71 C6** 49 30N 68 30W
Manicouagan, Rés., *Canada* **71 B6** 51 5N 68 40W
Maniema □, *Dem. Rep. of the Congo* **54 C2** 3 0S 26 0 E
Manīfah, *Si. Arabia* **45 E6** 27 44N 49 0 E
Manifold, C., *Australia* **62 C5** 22 41S 150 50 E
Manigotagan, *Canada* **73 C9** 51 6N 96 18W
Manigotagan →, *Canada* **73 C9** 51 7N 96 20W
Manihari, *India* **43 G12** 25 21N 87 38 E
Manihiki, *Cook Is.* **65 J11** 10 24S 161 1W
Manika, Plateau de la, *Dem. Rep. of the Congo* **55 E2** 10 0S 25 5 E
Manikpur, *India* **43 G9** 25 4N 81 7 E
Manila, *Phil.* **37 B6** 14 40N 121 3 E
Manila, *U.S.A.* **82 F9** 40 59N 109 43W
Manila B., *Phil.* **37 B6** 14 40N 120 35 E
Maningrida, *Australia* **62 A1** 12 3S 134 13 E
Manipur □, *India* **41 G19** 25 0N 94 0 E
Manipur →, *Burma* **41 H19** 23 45N 94 20 E
Manisa, *Turkey* **21 E12** 38 38N 27 30 E
Manistee, *U.S.A.* **76 C2** 44 15N 86 19W
Manistee →, *U.S.A.* **76 C2** 44 15N 86 21W
Manistique, *U.S.A.* **76 C2** 45 57N 86 15W
Manito L., *Canada* **73 C7** 52 43N 109 43W
Manitoba □, *Canada* **73 B9** 55 30N 97 0W
Manitoba, L., *Canada* **73 C9** 51 0N 98 45W
Manitou, *Canada* **73 D9** 49 15N 98 32W
Manitou, L., *Canada* **71 B6** 50 55N 65 17W
Manitou Is., *U.S.A.* **76 C3** 45 8N 86 0W
Manitou Springs, *U.S.A.* **80 F2** 38 52N 104 55W
Manitoulin I., *Canada* **70 C3** 45 40N 82 30W
Manitouwadge, *Canada* **70 C2** 49 8N 85 48W
Manitowoc, *U.S.A.* **76 C2** 44 5N 87 40W
Manizales, *Colombia* **92 B3** 5 5N 75 32W
Manja, *Madag.* **57 C7** 21 26S 44 20 E
Manjacaze, *Mozam.* **57 C5** 24 45S 34 0 E
Manjakandriana, *Madag.* **57 B8** 18 55S 47 47 E
Manjhand, *Pakistan* **42 G3** 25 50N 68 10 E
Manjil, *Iran* **45 B6** 36 46N 49 30 E
Manjimup, *Australia* **61 F2** 34 15S 116 6 E
Manjra →, *India* **40 K10** 18 49N 77 52 E
Mankato, *Kans., U.S.A.* **80 F5** 39 47N 98 13W
Mankato, *Minn., U.S.A.* **80 C8** 44 10N 94 0W
Mankayane, *Swaziland* **57 D5** 26 40S 31 4 E
Mankera, *Pakistan* **42 D4** 31 23N 71 26 E
Mankota, *Canada* **73 D7** 49 25N 107 5W
Manlay = Üydzin, *Mongolia* **34 B4** 44 9N 107 0 E
Manmad, *India* **40 J9** 20 18N 74 28 E
Mann Ranges, *Australia* **61 E5** 26 6S 130 5 E
Manna, *Indonesia* **36 E2** 4 25S 102 55 E
Mannar, *Sri Lanka* **40 Q11** 9 1N 79 54 E
Mannar, G. of, *Asia* **40 Q11** 8 30N 79 0 E
Mannar I., *Sri Lanka* **40 Q11** 9 5N 79 45 E
Mannheim, *Germany* **16 D5** 49 29N 8 29 E
Manning, *Canada* **72 B5** 56 53N 117 39W
Manning, *Oreg., U.S.A.* **84 E3** 45 45N 123 13W
Manning, *S.C., U.S.A.* **77 J5** 33 42N 80 13W
Manning Prov. Park, *Canada* **72 D4** 49 5N 120 45W
Manoharpur, *India* **43 H11** 22 23N 85 12 E
Manokwari, *Indonesia* **37 E8** 0 54S 134 0 E
Manombo, *Madag.* **57 C7** 22 57S 43 28 E
Manono, *Dem. Rep. of the Congo* **54 D2** 7 15S 27 25 E
Manosque, *France* **18 E6** 43 49N 5 47 E
Manotick, *Canada* **79 A9** 45 13N 75 41W
Manouane →, *Canada* **71 C5** 49 30N 71 10W
Manouane, L., *Canada* **71 B5** 50 45N 70 45W
Manp'o, *N. Korea* **35 D14** 41 6N 126 24 E
Manpojin = Manp'o, *N. Korea* **35 D14** 41 6N 126 24 E
Manpur, *Mad. P., India* **42 H6** 22 26N 75 37 E
Manpur, *Mad. P., India* **43 H10** 23 17N 83 35 E
Manresa, *Spain* **19 B6** 41 48N 1 50 E
Mansa, *Gujarat, India* **42 H5** 23 27N 72 45 E
Mansa, *Punjab, India* **42 E6** 30 0N 75 27 E
Mansa, *Zambia* **55 E2** 11 13S 28 55 E
Mansehra, *Pakistan* **42 B5** 34 20N 73 15 E
Mansel I., *Canada* **69 B11** 62 0N 80 0W
Mansfield, *U.K.* **10 D6** 53 9N 1 11W
Mansfield, *La., U.S.A.* **81 J8** 32 2N 93 43W
Mansfield, *Mass., U.S.A.* **79 D13** 42 2N 71 13W
Mansfield, *Ohio, U.S.A.* **78 F2** 40 45N 82 31W
Mansfield, *Pa., U.S.A.* **78 E7** 41 48N 77 5W
Mansfield, Mt., *U.S.A.* **79 B12** 44 33N 72 49W
Manson Creek, *Canada* **72 B4** 55 37N 124 32W
Manta, *Ecuador* **92 D2** 1 0S 80 40W
Mantalingajan, Mt., *Phil.* **36 C5** 8 55N 117 45 E
Mantare, *Tanzania* **54 C3** 2 42S 33 13 E
Manteca, *U.S.A.* **84 H5** 37 48N 121 13W
Manteo, *U.S.A.* **77 H8** 35 55N 75 40W
Mantes-la-Jolie, *France* **18 B4** 48 58N 1 41 E
Manthani, *India* **40 K11** 18 40N 79 35 E
Manti, *U.S.A.* **82 G8** 39 16N 111 38W
Mantiqueira, Serra da, *Brazil* **95 A7** 22 0S 44 0W
Manton, *U.S.A.* **76 C3** 44 25N 85 24W
Mántova, *Italy* **20 B4** 45 9N 10 48 E
Mänttä, *Finland* **9 E21** 62 0N 24 40 E
Mantua = Mántova, *Italy* **20 B4** 45 9N 10 48 E
Manu, *Peru* **92 F4** 12 10S 70 51W
Manu →, *Peru* **92 F4** 12 16S 70 55W
Manua Is., *Amer. Samoa* **59 B14** 14 13S 169 35W
Manuel Alves →, *Brazil* **93 F9** 11 19S 48 28W
Manui, *Indonesia* **37 E6** 3 35S 123 5 E
Manukau, *N.Z.* **59 G5** 40 43S 175 13 E
Manuripi →, *Bolivia* **92 F5** 11 6S 67 36W
Many, *U.S.A.* **81 K8** 31 34N 93 29W
Manyara, L., *Tanzania* **54 C4** 3 40S 35 50 E
Manych-Gudilo, Ozero, *Russia* **25 E7** 46 24N 42 38 E
Manyonga →, *Tanzania* **54 C3** 4 10S 34 15 E
Manyoni, *Tanzania* **54 D3** 5 45S 34 55 E
Manzai, *Pakistan* **42 C4** 32 12N 70 15 E
Manzanares, *Spain* **19 C4** 39 2N 3 22W
Manzanillo, *Cuba* **88 B4** 20 20N 77 31W
Manzanillo, *Mexico* **86 D4** 19 0N 104 20W
Manzanillo, Pta., *Panama* **88 E4** 9 30N 79 40W
Manzano Mts., *U.S.A.* **83 J10** 34 40N 106 20W
Manzarīyeh, *Iran* **45 C6** 34 53N 50 50 E
Manzhouli, *China* **33 B6** 49 35N 117 25 E
Manzini, *Swaziland* **57 D5** 26 30S 31 25 E
Mao, *Chad* **51 F9** 14 4N 15 19 E
Maó, *Spain* **22 B11** 39 53N 4 16 E
Maoke, Pegunungan, *Indonesia* **37 E9** 3 40S 137 30 E
Maolin, *China* **35 C12** 43 58N 123 30 E
Maoming, *China* **33 D6** 21 50N 110 54 E
Maoxing, *China* **35 B13** 45 28N 124 40 E
Mapam Yumco, *China* **32 C3** 30 45N 81 28 E
Mapastepec, *Mexico* **87 D6** 15 26N 92 54W
Mapia, Kepulauan, *Indonesia* **37 D8** 0 50N 134 20 E
Mapimí, *Mexico* **86 B4** 25 50N 103 50W
Mapimí, Bolsón de, *Mexico* **86 B4** 27 30N 104 15W
Mapinga, *Tanzania* **54 D4** 6 40S 39 12 E
Mapinhane, *Mozam.* **57 C6** 22 20S 35 0 E
Maple Creek, *Canada* **73 D7** 49 55N 109 29W
Maple Valley, *U.S.A.* **84 C4** 47 25N 122 3W
Mapleton, *U.S.A.* **82 D2** 44 2N 123 52W
Mapuera →, *Brazil* **92 D7** 1 5S 57 2W
Mapulanguene, *Mozam.* **57 C5** 24 29S 32 6 E
Maputo, *Mozam.* **57 D5** 25 58S 32 32 E
Maputo □, *Mozam.* **57 D5** 26 0S 32 25 E
Maputo, B. de, *Mozam.* **57 D5** 25 50S 32 45 E
Maqiaohe, *China* **35 B16** 44 40N 130 30 E
Maqnā, *Si. Arabia* **44 D2** 28 25N 34 50 E
Maquela do Zombo, *Angola* **52 F3** 6 0S 15 15 E
Maquinchao, *Argentina* **96 E3** 41 15S 68 50W
Maquoketa, *U.S.A.* **80 D9** 42 4N 90 40W
Mar, Serra do, *Brazil* **95 B6** 25 30S 49 0W
Mar Chiquita, L., *Argentina* **94 C3** 30 40S 62 50W
Mar del Plata, *Argentina* **94 D4** 38 0S 57 30W
Mar Menor, *Spain* **19 D5** 37 40N 0 45W
Mara, *Tanzania* **54 C3** 1 30S 34 32 E
Mara □, *Tanzania* **54 C3** 1 45S 34 20 E
Maraã, *Brazil* **92 D5** 1 52S 65 25W
Marabá, *Brazil* **93 E9** 5 20S 49 5W
Maracá, I. de, *Brazil* **93 C8** 2 10N 50 30W
Maracaibo, *Venezuela* **92 A4** 10 40N 71 37W
Maracaibo, L. de, *Venezuela* **92 B4** 9 40N 71 30W
Maracaju, *Brazil* **95 A4** 21 38S 55 9W
Maracay, *Venezuela* **92 A5** 10 15N 67 28W
Maradi, *Niger* **50 F7** 13 29N 7 20 E
Marāgheh, *Iran* **44 B5** 37 30N 46 12 E
Marāh, *Si. Arabia* **44 E5** 25 0N 45 35 E
Marajó, I. de, *Brazil* **93 D9** 1 0S 49 30W
Marākand, *Iran* **44 B5** 38 51N 45 16 E
Maralal, *Kenya* **54 B4** 1 0N 36 38 E
Maralinga, *Australia* **61 F5** 30 13S 131 32 E
Maran, *Malaysia* **39 L4** 3 35N 102 45 E
Marana, *U.S.A.* **83 K8** 32 27N 111 13W
Maranboy, *Australia* **60 B5** 14 40S 132 39 E
Marand, *Iran* **44 B5** 38 30N 45 45 E
Marang, *Malaysia* **39 K4** 5 12N 103 13 E
Maranguape, *Brazil* **93 D11** 3 55S 38 50W
Maranhão = São Luís, *Brazil* **93 D10** 2 39S 44 15W
Maranhão □, *Brazil* **93 E9** 5 0S 46 0W
Maranoa →, *Australia* **63 D4** 27 50S 148 37 E
Marañón →, *Peru* **92 D4** 4 30S 73 35W
Marão, *Mozam.* **57 C5** 24 18S 34 2 E
Maraş = Kahramanmaraş, *Turkey* **25 G6** 37 37N 36 53 E
Marathasa □, *Cyprus* **23 E11** 34 59N 32 51 E
Marathon, *Australia* **62 C3** 20 51S 143 32 E
Marathon, *Canada* **70 C2** 48 44N 86 23W
Marathon, *N.Y., U.S.A.* **79 D8** 42 27N 76 2W
Marathon, *Tex., U.S.A.* **81 K3** 30 12N 103 15W
Marathóvouno, *Cyprus* **23 D12** 35 13N 33 37 E
Maratua, *Indonesia* **37 D5** 2 10N 118 35 E
Maravatío, *Mexico* **86 D4** 19 51N 100 25W
Marāwih, *U.A.E.* **45 E7** 24 18N 53 18 E
Marbella, *Spain* **19 D3** 36 30N 4 57W
Marble Bar, *Australia* **60 D2** 21 9S 119 44 E
Marble Falls, *U.S.A.* **81 K5** 30 35N 98 16W
Marblehead, *U.S.A.* **79 D14** 42 30N 70 51W
Marburg, *Germany* **16 C5** 50 47N 8 46 E
March, *U.K.* **11 E8** 52 33N 0 5 E
Marche, *France* **18 C4** 46 5N 1 20 E
Marche-en-Famenne, *Belgium* **15 D5** 50 14N 5 19 E
Marchena, *Spain* **19 D3** 37 18N 5 23W
Marco, *U.S.A.* **77 N5** 25 58N 81 44W
Marcos Juárez, *Argentina* **94 C3** 32 42S 62 5W
Marcus I. = Minami-Tori-Shima, *Pac. Oc.* **64 E7** 24 20N 153 58 E
Marcus Necker Ridge, *Pac. Oc.* **64 F9** 20 0N 175 0 E
Marcy, Mt., *U.S.A.* **79 B11** 44 7N 73 56W
Mardan, *Pakistan* **42 B5** 34 20N 72 0 E
Mardin, *Turkey* **25 G7** 37 20N 40 43 E
Maree, L., *U.K.* **12 D3** 57 40N 5 26W
Mareeba, *Australia* **62 B4** 16 59S 145 28 E
Mareetsane, *S. Africa* **56 D4** 26 9S 25 25 E
Marek = Stanke Dimitrov, *Bulgaria* **21 C10** 42 17N 23 9 E
Marengo, *U.S.A.* **80 E8** 41 48N 92 4W
Marenyi, *Kenya* **54 C4** 4 22S 39 8 E
Marerano, *Madag.* **57 C7** 21 23S 44 52 E
Marfa, *U.S.A.* **81 K2** 30 19N 104 1W
Marfa Pt., *Malta* **23 D1** 35 59N 14 19 E
Margaret →, *Australia* **60 C4** 18 9S 125 41 E
Margaret Bay, *Canada* **72 C3** 51 20N 127 35W
Margaret L., *Canada* **72 B5** 58 56N 115 25W
Margaret River, *Australia* **61 F2** 33 57S 115 4 E
Margarita, I. de, *Venezuela* **92 A6** 11 0N 64 0W
Margaritovo, *Russia* **30 C7** 43 25N 134 45 E
Margate, *S. Africa* **57 E5** 30 50S 30 20 E
Margate, *U.K.* **11 F9** 51 23N 1 23 E
Mārgow, Dasht-e, *Afghan.* **40 D3** 30 40N 62 30 E
Marguerite, *Canada* **72 C4** 52 30N 122 25W
Mari El □, *Russia* **24 C8** 56 30N 48 0 E
Mari Indus, *Pakistan* **42 C4** 32 57N 71 34 E
Mari Republic = Mari El □, *Russia* **24 C8** 56 30N 48 0 E
María Elena, *Chile* **94 A2** 22 18S 69 40W
María Grande, *Argentina* **94 C4** 31 45S 59 55W
Maria I., *N. Terr., Australia* **62 A2** 14 52S 135 45 E
Maria I., *Tas., Australia* **62 G4** 42 35S 148 0 E
Maria van Diemen, C., *N.Z.* **59 F4** 34 29S 172 40 E
Mariakani, *Kenya* **54 C4** 3 50S 39 27 E
Marian, *Australia* **62 C4** 21 9S 148 57 E
Marian L., *Canada* **72 A5** 63 0N 116 15W
Mariana Trench, *Pac. Oc.* **28 H18** 13 0N 145 0 E
Marianao, *Cuba* **88 B3** 23 8N 82 24W
Marianna, *Ark., U.S.A.* **81 H9** 34 46N 90 46W
Marianna, *Fla., U.S.A.* **77 K3** 30 46N 85 14W
Marias →, *U.S.A.* **82 C8** 47 56N 110 30W
Mariato, Punta, *Panama* **88 E3** 7 12N 80 52W
Maribor, *Slovenia* **16 E8** 46 36N 15 40 E
Marico →, *Africa* **56 C4** 23 35S 26 57 E
Maricopa, *Ariz., U.S.A.* **83 K7** 33 4N 112 3W
Maricopa, *Calif., U.S.A.* **85 K7** 35 4N 119 24W
Marié →, *Brazil* **92 D5** 0 27S 66 26W
Marie Byrd Land, *Antarctica* **5 D14** 79 30S 125 0W
Marie-Galante, *Guadeloupe* **89 C7** 15 56N 61 16W
Mariecourt = Kangiqsujuaq, *Canada* **69 B12** 61 30N 72 0W
Mariembourg, *Belgium* **15 D4** 50 6N 4 31 E
Mariental, *Namibia* **56 C2** 24 36S 18 0 E
Marienville, *U.S.A.* **78 E5** 41 28N 79 8W
Mariestad, *Sweden* **9 G15** 58 43N 13 50 E
Marietta, *Ga., U.S.A.* **77 J3** 33 57N 84 33W
Marietta, *Ohio, U.S.A.* **76 F5** 39 25N 81 27W
Marieville, *Canada* **79 A11** 45 26N 73 10W
Mariinsk, *Russia* **26 D9** 56 10N 87 20 E
Marijampolė, *Lithuania* **9 J20** 54 33N 23 19 E
Marília, *Brazil* **95 A6** 22 13S 50 0W
Marín, *Spain* **19 A1** 42 23N 8 42W
Marina, *U.S.A.* **84 J5** 36 41N 121 48W
Marinduque, *Phil.* **37 B6** 13 25N 122 0 E
Marine City, *U.S.A.* **78 D2** 42 43N 82 30W
Marinette, *U.S.A.* **76 C2** 45 6N 87 38W
Maringá, *Brazil* **95 A5** 23 26S 52 2W
Marion, *Ala., U.S.A.* **77 J2** 32 38N 87 19W
Marion, *Ill., U.S.A.* **81 G10** 37 44N 88 56W
Marion, *Ind., U.S.A.* **76 E3** 40 32N 85 40W
Marion, *Iowa, U.S.A.* **80 D9** 42 2N 91 36W
Marion, *Kans., U.S.A.* **80 F6** 38 21N 97 1W
Marion, *N.C., U.S.A.* **77 H5** 35 41N 82 1W
Marion, *Ohio, U.S.A.* **76 E4** 40 35N 83 8W
Marion, *S.C., U.S.A.* **77 H6** 34 11N 79 24W
Marion, *Va., U.S.A.* **77 G5** 36 50N 81 31W
Marion, L., *U.S.A.* **77 J5** 33 28N 80 10W
Mariposa, *U.S.A.* **84 H7** 37 29N 119 58W
Mariscal Estigarribia, *Paraguay* **94 A3** 22 3S 60 40W
Maritime Alps = Maritimes, Alpes, *Europe* **18 D7** 44 10N 7 10 E
Maritimes, Alpes, *Europe* **18 D7** 44 10N 7 10 E
Maritsa = Évros →, *Greece* **21 D12** 41 40N 26 34 E
Maritsá, *Greece* **23 C10** 36 22N 28 8 E
Mariupol, *Ukraine* **25 E6** 47 5N 37 31 E
Marīvān, *Iran* **44 C5** 35 30N 46 25 E
Marj 'Uyūn, *Lebanon* **47 B4** 33 20N 35 35 E
Markazī □, *Iran* **45 C6** 35 0N 49 30 E
Markdale, *Canada* **78 B4** 44 19N 80 39W
Marked Tree, *U.S.A.* **81 H9** 35 32N 90 25W
Market Drayton, *U.K.* **10 E5** 52 54N 2 29W
Market Harborough, *U.K.* **11 E7** 52 29N 0 55W
Market Rasen, *U.K.* **10 D7** 53 24N 0 20W
Markham, *Canada* **78 C5** 43 52N 79 16W
Markham, Mt., *Antarctica* **5 E11** 83 0S 164 0 E
Markleeville, *U.S.A.* **84 G7** 38 42N 119 47W
Markovo, *Russia* **27 C17** 64 40N 170 24 E
Marks, *Russia* **24 D8** 51 45N 46 50 E
Marksville, *U.S.A.* **81 K8** 31 8N 92 4W
Marla, *Australia* **63 D1** 27 19S 133 33 E
Marlbank, *Canada* **78 B7** 44 26N 77 6W
Marlboro, *Mass., U.S.A.* **79 D13** 42 19N 71 33W
Marlboro, *N.Y., U.S.A.* **79 E11** 41 36N 73 59W
Marlborough, *Australia* **62 C4** 22 46S 149 52 E
Marlborough, *U.K.* **11 F6** 51 25N 1 43W
Marlborough Downs, *U.K.* **11 F6** 51 27N 1 53W

Medvezhi, Ostrava

Marlin, *U.S.A.* **81 K6** 31 18N 96 54W
Marlow, *U.S.A.* **81 H6** 34 39N 97 58W
Marmagao, *India* **40 M8** 15 25N 73 56 E
Marmara, *Turkey* **21 D12** 40 35N 27 34 E
Marmara, Sea of = Marmara Denizi, *Turkey* **21 D13** 40 45N 28 15 E
Marmara Denizi, *Turkey* **21 D13** 40 45N 28 15 E
Marmaris, *Turkey* **21 F13** 36 50N 28 14 E
Marmion, Mt., *Australia* **61 E2** 29 16S 119 50 E
Marmion L., *Canada* **70 C1** 48 55N 91 20W
Marmolada, Mte., *Italy* **20 A4** 46 26N 11 51 E
Marmora, *Canada* **78 B7** 44 28N 77 41W
Marne →, *France* **18 B5** 48 48N 2 24 E
Maroala, *Madag.* **57 B8** 15 23S 47 59 E
Maroantsetra, *Madag.* **57 B8** 15 26S 49 44 E
Maroelaboom, *Namibia* **56 B2** 19 15S 18 53 E
Marofandilia, *Madag.* **57 C7** 20 7S 44 34 E
Marolambo, *Madag.* **57 C8** 20 2S 48 7 E
Maromandia, *Madag.* **57 A8** 14 13S 48 5 E
Marondera, *Zimbabwe* **55 F3** 18 5S 31 42 E
Maroni →, *Fr. Guiana* **93 B8** 5 30N 54 0W
Maroochydore, *Australia* **63 D5** 26 29S 153 5 E
Marosakoa, *Madag.* **57 B8** 15 26S 46 38 E
Maroseranana, *Madag.* **57 B8** 18 32S 48 51 E
Marotandrano, *Madag.* **57 B8** 16 10S 48 50 E
Marotaolano, *Madag.* **57 A8** 12 47S 49 15 E
Maroua, *Cameroon* **51 F8** 10 40N 14 20 E
Marovato, *Madag.* **57 B8** 15 48S 48 5 E
Marovoay, *Madag.* **57 B8** 16 6S 46 39 E
Marquard, *S. Africa* **56 D4** 28 40S 27 28 E
Marquesas Is. = Marquises, Is., *Pac. Oc.* **65 H14** 9 30S 140 0W
Marquette, *U.S.A.* **76 B2** 46 33N 87 24W
Marquises, Is., *Pac. Oc.* **65 H14** 9 30S 140 0W
Marra, Djebel, *Sudan* **51 F10** 13 10N 24 22 E
Marracuene, *Mozam.* **57 D5** 25 45S 32 35 E
Marrakech, *Morocco* **50 B4** 31 9N 8 0W
Marrawah, *Australia* **62 G3** 40 55S 144 42 E
Marree, *Australia* **63 D2** 29 39S 138 1 E
Marrero, *U.S.A.* **81 L9** 29 54N 90 6W
Marrimane, *Mozam.* **57 C5** 22 58S 33 34 E
Marromeu, *Mozam.* **57 B6** 18 15S 36 25 E
Marrubane, *Mozam.* **55 F4** 18 0S 37 0 E
Marrupa, *Mozam.* **55 E4** 13 8S 37 30 E
Mars Hill, *U.S.A.* **77 B12** 46 31N 67 52W
Marsá Matrûh, *Egypt* **51 B11** 31 19N 27 9 E
Marsabit, *Kenya* **54 B4** 2 18N 38 0 E
Marsala, *Italy* **20 F5** 37 48N 12 26 E
Marsalforn, *Malta* **23 C1** 36 4N 14 15 E
Marseille, *France* **18 E6** 43 18N 5 23 E
Marseilles = Marseille, *France* **18 E6** 43 18N 5 23 E
Marsh I., *U.S.A.* **81 L9** 29 34N 91 53W
Marshall, *Ark., U.S.A.* **81 H8** 35 55N 92 38W
Marshall, *Mich., U.S.A.* **76 D3** 42 16N 84 58W
Marshall, *Minn., U.S.A.* **80 C7** 44 25N 95 45W
Marshall, *Mo., U.S.A.* **80 F8** 39 7N 93 12W
Marshall, *Tex., U.S.A.* **81 J7** 32 33N 94 23W
Marshall →, *Australia* **62 C2** 22 59S 136 59 E
Marshall Is. ■, *Pac. Oc.* **64 G9** 9 0N 171 0 E
Marshalltown, *U.S.A.* **80 D8** 42 3N 92 55W
Marshbrook, *Zimbabwe* **57 B5** 18 33S 31 9 E
Marshfield, *Mo., U.S.A.* **81 G8** 37 15N 92 54W
Marshfield, *Vt., U.S.A.* **79 B12** 44 20N 72 20W
Marshfield, *Wis., U.S.A.* **80 C9** 44 40N 90 10W
Marshūn, *Iran* **45 B6** 36 19N 49 23 E
Märsta, *Sweden* **9 G17** 59 37N 17 52 E
Mart, *U.S.A.* **81 K6** 31 33N 96 50W
Martaban, *Burma* **41 L20** 16 30N 97 35 E
Martaban, G. of, *Burma* **41 L20** 16 5N 96 30 E
Martapura, *Kalimantan, Indonesia* **36 E4** 3 22S 114 47 E
Martapura, *Sumatera, Indonesia* **36 E2** 4 19S 104 22 E
Martelange, *Belgium* **15 E5** 49 49N 5 43 E
Martha's Vineyard, *U.S.A.* **79 E14** 41 25N 70 38W
Martigny, *Switz.* **18 C7** 46 6N 7 3 E
Martigues, *France* **18 E6** 43 24N 5 4 E
Martin, *Slovak Rep.* **17 D10** 49 6N 18 58 E
Martin, *S. Dak., U.S.A.* **80 D4** 43 11N 101 44W
Martin, *Tenn., U.S.A.* **81 G10** 36 21N 88 51W
Martin, L., *U.S.A.* **77 J3** 32 41N 85 55W
Martina Franca, *Italy* **20 D7** 40 42N 17 20 E
Martinborough, *N.Z.* **59 J5** 41 14S 175 29 E
Martinez, *Calif., U.S.A.* **84 G4** 38 1N 122 8W
Martinez, *Ga., U.S.A.* **77 J4** 33 31N 82 4W
Martinique ■, *W. Indies* **89 D7** 14 40N 61 0W
Martinique Passage, *W. Indies* **89 C7** 15 15N 61 0W
Martinópolis, *Brazil* **95 A5** 22 11S 51 12W
Martins Ferry, *U.S.A.* **78 F4** 40 6N 80 44W
Martinsburg, *Pa., U.S.A.* **78 F6** 40 19N 78 20W
Martinsburg, *W. Va., U.S.A.* **76 F7** 39 27N 77 58W
Martinsville, *Ind., U.S.A.* **76 F2** 39 26N 86 25W
Martinsville, *Va., U.S.A.* **77 G6** 36 41N 79 52W
Marton, *N.Z.* **59 J5** 40 4S 175 23 E
Martos, *Spain* **19 D4** 37 44N 3 58W
Marudi, *Malaysia* **36 D4** 4 11N 114 19 E
Maruf, *Afghan.* **40 D5** 31 30N 67 6 E
Marugame, *Japan* **31 G6** 34 15N 133 40 E
Marunga, *Angola* **56 B3** 17 28S 20 2 E
Marungu, Mts., *Dem. Rep. of the Congo* **54 D3** 7 30S 30 0 E
Marv Dasht, *Iran* **45 D7** 29 50N 52 40 E
Marvast, *Iran* **45 D7** 30 30N 54 15 E
Marvel Loch, *Australia* **61 F2** 31 28S 119 29 E
Marwar, *India* **42 G5** 25 43N 73 45 E
Mary, *Turkmenistan* **26 F7** 37 40N 61 50 E
Maryborough = Port Laoise, *Ireland* **13 C4** 53 2N 7 18W
Maryborough, *Australia* **63 D5** 25 31S 152 37 E
Maryfield, *Canada* **73 D8** 49 50N 101 35W
Maryland □, *U.S.A.* **76 F7** 39 0N 76 30W
Maryland Junction, *Zimbabwe* **55 F3** 17 45S 30 31 E
Maryport, *U.K.* **10 C4** 54 44N 3 28W
Mary's Harbour, *Canada* **71 B8** 52 18N 55 51W
Marystown, *Canada* **71 C8** 47 10N 55 10W
Marysville, *Canada* **72 D5** 49 35N 116 0W
Marysville, *Calif., U.S.A.* **84 F5** 39 9N 121 35W
Marysville, *Kans., U.S.A.* **80 F6** 39 51N 96 39W
Marysville, *Mich., U.S.A.* **78 D2** 42 54N 82 29W
Marysville, *Ohio, U.S.A.* **76 E4** 40 14N 83 22W
Marysville, *Wash., U.S.A.* **84 B4** 48 3N 122 11W
Maryville, *Mo., U.S.A.* **80 E7** 40 21N 94 52W
Maryville, *Tenn., U.S.A.* **77 H4** 35 46N 83 58W
Marzūq, *Libya* **51 C8** 25 53N 13 57 E
Masahunga, *Tanzania* **54 C3** 2 6S 33 18 E
Masai Steppe, *Tanzania* **54 C4** 4 30S 36 30 E
Masaka, *Uganda* **54 C3** 0 21S 31 45 E
Masalembo, Kepulauan, *Indonesia* **36 F4** 5 35S 114 30 E
Masalima, Kepulauan, *Indonesia* **36 F5** 5 4S 117 5 E
Masamba, *Indonesia* **37 E6** 2 30S 120 15 E
Masan, *S. Korea* **35 G15** 35 11N 128 32 E
Masandam, Ra's, *Oman* **46 B6** 26 30N 56 30 E
Masasi, *Tanzania* **55 E4** 10 45S 38 52 E
Masaya, *Nic.* **88 D2** 12 0N 86 7W
Masbate, *Phil.* **37 B6** 12 21N 123 36 E
Mascara, *Algeria* **50 A6** 35 26N 0 6 E
Mascota, *Mexico* **86 C4** 20 30N 104 50W
Masela, *Indonesia* **37 F7** 8 9S 129 51 E
Maseru, *Lesotho* **56 D4** 29 18S 27 30 E
Mashaba, *Zimbabwe* **55 G3** 20 2S 30 29 E
Mashābih, *Si. Arabia* **44 E3** 25 35N 36 30 E
Masherbrum, *Pakistan* **43 B7** 35 38N 76 18 E
Mashhad, *Iran* **45 B8** 36 20N 59 35 E
Mashīz, *Iran* **45 D8** 29 56N 56 37 E
Māshkel, Hāmūn-i-, *Pakistan* **40 E3** 28 20N 62 56 E
Mashki Chāh, *Pakistan* **40 E3** 29 5N 62 30 E
Mashonaland, *Zimbabwe* **53 H6** 16 30S 31 0 E
Mashonaland Central □, *Zimbabwe* **57 B5** 17 30S 31 0 E
Mashonaland East □, *Zimbabwe* **57 B5** 18 0S 32 0 E
Mashonaland West □, *Zimbabwe* **57 B4** 17 30S 29 30 E
Mashrakh, *India* **43 F11** 26 7N 84 48 E
Masindi, *Uganda* **54 B3** 1 40N 31 43 E
Masindi Port, *Uganda* **54 B3** 1 43N 32 2 E
Maşīrah, *Oman* **46 C6** 21 0N 58 50 E
Maşīrah, Khalīj, *Oman* **46 C6** 20 10N 58 10 E
Masisi, *Dem. Rep. of the Congo* **54 C2** 1 23S 28 49 E
Masjed Soleyman, *Iran* **45 D6** 31 55N 49 18 E
Mask, L., *Ireland* **13 C2** 53 36N 9 22W
Maskin, *Oman* **45 F8** 23 30N 56 50 E
Masoala, Tanjon' i, *Madag.* **57 B9** 15 59S 50 13 E
Masoarivo, *Madag.* **57 B7** 19 3S 44 19 E
Masohi = Amahai, *Indonesia* **37 E7** 3 20S 128 55 E
Masomeloka, *Madag.* **57 C8** 20 17S 48 37 E
Mason, *Nev., U.S.A.* **84 G7** 38 56N 119 8W
Mason, *Tex., U.S.A.* **81 K5** 30 45N 99 14W
Mason City, *U.S.A.* **80 D8** 43 9N 93 12W
Maspalomas, *Canary Is.* **22 G4** 27 46N 15 35W
Maspalomas, Pta., *Canary Is.* **22 G4** 27 43N 15 36W
Masqat, *Oman* **46 C6** 23 37N 58 36 E
Massa, *Italy* **18 D9** 44 1N 10 9 E
Massachusetts □, *U.S.A.* **79 D13** 42 30N 72 0W
Massachusetts B., *U.S.A.* **79 D14** 42 20N 70 50W
Massakory, *Chad* **51 F9** 13 0N 15 49 E
Massanella, *Spain* **22 B9** 39 48N 2 51 E
Massangena, *Mozam.* **57 C5** 21 34S 33 0 E
Massango, *Angola* **52 F3** 8 2S 16 21 E
Massawa = Mitsiwa, *Eritrea* **46 D2** 15 35N 39 25 E
Massena, *U.S.A.* **79 B10** 44 56N 74 54W
Massénya, *Chad* **51 F9** 11 21N 16 9 E
Masset, *Canada* **72 C2** 54 2N 132 10W
Massif Central, *France* **18 D5** 44 55N 3 0 E
Massillon, *U.S.A.* **78 F3** 40 48N 81 32W
Massinga, *Mozam.* **57 C6** 23 15S 35 22 E
Massingir, *Mozam.* **57 C5** 23 51S 32 4 E
Masson, *Canada* **79 A9** 45 32N 75 25W
Masson I., *Antarctica* **5 C7** 66 10S 93 20 E
Mastanli = Momchilgrad, *Bulgaria* **21 D11** 41 33N 25 23 E
Masterton, *N.Z.* **59 J5** 40 56S 175 39 E
Mastic, *U.S.A.* **79 F12** 40 47N 72 54W
Mastuj, *Pakistan* **43 A5** 36 20N 72 36 E
Mastung, *Pakistan* **40 E5** 29 50N 66 56 E
Masty, *Belarus* **17 B13** 53 27N 24 38 E
Masuda, *Japan* **31 G5** 34 40N 131 51 E
Masvingo, *Zimbabwe* **55 G3** 20 8S 30 49 E
Masvingo □, *Zimbabwe* **55 G3** 21 0S 31 30 E
Maşyāf, *Syria* **44 C3** 35 4N 36 20 E
Matabeleland, *Zimbabwe* **53 H5** 18 0S 27 0 E
Matabeleland North □, *Zimbabwe* **55 F2** 19 0S 28 0 E
Matabeleland South □, *Zimbabwe* **55 G2** 21 0S 29 0 E
Matachewan, *Canada* **70 C3** 47 56N 80 39W
Matadi, *Dem. Rep. of the Congo* **52 F2** 5 52S 13 31 E
Matagalpa, *Nic.* **88 D2** 13 0N 85 58W
Matagami, *Canada* **70 C4** 49 45N 77 34W
Matagami, L., *Canada* **70 C4** 49 50N 77 40W
Matagorda B., *U.S.A.* **81 L6** 28 40N 96 0W
Matagorda I., *U.S.A.* **81 L6** 28 15N 96 30W
Matak, *Indonesia* **39 L6** 3 18N 106 16 E
Mátala, *Greece* **23 E6** 34 59N 24 45 E
Matam, *Senegal* **50 E3** 15 34N 13 17W
Matamoros, *Campeche, Mexico* **87 D6** 18 50N 90 50W
Matamoros, *Coahuila, Mexico* **86 B4** 25 33N 103 15W
Matamoros, *Tamaulipas, Mexico* **87 B5** 25 50N 97 30W
Ma'ţan as Sarra, *Libya* **51 D10** 21 45N 22 0 E
Matandu →, *Tanzania* **55 D3** 8 45S 34 19 E
Matane, *Canada* **71 C6** 48 50N 67 33W
Matanomadh, *India* **42 H3** 23 33N 68 57 E
Matanzas, *Cuba* **88 B3** 23 0N 81 40W
Matapa, *Botswana* **56 C3** 23 11S 24 39 E
Matapan, C. = Taínaron, Ákra, *Greece* **21 F10** 36 22N 22 27 E
Matapédia, *Canada* **71 C6** 48 0N 66 59W
Matara, *Sri Lanka* **40 S12** 5 58N 80 30 E
Mataram, *Indonesia* **36 F5** 8 41S 116 10 E
Matarani, *Peru* **92 G4** 17 0S 72 10W
Mataranka, *Australia* **60 B5** 14 55S 133 4 E
Matarma, Râs, *Egypt* **47 E1** 30 27N 32 44 E
Mataró, *Spain* **19 B7** 41 32N 2 29 E
Matatiele, *S. Africa* **57 E4** 30 20S 28 49 E
Mataura, *N.Z.* **59 M2** 46 11S 168 51 E
Matehuala, *Mexico* **86 C4** 23 40N 100 40W
Mateke Hills, *Zimbabwe* **55 G3** 21 48S 31 0 E
Matera, *Italy* **20 D7** 40 40N 16 36 E
Matetsi, *Zimbabwe* **55 F2** 18 12S 26 0 E
Mathis, *U.S.A.* **81 L6** 28 6N 97 50W
Mathráki, *Greece* **23 A3** 39 48N 19 31 E
Mathura, *India* **42 F7** 27 30N 77 40 E
Mati, *Phil.* **37 C7** 6 55N 126 15 E
Matiali, *India* **43 F13** 26 56N 88 49 E
Matías Romero, *Mexico* **87 D5** 16 53N 95 2W
Matibane, *Mozam.* **55 E5** 14 49S 40 45 E
Matima, *Botswana* **56 C3** 20 15S 24 26 E
Matiri Ra., *N.Z.* **59 J4** 41 38S 172 20 E
Matjiesfontein, *S. Africa* **56 E3** 33 14S 20 35 E
Matla →, *India* **43 J13** 21 40N 88 40 E
Matlamanyane, *Botswana* **56 B4** 19 33S 25 57 E
Matli, *Pakistan* **42 G3** 25 2N 68 39 E
Matlock, *U.K.* **10 D6** 53 9N 1 33W
Mato Grosso □, *Brazil* **93 F8** 14 0S 55 0W
Mato Grosso, Planalto do, *Brazil* **93 G8** 15 0S 55 0W
Mato Grosso do Sul □, *Brazil* **93 G8** 18 0S 55 0W
Matochkin Shar, *Russia* **26 B6** 73 10N 56 40 E
Matopo Hills, *Zimbabwe* **55 G2** 20 36S 28 20 E
Matopos, *Zimbabwe* **55 G2** 20 20S 28 29 E
Matosinhos, *Portugal* **19 B1** 41 11N 8 42W
Matroosberg, *S. Africa* **56 E2** 33 23S 19 40 E
Maţruḥ, *Oman* **46 C6** 23 37N 58 30 E
Matsue, *Japan* **31 G6** 35 25N 133 10 E
Matsumae, *Japan* **30 D10** 41 26N 140 7 E
Matsumoto, *Japan* **31 F9** 36 15N 138 0 E
Matsusaka, *Japan* **31 G8** 34 34N 136 32 E
Matsuura, *Japan* **31 H4** 33 20N 129 49 E
Matsuyama, *Japan* **31 H6** 33 45N 132 45 E
Mattagami →, *Canada* **70 B3** 50 43N 81 29W
Mattancheri, *India* **40 Q10** 9 50N 76 15 E
Mattawa, *Canada* **70 C4** 46 20N 78 45W
Matterhorn, *Switz.* **18 D7** 45 58N 7 39 E
Matthew Town, *Bahamas* **89 B5** 20 57N 73 40W
Matthew's Ridge, *Guyana* **92 B6** 7 37N 60 10W
Mattice, *Canada* **70 C3** 49 40N 83 20W
Mattituck, *U.S.A.* **79 F12** 40 59N 72 32W
Mattō, *Japan* **31 F8** 36 31N 136 34 E
Mattoon, *U.S.A.* **76 F1** 39 29N 88 23W
Matuba, *Mozam.* **57 C5** 24 28S 32 49 E
Matucana, *Peru* **92 F3** 11 55S 76 25W
Matūn = Khowst, *Afghan.* **42 C3** 33 22N 69 58 E
Maturín, *Venezuela* **92 B6** 9 45N 63 11W
Mau, *Mad. P., India* **43 F8** 26 17N 78 41 E
Mau, *Ut. P., India* **43 G10** 25 56N 83 33 E
Mau, *Ut. P., India* **43 G9** 25 17N 81 23 E
Mau Escarpment, *Kenya* **54 C4** 0 40S 36 0 E
Mau Ranipur, *India* **43 G8** 25 16N 79 8 E
Maubeuge, *France* **18 A6** 50 17N 3 57 E
Maud, Pt., *Australia* **60 D1** 23 6S 113 45 E
Maudin Sun, *Burma* **41 M19** 16 0N 94 30 E
Maués, *Brazil* **92 D7** 3 20S 57 45W
Mauganj, *India* **41 G12** 24 50N 81 55 E
Maughold Hd., *U.K.* **10 C3** 54 18N 4 18W
Maui, *U.S.A.* **74 H16** 20 48N 156 20W
Maulamyaing = Moulmein, *Burma* **41 L20** 16 30N 97 40 E
Maule □, *Chile* **94 D1** 36 5S 72 30W
Maumee, *U.S.A.* **76 E4** 41 34N 83 39W
Maumee →, *U.S.A.* **76 E4** 41 42N 83 28W
Maumere, *Indonesia* **37 F6** 8 38S 122 13 E
Maun, *Botswana* **56 C3** 20 0S 23 26 E
Mauna Kea, *U.S.A.* **74 J17** 19 50N 155 28W
Mauna Loa, *U.S.A.* **74 J17** 19 30N 155 35W
Maungmagan Kyunzu, *Burma* **38 E1** 14 0N 97 48 E
Maupin, *U.S.A.* **82 D3** 45 11N 121 5W
Maurepas, L., *U.S.A.* **81 K9** 30 15N 90 30W
Maurice, L., *Australia* **61 E5** 29 30S 131 0 E
Mauricie, Parc Nat. de la, *Canada* **70 C5** 46 45N 73 0W
Mauritania ■, *Africa* **50 E3** 20 50N 10 0W
Mauritius ■, *Ind. Oc.* **49 J9** 20 0S 57 0 E
Mauston, *U.S.A.* **80 D9** 43 48N 90 5W
Mavli, *India* **42 G5** 24 45N 73 55 E
Mavuradonha Mts., *Zimbabwe* **55 F3** 16 30S 31 30 E
Mawa, *Dem. Rep. of the Congo* **54 B2** 2 45N 26 40 E
Mawai, *India* **43 H9** 22 30N 81 4 E
Mawana, *India* **42 E7** 29 6N 77 58 E
Mawand, *Pakistan* **42 E3** 29 33N 68 38 E
Mawk Mai, *Burma* **41 J20** 20 14N 97 37 E
Mawlaik, *Burma* **41 H19** 23 40N 94 26 E
Mawlamyine = Moulmein, *Burma* **41 L20** 16 30N 97 40 E
Mawqaq, *Si. Arabia* **44 E4** 27 25N 41 8 E
Mawson Coast, *Antarctica* **5 C6** 68 30S 63 0 E
Max, *U.S.A.* **80 B4** 47 49N 101 18W
Maxcanú, *Mexico* **87 C6** 20 40N 92 0W
Maxesibeni, *S. Africa* **57 E4** 30 49S 29 23 E
Maxhamish L., *Canada* **72 B4** 59 50N 123 17W
Maxixe, *Mozam.* **57 C6** 23 54S 35 17 E
Maxville, *Canada* **79 A10** 45 17N 74 51W
Maxwell, *U.S.A.* **84 F4** 39 17N 122 11W
Maxwelton, *Australia* **62 C3** 20 43S 142 41 E
May, C., *U.S.A.* **76 F8** 38 56N 74 58W
May Pen, *Jamaica* **88 C4** 17 58N 77 15W
Maya →, *Russia* **27 D14** 60 28N 134 28 E
Maya Mts., *Belize* **87 D7** 16 30N 89 0W
Mayaguana, *Bahamas* **89 B5** 22 30N 72 44W
Mayagüez, *Puerto Rico* **89 C6** 18 12N 67 9W
Mayāmey, *Iran* **45 B7** 36 24N 55 42 E
Mayanup, *Australia* **61 F2** 33 57S 116 27 E
Mayapan, *Mexico* **87 C7** 20 30N 89 25W
Mayarí, *Cuba* **89 B4** 20 40N 75 41W
Maybell, *U.S.A.* **82 F9** 40 31N 108 5W
Maybole, *U.K.* **12 F4** 55 21N 4 42W
Maydān, *Iraq* **44 C5** 34 55N 45 37 E
Maydena, *Australia* **62 G4** 42 45S 146 30 E
Mayenne →, *France* **18 C3** 47 30N 0 32W
Mayer, *U.S.A.* **83 J7** 34 24N 112 14W
Mayerthorpe, *Canada* **72 C5** 53 57N 115 8W
Mayfield, *Ky., U.S.A.* **77 G1** 36 44N 88 38W
Mayfield, *N.Y., U.S.A.* **79 C10** 43 6N 74 16W
Mayhill, *U.S.A.* **83 K11** 32 53N 105 29W
Maykop, *Russia* **25 F7** 44 35N 40 10 E
Maymyo, *Burma* **38 A1** 22 2N 96 28 E
Maynard, *Mass., U.S.A.* **79 D13** 42 26N 71 27W
Maynard, *Wash., U.S.A.* **84 C4** 47 59N 122 55W
Maynard Hills, *Australia* **61 E2** 28 28S 119 49 E
Mayne →, *Australia* **62 C3** 23 40S 141 55 E
Maynooth, *Ireland* **13 C5** 53 23N 6 34W
Mayo, *Canada* **68 B6** 63 38N 135 57W
Mayo □, *Ireland* **13 C2** 53 53N 9 3W
Mayon Volcano, *Phil.* **37 B6** 13 15N 123 41 E
Mayor I., *N.Z.* **59 G6** 37 16S 176 17 E
Mayotte, *Ind. Oc.* **53 G9** 12 50S 45 10 E
Maysville, *U.S.A.* **76 F4** 38 39N 83 46W
Mayu, *Indonesia* **37 D7** 1 30N 126 30 E
Mayville, *N. Dak., U.S.A.* **80 B6** 47 30N 97 20W
Mayville, *N.Y., U.S.A.* **78 D5** 42 15N 79 30W
Mayya, *Russia* **27 C14** 61 44N 130 18 E
Mazabuka, *Zambia* **55 F2** 15 52S 27 44 E
Mazagán = El Jadida, *Morocco* **50 B4** 33 11N 8 17W
Mazagão, *Brazil* **93 D8** 0 7S 51 16W
Mazán, *Peru* **92 D4** 3 30S 73 0W
Māzandarān □, *Iran* **45 B7** 36 30N 52 0 E
Mazapil, *Mexico* **86 C4** 24 38N 101 34W
Mazara del Vallo, *Italy* **20 F5** 37 39N 12 35 E
Mazarrón, *Spain* **19 D5** 37 38N 1 19W
Mazaruni →, *Guyana* **92 B7** 6 25N 58 35W
Mazatán, *Mexico* **86 B2** 29 0N 110 8W
Mazatenango, *Guatemala* **88 D1** 14 35N 91 30W
Mazatlán, *Mexico* **86 C3** 23 13N 106 25W
Mažeikiai, *Lithuania* **9 H20** 56 20N 22 20 E
Māzhān, *Iran* **45 C8** 32 30N 59 0 E
Mazīnān, *Iran* **45 B8** 36 19N 56 56 E
Mazoe, *Mozam.* **55 F3** 16 42S 33 7 E
Mazoe →, *Mozam.* **55 F3** 16 20S 33 30 E
Mazowe, *Zimbabwe* **55 F3** 17 28S 30 58 E
Mazurian Lakes = Mazurski, Pojezierze, *Poland* **17 B11** 53 50N 21 0 E
Mazurski, Pojezierze, *Poland* **17 B11** 53 50N 21 0 E
Mazyr, *Belarus* **17 B15** 51 59N 29 15 E
Mbabane, *Swaziland* **57 D5** 26 18S 31 6 E
Mbaïki, *C.A.R.* **52 D3** 3 53N 18 1 E
Mbala, *Zambia* **55 D3** 8 46S 31 24 E
Mbalabala, *Zimbabwe* **57 C4** 20 27S 29 3 E
Mbale, *Uganda* **54 B3** 1 8N 34 12 E
Mbalmayo, *Cameroon* **52 D2** 3 33N 11 33 E
Mbamba Bay, *Tanzania* **55 E3** 11 13S 34 49 E
Mbandaka, *Dem. Rep. of the Congo* **52 D3** 0 1N 18 18 E
Mbanza Congo, *Angola* **52 F2** 6 18S 14 16 E
Mbanza Ngungu, *Dem. Rep. of the Congo* **52 F2** 5 12S 14 53 E
Mbarara, *Uganda* **54 C3** 0 35S 30 40 E
Mbashe →, *S. Africa* **57 E4** 32 15S 28 54 E
Mbenkuru →, *Tanzania* **55 D4** 9 25S 39 50 E
Mberengwa, *Zimbabwe* **55 G2** 20 29S 29 57 E
Mberengwa, Mt., *Zimbabwe* **55 G2** 20 37S 29 55 E
Mbesuma, *Zambia* **55 E3** 10 0S 32 2 E
Mbeya, *Tanzania* **55 D3** 8 54S 33 29 E
Mbeya □, *Tanzania* **54 D3** 8 15S 33 30 E
Mbinga, *Tanzania* **55 E4** 10 50S 35 0 E
Mbini □, *Eq. Guin.* **52 D2** 1 30N 10 0 E
Mbour, *Senegal* **50 F2** 14 22N 16 54W
Mbuji-Mayi, *Dem. Rep. of the Congo* **54 D1** 6 9S 23 40 E
Mbulu, *Tanzania* **54 C4** 3 45S 35 30 E
Mburucuyá, *Argentina* **94 B4** 28 1S 58 14W
Mchinja, *Tanzania* **55 D4** 9 44S 39 45 E
Mchinji, *Malawi* **55 E3** 13 47S 32 58 E
Mdantsane, *S. Africa* **53 L5** 32 56S 27 46 E
Mead, L., *U.S.A.* **85 J12** 36 1N 114 44W
Meade, *U.S.A.* **81 G4** 37 17N 100 20W
Meadow Lake, *Canada* **73 C7** 54 10N 108 26W
Meadow Lake Prov. Park, *Canada* **73 C7** 54 27N 109 0W
Meadow Valley Wash →, *U.S.A.* **85 J12** 36 40N 114 34W
Meadville, *U.S.A.* **78 E4** 41 39N 80 9W
Meaford, *Canada* **78 B4** 44 36N 80 35W
Mealy Mts., *Canada* **71 B8** 53 10N 58 0W
Meander River, *Canada* **72 B5** 59 2N 117 42W
Meares, C., *U.S.A.* **82 D2** 45 37N 124 0W
Mearim →, *Brazil* **93 D10** 3 4S 44 35W
Meath □, *Ireland* **13 C5** 53 40N 6 57W
Meath Park, *Canada* **73 C7** 53 27N 105 22W
Meaux, *France* **18 B5** 48 58N 2 50 E
Mebechi-Gawa →, *Japan* **30 D10** 40 31N 141 31 E
Mecanhelas, *Mozam.* **55 F4** 15 12S 35 54 E
Mecca = Makkah, *Si. Arabia* **46 C2** 21 30N 39 54 E
Mecca, *U.S.A.* **85 M10** 33 34N 116 5W
Mechanicsburg, *U.S.A.* **78 F8** 40 13N 77 1W
Mechanicville, *U.S.A.* **79 D11** 42 54N 73 41W
Mechelen, *Belgium* **15 C4** 51 2N 4 29 E
Mecheria, *Algeria* **50 B5** 33 35N 0 18W
Mecklenburg, *Germany* **16 B6** 53 33N 11 40 E
Mecklenburger Bucht, *Germany* **16 A6** 54 20N 11 40 E
Meconta, *Mozam.* **55 E4** 14 59S 39 50 E
Medan, *Indonesia* **36 D1** 3 40N 98 38 E
Medanosa, Pta., *Argentina* **96 F3** 48 8S 66 0W
Médéa, *Algeria* **50 A6** 36 12N 2 50 E
Medellín, *Colombia* **92 B3** 6 15N 75 35W
Medelpad, *Sweden* **9 E17** 62 33N 16 30 E
Medemblik, *Neths.* **15 B5** 52 46N 5 8 E
Medford, *Mass., U.S.A.* **79 D13** 42 25N 71 7W
Medford, *Oreg., U.S.A.* **82 E2** 42 19N 122 52W
Medford, *Wis., U.S.A.* **80 C9** 45 9N 90 20W
Medgidia, *Romania* **17 F15** 44 15N 28 19 E
Media Agua, *Argentina* **94 C2** 31 58S 68 25W
Media Luna, *Argentina* **94 C2** 34 45S 66 44W
Medianeira, *Brazil* **95 B5** 25 17S 54 5W
Mediaş, *Romania* **17 E13** 46 9N 24 22 E
Medicine Bow, *U.S.A.* **82 F10** 41 54N 106 12W
Medicine Bow Pk., *U.S.A.* **82 F10** 41 21N 106 19W
Medicine Bow Ra., *U.S.A.* **82 F10** 41 10N 106 25W
Medicine Hat, *Canada* **73 D6** 50 0N 110 45W
Medicine Lake, *U.S.A.* **80 A2** 48 30N 104 30W
Medicine Lodge, *U.S.A.* **81 G5** 37 17N 98 35W
Medina = Al Madīnah, *Si. Arabia* **46 C2** 24 35N 39 52 E
Medina, *N. Dak., U.S.A.* **80 B5** 46 54N 99 18W
Medina, *N.Y., U.S.A.* **78 C6** 43 13N 78 23W
Medina, *Ohio, U.S.A.* **78 E3** 41 8N 81 52W
Medina →, *U.S.A.* **81 L5** 29 16N 98 29W
Medina del Campo, *Spain* **19 B3** 41 18N 4 55W
Medina L., *U.S.A.* **81 L5** 29 32N 98 56W
Medina Sidonia, *Spain* **19 D3** 36 28N 5 57W
Medinipur, *India* **43 H12** 22 25N 87 21 E
Mediterranean Sea, *Europe* **49 C5** 35 0N 15 0 E
Médoc, *France* **18 D3** 45 10N 0 50W
Medveditsa →, *Russia* **25 E7** 49 35N 42 41 E
Medvezhi, Ostrava, *Russia* **27 B17** 71 0N 161 0 E

Montgomery

Mingäçevir Su Anbarı, Azerbaijan 25 F8 40 57N 46 50 E
Mingan, Canada 71 B7 50 20N 64 0W
Mingechaurskoye Vdkhr. = Mingäçevir Su Anbarı, Azerbaijan 25 F8 40 57N 46 50 E
Mingela, Australia 62 B4 19 52S 146 38 E
Mingenew, Australia 61 E2 29 12S 115 21 E
Mingera Cr. →, Australia 62 C2 20 38S 137 45 E
Mingin, Burma 41 H19 22 50N 94 30 E
Mingo Junction, U.S.A. 78 F4 40 19N 80 37W
Mingteke Daban = Mintaka Pass, Pakistan 43 A6 37 0N 74 58 E
Mingyuegue, China 35 C15 43 2N 128 50 E
Minho = Miño →, Spain 19 A2 41 52N 8 40W
Minho, Portugal 19 B1 41 25N 8 20W
Minidoka, U.S.A. 82 E7 42 45N 113 29W
Minigwal, L., Australia 61 E3 29 31S 123 14 E
Minilya →, Australia 61 D1 23 45S 114 0 E
Minilya Roadhouse, Australia 61 D1 23 55S 114 0 E
Minipi L., Canada 71 B7 52 25N 60 45W
Mink L., Canada 72 A5 61 54N 117 40W
Minna, Nigeria 50 G7 9 37N 6 30 E
Minneapolis, Kans., U.S.A. 80 F6 39 8N 97 42W
Minneapolis, Minn., U.S.A. 80 C8 44 59N 93 16W
Minnedosa, Canada 73 C9 50 14N 99 50W
Minnesota □, U.S.A. 80 B8 46 0N 94 15W
Minnesota →, U.S.A. 80 C8 44 54N 93 9W
Minnewaukan, U.S.A. 80 A5 48 4N 99 15W
Minnipa, Australia 63 E2 32 51S 135 9 E
Minnitaki L., Canada 70 C1 49 57N 92 10W
Mino, Japan 31 G8 35 32N 136 55 E
Miño →, Spain 19 A2 41 52N 8 40W
Minorca = Menorca, Spain 22 B11 40 0N 4 0 E
Minot, U.S.A. 80 A4 48 14N 101 18W
Minqin, China 34 E2 38 38N 103 20 E
Minsk, Belarus 17 B14 53 52N 27 30 E
Mińsk Mazowiecki, Poland 17 B11 52 10N 21 33 E
Mintabie, Australia 63 D1 27 15S 133 7 E
Mintaka Pass, Pakistan 43 A6 37 0N 74 58 E
Minto, Canada 71 C6 46 5N 66 5W
Minto, L., Canada 70 A5 57 13N 75 0W
Minton, Canada 73 D8 49 10N 104 35W
Minturn, U.S.A. 82 G10 39 35N 106 26W
Minusinsk, Russia 27 D10 53 43N 91 20 E
Minutang, India 41 E20 28 15N 96 30 E
Miquelon, Canada 70 C4 49 25N 76 27W
Miquelon, St- P. & M. 71 C8 47 8N 56 22W
Mīr Kūh, Iran 45 E8 26 22N 58 55 E
Mīr Shahdād, Iran 45 E8 26 15N 58 29 E
Mira, Italy 20 B5 45 26N 12 8 E
Mira por vos Cay, Bahamas 89 B5 22 9N 74 30W
Miraj, India 40 L9 16 50N 74 45 E
Miram Shah, Pakistan 42 C4 33 0N 70 2 E
Miramar, Argentina 94 D4 38 15S 57 50W
Miramar, Mozam. 57 C6 23 50S 35 35 E
Miramichi, Canada 71 C6 47 2N 65 28W
Miramichi B., Canada 71 C7 47 15N 65 0W
Miranda, Brazil 93 H7 20 10S 56 15W
Miranda →, Brazil 92 G7 19 25S 57 20W
Miranda de Ebro, Spain 19 A4 42 41N 2 57W
Miranda do Douro, Portugal 19 B2 41 30N 6 16W
Mirandópolis, Brazil 95 A5 21 9S 51 6W
Mirango, Malawi 55 E3 13 32S 34 58 E
Mirassol, Brazil 95 A6 20 46S 49 28W
Mirbāţ, Oman 46 D5 17 0N 54 45 E
Miri, Malaysia 36 D4 4 23N 113 59 E
Miriam Vale, Australia 62 C5 24 20S 151 33 E
Mirim, L., S. Amer. 95 C5 32 45S 52 50W
Mirnyy, Russia 27 C12 62 33N 113 53 E
Mirokhan, Pakistan 42 F3 27 46N 68 6 E
Mirond L., Canada 73 B8 55 6N 102 47W
Mirpur, Pakistan 43 C5 33 32N 73 56 E
Mirpur Batoro, Pakistan 42 G3 24 44N 68 16 E
Mirpur Bibiwari, Pakistan 42 E2 28 33N 67 44 E
Mirpur Khas, Pakistan 42 G3 25 30N 69 0 E
Mirpur Sakro, Pakistan 42 G2 24 33N 67 41 E
Mirtağ, Turkey 44 B4 38 23N 41 56 E
Miryang, S. Korea 35 G15 35 31N 128 44 E
Mirzapur, India 43 G10 25 10N 82 34 E
Mirzapur-cum-Vindhyachal = Mirzapur, India 43 G10 25 10N 82 34 E
Misantla, Mexico 87 D5 19 56N 96 50W
Misawa, Japan 30 D10 40 41N 141 24 E
Miscou I., Canada 71 C7 47 57N 64 31W
Mish'āb, Ra's al, Si. Arabia 45 D6 28 15N 48 43 E
Mishan, China 33 B8 45 37N 131 48 E
Mishawaka, U.S.A. 76 E2 41 40N 86 11W
Mishima, Japan 31 G9 35 10N 138 52 E
Misión, Mexico 85 N10 32 6N 116 53W
Misiones □, Argentina 95 B5 27 0S 55 0W
Misiones □, Paraguay 94 B4 27 0S 56 0W
Miskah, Si. Arabia 44 E4 24 49N 42 56 E
Miskitos, Cayos, Nic. 88 D3 14 26N 82 50W
Miskolc, Hungary 17 D11 48 7N 20 50 E
Misoke, Dem. Rep. of the Congo 54 C2 0 42S 28 2 E
Misool, Indonesia 37 E8 1 52S 130 10 E
Mişrātah, Libya 51 B9 32 24N 15 3 E
Missanabie, Canada 70 C3 48 20N 84 6W
Missinaibi →, Canada 70 B3 50 43N 81 29W
Missinaibi L., Canada 70 C3 48 23N 83 40W
Mission, Canada 72 D4 49 10N 122 15W
Mission, S. Dak., U.S.A. 80 D4 43 18N 100 39W
Mission, Tex., U.S.A. 81 M5 26 13N 98 20W
Mission Beach, Australia 62 B4 17 53S 146 6 E
Mission Viejo, U.S.A. 85 M9 33 36N 117 40W
Missisa L., Canada 70 B2 52 20N 85 7W
Missisicabi →, Canada 70 B4 51 14N 79 31W
Mississagi →, Canada 70 C3 46 15N 83 9W
Mississauga, Canada 78 C5 43 32N 79 35W
Mississippi □, U.S.A. 81 J10 33 0N 90 0W
Mississippi →, U.S.A. 81 L10 29 9N 89 15W
Mississippi L., Canada 79 A8 45 5N 76 10W
Mississippi River Delta, U.S.A. 81 L9 29 10N 89 15W
Mississippi Sd., U.S.A. 81 K10 30 20N 89 0W
Missoula, U.S.A. 82 C7 46 52N 114 1W
Missouri □, U.S.A. 80 F8 38 25N 92 30W
Missouri →, U.S.A. 80 F9 38 49N 90 7W
Missouri City, U.S.A. 81 L7 29 37N 95 32W
Missouri Valley, U.S.A. 80 E7 41 34N 95 53W
Mist, U.S.A. 84 E3 45 59N 123 15W
Mistassibi →, Canada 71 B5 48 53N 72 13W
Mistassini, Canada 71 C5 48 53N 72 12W
Mistassini →, Canada 71 C5 48 42N 72 20W
Mistassini, L., Canada 70 B5 51 0N 73 30W
Mistastin L., Canada 71 A7 55 57N 63 20W
Mistinibi, L., Canada 71 A7 55 56N 64 17W
Misty L., Canada 73 B8 58 53N 101 40W
Misurata = Mişrātah, Libya 51 B9 32 24N 15 3 E
Mitchell, Australia 63 D4 26 29S 147 58 E
Mitchell, Canada 78 C3 43 28N 81 12W
Mitchell, Nebr., U.S.A. 80 E3 41 57N 103 49W
Mitchell, Oreg., U.S.A. 82 D3 44 34N 120 9W
Mitchell, S. Dak., U.S.A. 80 D6 43 43N 98 2W
Mitchell →, Australia 62 B3 15 12S 141 35 E
Mitchell, Mt., U.S.A. 77 H4 35 46N 82 16W
Mitchell Ranges, Australia 62 A2 12 49S 135 36 E
Mitchelstown, Ireland 13 D3 52 15N 8 16W
Mitha Tiwana, Pakistan 42 C5 32 13N 72 6 E
Mithi, Pakistan 42 G3 24 44N 69 48 E
Mithrao, Pakistan 42 F3 27 28N 69 40 E
Mitilíni, Greece 21 E12 39 6N 26 35 E
Mito, Japan 31 F10 36 20N 140 30 E
Mitrovica = Kosovska Mitrovica, Kosovo, Yug. 21 C9 42 54N 20 52 E
Mitsinjo, Madag. 57 B8 16 1S 45 52 E
Mitsiwa, Eritrea 46 D2 15 35N 39 25 E
Mitsukaidō, Japan 31 F9 36 1N 139 59 E
Mittimatalik = Pond Inlet, Canada 69 A12 72 40N 77 0W
Mitú, Colombia 92 C4 1 15N 70 13W
Mitumba, Tanzania 54 D3 7 8S 31 2 E
Mitumba, Mts., Dem. Rep. of the Congo 54 D2 7 0S 27 30 E
Mitwaba, Dem. Rep. of the Congo 55 D2 8 2S 27 17 E
Mityana, Uganda 54 B3 0 23N 32 2 E
Mixteco →, Mexico 87 D5 18 11N 98 30W
Miyagi □, Japan 30 E10 38 15N 140 45 E
Miyāh, W. el →, Syria 44 C3 34 44N 39 57 E
Miyake-Jima, Japan 31 G9 34 5N 139 30 E
Miyako, Japan 30 E10 39 40N 141 59 E
Miyako-Jima, Japan 31 M2 24 45N 125 20 E
Miyako-Rettō, Japan 31 M2 24 24N 125 0 E
Miyakonojō, Japan 31 J5 31 40N 131 5 E
Miyani, India 42 J3 21 50N 69 26 E
Miyanoura-Dake, Japan 31 J5 30 20N 130 31 E
Miyazaki, Japan 31 J5 31 56N 131 30 E
Miyazaki □, Japan 31 H5 32 30N 131 30 E
Miyazu, Japan 31 G7 35 35N 135 10 E
Miyet, Bahr el = Dead Sea, Asia 47 D4 31 30N 35 30 E
Miyoshi, Japan 31 G6 34 48N 132 51 E
Miyun, China 34 D9 40 28N 116 50 E
Miyun Shuiku, China 35 D9 40 30N 117 0 E
Mizdah, Libya 51 B8 31 30N 13 0 E
Mizen Hd., Cork, Ireland 13 E2 51 27N 9 50W
Mizen Hd., Wick., Ireland 13 D5 52 51N 6 4W
Mizhi, China 34 F6 37 47N 110 12 E
Mizoram □, India 41 H18 23 30N 92 40 E
Mizpe Ramon, Israel 47 E3 30 34N 34 49 E
Mizusawa, Japan 30 E10 39 8N 141 8 E
Mjölby, Sweden 9 G16 58 20N 15 10 E
Mjøsa, Norway 9 F14 60 40N 11 0 E
Mkata, Tanzania 54 D4 5 45S 38 20 E
Mkokotoni, Tanzania 54 D4 5 55S 39 15 E
Mkomazi, Tanzania 54 C4 4 40S 38 7 E
Mkomazi →, S. Africa 57 E5 30 12S 30 50 E
Mkulwe, Tanzania 55 D3 8 37S 32 20 E
Mkumbi, Ras, Tanzania 54 D4 7 38S 39 55 E
Mkushi, Zambia 55 E2 14 25S 29 15 E
Mkushi River, Zambia 55 E2 13 32S 29 45 E
Mkuze, S. Africa 57 D5 27 10S 32 0 E
Mladá Boleslav, Czech Rep. 16 C8 50 27N 14 53 E
Mlala Hills, Tanzania 54 D3 6 50S 31 40 E
Mlange = Mulanje, Malawi 55 F4 16 2S 35 33 E
Mlanje, Pic, Malawi 53 H7 15 57S 35 38 E
Mława, Poland 17 B11 53 9N 20 25 E
Mljet, Croatia 20 C7 42 43N 17 30 E
Mmabatho, S. Africa 56 D4 25 49S 25 30 E
Mo i Rana, Norway 8 C16 66 20N 14 7 E
Moa, Cuba 89 B4 20 40N 74 56W
Moa, Indonesia 37 F7 8 0S 128 0 E
Moab, U.S.A. 83 G9 38 35N 109 33W
Moala, Fiji 59 D8 18 36S 179 53 E
Moama, Australia 63 F3 36 7S 144 46 E
Moamba, Mozam. 57 D5 25 36S 32 15 E
Moapa, U.S.A. 85 J12 36 40N 114 37W
Moate, Ireland 13 C4 53 24N 7 44W
Moba, Dem. Rep. of the Congo 54 D2 7 0S 29 48 E
Mobārakābād, Iran 45 D7 28 24N 53 20 E
Mobaye, C.A.R. 52 D4 4 25N 21 5 E
Mobayi, Dem. Rep. of the Congo 52 D4 4 15N 21 8 E
Moberley Lake, Canada 72 B4 55 50N 121 44W
Moberly, U.S.A. 80 F8 39 25N 92 26W
Mobile, U.S.A. 77 K1 30 41N 88 3W
Mobile B., U.S.A. 77 K2 30 30N 88 0W
Mobridge, U.S.A. 80 C4 45 32N 100 26W
Mobutu Sese Seko, L. = Albert, L., Africa 54 B3 1 30N 31 0 E
Moc Chau, Vietnam 38 B5 20 50N 104 38 E
Moc Hoa, Vietnam 39 G5 10 46N 105 56 E
Mocabe Kasari, Dem. Rep. of the Congo 55 D2 9 58S 26 12 E
Moçambique, Mozam. 55 F5 15 3S 40 42 E
Moçâmedes = Namibe, Angola 53 H2 15 7S 12 11 E
Mocanaqua, U.S.A. 79 E8 41 9N 76 8W
Mochudi, Botswana 56 C4 24 27S 26 7 E
Mocimboa da Praia, Mozam. 55 E5 11 25S 40 20 E
Moclips, U.S.A. 84 C2 47 14N 124 13W
Mocoa, Colombia 92 C3 1 7N 76 35W
Mococa, Brazil 95 A6 21 28S 47 0W
Mocorito, Mexico 86 B3 25 30N 107 53W
Moctezuma, Mexico 86 B3 29 50N 109 0W
Moctezuma →, Mexico 87 C5 21 59N 98 34W
Mocuba, Mozam. 55 F4 16 54S 36 57 E
Mocúzari, Presa, Mexico 86 B3 27 10N 109 10W
Modane, France 18 D7 45 12N 6 40 E
Modasa, India 42 H5 23 30N 73 21 E
Modder →, S. Africa 56 D3 29 2S 24 37 E
Modderrivier, S. Africa 56 D3 29 2S 24 38 E
Módena, Italy 20 B4 44 40N 10 55 E
Modena, U.S.A. 83 H7 37 48N 113 56W
Modesto, U.S.A. 84 H6 37 39N 121 0W
Módica, Italy 20 F6 36 52N 14 46 E
Moebase, Mozam. 55 F4 17 3S 38 41 E
Moengo, Surinam 93 B8 5 45N 54 20W
Moffat, U.K. 12 F5 55 21N 3 27W
Moga, India 42 D6 30 48N 75 8 E
Mogadishu = Muqdisho, Somali Rep. 46 G4 2 2N 45 25 E
Mogador = Essaouira, Morocco 50 B4 31 32N 9 42W
Mogalakwena →, S. Africa 57 C4 22 38S 28 40 E
Mogami-Gawa →, Japan 30 E10 38 45N 140 0 E
Mogán, Canary Is. 22 G4 27 53N 15 43W
Mogaung, Burma 41 G20 25 20N 97 0 E
Mogi das Cruzes, Brazil 95 A6 23 31S 46 11W
Mogi-Guaçu →, Brazil 95 A6 20 53S 48 10W
Mogi-Mirim, Brazil 95 A6 22 29S 47 0W
Mogilev = Mahilyow, Belarus 17 B16 53 55N 30 18 E
Mogilev-Podolskiy = Mohyliv-Podilskyy, Ukraine 17 D14 48 26N 27 48 E
Mogincual, Mozam. 55 F5 15 35S 40 25 E
Mogocha, Russia 27 D12 53 40N 119 50 E
Mogok, Burma 41 H20 23 0N 96 40 E
Mogollon Rim, U.S.A. 83 J8 34 10N 110 50W
Mogumber, Australia 61 F2 31 2S 116 3 E
Mohács, Hungary 17 F10 45 58N 18 41 E
Mohales Hoek, Lesotho 56 E4 30 7S 27 26 E
Mohall, U.S.A. 80 A4 48 46N 101 31W
Moḩammadābād, Iran 45 B8 37 52N 59 5 E
Mohammedia, Morocco 50 B4 33 44N 7 21W
Mohana →, India 43 G11 24 43N 85 0 E
Mohanlalganj, India 43 F9 26 41N 80 58 E
Mohave, L., U.S.A. 85 K12 35 12N 114 34W
Mohawk →, U.S.A. 79 D11 42 47N 73 41W
Mohenjodaro, Pakistan 42 F3 27 19N 68 7 E
Mohicanville Reservoir, U.S.A. 78 F3 40 45N 82 0W
Mohoro, Tanzania 54 D4 8 6S 39 8 E
Mohyliv-Podilskyy, Ukraine 17 D14 48 26N 27 48 E
Moidart, L., U.K. 12 E3 56 47N 5 52W
Moira →, Canada 78 B7 44 21N 77 24W
Moíres, Greece 23 D6 35 4N 24 56 E
Moisaküla, Estonia 9 G21 58 3N 25 12 E
Moisie, Canada 71 B6 50 12N 66 1W
Moisie →, Canada 71 B6 50 14N 66 5W
Mojave, U.S.A. 85 K8 35 3N 118 10W
Mojave Desert, U.S.A. 85 L10 35 0N 116 30W
Mojo, Bolivia 94 A2 21 48S 65 33W
Mojokerto, Indonesia 37 G15 7 28S 112 26 E
Mokai, N.Z. 59 H5 38 32S 175 56 E
Mokambo, Dem. Rep. of the Congo 55 E2 12 25S 28 20 E
Mokameh, India 43 G11 25 24N 85 55 E
Mokau, N.Z. 59 H5 38 42S 174 39 E
Mokelumne →, U.S.A. 84 G5 38 13N 121 28W
Mokelumne Hill, U.S.A. 84 G6 38 18N 120 43W
Mokhós, Greece 23 D7 35 16N 25 27 E
Mokhotlong, Lesotho 57 D4 29 22S 29 2 E
Mokokchung, India 41 F19 26 15N 94 30 E
Mokolo →, S. Africa 57 C4 23 14S 27 43 E
Mokp'o, S. Korea 35 G14 34 50N 126 25 E
Mokra Gora, Yugoslavia 21 C9 42 50N 20 30 E
Mol, Belgium 15 C5 51 11N 5 5 E
Molchanovo, Russia 26 D9 57 40N 83 50 E
Mold, U.K. 10 D4 53 9N 3 8W
Moldavia = Moldova ■, Europe 17 E15 47 0N 28 0 E
Molde, Norway 8 E12 62 45N 7 9 E
Moldova ■, Europe 17 E15 47 0N 28 0 E
Moldoveanu, Vf., Romania 17 F13 45 36N 24 45 E
Mole →, U.K. 11 F7 51 24N 0 21W
Mole Creek, Australia 62 G4 41 34S 146 24 E
Molepolole, Botswana 56 C4 24 28S 25 28 E
Molfetta, Italy 20 D7 41 12N 16 36 E
Moline, U.S.A. 80 E9 41 30N 90 31W
Molinos, Argentina 94 B2 25 28S 66 15W
Moliro, Dem. Rep. of the Congo 54 D3 8 12S 30 30 E
Mollendo, Peru 92 G4 17 0S 72 0W
Mollerin, L., Australia 61 F2 30 30S 117 35 E
Molodechno = Maladzyechna, Belarus 17 A14 54 20N 26 50 E
Molokai, U.S.A. 74 H16 21 8N 157 0W
Molopo →, Africa 56 D3 27 30S 20 13 E
Molotov = Perm, Russia 24 C10 58 0N 56 10 E
Molson L., Canada 73 C9 54 22N 96 40W
Molteno, S. Africa 56 E4 31 22S 26 22 E
Molu, Indonesia 37 F8 6 45S 131 40 E
Molucca Sea, Indonesia 37 E6 0 0 125 0 E
Moluccas = Maluku, Indonesia 37 E7 1 0S 127 0 E
Moma, Dem. Rep. of the Congo 54 C1 1 35S 23 52 E
Moma, Mozam. 55 F4 16 47S 39 4 E
Mombasa, Kenya 54 C4 4 2S 39 43 E
Mombetsu, Japan 30 B11 44 21N 143 22 E
Momchilgrad, Bulgaria 21 D11 41 33N 25 23 E
Momi, Dem. Rep. of the Congo 54 C2 1 42S 27 0 E
Mompós, Colombia 92 B4 9 14N 74 26W
Møn, Denmark 9 J15 54 57N 12 20 E
Mon □, Burma 41 L20 16 0N 97 30 E
Mona, Canal de la, W. Indies 89 C6 18 30N 67 45W
Mona, Isla, Puerto Rico 89 C6 18 5N 67 54W
Mona, Pta., Costa Rica 88 E3 9 37N 82 36W
Monaca, U.S.A. 78 F4 40 41N 80 17W
Monaco ■, Europe 18 E7 43 46N 7 23 E
Monadhliath Mts., U.K. 12 D4 57 10N 4 4W
Monadnock, Mt., U.S.A. 79 D12 42 52N 72 7W
Monaghan, Ireland 13 B5 54 15N 6 57W
Monaghan □, Ireland 13 B5 54 11N 6 56W
Monahans, U.S.A. 81 K3 31 36N 102 54W
Monapo, Mozam. 55 E5 14 56S 40 19 E
Monar, L., U.K. 12 D3 57 26N 5 8W
Monarch Mt., Canada 72 C3 51 55N 125 57W
Monashee Mts., Canada 72 C5 51 0N 118 43W
Monasterevin, Ireland 13 C4 53 8N 7 4W
Monastir = Bitola, Macedonia 21 D9 41 1N 21 20 E
Moncayo, Sierra del, Spain 19 B5 41 48N 1 50W
Monchegorsk, Russia 24 A5 67 54N 32 58 E
Mönchengladbach, Germany 16 C4 51 11N 6 27 E
Monchique, Portugal 19 D1 37 19N 8 38W
Moncks Corner, U.S.A. 77 J5 33 12N 80 1W
Monclova, Mexico 86 B4 26 50N 101 30W
Moncton, Canada 71 C7 46 7N 64 51W
Mondego →, Portugal 19 B1 40 9N 8 52W
Mondeodo, Indonesia 37 E6 3 34S 122 9 E
Mondovì, Italy 18 D7 44 23N 7 49 E
Mondrain I., Australia 61 F3 34 9S 122 14 E
Monessen, U.S.A. 78 F5 40 9N 79 54W
Monett, U.S.A. 81 G8 36 55N 93 55W
Moneymore, U.K. 13 B5 54 41N 6 40W
Monforte de Lemos, Spain 19 A2 42 31N 7 33W
Mong Hsu, Burma 41 J21 21 54N 98 30 E
Mong Kung, Burma 41 J20 21 35N 97 35 E
Mong Nai, Burma 41 J20 20 32N 97 46 E
Mong Pawk, Burma 41 H21 22 4N 99 16 E
Mong Ton, Burma 41 J21 20 17N 98 45 E
Mong Wa, Burma 41 J22 21 26N 100 27 E
Mong Yai, Burma 41 H21 22 21N 98 3 E
Mongalla, Sudan 51 G12 5 8N 31 42 E
Mongers, L., Australia 61 E2 29 25S 117 5 E
Monghyr = Munger, India 43 G12 25 23N 86 30 E
Mongibello = Etna, Italy 20 F6 37 50N 14 55 E
Mongo, Chad 51 F9 12 14N 18 43 E
Mongolia ■, Asia 27 E10 47 0N 103 0 E
Mongu, Zambia 53 H4 15 16S 23 12 E
Mônguá, Angola 56 B2 16 43S 15 20 E
Monifieth, U.K. 12 E6 56 30N 2 48W
Monkey Bay, Malawi 55 E4 14 7S 35 1 E
Monkey Mia, Australia 61 E1 25 48S 113 43 E
Monkey River, Belize 87 D7 16 22N 88 29W
Monkoto, Dem. Rep. of the Congo 52 E4 1 38S 20 35 E
Monkton, Canada 78 C3 43 35N 81 5W
Monmouth, U.K. 11 F5 51 48N 2 42W
Monmouth, Ill., U.S.A. 80 E9 40 55N 90 39W
Monmouth, Oreg., U.S.A. 82 D2 44 51N 123 14W
Monmouthshire □, U.K. 11 F5 51 48N 2 54W
Mono L., U.S.A. 84 H7 38 1N 119 1W
Monolith, U.S.A. 85 K8 35 7N 118 22W
Monólithos, Greece 23 C9 36 7N 27 45 E
Monongahela, U.S.A. 78 F5 40 12N 79 56W
Monópoli, Italy 20 D7 40 57N 17 18 E
Monroe, Ga., U.S.A. 77 J4 33 47N 83 43W
Monroe, La., U.S.A. 81 J8 32 30N 92 7W
Monroe, Mich., U.S.A. 76 E4 41 55N 83 24W
Monroe, N.C., U.S.A. 77 H5 34 59N 80 33W
Monroe, N.Y., U.S.A. 79 E10 41 20N 74 11W
Monroe, Utah, U.S.A. 83 G7 38 38N 112 7W
Monroe, Wash., U.S.A. 84 C5 47 51N 121 58W
Monroe, Wis., U.S.A. 80 D10 42 36N 89 38W
Monroe City, U.S.A. 80 F9 39 39N 91 44W
Monroeton, U.S.A. 79 E8 41 43N 76 29W
Monroeville, Ala., U.S.A. 77 K2 31 31N 87 20W
Monroeville, Pa., U.S.A. 78 F5 40 26N 79 45W
Monrovia, Liberia 50 G3 6 18N 10 47W
Mons, Belgium 15 D3 50 27N 3 58 E
Monse, Indonesia 37 E6 4 7S 123 15 E
Mont-de-Marsan, France 18 E3 43 54N 0 31W
Mont-Joli, Canada 71 C6 48 37N 68 10W
Mont-Laurier, Canada 70 C4 46 35N 75 30W
Mont-Louis, Canada 71 C6 49 15N 65 44W
Mont-St-Michel, Le = Le Mont-St-Michel, France 18 B3 48 40N 1 30W
Mont Tremblant, Parc Recr. du, Canada 70 C5 46 30N 74 30W
Montagu, S. Africa 56 E3 33 45S 20 8 E
Montagu I., Antarctica 5 B1 58 25S 26 20W
Montague, Canada 71 C7 46 10N 62 39W
Montague, I., Mexico 86 A2 31 40N 114 56W
Montague Ra., Australia 61 E2 27 15S 119 30 E
Montague Sd., Australia 60 B4 14 28S 125 20 E
Montalbán, Spain 19 B5 40 50N 0 45W
Montalvo, U.S.A. 85 L7 34 15N 119 12W
Montana, Bulgaria 21 C10 43 27N 23 16 E
Montaña, Peru 92 E4 6 0S 73 0W
Montana □, U.S.A. 82 C9 47 0N 110 0W
Montaña Clara, I., Canary Is. 22 E6 29 17N 13 33W
Montargis, France 18 C5 47 59N 2 43 E
Montauban, France 18 D4 44 2N 1 21 E
Montauk, U.S.A. 79 E13 41 3N 71 57W
Montauk Pt., U.S.A. 79 E13 41 4N 71 52W
Montbéliard, France 18 C7 47 31N 6 48 E
Montceau-les-Mines, France 18 C6 46 40N 4 23 E
Montclair, U.S.A. 79 F10 40 49N 74 13W
Monte Albán, Mexico 87 D5 17 2N 96 45W
Monte Alegre, Brazil 93 D8 2 0S 54 0W
Monte Azul, Brazil 93 G10 15 9S 42 53W
Monte Bello Is., Australia 60 D2 20 30S 115 45 E
Monte-Carlo, Monaco 18 E7 43 46N 7 23 E
Monte Caseros, Argentina 94 C4 30 10S 57 50W
Monte Comán, Argentina 94 C2 34 40S 67 53W
Monte Cristi, Dom. Rep. 89 C5 19 52N 71 39W
Monte Lindo →, Paraguay 94 A4 23 56S 57 12W
Monte Patria, Chile 94 C1 30 42S 70 58W
Monte Quemado, Argentina 94 B3 25 53S 62 41W
Monte Rio, U.S.A. 84 G4 38 28N 123 0W
Monte Santu, C. di, Italy 20 D3 40 5N 9 44 E
Monte Vista, U.S.A. 83 H10 37 35N 106 9W
Monteagudo, Argentina 95 B5 27 14S 54 8W
Montebello, Canada 70 C5 45 40N 74 55W
Montecito, U.S.A. 85 L7 34 26N 119 40W
Montecristo, Italy 20 C4 42 20N 10 19 E
Montego Bay, Jamaica 88 C4 18 30N 78 0W
Montélimar, France 18 D6 44 33N 4 45 E
Montello, U.S.A. 80 D10 43 48N 89 20W
Montemorelos, Mexico 87 B5 25 11N 99 42W
Montenegro, Brazil 95 B5 29 39S 51 29W
Montenegro □, Yugoslavia 21 C8 42 40N 19 20 E
Montepuez, Mozam. 55 E4 13 8S 38 59 E
Montepuez →, Mozam. 55 E5 12 32S 40 27 E
Monterey, U.S.A. 84 J5 36 37N 121 55W
Monterey B., U.S.A. 84 J5 36 45N 122 0W
Montería, Colombia 92 B3 8 46N 75 53W
Monteros, Argentina 94 B2 27 11S 65 30W
Monterrey, Mexico 86 B4 25 40N 100 30W
Montes Claros, Brazil 93 G10 16 30S 43 50W
Montesano, U.S.A. 84 D3 46 59N 123 36W
Montesilvano, Italy 20 C6 42 29N 14 8 E
Montevideo, Uruguay 95 C4 34 50S 56 11W
Montevideo, U.S.A. 80 C7 44 57N 95 43W
Montezuma, U.S.A. 80 E8 41 35N 92 32W
Montgomery = Sahiwal, Pakistan 42 D5 30 45N 73 8 E
Montgomery, U.K. 11 E4 52 34N 3 8W

Montgomery

Montgomery, Ala., U.S.A. **77 J2** 32 23N 86 19W
Montgomery, Pa., U.S.A. **78 E8** 41 10N 76 53W
Montgomery, W. Va., U.S.A. **76 F5** 38 11N 81 19W
Montgomery City, U.S.A. **80 F9** 38 59N 91 30W
Monticello, Ark., U.S.A. **81 J9** 33 38N 91 47W
Monticello, Fla., U.S.A. **77 K4** 30 33N 83 52W
Monticello, Ind., U.S.A. **76 E2** 40 45N 86 46W
Monticello, Iowa, U.S.A. **80 D9** 42 15N 91 12W
Monticello, Ky., U.S.A. **77 G3** 36 50N 84 51W
Monticello, Minn., U.S.A. **80 C8** 45 18N 93 48W
Monticello, Miss., U.S.A. **81 K9** 31 33N 90 7W
Monticello, N.Y., U.S.A. **79 E10** 41 39N 74 42W
Monticello, Utah, U.S.A. **83 H9** 37 52N 109 21W
Montijo, Portugal **19 C1** 38 41N 8 54W
Montilla, Spain **19 D3** 37 36N 4 40W
Montluçon, France **18 C5** 46 22N 2 36 E
Montmagny, Canada **71 C5** 46 58N 70 34W
Montmartre, Canada **73 C8** 50 14N 103 27W
Montmorillon, France **18 C4** 46 26N 0 50 E
Monto, Australia **62 C5** 24 52S 151 6 E
Montoro, Spain **19 C3** 38 1N 4 27W
Montour Falls, U.S.A. **78 D8** 42 21N 76 51W
Montoursville, U.S.A. **78 E8** 41 15N 76 55W
Montpelier, Idaho, U.S.A. **82 E8** 42 19N 111 18W
Montpelier, Vt., U.S.A. **79 B12** 44 16N 72 35W
Montpellier, France **18 E5** 43 37N 3 52 E
Montréal, Canada **79 A11** 45 31N 73 34W
Montreal →, Canada **70 C3** 47 14N 84 39W
Montreal L., Canada **73 C7** 54 20N 105 45W
Montreal Lake, Canada **73 C7** 54 3N 105 46W
Montreux, Switz. **18 C7** 46 26N 6 55 E
Montrose, U.K. **12 E6** 56 44N 2 27W
Montrose, Colo., U.S.A. **83 G10** 38 29N 107 53W
Montrose, Pa., U.S.A. **79 E9** 41 50N 75 53W
Monts, Pte. des, Canada **71 C6** 49 20N 67 12W
Montserrat ■, W. Indies **89 C7** 16 40N 62 10W
Montuiri, Spain **22 B9** 39 34N 2 59 E
Monywa, Burma **41 H19** 22 7N 95 11 E
Monza, Italy **18 D8** 45 35N 9 16 E
Monze, Zambia **55 F2** 16 17S 27 29 E
Monze, C., Pakistan **42 G2** 24 47N 66 37 E
Monzón, Spain **19 B6** 41 52N 0 10 E
Mooers, U.S.A. **79 B11** 44 58N 73 35W
Mooi →, S. Africa **57 D5** 28 45S 30 34 E
Mooi River, S. Africa **57 D4** 29 13S 29 50 E
Moonah →, Australia **62 C2** 22 3S 138 33 E
Moonda, L., Australia **62 D3** 25 52S 140 25 E
Moonie, Australia **63 D5** 27 46S 150 20 E
Moonie →, Australia **63 D4** 29 19S 148 43 E
Moora, Australia **61 F2** 30 37S 115 58 E
Moorcroft, U.S.A. **80 C2** 44 16N 104 57W
Moore →, Australia **61 F2** 31 22S 115 30 E
Moore, L., Australia **61 E2** 29 50S 117 35 E
Moore Park, Australia **62 C5** 24 43S 152 17 E
Moore Reefs, Australia **62 B4** 16 0S 149 5 E
Moorefield, U.S.A. **76 F6** 39 5N 78 59W
Moores Res., U.S.A. **79 B13** 44 45N 71 50W
Moorfoot Hills, U.K. **12 F5** 55 44N 3 8W
Moorhead, U.S.A. **80 B6** 46 53N 96 45W
Moorpark, U.S.A. **85 L8** 34 17N 118 53W
Moorreesburg, S. Africa **56 E2** 33 6S 18 38 E
Moose →, Canada **70 B3** 51 20N 80 25W
Moose →, U.S.A. **79 C9** 43 38N 75 24W
Moose Creek, Canada **79 A10** 45 15N 74 58W
Moose Factory, Canada **70 B3** 51 16N 80 32W
Moose Jaw, Canada **73 C7** 50 24N 105 30W
Moose Jaw →, Canada **73 C7** 50 34N 105 18W
Moose Lake, Canada **73 C8** 53 43N 100 20W
Moose Lake, U.S.A. **80 B8** 46 27N 92 46W
Moose Mountain Prov. Park, Canada **73 D8** 49 48N 102 25W
Moosehead L., U.S.A. **77 C11** 45 38N 69 40W
Mooselookmeguntic L., U.S.A. **77 C10** 44 55N 70 49W
Moosilauke, Mt., U.S.A. **79 B13** 44 3N 71 40W
Moosomin, Canada **73 C8** 50 9N 101 40W
Moosonee, Canada **70 B3** 51 17N 80 39W
Moosup, U.S.A. **79 E13** 41 43N 71 53W
Mopane, S. Africa **57 C4** 22 37S 29 52 E
Mopeia Velha, Mozam. **55 F4** 17 30S 35 40 E
Mopipi, Botswana **56 C3** 21 6S 24 55 E
Mopoi, C.A.R. **54 A2** 5 6N 26 54 E
Mopti, Mali **50 F5** 14 30N 4 0W
Moqor, Afghan. **42 C2** 32 50N 67 42 E
Moquegua, Peru **92 G4** 17 15S 70 46W
Mora, Sweden **9 F16** 61 2N 14 38 E
Mora, Minn., U.S.A. **80 C8** 45 53N 93 18W
Mora, N. Mex., U.S.A. **83 J11** 35 58N 105 20W
Mora →, U.S.A. **81 H2** 35 35N 104 25W
Moradabad, India **43 E8** 28 50N 78 50 E
Morafenobe, Madag. **57 B7** 17 50S 44 53 E
Moramanga, Madag. **57 B8** 18 56S 48 12 E
Moran, Kans., U.S.A. **81 G7** 37 55N 95 10W
Moran, Wyo., U.S.A. **82 E8** 43 53N 110 37W
Moranbah, Australia **62 C4** 22 1S 148 6 E
Morant Cays, Jamaica **88 C4** 17 22N 76 0W
Morant Pt., Jamaica **88 C4** 17 55N 76 12W
Morar, India **42 F8** 26 14N 78 14 E
Morar, L., U.K. **12 E3** 56 57N 5 40W
Moratuwa, Sri Lanka **40 R11** 6 45N 79 55 E
Morava →, Serbia, Yug. **21 B9** 44 36N 21 4 E
Morava →, Slovak Rep. **17 D9** 48 10N 16 59 E
Moravia, U.S.A. **79 D8** 42 43N 76 25W
Moravian Hts. = Českomoravská Vrchovina, Czech Rep. **16 D8** 49 30N 15 40 E
Morawa, Australia **61 E2** 29 13S 116 0 E
Morawhanna, Guyana **92 B7** 8 30N 59 40W
Moray □, U.K. **12 D5** 57 31N 3 18W
Moray Firth, U.K. **12 D5** 57 40N 3 52W
Morbi, India **42 H4** 22 50N 70 42 E
Morden, Canada **73 D9** 49 15N 98 10W
Mordovian Republic = Mordvinia □, Russia **24 D7** 54 20N 44 30 E
Mordvinia □, Russia **24 D7** 54 20N 44 30 E
Morea, Greece **6 H10** 37 45N 22 10 E
Moreau →, U.S.A. **80 C4** 45 18N 100 43W
Morecambe, U.K. **10 C5** 54 5N 2 52W
Morecambe B., U.K. **10 C5** 54 7N 3 0W
Moree, Australia **63 D4** 29 28S 149 54 E
Morehead, U.S.A. **76 F4** 38 11N 83 26W
Morehead City, U.S.A. **77 H7** 34 43N 76 43W
Morel →, India **42 F7** 26 13N 76 36 E
Morelia, Mexico **86 D4** 19 42N 101 7W
Morella, Australia **62 C3** 23 0S 143 52 E
Morella, Spain **19 B5** 40 35N 0 5W
Morelos, Mexico **86 B3** 26 42N 107 40W
Morelos □, Mexico **87 D5** 18 40N 99 10W
Morena, India **42 F8** 26 30N 78 4 E
Morena, Sierra, Spain **19 C3** 38 20N 4 0W
Moreno Valley, U.S.A. **85 M10** 33 56N 117 15W
Moresby I., Canada **72 C2** 52 30N 131 40W
Moreton I., Australia **63 D5** 27 10S 153 25 E
Morey, Spain **22 B10** 39 44N 3 20 E
Morgan, U.S.A. **82 F8** 41 2N 111 41W
Morgan City, U.S.A. **81 L9** 29 42N 91 12W
Morgan Hill, U.S.A. **84 H5** 37 8N 121 39W
Morganfield, U.S.A. **76 G2** 37 41N 87 55W
Morganton, U.S.A. **77 H5** 35 45N 81 41W
Morgantown, U.S.A. **76 F6** 39 38N 79 57W
Morgenzon, S. Africa **57 D4** 26 45S 29 36 E
Morghak, Iran **45 D8** 29 7N 57 54 E
Morhar →, India **43 G11** 25 29N 85 11 E
Moriarty, U.S.A. **83 J10** 34 59N 106 3W
Morice L., Canada **72 C3** 53 50N 127 40W
Morinville, Canada **72 C6** 53 49N 113 41W
Morioka, Japan **30 E10** 39 45N 141 8 E
Moris, Mexico **86 B3** 28 8N 108 32W
Morlaix, France **18 B2** 48 36N 3 52W
Mornington, I., Chile **96 F1** 49 50S 75 30W
Mornington I., Australia **62 B2** 16 30S 139 30 E
Moro, Pakistan **42 F2** 26 40N 68 0 E
Moro →, Pakistan **42 E2** 29 42N 67 22 E
Moro G., Phil. **37 C6** 6 30N 123 0 E
Morocco ■, N. Afr. **50 B4** 32 0N 5 50W
Morogoro, Tanzania **54 D4** 6 50S 37 40 E
Morogoro □, Tanzania **54 D4** 8 0S 37 0 E
Moroleón, Mexico **86 C4** 20 8N 101 32W
Morombe, Madag. **57 C7** 21 45S 43 22 E
Moron, Argentina **94 C4** 34 39S 58 37W
Morón, Cuba **88 B4** 22 8N 78 39W
Morón de la Frontera, Spain **19 D3** 37 6N 5 28W
Morona →, Peru **92 D3** 4 40S 77 10W
Morondava, Madag. **57 C7** 20 17S 44 17 E
Morongo Valley, U.S.A. **85 L10** 34 3N 116 37W
Moroni, Comoros Is. **49 H8** 11 40S 43 16 E
Moroni, U.S.A. **82 G8** 39 32N 111 35W
Morotai, Indonesia **37 D7** 2 10N 128 30 E
Moroto, Uganda **54 B3** 2 28N 34 42 E
Moroto Summit, Kenya **54 B3** 2 30N 34 43 E
Morpeth, U.K. **10 B6** 55 10N 1 41W
Morphou, Cyprus **23 D11** 35 12N 32 59 E
Morphou Bay, Cyprus **23 D11** 35 15N 32 50 E
Morrilton, U.S.A. **81 H8** 35 9N 92 44W
Morrinhos, Brazil **93 G9** 17 45S 49 10W
Morrinsville, N.Z. **59 G5** 37 40S 175 32 E
Morris, Canada **73 D9** 49 25N 97 22W
Morris, Ill., U.S.A. **80 E10** 41 22N 88 26W
Morris, Minn., U.S.A. **80 C7** 45 35N 95 55W
Morris, N.Y., U.S.A. **79 D9** 42 33N 75 15W
Morris, Pa., U.S.A. **78 E7** 41 35N 77 17W
Morris, Mt., Australia **61 E5** 26 9S 131 4 E
Morrisburg, Canada **79 B9** 44 55N 75 7W
Morristown, Ariz., U.S.A. **83 K7** 33 51N 112 37W
Morristown, N.J., U.S.A. **79 F10** 40 48N 74 29W
Morristown, N.Y., U.S.A. **79 B9** 44 35N 75 39W
Morristown, Tenn., U.S.A. **77 G4** 36 13N 83 18W
Morrisville, N.Y., U.S.A. **79 D9** 42 53N 75 35W
Morrisville, Pa., U.S.A. **79 F10** 40 13N 74 47W
Morrisville, Vt., U.S.A. **79 B12** 44 34N 72 36W
Morro, Pta., Chile **94 B1** 27 6S 71 0W
Morro Bay, U.S.A. **84 K6** 35 22N 120 51W
Morro del Jable, Canary Is. **22 F5** 28 3N 14 23W
Morro Jable, Pta. de, Canary Is. **22 F5** 28 2N 14 20W
Morrosquillo, G. de, Colombia **88 E4** 9 35N 75 40W
Morrumbene, Mozam. **57 C6** 23 31S 35 16 E
Morshansk, Russia **24 D7** 53 28N 41 50 E
Morteros, Argentina **94 C3** 30 50S 62 0W
Mortlach, Canada **73 C7** 50 27N 106 4W
Morton, Tex., U.S.A. **81 J3** 33 44N 102 46W
Morton, Wash., U.S.A. **84 D4** 46 34N 122 17W
Morvan, France **18 C6** 47 5N 4 3 E
Morven, Australia **63 D4** 26 22S 147 5 E
Morvern, U.K. **12 E3** 56 38N 5 44W
Morzhovets, Ostrov, Russia **24 A7** 66 44N 42 35 E
Moscos Is., Burma **38 E1** 14 0N 97 30 E
Moscow = Moskva, Russia **24 C6** 55 45N 37 35 E
Moscow, Idaho, U.S.A. **82 C5** 46 44N 117 0W
Moscow, Pa., U.S.A. **79 E9** 41 20N 75 31W
Mosel →, Europe **18 A7** 50 22N 7 36 E
Moselle = Mosel →, Europe **18 A7** 50 22N 7 36 E
Moses Lake, U.S.A. **82 C4** 47 8N 119 17W
Mosgiel, N.Z. **59 L3** 45 53S 170 21 E
Moshaweng →, S. Africa **56 D3** 26 35S 22 50 E
Moshi, Tanzania **54 C4** 3 22S 37 18 E
Moshupa, Botswana **56 C4** 24 46S 25 29 E
Mosjøen, Norway **8 D15** 65 51N 13 12 E
Moskenesøya, Norway **8 C15** 67 58N 13 0 E
Moskenstraumen, Norway **8 C15** 67 47N 12 45 E
Moskva, Russia **24 C6** 55 45N 37 35 E
Mosomane, Botswana **56 C4** 24 2S 26 19 E
Mosonmagyaróvár, Hungary **17 E9** 47 52N 17 18 E
Mosquera, Colombia **92 C3** 2 35N 78 24W
Mosquero, U.S.A. **81 H3** 35 47N 103 58W
Mosquitia, Honduras **88 C3** 15 20N 84 10W
Mosquito Coast = Mosquitia, Honduras **88 C3** 15 20N 84 10W
Mosquito Creek L., U.S.A. **78 E4** 41 18N 80 46W
Mosquito L., Canada **73 A8** 62 35N 103 20W
Mosquitos, G. de los, Panama **88 E3** 9 15N 81 10W
Moss, Norway **9 G14** 59 27N 10 40 E
Mossbank, Canada **73 D7** 49 56N 105 56W
Mossburn, N.Z. **59 L2** 45 41S 168 15 E
Mosselbaai, S. Africa **56 E3** 34 11S 22 8 E
Mossendjo, Congo **52 E2** 2 55S 12 42 E
Mossman, Australia **62 B4** 16 21S 145 15 E
Mossoró, Brazil **93 E11** 5 10S 37 15W
Mossuril, Mozam. **55 E5** 14 58S 40 42 E
Most, Czech Rep. **16 C7** 50 31N 13 38 E
Mosta, Malta **23 D1** 35 54N 14 24 E
Mostaganem, Algeria **50 A6** 35 54N 0 5 E
Mostar, Bos.-H. **21 C7** 43 22N 17 50 E
Mostardas, Brazil **95 C5** 31 2S 50 51W
Mostiska = Mostyska, Ukraine **17 D12** 49 48N 23 4 E
Mosty = Masty, Belarus **17 B13** 53 27N 24 38 E
Mostyska, Ukraine **17 D12** 49 48N 23 4 E
Mosul = Al Mawşil, Iraq **44 B4** 36 15N 43 5 E
Mosŭlpo, S. Korea **35 H14** 33 20N 126 17 E
Motagua →, Guatemala **88 C2** 15 44N 88 14W
Motala, Sweden **9 G16** 58 32N 15 1 E
Motaze, Mozam. **57 C5** 24 48S 32 52 E
Moth, India **43 G8** 25 43N 78 57 E
Motherwell, U.K. **12 F5** 55 47N 3 58W
Motihari, India **43 F11** 26 30N 84 55 E
Motozintla de Mendoza, Mexico **87 D6** 15 21N 92 14W
Motril, Spain **19 D4** 36 31N 3 37W
Mott, U.S.A. **80 B3** 46 23N 102 20W
Motueka, N.Z. **59 J4** 41 7S 173 1 E
Motueka →, N.Z. **59 J4** 41 5S 173 1 E
Motul, Mexico **87 C7** 21 0N 89 20W
Mouchalagane →, Canada **71 B6** 50 56N 68 41W
Moúdhros, Greece **21 E11** 39 50N 25 18 E
Mouila, Gabon **52 E2** 1 50S 11 0 E
Moulianá, Greece **23 D7** 35 10N 25 59 E
Moulins, France **18 C5** 46 35N 3 19 E
Moulmein, Burma **41 L20** 16 30N 97 40 E
Moulouya, O. →, Morocco **50 B5** 35 5N 2 25W
Moultrie, U.S.A. **77 K4** 31 11N 83 47W
Moultrie, L., U.S.A. **77 J5** 33 20N 80 5W
Mound City, Mo., U.S.A. **80 E7** 40 7N 95 14W
Mound City, S. Dak., U.S.A. **80 C4** 45 44N 100 4W
Moundou, Chad **51 G9** 8 40N 16 10 E
Moundsville, U.S.A. **78 G4** 39 55N 80 44W
Moung, Cambodia **38 F4** 12 46N 103 27 E
Mount Airy, U.S.A. **77 G5** 36 31N 80 37W
Mount Albert, Canada **78 B5** 44 8N 79 19W
Mount Barker, Australia **61 F2** 34 38S 117 40 E
Mount Brydges, Canada **78 D3** 42 54N 81 29W
Mount Burr, Australia **63 F3** 37 34S 140 26 E
Mount Carmel, Ill., U.S.A. **76 F2** 38 25N 87 46W
Mount Carmel, Pa., U.S.A. **79 F8** 40 47N 76 24W
Mount Charleston, U.S.A. **85 J11** 36 16N 115 37W
Mount Clemens, U.S.A. **78 D2** 42 35N 82 53W
Mount Coolon, Australia **62 C4** 21 25S 147 25 E
Mount Darwin, Zimbabwe **55 F3** 16 47S 31 38 E
Mount Desert I., U.S.A. **77 C11** 44 21N 68 20W
Mount Dora, U.S.A. **77 L5** 28 48N 81 38W
Mount Edziza Prov. Park, Canada **72 B2** 57 30N 130 45W
Mount Fletcher, S. Africa **57 E4** 30 40S 28 30 E
Mount Forest, Canada **78 C4** 43 59N 80 43W
Mount Garnet, Australia **62 B4** 17 37S 145 6 E
Mount Holly, U.S.A. **79 G10** 39 59N 74 47W
Mount Holly Springs, U.S.A. **78 F7** 40 7N 77 12W
Mount Hope, Australia **63 E2** 34 7S 135 23 E
Mount Isa, Australia **62 C2** 20 42S 139 26 E
Mount Jewett, U.S.A. **78 E6** 41 44N 78 39W
Mount Kisco, U.S.A. **79 E11** 41 12N 73 44W
Mount Laguna, U.S.A. **85 N10** 32 52N 116 25W
Mount Larcom, Australia **62 C5** 23 48S 150 59 E
Mount Magnet, Australia **61 E2** 28 2S 117 47 E
Mount Maunganui, N.Z. **59 G6** 37 40S 176 14 E
Mount Molloy, Australia **62 B4** 16 42S 145 20 E
Mount Morgan, Australia **62 C5** 23 40S 150 25 E
Mount Morris, U.S.A. **78 D7** 42 44N 77 52W
Mount Pearl, Canada **71 C9** 47 31N 52 47W
Mount Penn, U.S.A. **79 F9** 40 20N 75 54W
Mount Perry, Australia **63 D5** 25 13S 151 42 E
Mount Pleasant, Iowa, U.S.A. **80 E9** 40 58N 91 33W
Mount Pleasant, Mich., U.S.A. **76 D3** 43 36N 84 46W
Mount Pleasant, Pa., U.S.A. **78 F5** 40 9N 79 33W
Mount Pleasant, S.C., U.S.A. **77 J6** 32 47N 79 52W
Mount Pleasant, Tenn., U.S.A. **77 H2** 35 32N 87 12W
Mount Pleasant, Tex., U.S.A. **81 J7** 33 9N 94 58W
Mount Pleasant, Utah, U.S.A. **82 G8** 39 33N 111 27W
Mount Pocono, U.S.A. **79 E9** 41 7N 75 22W
Mount Rainier Nat. Park, U.S.A. **84 D5** 46 55N 121 50W
Mount Revelstoke Nat. Park, Canada **72 C5** 51 5N 118 30W
Mount Robson Prov. Park, Canada **72 C5** 53 0N 119 0W
Mount Selinda, Zimbabwe **57 C5** 20 24S 32 43 E
Mount Shasta, U.S.A. **82 F2** 41 19N 122 19W
Mount Signal, U.S.A. **85 N11** 32 39N 115 37W
Mount Sterling, Ill., U.S.A. **80 F9** 39 59N 90 45W
Mount Sterling, Ky., U.S.A. **76 F4** 38 4N 83 56W
Mount Surprise, Australia **62 B3** 18 10S 144 17 E
Mount Union, U.S.A. **78 F7** 40 23N 77 53W
Mount Upton, U.S.A. **79 D9** 42 26N 75 23W
Mount Vernon, Ill., U.S.A. **76 F1** 38 19N 88 55W
Mount Vernon, Ind., U.S.A. **80 F10** 38 17N 88 57W
Mount Vernon, N.Y., U.S.A. **79 F11** 40 55N 73 50W
Mount Vernon, Ohio, U.S.A. **78 F2** 40 23N 82 29W
Mount Vernon, Wash., U.S.A. **84 B4** 48 25N 122 20W
Mountain Ash, U.K. **11 F4** 51 40N 3 23W
Mountain Center, U.S.A. **85 M10** 33 42N 116 44W
Mountain City, Nev., U.S.A. **82 F6** 41 50N 115 58W
Mountain City, Tenn., U.S.A. **77 G5** 36 29N 81 48W
Mountain Dale, U.S.A. **79 E10** 41 41N 74 32W
Mountain Grove, U.S.A. **81 G8** 37 8N 92 16W
Mountain Home, Ark., U.S.A. **81 G8** 36 20N 92 23W
Mountain Home, Idaho, U.S.A. **82 E6** 43 8N 115 41W
Mountain Iron, U.S.A. **80 B8** 47 32N 92 37W
Mountain Pass, U.S.A. **85 K11** 35 29N 115 35W
Mountain View, Ark., U.S.A. **81 H8** 35 52N 92 7W
Mountain View, Calif., U.S.A. **84 H4** 37 23N 122 5W
Mountain View, Hawaii, U.S.A. **74 J17** 19 33N 155 7W
Mountainair, U.S.A. **83 J10** 34 31N 106 15W
Mountlake Terrace, U.S.A. **84 C4** 47 47N 122 19W
Mountmellick, Ireland **13 C4** 53 7N 7 20W
Mountrath, Ireland **13 D4** 53 0N 7 28W
Moura, Australia **62 C4** 24 35S 149 58 E
Moura, Brazil **92 D6** 1 32S 61 38W
Moura, Portugal **19 C2** 38 7N 7 30W
Mourdi, Dépression du, Chad **51 E10** 18 10N 23 0 E
Mourilyan, Australia **62 B4** 17 35S 146 3 E
Mourne →, U.K. **13 B4** 54 52N 7 26W
Mourne Mts., U.K. **13 B5** 54 10N 6 0W
Mourniai, Greece **23 D6** 35 29N 24 1 E
Mournies = Mourniai, Greece **23 D6** 35 29N 24 1 E
Mouscron, Belgium **15 D3** 50 45N 3 12 E
Moussoro, Chad **51 F9** 13 41N 16 35 E
Moutong, Indonesia **37 D6** 0 28N 121 13 E
Movas, Mexico **86 B3** 28 10N 109 25W
Moville, Ireland **13 A4** 55 11N 7 3W
Mowandjum, Australia **60 C3** 17 22S 123 40 E
Moy →, Ireland **13 B2** 54 8N 9 8W
Moyale, Kenya **54 B4** 3 30N 39 0 E
Moyen Atlas, Morocco **50 B4** 33 0N 5 0W
Moyne, L. le, Canada **71 A6** 56 45N 68 47W
Moyo, Indonesia **36 F5** 8 10S 117 40 E
Moyobamba, Peru **92 E3** 6 0S 77 0W
Moyyero →, Russia **27 C11** 68 44N 103 42 E
Moyynty, Kazakstan **26 E8** 47 10N 73 18 E
Mozambique = Moçambique, Mozam. **55 F5** 15 3S 40 42 E
Mozambique ■, Africa **55 F4** 19 0S 35 0 E
Mozambique Chan., Africa **57 B7** 17 30S 42 30 E
Mozdok, Russia **25 F7** 43 45N 44 48 E
Mozdūrān, Iran **45 B9** 36 9N 60 35 E
Mozhnābād, Iran **45 C9** 34 7N 60 6 E
Mozyr = Mazyr, Belarus **17 B15** 51 59N 29 15 E
Mpanda, Tanzania **54 D3** 6 23S 31 1 E
Mphoengs, Zimbabwe **57 C4** 21 10S 27 51 E
Mpika, Zambia **55 E3** 11 51S 31 25 E
Mpulungu, Zambia **55 D3** 8 51S 31 5 E
Mpumalanga, S. Africa **57 D5** 29 50S 30 33 E
Mpumalanga □, S. Africa **57 B5** 26 0S 30 0 E
Mpwapwa, Tanzania **54 D4** 6 23S 36 30 E
Mqanduli, S. Africa **57 E4** 31 49S 28 45 E
Msambansovu, Zimbabwe **55 F3** 15 50S 30 3 E
M'sila →, Algeria **50 A6** 35 30N 4 29 E
Msoro, Zambia **55 E3** 13 35S 31 50 E
Mstislavl = Mstsislaw, Belarus **17 A16** 54 0N 31 50 E
Mstsislaw, Belarus **17 A16** 54 0N 31 50 E
Mtama, Tanzania **55 E4** 10 17S 39 21 E
Mtamvuna →, S. Africa **57 E5** 31 6S 30 12 E
Mtilikwe →, Zimbabwe **55 G3** 21 9S 31 30 E
Mtubatuba, S. Africa **57 D5** 28 30S 32 8 E
Mtwalume, S. Africa **57 E5** 30 30S 30 38 E
Mtwara-Mikindani, Tanzania **55 E5** 10 20S 40 20 E
Mu Gia, Deo, Vietnam **38 D5** 17 40N 105 47 E
Mu Us Shamo, China **34 E5** 39 0N 109 0 E
Muang Chiang Rai = Chiang Rai, Thailand **38 C2** 19 52N 99 50 E
Muang Khong, Laos **38 E5** 14 7N 105 51 E
Muang Lamphun, Thailand **38 C2** 18 40N 99 2 E
Muang Pak Beng, Laos **38 C3** 19 54N 101 8 E
Muar, Malaysia **39 L4** 2 3N 102 34 E
Muarabungo, Indonesia **36 E2** 1 28S 102 52 E
Muaraenim, Indonesia **36 E2** 3 40S 103 50 E
Muarajuloi, Indonesia **36 E4** 0 12S 114 3 E
Muarakaman, Indonesia **36 E5** 0 2S 116 45 E
Muaratebo, Indonesia **36 E2** 1 30S 102 26 E
Muaratembesi, Indonesia **36 E2** 1 42S 103 8 E
Muaratewe, Indonesia **36 E4** 0 58S 114 52 E
Mubarakpur, India **43 F10** 26 6N 83 18 E
Mubarraz = Al Mubarraz, Si. Arabia **45 E6** 25 30N 49 40 E
Mubende, Uganda **54 B3** 0 33N 31 22 E
Mubi, Nigeria **51 F8** 10 18N 13 16 E
Mubur, Pulau, Indonesia **39 L6** 3 20N 106 12 E
Mucajaí →, Brazil **92 C6** 2 25N 60 52W
Muchachos, Roque de los, Canary Is. **22 F2** 28 44N 17 52W
Muchinga Mts., Zambia **55 E3** 11 30S 31 30 E
Muck, U.K. **12 E2** 56 50N 6 15W
Muckadilla, Australia **63 D4** 26 35S 148 23 E
Mucuri, Brazil **93 G11** 18 0S 39 36W
Mucusso, Angola **56 B3** 18 1S 21 25 E
Muda, Canary Is. **22 F6** 28 34N 13 57W
Mudanjiang, China **35 B15** 44 38N 129 30 E
Mudanya, Turkey **21 D13** 40 25N 28 50 E
Muddy Cr. →, U.S.A. **83 H8** 38 24N 110 42W
Mudjatik →, Canada **73 B7** 56 1N 107 36W
Muecate, Mozam. **55 E4** 14 55S 39 40 E
Mueda, Mozam. **55 E4** 11 36S 39 28 E
Mueller Ra., Australia **60 C4** 18 18S 126 46 E
Muende, Mozam. **55 E3** 14 28S 33 0 E
Muerto, Mar, Mexico **87 D6** 16 10N 94 10W
Mufulira, Zambia **55 E2** 12 32S 28 15 E
Mufumbiro Range, Africa **54 C2** 1 25S 29 30 E
Mughal Sarai, India **43 G10** 25 18N 83 7 E
Mughayrā', Si. Arabia **44 D3** 29 17N 37 41 E
Mugi, Japan **31 H7** 33 40N 134 25 E
Mugila, Mts., Dem. Rep. of the Congo **54 D2** 7 0S 28 50 E
Muğla, Turkey **21 F13** 37 15N 28 22 E
Mugu, Nepal **43 E10** 29 45N 82 30 E
Muhammad, Ras, Egypt **44 E2** 27 44N 34 16 E
Muhammad Qol, Sudan **51 D13** 20 53N 37 9 E
Muhammadabad, India **43 F10** 26 4N 83 25 E
Muhesi →, Tanzania **54 D4** 7 0S 35 20 E
Mühlhausen, Germany **16 C6** 51 12N 10 27 E
Mühlig Hofmann fjell, Antarctica **5 D3** 72 30S 5 0 E
Muhos, Finland **8 D22** 64 47N 25 59 E
Muhu, Estonia **9 G20** 58 36N 23 11 E
Muhutwe, Tanzania **54 C3** 1 35S 31 45 E
Muine Bheag, Ireland **13 D5** 52 42N 6 58W
Muir, L., Australia **61 F2** 34 30S 116 40 E
Mujnak = Muynak, Uzbekistan **26 E6** 43 44N 59 10 E
Mukacheve, Ukraine **17 D12** 48 27N 22 45 E
Mukachevo = Mukacheve, Ukraine **17 D12** 48 27N 22 45 E
Mukah, Malaysia **36 D4** 2 55N 112 5 E
Mukandwara, India **42 G6** 24 49N 75 59 E
Mukdahan, Thailand **38 D5** 16 32N 104 43 E
Mukden = Shenyang, China **35 D12** 41 48N 123 27 E
Mukerian, India **42 D6** 31 57N 75 37 E
Mukhtuya = Lensk, Russia **27 C12** 60 48N 114 55 E
Mukinbudin, Australia **61 F2** 30 55S 118 5 E
Mukishi, Dem. Rep. of the Congo **55 D1** 8 30S 24 44 E
Mukomuko, Indonesia **36 E2** 2 30S 101 10 E
Mukomwenze, Dem. Rep. of the Congo **54 D2** 6 49S 27 15 E

Namp'o

Muktsar, India 42 D6 30 30N 74 30 E
Mukur = Moqor, Afghan. 42 C2 32 50N 67 42 E
Mukutawa →, Canada 73 C9 53 10N 97 24W
Mukwela, Zambia 55 F2 17 0S 26 40 E
Mula, Spain 19 C5 38 3N 1 33W
Mula →, Pakistan 42 F2 27 57N 67 36 E
Mulange, Dem. Rep. of the Congo 54 C2 3 40S 27 10 E
Mulanje, Malawi 55 F4 16 2S 35 33 E
Mulchén, Chile 94 D1 37 45S 72 20W
Mulde →, Germany 16 C7 51 53N 12 15 E
Mule Creek Junction, U.S.A. 80 D2 43 19N 104 8W
Muleba, Tanzania 54 C3 1 50S 31 37 E
Mulejé, Mexico 86 B2 26 53N 112 1W
Muleshoe, U.S.A. 81 H3 34 13N 102 43W
Mulgrave, Canada 71 C7 45 38N 61 31W
Mulhacén, Spain 19 D4 37 4N 3 20W
Mülheim, Germany 33 C6 51 25N 6 54 E
Mulhouse, France 18 C7 47 40N 7 20 E
Muling, China 35 B16 44 35N 130 10 E
Mull, U.K. 12 E3 56 25N 5 56W
Mull, Sound of, U.K. 12 E3 56 30N 5 50W
Mullaittivu, Sri Lanka 40 Q12 9 15N 80 49 E
Mullen, U.S.A. 80 D4 42 3N 101 1W
Mullens, U.S.A. 76 G5 37 35N 81 23W
Muller, Pegunungan, Indonesia 36 D4 0 30N 113 30 E
Mullet Pen., Ireland 13 B1 54 13N 10 2W
Mullewa, Australia 61 E2 28 29S 115 30 E
Mulligan →, Australia 62 D2 25 0S 139 0 E
Mullingar, Ireland 13 C4 53 31N 7 21W
Mullins, U.S.A. 77 H6 34 12N 79 15W
Mullumbimby, Australia 63 D5 28 30S 153 30 E
Mulobezi, Zambia 55 F2 16 45S 25 7 E
Mulroy B., Ireland 13 A4 55 15N 7 46W
Multan, Pakistan 42 D4 30 15N 71 36 E
Mulumbe, Mts., Dem. Rep. of the Congo 55 D2 8 40S 27 30 E
Mulungushi Dam, Zambia 55 E2 14 48S 28 48 E
Mulvane, U.S.A. 81 G6 37 29N 97 15W
Mumbai, India 40 K8 18 55N 72 50 E
Mumbwa, Zambia 55 F2 15 0S 27 0 E
Mun →, Thailand 38 E5 15 19N 105 30 E
Muna, Indonesia 37 F6 5 0S 122 30 E
Munabao, India 42 G4 25 45N 70 17 E
Munamagi, Estonia 9 H22 57 43N 27 4 E
München, Germany 16 D6 48 8N 11 34 E
Munchen-Gladbach = Mönchengladbach, Germany 16 C4 51 11N 6 27 E
Muncho Lake, Canada 72 B3 59 0N 125 50W
Munch'ŏn, N. Korea 35 E14 39 14N 127 19 E
Muncie, U.S.A. 76 E3 40 12N 85 23W
Muncoonie, L., Australia 62 D2 25 12S 138 40 E
Mundabbera, Australia 63 D5 25 36S 151 18 E
Munday, U.S.A. 81 J5 33 27N 99 38W
Münden, Germany 16 C5 51 25N 9 38 E
Mundiwindi, Australia 60 D3 23 47S 120 9 E
Mundo Novo, Brazil 93 F10 11 50S 40 29W
Mundra, India 42 H3 22 54N 69 48 E
Mundrabilla, Australia 61 F4 31 52S 127 51 E
Mungallala, Australia 63 D4 26 28S 147 34 E
Mungallala Cr. →, Australia 63 D4 28 53S 147 5 E
Mungana, Australia 62 B3 17 8S 144 27 E
Mungaoli, India 42 G8 24 24N 78 7 E
Mungari, Mozam. 55 F3 17 12S 33 30 E
Mungbere, Dem. Rep. of the Congo 54 B2 2 36N 28 28 E
Mungeli, India 43 H9 22 4N 81 41 E
Munger, India 43 G12 25 23N 86 30 E
Munich = München, Germany 16 D6 48 8N 11 34 E
Munising, U.S.A. 76 B2 46 25N 86 40W
Munku-Sardyk, Russia 27 D11 51 45N 100 20 E
Muñoz Gamero, Pen., Chile 96 G2 52 30S 73 5W
Munroe L., Canada 73 B9 59 13N 98 35W
Munsan, S. Korea 35 F14 37 51N 126 48 E
Münster, Germany 16 C4 51 58N 7 37 E
Munster □, Ireland 13 D3 52 18N 8 44W
Muntadgin, Australia 61 F2 31 45S 118 33 E
Muntok, Indonesia 36 E3 2 5S 105 10 E
Munyama, Zambia 55 F2 16 5S 28 31 E
Muong Beng, Laos 38 B3 20 23N 101 46 E
Muong Boum, Vietnam 38 A4 22 24N 102 49 E
Muong Et, Laos 38 B5 20 49N 104 1 E
Muong Hai, Laos 38 B3 21 3N 101 49 E
Muong Hiem, Laos 38 B4 20 5N 103 22 E
Muong Houn, Laos 38 B3 20 8N 101 23 E
Muong Hung, Vietnam 38 B4 20 56N 103 53 E
Muong Kau, Laos 38 E5 15 6N 105 47 E
Muong Khao, Laos 38 C4 19 38N 103 32 E
Muong Khoua, Laos 38 B4 21 5N 102 31 E
Muong Liep, Laos 38 C3 18 29N 101 40 E
Muong May, Laos 38 E6 14 49N 106 56 E
Muong Ngeun, Laos 38 B3 20 36N 101 3 E
Muong Ngoi, Laos 38 B4 20 43N 102 41 E
Muong Nhie, Vietnam 38 A4 22 12N 102 28 E
Muong Nong, Laos 38 D6 16 22N 106 30 E
Muong Ou Tay, Laos 38 A3 22 7N 101 48 E
Muong Oua, Laos 38 C3 18 18N 101 20 E
Muong Peun, Laos 38 B4 20 13N 103 52 E
Muong Phalane, Laos 38 D5 16 39N 105 34 E
Muong Phieng, Laos 38 C3 19 6N 101 32 E
Muong Phine, Laos 38 D6 16 32N 106 2 E
Muong Sai, Laos 38 B3 20 42N 101 59 E
Muong Saiapoun, Laos 38 C3 18 24N 101 31 E
Muong Sen, Vietnam 38 C5 19 24N 104 8 E
Muong Sing, Laos 38 B3 21 11N 101 9 E
Muong Son, Laos 38 B4 20 27N 103 19 E
Muong Soui, Laos 38 C4 19 33N 102 52 E
Muong Va, Laos 38 B4 21 53N 102 19 E
Muong Xia, Vietnam 38 B5 20 19N 104 50 E
Muonio, Finland 8 C20 67 57N 23 40 E
Muonionjoki →, Finland 8 C20 67 11N 23 34 E
Muping, China 35 F11 37 22N 121 36 E
Muqdisho, Somali Rep. 46 G4 2 2N 45 25 E
Mur →, Austria 17 E9 46 18N 16 52 E
Murakami, Japan 30 E9 38 14N 139 29 E
Murallón, Cerro, Chile 96 F2 49 48S 73 30W
Muranda, Rwanda 54 C2 1 52S 29 20 E
Murang'a, Kenya 54 C4 0 45S 37 9 E
Murashi, Russia 24 C8 59 30N 49 0 E
Murat →, Turkey 25 G7 38 46N 40 0 E
Muratlı, Turkey 21 D12 41 10N 27 29 E
Murayama, Japan 30 E10 38 30N 140 25 E
Murchison →, Australia 61 E1 27 45S 114 0 E
Murchison, Mt., Antarctica 5 D11 73 0S 168 0 E
Murchison Falls, Uganda 54 B3 2 15N 31 30 E
Murchison Ra., Australia 62 C1 20 0S 134 10 E
Murchison Rapids, Malawi 55 F3 15 55S 34 35 E
Murcia, Spain 19 D5 38 5N 1 10W
Murcia □, Spain 19 D5 37 50N 1 30W
Murdo, U.S.A. 80 D4 43 53N 100 43W
Murdoch Pt., Australia 62 A3 14 37S 144 55 E
Mureş →, Romania 17 E11 46 15N 20 13 E
Mureşul = Mureş →, Romania 17 E11 46 15N 20 13 E
Murewa, Zimbabwe 57 B5 17 39S 31 47 E
Murfreesboro, N.C., U.S.A. 77 G7 36 27N 77 6W
Murfreesboro, Tenn., U.S.A. 77 H2 35 51N 86 24W
Murgab = Murghob, Tajikistan 26 F8 38 10N 74 2 E
Murgab →, Turkmenistan 45 B9 38 18N 61 12 E
Murgenella, Australia 60 B5 11 34S 132 56 E
Murgha Kibzai, Pakistan 42 D3 30 44N 69 25 E
Murghob, Tajikistan 26 F8 38 10N 74 2 E
Murgon, Australia 63 D5 26 15S 151 54 E
Muri, India 43 H11 23 22N 85 52 E
Muria, Indonesia 37 G14 6 36S 110 53 E
Muriaé, Brazil 95 A7 21 8S 42 23W
Muriel Mine, Zimbabwe 55 F3 17 14S 30 40 E
Müritz, Germany 16 B7 53 25N 12 42 E
Murka, Kenya 54 C4 3 27S 38 0 E
Murliganj, India 43 G12 25 54N 86 59 E
Murmansk, Russia 24 A5 68 57N 33 10 E
Muro, Spain 22 B10 39 44N 3 3 E
Murom, Russia 24 C7 55 35N 42 3 E
Muroran, Japan 30 C10 42 25N 141 0 E
Muroto, Japan 31 H7 33 18N 134 9 E
Muroto-Misaki, Japan 31 H7 33 15N 134 10 E
Murphy, U.S.A. 82 E5 43 13N 116 33W
Murphys, U.S.A. 84 G6 38 8N 120 28W
Murray, Ky., U.S.A. 77 G1 36 37N 88 19W
Murray, Utah, U.S.A. 82 F8 40 40N 111 53W
Murray, L., U.S.A. 77 H5 34 3N 81 13W
Murray Harbour, Canada 71 C7 46 0N 62 28W
Murraysburg, S. Africa 56 E3 31 58S 23 47 E
Murree, Pakistan 42 C5 33 56N 73 28 E
Murrieta, U.S.A. 85 M9 33 33N 117 13W
Murshidabad, India 43 G13 24 11N 88 19 E
Murtle L., Canada 72 C5 52 8N 119 38W
Murungu, Tanzania 54 C3 4 12S 31 10 E
Mururoa, Pac. Oc. 65 K14 21 52S 138 55W
Murwara, India 43 H9 23 46N 80 28 E
Murwillumbah, Australia 63 D5 28 18S 153 27 E
Mürzzuschlag, Austria 16 E8 47 36N 15 41 E
Muş, Turkey 25 G7 38 45N 41 30 E
Mûsa, Gebel, Egypt 44 D2 28 33N 33 59 E
Musa Khel, Pakistan 42 D3 30 59N 69 52 E
Mūsa Qal'eh, Afghan. 40 C4 32 20N 64 50 E
Musafirkhana, India 43 F9 26 22N 81 48 E
Musala, Bulgaria 21 C10 42 13N 23 37 E
Musala, Indonesia 36 D1 1 41N 98 28 E
Musan, N. Korea 35 C15 42 12N 129 12 E
Musangu, Dem. Rep. of the Congo 55 E1 10 28S 23 55 E
Musasa, Tanzania 54 C3 3 25S 31 30 E
Musay'īd, Qatar 45 E6 25 0N 51 33 E
Muscat = Masqat, Oman 46 C6 23 37N 58 36 E
Muscat & Oman = Oman ■, Asia 46 C6 23 0N 58 0 E
Muscatine, U.S.A. 80 E9 41 25N 91 3W
Musgrave Harbour, Canada 71 C9 49 27N 53 58W
Musgrave Ranges, Australia 61 E5 26 0S 132 0 E
Mushie, Dem. Rep. of the Congo 52 E3 2 56S 16 55 E
Musi →, Indonesia 36 E2 2 20S 104 56 E
Muskeg →, Canada 72 A4 60 20N 123 20W
Muskegon, U.S.A. 76 D2 43 14N 86 16W
Muskegon →, U.S.A. 76 D2 43 14N 86 21W
Muskegon Heights, U.S.A. 76 D2 43 12N 86 16W
Muskogee, U.S.A. 81 H7 35 45N 95 22W
Muskoka, L., Canada 78 B5 45 0N 79 25W
Muskwa →, Canada 72 B4 58 47N 122 48W
Muslimiyah, Syria 44 B3 36 19N 37 12 E
Musofu, Zambia 55 E2 13 30S 29 0 E
Musoma, Tanzania 54 C3 1 30S 33 48 E
Musquaro, L., Canada 71 B7 50 38N 61 5W
Musquodoboit Harbour, Canada 71 D7 44 50N 63 9W
Musselburgh, U.K. 12 F5 55 57N 3 2W
Musselshell →, U.S.A. 82 C10 47 21N 107 57W
Mussoorie, India 42 D8 30 27N 78 6 E
Mussuco, Angola 56 B2 17 2S 19 3 E
Mustafakemalpaşa, Turkey 21 D13 40 2N 28 24 E
Mustang, Nepal 43 E10 29 10N 83 55 E
Musters, L., Argentina 96 F3 45 20S 69 25W
Musudan, N. Korea 35 D15 40 50N 129 43 E
Mût, Egypt 51 C11 25 28N 28 58 E
Mut, Turkey 44 B2 36 40N 33 28 E
Mutanda, Mozam. 57 C5 21 0S 33 34 E
Mutanda, Zambia 55 E2 12 24S 26 13 E
Mutare, Zimbabwe 55 F3 18 58S 32 38 E
Muting, Indonesia 37 F10 7 23S 140 20 E
Mutoko, Zimbabwe 57 B5 17 24S 32 13 E
Mutoray, Russia 27 C11 60 56N 101 0 E
Mutshatsha, Dem. Rep. of the Congo 55 E1 10 35S 24 20 E
Mutsu, Japan 30 D10 41 5N 140 55 E
Mutsu-Wan, Japan 30 D10 41 5N 140 55 E
Muttaburra, Australia 62 C3 22 38S 144 29 E
Mutton I., Ireland 13 D2 52 49N 9 32W
Mutuáli, Mozam. 55 E4 14 55S 37 0 E
Muweilih, Egypt 47 E3 30 42N 34 19 E
Muy Muy, Nic. 88 D2 12 39N 85 36W
Muyinga, Burundi 54 C3 3 14S 30 33 E
Muynak, Uzbekistan 26 E6 43 44N 59 10 E
Muzaffarabad, Pakistan 43 B5 34 25N 73 30 E
Muzaffargarh, Pakistan 42 D4 30 5N 71 14 E
Muzaffarnagar, India 42 E7 29 26N 77 40 E
Muzaffarpur, India 43 F11 26 7N 85 23 E
Muzafirpur, Pakistan 42 D3 30 58N 69 9 E
Muzhi, Russia 24 A11 65 25N 64 40 E
Mvuma, Zimbabwe 55 F3 19 16S 30 30 E
Mvurwi, Zimbabwe 55 F3 17 0S 30 57 E
Mwadui, Tanzania 54 C3 3 26S 33 32 E
Mwambo, Tanzania 55 E5 10 30S 40 22 E
Mwandi, Zambia 55 F1 17 30S 24 51 E
Mwanza, Dem. Rep. of the Congo 54 D2 7 55S 26 43 E
Mwanza, Tanzania 54 C3 2 30S 32 58 E
Mwanza, Zambia 55 F1 16 58S 24 28 E
Mwanza □, Tanzania 54 C3 2 0S 33 0 E
Mwaya, Tanzania 55 D3 9 32S 33 55 E
Mweelrea, Ireland 13 C2 53 39N 9 49W
Mweka, Dem. Rep. of the Congo 52 E4 4 50S 21 34 E
Mwenezi, Zimbabwe 55 G3 21 15S 30 48 E
Mwenezi →, Mozam. 55 G3 22 40S 31 50 E
Mwenga, Dem. Rep. of the Congo 54 C2 3 1S 28 28 E
Mweru, L., Zambia 55 D2 9 0S 28 40 E
Mweza Range, Zimbabwe 55 G3 21 0S 30 0 E
Mwilambwe, Dem. Rep. of the Congo 54 D2 8 7S 25 5 E
Mwimbi, Tanzania 55 D3 8 38S 31 39 E
Mwinilunga, Zambia 55 E1 11 43S 24 25 E
My Tho, Vietnam 39 G6 10 29N 106 23 E
Myajlar, India 42 F4 26 15N 70 20 E
Myanaung, Burma 41 K19 18 18N 95 22 E
Myanmar = Burma ■, Asia 41 J20 21 0N 96 30 E
Myaungmya, Burma 41 L19 16 30N 94 40 E
Mycenæ, Greece 21 F10 37 39N 22 52 E
Myeik Kyunzu, Burma 39 G1 11 30N 97 30 E
Myers Chuck, U.S.A. 72 B2 55 44N 132 11W
Myerstown, U.S.A. 79 F8 40 22N 76 19W
Myingyan, Burma 41 J19 21 30N 95 20 E
Myitkyina, Burma 41 G20 25 24N 97 26 E
Mykines, Færoe Is. 8 E9 62 7N 7 35W
Mykolayiv, Ukraine 25 E5 46 58N 32 0 E
Mymensingh, Bangla. 41 G17 24 45N 90 24 E
Mynydd Du, U.K. 11 F4 51 52N 3 50W
Mýrdalsjökull, Iceland 8 E4 63 40N 19 6W
Myrtle Beach, U.S.A. 77 J6 33 42N 78 53W
Myrtle Creek, U.S.A. 82 E2 43 1N 123 17W
Myrtle Point, U.S.A. 82 E1 43 4N 124 8W
Myrtou, Cyprus 23 D12 35 18N 33 4 E
Mysia, Turkey 21 E12 39 50N 27 0 E
Mysore = Karnataka □, India 40 N10 13 15N 77 0 E
Mysore, India 40 N10 12 17N 76 41 E
Mystic, U.S.A. 79 E13 41 21N 71 58W
Myszków, Poland 17 C10 50 45N 19 22 E
Mytishchi, Russia 24 C6 55 50N 37 50 E
Mývatn, Iceland 8 D5 65 36N 17 0W
Mzimba, Malawi 55 E3 11 55S 33 39 E
Mzimkulu →, S. Africa 57 E5 30 44S 30 20 E
Mzimvubu →, S. Africa 57 E4 31 38S 29 33 E
Mzuzu, Malawi 55 E3 11 30S 33 55 E

N

Na Hearadh = Harris, U.K. 12 D2 57 50N 6 55W
Na Noi, Thailand 38 C3 18 19N 100 43 E
Na Phao, Laos 38 D5 17 35N 105 44 E
Na Sam, Vietnam 38 A6 22 3N 106 37 E
Na San, Vietnam 38 B5 21 12N 104 2 E
Naab →, Germany 16 D6 49 1N 12 2 E
Naantali, Finland 9 F19 60 29N 22 2 E
Naas, Ireland 13 C5 53 12N 6 40W
Nababeep, S. Africa 56 D2 29 36S 17 46 E
Nabadwip = Navadwip, India 43 H13 23 34N 88 20 E
Nabari, Japan 31 G8 34 37N 136 5 E
Nabawa, Australia 61 E1 28 30S 114 48 E
Nabberu, L., Australia 61 E3 25 50S 120 30 E
Naberezhnyye Chelny, Russia 24 C9 55 42N 52 19 E
Nabeul, Tunisia 51 A8 36 30N 10 44 E
Nabha, India 42 D7 30 26N 76 14 E
Nabīd, Iran 45 D8 29 40N 57 38 E
Nabire, Indonesia 37 E9 3 15S 135 26 E
Nabisar, Pakistan 42 G3 25 8N 69 40 E
Nabisipi →, Canada 71 B7 50 14N 62 13W
Nabiswera, Uganda 54 B3 1 27N 32 15 E
Nablus = Nābulus, West Bank 47 C4 32 14N 35 15 E
Naboomspruit, S. Africa 57 C4 24 32S 28 40 E
Nābulus, West Bank 47 C4 32 14N 35 15 E
Nacala, Mozam. 55 E5 14 31S 40 34 E
Nacala-Velha, Mozam. 55 E5 14 32S 40 34 E
Nacaome, Honduras 88 D2 13 31N 87 30W
Nacaroa, Mozam. 55 E4 14 22S 39 56 E
Naches, U.S.A. 82 C3 46 44N 120 42W
Naches →, U.S.A. 84 D6 46 38N 120 31W
Nachicapau, L., Canada 71 A6 56 40N 68 5W
Nachingwea, Tanzania 55 E4 10 23S 38 49 E
Nachna, India 42 F4 27 34N 71 41 E
Nacimiento L., U.S.A. 84 K6 35 46N 120 53W
Naco, Mexico 86 A3 31 20N 109 56W
Nacogdoches, U.S.A. 81 K7 31 36N 94 39W
Nácori Chico, Mexico 86 B3 29 39N 109 1W
Nacozari, Mexico 86 A3 30 24N 109 39W
Nadiad, India 42 H5 22 41N 72 56 E
Nador, Morocco 50 B5 35 14N 2 58W
Nadur, Malta 23 C1 36 2N 14 17 E
Nadūshan, Iran 45 C7 32 2N 53 35 E
Nadvirna, Ukraine 17 D13 48 37N 24 30 E
Nadvoitsy, Russia 24 B5 63 52N 34 14 E
Nadvornaya = Nadvirna, Ukraine 17 D13 48 37N 24 30 E
Nadym, Russia 26 C8 65 35N 72 42 E
Nadym →, Russia 26 C8 66 12N 72 0 E
Nærbø, Norway 9 G11 58 40N 5 39 E
Næstved, Denmark 9 J14 55 13N 11 44 E
Naft-e Safīd, Iran 45 D6 31 40N 49 17 E
Naftshahr, Iran 44 C5 34 0N 45 30 E
Nafud Desert = An Nafūd, Si. Arabia 44 D4 28 15N 41 0 E
Naga, Phil. 37 B6 13 38N 123 15 E
Nagahama, Japan 31 G8 35 23N 136 16 E
Nagai, Japan 30 E10 38 6N 140 2 E
Nagaland □, India 41 G19 26 0N 94 30 E
Nagano, Japan 31 F9 36 40N 138 10 E
Nagano □, Japan 31 F9 36 15N 138 0 E
Nagaoka, Japan 31 F9 37 27N 138 51 E
Nagappattinam, India 40 P11 10 46N 79 51 E
Nagar →, Bangla. 43 G13 24 27N 89 12 E
Nagar Parkar, Pakistan 42 G4 24 28N 70 46 E
Nagasaki, Japan 31 H4 32 47N 129 50 E
Nagasaki □, Japan 31 H4 32 50N 129 40 E
Nagato, Japan 31 G5 34 19N 131 5 E
Nagaur, India 42 F5 27 15N 73 45 E
Nagda, India 42 H6 23 27N 75 25 E
Nagercoil, India 40 Q10 8 12N 77 26 E
Nagina, India 43 E8 29 30N 78 30 E
Nagineh, Iran 45 C8 34 20N 57 15 E
Nagir, Pakistan 43 A6 36 12N 74 42 E
Nagod, India 43 G9 24 34N 80 36 E
Nagoorin, Australia 62 C5 24 17S 151 15 E
Nagorno-Karabakh, Azerbaijan 25 F8 39 55N 46 45 E
Nagornyy, Russia 27 D13 55 58N 124 57 E
Nagoya, Japan 31 G8 35 10N 136 50 E
Nagpur, India 40 J11 21 8N 79 10 E
Nagua, Dom. Rep. 89 C6 19 23N 69 50W
Nagykanizsa, Hungary 17 E9 46 28N 17 0 E
Nagykőrös, Hungary 17 E10 47 5N 19 48 E
Naha, Japan 31 L3 26 13N 127 42 E
Nahan, India 42 D7 30 33N 77 18 E
Nahanni Butte, Canada 72 A4 61 2N 123 31W
Nahanni Nat. Park, Canada 72 A4 61 15N 125 0W
Nahargarh, Mad. P., India 42 G6 24 10N 75 14 E
Nahargarh, Raj., India 42 G7 24 55N 76 50 E
Nahariyya, Israel 44 C2 33 1N 35 5 E
Nahāvand, Iran 45 C6 34 10N 48 22 E
Naicá, Mexico 86 B3 27 53N 105 31W
Naicam, Canada 73 C8 52 30N 104 30W
Naikoon Prov. Park, Canada 72 C2 53 55N 131 55W
Naimisharanya, India 43 F9 27 21N 80 30 E
Nain, Canada 71 A7 56 34N 61 40W
Nā'īn, Iran 45 C7 32 54N 53 0 E
Naini Tal, India 43 E8 29 30N 79 30 E
Nainpur, India 40 H12 22 30N 80 10 E
Nainwa, India 42 G6 25 46N 75 51 E
Nairn, U.K. 12 D5 57 35N 3 53W
Nairobi, Kenya 54 C4 1 17S 36 48 E
Naissaar, Estonia 9 G21 59 34N 24 29 E
Naivasha, Kenya 54 C4 0 40S 36 30 E
Naivasha, L., Kenya 54 C4 0 48S 36 20 E
Najafābād, Iran 45 C6 32 40N 51 15 E
Najd, Si. Arabia 46 B3 26 30N 42 0 E
Najibabad, India 42 E8 29 40N 78 20 E
Najin, N. Korea 35 C16 42 12N 130 15 E
Najmah, Si. Arabia 45 E6 26 42N 50 6 E
Naju, S. Korea 35 G14 35 3N 126 43 E
Nakadōri-Shima, Japan 31 H4 32 57N 129 4 E
Nakalagba, Dem. Rep. of the Congo 54 B2 2 50N 27 58 E
Nakaminato, Japan 31 F10 36 21N 140 36 E
Nakamura, Japan 31 H6 32 59N 132 56 E
Nakano, Japan 31 F9 36 45N 138 22 E
Nakano-Shima, Japan 31 K4 29 51N 129 52 E
Nakashibetsu, Japan 30 C12 43 33N 144 59 E
Nakfa, Eritrea 46 D2 16 40N 38 32 E
Nakhfar al Buşayyah, Iraq 44 D5 30 0N 46 10 E
Nakhichevan = Naxçıvan, Azerbaijan 25 G8 39 12N 45 15 E
Nakhichevan Republic = Naxçıvan □, Azerbaijan 25 G8 39 25N 45 26 E
Nakhl, Egypt 47 F2 29 55N 33 43 E
Nakhl-e Taqī, Iran 45 E7 27 28N 52 36 E
Nakhodka, Russia 27 E14 42 53N 132 54 E
Nakhon Nayok, Thailand 38 E3 14 12N 101 13 E
Nakhon Pathom, Thailand 38 F3 13 49N 100 3 E
Nakhon Phanom, Thailand 38 D5 17 23N 104 43 E
Nakhon Ratchasima, Thailand 38 E4 14 59N 102 12 E
Nakhon Sawan, Thailand 38 E3 15 35N 100 10 E
Nakhon Si Thammarat, Thailand 39 H3 8 29N 100 0 E
Nakhon Thai, Thailand 38 D3 17 5N 100 44 E
Nakhtarana, India 42 H3 23 20N 69 15 E
Nakina, Canada 70 B2 50 10N 86 40W
Nakodar, India 42 D6 31 8N 75 31 E
Nakskov, Denmark 9 J14 54 50N 11 8 E
Naktong →, S. Korea 35 G15 35 7N 128 57 E
Nakuru, Kenya 54 C4 0 15S 36 4 E
Nakuru, L., Kenya 54 C4 0 23S 36 5 E
Nakusp, Canada 72 C5 50 20N 117 45W
Nal, Pakistan 42 F2 27 40N 66 12 E
Nal →, Pakistan 42 G1 25 20N 65 30 E
Nalázi, Mozam. 57 C5 24 3S 33 20 E
Nalchik, Russia 25 F7 43 30N 43 33 E
Nalgonda, India 40 L11 17 6N 79 15 E
Nalhati, India 43 G12 24 17N 87 52 E
Naliya, India 42 H3 23 16N 68 50 E
Nallamalai Hills, India 40 M11 15 30N 78 50 E
Nam Can, Vietnam 39 H5 8 46N 104 59 E
Nam-ch'on, N. Korea 35 E14 38 15N 126 26 E
Nam Co, China 32 C4 30 30N 90 45 E
Nam Dinh, Vietnam 38 B6 20 25N 106 5 E
Nam Du, Hon, Vietnam 39 H5 9 41N 104 21 E
Nam Ngum Dam, Laos 38 C4 18 35N 102 34 E
Nam-Phan, Vietnam 39 G6 10 30N 106 0 E
Nam Phong, Thailand 38 D4 16 42N 102 52 E
Nam Tha, Laos 38 B3 20 58N 101 30 E
Nam Tok, Thailand 38 E2 14 21N 99 4 E
Namacunde, Angola 56 B2 17 18S 15 50 E
Namacurra, Mozam. 57 B6 17 30S 36 50 E
Namak, Daryācheh-ye, Iran 45 C7 34 30N 52 0 E
Namak, Kavir-e, Iran 45 C8 34 30N 57 30 E
Namakzār, Daryācheh-ye, Iran 45 C9 34 0N 60 30 E
Namaland, Namibia 56 C2 26 0S 17 0 E
Namangan, Uzbekistan 26 E8 41 0N 71 40 E
Namapa, Mozam. 55 E4 13 43S 39 50 E
Namaqualand, S. Africa 56 E2 30 0S 17 25 E
Namasagali, Uganda 54 B3 1 2N 33 0 E
Namber, Indonesia 37 E8 1 2S 134 49 E
Nambour, Australia 63 D5 26 32S 152 58 E
Namcha Barwa, China 32 D4 29 40N 95 10 E
Namche Bazar, Nepal 43 F12 27 51N 86 47 E
Namchonjŏm = Nam-ch'on, N. Korea 35 E14 38 15N 126 26 E
Namecunda, Mozam. 55 E4 14 54S 37 37 E
Nameponda, Mozam. 55 F4 15 50S 39 50 E
Nametil, Mozam. 55 F4 15 40S 39 21 E
Namew L., Canada 73 C8 54 14N 101 56W
Namgia, India 43 D8 31 48N 78 40 E
Namib Desert, Namibia 56 C2 22 30S 15 0 E
Namibe, Angola 53 H2 15 7S 12 11 E
Namibe □, Angola 56 B1 16 35S 12 30 E
Namibia ■, Africa 56 C2 22 0S 18 9 E
Namibwoestyn = Namib Desert, Namibia 56 C2 22 30S 15 0 E
Namlea, Indonesia 37 E7 3 18S 127 5 E
Namoi →, Australia 63 E4 30 12S 149 30 E
Nampa, U.S.A. 82 E5 43 34N 116 34W
Namp'o, N. Korea 35 E13 38 52N 125 10 E

North East Lincolnshire

New Philadelphia, *U.S.A.* . **78 F3** 40 30N 81 27W
New Plymouth, *N.Z.* ...... **59 H5** 39 4S 174 5 E
New Plymouth, *U.S.A.* **82 E5** 43 58N 116 49W
New Port Richey, *U.S.A.* .. **77 L4** 28 16N 82 43W
New Providence, *Bahamas* **88 A4** 25 25N 78 35W
New Quay, *U.K.* **11 E3** 52 13N 4 21W
New Radnor, *U.K.* **11 E4** 52 15N 3 9W
New Richmond, *Canada* .. **71 C6** 48 15N 65 45W
New Richmond, *U.S.A.* ... **80 C8** 45 7N 92 32W
New Roads, *U.S.A.* **81 K9** 30 42N 91 26W
New Rochelle, *U.S.A.* **79 F11** 40 55N 73 47W
New Rockford, *U.S.A.* **80 B5** 47 41N 99 8W
New Romney, *U.K.* .... **11 G8** 50 59N 0 57 E
New Ross, *Ireland* **13 D5** 52 23N 6 57W
New Salem, *U.S.A.* **80 B4** 46 51N 101 25W
New Scone, *U.K.* **12 E5** 56 25N 3 24W
New Siberian I. = Novaya Sibir, Ostrov, *Russia* .... **27 B16** 75 10N 150 0 E
New Siberian Is. = Novosibirskiye Ostrova, *Russia* .... **27 B15** 75 0N 142 0 E
New Smyrna Beach, *U.S.A.* **77 L5** 29 1N 80 56W
New Town, *U.S.A.* **80 B3** 47 59N 102 30W
New Tredegar, *U.K.* **11 F4** 51 44N 3 16W
New Ulm, *U.S.A.* **80 C7** 44 19N 94 28W
New Waterford, *Canada* .. **71 C7** 46 13N 60 4W
New Westminster, *Canada* **84 A4** 49 13N 122 55W
New York, *U.S.A.* **79 F11** 40 45N 74 0W
New York □, *U.S.A.* **79 D9** 43 0N 75 0W
New York Mts., *U.S.A.* **83 J6** 35 0N 115 20W
New Zealand ■, *Oceania* .. **59 J6** 40 0S 176 0 E
Newaj →, *India* .... **42 G7** 24 24N 76 49 E
Newala, *Tanzania* .... **55 E4** 10 58S 39 18 E
Newark, *Del., U.S.A.* **76 F8** 39 41N 75 46W
Newark, *N.J., U.S.A.* **79 F10** 40 44N 74 10W
Newark, *N.Y., U.S.A.* **78 C7** 43 3N 77 6W
Newark, *Ohio, U.S.A.* **78 F2** 40 3N 82 24W
Newark-on-Trent, *U.K.* **10 D7** 53 5N 0 48W
Newark Valley, *U.S.A.* **79 D8** 42 14N 76 11W
Newberg, *U.S.A.* **82 D2** 45 18N 122 58W
Newberry, *Mich., U.S.A.* .. **76 B3** 46 21N 85 30W
Newberry, *S.C., U.S.A.* **77 H5** 34 17N 81 37W
Newberry Springs, *U.S.A.* . **85 L10** 34 50N 116 41W
Newboro L., *Canada* **79 B8** 44 38N 76 20W
Newbridge = Droichead Nua, *Ireland* **13 C5** 53 11N 6 48W
Newburgh, *Canada* **78 B8** 44 19N 76 52W
Newburgh, *U.S.A.* **79 E10** 41 30N 74 1W
Newbury, *U.K.* **11 F6** 51 24N 1 20W
Newbury, *N.H., U.S.A.* **79 B12** 43 19N 72 3W
Newbury, *Vt., U.S.A.* **79 B12** 44 5N 72 4W
Newburyport, *U.S.A.* **77 D10** 42 49N 70 53W
Newcastle, *N.B., Canada* .. **71 C6** 47 1N 65 38W
Newcastle, *Ont., Canada* .. **70 D4** 43 55N 78 35W
Newcastle, *S. Africa* ...... **57 D4** 27 45S 29 58 E
Newcastle, *U.K.* **13 B6** 54 13N 5 54W
Newcastle, *Calif., U.S.A.* .. **84 G5** 38 53N 121 8W
Newcastle, *Wyo., U.S.A.* .. **80 D2** 43 50N 104 11W
Newcastle Emlyn, *U.K.* **11 E3** 52 2N 4 28W
Newcastle Ra., *Australia* .. **60 C5** 15 45S 130 15 E
Newcastle-under-Lyme, *U.K.* **10 D5** 53 1N 2 14W
Newcastle-upon-Tyne, *U.K.* **10 C6** 54 58N 1 36W
Newcastle Waters, *Australia* .... **62 B1** 17 30S 133 28 E
Newcastle West, *Ireland* .. **13 D2** 52 27N 9 3W
Newcomb, *U.S.A.* **79 C10** 43 58N 74 10W
Newcomerstown, *U.S.A.* .. **78 F3** 40 16N 81 36W
Newdegate, *Australia* .... **61 F2** 33 6S 119 0 E
Newell, *Australia* .... **62 B4** 16 20S 145 16 E
Newell, *U.S.A.* **80 C3** 44 43N 103 25W
Newfane, *U.S.A.* **78 C6** 43 17N 78 43W
Newfield, *U.S.A.* **79 D8** 42 18N 76 33W
Newfound L., *U.S.A.* **79 C13** 43 40N 71 47W
Newfoundland, *Canada* ... **66 E14** 49 0N 55 0W
Newfoundland, *U.S.A.* **79 E9** 41 18N 75 19W
Newfoundland □, *Canada* . **71 B8** 53 0N 58 0W
Newhall, *U.S.A.* **85 L8** 34 23N 118 32W
Newhaven, *U.K.* .... **11 G8** 50 47N 0 3 E
Newkirk, *U.S.A.* **81 G6** 36 53N 97 3W
Newlyn, *U.K.* **11 G2** 50 6N 5 34W
Newman, *Australia* .... **60 D2** 23 18S 119 45 E
Newman, *U.S.A.* **84 H5** 37 19N 121 1W
Newmarket, *Canada* **78 B5** 44 3N 79 28W
Newmarket, *Ireland* **13 D2** 52 13N 9 0W
Newmarket, *U.K.* .... **11 E8** 52 15N 0 25 E
Newmarket, *U.S.A.* **79 C14** 43 4N 70 56W
Newnan, *U.S.A.* **77 J3** 33 23N 84 48W
Newport, *Ireland* **13 C2** 53 53N 9 33W
Newport, *I. of W., U.K.* **11 G6** 50 42N 1 17W
Newport, *Newp., U.K.* **11 F5** 51 35N 3 0W
Newport, *Ark., U.S.A.* **81 H9** 35 37N 91 16W
Newport, *Ky., U.S.A.* **76 F3** 39 5N 84 30W
Newport, *N.H., U.S.A.* **79 C12** 43 22N 72 10W
Newport, *N.Y., U.S.A.* **79 C9** 43 11N 75 1W
Newport, *Oreg., U.S.A.* **82 D1** 44 39N 124 3W
Newport, *Pa., U.S.A.* **78 F7** 40 29N 77 8W
Newport, *R.I., U.S.A.* **79 E13** 41 29N 71 19W
Newport, *Tenn., U.S.A.* **77 H4** 35 58N 83 11W
Newport, *Vt., U.S.A.* **79 B12** 44 56N 72 13W
Newport, *Wash., U.S.A.* ... **82 B5** 48 11N 117 3W
Newport □, *U.K.* **11 F4** 51 33N 3 1W
Newport Beach, *U.S.A.* **85 M9** 33 37N 117 56W
Newport News, *U.S.A.* **76 G7** 36 59N 76 25W
Newport Pagnell, *U.K.* **11 E7** 52 5N 0 43W
Newquay, *U.K.* **11 G2** 50 25N 5 6W
Newry, *U.K.* **13 B5** 54 11N 6 21W
Newton, *Ill., U.S.A.* **80 F10** 38 59N 88 10W
Newton, *Iowa, U.S.A.* **80 E8** 41 42N 93 3W
Newton, *Kans., U.S.A.* **81 F6** 38 3N 97 21W
Newton, *Mass., U.S.A.* **79 D13** 42 21N 71 12W
Newton, *Miss., U.S.A.* **81 J10** 32 19N 89 10W
Newton, *N.C., U.S.A.* **77 H5** 35 40N 81 13W
Newton, *N.J., U.S.A.* **79 E10** 41 3N 74 45W
Newton, *Tex., U.S.A.* **81 K8** 30 51N 93 46W
Newton Abbot, *U.K.* **11 G4** 50 32N 3 37W
Newton Aycliffe, *U.K.* **10 C6** 54 37N 1 34W
Newton Falls, *U.S.A.* **78 E4** 41 11N 80 59W
Newton Stewart, *U.K.* **12 G4** 54 57N 4 30W
Newtonmore, *U.K.* **12 D4** 57 4N 4 8W
Newtown, *U.K.* **11 E4** 52 31N 3 19W
Newtownabbey, *U.K.* **13 B6** 54 40N 5 56W
Newtownards, *U.K.* **13 B6** 54 36N 5 42W
Newtownbarry = Bunclody, *Ireland* **13 D5** 52 39N 6 40W
Newtownstewart, *U.K.* **13 B4** 54 43N 7 23W
Newville, *U.S.A.* **78 F7** 40 10N 77 24W
Neya, *Russia* .... **24 C7** 58 21N 43 49 E
Neyriz, *Iran* .... **45 D7** 29 15N 54 19 E
Neyshābūr, *Iran* .... **45 B8** 36 10N 58 50 E
Nezhin = Nizhyn, *Ukraine* . **25 D5** 51 5N 31 55 E
Nezperce, *U.S.A.* **82 C5** 46 14N 116 14W
Ngabang, *Indonesia* ...... **36 D3** 0 23N 109 55 E
Ngabordamlu, Tanjung, *Indonesia* .... **37 F8** 6 56S 134 11 E
N'Gage, *Angola* .... **52 F3** 7 46S 15 16 E
Ngami Depression, *Botswana* .... **56 C3** 20 30S 22 46 E
Ngamo, *Zimbabwe* .... **55 F2** 19 3S 27 32 E
Nganglong Kangri, *China* . **41 C12** 33 0N 81 0 E
Ngao, *Thailand* .... **38 C2** 18 46N 99 59 E
Ngaoundéré, *Cameroon* .. **52 C2** 7 15N 13 35 E
Ngapara, *N.Z.* .... **59 L3** 44 57S 170 46 E
Ngara, *Tanzania* .... **54 C3** 2 29S 30 40 E
Ngawi, *Indonesia* .... **37 G14** 7 24S 111 26 E
Nghia Lo, *Vietnam* .... **38 B5** 21 33N 104 28 E
Ngoma, *Malawi* .... **55 E3** 13 8S 33 45 E
Ngomahura, *Zimbabwe* ... **55 G3** 20 26S 30 43 E
Ngomba, *Tanzania* .... **55 D3** 8 20S 32 53 E
Ngoring Hu, *China* .... **32 C4** 34 55N 97 5 E
Ngorongoro, *Tanzania* .... **54 C4** 3 11S 35 32 E
Ngozi, *Burundi* .... **54 C2** 2 54S 29 50 E
Ngudu, *Tanzania* .... **54 C3** 2 58S 33 25 E
Nguigmi, *Niger* .... **51 F8** 14 20N 13 20 E
Nguiu, *Australia* .... **60 B5** 11 46S 130 38 E
Ngukurr, *Australia* .... **62 A1** 14 44S 134 44 E
Ngulu Atoll, *Pac. Oc.* ..... **37 C9** 8 0N 137 30 E
Ngunga, *Tanzania* .... **54 C3** 3 37S 33 37 E
Nguru, *Nigeria* .... **51 F8** 12 56N 10 29 E
Nguru Mts., *Tanzania* ..... **54 D4** 6 0S 37 30 E
Nguyen Binh, *Vietnam* .... **38 A5** 22 39N 105 56 E
Nha Trang, *Vietnam* ...... **39 F7** 12 16N 109 10 E
Nhacoongo, *Mozam.* ..... **57 C6** 24 18S 35 14 E
Nhamaabué, *Mozam.* ..... **55 F4** 17 25S 35 5 E
Nhamundá →, *Brazil* **93 D7** 2 12S 56 41W
Nhangulaze, L., *Mozam.* .. **57 C5** 24 0S 34 30 E
Nho Quan, *Vietnam* ...... **38 B5** 20 18N 105 45 E
Nhulunbuy, *Australia* ..... **62 A2** 12 10S 137 20 E
Nia-nia, *Dem. Rep. of the Congo* .... **54 B2** 1 30N 27 40 E
Niagara Falls, *Canada* **78 C5** 43 7N 79 5W
Niagara Falls, *U.S.A.* **78 C6** 43 5N 79 4W
Niagara-on-the-Lake, *Canada* **78 C5** 43 15N 79 4W
Niah, *Malaysia* .... **36 D4** 3 58N 113 46 E
Niamey, *Niger* .... **50 F6** 13 27N 2 6 E
Niangara, *Dem. Rep. of the Congo* .... **54 B2** 3 42N 27 50 E
Niantic, *U.S.A.* **79 E12** 41 20N 72 11W
Nias, *Indonesia* .... **36 D1** 1 0N 97 30 E
Niassa □, *Mozam.* .... **55 E4** 13 30S 36 0 E
Nibāk, *Si. Arabia* .... **45 E7** 24 25N 50 50 E
Nicaragua ■, *Cent. Amer.* . **88 D2** 11 40N 85 30W
Nicaragua, L. de, *Nic.* **88 D2** 12 0N 85 30W
Nicastro, *Italy* .... **20 E7** 38 59N 16 19 E
Nice, *France* .... **18 E7** 43 42N 7 14 E
Niceville, *U.S.A.* **77 K2** 30 31N 86 30W
Nichicun, L., *Canada* **71 B5** 53 5N 71 0W
Nichinan, *Japan* .... **31 J5** 31 38N 131 23 E
Nicholás, Canal, *W. Indies* **88 B3** 23 30N 80 5W
Nicholasville, *U.S.A.* **76 G3** 37 53N 84 34W
Nichols, *U.S.A.* **79 D8** 42 1N 76 22W
Nicholson, *Australia* ..... **60 C4** 18 2S 128 54 E
Nicholson, *U.S.A.* **79 E9** 41 37N 75 47W
Nicholson →, *Australia* .. **62 B2** 17 31S 139 36 E
Nicholson L., *Canada* **73 A8** 62 40N 102 40W
Nicholson Ra., *Australia* .. **61 E2** 27 15S 116 45 E
Nicholville, *U.S.A.* **79 B10** 44 41N 74 39W
Nicobar Is., *Ind. Oc.* ...... **29 J13** 9 0N 93 0 E
Nicola, *Canada* **72 C4** 50 12N 120 40W
Nicolls Town, *Bahamas* ... **88 A4** 25 8N 78 0W
Nicosia, *Cyprus* .... **23 D12** 35 10N 33 25 E
Nicoya, *Costa Rica* **88 D2** 10 9N 85 27W
Nicoya, G. de, *Costa Rica* . **88 E3** 10 0N 85 0W
Nicoya, Pen. de, *Costa Rica* **88 E2** 9 45N 85 40W
Nidd →, *U.K.* **10 D6** 53 59N 1 23W
Niedersachsen □, *Germany* **16 B5** 52 50N 9 0 E
Niekerkshoop, *S. Africa* .. **56 D3** 29 19S 22 51 E
Niemba, *Dem. Rep. of the Congo* .... **54 D2** 5 58S 28 24 E
Niemen = Neman →, *Lithuania* .... **9 J19** 55 25N 21 10 E
Nienburg, *Germany* ...... **16 B5** 52 39N 9 13 E
Nieu Bethesda, *S. Africa* .. **56 E3** 31 51S 24 34 E
Nieuw Amsterdam, *Surinam* **93 B7** 5 53N 55 5W
Nieuw Nickerie, *Surinam* . **93 B7** 6 0N 56 59W
Nieuwoudtville, *S. Africa* . **56 E2** 31 23S 19 7 E
Nieuwpoort, *Belgium* ..... **15 C2** 51 8N 2 45 E
Nieves, Pico de las, *Canary Is.* **22 G4** 27 57N 15 35W
Niğde, *Turkey* .... **25 G5** 37 58N 34 40 E
Nigel, *S. Africa* .... **57 D4** 26 27S 28 25 E
Niger ■, *W. Afr.* .... **50 E7** 17 30N 10 0 E
Niger →, *W. Afr.* .... **50 G7** 5 33N 6 33 E
Nigeria ■, *W. Afr.* .... **50 G7** 8 30N 8 0 E
Nighasin, *India* .... **43 E9** 28 14N 80 52 E
Nightcaps, *N.Z.* .... **59 L2** 45 57S 168 2 E
Nii-Jima, *Japan* .... **31 G9** 34 20N 139 15 E
Niigata, *Japan* .... **30 F9** 37 58N 139 0 E
Niigata □, *Japan* .... **31 F9** 37 15N 138 45 E
Niihama, *Japan* .... **31 H6** 33 55N 133 16 E
Niihau, *U.S.A.* **74 H14** 21 54N 160 9W
Niimi, *Japan* .... **31 G6** 34 59N 133 28 E
Niitsu, *Japan* .... **30 F9** 37 48N 139 7 E
Nijil, *Jordan* .... **47 E4** 30 32N 35 33 E
Nijkerk, *Neths.* .... **15 B5** 52 13N 5 30 E
Nijmegen, *Neths.* .... **15 C5** 51 50N 5 52 E
Nijverdal, *Neths.* .... **15 B6** 52 22N 6 28 E
Nīk Pey, *Iran* .... **45 B6** 36 50N 48 10 E
Nikiniki, *Indonesia* .... **37 F6** 9 49S 124 30 E
Nikkō, *Japan* .... **31 F9** 36 45N 139 35 E
Nikolayev = Mykolayiv, *Ukraine* .... **25 E5** 46 58N 32 0 E
Nikolayevsk, *Russia* ...... **25 E8** 50 0N 45 35 E
Nikolayevsk-na-Amur, *Russia* .... **27 D15** 53 8N 140 44 E
Nikolskoye, *Russia* .... **27 D17** 55 12N 166 0 E
Nikopol, *Ukraine* .... **25 E5** 47 35N 34 25 E
Nīkshahr, *Iran* .... **45 E9** 26 15N 60 10 E
Nikšić, *Montenegro, Yug.* . **21 C8** 42 50N 18 57 E
Nîl, Nahr en →, *Africa* ... **51 B12** 30 10N 31 6 E
Nîl el Abyad →, *Sudan* ... **51 E12** 15 38N 32 31 E
Nîl el Azraq →, *Sudan* ... **51 E12** 15 38N 32 31 E
Nila, *Indonesia* .... **37 F7** 6 44S 129 31 E
Niland, *U.S.A.* **85 M11** 33 14N 115 31W
Nile = Nîl, Nahr en →, *Africa* .... **51 B12** 30 10N 31 6 E
Niles, *Mich., U.S.A.* **76 E2** 41 50N 86 15W
Niles, *Ohio, U.S.A.* **78 E4** 41 11N 80 46W
Nim Ka Thana, *India* ...... **42 F6** 27 44N 75 48 E
Nimach, *India* .... **42 G6** 24 30N 74 56 E
Nimbahera, *India* .... **42 G6** 24 37N 74 45 E
Nîmes, *France* .... **18 E6** 43 50N 4 23 E
Nimfaíon, Ákra = Pínnes, Ákra, *Greece* .... **21 D11** 40 5N 24 20 E
Ninawá, *Iraq* .... **44 B4** 36 25N 43 10 E
Nindigully, *Australia* ..... **63 D4** 28 21S 148 50 E
Nineveh = Ninawá, *Iraq* ... **44 B4** 36 25N 43 10 E
Ning Xian, *China* .... **34 G4** 35 30N 107 58 E
Ning'an, *China* .... **35 B15** 44 22N 129 20 E
Ningbo, *China* .... **33 D7** 29 51N 121 28 E
Ningcheng, *China* .... **35 D10** 41 32N 119 53 E
Ningjin, *China* .... **34 F8** 37 35N 114 57 E
Ningjing Shan, *China* ..... **32 D4** 30 0N 98 20 E
Ningling, *China* .... **34 G8** 34 25N 115 22 E
Ningpo = Ningbo, *China* .. **33 D7** 29 51N 121 28 E
Ningqiang, *China* .... **34 H4** 32 47N 106 15 E
Ningshan, *China* .... **34 H5** 33 21N 108 21 E
Ningsia Hui A.R. = Ningxia Huizu Zizhiqu □, *China* . **34 F4** 38 0N 106 0 E
Ningwu, *China* .... **34 E7** 39 0N 112 18 E
Ningxia Huizu Zizhiqu □, *China* .... **34 F4** 38 0N 106 0 E
Ningyang, *China* .... **34 G9** 35 47N 116 45 E
Ninh Binh, *Vietnam* .... **38 B5** 20 15N 105 55 E
Ninh Giang, *Vietnam* ..... **38 B6** 20 44N 106 24 E
Ninh Hoa, *Vietnam* .... **38 F7** 12 30N 109 7 E
Ninh Ma, *Vietnam* .... **38 F7** 12 48N 109 21 E
Ninove, *Belgium* .... **15 D4** 50 51N 4 2 E
Nioaque, *Brazil* **95 A4** 21 5S 55 50W
Niobrara, *U.S.A.* **80 D6** 42 45N 98 2W
Niobrara →, *U.S.A.* **80 D6** 42 46N 98 3W
Nioro du Sahel, *Mali* **50 E4** 15 15N 9 30W
Niort, *France* **18 C3** 46 19N 0 29W
Nipawin, *Canada* **73 C8** 53 20N 104 0W
Nipigon, *Canada* **70 C2** 49 0N 88 17W
Nipigon, L., *Canada* **70 C2** 49 50N 88 30W
Nipishish L., *Canada* **71 B7** 54 12N 60 45W
Nipissing, L., *Canada* **70 C4** 46 20N 80 0W
Nipomo, *U.S.A.* **85 K6** 35 3N 120 29W
Nipton, *U.S.A.* **85 K11** 35 28N 115 16W
Niquelândia, *Brazil* **93 F9** 14 33S 48 23W
Nīr, *Iran* .... **44 B5** 38 2N 47 59 E
Nirasaki, *Japan* .... **31 G9** 35 42N 138 27 E
Nirmal, *India* .... **40 K11** 19 3N 78 20 E
Nirmali, *India* .... **43 F12** 26 20N 86 35 E
Niš, *Serbia, Yug.* .... **21 C9** 43 19N 21 58 E
Nişāb, *Si. Arabia* .... **44 D5** 29 11N 44 43 E
Nişāb, *Yemen* .... **46 E4** 14 25N 46 29 E
Nishinomiya, *Japan* ...... **31 G7** 34 45N 135 20 E
Nishino'omote, *Japan* ..... **31 J5** 30 43N 130 59 E
Nishiwaki, *Japan* .... **31 G7** 34 59N 134 58 E
Niskibi →, *Canada* **70 A2** 56 29N 88 9W
Nisqually →, *U.S.A.* **84 C4** 47 6N 122 42W
Nissáki, *Greece* .... **23 A3** 39 43N 19 52 E
Nissum Bredning, *Denmark* **9 H13** 56 40N 8 20 E
Nistru = Dnister →, *Europe* **17 E16** 46 18N 30 17 E
Nisutlin →, *Canada* **72 A2** 60 14N 132 34W
Nitchequon, *Canada* **71 B5** 53 10N 70 58W
Niterói, *Brazil* **95 A7** 22 52S 43 0W
Nith →, *Canada* **78 C4** 43 12N 80 23W
Nith →, *U.K.* **12 F5** 55 14N 3 33W
Nitra, *Slovak Rep.* .... **17 D10** 48 19N 18 4 E
Nitra →, *Slovak Rep.* ..... **17 E10** 47 46N 18 10 E
Niuafo'ou, *Tonga* **59 B11** 15 30S 175 58W
Niue, *Cook Is.* **65 J11** 19 2S 169 54W
Niut, *Indonesia* .... **36 D4** 0 55N 110 6 E
Niuzhuang, *China* .... **35 D12** 40 58N 122 28 E
Nivala, *Finland* .... **8 E21** 63 56N 24 57 E
Nivelles, *Belgium* .... **15 D4** 50 35N 4 20 E
Nivernais, *France* .... **18 C5** 47 15N 3 30 E
Niwas, *India* .... **43 H9** 23 3N 80 26 E
Nixon, *U.S.A.* **81 L6** 29 16N 97 46W
Nizamabad, *India* .... **40 K11** 18 45N 78 7 E
Nizamghat, *India* .... **41 E19** 28 20N 95 45 E
Nizhne Kolymsk, *Russia* .. **27 C17** 68 34N 160 55 E
Nizhnekamsk, *Russia* ..... **24 C9** 55 38N 51 49 E
Nizhneudinsk, *Russia* ..... **27 D10** 54 54N 99 3 E
Nizhnevartovsk, *Russia* ... **26 C8** 60 56N 76 38 E
Nizhniy Novgorod, *Russia* . **24 C7** 56 20N 44 0 E
Nizhniy Tagil, *Russia* ..... **24 C10** 57 55N 59 57 E
Nizhyn, *Ukraine* .... **25 D5** 51 5N 31 55 E
Nizip, *Turkey* .... **44 B3** 37 5N 37 50 E
Nízké Tatry, *Slovak Rep.* .. **17 D10** 48 55N 19 30 E
Njakwa, *Malawi* .... **55 E3** 11 1S 33 56 E
Njanji, *Zambia* .... **55 E3** 14 25S 31 46 E
Njinjo, *Tanzania* .... **55 D4** 8 48S 38 54 E
Njombe, *Tanzania* .... **55 D3** 9 20S 34 50 E
Njombe →, *Tanzania* ..... **54 D4** 6 56S 35 6 E
Nkana, *Zambia* .... **55 E2** 12 50S 28 8 E
Nkandla, *S. Africa* .... **57 D5** 28 37S 31 5 E
Nkayi, *Zimbabwe* .... **55 F2** 19 41S 29 20 E
Nkhotakota, *Malawi* ...... **55 E3** 12 56S 34 15 E
Nkongsamba, *Cameroon* .. **52 D1** 4 55N 9 55 E
Nkurenkuru, *Namibia* ..... **56 B2** 17 42S 18 32 E
Nmai →, *Burma* .... **41 G20** 25 30N 97 25 E
Noakhali = Maijdi, *Bangla.* **41 H17** 22 48N 91 10 E
Nobel, *Canada* **78 A4** 45 25N 80 6W
Nobeoka, *Japan* .... **31 H5** 32 36N 131 41 E
Noblesville, *U.S.A.* **76 E3** 40 3N 86 1W
Nocera Inferiore, *Italy* .... **20 D6** 40 44N 14 38 E
Nocona, *U.S.A.* **81 J6** 33 47N 97 44W
Noda, *Japan* .... **31 G9** 35 56N 139 52 E
Nogales, *Mexico* **86 A2** 31 20N 110 56W
Nogales, *U.S.A.* **83 L8** 31 20N 110 56W
Nōgata, *Japan* .... **31 H5** 33 48N 130 44 E
Noggerup, *Australia* ...... **61 F2** 33 32S 116 5 E
Noginsk, *Russia* .... **27 C10** 64 30N 90 50 E
Nogoa →, *Australia* ...... **62 C4** 23 40S 147 55 E
Nogoyá, *Argentina* **94 C4** 32 24S 59 48W
Nohar, *India* .... **42 E6** 29 11N 74 49 E
Nohta, *India* .... **43 H8** 23 40N 79 34 E
Noires, Mts., *France* **18 B2** 48 7N 3 28W
Noirmoutier, Î. de, *France* . **18 C2** 46 58N 2 10W
Nojane, *Botswana* .... **56 C3** 23 15S 20 14 E
Nojima-Zaki, *Japan* .... **31 G9** 34 54N 139 53 E
Nok Kundi, *Pakistan* ...... **40 E3** 28 50N 62 45 E
Nokaneng, *Botswana* ..... **56 B3** 19 40S 22 17 E
Nokia, *Finland* .... **9 F20** 61 30N 23 30 E
Nokomis, *Canada* **73 C8** 51 35N 105 0W
Nokomis L., *Canada* **73 B8** 57 0N 103 0W
Nola, *C.A.R.* .... **52 D3** 3 35N 16 4 E
Noma Omuramba →, *Namibia* .... **56 B3** 18 52S 20 53 E
Nombre de Dios, *Panama* . **88 E4** 9 34N 79 28W
Nome, *U.S.A.* **68 B3** 64 30N 165 25W
Nomo-Zaki, *Japan* .... **31 H4** 32 35N 129 44 E
Nonacho L., *Canada* **73 A7** 61 42N 109 40W
Nonda, *Australia* .... **62 C3** 20 40S 142 28 E
Nong Chang, *Thailand* .... **38 E2** 15 23N 99 51 E
Nong Het, *Laos* .... **38 C4** 19 29N 103 59 E
Nong Khai, *Thailand* ...... **38 D4** 17 50N 102 46 E
Nong'an, *China* .... **35 B13** 44 25N 125 5 E
Nongoma, *S. Africa* ...... **57 D5** 27 58S 31 35 E
Nonoava, *Mexico* **86 B3** 27 28N 106 44W
Nonoava →, *Mexico* **86 B3** 27 29N 106 45W
Nonthaburi, *Thailand* ..... **38 F3** 13 51N 100 34 E
Noonamah, *Australia* ..... **60 B5** 12 40S 131 4 E
Noord Brabant □, *Neths.* .. **15 C5** 51 40N 5 0 E
Noord Holland □, *Neths.* .. **15 B4** 52 30N 4 45 E
Noordbeveland, *Neths.* ... **15 C3** 51 35N 3 50 E
Noordoostpolder, *Neths.* .. **15 B5** 52 45N 5 45 E
Noordwijk, *Neths.* .... **15 B4** 52 14N 4 26 E
Nootka I., *Canada* **72 D3** 49 32N 126 42W
Nopiming Prov. Park, *Canada* **73 C9** 50 30N 95 37W
Noralee, *Canada* **72 C3** 53 59N 126 26W
Noranda = Rouyn-Noranda, *Canada* **70 C4** 48 20N 79 0W
Norco, *U.S.A.* **85 M9** 33 56N 117 33W
Nord-Kivu □, *Dem. Rep. of the Congo* .... **54 C2** 1 0S 29 0 E
Nord-Ostsee-Kanal, *Germany* .... **16 A5** 54 12N 9 32 E
Nordaustlandet, *Svalbard* . **4 B9** 79 14N 23 0 E
Nordegg, *Canada* **72 C5** 52 29N 116 5W
Norderney, *Germany* ..... **16 B4** 53 42N 7 9 E
Norderstedt, *Germany* .... **16 B5** 53 42N 10 1 E
Nordfjord, *Norway* .... **9 F11** 61 55N 5 30 E
Nordfriesische Inseln, *Germany* .... **16 A5** 54 40N 8 20 E
Nordhausen, *Germany* .... **16 C6** 51 30N 10 47 E
Norðoyar, *Færoe Is.* **8 E9** 62 17N 6 35W
Nordkapp, *Norway* .... **8 A21** 71 10N 25 50 E
Nordkapp, *Svalbard* ...... **4 A9** 80 31N 20 0 E
Nordkinn = Kinnarodden, *Norway* .... **6 A11** 71 8N 27 40 E
Nordkinn-halvøya, *Norway* **8 A22** 70 55N 27 40 E
Nordrhein-Westfalen □, *Germany* .... **16 C4** 51 45N 7 30 E
Nordvik, *Russia* .... **27 B12** 74 2N 111 32 E
Nore →, *Ireland* **13 D4** 52 25N 6 58W
Norfolk, *Nebr., U.S.A.* **80 D6** 42 2N 97 25W
Norfolk, *Va., U.S.A.* **76 G7** 36 51N 76 17W
Norfolk □, *U.K.* .... **11 E8** 52 39N 0 54 E
Norfolk I., *Pac. Oc.* .... **64 K8** 28 58S 168 3 E
Norfork L., *U.S.A.* **81 G8** 36 15N 92 14W
Norilsk, *Russia* .... **27 C9** 69 20N 88 6 E
Norma, Mt., *Australia* .... **62 C3** 20 55S 140 42 E
Normal, *U.S.A.* **80 E10** 40 31N 88 59W
Norman, *U.S.A.* **81 H6** 35 13N 97 26W
Norman →, *Australia* ..... **62 B3** 19 18S 141 51 E
Norman Wells, *Canada* ... **68 B7** 65 17N 126 51W
Normanby →, *Australia* .. **62 A3** 14 23S 144 10 E
Normandie, *France* ...... **18 B4** 48 45N 0 10 E
Normandin, *Canada* **70 C5** 48 49N 72 31W
Normandy = Normandie, *France* .... **18 B4** 48 45N 0 10 E
Normanhurst, Mt., *Australia* **61 E3** 25 4S 122 30 E
Normanton, *Australia* .... **62 B3** 17 40S 141 10 E
Normétal, *Canada* **70 C4** 49 0N 79 22W
Norquay, *Canada* **73 C8** 51 53N 102 5W
Norquinco, *Argentina* **96 E2** 41 51S 70 55W
Norrbotten □, *Sweden* .... **8 C19** 66 30N 22 30 E
Norris Point, *Canada* **71 C8** 49 31N 57 53W
Norristown, *U.S.A.* **79 F9** 40 7N 75 21W
Norrköping, *Sweden* ...... **9 G17** 58 37N 16 11 E
Norrland, *Sweden* .... **9 E16** 62 15N 15 45 E
Norrtälje, *Sweden* .... **9 G18** 59 46N 18 42 E
Norseman, *Australia* ..... **61 F3** 32 8S 121 43 E
Norsk, *Russia* .... **27 D14** 52 30N 130 5 E
Norte, Pta. del, *Canary Is.* . **22 G2** 27 51N 17 57W
Norte, Serra do, *Brazil* **92 F7** 11 20S 59 0W
North, C., *Canada* **71 C7** 47 2N 60 20W
North Adams, *U.S.A.* **79 D11** 42 42N 73 7W
North Arm, *Canada* **72 A5** 62 0N 114 30W
North Augusta, *U.S.A.* **77 J5** 33 30N 81 59W
North Ayrshire □, *U.K.* ... **12 F4** 55 45N 4 44W
North Bass I., *U.S.A.* **78 E2** 41 43N 82 49W
North Battleford, *Canada* . **73 C7** 52 50N 108 17W
North Bay, *Canada* **70 C4** 46 20N 79 30W
North Belcher Is., *Canada* . **70 A4** 56 50N 79 50W
North Bend, *Oreg., U.S.A.* . **82 E1** 43 24N 124 14W
North Bend, *Pa., U.S.A.* ... **78 E7** 41 20N 77 42W
North Bend, *Wash., U.S.A.* **84 C5** 47 30N 121 47W
North Bennington, *U.S.A.* . **79 D11** 42 56N 73 15W
North Berwick, *U.K.* **12 E6** 56 4N 2 42W
North Berwick, *U.S.A.* **79 C14** 43 18N 70 44W
North C., *Canada* **71 C7** 47 5N 64 0W
North C., *N.Z.* .... **59 F4** 34 23S 173 4 E
North Canadian →, *U.S.A.* **81 H7** 35 16N 95 31W
North Canton, *U.S.A.* **78 F3** 40 53N 81 24W
North Cape = Nordkapp, *Norway* .... **8 A21** 71 10N 25 50 E
North Cape = Nordkapp, *Svalbard* .... **4 A9** 80 31N 20 0 E
North Caribou L., *Canada* . **70 B1** 52 50N 90 40W
North Carolina □, *U.S.A.* . **77 H6** 35 30N 80 0W
North Cascades National Park, *U.S.A.* **82 B3** 48 45N 121 10W
North Channel, *Canada* ... **70 C3** 46 0N 83 0W
North Channel, *U.K.* **12 F3** 55 13N 5 52W
North Charleston, *U.S.A.* . **77 J6** 32 53N 79 58W
North Chicago, *U.S.A.* **76 D2** 42 19N 87 51W
North Creek, *U.S.A.* **79 C11** 43 41N 73 59W
North Dakota □, *U.S.A.* ... **80 B5** 47 30N 100 15W
North Downs, *U.K.* .... **11 F8** 51 19N 0 21 E
North East, *U.S.A.* **78 D5** 42 13N 79 50W
North East Frontier Agency = Arunachal Pradesh □, *India* ...... **41 F19** 28 0N 95 0 E
North East Lincolnshire □, *U.K.* **10 D7** 53 34N 0 2W

O

Orūmīyeh, Daryācheh-ye

Odda, *Norway* 9 F12 60 3N 6 35 E
Odei →, *Canada* 73 B9 56 6N 96 54W
Ödemiş, *Turkey* 21 E13 38 15N 28 0 E
Odendaalsrus, *S. Africa* 56 D4 27 48S 26 45 E
Odense, *Denmark* 9 J14 55 22N 10 23 E
Oder →, *Europe* 16 B8 53 33N 14 38 E
Odesa, *Ukraine* 25 E5 46 30N 30 45 E
Odessa = Odesa, *Ukraine* 25 E5 46 30N 30 45 E
Odessa, *Canada* 79 B8 44 17N 76 43W
Odessa, *Tex., U.S.A.* 81 K3 31 52N 102 23W
Odessa, *Wash., U.S.A.* 82 C4 47 20N 118 41W
Odiakwe, *Botswana* 56 C4 20 12S 25 17 E
Odienné, *Ivory C.* 50 G4 9 30N 7 34W
Odintsovo, *Russia* 24 C6 55 39N 37 15 E
O'Donnell, *U.S.A.* 81 J4 32 58N 101 50W
Odorheiu Secuiesc, *Romania* 17 E13 46 21N 25 21 E
Odra = Oder →, *Europe* 16 B8 53 33N 14 38 E
Odzi, *Zimbabwe* 57 B5 19 0S 32 20 E
Odzi →, *Zimbabwe* 57 B5 19 45S 32 23 E
Oeiras, *Brazil* 93 E10 7 0S 42 8W
Oelrichs, *U.S.A.* 80 D3 43 11N 103 14W
Oelwein, *U.S.A.* 80 D9 42 41N 91 55W
Oenpelli, *Australia* 60 B5 12 20S 133 4 E
Ofanto →, *Italy* 20 D7 41 22N 16 13 E
Offa, *Nigeria* 50 G6 8 13N 4 42 E
Offaly □, *Ireland* 13 C4 53 15N 7 30W
Offenbach, *Germany* 16 C5 50 6N 8 44 E
Offenburg, *Germany* 16 D4 48 28N 7 56 E
Ofotfjorden, *Norway* 8 B17 68 27N 17 0 E
Ōfunato, *Japan* 30 E10 39 4N 141 43 E
Oga, *Japan* 30 E9 39 55N 139 50 E
Oga-Hantō, *Japan* 30 E9 39 58N 139 47 E
Ogaden, *Ethiopia* 46 F3 7 30N 45 30 E
Ōgaki, *Japan* 31 G8 35 21N 136 37 E
Ogallala, *U.S.A.* 80 E4 41 8N 101 43W
Ogasawara Gunto, *Pac. Oc.* 28 G18 27 0N 142 0 E
Ogbomosho, *Nigeria* 50 G6 8 1N 4 11 E
Ogden, *U.S.A.* 82 F7 41 13N 111 58W
Ogdensburg, *U.S.A.* 79 B9 44 42N 75 30W
Ogeechee →, *U.S.A.* 77 K5 31 50N 81 3W
Ogilby, *U.S.A.* 85 N12 32 49N 114 50W
Oglio →, *Italy* 20 B4 45 2N 10 39 E
Ogmore, *Australia* 62 C4 22 37S 149 35 E
Ogoki, *Canada* 70 B2 51 38N 85 58W
Ogoki →, *Canada* 70 B2 51 38N 85 57W
Ogoki L., *Canada* 70 B2 50 50N 87 10W
Ogoki Res., *Canada* 70 B2 50 45N 88 15W
Ogooué →, *Gabon* 52 E1 1 0S 9 0 E
Ogowe = Ogooué →, *Gabon* 52 E1 1 0S 9 0 E
Ogre, *Latvia* 9 H21 56 49N 24 36 E
Ogurchinskiy, Ostrov, *Turkmenistan* 45 B7 38 55N 53 2 E
Ohai, *N.Z.* 59 L2 45 55S 168 0 E
Ohakune, *N.Z.* 59 H5 39 24S 175 24 E
Ohata, *Japan* 30 D10 41 24N 141 10 E
Ohau, L., *N.Z.* 59 L2 44 15S 169 53 E
Ohio □, *U.S.A.* 78 F2 40 15N 82 45W
Ohio →, *U.S.A.* 76 G1 36 59N 89 8W
Ohře →, *Czech Rep.* 16 C8 50 30N 14 10 E
Ohrid, *Macedonia* 21 D9 41 8N 20 52 E
Ohridsko Jezero, *Macedonia* 21 D9 41 8N 20 52 E
Ohrigstad, *S. Africa* 57 C5 24 39S 30 36 E
Oiapoque, *Brazil* 93 3 50N 51 50W
Oikou, *China* 35 E9 38 35N 117 42 E
Oil City, *U.S.A.* 78 E5 41 26N 79 42W
Oil Springs, *Canada* 78 D2 42 47N 82 7W
Oildale, *U.S.A.* 85 K7 35 25N 119 1W
Oise →, *France* 18 B5 49 0N 2 4 E
Ōita, *Japan* 31 H5 33 14N 131 36 E
Ōita □, *Japan* 31 H5 33 15N 131 30 E
Oiticica, *Brazil* 93 E10 5 3S 41 5W
Ojacaliente, *Mexico* 86 C4 22 34N 102 15W
Ojai, *U.S.A.* 85 L7 34 27N 119 15W
Ojinaga, *Mexico* 86 B4 29 34N 104 25W
Ojiya, *Japan* 31 F9 37 18N 138 48 E
Ojos del Salado, Cerro, *Argentina* 94 B2 27 0S 68 40W
Oka →, *Russia* 24 C7 56 20N 43 59 E
Okaba, *Indonesia* 37 F9 8 6S 139 42 E
Okahandja, *Namibia* 56 C2 22 0S 16 59 E
Okanagan L., *Canada* 72 D5 50 0N 119 30W
Okanogan, *U.S.A.* 82 B4 48 22N 119 35W
Okanogan →, *U.S.A.* 82 B4 48 6N 119 44W
Okaputa, *Namibia* 56 C2 20 5S 17 0 E
Okara, *Pakistan* 42 D5 30 50N 73 31 E
Okaukuejo, *Namibia* 56 B2 19 10S 16 0 E
Okavango Swamps, *Botswana* 56 B3 18 45S 22 45 E
Okaya, *Japan* 31 F9 36 5N 138 10 E
Okayama, *Japan* 31 G6 34 40N 133 54 E
Okayama □, *Japan* 31 G6 35 0N 133 50 E
Okazaki, *Japan* 31 G8 34 57N 137 10 E
Okeechobee, *U.S.A.* 77 M5 27 15N 80 50W
Okeechobee, L., *U.S.A.* 77 M5 27 0N 80 50W
Okefenokee Swamp, *U.S.A.* 77 K4 30 40N 82 20W
Okehampton, *U.K.* 11 G4 50 44N 4 0W
Okha, *India* 42 H3 22 27N 69 4 E
Okha, *Russia* 27 D15 53 40N 143 0 E
Okhotsk, *Russia* 27 D15 59 20N 143 10 E
Okhotsk, Sea of, *Asia* 27 D15 55 0N 145 0 E
Okhotskiy Perevoz, *Russia* 27 C14 61 52N 135 35 E
Okhtyrka, *Ukraine* 25 D5 50 25N 35 0 E
Oki-Shotō, *Japan* 31 F6 36 5N 133 15 E
Okiep, *S. Africa* 56 D2 29 39S 17 53 E
Okinawa □, *Japan* 31 L4 26 40N 128 0 E
Okinawa-Guntō, *Japan* 31 L4 26 40N 128 0 E
Okinawa-Jima, *Japan* 31 L4 26 32N 128 0 E
Okino-erabu-Shima, *Japan* 31 L4 27 21N 128 33 E
Oklahoma □, *U.S.A.* 81 H6 35 20N 97 30W
Oklahoma City, *U.S.A.* 81 H6 35 30N 97 30W
Okmulgee, *U.S.A.* 81 H7 35 37N 95 58W
Oknitsa = Ocniţa, *Moldova* 17 D14 48 25N 27 30 E
Okolo, *Uganda* 54 B3 2 37N 31 8 E
Okolona, *U.S.A.* 81 J10 34 0N 88 45W
Okombahe, *Namibia* 56 C2 21 23S 15 22 E
Okotoks, *Canada* 72 C6 50 43N 113 58W
Oksibil, *Indonesia* 37 E10 4 59S 140 35 E
Oksovskiy, *Russia* 24 B6 62 33N 39 57 E
Oktabrsk = Oktyabrsk, *Kazakstan* 25 E10 49 28N 57 25 E
Oktyabrsk, *Kazakstan* 25 E10 49 28N 57 25 E
Oktyabrskiy = Aktsyabrski, *Belarus* 17 B15 52 38N 28 53 E
Oktyabrskiy, *Russia* 24 D9 54 28N 53 28 E
Oktyabrskoy Revolyutsii, Ostrov, *Russia* 27 B10 79 30N 97 0 E
Okuru, *N.Z.* 59 K2 43 55S 168 55 E
Okushiri-Tō, *Japan* 30 C9 42 15N 139 30 E
Okwa →, *Botswana* 56 C3 22 30S 23 0 E
Ola, *U.S.A.* 81 H8 35 2N 93 13W
Ólafsfjörður, *Iceland* 8 C4 66 4N 18 39W
Ólafsvík, *Iceland* 8 D2 64 53N 23 43W
Olancha, *U.S.A.* 85 J8 36 17N 118 1W
Olancha Pk., *U.S.A.* 85 J8 36 15N 118 7W
Olanchito, *Honduras* 88 C2 15 30N 86 30W
Öland, *Sweden* 9 H17 56 45N 16 38 E
Olascoaga, *Argentina* 94 D3 35 15S 60 39W
Olathe, *U.S.A.* 80 F7 38 53N 94 49W
Olavarría, *Argentina* 94 D3 36 55S 60 20W
Oława, *Poland* 17 C9 50 57N 17 20 E
Ólbia, *Italy* 20 D3 40 55N 9 31 E
Olcott, *U.S.A.* 78 C6 43 20N 78 42W
Old Bahama Chan. = Bahama, Canal Viejo de, *W. Indies* 88 B4 22 10N 77 30W
Old Baldy Pk. = San Antonio, Mt., *U.S.A.* 85 L9 34 17N 117 38W
Old Castile = Castilla y Leon □, *Spain* 19 B3 42 0N 5 0W
Old Crow, *Canada* 68 B6 67 30N 139 55W
Old Dale, *U.S.A.* 85 L11 34 8N 115 47W
Old Forge, *N.Y., U.S.A.* 79 C10 43 43N 74 58W
Old Forge, *Pa., U.S.A.* 79 E9 41 22N 75 45W
Old Perlican, *Canada* 71 C9 48 5N 53 1W
Old Shinyanga, *Tanzania* 54 C3 3 33S 33 27 E
Old Speck Mt., *U.S.A.* 79 B14 44 34N 70 57W
Old Town, *U.S.A.* 77 C11 44 56N 68 39W
Old Washington, *U.S.A.* 78 F3 40 2N 81 27W
Old Wives L., *Canada* 73 C7 50 5N 106 0W
Oldbury, *U.K.* 11 F5 51 38N 2 33W
Oldcastle, *Ireland* 13 C4 53 46N 7 10W
Oldeani, *Tanzania* 54 C4 3 22S 35 35 E
Oldenburg, *Germany* 16 B5 53 9N 8 13 E
Oldenzaal, *Neths.* 15 B6 52 19N 6 53 E
Oldham, *U.K.* 10 D5 53 33N 2 7W
Oldman →, *Canada* 72 D6 49 57N 111 42W
Oldmeldrum, *U.K.* 12 D6 57 20N 2 19W
Olds, *Canada* 72 C6 51 50N 114 10W
Oldziyt, *Mongolia* 34 B5 44 40N 109 1 E
Olean, *U.S.A.* 78 D6 42 5N 78 26W
Olekma →, *Russia* 27 C13 60 22N 120 42 E
Olekminsk, *Russia* 27 C13 60 25N 120 30 E
Oleksandriya, *Ukraine* 17 C14 50 37N 26 19 E
Olema, *U.S.A.* 84 G4 38 3N 122 47W
Olenegorsk, *Russia* 24 A5 68 9N 33 18 E
Olenek, *Russia* 27 C12 68 28N 112 18 E
Olenek →, *Russia* 27 B13 73 0N 120 10 E
Oléron, Î. d', *France* 18 D3 45 55N 1 15W
Oleśnica, *Poland* 17 C9 51 13N 17 22 E
Olevsk, *Ukraine* 17 C14 51 12N 27 39 E
Olga, *Russia* 27 E14 43 50N 135 14 E
Olga, L., *Canada* 70 C4 49 47N 77 15W
Olga, Mt., *Australia* 61 E5 25 20S 130 50 E
Olhão, *Portugal* 19 D2 37 3N 7 48W
Olifants →, *Africa* 57 C5 23 57S 31 58 E
Olifants →, *Namibia* 56 C2 25 30S 19 30 E
Olifantshoek, *S. Africa* 56 D3 27 57S 22 42 E
Ólimbos, Óros, *Greece* 21 D10 40 6N 22 23 E
Olímpia, *Brazil* 95 A6 20 44S 48 54W
Olinda, *Brazil* 93 E12 8 1S 34 51W
Oliva, *Argentina* 94 C3 32 0S 63 38W
Olivehurst, *U.S.A.* 84 F5 39 6N 121 34W
Olivenza, *Spain* 19 C2 38 41N 7 9W
Oliver, *Canada* 72 D5 49 13N 119 37W
Oliver L., *Canada* 73 B8 56 56N 103 22W
Ollagüe, *Chile* 94 A2 21 15S 68 10W
Olney, *Ill., U.S.A.* 76 F1 38 44N 88 5W
Olney, *Tex., U.S.A.* 81 J5 33 22N 98 45W
Olomane →, *Canada* 71 B7 50 14N 60 37W
Olomouc, *Czech Rep.* 17 D9 49 38N 17 12 E
Olonets, *Russia* 24 B5 61 0N 32 54 E
Olongapo, *Phil.* 37 B6 14 50N 120 18 E
Olot, *Spain* 19 A7 42 11N 2 30 E
Olovyannaya, *Russia* 27 D12 50 58N 115 35 E
Oloy →, *Russia* 27 C16 66 29N 159 29 E
Olsztyn, *Poland* 17 B11 53 48N 20 29 E
Olt →, *Romania* 17 G13 43 43N 24 51 E
Olteniţa, *Romania* 17 F14 44 7N 26 42 E
Olton, *U.S.A.* 81 H3 34 11N 102 8W
Olymbos, *Cyprus* 23 D12 35 21N 33 45 E
Olympia, *Greece* 21 F9 37 39N 21 39 E
Olympia, *U.S.A.* 84 D4 47 3N 122 53W
Olympic Dam, *Australia* 63 E2 30 30S 136 55 E
Olympic Mts., *U.S.A.* 84 C3 47 55N 123 45W
Olympic Nat. Park, *U.S.A.* 84 C3 47 48N 123 30W
Olympus, *Cyprus* 23 E11 34 56N 32 52 E
Olympus, Mt. = Ólimbos, Óros, *Greece* 21 D10 40 6N 22 23 E
Olympus, Mt. = Uludağ, *Turkey* 21 D13 40 4N 29 13 E
Olympus, Mt., *U.S.A.* 84 C3 47 48N 123 43W
Olyphant, *U.S.A.* 79 E9 41 27N 75 36W
Om →, *Russia* 26 D8 54 59N 73 22 E
Om Koi, *Thailand* 38 D2 17 48N 98 22 E
Ōma, *Japan* 30 D10 41 45N 141 5 E
Ōmachi, *Japan* 31 F8 36 30N 137 50 E
Omae-Zaki, *Japan* 31 G9 34 36N 138 14 E
Ōmagari, *Japan* 30 E10 39 27N 140 29 E
Omagh, *U.K.* 13 B4 54 36N 7 19W
Omagh □, *U.K.* 13 B4 54 35N 7 15W
Omaha, *U.S.A.* 80 E7 41 17N 95 58W
Omak, *U.S.A.* 82 B4 48 25N 119 31W
Omalos, *Greece* 23 D5 35 19N 23 55 E
Oman ■, *Asia* 46 C6 23 0N 58 0 E
Oman, G. of, *Asia* 45 E8 24 30N 58 30 E
Omaruru, *Namibia* 56 C2 21 26S 16 0 E
Omaruru →, *Namibia* 56 C1 22 7S 14 15 E
Omate, *Peru* 92 G4 16 45S 71 0W
Ombai, Selat, *Indonesia* 37 F6 8 30S 124 50 E
Omboué, *Gabon* 52 E1 1 35S 9 15 E
Ombrone →, *Italy* 20 C4 42 42N 11 5 E
Omdurmân, *Sudan* 51 E12 15 40N 32 28 E
Omemee, *Canada* 78 B6 44 18N 78 33W
Omeonga, *Dem. Rep. of the Congo* 54 C1 3 40S 24 22 E
Ometepe, I. de, *Nic.* 88 D2 11 32N 85 35W
Ometepec, *Mexico* 87 D5 16 39N 98 23W
Ominato, *Japan* 30 D10 41 17N 141 10 E
Omineca →, *Canada* 72 B4 56 3N 124 16W
Omitara, *Namibia* 56 C2 22 16S 18 2 E
Ōmiya, *Japan* 31 G9 35 54N 139 38 E
Ommen, *Neths.* 15 B6 52 31N 6 26 E
Ömnögovĭ □, *Mongolia* 34 C3 43 15N 104 0 E
Omo →, *Ethiopia* 46 F2 6 25N 36 10 E
Omodhos, *Cyprus* 23 E11 34 51N 32 48 E
Omolon →, *Russia* 27 C16 68 42N 158 36 E
Omono-Gawa →, *Japan* 30 E10 39 46N 140 3 E
Omsk, *Russia* 26 D8 55 0N 73 12 E
Omsukchan, *Russia* 27 C16 62 32N 155 48 E
Ōmu, *Japan* 30 B11 44 34N 142 58 E
Omul, Vf., *Romania* 17 F13 45 27N 25 29 E
Ōmura, *Japan* 31 H4 32 56N 129 57 E
Omuramba Omatako →, *Namibia* 56 B2 17 45S 20 25 E
Omuramba Ovambo →, *Namibia* 56 B2 18 45S 16 59 E
Ōmuta, *Japan* 31 H5 33 5N 130 26 E
Onaga, *U.S.A.* 80 F6 39 29N 96 10W
Onalaska, *U.S.A.* 80 D9 43 53N 91 14W
Onancock, *U.S.A.* 76 G8 37 43N 75 45W
Onang, *Indonesia* 37 E5 3 2S 118 49 E
Onaping L., *Canada* 70 C3 47 3N 81 30W
Onavas, *Mexico* 86 B3 28 28N 109 30W
Onawa, *U.S.A.* 80 D6 42 2N 96 6W
Oncócua, *Angola* 56 B1 16 30S 13 25 E
Onda, *Spain* 19 C5 39 55N 0 17W
Ondaejin, *N. Korea* 35 D15 41 34N 129 40 E
Ondangwa, *Namibia* 56 B2 17 57S 16 4 E
Ondjiva, *Angola* 56 B2 16 48S 15 50 E
Öndörshil, *Mongolia* 34 B5 45 13N 108 5 E
Öndverðarnes, *Iceland* 8 D1 64 52N 24 0W
One Tree, *Australia* 63 E3 34 11S 144 43 E
Onega, *Russia* 24 B6 64 0N 38 10 E
Onega →, *Russia* 24 B6 63 58N 38 2 E
Onega, G. of = Onezhskaya Guba, *Russia* 24 B6 64 24N 36 38 E
Onega, L. = Onezhskoye Ozero, *Russia* 24 B6 61 44N 35 22 E
Oneida, *U.S.A.* 79 C9 43 6N 75 39W
Oneida L., *U.S.A.* 79 C9 43 12N 75 54W
O'Neill, *U.S.A.* 80 D5 42 27N 98 39W
Onekotan, Ostrov, *Russia* 27 E16 49 25N 154 45 E
Onema, *Dem. Rep. of the Congo* 54 C1 4 35S 24 30 E
Oneonta, *U.S.A.* 79 D9 42 27N 75 4W
Oneşti, *Romania* 17 E14 46 17N 26 47 E
Onezhskaya Guba, *Russia* 24 B6 64 24N 36 38 E
Onezhskoye Ozero, *Russia* 24 B6 61 44N 35 22 E
Ongarue, *N.Z.* 59 H5 38 42S 175 19 E
Ongers →, *S. Africa* 56 E3 31 4S 23 13 E
Ongerup, *Australia* 61 F2 33 58S 118 28 E
Ongjin, *N. Korea* 35 F13 37 56N 125 21 E
Ongkharak, *Thailand* 38 E3 14 8N 101 1 E
Ongniud Qi, *China* 35 C10 43 0N 118 38 E
Ongoka, *Dem. Rep. of the Congo* 54 C2 1 20S 26 0 E
Ongole, *India* 40 M12 15 33N 80 2 E
Ongon = Havirga, *Mongolia* 34 B7 45 41N 113 5 E
Onida, *U.S.A.* 80 C4 44 42N 100 4W
Onilahy →, *Madag.* 57 C7 23 34S 43 45 E
Onitsha, *Nigeria* 50 G7 6 6N 6 42 E
Onoda, *Japan* 31 G5 33 59N 131 11 E
Onpyŏng-ni, *S. Korea* 35 H14 33 25N 126 55 E
Onslow, *Australia* 60 D2 21 40S 115 12 E
Onslow B., *U.S.A.* 77 H7 34 20N 77 15W
Ontake-San, *Japan* 31 G8 35 53N 137 29 E
Ontario, *Calif., U.S.A.* 85 L9 34 4N 117 39W
Ontario, *Oreg., U.S.A.* 82 D5 44 2N 116 58W
Ontario □, *Canada* 70 B2 48 0N 83 0W
Ontario, L., *N. Amer.* 78 C7 43 20N 78 0W
Ontonagon, *U.S.A.* 80 B10 46 52N 89 19W
Onyx, *U.S.A.* 85 K8 35 41N 118 14W
Oodnadatta, *Australia* 63 D2 27 33S 135 30 E
Ooldea, *Australia* 61 F5 30 27S 131 50 E
Oombulgurri, *Australia* 60 C4 15 15S 127 45 E
Oorindi, *Australia* 62 C3 20 40S 141 1 E
Oost-Vlaanderen □, *Belgium* 15 C3 51 5N 3 50 E
Oostende, *Belgium* 15 C2 51 15N 2 54 E
Oosterhout, *Neths.* 15 C4 51 39N 4 47 E
Oosterschelde →, *Neths.* 15 C4 51 33N 4 0 E
Oosterwolde, *Neths.* 15 B6 53 0N 6 17 E
Ootacamund = Udagamandalam, *India* 40 P10 11 30N 76 44 E
Ootsa L., *Canada* 72 C3 53 50N 126 2W
Opala, *Dem. Rep. of the Congo* 54 C1 0 40S 24 20 E
Opanake, *Sri Lanka* 40 R12 6 35N 80 40 E
Opasatika, *Canada* 70 C3 49 30N 82 50W
Opasquia Prov. Park, *Canada* 70 B1 53 33N 93 5W
Opava, *Czech Rep.* 17 D9 49 57N 17 58 E
Opelika, *U.S.A.* 77 J3 32 39N 85 23W
Opelousas, *U.S.A.* 81 K8 30 32N 92 5W
Opémisca, L., *Canada* 70 C5 49 56N 74 52W
Opheim, *U.S.A.* 82 B10 48 51N 106 24W
Ophthalmia Ra., *Australia* 60 D2 23 15S 119 30 E
Opinaca →, *Canada* 70 B4 52 15N 78 2W
Opinaca, Rés., *Canada* 70 B4 52 39N 76 20W
Opinnagau →, *Canada* 70 B3 54 12N 82 25W
Opiscoteo, L., *Canada* 71 B6 53 10N 68 10W
Opole, *Poland* 17 C9 50 42N 17 58 E
Oponono L., *Namibia* 56 B2 18 8S 15 45 E
Oporto = Porto, *Portugal* 19 B1 41 8N 8 40W
Opotiki, *N.Z.* 59 H6 38 1S 177 19 E
Opp, *U.S.A.* 77 K2 31 17N 86 16W
Oppdal, *Norway* 9 E13 62 35N 9 41 E
Opportunity, *U.S.A.* 82 C5 47 39N 117 15W
Opua, *N.Z.* 59 F5 35 19S 174 9 E
Opunake, *N.Z.* 59 H4 39 26S 173 52 E
Opuwo, *Namibia* 56 B1 18 3S 13 45 E
Ora, *Cyprus* 23 E12 34 51N 33 12 E
Oracle, *U.S.A.* 83 K8 32 37N 110 46W
Oradea, *Romania* 17 E11 47 2N 21 58 E
Öræfajökull, *Iceland* 8 D5 64 2N 16 39W
Orai, *India* 43 G8 25 58N 79 30 E
Oral = Zhayyq →, *Kazakstan* 25 E9 47 0N 51 48 E
Oral, *Kazakstan* 25 D9 51 20N 51 20 E
Oran, *Algeria* 50 A5 35 45N 0 39W
Orange, *France* 18 D6 44 8N 4 47 E
Orange, *Calif., U.S.A.* 85 M9 33 47N 117 51W
Orange, *Mass., U.S.A.* 79 D12 42 35N 72 19W
Orange, *Tex., U.S.A.* 81 K8 30 6N 93 44W
Orange, *Va., U.S.A.* 76 F6 38 15N 78 7W
Orange →, *S. Africa* 56 D2 28 41S 16 28 E
Orange, C., *Brazil* 93 C8 4 20N 51 30W
Orange Cove, *U.S.A.* 84 J7 36 38N 119 19W
Orange Free State = Free State □, *S. Africa* 56 D4 28 30S 27 0 E
Orange Grove, *U.S.A.* 81 M6 27 58N 97 56W
Orange Walk, *Belize* 87 D7 18 6N 88 33W
Orangeburg, *U.S.A.* 77 J5 33 30N 80 52W
Orangeville, *Canada* 78 C4 43 55N 80 5W
Oranienburg, *Germany* 16 B7 52 45N 13 14 E
Oranje = Orange →, *S. Africa* 56 D2 28 41S 16 28 E
Oranje Vrystaat = Free State □, *S. Africa* 56 D4 28 30S 27 0 E
Oranjemund, *Namibia* 56 D2 28 38S 16 29 E
Oranjerivier, *S. Africa* 56 D3 29 40S 24 12 E
Orapa, *Botswana* 53 J5 21 15S 25 30 E
Oras, *Phil.* 37 B7 12 9N 125 28 E
Oraşul Stalin = Braşov, *Romania* 17 F13 45 38N 25 35 E
Orbetello, *Italy* 20 C4 42 27N 11 13 E
Orbisonia, *U.S.A.* 78 F7 40 15N 77 54W
Orcas I., *U.S.A.* 84 B4 48 42N 122 56W
Orchard City, *U.S.A.* 83 G10 38 50N 107 58W
Orchila, I., *Venezuela* 89 D6 11 48N 66 10W
Orcutt, *U.S.A.* 85 L6 34 52N 120 27W
Ord, *U.S.A.* 80 E5 41 36N 98 56W
Ord →, *Australia* 60 C4 15 33S 128 15 E
Ord, Mt., *Australia* 60 C4 17 20S 125 34 E
Orderville, *U.S.A.* 83 H7 37 17N 112 38W
Ordos = Mu Us Shamo, *China* 34 E5 39 0N 109 0 E
Ordu, *Turkey* 25 F6 40 55N 37 53 E
Ordway, *U.S.A.* 80 F3 38 13N 103 46W
Ordzhonikidze = Vladikavkaz, *Russia* 25 F7 43 0N 44 35 E
Ore, *Dem. Rep. of the Congo* 54 B2 3 17N 29 30 E
Ore Mts. = Erzgebirge, *Germany* 16 C7 50 27N 12 55 E
Örebro, *Sweden* 9 G16 59 20N 15 18 E
Oregon, *U.S.A.* 80 D10 42 1N 89 20W
Oregon □, *U.S.A.* 82 E3 44 0N 121 0W
Oregon City, *U.S.A.* 84 E4 45 21N 122 36W
Orekhovo-Zuyevo, *Russia* 24 C6 55 50N 38 55 E
Orel, *Russia* 24 D6 52 57N 36 3 E
Orem, *U.S.A.* 82 F8 40 19N 111 42W
Ören, *Turkey* 21 F12 37 3N 27 57 E
Orenburg, *Russia* 24 D10 51 45N 55 6 E
Orense = Ourense, *Spain* 19 A2 42 19N 7 55W
Orepuki, *N.Z.* 59 M1 46 19S 167 46 E
Orestiás, *Greece* 21 D12 41 30N 26 33 E
Orestos Pereyra, *Mexico* 86 B3 26 31N 105 40W
Orford Ness, *U.K.* 11 E9 52 5N 1 35 E
Organos, Pta. de los, *Canary Is.* 22 F2 28 12N 17 17W
Orgaz, *Spain* 19 C4 39 39N 3 53W
Orgeyev = Orhei, *Moldova* 17 E15 47 24N 28 50 E
Orhaneli, *Turkey* 21 E13 39 54N 28 59 E
Orhangazi, *Turkey* 21 D13 40 29N 29 18 E
Orhei, *Moldova* 17 E15 47 24N 28 50 E
Orhon Gol →, *Mongolia* 32 A5 50 21N 106 0 E
Oriental, Cordillera, *Colombia* 92 B4 6 0N 73 0W
Orientale □, *Dem. Rep. of the Congo* 54 B2 2 20N 26 0 E
Oriente, *Argentina* 94 D3 38 44S 60 37W
Orihuela, *Spain* 19 C5 38 7N 0 55W
Orillia, *Canada* 78 B5 44 40N 79 24W
Orinoco →, *Venezuela* 92 B6 9 15N 61 30W
Orion, *Canada* 73 D6 49 27N 110 49W
Oriskany, *U.S.A.* 79 C9 43 10N 75 20W
Orissa □, *India* 41 K14 20 0N 84 0 E
Orissaare, *Estonia* 9 G20 58 34N 23 5 E
Oristano, *Italy* 20 E3 39 54N 8 36 E
Oristano, G. di, *Italy* 20 E3 39 50N 8 29 E
Orizaba, *Mexico* 87 D5 18 51N 97 6W
Orkanger, *Norway* 8 E13 63 18N 9 52 E
Orkla →, *Norway* 8 E13 63 18N 9 51 E
Orkney, *S. Africa* 56 D4 26 58S 26 40 E
Orkney □, *U.K.* 12 B5 59 2N 3 13W
Orkney Is., *U.K.* 12 B6 59 0N 3 0W
Orland, *U.S.A.* 84 F4 39 45N 122 12W
Orlando, *U.S.A.* 77 L5 28 33N 81 23W
Orléanais, *France* 18 C5 48 0N 2 0 E
Orléans, *France* 18 C4 47 54N 1 52 E
Orleans, *U.S.A.* 79 B12 44 49N 72 12W
Orléans, I. d', *Canada* 71 C5 46 54N 70 58W
Ormara, *Pakistan* 40 G4 25 16N 64 33 E
Ormoc, *Phil.* 37 B6 11 0N 124 37 E
Ormond, *N.Z.* 59 H6 38 33S 177 56 E
Ormond Beach, *U.S.A.* 77 L5 29 17N 81 3W
Ormskirk, *U.K.* 10 D5 53 35N 2 54W
Ormstown, *Canada* 79 A11 45 8N 74 0W
Örnsköldsvik, *Sweden* 8 E18 63 17N 18 40 E
Oro, *N. Korea* 35 D14 40 1N 127 27 E
Oro →, *Mexico* 86 B3 25 35N 105 2W
Oro Grande, *U.S.A.* 85 L9 34 36N 117 20W
Oro Valley, *U.S.A.* 83 K8 32 26N 110 58W
Orocué, *Colombia* 92 C4 4 48N 71 20W
Orofino, *U.S.A.* 82 C5 46 29N 116 15W
Orol Dengizi = Aral Sea, *Asia* 26 E7 44 30N 60 0 E
Oromocto, *Canada* 71 C6 45 54N 66 29W
Orono, *Canada* 78 C6 43 59N 78 37W
Orono, *U.S.A.* 77 C11 44 53N 68 40W
Oronsay, *U.K.* 12 E2 56 1N 6 15W
Oroqen Zizhiqi, *China* 33 A7 50 34N 123 43 E
Oroquieta, *Phil.* 37 C6 8 32N 123 44 E
Orosháza, *Hungary* 17 E11 46 32N 20 42 E
Orotukan, *Russia* 27 C16 62 16N 151 42 E
Oroville, *Calif., U.S.A.* 84 F5 39 31N 121 33W
Oroville, *Wash., U.S.A.* 82 B4 48 56N 119 26W
Oroville, L., *U.S.A.* 84 F5 39 33N 121 29W
Orrville, *U.S.A.* 78 F3 40 50N 81 46W
Orsha, *Belarus* 24 D5 54 30N 30 25 E
Orsk, *Russia* 26 D6 51 12N 58 34 E
Orşova, *Romania* 17 F12 44 41N 22 25 E
Ortaca, *Turkey* 21 F13 36 49N 28 45 E
Ortegal, C., *Spain* 19 A2 43 43N 7 52W
Orthez, *France* 18 E3 43 29N 0 48W
Ortigueira, *Spain* 19 A2 43 40N 7 50W
Orting, *U.S.A.* 84 C4 47 6N 122 12W
Ortles, *Italy* 18 C9 46 31N 10 33 E
Ortón →, *Bolivia* 92 F5 10 50S 67 0W
Ortonville, *U.S.A.* 80 C6 45 19N 96 27W
Orūmīyeh, *Iran* 44 B5 37 40N 45 0 E
Orūmīyeh, Daryācheh-ye, *Iran* 44 B5 37 50N 45 30 E

Oruro

Oruro, *Bolivia* **92 G5** 18 0S 67 9W
Orust, *Sweden* **9 G14** 58 10N 11 40 E
Oruzgān □, *Afghan.* **40 C5** 33 30N 66 0 E
Orvieto, *Italy* **20 C5** 42 43N 12 7 E
Orwell, *N.Y., U.S.A.* **79 C9** 43 35N 75 50W
Orwell, *Ohio, U.S.A.* **78 E4** 41 32N 80 52W
Orwell →, *U.K.* **11 F9** 51 59N 1 18 E
Orwigsburg, *U.S.A.* **79 F8** 40 38N 76 6W
Oryakhovo, *Bulgaria* **21 C10** 43 40N 23 57 E
Osa, *Russia* **24 C10** 57 17N 55 26 E
Osa, Pen. de, *Costa Rica* **88 E3** 8 0N 84 0W
Osage, *U.S.A.* **80 D8** 43 17N 92 49W
Osage →, *U.S.A.* **80 F9** 38 35N 91 57W
Osage City, *U.S.A.* **80 F7** 38 38N 95 50W
Ōsaka, *Japan* **31 G7** 34 40N 135 30 E
Osan, *S. Korea* **35 F14** 37 11N 127 4 E
Osawatomie, *U.S.A.* **80 F7** 38 31N 94 57W
Osborne, *U.S.A.* **80 F5** 39 26N 98 42W
Osceola, *Ark., U.S.A.* **81 H10** 35 42N 89 58W
Osceola, *Iowa, U.S.A.* **80 E8** 41 2N 93 46W
Oscoda, *U.S.A.* **78 B1** 44 26N 83 20W
Ösel = Saaremaa, *Estonia* **9 G20** 58 30N 22 30 E
Osgoode, *Canada* **79 A9** 45 8N 75 36W
Osh, *Kyrgyzstan* **26 E8** 40 37N 72 49 E
Oshakati, *Namibia* **53 H3** 17 45S 15 40 E
Oshawa, *Canada* **78 C6** 43 50N 78 50W
Oshigambo, *Namibia* **56 B2** 17 45S 16 5 E
Oshkosh, *Nebr., U.S.A.* **80 E3** 41 24N 102 21W
Oshkosh, *Wis., U.S.A.* **80 C10** 44 1N 88 33W
Oshmyany = Ashmyany, *Belarus* **9 J21** 54 26N 25 52 E
Oshnovīyeh, *Iran* **44 B5** 37 2N 45 6 E
Oshogbo, *Nigeria* **50 G6** 7 48N 4 37 E
Oshtorīnān, *Iran* **45 C6** 34 1N 48 38 E
Oshwe, *Dem. Rep. of the Congo* **52 E3** 3 25S 19 28 E
Osijek, *Croatia* **21 B8** 45 34N 18 41 E
Osipenko = Berdyansk, *Ukraine* **25 E6** 46 45N 36 50 E
Osipovichi = Asipovichy, *Belarus* **17 B15** 53 19N 28 33 E
Osiyan, *India* **42 F5** 26 43N 72 55 E
Osizweni, *S. Africa* **57 D5** 27 49S 30 7 E
Oskaloosa, *U.S.A.* **80 E8** 41 18N 92 39W
Oskarshamn, *Sweden* **9 H17** 57 15N 16 27 E
Oskélanéo, *Canada* **70 C4** 48 5N 75 15W
Öskemen, *Kazakstan* **26 E9** 50 0N 82 36 E
Oslo, *Norway* **9 G14** 59 55N 10 45 E
Oslofjorden, *Norway* **9 G14** 59 20N 10 35 E
Osmanabad, *India* **40 K10** 18 5N 76 10 E
Osmaniye, *Turkey* **25 G6** 37 5N 36 10 E
Osnabrück, *Germany* **16 B5** 52 17N 8 3 E
Osorio, *Brazil* **95 B5** 29 53S 50 17W
Osorno, *Chile* **96 E2** 40 25S 73 0W
Osoyoos, *Canada* **72 D5** 49 0N 119 30W
Osøyro, *Norway* **9 F11** 60 9N 5 30 E
Ospika →, *Canada* **72 B4** 56 20N 124 0W
Osprey Reef, *Australia* **62 A4** 13 52S 146 36 E
Oss, *Neths.* **15 C5** 51 46N 5 32 E
Ossa, Mt., *Australia* **62 G4** 41 52S 146 3 E
Óssa, Óros, *Greece* **21 E10** 39 47N 22 42 E
Ossabaw I., *U.S.A.* **77 K5** 31 50N 81 5W
Ossining, *U.S.A.* **79 E11** 41 10N 73 55W
Ossipee, *U.S.A.* **79 C13** 43 41N 71 7W
Ossokmanuan L., *Canada* **71 B7** 53 25N 65 0W
Ossora, *Russia* **27 D17** 59 20N 163 13 E
Ostend = Oostende, *Belgium* **15 C2** 51 15N 2 54 E
Oster, *Ukraine* **17 C16** 50 57N 30 53 E
Osterburg, *U.S.A.* **78 F6** 40 16N 78 31W
Österdalälven, *Sweden* **9 F16** 61 30N 13 45 E
Østerdalen, *Norway* **9 F14** 61 40N 10 50 E
Östersund, *Sweden* **8 E16** 63 10N 14 38 E
Ostfriesische Inseln, *Germany* **16 B4** 53 42N 7 0 E
Ostrava, *Czech Rep.* **17 D10** 49 51N 18 18 E
Ostróda, *Poland* **17 B10** 53 42N 19 58 E
Ostroh, *Ukraine* **17 C14** 50 20N 26 30 E
Ostrołęka, *Poland* **17 B11** 53 4N 21 32 E
Ostrów Mazowiecka, *Poland* **17 B11** 52 50N 21 51 E
Ostrów Wielkopolski, *Poland* **17 C9** 51 36N 17 44 E
Ostrowiec-Świętokrzyski, *Poland* **17 C11** 50 55N 21 22 E
Ostuni, *Italy* **21 D7** 40 44N 17 35 E
Ōsumi-Kaikyō, *Japan* **31 J5** 30 55N 131 0 E
Ōsumi-Shotō, *Japan* **31 J5** 30 30N 130 0 E
Osuna, *Spain* **19 D3** 37 14N 5 8W
Oswegatchie →, *U.S.A.* **79 B9** 44 42N 75 30W
Oswego, *U.S.A.* **79 C8** 43 27N 76 31W
Oswego →, *U.S.A.* **79 C8** 43 27N 76 30W
Oswestry, *U.K.* **10 E4** 52 52N 3 3W
Oświęcim, *Poland* **17 C10** 50 2N 19 11 E
Otago □, *N.Z.* **59 L2** 45 15S 170 0 E
Otago Harbour, *N.Z.* **59 L3** 45 47S 170 42 E
Ōtake, *Japan* **31 G6** 34 12N 132 13 E
Otaki, *N.Z.* **59 J5** 40 45S 175 10 E
Otaru, *Japan* **30 C10** 43 10N 141 0 E
Otaru-Wan = Ishikari-Wan, *Japan* **30 C10** 43 25N 141 1 E
Otavalo, *Ecuador* **92 C3** 0 13N 78 20W
Otavi, *Namibia* **56 B2** 19 40S 17 24 E
Otchinjau, *Angola* **56 B1** 16 30S 13 56 E
Otelnuk L., *Canada* **71 A6** 56 9N 68 12W
Othello, *U.S.A.* **82 C4** 46 50N 119 10W
Otjiwarongo, *Namibia* **56 C2** 20 30S 16 33 E
Otoineppu, *Japan* **30 B11** 44 44N 142 16 E
Otorohanga, *N.Z.* **59 H5** 38 12S 175 14 E
Otoskwin →, *Canada* **70 B2** 52 13N 88 6W
Otra →, *Norway* **9 G13** 58 9N 8 1 E
Otranto, *Italy* **21 D8** 40 9N 18 28 E
Otranto, C. d', *Italy* **21 D8** 40 7N 18 30 E
Otranto, Str. of, *Italy* **21 D8** 40 15N 18 40 E
Otse, *S. Africa* **56 D4** 25 2S 25 45 E
Ōtsu, *Japan* **31 G7** 35 0N 135 50 E
Ōtsuki, *Japan* **31 G9** 35 36N 138 57 E
Ottawa = Outaouais →, *Canada* **70 C5** 45 27N 74 8W
Ottawa, *Canada* **79 A9** 45 27N 75 42W
Ottawa, *Ill., U.S.A.* **80 E10** 41 21N 88 51W
Ottawa, *Kans., U.S.A.* **80 F7** 38 37N 95 16W
Ottawa Is., *Canada* **69 C11** 59 35N 80 10W
Otter Cr. →, *U.S.A.* **79 B11** 44 13N 73 17W
Otter L., *Canada* **73 B8** 55 35N 104 39W
Otterville, *Canada* **78 D4** 42 55N 80 36W
Ottery St. Mary, *U.K.* **11 G4** 50 44N 3 17W
Otto Beit Bridge, *Zimbabwe* **55 F2** 15 59S 28 56 E
Ottosdal, *S. Africa* **56 D4** 26 46S 25 59 E
Ottumwa, *U.S.A.* **80 E8** 41 1N 92 25W
Oturkpo, *Nigeria* **50 G7** 7 16N 8 8 E
Otway, B., *Chile* **96 G2** 53 30S 74 0W
Otwock, *Poland* **17 B11** 52 5N 21 20 E
Ou →, *Laos* **38 B4** 20 4N 102 13 E
Ou Neua, *Laos* **38 A3** 22 18N 101 48 E
Ou-Sammyaku, *Japan* **30 E10** 39 20N 140 35 E
Ouachita →, *U.S.A.* **81 K9** 31 38N 91 49W
Ouachita, L., *U.S.A.* **81 H8** 34 34N 93 12W
Ouachita Mts., *U.S.A.* **81 H7** 34 40N 94 25W
Ouagadougou, *Burkina Faso* **50 F5** 12 25N 1 30W
Ouahran = Oran, *Algeria* **50 A5** 35 45N 0 39W
Ouallene, *Algeria* **50 D6** 24 41N 1 11 E
Ouargla, *Algeria* **50 B7** 31 59N 5 16 E
Ouarzazate, *Morocco* **50 B4** 30 55N 6 50W
Oubangi →, *Dem. Rep. of the Congo* **52 E3** 0 30S 17 50 E
Ouddorp, *Neths.* **15 C3** 51 50N 3 57 E
Oude Rijn →, *Neths.* **15 B4** 52 12N 4 24 E
Oudenaarde, *Belgium* **15 D3** 50 50N 3 37 E
Oudtshoorn, *S. Africa* **56 E3** 33 35S 22 14 E
Ouessant, Î. d', *France* **18 B1** 48 28N 5 6W
Ouesso, *Congo* **52 D3** 1 37N 16 5 E
Ouest, Pte. de l', *Canada* **71 C7** 49 52N 64 40W
Ouezzane, *Morocco* **50 B4** 34 51N 5 35W
Oughterard, *Ireland* **13 C2** 53 26N 9 18W
Oujda, *Morocco* **50 B5** 34 41N 1 55W
Oulainen, *Finland* **8 D21** 64 17N 24 47 E
Oulu, *Finland* **8 D21** 65 1N 25 29 E
Oulujärvi, *Finland* **8 D22** 64 25N 27 15 E
Oulujoki →, *Finland* **8 D21** 65 1N 25 30 E
Oum Chalouba, *Chad* **51 E10** 15 48N 20 46 E
Oum Hadjer, *Chad* **51 F9** 13 18N 19 41 E
Ounasjoki →, *Finland* **8 C21** 66 31N 25 40 E
Ounguati, *Namibia* **56 C2** 22 0S 15 46 E
Ounianga Sérir, *Chad* **51 E10** 18 54N 20 51 E
Our →, *Lux.* **15 E6** 49 55N 6 5 E
Ouray, *U.S.A.* **83 G10** 38 1N 107 40W
Ourense, *Spain* **19 A2** 42 19N 7 55W
Ouricuri, *Brazil* **93 E10** 7 53S 40 5W
Ourinhos, *Brazil* **95 A6** 23 0S 49 54W
Ouro Fino, *Brazil* **95 A6** 22 16S 46 25W
Ouro Prêto, *Brazil* **95 A7** 20 20S 43 30W
Ourthe →, *Belgium* **15 D5** 50 29N 5 35 E
Ouse →, *E. Susx., U.K.* **11 G8** 50 47N 0 4 E
Ouse →, *N. Yorks., U.K.* **10 D7** 53 44N 0 55W
Outaouais →, *Canada* **70 C5** 45 27N 74 8W
Outardes →, *Canada* **71 C6** 49 24N 69 30W
Outer Hebrides, *U.K.* **12 D1** 57 30N 7 40W
Outjo, *Namibia* **56 C2** 20 5S 16 7 E
Outlook, *Canada* **73 C7** 51 30N 107 0W
Outokumpu, *Finland* **8 E23** 62 43N 29 1 E
Ovalau, *Fiji* **59 C8** 17 40S 178 48 E
Ovalle, *Chile* **94 C1** 30 33S 71 18W
Ovamboland, *Namibia* **56 B2** 18 30S 16 0 E
Overflakkee, *Neths.* **15 C4** 51 44N 4 10 E
Overijssel □, *Neths.* **15 B6** 52 25N 6 35 E
Overland Park, *U.S.A.* **80 F7** 38 55N 94 50W
Overton, *U.S.A.* **85 J12** 36 33N 114 27W
Övertorneå, *Sweden* **8 C20** 66 23N 23 38 E
Ovid, *U.S.A.* **79 D8** 42 41N 76 49W
Oviedo, *Spain* **19 A3** 43 25N 5 50W
Oviši, *Latvia* **9 H19** 57 33N 21 44 E
Ovoot, *Mongolia* **34 B7** 45 21N 113 45 E
Övör Hangay □, *Mongolia* **34 B2** 45 0N 102 30 E
Øvre Årdal, *Norway* **9 F12** 61 19N 7 48 E
Ovruch, *Ukraine* **17 C15** 51 25N 28 45 E
Owaka, *N.Z.* **59 M2** 46 27S 169 40 E
Owambo = Ovamboland, *Namibia* **56 B2** 18 30S 16 0 E
Owasco L., *U.S.A.* **79 D8** 42 50N 76 31W
Owase, *Japan* **31 G8** 34 7N 136 12 E
Owatonna, *U.S.A.* **80 C8** 44 5N 93 14W
Owbeh, *Afghan.* **40 B3** 34 28N 63 10 E
Owego, *U.S.A.* **79 D8** 42 6N 76 16W
Owen Falls Dam, *Uganda* **54 B3** 0 30N 33 5 E
Owen Sound, *Canada* **78 B4** 44 35N 80 55W
Owens →, *U.S.A.* **84 J9** 36 32N 117 59W
Owens L., *U.S.A.* **85 J9** 36 26N 117 57W
Owensboro, *U.S.A.* **76 G2** 37 46N 87 7W
Owl →, *Canada* **73 B10** 57 51N 92 44W
Owo, *Nigeria* **50 G7** 7 10N 5 39 E
Owosso, *U.S.A.* **76 D3** 43 0N 84 10W
Owyhee, *U.S.A.* **82 F5** 41 57N 116 6W
Owyhee →, *U.S.A.* **82 E5** 43 49N 117 2W
Owyhee, L., *U.S.A.* **82 E5** 43 38N 117 14W
Ox Mts. = Slieve Gamph, *Ireland* **13 B3** 54 6N 9 0W
Öxarfjörður, *Iceland* **8 C5** 66 15N 16 45W
Oxbow, *Canada* **73 D8** 49 14N 102 10W
Oxelösund, *Sweden* **9 G17** 58 43N 17 5 E
Oxford, *N.Z.* **59 K4** 43 18S 172 11 E
Oxford, *U.K.* **11 F6** 51 46N 1 15W
Oxford, *Mass., U.S.A.* **79 D13** 42 7N 71 52W
Oxford, *Miss., U.S.A.* **81 H10** 34 22N 89 31W
Oxford, *N.C., U.S.A.* **77 G6** 36 19N 78 35W
Oxford, *N.Y., U.S.A.* **79 D9** 42 27N 75 36W
Oxford, *Ohio, U.S.A.* **76 F3** 39 31N 84 45W
Oxford L., *Canada* **73 C9** 54 51N 95 37W
Oxfordshire □, *U.K.* **11 F6** 51 48N 1 16W
Oxnard, *U.S.A.* **85 L7** 34 12N 119 11W
Oxus = Amudarya →, *Uzbekistan* **26 E6** 43 58N 59 34 E
Oya, *Malaysia* **36 D4** 2 55N 111 55 E
Oyama, *Japan* **31 F9** 36 18N 139 48 E
Oyem, *Gabon* **52 D2** 1 34N 11 31 E
Oyen, *Canada* **73 C6** 51 22N 110 28W
Oykel →, *U.K.* **12 D4** 57 56N 4 26W
Oymyakon, *Russia* **27 C15** 63 25N 142 44 E
Oyo, *Nigeria* **50 G6** 7 46N 3 56 E
Oyster Bay, *U.S.A.* **79 F11** 40 52N 73 32W
Ōyūbari, *Japan* **30 C11** 43 1N 142 5 E
Ozamiz, *Phil.* **37 C6** 8 15N 123 50 E
Ozark, *Ala., U.S.A.* **77 K3** 31 28N 85 39W
Ozark, *Ark., U.S.A.* **81 H8** 35 29N 93 50W
Ozark, *Mo., U.S.A.* **81 G8** 37 1N 93 12W
Ozark Plateau, *U.S.A.* **81 G9** 37 20N 91 40W
Ozarks, L. of the, *U.S.A.* **80 F8** 38 12N 92 38W
Ózd, *Hungary* **17 D11** 48 14N 20 15 E
Ozette L., *U.S.A.* **84 B2** 48 6N 124 38W
Ozona, *U.S.A.* **81 K4** 30 43N 101 12W
Ozuluama, *Mexico* **87 C5** 21 40N 97 50W

P

Pa-an, *Burma* **41 L20** 16 51N 97 40 E
Pa Mong Dam, *Thailand* **38 D4** 18 0N 102 22 E
Pa Sak →, *Thailand* **36 B2** 15 30N 101 0 E
Paamiut, *Greenland* **4 C5** 62 0N 49 43W
Paarl, *S. Africa* **56 E2** 33 45S 18 56 E
Pab Hills, *Pakistan* **42 F2** 26 30N 66 45 E
Pabbay, *U.K.* **12 D1** 57 46N 7 14W
Pabianice, *Poland* **17 C10** 51 40N 19 20 E
Pabna, *Bangla.* **41 G16** 24 1N 89 18 E
Pabo, *Uganda* **54 B3** 3 1N 32 10 E
Pacaja →, *Brazil* **93 D8** 1 56S 50 50W
Pacaraima, Sa., *S. Amer.* **92 C6** 4 0N 62 30W
Pacasmayo, *Peru* **92 E3** 7 20S 79 35W
Pachhar, *India* **42 G7** 24 40N 77 42 E
Pachitea →, *Peru* **92 E4** 8 46S 74 33W
Pachmarhi, *India* **43 H8** 22 28N 78 26 E
Pachpadra, *India* **40 G8** 25 58N 72 10 E
Pachuca, *Mexico* **87 C5** 20 10N 98 40W
Pacific, *Canada* **72 C3** 54 48N 128 28W
Pacific-Antarctic Ridge, *Pac. Oc.* **65 M16** 43 0S 115 0W
Pacific Grove, *U.S.A.* **84 J5** 36 38N 121 56W
Pacific Ocean, *Pac. Oc.* **65 G14** 10 0N 140 0W
Pacific Rim Nat. Park, *Canada* **84 B2** 48 40N 124 45W
Pacifica, *U.S.A.* **84 H4** 37 36N 122 30W
Pacitan, *Indonesia* **37 H14** 8 12S 111 7 E
Packwood, *U.S.A.* **84 D5** 46 36N 121 40W
Padaido, Kepulauan, *Indonesia* **37 E9** 1 15S 136 30 E
Padang, *Indonesia* **36 E2** 1 0S 100 20 E
Padang Endau, *Malaysia* **39 L4** 2 40N 103 38 E
Padangpanjang, *Indonesia* **36 E2** 0 40S 100 20 E
Padangsidempuan, *Indonesia* **36 D1** 1 30N 99 15 E
Paddle Prairie, *Canada* **72 B5** 57 57N 117 29W
Paddockwood, *Canada* **73 C7** 53 30N 105 30W
Paderborn, *Germany* **16 C5** 51 42N 8 45 E
Padma, *India* **43 G11** 24 12N 85 22 E
Pádova, *Italy* **20 B4** 45 25N 11 53 E
Padra, *India* **42 H5** 22 15N 73 7 E
Padrauna, *India* **43 F10** 26 54N 83 59 E
Padre I., *U.S.A.* **81 M6** 27 10N 97 25W
Padstow, *U.K.* **11 G3** 50 33N 4 58W
Padua = Pádova, *Italy* **20 B4** 45 25N 11 53 E
Paducah, *Ky., U.S.A.* **76 G1** 37 5N 88 37W
Paducah, *Tex., U.S.A.* **81 H4** 34 1N 100 18W
Paengnyŏng-do, *S. Korea* **35 F13** 37 57N 124 40 E
Paeroa, *N.Z.* **59 G5** 37 23S 175 41 E
Pafúri, *Mozam.* **57 C5** 22 28S 31 17 E
Pag, *Croatia* **16 F8** 44 25N 15 3 E
Pagadian, *Phil.* **37 C6** 7 55N 123 30 E
Pagai Selatan, Pulau, *Indonesia* **36 E2** 3 0S 100 15 E
Pagai Utara, Pulau, *Indonesia* **36 E2** 2 35S 100 0 E
Pagalu = Annobón, *Atl. Oc.* **49 G4** 1 25S 5 36 E
Pagara, *India* **43 G9** 24 22N 80 1 E
Pagastikós Kólpos, *Greece* **21 E10** 39 15N 23 0 E
Pagatan, *Indonesia* **36 E5** 3 33S 115 59 E
Page, *U.S.A.* **83 H8** 36 57N 111 27W
Pago Pago, *Amer. Samoa* **59 B13** 14 16S 170 43W
Pagosa Springs, *U.S.A.* **83 H10** 37 16N 107 1W
Pagwa River, *Canada* **70 B2** 50 2N 85 14W
Pahala, *U.S.A.* **74 J17** 19 12N 155 29W
Pahang →, *Malaysia* **39 L4** 3 30N 103 9 E
Pahiatua, *N.Z.* **59 J5** 40 27S 175 50 E
Pahokee, *U.S.A.* **77 M5** 26 50N 80 40W
Pahrump, *U.S.A.* **85 J11** 36 12N 115 59W
Pahute Mesa, *U.S.A.* **84 H10** 37 20N 116 45W
Pai, *Thailand* **38 C2** 19 19N 98 27 E
Paicines, *U.S.A.* **84 J5** 36 44N 121 17W
Paide, *Estonia* **9 G21** 58 57N 25 31 E
Paignton, *U.K.* **11 G4** 50 26N 3 35W
Päijänne, *Finland* **9 F21** 61 30N 25 30 E
Pailani, *India* **43 G9** 25 45N 80 26 E
Pailin, *Cambodia* **38 F4** 12 46N 102 36 E
Painan, *Indonesia* **36 E2** 1 21S 100 34 E
Painesville, *U.S.A.* **78 E3** 41 43N 81 15W
Paint Hills = Wemindji, *Canada* **70 B4** 53 0N 78 49W
Paint L., *Canada* **73 B9** 55 28N 97 57W
Painted Desert, *U.S.A.* **83 J8** 36 0N 111 0W
Paintsville, *U.S.A.* **76 G4** 37 49N 82 48W
País Vasco □, *Spain* **19 A4** 42 50N 2 45W
Paisley, *Canada* **78 B3** 44 18N 81 16W
Paisley, *U.K.* **12 F4** 55 50N 4 25W
Paisley, *U.S.A.* **82 E3** 42 42N 120 32W
Paita, *Peru* **92 E2** 5 11S 81 9W
Pajares, Puerto de, *Spain* **19 A3** 42 58N 5 46W
Pak Lay, *Laos* **38 C3** 18 15N 101 27 E
Pak Phanang, *Thailand* **39 H3** 8 21N 100 12 E
Pak Sane, *Laos* **38 C4** 18 22N 103 39 E
Pak Song, *Laos* **38 E6** 15 11N 106 14 E
Pak Suong, *Laos* **38 C4** 19 58N 102 15 E
Pakaur, *India* **43 G12** 24 38N 87 51 E
Pakenham, *Canada* **79 A8** 45 18N 76 18W
Pákhnes, *Greece* **23 D6** 35 16N 24 4 E
Pakhuis, *S. Africa* **56 E2** 32 9S 19 5 E
Pakistan ■, *Asia* **42 E4** 30 0N 70 0 E
Pakkading, *Laos* **38 C4** 18 19N 103 59 E
Pakokku, *Burma* **41 J19** 21 20N 95 0 E
Pakowki L., *Canada* **73 D6** 49 20N 111 0W
Pakpattan, *Pakistan* **42 D5** 30 25N 73 27 E
Paktīā □, *Afghan.* **40 C6** 33 0N 69 15 E
Pakwach, *Uganda* **54 B3** 2 28N 31 27 E
Pakxe, *Laos* **38 E5** 15 5N 105 52 E
Pal Lahara, *India* **43 J11** 21 27N 85 11 E
Pala, *Chad* **51 G9** 9 25N 15 5 E
Pala, *Dem. Rep. of the Congo* **54 D2** 6 45S 29 30 E
Pala, *U.S.A.* **85 M9** 33 22N 117 5W
Palabek, *Uganda* **54 B3** 3 22N 32 33 E
Palacios, *U.S.A.* **81 L6** 28 42N 96 13W
Palagruža, *Croatia* **20 C7** 42 24N 16 15 E
Palaiókastron, *Greece* **23 D8** 35 12N 26 15 E
Palaiokhóra, *Greece* **23 D5** 35 16N 23 39 E
Palam, *India* **40 K10** 19 0N 77 0 E
Palampur, *India* **42 C7** 32 10N 76 30 E
Palana, *Australia* **62 F4** 39 45S 147 55 E
Palana, *Russia* **27 D16** 59 10N 159 59 E
Palanan, *Phil.* **37 A6** 17 8N 122 29 E
Palanan Pt., *Phil.* **37 A6** 17 17N 122 30 E
Palandri, *Pakistan* **43 C5** 33 42N 73 40 E
Palanga, *Lithuania* **9 J19** 55 58N 21 3 E
Palangkaraya, *Indonesia* **36 E4** 2 16S 113 56 E
Palani Hills, *India* **40 P10** 10 14N 77 33 E
Palanpur, *India* **42 G5** 24 10N 72 25 E
Palapye, *Botswana* **56 C4** 22 30S 27 7 E
Palas, *Pakistan* **43 B5** 35 4N 73 14 E
Palashi, *India* **43 H13** 23 47N 88 15 E
Palasponga, *India* **43 J11** 21 47N 85 34 E
Palatka, *Russia* **27 C16** 60 6N 150 54 E
Palatka, *U.S.A.* **77 L5** 29 39N 81 38W
Palau ■, *Pac. Oc.* **28 J17** 7 30N 134 30 E
Palauk, *Burma* **38 F2** 13 10N 98 40 E
Palawan, *Phil.* **36 C5** 9 30N 118 30 E
Palayankottai, *India* **40 Q10** 8 45N 77 45 E
Paldiski, *Estonia* **9 G21** 59 23N 24 9 E
Paleleh, *Indonesia* **37 D6** 1 10N 121 50 E
Palembang, *Indonesia* **36 E2** 3 0S 104 50 E
Palencia, *Spain* **19 A3** 42 1N 4 34W
Palenque, *Mexico* **87 D6** 17 31N 91 58W
Paleokastrítsa, *Greece* **23 A3** 39 40N 19 41 E
Paleometokho, *Cyprus* **23 D12** 35 7N 33 11 E
Palermo, *Italy* **20 E5** 38 7N 13 22 E
Palermo, *U.S.A.* **82 G3** 39 26N 121 33W
Palestina, *Chile* **96 A3** 23 50S 69 47W
Palestine, *Asia* **47 D4** 32 0N 35 0 E
Palestine, *U.S.A.* **81 K7** 31 46N 95 38W
Paletwa, *Burma* **41 J18** 21 10N 92 50 E
Palghat, *India* **40 P10** 10 46N 76 42 E
Palgrave, Mt., *Australia* **60 D2** 23 22S 115 58 E
Pali, *India* **42 G5** 25 50N 73 20 E
Palikir, *Micronesia* **64 G7** 6 55N 158 9 E
Palioúrion, Ákra, *Greece* **21 E10** 39 57N 23 45 E
Palisades Reservoir, *U.S.A.* **82 E8** 43 20N 111 12W
Paliseul, *Belgium* **15 E5** 49 54N 5 8 E
Palitana, *India* **42 J4** 21 32N 71 49 E
Palizada, *Mexico* **87 D6** 18 18N 92 8W
Palk Bay, *Asia* **40 Q11** 9 30N 79 15 E
Palk Strait, *Asia* **40 Q11** 10 0N 79 45 E
Palkānah, *Iraq* **44 C5** 35 49N 44 26 E
Palkot, *India* **43 H11** 22 53N 84 39 E
Palla Road = Dinokwe, *Botswana* **56 C4** 23 29S 26 37 E
Pallanza = Verbánia, *Italy* **18 D8** 45 56N 8 33 E
Pallarenda, *Australia* **62 B4** 19 12S 146 46 E
Pallinup →, *Australia* **61 F2** 34 27S 118 50 E
Pallisa, *Uganda* **54 B3** 1 12N 33 43 E
Pallu, *India* **42 E6** 28 59N 74 14 E
Palm Bay, *U.S.A.* **77 L5** 28 2N 80 35W
Palm Beach, *U.S.A.* **77 M6** 26 43N 80 2W
Palm Coast, *U.S.A.* **77 L5** 29 32N 81 10W
Palm Desert, *U.S.A.* **85 M10** 33 43N 116 22W
Palm Is., *Australia* **62 B4** 18 40S 146 35 E
Palm Springs, *U.S.A.* **85 M10** 33 50N 116 33W
Palma, *Mozam.* **55 E5** 10 46S 40 29 E
Palma, B. de, *Spain* **22 B9** 39 30N 2 39 E
Palma de Mallorca, *Spain* **22 B9** 39 35N 2 39 E
Palma Soriano, *Cuba* **88 B4** 20 15N 76 0W
Palmares, *Brazil* **93 E11** 8 41S 35 28W
Palmas, *Brazil* **95 B5** 26 29S 52 0W
Palmas, C., *Liberia* **50 H4** 4 27N 7 46W
Pálmas, G. di, *Italy* **20 E3** 39 0N 8 30 E
Palmdale, *U.S.A.* **85 L8** 34 35N 118 7W
Palmeira das Missões, *Brazil* **95 B5** 27 55S 53 17W
Palmeira dos Índios, *Brazil* **93 E11** 9 25S 36 37W
Palmer, *U.S.A.* **68 B5** 61 36N 149 7W
Palmer →, *Australia* **62 B3** 16 0S 142 26 E
Palmer Arch., *Antarctica* **5 C17** 64 15S 65 0W
Palmer Lake, *U.S.A.* **80 F2** 39 7N 104 55W
Palmer Land, *Antarctica* **5 D18** 73 0S 63 0W
Palmerston, *Canada* **78 C4** 43 50N 80 51W
Palmerston, *N.Z.* **59 L3** 45 29S 170 43 E
Palmerston North, *N.Z.* **59 J5** 40 21S 175 39 E
Palmerton, *U.S.A.* **79 F9** 40 48N 75 37W
Palmetto, *U.S.A.* **77 M4** 27 31N 82 34W
Palmi, *Italy* **20 E6** 38 21N 15 51 E
Palmira, *Argentina* **94 C2** 32 59S 68 34W
Palmira, *Colombia* **92 C3** 3 32N 76 16W
Palmyra = Tudmur, *Syria* **44 C3** 34 36N 38 15 E
Palmyra, *Mo., U.S.A.* **80 F9** 39 48N 91 32W
Palmyra, *N.J., U.S.A.* **79 F9** 40 1N 75 1W
Palmyra, *N.Y., U.S.A.* **78 C7** 43 5N 77 18W
Palmyra, *Pa., U.S.A.* **79 F8** 40 18N 76 36W
Palmyra Is., *Pac. Oc.* **65 G11** 5 52N 162 5W
Palo Alto, *U.S.A.* **84 H4** 37 27N 122 10W
Palo Verde, *U.S.A.* **85 M12** 33 26N 114 44W
Palopo, *Indonesia* **37 E6** 3 0S 120 16 E
Palos, C. de, *Spain* **19 D5** 37 38N 0 40W
Palos Verdes, *U.S.A.* **85 M8** 33 48N 118 23W
Palos Verdes, Pt., *U.S.A.* **85 M8** 33 43N 118 26W
Palu, *Indonesia* **37 E5** 1 0S 119 52 E
Palu, *Turkey* **25 G7** 38 45N 40 0 E
Palwal, *India* **42 E7** 28 8N 77 19 E
Pamanukan, *Indonesia* **37 G12** 6 16S 107 49 E
Pamiers, *France* **18 E4** 43 7N 1 39 E
Pamir, *Tajikistan* **26 F8** 37 40N 73 0 E
Pamlico →, *U.S.A.* **77 H7** 35 20N 76 28W
Pamlico Sd., *U.S.A.* **77 H8** 35 20N 76 0W
Pampa, *U.S.A.* **81 H4** 35 32N 100 58W
Pampa de las Salinas, *Argentina* **94 C2** 32 1S 66 58W
Pampanua, *Indonesia* **37 E6** 4 16S 120 8 E
Pampas, *Argentina* **94 D3** 35 0S 63 0W
Pampas, *Peru* **92 F4** 12 20S 74 50W
Pamplona, *Colombia* **92 B4** 7 23N 72 39W
Pamplona, *Spain* **19 A5** 42 48N 1 38W
Pampoenpoort, *S. Africa* **56 E3** 31 3S 22 40 E
Pana, *U.S.A.* **80 F10** 39 23N 89 5W
Panaca, *U.S.A.* **83 H6** 37 47N 114 23W
Panaitan, *Indonesia* **37 G11** 6 36S 105 12 E
Panaji, *India* **40 M8** 15 25N 73 50 E
Panamá, *Panama* **88 E4** 9 0N 79 25W
Panama ■, *Cent. Amer.* **88 E4** 8 48N 79 55W
Panamá, G. de, *Panama* **88 E4** 8 4N 79 20W
Panama Canal, *Panama* **88 E4** 9 10N 79 37W
Panama City, *U.S.A.* **77 K3** 30 10N 85 40W
Panamint Range, *U.S.A.* **85 J9** 36 20N 117 20W
Panamint Springs, *U.S.A.* **85 J9** 36 20N 117 28W
Panão, *Peru* **92 E3** 9 55S 75 55W
Panare, *Thailand* **39 J3** 6 51N 101 30 E
Panay, *Phil.* **37 B6** 11 10N 122 30 E
Panay, G., *Phil.* **37 B6** 11 0N 122 30 E
Pančevo, *Serbia, Yug.* **21 B9** 44 52N 20 41 E
Panda, *Mozam.* **57 C5** 24 2S 34 45 E
Pandan, *Phil.* **37 B6** 11 45N 122 10 E

Q

Raquette

Qahar Youyi Zhongqi, *China* **34 D7** 41 12N 112 40 E
Qahremānshahr = Bākhtarān, *Iran* **44 C5** 34 23N 47 0 E
Qaidam Pendi, *China* **32 C4** 37 0N 95 0 E
Qajarīyeh, *Iran* **45 D6** 31 1N 48 22 E
Qala, Ras il, *Malta* **23 C1** 36 1N 14 20 E
Qala-i-Jadid = Spīn Búldak, *Afghan.* **42 D2** 31 1N 66 25 E
Qala Viala, *Pakistan* **42 D2** 30 49N 67 17 E
Qala Yangi, *Afghan.* **42 B2** 34 20N 66 30 E
Qal'at al Akhḑar, *Si. Arabia* **44 E3** 28 0N 37 10 E
Qal'at Dīzah, *Iraq* **44 B5** 36 11N 45 7 E
Qal'at Şaliḩ, *Iraq* **44 D5** 31 31N 47 16 E
Qal'at Sukkar, *Iraq* **44 D5** 31 51N 46 5 E
Qamani'tuaq = Baker Lake, *Canada* **68 B10** 64 20N 96 3W
Qamdo, *China* **32 C4** 31 15N 97 6 E
Qamruddin Karez, *Pakistan* **42 D3** 31 45N 68 20 E
Qandahār, *Afghan.* **40 D4** 31 32N 65 30 E
Qandahār □, *Afghan.* **40 D4** 31 0N 65 0 E
Qapān, *Iran* **45 B7** 37 40N 55 47 E
Qapshaghay, *Kazakstan* **26 E8** 43 51N 77 14 E
Qaqortoq, *Greenland* **69 B6** 60 43N 46 0W
Qara Qash →, *India* **43 B8** 35 0N 78 30 E
Qarabutaq, *Kazakstan* **26 E7** 49 59N 60 14 E
Qaraghandy, *Kazakstan* **26 E8** 49 50N 73 10 E
Qārah, *Si. Arabia* **44 D4** 29 55N 40 3 E
Qarataū, *Kazakstan* **26 E8** 43 10N 70 28 E
Qarataū, *Kazakstan* **26 E7** 43 30N 69 30 E
Qareh →, *Iran* **44 B5** 39 25N 47 22 E
Qareh Tekān, *Iran* **45 B6** 36 38N 49 29 E
Qarqan He →, *China* **32 C3** 39 30N 88 30 E
Qarqaraly, *Kazakstan* **26 E8** 49 26N 75 30 E
Qarshi, *Uzbekistan* **26 F7** 38 53N 65 48 E
Qartabā, *Lebanon* **47 A4** 34 4N 35 50 E
Qaryat al Gharab, *Iraq* **44 D5** 31 27N 44 48 E
Qaryat al 'Ulyā, *Si. Arabia* **44 E5** 27 33N 47 42 E
Qasr 'Amra, *Jordan* **44 D3** 31 48N 36 35 E
Qaşr-e Qand, *Iran* **45 E9** 26 15N 60 45 E
Qasr Farâfra, *Egypt* **51 C11** 27 0N 28 1 E
Qatanā, *Syria* **47 B5** 33 26N 36 4 E
Qatar ■, *Asia* **46 B5** 25 30N 51 15 E
Qatlīsh, *Iran* **45 B8** 37 50N 57 19 E
Qattâra, Munkhafed el, *Egypt* **51 C11** 29 30N 27 30 E
Qattâra Depression = Qattâra, Munkhafed el, *Egypt* **51 C11** 29 30N 27 30 E
Qawām al Ḩamzah, *Iraq* **44 D5** 31 43N 44 58 E
Qāyen, *Iran* **45 C8** 33 40N 59 10 E
Qazaqstan = Kazakstan ■, *Asia* **26 E7** 50 0N 70 0 E
Qazimämmäd, *Azerbaijan* **45 A6** 40 3N 49 0 E
Qazvin, *Iran* **45 B6** 36 15N 50 0 E
Qena, *Egypt* **51 C12** 26 10N 32 43 E
Qeqertarsuaq, *Greenland* **4 C5** 69 15N 53 38W
Qeqertarsuaq, *Greenland* **69 B5** 69 45N 53 30W
Qeshlāq, *Iran* **44 C5** 34 55N 46 28 E
Qeshm, *Iran* **45 E8** 26 55N 56 10 E
Qeys, *Iran* **45 E7** 26 32N 53 58 E
Qezel Owzen →, *Iran* **45 B6** 36 45N 49 22 E
Qezi'ot, *Israel* **47 E3** 30 52N 34 26 E
Qi Xian, *China* **34 G8** 34 40N 114 48 E
Qian Gorlos, *China* **35 B13** 45 5N 124 42 E
Qian Xian, *China* **34 G5** 34 31N 108 15 E
Qianyang, *China* **34 G4** 34 40N 107 8 E
Qikiqtarjuaq, *Canada* **69 B13** 67 33N 63 0W
Qila Safed, *Pakistan* **40 E2** 29 0N 61 30 E
Qila Saifullāh, *Pakistan* **42 D3** 30 45N 68 17 E
Qilian Shan, *China* **32 C4** 38 30N 96 0 E
Qin He →, *China* **34 G7** 35 1N 113 22 E
Qin Ling = Qinling Shandi, *China* **34 H5** 33 50N 108 10 E
Qin'an, *China* **34 G3** 34 48N 105 40 E
Qing Xian, *China* **34 E9** 38 35N 116 45 E
Qingcheng, *China* **35 F9** 37 15N 117 40 E
Qingdao, *China* **35 F11** 36 5N 120 20 E
Qingfeng, *China* **34 G8** 35 52N 115 8 E
Qinghai □, *China* **32 C4** 36 0N 98 0 E
Qinghai Hu, *China* **32 C5** 36 40N 100 10 E
Qinghecheng, *China* **35 D13** 41 28N 124 15 E
Qinghemen, *China* **35 D11** 41 48N 121 25 E
Qingjian, *China* **34 F6** 37 8N 110 8 E
Qingjiang = Huaiyin, *China* **35 H10** 33 30N 119 2 E
Qingshui, *China* **34 G4** 34 48N 106 8 E
Qingshuihe, *China* **34 E6** 39 55N 111 35 E
Qingtongxia Shuiku, *China* **34 F3** 37 50N 105 58 E
Qingxu, *China* **34 F7** 37 34N 112 22 E
Qingyang, *China* **34 F4** 36 2N 107 55 E
Qingyuan, *China* **35 C13** 42 10N 124 55 E
Qingyun, *China* **35 F9** 37 45N 117 20 E
Qinhuangdao, *China* **35 E10** 39 56N 119 30 E
Qinling Shandi, *China* **34 H5** 33 50N 108 10 E
Qinshui, *China* **34 G7** 35 40N 112 8 E
Qinyang = Jiyuan, *China* **34 G7** 35 7N 112 57 E
Qinyuan, *China* **34 F7** 36 29N 112 20 E
Qinzhou, *China* **32 D5** 21 58N 108 38 E
Qionghai, *China* **38 C8** 19 15N 110 26 E
Qiongzhou Haixia, *China* **38 B8** 20 10N 110 15 E
Qiqihar, *China* **27 E13** 47 26N 124 0 E
Qirâiya, W. →, *Egypt* **47 E3** 30 27N 34 0 E
Qiryat Ata, *Israel* **47 C4** 32 47N 35 6 E
Qiryat Gat, *Israel* **47 D3** 31 32N 34 46 E
Qiryat Mal'akhi, *Israel* **47 D3** 31 44N 34 44 E
Qiryat Shemona, *Israel* **47 B4** 33 13N 35 35 E
Qiryat Yam, *Israel* **47 C4** 32 51N 35 4 E
Qishan, *China* **34 G4** 34 25N 107 38 E
Qitai, *China* **32 B3** 44 2N 89 35 E
Qixia, *China* **35 F11** 37 17N 120 52 E
Qızılağac Körfäzi, *Azerbaijan* **45 B6** 39 9N 49 0 E
Qojūr, *Iran* **44 B5** 36 12N 47 55 E
Qom, *Iran* **45 C6** 34 40N 51 0 E
Qomolangma Feng = Everest, Mt., *Nepal* **43 E12** 28 5N 86 58 E
Qomsheh, *Iran* **45 D6** 32 0N 51 55 E
Qoraqalpoghistan □, *Uzbekistan* **26 E6** 43 0N 58 0 E
Qostanay, *Kazakstan* **26 D7** 53 10N 63 35 E
Quabbin Reservoir, *U.S.A.* **79 D12** 42 20N 72 20W
Quairading, *Australia* **61 F2** 32 0S 117 21 E
Quakertown, *U.S.A.* **79 F9** 40 26N 75 21W
Qualicum Beach, *Canada* **72 D4** 49 22N 124 26W
Quamby, *Australia* **62 C3** 20 22S 140 17 E
Quan Long = Ca Mau, *Vietnam* **39 H5** 9 7N 105 8 E
Quanah, *U.S.A.* **81 H5** 34 18N 99 44W
Quang Ngai, *Vietnam* **38 E7** 15 13N 108 58 E
Quang Tri, *Vietnam* **38 D6** 16 45N 107 13 E
Quang Yen, *Vietnam* **38 B6** 20 56N 106 52 E
Quantock Hills, *U.K.* **11 F4** 51 8N 3 10W
Quanzhou, *China* **33 D6** 24 55N 118 34 E
Qu'Appelle, *Canada* **73 C8** 50 33N 103 53W
Quaqtaq, *Canada* **69 B13** 60 55N 69 40W
Quaraí, *Brazil* **94 C4** 30 15S 56 20W
Quartu Sant'Elena, *Italy* **20 E3** 39 15N 9 10 E
Quartzsite, *U.S.A.* **85 M12** 33 40N 114 13W
Quatsino Sd., *Canada* **72 C3** 50 25N 127 58W
Quba, *Azerbaijan* **25 F8** 41 21N 48 32 E
Qūchān, *Iran* **45 B8** 37 10N 58 27 E
Québec, *Canada* **71 C5** 46 52N 71 13W
Québec □, *Canada* **71 C6** 48 0N 74 0W
Queen Alexandra Ra., *Antarctica* **5 E11** 85 0S 170 0 E
Queen Charlotte City, *Canada* **72 C2** 53 15N 132 2W
Queen Charlotte Is., *Canada* **72 C2** 53 20N 132 10W
Queen Charlotte Sd., *Canada* **72 C3** 51 0N 128 0W
Queen Charlotte Strait, *Canada* **72 C3** 50 45N 127 10W
Queen Elizabeth Is., *Canada* **66 B10** 76 0N 95 0W
Queen Elizabeth Nat. Park, *Uganda* **54 C3** 0 0 30 0 E
Queen Mary Land, *Antarctica* **5 D7** 70 0S 95 0 E
Queen Maud G., *Canada* **68 B9** 68 15N 102 30W
Queen Maud Land, *Antarctica* **5 D3** 72 30S 12 0 E
Queen Maud Mts., *Antarctica* **5 E13** 86 0S 160 0W
Queens Chan., *Australia* **60 C4** 15 0S 129 30 E
Queensland □, *Australia* **62 C3** 22 0S 142 0 E
Queenstown, *Australia* **62 G4** 42 4S 145 35 E
Queenstown, *N.Z.* **59 L2** 45 1S 168 40 E
Queenstown, *S. Africa* **56 E4** 31 52S 26 52 E
Queets, *U.S.A.* **84 C2** 47 32N 124 20W
Queguay Grande →, *Uruguay* **94 C4** 32 9S 58 9W
Queimadas, *Brazil* **93 F11** 11 0S 39 38W
Quelimane, *Mozam.* **55 F4** 17 53S 36 58 E
Quellón, *Chile* **96 E2** 43 7S 73 37W
Quelpart = Cheju do, *S. Korea* **35 H14** 33 29N 126 34 E
Quemado, *N. Mex., U.S.A.* **83 J9** 34 20N 108 30W
Quemado, *Tex., U.S.A.* **81 L4** 28 58N 100 35W
Quemú-Quemú, *Argentina* **94 D3** 36 3S 63 36W
Quequén, *Argentina* **94 D4** 38 30S 58 30W
Querétaro, *Mexico* **86 C4** 20 36N 100 23W
Querétaro □, *Mexico* **86 C5** 20 30N 100 0W
Queshan, *China* **34 H8** 32 55N 114 2 E
Quesnel, *Canada* **72 C4** 53 0N 122 30W
Quesnel →, *Canada* **72 C4** 52 58N 122 29W
Quesnel L., *Canada* **72 C4** 52 30N 121 20W
Questa, *U.S.A.* **83 H11** 36 42N 105 36W
Quetico Prov. Park, *Canada* **70 C1** 48 30N 91 45W
Quetta, *Pakistan* **42 D2** 30 15N 66 55 E
Quezaltenango, *Guatemala* **88 D1** 14 50N 91 30W
Quezon City, *Phil.* **37 B6** 14 38N 121 0 E
Qufār, *Si. Arabia* **44 E4** 27 26N 41 37 E
Qui Nhon, *Vietnam* **38 F7** 13 40N 109 13 E
Quibaxe, *Angola* **52 F2** 8 24S 14 27 E
Quibdo, *Colombia* **92 B3** 5 42N 76 40W
Quiberon, *France* **18 C2** 47 29N 3 9W
Quiet L., *Canada* **72 A2** 61 5N 133 5W
Quiindy, *Paraguay* **94 B4** 25 58S 57 14W
Quila, *Mexico* **86 C3** 24 23N 107 13W
Quilán, C., *Chile* **96 E2** 43 15S 74 30W
Quilcene, *U.S.A.* **84 C4** 47 49N 122 53W
Quilimarí, *Chile* **94 C1** 32 5S 71 30W
Quilino, *Argentina* **94 C3** 30 14S 64 29W
Quill Lakes, *Canada* **73 C8** 51 55N 104 13W
Quillabamba, *Peru* **92 F4** 12 50S 72 50W
Quillagua, *Chile* **94 A2** 21 40S 69 40W
Quillaicillo, *Chile* **94 C1** 31 17S 71 40W
Quillota, *Chile* **94 C1** 32 54S 71 16W
Quilmes, *Argentina* **94 C4** 34 43S 58 15W
Quilon, *India* **40 Q10** 8 50N 76 38 E
Quilpie, *Australia* **63 D3** 26 35S 144 11 E
Quilpué, *Chile* **94 C1** 33 5S 71 33W
Quilua, *Mozam.* **55 F4** 16 17S 39 54 E
Quimilí, *Argentina* **94 B3** 27 40S 62 30W
Quimper, *France* **18 B1** 48 0N 4 9W
Quimperlé, *France* **18 C2** 47 53N 3 33W
Quinault →, *U.S.A.* **84 C2** 47 21N 124 18W
Quincy, *Calif., U.S.A.* **84 F6** 39 56N 120 57W
Quincy, *Fla., U.S.A.* **77 K3** 30 35N 84 34W
Quincy, *Ill., U.S.A.* **80 F9** 39 56N 91 23W
Quincy, *Mass., U.S.A.* **79 D14** 42 15N 71 0W
Quincy, *Wash., U.S.A.* **82 C4** 47 22N 119 56W
Quines, *Argentina* **94 C2** 32 13S 65 48W
Quinga, *Mozam.* **55 F5** 15 49S 40 15 E
Quinns Rocks, *Australia* **61 F2** 31 40S 115 42 E
Quintana Roo □, *Mexico* **87 D7** 19 0N 88 0W
Quintanar de la Orden, *Spain* **19 C4** 39 36N 3 5W
Quintero, *Chile* **94 C1** 32 45S 71 30W
Quirihue, *Chile* **94 D1** 36 15S 72 35W
Quirinópolis, *Brazil* **93 G8** 18 32S 50 30W
Quissanga, *Mozam.* **55 E5** 12 24S 40 28 E
Quissico, *Mozam.* **57 C5** 24 42S 34 44 E
Quitilipi, *Argentina* **94 B3** 26 50S 60 13W
Quitman, *U.S.A.* **77 K4** 30 47N 83 34W
Quito, *Ecuador* **92 D3** 0 15S 78 35W
Quixadá, *Brazil* **93 D11** 4 55S 39 0W
Quixaxe, *Mozam.* **55 F5** 15 17S 40 4 E
Qulan, *Kazakstan* **26 E8** 42 55N 72 43 E
Qul'ân, Jazâ'ir, *Egypt* **44 E2** 24 22N 35 31 E
Qumbu, *S. Africa* **57 E4** 31 10S 28 48 E
Quneitra, *Syria* **47 B4** 33 7N 35 48 E
Qŭnghirot, *Uzbekistan* **26 E6** 43 6N 58 54 E
Quoin I., *Australia* **60 B4** 14 54S 129 32 E
Quoin Pt., *S. Africa* **56 E2** 34 46S 19 37 E
Qŭqon, *Uzbekistan* **26 E8** 40 30N 70 57 E
Qurnat as Sawdā', *Lebanon* **47 A5** 34 18N 36 6 E
Quşaybā', *Si. Arabia* **44 E4** 26 53N 43 35 E
Qusaybah, *Iraq* **44 C4** 34 24N 40 59 E
Quseir, *Egypt* **44 E2** 26 7N 34 16 E
Qūshchī, *Iran* **44 B5** 37 59N 45 3 E
Quthing, *Lesotho* **57 E4** 30 25S 27 36 E
Qūţīābād, *Iran* **45 C6** 35 47N 48 30 E
Quwo, *China* **34 G6** 35 38N 111 25 E
Quyang, *China* **34 E8** 38 35N 114 40 E
Quynh Nhai, *Vietnam* **38 B4** 21 49N 103 33 E
Quyon, *Canada* **79 A8** 45 31N 76 14W
Quzhou, *China* **33 D6** 28 57N 118 54 E
Quzi, *China* **34 F4** 36 20N 107 20 E
Qyzylorda, *Kazakstan* **26 E7** 44 48N 65 28 E

R

Ra, Ko, *Thailand* **39 H2** 9 13N 98 16 E
Raahe, *Finland* **8 D21** 64 40N 24 28 E
Raalte, *Neths.* **15 B6** 52 23N 6 16 E
Raasay, *U.K.* **12 D2** 57 25N 6 4W
Raasay, Sd. of, *U.K.* **12 D2** 57 30N 6 8W
Raba, *Indonesia* **37 F5** 8 36S 118 55 E
Rába →, *Hungary* **17 E9** 47 38N 17 38 E
Rabai, *Kenya* **54 C4** 3 50S 39 31 E
Rabat, *Malta* **23 D1** 35 53N 14 25 E
Rabat, *Morocco* **50 B4** 34 2N 6 48W
Rabaul, *Papua N. G.* **64 H7** 4 24S 152 18 E
Rābigh, *Si. Arabia* **46 C2** 22 50N 39 5 E
Râbniţa, *Moldova* **17 E15** 47 45N 29 0 E
Rābor, *Iran* **45 D8** 29 17N 56 55 E
Race, C., *Canada* **71 C9** 46 40N 53 5W
Rach Gia, *Vietnam* **39 G5** 10 5N 105 5 E
Rachid, *Mauritania* **50 E3** 18 45N 11 35W
Racibórz, *Poland* **17 C10** 50 7N 18 18 E
Racine, *U.S.A.* **76 D2** 42 41N 87 51W
Rackerby, *U.S.A.* **84 F5** 39 26N 121 22W
Radama, Nosy, *Madag.* **57 A8** 14 0S 47 47 E
Radama, Saikanosy, *Madag.* **57 A8** 14 16S 47 53 E
Rădăuţi, *Romania* **17 E13** 47 50N 25 59 E
Radcliff, *U.S.A.* **76 G3** 37 51N 85 57W
Radekhiv, *Ukraine* **17 C13** 50 25N 24 32 E
Radekhov = Radekhiv, *Ukraine* **17 C13** 50 25N 24 32 E
Radford, *U.S.A.* **76 G5** 37 8N 80 34W
Radhanpur, *India* **42 H4** 23 50N 71 38 E
Radhwa, Jabal, *Si. Arabia* **44 E3** 24 34N 38 18 E
Radisson, *Qué., Canada* **70 B4** 53 47N 77 37W
Radisson, *Sask., Canada* **73 C7** 52 30N 107 20W
Radium Hot Springs, *Canada* **72 C5** 50 35N 116 2W
Radnor Forest, *U.K.* **11 E4** 52 17N 3 10W
Radom, *Poland* **17 C11** 51 23N 21 12 E
Radomsko, *Poland* **17 C10** 51 5N 19 28 E
Radomyshl, *Ukraine* **17 C15** 50 30N 29 12 E
Radstock, C., *Australia* **63 E1** 33 12S 134 20 E
Radviliškis, *Lithuania* **9 J20** 55 49N 23 33 E
Radville, *Canada* **73 D8** 49 30N 104 15W
Rae, *Canada* **72 A5** 62 50N 116 3W
Rae Bareli, *India* **43 F9** 26 18N 81 20 E
Rae Isthmus, *Canada* **69 B11** 66 40N 87 30W
Raeren, *Belgium* **15 D6** 50 41N 6 7 E
Raeside, L., *Australia* **61 E3** 29 20S 122 0 E
Raetihi, *N.Z.* **59 H5** 39 25S 175 17 E
Rafaela, *Argentina* **94 C3** 31 10S 61 30W
Rafah, *Gaza Strip* **47 D3** 31 18N 34 14 E
Rafai, *C.A.R.* **54 B1** 4 59N 23 58 E
Rafḩā, *Si. Arabia* **44 D4** 29 35N 43 35 E
Rafsanjān, *Iran* **45 D8** 30 30N 56 5 E
Raft Pt., *Australia* **60 C3** 16 4S 124 26 E
Râgâ, *Sudan* **51 G11** 8 28N 25 41 E
Ragachow, *Belarus* **17 B16** 53 8N 30 5 E
Ragama, *Sri Lanka* **40 R11** 7 0N 79 50 E
Ragged, Mt., *Australia* **61 F3** 33 27S 123 25 E
Raghunathpalli, *India* **43 H11** 22 14N 84 48 E
Raghunathpur, *India* **43 H12** 23 33N 86 40 E
Raglan, *N.Z.* **59 G5** 37 55S 174 55 E
Ragusa, *Italy* **20 F6** 36 55N 14 44 E
Raha, *Indonesia* **37 E6** 4 55S 123 0 E
Rahaeng = Tak, *Thailand* **38 D2** 16 52N 99 8 E
Rahatgarh, *India* **43 H8** 23 47N 78 22 E
Rahimyar Khan, *Pakistan* **42 E4** 28 30N 70 25 E
Rāhjerd, *Iran* **45 C6** 34 22N 50 22 E
Rahon, *India* **42 D7** 31 3N 76 7 E
Raichur, *India* **40 L10** 16 10N 77 20 E
Raiganj, *India* **43 G13** 25 37N 88 10 E
Raigarh, *India* **41 J13** 21 56N 83 25 E
Raijua, *Indonesia* **37 F6** 10 37S 121 36 E
Raikot, *India* **42 D6** 30 41N 75 42 E
Railton, *Australia* **62 G4** 41 25S 146 28 E
Rainbow Lake, *Canada* **72 B5** 58 30N 119 23W
Rainier, *U.S.A.* **84 D4** 46 53N 122 41W
Rainier, Mt., *U.S.A.* **84 D5** 46 52N 121 46W
Rainy L., *Canada* **73 D10** 48 42N 93 10W
Rainy River, *Canada* **73 D10** 48 43N 94 29W
Raippaluoto, *Finland* **8 E19** 63 13N 21 14 E
Raipur, *India* **41 J12** 21 17N 81 45 E
Raisen, *India* **42 H8** 23 20N 77 48 E
Raisio, *Finland* **9 F20** 60 28N 22 11 E
Raj Nandgaon, *India* **41 J12** 21 5N 81 5 E
Raj Nilgiri, *India* **43 J12** 21 28N 86 46 E
Raja, Ujung, *Indonesia* **36 D1** 3 40N 96 25 E
Raja Ampat, Kepulauan, *Indonesia* **37 E7** 0 30S 130 0 E
Rajahmundry, *India* **41 L12** 17 1N 81 48 E
Rajang →, *Malaysia* **36 D4** 2 30N 112 0 E
Rajanpur, *Pakistan* **42 E4** 29 6N 70 19 E
Rajapalaiyam, *India* **40 Q10** 9 25N 77 35 E
Rajasthan □, *India* **42 F5** 26 45N 73 30 E
Rajasthan Canal, *India* **42 F5** 28 0N 72 0 E
Rajauri, *India* **43 C6** 33 25N 74 21 E
Rajgarh, *Mad. P., India* **42 G7** 24 2N 76 45 E
Rajgarh, *Raj., India* **42 F7** 27 14N 76 38 E
Rajgarh, *Raj., India* **42 E6** 28 40N 75 25 E
Rajgir, *India* **43 G11** 25 2N 85 25 E
Rajkot, *India* **42 H4** 22 15N 70 56 E
Rajmahal Hills, *India* **43 G12** 24 30N 87 30 E
Rajpipla, *India* **40 J8** 21 50N 73 30 E
Rajpur, *India* **42 H6** 22 18N 74 21 E
Rajpura, *India* **42 D7** 30 25N 76 32 E
Rajshahi, *Bangla.* **41 G16** 24 22N 88 39 E
Rajshahi □, *Bangla.* **43 G13** 25 0N 89 0 E
Rajula, *India* **42 J4** 21 3N 71 26 E
Rakaia, *N.Z.* **59 K4** 43 45S 172 1 E
Rakaia →, *N.Z.* **59 K4** 43 36S 172 15 E
Rakan, Ra's, *Qatar* **45 E6** 26 10N 51 20 E
Rakaposhi, *Pakistan* **43 A6** 36 10N 74 25 E
Rakata, Pulau, *Indonesia* **36 F3** 6 10S 105 20 E
Rakhiv, *Ukraine* **17 D13** 48 3N 24 12 E
Rakhni, *Pakistan* **42 D3** 30 4N 69 56 E
Rakhni →, *Pakistan* **42 E3** 29 31N 69 36 E
Rakitnoye, *Russia* **30 B7** 45 36N 134 17 E
Rakops, *Botswana* **56 C3** 21 1S 24 28 E
Rakvere, *Estonia* **9 G22** 59 20N 26 25 E
Raleigh, *U.S.A.* **77 H6** 35 47N 78 39W
Ralls, *U.S.A.* **81 J4** 33 41N 101 24W
Ralston, *U.S.A.* **78 E8** 41 30N 76 57W
Ram →, *Canada* **72 A4** 62 1N 123 41W
Rām Allāh, *West Bank* **47 D4** 31 55N 35 10 E
Rama, *Nic.* **88 D3** 12 9N 84 15W
Ramakona, *India* **43 J8** 21 43N 78 50 E
Raman, *Thailand* **39 J3** 6 29N 101 18 E
Ramanathapuram, *India* **40 Q11** 9 25N 78 55 E
Ramanetaka, B. de, *Madag.* **57 A8** 14 13S 47 52 E
Ramanujganj, *India* **43 H10** 23 48N 83 42 E
Ramat Gan, *Israel* **47 C3** 32 4N 34 48 E
Ramatlhabama, *S. Africa* **56 D4** 25 37S 25 33 E
Ramban, *India* **43 C6** 33 14N 75 12 E
Rambipuji, *Indonesia* **37 H15** 8 12S 113 37 E
Ramechhap, *Nepal* **43 F12** 27 25N 86 10 E
Ramganga →, *India* **43 F8** 27 5N 79 58 E
Ramgarh, *Bihar, India* **43 H11** 23 40N 85 35 E
Ramgarh, *Raj., India* **42 F6** 27 16N 75 14 E
Ramgarh, *Raj., India* **42 F4** 27 30N 70 36 E
Rāmhormoz, *Iran* **45 D6** 31 15N 49 35 E
Ramīān, *Iran* **45 B7** 37 3N 55 16 E
Ramingining, *Australia* **62 A2** 12 19S 135 3 E
Ramla, *Israel* **47 D3** 31 55N 34 52 E
Ramnad = Ramanathapuram, *India* **40 Q11** 9 25N 78 55 E
Ramnagar, *Jammu & Kashmir, India* **43 C6** 32 47N 75 18 E
Ramnagar, *Ut. P., India* **43 E8** 29 24N 79 7 E
Râmnicu Sărat, *Romania* **17 F14** 45 26N 27 3 E
Râmnicu Vâlcea, *Romania* **17 F13** 45 9N 24 21 E
Ramona, *U.S.A.* **85 M10** 33 2N 116 52W
Ramore, *Canada* **70 C3** 48 30N 80 25W
Ramotswa, *Botswana* **56 C4** 24 50S 25 52 E
Rampur, *H.P., India* **42 D7** 31 26N 77 43 E
Rampur, *Mad. P., India* **42 H5** 23 25N 73 53 E
Rampur, *Ut. P., India* **43 E8** 28 50N 79 5 E
Rampur Hat, *India* **43 G12** 24 10N 87 50 E
Rampura, *India* **42 G6** 24 30N 75 27 E
Ramrama Tola, *India* **43 J8** 21 52N 79 55 E
Ramree I., *Burma* **41 K19** 19 0N 94 0 E
Rāmsar, *Iran* **45 B6** 36 53N 50 41 E
Ramsey, *U.K.* **10 C3** 54 20N 4 22W
Ramsey, *U.S.A.* **79 E10** 41 4N 74 9W
Ramsey L., *Canada* **70 C3** 47 13N 82 15W
Ramsgate, *U.K.* **11 F9** 51 20N 1 25 E
Ramtek, *India* **40 J11** 21 20N 79 15 E
Rana Pratap Sagar Dam, *India* **42 G6** 24 58N 75 38 E
Ranaghat, *India* **43 H13** 23 15N 88 35 E
Ranahu, *Pakistan* **42 G3** 25 55N 69 45 E
Ranau, *Malaysia* **36 C5** 6 2N 116 40 E
Rancagua, *Chile* **94 C1** 34 10S 70 50W
Rancheria →, *Canada* **72 A3** 60 13N 129 7W
Ranchester, *U.S.A.* **82 D10** 44 54N 107 10W
Ranchi, *India* **43 H11** 23 19N 85 27 E
Rancho Cucamonga, *U.S.A.* **85 L9** 34 10N 117 30W
Randalstown, *U.K.* **13 B5** 54 45N 6 19W
Randers, *Denmark* **9 H14** 56 29N 10 1 E
Randfontein, *S. Africa* **57 D4** 26 8S 27 45 E
Randle, *U.S.A.* **84 D5** 46 32N 121 57W
Randolph, *Mass., U.S.A.* **79 D13** 42 10N 71 2W
Randolph, *N.Y., U.S.A.* **78 D6** 42 10N 78 59W
Randolph, *Utah, U.S.A.* **82 F8** 41 40N 111 11W
Randolph, *Vt., U.S.A.* **79 C12** 43 55N 72 40W
Randsburg, *U.S.A.* **85 K9** 35 22N 117 39W
Råne älv →, *Sweden* **8 D20** 65 50N 22 20 E
Rangae, *Thailand* **39 J3** 6 19N 101 44 E
Rangaunu B., *N.Z.* **59 F4** 34 51S 173 15 E
Rangeley, *U.S.A.* **79 B14** 44 58N 70 39W
Rangeley L., *U.S.A.* **79 B14** 44 55N 70 43W
Rangely, *U.S.A.* **82 F9** 40 5N 108 48W
Ranger, *U.S.A.* **81 J5** 32 28N 98 41W
Rangia, *India* **41 F17** 26 28N 91 38 E
Rangiora, *N.Z.* **59 K4** 43 19S 172 36 E
Rangitaiki →, *N.Z.* **59 G6** 37 54S 176 49 E
Rangitata →, *N.Z.* **59 K3** 43 45S 171 15 E
Rangkasbitung, *Indonesia* **37 G12** 6 21S 106 15 E
Rangon →, *Burma* **41 L20** 16 28N 96 40 E
Rangoon, *Burma* **41 L20** 16 45N 96 20 E
Rangpur, *Bangla.* **41 G16** 25 42N 89 22 E
Rangsit, *Thailand* **38 F3** 13 59N 100 37 E
Ranibennur, *India* **40 M9** 14 35N 75 30 E
Raniganj, *Ut. P., India* **43 F9** 27 3N 82 13 E
Raniganj, *W. Bengal, India* **41 H15** 23 40N 87 5 E
Ranikhet, *India* **43 E8** 29 39N 79 25 E
Raniwara, *India* **40 G8** 24 50N 72 10 E
Rāniyah, *Iraq* **44 B5** 36 15N 44 53 E
Ranka, *India* **43 H10** 23 59N 83 47 E
Ranken →, *Australia* **62 C2** 20 31S 137 36 E
Rankin, *U.S.A.* **81 K4** 31 13N 101 56W
Rankin Inlet, *Canada* **68 B10** 62 30N 93 0W
Rannoch, L., *U.K.* **12 E4** 56 41N 4 20W
Rannoch Moor, *U.K.* **12 E4** 56 38N 4 48W
Ranobe, Helodranon' i, *Madag.* **57 C7** 23 3S 43 33 E
Ranohira, *Madag.* **57 C8** 22 29S 45 24 E
Ranomafana, *Toamasina, Madag.* **57 B8** 18 57S 48 50 E
Ranomafana, *Toliara, Madag.* **57 C8** 24 34S 47 0 E
Ranomena, *Madag.* **57 C8** 23 25S 47 17 E
Ranong, *Thailand* **39 H2** 9 56N 98 40 E
Ranotsara Nord, *Madag.* **57 C8** 22 48S 46 36 E
Rānsa, *Iran* **45 C6** 33 39N 48 18 E
Ransiki, *Indonesia* **37 E8** 1 30S 134 10 E
Rantabe, *Madag.* **57 B8** 15 42S 49 39 E
Rantauprapat, *Indonesia* **36 D1** 2 15N 99 50 E
Rantemario, *Indonesia* **37 E5** 3 15S 119 57 E
Rantoul, *U.S.A.* **76 E1** 40 19N 88 9W
Raoyang, *China* **34 E8** 38 15N 115 45 E
Rapa, *Pac. Oc.* **65 K13** 27 35S 144 20W
Rapallo, *Italy* **18 D8** 44 21N 9 14 E
Rapar, *India* **42 H4** 23 34N 70 38 E
Rāpch, *Iran* **45 E8** 25 40N 59 15 E
Raper, C., *Canada* **69 B13** 69 44N 67 6W
Rapid City, *U.S.A.* **80 D3** 44 5N 103 14W
Rapid River, *U.S.A.* **76 C2** 45 55N 86 58W
Rapla, *Estonia* **9 G21** 59 1N 24 52 E
Rapti →, *India* **43 F10** 26 18N 83 41 E
Raquette →, *U.S.A.* **79 B10** 45 0N 74 42W

Raquette Lake

Raquette Lake, *U.S.A.* **79 C10** 43 49N 74 40W
Rarotonga, *Cook Is.* **65 K12** 21 30S 160 0W
Ra's al 'Ayn, *Syria* **44 B4** 36 45N 40 12 E
Ra's al Khaymah, *U.A.E.* **46 B6** 25 50N 55 59 E
Rasca, Pta. de la, *Canary Is.* **22 G3** 27 59N 16 41W
Raseiniai, *Lithuania* **9 J20** 55 25N 23 5 E
Rashmi, *India* **42 G6** 25 4N 74 22 E
Rasht, *Iran* **45 B6** 37 20N 49 40 E
Rasi Salai, *Thailand* **38 E5** 15 20N 104 9 E
Rason L., *Australia* **61 E3** 28 45S 124 25 E
Rasra, *India* **43 G10** 25 50N 83 50 E
Rasul, *Pakistan* **42 C5** 32 42N 73 34 E
Rat Buri, *Thailand* **38 F2** 13 30N 99 54 E
Rat Islands, *U.S.A.* **68 C1** 52 0N 178 0 E
Rat L., *Canada* **73 B9** 56 10N 99 40W
Ratangarh, *India* **42 E6** 28 5N 74 35 E
Raṭāwī, *Iraq* **44 D5** 30 38N 47 13 E
Rath, *India* **43 G8** 25 36N 79 37 E
Rath Luirc, *Ireland* **13 D3** 52 21N 8 40W
Rathdrum, *Ireland* **13 D5** 52 56N 6 14W
Rathenow, *Germany* **16 B7** 52 37N 12 19 E
Rathkeale, *Ireland* **13 D3** 52 32N 8 56W
Rathlin I., *U.K.* **13 A5** 55 18N 6 14W
Rathmelton, *Ireland* **13 A4** 55 2N 7 38W
Ratibor = Racibórz, *Poland* **17 C10** 50 7N 18 18 E
Ratlam, *India* **42 H6** 23 20N 75 0 E
Ratnagiri, *India* **40 L8** 16 57N 73 18 E
Ratodero, *Pakistan* **42 F3** 27 48N 68 18 E
Raton, *U.S.A.* **81 G2** 36 54N 104 24W
Rattaphum, *Thailand* **39 J3** 7 8N 100 16 E
Rattray Hd., *U.K.* **12 D7** 57 38N 1 50W
Ratz, Mt., *Canada* **72 B2** 57 23N 132 12W
Raub, *Malaysia* **39 L3** 3 47N 101 52 E
Rauch, *Argentina* **94 D4** 36 45S 59 5W
Raudales de Malpaso, *Mexico* **87 D6** 17 30N 23 30W
Raufarhöfn, *Iceland* **8 C6** 66 27N 15 57W
Raufoss, *Norway* **9 F14** 60 44N 10 37 E
Raukumara Ra., *N.Z.* **59 H6** 38 5S 177 55 E
Rauma, *Finland* **9 F19** 61 10N 21 30 E
Raurkela, *India* **43 H11** 22 14N 84 50 E
Rausu-Dake, *Japan* **30 B12** 44 4N 145 7 E
Rava-Ruska, *Poland* **17 C12** 50 15N 23 42 E
Rava Russkaya = Rava-Ruska, *Poland* **17 C12** 50 15N 23 42 E
Ravalli, *U.S.A.* **82 C6** 47 17N 114 11W
Ravānsar, *Iran* **44 C5** 34 43N 46 40 E
Rāvar, *Iran* **45 D8** 31 20N 56 51 E
Ravena, *U.S.A.* **79 D11** 42 28N 73 49W
Ravenna, *Italy* **20 B5** 44 25N 12 12 E
Ravenna, *Nebr., U.S.A.* **80 E5** 41 1N 98 55W
Ravenna, *Ohio, U.S.A.* **78 E3** 41 9N 81 15W
Ravensburg, *Germany* **16 E5** 47 46N 9 36 E
Ravenshoe, *Australia* **62 B4** 17 37S 145 29 E
Ravensthorpe, *Australia* **61 F3** 33 35S 120 2 E
Ravenswood, *Australia* **62 C4** 20 6S 146 54 E
Ravenswood, *U.S.A.* **76 F5** 38 57N 81 46W
Ravi →, *Pakistan* **42 D4** 30 35N 71 49 E
Rawalpindi, *Pakistan* **42 C5** 33 38N 73 8 E
Rawāndūz, *Iraq* **44 B5** 36 40N 44 30 E
Rawang, *Malaysia* **39 L3** 3 20N 101 35 E
Rawene, *N.Z.* **59 F4** 35 25S 173 32 E
Rawlinna, *Australia* **61 F4** 30 58S 125 28 E
Rawlins, *U.S.A.* **82 F10** 41 47N 107 14W
Rawlinson Ra., *Australia* **61 D4** 24 40S 128 30 E
Rawson, *Argentina* **96 E3** 43 15S 65 5W
Raxaul, *India* **43 F11** 26 59N 84 51 E
Ray, *U.S.A.* **80 A3** 48 21N 103 10W
Ray, C., *Canada* **71 C8** 47 33N 59 15W
Rayadurg, *India* **40 M10** 14 40N 76 50 E
Rayagada, *India* **41 K13** 19 15N 83 20 E
Raychikhinsk, *Russia* **27 E13** 49 46N 129 25 E
Rāyen, *Iran* **45 D8** 29 34N 57 26 E
Rayleigh, *U.K.* **11 F8** 51 36N 0 37 E
Raymond, *Canada* **72 D6** 49 30N 112 35W
Raymond, *Calif., U.S.A.* **84 H7** 37 13N 119 54W
Raymond, *N.H., U.S.A.* **79 C13** 43 2N 71 11W
Raymond, *Wash., U.S.A.* **84 D3** 46 41N 123 44W
Raymondville, *U.S.A.* **81 M6** 26 29N 97 47W
Raymore, *Canada* **73 C8** 51 25N 104 31W
Rayón, *Mexico* **86 B2** 29 43N 110 35W
Rayong, *Thailand* **38 F3** 12 40N 101 20 E
Rayville, *U.S.A.* **81 J9** 32 29N 91 46W
Raz, Pte. du, *France* **18 C1** 48 2N 4 47W
Razan, *Iran* **45 C6** 35 23N 49 2 E
Razdel'naya = Rozdilna, *Ukraine* **17 E16** 46 50N 30 2 E
Razdolnoye, *Russia* **30 C5** 43 30N 131 52 E
Razeh, *Iran* **45 C6** 32 47N 48 9 E
Razgrad, *Bulgaria* **21 C12** 43 33N 26 34 E
Razim, Lacul, *Romania* **17 F15** 44 50N 29 0 E
Razmak, *Pakistan* **42 C3** 32 45N 69 50 E
Ré, Î. de, *France* **18 C3** 46 12N 1 30W
Reading, *U.K.* **11 F7** 51 27N 0 58W
Reading, *U.S.A.* **79 F9** 40 20N 75 56W
Reading □, *U.K.* **11 F7** 51 27N 0 58W
Realicó, *Argentina* **94 D3** 35 0S 64 15W
Ream, *Cambodia* **39 G4** 10 34N 103 39 E
Reata, *Mexico* **86 B4** 26 8N 101 5W
Reay Forest, *U.K.* **12 C4** 58 22N 4 55W
Rebi, *Indonesia* **37 F8** 6 23S 134 7 E
Rebiana, *Libya* **51 D10** 24 12N 22 10 E
Rebun-Tō, *Japan* **30 B10** 45 23N 141 2 E
Recherche, Arch. of the, *Australia* **61 F3** 34 15S 122 50 E
Rechna Doab, *Pakistan* **42 D5** 31 35N 73 30 E
Rechytsa, *Belarus* **17 B16** 52 21N 30 24 E
Recife, *Brazil* **93 E12** 8 0S 35 0W
Recklinghausen, *Germany* **15 C7** 51 37N 7 12 E
Reconquista, *Argentina* **94 B4** 29 10S 59 45W
Recreo, *Argentina* **94 B2** 29 25S 65 10W
Red →, *La., U.S.A.* **81 K9** 31 1N 91 45W
Red →, *N. Dak., U.S.A.* **68 C10** 49 0N 97 15W
Red Bank, *U.S.A.* **79 F10** 40 21N 74 5W
Red Bay, *Canada* **71 B8** 51 44N 56 25W
Red Bluff, *U.S.A.* **82 F2** 40 11N 122 15W
Red Bluff L., *U.S.A.* **81 K3** 31 54N 103 55W
Red Cloud, *U.S.A.* **80 E5** 40 5N 98 32W
Red Creek, *U.S.A.* **79 C8** 43 14N 76 45W
Red Deer, *Canada* **72 C6** 52 20N 113 50W
Red Deer →, *Alta., Canada* **73 C7** 50 58N 110 0W
Red Deer →, *Man., Canada* **73 C8** 52 53N 101 1W
Red Deer L., *Canada* **73 C8** 52 55N 101 20W
Red Hook, *U.S.A.* **79 E11** 41 55N 73 53W
Red Indian L., *Canada* **71 C8** 48 35N 57 0W
Red L., *Canada* **73 C10** 51 3N 93 49W
Red Lake, *Canada* **73 C10** 51 3N 93 49W
Red Lake Falls, *U.S.A.* **80 B6** 47 53N 96 16W
Red Lake Road, *Canada* **73 C10** 49 59N 93 25W
Red Lodge, *U.S.A.* **82 D9** 45 11N 109 15W
Red Mountain, *U.S.A.* **85 K9** 35 37N 117 38W
Red Oak, *U.S.A.* **80 E7** 41 1N 95 14W
Red Rock, *Canada* **70 C2** 48 55N 88 15W
Red Rock, L., *U.S.A.* **80 E8** 41 22N 92 59W
Red Rocks Pt., *Australia* **61 F4** 32 13S 127 32 E
Red Sea, *Asia* **46 C2** 25 0N 36 0 E
Red Slate Mt., *U.S.A.* **84 H8** 37 31N 118 52W
Red Sucker L., *Canada* **70 B1** 54 9N 93 40W
Red Tower Pass = Turnu Roşu, P., *Romania* **17 F13** 45 33N 24 17 E
Red Wing, *U.S.A.* **80 C8** 44 34N 92 31W
Redang, *Malaysia* **36 C2** 5 49N 103 2 E
Redange, *Lux.* **15 E5** 49 46N 5 52 E
Redcar, *U.K.* **10 C6** 54 37N 1 4W
Redcar & Cleveland □, *U.K.* **10 C7** 54 29N 1 0W
Redcliff, *Canada* **73 C6** 50 10N 110 50W
Redcliffe, *Australia* **63 D5** 27 12S 153 0 E
Redcliffe, Mt., *Australia* **61 E3** 28 30S 121 30 E
Reddersburg, *S. Africa* **56 D4** 29 41S 26 10 E
Redding, *U.S.A.* **82 F2** 40 35N 122 24W
Redditch, *U.K.* **11 E6** 52 18N 1 55W
Redfield, *U.S.A.* **80 C5** 44 53N 98 31W
Redford, *U.S.A.* **79 B11** 44 38N 73 48W
Redlands, *U.S.A.* **85 M9** 34 4N 117 11W
Redmond, *Oreg., U.S.A.* **82 D3** 44 17N 121 11W
Redmond, *Wash., U.S.A.* **84 C4** 47 41N 122 7W
Redon, *France* **18 C2** 47 40N 2 6W
Redonda, *Antigua* **89 C7** 16 58N 62 19W
Redondela, *Spain* **19 A1** 42 15N 8 38W
Redondo Beach, *U.S.A.* **85 M8** 33 50N 118 23W
Redruth, *U.K.* **11 G2** 50 14N 5 14W
Redvers, *Canada* **73 D8** 49 35N 101 40W
Redwater, *Canada* **72 C6** 53 55N 113 6W
Redwood, *U.S.A.* **79 B9** 44 18N 75 48W
Redwood City, *U.S.A.* **84 H4** 37 30N 122 15W
Redwood Falls, *U.S.A.* **80 C7** 44 32N 95 7W
Redwood National Park, *U.S.A.* **82 F1** 41 40N 124 5W
Ree, L., *Ireland* **13 C3** 53 35N 8 0W
Reed, L., *Canada* **73 C8** 54 38N 100 30W
Reed City, *U.S.A.* **76 D3** 43 53N 85 31W
Reedley, *U.S.A.* **84 J7** 36 36N 119 27W
Reedsburg, *U.S.A.* **80 D9** 43 32N 90 0W
Reedsport, *U.S.A.* **82 E1** 43 42N 124 6W
Reedsville, *U.S.A.* **78 F7** 40 39N 77 35W
Reefton, *N.Z.* **59 K3** 42 6S 171 51 E
Reese →, *U.S.A.* **82 F5** 40 48N 117 4W
Refugio, *U.S.A.* **81 L6** 28 18N 97 17W
Regensburg, *Germany* **16 D7** 49 1N 12 6 E
Reggâne = Zaouiet Reggâne, *Algeria* **50 C6** 26 32N 0 3 E
Réggio di Calábria, *Italy* **20 E6** 38 6N 15 39 E
Réggio nell'Emília, *Italy* **20 B4** 44 43N 10 36 E
Reghin, *Romania* **17 E13** 46 46N 24 42 E
Regina, *Canada* **73 C8** 50 27N 104 35W
Regina Beach, *Canada* **73 C8** 50 47N 105 0W
Registro, *Brazil* **95 A6** 24 29S 47 49W
Rehar →, *India* **43 H10** 23 55N 82 40 E
Rehli, *India* **43 H8** 23 38N 79 5 E
Rehoboth, *Namibia* **56 C2** 23 15S 17 4 E
Rehovot, *Israel* **47 D3** 31 54N 34 48 E
Reichenbach, *Germany* **16 C7** 50 37N 12 17 E
Reid, *Australia* **61 F4** 30 49S 128 26 E
Reidsville, *U.S.A.* **77 G6** 36 21N 79 40W
Reigate, *U.K.* **11 F7** 51 14N 0 12W
Reims, *France* **18 B6** 49 15N 4 1 E
Reina Adelaida, Arch., *Chile* **96 G2** 52 20S 74 0W
Reindeer →, *Canada* **73 B8** 55 36N 103 11W
Reindeer I., *Canada* **73 C9** 52 30N 98 0W
Reindeer L., *Canada* **73 B8** 57 15N 102 15W
Reinga, C., *N.Z.* **59 F4** 34 25S 172 43 E
Reinosa, *Spain* **19 A3** 43 2N 4 15W
Reitz, *S. Africa* **57 D4** 27 48S 28 29 E
Reivilo, *S. Africa* **56 D3** 27 36S 24 8 E
Reliance, *Canada* **73 A7** 63 0N 109 20W
Rembang, *Indonesia* **37 G14** 6 42S 111 21 E
Remedios, *Panama* **88 E3** 8 15N 81 50W
Remeshk, *Iran* **45 E8** 26 55N 58 50 E
Remich, *Lux.* **15 E6** 49 32N 6 22 E
Remscheid, *Germany* **15 C7** 51 11N 7 12 E
Ren Xian, *China* **34 F8** 37 8N 114 40 E
Rendsburg, *Germany* **16 A5** 54 17N 9 39 E
Renfrew, *Canada* **79 A8** 45 30N 76 40W
Renfrewshire □, *U.K.* **12 F4** 55 49N 4 38W
Rengat, *Indonesia* **36 E2** 0 30S 102 45 E
Rengo, *Chile* **94 C1** 34 24S 70 50W
Reni, *Ukraine* **17 F15** 45 28N 28 15 E
Rennell Sd., *Canada* **72 C2** 53 23N 132 35W
Renner Springs, *Australia* **62 B1** 18 20S 133 47 E
Rennes, *France* **18 B3** 48 7N 1 41W
Rennie L., *Canada* **73 A7** 61 32N 105 35W
Reno, *U.S.A.* **84 F7** 39 31N 119 48W
Reno →, *Italy* **20 B5** 44 38N 12 16 E
Renovo, *U.S.A.* **78 E7** 41 20N 77 45W
Renqiu, *China* **34 E9** 38 43N 116 5 E
Rensselaer, *Ind., U.S.A.* **76 E2** 40 57N 87 9W
Rensselaer, *N.Y., U.S.A.* **79 D11** 42 38N 73 45W
Rentería, *Spain* **19 A5** 43 19N 1 54W
Renton, *U.S.A.* **84 C4** 47 29N 122 12W
Reotipur, *India* **43 G10** 25 33N 83 45 E
Republic, *Mo., U.S.A.* **81 G8** 37 7N 93 29W
Republic, *Wash., U.S.A.* **82 B4** 48 39N 118 44W
Republican →, *U.S.A.* **80 F6** 39 4N 96 48W
Repulse Bay, *Canada* **69 B11** 66 30N 86 30W
Requena, *Peru* **92 E4** 5 5S 73 52W
Requena, *Spain* **19 C5** 39 30N 1 4W
Reşadiye = Datça, *Turkey* **21 F12** 36 46N 27 40 E
Reserve, *U.S.A.* **83 K9** 33 43N 108 45W
Resht = Rasht, *Iran* **45 B6** 37 20N 49 40 E
Resistencia, *Argentina* **94 B4** 27 30S 59 0W
Reşiţa, *Romania* **17 F11** 45 18N 21 53 E
Resolution I., *Canada* **69 B13** 61 30N 65 0W
Resolution I., *N.Z.* **59 L1** 45 40S 166 40 E
Ressano Garcia, *Mozam.* **57 D5** 25 25S 32 0 E
Reston, *Canada* **73 D8** 49 33N 101 6W
Retalhuleu, *Guatemala* **88 D1** 14 33N 91 46W
Retenue, L. de, *Dem. Rep. of the Congo* **55 E2** 11 0S 27 0 E
Retford, *U.K.* **10 D7** 53 19N 0 56W
Réthímnon, *Greece* **23 D6** 35 18N 24 30 E
Réthímnon □, *Greece* **23 D6** 35 23N 24 28 E
Reti, *Pakistan* **42 E3** 28 5N 69 48 E
Réunion ■, *Ind. Oc.* **49 J9** 21 0S 56 0 E
Reus, *Spain* **19 B6** 41 10N 1 5 E
Reutlingen, *Germany* **16 D5** 48 29N 9 12 E
Reval = Tallinn, *Estonia* **9 G21** 59 22N 24 48 E
Revda, *Russia* **24 C10** 56 48N 59 57 E
Revelganj, *India* **43 G11** 25 50N 84 40 E
Revelstoke, *Canada* **72 C5** 51 0N 118 10W
Reventazón, *Peru* **92 E2** 6 10S 80 58W
Revillagigedo, Is. de, *Pac. Oc.* **86 D2** 18 40N 112 0W
Revuè →, *Mozam.* **55 F3** 19 50S 34 0 E
Rewa, *India* **43 G9** 24 33N 81 25 E
Rewari, *India* **42 E7** 28 15N 76 40 E
Rexburg, *U.S.A.* **82 E8** 43 49N 111 47W
Rey, *Iran* **45 C6** 35 35N 51 25 E
Rey, I. del, *Panama* **88 E4** 8 20N 78 30W
Rey Malabo, *Eq. Guin.* **52 D1** 3 45N 8 50 E
Reyðarfjörður, *Iceland* **8 D6** 65 2N 14 13W
Reyes, Pt., *U.S.A.* **84 H3** 38 0N 123 0W
Reykjahlið, *Iceland* **8 D5** 65 40N 16 55W
Reykjanes, *Iceland* **8 E2** 63 48N 22 40W
Reykjavík, *Iceland* **8 D3** 64 10N 21 57W
Reynolds Ra., *Australia* **60 D5** 22 30S 133 0 E
Reynoldsville, *U.S.A.* **78 E6** 41 5N 78 58W
Reynosa, *Mexico* **87 B5** 26 5N 98 18W
Rēzekne, *Latvia* **9 H22** 56 30N 27 17 E
Rezvān, *Iran* **45 E8** 27 34N 56 6 E
Rhayader, *U.K.* **11 E4** 52 18N 3 29W
Rhein →, *Europe* **15 C6** 51 52N 6 2 E
Rhein-Main-Donau-Kanal, *Germany* **16 D6** 49 1N 11 27 E
Rheine, *Germany* **16 B4** 52 17N 7 26 E
Rheinland-Pfalz □, *Germany* **16 C4** 50 0N 7 0 E
Rhin = Rhein →, *Europe* **15 C6** 51 52N 6 2 E
Rhine = Rhein →, *Europe* **15 C6** 51 52N 6 2 E
Rhinebeck, *U.S.A.* **79 E11** 41 56N 73 55W
Rhineland-Palatinate = Rheinland-Pfalz □, *Germany* **16 C4** 50 0N 7 0 E
Rhinelander, *U.S.A.* **80 C10** 45 38N 89 25W
Rhinns Pt., *U.K.* **12 F2** 55 40N 6 29W
Rhino Camp, *Uganda* **54 B3** 3 0N 31 22 E
Rhir, Cap, *Morocco* **50 B4** 30 38N 9 54W
Rhode Island □, *U.S.A.* **79 E13** 41 40N 71 30W
Rhodes = Ródhos, *Greece* **23 C10** 36 15N 28 10 E
Rhodesia = Zimbabwe ■, *Africa* **55 F3** 19 0S 30 0 E
Rhodope Mts. = Rhodopi Planina, *Bulgaria* **21 D11** 41 40N 24 20 E
Rhodopi Planina, *Bulgaria* **21 D11** 41 40N 24 20 E
Rhön, *Germany* **16 C5** 50 24N 9 58 E
Rhondda, *U.K.* **11 F4** 51 39N 3 31W
Rhondda Cynon Taff □, *U.K.* **11 F4** 51 42N 3 27W
Rhône →, *France* **18 E6** 43 28N 4 42 E
Rhum, *U.K.* **12 E2** 57 0N 6 20W
Rhyl, *U.K.* **10 D4** 53 20N 3 29W
Riachão, *Brazil* **93 E9** 7 20S 46 37W
Riasi, *India* **43 C6** 33 10N 74 50 E
Riau □, *Indonesia* **36 D2** 0 0 102 35 E
Riau, Kepulauan, *Indonesia* **36 D2** 0 30N 104 20 E
Riau Arch. = Riau, Kepulauan, *Indonesia* **36 D2** 0 30N 104 20 E
Ribadeo, *Spain* **19 A2** 43 35N 7 5W
Ribas do Rio Pardo, *Brazil* **93 H8** 20 27S 53 46W
Ribble →, *U.K.* **10 D5** 53 52N 2 25W
Ribe, *Denmark* **9 J13** 55 19N 8 44 E
Ribeira Brava, *Madeira* **22 D2** 32 41N 17 4W
Ribeirão Prêto, *Brazil* **95 A6** 21 10S 47 50W
Riberalta, *Bolivia* **92 F5** 11 0S 66 0W
Riccarton, *N.Z.* **59 K4** 43 32S 172 37 E
Rice, *U.S.A.* **85 L12** 34 5N 114 51W
Rice L., *Canada* **78 B6** 44 12N 78 10W
Rice Lake, *U.S.A.* **80 C9** 45 30N 91 44W
Rich, C., *Canada* **78 B4** 44 43N 80 38W
Richards Bay, *S. Africa* **57 D5** 28 48S 32 6 E
Richardson →, *Canada* **73 B6** 58 25N 111 14W
Richardson Lakes, *U.S.A.* **76 C10** 44 46N 70 58W
Richardson Springs, *U.S.A.* **84 F5** 39 51N 121 46W
Riche, C., *Australia* **61 F2** 34 36S 118 47 E
Richey, *U.S.A.* **80 B2** 47 39N 105 4W
Richfield, *U.S.A.* **83 G8** 38 46N 112 5W
Richfield Springs, *U.S.A.* **79 D10** 42 51N 74 59W
Richford, *U.S.A.* **79 B12** 45 0N 72 40W
Richibucto, *Canada* **71 C7** 46 42N 64 54W
Richland, *Ga., U.S.A.* **77 J3** 32 5N 84 40W
Richland, *Wash., U.S.A.* **82 C4** 46 17N 119 18W
Richland Center, *U.S.A.* **80 D9** 43 21N 90 23W
Richlands, *U.S.A.* **76 G5** 37 6N 81 48W
Richmond, *Australia* **62 C3** 20 43S 143 8 E
Richmond, *N.Z.* **59 J4** 41 20S 173 12 E
Richmond, *U.K.* **10 C6** 54 25N 1 43W
Richmond, *Calif., U.S.A.* **84 H4** 37 56N 122 21W
Richmond, *Ind., U.S.A.* **76 F3** 39 50N 84 53W
Richmond, *Ky., U.S.A.* **76 G3** 37 45N 84 18W
Richmond, *Mich., U.S.A.* **78 D2** 42 49N 82 45W
Richmond, *Mo., U.S.A.* **80 F8** 39 17N 93 58W
Richmond, *Tex., U.S.A.* **81 L7** 29 35N 95 46W
Richmond, *Utah, U.S.A.* **82 F8** 41 56N 111 48W
Richmond, *Va., U.S.A.* **76 G7** 37 33N 77 27W
Richmond, *Vt., U.S.A.* **79 B12** 44 24N 72 59W
Richmond Hill, *Canada* **78 C5** 43 52N 79 27W
Richmond Ra., *Australia* **63 D5** 29 0S 152 45 E
Richwood, *U.S.A.* **76 F5** 38 14N 80 32W
Ridder = Leninogorsk, *Kazakstan* **26 D9** 50 20N 83 30 E
Riddlesburg, *U.S.A.* **78 F6** 40 9N 78 15W
Ridgecrest, *U.S.A.* **85 K9** 35 38N 117 40W
Ridgefield, *Conn., U.S.A.* **79 E11** 41 17N 73 30W
Ridgefield, *Wash., U.S.A.* **84 E4** 45 49N 122 45W
Ridgeland, *U.S.A.* **77 J5** 32 29N 80 59W
Ridgetown, *Canada* **78 D3** 42 26N 81 52W
Ridgewood, *U.S.A.* **79 F10** 40 59N 74 7W
Ridgway, *U.S.A.* **78 E6** 41 25N 78 44W
Riding Mountain Nat. Park, *Canada* **73 C9** 50 50N 100 0W
Ridley, Mt., *Australia* **61 F3** 33 12S 122 7 E
Riebeek-Oos, *S. Africa* **56 E4** 33 10S 26 10 E
Ried, *Austria* **16 D7** 48 14N 13 30 E
Riesa, *Germany* **16 C7** 51 17N 13 17 E
Riet →, *S. Africa* **56 D3** 29 0S 23 54 E
Rietbron, *S. Africa* **56 E3** 32 54S 23 10 E
Rietfontein, *Namibia* **56 C3** 21 58S 20 58 E
Rieti, *Italy* **20 C5** 42 24N 12 51 E
Riffe L., *U.S.A.* **84 D4** 46 32N 122 26W
Rifle, *U.S.A.* **82 G10** 39 32N 107 47W
Rift Valley □, *Kenya* **54 B4** 0 20N 36 0 E
Rīga, *Latvia* **9 H21** 56 53N 24 8 E
Riga, G. of, *Latvia* **9 H20** 57 40N 23 45 E
Rīgān, *Iran* **45 D8** 28 37N 58 58 E
Rīgas Jūras Līcis = Riga, G. of, *Latvia* **9 H20** 57 40N 23 45 E
Rigaud, *Canada* **79 A10** 45 29N 74 18W
Rigby, *U.S.A.* **82 E8** 43 40N 111 55W
Rīgestān, *Afghan.* **40 D4** 30 15N 65 0 E
Riggins, *U.S.A.* **82 D5** 45 25N 116 19W
Rigolet, *Canada* **71 B8** 54 10N 58 23W
Rihand Dam, *India* **43 G10** 24 9N 83 2 E
Riihimäki, *Finland* **9 F21** 60 45N 24 48 E
Riiser-Larsen-halvøya, *Antarctica* **5 C4** 68 0S 35 0 E
Rijeka, *Croatia* **16 F8** 45 20N 14 21 E
Rijssen, *Neths.* **15 B6** 52 19N 6 31 E
Rikuzentakada, *Japan* **30 E10** 39 0N 141 40 E
Riley, *U.S.A.* **82 E4** 43 32N 119 28W
Rimah, Wadi ar →, *Si. Arabia* **44 E4** 26 5N 41 30 E
Rimbey, *Canada* **72 C6** 52 35N 114 15W
Rimersburg, *U.S.A.* **78 E5** 41 3N 79 30W
Rímini, *Italy* **20 B5** 44 3N 12 33 E
Rimouski, *Canada* **71 C6** 48 27N 68 30W
Rimrock, *U.S.A.* **84 D5** 46 38N 121 10W
Rinca, *Indonesia* **37 F5** 8 45S 119 35 E
Rincón de Romos, *Mexico* **86 C4** 22 14N 102 18W
Rinconada, *Argentina* **94 A2** 22 26S 66 10W
Rind →, *India* **43 G9** 25 53N 80 33 E
Ringas, *India* **42 F6** 27 21N 75 34 E
Ringkøbing, *Denmark* **9 H13** 56 5N 8 15 E
Ringvassøy, *Norway* **8 B18** 69 56N 19 15 E
Ringwood, *U.S.A.* **79 E10** 41 7N 74 15W
Rinjani, *Indonesia* **36 F5** 8 24S 116 28 E
Rio Branco, *Brazil* **92 E5** 9 58S 67 49W
Río Branco, *Uruguay* **95 C5** 32 40S 53 40W
Río Bravo del Norte →, *Mexico* **87 B5** 25 57N 97 9W
Rio Brilhante, *Brazil* **95 A5** 21 48S 54 33W
Rio Claro, *Brazil* **95 A6** 22 19S 47 35W
Rio Claro, *Trin. & Tob.* **89 D7** 10 20N 61 25W
Río Colorado, *Argentina* **96 D4** 39 0S 64 0W
Río Cuarto, *Argentina* **94 C3** 33 10S 64 25W
Rio das Pedras, *Mozam.* **57 C6** 23 8S 35 28 E
Rio de Janeiro, *Brazil* **95 A7** 23 0S 43 12W
Rio de Janeiro □, *Brazil* **95 A7** 22 50S 43 0W
Rio do Sul, *Brazil* **95 B6** 27 13S 49 37W
Río Gallegos, *Argentina* **96 G3** 51 35S 69 15W
Río Grande = Grande, Rio →, *U.S.A.* **81 N6** 25 58N 97 9W
Río Grande, *Argentina* **96 G3** 53 50S 67 45W
Rio Grande, *Brazil* **95 C5** 32 0S 52 20W
Río Grande, *Mexico* **86 C4** 23 50N 103 2W
Río Grande, *Nic.* **88 D3** 12 54N 83 33W
Rio Grande City, *U.S.A.* **81 M5** 26 23N 98 49W
Río Grande de Santiago →, *Mexico* **86 C3** 21 36N 105 26W
Rio Grande do Norte □, *Brazil* **93 E11** 5 40S 36 0W
Rio Grande do Sul □, *Brazil* **95 C5** 30 0S 53 0W
Río Hato, *Panama* **88 E3** 8 22N 80 10W
Río Lagartos, *Mexico* **87 C7** 21 36N 88 10W
Rio Largo, *Brazil* **93 E11** 9 28S 35 50W
Río Mulatos, *Bolivia* **92 G5** 19 40S 66 50W
Río Muni = Mbini □, *Eq. Guin.* **52 D2** 1 30N 10 0 E
Rio Negro, *Brazil* **95 B6** 26 0S 49 55W
Rio Pardo, *Brazil* **95 C5** 30 0S 52 30W
Rio Rancho, *U.S.A.* **83 J10** 35 14N 106 38W
Río Segundo, *Argentina* **94 C3** 31 40S 63 59W
Río Tercero, *Argentina* **94 C3** 32 15S 64 8W
Rio Verde, *Brazil* **93 G8** 17 50S 51 0W
Río Verde, *Mexico* **87 C5** 21 56N 99 59W
Rio Vista, *U.S.A.* **84 G5** 38 10N 121 42W
Riobamba, *Ecuador* **92 D3** 1 50S 78 45W
Ríohacha, *Colombia* **92 A4** 11 33N 72 55W
Ríosucio, *Colombia* **92 B3** 7 27N 77 7W
Riou L., *Canada* **73 B7** 59 7N 106 25W
Ripley, *Canada* **78 B3** 44 4N 81 35W
Ripley, *Calif., U.S.A.* **85 M12** 33 32N 114 39W
Ripley, *N.Y., U.S.A.* **78 D5** 42 16N 79 43W
Ripley, *Tenn., U.S.A.* **81 H10** 35 45N 89 32W
Ripley, *W. Va., U.S.A.* **76 F5** 38 49N 81 43W
Ripon, *U.K.* **10 C6** 54 9N 1 31W
Ripon, *Calif., U.S.A.* **84 H5** 37 44N 121 7W
Ripon, *Wis., U.S.A.* **76 D1** 43 51N 88 50W
Rishā', W. ar →, *Si. Arabia* **44 E5** 25 33N 44 5 E
Rishiri-Tō, *Japan* **30 B10** 45 11N 141 15 E
Rishon le Ẕiyyon, *Israel* **47 D3** 31 58N 34 48 E
Rison, *U.S.A.* **81 J8** 33 58N 92 11W
Risør, *Norway* **9 G13** 58 43N 9 13 E
Rita Blanca Cr. →, *U.S.A.* **81 H3** 35 40N 102 29W
Ritter, Mt., *U.S.A.* **84 H7** 37 41N 119 12W
Rittman, *U.S.A.* **78 F3** 40 58N 81 47W
Ritzville, *U.S.A.* **82 C4** 47 8N 118 23W
Riva del Garda, *Italy* **20 B4** 45 53N 10 50 E
Rivadavia, *Buenos Aires, Argentina* **94 D3** 35 29S 62 59W
Rivadavia, *Mendoza, Argentina* **94 C2** 33 13S 68 30W
Rivadavia, *Salta, Argentina* **94 A3** 24 5S 62 54W
Rivadavia, *Chile* **94 B1** 29 57S 70 35W
Rivas, *Nic.* **88 D2** 11 30N 85 50W
River Cess, *Liberia* **50 G4** 5 30N 9 32W
River Jordan, *Canada* **84 B2** 48 26N 124 3W
Rivera, *Argentina* **94 D3** 37 12S 63 14W
Rivera, *Uruguay* **95 C4** 31 0S 55 50W
Riverbank, *U.S.A.* **84 H6** 37 44N 120 56W
Riverdale, *U.S.A.* **84 J7** 36 26N 119 52W
Riverhead, *U.S.A.* **79 F12** 40 55N 72 40W
Riverhurst, *Canada* **73 C7** 50 55N 106 50W
Rivers, *Canada* **73 C8** 50 2N 100 14W
Rivers Inlet, *Canada* **72 C3** 51 42N 127 15W
Riversdale, *S. Africa* **56 E3** 34 7S 21 15 E
Riverside, *U.S.A.* **85 M9** 33 59N 117 22W
Riverton, *Canada* **73 C9** 51 1N 97 0W
Riverton, *N.Z.* **59 M2** 46 21S 168 0 E
Riverton, *U.S.A.* **82 E9** 43 2N 108 23W
Riverton Heights, *U.S.A.* **84 C4** 47 28N 122 17W
Riviera, *U.S.A.* **85 K12** 35 4N 114 35W
Riviera di Levante, *Italy* **18 D8** 44 15N 9 30 E
Riviera di Ponente, *Italy* **18 D8** 44 10N 8 20 E
Rivière-au-Renard, *Canada* **71 C7** 48 59N 64 23W
Rivière-du-Loup, *Canada* **71 C6** 47 50N 69 30W

Rzhev

Rivière-Pentecôte, *Canada* **71 C6** 49 57N 67 1W
Rivière-Pilote, *Martinique* . **89 D7** 14 26N 60 53W
Rivière St. Paul, *Canada* .. **71 B8** 51 28N 57 45W
Rivne, *Ukraine* .... **17 C14** 50 40N 26 10 E
Rivoli, *Italy* .... **18 D7** 45 3N 7 31 E
Riyadh = Ar Riyāḍ,
Si. Arabia .... **46 C4** 24 41N 46 42 E
Rize, *Turkey* .... **25 F7** 41 0N 40 30 E
Rizhao, *China* .... **35 G10** 35 25N 119 30 E
Rizokarpaso, *Cyprus* ..... **23 D13** 35 36N 34 23 E
Rizzuto, C., *Italy* .... **20 E7** 38 53N 17 5 E
Rjukan, *Norway* .... **9 G13** 59 54N 8 33 E
Road Town, *Br. Virgin Is.* .. **89 C7** 18 27N 64 37W
Roan Plateau, *U.S.A.* **82 G9** 39 20N 109 20W
Roanne, *France* .... **18 C6** 46 3N 4 4 E
Roanoke, *Ala., U.S.A.* **77 J3** 33 9N 85 22W
Roanoke, *Va., U.S.A.* **76 G6** 37 16N 79 56W
Roanoke →, *U.S.A.* **77 H7** 35 57N 76 42W
Roanoke I., *U.S.A.* **77 H8** 35 55N 75 40W
Roanoke Rapids, *U.S.A.* **77 G7** 36 28N 77 40W
Roatán, *Honduras* **88 C2** 16 18N 86 35W
Robāt Sang, *Iran* .... **45 C8** 35 35N 59 10 E
Robbins I., *Australia* ...... **62 G4** 40 42S 145 0 E
Robe →, *Australia* .... **60 D2** 21 42S 116 15 E
Robert Lee, *U.S.A.* **81 K4** 31 54N 100 29W
Robertsdale, *U.S.A.* **78 F6** 40 11N 78 6W
Robertsganj, *India* .... **43 G10** 24 44N 83 4 E
Robertson, *S. Africa* ...... **56 E2** 33 46S 19 50 E
Robertson I., *Antarctica* ... **5 C18** 65 15S 59 30W
Robertson Ra., *Australia* .. **60 D3** 23 15S 121 0 E
Roberval, *Canada* **71 C5** 48 32N 72 15W
Robeson Chan., *Greenland* **4 A4** 82 0N 61 30W
Robesonia, *U.S.A.* **79 F8** 40 21N 76 8W
Robinson, *U.S.A.* **76 F2** 39 0N 87 44W
Robinson →, *Australia* ... **62 B2** 16 3S 137 16 E
Robinson Ra., *Australia* ... **61 E2** 25 40S 119 0 E
Roblin, *Canada* **73 C8** 51 14N 101 21W
Roboré, *Bolivia* **92 G7** 18 10S 59 45W
Robson, *Canada* **72 D5** 49 20N 117 41W
Robson, Mt., *Canada* **72 C5** 53 10N 119 10W
Robstown, *U.S.A.* **81 M6** 27 47N 97 40W
Roca, C. da, *Portugal* **19 C1** 38 40N 9 31W
Roca Partida, I., *Mexico* ... **86 D2** 19 1N 112 2W
Rocas, I., *Brazil* **93 D12** 4 0S 34 1W
Rocha, *Uruguay* **95 C5** 34 30S 54 25W
Rochdale, *U.K.* **10 D5** 53 38N 2 9W
Rochefort, *Belgium* .... **15 D5** 50 9N 5 12 E
Rochefort, *France* **18 D3** 45 56N 0 57W
Rochelle, *U.S.A.* **80 E10** 41 56N 89 4W
Rocher River, *Canada* **72 A6** 61 23N 112 44W
Rochester, *U.K.* .... **11 F8** 51 23N 0 31 E
Rochester, *Ind., U.S.A.* **76 E2** 41 4N 86 13W
Rochester, *Minn., U.S.A.* ... **80 C8** 44 1N 92 28W
Rochester, *N.H., U.S.A.* ... **79 C14** 43 18N 70 59W
Rochester, *N.Y., U.S.A.* ... **78 C7** 43 10N 77 37W
Rock →, *Canada* **72 A3** 60 7N 127 7W
Rock Creek, *U.S.A.* **78 E4** 41 40N 80 52W
Rock Falls, *U.S.A.* **80 E10** 41 47N 89 41W
Rock Hill, *U.S.A.* **77 H5** 34 56N 81 1W
Rock Island, *U.S.A.* **80 E9** 41 30N 90 34W
Rock Rapids, *U.S.A.* **80 D6** 43 26N 96 10W
Rock Sound, *Bahamas* **88 B4** 24 54N 76 12W
Rock Springs, *Mont., U.S.A.* **82 C10** 46 49N 106 15W
Rock Springs, *Wyo., U.S.A.* **82 F9** 41 35N 109 14W
Rock Valley, *U.S.A.* **80 D6** 43 12N 96 18W
Rockall, *Atl. Oc.* **6 D3** 57 37N 13 42W
Rockdale, *Tex., U.S.A.* **81 K6** 30 39N 97 0W
Rockdale, *Wash., U.S.A.* ... **84 C5** 47 22N 121 28W
Rockefeller Plateau,
Antarctica **5 E14** 80 0S 140 0W
Rockford, *U.S.A.* **80 D10** 42 16N 89 6W
Rockglen, *Canada* **73 D7** 49 11N 105 57W
Rockhampton, *Australia* .. **62 C5** 23 22S 150 32 E
Rockingham, *Australia* .... **61 F2** 32 15S 115 38 E
Rockingham, *U.S.A.* **77 H6** 34 57N 79 46W
Rockingham B., *Australia* . **62 B4** 18 5S 146 10 E
Rocklake, *U.S.A.* **80 A5** 48 47N 99 15W
Rockland, *Canada* **79 A9** 45 33N 75 17W
Rockland, *Idaho, U.S.A.* ... **82 E7** 42 34N 112 53W
Rockland, *Maine, U.S.A.* ... **77 C11** 44 6N 69 7W
Rockland, *Mich., U.S.A.* ... **80 B10** 46 44N 89 11W
Rocklin, *U.S.A.* **84 G5** 38 48N 121 14W
Rockmart, *U.S.A.* **77 H3** 34 0N 85 3W
Rockport, *Mass., U.S.A.* ... **79 D14** 42 39N 70 37W
Rockport, *Mo., U.S.A.* **80 E7** 40 25N 95 31W
Rockport, *Tex., U.S.A.* **81 L6** 28 2N 97 3W
Rocksprings, *U.S.A.* **81 K4** 30 1N 100 13W
Rockville, *Conn., U.S.A.* ... **79 E12** 41 52N 72 28W
Rockville, *Md., U.S.A.* **76 F7** 39 5N 77 9W
Rockwall, *U.S.A.* **81 J6** 32 56N 96 28W
Rockwell City, *U.S.A.* **80 D7** 42 24N 94 38W
Rockwood, *Canada* **78 C4** 43 37N 80 8W
Rockwood, *Maine, U.S.A.* . **77 C11** 45 41N 69 45W
Rockwood, *Tenn., U.S.A.* .. **77 H3** 35 52N 84 41W
Rocky Ford, *U.S.A.* **80 F3** 38 3N 103 43W
Rocky Gully, *Australia* .... **61 F2** 34 30S 116 57 E
Rocky Harbour, *Canada* ... **71 C8** 49 36N 57 55W
Rocky Island L., *Canada* ... **70 C3** 46 55N 83 0W
Rocky Lane, *Canada* **72 B5** 58 31N 116 22W
Rocky Mount, *U.S.A.* **77 H7** 35 57N 77 48W
Rocky Mountain House,
Canada **72 C6** 52 22N 114 55W
Rocky Mountain National
Park, *U.S.A.* **82 F11** 40 25N 105 45W
Rocky Mts., *N. Amer.* **82 G10** 49 0N 115 0W
Rocky Point, *Namibia* ..... **56 B2** 19 3S 12 30 E
Rod, *Pakistan* .... **40 E3** 28 10N 63 5 E
Rødbyhavn, *Denmark* ..... **9 J14** 54 39N 11 22 E
Roddickton, *Canada* **71 B8** 50 51N 56 8W
Rodez, *France* .... **18 D5** 44 21N 2 33 E
Rodhopoú, *Greece* .... **23 D5** 35 34N 23 45 E
Ródhos, *Greece* .... **23 C10** 36 15N 28 10 E
Rodney, *Canada* **78 D3** 42 34N 81 41W
Rodney, C., *N.Z.* .... **59 G5** 36 17S 174 50 E
Rodriguez, *Ind. Oc.* .... **3 E13** 19 45S 63 20 E
Roe →, *U.K.* **13 A5** 55 6N 6 59W
Roebling, *U.S.A.* **79 F10** 40 7N 74 47W
Roebourne, *Australia* ..... **60 D2** 20 44S 117 9 E
Roebuck B., *Australia* ..... **60 C3** 18 5S 122 20 E
Roermond, *Neths.* .... **15 C6** 51 12N 6 0 E
Roes Welcome Sd., *Canada* **69 B11** 65 0N 87 0W
Roeselare, *Belgium* .... **15 D3** 50 57N 3 7 E
Rogachev = Ragachow,
Belarus .... **17 B16** 53 8N 30 5 E
Rogagua, L., *Bolivia* **92 F5** 13 43S 66 50W
Rogatyn, *Ukraine* .... **17 D13** 49 24N 24 36 E
Rogdhia, *Greece* .... **23 D7** 35 22N 25 1 E
Rogers, *U.S.A.* **81 G7** 36 20N 94 7W
Rogers City, *U.S.A.* **76 C4** 45 25N 83 49W
Rogersville, *Canada* **71 C6** 46 44N 65 26W
Roggan →, *Canada* **70 B4** 54 24N 79 25W
Roggan L., *Canada* **70 B4** 54 8N 77 50W
Roggeveldberge, *S. Africa* **56 E3** 32 10S 20 10 E
Rogoaguado, L., *Bolivia* ... **92 F5** 13 0S 65 30W
Rogue →, *U.S.A.* **82 E1** 42 26N 124 26W
Róhda, *Greece* .... **23 A3** 39 48N 19 46 E
Rohnert Park, *U.S.A.* **84 G4** 38 16N 122 40W
Rohri, *Pakistan* .... **42 F3** 27 45N 68 51 E
Rohri Canal, *Pakistan* ..... **42 F3** 26 15N 68 27 E
Rohtak, *India* .... **42 E7** 28 55N 76 43 E
Roi Et, *Thailand* .... **38 D4** 16 4N 103 40 E
Roja, *Latvia* .... **9 H20** 57 29N 22 43 E
Rojas, *Argentina* **94 C3** 34 10S 60 45W
Rojo, C., *Mexico* **87 C5** 21 33N 97 20W
Rokan →, *Indonesia* ..... **36 D2** 2 0N 100 50 E
Rokiškis, *Lithuania* .... **9 J21** 55 55N 25 35 E
Rolândia, *Brazil* **95 A5** 23 18S 51 23W
Rolla, *U.S.A.* **81 G9** 37 57N 91 46W
Rolleston, *Australia* ...... **62 C4** 24 28S 148 35 E
Rollingstone, *Australia* ... **62 B4** 19 2S 146 24 E
Roma, *Australia* .... **63 D4** 26 32S 148 49 E
Roma, *Italy* .... **20 D5** 41 54N 12 29 E
Roma, *Sweden* .... **9 H18** 57 32N 18 26 E
Roma, *U.S.A.* **81 M5** 26 25N 99 1W
Romain C., *U.S.A.* **77 J6** 33 0N 79 22W
Romaine, *Canada* **71 B7** 50 13N 60 40W
Romaine →, *Canada* **71 B7** 50 18N 63 47W
Roman, *Romania* .... **17 E14** 46 57N 26 55 E
Romang, *Indonesia* .... **37 F7** 7 30S 127 20 E
Români, *Egypt* .... **47 E1** 30 59N 32 38 E
Romania ■, *Europe* .... **17 F12** 46 0N 25 0 E
Romano, Cayo, *Cuba* **88 B4** 22 0N 77 30W
Romanovka =
Basarabeasca, *Moldova* . **17 E15** 46 21N 28 58 E
Romans-sur-Isère, *France* . **18 D6** 45 3N 5 3 E
Romblon, *Phil.* .... **37 B6** 12 33N 122 17 E
Rome = Roma, *Italy* .... **20 D5** 41 54N 12 29 E
Rome, *Ga., U.S.A.* **77 H3** 34 15N 85 10W
Rome, *N.Y., U.S.A.* **79 C9** 43 13N 75 27W
Rome, *Pa., U.S.A.* **79 E8** 41 51N 76 21W
Romney, *U.S.A.* **76 F6** 39 21N 78 45W
Romney Marsh, *U.K.* ...... **11 F8** 51 2N 0 54 E
Rømø, *Denmark* .... **9 J13** 55 10N 8 30 E
Romorantin-Lanthenay,
France .... **18 C4** 47 21N 1 45 E
Romsdalen, *Norway* ...... **9 E12** 62 25N 7 52 E
Romsey, *U.K.* **11 G6** 51 0N 1 29W
Ron, *Vietnam* .... **38 D6** 17 53N 106 27 E
Rona, *U.K.* **12 D3** 57 34N 5 59W
Ronan, *U.S.A.* **82 C6** 47 32N 114 6W
Roncador, Cayos,
Caribbean **88 D3** 13 32N 80 4W
Roncador, Serra do, *Brazil* **93 F8** 12 30S 52 30W
Ronda, *Spain* **19 D3** 36 46N 5 12W
Rondane, *Norway* .... **9 F13** 61 57N 9 50 E
Rondônia □, *Brazil* **92 F6** 11 0S 63 0W
Rondonópolis, *Brazil* **93 G8** 16 28S 54 38W
Rong, Koh, *Cambodia* ..... **39 G4** 10 45N 103 15 E
Ronge, L. la, *Canada* **73 B7** 55 6N 105 17W
Rønne, *Denmark* .... **9 J16** 55 6N 14 43 E
Ronne Ice Shelf, *Antarctica* **5 D18** 78 0S 60 0W
Ronsard, C., *Australia* .... **61 D1** 24 46S 113 10 E
Ronse, *Belgium* .... **15 D3** 50 45N 3 35 E
Roodepoort, *S. Africa* .... **57 D4** 26 11S 27 54 E
Roof Butte, *U.S.A.* **83 H9** 36 28N 109 5W
Rooiboklaagte →, *Namibia* **56 C3** 20 50S 21 0 E
Roorkee, *India* .... **42 E7** 29 52N 77 59 E
Roosendaal, *Neths.* .... **15 C4** 51 32N 4 29 E
Roosevelt, *U.S.A.* **82 F8** 40 18N 109 59W
Roosevelt →, *Brazil* **92 E6** 7 35S 60 20W
Roosevelt, Mt., *Canada* **72 B3** 58 26N 125 20W
Roosevelt I., *Antarctica* ... **5 D12** 79 30S 162 0W
Roper →, *Australia* ...... **62 A2** 14 43S 135 27 E
Roper Bar, *Australia* ...... **62 A1** 14 44S 134 44 E
Roque Pérez, *Argentina* ... **94 D4** 35 25S 59 24W
Roquetas de Mar, *Spain* ... **19 D4** 36 46N 2 36W
Roraima □, *Brazil* **92 C6** 2 0N 61 30W
Roraima, Mt., *Venezuela* .. **92 B6** 5 10N 60 40W
Røros, *Norway* .... **9 E14** 62 35N 11 23 E
Rosa, *Zambia* .... **55 D3** 9 33S 31 15 E
Rosa, L., *Bahamas* **89 B5** 21 0N 73 30W
Rosa, Monte, *Europe* ...... **18 D7** 45 57N 7 53 E
Rosalia, *U.S.A.* **82 C5** 47 14N 117 22W
Rosamond, *U.S.A.* **85 L8** 34 52N 118 10W
Rosario, *Argentina* **94 C3** 33 0S 60 40W
Rosário, *Brazil* **93 D10** 3 0S 44 15W
Rosario, *Baja Calif., Mexico* **86 B1** 30 0N 115 50W
Rosario, *Sinaloa, Mexico* .. **86 C3** 23 0N 105 52W
Rosario, *Paraguay* **94 A4** 24 30S 57 35W
Rosario de la Frontera,
Argentina **94 B3** 25 50S 65 0W
Rosario de Lerma,
Argentina **94 A2** 24 59S 65 35W
Rosario del Tala, *Argentina* **94 C4** 32 20S 59 10W
Rosário do Sul, *Brazil* **95 C5** 30 15S 54 55W
Rosarito, *Mexico* **85 N9** 32 18N 117 4W
Roscoe, *U.S.A.* **79 E10** 41 56N 74 55W
Roscommon, *Ireland* **13 C3** 53 38N 8 11W
Roscommon □, *Ireland* **13 C3** 53 49N 8 23W
Roscrea, *Ireland* **13 D4** 52 57N 7 49W
Rose →, *Australia* .... **62 A2** 14 16S 135 45 E
Rose Blanche, *Canada* **71 C8** 47 38N 58 45W
Rose Pt., *Canada* **72 C2** 54 11N 131 39W
Rose Valley, *Canada* **73 C8** 52 19N 103 49W
Roseau, *Domin.* **89 C7** 15 20N 61 24W
Roseau, *U.S.A.* **80 A7** 48 51N 95 46W
Rosebery, *Australia* .... **62 G4** 41 46S 145 33 E
Rosebud, *S. Dak., U.S.A.* .. **80 D4** 43 14N 100 51W
Rosebud, *Tex., U.S.A.* **81 K6** 31 4N 96 59W
Roseburg, *U.S.A.* **82 E2** 43 13N 123 20W
Rosedale, *U.S.A.* **81 J9** 33 51N 91 2W
Roseland, *U.S.A.* **84 G4** 38 25N 122 43W
Rosemary, *Canada* **72 C6** 50 46N 112 5W
Rosenberg, *U.S.A.* **81 L7** 29 34N 95 49W
Rosenheim, *Germany* ...... **16 E7** 47 51N 12 7 E
Roses, G. de, *Spain* .... **19 A7** 42 10N 3 15 E
Rosetown, *Canada* **73 C7** 51 35N 107 59W
Roseville, *Calif., U.S.A.* ... **84 G5** 38 45N 121 17W
Roseville, *Mich., U.S.A.* ... **78 D2** 42 30N 82 56W
Rosewood, *Australia* ...... **63 D5** 27 38S 152 36 E
Roshkhvār, *Iran* .... **45 C8** 34 58N 59 37 E
Rosignano Maríttimo, *Italy* **20 C4** 43 24N 10 28 E
Rosignol, *Guyana* **92 B7** 6 15N 57 30W
Roşiori de Vede, *Romania* . **17 F13** 44 9N 25 0 E
Roskilde, *Denmark* .... **9 J15** 55 38N 12 3 E
Roslavl, *Russia* .... **24 D5** 53 57N 32 55 E
Rosmead, *S. Africa* .... **56 E4** 31 29S 25 8 E
Ross, *Australia* .... **62 G4** 42 2S 147 30 E
Ross, *N.Z.* .... **59 K3** 42 53S 170 49 E
Ross I., *Antarctica* .... **5 D11** 77 30S 168 0 E
Ross Ice Shelf, *Antarctica* . **5 E12** 80 0S 180 0 E
Ross L., *U.S.A.* **82 B3** 48 44N 121 4W
Ross-on-Wye, *U.K.* **11 F5** 51 54N 2 34W
Ross River, *Australia* ..... **62 C1** 23 44S 134 30 E
Ross River, *Canada* **72 A2** 62 30N 131 30W
Ross Sea, *Antarctica* ...... **5 D11** 74 0S 178 0 E
Rossall Pt., *U.K.* **10 D4** 53 55N 3 3W
Rossan Pt., *Ireland* **13 B3** 54 42N 8 47W
Rossano, *Italy* .... **20 E7** 39 36N 16 39 E
Rossburn, *Canada* **73 C8** 50 40N 100 49W
Rosseau, *Canada* **78 A5** 45 16N 79 39W
Rosseau L., *Canada* **78 A5** 45 10N 79 35W
Rosses, The, *Ireland* **13 A3** 55 2N 8 20W
Rossignol, L., *Canada* **70 B5** 52 43N 73 40W
Rossignol Res., *Canada* ... **71 D6** 44 12N 65 10W
Rossland, *Canada* **72 D5** 49 6N 117 50W
Rosslare, *Ireland* **13 D5** 52 17N 6 24W
Rosso, *Mauritania* **50 E2** 16 40N 15 45W
Rossosh, *Russia* .... **25 D6** 50 15N 39 28 E
Røssvatnet, *Norway* ...... **8 D16** 65 45N 14 5 E
Røst, *Norway* .... **8 C15** 67 32N 12 0 E
Rosthern, *Canada* **73 C7** 52 40N 106 20W
Rostock, *Germany* .... **16 A7** 54 5N 12 8 E
Rostov, *Don, Russia* ...... **25 E6** 47 15N 39 45 E
Rostov, *Yaroslavl, Russia* . **24 C6** 57 14N 39 25 E
Roswell, *Ga., U.S.A.* **77 H3** 34 2N 84 22W
Roswell, *N. Mex., U.S.A.* .. **81 J2** 33 24N 104 32W
Rotan, *U.S.A.* **81 J4** 32 51N 100 28W
Rother →, *U.K.* .... **11 G8** 50 59N 0 45 E
Rotherham, *U.K.* **10 D6** 53 26N 1 20W
Rothes, *U.K.* **12 D5** 57 32N 3 13W
Rothesay, *Canada* **71 C6** 45 23N 66 0W
Rothesay, *U.K.* **12 F3** 55 50N 5 3W
Roti, *Indonesia* .... **37 F6** 10 50S 123 0 E
Rotondo, Mte., *France* .... **18 E8** 42 14N 9 8 E
Rotoroa, L., *N.Z.* .... **59 J4** 41 55S 172 39 E
Rotorua, *N.Z.* .... **59 H6** 38 9S 176 16 E
Rotorua, L., *N.Z.* .... **59 H6** 38 5S 176 18 E
Rotterdam, *Neths.* .... **15 C4** 51 55N 4 30 E
Rotterdam, *U.S.A.* **79 D10** 42 48N 74 1W
Rottnest I., *Australia* ..... **61 F2** 32 0S 115 27 E
Rottumeroog, *Neths.* ...... **15 A6** 53 33N 6 34 E
Rottweil, *Germany* .... **16 D5** 48 9N 8 37 E
Rotuma, *Fiji* .... **64 J9** 12 25S 177 5 E
Roubaix, *France* .... **18 A5** 50 40N 3 10 E
Rouen, *France* .... **18 B4** 49 27N 1 4 E
Rouleau, *Canada* **73 C8** 50 10N 104 56W
Round Mountain, *U.S.A.* ... **82 G5** 38 43N 117 4W
Round Mt., *Australia* ...... **63 E5** 30 26S 152 16 E
Round Rock, *U.S.A.* **81 K6** 30 31N 97 41W
Roundup, *U.S.A.* **82 C9** 46 27N 108 33W
Rousay, *U.K.* **12 B5** 59 10N 3 2W
Rouses Point, *U.S.A.* **79 B11** 44 59N 73 22W
Rouseville, *U.S.A.* **78 E5** 41 28N 79 42W
Roussillon, *France* .... **18 E5** 42 30N 2 35 E
Rouxville, *S. Africa* .... **56 E4** 30 25S 26 50 E
Rouyn-Noranda, *Canada* ... **70 C4** 48 20N 79 0W
Rovaniemi, *Finland* .... **8 C21** 66 29N 25 41 E
Rovereto, *Italy* .... **20 B4** 45 53N 11 3 E
Rovigo, *Italy* .... **20 B4** 45 4N 11 47 E
Rovinj, *Croatia* .... **16 F7** 45 5N 13 40 E
Rovno = Rivne, *Ukraine* ... **17 C14** 50 40N 26 10 E
Rovuma = Ruvuma →,
Tanzania .... **55 E5** 10 29S 40 28 E
Row'ān, *Iran* .... **45 C6** 35 8N 48 51 E
Rowena, *Australia* .... **63 D4** 29 48S 148 55 E
Rowley Shoals, *Australia* . **60 C2** 17 30S 119 0 E
Roxas, *Phil.* .... **37 B6** 11 36N 122 49 E
Roxboro, *U.S.A.* **77 G6** 36 24N 78 59W
Roxburgh, *N.Z.* .... **59 L2** 45 33S 169 19 E
Roxbury, *U.S.A.* **78 F7** 40 6N 77 39W
Roy, *Mont., U.S.A.* **82 C9** 47 20N 108 58W
Roy, *N. Mex., U.S.A.* **81 H2** 35 57N 104 12W
Roy, *Utah, U.S.A.* **82 F7** 41 10N 112 2W
Royal Canal, *Ireland* **13 C4** 53 30N 7 13W
Royal Leamington Spa,
U.K. **11 E6** 52 18N 1 31W
Royal Tunbridge Wells,
U.K. .... **11 F8** 51 7N 0 16 E
Royan, *France* **18 D3** 45 37N 1 2W
Royston, *U.K.* **11 E7** 52 3N 0 0W
Rozdilna, *Ukraine* .... **17 E16** 46 50N 30 2 E
Rozhyshche, *Ukraine* ..... **17 C13** 50 54N 25 15 E
Rtishchevo, *Russia* .... **24 C7** 52 18N 43 46 E
Ruacaná, *Namibia* .... **56 B1** 17 27S 14 21 E
Ruahine Ra., *N.Z.* .... **59 H6** 39 55S 176 2 E
Ruapehu, *N.Z.* .... **59 H5** 39 17S 175 35 E
Ruapuke I., *N.Z.* .... **59 M2** 46 46S 168 31 E
Ruâq, W. →, *Egypt* ...... **47 F2** 30 0N 33 49 E
Rub' al Khālī, *Si. Arabia* .. **46 D4** 18 0N 48 0 E
Rubeho Mts., *Tanzania* .... **54 D4** 6 50S 36 25 E
Rubh a' Mhail, *U.K.* **12 F2** 55 56N 6 8W
Rubha Hunish, *U.K.* **12 D2** 57 42N 6 20W
Rubha Robhanais = Lewis,
Butt of, *U.K.* **12 C2** 58 31N 6 16W
Rubicon →, *U.S.A.* **84 G5** 38 53N 121 4W
Rubio, *Venezuela* **92 B4** 7 43N 72 22W
Rubtsovsk, *Russia* .... **26 D9** 51 30N 81 10 E
Ruby L., *U.S.A.* **82 F6** 40 10N 115 28W
Ruby Mts., *U.S.A.* **82 F6** 40 30N 115 20W
Rubyvale, *Australia* ...... **62 C4** 23 25S 147 42 E
Rūd Sar, *Iran* .... **45 B6** 37 8N 50 18 E
Rudall →, *Australia* ..... **60 D3** 22 34S 122 13 E
Rudewa, *Tanzania* .... **55 E3** 10 7S 34 40 E
Rudnyy, *Kazakstan* .... **26 D7** 52 57N 63 7 E
Rudolfa, Ostrov, *Russia* ... **26 A6** 81 45N 58 30 E
Rudyard, *U.S.A.* **76 B3** 46 14N 84 36W
Rufiji →, *Tanzania* .... **54 D4** 7 50S 39 15 E
Rufino, *Argentina* **94 C3** 34 20S 62 50W
Rufunsa, *Zambia* .... **55 F2** 15 4S 29 34 E
Rugby, *U.K.* **11 E6** 52 23N 1 16W
Rugby, *U.S.A.* **80 A5** 48 22N 100 0W
Rügen, *Germany* .... **16 A7** 54 22N 13 24 E
Ruhengeri, *Rwanda* .... **54 C2** 1 30S 29 36 E
Ruhnu, *Estonia* .... **9 H20** 57 48N 23 15 E
Ruhr →, *Germany* .... **16 C4** 51 27N 6 43 E
Ruhuhu →, *Tanzania* ..... **55 E3** 10 31S 34 34 E
Ruidoso, *U.S.A.* **83 K11** 33 20N 105 41W
Ruivo, Pico, *Madeira* **22 D3** 32 45N 16 56W
Rujm Tal'at al Jamā'ah,
Jordan .... **47 E4** 30 24N 35 30 E
Ruk, *Pakistan* .... **42 F3** 27 50N 68 42 E
Rukhla, *Pakistan* .... **42 C4** 32 27N 71 57 E
Ruki →, *Dem. Rep. of
the Congo* .... **52 E3** 0 5N 18 17 E
Rukwa □, *Tanzania* .... **54 D3** 7 0S 31 30 E
Rukwa, L., *Tanzania* ...... **54 D3** 8 0S 32 20 E
Rulhieres, C., *Australia* .... **60 B4** 13 56S 127 22 E
Rum = Rhum, *U.K.* **12 E2** 57 0N 6 20W
Rum Cay, *Bahamas* **89 B5** 23 40N 74 58W
Rum Jungle, *Australia* .... **60 B5** 13 0S 130 59 E
Rumāḥ, *Si. Arabia* .... **44 E5** 25 29N 47 10 E
Rumania = Romania ■,
Europe .... **17 F12** 46 0N 25 0 E
Rumaylah, *Iraq* .... **44 D5** 30 47N 47 37 E
Rumbêk, *Sudan* .... **51 G11** 6 54N 29 37 E
Rumford, *U.S.A.* **77 C10** 44 33N 70 33W
Rumia, *Poland* .... **17 A10** 54 37N 18 25 E
Rumoi, *Japan* .... **30 C10** 43 56N 141 39 E
Rumonge, *Burundi* .... **54 C2** 3 59S 29 26 E
Rumson, *U.S.A.* **79 F11** 40 23N 74 0W
Rumuruti, *Kenya* .... **54 B4** 0 17N 36 32 E
Runan, *China* .... **34 H8** 33 0N 114 30 E
Runanga, *N.Z.* .... **59 K3** 42 25S 171 15 E
Runaway, C., *N.Z.* .... **59 G6** 37 32S 177 59 E
Runcorn, *U.K.* **10 D5** 53 21N 2 44W
Rundu, *Namibia* .... **56 B2** 17 52S 19 43 E
Rungwa, *Tanzania* .... **54 D3** 6 55S 33 32 E
Rungwa →, *Tanzania* .... **54 D3** 7 36S 31 50 E
Rungwe, *Tanzania* .... **55 D3** 9 11S 33 32 E
Rungwe, Mt., *Tanzania* .... **52 F6** 9 8S 33 40 E
Runton Ra., *Australia* ..... **60 D3** 23 31S 123 6 E
Ruoqiang, *China* .... **32 C3** 38 55N 88 10 E
Rupa, *India* .... **41 F18** 27 15N 92 21 E
Rupar, *India* .... **42 D7** 31 2N 76 38 E
Rupat, *Indonesia* .... **36 D2** 1 45N 101 40 E
Rupen →, *India* .... **42 H4** 23 28N 71 31 E
Rupert, *U.S.A.* **82 E7** 42 37N 113 41W
Rupert →, *Canada* **70 B4** 51 29N 78 45W
Rupert B., *Canada* **70 B4** 51 35N 79 0W
Rupert House =
Waskaganish, *Canada* .. **70 B4** 51 30N 78 40W
Rupsa, *India* .... **43 J12** 21 37N 87 1 E
Rurrenabaque, *Bolivia* **92 F5** 14 30S 67 32W
Rusambo, *Zimbabwe* ..... **55 F3** 16 30S 32 4 E
Rusape, *Zimbabwe* .... **55 F3** 18 35S 32 8 E
Ruschuk = Ruse, *Bulgaria* . **21 C12** 43 48N 25 59 E
Ruse, *Bulgaria* .... **21 C12** 43 48N 25 59 E
Rush, *Ireland* **13 C5** 53 31N 6 6W
Rushan, *China* .... **35 F11** 36 56N 121 30 E
Rushden, *U.K.* **11 E7** 52 18N 0 35W
Rushmore, Mt., *U.S.A.* **80 D3** 43 53N 103 28W
Rushville, *Ill., U.S.A.* **80 E9** 40 7N 90 34W
Rushville, *Ind., U.S.A.* **76 F3** 39 37N 85 27W
Rushville, *Nebr., U.S.A.* ... **80 D3** 42 43N 102 28W
Russas, *Brazil* **93 D11** 4 55S 37 50W
Russell, *Canada* **73 C8** 50 50N 101 20W
Russell, *Kans., U.S.A.* **80 F5** 38 54N 98 52W
Russell, *N.Y., U.S.A.* **79 B9** 44 27N 75 9W
Russell, *Pa., U.S.A.* **78 E5** 41 56N 79 8W
Russell L., *Man., Canada* .. **73 B8** 56 15N 101 30W
Russell L., *N.W.T., Canada* **72 A5** 63 5N 115 44W
Russellkonda, *India* ...... **41 K14** 19 57N 84 42 E
Russellville, *Ala., U.S.A.* .. **77 H2** 34 30N 87 44W
Russellville, *Ark., U.S.A.* .. **81 H8** 35 17N 93 8W
Russellville, *Ky., U.S.A.* .. **77 G2** 36 51N 86 53W
Russia ■, *Eurasia* .... **27 C11** 62 0N 105 0 E
Russian →, *U.S.A.* **84 G3** 38 27N 123 8W
Russkoye Ustie, *Russia* ... **4 B15** 71 0N 149 0 E
Rustam, *Pakistan* .... **42 B5** 34 25N 72 13 E
Rustam Shahr, *Pakistan* ... **42 F2** 26 58N 66 6 E
Rustavi, *Georgia* .... **25 F8** 41 30N 45 0 E
Rustenburg, *S. Africa* ..... **56 D4** 25 41S 27 14 E
Ruston, *U.S.A.* **81 J8** 32 32N 92 38W
Rutana, *Burundi* .... **54 C3** 3 55S 30 0 E
Ruteng, *Indonesia* .... **37 F6** 8 35S 120 30 E
Ruth, *U.S.A.* **78 C2** 43 42N 82 45W
Rutherford, *U.S.A.* **84 G4** 38 26N 122 24W
Rutland, *U.S.A.* **79 C12** 43 37N 72 58W
Rutland □, *U.K.* **11 E7** 52 38N 0 40W
Rutland Water, *U.K.* **11 E7** 52 39N 0 38W
Rutledge →, *Canada* **73 A6** 61 4N 112 0W
Rutledge L., *Canada* **73 A6** 61 33N 110 47W
Rutshuru, *Dem. Rep. of
the Congo* .... **54 C2** 1 13S 29 25 E
Ruvu, *Tanzania* .... **54 D4** 6 49S 38 43 E
Ruvu →, *Tanzania* .... **54 D4** 6 23S 38 52 E
Ruvuma □, *Tanzania* ..... **55 E4** 10 20S 36 0 E
Ruvuma →, *Tanzania* .... **55 E5** 10 29S 40 28 E
Ruwais, *U.A.E.* .... **45 E7** 24 5N 52 50 E
Ruwenzori, *Africa* .... **54 B2** 0 30N 29 55 E
Ruya →, *Zimbabwe* ...... **57 B5** 16 27S 32 5 E
Ruyigi, *Burundi* .... **54 C3** 3 29S 30 15 E
Ružomberok, *Slovak Rep.* . **17 D10** 49 3N 19 17 E
Rwanda ■, *Africa* .... **54 C3** 2 0S 30 0 E
Ryan, L., *U.K.* **12 G3** 55 0N 5 2W
Ryazan, *Russia* .... **24 D6** 54 40N 39 40 E
Ryazhsk, *Russia* .... **24 D7** 53 45N 40 3 E
Rybache = Rybachye,
Kazakstan .... **26 E9** 46 40N 81 20 E
Rybachiy Poluostrov,
Russia .... **24 A5** 69 43N 32 0 E
Rybachye, *Kazakstan* ..... **26 E9** 46 40N 81 20 E
Rybinsk, *Russia* .... **24 C6** 58 5N 38 50 E
Rybinskoye Vdkhr., *Russia* **24 C6** 58 30N 38 25 E
Rybnitsa = Râbniţa,
Moldova .... **17 E15** 47 45N 29 0 E
Rycroft, *Canada* **72 B5** 55 45N 118 40W
Ryde, *U.K.* **11 G6** 50 43N 1 9W
Ryderwood, *U.S.A.* **84 D3** 46 23N 123 3W
Rye, *U.K.* .... **11 G8** 50 57N 0 45 E
Rye →, *U.K.* **10 C7** 54 11N 0 44W
Rye Bay, *U.K.* .... **11 G8** 50 52N 0 49 E
Rye Patch Reservoir, *U.S.A.* **82 F4** 40 28N 118 19W
Ryegate, *U.S.A.* **82 C9** 46 18N 109 15W
Ryley, *Canada* **72 C6** 53 17N 112 26W
Ryōtsu, *Japan* .... **30 E9** 38 5N 138 26 E
Rypin, *Poland* .... **17 B10** 53 3N 19 25 E
Ryūgasaki, *Japan* .... **31 G10** 35 54N 140 11 E
Ryūkyū Is. = Ryūkyū-rettō,
Japan .... **31 M3** 26 0N 126 0 E
Ryūkyū-rettō, *Japan* ...... **31 M3** 26 0N 126 0 E
Rzeszów, *Poland* .... **17 C11** 50 5N 21 58 E
Rzhev, *Russia* .... **24 C5** 56 20N 34 20 E

S

Sa, *Thailand* **38 C3** 18 34N 100 45 E
Sa Canal, *Spain* **22 C7** 38 51N 1 23 E
Sa Conillera, *Spain* **22 C7** 38 59N 1 13 E
Sa Dec, *Vietnam* **39 G5** 10 20N 105 46 E
Sa Dragonera, *Spain* **22 B9** 39 35N 2 19 E
Sa Mesquida, *Spain* **22 B11** 39 55N 4 16 E
Sa Savina, *Spain* **22 C7** 38 44N 1 25 E
Sa'ādatābād, *Fārs, Iran* **45 D7** 30 10N 53 5 E
Sa'ādatābād, *Hormozgān, Iran* **45 D7** 28 3N 55 53 E
Sa'ādatābād, *Kermān, Iran* **45 D7** 29 40N 55 51 E
Saale →, *Germany* **16 C6** 51 56N 11 54 E
Saalfeld, *Germany* **16 C6** 50 38N 11 21 E
Saar →, *Europe* **18 B7** 49 41N 6 32 E
Saarbrücken, *Germany* **16 D4** 49 14N 6 59 E
Saaremaa, *Estonia* **9 G20** 58 30N 22 30 E
Saarijärvi, *Finland* **9 E21** 62 43N 25 16 E
Saariselkä, *Finland* **8 B23** 68 16N 28 15 E
Sab 'Ābar, *Syria* **44 C3** 33 46N 37 41 E
Saba, *W. Indies* **89 C7** 17 42N 63 26W
Šabac, *Serbia, Yug.* **21 B8** 44 48N 19 42 E
Sabadell, *Spain* **19 B7** 41 28N 2 7 E
Sabah □, *Malaysia* **36 C5** 6 0N 117 0 E
Sabak Bernam, *Malaysia* **39 L3** 3 46N 100 58 E
Sabalān, Kūhhā-ye, *Iran* **44 B5** 38 15N 47 45 E
Sabalana, Kepulauan, *Indonesia* **37 F5** 6 45S 118 50 E
Sábana de la Mar, *Dom. Rep.* **89 C6** 19 7N 69 24W
Sábanalarga, *Colombia* **92 A4** 10 38N 74 55W
Sabang, *Indonesia* **36 C1** 5 50N 95 15 E
Sabará, *Brazil* **93 G10** 19 55S 43 46W
Sabarmati →, *India* **42 H5** 22 18N 72 22 E
Sabattis, *U.S.A.* **79 B10** 44 6N 74 40W
Saberania, *Indonesia* **37 E9** 2 5S 138 18 E
Sabhah, *Libya* **51 C8** 27 9N 14 29 E
Sabi →, *India* **42 E7** 28 29N 76 44 E
Sabie, *S. Africa* **57 D5** 25 10S 30 48 E
Sabinal, *Mexico* **86 A3** 30 58N 107 25W
Sabinal, *U.S.A.* **81 L5** 29 19N 99 28W
Sabinas, *Mexico* **86 B4** 27 50N 101 10W
Sabinas →, *Mexico* **86 B4** 27 37N 100 42W
Sabinas Hidalgo, *Mexico* **86 B4** 26 33N 100 10W
Sabine →, *U.S.A.* **81 L8** 29 59N 93 47W
Sabine L., *U.S.A.* **81 L8** 29 53N 93 51W
Sabine Pass, *U.S.A.* **81 L8** 29 44N 93 54W
Sabinsville, *U.S.A.* **78 E7** 41 52N 77 31W
Sabkhet el Bardawîl, *Egypt* **47 D2** 31 10N 33 15 E
Sablayan, *Phil.* **37 B6** 12 50N 120 50 E
Sable, *Canada* **71 A6** 55 30N 68 21W
Sable, C., *Canada* **71 D6** 43 29N 65 38W
Sable, C., *U.S.A.* **75 E10** 25 9N 81 8W
Sable I., *Canada* **71 D8** 44 0N 60 0W
Sabrina Coast, *Antarctica* **5 C9** 68 0S 120 0 E
Sabulubbek, *Indonesia* **36 E1** 1 36S 98 40 E
Sabzevār, *Iran* **45 B8** 36 15N 57 40 E
Sabzvārān, *Iran* **45 D8** 28 45N 57 50 E
Sac City, *U.S.A.* **80 D7** 42 25N 95 0W
Săcele, *Romania* **17 F13** 45 37N 25 41 E
Sachigo →, *Canada* **70 A2** 55 6N 88 58W
Sachigo, L., *Canada* **70 B1** 53 50N 92 12W
Sachsen □, *Germany* **16 C7** 50 55N 13 10 E
Sachsen-Anhalt □, *Germany* **16 C7** 52 0N 12 0 E
Sackets Harbor, *U.S.A.* **79 C8** 43 57N 76 7W
Sackville, *Canada* **71 C7** 45 54N 64 22W
Saco, *Maine, U.S.A.* **77 D10** 43 30N 70 27W
Saco, *Mont., U.S.A.* **82 B10** 48 28N 107 21W
Sacramento, *U.S.A.* **84 G5** 38 35N 121 29W
Sacramento →, *U.S.A.* **84 G5** 38 3N 121 56W
Sacramento Mts., *U.S.A.* **83 K11** 32 30N 105 30W
Sacramento Valley, *U.S.A.* **84 G5** 39 30N 122 0W
Sada-Misaki, *Japan* **31 H6** 33 20N 132 1 E
Sadabad, *India* **42 F8** 27 27N 78 3 E
Sadani, *Tanzania* **54 D4** 5 58S 38 35 E
Sadao, *Thailand* **39 J3** 6 38N 100 26 E
Sadd el Aali, *Egypt* **51 D12** 23 54N 32 54 E
Saddle Mt., *U.S.A.* **84 E3** 45 58N 123 41W
Sadimi, *Dem. Rep. of the Congo* **55 D1** 9 25S 23 32 E
Sado, *Japan* **30 F9** 38 0N 138 25 E
Sadon, *Burma* **41 G20** 25 28N 97 55 E
Sadra, *India* **42 H5** 23 21N 72 43 E
Sadri, *India* **42 G5** 25 11N 73 26 E
Sæby, *Denmark* **9 H14** 57 21N 10 30 E
Saegertown, *U.S.A.* **78 E4** 41 43N 80 9W
Şafājah, *Si. Arabia* **44 E3** 26 25N 39 0 E
Säffle, *Sweden* **9 G15** 59 8N 12 55 E
Safford, *U.S.A.* **83 K9** 32 50N 109 43W
Saffron Walden, *U.K.* **11 E8** 52 1N 0 16 E
Safi, *Morocco* **50 B4** 32 18N 9 20W
Şafīābād, *Iran* **45 B8** 36 45N 57 58 E
Safīd Dasht, *Iran* **45 C6** 33 27N 48 11 E
Safīd Kūh, *Afghan.* **40 B3** 34 45N 63 0 E
Safīd Rūd →, *Iran* **45 B6** 37 23N 50 11 E
Safipur, *India* **43 F9** 26 44N 80 21 E
Safwān, *Iraq* **44 D5** 30 7N 47 43 E
Sag Harbor, *U.S.A.* **79 F12** 41 0N 72 18W
Saga, *Japan* **31 H5** 33 15N 130 16 E
Saga □, *Japan* **31 H5** 33 15N 130 20 E
Sagae, *Japan* **30 E10** 38 22N 140 17 E
Sagamore, *U.S.A.* **78 F5** 40 46N 79 14W
Sagar, *Karnataka, India* **40 M9** 14 14N 75 6 E
Sagar, *Mad. P., India* **43 H8** 23 50N 78 44 E
Sagara, L., *Tanzania* **54 D3** 5 20S 31 0 E
Saginaw, *U.S.A.* **76 D4** 43 26N 83 56W
Saginaw →, *U.S.A.* **76 D4** 43 39N 83 51W
Saginaw B., *U.S.A.* **76 D4** 43 50N 83 40W
Saglouc = Salluit, *Canada* **69 B12** 62 14N 75 38W
Sagŏ-ri, *S. Korea* **35 G14** 35 25N 126 49 E
Sagua la Grande, *Cuba* **88 B3** 22 50N 80 10W
Saguache, *U.S.A.* **83 G10** 38 5N 106 8W
Saguaro Nat. Park, *U.S.A.* **83 K8** 32 12N 110 38W
Saguenay →, *Canada* **71 C5** 48 22N 71 0W
Sagunt, *Spain* **19 C5** 39 42N 0 18W
Sagunto = Sagunt, *Spain* **19 C5** 39 42N 0 18W
Sagwara, *India* **42 H6** 23 41N 74 1 E
Sahagún, *Spain* **19 A3** 42 18N 5 2W
Saḥam al Jawlān, *Syria* **47 C4** 32 45N 35 55 E
Sahamandrevo, *Madag.* **57 C8** 23 15S 45 35 E
Sahand, Kūh-e, *Iran* **44 B5** 37 44N 46 27 E
Sahara, *Africa* **50 D6** 23 0N 5 0 E
Saharan Atlas = Saharien, Atlas, *Algeria* **50 B6** 33 30N 1 0 E
Saharanpur, *India* **42 E7** 29 58N 77 33 E
Saharien, Atlas, *Algeria* **50 B6** 33 30N 1 0 E
Saharsa, *India* **43 G12** 25 53N 86 36 E
Sahasinaka, *Madag.* **57 C8** 21 49S 47 49 E
Sahaswan, *India* **43 E8** 28 5N 78 45 E
Sahel, *Africa* **50 E5** 16 0N 5 0 E
Sahibganj, *India* **43 G12** 25 12N 87 40 E
Sāḥilīyah, *Iraq* **44 C4** 33 43N 42 42 E
Sahiwal, *Pakistan* **42 D5** 30 45N 73 8 E
Şaḥneh, *Iran* **44 C5** 34 29N 47 41 E
Sahuaripa, *Mexico* **86 B3** 29 0N 109 13W
Sahuarita, *U.S.A.* **83 L8** 31 57N 110 58W
Sahuayo, *Mexico* **86 C4** 20 4N 102 43W
Sai →, *India* **43 G10** 25 39N 82 47 E
Sai Buri, *Thailand* **39 J3** 6 43N 101 45 E
Sa'id Bundas, *Sudan* **51 G10** 8 24N 24 48 E
Sa'īdābād, *Kermān, Iran* **45 D7** 29 30N 55 45 E
Sa'īdābād, *Semnān, Iran* **45 B7** 36 8N 54 11 E
Sa'īdīyeh, *Iran* **45 B6** 36 20N 48 55 E
Saidpur, *Bangla.* **41 G16** 25 48N 89 0 E
Saidpur, *India* **43 G10** 25 33N 83 11 E
Saidu, *Pakistan* **43 B5** 34 43N 72 24 E
Saigon = Thanh Pho Ho Chi Minh, *Vietnam* **39 G6** 10 58N 106 40 E
Saijō, *Japan* **31 H6** 33 55N 133 11 E
Saikanosy Masoala, *Madag.* **57 B9** 15 45S 50 10 E
Saikhoa Ghat, *India* **41 F19** 27 50N 95 40 E
Saiki, *Japan* **31 H5** 32 58N 131 51 E
Sailana, *India* **42 H6** 23 28N 74 55 E
Sailolof, *Indonesia* **37 E8** 1 15S 130 46 E
Saimaa, *Finland* **9 F23** 61 15N 28 15 E
Şa'in Dezh, *Iran* **44 B5** 36 40N 46 25 E
St. Abb's Head, *U.K.* **12 F6** 55 55N 2 8W
St. Alban's, *Canada* **71 C8** 47 51N 55 50W
St. Albans, *U.K.* **11 F7** 51 45N 0 19W
St. Albans, *Vt., U.S.A.* **79 B11** 44 49N 73 5W
St. Albans, *W. Va., U.S.A.* **76 F5** 38 23N 81 50W
St. Alban's Head, *U.K.* **11 G5** 50 34N 2 4W
St. Albert, *Canada* **72 C6** 53 37N 113 32W
St. Andrew's, *Canada* **71 C8** 47 45N 59 15W
St. Andrews, *U.K.* **12 E6** 56 20N 2 47W
St-Anicet, *Canada* **79 A10** 45 8N 74 22W
St. Ann B., *Canada* **71 C7** 46 22N 60 25W
St. Ann's Bay, *Jamaica* **88 C4** 18 26N 77 15W
St. Anthony, *Canada* **71 B8** 51 22N 55 35W
St. Anthony, *U.S.A.* **82 E8** 43 58N 111 41W
St. Antoine, *Canada* **71 C7** 46 22N 64 45W
St-Augustin →, *Canada* **71 B8** 51 16N 58 40W
St-Augustin-Saguenay, *Canada* **71 B8** 51 13N 58 38W
St. Augustine, *U.S.A.* **77 L5** 29 54N 81 19W
St. Austell, *U.K.* **11 G3** 50 20N 4 47W
St. Barbe, *Canada* **71 B8** 51 12N 56 46W
St-Barthélemy, *W. Indies* **89 C7** 17 50N 62 50W
St. Bees Hd., *U.K.* **10 C4** 54 31N 3 38W
St. Bride's, *Canada* **71 C9** 46 56N 54 10W
St. Brides B., *U.K.* **11 F2** 51 49N 5 9W
St-Brieuc, *France* **18 B2** 48 30N 2 46W
St. Catharines, *Canada* **78 C5** 43 10N 79 15W
St. Catherines I., *U.S.A.* **77 K5** 31 40N 81 10W
St. Catherine's Pt., *U.K.* **11 G6** 50 34N 1 18W
St-Chamond, *France* **18 D6** 45 28N 4 31 E
St. Charles, *Ill., U.S.A.* **76 E1** 41 54N 88 19W
St. Charles, *Mo., U.S.A.* **80 F9** 38 47N 90 29W
St. Charles, *Va., U.S.A.* **76 F7** 36 48N 83 4W
St. Christopher-Nevis = St. Kitts & Nevis ■, *W. Indies* **89 C7** 17 20N 62 40W
St. Clair, *Mich., U.S.A.* **78 D2** 42 50N 82 30W
St. Clair, *Pa., U.S.A.* **79 F8** 40 43N 76 12W
St. Clair →, *U.S.A.* **78 D2** 42 38N 82 31W
St. Clair, L., *Canada* **70 D3** 42 30N 82 45W
St. Clair, L., *U.S.A.* **78 D2** 42 27N 82 39W
St. Clairsville, *U.S.A.* **78 F4** 40 5N 80 54W
St. Claude, *Canada* **73 D9** 49 40N 98 20W
St-Clet, *Canada* **79 A10** 45 21N 74 13W
St. Cloud, *Fla., U.S.A.* **77 L5** 28 15N 81 17W
St. Cloud, *Minn., U.S.A.* **80 C7** 45 34N 94 10W
St. Cricq, C., *Australia* **61 E1** 25 17S 113 6 E
St. Croix, *U.S. Virgin Is.* **89 C7** 17 45N 64 45W
St. Croix →, *U.S.A.* **80 C8** 44 45N 92 48W
St. Croix Falls, *U.S.A.* **80 C8** 45 24N 92 38W
St. David's, *Canada* **71 C8** 48 12N 58 52W
St. David's, *U.K.* **11 F2** 51 53N 5 16W
St. David's Head, *U.K.* **11 F2** 51 54N 5 19W
St-Denis, *France* **18 B5** 48 56N 2 22 E
St-Dizier, *France* **18 B6** 48 38N 4 56 E
St. Elias, Mt., *U.S.A.* **68 B5** 60 18N 140 56W
St. Elias Mts., *Canada* **72 A1** 60 33N 139 28W
St. Elias Mts., *U.S.A.* **68 C6** 60 0N 138 0W
St-Étienne, *France* **18 D6** 45 27N 4 22 E
St. Eugène, *Canada* **79 A10** 45 30N 74 28W
St. Eustatius, *W. Indies* **89 C7** 17 20N 63 0W
St-Félicien, *Canada* **70 C5** 48 40N 72 25W
St-Flour, *France* **18 D5** 45 2N 3 6 E
St. Francis, *U.S.A.* **80 F4** 39 47N 101 48W
St. Francis →, *U.S.A.* **81 H9** 34 38N 90 36W
St. Francis, C., *S. Africa* **56 E3** 34 14S 24 49 E
St. Francisville, *U.S.A.* **81 K9** 30 47N 91 23W
St-François, L., *Canada* **79 A10** 45 10N 74 22W
St-Gabriel, *Canada* **70 C5** 46 17N 73 24W
St. Gallen = Sankt Gallen, *Switz.* **18 C8** 47 26N 9 22 E
St-Gaudens, *France* **18 E4** 43 6N 0 44 E
St. George, *Australia* **63 D4** 28 1S 148 30 E
St. George, *Canada* **71 C6** 45 11N 66 50W
St. George, *S.C., U.S.A.* **77 J5** 33 11N 80 35W
St. George, *Utah, U.S.A.* **83 H7** 37 6N 113 35W
St. George, C., *Canada* **71 C8** 48 30N 59 16W
St. George, C., *U.S.A.* **77 L3** 29 40N 85 5W
St. George Ra., *Australia* **60 C4** 18 40S 125 0 E
St. George's, *Canada* **71 C8** 48 26N 58 31W
St-Georges, *Canada* **71 C5** 46 8N 70 40W
St. George's, *Grenada* **89 D7** 12 5N 61 43W
St. George's B., *Canada* **71 C8** 48 24N 58 53W
St. Georges Basin, *N.S.W., Australia* **63 F5** 35 7S 150 36 E
St. Georges Basin, *W. Austral., Australia* **60 C4** 15 23S 125 2 E
St. George's Channel, *Europe* **13 E6** 52 0N 6 0W
St. Gotthard P. = San Gottardo, P. del, *Switz.* **18 C8** 46 33N 8 33 E
St. Helena, *U.S.A.* **82 G2** 38 30N 122 28W
St. Helena ■, *Atl. Oc.* **48 H3** 15 55S 5 44W
St. Helena, Mt., *U.S.A.* **84 G4** 38 40N 122 36W
St. Helena B., *S. Africa* **56 E2** 32 40S 18 10 E
St. Helens, *Australia* **62 G4** 41 20S 148 15 E
St. Helens, *U.K.* **10 D5** 53 27N 2 44W
St. Helens, *U.S.A.* **84 E4** 45 52N 122 48W
St. Helens, Mt., *U.S.A.* **84 D4** 46 12N 122 12W
St. Helier, *U.K.* **11 H5** 49 10N 2 7W
St-Hubert, *Belgium* **15 D5** 50 2N 5 23 E
St-Hyacinthe, *Canada* **70 C5** 45 40N 72 58W
St. Ignace, *U.S.A.* **76 C3** 45 52N 84 44W
St. Ignace I., *Canada* **70 C2** 48 45N 88 0W
St. Ignatius, *U.S.A.* **82 C6** 47 19N 114 6W
St. Ives, *U.K.* **11 G2** 50 12N 5 30W
St. James, *U.S.A.* **80 D7** 43 59N 94 38W
St-Jean →, *Canada* **71 B7** 50 17N 64 20W
St-Jean, L., *Canada* **71 C5** 48 40N 72 0W
St-Jean-Port-Joli, *Canada* **71 C5** 47 15N 70 13W
St-Jean-sur-Richelieu, *Canada* **79 A11** 45 20N 73 20W
St-Jérôme, *Canada* **70 C5** 45 47N 74 0W
St. John, *Canada* **71 C6** 45 20N 66 8W
St. John, *U.S.A.* **81 G5** 38 0N 98 46W
St. John →, *U.S.A.* **77 C12** 45 12N 66 5W
St. John, C., *Canada* **71 C8** 50 0N 55 32W
St. John's, *Antigua* **89 C7** 17 6N 61 51W
St. John's, *Canada* **71 C9** 47 35N 52 40W
St. Johns, *Ariz., U.S.A.* **83 J9** 34 30N 109 22W
St. Johns, *Mich., U.S.A.* **76 D3** 43 0N 84 33W
St. Johns →, *U.S.A.* **77 K5** 30 24N 81 24W
St. John's Pt., *Ireland* **13 B3** 54 34N 8 27W
St. Johnsbury, *U.S.A.* **79 B12** 44 25N 72 1W
St. Johnsville, *U.S.A.* **79 D10** 43 0N 74 43W
St. Joseph, *La., U.S.A.* **81 K9** 31 55N 91 14W
St. Joseph, *Mo., U.S.A.* **80 F7** 39 46N 94 50W
St. Joseph →, *U.S.A.* **76 D2** 42 7N 86 29W
St. Joseph, I., *Canada* **70 C3** 46 12N 83 58W
St. Joseph, L., *Canada* **70 B1** 51 10N 90 35W
St-Jovite, *Canada* **70 C5** 46 8N 74 38W
St. Kitts & Nevis ■, *W. Indies* **89 C7** 17 20N 62 40W
St. Laurent, *Canada* **73 C9** 50 25N 97 58W
St. Lawrence, *Australia* **62 C4** 22 16S 149 31 E
St. Lawrence, *Canada* **71 C8** 46 54N 55 23W
St. Lawrence →, *Canada* **71 C6** 49 30N 66 0W
St. Lawrence, Gulf of, *Canada* **71 C7** 48 25N 62 0W
St. Lawrence I., *U.S.A.* **68 B3** 63 30N 170 30W
St. Leonard, *Canada* **71 C6** 47 12N 67 58W
St. Lewis →, *Canada* **71 B8** 52 26N 56 11W
St-Lô, *France* **18 B3** 49 7N 1 5W
St. Louis, *Senegal* **50 E2** 16 8N 16 27W
St. Louis, *U.S.A.* **80 F9** 38 37N 90 12W
St. Louis →, *U.S.A.* **80 B8** 47 15N 92 45W
St. Lucia ■, *W. Indies* **89 D7** 14 0N 60 50W
St. Lucia, L., *S. Africa* **57 D5** 28 5S 32 30 E
St. Lucia Channel, *W. Indies* **89 D7** 14 15N 61 0W
St. Maarten, *W. Indies* **89 C7** 18 0N 63 5W
St. Magnus B., *U.K.* **12 A7** 60 25N 1 35W
St-Malo, *France* **18 B2** 48 39N 2 1W
St-Marc, *Haiti* **89 C5** 19 10N 72 41W
St. Maries, *U.S.A.* **82 C5** 47 19N 116 35W
St-Martin, *W. Indies* **89 C7** 18 0N 63 0W
St. Martin, L., *Canada* **73 C9** 51 40N 98 30W
St. Marys, *Australia* **62 G4** 41 35S 148 11 E
St. Marys, *Canada* **78 C3** 43 20N 81 10W
St. Mary's, *Corn., U.K.* **11 H1** 49 55N 6 18W
St. Mary's, *Orkney, U.K.* **12 C6** 58 54N 2 54W
St. Marys, *Ga., U.S.A.* **77 K5** 30 44N 81 33W
St. Marys, *Pa., U.S.A.* **78 E6** 41 26N 78 34W
St. Mary's, C., *Canada* **71 C9** 46 50N 54 12W
St. Mary's B., *Canada* **71 C9** 46 50N 53 50W
St. Marys Bay, *Canada* **71 D6** 44 25N 66 10W
St-Mathieu, Pte., *France* **18 B1** 48 20N 4 45W
St. Matthew I., *U.S.A.* **68 B2** 60 24N 172 42W
St. Matthews, I. = Zadetkyi Kyun, *Burma* **39 G1** 10 0N 98 25 E
St-Maurice →, *Canada* **70 C5** 46 21N 72 31W
St-Nazaire, *France* **18 C2** 47 17N 2 12W
St. Neots, *U.K.* **11 E7** 52 14N 0 15W
St-Niklaas, *Belgium* **15 C4** 51 10N 4 8 E
St-Omer, *France* **18 A5** 50 45N 2 15 E
St-Pamphile, *Canada* **71 C6** 46 58N 69 48W
St. Pascal, *Canada* **71 C6** 47 32N 69 48W
St. Paul, *Canada* **72 C6** 54 0N 111 17W
St. Paul, *Minn., U.S.A.* **80 C8** 44 57N 93 6W
St. Paul, *Nebr., U.S.A.* **80 E5** 41 13N 98 27W
St-Paul →, *Canada* **71 B8** 51 27N 57 42W
St. Paul, I., *Ind. Oc.* **3 F13** 38 55S 77 34 E
St. Paul I., *Canada* **71 C7** 47 12N 60 9W
St. Peter, *U.S.A.* **80 C8** 44 20N 93 57W
St. Peter Port, *U.K.* **11 H5** 49 26N 2 33W
St. Peters, *N.S., Canada* **71 C7** 45 40N 60 53W
St. Peters, *P.E.I., Canada* **71 C7** 46 25N 62 35W
St. Petersburg = Sankt-Peterburg, *Russia* **24 C5** 59 55N 30 20 E
St. Petersburg, *U.S.A.* **77 M4** 27 46N 82 39W
St-Pie, *Canada* **79 A12** 45 30N 72 54W
St-Pierre, *St- P. & M.* **71 C8** 46 46N 56 12W
St-Pierre, L., *Canada* **70 C5** 46 12N 72 52W
St-Pierre et Miquelon □, *St- P. & M.* **71 C8** 46 55N 56 10W
St-Quentin, *Canada* **71 C6** 47 30N 67 23W
St-Quentin, *France* **18 B5** 49 50N 3 16 E
St. Regis, *U.S.A.* **82 C6** 47 18N 115 6W
St. Sebastien, Tanjon' i, *Madag.* **57 A8** 12 26S 48 44 E
St-Siméon, *Canada* **71 C6** 47 51N 69 54W
St. Simons I., *U.S.A.* **77 K5** 31 12N 81 15W
St. Simons Island, *U.S.A.* **77 K5** 31 9N 81 22W
St. Stephen, *Canada* **71 C6** 45 16N 67 17W
St. Thomas, *Canada* **78 D3** 42 45N 81 10W
St. Thomas I., *U.S. Virgin Is.* **89 C7** 18 20N 64 55W
St-Tite, *Canada* **70 C5** 46 45N 72 34W
St-Tropez, *France* **18 E7** 43 17N 6 38 E
St. Troud = St. Truiden, *Belgium* **15 D5** 50 48N 5 10 E
St. Truiden, *Belgium* **15 D5** 50 48N 5 10 E
St. Vincent & the Grenadines ■, *W. Indies* **89 D7** 13 0N 61 10W
St. Vincent Passage, *W. Indies* **89 D7** 13 30N 61 0W
St-Vith, *Belgium* **15 D6** 50 17N 6 9 E
St. Walburg, *Canada* **73 C7** 53 39N 109 12W
Ste-Agathe-des-Monts, *Canada* **70 C5** 46 3N 74 17W
Ste-Anne, L., *Canada* **71 B6** 50 0N 67 42W
Ste-Anne-des-Monts, *Canada* **71 C6** 49 8N 66 30W
Ste. Genevieve, *U.S.A.* **80 G9** 37 59N 90 2W
Ste-Marguerite →, *Canada* **71 B6** 50 9N 66 36W
Ste-Marie, *Martinique* **89 D7** 14 48N 61 1W
Ste-Marie de la Madeleine, *Canada* **71 C5** 46 26N 71 0W
Ste-Rose, *Guadeloupe* **89 C7** 16 20N 61 45W
Ste. Rose du Lac, *Canada* **73 C9** 51 4N 99 30W
Saintes, *France* **18 D3** 45 45N 0 37W
Saintes, I. des, *Guadeloupe* **89 C7** 15 50N 61 35W
Saintfield, *U.K.* **13 B6** 54 28N 5 49W
Saintonge, *France* **18 D3** 45 40N 0 50W
Saipan, *Pac. Oc.* **64 F6** 15 12N 145 45 E
Sairang, *India* **41 H18** 23 50N 92 45 E
Sairecábur, Cerro, *Bolivia* **94 A2** 22 43S 67 54W
Saitama □, *Japan* **31 F9** 36 25N 139 30 E
Saiyid, *Pakistan* **42 C5** 33 7N 73 2 E
Sajama, *Bolivia* **92 G5** 18 7S 69 0W
Sajószentpéter, *Hungary* **17 D11** 48 12N 20 44 E
Sajum, *India* **43 C8** 33 20N 79 0 E
Sak →, *S. Africa* **56 E3** 30 52S 20 25 E
Sakai, *Japan* **31 G7** 34 30N 135 30 E
Sakaide, *Japan* **31 G6** 34 19N 133 50 E
Sakaiminato, *Japan* **31 G6** 35 38N 133 11 E
Sakākah, *Si. Arabia* **44 D4** 30 0N 40 8 E
Sakakawea, L., *U.S.A.* **80 B4** 47 30N 101 25W
Sakami →, *Canada* **70 B4** 53 40N 76 40W
Sakami, L., *Canada* **70 B4** 53 15N 77 0W
Sakania, *Dem. Rep. of the Congo* **55 E2** 12 43S 28 30 E
Sakaraha, *Madag.* **57 C7** 22 55S 44 32 E
Sakarya, *Turkey* **25 F5** 40 48N 30 25 E
Sakashima-Guntō, *Japan* **31 M2** 24 46N 124 0 E
Sakata, *Japan* **30 E9** 38 55N 139 50 E
Sakchu, *N. Korea* **35 D13** 40 23N 125 2 E
Sakeny →, *Madag.* **57 C8** 20 0S 45 25 E
Sakha □, *Russia* **27 C13** 66 0N 130 0 E
Sakhalin, *Russia* **27 D15** 51 0N 143 0 E
Sakhalinskiy Zaliv, *Russia* **27 D15** 54 0N 141 0 E
Šakiai, *Lithuania* **9 J20** 54 59N 23 2 E
Sakon Nakhon, *Thailand* **38 D5** 17 10N 104 9 E
Sakrand, *Pakistan* **42 F3** 26 10N 68 15 E
Sakri, *India* **43 F12** 26 13N 86 5 E
Sakrivier, *S. Africa* **56 E3** 30 54S 20 28 E
Sakti, *India* **43 H10** 22 2N 82 58 E
Sakuma, *Japan* **31 G8** 35 3N 137 49 E
Sakurai, *Japan* **31 G7** 34 30N 135 51 E
Sala, *Sweden* **9 G17** 59 58N 16 35 E
Sala Consilina, *Italy* **20 D6** 40 23N 15 36 E
Sala-y-Gómez, *Pac. Oc.* **65 K17** 26 28S 105 28W
Salaberry-de-Valleyfield, *Canada* **79 A10** 45 15N 74 8W
Saladas, *Argentina* **94 B4** 28 15S 58 40W
Saladillo, *Argentina* **94 D4** 35 40S 59 55W
Salado →, *Buenos Aires, Argentina* **94 D4** 35 44S 57 22W
Salado →, *La Pampa, Argentina* **96 D3** 37 30S 67 0W
Salado →, *Santa Fe, Argentina* **94 C3** 31 40S 60 41W
Salado →, *Mexico* **81 M5** 26 52N 99 19W
Salaga, *Ghana* **50 G5** 8 31N 0 31W
Sālah, *Syria* **47 C5** 32 40N 36 45 E
Sálakhos, *Greece* **23 C9** 36 17N 27 57 E
Salālah, *Oman* **46 D5** 16 56N 53 59 E
Salamanca, *Chile* **94 C1** 31 46S 70 59W
Salamanca, *Spain* **19 B3** 40 58N 5 39W
Salamanca, *U.S.A.* **78 D6** 42 10N 78 43W
Salāmatābād, *Iran* **44 C5** 35 39N 47 50 E
Salamis, *Cyprus* **23 D12** 35 11N 33 54 E
Salamís, *Greece* **21 F10** 37 56N 23 30 E
Salar de Atacama, *Chile* **94 A2** 23 30S 68 25W
Salar de Uyuni, *Bolivia* **92 H5** 20 30S 67 45W
Salatiga, *Indonesia* **37 G14** 7 19S 110 30 E
Salavat, *Russia* **24 D10** 53 21N 55 55 E
Salaverry, *Peru* **92 E3** 8 15S 79 0W
Salawati, *Indonesia* **37 E8** 1 7S 130 52 E
Salaya, *India* **42 H3** 22 19N 69 35 E
Salayar, *Indonesia* **37 F6** 6 7S 120 30 E
Salcombe, *U.K.* **11 G4** 50 14N 3 47W
Saldanha, *S. Africa* **56 E2** 33 0S 17 58 E
Saldanha B., *S. Africa* **56 E2** 33 6S 18 0 E
Saldus, *Latvia* **9 H20** 56 38N 22 30 E
Salé, *Morocco* **50 B4** 34 3N 6 48W
Sale, *U.K.* **10 D5** 53 26N 2 19W
Salekhard, *Russia* **26 C7** 66 30N 66 35 E
Salem, *India* **40 P11** 11 40N 78 11 E
Salem, *Ill., U.S.A.* **76 F1** 38 38N 88 57W
Salem, *Ind., U.S.A.* **76 F2** 38 36N 86 6W
Salem, *Mass., U.S.A.* **79 D14** 42 31N 70 53W
Salem, *Mo., U.S.A.* **81 G9** 37 39N 91 32W
Salem, *N.H., U.S.A.* **79 D13** 42 45N 71 12W
Salem, *N.J., U.S.A.* **76 F8** 39 34N 75 28W
Salem, *N.Y., U.S.A.* **79 C11** 43 10N 73 20W
Salem, *Ohio, U.S.A.* **78 F4** 40 54N 80 52W
Salem, *Oreg., U.S.A.* **82 D2** 44 56N 123 2W
Salem, *S. Dak., U.S.A.* **80 D6** 43 44N 97 23W
Salem, *Va., U.S.A.* **76 G5** 37 18N 80 3W
Salerno, *Italy* **20 D6** 40 41N 14 47 E
Salford, *U.K.* **10 D5** 53 30N 2 18W
Salgótarján, *Hungary* **17 D10** 48 5N 19 47 E
Salgueiro, *Brazil* **93 E11** 8 4S 39 6W
Salibabu, *Indonesia* **37 D7** 3 51N 126 40 E
Salida, *U.S.A.* **74 C5** 38 32N 106 0W
Salihli, *Turkey* **21 E13** 38 28N 28 8 E
Salihorsk, *Belarus* **17 B14** 52 51N 27 27 E
Salima, *Malawi* **53 G6** 13 47S 34 28 E
Salina, *Italy* **20 E6** 38 34N 14 50 E
Salina, *Kans., U.S.A.* **80 F6** 38 50N 97 37W
Salina, *Utah, U.S.A.* **83 G8** 38 58N 111 51W
Salina Cruz, *Mexico* **87 D5** 16 10N 95 10W
Salinas, *Brazil* **93 G10** 16 10S 42 10W
Salinas, *Chile* **94 A2** 23 31S 69 29W
Salinas, *Ecuador* **92 D2** 2 10S 80 58W
Salinas, *U.S.A.* **84 J5** 36 40N 121 39W
Salinas →, *Guatemala* **87 D6** 16 28N 90 31W
Salinas →, *U.S.A.* **84 J5** 36 45N 121 48W
Salinas, B. de, *Nic.* **88 D2** 11 4N 85 45W
Salinas, Pampa de las, *Argentina* **94 C2** 31 58S 66 42W
Salinas Ambargasta, *Argentina* **94 B3** 29 0S 65 0W
Salinas de Hidalgo, *Mexico* **86 C4** 22 30N 101 40W
Salinas Grandes, *Argentina* **94 C3** 30 0S 65 0W
Saline →, *Ark., U.S.A.* **81 J8** 33 10N 92 8W

Sanand

Saline →, Kans., U.S.A. 80 F6 38 52N 97 30W
Salines, Spain 22 B10 39 21N 3 3 E
Salines, C. de ses, Spain 22 B10 39 16N 3 4 E
Salinópolis, Brazil 93 D9 0 40S 47 20W
Salisbury = Harare, Zimbabwe 55 F3 17 43S 31 2 E
Salisbury, U.K. 11 F6 51 4N 1 47W
Salisbury, Md., U.S.A. 76 F8 38 22N 75 36W
Salisbury, N.C., U.S.A. 77 H5 35 40N 80 29W
Salisbury I., Canada 69 B12 63 30N 77 0W
Salisbury Plain, U.K. 11 F6 51 14N 1 55W
Şalkhad, Syria 47 C5 32 29N 36 43 E
Salla, Finland 8 C23 66 50N 28 49 E
Salliq, Canada 69 B11 64 8N 83 10W
Sallisaw, U.S.A. 81 H7 35 28N 94 47W
Salluit, Canada 69 B12 62 14N 75 38W
Salmās, Iran 44 B5 38 11N 44 47 E
Salmo, Canada 72 D5 49 10N 117 20W
Salmon, U.S.A. 82 D7 45 11N 113 54W
Salmon →, Canada 72 C4 54 3N 122 40W
Salmon →, U.S.A. 82 D5 45 51N 116 47W
Salmon Arm, Canada 72 C5 50 40N 119 15W
Salmon Gums, Australia 61 F3 32 59S 121 38 E
Salmon River Mts., U.S.A. 82 D6 45 0N 114 30W
Salo, Finland 9 F20 60 22N 23 10 E
Salome, U.S.A. 85 M13 33 47N 113 37W
Salon, India 43 F9 26 2N 81 27 E
Salon-de-Provence, France 18 E6 43 39N 5 6 E
Salonica = Thessaloníki, Greece 21 D10 40 38N 22 58 E
Salonta, Romania 17 E11 46 49N 21 42 E
Salpausselkä, Finland 9 F22 61 0N 27 0 E
Salsacate, Argentina 94 C2 31 20S 65 5W
Salsk, Russia 25 E7 46 28N 41 30 E
Salso →, Italy 20 F5 37 6N 13 57 E
Salt →, Canada 72 B6 60 0N 112 25W
Salt →, U.S.A. 83 K7 33 23N 112 19W
Salt Lake City, U.S.A. 82 F8 40 45N 111 53W
Salt Range, Pakistan 42 C5 32 30N 72 25 E
Salta, Argentina 94 A2 24 57S 65 25W
Salta □, Argentina 94 A2 24 48S 65 30W
Saltash, U.K. 11 G3 50 24N 4 14W
Saltburn by the Sea, U.K. 10 C7 54 35N 0 58W
Saltcoats, U.K. 12 F4 55 38N 4 47W
Saltee Is., Ireland 13 D5 52 7N 6 37W
Saltfjellet, Norway 8 C16 66 40N 15 15 E
Saltfjorden, Norway 8 C16 67 15N 14 10 E
Saltillo, Mexico 86 B4 25 25N 101 0W
Salto, Argentina 94 C3 34 20S 60 15W
Salto, Uruguay 94 C4 31 27S 57 50W
Salto →, Italy 20 C5 42 26N 12 25 E
Salto del Guaíra, Paraguay 95 A5 24 3S 54 17W
Salton City, U.S.A. 85 M11 33 29N 115 51W
Salton Sea, U.S.A. 85 M11 33 15N 115 45W
Saltsburg, U.S.A. 78 F5 40 29N 79 27W
Saluda →, U.S.A. 77 J5 34 1N 81 4W
Salûm, Egypt 51 B11 31 31N 25 7 E
Salur, India 41 K13 18 27N 83 18 E
Salvador, Brazil 93 F11 13 0S 38 30W
Salvador, Canada 73 C7 52 10N 109 32W
Salvador, L., U.S.A. 81 L9 29 43N 90 15W
Salween →, Burma 41 L20 16 31N 97 37 E
Salyan, Azerbaijan 25 G8 39 33N 48 59 E
Salzach →, Austria 16 D7 48 12N 12 56 E
Salzburg, Austria 16 E7 47 48N 13 2 E
Salzgitter, Germany 16 B6 52 9N 10 19 E
Salzwedel, Germany 16 B6 52 52N 11 10 E
Sam, India 42 F4 26 50N 70 31 E
Sam Neua, Laos 38 B5 20 29N 104 5 E
Sam Ngao, Thailand 38 D2 17 18N 99 0 E
Sam Rayburn Reservoir, U.S.A. 81 K7 31 4N 94 5W
Sam Son, Vietnam 38 C5 19 44N 105 54 E
Sam Teu, Laos 38 C5 19 59N 104 38 E
Sama de Langreo = Langreo, Spain 19 A3 43 18N 5 40W
Samagaltay, Russia 27 D10 50 36N 95 3 E
Samales Group, Phil. 37 C6 6 0N 122 0 E
Samana, India 42 D7 30 10N 76 13 E
Samana Cay, Bahamas 89 B5 23 3N 73 45W
Samanga, Tanzania 55 D4 8 20S 39 13 E
Samangwa, Dem. Rep. of the Congo 54 C1 4 23S 24 10 E
Samani, Japan 30 C11 42 7N 142 56 E
Samar, Phil. 37 B7 12 0N 125 0 E
Samara, Russia 24 D9 53 8N 50 6 E
Samaria = Shōmrōn, West Bank 47 C4 32 15N 35 13 E
Samariá, Greece 23 D5 35 17N 23 58 E
Samarinda, Indonesia 36 E5 0 30S 117 9 E
Samarkand = Samarqand, Uzbekistan 26 F7 39 40N 66 55 E
Samarqand, Uzbekistan 26 F7 39 40N 66 55 E
Sāmarrā, Iraq 44 C4 34 12N 43 52 E
Samastipur, India 43 G11 25 50N 85 50 E
Samba, Dem. Rep. of the Congo 54 C2 4 38S 26 22 E
Samba, India 43 C6 32 32N 75 10 E
Sambalpur, India 41 J14 21 28N 84 4 E
Sambar, Tanjung, Indonesia 36 E4 2 59S 110 19 E
Sambas, Indonesia 36 D3 1 20N 109 20 E
Sambava, Madag. 57 A9 14 16S 50 10 E
Sambawizi, Zimbabwe 55 F2 18 24S 26 13 E
Sambhal, India 43 E8 28 35N 78 37 E
Sambhar, India 42 F6 26 52N 75 6 E
Sambhar L., India 42 F6 26 55N 75 12 E
Sambiase, Italy 20 E7 38 58N 16 17 E
Sambir, Ukraine 17 D12 49 30N 23 10 E
Sambor, Cambodia 38 F6 12 46N 106 0 E
Samborombón, B., Argentina 94 D4 36 5S 57 20W
Samch'ŏk, S. Korea 35 F15 37 30N 129 10 E
Samch'onp'o, S. Korea 35 G15 35 0N 128 6 E
Same, Tanzania 54 C4 4 2S 37 38 E
Samfya, Zambia 55 E2 11 22S 29 31 E
Samnah, Si. Arabia 44 E3 25 10N 37 15 E
Samo Alto, Chile 94 C1 30 22S 71 0W
Samoa ■, Pac. Oc. 59 B13 14 0S 172 0W
Samokov, Bulgaria 21 C10 42 18N 23 35 E
Sámos, Greece 21 F12 37 45N 26 50 E
Samothráki = Mathráki, Greece 23 A3 39 48N 19 31 E
Samothráki, Greece 21 D11 40 28N 25 28 E
Sampacho, Argentina 94 C3 33 20S 64 50W
Sampang, Indonesia 37 G15 7 11S 113 13 E
Sampit, Indonesia 36 E4 2 34S 113 0 E
Sampit, Teluk, Indonesia 36 E4 3 5S 113 3 E
Samrong, Cambodia 38 E4 14 15N 103 30 E
Samrong, Thailand 38 E3 15 10N 100 40 E
Samsø, Denmark 9 J14 55 50N 10 35 E
Samsun, Turkey 25 F6 41 15N 36 22 E
Samui, Ko, Thailand 39 H3 9 30N 100 0 E
Samusole, Dem. Rep. of the Congo 55 E1 10 2S 24 0 E
Samut Prakan, Thailand 38 F3 13 32N 100 40 E
Samut Songkhram →, Thailand 36 B1 13 24N 100 1 E
Samwari, Pakistan 42 E2 28 30N 66 46 E
San, Mali 50 F5 13 15N 4 57W
San →, Cambodia 38 F5 13 32N 105 57 E
San →, Poland 17 C11 50 45N 21 51 E
San Agustin, C., Phil. 37 C7 6 20N 126 13 E
San Agustín de Valle Fértil, Argentina 94 C2 30 35S 67 30W
San Ambrosio, Pac. Oc. 90 F3 26 28S 79 53W
San Andreas, U.S.A. 84 G6 38 12N 120 41W
San Andrés, I. de, Caribbean 88 D3 12 42N 81 46W
San Andres Mts., U.S.A. 83 K10 33 0N 106 30W
San Andrés Tuxtla, Mexico 87 D5 18 30N 95 20W
San Angelo, U.S.A. 81 K4 31 28N 100 26W
San Anselmo, U.S.A. 84 H4 37 59N 122 34W
San Antonio, Belize 87 D7 16 15N 89 2W
San Antonio, Chile 94 C1 33 40S 71 40W
San Antonio, N. Mex., U.S.A. 83 K10 33 55N 106 52W
San Antonio, Tex., U.S.A. 81 L5 29 25N 98 30W
San Antonio →, U.S.A. 81 L6 28 30N 96 54W
San Antonio, C., Argentina 94 D4 36 15S 56 40W
San Antonio, C., Cuba 88 B3 21 50N 84 57W
San Antonio, Mt., U.S.A. 85 L9 34 17N 117 38W
San Antonio de los Baños, Cuba 88 B3 22 54N 82 31W
San Antonio de los Cobres, Argentina 94 A2 24 10S 66 17W
San Antonio Oeste, Argentina 96 E4 40 40S 65 0W
San Ardo, U.S.A. 84 J6 36 1N 120 54W
San Augustin, Canary Is. 22 G4 27 47N 15 32W
San Augustine, U.S.A. 81 K7 31 30N 94 7W
San Bartolomé, Canary Is. 22 F6 28 59N 13 37W
San Bartolomé de Tirajana, Canary Is. 22 G4 27 54N 15 34W
San Benedetto del Tronto, Italy 20 C5 42 57N 13 53 E
San Benedicto, I., Mexico 86 D2 19 18N 110 49W
San Benito, U.S.A. 81 M6 26 8N 97 38W
San Benito →, U.S.A. 84 J5 36 53N 121 34W
San Benito Mt., U.S.A. 84 J6 36 22N 120 37W
San Bernardino, U.S.A. 85 L9 34 7N 117 19W
San Bernardino Mts., U.S.A. 85 L10 34 10N 116 45W
San Bernardino Str., Phil. 37 B6 13 0N 125 0 E
San Bernardo, Chile 94 C1 33 40S 70 50W
San Bernardo, I. de, Colombia 92 B3 9 45N 75 50W
San Blas, Mexico 86 B3 26 4N 108 46W
San Blas, Arch. de, Panama 88 E4 9 50N 78 31W
San Blas, C., U.S.A. 77 L3 29 40N 85 21W
San Borja, Bolivia 92 F5 14 50S 66 52W
San Buenaventura, Mexico 86 B4 27 5N 101 32W
San Carlos = Sant Carles, Spain 22 B8 39 3N 1 34 E
San Carlos, Argentina 94 C2 33 50S 69 0W
San Carlos, Chile 94 D1 36 10S 72 0W
San Carlos, Baja Calif. S., Mexico 86 C2 24 47N 112 6W
San Carlos, Coahuila, Mexico 86 B4 29 0N 100 54W
San Carlos, Nic. 88 D3 11 12N 84 50W
San Carlos, Phil. 37 B6 10 29N 123 25 E
San Carlos, Uruguay 95 C5 34 46S 54 58W
San Carlos, U.S.A. 83 K8 33 21N 110 27W
San Carlos, Venezuela 92 B5 9 40N 68 36W
San Carlos de Bariloche, Argentina 96 E2 41 10S 71 25W
San Carlos de Bolívar, Argentina 96 D4 36 15S 61 6W
San Carlos del Zulia, Venezuela 92 B4 9 1N 71 55W
San Carlos L., U.S.A. 83 K8 33 11N 110 32W
San Clemente, Chile 94 D1 35 30S 71 29W
San Clemente, U.S.A. 85 M9 33 26N 117 37W
San Clemente I., U.S.A. 85 N8 32 53N 118 29W
San Cristóbal = Es Migjorn Gran, Spain 22 B11 39 57N 4 3 E
San Cristóbal, Argentina 94 C3 30 20S 61 10W
San Cristóbal, Dom. Rep. 89 C5 18 25N 70 6W
San Cristóbal, Venezuela 92 B4 7 46N 72 14W
San Cristóbal de la Casas, Mexico 87 D6 16 50N 92 33W
San Diego, Calif., U.S.A. 85 N9 32 43N 117 9W
San Diego, Tex., U.S.A. 81 M5 27 46N 98 14W
San Diego, C., Argentina 96 G3 54 40S 65 10W
San Diego de la Unión, Mexico 86 C4 21 28N 100 52W
San Dimitri, Ras, Malta 23 C1 36 4N 14 11 E
San Estanislao, Paraguay 94 A4 24 39S 56 26W
San Felipe, Chile 94 C1 32 43S 70 42W
San Felipe, Mexico 86 A2 31 0N 114 52W
San Felipe, Venezuela 92 A5 10 20N 68 44W
San Felipe →, U.S.A. 85 M11 33 12N 115 49W
San Felix, Chile 94 B1 28 56S 70 28W
San Félix, Pac. Oc. 90 F2 26 23S 80 0W
San Fernando = Sant Ferran, Spain 22 C7 38 42N 1 28 E
San Fernando, Chile 94 C1 34 30S 71 0W
San Fernando, Baja Calif., Mexico 86 B1 29 55N 115 10W
San Fernando, Tamaulipas, Mexico 87 C5 24 51N 98 10W
San Fernando, La Union, Phil. 37 A6 16 40N 120 23 E
San Fernando, Pampanga, Phil. 37 A6 15 5N 120 37 E
San Fernando, Spain 19 D2 36 28N 6 17W
San Fernando, Trin. & Tob. 89 D7 10 20N 61 30W
San Fernando, U.S.A. 85 L8 34 17N 118 26W
San Fernando de Apure, Venezuela 92 B5 7 54N 67 15W
San Fernando de Atabapo, Venezuela 92 C5 4 3N 67 42W
San Francisco, Argentina 94 C3 31 30S 62 5W
San Francisco, U.S.A. 84 H4 37 47N 122 25W
San Francisco →, U.S.A. 83 K9 32 59N 109 22W
San Francisco, Paso de, S. Amer. 94 B2 27 0S 68 0W
San Francisco de Macorís, Dom. Rep. 89 C5 19 19N 70 15W
San Francisco del Monte de Oro, Argentina 94 C2 32 36S 66 8W
San Francisco del Oro, Mexico 86 B3 26 52N 105 50W
San Francisco Javier = Sant Francesc de Formentera, Spain 22 C7 38 42N 1 26 E
San Francisco Solano, Pta., Colombia 90 C3 6 18N 77 29W
San Gabriel, Chile 94 C1 33 47S 70 15W
San Gabriel Mts., U.S.A. 85 L9 34 20N 118 0W
San Gorgonio Mt., U.S.A. 85 L10 34 7N 116 51W
San Gottardo, P. del, Switz. 18 C8 46 33N 8 33 E
San Gregorio, Uruguay 95 C4 32 37S 55 40W
San Gregorio, U.S.A. 84 H4 37 20N 122 23W
San Ignacio, Belize 87 D7 17 10N 89 0W
San Ignacio, Bolivia 92 G6 16 20S 60 55W
San Ignacio, Mexico 86 B2 27 27N 113 0W
San Ignacio, Paraguay 88 C2 26 52S 57 3W
San Ignacio, L., Mexico 86 B2 26 50N 113 11W
San Ildefonso, C., Phil. 37 A6 16 0N 122 1 E
San Isidro, Argentina 94 C4 34 29S 58 31W
San Jacinto, U.S.A. 85 M10 33 47N 116 57W
San Jaime = Sant Jaume, Spain 22 B11 39 54N 4 4 E
San Javier, Misiones, Argentina 95 B4 27 55S 55 5W
San Javier, Santa Fe, Argentina 94 C4 30 40S 59 55W
San Javier, Bolivia 92 G6 16 18S 62 30W
San Javier, Chile 94 D1 35 40S 71 45W
San Jeronimo Taviche, Mexico 87 D5 16 38N 96 32W
San Joaquin, U.S.A. 84 J6 36 36N 120 11W
San Joaquin →, U.S.A. 84 G5 38 4N 121 51W
San Joaquin Valley, U.S.A. 84 J6 37 20N 121 0W
San Jon, U.S.A. 81 H3 35 6N 103 20W
San Jordi = Sant Jordi, Spain 22 B9 39 33N 2 46 E
San Jorge, Argentina 94 C3 31 54S 61 50W
San Jorge, Spain 22 C7 38 54N 1 24 E
San Jorge, B. de, Mexico 86 A2 31 20N 113 20W
San Jorge, G., Argentina 96 F3 46 0S 66 0W
San Jorge, G. of, Argentina 90 H4 46 0S 66 0W
San José = San Josep, Spain 22 C7 38 55N 1 18 E
San José, Costa Rica 88 E3 9 55N 84 2W
San José, Guatemala 88 D1 14 0N 90 50W
San José, Mexico 86 C2 25 0N 110 50W
San Jose, Mind. Occ., Phil. 37 B6 12 27N 121 4 E
San Jose, Nueva Ecija, Phil. 37 A6 15 45N 120 55 E
San Jose, U.S.A. 84 H5 37 20N 121 53W
San Jose →, U.S.A. 83 J10 34 25N 106 45W
San Jose de Buenavista, Phil. 37 B6 10 45N 121 56 E
San José de Chiquitos, Bolivia 92 G6 17 53S 60 50W
San José de Feliciano, Argentina 94 C4 30 26S 58 46W
San José de Jáchal, Argentina 94 C2 30 15S 68 46W
San José de Mayo, Uruguay 94 C4 34 27S 56 40W
San José del Cabo, Mexico 86 C3 23 0N 109 40W
San José del Guaviare, Colombia 92 C4 2 35N 72 38W
San Josep, Spain 22 C7 38 55N 1 18 E
San Juan, Argentina 94 C2 31 30S 68 30W
San Juan, Mexico 86 C4 21 20N 102 50W
San Juan, Puerto Rico 89 C6 18 28N 66 7W
San Juan □, Argentina 94 C2 31 9S 69 0W
San Juan →, Argentina 94 C2 32 20S 67 25W
San Juan →, Nic. 88 D3 10 56N 83 42W
San Juan →, U.S.A. 83 H8 37 16N 110 26W
San Juan Bautista = Sant Joan Baptista, Spain 22 B8 39 5N 1 31 E
San Juan Bautista, Paraguay 94 B4 26 37S 57 6W
San Juan Bautista, U.S.A. 84 J5 36 51N 121 32W
San Juan Bautista Valle Nacional, Mexico 87 D5 17 47N 96 19W
San Juan Capistrano, U.S.A. 85 M9 33 30N 117 40W
San Juan Cr. →, U.S.A. 84 J5 35 40N 120 22W
San Juan de Guadalupe, Mexico 86 C4 24 38N 102 44W
San Juan de la Costa, Mexico 86 C2 24 23N 110 45W
San Juan de los Morros, Venezuela 92 B5 9 55N 67 21W
San Juan del Norte, Nic. 88 D3 10 58N 83 40W
San Juan del Norte, B. de, Nic. 88 D3 11 0N 83 40W
San Juan del Río, Mexico 87 C5 20 25N 100 0W
San Juan del Sur, Nic. 88 D2 11 20N 85 51W
San Juan I., U.S.A. 84 B3 48 32N 123 5W
San Juan Mts., U.S.A. 83 H10 37 30N 107 0W
San Justo, Argentina 94 C3 30 47S 60 30W
San Kamphaeng, Thailand 38 C2 18 45N 99 8 E
San Lázaro, C., Mexico 86 C2 24 50N 112 18W
San Lázaro, Sa., Mexico 86 C3 23 25N 110 0W
San Leandro, U.S.A. 84 H4 37 44N 122 9W
San Lorenzo = Sant Llorenç des Cardassar, Spain 22 B10 39 37N 3 17 E
San Lorenzo, Argentina 94 C3 32 45S 60 45W
San Lorenzo, Ecuador 92 C3 1 15N 78 50W
San Lorenzo, Paraguay 94 B4 25 20S 57 32W
San Lorenzo →, Mexico 86 C3 24 15N 107 24W
San Lorenzo, I., Mexico 86 B2 28 35N 112 50W
San Lorenzo, Mte., Argentina 96 F2 47 40S 72 20W
San Lucas, Bolivia 92 H5 20 5S 65 7W
San Lucas, Baja Calif. S., Mexico 86 C3 22 53N 109 54W
San Lucas, Baja Calif. S., Mexico 86 B2 27 10N 112 14W
San Lucas, U.S.A. 84 J5 36 8N 121 1W
San Lucas, C., Mexico 86 C3 22 50N 110 0W
San Luis, Argentina 94 C2 33 20S 66 20W
San Luis, Cuba 88 B3 22 17N 83 46W
San Luis, Guatemala 88 C2 16 14N 89 27W
San Luis, Ariz., U.S.A. 83 K6 32 29N 114 47W
San Luis, Colo., U.S.A. 83 H11 37 12N 105 25W
San Luis □, Argentina 94 C2 34 0S 66 0W
San Luis, I., Mexico 86 B2 29 58N 114 26W
San Luis, Sierra de, Argentina 94 C2 32 30S 66 10W
San Luis de la Paz, Mexico 86 C4 21 19N 100 32W
San Luis Obispo, U.S.A. 85 K6 35 17N 120 40W
San Luis Potosí, Mexico 86 C4 22 9N 100 59W
San Luis Potosí □, Mexico 86 C4 22 10N 101 0W
San Luis Reservoir, U.S.A. 84 H5 37 4N 121 5W
San Luis Río Colorado, Mexico 86 A2 32 29N 114 58W
San Manuel, U.S.A. 83 K8 32 36N 110 38W
San Marcos, Guatemala 88 D1 14 59N 91 52W
San Marcos, Mexico 86 B2 27 13N 112 6W
San Marcos, Calif., U.S.A. 85 M9 33 9N 117 10W
San Marcos, Tex., U.S.A. 81 L6 29 53N 97 56W
San Marino, San Marino 16 G7 43 55N 12 30 E
San Marino ■, Europe 20 C5 43 56N 12 25 E
San Martín, Argentina 94 C2 33 5S 68 28W
San Martín →, Bolivia 92 F6 13 8S 63 43W
San Martín, L., Argentina 96 F2 48 50S 72 50W
San Martín de los Andes, Argentina 96 E2 40 10S 71 20W
San Mateo = Sant Mateu, Spain 22 B7 39 3N 1 23 E
San Mateo, U.S.A. 84 H4 37 34N 122 19W
San Matías, Bolivia 92 G7 16 25S 58 20W
San Matías, G., Argentina 96 E4 41 30S 64 0W
San Miguel = Sant Miquel, Spain 22 B7 39 3N 1 26 E
San Miguel, El Salv. 88 D2 13 30N 88 12W
San Miguel, Panama 88 E4 8 27N 78 55W
San Miguel, U.S.A. 84 K6 35 45N 120 42W
San Miguel →, Bolivia 92 F6 13 52S 63 56W
San Miguel de Tucumán, Argentina 94 B2 26 50S 65 20W
San Miguel del Monte, Argentina 94 D4 35 23S 58 50W
San Miguel I., U.S.A. 85 L6 34 2N 120 23W
San Nicolás, Canary Is. 22 G4 27 58N 15 47W
San Nicolás de los Arroyas, Argentina 94 C3 33 25S 60 10W
San Nicolas I., U.S.A. 85 M7 33 15N 119 30W
San Onofre, U.S.A. 85 M9 33 22N 117 34W
San Pablo, Bolivia 94 A2 21 43S 66 38W
San Pablo, U.S.A. 84 H4 37 58N 122 21W
San Pedro, Buenos Aires, Argentina 94 C4 33 40S 59 40W
San Pedro, Misiones, Argentina 95 B5 26 30S 54 10W
San Pedro, Chile 94 C1 33 54S 71 28W
San Pédro, Ivory C. 50 H4 4 50N 6 33W
San Pedro, Mexico 86 C2 23 55N 110 17W
San Pedro □, Paraguay 94 A4 24 0S 57 0W
San Pedro →, Chihuahua, Mexico 86 B3 28 20N 106 10W
San Pedro →, Nayarit, Mexico 86 C3 21 45N 105 30W
San Pedro →, U.S.A. 83 K8 32 59N 110 47W
San Pedro, Pta., Chile 94 B1 25 30S 70 38W
San Pedro Channel, U.S.A. 85 M8 33 30N 118 25W
San Pedro de Atacama, Chile 94 A2 22 55S 68 15W
San Pedro de Jujuy, Argentina 94 A3 24 12S 64 55W
San Pedro de las Colonias, Mexico 86 B4 25 50N 102 59W
San Pedro de Macorís, Dom. Rep. 89 C6 18 30N 69 18W
San Pedro del Norte, Nic. 88 D3 13 4N 84 33W
San Pedro del Paraná, Paraguay 94 B4 26 43S 56 13W
San Pedro Mártir, Sierra, Mexico 86 A1 31 0N 115 30W
San Pedro Mixtepec, Mexico 87 D5 16 2N 97 7W
San Pedro Ocampo = Melchor Ocampo, Mexico 86 C4 24 52N 101 40W
San Pedro Sula, Honduras 88 C2 15 30N 88 0W
San Pietro, Italy 20 E3 39 8N 8 17 E
San Quintín, Mexico 86 A1 30 29N 115 57W
San Rafael, Argentina 94 C2 34 40S 68 21W
San Rafael, Calif., U.S.A. 84 H4 37 58N 122 32W
San Rafael, N. Mex., U.S.A. 83 J10 35 7N 107 53W
San Rafael Mt., U.S.A. 85 L7 34 41N 119 52W
San Rafael Mts., U.S.A. 85 L7 34 40N 119 50W
San Ramón de la Nueva Orán, Argentina 94 A3 23 10S 64 20W
San Remo, Italy 18 E7 43 49N 7 46 E
San Roque, Argentina 94 B4 28 25S 58 45W
San Roque, Spain 19 D3 36 17N 5 21W
San Rosendo, Chile 94 D1 37 16S 72 43W
San Saba, U.S.A. 81 K5 31 12N 98 43W
San Salvador, El Salv. 88 D2 13 40N 89 10W
San Salvador, Spain 22 B10 39 27N 3 11 E
San Salvador de Jujuy, Argentina 94 A3 24 10S 64 48W
San Salvador I., Bahamas 89 B5 24 0N 74 40W
San Sebastián = Donostia-San Sebastián, Spain 19 A5 43 17N 1 58W
San Sebastián, Argentina 96 G3 53 10S 68 30W
San Sebastian de la Gomera, Canary Is. 22 F2 28 5N 17 7W
San Serra = Son Serra, Spain 22 B10 39 43N 3 13 E
San Severo, Italy 20 D6 41 41N 15 23 E
San Simeon, U.S.A. 84 K5 35 39N 121 11W
San Simon, U.S.A. 83 K9 32 16N 109 14W
San Telmo = Sant Telm, Spain 22 B9 39 35N 2 21 E
San Telmo, Mexico 86 A1 30 58N 116 6W
San Tiburcio, Mexico 86 C4 24 8N 101 32W
San Valentin, Mte., Chile 96 F2 46 30S 73 30W
San Vicente de la Barquera, Spain 19 A3 43 23N 4 29W
San Vito, Costa Rica 88 E3 8 50N 82 58W
Sana', Yemen 46 D3 15 27N 44 12 E
Sana →, Bos.-H. 16 F9 45 3N 16 23 E
Sanaga →, Cameroon 52 D1 3 35N 9 38 E
Sanaloa, Presa, Mexico 86 C3 24 50N 107 20W
Sanana, Indonesia 37 E7 2 4S 125 58 E
Sanand, India 42 H5 22 59N 72 25 E

Seyhan

Sasyk, Ozero, *Ukraine* **17 F15** 45 45N 29 20 E
Sata-Misaki, *Japan* **31 J5** 31 0N 130 40 E
Satadougou, *Mali* **50 F3** 12 25N 11 25W
Satakunta, *Finland* **9 F20** 61 45N 23 0 E
Satara, *India* **40 L8** 17 44N 73 58 E
Satara, *S. Africa* **57 C5** 24 29S 31 47 E
Satbarwa, *India* **43 H11** 23 55N 84 16 E
Satevó, *Mexico* **86 B3** 27 57N 106 7W
Satilla →, *U.S.A.* **77 K5** 30 59N 81 29W
Satka, *Russia* **24 C10** 55 3N 59 1 E
Satmala Hills, *India* **40 J9** 20 15N 74 40 E
Satna, *India* **43 G9** 24 35N 80 50 E
Sátoraljaújhely, *Hungary* **17 D11** 48 25N 21 41 E
Satpura Ra., *India* **40 J10** 21 25N 76 10 E
Satsuna-Shotō, *Japan* **31 K5** 30 0N 130 0 E
Sattahip, *Thailand* **38 F3** 12 41N 100 54 E
Satu Mare, *Romania* **17 E12** 47 46N 22 55 E
Satui, *Indonesia* **36 E5** 3 50S 115 27 E
Satun, *Thailand* **39 J3** 6 43N 100 2 E
Saturnina →, *Brazil* **92 F7** 12 15S 58 10W
Sauce, *Argentina* **94 C4** 30 5S 58 46W
Sauceda, *Mexico* **86 B4** 25 55N 101 18W
Saucillo, *Mexico* **86 B3** 28 1N 105 17W
Sauda, *Norway* **9 G12** 59 40N 6 20 E
Sauðarkrókur, *Iceland* **8 D4** 65 45N 19 40W
Saudi Arabia ■, *Asia* **46 B3** 26 0N 44 0 E
Sauerland, *Germany* **16 C4** 51 12N 7 59 E
Saugeen →, *Canada* **78 B3** 44 30N 81 22W
Saugerties, *U.S.A.* **79 D11** 42 5N 73 57W
Saugus, *U.S.A.* **85 L8** 34 25N 118 32W
Sauk Centre, *U.S.A.* **80 C7** 45 44N 94 57W
Sauk Rapids, *U.S.A.* **80 C7** 45 35N 94 10W
Sault Ste. Marie, *Canada* **70 C3** 46 30N 84 20W
Sault Ste. Marie, *U.S.A.* **69 D11** 46 30N 84 21W
Saumlaki, *Indonesia* **37 F8** 7 55S 131 20 E
Saumur, *France* **18 C3** 47 15N 0 5W
Saunders C., *N.Z.* **59 L3** 45 53S 170 45 E
Saunders I., *Antarctica* **5 B1** 57 48S 26 28W
Saunders Point, *Australia* **61 E4** 27 52S 125 38 E
Saurimo, *Angola* **52 F4** 9 40S 20 12 E
Sausalito, *U.S.A.* **84 H4** 37 51N 122 29W
Savá, *Honduras* **88 C2** 15 32N 86 15W
Sava →, *Serbia, Yug.* **21 B9** 44 50N 20 26 E
Savage, *U.S.A.* **80 B2** 47 27N 104 21W
Savage I. = Niue, *Cook Is.* **65 J11** 19 2S 169 54W
Savage River, *Australia* **62 G4** 41 31S 145 14 E
Savai'i, *Samoa* **59 A12** 13 28S 172 24W
Savalou, *Benin* **50 G6** 7 57N 1 58 E
Savane, *Mozam.* **55 F4** 19 37S 35 8 E
Savanna, *U.S.A.* **80 D9** 42 5N 90 8W
Savanna-la-Mar, *Jamaica* **88 C4** 18 10N 78 10W
Savannah, *Ga., U.S.A.* **77 J5** 32 5N 81 6W
Savannah, *Mo., U.S.A.* **80 F7** 39 56N 94 50W
Savannah, *Tenn., U.S.A.* **77 H1** 35 14N 88 15W
Savannah →, *U.S.A.* **77 J5** 32 2N 80 53W
Savannakhet, *Laos* **38 D5** 16 30N 104 49 E
Savant L., *Canada* **70 B1** 50 16N 90 44W
Savant Lake, *Canada* **70 B1** 50 14N 90 40W
Save →, *Mozam.* **57 C5** 21 16S 34 0 E
Sāveh, *Iran* **45 C6** 35 2N 50 20 E
Savelugu, *Ghana* **50 G5** 9 38N 0 54W
Savo, *Finland* **8 E22** 62 45N 27 30 E
Savoie □, *France* **18 D7** 45 26N 6 25 E
Savona, *Italy* **18 D8** 44 17N 8 30 E
Savona, *U.S.A.* **78 D7** 42 17N 77 13W
Savonlinna, *Finland* **24 B4** 61 52N 28 53 E
Savoy = Savoie □, *France* **18 D7** 45 26N 6 25 E
Savur, *Turkey* **44 B4** 37 34N 40 53 E
Sawahlunto, *Indonesia* **36 E2** 0 40S 100 52 E
Sawai, *Indonesia* **37 E7** 3 0S 129 5 E
Sawai Madhopur, *India* **42 G7** 26 0N 76 25 E
Sawang Daen Din, *Thailand* **38 D4** 17 28N 103 28 E
Sawankhalok, *Thailand* **38 D2** 17 19N 99 50 E
Sawara, *Japan* **31 G10** 35 55N 140 30 E
Sawatch Range, *U.S.A.* **83 G10** 38 30N 106 30W
Sawel Mt., *U.K.* **13 B4** 54 50N 7 2W
Sawi, *Thailand* **39 G2** 10 14N 99 5 E
Sawmills, *Zimbabwe* **55 F2** 19 30S 28 2 E
Sawtooth Range, *U.S.A.* **82 E6** 44 3N 114 58W
Sawu, *Indonesia* **37 F6** 10 35S 121 50 E
Sawu Sea, *Indonesia* **37 F6** 9 30S 121 50 E
Saxby →, *Australia* **62 B3** 18 25S 140 53 E
Saxmundham, *U.K.* **11 E9** 52 13N 1 30 E
Saxony = Sachsen □, *Germany* **16 C7** 50 55N 13 10 E
Saxony, Lower = Niedersachsen □, *Germany* **16 B5** 52 50N 9 0 E
Saxton, *U.S.A.* **78 F6** 40 13N 78 15W
Sayabec, *Canada* **71 C6** 48 35N 67 41W
Sayaboury, *Laos* **38 C3** 19 15N 101 45 E
Sayán, *Peru* **92 F3** 11 8S 77 12W
Sayan, Vostochnyy, *Russia* **27 D10** 54 0N 96 0 E
Sayan, Zapadnyy, *Russia* **27 D10** 52 30N 94 0 E
Saydā, *Lebanon* **47 B4** 33 35N 35 25 E
Sayhandulaan = Oldziyt, *Mongolia* **34 B5** 44 40N 109 1 E
Sayhūt, *Yemen* **46 D5** 15 12N 51 10 E
Saynshand, *Mongolia* **33 B6** 44 55N 110 11 E
Sayre, *Okla., U.S.A.* **81 H5** 35 18N 99 38W
Sayre, *Pa., U.S.A.* **79 E8** 41 59N 76 32W
Sayreville, *U.S.A.* **79 F10** 40 28N 74 22W
Sayula, *Mexico* **86 D4** 19 50N 103 40W
Sayward, *Canada* **72 C3** 50 21N 125 55W
Sazanit, *Albania* **21 D8** 40 30N 19 20 E
Sázava →, *Czech Rep.* **16 D8** 49 53N 14 24 E
Sazin, *Pakistan* **43 B5** 35 35N 73 30 E
Scafell Pike, *U.K.* **10 C4** 54 27N 3 14W
Scalloway, *U.K.* **12 A7** 60 9N 1 17W
Scalpay, *U.K.* **12 D3** 57 18N 6 0W
Scandia, *Canada* **72 C6** 50 20N 112 0W
Scandicci, *Italy* **20 C4** 43 45N 11 11 E
Scandinavia, *Europe* **8 E16** 64 0N 12 0 E
Scapa Flow, *U.K.* **12 C5** 58 53N 3 3W
Scappoose, *U.S.A.* **84 E4** 45 45N 122 53W
Scarba, *U.K.* **12 E3** 56 11N 5 43W
Scarborough, *Trin. & Tob.* **89 D7** 11 11N 60 42W
Scarborough, *U.K.* **10 C7** 54 17N 0 24W
Scariff I., *Ireland* **13 E1** 51 44N 10 15W
Scarp, *U.K.* **12 C1** 58 1N 7 8W
Scebeli, Wabi →, *Somali Rep.* **46 G3** 2 0N 44 0 E
Schaffhausen, *Switz.* **18 C8** 47 42N 8 39 E
Schagen, *Neths.* **15 B4** 52 49N 4 48 E
Schaghticoke, *U.S.A.* **79 D11** 42 54N 73 35W
Schefferville, *Canada* **71 B6** 54 48N 66 50W
Schelde →, *Belgium* **15 C4** 51 15N 4 16 E
Schell Creek Ra., *U.S.A.* **82 G6** 39 15N 114 30W
Schellsburg, *U.S.A.* **78 F6** 40 3N 78 39W
Schenectady, *U.S.A.* **79 D11** 42 49N 73 57W
Schenevus, *U.S.A.* **79 D10** 42 33N 74 50W
Schiedam, *Neths.* **15 C4** 51 55N 4 25 E
Schiermonnikoog, *Neths.* **15 A6** 53 30N 6 15 E
Schio, *Italy* **20 B4** 45 43N 11 21 E
Schleswig, *Germany* **16 A5** 54 31N 9 34 E
Schleswig-Holstein □, *Germany* **16 A5** 54 30N 9 30 E
Schoharie, *U.S.A.* **79 D10** 42 40N 74 19W
Schoharie →, *U.S.A.* **79 D10** 42 57N 74 18W
Scholls, *U.S.A.* **84 E4** 45 24N 122 56W
Schouten I., *Australia* **62 G4** 42 20S 148 20 E
Schouten Is. = Supiori, *Indonesia* **37 E9** 1 0S 136 0 E
Schouwen, *Neths.* **15 C3** 51 43N 3 45 E
Schreiber, *Canada* **70 C2** 48 45N 87 20W
Schroffenstein, *Namibia* **56 D2** 27 11S 18 42 E
Schroon Lake, *U.S.A.* **79 C11** 43 50N 73 46W
Schuler, *Canada* **73 C6** 50 20N 110 6W
Schumacher, *Canada* **70 C3** 48 30N 81 16W
Schurz, *U.S.A.* **82 G4** 38 57N 118 49W
Schuyler, *U.S.A.* **80 E6** 41 27N 97 4W
Schuylerville, *U.S.A.* **79 C11** 43 6N 73 35W
Schuylkill →, *U.S.A.* **79 G9** 39 53N 75 12W
Schuylkill Haven, *U.S.A.* **79 F8** 40 37N 76 11W
Schwäbische Alb, *Germany* **16 D5** 48 20N 9 30 E
Schwaner, Pegunungan, *Indonesia* **36 E4** 1 0S 112 30 E
Schwarzrand, *Namibia* **56 D2** 25 37S 16 50 E
Schwarzwald, *Germany* **16 D5** 48 30N 8 20 E
Schwedt, *Germany* **16 B8** 53 3N 14 16 E
Schweinfurt, *Germany* **16 C6** 50 3N 10 14 E
Schweizer-Reneke, *S. Africa* **56 D4** 27 11S 25 18 E
Schwenningen = Villingen-Schwenningen, *Germany* **16 D5** 48 3N 8 26 E
Schwerin, *Germany* **16 B6** 53 36N 11 22 E
Schwyz, *Switz.* **18 C8** 47 2N 8 39 E
Sciacca, *Italy* **20 F5** 37 31N 13 3 E
Scilla, *Italy* **20 E6** 38 15N 15 43 E
Scilly, Isles of, *U.K.* **11 H1** 49 56N 6 22W
Scioto →, *U.S.A.* **76 F4** 38 44N 83 1W
Scituate, *U.S.A.* **79 D14** 42 12N 70 44W
Scobey, *U.S.A.* **80 A2** 48 47N 105 25W
Scoresbysund = Ittoqqortoormiit, *Greenland* **4 B6** 70 20N 23 0W
Scotia, *Calif., U.S.A.* **82 F1** 40 29N 124 6W
Scotia, *N.Y., U.S.A.* **79 D11** 42 50N 73 58W
Scotia Sea, *Antarctica* **5 B18** 56 5S 56 0W
Scotland, *Canada* **78 C4** 43 1N 80 22W
Scotland □, *U.K.* **12 E5** 57 0N 4 0W
Scott, C., *Australia* **60 B4** 13 30S 129 49 E
Scott City, *U.S.A.* **80 F4** 38 29N 100 54W
Scott Glacier, *Antarctica* **5 C8** 66 15S 100 5 E
Scott I., *Antarctica* **5 C11** 67 0S 179 0 E
Scott Is., *Canada* **72 C3** 50 48N 128 40W
Scott L., *Canada* **73 B7** 59 55N 106 18W
Scott Reef, *Australia* **60 B3** 14 0S 121 50 E
Scottburgh, *S. Africa* **57 E5** 30 15S 30 47 E
Scottdale, *U.S.A.* **78 F5** 40 6N 79 35W
Scottish Borders □, *U.K.* **12 F6** 55 35N 2 50W
Scottsbluff, *U.S.A.* **80 E3** 41 52N 103 40W
Scottsboro, *U.S.A.* **77 H3** 34 40N 86 2W
Scottsburg, *U.S.A.* **76 F3** 38 41N 85 47W
Scottsdale, *Australia* **62 G4** 41 9S 147 31 E
Scottsdale, *U.S.A.* **83 K7** 33 29N 111 56W
Scottsville, *Ky., U.S.A.* **77 G2** 36 45N 86 11W
Scottsville, *N.Y., U.S.A.* **78 C7** 43 2N 77 47W
Scottville, *U.S.A.* **76 D2** 43 58N 86 17W
Scranton, *U.S.A.* **79 E9** 41 25N 75 40W
Scugog, L., *Canada* **78 B6** 44 10N 78 55W
Scunthorpe, *U.K.* **10 D7** 53 36N 0 39W
Seabrook, L., *Australia* **61 F2** 30 55S 119 40 E
Seaford, *U.K.* **11 G8** 50 47N 0 7 E
Seaford, *U.S.A.* **76 F8** 38 39N 75 37W
Seaforth, *Australia* **62 C4** 20 55S 148 57 E
Seaforth, *Canada* **78 C3** 43 35N 81 25W
Seaforth, L., *U.K.* **12 D2** 57 52N 6 36W
Seagraves, *U.S.A.* **81 J3** 32 57N 102 34W
Seaham, *U.K.* **10 C6** 54 50N 1 20W
Seal →, *Canada* **73 B10** 59 4N 94 48W
Seal L., *Canada* **71 B7** 54 20N 61 30W
Sealy, *U.S.A.* **81 L6** 29 47N 96 9W
Searchlight, *U.S.A.* **85 K12** 35 28N 114 55W
Searcy, *U.S.A.* **81 H9** 35 15N 91 44W
Searles L., *U.S.A.* **85 K9** 35 44N 117 21W
Seascale, *U.K.* **10 C4** 54 24N 3 29W
Seaside, *Calif., U.S.A.* **84 J5** 36 37N 121 50W
Seaside, *Oreg., U.S.A.* **84 E3** 46 0N 123 56W
Seaspray, *Australia* **63 F4** 38 25S 147 15 E
Seattle, *U.S.A.* **84 C4** 47 36N 122 20W
Seaview Ra., *Australia* **62 B4** 18 40S 145 45 E
Sebago L., *U.S.A.* **79 C14** 43 52N 70 34W
Sebago Lake, *U.S.A.* **79 C14** 43 51N 70 34W
Sebastián Vizcaíno, B., *Mexico* **86 B2** 28 0N 114 30W
Sebastopol = Sevastopol, *Ukraine* **25 F5** 44 35N 33 30 E
Sebastopol, *U.S.A.* **84 G4** 38 24N 122 49W
Sebewaing, *U.S.A.* **76 D4** 43 44N 83 27W
Sebha = Sabhah, *Libya* **51 C8** 27 9N 14 29 E
Şebinkarahisar, *Turkey* **25 F6** 40 22N 38 28 E
Sebring, *Fla., U.S.A.* **77 M5** 27 30N 81 27W
Sebring, *Ohio, U.S.A.* **78 F3** 40 55N 81 2W
Sebringville, *Canada* **78 C3** 43 24N 81 4W
Sebta = Ceuta, *N. Afr.* **19 E3** 35 52N 5 18W
Sebuku, *Indonesia* **36 E5** 3 30S 116 25 E
Sebuku, Teluk, *Malaysia* **36 D5** 4 0N 118 10 E
Sechelt, *Canada* **72 D4** 49 25N 123 42W
Sechura, Desierto de, *Peru* **92 E2** 6 0S 80 30W
Secretary I., *N.Z.* **59 L1** 45 15S 166 56 E
Secunderabad, *India* **40 L11** 17 28N 78 30 E
Security-Widefield, *U.S.A.* **80 F2** 38 45N 104 45W
Sedalia, *U.S.A.* **80 F8** 38 42N 93 14W
Sedan, *France* **18 B6** 49 43N 4 57 E
Sedan, *U.S.A.* **81 G6** 37 8N 96 11W
Seddon, *N.Z.* **59 J5** 41 40S 174 7 E
Seddonville, *N.Z.* **59 J4** 41 33S 172 1 E
Sedé Boqér, *Israel* **47 E3** 30 52N 34 47 E
Sedeh, *Fārs, Iran* **45 D7** 30 45N 52 11 E
Sedeh, *Khorāsān, Iran* **45 C8** 33 20N 59 14 E
Sederot, *Israel* **47 D3** 31 32N 34 37 E
Sédhiou, *Senegal* **50 F2** 12 44N 15 30W
Sedley, *Canada* **73 C8** 50 10N 104 0W
Sedona, *U.S.A.* **83 J8** 34 52N 111 46W
Sedova, Pik, *Russia* **26 B6** 73 29N 54 58 E
Sedro Woolley, *U.S.A.* **84 B4** 48 30N 122 14W
Seeheim, *Namibia* **56 D2** 26 50S 17 45 E
Seeis, *Namibia* **56 C2** 22 29S 17 39 E
Seekoei →, *S. Africa* **56 E4** 30 18S 25 1 E
Seeley's Bay, *Canada* **79 B8** 44 29N 76 14W
Seferihisar, *Turkey* **21 E12** 38 10N 26 50 E
Seg-ozero, *Russia* **24 B5** 63 20N 33 46 E
Segamat, *Malaysia* **39 L4** 2 30N 102 50 E
Segesta, *Italy* **20 F5** 37 56N 12 50 E
Seget, *Indonesia* **37 E8** 1 24S 130 58 E
Segezha, *Russia* **24 B5** 63 44N 34 19 E
Ségou, *Mali* **50 F4** 13 30N 6 16W
Segovia = Coco →, *Cent. Amer.* **88 D3** 15 0N 83 8W
Segovia, *Spain* **19 B3** 40 57N 4 10W
Segre →, *Spain* **19 B6** 41 40N 0 43 E
Séguéla, *Ivory C.* **50 G4** 7 55N 6 40W
Seguin, *U.S.A.* **81 L6** 29 34N 97 58W
Segundo →, *Argentina* **94 C3** 30 53S 62 44W
Segura →, *Spain* **19 C5** 38 3N 0 44W
Seh Konj, Kūh-e, *Iran* **45 D8** 30 6N 57 30 E
Seh Qal'eh, *Iran* **45 C8** 33 40N 58 24 E
Sehitwa, *Botswana* **56 C3** 20 30S 22 30 E
Sehore, *India* **42 H7** 23 10N 77 5 E
Sehwan, *Pakistan* **42 F2** 26 28N 67 53 E
Seil, *U.K.* **12 E3** 56 18N 5 38W
Seiland, *Norway* **8 A20** 70 25N 23 15 E
Seiling, *U.S.A.* **81 G5** 36 9N 98 56W
Seinäjoki, *Finland* **9 E20** 62 40N 22 51 E
Seine →, *France* **18 B4** 49 26N 0 26 E
Seistan = Sīstān, *Asia* **45 D9** 30 50N 61 0 E
Seistan, Daryācheh-ye = Sīstān, Daryācheh-ye, *Iran* **45 D9** 31 0N 61 0 E
Sekayu, *Indonesia* **36 E2** 2 51S 103 51 E
Seke, *Tanzania* **54 C3** 3 20S 33 31 E
Sekenke, *Tanzania* **54 C3** 4 18S 34 11 E
Sekondi-Takoradi, *Ghana* **50 H5** 4 58N 1 45W
Sekuma, *Botswana* **56 C3** 24 36S 23 50 E
Selah, *U.S.A.* **82 C3** 46 39N 120 32W
Selama, *Malaysia* **39 K3** 5 12N 100 42 E
Selaru, *Indonesia* **37 F8** 8 9S 131 0 E
Selby, *U.K.* **10 D6** 53 47N 1 5W
Selby, *U.S.A.* **80 C4** 45 31N 100 2W
Selçuk, *Turkey* **21 F12** 37 56N 27 22 E
Selden, *U.S.A.* **80 F4** 39 33N 100 34W
Sele →, *Italy* **20 D6** 40 29N 14 56 E
Selebi-Pikwe, *Botswana* **57 C4** 21 58S 27 48 E
Selemdzha →, *Russia* **27 D13** 51 42N 128 53 E
Selenga = Selenge Mörön →, *Asia* **32 A5** 52 16N 106 16 E
Selenge Mörön →, *Asia* **32 A5** 52 16N 106 16 E
Seletan, Tanjung, *Indonesia* **36 E4** 4 10S 114 40 E
Sélibabi, *Mauritania* **50 E3** 15 10N 12 15W
Seligman, *U.S.A.* **83 J7** 35 20N 112 53W
Selîma, El Wâhât el, *Sudan* **51 D11** 21 22N 29 19 E
Selinda Spillway →, *Botswana* **56 B3** 18 35S 23 10 E
Selinsgrove, *U.S.A.* **78 F8** 40 48N 76 52W
Selkirk, *Canada* **73 C9** 50 10N 96 55W
Selkirk, *U.K.* **12 F6** 55 33N 2 50W
Selkirk I., *Canada* **73 C9** 53 20N 99 6W
Selkirk Mts., *Canada* **68 C8** 51 15N 117 40W
Selliá, *Greece* **23 D6** 35 12N 24 23 E
Sells, *U.S.A.* **83 L8** 31 55N 111 53W
Selma, *Ala., U.S.A.* **77 J2** 32 25N 87 1W
Selma, *Calif., U.S.A.* **84 J7** 36 34N 119 37W
Selma, *N.C., U.S.A.* **77 H6** 35 32N 78 17W
Selmer, *U.S.A.* **77 H1** 35 10N 88 36W
Selowandoma Falls, *Zimbabwe* **55 G3** 21 15S 31 50 E
Selpele, *Indonesia* **37 E8** 0 1S 130 5 E
Selsey Bill, *U.K.* **11 G7** 50 43N 0 47W
Seltso, *Russia* **24 D5** 53 22N 34 4 E
Selu, *Indonesia* **37 F8** 7 32S 130 55 E
Selva, *Argentina* **94 B3** 29 50S 62 0W
Selvas, *Brazil* **92 E5** 6 30S 67 0W
Selwyn L., *Canada* **73 B8** 60 0N 104 30W
Selwyn Mts., *Canada* **68 B6** 63 0N 130 0W
Selwyn Ra., *Australia* **62 C3** 21 10S 140 0 E
Seman →, *Albania* **21 D8** 40 47N 19 30 E
Semarang, *Indonesia* **36 F4** 7 0S 110 26 E
Sembabule, *Uganda* **54 C3** 0 4S 31 25 E
Semeru, *Indonesia* **37 H15** 8 4S 112 55 E
Semey, *Kazakstan* **26 D9** 50 30N 80 10 E
Seminoe Reservoir, *U.S.A.* **82 F10** 42 9N 106 55W
Seminole, *Okla., U.S.A.* **81 H6** 35 14N 96 41W
Seminole, *Tex., U.S.A.* **81 J3** 32 43N 102 39W
Seminole Draw →, *U.S.A.* **81 J3** 32 27N 102 20W
Semipalatinsk = Semey, *Kazakstan* **26 D9** 50 30N 80 10 E
Semirara Is., *Phil.* **37 B6** 12 0N 121 20 E
Semitau, *Indonesia* **36 D4** 0 29N 111 57 E
Semiyarka, *Kazakstan* **26 D8** 50 55N 78 23 E
Semiyarskoye = Semiyarka, *Kazakstan* **26 D8** 50 55N 78 23 E
Semmering P., *Austria* **16 E8** 47 41N 15 45 E
Semnān, *Iran* **45 C7** 35 40N 53 23 E
Semnān □, *Iran* **45 C7** 36 0N 54 0 E
Semporna, *Malaysia* **37 D5** 4 30N 118 33 E
Semuda, *Indonesia* **36 E4** 2 51S 112 58 E
Sen →, *Cambodia* **36 B3** 13 45N 105 12 E
Senā, *Iran* **45 D6** 28 27N 51 36 E
Sena, *Mozam.* **55 F4** 17 25S 35 0 E
Sena Madureira, *Brazil* **92 E5** 9 5S 68 45W
Senador Pompeu, *Brazil* **93 E11** 5 40S 39 20W
Senanga, *Zambia* **53 H4** 16 7S 23 16 E
Senatobia, *U.S.A.* **81 H10** 34 37N 89 58W
Sencelles, *Spain* **22 B9** 39 39N 2 54 E
Sendai, *Kagoshima, Japan* **31 J5** 31 50N 130 20 E
Sendai, *Miyagi, Japan* **30 E10** 38 15N 140 53 E
Sendai-Wan, *Japan* **30 E10** 38 15N 141 0 E
Sendhwa, *India* **42 J6** 21 41N 75 6 E
Seneca, *U.S.A.* **77 H4** 34 41N 82 57W
Seneca Falls, *U.S.A.* **79 D8** 42 55N 76 48W
Seneca L., *U.S.A.* **78 D8** 42 40N 76 54W
Senecaville L., *U.S.A.* **78 G3** 39 55N 81 25W
Senegal ■, *W. Afr.* **50 F3** 14 30N 14 30W
Sénégal →, *W. Afr.* **50 E2** 15 48N 16 32W
Senegambia, *Africa* **48 E2** 12 45N 12 0W
Senekal, *S. Africa* **57 D4** 28 20S 27 36 E
Senga Hill, *Zambia* **55 D3** 9 19S 31 11 E
Senge Khambab = Indus →, *Pakistan* **42 G2** 24 20N 67 47 E
Sengua →, *Zimbabwe* **55 F2** 17 7S 28 5 E
Senhor-do-Bonfim, *Brazil* **93 F10** 10 30S 40 10W
Senigállia, *Italy* **20 C5** 43 43N 13 13 E
Senj, *Croatia* **16 F8** 45 0N 14 58 E
Senja, *Norway* **8 B17** 69 25N 17 30 E
Senkaku-Shotō, *Japan* **31 L1** 25 45N 124 0 E
Senlis, *France* **18 B5** 49 13N 2 35 E
Senmonorom, *Cambodia* **38 F6** 12 27N 107 12 E
Senneterre, *Canada* **70 C4** 48 25N 77 15W
Seno, *Laos* **38 D5** 16 35N 104 50 E
Sens, *France* **18 B5** 48 11N 3 15 E
Senta, *Serbia, Yug.* **21 B9** 45 55N 20 3 E
Sentani, *Indonesia* **37 E10** 2 36S 140 37 E
Sentery, *Dem. Rep. of the Congo* **54 D2** 5 17S 25 42 E
Sentinel, *U.S.A.* **83 K7** 32 52N 113 13W
Seo de Urgel = La Seu d'Urgell, *Spain* **19 A6** 42 22N 1 23 E
Seohara, *India* **43 E8** 29 15N 78 33 E
Seonath →, *India* **43 J10** 21 44N 82 28 E
Seondha, *India* **43 F8** 26 9N 78 48 E
Seoni, *India* **43 H8** 22 5N 79 30 E
Seoni Malwa, *India* **42 H8** 22 27N 77 28 E
Seoul = Sŏul, *S. Korea* **35 F14** 37 31N 126 58 E
Sepīdān, *Iran* **45 D7** 30 20N 52 5 E
Sepo-ri, *N. Korea* **35 E14** 38 57N 127 25 E
Sepone, *Laos* **38 D6** 16 45N 106 13 E
Sept-Îles, *Canada* **71 B6** 50 13N 66 22W
Sequim, *U.S.A.* **84 B3** 48 5N 123 6W
Sequoia National Park, *U.S.A.* **84 J8** 36 30N 118 30W
Seraing, *Belgium* **15 D5** 50 35N 5 32 E
Seraja, *Indonesia* **39 L7** 2 41N 108 35 E
Serakhis →, *Cyprus* **23 D11** 35 13N 32 55 E
Seram, *Indonesia* **37 E7** 3 10S 129 0 E
Seram Sea, *Indonesia* **37 E7** 2 30S 128 30 E
Seranantsara, *Madag.* **57 B8** 18 30S 49 5 E
Serang, *Indonesia* **37 G12** 6 8S 106 10 E
Serasan, *Indonesia* **39 L7** 2 29N 109 4 E
Serbia □, *Yugoslavia* **21 C9** 43 30N 21 0 E
Serdobsk, *Russia* **24 D7** 52 28N 44 10 E
Seremban, *Malaysia* **39 L3** 2 43N 101 53 E
Serengeti Plain, *Tanzania* **54 C4** 2 40S 35 0 E
Serenje, *Zambia* **55 E3** 13 14S 30 15 E
Sereth = Siret →, *Romania* **17 F14** 45 24N 28 1 E
Sergino, *Russia* **26 C7** 62 25N 65 12 E
Sergipe □, *Brazil* **93 F11** 10 30S 37 30W
Sergiyev Posad, *Russia* **24 C6** 56 20N 38 10 E
Seria, *Brunei* **36 D4** 4 37N 114 23 E
Serian, *Malaysia* **36 D4** 1 10N 110 31 E
Seribu, Kepulauan, *Indonesia* **36 F3** 5 36S 106 33 E
Sérifos, *Greece* **21 F11** 37 9N 24 30 E
Sérigny →, *Canada* **71 A6** 56 47N 66 0W
Seringapatam Reef, *Australia* **60 B3** 13 38S 122 5 E
Sermata, *Indonesia* **37 F7** 8 15S 128 50 E
Serov, *Russia* **24 C11** 59 29N 60 35 E
Serowe, *Botswana* **56 C4** 22 25S 26 43 E
Serpentine Lakes, *Australia* **61 E4** 28 30S 129 10 E
Serpukhov, *Russia* **24 D6** 54 55N 37 28 E
Serra do Navio, *Brazil* **93 C8** 0 59N 52 3W
Sérrai, *Greece* **21 D10** 41 5N 23 31 E
Serrezuela, *Argentina* **94 C2** 30 40S 65 20W
Serrinha, *Brazil* **93 F11** 11 39S 39 0W
Sertanópolis, *Brazil* **95 A5** 23 4S 51 2W
Serua, *Indonesia* **37 F8** 6 18S 130 1 E
Serui, *Indonesia* **37 E9** 1 53S 136 10 E
Serule, *Botswana* **56 C4** 21 57S 27 20 E
Sese Is., *Uganda* **54 C3** 0 20S 32 20 E
Sesepe, *Indonesia* **37 E7** 1 30S 127 59 E
Sesfontein, *Namibia* **56 B1** 19 7S 13 39 E
Sesheke, *Zambia* **56 B3** 17 29S 24 13 E
S'Espalmador, *Spain* **22 C7** 38 47N 1 26 E
S'Espardell, *Spain* **22 C7** 38 48N 1 29 E
S'Estanyol, *Spain* **22 B9** 39 22N 2 54 E
Setana, *Japan* **30 C9** 42 26N 139 51 E
Sète, *France* **18 E5** 43 25N 3 42 E
Sete Lagôas, *Brazil* **93 G10** 19 27S 44 16W
Sétif, *Algeria* **50 A7** 36 9N 5 26 E
Seto, *Japan* **31 G8** 35 14N 137 6 E
Setonaikai, *Japan* **31 G6** 34 20N 133 30 E
Settat, *Morocco* **50 B4** 33 0N 7 40W
Setting L., *Canada* **73 C9** 55 0N 98 38W
Settle, *U.K.* **10 C5** 54 5N 2 16W
Settlement Pt., *Bahamas* **77 M6** 26 40N 79 0W
Settlers, *S. Africa* **57 C4** 25 2S 28 30 E
Setúbal, *Portugal* **19 C1** 38 30N 8 58W
Setúbal, B. de, *Portugal* **19 C1** 38 40N 8 56W
Seul, Lac, *Canada* **70 B1** 50 20N 92 30W
Sevan, Ozero = Sevana Lich, *Armenia* **25 F8** 40 30N 45 20 E
Sevana Lich, *Armenia* **25 F8** 40 30N 45 20 E
Sevastopol, *Ukraine* **25 F5** 44 35N 33 30 E
Seven Sisters, *Canada* **72 C3** 54 56N 128 10W
Severn →, *Canada* **70 A2** 56 2N 87 36W
Severn →, *U.K.* **11 F5** 51 35N 2 40W
Severn L., *Canada* **70 B1** 53 54N 90 48W
Severnaya Zemlya, *Russia* **27 B10** 79 0N 100 0 E
Severnyye Uvaly, *Russia* **24 C8** 60 0N 50 0 E
Severo-Kurilsk, *Russia* **27 D16** 50 40N 156 8 E
Severo-Yeniseyskiy, *Russia* **27 C10** 60 22N 93 1 E
Severodvinsk, *Russia* **24 B6** 64 27N 39 58 E
Severomorsk, *Russia* **24 A5** 69 5N 33 27 E
Severouralsk, *Russia* **24 B10** 60 9N 59 57 E
Sevier, *U.S.A.* **83 G7** 38 39N 112 11W
Sevier →, *U.S.A.* **83 G7** 39 4N 113 6W
Sevier Desert, *U.S.A.* **82 G7** 39 40N 112 45W
Sevier L., *U.S.A.* **82 G7** 38 54N 113 9W
Sevilla, *Spain* **19 D2** 37 23N 5 58W
Seville = Sevilla, *Spain* **19 D2** 37 23N 5 58W
Sevlievo, *Bulgaria* **21 C11** 43 2N 25 6 E
Sewani, *India* **42 E6** 28 58N 75 39 E
Seward, *Alaska, U.S.A.* **68 B5** 60 7N 149 27W
Seward, *Nebr., U.S.A.* **80 E6** 40 55N 97 6W
Seward, *Pa., U.S.A.* **78 F5** 40 25N 79 1W
Seward Peninsula, *U.S.A.* **68 B3** 65 30N 166 0W
Sewell, *Chile* **94 C1** 34 10S 70 23W
Sewer, *Indonesia* **37 F8** 5 53S 134 40 E
Sewickley, *U.S.A.* **78 F4** 40 32N 80 12W
Sexsmith, *Canada* **72 B5** 55 21N 118 47W
Seychelles ■, *Ind. Oc.* **29 K9** 5 0S 56 0 E
Seyðisfjörður, *Iceland* **8 D6** 65 16N 13 57W
Seydişehir, *Turkey* **25 G5** 37 25N 31 51 E
Seydvān, *Iran* **44 B5** 38 34N 45 2 E
Seyhan →, *Turkey* **44 B2** 36 43N 34 53 E

Seym →, *Ukraine* 25 D5 51 27N 32 34 E
Seymour, *S. Africa* 57 E4 32 33S 26 46 E
Seymour, *Conn., U.S.A.* 79 E11 41 24N 73 4W
Seymour, *Ind., U.S.A.* 76 F3 38 58N 85 53W
Seymour, *Tex., U.S.A.* 81 J5 33 35N 99 16W
Sfântu Gheorghe, *Romania* 17 F13 45 52N 25 48 E
Sfax, *Tunisia* 51 B8 34 49N 10 48 E
Shaanxi □, *China* 34 G5 35 0N 109 0 E
Shaba = Katanga □, *Dem. Rep. of the Congo* 54 D2 8 0S 25 0 E
Shabogamo L., *Canada* 71 B6 53 15N 66 30W
Shabunda, *Dem. Rep. of the Congo* 54 C2 2 40S 27 16 E
Shache, *China* 32 C2 38 20N 77 10 E
Shackleton Ice Shelf, *Antarctica* 5 C8 66 0S 100 0 E
Shackleton Inlet, *Antarctica* 5 E11 83 0S 160 0 E
Shādegān, *Iran* 45 D6 30 40N 48 38 E
Shadi, *India* 43 C7 33 24N 77 14 E
Shadrinsk, *Russia* 26 D7 56 5N 63 32 E
Shadyside, *U.S.A.* 78 G4 39 58N 80 45W
Shafter, *U.S.A.* 85 K7 35 30N 119 16W
Shaftesbury, *U.K.* 11 F5 51 0N 2 11W
Shagram, *Pakistan* 43 A5 36 24N 72 20 E
Shah Alizai, *Pakistan* 42 E2 29 25N 66 33 E
Shah Bunder, *Pakistan* 42 G2 24 13N 67 56 E
Shahabad, *Punjab, India* 42 D7 30 10N 76 55 E
Shahabad, *Raj., India* 42 G7 25 15N 77 11 E
Shahabad, *Ut. P., India* 43 F8 27 36N 79 56 E
Shahadpur, *Pakistan* 42 G3 25 55N 68 35 E
Shahba, *Syria* 47 C5 32 52N 36 38 E
Shahdād, *Iran* 45 D8 30 30N 57 40 E
Shahdād, Namakzār-e, *Iran* 45 D8 30 20N 58 20 E
Shahdadkot, *Pakistan* 42 F2 27 50N 67 55 E
Shahdol, *India* 43 H9 23 19N 81 26 E
Shahe, *China* 34 F8 37 0N 114 32 E
Shahganj, *India* 43 F10 26 3N 82 44 E
Shahgarh, *India* 40 F6 27 15N 69 50 E
Shahjahanpur, *India* 43 F8 27 54N 79 57 E
Shahpur, *India* 42 H7 22 12N 77 58 E
Shahpur, *Baluchistan, Pakistan* 42 E3 28 46N 68 27 E
Shahpur, *Punjab, Pakistan* 42 C5 32 17N 72 26 E
Shahpur Chakar, *Pakistan* 42 F3 26 9N 68 39 E
Shahpura, *Mad. P., India* 43 H9 23 10N 80 45 E
Shahpura, *Raj., India* 42 G6 25 38N 74 56 E
Shahr-e Bābak, *Iran* 45 D7 30 7N 55 9 E
Shahr-e Kord, *Iran* 45 C6 32 15N 50 55 E
Shāhrakht, *Iran* 45 C9 33 38N 60 16 E
Shahrig, *Pakistan* 42 D2 30 15N 67 40 E
Shahukou, *China* 34 D7 40 20N 112 18 E
Shaikhabad, *Afghan.* 42 B3 34 2N 68 45 E
Shajapur, *India* 42 H7 23 27N 76 21 E
Shakargarh, *Pakistan* 42 C6 32 17N 75 10 E
Shakawe, *Botswana* 56 B3 18 28S 21 49 E
Shaker Heights, *U.S.A.* 78 E3 41 29N 81 32W
Shakhty, *Russia* 25 E7 47 40N 40 16 E
Shakhunya, *Russia* 24 C8 57 40N 46 46 E
Shaki, *Nigeria* 50 G6 8 41N 3 21 E
Shallow Lake, *Canada* 78 B3 44 36N 81 5W
Shalqar, *Kazakstan* 26 E6 47 48N 59 39 E
Shaluli Shan, *China* 32 C4 30 40N 99 55 E
Shām, *Iran* 45 E8 26 39N 57 21 E
Shām, Bādiyat ash, *Asia* 44 C3 32 0N 40 0 E
Shamâl Kordofân □, *Sudan* 48 E6 15 0N 30 0 E
Shamattawa, *Canada* 70 A1 55 51N 92 5W
Shamattawa →, *Canada* 70 A2 55 1N 85 23W
Shamīl, *Iran* 45 E8 27 30N 56 55 E
Shāmkūh, *Iran* 45 C8 35 47N 57 50 E
Shamli, *India* 42 E7 29 32N 77 18 E
Shammar, Jabal, *Si. Arabia* 44 E4 27 40N 41 0 E
Shamo = Gobi, *Asia* 34 C6 44 0N 110 0 E
Shamo, L., *Ethiopia* 46 F2 5 45N 37 30 E
Shamokin, *U.S.A.* 79 F8 40 47N 76 34W
Shamrock, *U.S.A.* 81 H4 35 13N 100 15W
Shamva, *Zimbabwe* 55 F3 17 20S 31 32 E
Shan □, *Burma* 41 J21 21 30N 98 30 E
Shan Xian, *China* 34 G9 34 50N 116 5 E
Shanchengzhen, *China* 35 C13 42 20N 125 20 E
Shāndak, *Iran* 45 D9 28 28N 60 27 E
Shandon, *U.S.A.* 84 K6 35 39N 120 23W
Shandong □, *China* 35 G10 36 0N 118 0 E
Shandong Bandao, *China* 35 F11 37 0N 121 0 E
Shang Xian = Shangzhou, *China* 34 H5 33 50N 109 58 E
Shanga, *Nigeria* 50 F6 11 12N 4 33 E
Shangalowe, *Dem. Rep. of the Congo* 55 E2 10 50S 26 30 E
Shangani, *Zimbabwe* 57 B4 19 41S 29 20 E
Shangani →, *Zimbabwe* 55 F2 18 41S 27 10 E
Shangbancheng, *China* 35 D10 40 50N 118 1 E
Shangdu, *China* 34 D7 41 30N 113 30 E
Shanghai, *China* 33 C7 31 15N 121 26 E
Shanghe, *China* 35 F9 37 20N 117 10 E
Shangnan, *China* 34 H6 33 32N 110 50 E
Shangqiu, *China* 34 G8 34 26N 115 36 E
Shangrao, *China* 33 D6 28 25N 117 59 E
Shangshui, *China* 33 C6 33 42N 114 35 E
Shangzhi, *China* 35 B14 45 22N 127 56 E
Shangzhou, *China* 34 H5 33 50N 109 58 E
Shanhetun, *China* 35 B14 44 33N 127 15 E
Shannon, *N.Z.* 59 J5 40 33S 175 25 E
Shannon →, *Ireland* 13 D2 52 35N 9 30W
Shannon, Mouth of the, *Ireland* 13 D2 52 30N 9 55W
Shannon Airport, *Ireland* 13 D3 52 42N 8 57W
Shansi = Shanxi □, *China* 34 F7 37 0N 112 0 E
Shantar, Ostrov Bolshoy, *Russia* 27 D14 55 9N 137 40 E
Shantipur, *India* 43 H13 23 17N 88 25 E
Shantou, *China* 33 D6 23 18N 116 40 E
Shantung = Shandong □, *China* 35 G10 36 0N 118 0 E
Shanxi □, *China* 34 F7 37 0N 112 0 E
Shanyang, *China* 34 H5 33 31N 109 55 E
Shanyin, *China* 34 E7 39 25N 112 56 E
Shaoguan, *China* 33 D6 24 48N 113 35 E
Shaoxing, *China* 33 D7 30 0N 120 35 E
Shaoyang, *China* 33 D6 27 14N 111 25 E
Shap, *U.K.* 10 C5 54 32N 2 40W
Shapinsay, *U.K.* 12 B6 59 3N 2 51W
Shaqra', *Si. Arabia* 44 E5 25 15N 45 16 E
Shaqrā', *Yemen* 46 E4 13 22N 45 44 E
Sharafkhāneh, *Iran* 44 B5 38 11N 45 29 E
Sharbot Lake, *Canada* 79 B8 44 46N 76 41W
Shari, *Japan* 30 C12 43 55N 144 40 E
Sharjah = Ash Shāriqah, *U.A.E.* 46 B6 25 23N 55 26 E
Shark B., *Australia* 61 E1 25 30S 113 32 E
Sharon, *Mass., U.S.A.* 79 D13 42 7N 71 11W
Sharon, *Pa., U.S.A.* 78 E4 41 14N 80 31W
Sharon Springs, *Kans., U.S.A.* 80 F4 38 54N 101 45W
Sharon Springs, *N.Y., U.S.A.* 79 D10 42 48N 74 37W
Sharp Pt., *Australia* 62 A3 10 58S 142 43 E
Sharpe L., *Canada* 70 B1 54 24N 93 40W
Sharpsville, *U.S.A.* 78 E4 41 15N 80 29W
Sharya, *Russia* 24 C8 58 22N 45 20 E
Shashemene, *Ethiopia* 46 F2 7 13N 38 33 E
Shashi, *Botswana* 57 C4 21 15S 27 27 E
Shashi, *China* 33 C6 30 25N 112 14 E
Shashi →, *Africa* 55 G2 21 14S 29 20 E
Shasta, Mt., *U.S.A.* 82 F2 41 25N 122 12W
Shasta L., *U.S.A.* 82 F2 40 43N 122 25W
Shatt al Arab = Arab, Shatt al →, *Asia* 45 D6 30 0N 48 31 E
Shaunavon, *Canada* 73 D7 49 35N 108 25W
Shaver L., *U.S.A.* 84 H7 37 9N 119 18W
Shaw →, *Australia* 60 D2 20 21S 119 17 E
Shaw I., *Australia* 62 C4 20 30S 149 2 E
Shawanaga, *Canada* 78 A4 45 31N 80 17W
Shawangunk Mts., *U.S.A.* 79 E10 41 35N 74 30W
Shawano, *U.S.A.* 76 C1 44 47N 88 36W
Shawinigan, *Canada* 70 C5 46 35N 72 50W
Shawnee, *U.S.A.* 81 H6 35 20N 96 55W
Shay Gap, *Australia* 60 D3 20 30S 120 10 E
Shaybārā, *Si. Arabia* 44 E3 25 26N 36 47 E
Shaykh, J. ash, *Lebanon* 47 B4 33 25N 35 50 E
Shaykh Miskīn, *Syria* 47 C5 32 49N 36 9 E
Shaykh Sa'īd, *Iraq* 44 C5 32 34N 46 17 E
Shcherbakov = Rybinsk, *Russia* 24 C6 58 5N 38 50 E
Shchuchinsk, *Kazakstan* 26 D8 52 56N 70 12 E
She Xian, *China* 34 F7 36 30N 113 40 E
Shebele = Scebeli, Wabi →, *Somali Rep.* 46 G3 2 0N 44 0 E
Sheboygan, *U.S.A.* 76 D2 43 46N 87 45W
Shediac, *Canada* 71 C7 46 14N 64 32W
Sheelin, L., *Ireland* 13 C4 53 48N 7 20W
Sheep Haven, *Ireland* 13 A4 55 11N 7 52W
Sheerness, *U.K.* 11 F8 51 26N 0 47 E
Sheet Harbour, *Canada* 71 D7 44 56N 62 31W
Sheffield, *U.K.* 10 D6 53 23N 1 28W
Sheffield, *Ala., U.S.A.* 77 H2 34 46N 87 41W
Sheffield, *Mass., U.S.A.* 79 D11 42 5N 73 21W
Sheffield, *Pa., U.S.A.* 78 E5 41 42N 79 3W
Sheikhpura, *India* 43 G11 25 9N 85 53 E
Shekhupura, *Pakistan* 42 D5 31 42N 73 58 E
Shelburne, *N.S., Canada* 71 D6 43 47N 65 20W
Shelburne, *Ont., Canada* 78 B4 44 4N 80 15W
Shelburne, *U.S.A.* 79 B11 44 23N 73 14W
Shelburne B., *Australia* 62 A3 11 50S 142 50 E
Shelburne Falls, *U.S.A.* 79 D12 42 36N 72 45W
Shelby, *Mich., U.S.A.* 76 D2 43 37N 86 22W
Shelby, *Miss., U.S.A.* 81 J9 33 57N 90 46W
Shelby, *Mont., U.S.A.* 82 B8 48 30N 111 51W
Shelby, *N.C., U.S.A.* 77 H5 35 17N 81 32W
Shelby, *Ohio, U.S.A.* 78 F2 40 53N 82 40W
Shelbyville, *Ill., U.S.A.* 80 F10 39 24N 88 48W
Shelbyville, *Ind., U.S.A.* 76 F3 39 31N 85 47W
Shelbyville, *Ky., U.S.A.* 76 F3 38 13N 85 14W
Shelbyville, *Tenn., U.S.A.* 77 H2 35 29N 86 28W
Sheldon, *U.S.A.* 80 D7 43 11N 95 51W
Sheldrake, *Canada* 71 B7 50 20N 64 51W
Shelikhova, Zaliv, *Russia* 27 D16 59 30N 157 0 E
Shell Lakes, *Australia* 61 E4 29 20S 127 30 E
Shellbrook, *Canada* 73 C7 53 13N 106 24W
Shelter I, *U.S.A.* 79 E12 41 5N 72 21W
Shelton, *Conn., U.S.A.* 79 E11 41 19N 73 5W
Shelton, *Wash., U.S.A.* 84 C3 47 13N 123 6W
Shen Xian, *China* 34 F8 36 15N 115 40 E
Shenandoah, *Iowa, U.S.A.* 80 E7 40 46N 95 22W
Shenandoah, *Pa., U.S.A.* 79 F8 40 49N 76 12W
Shenandoah, *Va., U.S.A.* 76 F6 38 29N 78 37W
Shenandoah →, *U.S.A.* 76 F7 39 19N 77 44W
Shenandoah National Park, *U.S.A.* 76 F6 38 35N 78 22W
Shenchi, *China* 34 E7 39 8N 112 10 E
Shendam, *Nigeria* 50 G7 8 49N 9 30 E
Shendī, *Sudan* 51 E12 16 46N 33 22 E
Shengfang, *China* 34 E9 39 3N 116 42 E
Shenjingzi, *China* 35 B13 44 40N 124 30 E
Shenmu, *China* 34 E6 38 50N 110 29 E
Shenqiu, *China* 34 H8 33 25N 115 5 E
Shensi = Shaanxi □, *China* 34 G5 35 0N 109 0 E
Shenyang, *China* 35 D12 41 48N 123 27 E
Sheo, *India* 42 F4 26 11N 71 15 E
Sheopur Kalan, *India* 40 G10 25 40N 76 40 E
Shepetivka, *Ukraine* 17 C14 50 10N 27 10 E
Shepetovka = Shepetivka, *Ukraine* 17 C14 50 10N 27 10 E
Sheppey, I. of, *U.K.* 11 F8 51 25N 0 48 E
Shepton Mallet, *U.K.* 11 F5 51 11N 2 33W
Sheqi, *China* 34 H7 33 12N 112 57 E
Sher Qila, *Pakistan* 43 A6 36 7N 74 2 E
Sherborne, *U.K.* 11 G5 50 57N 2 31W
Sherbro I., *S. Leone* 50 G3 7 30N 12 40W
Sherbrooke, *N.S., Canada* 71 C7 45 8N 61 59W
Sherbrooke, *Qué., Canada* 79 A13 45 28N 71 57W
Sherburne, *U.S.A.* 79 D9 42 41N 75 30W
Shergarh, *India* 42 F5 26 20N 72 18 E
Sherghati, *India* 43 G11 24 34N 84 47 E
Sheridan, *Ark., U.S.A.* 81 H8 34 19N 92 24W
Sheridan, *Wyo., U.S.A.* 82 D10 44 48N 106 58W
Sheringham, *U.K.* 10 E9 52 56N 1 13 E
Sherkin I., *Ireland* 13 E2 51 28N 9 26W
Sherkot, *India* 43 E8 29 22N 78 35 E
Sherman, *U.S.A.* 81 J6 33 40N 96 35W
Sherpur, *India* 43 G10 25 34N 83 47 E
Sherridon, *Canada* 73 B8 55 8N 101 5W
Sherwood Forest, *U.K.* 10 D6 53 6N 1 7W
Sherwood Park, *Canada* 72 C6 53 31N 113 19W
Sheslay →, *Canada* 72 B2 58 48N 132 5W
Shethanei L., *Canada* 73 B9 58 48N 97 50W
Shetland □, *U.K.* 12 A7 60 30N 1 30W
Shetland Is., *U.K.* 12 A7 60 30N 1 30W
Shetrunji →, *India* 42 J5 21 19N 72 7 E
Sheyenne →, *U.S.A.* 80 B6 47 2N 96 50W
Shibām, *Yemen* 46 D4 16 0N 48 36 E
Shibata, *Japan* 30 F9 37 57N 139 20 E
Shibecha, *Japan* 30 C12 43 17N 144 36 E
Shibetsu, *Japan* 30 B11 44 10N 142 23 E
Shibogama L., *Canada* 70 B2 53 35N 88 15W
Shibushi, *Japan* 31 J5 31 25N 131 8 E
Shickshinny, *U.S.A.* 79 E8 41 9N 76 9W
Shickshock Mts. = Chic-Chocs, Mts., *Canada* 71 C6 48 55N 66 0W
Shidao, *China* 35 F12 36 50N 122 25 E
Shido, *Japan* 31 G7 34 19N 134 10 E
Shiel, L., *U.K.* 12 E3 56 48N 5 34W
Shield, C., *Australia* 62 A2 13 20S 136 20 E
Shīeli, *Kazakstan* 26 E7 44 20N 66 15 E
Shiga □, *Japan* 31 G8 35 20N 136 0 E
Shiguaigou, *China* 34 D6 40 52N 110 15 E
Shihchiachuangi = Shijiazhuang, *China* 34 E8 38 2N 114 28 E
Shijiazhuang, *China* 34 E8 38 2N 114 28 E
Shikarpur, *India* 42 E8 28 17N 78 7 E
Shikarpur, *Pakistan* 42 F3 27 57N 68 39 E
Shikohabad, *India* 43 F8 27 6N 78 36 E
Shikoku □, *Japan* 31 H6 33 30N 133 30 E
Shikoku-Sanchi, *Japan* 31 H6 33 30N 133 30 E
Shiliguri, *India* 41 F16 26 45N 88 25 E
Shilka, *Russia* 27 D12 52 0N 115 55 E
Shilka →, *Russia* 27 D13 53 20N 121 26 E
Shillelagh, *Ireland* 13 D5 52 45N 6 32W
Shillington, *U.S.A.* 79 F9 40 18N 75 58W
Shillong, *India* 41 G17 25 35N 91 53 E
Shilo, *West Bank* 47 C4 32 4N 35 18 E
Shilou, *China* 34 F6 37 0N 110 48 E
Shimabara, *Japan* 31 H5 32 48N 130 20 E
Shimada, *Japan* 31 G9 34 49N 138 10 E
Shimane □, *Japan* 31 G6 35 0N 132 30 E
Shimanovsk, *Russia* 27 D13 52 15N 127 30 E
Shimizu, *Japan* 31 G9 35 0N 138 30 E
Shimodate, *Japan* 31 F9 36 20N 139 55 E
Shimoga, *India* 40 N9 13 57N 75 32 E
Shimoni, *Kenya* 54 C4 4 38S 39 20 E
Shimonoseki, *Japan* 31 H5 33 58N 130 55 E
Shimpuru Rapids, *Angola* 56 B2 17 45S 19 55 E
Shin, L., *U.K.* 12 C4 58 5N 4 30W
Shinano-Gawa →, *Japan* 31 F9 36 50N 138 30 E
Shināş, *Oman* 45 E8 24 46N 56 28 E
Shīndand, *Afghan.* 40 C3 33 12N 62 8 E
Shinglehouse, *U.S.A.* 78 E6 41 58N 78 12W
Shingū, *Japan* 31 H7 33 40N 135 55 E
Shingwidzi, *S. Africa* 57 C5 23 5S 31 25 E
Shinjō, *Japan* 30 E10 38 46N 140 18 E
Shinshār, *Syria* 47 A5 34 36N 36 43 E
Shinyanga, *Tanzania* 54 C3 3 45S 33 27 E
Shinyanga □, *Tanzania* 54 C3 3 50S 34 0 E
Shio-no-Misaki, *Japan* 31 H7 33 25N 135 45 E
Shiogama, *Japan* 30 E10 38 19N 141 1 E
Shiojiri, *Japan* 31 F8 36 6N 137 58 E
Shipchenski Prokhod, *Bulgaria* 21 C11 42 45N 25 15 E
Shiping, *China* 32 D5 23 45N 102 23 E
Shippegan, *Canada* 71 C7 47 45N 64 45W
Shippensburg, *U.S.A.* 78 F7 40 3N 77 31W
Shippenville, *U.S.A.* 78 E5 41 15N 79 28W
Shiprock, *U.S.A.* 83 H9 36 47N 108 41W
Shiqma, N. →, *Israel* 47 D3 31 37N 34 30 E
Shiquan, *China* 34 H5 33 5N 108 15 E
Shiquan He = Indus →, *Pakistan* 42 G2 24 20N 67 47 E
Shīr Kūh, *Iran* 45 D7 31 39N 54 3 E
Shiragami-Misaki, *Japan* 30 D10 41 24N 140 12 E
Shirakawa, *Fukushima, Japan* 31 F10 37 7N 140 13 E
Shirakawa, *Gifu, Japan* 31 F8 36 17N 136 56 E
Shirane-San, *Gumma, Japan* 31 F9 36 48N 139 22 E
Shirane-San, *Yamanashi, Japan* 31 G9 35 42N 138 9 E
Shiraoi, *Japan* 30 C10 42 33N 141 21 E
Shīrāz, *Iran* 45 D7 29 42N 52 30 E
Shire →, *Africa* 55 F4 17 42S 35 19 E
Shiretoko-Misaki, *Japan* 30 B12 44 21N 145 20 E
Shirinab →, *Pakistan* 42 D2 30 15N 66 28 E
Shiriya-Zaki, *Japan* 30 D10 41 25N 141 30 E
Shiroishi, *Japan* 30 F10 38 0N 140 37 E
Shīrvān, *Iran* 45 B8 37 30N 57 50 E
Shirwa, L. = Chilwa, L., *Malawi* 55 F4 15 15S 35 40 E
Shivpuri, *India* 42 G7 25 26N 77 42 E
Shixian, *China* 35 C15 43 5N 129 50 E
Shizuishan, *China* 34 E4 39 15N 106 50 E
Shizuoka, *Japan* 31 G9 34 57N 138 24 E
Shizuoka □, *Japan* 31 G9 35 15N 138 40 E
Shklov = Shklow, *Belarus* 17 A16 54 16N 30 15 E
Shklow, *Belarus* 17 A16 54 16N 30 15 E
Shkoder = Shkodër, *Albania* 21 C8 42 4N 19 32 E
Shkodër, *Albania* 21 C8 42 4N 19 32 E
Shkumbini →, *Albania* 21 D8 41 2N 19 31 E
Shmidta, Ostrov, *Russia* 27 A10 81 0N 91 0 E
Shō-Gawa →, *Japan* 31 F8 36 47N 137 4 E
Shoal L., *Canada* 73 D9 49 33N 95 1W
Shoal Lake, *Canada* 73 C8 50 30N 100 35W
Shōdo-Shima, *Japan* 31 G7 34 30N 134 15 E
Sholapur = Solapur, *India* 40 L9 17 43N 75 56 E
Shologontsy, *Russia* 27 C12 66 13N 114 0 E
Shōmrōn, *West Bank* 47 C4 32 15N 35 13 E
Shoreham by Sea, *U.K.* 11 G7 50 50N 0 16W
Shori →, *Pakistan* 42 E3 28 29N 69 44 E
Shorkot Road, *Pakistan* 42 D5 30 47N 72 15 E
Shoshone, *Calif., U.S.A.* 85 K10 35 58N 116 16W
Shoshone, *Idaho, U.S.A.* 82 E6 42 56N 114 25W
Shoshone L., *U.S.A.* 82 D8 44 22N 110 43W
Shoshone Mts., *U.S.A.* 82 G5 39 20N 117 25W
Shoshong, *Botswana* 56 C4 22 56S 26 31 E
Shoshoni, *U.S.A.* 82 E9 43 14N 108 7W
Shouguang, *China* 35 F10 37 52N 118 45 E
Shouyang, *China* 34 F7 37 54N 113 8 E
Show Low, *U.S.A.* 83 J9 34 15N 110 2W
Shreveport, *U.S.A.* 81 J8 32 31N 93 45W
Shrewsbury, *U.K.* 11 E5 52 43N 2 45W
Shri Mohangarh, *India* 42 F4 27 17N 71 18 E
Shrirampur, *India* 43 H13 22 44N 88 21 E
Shropshire □, *U.K.* 11 E5 52 36N 2 45W
Shū, *Kazakstan* 26 E8 43 36N 73 42 E
Shū →, *Kazakstan* 28 E10 45 0N 67 44 E
Shuangcheng, *China* 35 B14 45 20N 126 15 E
Shuanggou, *China* 35 G9 34 2N 117 30 E
Shuangliao, *China* 35 C12 43 29N 123 30 E
Shuangshanzi, *China* 35 D10 40 20N 119 8 E
Shuangyang, *China* 35 C13 43 28N 125 40 E
Shuangyashan, *China* 33 B8 46 28N 131 5 E
Shuguri Falls, *Tanzania* 55 D4 8 33S 37 22 E
Shuiye, *China* 34 F8 36 7N 114 8 E
Shujalpur, *India* 42 H7 23 18N 76 46 E
Shukpa Kunzang, *India* 43 B8 34 22N 78 22 E
Shulan, *China* 35 B14 44 28N 127 0 E
Shule, *China* 32 C2 39 25N 76 3 E
Shumagin Is., *U.S.A.* 68 C4 55 7N 160 30W
Shumen, *Bulgaria* 21 C12 43 18N 26 55 E
Shumikha, *Russia* 26 D7 55 10N 63 15 E
Shuo Xian = Shuozhou, *China* 34 E7 39 20N 112 33 E
Shuozhou, *China* 34 E7 39 20N 112 33 E
Shūr →, *Fārs, Iran* 45 D7 28 30N 55 0 E
Shūr →, *Kermān, Iran* 45 D8 30 52N 57 37 E
Shūr →, *Yazd, Iran* 45 D7 31 45N 55 15 E
Shūr Āb, *Iran* 45 C6 34 23N 51 11 E
Shūr Gaz, *Iran* 45 D8 29 10N 59 20 E
Shūrāb, *Iran* 45 C8 33 43N 56 29 E
Shūrjestān, *Iran* 45 D7 31 24N 52 25 E
Shurugwi, *Zimbabwe* 55 F3 19 40S 30 0 E
Shūsf, *Iran* 45 D9 31 50N 60 5 E
Shūshtar, *Iran* 45 D6 32 0N 48 50 E
Shuswap L., *Canada* 72 C5 50 55N 119 3W
Shuyang, *China* 35 G10 34 10N 118 42 E
Shūzū, *Iran* 45 D7 29 52N 54 30 E
Shwebo, *Burma* 41 H19 22 30N 95 45 E
Shwegu, *Burma* 41 G20 24 15N 96 26 E
Shweli →, *Burma* 41 H20 23 45N 96 45 E
Shymkent, *Kazakstan* 26 E7 42 18N 69 36 E
Shyok, *India* 43 B8 34 13N 78 12 E
Shyok →, *Pakistan* 43 B6 35 13N 75 53 E
Si Chon, *Thailand* 39 H2 9 0N 99 54 E
Si Kiang = Xi Jiang →, *China* 33 D6 22 5N 113 20 E
Si-ngan = Xi'an, *China* 34 G5 34 15N 109 0 E
Si Prachan, *Thailand* 38 E3 14 37N 100 9 E
Si Racha, *Thailand* 38 F3 13 10N 100 48 E
Si Xian, *China* 35 H9 33 30N 117 50 E
Siahaf →, *Pakistan* 42 E3 29 3N 68 57 E
Siahan Range, *Pakistan* 40 F4 27 30N 64 40 E
Siaksriindrapura, *Indonesia* 36 D2 0 51N 102 0 E
Sialkot, *Pakistan* 42 C6 32 32N 74 30 E
Siam = Thailand ■, *Asia* 38 E4 16 0N 102 0 E
Sian = Xi'an, *China* 34 G5 34 15N 109 0 E
Siantan, *Indonesia* 36 D3 3 10N 106 15 E
Sīāreh, *Iran* 45 D9 28 5N 60 14 E
Siargao I., *Phil.* 37 C7 9 52N 126 3 E
Siari, *Pakistan* 43 B7 34 55N 76 40 E
Siasi, *Phil.* 37 C6 5 34N 120 50 E
Siau, *Indonesia* 37 D7 2 50N 125 25 E
Šiauliai, *Lithuania* 9 J20 55 56N 23 15 E
Sibâi, Gebel el, *Egypt* 44 E2 25 45N 34 10 E
Sibay, *Russia* 24 D10 52 42N 58 39 E
Sibayi, L., *S. Africa* 57 D5 27 20S 32 45 E
Šibenik, *Croatia* 20 C6 43 48N 15 54 E
Siberia, *Russia* 4 D13 60 0N 100 0 E
Siberut, *Indonesia* 36 E1 1 30S 99 0 E
Sibi, *Pakistan* 42 E2 29 30N 67 54 E
Sibil = Oksibil, *Indonesia* 37 E10 4 59S 140 35 E
Sibiti, *Congo* 52 E2 3 38S 13 19 E
Sibiu, *Romania* 17 F13 45 45N 24 9 E
Sibley, *U.S.A.* 80 D7 43 24N 95 45W
Sibolga, *Indonesia* 36 D1 1 42N 98 45 E
Sibsagar, *India* 41 F19 27 0N 94 36 E
Sibu, *Malaysia* 36 D4 2 18N 111 49 E
Sibuco, *Phil.* 37 C6 7 20N 122 10 E
Sibuguey B., *Phil.* 37 C6 7 50N 122 45 E
Sibut, *C.A.R.* 52 C3 5 46N 19 10 E
Sibutu, *Phil.* 37 D5 4 45N 119 30 E
Sibutu Passage, *E. Indies* 37 D5 4 50N 120 0 E
Sibuyan I., *Phil.* 37 B6 12 25N 122 40 E
Sibuyan Sea, *Phil.* 37 B6 12 30N 122 20 E
Sicamous, *Canada* 72 C5 50 49N 119 0W
Siccus →, *Australia* 63 E2 31 26S 139 30 E
Sichuan □, *China* 32 C5 30 30N 103 0 E
Sicilia, *Italy* 20 F6 37 30N 14 30 E
Sicily = Sicilia, *Italy* 20 F6 37 30N 14 30 E
Sicuani, *Peru* 92 F4 14 21S 71 10W
Sidári, *Greece* 23 A3 39 47N 19 41 E
Siddhapur, *India* 42 H5 23 56N 72 25 E
Siddipet, *India* 40 K11 18 5N 78 51 E
Sidhauli, *India* 43 F9 27 17N 80 50 E
Sidheros, Ákra, *Greece* 23 D8 35 19N 26 19 E
Sidhi, *India* 43 G9 24 25N 81 53 E
Sidi-bel-Abbès, *Algeria* 50 A5 35 13N 0 39W
Sidi Ifni, *Morocco* 50 C3 29 29N 10 12W
Sidlaw Hills, *U.K.* 12 E5 56 32N 3 2W
Sidley, Mt., *Antarctica* 5 D14 77 2S 126 2W
Sidmouth, *U.K.* 11 G4 50 40N 3 15W
Sidmouth, C., *Australia* 62 A3 13 25S 143 36 E
Sidney, *Canada* 72 D4 48 39N 123 24W
Sidney, *Mont., U.S.A.* 80 B2 47 43N 104 9W
Sidney, *N.Y., U.S.A.* 79 D9 42 19N 75 24W
Sidney, *Nebr., U.S.A.* 80 E3 41 8N 102 59W
Sidney, *Ohio, U.S.A.* 76 E3 40 17N 84 9W
Sidney Lanier, L., *U.S.A.* 77 H4 34 10N 84 4W
Sidoarjo, *Indonesia* 37 G15 7 27S 112 43 E
Sidon = Saydā, *Lebanon* 47 B4 33 35N 35 25 E
Sidra, G. of = Surt, Khalīj, *Libya* 51 B9 31 40N 18 30 E
Siedlce, *Poland* 17 B12 52 10N 22 20 E
Sieg →, *Germany* 16 C4 50 46N 7 6 E
Siegen, *Germany* 16 C5 50 51N 8 0 E
Siem Pang, *Cambodia* 38 E6 14 7N 106 23 E
Siem Reap = Siemreab, *Cambodia* 38 F4 13 20N 103 52 E
Siemreab, *Cambodia* 38 F4 13 20N 103 52 E
Siena, *Italy* 20 C4 43 19N 11 21 E
Sieradz, *Poland* 17 C10 51 37N 18 41 E
Sierra Blanca, *U.S.A.* 83 L11 31 11N 105 22W
Sierra Blanca Peak, *U.S.A.* 83 K11 33 23N 105 49W
Sierra City, *U.S.A.* 84 F6 39 34N 120 38W
Sierra Colorada, *Argentina* 96 E3 40 35S 67 50W
Sierra Gorda, *Chile* 94 A2 22 50S 69 15W
Sierra Leone ■, *W. Afr.* 50 G3 9 0N 12 0W
Sierra Madre, *Mexico* 87 D6 16 0N 93 0W
Sierra Mojada, *Mexico* 86 B4 27 19N 103 42W
Sierra Nevada, *Spain* 19 D4 37 3N 3 15W
Sierra Nevada, *U.S.A.* 84 H8 39 0N 120 30W
Sierra Vista, *U.S.A.* 83 L8 31 33N 110 18W
Sierraville, *U.S.A.* 84 F6 39 36N 120 22W
Sífnos, *Greece* 21 F11 37 0N 24 45 E
Sifton, *Canada* 73 C8 51 21N 100 8W
Sifton Pass, *Canada* 72 B3 57 52N 126 15W
Sighetu-Marmaţiei, *Romania* 17 E12 47 57N 23 52 E

Suphan Dağı

Stanley, *Falk. Is.* **96 G5** 51 40S 59 51W
Stanley, *U.K.* **10 C6** 54 53N 1 41W
Stanley, *Idaho, U.S.A.* **82 D6** 44 13N 114 56W
Stanley, *N. Dak., U.S.A.* **80 A3** 48 19N 102 23W
Stanley, *N.Y., U.S.A.* **78 D7** 42 48N 77 6W
Stanovoy Khrebet, *Russia* **27 D13** 55 0N 130 0 E
Stanovoy Ra. = Stanovoy Khrebet, *Russia* **27 D13** 55 0N 130 0 E
Stansmore Ra., *Australia* **60 D4** 21 23S 128 33 E
Stanthorpe, *Australia* **63 D5** 28 36S 151 59 E
Stanton, *U.S.A.* **81 J4** 32 8N 101 48W
Stanwood, *U.S.A.* **84 B4** 48 15N 122 23W
Staples, *U.S.A.* **80 B7** 46 21N 94 48W
Star City, *Canada* **73 C8** 52 50N 104 20W
Star Lake, *U.S.A.* **79 B9** 44 10N 75 2W
Stara Planina, *Bulgaria* **21 C10** 43 15N 23 0 E
Stara Zagora, *Bulgaria* **21 C11** 42 26N 25 39 E
Starachowice, *Poland* **17 C11** 51 3N 21 2 E
Staraya Russa, *Russia* **24 C5** 57 58N 31 23 E
Starbuck I., *Kiribati* **65 H12** 5 37S 155 55W
Stargard Szczeciński, *Poland* **16 B8** 53 20N 15 0 E
Staritsa, *Russia* **24 C5** 56 33N 34 55 E
Starke, *U.S.A.* **77 L4** 29 57N 82 7W
Starogard Gdański, *Poland* **17 B10** 53 59N 18 30 E
Starokonstantinov = Starokonstyantyniv, *Ukraine* **17 D14** 49 48N 27 10 E
Starokonstyantyniv, *Ukraine* **17 D14** 49 48N 27 10 E
Start Pt., *U.K.* **11 G4** 50 13N 3 39W
Staryy Chartoriysk, *Ukraine* **17 C13** 51 15N 25 54 E
Staryy Oskol, *Russia* **25 D6** 51 19N 37 55 E
State College, *U.S.A.* **78 F7** 40 48N 77 52W
Stateline, *U.S.A.* **84 G7** 38 57N 119 56W
Staten, I. = Estados, I. de Los, *Argentina* **96 G4** 54 40S 64 30W
Staten I., *U.S.A.* **79 F10** 40 35N 74 9W
Statesboro, *U.S.A.* **77 J5** 32 27N 81 47W
Statesville, *U.S.A.* **77 H5** 35 47N 80 53W
Stauffer, *U.S.A.* **85 L7** 34 45N 119 3W
Staunton, *Ill., U.S.A.* **80 F10** 39 1N 89 47W
Staunton, *Va., U.S.A.* **76 F6** 38 9N 79 4W
Stavanger, *Norway* **9 G11** 58 57N 5 40 E
Staveley, *N.Z.* **59 K3** 43 40S 171 32 E
Stavelot, *Belgium* **15 D5** 50 23N 5 55 E
Stavern, *Norway* **9 G14** 59 0N 10 1 E
Stavoren, *Neths.* **15 B5** 52 53N 5 22 E
Stavropol, *Russia* **25 E7** 45 5N 42 0 E
Stavros, *Cyprus* **23 D11** 35 1N 32 38 E
Stavrós, *Greece* **23 D6** 35 12N 24 45 E
Stavrós, Ákra, *Greece* **23 D6** 35 26N 24 58 E
Stawell →, *Australia* **62 C3** 20 20S 142 55 E
Stayner, *Canada* **78 B4** 44 25N 80 5W
Stayton, *U.S.A.* **82 D2** 44 48N 122 48W
Steamboat Springs, *U.S.A.* **82 F10** 40 29N 106 50W
Steele, *U.S.A.* **80 B5** 46 51N 99 55W
Steelton, *U.S.A.* **78 F8** 40 14N 76 50W
Steen River, *Canada* **72 B5** 59 40N 117 12W
Steenkool = Bintuni, *Indonesia* **37 E8** 2 7S 133 32 E
Steens Mt., *U.S.A.* **82 E4** 42 35N 118 40W
Steenwijk, *Neths.* **15 B6** 52 47N 6 7 E
Steep Pt., *Australia* **61 E1** 26 8S 113 8 E
Steep Rock, *Canada* **73 C9** 51 30N 98 48W
Stefanie L. = Chew Bahir, *Ethiopia* **46 G2** 4 40N 36 50 E
Stefansson Bay, *Antarctica* **5 C5** 67 20S 59 8 E
Steiermark □, *Austria* **16 E8** 47 26N 15 0 E
Steilacoom, *U.S.A.* **84 C4** 47 10N 122 36W
Steilrandberge, *Namibia* **56 B1** 17 45S 13 20 E
Steinbach, *Canada* **73 D9** 49 32N 96 40W
Steinhausen, *Namibia* **56 C2** 21 49S 18 20 E
Steinkjer, *Norway* **8 D14** 64 1N 11 31 E
Steinkopf, *S. Africa* **56 D2** 29 18S 17 43 E
Stellarton, *Canada* **71 C7** 45 32N 62 30W
Stellenbosch, *S. Africa* **56 E2** 33 58S 18 50 E
Stendal, *Germany* **16 B6** 52 36N 11 53 E
Steornabhaigh = Stornoway, *U.K.* **12 C2** 58 13N 6 23W
Stepanakert = Xankändi, *Azerbaijan* **25 G8** 39 52N 46 49 E
Stephens I., *Canada* **72 C2** 54 10N 130 45W
Stephens L., *Canada* **73 B9** 56 32N 95 0W
Stephenville, *Canada* **71 C8** 48 31N 58 35W
Stephenville, *U.S.A.* **81 J5** 32 13N 98 12W
Stepnoi = Elista, *Russia* **25 E7** 46 16N 44 14 E
Steppe, *Asia* **28 D9** 50 0N 50 0 E
Sterkstroom, *S. Africa* **56 E4** 31 32S 26 32 E
Sterling, *Colo., U.S.A.* **80 E3** 40 37N 103 13W
Sterling, *Ill., U.S.A.* **80 E10** 41 48N 89 42W
Sterling, *Kans., U.S.A.* **80 F5** 38 13N 98 12W
Sterling City, *U.S.A.* **81 K4** 31 51N 101 0W
Sterling Heights, *U.S.A.* **76 D4** 42 35N 83 0W
Sterling Run, *U.S.A.* **78 E6** 41 25N 78 12W
Sterlitamak, *Russia* **24 D10** 53 40N 56 0 E
Stérnes, *Greece* **23 D6** 35 30N 24 9 E
Stettin = Szczecin, *Poland* **16 B8** 53 27N 14 27 E
Stettiner Haff, *Germany* **16 B8** 53 47N 14 15 E
Stettler, *Canada* **72 C6** 52 19N 112 40W
Steubenville, *U.S.A.* **78 F4** 40 22N 80 37W
Stevenage, *U.K.* **11 F7** 51 55N 0 13W
Stevens Point, *U.S.A.* **80 C10** 44 31N 89 34W
Stevenson, *U.S.A.* **84 E5** 45 42N 121 53W
Stevenson L., *Canada* **73 C9** 53 55N 96 0W
Stevensville, *U.S.A.* **82 C6** 46 30N 114 5W
Stewart, *Canada* **72 B3** 55 56N 129 57W
Stewart, *U.S.A.* **84 F7** 39 5N 119 46W
Stewart →, *Canada* **68 B6** 63 19N 139 26W
Stewart, C., *Australia* **62 A1** 11 57S 134 56 E
Stewart, I., *Chile* **96 G2** 54 50S 71 15W
Stewart I., *N.Z.* **59 M1** 46 58S 167 54 E
Stewarts Point, *U.S.A.* **84 G3** 38 39N 123 24W
Stewartville, *U.S.A.* **80 D8** 43 51N 92 29W
Stewiacke, *Canada* **71 C7** 45 9N 63 22W
Steynsburg, *S. Africa* **56 E4** 31 15S 25 49 E
Steyr, *Austria* **16 D8** 48 3N 14 25 E
Steytlerville, *S. Africa* **56 E3** 33 17S 24 19 E
Stigler, *U.S.A.* **81 H7** 35 15N 95 8W
Stikine →, *Canada* **72 B2** 56 40N 132 30W
Stilfontein, *S. Africa* **56 D4** 26 51S 26 50 E
Stillwater, *N.Z.* **59 K3** 42 27S 171 20 E
Stillwater, *Minn., U.S.A.* **80 C8** 45 3N 92 49W
Stillwater, *N.Y., U.S.A.* **79 D11** 42 55N 73 41W
Stillwater, *Okla., U.S.A.* **81 G6** 36 7N 97 4W
Stillwater Range, *U.S.A.* **82 G4** 39 50N 118 5W
Stillwater Reservoir, *U.S.A.* **79 C9** 43 54N 75 3W
Stilwell, *U.S.A.* **81 H7** 35 49N 94 38W
Štip, *Macedonia* **21 D10** 41 42N 22 10 E
Stirling, *Canada* **78 B7** 44 18N 77 33W
Stirling, *U.K.* **12 E5** 56 8N 3 57W
Stirling □, *U.K.* **12 E4** 56 12N 4 18W
Stirling Ra., *Australia* **61 F2** 34 23S 118 0 E
Stittsville, *Canada* **79 A9** 45 15N 75 55W
Stjernøya, *Norway* **8 A20** 70 20N 22 40 E
Stjørdalshalsen, *Norway* **8 E14** 63 29N 10 51 E
Stockerau, *Austria* **16 D9** 48 24N 16 12 E
Stockholm, *Sweden* **9 G18** 59 20N 18 3 E
Stockport, *U.K.* **10 D5** 53 25N 2 9W
Stocksbridge, *U.K.* **10 D6** 53 29N 1 35W
Stockton, *Calif., U.S.A.* **84 H5** 37 58N 121 17W
Stockton, *Kans., U.S.A.* **80 F5** 39 26N 99 16W
Stockton, *Mo., U.S.A.* **81 G8** 37 42N 93 48W
Stockton-on-Tees, *U.K.* **10 C6** 54 35N 1 19W
Stockton-on-Tees □, *U.K.* **10 C6** 54 35N 1 19W
Stockton Plateau, *U.S.A.* **81 K3** 30 30N 102 30W
Stoeng Treng, *Cambodia* **38 F5** 13 31N 105 58 E
Stoer, Pt. of, *U.K.* **12 C3** 58 16N 5 23W
Stoke-on-Trent, *U.K.* **10 D5** 53 1N 2 11W
Stoke-on-Trent □, *U.K.* **10 D5** 53 1N 2 11W
Stokes Pt., *Australia* **62 G3** 40 10S 143 56 E
Stokes Ra., *Australia* **60 C5** 15 50S 130 50 E
Stokksnes, *Iceland* **8 D6** 64 14N 14 58W
Stokmarknes, *Norway* **8 B16** 68 34N 14 54 E
Stolac, *Bos.-H.* **21 C7** 43 5N 17 59 E
Stolbovoy, Ostrov, *Russia* **27 B14** 74 44N 135 14 E
Stolbtsy = Stowbtsy, *Belarus* **17 B14** 53 30N 26 43 E
Stolin, *Belarus* **17 C14** 51 53N 26 50 E
Stomíon, *Greece* **23 D5** 35 21N 23 32 E
Stone, *U.K.* **10 E5** 52 55N 2 9W
Stoneboro, *U.S.A.* **78 E4** 41 20N 80 7W
Stonehaven, *U.K.* **12 E6** 56 59N 2 12W
Stonehenge, *Australia* **62 C3** 24 22S 143 17 E
Stonehenge, *U.K.* **11 F6** 51 9N 1 45W
Stonewall, *Canada* **73 C9** 50 10N 97 19W
Stony L., *Man., Canada* **73 B9** 58 51N 98 40W
Stony L., *Ont., Canada* **78 B6** 44 30N 78 5W
Stony Point, *U.S.A.* **79 E11** 41 14N 73 59W
Stony Pt., *U.S.A.* **79 C8** 43 50N 76 18W
Stony Rapids, *Canada* **73 B7** 59 16N 105 50W
Stony Tunguska = Tunguska, Podkamennaya →, *Russia* **27 C10** 61 50N 90 13 E
Stonyford, *U.S.A.* **84 F4** 39 23N 122 33W
Stora Lulevatten, *Sweden* **8 C18** 67 10N 19 30 E
Storavan, *Sweden* **8 D18** 65 45N 18 10 E
Stord, *Norway* **9 G11** 59 52N 5 23 E
Store Bælt, *Denmark* **9 J14** 55 20N 11 0 E
Storm B., *Australia* **62 G4** 43 10S 147 30 E
Storm Lake, *U.S.A.* **80 D7** 42 39N 95 13W
Stormberge, *S. Africa* **56 E4** 31 16S 26 17 E
Stormsrivier, *S. Africa* **56 E3** 33 59S 23 52 E
Stornoway, *U.K.* **12 C2** 58 13N 6 23W
Storozhinets = Storozhynets, *Ukraine* **17 D13** 48 14N 25 45 E
Storozhynets, *Ukraine* **17 D13** 48 14N 25 45 E
Storrs, *U.S.A.* **79 E12** 41 49N 72 15W
Storsjön, *Sweden* **8 E16** 63 9N 14 30 E
Storuman, *Sweden* **8 D17** 65 5N 17 10 E
Storuman, sjö, *Sweden* **8 D17** 65 13N 16 50 E
Stouffville, *Canada* **78 C5** 43 58N 79 15W
Stoughton, *Canada* **73 D8** 49 40N 103 0W
Stour →, *Dorset, U.K.* **11 G6** 50 43N 1 47W
Stour →, *Kent, U.K.* **11 F9** 51 18N 1 22 E
Stour →, *Suffolk, U.K.* **11 F9** 51 57N 1 4 E
Stourbridge, *U.K.* **11 E5** 52 28N 2 8W
Stout L., *Canada* **73 C10** 52 0N 94 40W
Stove Pipe Wells Village, *U.S.A.* **85 J9** 36 35N 117 11W
Stow, *U.S.A.* **78 E3** 41 10N 81 27W
Stowbtsy, *Belarus* **17 B14** 53 30N 26 43 E
Stowmarket, *U.K.* **11 E9** 52 12N 1 0 E
Strabane, *U.K.* **13 B4** 54 50N 7 27W
Strahan, *Australia* **62 G4** 42 9S 145 20 E
Stralsund, *Germany* **16 A7** 54 18N 13 4 E
Strand, *S. Africa* **56 E2** 34 9S 18 48 E
Stranda, *Møre og Romsdal, Norway* **9 E12** 62 19N 6 58 E
Stranda, *Nord-Trøndelag, Norway* **8 E14** 63 33N 10 14 E
Strangford L., *U.K.* **13 B6** 54 30N 5 37W
Stranraer, *U.K.* **12 G3** 54 54N 5 1W
Strasbourg, *Canada* **73 C8** 51 4N 104 55W
Strasbourg, *France* **18 B7** 48 35N 7 42 E
Stratford, *Canada* **78 C4** 43 23N 81 0W
Stratford, *N.Z.* **59 H5** 39 20S 174 19 E
Stratford, *Calif., U.S.A.* **84 J7** 36 11N 119 49W
Stratford, *Conn., U.S.A.* **79 E11** 41 12N 73 8W
Stratford, *Tex., U.S.A.* **81 G3** 36 20N 102 4W
Stratford-upon-Avon, *U.K.* **11 E6** 52 12N 1 42W
Strath Spey, *U.K.* **12 D5** 57 9N 3 49W
Strathaven, *U.K.* **12 F4** 55 40N 4 5W
Strathcona Prov. Park, *Canada* **72 D3** 49 38N 125 40W
Strathmore, *Canada* **72 C6** 51 5N 113 18W
Strathmore, *U.K.* **12 E5** 56 37N 3 7W
Strathmore, *U.S.A.* **84 J7** 36 9N 119 4W
Strathnaver, *Canada* **72 C4** 53 20N 122 33W
Strathpeffer, *U.K.* **12 D4** 57 35N 4 32W
Strathroy, *Canada* **78 D3** 42 58N 81 38W
Strathy Pt., *U.K.* **12 C4** 58 36N 4 1W
Strattanville, *U.S.A.* **78 E5** 41 12N 79 19W
Stratton, *U.S.A.* **79 A14** 45 8N 70 26W
Stratton Mt., *U.S.A.* **79 C12** 43 4N 72 55W
Straubing, *Germany* **16 D7** 48 52N 12 34 E
Straumnes, *Iceland* **8 C2** 66 26N 23 8W
Strawberry →, *U.S.A.* **82 F8** 40 10N 110 24W
Streaky B., *Australia* **63 E1** 32 48S 134 13 E
Streaky Bay, *Australia* **63 E1** 32 51S 134 18 E
Streator, *U.S.A.* **80 E10** 41 8N 88 50W
Streetsboro, *U.S.A.* **78 E3** 41 14N 81 21W
Streetsville, *Canada* **78 C5** 43 35N 79 42W
Strelka, *Russia* **27 D10** 58 5N 93 3 E
Streng →, *Cambodia* **38 F4** 13 12N 103 37 E
Streymoy, *Færoe Is.* **8 E9** 62 8N 7 5W
Strezhevoy, *Russia* **26 C8** 60 42N 77 34 E
Strimón →, *Greece* **21 D10** 40 46N 23 51 E
Strimonikós Kólpos, *Greece* **21 D11** 40 33N 24 0 E
Stroma, *U.K.* **12 C5** 58 41N 3 7W
Strómboli, *Italy* **20 E6** 38 47N 15 13 E
Stromeferry, *U.K.* **12 D3** 57 21N 5 33W
Stromness, *U.K.* **12 C5** 58 58N 3 17W
Stromsburg, *U.S.A.* **80 E6** 41 7N 97 36W
Strömstad, *Sweden* **9 G14** 58 56N 11 10 E
Strömsund, *Sweden* **8 E16** 63 51N 15 33 E
Strongsville, *U.S.A.* **78 E3** 41 19N 81 50W
Stronsay, *U.K.* **12 B6** 59 7N 2 35W
Stroud, *U.K.* **11 F5** 51 45N 2 13W
Stroudsburg, *U.S.A.* **79 F9** 40 59N 75 12W
Stroumbi, *Cyprus* **23 E11** 34 53N 32 29 E
Struer, *Denmark* **9 H13** 56 30N 8 35 E
Strumica, *Macedonia* **21 D10** 41 28N 22 41 E
Struthers, *Canada* **70 C2** 48 41N 85 51W
Struthers, *U.S.A.* **78 E4** 41 4N 80 39W
Stryker, *U.S.A.* **82 B6** 48 41N 114 46W
Stryy, *Ukraine* **17 D12** 49 16N 23 48 E
Strzelecki Cr. →, *Australia* **63 D2** 29 37S 139 59 E
Stuart, *Fla., U.S.A.* **77 M5** 27 12N 80 15W
Stuart, *Nebr., U.S.A.* **80 D5** 42 36N 99 8W
Stuart →, *Canada* **72 C4** 54 0N 123 35W
Stuart Bluff Ra., *Australia* **60 D5** 22 50S 131 52 E
Stuart L., *Canada* **72 C4** 54 30N 124 30W
Stuart Ra., *Australia* **63 D1** 29 10S 134 56 E
Stull L., *Canada* **70 B1** 54 24N 92 34W
Stung Treng = Stoeng Treng, *Cambodia* **38 F5** 13 31N 105 58 E
Stupart →, *Canada* **70 A1** 56 0N 93 25W
Sturgeon B., *Canada* **73 C9** 52 0N 97 50W
Sturgeon Bay, *U.S.A.* **76 C2** 44 50N 87 23W
Sturgeon Falls, *Canada* **70 C4** 46 25N 79 57W
Sturgeon L., *Alta., Canada* **72 B5** 55 6N 117 32W
Sturgeon L., *Ont., Canada* **70 C1** 50 0N 90 45W
Sturgeon L., *Ont., Canada* **78 B6** 44 28N 78 43W
Sturgis, *Canada* **73 C8** 51 56N 102 36W
Sturgis, *Mich., U.S.A.* **76 E3** 41 48N 85 25W
Sturgis, *S. Dak., U.S.A.* **80 C3** 44 25N 103 31W
Sturt Cr. →, *Australia* **60 C4** 19 8S 127 50 E
Stutterheim, *S. Africa* **56 E4** 32 33S 27 28 E
Stuttgart, *Germany* **16 D5** 48 48N 9 11 E
Stuttgart, *U.S.A.* **81 H9** 34 30N 91 33W
Stuyvesant, *U.S.A.* **79 D11** 42 23N 73 45W
Stykkishólmur, *Iceland* **8 D2** 65 2N 22 40W
Styria = Steiermark □, *Austria* **16 E8** 47 26N 15 0 E
Su Xian = Suzhou, *China* **34 H9** 33 41N 116 59 E
Suakin, *Sudan* **51 E13** 19 8N 37 20 E
Suan, *N. Korea* **35 E14** 38 42N 126 22 E
Suaqui, *Mexico* **86 B3** 29 12N 109 41W
Suar, *India* **43 E8** 29 2N 79 3 E
Subang, *Indonesia* **37 G12** 6 34S 107 45 E
Subansiri →, *India* **41 F18** 26 48N 93 50 E
Subarnarekha →, *India* **43 H12** 22 34N 87 24 E
Subayhah, *Si. Arabia* **44 D3** 30 2N 38 50 E
Subi, *Indonesia* **39 L7** 2 58N 108 50 E
Subotica, *Serbia, Yug.* **21 A8** 46 6N 19 39 E
Suceava, *Romania* **17 E14** 47 38N 26 16 E
Suchan, *Russia* **30 C6** 43 8N 133 9 E
Suchitoto, *El Salv.* **88 D2** 13 56N 89 0W
Suchou = Suzhou, *China* **33 C7** 31 19N 120 38 E
Süchow = Xuzhou, *China* **35 G9** 34 18N 117 10 E
Suck →, *Ireland* **13 C3** 53 17N 8 3W
Sucre, *Bolivia* **92 G5** 19 0S 65 15W
Sucuriú →, *Brazil* **93 H8** 20 47S 51 38W
Sud, Pte. du, *Canada* **71 C7** 49 3N 62 14W
Sud-Kivu □, *Dem. Rep. of the Congo* **54 C2** 3 30S 28 0 E
Sud-Ouest, Pte. du, *Canada* **71 C7** 49 23N 63 36W
Sudan, *U.S.A.* **81 H3** 34 4N 102 32W
Sudan ■, *Africa* **51 E11** 15 0N 30 0 E
Sudbury, *Canada* **70 C3** 46 30N 81 0W
Sudbury, *U.K.* **11 E8** 52 2N 0 45 E
Sûdd, *Sudan* **51 G12** 8 20N 30 0 E
Sudeten Mts. = Sudety, *Europe* **17 C9** 50 20N 16 45 E
Sudety, *Europe* **17 C9** 50 20N 16 45 E
Suðuroy, *Færoe Is.* **8 F9** 61 32N 6 50W
Sudi, *Tanzania* **55 E4** 10 11S 39 57 E
Sudirman, Pegunungan, *Indonesia* **37 E9** 4 30S 137 0 E
Sueca, *Spain* **19 C5** 39 12N 0 21W
Suemez I., *U.S.A.* **72 B2** 55 15N 133 20W
Suez = El Suweis, *Egypt* **51 C12** 29 58N 32 31 E
Suez, G. of = Suweis, Khalîg el, *Egypt* **51 C12** 28 40N 33 0 E
Suez Canal = Suweis, Qanâ es, *Egypt* **51 B12** 31 0N 32 20 E
Suffield, *Canada* **72 C6** 50 12N 111 10W
Suffolk, *U.S.A.* **76 G7** 36 44N 76 35W
Suffolk □, *U.K.* **11 E9** 52 16N 1 0 E
Sugargrove, *U.S.A.* **78 E5** 41 59N 79 21W
Sugarive →, *India* **43 F12** 26 16N 86 24 E
Sugluk = Salluit, *Canada* **69 B12** 62 14N 75 38W
Şuḥār, *Oman* **46 C6** 24 20N 56 40 E
Sühbaatar □, *Mongolia* **34 B8** 45 30N 114 0 E
Suhl, *Germany* **16 C6** 50 36N 10 42 E
Sui, *Pakistan* **42 E3** 28 37N 69 19 E
Sui Xian, *China* **34 G8** 34 25N 115 2 E
Suide, *China* **34 F6** 37 30N 110 12 E
Suifenhe, *China* **35 B16** 44 25N 131 10 E
Suihua, *China* **33 B7** 46 32N 126 55 E
Suining, *China* **35 H9** 33 56N 117 58 E
Suiping, *China* **34 H7** 33 10N 113 59 E
Suir →, *Ireland* **13 D4** 52 16N 7 9W
Suisun City, *U.S.A.* **84 G4** 38 15N 122 2W
Suiyang, *China* **35 B16** 44 30N 130 56 E
Suizhong, *China* **35 D11** 40 21N 120 20 E
Sujangarh, *India* **42 F6** 27 42N 74 31 E
Sukabumi, *Indonesia* **37 G12** 6 56S 106 50 E
Sukadana, *Indonesia* **36 E3** 1 10S 110 0 E
Sukagawa, *Japan* **31 F10** 37 17N 140 23 E
Sukaraja, *Indonesia* **36 E4** 2 28S 110 25 E
Sukarnapura = Jayapura, *Indonesia* **37 E10** 2 28S 140 38 E
Sukch'ŏn, *N. Korea* **35 E13** 39 22N 125 35 E
Sukhona →, *Russia* **24 C6** 61 15N 46 39 E
Sukhothai, *Thailand* **38 D2** 17 1N 99 49 E
Sukhumi = Sokhumi, *Georgia* **25 F7** 43 0N 41 0 E
Sukkur, *Pakistan* **42 F3** 27 42N 68 54 E
Sukkur Barrage, *Pakistan* **42 F3** 27 40N 68 50 E
Sukri →, *India* **42 G4** 25 4N 71 43 E
Sukumo, *Japan* **31 H6** 32 56N 132 44 E
Sukunka →, *Canada* **72 B4** 55 45N 121 15W
Sula, Kepulauan, *Indonesia* **37 E7** 1 45S 125 0 E
Sulaco →, *Honduras* **88 C2** 15 2N 87 44W
Sulaiman Range, *Pakistan* **42 D3** 30 30N 69 50 E
Sūlār, *Iran* **45 D6** 31 53N 51 54 E
Sulawesi Sea = Celebes Sea, *Indonesia* **37 D6** 3 0N 123 0 E
Sulawesi Selatan □, *Indonesia* **37 E6** 2 30S 125 0 E
Sulawesi Utara □, *Indonesia* **37 D6** 1 0N 122 30 E
Sulima, *S. Leone* **50 G3** 6 58N 11 32W
Sulina, *Romania* **17 F15** 45 10N 29 40 E
Sulitjelma, *Norway* **8 C17** 67 9N 16 3 E
Sullana, *Peru* **92 D2** 4 52S 80 39W
Sullivan, *Ill., U.S.A.* **80 F10** 39 36N 88 37W
Sullivan, *Ind., U.S.A.* **76 F2** 39 6N 87 24W
Sullivan, *Mo., U.S.A.* **80 F9** 38 13N 91 10W
Sullivan Bay, *Canada* **72 C3** 50 55N 126 50W
Sullivan I. = Lanbi Kyun, *Burma* **39 G2** 10 50N 98 20 E
Sulphur, *La., U.S.A.* **81 K8** 30 14N 93 23W
Sulphur, *Okla., U.S.A.* **81 H6** 34 31N 96 58W
Sulphur Pt., *Canada* **72 A6** 60 56N 114 48W
Sulphur Springs, *U.S.A.* **81 J7** 33 8N 95 36W
Sultan, *Canada* **70 C3** 47 36N 82 47W
Sultan, *U.S.A.* **84 C5** 47 52N 121 49W
Sultanpur, *Mad. P., India* **42 H8** 23 9N 77 56 E
Sultanpur, *Punjab, India* **42 D6** 31 13N 75 11 E
Sultanpur, *Ut. P., India* **43 F10** 26 18N 82 4 E
Sulu Arch., *Phil.* **37 C6** 6 0N 121 0 E
Sulu Sea, *E. Indies* **37 C6** 8 0N 120 0 E
Suluq, *Libya* **51 B10** 31 44N 20 14 E
Sulzberger Ice Shelf, *Antarctica* **5 D10** 78 0S 150 0 E
Sumalata, *Indonesia* **37 D6** 1 0N 122 31 E
Sumampa, *Argentina* **94 B3** 29 25S 63 29W
Sumatera □, *Indonesia* **36 D2** 0 40N 100 20 E
Sumatera Barat □, *Indonesia* **36 E2** 1 0S 101 0 E
Sumatera Utara □, *Indonesia* **36 D1** 2 30N 98 0 E
Sumatra = Sumatera □, *Indonesia* **36 D2** 0 40N 100 20 E
Sumba, *Indonesia* **37 F5** 9 45S 119 35 E
Sumba, Selat, *Indonesia* **37 F5** 9 0S 118 40 E
Sumbawa, *Indonesia* **36 F5** 8 26S 117 30 E
Sumbawa Besar, *Indonesia* **36 F5** 8 30S 117 26 E
Sumbawanga □, *Tanzania* **52 F6** 8 0S 31 30 E
Sumbe, *Angola* **52 G2** 11 10S 13 48 E
Sumburgh Hd., *U.K.* **12 D7** 59 52N 1 17W
Sumdeo, *India* **43 D8** 31 26N 78 44 E
Sumdo, *India* **43 B8** 35 6N 78 41 E
Sumedang, *Indonesia* **37 G12** 6 52S 107 55 E
Šumen = Shumen, *Bulgaria* **21 C12** 43 18N 26 55 E
Sumenep, *Indonesia* **37 G15** 7 1S 113 52 E
Sumgait = Sumqayıt, *Azerbaijan* **25 F8** 40 34N 49 38 E
Summer L., *U.S.A.* **82 E3** 42 50N 120 45W
Summerland, *Canada* **72 D5** 49 32N 119 41W
Summerside, *Canada* **71 C7** 46 24N 63 47W
Summersville, *U.S.A.* **76 F5** 38 17N 80 51W
Summerville, *Ga., U.S.A.* **77 H3** 34 29N 85 21W
Summerville, *S.C., U.S.A.* **77 J5** 33 1N 80 11W
Summit Lake, *Canada* **72 C4** 54 20N 122 40W
Summit Peak, *U.S.A.* **83 H10** 37 21N 106 42W
Sumner, *Iowa, U.S.A.* **80 D8** 42 51N 92 6W
Sumner, *Wash., U.S.A.* **84 C4** 47 12N 122 14W
Sumoto, *Japan* **31 G7** 34 21N 134 54 E
Šumperk, *Czech Rep.* **17 D9** 49 59N 16 59 E
Sumqayıt, *Azerbaijan* **25 F8** 40 34N 49 38 E
Sumter, *U.S.A.* **77 J5** 33 55N 80 21W
Sumy, *Ukraine* **25 D5** 50 57N 34 50 E
Sun City, *Ariz., U.S.A.* **85 K7** 33 36N 112 17W
Sun City, *Calif., U.S.A.* **85 M9** 33 42N 117 11W
Sun City Center, *U.S.A.* **77 M4** 27 43N 82 18W
Sun Lakes, *U.S.A.* **83 K8** 33 10N 111 52W
Sun Valley, *U.S.A.* **82 E6** 43 42N 114 21W
Sunagawa, *Japan* **30 C10** 43 29N 141 55 E
Sunan, *N. Korea* **35 E13** 39 15N 125 40 E
Sunart, L., *U.K.* **12 E3** 56 42N 5 43W
Sunburst, *U.S.A.* **82 B8** 48 53N 111 55W
Sunbury, *U.S.A.* **79 F8** 40 52N 76 48W
Sunchales, *Argentina* **94 C3** 30 58S 61 35W
Suncho Corral, *Argentina* **94 B3** 27 55S 63 27W
Sunch'ŏn, *S. Korea* **35 G14** 34 52N 127 31 E
Suncook, *U.S.A.* **79 C13** 43 8N 71 27W
Sunda, Selat, *Indonesia* **36 F3** 6 20S 105 30 E
Sunda Is., *Indonesia* **28 K14** 5 0S 105 0 E
Sunda Str. = Sunda, Selat, *Indonesia* **36 F3** 6 20S 105 30 E
Sundance, *Canada* **73 B10** 56 32N 94 4W
Sundance, *U.S.A.* **80 C2** 44 24N 104 23W
Sundar Nagar, *India* **42 D7** 31 32N 76 53 E
Sundarbans, The, *Asia* **41 J16** 22 0N 89 0 E
Sundargarh, *India* **41 H14** 22 4N 84 5 E
Sundays = Sondags →, *S. Africa* **56 E4** 33 44S 25 51 E
Sunderland, *Canada* **78 B5** 44 16N 79 4W
Sunderland, *U.K.* **10 C6** 54 55N 1 23W
Sundre, *Canada* **72 C6** 51 49N 114 38W
Sundsvall, *Sweden* **9 E17** 62 23N 17 17 E
Sung Hei, *Vietnam* **39 G6** 10 20N 106 2 E
Sungai Kolok, *Thailand* **39 J3** 6 2N 101 58 E
Sungai Lembing, *Malaysia* **39 L4** 3 55N 103 3 E
Sungai Petani, *Malaysia* **39 K3** 5 37N 100 30 E
Sungaigerong, *Indonesia* **36 E2** 2 59S 104 52 E
Sungailiat, *Indonesia* **36 E3** 1 51S 106 8 E
Sungaipenuh, *Indonesia* **36 E2** 2 1S 101 20 E
Sungari = Songhua Jiang →, *China* **33 B8** 47 45N 132 30 E
Sunghua Chiang = Songhua Jiang →, *China* **33 B8** 47 45N 132 30 E
Sunland Park, *U.S.A.* **83 L10** 31 50N 106 40W
Sunndalsøra, *Norway* **9 E13** 62 40N 8 33 E
Sunnyside, *U.S.A.* **82 C3** 46 20N 120 0W
Sunnyvale, *U.S.A.* **84 H4** 37 23N 122 2W
Suntar, *Russia* **27 C12** 62 15N 117 30 E
Suomenselkä, *Finland* **8 E21** 62 52N 24 0 E
Suomussalmi, *Finland* **8 D23** 64 54N 29 10 E
Suoyarvi, *Russia* **24 B5** 62 3N 32 20 E
Supai, *U.S.A.* **83 H7** 36 15N 112 41W
Supaul, *India* **43 F12** 26 10N 86 40 E
Superior, *Ariz., U.S.A.* **83 K8** 33 18N 111 6W
Superior, *Mont., U.S.A.* **82 C6** 47 12N 114 53W
Superior, *Nebr., U.S.A.* **80 E5** 40 1N 98 4W
Superior, *Wis., U.S.A.* **80 B8** 46 44N 92 6W
Superior, L., *N. Amer.* **70 C2** 47 0N 87 0W
Suphan Buri, *Thailand* **38 E3** 14 14N 100 10 E
Suphan Dağı, *Turkey* **44 B4** 38 54N 42 48 E

Supiori

Supiori, *Indonesia* **37 E9** 1 0S 136 0 E
Supung Shuiku, *China* **35 D13** 40 35N 124 50 E
Sūq Suwayq, *Si. Arabia* **44 E3** 24 23N 38 27 E
Suqian, *China* **35 H10** 33 54N 118 8 E
Sūr, *Lebanon* **47 B4** 33 19N 35 16 E
Şūr, *Oman* **46 C6** 22 34N 59 32 E
Sur, Pt., *U.S.A.* **84 J5** 36 18N 121 54W
Sura →, *Russia* **24 C8** 56 6N 46 0 E
Surab, *Pakistan* **42 E2** 28 25N 66 15 E
Surabaja = Surabaya, *Indonesia* **36 F4** 7 17S 112 45 E
Surabaya, *Indonesia* **36 F4** 7 17S 112 45 E
Surakarta, *Indonesia* **36 F4** 7 35S 110 48 E
Surat, *Australia* **63 D4** 27 10S 149 6 E
Surat, *India* **40 J8** 21 12N 72 55 E
Surat Thani, *Thailand* **39 H2** 9 6N 99 20 E
Suratgarh, *India* **42 E5** 29 18N 73 55 E
Surendranagar, *India* **42 H4** 22 45N 71 40 E
Surf, *U.S.A.* **85 L6** 34 41N 120 36W
Surgut, *Russia* **26 C8** 61 14N 73 20 E
Suriapet, *India* **40 L11** 17 10N 79 40 E
Surigao, *Phil.* **37 C7** 9 47N 125 29 E
Surin, *Thailand* **38 E4** 14 50N 103 34 E
Surin Nua, Ko, *Thailand* **39 H1** 9 30N 97 55 E
Surinam ■, *S. Amer.* **93 C7** 4 0N 56 0W
Suriname = Surinam ■, *S. Amer.* **93 C7** 4 0N 56 0W
Suriname →, *Surinam* **93 B7** 5 50N 55 15W
Sūrmaq, *Iran* **45 D7** 31 3N 52 48 E
Surrey □, *U.K.* **11 F7** 51 15N 0 31W
Sursand, *India* **43 F11** 26 39N 85 43 E
Sursar →, *India* **43 F12** 26 14N 87 3 E
Surt, *Libya* **51 B9** 31 11N 16 39 E
Surt, Khalīj, *Libya* **51 B9** 31 40N 18 30 E
Surtanahu, *Pakistan* **42 F4** 26 22N 70 0 E
Surtsey, *Iceland* **8 E3** 63 20N 20 30W
Suruga-Wan, *Japan* **31 G9** 34 45N 138 30 E
Susaki, *Japan* **31 H6** 33 22N 133 17 E
Sūsangerd, *Iran* **45 D6** 31 35N 48 6 E
Susanville, *U.S.A.* **82 F3** 40 25N 120 39W
Susner, *India* **42 H7** 23 57N 76 5 E
Susquehanna, *U.S.A.* **79 E9** 41 57N 75 36W
Susquehanna →, *U.S.A.* **79 G8** 39 33N 76 5W
Susques, *Argentina* **94 A2** 23 35S 66 25W
Sussex, *Canada* **71 C6** 45 45N 65 37W
Sussex, *U.S.A.* **79 E10** 41 13N 74 37W
Sussex, E. □, *U.K.* **11 G8** 51 0N 0 20 E
Sussex, W. □, *U.K.* **11 G7** 51 0N 0 30W
Sustut →, *Canada* **72 B3** 56 20N 127 30W
Susuman, *Russia* **27 C15** 62 47N 148 10 E
Susunu, *Indonesia* **37 E8** 3 7S 133 39 E
Susurluk, *Turkey* **21 E13** 39 54N 28 8 E
Sutherland, *S. Africa* **56 E3** 32 24S 20 40 E
Sutherland, *U.S.A.* **80 E4** 41 10N 101 8W
Sutherland Falls, *N.Z.* **59 L1** 44 48S 167 46 E
Sutherlin, *U.S.A.* **82 E2** 43 23N 123 19W
Suthri, *India* **42 H3** 23 3N 68 55 E
Sutlej →, *Pakistan* **42 E4** 29 23N 71 3 E
Sutter, *U.S.A.* **84 F5** 39 10N 121 45W
Sutter Creek, *U.S.A.* **84 G6** 38 24N 120 48W
Sutton, *Canada* **79 A12** 45 6N 72 37W
Sutton, *Nebr., U.S.A.* **80 E6** 40 36N 97 52W
Sutton, *W. Va., U.S.A.* **76 F5** 38 40N 80 43W
Sutton →, *Canada* **70 A3** 55 15N 83 45W
Sutton Coldfield, *U.K.* **11 E6** 52 35N 1 49W
Sutton in Ashfield, *U.K.* **10 D6** 53 8N 1 16W
Sutton L., *Canada* **70 B3** 54 15N 84 42W
Suttor →, *Australia* **62 C4** 21 36S 147 2 E
Suttsu, *Japan* **30 C10** 42 48N 140 14 E
Suva, *Fiji* **59 D8** 18 6S 178 30 E
Suva Planina, *Serbia, Yug.* **21 C10** 43 10N 22 5 E
Suvorov Is. = Suwarrow Is., *Cook Is.* **65 J11** 15 0S 163 0W
Suwałki, *Poland* **17 A12** 54 8N 22 59 E
Suwannaphum, *Thailand* **38 E4** 15 33N 103 47 E
Suwannee →, *U.S.A.* **77 L4** 29 17N 83 10W
Suwanose-Jima, *Japan* **31 K4** 29 38N 129 43 E
Suwarrow Is., *Cook Is.* **65 J11** 15 0S 163 0W
Suwayq aş Şuqban, *Iraq* **44 D5** 31 32N 46 7 E
Suweis, Khalîg el, *Egypt* **51 C12** 28 40N 33 0 E
Suweis, Qanâ es, *Egypt* **51 B12** 31 0N 32 20 E
Suwŏn, *S. Korea* **35 F14** 37 17N 127 1 E
Suzdal, *Russia* **24 C7** 56 29N 40 26 E
Suzhou, *Anhui, China* **34 H9** 33 41N 116 59 E
Suzhou, *Jiangsu, China* **33 C7** 31 19N 120 38 E
Suzu, *Japan* **31 F8** 37 25N 137 17 E
Suzu-Misaki, *Japan* **31 F8** 37 31N 137 21 E
Suzuka, *Japan* **31 G8** 34 55N 136 36 E
Svalbard, *Arctic* **4 B8** 78 0N 17 0 E
Svappavaara, *Sweden* **8 C19** 67 40N 21 3 E
Svartisen, *Norway* **8 C15** 66 40N 13 50 E
Svay Chek, *Cambodia* **38 F4** 13 48N 102 58 E
Svay Rieng, *Cambodia* **39 G5** 11 9N 105 45 E
Svealand □, *Sweden* **9 G16** 60 20N 15 0 E
Sveg, *Sweden* **9 E16** 62 2N 14 21 E
Svendborg, *Denmark* **9 J14** 55 4N 10 35 E
Sverdlovsk = Yekaterinburg, *Russia* **26 D7** 56 50N 60 30 E
Sverdrup Is., *Canada* **4 B3** 79 0N 97 0W
Svetlaya, *Russia* **30 A9** 46 33N 138 18 E
Svetlogorsk = Svyetlahorsk, *Belarus* **17 B15** 52 38N 29 46 E
Svir →, *Russia* **24 B5** 60 30N 32 48 E
Svishtov, *Bulgaria* **21 C11** 43 36N 25 23 E
Svislach, *Belarus* **17 B13** 53 3N 24 2 E
Svobodnyy, *Russia* **27 D13** 51 20N 128 0 E
Svolvær, *Norway* **8 B16** 68 15N 14 34 E
Svyetlahorsk, *Belarus* **17 B15** 52 38N 29 46 E
Swabian Alps = Schwäbische Alb, *Germany* **16 D5** 48 20N 9 30 E
Swainsboro, *U.S.A.* **77 J4** 32 36N 82 20W
Swakop →, *Namibia* **56 C2** 22 38S 14 36 E
Swakopmund, *Namibia* **56 C1** 22 37S 14 30 E
Swale →, *U.K.* **10 C6** 54 5N 1 20W
Swan →, *Australia* **61 F2** 32 3S 115 45 E
Swan →, *Canada* **73 C8** 52 30N 100 45W
Swan Hills, *Canada* **72 C5** 54 43N 115 24W
Swan Is., *W. Indies* **88 C3** 17 22N 83 57W
Swan L., *Canada* **73 C8** 52 30N 100 40W
Swan Peak, *U.S.A.* **82 C7** 47 43N 113 38W
Swan Ra., *U.S.A.* **82 C7** 48 0N 113 45W
Swan River, *Canada* **73 C8** 52 10N 101 16W
Swanage, *U.K.* **11 G6** 50 36N 1 58W
Swansea, *Australia* **62 G4** 42 8S 148 4 E
Swansea, *Canada* **78 C5** 43 38N 79 28W
Swansea, *U.K.* **11 F4** 51 37N 3 57W
Swansea □, *U.K.* **11 F3** 51 38N 4 3W
Swar →, *Pakistan* **43 B5** 34 40N 72 5 E
Swartberge, *S. Africa* **56 E3** 33 20S 22 0 E
Swartmodder, *S. Africa* **56 D3** 28 1S 20 32 E
Swartnossob →, *Namibia* **56 C2** 23 8S 18 42 E
Swartruggens, *S. Africa* **56 D4** 25 39S 26 42 E
Swastika, *Canada* **70 C3** 48 7N 80 6W
Swatow = Shantou, *China* **33 D6** 23 18N 116 40 E
Swaziland ■, *Africa* **57 D5** 26 30S 31 30 E
Sweden ■, *Europe* **9 G16** 57 0N 15 0 E
Sweet Home, *U.S.A.* **82 D2** 44 24N 122 44W
Sweetgrass, *U.S.A.* **82 B8** 48 59N 111 58W
Sweetwater, *Nev., U.S.A.* **84 G7** 38 27N 119 9W
Sweetwater, *Tenn., U.S.A.* **77 H3** 35 36N 84 28W
Sweetwater, *Tex., U.S.A.* **81 J4** 32 28N 100 25W
Sweetwater →, *U.S.A.* **82 E10** 42 31N 107 2W
Swellendam, *S. Africa* **56 E3** 34 1S 20 26 E
Świdnica, *Poland* **17 C9** 50 50N 16 30 E
Świdnik, *Poland* **17 C12** 51 13N 22 39 E
Świebodzin, *Poland* **16 B8** 52 15N 15 31 E
Świecie, *Poland* **17 B10** 53 25N 18 30 E
Swift Current, *Canada* **73 C7** 50 20N 107 45W
Swiftcurrent →, *Canada* **73 C7** 50 38N 107 44W
Swilly, L., *Ireland* **13 A4** 55 12N 7 33W
Swindon, *U.K.* **11 F6** 51 34N 1 46W
Swindon □, *U.K.* **11 F6** 51 34N 1 46W
Swinemünde = Świnoujście, *Poland* **16 B8** 53 54N 14 16 E
Swinford, *Ireland* **13 C3** 53 57N 8 58W
Świnoujście, *Poland* **16 B8** 53 54N 14 16 E
Switzerland ■, *Europe* **18 C8** 46 30N 8 0 E
Swords, *Ireland* **13 C5** 53 28N 6 13W
Swoyerville, *U.S.A.* **79 E9** 41 18N 75 53W
Sydenham →, *Canada* **78 D2** 42 33N 82 25W
Sydney, *Canada* **71 C7** 46 7N 60 7W
Sydney L., *Canada* **73 C10** 50 41N 94 25W
Sydney Mines, *Canada* **71 C7** 46 18N 60 15W
Sydprøven = Alluitsup Paa, *Greenland* **4 C5** 60 30N 45 35W
Sydra, G. of = Surt, Khalīj, *Libya* **51 B9** 31 40N 18 30 E
Sykesville, *U.S.A.* **78 E6** 41 3N 78 50W
Syktyvkar, *Russia* **24 B9** 61 45N 50 40 E
Sylacauga, *U.S.A.* **77 J2** 33 10N 86 15W
Sylarna, *Sweden* **8 E15** 63 2N 12 13 E
Sylhet, *Bangla.* **41 G17** 24 54N 91 52 E
Sylhet □, *Bangla.* **41 G17** 24 50N 91 50 E
Sylt, *Germany* **16 A5** 54 54N 8 22 E
Sylvan Beach, *U.S.A.* **79 C9** 43 12N 75 44W
Sylvan Lake, *Canada* **72 C6** 52 20N 114 3W
Sylvania, *U.S.A.* **77 J5** 32 45N 81 38W
Sylvester, *U.S.A.* **77 K4** 31 32N 83 50W
Sym, *Russia* **26 C9** 60 20N 88 18 E
Symón, *Mexico* **86 C4** 24 42N 102 35W
Synnott Ra., *Australia* **60 C4** 16 30S 125 20 E
Syracuse, *Kans., U.S.A.* **81 G4** 37 59N 101 45W
Syracuse, *N.Y., U.S.A.* **79 C8** 43 3N 76 9W
Syracuse, *Nebr., U.S.A.* **80 E6** 40 39N 96 11W
Syrdarya →, *Kazakstan* **26 E7** 46 3N 61 0 E
Syria ■, *Asia* **44 C3** 35 0N 38 0 E
Syrian Desert = Shām, Bādiyat ash, *Asia* **44 C3** 32 0N 40 0 E
Syzran, *Russia* **24 D8** 53 12N 48 30 E
Szczecin, *Poland* **16 B8** 53 27N 14 27 E
Szczecinek, *Poland* **17 B9** 53 43N 16 41 E
Szczeciński, Zalew = Stettiner Haff, *Germany* **16 B8** 53 47N 14 15 E
Szczytno, *Poland* **17 B11** 53 33N 21 0 E
Szechwan = Sichuan □, *China* **32 C5** 30 30N 103 0 E
Szeged, *Hungary* **17 E11** 46 16N 20 10 E
Székesfehérvár, *Hungary* **17 E10** 47 15N 18 25 E
Szekszárd, *Hungary* **17 E10** 46 22N 18 42 E
Szentes, *Hungary* **17 E11** 46 39N 20 21 E
Szolnok, *Hungary* **17 E11** 47 10N 20 15 E
Szombathely, *Hungary* **17 E9** 47 14N 16 38 E

T

Ta Khli Khok, *Thailand* **38 E3** 15 18N 100 20 E
Ta Lai, *Vietnam* **39 G6** 11 24N 107 23 E
Tabacal, *Argentina* **94 A3** 23 15S 64 15W
Tabaco, *Phil.* **37 B6** 13 22N 123 44 E
Ţābah, *Si. Arabia* **44 E4** 26 55N 42 38 E
Ţabas, *Khorāsān, Iran* **45 C9** 32 48N 60 12 E
Ţabas, *Khorāsān, Iran* **45 C8** 33 35N 56 55 E
Tabasará, Serranía de, *Panama* **88 E3** 8 35N 81 40W
Tabasco □, *Mexico* **87 D6** 17 45N 93 30W
Tabāsīn, *Iran* **45 D8** 31 12N 57 54 E
Tabatinga, Serra da, *Brazil* **93 F10** 10 30S 44 0W
Taber, *Canada* **72 D6** 49 47N 112 8W
Taberg, *U.S.A.* **79 C9** 43 18N 75 37W
Tablas I., *Phil.* **37 B6** 12 25N 122 2 E
Table B. = Tafelbaai, *S. Africa* **56 E2** 33 35S 18 25 E
Table B., *Canada* **71 B8** 53 40N 56 25W
Table Mt., *S. Africa* **56 E2** 34 0S 18 22 E
Table Rock L., *U.S.A.* **81 G8** 36 36N 93 19W
Tabletop, Mt., *Australia* **62 C4** 23 24S 147 11 E
Tábor, *Czech Rep.* **16 D8** 49 25N 14 39 E
Tabora, *Tanzania* **54 D3** 5 2S 32 50 E
Tabora □, *Tanzania* **54 D3** 5 0S 33 0 E
Tabou, *Ivory C.* **50 H4** 4 30N 7 20W
Tabrīz, *Iran* **44 B5** 38 7N 46 20 E
Tabuaeran, *Kiribati* **65 G12** 3 51N 159 22W
Tabūk, *Si. Arabia* **44 D3** 28 23N 36 36 E
Tacámbaro de Codallos, *Mexico* **86 D4** 19 14N 101 28W
Tacheng, *China* **32 B3** 46 40N 82 58 E
Tach'ing Shan = Daqing Shan, *China* **34 D6** 40 40N 111 0 E
Tacloban, *Phil.* **37 B6** 11 15N 124 58 E
Tacna, *Peru* **92 G4** 18 0S 70 20W
Tacoma, *U.S.A.* **84 C4** 47 14N 122 26W
Tacuarembó, *Uruguay* **95 C4** 31 45S 56 0W
Tademaït, Plateau du, *Algeria* **50 C6** 28 30N 2 30 E
Tadjoura, *Djibouti* **46 E3** 11 50N 42 55 E
Tadmor, *N.Z.* **59 J4** 41 27S 172 45 E
Tadoule, L., *Canada* **73 B9** 58 36N 98 20W
Tadoussac, *Canada* **71 C6** 48 11N 69 42W
Tadzhikistan = Tajikistan ■, *Asia* **26 F8** 38 30N 70 0 E
Taechŏn-ni, *S. Korea* **35 F14** 36 21N 126 36 E
Taegu, *S. Korea* **35 G15** 35 50N 128 37 E
Taegwan, *N. Korea* **35 D13** 40 13N 125 12 E
Taejŏn, *S. Korea* **35 F14** 36 20N 127 28 E
Tafalla, *Spain* **19 A5** 42 30N 1 41W
Tafelbaai, *S. Africa* **56 E2** 33 35S 18 25 E
Tafermaar, *Indonesia* **37 F8** 6 47S 134 10 E
Tafí Viejo, *Argentina* **94 B2** 26 43S 65 17W
Tafihān, *Iran* **45 D7** 29 25N 52 39 E
Tafresh, *Iran* **45 C6** 34 45N 49 57 E
Taft, *Iran* **45 D7** 31 45N 54 14 E
Taft, *Phil.* **37 B7** 11 57N 125 30 E
Taft, *U.S.A.* **85 K7** 35 8N 119 28W
Taftān, Kūh-e, *Iran* **45 D9** 28 40N 61 0 E
Taga Dzong, *Bhutan* **41 F16** 27 5N 89 55 E
Taganrog, *Russia* **25 E6** 47 12N 38 50 E
Tagbilaran, *Phil.* **37 C6** 9 39N 123 51 E
Tagish, *Canada* **72 A2** 60 19N 134 16W
Tagish L., *Canada* **72 A2** 60 10N 134 20W
Tagliamento →, *Italy* **20 B5** 45 38N 13 6 E
Tagomago, *Spain* **22 B8** 39 2N 1 39 E
Taguatinga, *Brazil* **93 F10** 12 16S 42 26W
Tagum, *Phil.* **37 C7** 7 33N 125 53 E
Tagus = Tejo →, *Europe* **19 C1** 38 40N 9 24W
Tahakopa, *N.Z.* **59 M2** 46 30S 169 23 E
Tahan, Gunong, *Malaysia* **39 K4** 4 34N 102 17 E
Tahat, *Algeria* **50 D7** 23 18N 5 33 E
Tāherī, *Iran* **45 E7** 27 43N 52 20 E
Tahiti, *Pac. Oc.* **65 J13** 17 37S 149 27W
Tahlequah, *U.S.A.* **81 H7** 35 55N 94 58W
Tahoe, L., *U.S.A.* **84 G6** 39 6N 120 2W
Tahoe City, *U.S.A.* **84 F6** 39 10N 120 9W
Tahoka, *U.S.A.* **81 J4** 33 10N 101 48W
Taholah, *U.S.A.* **84 C2** 47 21N 124 17W
Tahoua, *Niger* **50 F7** 14 57N 5 16 E
Tahrūd, *Iran* **45 D8** 29 26N 57 49 E
Tahsis, *Canada* **72 D3** 49 55N 126 40W
Tahta, *Egypt* **51 C12** 26 44N 31 32 E
Tahulandang, *Indonesia* **37 D7** 2 27N 125 23 E
Tahuna, *Indonesia* **37 D7** 3 38N 125 30 E
Tai Shan, *China* **35 F9** 36 25N 117 20 E
Tai'an, *China* **35 F9** 36 12N 117 8 E
Taibei = T'aipei, *Taiwan* **33 D7** 25 2N 121 30 E
Taibique, *Canary Is.* **22 G2** 27 42N 17 58W
Taibus Qi, *China* **34 D8** 41 54N 115 22 E
T'aichung, *Taiwan* **33 D7** 24 9N 120 37 E
Taieri →, *N.Z.* **59 M3** 46 3S 170 12 E
Taigu, *China* **34 F7** 37 28N 112 30 E
Taihang Shan, *China* **34 G7** 36 0N 113 30 E
Taihape, *N.Z.* **59 H5** 39 41S 175 48 E
Taihe, *China* **34 H8** 33 20N 115 42 E
Taikang, *China* **34 G8** 34 5N 114 50 E
Taimyr Peninsula = Taymyr, Poluostrov, *Russia* **27 B11** 75 0N 100 0 E
Tain, *U.K.* **12 D4** 57 49N 4 4W
T'ainan, *Taiwan* **33 D7** 23 0N 120 10 E
Tainaron, Ákra, *Greece* **21 F10** 36 22N 22 27 E
T'aipei, *Taiwan* **33 D7** 25 2N 121 30 E
Taiping, *Malaysia* **39 K3** 4 51N 100 44 E
Taipingzhen, *China* **34 H6** 33 35N 111 42 E
Tairbeart = Tarbert, *U.K.* **12 D2** 57 54N 6 49W
Taita Hills, *Kenya* **54 C4** 3 25S 38 15 E
Taitao, Pen. de, *Chile* **96 F2** 46 30S 75 0W
T'aitung, *Taiwan* **33 D7** 22 43N 121 4 E
Taivalkoski, *Finland* **8 D23** 65 33N 28 12 E
Taiwan ■, *Asia* **33 D7** 23 30N 121 0 E
Taïyetos Óros, *Greece* **21 F10** 37 0N 22 23 E
Taiyiba, *Israel* **47 C4** 32 36N 35 27 E
Taiyuan, *China* **34 F7** 37 52N 112 33 E
Taizhong = T'aichung, *Taiwan* **33 D7** 24 9N 120 37 E
Ta'izz, *Yemen* **46 E3** 13 35N 44 2 E
Tājābād, *Iran* **45 D7** 30 2N 54 24 E
Tajikistan ■, *Asia* **26 F8** 38 30N 70 0 E
Tajima, *Japan* **31 F9** 37 12N 139 46 E
Tajo = Tejo →, *Europe* **19 C1** 38 40N 9 24W
Tajrish, *Iran* **45 C6** 35 48N 51 25 E
Tak, *Thailand* **38 D2** 16 52N 99 8 E
Takāb, *Iran* **44 B5** 36 24N 47 7 E
Takachiho, *Japan* **31 H5** 32 42N 131 18 E
Takachu, *Botswana* **56 C3** 22 37S 21 58 E
Takada, *Japan* **31 F9** 37 7N 138 15 E
Takahagi, *Japan* **31 F10** 36 43N 140 45 E
Takaka, *N.Z.* **59 J4** 40 51S 172 50 E
Takamatsu, *Japan* **31 G7** 34 20N 134 5 E
Takaoka, *Japan* **31 F8** 36 47N 137 0 E
Takapuna, *N.Z.* **59 G5** 36 47S 174 47 E
Takasaki, *Japan* **31 F9** 36 20N 139 0 E
Takatsuki, *Japan* **31 G7** 34 51N 135 37 E
Takaungu, *Kenya* **54 C4** 3 38S 39 52 E
Takayama, *Japan* **31 F8** 36 18N 137 11 E
Take-Shima, *Japan* **31 J5** 30 49N 130 26 E
Takefu, *Japan* **31 G8** 35 50N 136 10 E
Takengon, *Indonesia* **36 D1** 4 45N 96 50 E
Takeo, *Japan* **31 H5** 33 12N 130 1 E
Tākestān, *Iran* **45 C6** 36 0N 49 40 E
Taketa, *Japan* **31 H5** 32 58N 131 24 E
Takev, *Cambodia* **39 G5** 10 59N 104 47 E
Takh, *India* **43 C7** 33 6N 77 32 E
Takht-Sulaiman, *Pakistan* **42 D3** 31 40N 69 58 E
Takikawa, *Japan* **30 C10** 43 33N 141 54 E
Takla L., *Canada* **72 B3** 55 15N 125 45W
Takla Landing, *Canada* **72 B3** 55 30N 125 50W
Takla Makan = Taklamakan Shamo, *China* **32 C3** 38 0N 83 0 E
Taklamakan Shamo, *China* **32 C3** 38 0N 83 0 E
Taku →, *Canada* **72 B2** 58 30N 133 50W
Tal Halāl, *Iran* **45 D7** 28 54N 55 1 E
Tala, *Uruguay* **95 C4** 34 21S 55 46W
Talagang, *Pakistan* **42 C5** 32 55N 72 25 E
Talagante, *Chile* **94 C1** 33 40S 70 50W
Talamanca, Cordillera de, *Cent. Amer.* **88 E3** 9 20N 83 20W
Talara, *Peru* **92 D2** 4 38S 81 18W
Talas, *Kyrgyzstan* **26 E8** 42 30N 72 13 E
Talâta, *Egypt* **47 E1** 30 36N 32 20 E
Talaud, Kepulauan, *Indonesia* **37 D7** 4 30N 126 50 E
Talaud Is. = Talaud, Kepulauan, *Indonesia* **37 D7** 4 30N 126 50 E
Talavera de la Reina, *Spain* **19 C3** 39 55N 4 46W
Talayan, *Phil.* **37 C6** 6 52N 124 24 E
Talbandh, *India* **43 H12** 22 3N 86 20 E
Talbot, C., *Australia* **60 B4** 13 48S 126 43 E
Talca, *Chile* **94 D1** 35 28S 71 40W
Talcahuano, *Chile* **94 D1** 36 40S 73 10W
Talcher, *India* **41 J14** 21 0N 85 18 E
Taldy Kurgan = Taldyqorghan, *Kazakstan* **26 E8** 45 10N 78 45 E
Taldyqorghan, *Kazakstan* **26 E8** 45 10N 78 45 E
Tālesh, *Iran* **45 B6** 37 58N 48 58 E
Tālesh, Kūhhā-ye, *Iran* **45 B6** 37 42N 48 55 E
Tali Post, *Sudan* **51 G12** 5 55N 30 44 E
Taliabu, *Indonesia* **37 E6** 1 50S 125 0 E
Talibon, *Phil.* **37 B6** 10 9N 124 20 E
Talibong, Ko, *Thailand* **39 J2** 7 15N 99 23 E
Talihina, *U.S.A.* **81 H7** 34 45N 95 3W
Taliwang, *Indonesia* **36 F5** 8 50S 116 55 E
Tall 'Afar, *Iraq* **44 B4** 36 22N 42 27 E
Tall Kalakh, *Syria* **47 A5** 34 41N 36 15 E
Talladega, *U.S.A.* **77 J2** 33 26N 86 6W
Tallahassee, *U.S.A.* **77 K3** 30 27N 84 17W
Tallering Pk., *Australia* **61 E2** 28 6S 115 37 E
Talli, *Pakistan* **42 E3** 29 32N 68 8 E
Tallinn, *Estonia* **9 G21** 59 22N 24 48 E
Tallmadge, *U.S.A.* **78 E3** 41 6N 81 27W
Tallulah, *U.S.A.* **81 J9** 32 25N 91 11W
Taloyoak, *Canada* **68 B10** 69 32N 93 32W
Talpa de Allende, *Mexico* **86 C4** 20 23N 104 51W
Talsi, *Latvia* **9 H20** 57 10N 22 30 E
Taltal, *Chile* **94 B1** 25 23S 70 33W
Taltson →, *Canada* **72 A6** 61 24N 112 46W
Talurqjuak = Taloyoak, *Canada* **68 B10** 69 32N 93 32W
Talwood, *Australia* **63 D4** 28 29S 149 29 E
Tam Chau, *Vietnam* **39 G5** 10 48N 105 12 E
Tam Ky, *Vietnam* **38 E7** 15 34N 108 29 E
Tam Quan, *Vietnam* **38 E7** 14 35N 109 3 E
Tama, *U.S.A.* **80 E8** 41 58N 92 35W
Tamale, *Ghana* **50 G5** 9 22N 0 50W
Tamano, *Japan* **31 G6** 34 29N 133 59 E
Tamanrasset, *Algeria* **50 D7** 22 50N 5 30 E
Tamaqua, *U.S.A.* **79 F9** 40 48N 75 58W
Tamar →, *U.K.* **11 G3** 50 27N 4 15W
Tamarinda, *Spain* **22 B10** 39 55N 3 49 E
Tamashima, *Japan* **31 G6** 34 32N 133 40 E
Tamaulipas □, *Mexico* **87 C5** 24 0N 99 0W
Tamaulipas, Sierra de, *Mexico* **87 C5** 23 30N 98 20W
Tamazula, *Mexico* **86 C3** 24 55N 106 58W
Tamazunchale, *Mexico* **87 C5** 21 16N 98 47W
Tambacounda, *Senegal* **50 F3** 13 45N 13 40W
Tambelan, Kepulauan, *Indonesia* **36 D3** 1 0N 107 30 E
Tambellup, *Australia* **61 F2** 34 4S 117 37 E
Tambo, *Australia* **62 C4** 24 54S 146 14 E
Tambo de Mora, *Peru* **92 F3** 13 30S 76 8W
Tambohorano, *Madag.* **57 B7** 17 30S 43 58 E
Tambora, *Indonesia* **36 F5** 8 12S 118 5 E
Tambov, *Russia* **24 D7** 52 45N 41 28 E
Tambuku, *Indonesia* **37 G15** 7 8S 113 40 E
Tâmega →, *Portugal* **19 B1** 41 5N 8 21W
Tamenglong, *India* **41 G18** 25 0N 93 35 E
Tamiahua, L. de, *Mexico* **87 C5** 21 30N 97 30W
Tamil Nadu □, *India* **40 P10** 11 0N 77 0 E
Tamluk, *India* **43 H12** 22 18N 87 58 E
Tammerfors = Tampere, *Finland* **9 F20** 61 30N 23 50 E
Tammisaari, *Finland* **9 F20** 60 0N 23 26 E
Tamo Abu, Pegunungan, *Malaysia* **36 D5** 3 10N 115 5 E
Tampa, *U.S.A.* **77 M4** 27 57N 82 27W
Tampa B., *U.S.A.* **77 M4** 27 50N 82 30W
Tampere, *Finland* **9 F20** 61 30N 23 50 E
Tampico, *Mexico* **87 C5** 22 20N 97 50W
Tampin, *Malaysia* **39 L4** 2 28N 102 13 E
Tamu, *Burma* **41 G19** 24 13N 94 12 E
Tamworth, *Canada* **78 B8** 44 29N 77 0W
Tamworth, *U.K.* **11 E6** 52 39N 1 41W
Tamyang, *S. Korea* **35 G14** 35 19N 126 59 E
Tan An, *Vietnam* **39 G6** 10 32N 106 25 E
Tan-Tan, *Morocco* **50 C3** 28 29N 11 1W
Tana →, *Kenya* **54 C5** 2 32S 40 31 E
Tana →, *Norway* **8 A23** 70 30N 28 14 E
Tana, L., *Ethiopia* **46 E2** 13 5N 37 30 E
Tana River, *Kenya* **54 C4** 2 0S 39 30 E
Tanabe, *Japan* **31 H7** 33 44N 135 22 E
Tanafjorden, *Norway* **8 A23** 70 45N 28 25 E
Tanaga, Pta., *Canary Is.* **22 G1** 27 42N 18 10W
Tanahbala, *Indonesia* **36 E1** 0 30S 98 30 E
Tanahgrogot, *Indonesia* **36 E5** 1 55S 116 15 E
Tanahjampea, *Indonesia* **37 F6** 7 10S 120 35 E
Tanahmasa, *Indonesia* **36 E1** 0 12S 98 39 E
Tanahmerah, *Indonesia* **37 F10** 6 5S 140 16 E
Tanakpur, *India* **43 E9** 29 5N 80 7 E
Tanakura, *Japan* **31 F10** 37 10N 140 20 E
Tanami, *Australia* **60 C4** 19 59S 129 43 E
Tanami Desert, *Australia* **60 C5** 18 50S 132 0 E
Tanana →, *U.S.A.* **68 B4** 65 10N 151 58W
Tananarive = Antananarivo, *Madag.* **57 B8** 18 55S 47 31 E
Tánaro →, *Italy* **18 D8** 44 55N 8 40 E
Tancheng, *China* **35 G10** 34 25N 118 20 E
Tanch'ŏn, *N. Korea* **35 D15** 40 27N 128 54 E
Tanda, *Ut. P., India* **43 F10** 26 33N 82 35 E
Tanda, *Ut. P., India* **43 E8** 28 57N 78 56 E
Tandag, *Phil.* **37 C7** 9 4N 126 9 E
Tandaia, *Tanzania* **55 D3** 9 25S 34 15 E
Tandaué, *Angola* **56 B2** 16 58S 18 5 E
Tandil, *Argentina* **94 D4** 37 15S 59 6W
Tandil, Sa. del, *Argentina* **94 D4** 37 30S 59 0W
Tandlianwala, *Pakistan* **42 D5** 31 3N 73 9 E
Tando Adam, *Pakistan* **42 G3** 25 45N 68 40 E
Tando Allahyar, *Pakistan* **42 G3** 25 28N 68 43 E
Tando Bago, *Pakistan* **42 G3** 24 47N 68 58 E
Tando Mohommed Khan, *Pakistan* **42 G3** 25 8N 68 32 E
Tandragee, *U.K.* **13 B5** 54 21N 6 24W
Tane-ga-Shima, *Japan* **31 J5** 30 30N 131 0 E
Taneatua, *N.Z.* **59 H6** 38 4S 177 1 E
Tanen Tong Dan = Dawna Ra., *Burma* **38 D2** 16 30N 98 30 E
Tanezrouft, *Algeria* **50 D6** 23 9N 0 11 E
Tang, Koh, *Cambodia* **39 G4** 10 16N 103 7 E
Tang, Ra's-e, *Iran* **45 E8** 25 21N 59 52 E
Tang Krasang, *Cambodia* **38 F5** 12 34N 105 3 E
Tanga, *Tanzania* **54 D4** 5 5S 39 2 E
Tanga □, *Tanzania* **54 D4** 5 20S 38 0 E
Tanganyika, L., *Africa* **54 D3** 6 40S 30 0 E
Tanger, *Morocco* **50 A4** 35 50N 5 49W
Tangerang, *Indonesia* **37 G12** 6 11S 106 37 E

Teuco

Tanggu, China 35 E9 39 2N 117 40 E
Tanggula Shan, China 32 C4 32 40N 92 10 E
Tanghe, China 34 H7 32 47N 112 50 E
Tangier = Tanger, Morocco 50 A4 35 50N 5 49W
Tangorin, Australia 62 C3 21 47S 144 12 E
Tangorombohitr'i Makay, Madag. 57 C8 21 0S 45 15 E
Tangshan, China 35 E10 39 38N 118 10 E
Tangtou, China 35 G10 35 28N 118 30 E
Tanimbar, Kepulauan, Indonesia 37 F8 7 30S 131 30 E
Tanimbar Is. = Tanimbar, Kepulauan, Indonesia 37 F8 7 30S 131 30 E
Taninthari = Tenasserim □, Burma 38 F2 14 0N 98 30 E
Tanjay, Phil. 37 C6 9 30N 123 5 E
Tanjong Malim, Malaysia 39 L3 3 42N 101 31 E
Tanjore = Thanjavur, India 40 P11 10 48N 79 12 E
Tanjung, Indonesia 36 E5 2 10S 115 25 E
Tanjungbalai, Indonesia 36 D1 2 55N 99 44 E
Tanjungbatu, Indonesia 36 D5 2 23N 118 3 E
Tanjungkarang Telukbetung, Indonesia 36 F3 5 20S 105 10 E
Tanjungpandan, Indonesia 36 E3 2 43S 107 38 E
Tanjungpinang, Indonesia 36 D2 1 5N 104 30 E
Tanjungredeb, Indonesia 36 D5 2 9N 117 29 E
Tanjungselor, Indonesia 36 D5 2 55N 117 25 E
Tank, Pakistan 42 C4 32 14N 70 25 E
Tankhala, India 42 J5 21 58N 73 47 E
Tannersville, U.S.A. 79 E9 41 3N 75 18W
Tannu-Ola, Russia 27 D10 51 0N 94 0 E
Tannum Sands, Australia 62 C5 23 57S 151 22 E
Tanout, Niger 50 F7 14 50N 8 55 E
Tanta, Egypt 51 B12 30 45N 30 57 E
Tantoyuca, Mexico 87 C5 21 21N 98 10W
Tantung = Dandong, China 35 D13 40 10N 124 20 E
Tanzania ■, Africa 54 D3 6 0S 34 0 E
Tanzilla →, Canada 72 B2 58 8N 130 43W
Tao, Ko, Thailand 39 G2 10 5N 99 52 E
Tao'an = Taonan, China 35 B12 45 22N 122 40 E
Tao'er He →, China 35 B13 45 45N 124 5 E
Taolanaro, Madag. 57 D8 25 2S 47 0 E
Taole, China 34 E4 38 48N 106 40 E
Taonan, China 35 B12 45 22N 122 40 E
Taos, U.S.A. 83 H11 36 24N 105 35W
Taoudenni, Mali 50 D5 22 40N 3 55W
Tapa, Estonia 9 G21 59 16N 25 50 E
Tapa Shan = Daba Shan, China 33 C5 32 0N 109 0 E
Tapachula, Mexico 87 E6 14 54N 92 17W
Tapah, Malaysia 39 K3 4 12N 101 15 E
Tapajós →, Brazil 93 D8 2 24S 54 41W
Tapaktuan, Indonesia 36 D1 3 15N 97 10 E
Tapanahoni →, Surinam 93 C8 4 20N 54 25W
Tapanui, N.Z. 59 L2 45 56S 169 18 E
Tapauá →, Brazil 92 E6 5 40S 64 21W
Tapes, Brazil 95 C5 30 40S 51 23W
Tapeta, Liberia 50 G4 6 29N 8 52W
Taphan Hin, Thailand 38 D3 16 13N 100 26 E
Tapi →, India 40 J8 21 8N 72 41 E
Tapirapecó, Serra, Venezuela 92 C6 1 10N 65 0W
Tapuaenuku, Mt., N.Z. 59 K4 42 0S 173 39 E
Tapul Group, Phil. 37 C6 5 35N 120 50 E
Tapurucuará, Brazil 92 D5 0 24S 65 2W
Ţaqţaq, Iraq 44 C5 35 53N 44 35 E
Taquara, Brazil 95 B5 29 36S 50 46W
Taquari →, Brazil 92 G7 19 15S 57 17W
Tara, Australia 63 D5 27 17S 150 31 E
Tara, Canada 78 B3 44 28N 81 9W
Tara, Russia 26 D8 56 55N 74 24 E
Tara, Zambia 55 F2 16 58S 26 45 E
Tara →, Montenegro, Yug. 21 C8 43 21N 18 51 E
Tarabagatay, Khrebet, Kazakstan 26 E9 48 0N 83 0 E
Tarābulus, Lebanon 47 A4 34 31N 35 50 E
Tarābulus, Libya 51 B8 32 49N 13 7 E
Taradehi, India 43 H8 23 18N 79 21 E
Tarajalejo, Canary Is. 22 F5 28 12N 14 7W
Tarakan, Indonesia 36 D5 3 20N 117 35 E
Tarakit, Mt., Kenya 54 B4 2 2N 35 10 E
Tarama-Jima, Japan 31 M2 24 39N 124 42 E
Taran, Mys, Russia 9 J18 54 56N 19 59 E
Taranagar, India 42 E6 28 43N 74 50 E
Taranaki □, N.Z. 59 H5 39 25S 174 30 E
Taranaki, Mt., N.Z. 59 H5 39 17S 174 5 E
Tarancón, Spain 19 B4 40 1N 3 0W
Taransay, U.K. 12 D1 57 54N 7 0W
Táranto, Italy 20 D7 40 28N 17 14 E
Táranto, G. di, Italy 20 D7 40 8N 17 20 E
Tarapacá, Colombia 92 D5 2 56S 69 46W
Tarapacá □, Chile 94 A2 20 45S 69 30W
Tarapoto, Peru 92 E3 6 30S 76 20W
Tararua Ra., N.Z. 59 J5 40 45S 175 25 E
Tarashcha, Ukraine 17 D16 49 30N 30 31 E
Tarauacá, Brazil 92 E4 8 6S 70 48W
Tarauacá →, Brazil 92 E5 6 42S 69 48W
Tarawa, Kiribati 64 G9 1 30N 173 0 E
Tarawera, N.Z. 59 H6 39 2S 176 36 E
Tarawera L., N.Z. 59 H6 38 13S 176 27 E
Taraz, Kazakstan 26 E8 42 54N 71 22 E
Tarazona, Spain 19 B5 41 55N 1 43W
Tarbat Ness, U.K. 12 D5 57 52N 3 47W
Tarbela Dam, Pakistan 42 B5 34 8N 72 52 E
Tarbert, Arg. & Bute, U.K. 12 F3 55 52N 5 25W
Tarbert, W. Isles, U.K. 12 D2 57 54N 6 49W
Tarbes, France 18 E4 43 15N 0 3 E
Tarboro, U.S.A. 77 H7 35 54N 77 32W
Tarcoola, Australia 63 E1 30 44S 134 36 E
Tarcoon, Australia 63 E4 30 15S 146 43 E
Tarfaya, Morocco 50 C3 27 55N 12 55W
Târgovişte, Romania 17 F13 44 55N 25 27 E
Târgu-Jiu, Romania 17 F12 45 5N 23 19 E
Târgu Mureş, Romania 17 E13 46 31N 24 38 E
Ţarif, U.A.E. 45 E7 24 3N 53 46 E
Tarifa, Spain 19 D3 36 1N 5 36W
Tarija, Bolivia 94 A3 21 30S 64 40W
Tarija □, Bolivia 94 A3 21 30S 63 30W
Tariku →, Indonesia 37 E9 2 55S 138 26 E
Tarim Basin = Tarim Pendi, China 32 B3 40 0N 84 0 E
Tarim He →, China 32 C3 39 30N 88 30 E
Tarim Pendi, China 32 B3 40 0N 84 0 E
Taritatu →, Indonesia 37 E9 2 54S 138 27 E
Tarka →, S. Africa 56 E4 32 10S 26 0 E
Tarkastad, S. Africa 56 E4 32 0S 26 16 E
Tarkhankut, Mys, Ukraine 25 E5 45 25N 32 30 E
Tarko Sale, Russia 26 C8 64 55N 77 50 E
Tarkwa, Ghana 50 G5 5 20N 2 0W
Tarlac, Phil. 37 A6 15 29N 120 35 E
Tarma, Peru 92 F3 11 25S 75 45W
Tarn →, France 18 E4 44 5N 1 6 E
Târnăveni, Romania 17 E13 46 19N 24 13 E
Tarnobrzeg, Poland 17 C11 50 35N 21 41 E
Tarnów, Poland 17 C11 50 3N 21 0 E
Tarnowskie Góry, Poland 17 C10 50 27N 18 54 E
Ţārom, Iran 45 D7 28 11N 55 46 E
Taroom, Australia 63 D4 25 36S 149 48 E
Taroudannt, Morocco 50 B4 30 30N 8 52W
Tarpon Springs, U.S.A. 77 L4 28 9N 82 45W
Tarragona, Spain 19 B6 41 5N 1 17 E
Tarraleah, Australia 62 G4 42 17S 146 26 E
Tarrasa = Terrassa, Spain 19 B7 41 34N 2 1 E
Tarrytown, U.S.A. 79 E11 41 4N 73 52W
Tarshiha = Me'ona, Israel 47 B4 33 1N 35 15 E
Tarso Emissi, Chad 51 D9 21 27N 18 36 E
Tarsus, Turkey 25 G5 36 58N 34 55 E
Tartagal, Argentina 94 A3 22 30S 63 50W
Tartu, Estonia 9 G22 58 20N 26 44 E
Ţarţūs, Syria 44 C2 34 55N 35 55 E
Tarumizu, Japan 31 J5 31 29N 130 42 E
Tarutao, Ko, Thailand 39 J2 6 33N 99 40 E
Tarutung, Indonesia 36 D1 2 0N 98 54 E
Taseko →, Canada 72 C4 52 8N 123 45W
Tash-Kömür, Kyrgyzstan 26 E8 41 40N 72 10 E
Tash-Kumyr = Tash-Kömür, Kyrgyzstan 26 E8 41 40N 72 10 E
Tashauz = Dashhowuz, Turkmenistan 26 E6 41 49N 59 58 E
Tashi Chho Dzong = Thimphu, Bhutan 41 F16 27 31N 89 45 E
Ţashk, Daryācheh-ye, Iran 45 D7 29 45N 53 35 E
Tashkent = Toshkent, Uzbekistan 26 E7 41 20N 69 10 E
Tashtagol, Russia 26 D9 52 47N 87 53 E
Tasiilaq, Greenland 4 C6 65 40N 37 20W
Tasikmalaya, Indonesia 37 G13 7 18S 108 12 E
Tåsjön, Sweden 8 D16 64 15N 15 40 E
Taskan, Russia 27 C16 62 59N 150 20 E
Tasman B., N.Z. 59 J4 40 59S 173 25 E
Tasman Mts., N.Z. 59 J4 41 3S 172 25 E
Tasman Pen., Australia 62 G4 43 10S 148 0 E
Tasman Sea, Pac. Oc. 64 L8 36 0S 160 0 E
Tasmania □, Australia 62 G4 42 0S 146 30 E
Tassili n'Ajjer, Algeria 50 C7 25 47N 8 1 E
Tatabánya, Hungary 17 E10 47 32N 18 25 E
Tatahouine, Tunisia 51 B8 32 56N 10 27 E
Tatar Republic = Tatarstan □, Russia 24 C9 55 30N 51 30 E
Tatarbunary, Ukraine 17 F15 45 50N 29 39 E
Tatarsk, Russia 26 D8 55 14N 76 0 E
Tatarstan □, Russia 24 C9 55 30N 51 30 E
Tateyama, Japan 31 G9 35 0N 139 50 E
Tathlina L., Canada 72 A5 60 33N 117 39W
Tatinnai L., Canada 73 A9 60 55N 97 40W
Tatla L., Canada 72 C4 52 0N 124 20W
Tatnam, C., Canada 73 B10 57 16N 91 0W
Tatra = Tatry, Slovak Rep. 17 D11 49 20N 20 0 E
Tatry, Slovak Rep. 17 D11 49 20N 20 0 E
Tatshenshini →, Canada 72 B1 59 28N 137 45W
Tatsuno, Japan 31 G7 34 52N 134 33 E
Tatta, Pakistan 42 G2 24 42N 67 55 E
Tatuí, Brazil 95 A6 23 25S 47 53W
Tatum, U.S.A. 81 J3 33 16N 103 19W
Tat'ung = Datong, China 34 D7 40 6N 113 18 E
Tatvan, Turkey 25 G7 38 31N 42 15 E
Taubaté, Brazil 95 A6 23 0S 45 36W
Tauern, Austria 16 E7 47 15N 12 40 E
Taumarunui, N.Z. 59 H5 38 53S 175 15 E
Taumaturgo, Brazil 92 E4 8 54S 72 51W
Taung, S. Africa 56 D3 27 33S 24 47 E
Taungdwingyi, Burma 41 J19 20 1N 95 40 E
Taunggyi, Burma 41 J20 20 50N 97 0 E
Taungup, Burma 41 K19 18 51N 94 14 E
Taungup Taunggya, Burma 41 K18 18 20N 93 40 E
Taunsa, Pakistan 42 D4 30 42N 70 39 E
Taunsa Barrage, Pakistan 42 D4 30 42N 70 50 E
Taunton, U.K. 11 F4 51 1N 3 5W
Taunton, U.S.A. 79 E13 41 54N 71 6W
Taunus, Germany 16 C5 50 13N 8 34 E
Taupo, N.Z. 59 H6 38 41S 176 7 E
Taupo, L., N.Z. 59 H5 38 46S 175 55 E
Tauragė, Lithuania 9 J20 55 14N 22 16 E
Tauranga, N.Z. 59 G6 37 42S 176 11 E
Tauranga Harb., N.Z. 59 G6 37 30S 176 5 E
Taureau, Rés., Canada 70 C5 46 46N 73 50W
Taurianova, Italy 20 E7 38 21N 16 1 E
Taurus Mts. = Toros Dağları, Turkey 25 G5 37 0N 32 30 E
Tavda, Russia 26 D7 58 7N 65 8 E
Tavda →, Russia 26 D7 57 47N 67 18 E
Taveta, Tanzania 54 C4 3 23S 37 37 E
Taveuni, Fiji 59 C9 16 51S 179 58W
Tavira, Portugal 19 D2 37 8N 7 40W
Tavistock, Canada 78 C4 43 19N 80 50W
Tavistock, U.K. 11 G3 50 33N 4 9W
Tavoy = Dawei, Burma 38 E2 14 2N 98 12 E
Taw →, U.K. 11 F3 51 4N 4 4W
Tawa →, India 42 H8 22 48N 77 48 E
Tawas City, U.S.A. 76 C4 44 16N 83 31W
Tawau, Malaysia 36 D5 4 20N 117 55 E
Tawitawi, Phil. 37 B6 5 10N 120 0 E
Taxco de Alarcón, Mexico 87 D5 18 33N 99 36W
Taxila, Pakistan 42 C5 33 42N 72 52 E
Tay →, U.K. 12 E5 56 37N 3 38W
Tay, Firth of, U.K. 12 E5 56 25N 3 8W
Tay, L., Australia 61 F3 32 55S 120 48 E
Tay, L., U.K. 12 E4 56 32N 4 8W
Tay Ninh, Vietnam 39 G6 11 20N 106 5 E
Tayabamba, Peru 92 E3 8 15S 77 16W
Taylakova, Russia 26 D8 59 13N 74 0 E
Taylakovy = Taylakova, Russia 26 D8 59 13N 74 0 E
Taylor, Canada 72 B4 56 13N 120 40W
Taylor, Nebr., U.S.A. 80 E5 41 46N 99 23W
Taylor, Pa., U.S.A. 79 E9 41 23N 75 43W
Taylor, Tex., U.S.A. 81 K6 30 34N 97 25W
Taylor, Mt., U.S.A. 83 J10 35 14N 107 37W
Taylorville, U.S.A. 80 F10 39 33N 89 18W
Taymā, Si. Arabia 44 E3 27 35N 38 45 E
Taymyr, Oz., Russia 27 B11 74 20N 102 0 E
Taymyr, Poluostrov, Russia 27 B11 75 0N 100 0 E
Tayport, U.K. 12 E6 56 27N 2 52W
Tayshet, Russia 27 D10 55 58N 98 1 E
Taytay, Phil. 37 B5 10 45N 119 30 E
Taz →, Russia 26 C8 67 32N 78 40 E
Taza, Morocco 50 B5 34 16N 4 6W
Tāzah Khurmātū, Iraq 44 C5 35 18N 44 20 E
Tazawa-Ko, Japan 30 E10 39 43N 140 40 E
Tazin, Canada 73 B7 59 48N 109 55W
Tazin L., Canada 73 B7 59 44N 108 42W
Tazovskiy, Russia 26 C8 67 30N 78 44 E
Tbilisi, Georgia 25 F7 41 43N 44 50 E
Tchad = Chad ■, Africa 51 F8 15 0N 17 15 E
Tchad, L., Chad 51 F8 13 30N 14 30 E
Tch'eng-tou = Chengdu, China 32 C5 30 38N 104 2 E
Tchentlo L., Canada 72 B4 55 15N 125 0W
Tchibanga, Gabon 52 E2 2 45S 11 0 E
Tch'ong-k'ing = Chongqing, China 32 D5 29 35N 106 25 E
Tczew, Poland 17 A10 54 8N 18 50 E
Te Anau, N.Z. 59 L1 45 25S 167 43 E
Te Anau, L., N.Z. 59 L1 45 15S 167 45 E
Te Aroha, N.Z. 59 G5 37 32S 175 44 E
Te Awamutu, N.Z. 59 H5 38 1S 175 20 E
Te Kuiti, N.Z. 59 H5 38 20S 175 11 E
Te Puke, N.Z. 59 G6 37 46S 176 22 E
Te Waewae B., N.Z. 59 M1 46 13S 167 33 E
Teague, U.S.A. 81 K6 31 38N 96 17W
Teapa, Mexico 87 D6 18 35N 92 56W
Tebakang, Malaysia 36 D4 1 6N 110 30 E
Tébessa, Algeria 50 A7 35 22N 8 8 E
Tebicuary →, Paraguay 94 B4 26 36S 58 16W
Tebingtinggi, Indonesia 36 D1 3 20N 99 9 E
Tebintingii, Indonesia 36 E2 1 0N 102 45 E
Tecate, Mexico 85 N10 32 34N 116 38W
Tecka, Argentina 96 E2 43 29S 70 48W
Tecomán, Mexico 86 D4 18 55N 103 53W
Tecopa, U.S.A. 85 K10 35 51N 116 13W
Tecoripa, Mexico 86 B3 28 37N 109 57W
Tecuala, Mexico 86 C3 22 23N 105 27W
Tecuci, Romania 17 F14 45 51N 27 27 E
Tecumseh, Canada 78 D2 42 19N 82 54W
Tecumseh, Mich., U.S.A. 76 D4 42 0N 83 57W
Tecumseh, Okla., U.S.A. 81 H6 35 15N 96 56W
Tedzhen = Tejen, Turkmenistan 26 F7 37 23N 60 31 E
Tees →, U.K. 10 C6 54 37N 1 10W
Tees B., U.K. 10 C6 54 40N 1 9W
Teeswater, Canada 78 C3 43 59N 81 17W
Tefé, Brazil 92 D6 3 25S 64 50W
Tegal, Indonesia 36 F3 6 52S 109 8 E
Tegid, L. = Bala, L., U.K. 10 E4 52 53N 3 37W
Tegucigalpa, Honduras 88 D2 14 5N 87 14W
Tehachapi, U.S.A. 85 K8 35 8N 118 27W
Tehachapi Mts., U.S.A. 85 L8 35 0N 118 30W
Tehoru, Indonesia 37 E7 3 23S 129 30 E
Tehrān, Iran 45 C6 35 44N 51 30 E
Tehri, India 43 D8 30 23N 78 29 E
Tehuacán, Mexico 87 D5 18 30N 97 30W
Tehuantepec, Mexico 87 D5 16 21N 95 13W
Tehuantepec, G. de, Mexico 87 D5 15 50N 95 12W
Tehuantepec, Istmo de, Mexico 87 D6 17 0N 94 30W
Teide, Canary Is. 22 F3 28 15N 16 38W
Teifi →, U.K. 11 E3 52 5N 4 41W
Teign →, U.K. 11 G4 50 32N 3 32W
Teignmouth, U.K. 11 G4 50 33N 3 31W
Tejam, India 43 E9 29 57N 80 11 E
Tejen, Turkmenistan 26 F7 37 23N 60 31 E
Tejen →, Turkmenistan 45 B9 37 24N 60 38 E
Tejo →, Europe 19 C1 38 40N 9 24W
Tejon Pass, U.S.A. 85 L8 34 49N 118 53W
Tekamah, U.S.A. 80 E6 41 47N 96 13W
Tekapo, L., N.Z. 59 K3 43 53S 170 33 E
Tekax, Mexico 87 C7 20 11N 89 18W
Tekeli, Kazakstan 26 E8 44 50N 79 0 E
Tekirdağ, Turkey 21 D12 40 58N 27 30 E
Tekkali, India 41 K14 18 37N 84 15 E
Tekoa, U.S.A. 82 C5 47 14N 117 4W
Tel Aviv-Yafo, Israel 47 C3 32 4N 34 48 E
Tel Lakhish, Israel 47 D3 31 34N 34 51 E
Tel Megiddo, Israel 47 C4 32 35N 35 11 E
Tela, Honduras 88 C2 15 40N 87 28W
Telanaipura = Jambi, Indonesia 36 E2 1 38S 103 30 E
Telavi, Georgia 25 F8 42 0N 45 30 E
Telde, Canary Is. 22 G4 27 59N 15 25W
Telegraph Creek, Canada 72 B2 58 0N 131 10W
Telekhany = Tsyelyakhany, Belarus 17 B13 52 30N 25 46 E
Telemark, Norway 9 G12 59 15N 7 40 E
Telén, Argentina 94 D2 36 15S 65 31W
Teleng, Iran 45 E9 25 47N 61 3 E
Teles Pires →, Brazil 92 E7 7 21S 58 3W
Telescope Pk., U.S.A. 85 J9 36 10N 117 5W
Telfer Mine, Australia 60 C3 21 40S 122 12 E
Telford, U.K. 11 E5 52 40N 2 27W
Telford and Wrekin □, U.K. 10 E5 52 45N 2 27W
Telkwa, Canada 72 C3 54 41N 127 5W
Tell City, U.S.A. 76 G2 37 57N 86 46W
Tellicherry, India 40 P9 11 45N 75 30 E
Telluride, U.S.A. 83 H10 37 56N 107 49W
Teloloapán, Mexico 87 D5 18 21N 99 51W
Telpos Iz, Russia 24 B10 63 16N 59 13 E
Telsen, Argentina 96 E3 42 30S 66 50W
Telšiai, Lithuania 9 H20 55 59N 22 14 E
Teluk Anson = Teluk Intan, Malaysia 39 K3 4 3N 101 0 E
Teluk Betung = Tanjungkarang Telukbetung, Indonesia 36 F3 5 20S 105 10 E
Teluk Intan, Malaysia 39 K3 4 3N 101 0 E
Telukbutun, Indonesia 39 K7 4 13N 108 12 E
Telukdalem, Indonesia 36 D1 0 33N 97 50 E
Tema, Ghana 50 G5 5 41N 0 0W
Temax, Mexico 87 C7 21 10N 88 50W
Temba, S. Africa 57 D4 25 20S 28 17 E
Tembagapura, Indonesia 37 E9 4 20S 137 0 E
Tembe, Dem. Rep. of the Congo 54 C2 0 16S 28 14 E
Temblor Range, U.S.A. 85 K7 35 20N 119 50W
Teme →, U.K. 11 E5 52 11N 2 13W
Temecula, U.S.A. 85 M9 33 30N 117 9W
Temerloh, Malaysia 36 D2 3 27N 102 25 E
Teminabuan, Indonesia 37 E8 1 26S 132 1 E
Temir, Kazakstan 25 E10 49 1N 57 14 E
Temirtau, Kazakstan 26 D8 50 5N 72 56 E
Temirtau, Russia 26 D9 53 10N 87 30 E
Temiscamie →, Canada 71 B5 50 59N 73 5W
Témiscaming, Canada 70 C4 46 44N 79 5W
Témiscamingue, L., Canada 70 C4 47 10N 79 25W
Temosachic, Mexico 86 B3 28 58N 107 50W
Tempe, U.S.A. 83 K8 33 25N 111 56W
Tempiute, U.S.A. 84 H11 37 39N 115 38W
Temple, U.S.A. 81 K6 31 6N 97 21W
Temple B., Australia 62 A3 12 15S 143 3 E
Templemore, Ireland 13 D4 52 47N 7 51W
Templeton, U.S.A. 84 K6 35 33N 120 42W
Templeton →, Australia 62 C2 21 0S 138 40 E
Tempoal, Mexico 87 C5 21 31N 98 23W
Temuco, Chile 96 D2 38 45S 72 40W
Temuka, N.Z. 59 L3 44 14S 171 17 E
Tenabo, Mexico 87 C6 20 2N 90 12W
Tenaha, U.S.A. 81 K7 31 57N 94 15W
Tenakee Springs, U.S.A. 72 B1 57 47N 135 13W
Tenali, India 41 L12 16 15N 80 35 E
Tenancingo, Mexico 87 D5 19 0N 99 33W
Tenango, Mexico 87 D5 19 7N 99 33W
Tenasserim, Burma 39 F2 12 6N 99 3 E
Tenasserim □, Burma 38 F2 14 0N 98 30 E
Tenby, U.K. 11 F3 51 40N 4 42W
Tenda, Colle di, France 18 D7 44 7N 7 36 E
Tendaho, Ethiopia 46 E3 11 48N 40 54 E
Tendukhera, India 43 H8 23 24N 79 33 E
Tenerife, Canary Is. 22 F3 28 15N 16 35W
Tenerife, Pico, Canary Is. 22 G1 27 43N 18 1W
Teng Xian, China 35 G9 35 5N 117 10 E
Tengah □, Indonesia 37 E6 1 30S 121 0 E
Tengah, Kepulauan, Indonesia 36 F5 7 5S 118 15 E
Tengchong, China 32 D4 25 0N 98 28 E
Tengchowfu = Penglai, China 35 F11 37 48N 120 42 E
Tenggara □, Indonesia 37 E6 3 50S 122 0 E
Tenggarong, Indonesia 36 E5 0 24S 116 58 E
Tenggol, Pulau, Malaysia 39 K4 4 48N 103 41 E
Tengiz, Ozero, Kazakstan 26 D7 50 30N 69 0 E
Tenino, U.S.A. 84 D4 46 51N 122 51W
Tenkasi, India 40 Q10 8 55N 77 20 E
Tenke, Katanga, Dem. Rep. of the Congo 55 E2 11 22S 26 40 E
Tenke, Katanga, Dem. Rep. of the Congo 55 E2 10 32S 26 7 E
Tennant Creek, Australia 62 B1 19 30S 134 15 E
Tennessee □, U.S.A. 77 H2 36 0N 86 30W
Tennessee →, U.S.A. 76 G1 37 4N 88 34W
Teno, Pta. de, Canary Is. 22 F3 28 21N 16 55W
Tenom, Malaysia 36 C5 5 4N 115 57 E
Tenosique, Mexico 87 D6 17 30N 91 24W
Tenryū-Gawa →, Japan 31 G8 35 39N 137 48 E
Tenterden, U.K. 11 F8 51 4N 0 42 E
Tenterfield, Australia 63 D5 29 0S 152 0 E
Teófilo Otoni, Brazil 93 G10 17 50S 41 30W
Tepa, Indonesia 37 F7 7 52S 129 31 E
Tepalcatepec →, Mexico 86 D4 18 35N 101 59W
Tepehuanes, Mexico 86 B3 25 21N 105 44W
Tepetongo, Mexico 86 C4 22 28N 103 9W
Tepic, Mexico 86 C4 21 30N 104 54W
Teplice, Czech Rep. 16 C7 50 40N 13 48 E
Tepoca, C., Mexico 86 A2 30 20N 112 25W
Tequila, Mexico 86 C4 20 54N 103 47W
Ter →, Spain 19 A7 42 2N 3 12 E
Ter Apel, Neths. 15 B7 52 53N 7 5 E
Teraina, Kiribati 65 G11 4 43N 160 25W
Téramo, Italy 20 C5 42 39N 13 42 E
Tercero →, Argentina 94 C3 32 58S 61 47W
Terebovlya, Ukraine 17 D13 49 18N 25 44 E
Terek →, Russia 25 F8 44 0N 47 30 E
Teresina, Brazil 93 E10 5 9S 42 45W
Terewah, L., Australia 63 D4 29 52S 147 35 E
Termez = Termiz, Uzbekistan 26 F7 37 15N 67 15 E
Términi Imerese, Italy 20 F5 37 59N 13 42 E
Términos, L. de, Mexico 87 D6 18 35N 91 30W
Termiz, Uzbekistan 26 F7 37 15N 67 15 E
Térmoli, Italy 20 C6 42 0N 15 0 E
Ternate, Indonesia 37 D7 0 45N 127 25 E
Terneuzen, Neths. 15 C3 51 20N 3 50 E
Terney, Russia 27 E14 45 3N 136 37 E
Terni, Italy 20 C5 42 34N 12 37 E
Ternopil, Ukraine 17 D13 49 30N 25 40 E
Ternopol = Ternopil, Ukraine 17 D13 49 30N 25 40 E
Terra Bella, U.S.A. 85 K7 35 58N 119 3W
Terra Nova Nat. Park, Canada 71 C9 48 33N 53 55W
Terrace, Canada 72 C3 54 30N 128 35W
Terrace Bay, Canada 70 C2 48 47N 87 5W
Terracina, Italy 20 D5 41 17N 13 15 E
Terralba, Italy 20 E3 39 43N 8 39 E
Terranova = Ólbia, Italy 20 D3 40 55N 9 31 E
Terrassa, Spain 19 B7 41 34N 2 1 E
Terre Haute, U.S.A. 76 F2 39 28N 87 25W
Terrebonne B., U.S.A. 81 L9 29 5N 90 35W
Terrell, U.S.A. 81 J6 32 44N 96 17W
Terrenceville, Canada 71 C9 47 40N 54 44W
Terry, U.S.A. 80 B2 46 47N 105 19W
Terryville, U.S.A. 79 E11 41 41N 73 3W
Terschelling, Neths. 15 A5 53 25N 5 20 E
Teruel, Spain 19 B5 40 22N 1 8W
Tervola, Finland 8 C21 66 6N 24 49 E
Teshio, Japan 30 B10 44 53N 141 44 E
Teshio-Gawa →, Japan 30 B10 44 53N 141 45 E
Tesiyn Gol →, Mongolia 32 A4 50 40N 93 20 E
Teslin, Canada 72 A2 60 10N 132 43W
Teslin →, Canada 72 A2 61 34N 134 35W
Teslin L., Canada 72 A2 60 15N 132 57W
Tessalit, Mali 50 D6 20 12N 1 0 E
Test →, U.K. 11 G6 50 56N 1 29W
Testigos, Is. Las, Venezuela 89 D7 11 23N 63 7W
Tetachuck L., Canada 72 C3 53 18N 125 55W
Tetas, Pta., Chile 94 A1 23 31S 70 38W
Tete, Mozam. 55 F3 16 13S 33 33 E
Tete □, Mozam. 55 F3 15 15S 32 40 E
Teterev →, Ukraine 17 C16 51 1N 30 5 E
Teteven, Bulgaria 21 C11 42 58N 24 17 E
Tethul →, Canada 72 A6 60 35N 112 12W
Tetiyev, Ukraine 17 D15 49 22N 29 38 E
Teton →, U.S.A. 82 C8 47 56N 110 31W
Tétouan, Morocco 50 A4 35 35N 5 21W
Tetovo, Macedonia 21 C9 42 1N 20 59 E
Teuco →, Argentina 94 B3 25 35S 60 11W

Tsuyama

Toledo, Brazil 95 A5 24 44S 53 45W
Toledo, Spain 19 C3 39 50N 4 2W
Toledo, Ohio, U.S.A. 76 E4 41 39N 83 33W
Toledo, Oreg., U.S.A. 82 D2 44 37N 123 56W
Toledo, Wash., U.S.A. 82 C2 46 26N 122 51W
Toledo, Montes de, Spain 19 C3 39 33N 4 20W
Toledo Bend Reservoir, U.S.A. 81 K8 31 11N 93 34W
Tolga, Australia 62 B4 17 15S 145 29 E
Toliara, Madag. 57 C7 23 21S 43 40 E
Toliara □, Madag. 57 C8 21 0S 45 0 E
Tolima, Colombia 92 C3 4 40N 75 19W
Tolitoli, Indonesia 37 D6 1 5N 120 50 E
Tollhouse, U.S.A. 84 H7 37 1N 119 24W
Tolo, Teluk, Indonesia 37 E6 2 20S 122 10 E
Toluca, Mexico 87 D5 19 20N 99 40W
Tom Burke, S. Africa 57 C4 23 5S 28 0 E
Tom Price, Australia 60 D2 22 40S 117 48 E
Tomah, U.S.A. 80 D9 43 59N 90 30W
Tomahawk, U.S.A. 80 C10 45 28N 89 44W
Tomakomai, Japan 30 C10 42 38N 141 36 E
Tomales, U.S.A. 84 G4 38 15N 122 53W
Tomales B., U.S.A. 84 G3 38 15N 123 58W
Tomar, Portugal 19 C1 39 36N 8 25W
Tomaszów Mazowiecki, Poland 17 C10 51 30N 20 2 E
Tomatlán, Mexico 86 D3 19 56N 105 15W
Tombador, Serra do, Brazil 92 F7 12 0S 58 0W
Tombigbee →, U.S.A. 77 K2 31 8N 87 57W
Tombouctou, Mali 50 E5 16 50N 3 0W
Tombstone, U.S.A. 83 L8 31 43N 110 4W
Tombua, Angola 56 B1 15 55S 11 55 E
Tomé, Chile 94 D1 36 36S 72 57W
Tomelloso, Spain 19 C4 39 10N 3 2W
Tomini, Indonesia 37 D6 0 30N 120 30 E
Tomini, Teluk, Indonesia 37 E6 0 10S 121 0 E
Tomintoul, U.K. 12 D5 57 15N 3 23W
Tomkinson Ranges, Australia 61 E4 26 11S 129 5 E
Tommot, Russia 27 D13 59 4N 126 20 E
Tomnop Ta Suos, Cambodia 39 G5 11 20N 104 15 E
Tomo →, Colombia 92 B5 5 20N 67 48W
Toms Place, U.S.A. 84 H8 37 34N 118 41W
Toms River, U.S.A. 79 G10 39 58N 74 12W
Tomsk, Russia 26 D9 56 30N 85 5 E
Tonalá, Mexico 87 D6 16 8N 93 41W
Tonantins, Brazil 92 D5 2 45S 67 45W
Tonasket, U.S.A. 82 B4 48 42N 119 26W
Tonawanda, U.S.A. 78 D6 43 1N 78 53W
Tonbridge, U.K. 11 F8 51 11N 0 17 E
Tondano, Indonesia 37 D6 1 35N 124 54 E
Tondoro, Namibia 56 B2 17 45S 18 50 E
Tone →, Australia 61 F2 34 25S 116 25 E
Tone-Gawa →, Japan 31 F9 35 44N 140 51 E
Tonekābon, Iran 45 B6 36 45N 51 12 E
Tong Xian, China 34 E9 39 55N 116 35 E
Tonga ■, Pac. Oc. 59 D11 19 50S 174 30W
Tonga Trench, Pac. Oc. 64 J10 18 0S 173 0W
Tongaat, S. Africa 57 D5 29 33S 31 9 E
Tongareva, Cook Is. 65 H12 9 0S 158 0W
Tongatapu Group, Tonga 59 E12 21 0S 175 0W
Tongchŏn-ni, N. Korea 35 E14 39 50N 127 25 E
Tongchuan, China 34 G5 35 6N 109 3 E
Tongeren, Belgium 15 D5 50 47N 5 28 E
Tongguan, China 34 G6 34 40N 110 25 E
Tonghua, China 35 D13 41 42N 125 58 E
Tongjosŏn Man, N. Korea 35 E15 39 30N 128 0 E
Tongking, G. of = Tonkin, G. of, Asia 32 E5 20 0N 108 0 E
Tongliao, China 35 C12 43 38N 122 18 E
Tongling, China 33 C6 30 55N 117 48 E
Tongnae, S. Korea 35 G15 35 12N 129 5 E
Tongobory, Madag. 57 C7 23 32S 44 20 E
Tongoy, Chile 94 C1 30 16S 71 31W
Tongres = Tongeren, Belgium 15 D5 50 47N 5 28 E
Tongsa Dzong, Bhutan 41 F17 27 31N 90 31 E
Tongue, U.K. 12 C4 58 29N 4 25W
Tongue →, U.S.A. 80 B2 46 25N 105 52W
Tongwei, China 34 G3 35 0N 105 5 E
Tongxin, China 34 F3 36 59N 105 58 E
Tongyang, N. Korea 35 E14 39 9N 126 53 E
Tongyu, China 35 B12 44 45N 123 4 E
Tonj, Sudan 51 G11 7 20N 28 44 E
Tonk, India 42 F6 26 6N 75 54 E
Tonkawa, U.S.A. 81 G6 36 41N 97 18W
Tonkin = Bac Phan, Vietnam 38 B5 22 0N 105 0 E
Tonkin, G. of, Asia 32 E5 20 0N 108 0 E
Tonle Sap, Cambodia 38 F4 13 0N 104 0 E
Tono, Japan 30 E10 39 19N 141 32 E
Tonopah, U.S.A. 83 G5 38 4N 117 14W
Tonosí, Panama 88 E3 7 20N 80 20W
Tons →, Haryana, India 42 D7 30 30N 77 39 E
Tons →, Ut. P., India 43 F10 26 1N 83 33 E
Tønsberg, Norway 9 G14 59 19N 10 25 E
Toobanna, Australia 62 B4 18 42S 146 9 E
Toodyay, Australia 61 F2 31 34S 116 28 E
Tooele, U.S.A. 82 F7 40 32N 112 18W
Toompine, Australia 63 D3 27 15S 144 19 E
Toora-Khem, Russia 27 D10 52 28N 96 17 E
Toowoomba, Australia 63 D5 27 32S 151 56 E
Top-ozero, Russia 24 A5 65 35N 32 0 E
Top Springs, Australia 60 C5 16 37S 131 51 E
Topaz, U.S.A. 84 G7 38 41N 119 30W
Topeka, U.S.A. 80 F7 39 3N 95 40W
Topley, Canada 72 C3 54 49N 126 18W
Topocalma, Pta., Chile 94 C1 34 10S 72 2W
Topock, U.S.A. 85 L12 34 46N 114 29W
Topol'čany, Slovak Rep. 17 D10 48 35N 18 12 E
Topolobampo, Mexico 86 B3 25 40N 109 4W
Toppenish, U.S.A. 82 C3 46 23N 120 19W
Toraka Vestale, Madag. 57 B7 16 20S 43 58 E
Torata, Peru 92 G4 17 23S 70 1W
Torbalı, Turkey 21 E12 38 10N 27 21 E
Torbat-e Heydārīyeh, Iran 45 C8 35 15N 59 12 E
Torbat-e Jām, Iran 45 C9 35 16N 60 35 E
Torbay, Canada 71 C9 47 40N 52 42W
Torbay □, U.K. 11 G4 50 26N 3 31W
Tordesillas, Spain 19 B3 41 30N 5 0W
Torfaen □, U.K. 11 F4 51 43N 3 3W
Torgau, Germany 16 C7 51 34N 13 0 E
Torhout, Belgium 15 C3 51 5N 3 7 E
Tori-Shima, Japan 31 J10 30 29N 140 19 E
Torin, Mexico 86 B2 27 33N 110 15W
Torino, Italy 18 D7 45 3N 7 40 E
Torit, Sudan 51 H12 4 27N 32 31 E
Torkamān, Iran 44 B5 37 35N 47 23 E
Tormes →, Spain 19 B2 41 18N 6 29W
Tornado Mt., Canada 72 D6 49 55N 114 40W
Torne älv →, Sweden 8 D21 65 50N 24 12 E
Torneå = Tornio, Finland 8 D21 65 50N 24 12 E
Torneträsk, Sweden 8 B18 68 24N 19 15 E
Tornio, Finland 8 D21 65 50N 24 12 E
Tornionjoki →, Finland 8 D21 65 50N 24 12 E
Tornquist, Argentina 94 D3 38 8S 62 15W
Toro, Spain 22 B11 39 59N 4 8 E
Toro, Cerro del, Chile 94 B2 29 10S 69 50W
Toro Pk., U.S.A. 85 M10 33 34N 116 24W
Toroníos Kólpos, Greece 21 D10 40 5N 23 30 E
Toronto, Canada 78 C5 43 39N 79 20W
Toronto, U.S.A. 78 F4 40 28N 80 36W
Toropets, Russia 24 C5 56 30N 31 40 E
Tororo, Uganda 54 B3 0 45N 34 12 E
Toros Dağları, Turkey 25 G5 37 0N 32 30 E
Torpa, India 43 H11 22 57N 85 6 E
Torquay, U.K. 11 G4 50 27N 3 32W
Torrance, U.S.A. 85 M8 33 50N 118 19W
Torre de Moncorvo, Portugal 19 B2 41 12N 7 8W
Torre del Greco, Italy 20 D6 40 47N 14 22 E
Torrejón de Ardoz, Spain 19 B4 40 27N 3 29W
Torrelavega, Spain 19 A3 43 20N 4 5W
Torremolinos, Spain 19 D3 36 38N 4 30W
Torrens Cr. →, Australia 62 C4 22 23S 145 9 E
Torrens Creek, Australia 62 C4 20 48S 145 3 E
Torrent, Spain 19 C5 39 27N 0 28W
Torreón, Mexico 86 B4 25 33N 103 26W
Torres, Brazil 95 B5 29 21S 49 44W
Torres, Mexico 86 B2 28 46N 110 47W
Torres Strait, Australia 64 H6 9 50S 142 20 E
Torres Vedras, Portugal 19 C1 39 5N 9 15W
Torrevieja, Spain 19 D5 37 59N 0 42W
Torrey, U.S.A. 83 G8 38 18N 111 25W
Torridge →, U.K. 11 G3 51 0N 4 13W
Torridon, L., U.K. 12 D3 57 35N 5 50W
Torrington, Conn., U.S.A. 79 E11 41 48N 73 7W
Torrington, Wyo., U.S.A. 80 D2 42 4N 104 11W
Tórshavn, Færoe Is. 8 E9 62 5N 6 56W
Tortola, Br. Virgin Is. 89 C7 18 19N 64 45W
Tortosa, Spain 19 B6 40 49N 0 31 E
Tortosa, C., Spain 19 B6 40 41N 0 52 E
Tortue, I. de la, Haiti 89 B5 20 5N 72 57W
Torūd, Iran 45 C7 35 25N 55 5 E
Toruń, Poland 17 B10 53 2N 18 39 E
Tory I., Ireland 13 A3 55 16N 8 14W
Tosa, Japan 31 H6 33 24N 133 23 E
Tosa-Shimizu, Japan 31 H6 32 52N 132 58 E
Tosa-Wan, Japan 31 H6 33 15N 133 30 E
Toscana □, Italy 20 C4 43 25N 11 0 E
Toshkent, Uzbekistan 26 E7 41 20N 69 10 E
Tostado, Argentina 94 B3 29 15S 61 50W
Tostón, Pta. de, Canary Is. 22 F5 28 42N 14 2W
Tosu, Japan 31 H5 33 22N 130 31 E
Toteng, Botswana 56 C3 20 22S 22 58 E
Totma, Russia 24 C7 60 0N 42 40 E
Totnes, U.K. 11 G4 50 26N 3 42W
Totness, Surinam 93 B7 5 53N 56 19W
Totonicapán, Guatemala 88 D1 14 58N 91 12W
Totten Glacier, Antarctica 5 C8 66 45S 116 10 E
Tottenham, Canada 78 B5 44 1N 79 49W
Tottori, Japan 31 G7 35 30N 134 15 E
Tottori □, Japan 31 G7 35 30N 134 12 E
Toubkal, Djebel, Morocco 50 B4 31 0N 8 0W
Tougan, Burkina Faso 50 F5 13 11N 2 58W
Touggourt, Algeria 50 B7 33 6N 6 4 E
Toul, France 18 B6 48 40N 5 53 E
Toulon, France 18 E6 43 10N 5 55 E
Toulouse, France 18 E4 43 37N 1 27 E
Toummo, Niger 51 D8 22 45N 14 8 E
Toungoo, Burma 41 K20 19 0N 96 30 E
Touraine, France 18 C4 47 20N 0 30 E
Tourane = Da Nang, Vietnam 38 D7 16 4N 108 13 E
Tourcoing, France 18 A5 50 42N 3 10 E
Touriñán, C., Spain 19 A1 43 3N 9 18W
Tournai, Belgium 15 D3 50 35N 3 25 E
Tournon-sur-Rhône, France 18 D6 45 4N 4 50 E
Tours, France 18 C4 47 22N 0 40 E
Toussora, Mt., C.A.R. 52 C4 9 7N 23 14 E
Touws →, S. Africa 56 E3 33 45S 21 11 E
Touwsrivier, S. Africa 56 E3 33 20S 20 2 E
Towada, Japan 30 D10 40 37N 141 13 E
Towada-Ko, Japan 30 D10 40 28N 140 55 E
Towanda, U.S.A. 79 E8 41 46N 76 27W
Towang, India 41 F17 27 37N 91 50 E
Tower, U.S.A. 80 B8 47 48N 92 17W
Towerhill Cr. →, Australia 62 C3 22 28S 144 35 E
Towner, U.S.A. 80 A4 48 21N 100 25W
Townsend, U.S.A. 82 C8 46 19N 111 31W
Townshend I., Australia 62 C5 22 10S 150 31 E
Townsville, Australia 62 B4 19 15S 146 45 E
Towson, U.S.A. 76 F7 39 24N 76 36W
Towuti, Danau, Indonesia 37 E6 2 45S 121 32 E
Toya-Ko, Japan 30 C10 42 35N 140 51 E
Toyama, Japan 31 F8 36 40N 137 15 E
Toyama □, Japan 31 F8 36 45N 137 30 E
Toyama-Wan, Japan 31 F8 37 0N 137 30 E
Toyohashi, Japan 31 G8 34 45N 137 25 E
Toyokawa, Japan 31 G8 34 48N 137 27 E
Toyonaka, Japan 31 G7 34 50N 135 28 E
Toyooka, Japan 31 G7 35 35N 134 48 E
Toyota, Japan 31 G8 35 3N 137 7 E
Tozeur, Tunisia 50 B7 33 56N 8 8 E
Trá Li = Tralee, Ireland 13 D2 52 16N 9 42W
Tra On, Vietnam 39 H5 9 58N 105 55 E
Trabzon, Turkey 25 F6 41 0N 39 45 E
Tracadie, Canada 71 C7 47 30N 64 55W
Tracy, Calif., U.S.A. 84 H5 37 44N 121 26W
Tracy, Minn., U.S.A. 80 C7 44 14N 95 37W
Trafalgar, C., Spain 19 D2 36 10N 6 2W
Trail, Canada 72 D5 49 5N 117 40W
Trainor L., Canada 72 A4 60 24N 120 17W
Trákhonas, Cyprus 23 D12 35 12N 33 21 E
Tralee, Ireland 13 D2 52 16N 9 42W
Tralee B., Ireland 13 D2 52 17N 9 55W
Tramore, Ireland 13 D4 52 10N 7 10W
Tramore B., Ireland 13 D4 52 9N 7 10W
Tran Ninh, Cao Nguyen, Laos 38 C4 19 30N 103 10 E
Tranås, Sweden 9 G16 58 3N 14 59 E
Trancas, Argentina 94 B2 26 11S 65 20W
Trang, Thailand 39 J2 7 33N 99 38 E
Trangahy, Madag. 57 B7 19 7S 44 31 E
Trangan, Indonesia 37 F8 6 40S 134 20 E
Trani, Italy 20 D7 41 17N 16 25 E
Tranoroa, Madag. 57 C8 24 42S 45 4 E
Tranqueras, Uruguay 95 C4 31 13S 55 45W
Transantarctic Mts., Antarctica 5 E12 85 0S 170 0W
Transilvania, Romania 17 E12 46 30N 24 0 E
Transilvanian Alps = Carpaţii Meridionali, Romania 17 F13 45 30N 25 0 E
Transvaal, S. Africa 53 K5 25 0S 29 0 E
Transylvania = Transilvania, Romania 17 E12 46 30N 24 0 E
Trápani, Italy 20 E5 38 1N 12 29 E
Trapper Pk., U.S.A. 82 D6 45 54N 114 18W
Trasimeno, L., Italy 20 C5 43 8N 12 6 E
Trat, Thailand 39 F4 12 14N 102 33 E
Tratani →, Pakistan 42 E3 29 19N 68 20 E
Traun, Austria 16 D8 48 14N 14 15 E
Travemünde, Germany 16 B6 53 57N 10 52 E
Travers, Mt., N.Z. 59 K4 42 1S 172 45 E
Traverse City, U.S.A. 76 C3 44 46N 85 38W
Travis, L., U.S.A. 81 K5 30 24N 97 55W
Travnik, Bos.-H. 21 B7 44 17N 17 39 E
Trébbia →, Italy 18 D8 45 4N 9 41 E
Třebíč, Czech Rep. 16 D8 49 14N 15 55 E
Trebinje, Bos.-H. 21 C8 42 44N 18 22 E
Trebonne, Australia 62 B4 18 37S 146 5 E
Tregaron, U.K. 11 E4 52 14N 3 56W
Tregrosse Is., Australia 62 B5 17 41S 150 43 E
Treherne, Canada 73 D9 49 38N 98 42W
Treinta y Tres, Uruguay 95 C5 33 16S 54 17W
Trelawney, Zimbabwe 57 B5 17 30S 30 30 E
Trelew, Argentina 96 E3 43 10S 65 20W
Trelleborg, Sweden 9 J15 55 20N 13 10 E
Tremadog Bay, U.K. 10 E3 52 51N 4 18W
Tremonton, U.S.A. 82 F7 41 43N 112 10W
Tremp, Spain 19 A6 42 10N 0 52 E
Trenche →, Canada 70 C5 47 46N 72 53W
Trenčín, Slovak Rep. 17 D10 48 52N 18 4 E
Trenggalek, Indonesia 37 H14 8 3S 111 43 E
Trenque Lauquen, Argentina 94 D3 36 5S 62 45W
Trent →, Canada 78 B7 44 6N 77 34W
Trent →, U.K. 10 D7 53 41N 0 42W
Trento, Italy 20 A4 46 4N 11 8 E
Trenton, Canada 78 B7 44 10N 77 34W
Trenton, Mo., U.S.A. 80 E8 40 5N 93 37W
Trenton, N.J., U.S.A. 79 F10 40 14N 74 46W
Trenton, Nebr., U.S.A. 80 E4 40 11N 101 1W
Trepassey, Canada 71 C9 46 43N 53 25W
Tres Arroyos, Argentina 94 D3 38 26S 60 20W
Três Corações, Brazil 95 A6 21 44S 45 15W
Três Lagoas, Brazil 93 H8 20 50S 51 43W
Tres Lomas, Argentina 94 D3 36 27S 62 51W
Tres Marías, Islas, Mexico 86 C3 21 25N 106 28W
Tres Montes, C., Chile 96 F1 46 50S 75 30W
Tres Pinos, U.S.A. 84 J5 36 48N 121 19W
Três Pontas, Brazil 95 A6 21 23S 45 29W
Tres Puentes, Chile 94 B1 27 50S 70 15W
Tres Puntas, C., Argentina 96 F3 47 0S 66 0W
Três Rios, Brazil 95 A7 22 6S 43 15W
Tres Valles, Mexico 87 D5 18 15N 96 8W
Tresco, U.K. 11 H1 49 57N 6 20W
Treviso, Italy 20 B5 45 40N 12 15 E
Triabunna, Australia 62 G4 42 30S 147 55 E
Triánda, Greece 23 C10 36 25N 28 10 E
Triangle, Zimbabwe 57 C5 21 2S 31 28 E
Tribal Areas □, Pakistan 42 C4 33 0N 70 0 E
Tribulation, C., Australia 62 B4 16 5S 145 29 E
Tribune, U.S.A. 80 F4 38 28N 101 45W
Trichinopoly = Tiruchchirappalli, India 40 P11 10 45N 78 45 E
Trichur, India 40 P10 10 30N 76 18 E
Trier, Germany 16 D4 49 45N 6 38 E
Trieste, Italy 20 B5 45 40N 13 46 E
Triglav, Slovenia 16 E7 46 21N 13 50 E
Tríkkala, Greece 21 E9 39 34N 21 47 E
Trikomo, Cyprus 23 D12 35 17N 33 52 E
Trikora, Puncak, Indonesia 37 E9 4 15S 138 45 E
Trim, Ireland 13 C5 53 33N 6 48W
Trincomalee, Sri Lanka 40 Q12 8 38N 81 15 E
Trindade, Brazil 93 G9 16 40S 49 30W
Trindade, I., Atl. Oc. 2 F8 20 20S 29 50W
Trinidad, Bolivia 92 F6 14 46S 64 50W
Trinidad, Cuba 88 B4 21 48N 80 0W
Trinidad, Trin. & Tob. 89 D7 10 30N 61 15W
Trinidad, Uruguay 94 C4 33 30S 56 50W
Trinidad, U.S.A. 81 G2 37 10N 104 31W
Trinidad →, Mexico 87 D5 17 49N 95 9W
Trinidad & Tobago ■, W. Indies 89 D7 10 30N 61 20W
Trinity, Canada 71 C9 48 59N 53 55W
Trinity, U.S.A. 81 K7 30 57N 95 22W
Trinity →, Calif., U.S.A. 82 F2 41 11N 123 42W
Trinity →, Tex., U.S.A. 81 L7 29 45N 94 43W
Trinity B., Canada 71 C9 48 20N 53 10W
Trinity Is., U.S.A. 68 C4 56 33N 154 25W
Trinity Range, U.S.A. 82 F4 40 15N 118 45W
Trinkitat, Sudan 51 E13 18 45N 37 51 E
Trinway, U.S.A. 78 F2 40 9N 82 1W
Tripoli = Tarābulus, Lebanon 47 A4 34 31N 35 50 E
Tripoli = Tarābulus, Libya 51 B8 32 49N 13 7 E
Trípolis, Greece 21 F10 37 31N 22 25 E
Tripolitania, N. Afr. 51 B8 31 0N 13 0 E
Tripura □, India 41 H18 24 0N 92 0 E
Tripylos, Cyprus 23 E11 34 59N 32 41 E
Tristan da Cunha, Atl. Oc. 49 K2 37 6S 12 20W
Trisul, India 43 D8 30 19N 79 47 E
Trivandrum, India 40 Q10 8 41N 77 0 E
Trnava, Slovak Rep. 17 D9 48 23N 17 35 E
Trochu, Canada 72 C6 51 50N 113 13W
Trodely I., Canada 70 B4 52 15N 79 26W
Troglav, Croatia 20 C7 43 56N 16 36 E
Troilus, L., Canada 70 B5 50 50N 74 35W
Trois-Pistoles, Canada 71 C6 48 5N 69 10W
Trois-Rivières, Canada 70 C5 46 25N 72 34W
Troitsk, Russia 26 D7 54 10N 61 35 E
Troitsko Pechorsk, Russia 24 B10 62 40N 56 10 E
Trölladyngja, Iceland 8 D5 64 54N 17 16W
Trollhättan, Sweden 9 G15 58 17N 12 20 E
Trollheimen, Norway 8 E13 62 46N 9 1 E
Trombetas →, Brazil 93 D7 1 55S 55 35W
Tromsø, Norway 8 B18 69 40N 18 56 E
Trona, U.S.A. 85 K9 35 46N 117 23W
Tronador, Mte., Argentina 96 E2 41 10S 71 50W
Trøndelag, Norway 8 D14 64 17N 11 50 E
Trondheim, Norway 8 E14 63 36N 10 25 E
Trondheimsfjorden, Norway 8 E14 63 35N 10 30 E
Troodos, Cyprus 23 E11 34 55N 32 52 E
Troon, U.K. 12 F4 55 33N 4 39W
Tropic, U.S.A. 83 H7 37 37N 112 5W
Trostan, U.K. 13 A5 55 3N 6 10W
Trout →, Canada 72 A5 61 19N 119 51W
Trout L., N.W.T., Canada 72 A4 60 40N 121 14W
Trout L., Ont., Canada 73 C10 51 20N 93 15W
Trout Lake, Canada 72 B6 56 30N 114 32W
Trout Lake, U.S.A. 84 E5 46 0N 121 32W
Trout River, Canada 71 C8 49 29N 58 8W
Trout Run, U.S.A. 78 E7 41 23N 77 3W
Trouville-sur-Mer, France 18 B4 49 21N 0 5 E
Trowbridge, U.K. 11 F5 51 18N 2 12W
Troy, Turkey 21 E12 39 57N 26 12 E
Troy, Ala., U.S.A. 77 K3 31 48N 85 58W
Troy, Kans., U.S.A. 80 F7 39 47N 95 5W
Troy, Mo., U.S.A. 80 F9 38 59N 90 59W
Troy, Mont., U.S.A. 82 B6 48 28N 115 53W
Troy, N.Y., U.S.A. 79 D11 42 44N 73 41W
Troy, Ohio, U.S.A. 76 E3 40 2N 84 12W
Troy, Pa., U.S.A. 79 E8 41 47N 76 47W
Troyes, France 18 B6 48 19N 4 3 E
Truchas Peak, U.S.A. 81 H2 35 58N 105 39W
Trucial States = United Arab Emirates ■, Asia 46 C5 23 50N 54 0 E
Truckee, U.S.A. 84 F6 39 20N 120 11W
Trudovoye, Russia 30 C6 43 17N 132 5 E
Trujillo, Honduras 88 C2 16 0N 86 0W
Trujillo, Peru 92 E3 8 6S 79 0W
Trujillo, Spain 19 C3 39 28N 5 55W
Trujillo, U.S.A. 81 H2 35 32N 104 42W
Trujillo, Venezuela 92 B4 9 22N 70 38W
Truk, Micronesia 64 G7 7 25N 151 46 E
Trumann, U.S.A. 81 H9 35 41N 90 31W
Trumansburg, U.S.A. 79 D8 42 33N 76 40W
Trumbull, Mt., U.S.A. 83 H7 36 25N 113 8W
Trung-Phan = Annam, Vietnam 38 E7 16 0N 108 0 E
Truro, Canada 71 C7 45 21N 63 14W
Truro, U.K. 11 G2 50 16N 5 4W
Truskavets, Ukraine 17 D12 49 17N 23 30 E
Trutch, Canada 72 B4 57 44N 122 57W
Truth or Consequences, U.S.A. 83 K10 33 8N 107 15W
Trutnov, Czech Rep. 16 C8 50 37N 15 54 E
Truxton, U.S.A. 79 D8 42 45N 76 2W
Tryonville, U.S.A. 78 E5 41 42N 79 48W
Tsandi, Namibia 56 B1 17 42S 14 50 E
Tsaratanana, Madag. 57 B8 16 47S 47 39 E
Tsaratanana, Mt. de, Madag. 57 A8 14 0S 49 0 E
Tsarevo = Michurin, Bulgaria 21 C12 42 9N 27 51 E
Tsau, Botswana 56 C3 20 8S 22 22 E
Tselinograd = Astana, Kazakstan 26 D8 51 10N 71 30 E
Tses, Namibia 56 D2 25 58S 18 8 E
Tsetserleg, Mongolia 32 B5 47 36N 101 32 E
Tshabong, Botswana 56 D3 26 2S 22 29 E
Tshane, Botswana 56 C3 24 5S 21 54 E
Tshela, Dem. Rep. of the Congo 52 E2 4 57S 13 4 E
Tshesebe, Botswana 57 C4 21 51S 27 32 E
Tshibeke, Dem. Rep. of the Congo 54 C2 2 40S 28 35 E
Tshibinda, Dem. Rep. of the Congo 54 C2 2 23S 28 43 E
Tshikapa, Dem. Rep. of the Congo 52 F4 6 28S 20 48 E
Tshilenge, Dem. Rep. of the Congo 54 D1 6 17S 23 48 E
Tshinsenda, Dem. Rep. of the Congo 55 E2 12 20S 28 0 E
Tshofa, Dem. Rep. of the Congo 54 D2 5 13S 25 16 E
Tshwane, Botswana 56 C3 22 24S 22 1 E
Tsigara, Botswana 56 C4 20 22S 25 54 E
Tsihombe, Madag. 57 D8 25 10S 45 41 E
Tsiigehtchic, Canada 68 B6 67 15N 134 0W
Tsimlyansk Res. = Tsimlyanskoye Vdkhr., Russia 25 E7 48 0N 43 0 E
Tsimlyanskoye Vdkhr., Russia 25 E7 48 0N 43 0 E
Tsinan = Jinan, China 34 F9 36 38N 117 1 E
Tsineng, S. Africa 56 D3 27 5S 23 5 E
Tsinghai = Qinghai □, China 32 C4 36 0N 98 0 E
Tsingtao = Qingdao, China 35 F11 36 5N 120 20 E
Tsinjoarivo, Madag. 57 B8 19 37S 47 40 E
Tsinjomitondraka, Madag. 57 B8 15 40S 47 8 E
Tsiroanomandidy, Madag. 57 B8 18 46S 46 2 E
Tsitondroina, Madag. 57 C8 21 19S 46 0 E
Tsivory, Madag. 57 C8 24 4S 46 5 E
Tskhinvali, Georgia 25 F7 42 14N 44 1 E
Tsna →, Russia 24 D7 54 55N 41 58 E
Tso Moriri, L., India 43 C8 32 50N 78 20 E
Tsobis, Namibia 56 B2 19 27S 17 30 E
Tsodilo Hill, Botswana 56 B3 18 49S 21 43 E
Tsogttsetsiy = Baruunsuu, Mongolia 34 C3 43 43N 105 35 E
Tsolo, S. Africa 57 E4 31 18S 28 37 E
Tsomo, S. Africa 57 E4 32 0S 27 42 E
Tsu, Japan 31 G8 34 45N 136 25 E
Tsu L., Canada 72 A6 60 40N 111 52W
Tsuchiura, Japan 31 F10 36 5N 140 15 E
Tsugaru-Kaikyō, Japan 30 D10 41 35N 141 0 E
Tsumeb, Namibia 56 B2 19 9S 17 44 E
Tsumis, Namibia 56 C2 23 39S 17 29 E
Tsuruga, Japan 31 G8 35 45N 136 2 E
Tsurugi-San, Japan 31 H7 33 51N 134 6 E
Tsuruoka, Japan 30 E9 38 44N 139 50 E
Tsushima, Gifu, Japan 31 G8 35 10N 136 43 E
Tsushima, Nagasaki, Japan 31 G4 34 20N 129 20 E
Tsuyama, Japan 31 G7 35 3N 134 0 E

Tsyelyakhany

Tsyelyakhany, *Belarus* **17 B13** 52 30N 25 46 E
Tual, *Indonesia* **37 F8** 5 38S 132 44 E
Tuam, *Ireland* **13 C3** 53 31N 8 51W
Tuamotu Arch. = Tuamotu Is., *Pac. Oc.* **65 J13** 17 0S 144 0W
Tuamotu Is., *Pac. Oc.* **65 J13** 17 0S 144 0W
Tuamotu Ridge, *Pac. Oc.* **65 K14** 20 0S 138 0W
Tuao, *Phil.* **37 A6** 17 55N 121 22 E
Tuapse, *Russia* **25 F6** 44 5N 39 10 E
Tuatapere, *N.Z.* **59 M1** 46 8S 167 41 E
Tuba City, *U.S.A.* **83 H8** 36 8N 111 14W
Tuban, *Indonesia* **37 G15** 6 54S 112 3 E
Tubani, *Botswana* **56 C3** 24 46S 24 18 E
Tubarão, *Brazil* **95 B6** 28 30S 49 0W
Tūbās, *West Bank* **47 C4** 32 20N 35 22 E
Tubas →, *Namibia* **56 C2** 22 54S 14 35 E
Tübingen, *Germany* **16 D5** 48 31N 9 4 E
Tubruq, *Libya* **51 B10** 32 7N 23 55 E
Tubuai Is., *Pac. Oc.* **65 K13** 25 0S 150 0W
Tuc Trung, *Vietnam* **39 G6** 11 1N 107 12 E
Tucacas, *Venezuela* **92 A5** 10 48N 68 19W
Tuchodi →, *Canada* **72 B4** 58 17N 123 42W
Tuckanarra, *Australia* **61 E2** 27 7S 118 5 E
Tucson, *U.S.A.* **83 K8** 32 13N 110 58W
Tucumán □, *Argentina* **94 B2** 26 48S 66 2W
Tucumcari, *U.S.A.* **81 H3** 35 10N 103 44W
Tucupita, *Venezuela* **92 B6** 9 2N 62 3W
Tucuruí, *Brazil* **93 D9** 3 42S 49 44W
Tucuruí, Represa de, *Brazil* **93 D9** 4 0S 49 30W
Tudela, *Spain* **19 A5** 42 4N 1 39W
Tudmur, *Syria* **44 C3** 34 36N 38 15 E
Tudor, L., *Canada* **71 A6** 55 50N 65 25W
Tugela →, *S. Africa* **57 D5** 29 14S 31 30 E
Tuguegarao, *Phil.* **37 A6** 17 35N 121 42 E
Tugur, *Russia* **27 D14** 53 44N 136 45 E
Tui, *Spain* **19 A1** 42 3N 8 39W
Tuineje, *Canary Is.* **22 F5** 28 19N 14 3W
Tukangbesi, Kepulauan, *Indonesia* **37 F6** 6 0S 124 0 E
Tukarak I., *Canada* **70 A4** 56 15N 78 45W
Tukayyid, *Iraq* **44 D5** 29 47N 45 36 E
Tuktoyaktuk, *Canada* **68 B6** 69 27N 133 2W
Tukums, *Latvia* **9 H20** 56 58N 23 10 E
Tukuyu, *Tanzania* **55 D3** 9 17S 33 35 E
Tula, *Hidalgo, Mexico* **87 C5** 20 5N 99 20W
Tula, *Tamaulipas, Mexico* **87 C5** 23 0N 99 40W
Tula, *Russia* **24 D6** 54 13N 37 38 E
Tulancingo, *Mexico* **87 C5** 20 5N 99 22W
Tulare, *U.S.A.* **84 J7** 36 13N 119 21W
Tulare Lake Bed, *U.S.A.* **84 K7** 36 0N 119 48W
Tularosa, *U.S.A.* **83 K10** 33 5N 106 1W
Tulbagh, *S. Africa* **56 E2** 33 16S 19 6 E
Tulcán, *Ecuador* **92 C3** 0 48N 77 43W
Tulcea, *Romania* **17 F15** 45 13N 28 46 E
Tulchyn, *Ukraine* **17 D15** 48 41N 28 49 E
Tuleh, *Iran* **45 C7** 34 35N 52 33 E
Tulemalu L., *Canada* **73 A9** 62 58N 99 25W
Tuli, *Zimbabwe* **55 G2** 21 58S 29 13 E
Tulia, *U.S.A.* **81 H4** 34 32N 101 46W
Tulita, *Canada* **68 B7** 64 57N 125 30W
Ţūlkarm, *West Bank* **47 C4** 32 19N 35 2 E
Tulla, *Ireland* **13 D3** 52 53N 8 46W
Tullahoma, *U.S.A.* **77 H2** 35 22N 86 13W
Tullamore, *Ireland* **13 C4** 53 16N 7 31W
Tulle, *France* **18 D4** 45 16N 1 46 E
Tullow, *Ireland* **13 D5** 52 49N 6 45W
Tully, *Australia* **62 B4** 17 56S 145 55 E
Tully, *U.S.A.* **79 D8** 42 48N 76 7W
Tulsa, *U.S.A.* **81 G7** 36 10N 95 55W
Tulsequah, *Canada* **72 B2** 58 39N 133 35W
Tulua, *Colombia* **92 C3** 4 6N 76 11W
Tulun, *Russia* **27 D11** 54 32N 100 35 E
Tulungagung, *Indonesia* **37 H14** 8 5S 111 54 E
Tuma →, *Nic.* **88 D3** 13 6N 84 35W
Tumaco, *Colombia* **92 C3** 1 50N 78 45W
Tumatumari, *Guyana* **92 B7** 5 20N 58 55W
Tumba, *Sweden* **9 G17** 59 12N 17 48 E
Tumba, L., *Dem. Rep. of the Congo* **52 E3** 0 50S 18 0 E
Tumbarumba, *Australia* **63 F4** 35 44S 148 0 E
Tumbaya, *Argentina* **94 A2** 23 50S 65 26W
Tumbes, *Peru* **92 D2** 3 37S 80 27W
Tumbwe, *Dem. Rep. of the Congo* **55 E2** 11 25S 27 15 E
Tumd Youqi, *China* **34 D6** 40 30N 110 30 E
Tumen, *China* **35 C15** 43 0N 129 50 E
Tumen Jiang →, *China* **35 C16** 42 20N 130 35 E
Tumeremo, *Venezuela* **92 B6** 7 18N 61 30W
Tumkur, *India* **40 N10** 13 18N 77 6 E
Tump, *Pakistan* **40 F3** 26 7N 62 16 E
Tumpat, *Malaysia* **39 J4** 6 11N 102 10 E
Tumu, *Ghana* **50 F5** 10 56N 1 56W
Tumucumaque, Serra, *Brazil* **93 C8** 2 0N 55 0W
Tumut, *Australia* **63 F4** 35 16S 148 13 E
Tumwater, *U.S.A.* **84 C4** 47 1N 122 54W
Tuna, *India* **42 H4** 22 59N 70 5 E
Tunas de Zaza, *Cuba* **88 B4** 21 39N 79 34W
Tunbridge Wells = Royal Tunbridge Wells, *U.K.* **11 F8** 51 7N 0 16 E
Tundla, *India* **42 F8** 27 12N 78 17 E
Tunduru, *Tanzania* **55 E4** 11 8S 37 25 E
Tundzha →, *Bulgaria* **21 C11** 41 40N 26 35 E
Tungabhadra →, *India* **40 M11** 15 57N 78 15 E
Tungla, *Nic.* **88 D3** 13 24N 84 21W
Tungsten, *Canada* **72 A3** 61 57N 128 16W
Tunguska, Nizhnyaya →, *Russia* **27 C9** 65 48N 88 4 E
Tunguska, Podkamennaya →, *Russia* **27 C10** 61 50N 90 13 E
Tunica, *U.S.A.* **81 H9** 34 41N 90 23W
Tunis, *Tunisia* **50 A7** 36 50N 10 11 E
Tunisia ■, *Africa* **50 B6** 33 30N 9 10 E
Tunja, *Colombia* **92 B4** 5 33N 73 25W
Tunkhannock, *U.S.A.* **79 E9** 41 32N 75 57W
Tunliu, *China* **34 F7** 36 13N 112 52 E
Tunnsjøen, *Norway* **8 D15** 64 45N 13 25 E
Tunungayualok I., *Canada* **71 A7** 56 0N 61 0W
Tununirusiq = Arctic Bay, *Canada* **69 A11** 73 1N 85 7W
Tunuyán, *Argentina* **94 C2** 33 35S 69 0W
Tunuyán →, *Argentina* **94 C2** 33 33S 67 30W
Tuolumne, *U.S.A.* **84 H6** 37 58N 120 15W
Tuolumne →, *U.S.A.* **84 H5** 37 36N 121 13W
Tūp Āghāj, *Iran* **44 B5** 36 3N 47 50 E
Tupã, *Brazil* **95 A5** 21 57S 50 28W
Tupelo, *U.S.A.* **77 H1** 34 16N 88 43W
Tupinambaranas, *Brazil* **92 D7** 3 0S 58 0W
Tupiza, *Bolivia* **94 A2** 21 30S 65 40W
Tupman, *U.S.A.* **85 K7** 35 18N 119 21W
Tupper, *Canada* **72 B4** 55 32N 120 1W
Tupper Lake, *U.S.A.* **79 B10** 44 14N 74 28W
Tupungato, Cerro, *S. Amer.* **94 C2** 33 15S 69 50W
Tuquan, *China* **35 B11** 45 18N 121 38 E
Túquerres, *Colombia* **92 C3** 1 5N 77 37W
Tura, *Russia* **27 C11** 64 20N 100 17 E
Turabah, *Si. Arabia* **46 C3** 28 20N 43 15 E
Tūrān, *Iran* **45 C8** 35 39N 56 42 E
Turan, *Russia* **27 D10** 51 55N 95 0 E
Ţurayf, *Si. Arabia* **44 D3** 31 41N 38 39 E
Turda, *Romania* **17 E12** 46 34N 23 47 E
Turek, *Poland* **17 B10** 52 3N 18 30 E
Turen, *Venezuela* **92 B5** 9 17N 69 6W
Turfan = Turpan, *China* **32 B3** 43 58N 89 10 E
Turfan Depression = Turpan Hami, *China* **28 E12** 42 40N 89 25 E
Turgeon →, *Canada* **70 C4** 50 0N 78 56W
Tŭrgovishte, *Bulgaria* **21 C12** 43 17N 26 38 E
Turgutlu, *Turkey* **21 E12** 38 30N 27 43 E
Turgwe →, *Zimbabwe* **57 C5** 21 31S 32 15 E
Turia →, *Spain* **19 C5** 39 27N 0 19W
Turiaçu, *Brazil* **93 D9** 1 40S 45 19W
Turiaçu →, *Brazil* **93 D9** 1 36S 45 19W
Turin = Torino, *Italy* **18 D7** 45 3N 7 40 E
Turkana, L., *Africa* **54 B4** 3 30N 36 5 E
Turkestan = Türkistan, *Kazakstan* **26 E7** 43 17N 68 16 E
Turkey ■, *Eurasia* **25 G6** 39 0N 36 0 E
Turkey Creek, *Australia* **60 C4** 17 2S 128 12 E
Türkistan, *Kazakstan* **26 E7** 43 17N 68 16 E
Türkmenbashi, *Turkmenistan* **25 G9** 40 5N 53 5 E
Turkmenistan ■, *Asia* **26 F6** 39 0N 59 0 E
Turks & Caicos Is. ■, *W. Indies* **89 B5** 21 20N 71 20W
Turks Island Passage, *W. Indies* **89 B5** 21 30N 71 30W
Turku, *Finland* **9 F20** 60 30N 22 19 E
Turkwel →, *Kenya* **54 B4** 3 6N 36 6 E
Turlock, *U.S.A.* **84 H6** 37 30N 120 51W
Turnagain →, *Canada* **72 B3** 59 12N 127 35W
Turnagain, C., *N.Z.* **59 J6** 40 28S 176 38 E
Turneffe Is., *Belize* **87 D7** 17 20N 87 50W
Turner, *U.S.A.* **82 B9** 48 51N 108 24W
Turner Pt., *Australia* **62 A1** 11 47S 133 32 E
Turner Valley, *Canada* **72 C6** 50 40N 114 17W
Turners Falls, *U.S.A.* **79 D12** 42 36N 72 33W
Turnhout, *Belgium* **15 C4** 51 19N 4 57 E
Turnor L., *Canada* **73 B7** 56 35N 108 35W
Tŭrnovo = Veliko Tŭrnovo, *Bulgaria* **21 C11** 43 5N 25 41 E
Turnu Măgurele, *Romania* **17 G13** 43 46N 24 56 E
Turnu Roşu, P., *Romania* **17 F13** 45 33N 24 17 E
Turpan, *China* **32 B3** 43 58N 89 10 E
Turpan Hami, *China* **28 E12** 42 40N 89 25 E
Turriff, *U.K.* **12 D6** 57 32N 2 27W
Tursāq, *Iraq* **44 C5** 33 27N 45 47 E
Turtle Head I., *Australia* **62 A3** 10 56S 142 37 E
Turtle L., *Canada* **73 C7** 53 36N 108 38W
Turtle Lake, *U.S.A.* **80 B4** 47 31N 100 53W
Turtleford, *Canada* **73 C7** 53 23N 108 57W
Turukhansk, *Russia* **27 C9** 65 21N 88 5 E
Tuscaloosa, *U.S.A.* **77 J2** 33 12N 87 34W
Tuscany = Toscana □, *Italy* **20 C4** 43 25N 11 0 E
Tuscarawas →, *U.S.A.* **78 F3** 40 24N 81 25W
Tuscarora Mt., *U.S.A.* **78 F7** 40 55N 77 55W
Tuscola, *Ill., U.S.A.* **76 F1** 39 48N 88 17W
Tuscola, *Tex., U.S.A.* **81 J5** 32 12N 99 48W
Tuscumbia, *U.S.A.* **77 H2** 34 44N 87 42W
Tuskegee, *U.S.A.* **77 J3** 32 25N 85 42W
Tustin, *U.S.A.* **85 M9** 33 44N 117 49W
Tuticorin, *India* **40 Q11** 8 50N 78 12 E
Tutóia, *Brazil* **93 D10** 2 45S 42 20W
Tutong, *Brunei* **36 D4** 4 47N 114 40 E
Tutrakan, *Bulgaria* **21 B12** 44 2N 26 40 E
Tuttle Creek L., *U.S.A.* **80 F6** 39 22N 96 40W
Tuttlingen, *Germany* **16 E5** 47 58N 8 48 E
Tutuala, *Indonesia* **37 F7** 8 25S 127 15 E
Tutuila, *Amer. Samoa* **59 B13** 14 19S 170 50W
Tutume, *Botswana* **53 J5** 20 30S 27 5 E
Tututepec, *Mexico* **87 D5** 16 9N 97 38W
Tuva □, *Russia* **27 D10** 51 30N 95 0 E
Tuvalu ■, *Pac. Oc.* **64 H9** 8 0S 178 0 E
Tuxpan, *Mexico* **87 C5** 20 58N 97 23W
Tuxtla Gutiérrez, *Mexico* **87 D6** 16 50N 93 10W
Tuy = Tui, *Spain* **19 A1** 42 3N 8 39W
Tuy An, *Vietnam* **38 F7** 13 17N 109 16 E
Tuy Duc, *Vietnam* **39 F6** 12 15N 107 27 E
Tuy Hoa, *Vietnam* **38 F7** 13 5N 109 10 E
Tuy Phong, *Vietnam* **39 G7** 11 14N 108 43 E
Tuya L., *Canada* **72 B2** 59 7N 130 35W
Tuyen Hoa, *Vietnam* **38 D6** 17 50N 106 10 E
Tuyen Quang, *Vietnam* **38 B5** 21 50N 105 10 E
Tūysarkān, *Iran* **45 C6** 34 33N 48 27 E
Tuz Gölü, *Turkey* **25 G5** 38 42N 33 18 E
Ţūz Khurmātū, *Iraq* **44 C5** 34 56N 44 38 E
Tuzla, *Bos.-H.* **21 B8** 44 34N 18 41 E
Tver, *Russia* **24 C6** 56 55N 35 55 E
Twain, *U.S.A.* **84 E5** 40 1N 121 3W
Twain Harte, *U.S.A.* **84 G6** 38 2N 120 14W
Tweed, *Canada* **78 B7** 44 29N 77 19W
Tweed →, *U.K.* **12 F6** 55 45N 2 0W
Tweed Heads, *Australia* **63 D5** 28 10S 153 31 E
Tweedsmuir Prov. Park, *Canada* **72 C3** 53 0N 126 20W
Twentynine Palms, *U.S.A.* **85 L10** 34 8N 116 3W
Twillingate, *Canada* **71 C9** 49 42N 54 45W
Twin Bridges, *U.S.A.* **82 D7** 45 33N 112 20W
Twin Falls, *Canada* **71 B7** 53 30N 64 32W
Twin Falls, *U.S.A.* **82 E6** 42 34N 114 28W
Twin Valley, *U.S.A.* **80 B6** 47 16N 96 16W
Twinsburg, *U.S.A.* **78 E3** 41 18N 81 26W
Twitchell Reservoir, *U.S.A.* **85 L6** 34 59N 120 19W
Two Harbors, *U.S.A.* **80 B9** 47 2N 91 40W
Two Hills, *Canada* **72 C6** 53 43N 111 52W
Two Rivers, *U.S.A.* **76 C2** 44 9N 87 34W
Two Rocks, *Australia* **61 F2** 31 30S 115 35 E
Tyachiv, *Ukraine* **17 D12** 48 1N 23 35 E
Tychy, *Poland* **17 C10** 50 9N 18 59 E
Tyler, *Minn., U.S.A.* **80 C6** 44 18N 96 8W
Tyler, *Tex., U.S.A.* **81 J7** 32 21N 95 18W
Tynda, *Russia* **27 D13** 55 10N 124 43 E
Tyndall, *U.S.A.* **80 D6** 43 0N 97 50W
Tyne →, *U.K.* **10 C6** 54 59N 1 32W
Tyne & Wear □, *U.K.* **10 B6** 55 6N 1 17W
Tynemouth, *U.K.* **10 B6** 55 1N 1 26W
Tyre = Sūr, *Lebanon* **47 B4** 33 19N 35 16 E
Tyrifjorden, *Norway* **9 F14** 60 2N 10 8 E
Tyrol = Tirol □, *Austria* **16 E6** 47 3N 10 43 E
Tyrone, *U.S.A.* **78 F6** 40 40N 78 14W
Tyrone □, *U.K.* **13 B4** 54 38N 7 11W
Tyrrell L., *Canada* **73 A7** 63 7N 105 27W
Tyrrhenian Sea, *Medit. S.* **20 E5** 40 0N 12 30 E
Tysfjorden, *Norway* **8 B17** 68 7N 16 25 E
Tyulgan, *Russia* **24 D10** 52 22N 56 12 E
Tyumen, *Russia* **26 D7** 57 11N 65 29 E
Tywi →, *U.K.* **11 F3** 51 48N 4 21W
Tywyn, *U.K.* **11 E3** 52 35N 4 5W
Tzaneen, *S. Africa* **57 C5** 23 47S 30 9 E
Tzermiádhes, *Greece* **23 D7** 35 12N 25 29 E
Tzukong = Zigong, *China* **32 D5** 29 15N 104 48 E

U

U Taphao, *Thailand* **38 F3** 12 35N 101 0 E
U.S.A. = United States of America ■, *N. Amer.* **74 C7** 37 0N 96 0W
Uatumã →, *Brazil* **92 D7** 2 26S 57 37W
Uaupés, *Brazil* **92 D5** 0 8S 67 5W
Uaupés →, *Brazil* **92 C5** 0 2N 67 16W
Uaxactún, *Guatemala* **88 C2** 17 25N 89 29W
Ubá, *Brazil* **95 A7** 21 8S 43 0W
Ubaitaba, *Brazil* **93 F11** 14 18S 39 20W
Ubangi = Oubangi →, *Dem. Rep. of the Congo* **52 E3** 0 30S 17 50 E
Ubauro, *Pakistan* **42 E3** 28 15N 69 45 E
Ubayyiḍ, W. al →, *Iraq* **44 C4** 32 34N 43 48 E
Ube, *Japan* **31 H5** 33 56N 131 15 E
Úbeda, *Spain* **19 C4** 38 3N 3 23W
Uberaba, *Brazil* **93 G9** 19 50S 47 55W
Uberlândia, *Brazil* **93 G9** 19 0S 48 20W
Ubolratna Res., *Thailand* **38 D4** 16 45N 102 30 E
Ubombo, *S. Africa* **57 D5** 27 31S 32 4 E
Ubon Ratchathani, *Thailand* **38 E5** 15 15N 104 50 E
Ubondo, *Dem. Rep. of the Congo* **54 C2** 0 55S 25 42 E
Ubort →, *Belarus* **17 B15** 52 6N 28 30 E
Ubundu, *Dem. Rep. of the Congo* **54 C2** 0 22S 25 30 E
Ucayali →, *Peru* **92 D4** 4 30S 73 30W
Uchab, *Namibia* **56 B2** 19 47S 17 42 E
Uchiura-Wan, *Japan* **30 C10** 42 25N 140 40 E
Uchquduq, *Uzbekistan* **26 E7** 41 50N 62 50 E
Uchur →, *Russia* **27 D14** 58 48N 130 35 E
Ucluelet, *Canada* **72 D3** 48 57N 125 32W
Uda →, *Russia* **27 D14** 54 42N 135 14 E
Udagamandalam, *India* **40 P10** 11 30N 76 44 E
Udainagar, *India* **42 H7** 22 33N 76 13 E
Udaipur, *India* **42 G5** 24 36N 73 44 E
Udaipur Garhi, *Nepal* **43 F12** 27 0N 86 35 E
Udala, *India* **43 J12** 21 35N 86 34 E
Uddevalla, *Sweden* **9 G14** 58 21N 11 55 E
Uddjaur, *Sweden* **8 D17** 65 56N 17 49 E
Uden, *Neths.* **15 C5** 51 40N 5 37 E
Udgir, *India* **40 K10** 18 25N 77 5 E
Udhampur, *India* **43 C6** 33 0N 75 5 E
Údine, *Italy* **20 A5** 46 3N 13 14 E
Udmurtia □, *Russia* **24 C9** 57 30N 52 30 E
Udon Thani, *Thailand* **38 D4** 17 29N 102 46 E
Udupi, *India* **40 N9** 13 25N 74 42 E
Udzungwa Range, *Tanzania* **55 D4** 9 30S 35 10 E
Ueda, *Japan* **31 F9** 36 24N 138 16 E
Uedineniya, Os., *Russia* **4 B12** 78 0N 85 0 E
Uele →, *Dem. Rep. of the Congo* **52 D4** 3 45N 24 45 E
Uelen, *Russia* **27 C19** 66 10N 170 0W
Uelzen, *Germany* **16 B6** 52 57N 10 32 E
Ufa, *Russia* **24 D10** 54 45N 55 55 E
Ufa →, *Russia* **24 D10** 54 40N 56 0 E
Ugab →, *Namibia* **56 C1** 20 55S 13 30 E
Ugalla →, *Tanzania* **54 D3** 5 8S 30 42 E
Uganda ■, *Africa* **54 B3** 2 0N 32 0 E
Ugie, *S. Africa* **57 E4** 31 10S 28 13 E
Uglegorsk, *Russia* **27 E15** 49 5N 142 2 E
Ugljan, *Croatia* **16 F8** 44 12N 15 10 E
Uhlenhorst, *Namibia* **56 C2** 23 45S 17 55 E
Uhrichsville, *U.S.A.* **78 F3** 40 24N 81 21W
Uibhist a Deas = South Uist, *U.K.* **12 D1** 57 20N 7 15W
Uibhist a Tuath = North Uist, *U.K.* **12 D1** 57 40N 7 15W
Uig, *U.K.* **12 D2** 57 35N 6 21W
Uíge, *Angola* **52 F2** 7 30S 14 40 E
Uijŏngbu, *S. Korea* **35 F14** 37 48N 127 0 E
Ŭiju, *N. Korea* **35 D13** 40 15N 124 35 E
Uinta Mts., *U.S.A.* **82 F8** 40 45N 110 30W
Uis, *Namibia* **56 B2** 21 8S 14 49 E
Uitenhage, *S. Africa* **56 E4** 33 40S 25 28 E
Uithuizen, *Neths.* **15 A6** 53 24N 6 41 E
Ujh →, *India* **42 C6** 32 10N 75 18 E
Ujhani, *India* **43 F8** 28 0N 79 6 E
Uji-guntō, *Japan* **31 J4** 31 15N 129 25 E
Ujjain, *India* **42 H6** 23 9N 75 43 E
Ujung Pandang, *Indonesia* **37 F5** 5 10S 119 20 E
Uka, *Russia* **27 D17** 57 50N 162 0 E
Ukara I., *Tanzania* **54 C3** 1 50S 33 0 E
Uke-Shima, *Japan* **31 K4** 28 2N 129 14 E
Ukerewe I., *Tanzania* **54 C3** 2 0S 33 0 E
Ukhrul, *India* **41 G19** 25 10N 94 25 E
Ukhta, *Russia* **24 B9** 63 34N 53 41 E
Ukiah, *U.S.A.* **84 F3** 39 9N 123 13W
Ukki Fort, *India* **43 C7** 33 28N 76 54 E
Ukmergė, *Lithuania* **9 J21** 55 15N 24 45 E
Ukraine ■, *Europe* **25 E5** 49 0N 32 0 E
Ukwi, *Botswana* **56 C3** 23 29S 20 30 E
Ulaan-Uul, *Mongolia* **34 B6** 44 13N 111 10 E
Ulaanbaatar, *Mongolia* **27 E11** 47 55N 106 53 E
Ulaangom, *Mongolia* **32 A4** 50 5N 92 10 E
Ulaanjirem, *Mongolia* **34 B3** 45 5N 105 30 E
Ulamba, *Dem. Rep. of the Congo* **55 D1** 9 3S 23 38 E
Ulan Bator = Ulaanbaatar, *Mongolia* **27 E11** 47 55N 106 53 E
Ulan Ude, *Russia* **27 D11** 51 45N 107 40 E
Ulaya, *Morogoro, Tanzania* **54 D4** 7 3S 36 55 E
Ulaya, *Tabora, Tanzania* **54 C3** 4 25S 33 30 E
Ulcinj, *Montenegro, Yug.* **21 D8** 41 58N 19 10 E
Ulco, *S. Africa* **56 D3** 28 21S 24 15 E
Ulefoss, *Norway* **9 G13** 59 17N 9 16 E
Ulhasnagar, *India* **40 K8** 19 15N 73 10 E
Uliastay = Ulyasutay, *Mongolia* **32 B4** 47 56N 97 28 E
Ulithi Atoll, *Pac. Oc.* **37 B9** 10 0N 139 30 E
Ullapool, *U.K.* **12 D3** 57 54N 5 9W
Ullswater, *U.K.* **10 C5** 54 34N 2 52W
Ullŭng-do, *S. Korea* **31 F5** 37 30N 130 30 E
Ulm, *Germany* **16 D5** 48 23N 9 58 E
Ulmarra, *Australia* **63 D5** 29 37S 153 4 E
Ulonguè, *Mozam.* **55 E3** 14 37S 34 19 E
Ulricehamn, *Sweden* **9 H15** 57 46N 13 26 E
Ulsan, *S. Korea* **35 G15** 35 20N 129 15 E
Ulsta, *U.K.* **12 A7** 60 30N 1 9W
Ulster □, *U.K.* **13 B5** 54 35N 6 30W
Ulubat Gölü, *Turkey* **21 D13** 40 9N 28 35 E
Uludağ, *Turkey* **21 D13** 40 4N 29 13 E
Uluguru Mts., *Tanzania* **54 D4** 7 15S 37 40 E
Ulungur He →, *China* **32 B3** 47 1N 87 24 E
Uluru = Ayers Rock, *Australia* **61 E5** 25 23S 131 5 E
Uluru Nat. Park, *Australia* **61 E5** 25 15S 131 20 E
Ulutau, *Kazakstan* **26 E7** 48 39N 67 1 E
Ulva, *U.K.* **12 E2** 56 29N 6 13W
Ulverston, *U.K.* **10 C4** 54 13N 3 5W
Ulverstone, *Australia* **62 G4** 41 11S 146 11 E
Ulya, *Russia* **27 D15** 59 10N 142 0 E
Ulyanovsk = Simbirsk, *Russia* **24 D8** 54 20N 48 25 E
Ulyasutay, *Mongolia* **32 B4** 47 56N 97 28 E
Ulysses, *U.S.A.* **81 G4** 37 35N 101 22W
Umala, *Bolivia* **92 G5** 17 25S 68 5W
Uman, *Ukraine* **17 D16** 48 40N 30 12 E
Umaria, *India* **41 H12** 23 35N 80 50 E
Umarkot, *Pakistan* **40 G6** 25 15N 69 40 E
Umarpada, *India* **42 J5** 21 27N 73 30 E
Umatilla, *U.S.A.* **82 D4** 45 55N 119 21W
Umba, *Russia* **24 A5** 66 42N 34 11 E
Umbagog L., *U.S.A.* **79 B13** 44 46N 71 3W
Umbakumba, *Australia* **62 A2** 13 47S 136 50 E
Umbrella Mts., *N.Z.* **59 L2** 45 35S 169 5 E
Ume älv →, *Sweden* **8 E19** 63 45N 20 20 E
Umeå, *Sweden* **8 E19** 63 45N 20 20 E
Umera, *Indonesia* **37 E7** 0 12S 129 37 E
Umfuli →, *Zimbabwe* **55 F2** 17 30S 29 23 E
Umgusa, *Zimbabwe* **55 F2** 19 29S 27 52 E
Umkomaas, *S. Africa* **57 E5** 30 13S 30 48 E
Umlazi, *S. Africa* **53 L6** 29 59S 30 54 E
Umm ad Daraj, J., *Jordan* **47 C4** 32 18N 35 48 E
Umm al Qaywayn, *U.A.E.* **45 E7** 25 30N 55 35 E
Umm al Qittayn, *Jordan* **47 C5** 32 18N 36 40 E
Umm Bāb, *Qatar* **45 E6** 25 12N 50 48 E
Umm el Fahm, *Israel* **47 C4** 32 31N 35 9 E
Umm Keddada, *Sudan* **51 F11** 13 33N 26 35 E
Umm Lajj, *Si. Arabia* **44 E3** 25 0N 37 23 E
Umm Ruwaba, *Sudan* **51 F12** 12 50N 31 20 E
Umnak I., *U.S.A.* **68 C3** 53 15N 168 20W
Umniati →, *Zimbabwe* **55 F2** 16 49S 28 45 E
Umpqua →, *U.S.A.* **82 E1** 43 40N 124 12W
Umreth, *India* **42 H5** 22 41N 73 4 E
Umtata, *S. Africa* **57 E4** 31 36S 28 49 E
Umuarama, *Brazil* **95 A5** 23 45S 53 20W
Umvukwe Ra., *Zimbabwe* **55 F3** 16 45S 30 45 E
Umzimvubu, *S. Africa* **57 E4** 31 38S 29 33 E
Umzingwane →, *Zimbabwe* **55 G2** 22 12S 29 56 E
Umzinto, *S. Africa* **57 E5** 30 15S 30 45 E
Una, *India* **42 J4** 20 46N 71 8 E
Una →, *Bos.-H.* **16 F9** 45 0N 16 20 E
Unadilla, *U.S.A.* **79 D9** 42 20N 75 19W
Unalakleet, *U.S.A.* **68 B3** 63 52N 160 47W
Unalaska, *U.S.A.* **68 C3** 53 53N 166 32W
Unalaska I., *U.S.A.* **68 C3** 53 35N 166 50W
'Unayzah, *Si. Arabia* **44 E4** 26 6N 43 58 E
'Unāzah, J., *Asia* **44 C3** 32 12N 39 18 E
Uncía, *Bolivia* **92 G5** 18 25S 66 40W
Uncompahgre Peak, *U.S.A.* **83 G10** 38 4N 107 28W
Uncompahgre Plateau, *U.S.A.* **83 G9** 38 20N 108 15W
Ungava, Pén. d', *Canada* **69 C12** 60 0N 74 0W
Ungava B., *Canada* **69 C13** 59 30N 67 30W
Ungeny = Ungheni, *Moldova* **17 E14** 47 11N 27 51 E
Unggi, *N. Korea* **35 C16** 42 16N 130 28 E
Ungheni, *Moldova* **17 E14** 47 11N 27 51 E
União da Vitória, *Brazil* **95 B5** 26 13S 51 5W
Unimak I., *U.S.A.* **68 C3** 54 45N 164 0W
Union, *Miss., U.S.A.* **81 J10** 32 34N 89 7W
Union, *Mo., U.S.A.* **80 F9** 38 27N 91 0W
Union, *S.C., U.S.A.* **77 H5** 34 43N 81 37W
Union City, *Calif., U.S.A.* **84 H4** 37 36N 122 1W
Union City, *N.J., U.S.A.* **79 F10** 40 45N 74 2W
Union City, *Pa., U.S.A.* **78 E5** 41 54N 79 51W
Union City, *Tenn., U.S.A.* **81 G10** 36 26N 89 3W
Union Gap, *U.S.A.* **82 C3** 46 33N 120 28W
Union Springs, *U.S.A.* **77 J3** 32 9N 85 43W
Uniondale, *S. Africa* **56 E3** 33 39S 23 7 E
Uniontown, *U.S.A.* **76 F6** 39 54N 79 44W
Unionville, *U.S.A.* **80 E8** 40 29N 93 1W
United Arab Emirates ■, *Asia* **46 C5** 23 50N 54 0 E
United Kingdom ■, *Europe* **7 E5** 53 0N 2 0W
United States of America ■, *N. Amer.* **74 C7** 37 0N 96 0W
Unity, *Canada* **73 C7** 52 30N 109 5W
University Park, *U.S.A.* **83 K10** 32 17N 106 45W
Unjha, *India* **42 H5** 23 46N 72 24 E
Unnao, *India* **43 F9** 26 35N 80 30 E
Unst, *U.K.* **12 A8** 60 44N 0 53W
Unuk →, *Canada* **72 B2** 56 5N 131 3W
Uozu, *Japan* **31 F8** 36 48N 137 24 E
Upata, *Venezuela* **92 B6** 8 1N 62 24W
Upemba, L., *Dem. Rep. of the Congo* **55 D2** 8 30S 26 20 E
Upernavik, *Greenland* **4 B5** 72 49N 56 20W
Upington, *S. Africa* **56 D3** 28 25S 21 15 E
Upleta, *India* **42 J4** 21 46N 70 16 E
Upolu, *Samoa* **59 A13** 13 58S 172 0W
Upper Alkali L., *U.S.A.* **82 F3** 41 47N 120 8W
Upper Arrow L., *Canada* **72 C5** 50 30N 117 50W
Upper Foster L., *Canada* **73 B7** 56 47N 105 20W

Vergara

Upper Hutt, N.Z. 59 J5 41 8S 175 5 E
Upper Klamath L., U.S.A. 82 E3 42 25N 121 55W
Upper Lake, U.S.A. 84 F4 39 10N 122 54W
Upper Musquodoboit, Canada 71 C7 45 10N 62 58W
Upper Red L., U.S.A. 80 A7 48 8N 94 45W
Upper Sandusky, U.S.A. 76 E4 40 50N 83 17W
Upper Volta = Burkina Faso ■, Africa 50 F5 12 0N 1 0W
Uppland, Sweden 9 F17 59 59N 17 48 E
Uppsala, Sweden 9 G17 59 53N 17 38 E
Upshi, India 43 C7 33 48N 77 52 E
Upstart, C., Australia 62 B4 19 41S 147 45 E
Upton, U.S.A. 80 C2 44 6N 104 38W
Ur, Iraq 44 D5 30 55N 46 25 E
Urad Qianqi, China 34 D5 40 40N 108 30 E
Urakawa, Japan 30 C11 42 9N 142 47 E
Ural = Zhayyq →, Kazakstan 25 E9 47 0N 51 48 E
Ural Mts. = Uralskie Gory, Eurasia 24 C10 60 0N 59 0 E
Uralsk = Oral, Kazakstan 25 D9 51 20N 51 20 E
Uralskie Gory, Eurasia 24 C10 60 0N 59 0 E
Urambo, Tanzania 54 D3 5 4S 32 0 E
Urandangi, Australia 62 C2 21 32S 138 14 E
Uranium City, Canada 73 B7 59 34N 108 37W
Uraricoera →, Brazil 92 C6 3 2N 60 30W
Urawa, Japan 31 G9 35 50N 139 40 E
Uray, Russia 26 C7 60 5N 65 15 E
'Uray'irah, Si. Arabia 45 E6 25 57N 48 53 E
Urbana, Ill., U.S.A. 76 E1 40 7N 88 12W
Urbana, Ohio, U.S.A. 76 E4 40 7N 83 45W
Urbino, Italy 20 C5 43 43N 12 38 E
Urbión, Picos de, Spain 19 A4 42 1N 2 52W
Urcos, Peru 92 F4 13 40S 71 38W
Urdinarrain, Argentina 94 C4 32 37S 58 52W
Urdzhar, Kazakstan 26 E9 47 5N 81 38 E
Ure →, U.K. 10 C6 54 5N 1 20W
Ures, Mexico 86 B2 29 30N 110 30W
Urfa = Sanliurfa, Turkey 25 G6 37 12N 38 50 E
Urganch, Uzbekistan 26 E7 41 40N 60 41 E
Urgench = Urganch, Uzbekistan 26 E7 41 40N 60 41 E
Ürgüp, Turkey 44 B2 38 38N 34 56 E
Uri, India 43 B6 34 8N 74 2 E
Uribia, Colombia 92 A4 11 43N 72 16W
Uriondo, Bolivia 94 A3 21 41S 64 41W
Urique, Mexico 86 B3 27 13N 107 55W
Urique →, Mexico 86 B3 26 29N 107 58W
Urk, Neths. 15 B5 52 39N 5 36 E
Urla, Turkey 21 E12 38 20N 26 47 E
Urmia = Orūmīyeh, Iran 44 B5 37 40N 45 0 E
Urmia, L. = Orūmīyeh, Daryācheh-ye, Iran 44 B5 37 50N 45 30 E
Uroševac, Kosovo, Yug. 21 C9 42 23N 21 10 E
Uruaçu, Brazil 93 F9 14 30S 49 10W
Uruapan, Mexico 86 D4 19 30N 102 0W
Urubamba →, Peru 92 F4 10 43S 73 48W
Uruçara, Brazil 92 D7 2 32S 57 45W
Uruçuí, Brazil 93 E10 7 20S 44 28W
Uruguai →, Brazil 95 B5 26 0S 53 30W
Uruguaiana, Brazil 94 B4 29 50S 57 0W
Uruguay ■, S. Amer. 94 C4 32 30S 56 30W
Uruguay →, S. Amer. 94 C4 34 12S 58 18W
Urumchi = Ürümqi, China 26 E9 43 45N 87 45 E
Ürümqi, China 26 E9 43 45N 87 45 E
Urup, Ostrov, Russia 27 E16 46 0N 151 0 E
Usa →, Russia 24 A10 66 16N 59 49 E
Uşak, Turkey 25 G4 38 43N 29 28 E
Usakos, Namibia 56 C2 21 54S 15 31 E
Usedom, Germany 16 B8 53 55N 14 2 E
Useless Loop, Australia 61 E1 26 8S 113 23 E
Ush-Tobe, Kazakstan 26 E8 45 16N 78 0 E
Ushakova, Ostrov, Russia 4 A12 82 0N 80 0 E
Ushant = Ouessant, Î. d', France 18 B1 48 28N 5 6W
Ushashi, Tanzania 54 C3 1 59S 33 57 E
Ushibuka, Japan 31 H5 32 11N 130 1 E
Ushuaia, Argentina 96 G3 54 50S 68 23W
Ushumun, Russia 27 D13 52 47N 126 32 E
Usk, Canada 72 C3 54 38N 128 26W
Usk →, U.K. 11 F5 51 33N 2 58W
Uska, India 43 F10 27 12N 83 7 E
Usman, Russia 24 D6 52 5N 39 48 E
Usoke, Tanzania 54 D3 5 8S 32 24 E
Usolye Sibirskoye, Russia 27 D11 52 48N 103 40 E
Uspallata, P. de, Argentina 94 C2 32 37S 69 22W
Uspenskiy, Kazakstan 26 E8 48 41N 72 43 E
Ussuri →, Asia 30 A7 48 27N 135 0 E
Ussuriysk, Russia 27 E14 43 48N 131 59 E
Ussurka, Russia 30 B6 45 12N 133 31 E
Ust-Aldan = Batamay, Russia 27 C13 63 30N 129 15 E
Ust-Amginskoye = Khandyga, Russia 27 C14 62 42N 135 35 E
Ust-Bolsheretsk, Russia 27 D16 52 50N 156 15 E
Ust-Chaun, Russia 27 C18 68 47N 170 30 E
Ust-Ilimpeya = Yukta, Russia 27 C11 63 26N 105 42 E
Ust-Ilimsk, Russia 27 D11 58 3N 102 39 E
Ust-Ishim, Russia 26 D8 57 45N 71 10 E
Ust-Kamchatsk, Russia 27 D17 56 10N 162 28 E
Ust-Kamenogorsk = Öskemen, Kazakstan 26 E9 50 0N 82 36 E
Ust-Khayryuzovo, Russia 27 D16 57 15N 156 45 E
Ust-Kut, Russia 27 D11 56 50N 105 42 E
Ust-Kuyga, Russia 27 B14 70 1N 135 43 E
Ust-Maya, Russia 27 C14 60 30N 134 28 E
Ust-Mil, Russia 27 D14 59 40N 133 11 E
Ust-Nera, Russia 27 C15 64 35N 143 15 E
Ust-Nyukzha, Russia 27 D13 56 34N 121 37 E
Ust-Olenek, Russia 27 B12 73 0N 120 5 E
Ust-Omchug, Russia 27 C15 61 9N 149 38 E
Ust-Port, Russia 26 C9 69 40N 84 26 E
Ust-Tsilma, Russia 24 A9 65 28N 52 11 E
Ust Urt = Ustyurt Plateau, Asia 26 E6 44 0N 55 0 E
Ust-Usa, Russia 24 A10 66 2N 56 57 E
Ust-Vorkuta, Russia 24 A11 67 24N 64 0 E
Ústí nad Labem, Czech Rep. 16 C8 50 41N 14 3 E
Ústica, Italy 20 E5 38 42N 13 11 E
Ustinov = Izhevsk, Russia 24 C9 56 51N 53 14 E
Ustyurt Plateau, Asia 26 E6 44 0N 55 0 E
Usu, China 32 B3 44 27N 84 40 E
Usuki, Japan 31 H5 33 8N 131 49 E
Usulután, El Salv. 88 D2 13 25N 88 28W
Usumacinta →, Mexico 87 D6 17 0N 91 0W
Usumbura = Bujumbura, Burundi 54 C2 3 16S 29 18 E
Usure, Tanzania 54 C3 4 40S 34 22 E
Usutuo →, Mozam. 57 D5 26 48S 32 7 E
Uta, Indonesia 37 E9 4 33S 136 0 E
Utah □, U.S.A. 82 G8 39 20N 111 30W
Utah L., U.S.A. 82 F8 40 10N 111 58W
Utarni, India 42 F4 26 5N 71 58 E
Utatlan, Guatemala 88 C1 15 2N 91 11W
Ute Creek →, U.S.A. 81 H3 35 21N 103 50W
Utena, Lithuania 9 J21 55 27N 25 40 E
Utete, Tanzania 54 D4 8 0S 38 45 E
Uthai Thani, Thailand 38 E3 15 22N 100 3 E
Uthal, Pakistan 42 G2 25 44N 66 40 E
Utiariti, Brazil 92 F7 13 0S 58 10W
Utica, N.Y., U.S.A. 79 C9 43 6N 75 14W
Utica, Ohio, U.S.A. 78 F2 40 14N 82 27W
Utikuma L., Canada 72 B5 55 50N 115 30W
Utopia, Australia 62 C1 22 14S 134 33 E
Utraula, India 43 F10 27 19N 82 25 E
Utrecht, Neths. 15 B5 52 5N 5 8 E
Utrecht, S. Africa 57 D5 27 38S 30 20 E
Utrecht □, Neths. 15 B5 52 6N 5 7 E
Utrera, Spain 19 D3 37 12N 5 48W
Utsjoki, Finland 8 B22 69 51N 26 59 E
Utsunomiya, Japan 31 F9 36 30N 139 50 E
Uttar Pradesh □, India 43 F9 27 0N 80 0 E
Uttaradit, Thailand 38 D3 17 36N 100 5 E
Uttaranchal □, India 43 D8 30 0N 79 30 E
Uttoxeter, U.K. 10 E6 52 54N 1 52W
Uummannarsuaq = Nunap Isua, Greenland 69 C15 59 48N 43 55W
Uusikaarlepyy, Finland 8 E20 63 32N 22 31 E
Uusikaupunki, Finland 9 F19 60 47N 21 25 E
Uva, Russia 24 C9 56 59N 52 13 E
Uvalde, U.S.A. 81 L5 29 13N 99 47W
Uvat, Russia 26 D7 59 5N 68 50 E
Uvinza, Tanzania 54 D3 5 5S 30 24 E
Uvira, Dem. Rep. of the Congo 54 C2 3 22S 29 3 E
Uvs Nuur, Mongolia 32 A4 50 20N 92 30 E
'Uwairidh, Ḥarrat al, Si. Arabia 44 E3 26 50N 38 0 E
Uwajima, Japan 31 H6 33 10N 132 35 E
Uweinat, Jebel, Sudan 51 D10 21 54N 24 58 E
Uxbridge, Canada 78 B5 44 6N 79 7W
Uxin Qi, China 34 E5 38 50N 109 5 E
Uxmal, Mexico 87 C7 20 22N 89 46W
Üydzin, Mongolia 34 B4 44 9N 107 0 E
Uyo, Nigeria 50 G7 5 1N 7 53 E
Uyûn Mûsa, Egypt 47 F1 29 53N 32 40 E
Uyuni, Bolivia 92 H5 20 28S 66 47W
Uzbekistan ■, Asia 26 E7 41 30N 65 0 E
Uzen, Kazakstan 25 F9 43 29N 52 54 E
Uzen, Mal →, Kazakstan 25 E8 49 4N 49 44 E
Uzerche, France 18 D4 45 25N 1 34 E
Uzh →, Ukraine 17 C16 51 15N 30 12 E
Uzhgorod = Uzhhorod, Ukraine 17 D12 48 36N 22 18 E
Uzhhorod, Ukraine 17 D12 48 36N 22 18 E
Užice, Serbia, Yug. 21 C8 43 55N 19 50 E
Uzunköprü, Turkey 21 D12 41 16N 26 43 E

V

Vaal →, S. Africa 56 D3 29 4S 23 38 E
Vaal Dam, S. Africa 57 D4 27 0S 28 14 E
Vaalwater, S. Africa 57 C4 24 15S 28 8 E
Vaasa, Finland 8 E19 63 6N 21 38 E
Vác, Hungary 17 E10 47 49N 19 10 E
Vacaria, Brazil 95 B5 28 31S 50 52W
Vacaville, U.S.A. 84 G5 38 21N 121 59W
Vach = Vakh →, Russia 26 C8 60 45N 76 45 E
Vache, Î. à, Haiti 89 C5 18 2N 73 35W
Vadnagar, India 42 H5 23 47N 72 40 E
Vadodara, India 42 H5 22 20N 73 10 E
Vadsø, Norway 8 A23 70 3N 29 50 E
Vaduz, Liech. 18 C8 47 8N 9 31 E
Værøy, Norway 8 C15 67 40N 12 40 E
Vágar, Færoe Is. 8 E9 62 5N 7 15W
Vågsfjorden, Norway 8 B17 68 50N 16 50 E
Váh →, Slovak Rep. 17 D9 47 43N 18 7 E
Vahsel B., Antarctica 5 D1 75 0S 35 0W
Vaï, Greece 23 D8 35 15N 26 18 E
Vaigach, Russia 26 B6 70 10N 59 0 E
Vail, U.S.A. 74 C5 39 40N 106 20W
Vaisali →, India 43 F8 26 28N 78 53 E
Vakh →, Russia 26 C8 60 45N 76 45 E
Val-d'Or, Canada 70 C4 48 7N 77 47W
Val Marie, Canada 73 D7 49 15N 107 45W
Valahia, Romania 17 F13 44 35N 25 0 E
Valandovo, Macedonia 21 D10 41 19N 22 34 E
Valcheta, Argentina 96 E3 40 40S 66 8W
Valdayskaya Vozvyshennost, Russia 24 C5 57 0N 33 30 E
Valdepeñas, Spain 19 C4 38 43N 3 25W
Valdés, Pen., Argentina 96 E4 42 30S 63 45W
Valdez, U.S.A. 68 B5 61 7N 146 16W
Valdivia, Chile 96 D2 39 50S 73 14W
Valdosta, U.S.A. 77 K4 30 50N 83 17W
Valdres, Norway 9 F13 61 5N 9 5 E
Vale, U.S.A. 82 E5 43 59N 117 15W
Vale of Glamorgan □, U.K. 11 F4 51 28N 3 25W
Valemount, Canada 72 C5 52 50N 119 15W
Valença, Brazil 93 F11 13 20S 39 5W
Valença do Piauí, Brazil 93 E10 6 20S 41 45W
Valence, France 18 D6 44 57N 4 54 E
Valencia, Spain 19 C5 39 27N 0 23W
Valencia, U.S.A. 83 J10 34 48N 106 43W
Valencia, Venezuela 92 A5 10 11N 68 0W
Valencia □, Spain 19 C5 39 20N 0 40W
Valencia, G. de, Spain 19 C6 39 30N 0 20 E
Valencia de Alcántara, Spain 19 C2 39 25N 7 14W
Valencia I., Ireland 13 E1 51 54N 10 22W
Valenciennes, France 18 A5 50 20N 3 34 E
Valentim, Sa. do, Brazil 93 E10 6 0S 43 30W
Valentin, Russia 30 C7 43 8N 134 17 E
Valentine, U.S.A. 81 K2 30 35N 104 30W
Valera, Venezuela 92 B4 9 19N 70 37W
Valga, Estonia 9 H22 57 47N 26 2 E
Valier, U.S.A. 82 B7 48 18N 112 16W
Valjevo, Serbia, Yug. 21 B8 44 18N 19 53 E
Valka, Latvia 9 H21 57 42N 25 57 E
Valkeakoski, Finland 9 F20 61 16N 24 2 E
Valkenswaard, Neths. 15 C5 51 21N 5 29 E
Vall de Uxó = La Vall d'Uixó, Spain 19 C5 39 49N 0 15W
Valladolid, Mexico 87 C7 20 40N 88 11W
Valladolid, Spain 19 B3 41 38N 4 43W
Valldemossa, Spain 22 B9 39 43N 2 37 E
Valle de la Pascua, Venezuela 92 B5 9 13N 66 0W
Valle de las Palmas, Mexico 85 N10 32 20N 116 43W
Valle de Santiago, Mexico 86 C4 20 25N 101 15W
Valle de Suchil, Mexico 86 C4 23 38N 103 55W
Valle de Zaragoza, Mexico 86 B3 27 28N 105 49W
Valle Fértil, Sierra del, Argentina 94 C2 30 20S 68 0W
Valle Hermoso, Mexico 87 B5 25 35N 97 40W
Valledupar, Colombia 92 A4 10 29N 73 15W
Vallehermoso, Canary Is. 22 F2 28 10N 17 15W
Vallejo, U.S.A. 84 G4 38 7N 122 14W
Vallenar, Chile 94 B1 28 30S 70 50W
Valletta, Malta 23 D2 35 54N 14 31 E
Valley Center, U.S.A. 85 M9 33 13N 117 2W
Valley City, U.S.A. 80 B6 46 55N 98 0W
Valley Falls, Oreg., U.S.A. 82 E3 42 29N 120 17W
Valley Falls, R.I., U.S.A. 79 E13 41 54N 71 24W
Valley Springs, U.S.A. 84 G6 38 12N 120 50W
Valley View, U.S.A. 79 F8 40 39N 76 33W
Valley Wells, U.S.A. 85 K11 35 27N 115 46W
Valleyview, Canada 72 B5 55 5N 117 17W
Vallimanca, Arroyo, Argentina 94 D4 35 40S 59 10W
Valls, Spain 19 B6 41 18N 1 15 E
Valmiera, Latvia 9 H21 57 37N 25 29 E
Valognes, France 18 B3 49 30N 1 28W
Valona = Vlorë, Albania 21 D8 40 32N 19 28 E
Valozhyn, Belarus 17 A14 54 3N 26 30 E
Valparaíso, Chile 94 C1 33 2S 71 40W
Valparaíso, Mexico 86 C4 22 50N 103 32W
Valparaiso, U.S.A. 76 E2 41 28N 87 4W
Valparaíso □, Chile 94 C1 33 2S 71 40W
Vals →, S. Africa 56 D4 27 23S 26 30 E
Vals, Tanjung, Indonesia 37 F9 8 26S 137 25 E
Valsad, India 40 J8 20 40N 72 58 E
Valverde, Canary Is. 22 G2 27 48N 17 55W
Valverde del Camino, Spain 19 D2 37 35N 6 47W
Vammala, Finland 9 F20 61 20N 22 54 E
Vámos, Greece 23 D6 35 24N 24 13 E
Van, Turkey 25 G7 38 30N 43 20 E
Van, L. = Van Gölü, Turkey 25 G7 38 30N 43 0 E
Van Alstyne, U.S.A. 81 J6 33 25N 96 35W
Van Blommestein Meer, Surinam 93 C7 4 45N 55 5W
Van Buren, Canada 71 C6 47 10N 67 55W
Van Buren, Ark., U.S.A. 81 H7 35 26N 94 21W
Van Buren, Maine, U.S.A. 77 B11 47 10N 67 58W
Van Buren, Mo., U.S.A. 81 G9 37 0N 91 1W
Van Canh, Vietnam 38 F7 13 37N 109 0 E
Van Diemen, C., N. Terr., Australia 60 B5 11 9S 130 24 E
Van Diemen, C., Queens., Australia 62 B2 16 30S 139 46 E
Van Diemen G., Australia 60 B5 11 45S 132 0 E
Van Gölü, Turkey 25 G7 38 30N 43 0 E
Van Horn, U.S.A. 81 K2 31 3N 104 50W
Van Ninh, Vietnam 38 F7 12 42N 109 14 E
Van Rees, Pegunungan, Indonesia 37 E9 2 35S 138 15 E
Van Wert, U.S.A. 76 E3 40 52N 84 35W
Van Yen, Vietnam 38 B5 21 4N 104 42 E
Vanadzor, Armenia 25 F7 40 48N 44 30 E
Vanavara, Russia 27 C11 60 22N 102 16 E
Vancouver, Canada 72 D4 49 15N 123 10W
Vancouver, U.S.A. 84 E4 45 38N 122 40W
Vancouver, C., Australia 61 G2 35 2S 118 11 E
Vancouver I., Canada 72 D3 49 50N 126 0W
Vandalia, Ill., U.S.A. 80 F10 38 58N 89 6W
Vandalia, Mo., U.S.A. 80 F9 39 19N 91 29W
Vandenburg, U.S.A. 85 L6 34 35N 120 33W
Vanderbijlpark, S. Africa 57 D4 26 42S 27 54 E
Vandergrift, U.S.A. 78 F5 40 36N 79 34W
Vanderhoof, Canada 72 C4 54 0N 124 0W
Vanderkloof Dam, S. Africa 56 E3 30 4S 24 40 E
Vanderlin I., Australia 62 B2 15 44S 137 2 E
Vänern, Sweden 9 G15 58 47N 13 30 E
Vänersborg, Sweden 9 G15 58 26N 12 19 E
Vang Vieng, Laos 38 C4 18 58N 102 32 E
Vanga, Kenya 54 C4 4 35S 39 12 E
Vangaindrano, Madag. 57 C8 23 21S 47 36 E
Vanguard, Canada 73 D7 49 55N 107 20W
Vanino, Russia 27 E15 48 50N 140 5 E
Vanna, Norway 8 A18 70 6N 19 50 E
Vännäs, Sweden 8 E18 63 58N 19 48 E
Vannes, France 18 C2 47 40N 2 47W
Vanrhynsdorp, S. Africa 56 E2 31 36S 18 44 E
Vansbro, Sweden 9 F16 60 32N 14 15 E
Vansittart B., Australia 60 B4 14 3S 126 17 E
Vantaa, Finland 9 F21 60 18N 24 58 E
Vanua Balavu, Fiji 59 C9 17 40S 178 57W
Vanua Levu, Fiji 59 C8 16 33S 179 15 E
Vanuatu ■, Pac. Oc. 64 J8 15 0S 168 0 E
Vanwyksvlei, S. Africa 56 E3 30 18S 21 49 E
Vanzylsrus, S. Africa 56 D3 26 52S 22 4 E
Vapnyarka, Ukraine 17 D15 48 32N 28 45 E
Varanasi, India 43 G10 25 22N 83 0 E
Varangerfjorden, Norway 8 A23 70 3N 29 25 E
Varangerhalvøya, Norway 8 A23 70 25N 29 30 E
Varaždin, Croatia 16 E9 46 20N 16 20 E
Varberg, Sweden 9 H15 57 6N 12 20 E
Vardar = Axiós →, Greece 21 D10 40 57N 22 35 E
Varde, Denmark 9 J13 55 38N 8 29 E
Vardø, Norway 8 A24 70 23N 31 5 E
Varella, Mui, Vietnam 38 F7 12 54N 109 26 E
Varėna, Lithuania 9 J21 54 12N 24 30 E
Varese, Italy 18 D8 45 48N 8 50 E
Varginha, Brazil 95 A6 21 33S 45 25W
Varillas, Chile 94 A1 24 0S 70 10W
Varkaus, Finland 9 E22 62 19N 27 50 E
Varna, Bulgaria 21 C12 43 13N 27 56 E
Värnamo, Sweden 9 H16 57 10N 14 3 E
Vars, Canada 79 A9 45 21N 75 21W
Varysburg, U.S.A. 78 D6 42 46N 78 19W
Varzaneh, Iran 45 C7 32 25N 52 40 E
Vasa Barris →, Brazil 93 F11 11 10S 37 10W
Vascongadas = País Vasco □, Spain 19 A4 42 50N 2 45W
Vasht = Khāsh, Iran 40 E2 28 15N 61 15 E
Vasilevichi, Belarus 17 B15 52 15N 29 50 E
Vasilkov = Vasylkiv, Ukraine 17 C16 50 7N 30 15 E
Vaslui, Romania 17 E14 46 38N 27 42 E
Vassar, Canada 73 D9 49 10N 95 55W
Vassar, U.S.A. 76 D4 43 22N 83 35W
Västerås, Sweden 9 G17 59 37N 16 38 E
Västerbotten, Sweden 8 D18 64 36N 20 4 E
Västerdalälven →, Sweden 9 F16 60 30N 14 7 E
Västervik, Sweden 9 H17 57 43N 16 33 E
Västmanland, Sweden 9 G16 59 45N 16 20 E
Vasto, Italy 20 C6 42 8N 14 40 E
Vasylkiv, Ukraine 17 C16 50 7N 30 15 E
Vatersay, U.K. 12 E1 56 55N 7 32W
Vatican City ■, Europe 20 D5 41 54N 12 27 E
Vatili, Cyprus 23 D12 35 6N 33 40 E
Vatnajökull, Iceland 8 D5 64 30N 16 48W
Vatoa, Fiji 59 D9 19 50S 178 13W
Vatólakkos, Greece 23 D5 35 27N 23 53 E
Vatoloha, Madag. 57 B8 17 52S 47 48 E
Vatomandry, Madag. 57 B8 19 20S 48 59 E
Vatra-Dornei, Romania 17 E13 47 22N 25 22 E
Vatrak →, India 42 H5 23 9N 73 2 E
Vättern, Sweden 9 G16 58 25N 14 30 E
Vaughn, Mont., U.S.A. 82 C8 47 33N 111 33W
Vaughn, N. Mex., U.S.A. 83 J11 34 36N 105 13W
Vaujours L., Canada 70 A5 55 27N 74 15W
Vaupés = Uaupés →, Brazil 92 C5 0 2N 67 16W
Vaupes □, Colombia 92 C4 1 0N 71 0W
Vauxhall, Canada 72 C6 50 5N 112 9W
Vav, India 42 G4 24 22N 71 31 E
Vavatenina, Madag. 57 B8 17 28S 49 12 E
Vava'u, Tonga 59 D12 18 36S 174 0W
Vawkavysk, Belarus 17 B13 53 9N 24 30 E
Växjö, Sweden 9 H16 56 52N 14 50 E
Vaygach, Ostrov, Russia 26 C6 70 0N 60 0 E
Váyia, Ákra, Greece 23 C10 36 15N 28 11 E
Vechte →, Neths. 15 B6 52 34N 6 6 E
Vedea →, Romania 17 G13 43 42N 25 41 E
Vedia, Argentina 94 C3 34 30S 61 31W
Veendam, Neths. 15 A6 53 5N 6 52 E
Veenendaal, Neths. 15 B5 52 2N 5 34 E
Vefsna →, Norway 8 D15 65 48N 13 10 E
Vega, Norway 8 D14 65 40N 11 55 E
Vega, U.S.A. 81 H3 35 15N 102 26W
Vegreville, Canada 72 C6 53 30N 112 5W
Vejer de la Frontera, Spain 19 D3 36 15N 5 59W
Vejle, Denmark 9 J13 55 43N 9 30 E
Velas, C., Costa Rica 88 D2 10 21N 85 52W
Velasco, Sierra de, Argentina 94 B2 29 20S 67 10W
Velddrif, S. Africa 56 E2 32 42S 18 11 E
Velebit Planina, Croatia 16 F8 44 50N 15 20 E
Veles, Macedonia 21 D9 41 46N 21 47 E
Vélez-Málaga, Spain 19 D3 36 48N 4 5W
Vélez Rubio, Spain 19 D4 37 41N 2 5W
Velhas →, Brazil 93 G10 17 13S 44 49W
Velika Kapela, Croatia 16 F8 45 10N 15 5 E
Velikaya →, Russia 24 C4 57 48N 28 10 E
Velikaya Kema, Russia 30 B8 45 30N 137 12 E
Veliki Ustyug, Russia 24 B8 60 47N 46 20 E
Velikiye Luki, Russia 24 C5 56 25N 30 32 E
Veliko Tŭrnovo, Bulgaria 21 C11 43 5N 25 41 E
Velikonda Range, India 40 M11 14 45N 79 10 E
Velletri, Italy 20 D5 41 41N 12 47 E
Vellore, India 40 N11 12 57N 79 10 E
Velsk, Russia 24 B7 61 10N 42 5 E
Velva, U.S.A. 80 A4 48 4N 100 56W
Venado Tuerto, Argentina 94 C3 33 50S 62 0W
Vendée □, France 18 C3 46 50N 1 35W
Vendôme, France 18 C4 47 47N 1 3 E
Venézia, Italy 20 B5 45 27N 12 21 E
Venézia, G. di, Italy 20 B5 45 15N 13 0 E
Venezuela ■, S. Amer. 92 B5 8 0N 66 0W
Venezuela, G. de, Venezuela 92 A4 11 30N 71 0W
Vengurla, India 40 M8 15 53N 73 45 E
Venice = Venézia, Italy 20 B5 45 27N 12 21 E
Venice, U.S.A. 77 M4 27 6N 82 27W
Venkatapuram, India 41 K12 18 20N 80 30 E
Venlo, Neths. 15 C6 51 22N 6 11 E
Vennesla, Norway 9 G12 58 15N 7 59 E
Venray, Neths. 15 C6 51 31N 6 0 E
Ventana, Punta de la, Mexico 86 C3 24 4N 109 48W
Ventana, Sa. de la, Argentina 94 D3 38 0S 62 30W
Ventersburg, S. Africa 56 D4 28 7S 27 9 E
Venterstad, S. Africa 56 E4 30 47S 25 48 E
Ventnor, U.K. 11 G6 50 36N 1 12W
Ventotène, Italy 20 D5 40 47N 13 25 E
Ventoux, Mt., France 18 D6 44 10N 5 17 E
Ventspils, Latvia 9 H19 57 25N 21 32 E
Ventuarí →, Venezuela 92 C5 3 58N 67 2W
Ventucopa, U.S.A. 85 L7 34 50N 119 29W
Ventura, U.S.A. 85 L7 34 17N 119 18W
Vera, Argentina 94 B3 29 30S 60 20W
Vera, Spain 19 D5 37 15N 1 51W
Veracruz, Mexico 87 D5 19 10N 96 10W
Veracruz □, Mexico 87 D5 19 0N 96 15W
Veraval, India 42 J4 20 53N 70 27 E
Verbánia, Italy 18 D8 45 56N 8 33 E
Vercelli, Italy 18 D8 45 19N 8 25 E
Verdalsøra, Norway 8 E14 63 48N 11 30 E
Verde →, Argentina 96 E3 41 56S 65 5W
Verde →, Goiás, Brazil 93 G8 18 1S 50 14W
Verde →, Mato Grosso do Sul, Brazil 93 H8 21 25S 52 20W
Verde →, Chihuahua, Mexico 86 B3 26 29N 107 58W
Verde →, Oaxaca, Mexico 87 D5 15 59N 97 50W
Verde →, Veracruz, Mexico 86 C4 21 10N 102 50W
Verde →, Paraguay 94 A4 23 9S 57 37W
Verde →, U.S.A. 74 D4 33 33N 111 40W
Verde, Cay, Bahamas 88 B4 23 0N 75 5W
Verden, Germany 16 B5 52 55N 9 14 E
Verdi, U.S.A. 84 F7 39 31N 119 59W
Verdun, France 18 B6 49 9N 5 24 E
Vereeniging, S. Africa 57 D4 26 38S 27 57 E
Verga, C., Guinea 50 F3 10 30N 14 10W
Vergara, Uruguay 95 C5 32 56S 53 57W

Vergemont Cr.

Vergemont Cr. →, *Australia* **62 C3** 24 16S 143 16 E
Vergennes, *U.S.A.* **79 B11** 44 10N 73 15W
Verín, *Spain* **19 B2** 41 57N 7 27W
Verkhnevilyuysk, *Russia* **27 C13** 63 27N 120 18 E
Verkhniy Baskunchak, *Russia* **25 E8** 48 14N 46 44 E
Verkhoyansk, *Russia* **27 C14** 67 35N 133 25 E
Verkhoyansk Ra. = Verkhoyanskiy Khrebet, *Russia* **27 C13** 66 0N 129 0 E
Verkhoyanskiy Khrebet, *Russia* **27 C13** 66 0N 129 0 E
Vermilion, *Canada* **73 C6** 53 20N 110 50W
Vermilion, *U.S.A.* **78 E2** 41 25N 82 22W
Vermilion →, *Alta., Canada* **73 C6** 53 22N 110 51W
Vermilion →, *Qué., Canada* **70 C5** 47 38N 72 56W
Vermilion, B., *U.S.A.* **81 L9** 29 45N 91 55W
Vermilion Bay, *Canada* **73 D10** 49 51N 93 34W
Vermilion L., *U.S.A.* **80 B8** 47 53N 92 26W
Vermillion, *U.S.A.* **80 D6** 42 47N 96 56W
Vermont □, *U.S.A.* **79 C12** 44 0N 73 0W
Vernal, *U.S.A.* **82 F9** 40 27N 109 32W
Vernalis, *U.S.A.* **84 H5** 37 36N 121 17W
Verner, *Canada* **70 C3** 46 25N 80 8W
Verneukpan, *S. Africa* **56 E3** 30 0S 21 0 E
Vernon, *Canada* **72 C5** 50 20N 119 15W
Vernon, *U.S.A.* **81 H5** 34 9N 99 17W
Vernonia, *U.S.A.* **84 E3** 45 52N 123 11W
Vero Beach, *U.S.A.* **77 M5** 27 38N 80 24W
Véroia, *Greece* **21 D10** 40 34N 22 12 E
Verona, *Canada* **79 B8** 44 29N 76 42W
Verona, *Italy* **20 B4** 45 27N 10 59 E
Verona, *U.S.A.* **80 D10** 42 59N 89 32W
Versailles, *France* **18 B5** 48 48N 2 8 E
Vert, C., *Senegal* **50 F2** 14 45N 17 30W
Verulam, *S. Africa* **57 D5** 29 38S 31 2 E
Verviers, *Belgium* **15 D5** 50 37N 5 52 E
Veselovskoye Vdkhr., *Russia* **25 E7** 46 58N 41 25 E
Vesoul, *France* **18 C7** 47 40N 6 11 E
Vesterålen, *Norway* **8 B16** 68 45N 15 0 E
Vestfjorden, *Norway* **8 C15** 67 55N 14 0 E
Vestmannaeyjar, *Iceland* **8 E3** 63 27N 20 15W
Vestspitsbergen, *Svalbard* **4 B8** 78 40N 17 0 E
Vestvågøy, *Norway* **8 B15** 68 18N 13 50 E
Vesuvio, *Italy* **20 D6** 40 49N 14 26 E
Vesuvius, Mt. = Vesuvio, *Italy* **20 D6** 40 49N 14 26 E
Veszprém, *Hungary* **17 E9** 47 8N 17 57 E
Vetlanda, *Sweden* **9 H16** 57 24N 15 3 E
Vetlugu →, *Russia* **24 C8** 56 36N 46 4 E
Vettore, Mte., *Italy* **20 C5** 42 49N 13 16 E
Veurne, *Belgium* **15 C2** 51 5N 2 40 E
Veys, *Iran* **45 D6** 31 30N 49 0 E
Vezhen, *Bulgaria* **21 C11** 42 50N 24 20 E
Vi Thanh, *Vietnam* **39 H5** 9 42N 105 26 E
Viacha, *Bolivia* **92 G5** 16 39S 68 18W
Viamão, *Brazil* **95 C5** 30 5S 51 0W
Viana, *Brazil* **93 D10** 3 13S 44 55W
Viana do Alentejo, *Portugal* **19 C2** 38 17N 7 59W
Viana do Castelo, *Portugal* **19 B1** 41 42N 8 50W
Vianden, *Lux.* **15 E6** 49 56N 6 12 E
Viangchan = Vientiane, *Laos* **38 D4** 17 58N 102 36 E
Vianópolis, *Brazil* **93 G9** 16 40S 48 35W
Viaréggio, *Italy* **20 C4** 43 52N 10 14 E
Vibo Valéntia, *Italy* **20 E7** 38 40N 16 6 E
Viborg, *Denmark* **9 H13** 56 27N 9 23 E
Vic, *Spain* **19 B7** 41 58N 2 19 E
Vicenza, *Italy* **20 B4** 45 33N 11 33 E
Vich = Vic, *Spain* **19 B7** 41 58N 2 19 E
Vichada →, *Colombia* **92 C5** 4 55N 67 50W
Vichy, *France* **18 C5** 46 9N 3 26 E
Vicksburg, *Ariz., U.S.A.* **85 M13** 33 45N 113 45W
Vicksburg, *Miss., U.S.A.* **81 J9** 32 21N 90 53W
Victor, *India* **42 J4** 21 0N 71 30 E
Victor, *U.S.A.* **78 D7** 42 58N 77 24W
Victoria = Labuan, *Malaysia* **36 C5** 5 20N 115 14 E
Victoria, *Argentina* **94 C3** 32 40S 60 10W
Victoria, *Canada* **72 D4** 48 30N 123 25W
Victoria, *Chile* **96 D2** 38 13S 72 20W
Victoria, *Malta* **23 C1** 36 2N 14 14 E
Victoria, *Kans., U.S.A.* **80 F5** 38 52N 99 9W
Victoria, *Tex., U.S.A.* **81 L6** 28 48N 97 0W
Victoria →, *Australia* **60 C4** 15 10S 129 40 E
Victoria, Grand L., *Canada* **70 C4** 47 31N 77 30W
Victoria, L., *Africa* **54 C3** 1 0S 33 0 E
Victoria, Mt., *Burma* **41 J18** 21 15N 93 55 E
Victoria Beach, *Canada* **73 C9** 50 40N 96 35W
Victoria de Durango = Durango, *Mexico* **86 C4** 24 3N 104 39W
Victoria de las Tunas, *Cuba* **88 B4** 20 58N 76 59W
Victoria Falls, *Zimbabwe* **55 F2** 17 58S 25 52 E
Victoria Harbour, *Canada* **78 B5** 44 45N 79 45W
Victoria I., *Canada* **68 A8** 71 0N 111 0W
Victoria L., *Canada* **71 C8** 48 20N 57 27W
Victoria Ld., *Antarctica* **5 D11** 75 0S 160 0 E
Victoria Nile →, *Uganda* **54 B3** 2 14N 31 26 E
Victoria River, *Australia* **60 C5** 16 25S 131 0 E
Victoria Str., *Canada* **68 B9** 69 30N 100 0W
Victoria West, *S. Africa* **56 E3** 31 25S 23 4 E
Victoriaville, *Canada* **71 C5** 46 4N 71 56W
Victorica, *Argentina* **94 D2** 36 20S 65 30W
Victorville, *U.S.A.* **85 L9** 34 32N 117 18W
Vicuña, *Chile* **94 C1** 30 0S 70 50W
Vicuña Mackenna, *Argentina* **94 C3** 33 53S 64 25W
Vidal, *U.S.A.* **85 L12** 34 7N 114 31W
Vidal Junction, *U.S.A.* **85 L12** 34 11N 114 34W
Vidalia, *U.S.A.* **77 J4** 32 13N 82 25W
Vídho, *Greece* **23 A3** 39 38N 19 55 E
Vidin, *Bulgaria* **21 C10** 43 59N 22 50 E
Vidisha, *India* **42 H7** 23 28N 77 53 E
Vidzy, *Belarus* **9 J22** 55 23N 26 37 E
Viedma, *Argentina* **96 E4** 40 50S 63 0W
Viedma, L., *Argentina* **96 F2** 49 30S 72 30W
Vielsalm, *Belgium* **15 D5** 50 17N 5 54 E
Vieng Pou Kha, *Laos* **38 B3** 20 41N 101 4 E
Vienna = Wien, *Austria* **16 D9** 48 12N 16 22 E
Vienna, *Ill., U.S.A.* **81 G10** 37 25N 88 54W
Vienna, *Mo., U.S.A.* **80 F9** 38 11N 91 57W
Vienne, *France* **18 D6** 45 31N 4 53 E
Vienne →, *France* **18 C4** 47 13N 0 5 E
Vientiane, *Laos* **38 D4** 17 58N 102 36 E
Vientos, Paso de los, *Caribbean* **89 C5** 20 0N 74 0W
Vierzon, *France* **18 C5** 47 13N 2 5 E
Vietnam ■, *Asia* **38 C6** 19 0N 106 0 E
Vigan, *Phil.* **37 A6** 17 35N 120 28 E
Vigévano, *Italy* **18 D8** 45 19N 8 51 E
Vigia, *Brazil* **93 D9** 0 50S 48 5W
Vigía Chico, *Mexico* **87 D7** 19 46N 87 35W
Víglas, Ákra, *Greece* **23 D9** 35 54N 27 51 E
Vigo, *Spain* **19 A1** 42 12N 8 41W
Vihowa, *Pakistan* **42 D4** 31 8N 70 30 E
Vihowa →, *Pakistan* **42 D4** 31 8N 70 41 E
Vijayawada, *India* **41 L12** 16 31N 80 39 E
Vijosë →, *Albania* **21 D8** 40 37N 19 24 E
Vík, *Iceland* **8 E4** 63 25N 19 1W
Vikeke, *E. Timor* **37 F7** 8 52S 126 23 E
Viking, *Canada* **72 C6** 53 7N 111 50W
Vikna, *Norway* **8 D14** 64 55N 10 58 E
Vila da Maganja, *Mozam.* **55 F4** 17 18S 37 30 E
Vila de João Belo = Xai-Xai, *Mozam.* **57 D5** 25 6S 33 31 E
Vila do Bispo, *Portugal* **19 D1** 37 5N 8 53W
Vila Franca de Xira, *Portugal* **19 C1** 38 57N 8 59W
Vila Gamito, *Mozam.* **55 E3** 14 12S 33 0 E
Vila Gomes da Costa, *Mozam.* **57 C5** 24 20S 33 37 E
Vila Machado, *Mozam.* **55 F3** 19 15S 34 14 E
Vila Mouzinho, *Mozam.* **55 E3** 14 48S 34 25 E
Vila Nova de Gaia, *Portugal* **19 B1** 41 8N 8 37W
Vila Real, *Portugal* **19 B2** 41 17N 7 48W
Vila-real de los Infantes, *Spain* **19 C5** 39 55N 0 3W
Vila Real de Santo António, *Portugal* **19 D2** 37 10N 7 28W
Vila Vasco da Gama, *Mozam.* **55 E3** 14 54S 32 14 E
Vila Velha, *Brazil* **95 A7** 20 20S 40 17W
Vilagarcía de Arousa, *Spain* **19 A1** 42 34N 8 46W
Vilaine →, *France* **18 C2** 47 30N 2 27W
Vilanandro, Tanjona, *Madag.* **57 B7** 16 11S 44 27 E
Vilanculos, *Mozam.* **57 C6** 22 1S 35 17 E
Vilanova i la Geltrú, *Spain* **19 B6** 41 13N 1 40 E
Vileyka, *Belarus* **17 A14** 54 30N 26 53 E
Vilhelmina, *Sweden* **8 D17** 64 35N 16 39 E
Vilhena, *Brazil* **92 F6** 12 40S 60 5W
Viliga, *Russia* **27 C16** 61 36N 156 56 E
Viliya →, *Lithuania* **9 J21** 55 8N 24 16 E
Viljandi, *Estonia* **9 G21** 58 28N 25 30 E
Vilkitskogo, Proliv, *Russia* **27 B11** 78 0N 103 0 E
Vilkovo = Vylkove, *Ukraine* **17 F15** 45 28N 29 32 E
Villa Abecia, *Bolivia* **94 A2** 21 0S 68 18W
Villa Ahumada, *Mexico* **86 A3** 30 38N 106 30W
Villa Ana, *Argentina* **94 B4** 28 28S 59 40W
Villa Ángela, *Argentina* **94 B3** 27 34S 60 45W
Villa Bella, *Bolivia* **92 F5** 10 25S 65 22W
Villa Bens = Tarfaya, *Morocco* **50 C3** 27 55N 12 55W
Villa Cañás, *Argentina* **94 C3** 34 0S 61 35W
Villa Cisneros = Dakhla, *W. Sahara* **50 D2** 23 50N 15 53W
Villa Colón, *Argentina* **94 C2** 31 38S 68 20W
Villa Constitución, *Argentina* **94 C3** 33 15S 60 20W
Villa de María, *Argentina* **94 B3** 29 55S 63 43W
Villa Dolores, *Argentina* **94 C2** 31 58S 65 15W
Villa Frontera, *Mexico* **86 B4** 26 56N 101 27W
Villa Guillermina, *Argentina* **94 B4** 28 15S 59 29W
Villa Hayes, *Paraguay* **94 B4** 25 5S 57 20W
Villa Iris, *Argentina* **94 D3** 38 12S 63 12W
Villa Juárez, *Mexico* **86 B4** 27 37N 100 44W
Villa María, *Argentina* **94 C3** 32 20S 63 10W
Villa Mazán, *Argentina* **94 B2** 28 40S 66 30W
Villa Montes, *Bolivia* **94 A3** 21 10S 63 30W
Villa Ocampo, *Argentina* **94 B4** 28 30S 59 20W
Villa Ocampo, *Mexico* **86 B3** 26 29N 105 30W
Villa Ojo de Agua, *Argentina* **94 B3** 29 30S 63 44W
Villa San José, *Argentina* **94 C4** 32 12S 58 15W
Villa San Martín, *Argentina* **94 B3** 28 15S 64 9W
Villa Unión, *Mexico* **86 C3** 23 12N 106 14W
Villacarlos, *Spain* **22 B11** 39 53N 4 17 E
Villacarrillo, *Spain* **19 C4** 38 7N 3 3W
Villach, *Austria* **16 E7** 46 37N 13 51 E
Villafranca de los Caballeros, *Spain* **22 B10** 39 34N 3 25 E
Villagrán, *Mexico* **87 C5** 24 29N 99 29W
Villaguay, *Argentina* **94 C4** 32 0S 59 0W
Villahermosa, *Mexico* **87 D6** 17 59N 92 55W
Villajoyosa, *Spain* **19 C5** 38 30N 0 12W
Villalba, *Spain* **19 A2** 43 26N 7 40W
Villanueva, *U.S.A.* **81 H2** 35 16N 105 22W
Villanueva de la Serena, *Spain* **19 C3** 38 59N 5 50W
Villanueva y Geltrú = Vilanova i la Geltrú, *Spain* **19 B6** 41 13N 1 40 E
Villarreal = Vila-real de los Infantes, *Spain* **19 C5** 39 55N 0 3W
Villarrica, *Chile* **96 D2** 39 15S 72 15W
Villarrica, *Paraguay* **94 B4** 25 40S 56 30W
Villarrobledo, *Spain* **19 C4** 39 18N 2 36W
Villavicencio, *Argentina* **94 C2** 32 28S 69 0W
Villavicencio, *Colombia* **92 C4** 4 9N 73 37W
Villaviciosa, *Spain* **19 A3** 43 32N 5 27W
Villazón, *Bolivia* **94 A2** 22 0S 65 35W
Ville-Marie, *Canada* **70 C4** 47 20N 79 30W
Ville Platte, *U.S.A.* **81 K8** 30 41N 92 17W
Villena, *Spain* **19 C5** 38 39N 0 52W
Villeneuve-d'Ascq, *France* **18 A5** 50 38N 3 9 E
Villeneuve-sur-Lot, *France* **18 D4** 44 24N 0 42 E
Villiers, *S. Africa* **57 D4** 27 2S 28 36 E
Villingen-Schwenningen, *Germany* **16 D5** 48 3N 8 26 E
Vilna, *Canada* **72 C6** 54 7N 111 55W
Vilnius, *Lithuania* **9 J21** 54 38N 25 19 E
Vilvoorde, *Belgium* **15 D4** 50 56N 4 26 E
Vilyuy →, *Russia* **27 C13** 64 24N 126 26 E
Vilyuysk, *Russia* **27 C13** 63 40N 121 35 E
Viña del Mar, *Chile* **94 C1** 33 0S 71 30W
Vinarós, *Spain* **19 B6** 40 30N 0 27 E
Vincennes, *U.S.A.* **76 F2** 38 41N 87 32W
Vincent, *U.S.A.* **85 L8** 34 33N 118 11W
Vinchina, *Argentina* **94 B2** 28 45S 68 15W
Vindelälven →, *Sweden* **8 E18** 63 55N 19 50 E
Vindeln, *Sweden* **8 D18** 64 12N 19 43 E
Vindhya Ra., *India* **42 H7** 22 50N 77 0 E
Vineland, *U.S.A.* **76 F8** 39 29N 75 2W
Vinh, *Vietnam* **38 C5** 18 45N 105 38 E
Vinh Linh, *Vietnam* **38 D6** 17 4N 107 2 E
Vinh Long, *Vietnam* **39 G5** 10 16N 105 57 E
Vinh Yen, *Vietnam* **38 B5** 21 21N 105 35 E
Vinita, *U.S.A.* **81 G7** 36 39N 95 9W
Vinkovci, *Croatia* **21 B8** 45 19N 18 48 E
Vinnitsa = Vinnytsya, *Ukraine* **17 D15** 49 15N 28 30 E
Vinnytsya, *Ukraine* **17 D15** 49 15N 28 30 E
Vinton, *Calif., U.S.A.* **84 F6** 39 48N 120 10W
Vinton, *Iowa, U.S.A.* **80 D8** 42 10N 92 1W
Vinton, *La., U.S.A.* **81 K8** 30 11N 93 35W
Virac, *Phil.* **37 B6** 13 30N 124 20 E
Virachei, *Cambodia* **38 F6** 13 59N 106 49 E
Virago Sd., *Canada* **72 C2** 54 0N 132 30W
Viramgam, *India* **42 H5** 23 5N 72 0 E
Viranşehir, *Turkey* **44 B3** 37 13N 39 45 E
Virawah, *Pakistan* **42 G4** 24 31N 70 46 E
Virden, *Canada* **73 D8** 49 50N 100 56W
Vire, *France* **18 B3** 48 50N 0 53W
Vírgenes, C., *Argentina* **96 G3** 52 19S 68 21W
Virgin →, *U.S.A.* **83 H6** 36 28N 114 21W
Virgin Gorda, *Br. Virgin Is.* **89 C7** 18 30N 64 26W
Virgin Is. (British) ■, *W. Indies* **89 C7** 18 30N 64 30W
Virgin Is. (U.S.) ■, *W. Indies* **89 C7** 18 20N 65 0W
Virginia, *S. Africa* **56 D4** 28 8S 26 55 E
Virginia, *U.S.A.* **80 B8** 47 31N 92 32W
Virginia □, *U.S.A.* **76 G7** 37 30N 78 45W
Virginia Beach, *U.S.A.* **76 G8** 36 51N 75 59W
Virginia City, *Mont., U.S.A.* **82 D8** 45 18N 111 56W
Virginia City, *Nev., U.S.A.* **84 F7** 39 19N 119 39W
Virginia Falls, *Canada* **72 A3** 61 38N 125 42W
Virginiatown, *Canada* **70 C4** 48 9N 79 36W
Viroqua, *U.S.A.* **80 D9** 43 34N 90 53W
Virovitica, *Croatia* **20 B7** 45 51N 17 21 E
Virpur, *India* **42 J4** 21 51N 70 42 E
Virton, *Belgium* **15 E5** 49 35N 5 32 E
Virudunagar, *India* **40 Q10** 9 30N 77 58 E
Vis, *Croatia* **20 C7** 43 4N 16 10 E
Visalia, *U.S.A.* **84 J7** 36 20N 119 18W
Visayan Sea, *Phil.* **37 B6** 11 30N 123 30 E
Visby, *Sweden* **9 H18** 57 37N 18 18 E
Viscount Melville Sd., *Canada* **4 B2** 74 10N 108 0W
Visé, *Belgium* **15 D5** 50 44N 5 41 E
Višegrad, *Bos.-H.* **21 C8** 43 47N 19 17 E
Viseu, *Brazil* **93 D9** 1 10S 46 5W
Viseu, *Portugal* **19 B2** 40 40N 7 55W
Vishakhapatnam, *India* **41 L13** 17 45N 83 20 E
Visnagar, *India* **42 H5** 23 45N 72 32 E
Viso, Mte., *Italy* **18 D7** 44 38N 7 5 E
Visokoi I., *Antarctica* **5 B1** 56 43S 27 15W
Vista, *U.S.A.* **85 M9** 33 12N 117 14W
Vistula = Wisła →, *Poland* **17 A10** 54 22N 18 55 E
Vitebsk = Vitsyebsk, *Belarus* **24 C5** 55 10N 30 15 E
Viterbo, *Italy* **20 C5** 42 25N 12 6 E
Viti Levu, *Fiji* **59 C7** 17 30S 177 30 E
Vitigudino, *Spain* **19 B2** 41 1N 6 26W
Vitim, *Russia* **27 D12** 59 28N 112 35 E
Vitim →, *Russia* **27 D12** 59 26N 112 34 E
Vitória, *Brazil* **93 H10** 20 20S 40 22W
Vitória da Conquista, *Brazil* **93 F10** 14 51S 40 51W
Vitória de São Antão, *Brazil* **93 E11** 8 10S 35 20W
Vitoria-Gasteiz, *Spain* **19 A4** 42 50N 2 41W
Vitsyebsk, *Belarus* **24 C5** 55 10N 30 15 E
Vittória, *Italy* **20 F6** 36 57N 14 32 E
Vittório Véneto, *Italy* **20 B5** 45 59N 12 18 E
Viveiro, *Spain* **19 A2** 43 39N 7 38W
Vivian, *U.S.A.* **81 J8** 32 53N 93 59W
Vizcaíno, Desierto de, *Mexico* **86 B2** 27 40N 113 50W
Vizcaíno, Sierra, *Mexico* **86 B2** 27 30N 114 0W
Vize, *Turkey* **21 D12** 41 34N 27 45 E
Vizianagaram, *India* **41 K13** 18 6N 83 30 E
Vlaardingen, *Neths.* **15 C4** 51 55N 4 21 E
Vladikavkaz, *Russia* **25 F7** 43 0N 44 35 E
Vladimir, *Russia* **24 C7** 56 15N 40 30 E
Vladimir Volynskiy = Volodymyr-Volynskyy, *Ukraine* **17 C13** 50 50N 24 18 E
Vladivostok, *Russia* **27 E14** 43 10N 131 53 E
Vlieland, *Neths.* **15 A4** 53 16N 4 55 E
Vlissingen, *Neths.* **15 C3** 51 26N 3 34 E
Vlorë, *Albania* **21 D8** 40 32N 19 28 E
Vltava →, *Czech Rep.* **16 D8** 50 21N 14 30 E
Vo Dat, *Vietnam* **39 G6** 11 9N 107 31 E
Voe, *U.K.* **12 A7** 60 21N 1 16W
Vogelkop = Doberai, Jazirah, *Indonesia* **37 E8** 1 25S 133 0 E
Vogelsberg, *Germany* **16 C5** 50 31N 9 12 E
Voghera, *Italy* **18 D8** 44 59N 9 1 E
Vohibinany, *Madag.* **57 B8** 18 49S 49 4 E
Vohilava, *Madag.* **57 C8** 21 4S 48 0 E
Vohimarina = Iharana, *Madag.* **57 A9** 13 25S 50 0 E
Vohimena, Tanjon' i, *Madag.* **57 D8** 25 36S 45 8 E
Vohipeno, *Madag.* **57 C8** 22 22S 47 51 E
Voi, *Kenya* **54 C4** 3 25S 38 32 E
Voiron, *France* **18 D6** 45 22N 5 35 E
Voisey B., *Canada* **71 A7** 56 15N 61 50W
Vojmsjön, *Sweden* **8 D17** 64 55N 16 40 E
Vojvodina □, *Serbia, Yug.* **21 B9** 45 20N 20 0 E
Volborg, *U.S.A.* **80 C2** 45 51N 105 41W
Volcano Is. = Kazan-Rettō, *Pac. Oc.* **64 E6** 25 0N 141 0 E
Volda, *Norway* **9 E12** 62 9N 6 5 E
Volga →, *Russia* **25 E8** 46 0N 48 30 E
Volga Hts. = Privolzhskaya Vozvyshennost, *Russia* **25 D8** 51 0N 46 0 E
Volgodonsk, *Russia* **25 E7** 47 33N 42 5 E
Volgograd, *Russia* **25 E7** 48 40N 44 25 E
Volgogradskoye Vdkhr., *Russia* **25 D8** 50 0N 45 20 E
Volkhov →, *Russia* **24 B5** 60 8N 32 20 E
Volkovysk = Vawkavysk, *Belarus* **17 B13** 53 9N 24 30 E
Volksrust, *S. Africa* **57 D4** 27 24S 29 53 E
Volochanka, *Russia* **27 B10** 71 0N 94 28 E
Volodymyr-Volynskyy, *Ukraine* **17 C13** 50 50N 24 18 E
Vologda, *Russia* **24 C6** 59 10N 39 45 E
Vólos, *Greece* **21 E10** 39 24N 22 59 E
Volovets, *Ukraine* **17 D12** 48 43N 23 11 E
Volozhin = Valozhyn, *Belarus* **17 A14** 54 3N 26 30 E
Volsk, *Russia* **24 D8** 52 5N 47 22 E
Volta →, *Ghana* **48 F4** 5 46N 0 41 E
Volta, L., *Ghana* **50 G6** 7 30N 0 0W
Volta Redonda, *Brazil* **95 A7** 22 31S 44 5W
Voltaire, C., *Australia* **60 B4** 14 16S 125 35 E
Volterra, *Italy* **20 C4** 43 24N 10 51 E
Volturno →, *Italy* **20 D5** 41 1N 13 55 E
Volzhskiy, *Russia* **25 E7** 48 56N 44 46 E
Vondrozo, *Madag.* **57 C8** 22 49S 47 20 E
Vopnafjörður, *Iceland* **8 D6** 65 45N 14 50W
Vóriai Sporádhes, *Greece* **21 E10** 39 15N 23 30 E
Vorkuta, *Russia* **24 A11** 67 48N 64 20 E
Vormsi, *Estonia* **9 G20** 59 1N 23 13 E
Voronezh, *Russia* **25 D6** 51 40N 39 10 E
Voroshilovgrad = Luhansk, *Ukraine* **25 E6** 48 38N 39 15 E
Voroshilovsk = Alchevsk, *Ukraine* **25 E6** 48 30N 38 45 E
Võrts Järv, *Estonia* **9 G22** 58 16N 26 3 E
Võru, *Estonia* **9 H22** 57 48N 26 54 E
Vosges, *France* **18 B7** 48 20N 7 10 E
Voss, *Norway* **9 F12** 60 38N 6 26 E
Vostok I., *Kiribati* **65 J12** 10 5S 152 23W
Votkinsk, *Russia* **24 C9** 57 0N 53 55 E
Votkinskoye Vdkhr., *Russia* **24 C10** 57 22N 55 12 E
Votsuri-Shima, *Japan* **31 M1** 25 45N 123 29 E
Vouga →, *Portugal* **19 B1** 40 41N 8 40W
Voúxa, Ákra, *Greece* **23 D5** 35 37N 23 32 E
Vozhe, Ozero, *Russia* **24 B6** 60 45N 39 0 E
Voznesensk, *Ukraine* **25 E5** 47 35N 31 21 E
Voznesenye, *Russia* **24 B6** 61 0N 35 28 E
Vrangelya, Ostrov, *Russia* **27 B19** 71 0N 180 0 E
Vranje, *Serbia, Yug.* **21 C9** 42 34N 21 54 E
Vratsa, *Bulgaria* **21 C10** 43 15N 23 30 E
Vrbas →, *Bos.-H.* **20 B7** 45 8N 17 29 E
Vrede, *S. Africa* **57 D4** 27 24S 29 6 E
Vredefort, *S. Africa* **56 D4** 27 0S 27 22 E
Vredenburg, *S. Africa* **56 E2** 32 56S 18 0 E
Vredendal, *S. Africa* **56 E2** 31 41S 18 35 E
Vrindavan, *India* **42 F7** 27 37N 77 40 E
Vríses, *Greece* **23 D6** 35 23N 24 13 E
Vršac, *Serbia, Yug.* **21 B9** 45 8N 21 20 E
Vryburg, *S. Africa* **56 D3** 26 55S 24 45 E
Vryheid, *S. Africa* **57 D5** 27 45S 30 47 E
Vu Liet, *Vietnam* **38 C5** 18 43N 105 23 E
Vukovar, *Croatia* **21 B8** 45 21N 18 59 E
Vulcan, *Canada* **72 C6** 50 25N 113 15W
Vulcan, *Romania* **17 F12** 45 23N 23 17 E
Vulcaneşti, *Moldova* **17 F15** 45 41N 28 18 E
Vulcano, *Italy* **20 E6** 38 24N 14 58 E
Vulkaneshty = Vulcaneşti, *Moldova* **17 F15** 45 41N 28 18 E
Vunduzi →, *Mozam.* **55 F3** 18 56S 34 1 E
Vung Tau, *Vietnam* **39 G6** 10 21N 107 4 E
Vyatka = Kirov, *Russia* **24 C8** 58 35N 49 40 E
Vyatka →, *Russia* **24 C9** 55 37N 51 28 E
Vyatskiye Polyany, *Russia* **24 C9** 56 14N 51 5 E
Vyazemskiy, *Russia* **27 E14** 47 32N 134 45 E
Vyazma, *Russia* **24 C5** 55 10N 34 15 E
Vyborg, *Russia* **24 B4** 60 43N 28 47 E
Vychegda →, *Russia* **24 B8** 61 18N 46 36 E
Vychodné Beskydy, *Europe* **17 D11** 49 20N 22 0 E
Vyg-ozero, *Russia* **24 B5** 63 47N 34 29 E
Vylkove, *Ukraine* **17 F15** 45 28N 29 32 E
Vynohradiv, *Ukraine* **17 D12** 48 9N 23 2 E
Vyrnwy, L., *U.K.* **10 E4** 52 48N 3 31W
Vyshniy Volochek, *Russia* **24 C5** 57 30N 34 30 E
Vyshzha = imeni 26 Bakinskikh Komissarov, *Turkmenistan* **45 B7** 39 22N 54 10 E
Vyškov, *Czech Rep.* **17 D9** 49 17N 17 0 E
Vytegra, *Russia* **24 B6** 61 0N 36 27 E

W

W.A.C. Bennett Dam, *Canada* **72 B4** 56 2N 122 6W
Waal →, *Neths.* **15 C5** 51 37N 5 0 E
Waalwijk, *Neths.* **15 C5** 51 42N 5 4 E
Wabana, *Canada* **71 C9** 47 40N 53 0W
Wabasca →, *Canada* **72 B5** 58 22N 115 20W
Wabasca-Desmarais, *Canada* **72 B6** 55 57N 113 56W
Wabash, *U.S.A.* **76 E3** 40 48N 85 49W
Wabash →, *U.S.A.* **76 G1** 37 48N 88 2W
Wabigoon L., *Canada* **73 D10** 49 44N 92 44W
Wabowden, *Canada* **73 C9** 54 55N 98 38W
Wabuk Pt., *Canada* **70 A2** 55 20N 85 5W
Wabush, *Canada* **71 B6** 52 55N 66 52W
Waco, *U.S.A.* **81 K6** 31 33N 97 9W
Waconichi, L., *Canada* **70 B5** 50 8N 74 0W
Wad Hamid, *Sudan* **51 E12** 16 30N 32 45 E
Wad Medanî, *Sudan* **51 F12** 14 28N 33 30 E
Wad Thana, *Pakistan* **42 F2** 27 22N 66 23 E
Wadai, *Africa* **48 E5** 12 0N 19 0 E
Wadayama, *Japan* **31 G7** 35 19N 134 52 E
Waddeneilanden, *Neths.* **15 A5** 53 20N 5 10 E
Waddenzee, *Neths.* **15 A5** 53 6N 5 10 E
Waddington, *U.S.A.* **79 B9** 44 52N 75 12W
Waddington, Mt., *Canada* **72 C3** 51 23N 125 15W
Waddy Pt., *Australia* **63 C5** 24 58S 153 21 E
Wadebridge, *U.K.* **11 G3** 50 31N 4 51W
Wadena, *Canada* **73 C8** 51 57N 103 47W
Wadena, *U.S.A.* **80 B7** 46 26N 95 8W
Wadeye, *Australia* **60 B4** 14 28S 129 52 E
Wadhams, *Canada* **72 C3** 51 30N 127 30W
Wādī as Sīr, *Jordan* **47 D4** 31 56N 35 49 E
Wadi Halfa, *Sudan* **51 D12** 21 53N 31 19 E
Wadsworth, *Nev., U.S.A.* **82 G4** 39 38N 119 17W
Wadsworth, *Ohio, U.S.A.* **78 E3** 41 2N 81 44W
Waegwan, *S. Korea* **35 G15** 35 59N 128 23 E
Wafangdian, *China* **35 E11** 39 38N 121 58 E
Wafrah, *Si. Arabia* **44 D5** 28 33N 47 56 E
Wageningen, *Neths.* **15 C5** 51 58N 5 40 E
Wager B., *Canada* **69 B11** 65 26N 88 40W
Waghete, *Indonesia* **37 E9** 4 10S 135 50 E
Wagin, *Australia* **61 F2** 33 17S 117 25 E
Wagner, *U.S.A.* **80 D5** 43 5N 98 18W
Wagon Mound, *U.S.A.* **81 G2** 36 1N 104 42W

West Beskids

Wagoner, *U.S.A.* **81 H7** 35 58N 95 22W
Wah, *Pakistan* **42 C5** 33 45N 72 40 E
Wahai, *Indonesia* **37 E7** 2 48S 129 35 E
Wahiawa, *U.S.A.* **74 H15** 21 30N 158 2W
Wâḥid, *Egypt* **47 E1** 30 48N 32 21 E
Wahnai, *Afghan.* **42 C1** 32 40N 65 50 E
Wahoo, *U.S.A.* **80 E6** 41 13N 96 37W
Wahpeton, *U.S.A.* **80 B6** 46 16N 96 36W
Waiau →, *N.Z.* **59 K4** 42 47S 173 22 E
Waibeem, *Indonesia* **37 E8** 0 30S 132 59 E
Waigeo, *Indonesia* **37 E8** 0 20S 130 40 E
Waihi, *N.Z.* **59 G5** 37 23S 175 52 E
Waihou →, *N.Z.* **59 G5** 37 15S 175 40 E
Waika, *Dem. Rep. of the Congo* **54 C2** 2 22S 25 42 E
Waikabubak, *Indonesia* **37 F5** 9 45S 119 25 E
Waikari, *N.Z.* **59 K4** 42 58S 172 41 E
Waikato →, *N.Z.* **59 G5** 37 23S 174 43 E
Waikokopu, *N.Z.* **59 H6** 39 3S 177 52 E
Waikouaiti, *N.Z.* **59 L3** 45 36S 170 41 E
Wailuku, *U.S.A.* **74 H16** 20 53N 156 30W
Waimakariri →, *N.Z.* **59 K4** 43 24S 172 42 E
Waimate, *N.Z.* **59 L3** 44 45S 171 3 E
Wainganga →, *India* **40 K11** 18 50N 79 55 E
Waingapu, *Indonesia* **37 F6** 9 35S 120 11 E
Waini →, *Guyana* **92 B7** 8 20N 59 50W
Wainwright, *Canada* **73 C6** 52 50N 110 50W
Waiouru, *N.Z.* **59 H5** 39 28S 175 41 E
Waipara, *N.Z.* **59 K4** 43 3S 172 46 E
Waipawa, *N.Z.* **59 H6** 39 56S 176 38 E
Waipiro, *N.Z.* **59 H7** 38 2S 178 22 E
Waipu, *N.Z.* **59 F5** 35 59S 174 29 E
Waipukurau, *N.Z.* **59 J6** 40 1S 176 33 E
Wairakei, *N.Z.* **59 H6** 38 37S 176 6 E
Wairarapa, L., *N.Z.* **59 J5** 41 14S 175 15 E
Wairoa, *N.Z.* **59 H6** 39 3S 177 25 E
Waitaki →, *N.Z.* **59 L3** 44 56S 171 7 E
Waitara, *N.Z.* **59 H5** 38 59S 174 15 E
Waitsburg, *U.S.A.* **82 C5** 46 16N 118 9W
Waiuku, *N.Z.* **59 G5** 37 15S 174 45 E
Wajima, *Japan* **31 F8** 37 30N 137 0 E
Wajir, *Kenya* **54 B5** 1 42N 40 5 E
Wakasa, *Japan* **31 G7** 35 20N 134 24 E
Wakasa-Wan, *Japan* **31 G7** 35 40N 135 30 E
Wakatipu, L., *N.Z.* **59 L2** 45 5S 168 33 E
Wakaw, *Canada* **73 C7** 52 39N 105 44W
Wakayama, *Japan* **31 G7** 34 15N 135 15 E
Wakayama □, *Japan* **31 H7** 33 50N 135 30 E
Wake Forest, *U.S.A.* **77 H6** 35 59N 78 30W
Wake I., *Pac. Oc.* **64 F8** 19 18N 166 36 E
WaKeeney, *U.S.A.* **80 F5** 39 1N 99 53W
Wakefield, *N.Z.* **59 J4** 41 24S 173 5 E
Wakefield, *U.K.* **10 D6** 53 41N 1 29W
Wakefield, *Mass., U.S.A.* **79 D13** 42 30N 71 4W
Wakefield, *Mich., U.S.A.* **80 B10** 46 29N 89 56W
Wakkanai, *Japan* **30 B10** 45 28N 141 35 E
Wakkerstroom, *S. Africa* **57 D5** 27 24S 30 10 E
Wakre, *Indonesia* **37 E8** 0 19S 131 5 E
Wakuach, L., *Canada* **71 A6** 55 34N 67 32W
Walamba, *Zambia* **55 E2** 13 30S 28 42 E
Wałbrzych, *Poland* **16 C9** 50 45N 16 18 E
Walbury Hill, *U.K.* **11 F6** 51 21N 1 28W
Walcheren, *Neths.* **15 C3** 51 30N 3 35 E
Walcott, *U.S.A.* **82 F10** 41 46N 106 51W
Wałcz, *Poland* **16 B9** 53 17N 16 27 E
Waldburg Ra., *Australia* **61 D2** 24 40S 117 35 E
Walden, *Colo., U.S.A.* **82 F10** 40 44N 106 17W
Walden, *N.Y., U.S.A.* **79 E10** 41 34N 74 11W
Waldport, *U.S.A.* **82 D1** 44 26N 124 4W
Waldron, *U.S.A.* **81 H7** 34 54N 94 5W
Walebing, *Australia* **61 F2** 30 41S 116 13 E
Wales □, *U.K.* **11 E3** 52 19N 4 43W
Walgett, *Australia* **63 E4** 30 0S 148 5 E
Walgreen Coast, *Antarctica* **5 D15** 75 15S 105 0W
Walker, *U.S.A.* **80 B7** 47 6N 94 35W
Walker, L., *Canada* **71 B6** 50 20N 67 11W
Walker L., *Canada* **73 C9** 54 42N 95 57W
Walker L., *U.S.A.* **82 G4** 38 42N 118 43W
Walkerston, *Australia* **62 C4** 21 11S 149 8 E
Walkerton, *Canada* **78 B3** 44 10N 81 10W
Wall, *U.S.A.* **80 D3** 44 0N 102 8W
Walla Walla, *U.S.A.* **82 C4** 46 4N 118 20W
Wallace, *Idaho, U.S.A.* **82 C6** 47 28N 115 56W
Wallace, *N.C., U.S.A.* **77 H7** 34 44N 77 59W
Wallaceburg, *Canada* **78 D2** 42 34N 82 23W
Wallachia = Valahia, *Romania* **17 F13** 44 35N 25 0 E
Wallal, *Australia* **63 D4** 26 32S 146 7 E
Wallam Cr. →, *Australia* **63 D4** 28 40S 147 20 E
Wallambin, L., *Australia* **61 F2** 30 57S 117 35 E
Wallangarra, *Australia* **63 D5** 28 56S 151 58 E
Wallenpaupack, L., *U.S.A.* **79 E9** 41 25N 75 15W
Wallingford, *U.S.A.* **79 E12** 41 27N 72 50W
Wallis & Futuna, Is., *Pac. Oc.* **64 J10** 13 18S 176 10W
Wallowa, *U.S.A.* **82 D5** 45 34N 117 32W
Wallowa Mts., *U.S.A.* **82 D5** 45 20N 117 30W
Walls, *U.K.* **12 A7** 60 14N 1 33W
Wallula, *U.S.A.* **82 C4** 46 5N 118 54W
Wallumbilla, *Australia* **63 D4** 26 33S 149 9 E
Walmsley, L., *Canada* **73 A7** 63 25N 108 36W
Walney, I. of, *U.K.* **10 C4** 54 6N 3 15W
Walnut Creek, *U.S.A.* **84 H4** 37 54N 122 4W
Walnut Ridge, *U.S.A.* **81 G9** 36 4N 90 57W
Walpole, *Australia* **61 F2** 34 58S 116 44 E
Walpole, *U.S.A.* **79 D13** 42 9N 71 15W
Walsall, *U.K.* **11 E6** 52 35N 1 58W
Walsenburg, *U.S.A.* **81 G2** 37 38N 104 47W
Walsh, *U.S.A.* **81 G3** 37 23N 102 17W
Walsh →, *Australia* **62 B3** 16 31S 143 42 E
Walterboro, *U.S.A.* **77 J5** 32 55N 80 40W
Walters, *U.S.A.* **81 H5** 34 22N 98 19W
Waltham, *U.S.A.* **79 D13** 42 23N 71 14W
Waltman, *U.S.A.* **82 E10** 43 4N 107 12W
Walton, *U.S.A.* **79 D9** 42 10N 75 8W
Walton-on-the-Naze, *U.K.* **11 F9** 51 51N 1 17 E
Walvis Bay, *Namibia* **56 C1** 23 0S 14 28 E
Walvisbaai = Walvis Bay, *Namibia* **56 C1** 23 0S 14 28 E
Wamba, *Dem. Rep. of the Congo* **54 B2** 2 10N 27 57 E
Wamba, *Kenya* **54 B4** 0 58N 37 19 E
Wamego, *U.S.A.* **80 F6** 39 12N 96 18W
Wamena, *Indonesia* **37 E9** 4 4S 138 57 E
Wamsutter, *U.S.A.* **82 F9** 41 40N 107 58W
Wamulan, *Indonesia* **37 E7** 3 27S 126 7 E
Wan Xian, *China* **34 E8** 38 47N 115 7 E
Wana, *Pakistan* **42 C3** 32 20N 69 32 E
Wanaaring, *Australia* **63 D3** 29 38S 144 9 E
Wanaka, *N.Z.* **59 L2** 44 42S 169 9 E
Wanaka L., *N.Z.* **59 L2** 44 33S 169 7 E
Wanapitei L., *Canada* **70 C3** 46 45N 80 40W
Wandel Sea = McKinley Sea, *Arctic* **4 A7** 82 0N 0 0W
Wanderer, *Zimbabwe* **55 F3** 19 36S 30 1 E
Wandhari, *Pakistan* **42 F2** 27 42N 66 48 E
Wandoan, *Australia* **63 D4** 26 5S 149 55 E
Wanfu, *China* **35 D12** 40 8N 122 38 E
Wang →, *Thailand* **38 D2** 17 8N 99 2 E
Wang Noi, *Thailand* **38 E3** 14 13N 100 44 E
Wang Saphung, *Thailand* **38 D3** 17 18N 101 46 E
Wang Thong, *Thailand* **38 D3** 16 50N 100 26 E
Wanga, *Dem. Rep. of the Congo* **54 B2** 2 58N 29 12 E
Wangal, *Indonesia* **37 F8** 6 8S 134 9 E
Wanganui, *N.Z.* **59 H5** 39 56S 175 3 E
Wangary, *Australia* **63 E2** 34 35S 135 29 E
Wangdu, *China* **34 E8** 38 40N 115 7 E
Wangerooge, *Germany* **16 B4** 53 47N 7 54 E
Wangi, *Kenya* **54 C5** 1 58S 40 58 E
Wangiwangi, *Indonesia* **37 F6** 5 22S 123 37 E
Wangqing, *China* **35 C15** 43 12N 129 42 E
Wankaner, *India* **42 H4** 22 35N 71 0 E
Wanless, *Canada* **73 C8** 54 11N 101 21W
Wanning, *China* **38 C8** 18 48N 110 22 E
Wanon Niwat, *Thailand* **38 D4** 17 38N 103 46 E
Wanquan, *China* **34 D8** 40 50N 114 40 E
Wanrong, *China* **34 G6** 35 25N 110 50 E
Wantage, *U.K.* **11 F6** 51 35N 1 25W
Wapakoneta, *U.S.A.* **76 E3** 40 34N 84 12W
Wapato, *U.S.A.* **82 C3** 46 27N 120 25W
Wapawekka L., *Canada* **73 C8** 54 55N 104 40W
Wapikopa L., *Canada* **70 B2** 52 56N 87 53W
Wapiti →, *Canada* **72 B5** 55 5N 118 18W
Wappingers Falls, *U.S.A.* **79 E11** 41 36N 73 55W
Wapsipinicon →, *U.S.A.* **80 E9** 41 44N 90 19W
Warangal, *India* **40 L11** 17 58N 79 35 E
Waraseoni, *India* **43 J9** 21 45N 80 2 E
Waratah, *Australia* **62 G4** 41 30S 145 30 E
Warburton, *Australia* **61 E4** 26 8S 126 35 E
Warburton Ra., *Australia* **61 E4** 25 55S 126 28 E
Ward, *N.Z.* **59 J5** 41 49S 174 11 E
Ward →, *Australia* **63 D4** 26 28S 146 6 E
Ward Mt., *U.S.A.* **84 H8** 37 12N 118 54W
Warden, *S. Africa* **57 D4** 27 50S 29 0 E
Wardha, *India* **40 J11** 20 45N 78 39 E
Wardha →, *India* **40 K11** 19 57N 79 11 E
Ware, *Canada* **72 B3** 57 26N 125 41W
Ware, *U.S.A.* **79 D12** 42 16N 72 14W
Waregem, *Belgium* **15 D3** 50 53N 3 27 E
Wareham, *U.S.A.* **79 E14** 41 46N 70 43W
Waremme, *Belgium* **15 D5** 50 43N 5 15 E
Warialda, *Australia* **63 D5** 29 29S 150 33 E
Wariap, *Indonesia* **37 E8** 1 30S 134 5 E
Warin Chamrap, *Thailand* **38 E5** 15 12N 104 53 E
Warkopi, *Indonesia* **37 E8** 1 12S 134 9 E
Warm Springs, *U.S.A.* **83 G5** 38 10N 116 20W
Warman, *Canada* **73 C7** 52 19N 106 30W
Warmbad, *Namibia* **56 D2** 28 25S 18 42 E
Warmbad, *S. Africa* **57 C4** 24 51S 28 19 E
Warminster, *U.K.* **11 F5** 51 12N 2 10W
Warminster, *U.S.A.* **79 F9** 40 12N 75 6W
Warner Mts., *U.S.A.* **82 F3** 41 40N 120 15W
Warner Robins, *U.S.A.* **77 J4** 32 37N 83 36W
Waroona, *Australia* **61 F2** 32 50S 115 58 E
Warrego →, *Australia* **63 E4** 30 24S 145 21 E
Warrego Ra., *Australia* **62 C4** 24 58S 146 0 E
Warren, *Ark., U.S.A.* **81 J8** 33 37N 92 4W
Warren, *Mich., U.S.A.* **76 D4** 42 30N 83 0W
Warren, *Minn., U.S.A.* **80 A6** 48 12N 96 46W
Warren, *Ohio, U.S.A.* **78 E4** 41 14N 80 49W
Warren, *Pa., U.S.A.* **78 E5** 41 51N 79 9W
Warrenpoint, *U.K.* **13 B5** 54 6N 6 15W
Warrensburg, *Mo., U.S.A.* **80 F8** 38 46N 93 44W
Warrensburg, *N.Y., U.S.A.* **79 C11** 43 29N 73 46W
Warrenton, *S. Africa* **56 D3** 28 9S 24 47 E
Warrenton, *U.S.A.* **84 D3** 46 10N 123 56W
Warri, *Nigeria* **50 G7** 5 30N 5 41 E
Warrina, *Australia* **63 D2** 28 12S 135 50 E
Warrington, *U.K.* **10 D5** 53 24N 2 35W
Warrington, *U.S.A.* **77 K2** 30 23N 87 17W
Warrington □, *U.K.* **10 D5** 53 24N 2 35W
Warroad, *U.S.A.* **80 A7** 48 54N 95 19W
Warruwi, *Australia* **62 A1** 11 36S 133 20 E
Warsa, *Indonesia* **37 E9** 0 47S 135 55 E
Warsak Dam, *Pakistan* **42 B4** 34 11N 71 19 E
Warsaw = Warszawa, *Poland* **17 B11** 52 13N 21 0 E
Warsaw, *Ind., U.S.A.* **76 E3** 41 14N 85 51W
Warsaw, *N.Y., U.S.A.* **78 D6** 42 45N 78 8W
Warsaw, *Ohio, U.S.A.* **78 F3** 40 20N 82 0W
Warszawa, *Poland* **17 B11** 52 13N 21 0 E
Warta →, *Poland* **16 B8** 52 35N 14 39 E
Warthe = Warta →, *Poland* **16 B8** 52 35N 14 39 E
Waru, *Indonesia* **37 E8** 3 30S 130 36 E
Warwick, *Australia* **63 D5** 28 10S 152 1 E
Warwick, *U.K.* **11 E6** 52 18N 1 35W
Warwick, *N.Y., U.S.A.* **79 E10** 41 16N 74 22W
Warwick, *R.I., U.S.A.* **79 E13** 41 42N 71 28W
Warwickshire □, *U.K.* **11 E6** 52 14N 1 38W
Wasaga Beach, *Canada* **78 B4** 44 31N 80 1W
Wasagaming, *Canada* **73 C9** 50 39N 99 58W
Wasatch Ra., *U.S.A.* **82 F8** 40 30N 111 15W
Wasbank, *S. Africa* **57 D5** 28 15S 30 9 E
Wasco, *Calif., U.S.A.* **85 K7** 35 36N 119 20W
Wasco, *Oreg., U.S.A.* **82 D3** 45 36N 120 42W
Waseca, *U.S.A.* **80 C8** 44 5N 93 30W
Wasekamio L., *Canada* **73 B7** 56 45N 108 45W
Wash, The, *U.K.* **10 E8** 52 58N 0 20 E
Washago, *Canada* **78 B5** 44 45N 79 20W
Washburn, *N. Dak., U.S.A.* **80 B4** 47 17N 101 2W
Washburn, *Wis., U.S.A.* **80 B9** 46 40N 90 54W
Washim, *India* **40 J10** 20 3N 77 0 E
Washington, *U.K.* **10 C6** 54 55N 1 30W
Washington, *D.C., U.S.A.* **76 F7** 38 54N 77 2W
Washington, *Ga., U.S.A.* **77 J4** 33 44N 82 44W
Washington, *Ind., U.S.A.* **76 F2** 38 40N 87 10W
Washington, *Iowa, U.S.A.* **80 E9** 41 18N 91 42W
Washington, *Mo., U.S.A.* **80 F9** 38 33N 91 1W
Washington, *N.C., U.S.A.* **77 H7** 35 33N 77 3W
Washington, *N.J., U.S.A.* **79 F10** 40 46N 74 59W
Washington, *Pa., U.S.A.* **78 F4** 40 10N 80 15W
Washington, *Utah, U.S.A.* **83 H7** 37 8N 113 31W
Washington □, *U.S.A.* **82 C3** 47 30N 120 30W
Washington, Mt., *U.S.A.* **79 B13** 44 16N 71 18W
Washington Court House, *U.S.A.* **76 F4** 39 32N 83 26W
Washington I., *U.S.A.* **76 C2** 45 23N 86 54W
Washougal, *U.S.A.* **84 E4** 45 35N 122 21W
Wasian, *Indonesia* **37 E8** 1 47S 133 19 E
Wasilla, *U.S.A.* **68 B5** 61 35N 149 26W
Wasior, *Indonesia* **37 E8** 2 43S 134 30 E
Waskaganish, *Canada* **70 B4** 51 30N 78 40W
Waskaiowaka, L., *Canada* **73 B9** 56 33N 96 23W
Waskesiu Lake, *Canada* **73 C7** 53 55N 106 5W
Wasserkuppe, *Germany* **16 C5** 50 29N 9 55 E
Waswanipi, *Canada* **70 C4** 49 40N 76 29W
Waswanipi, L., *Canada* **70 C4** 49 35N 76 40W
Watampone, *Indonesia* **37 E6** 4 29S 120 25 E
Water Park Pt., *Australia* **62 C5** 22 56S 150 47 E
Water Valley, *U.S.A.* **81 H10** 34 10N 89 38W
Waterberge, *S. Africa* **57 C4** 24 10S 28 0 E
Waterbury, *Conn., U.S.A.* **79 E11** 41 33N 73 3W
Waterbury, *Vt., U.S.A.* **79 B12** 44 20N 72 46W
Waterbury L., *Canada* **73 B8** 58 10N 104 22W
Waterdown, *Canada* **78 C5** 43 20N 79 53W
Waterford, *Canada* **78 D4** 42 56N 80 17W
Waterford, *Ireland* **13 D4** 52 15N 7 8W
Waterford, *Calif., U.S.A.* **84 H6** 37 38N 120 46W
Waterford, *Pa., U.S.A.* **78 E5** 41 57N 79 59W
Waterford □, *Ireland* **13 D4** 52 10N 7 40W
Waterford Harbour, *Ireland* **13 D5** 52 8N 6 58W
Waterhen L., *Canada* **73 C9** 52 10N 99 40W
Waterloo, *Belgium* **15 D4** 50 43N 4 25 E
Waterloo, *Ont., Canada* **78 C4** 43 30N 80 32W
Waterloo, *Qué., Canada* **79 A12** 45 22N 72 32W
Waterloo, *Ill., U.S.A.* **80 F9** 38 20N 90 9W
Waterloo, *Iowa, U.S.A.* **80 D8** 42 30N 92 21W
Waterloo, *N.Y., U.S.A.* **78 D8** 42 54N 76 52W
Watersmeet, *U.S.A.* **80 B10** 46 16N 89 11W
Waterton Lakes Nat. Park, *U.S.A.* **82 B7** 48 45N 115 0W
Watertown, *Conn., U.S.A.* **79 E11** 41 36N 73 7W
Watertown, *N.Y., U.S.A.* **79 C9** 43 59N 75 55W
Watertown, *S. Dak., U.S.A.* **80 C6** 44 54N 97 7W
Watertown, *Wis., U.S.A.* **80 D10** 43 12N 88 43W
Waterval-Boven, *S. Africa* **57 D5** 25 40S 30 18 E
Waterville, *Canada* **79 A13** 45 16N 71 54W
Waterville, *Maine, U.S.A.* **77 C11** 44 33N 69 38W
Waterville, *N.Y., U.S.A.* **79 D9** 42 56N 75 23W
Waterville, *Pa., U.S.A.* **78 E7** 41 19N 77 21W
Waterville, *Wash., U.S.A.* **82 C3** 47 39N 120 4W
Watervliet, *U.S.A.* **79 D11** 42 44N 73 42W
Wates, *Indonesia* **37 G14** 7 51S 110 10 E
Watford, *Canada* **78 D3** 42 57N 81 53W
Watford, *U.K.* **11 F7** 51 40N 0 24W
Watford City, *U.S.A.* **80 B3** 47 48N 103 17W
Wathaman →, *Canada* **73 B8** 57 16N 102 59W
Wathaman L., *Canada* **73 B8** 56 58N 103 44W
Watheroo, *Australia* **61 F2** 30 15S 116 0 E
Wating, *China* **34 G4** 35 40N 106 38 E
Watkins Glen, *U.S.A.* **78 D8** 42 23N 76 52W
Watling I. = San Salvador I., *Bahamas* **89 B5** 24 0N 74 40W
Watonga, *U.S.A.* **81 H5** 35 51N 98 25W
Watrous, *Canada* **73 C7** 51 40N 105 25W
Watrous, *U.S.A.* **81 H2** 35 48N 104 59W
Watsa, *Dem. Rep. of the Congo* **54 B2** 3 4N 29 30 E
Watseka, *U.S.A.* **76 E2** 40 47N 87 44W
Watson, *Australia* **61 F5** 30 29S 131 31 E
Watson, *Canada* **73 C8** 52 10N 104 30W
Watson Lake, *Canada* **72 A3** 60 6N 128 49W
Watsontown, *U.S.A.* **78 E8** 41 5N 76 52W
Watsonville, *U.S.A.* **84 J5** 36 55N 121 45W
Wattiwarriganna Cr. →, *Australia* **63 D2** 28 57S 136 10 E
Watuata = Batuata, *Indonesia* **37 F6** 6 12S 122 42 E
Watubela, Kepulauan, *Indonesia* **37 E8** 4 28S 131 35 E
Watubela Is. = Watubela, Kepulauan, *Indonesia* **37 E8** 4 28S 131 35 E
Wau = Wâw, *Sudan* **51 G11** 7 45N 28 1 E
Waubamik, *Canada* **78 A4** 45 27N 80 1W
Waubay, *U.S.A.* **80 C6** 45 20N 97 18W
Wauchope, *Australia* **62 C1** 20 36S 134 15 E
Wauchula, *U.S.A.* **77 M5** 27 33N 81 49W
Waukarlycarly, L., *Australia* **60 D3** 21 18S 121 56 E
Waukegan, *U.S.A.* **76 D2** 42 22N 87 50W
Waukesha, *U.S.A.* **76 D1** 43 1N 88 14W
Waukon, *U.S.A.* **80 D9** 43 16N 91 29W
Waupaca, *U.S.A.* **80 C10** 44 21N 89 5W
Waupun, *U.S.A.* **80 D10** 43 38N 88 44W
Waurika, *U.S.A.* **81 H6** 34 10N 98 0W
Wausau, *U.S.A.* **80 C10** 44 58N 89 38W
Wautoma, *U.S.A.* **80 C10** 44 4N 89 18W
Wauwatosa, *U.S.A.* **76 D2** 43 3N 88 0W
Waveney →, *U.K.* **11 E9** 52 35N 1 39 E
Waverley, *N.Z.* **59 H5** 39 46S 174 37 E
Waverly, *Iowa, U.S.A.* **80 D8** 42 44N 92 29W
Waverly, *N.Y., U.S.A.* **79 E8** 42 1N 76 32W
Wavre, *Belgium* **15 D4** 50 43N 4 38 E
Wâw, *Sudan* **51 G11** 7 45N 28 1 E
Wāw al Kabīr, *Libya* **51 C9** 25 20N 16 43 E
Wawa, *Canada* **70 C3** 47 59N 84 47W
Wawanesa, *Canada* **73 D9** 49 36N 99 40W
Wawona, *U.S.A.* **84 H7** 37 32N 119 39W
Waxahachie, *U.S.A.* **81 J6** 32 24N 96 51W
Way, L., *Australia* **61 E3** 26 45S 120 16 E
Waycross, *U.S.A.* **77 K4** 31 13N 82 21W
Wayland, *U.S.A.* **78 D7** 42 34N 77 35W
Wayne, *Nebr., U.S.A.* **80 D6** 42 14N 97 1W
Wayne, *W. Va., U.S.A.* **76 F4** 38 13N 82 27W
Waynesboro, *Ga., U.S.A.* **77 J4** 33 6N 82 1W
Waynesboro, *Miss., U.S.A.* **77 K1** 31 40N 88 39W
Waynesboro, *Pa., U.S.A.* **76 F7** 39 45N 77 35W
Waynesboro, *Va., U.S.A.* **76 F6** 38 4N 78 53W
Waynesburg, *U.S.A.* **76 F5** 39 54N 80 11W
Waynesville, *U.S.A.* **77 H4** 35 28N 82 58W
Waynoka, *U.S.A.* **81 G5** 36 35N 98 53W
Wazirabad, *Pakistan* **42 C6** 32 30N 74 8 E
We, *Indonesia* **36 C1** 5 51N 95 18 E
Weald, The, *U.K.* **11 F8** 51 4N 0 20 E
Wear →, *U.K.* **10 C6** 54 55N 1 23W
Weatherford, *Okla., U.S.A.* **81 H5** 35 32N 98 43W
Weatherford, *Tex., U.S.A.* **81 J6** 32 46N 97 48W
Weaverville, *U.S.A.* **82 F2** 40 44N 122 56W
Webb City, *U.S.A.* **81 G7** 37 9N 94 28W
Webequie, *Canada* **70 B2** 52 59N 87 21W
Webster, *Mass., U.S.A.* **79 D13** 42 3N 71 53W
Webster, *N.Y., U.S.A.* **78 C7** 43 13N 77 26W
Webster, *S. Dak., U.S.A.* **80 C6** 45 20N 97 31W
Webster City, *U.S.A.* **80 D8** 42 28N 93 49W
Webster Springs, *U.S.A.* **76 F5** 38 29N 80 25W
Weda, *Indonesia* **37 D7** 0 21N 127 50 E
Weda, Teluk, *Indonesia* **37 D7** 0 20N 128 0 E
Weddell I., *Falk. Is.* **96 G4** 51 50S 61 0W
Weddell Sea, *Antarctica* **5 D1** 72 30S 40 0W
Wedgeport, *Canada* **71 D6** 43 44N 65 59W
Wedza, *Zimbabwe* **55 F3** 18 40S 31 33 E
Wee Waa, *Australia* **63 E4** 30 11S 149 26 E
Weed, *U.S.A.* **82 F2** 41 25N 122 23W
Weed Heights, *U.S.A.* **84 G7** 38 59N 119 13W
Weedsport, *U.S.A.* **79 C8** 43 3N 76 35W
Weedville, *U.S.A.* **78 E6** 41 17N 78 30W
Weenen, *S. Africa* **57 D5** 28 48S 30 7 E
Weert, *Neths.* **15 C5** 51 15N 5 43 E
Wei He →, *Hebei, China* **34 F8** 36 10N 115 45 E
Wei He →, *Shaanxi, China* **34 G6** 34 38N 110 15 E
Weichang, *China* **35 D9** 41 58N 117 49 E
Weichuan, *China* **34 G7** 34 20N 113 59 E
Weiden, *Germany* **16 D7** 49 41N 12 10 E
Weifang, *China* **35 F10** 36 44N 119 7 E
Weihai, *China* **35 F12** 37 30N 122 6 E
Weimar, *Germany* **16 C6** 50 58N 11 19 E
Weinan, *China* **34 G5** 34 31N 109 29 E
Weipa, *Australia* **62 A3** 12 40S 141 50 E
Weir →, *Australia* **63 D4** 28 20S 149 50 E
Weir →, *Canada* **73 B10** 56 54N 93 21W
Weir River, *Canada* **73 B10** 56 49N 94 6W
Weirton, *U.S.A.* **78 F4** 40 24N 80 35W
Weiser, *U.S.A.* **82 D5** 44 10N 117 0W
Weishan, *China* **35 G9** 34 47N 117 5 E
Weiyuan, *China* **34 G3** 35 7N 104 10 E
Wejherowo, *Poland* **17 A10** 54 35N 18 12 E
Wekusko L., *Canada* **73 C9** 54 40N 99 50W
Welch, *U.S.A.* **76 G5** 37 26N 81 35W
Welkom, *S. Africa* **56 D4** 28 0S 26 46 E
Welland, *Canada* **78 D5** 43 0N 79 15W
Welland →, *U.K.* **11 E7** 52 51N 0 5W
Wellesley Is., *Australia* **62 B2** 16 42S 139 30 E
Wellingborough, *U.K.* **11 E7** 52 19N 0 41W
Wellington, *Canada* **78 C7** 43 57N 77 20W
Wellington, *N.Z.* **59 J5** 41 19S 174 46 E
Wellington, *S. Africa* **56 E2** 33 38S 19 1 E
Wellington, *Somst., U.K.* **11 G4** 50 58N 3 13W
Wellington, *Telford & Wrekin, U.K.* **11 E5** 52 42N 2 30W
Wellington, *Colo., U.S.A.* **80 E2** 40 42N 105 0W
Wellington, *Kans., U.S.A.* **81 G6** 37 16N 97 24W
Wellington, *Nev., U.S.A.* **84 G7** 38 45N 119 23W
Wellington, *Ohio, U.S.A.* **78 E2** 41 10N 82 13W
Wellington, *Tex., U.S.A.* **81 H4** 34 51N 100 13W
Wellington, I., *Chile* **96 F2** 49 30S 75 0W
Wells, *U.K.* **11 F5** 51 13N 2 39W
Wells, *Maine, U.S.A.* **79 C14** 43 20N 70 35W
Wells, *N.Y., U.S.A.* **79 C10** 43 24N 74 17W
Wells, *Nev., U.S.A.* **82 F6** 41 7N 114 58W
Wells, L., *Australia* **61 E3** 26 44S 123 15 E
Wells, Mt., *Australia* **60 C4** 17 25S 127 8 E
Wells Gray Prov. Park, *Canada* **72 C4** 52 30N 120 15W
Wells-next-the-Sea, *U.K.* **10 E8** 52 57N 0 51 E
Wells River, *U.S.A.* **79 B12** 44 9N 72 4W
Wellsboro, *U.S.A.* **78 E7** 41 45N 77 18W
Wellsburg, *U.S.A.* **78 F4** 40 16N 80 37W
Wellsville, *N.Y., U.S.A.* **78 D7** 42 7N 77 57W
Wellsville, *Ohio, U.S.A.* **78 F4** 40 36N 80 39W
Wellsville, *Utah, U.S.A.* **82 F8** 41 38N 111 56W
Wellton, *U.S.A.* **83 K6** 32 40N 114 8W
Wels, *Austria* **16 D8** 48 9N 14 1 E
Welshpool, *U.K.* **11 E4** 52 39N 3 8W
Welwyn Garden City, *U.K.* **11 F7** 51 48N 0 12W
Wem, *U.K.* **10 E5** 52 52N 2 44W
Wembere →, *Tanzania* **54 C3** 4 10S 34 15 E
Wemindji, *Canada* **70 B4** 53 0N 78 49W
Wen Xian, *China* **34 G7** 34 55N 113 5 E
Wenatchee, *U.S.A.* **82 C3** 47 25N 120 19W
Wenchang, *China* **38 C8** 19 38N 110 42 E
Wenchi, *Ghana* **50 G5** 7 46N 2 8W
Wenchow = Wenzhou, *China* **33 D7** 28 0N 120 38 E
Wenden, *U.S.A.* **85 M13** 33 49N 113 33W
Wendeng, *China* **35 F12** 37 15N 122 5 E
Wendesi, *Indonesia* **37 E8** 2 30S 134 17 E
Wendover, *U.S.A.* **82 F6** 40 44N 114 2W
Wenlock →, *Australia* **62 A3** 12 2S 141 55 E
Wenshan, *China* **32 D5** 23 20N 104 18 E
Wenshang, *China* **34 G9** 35 45N 116 30 E
Wenshui, *China* **34 F7** 37 26N 112 1 E
Wensleydale, *U.K.* **10 C6** 54 17N 2 0W
Wensu, *China* **32 B3** 41 15N 80 10 E
Wensum →, *U.K.* **10 E8** 52 40N 1 15 E
Wentzel L., *Canada* **72 B6** 59 2N 114 28W
Wenut, *Indonesia* **37 E8** 3 11S 133 19 E
Wenxi, *China* **34 G6** 35 20N 111 10 E
Wenxian, *China* **34 H3** 32 43N 104 36 E
Wenzhou, *China* **33 D7** 28 0N 120 38 E
Weott, *U.S.A.* **82 F2** 40 20N 123 55W
Wepener, *S. Africa* **56 D4** 29 42S 27 3 E
Werda, *Botswana* **56 D3** 25 24S 23 15 E
Weri, *Indonesia* **37 E8** 3 10S 132 38 E
Werra →, *Germany* **16 C5** 51 24N 9 39 E
Weser →, *Germany* **16 B5** 53 36N 8 28 E
Wesiri, *Indonesia* **37 F7** 7 30S 126 30 E
Weslemkoon L., *Canada* **78 A7** 45 2N 77 25W
Wesleyville, *Canada* **71 C9** 49 8N 53 36W
Wesleyville, *U.S.A.* **78 D4** 42 9N 80 0W
Wessel, C., *Australia* **62 A2** 10 59S 136 46 E
Wessel Is., *Australia* **62 A2** 11 10S 136 45 E
Wessington Springs, *U.S.A.* **80 C5** 44 5N 98 34W
West, *U.S.A.* **81 K6** 31 48N 97 6W
West →, *U.S.A.* **79 D12** 42 52N 72 33W
West Baines →, *Australia* **60 C4** 15 38S 129 59 E
West Bank □, *Asia* **47 C4** 32 6N 35 13 E
West Bend, *U.S.A.* **76 D1** 43 25N 88 11W
West Bengal □, *India* **43 H13** 23 0N 88 0 E
West Berkshire □, *U.K.* **11 F6** 51 25N 1 17W
West Beskids = Západné Beskydy, *Europe* **17 D10** 49 30N 19 0 E

West Branch

Yevpatoriya, *Ukraine* **25 E5** 45 15N 33 20 E
Yeysk, *Russia* **25 E6** 46 40N 38 12 E
Yezd = Yazd, *Iran* **45 D7** 31 55N 54 27 E
Yhati, *Paraguay* **94 B4** 25 45S 56 35W
Yhú, *Paraguay* **95 B4** 25 0S 56 0W
Yi →, *Uruguay* **94 C4** 33 7S 57 8W
Yi 'Allaq, G., *Egypt* **47 E2** 30 22N 33 32 E
Yi He →, *China* **35 G10** 34 10N 118 8 E
Yi Xian, *Hebei, China* **34 E8** 39 20N 115 30 E
Yi Xian, *Liaoning, China* **35 D11** 41 30N 121 22 E
Yialiás →, *Cyprus* **23 D12** 35 9N 33 44 E
Yialousa, *Cyprus* **23 D13** 35 32N 34 10 E
Yianisádhes, *Greece* **23 D8** 35 20N 26 10 E
Yiannitsa, *Greece* **21 D10** 40 46N 22 24 E
Yibin, *China* **32 D5** 28 45N 104 32 E
Yichang, *China* **33 C6** 30 40N 111 20 E
Yicheng, *China* **34 G6** 35 42N 111 40 E
Yichuan, *China* **34 F6** 36 2N 110 10 E
Yichun, *China* **33 B7** 47 44N 128 52 E
Yidu, *China* **35 F10** 36 43N 118 28 E
Yijun, *China* **34 G5** 35 28N 109 8 E
Yıldız Dağları, *Turkey* **21 D12** 41 48N 27 36 E
Yilehuli Shan, *China* **33 A7** 51 20N 124 20 E
Yimianpo, *China* **35 B15** 45 7N 128 2 E
Yinchuan, *China* **34 E4** 38 30N 106 15 E
Yindarlgooda, L., *Australia* **61 F3** 30 40S 121 52 E
Ying He →, *China* **34 H9** 32 30N 116 30 E
Ying Xian, *China* **34 E7** 39 32N 113 10 E
Yingkou, *China* **35 D12** 40 37N 122 18 E
Yining, *China* **26 E9** 43 58N 81 10 E
Yinmabin, *Burma* **41 H19** 22 10N 94 55 E
Yiofiros →, *Greece* **23 D7** 35 20N 25 6 E
Yirga Alem, *Ethiopia* **46 F2** 6 48N 38 22 E
Yirrkala, *Australia* **62 A2** 12 14S 136 56 E
Yishan, *China* **32 D5** 24 28N 108 38 E
Yishui, *China* **35 G10** 35 47N 118 30 E
Yíthion, *Greece* **21 F10** 36 46N 22 34 E
Yitong, *China* **35 C13** 43 13N 125 20 E
Yiyang, *Henan, China* **34 G7** 34 27N 112 10 E
Yiyang, *Hunan, China* **33 D6** 28 35N 112 18 E
Yli-Kitka, *Finland* **8 C23** 66 8N 28 30 E
Ylitornio, *Finland* **8 C20** 66 19N 23 39 E
Ylivieska, *Finland* **8 D21** 64 4N 24 28 E
Yoakum, *U.S.A.* **81 L6** 29 17N 97 9W
Yog Pt., *Phil.* **37 B6** 14 6N 124 12 E
Yogyakarta, *Indonesia* **36 F4** 7 49S 110 22 E
Yoho Nat. Park, *Canada* **72 C5** 51 25N 116 30W
Yojoa, L. de, *Honduras* **88 D2** 14 53N 88 0W
Yŏju, *S. Korea* **35 F14** 37 20N 127 35 E
Yokadouma, *Cameroon* **52 D2** 3 26N 14 55 E
Yokkaichi, *Japan* **31 G8** 34 55N 136 38 E
Yoko, *Cameroon* **52 C2** 5 32N 12 20 E
Yokohama, *Japan* **31 G9** 35 27N 139 28 E
Yokosuka, *Japan* **31 G9** 35 20N 139 40 E
Yokote, *Japan* **30 E10** 39 20N 140 30 E
Yola, *Nigeria* **51 G8** 9 10N 12 29 E
Yolaina, Cordillera de, *Nic.* **88 D3** 11 30N 84 0W
Yoloten, *Turkmenistan* **45 B9** 37 18N 62 21 E
Yom →, *Thailand* **36 A2** 15 35N 100 1 E
Yonago, *Japan* **31 G6** 35 25N 133 19 E
Yonaguni-Jima, *Japan* **31 M1** 24 27N 123 0 E
Yŏnan, *N. Korea* **35 F14** 37 55N 126 11 E
Yonezawa, *Japan* **30 F10** 37 57N 140 4 E
Yong Peng, *Malaysia* **39 L4** 2 0N 103 3 E
Yong Sata, *Thailand* **39 J2** 7 8N 99 41 E
Yongamp'o, *N. Korea* **35 E13** 39 56N 124 23 E
Yongcheng, *China* **34 H9** 33 55N 116 20 E
Yŏngch'ŏn, *S. Korea* **35 G15** 35 58N 128 56 E
Yongdeng, *China* **34 F2** 36 38N 103 25 E
Yŏngdŏk, *S. Korea* **35 F15** 36 24N 129 22 E
Yŏngdŭngpo, *S. Korea* **35 F14** 37 31N 126 54 E
Yonghe, *China* **34 F6** 36 46N 110 38 E
Yŏnghŭng, *N. Korea* **35 E14** 39 31N 127 18 E
Yongji, *China* **34 G6** 34 52N 110 28 E
Yŏngju, *S. Korea* **35 F15** 36 50N 128 40 E
Yongnian, *China* **34 F8** 36 47N 114 29 E
Yongning, *China* **34 E4** 38 15N 106 14 E
Yongqing, *China* **34 E9** 39 25N 116 28 E
Yŏngwŏl, *S. Korea* **35 F15** 37 11N 128 28 E
Yonibana, *S. Leone* **50 G3** 8 30N 12 19W
Yonkers, *U.S.A.* **79 F11** 40 56N 73 54W
Yonne →, *France* **18 B5** 48 23N 2 58 E
York, *Australia* **61 F2** 31 52S 116 47 E
York, *U.K.* **10 D6** 53 58N 1 6W
York, *Ala., U.S.A.* **81 J10** 32 29N 88 18W
York, *Nebr., U.S.A.* **80 E6** 40 52N 97 36W
York, *Pa., U.S.A.* **76 F7** 39 58N 76 44W
York, C., *Australia* **62 A3** 10 42S 142 31 E
York, City of □, *U.K.* **10 D6** 53 58N 1 6W
York, Kap, *Greenland* **4 B4** 75 55N 66 25W
York, Vale of, *U.K.* **10 C6** 54 15N 1 25W
York Haven, *U.S.A.* **78 F8** 40 7N 76 46W
York Sd., *Australia* **60 C4** 15 0S 125 5 E
Yorkshire Wolds, *U.K.* **10 C7** 54 8N 0 31W
Yorkton, *Canada* **73 C8** 51 11N 102 28W
Yorkville, *U.S.A.* **84 G3** 38 52N 123 13W
Yoro, *Honduras* **88 C2** 15 9N 87 7W
Yoron-Jima, *Japan* **31 L4** 27 2N 128 26 E
Yos Sudarso, Pulau = Dolak, Pulau, *Indonesia* **37 F9** 8 0S 138 30 E
Yosemite National Park, *U.S.A.* **84 H7** 37 45N 119 40W
Yosemite Village, *U.S.A.* **84 H7** 37 45N 119 35W
Yoshkar Ola, *Russia* **24 C8** 56 38N 47 55 E
Yŏsu, *S. Korea* **35 G14** 34 47N 127 45 E
Yotvata, *Israel* **47 F4** 29 55N 35 2 E
Youbou, *Canada* **84 B2** 48 53N 124 13W
Youghal, *Ireland* **13 E4** 51 56N 7 52W
Youghal B., *Ireland* **13 E4** 51 55N 7 49W
Young, *Canada* **73 C7** 51 47N 105 45W
Young, *Uruguay* **94 C4** 32 44S 57 36W
Youngstown, *Canada* **73 C6** 51 35N 111 10W
Youngstown, *N.Y., U.S.A.* **78 C5** 43 15N 79 3W
Youngstown, *Ohio, U.S.A.* **78 E4** 41 6N 80 39W
Youngsville, *U.S.A.* **78 E5** 41 51N 79 19W
Youngwood, *U.S.A.* **78 F5** 40 14N 79 34W
Youyu, *China* **34 D7** 40 10N 112 20 E
Yozgat, *Turkey* **25 G5** 39 51N 34 47 E
Ypané →, *Paraguay* **94 A4** 23 29S 57 19W
Ypres = Ieper, *Belgium* **15 D2** 50 51N 2 53 E
Yreka, *U.S.A.* **82 F2** 41 44N 122 38W
Ystad, *Sweden* **9 J15** 55 26N 13 50 E
Ysyk-Köl, *Kyrgyzstan* **26 E8** 42 25N 77 15 E
Ythan →, *U.K.* **12 D7** 57 19N 1 59W
Ytyk-Kyuyel, *Russia* **27 C14** 62 30N 133 45 E
Yu Jiang →, *China* **33 D6** 23 22N 110 3 E
Yu Xian = Yuzhou, *China* **34 G7** 34 10N 113 28 E
Yu Xian, *Hebei, China* **34 E8** 39 50N 114 35 E
Yu Xian, *Shanxi, China* **34 E7** 38 5N 113 20 E
Yuan Jiang →, *China* **33 D6** 28 55N 111 50 E
Yuanqu, *China* **34 G6** 35 18N 111 40 E
Yuanyang, *China* **34 G7** 35 3N 113 58 E
Yuba →, *U.S.A.* **84 F5** 39 8N 121 36W
Yuba City, *U.S.A.* **84 F5** 39 8N 121 37W
Yūbari, *Japan* **30 C10** 43 4N 141 59 E
Yūbetsu, *Japan* **30 B11** 44 13N 143 50 E
Yucatán □, *Mexico* **87 C7** 21 30N 86 30W
Yucatán, Canal de, *Caribbean* **88 B2** 22 0N 86 30W
Yucatán, Península de, *Mexico* **66 H11** 19 30N 89 0W
Yucatán Basin, *Cent. Amer.* **66 H11** 19 0N 86 0W
Yucatan Str. = Yucatán, Canal de, *Caribbean* **88 B2** 22 0N 86 30W
Yucca, *U.S.A.* **85 L12** 34 52N 114 9W
Yucca Valley, *U.S.A.* **85 L10** 34 8N 116 27W
Yucheng, *China* **34 F9** 36 55N 116 32 E
Yuci, *China* **34 F7** 37 42N 112 46 E
Yuendumu, *Australia* **60 D5** 22 16S 131 49 E
Yugoslavia ■, *Europe* **21 B9** 43 20N 20 0 E
Yukon →, *U.S.A.* **68 B3** 62 32N 163 54W
Yukon Territory □, *Canada* **68 B6** 63 0N 135 0W
Yukta, *Russia* **27 C11** 63 26N 105 42 E
Yukuhashi, *Japan* **31 H5** 33 44N 130 59 E
Yulara, *Australia* **61 E5** 25 10S 130 55 E
Yule →, *Australia* **60 D2** 20 41S 118 17 E
Yuleba, *Australia* **63 D4** 26 37S 149 24 E
Yülin, *Hainan, China* **39 C7** 18 10N 109 31 E
Yulin, *Shaanxi, China* **34 E5** 38 20N 109 30 E
Yuma, *Ariz., U.S.A.* **85 N12** 32 43N 114 37W
Yuma, *Colo., U.S.A.* **80 E3** 40 8N 102 43W
Yuma, B. de, *Dom. Rep.* **89 C6** 18 20N 68 35W
Yumbe, *Uganda* **54 B3** 3 28N 31 15 E
Yumbi, *Dem. Rep. of the Congo* **54 C2** 1 12S 26 15 E
Yumen, *China* **32 C4** 39 50N 97 30 E
Yun Ho →, *China* **35 E9** 39 10N 117 10 E
Yuna, *Australia* **61 E2** 28 20S 115 0 E
Yuncheng, *Henan, China* **34 G8** 35 36N 115 57 E
Yuncheng, *Shanxi, China* **34 G6** 35 2N 111 0 E
Yungas, *Bolivia* **92 G5** 17 0S 66 0W
Yungay, *Chile* **94 D1** 37 10S 72 5W
Yunnan □, *China* **32 D5** 25 0N 102 0 E
Yunxi, *China* **34 H6** 33 0N 110 22 E
Yupyongdong, *N. Korea* **35 D15** 41 49N 128 53 E
Yurga, *Russia* **26 D9** 55 42N 84 51 E
Yurimaguas, *Peru* **92 E3** 5 55S 76 7W
Yuscarán, *Honduras* **88 D2** 13 58N 86 45W
Yushe, *China* **34 F7** 37 4N 112 58 E
Yushu, *Jilin, China* **35 B14** 44 43N 126 38 E
Yushu, *Qinghai, China* **32 C4** 33 5N 96 55 E
Yutai, *China* **34 G9** 35 0N 116 45 E
Yutian, *China* **35 E9** 39 53N 117 45 E
Yuxarı Qarabağ = Nagorno-Karabakh, *Azerbaijan* **25 F8** 39 55N 46 45 E
Yuxi, *China* **32 D5** 24 30N 102 35 E
Yuzawa, *Japan* **30 E10** 39 10N 140 30 E
Yuzhno-Sakhalinsk, *Russia* **27 E15** 46 58N 142 45 E
Yuzhou, *China* **34 G7** 34 10N 113 28 E
Yvetot, *France* **18 B4** 49 37N 0 44 E

Z

Zaanstad, *Neths.* **15 B4** 52 27N 4 50 E
Zāb al Kabīr →, *Iraq* **44 C4** 36 1N 43 24 E
Zāb aş Şagīr →, *Iraq* **44 C4** 35 17N 43 29 E
Zabaykalsk, *Russia* **27 E12** 49 40N 117 25 E
Zābol, *Iran* **45 D9** 31 0N 61 32 E
Zābolī, *Iran* **45 E9** 27 10N 61 35 E
Zabrze, *Poland* **17 C10** 50 18N 18 50 E
Zacapa, *Guatemala* **88 D2** 14 59N 89 31W
Zacapu, *Mexico* **86 D4** 19 50N 101 43W
Zacatecas, *Mexico* **86 C4** 22 49N 102 34W
Zacatecas □, *Mexico* **86 C4** 23 30N 103 0W
Zacatecoluca, *El Salv.* **88 D2** 13 29N 88 51W
Zachary, *U.S.A.* **81 K9** 30 39N 91 9W
Zacoalco, *Mexico* **86 C4** 20 14N 103 33W
Zacualtipán, *Mexico* **87 C5** 20 39N 98 36W
Zadar, *Croatia* **16 F8** 44 8N 15 14 E
Zadetkyi Kyun, *Burma* **39 G1** 10 0N 98 25 E
Zafarqand, *Iran* **45 C7** 33 11N 52 29 E
Zafra, *Spain* **19 C2** 38 26N 6 30W
Żagań, *Poland* **16 C8** 51 39N 15 22 E
Zagaoua, *Chad* **51 E10** 15 30N 22 24 E
Zagazig, *Egypt* **51 B12** 30 40N 31 30 E
Zāgheh, *Iran* **45 C6** 33 30N 48 42 E
Zagorsk = Sergiyev Posad, *Russia* **24 C6** 56 20N 38 10 E
Zagreb, *Croatia* **16 F9** 45 50N 15 58 E
Zāgros, Kūhhā-ye, *Iran* **45 C6** 33 45N 48 5 E
Zagros Mts. = Zāgros, Kūhhā-ye, *Iran* **45 C6** 33 45N 48 5 E
Zāhedān, *Fārs, Iran* **45 D7** 28 46N 53 52 E
Zāhedān, *Sīstān va Balūchestān, Iran* **45 D9** 29 30N 60 50 E
Zahlah, *Lebanon* **47 B4** 33 52N 35 50 E
Zaïre = Congo →, *Africa* **52 F2** 6 4S 12 24 E
Zaječar, *Serbia, Yug.* **21 C10** 43 53N 22 18 E
Zaka, *Zimbabwe* **57 C5** 20 20S 31 29 E
Zakamensk, *Russia* **27 D11** 50 23N 103 17 E
Zakhodnaya Dzvina = Daugava →, *Latvia* **9 H21** 57 4N 24 3 E
Zākhū, *Iraq* **44 B4** 37 10N 42 50 E
Zákinthos, *Greece* **21 F9** 37 47N 20 57 E
Zakopane, *Poland* **17 D10** 49 18N 19 57 E
Zákros, *Greece* **23 D8** 35 6N 26 10 E
Zalaegerszeg, *Hungary* **17 E9** 46 53N 16 47 E
Zalău, *Romania* **17 E12** 47 12N 23 3 E
Zaleshchiki = Zalishchyky, *Ukraine* **17 D13** 48 45N 25 45 E
Zalew Wiślany, *Poland* **17 A10** 54 20N 19 50 E
Zalingei, *Sudan* **51 F10** 12 51N 23 29 E
Zalishchyky, *Ukraine* **17 D13** 48 45N 25 45 E
Zama L., *Canada* **72 B5** 58 45N 119 5W
Zambeke, *Dem. Rep. of the Congo* **54 B2** 2 8N 25 17 E
Zambeze →, *Africa* **55 F4** 18 35S 36 20 E
Zambezi = Zambeze →, *Africa* **55 F4** 18 35S 36 20 E
Zambezi, *Zambia* **53 G4** 13 30S 23 15 E
Zambezia □, *Mozam.* **55 F4** 16 15S 37 30 E
Zambia ■, *Africa* **55 F2** 15 0S 28 0 E
Zamboanga, *Phil.* **37 C6** 6 59N 122 3 E
Zamora, *Mexico* **86 D4** 20 0N 102 21W
Zamora, *Spain* **19 B3** 41 30N 5 45W
Zamość, *Poland* **17 C12** 50 43N 23 15 E
Zandvoort, *Neths.* **15 B4** 52 22N 4 32 E
Zanesville, *U.S.A.* **78 G2** 39 56N 82 1W
Zangābād, *Iran* **44 B5** 38 26N 46 44 E
Zangue →, *Mozam.* **55 F4** 17 50S 35 21 E
Zanjān, *Iran* **45 B6** 36 40N 48 35 E
Zanjān □, *Iran* **45 B6** 37 20N 49 30 E
Zanjān →, *Iran* **45 B6** 37 8N 47 47 E
Zante = Zákinthos, *Greece* **21 F9** 37 47N 20 57 E
Zanthus, *Australia* **61 F3** 31 2S 123 34 E
Zanzibar, *Tanzania* **54 D4** 6 12S 39 12 E
Zaouiet El-Kala = Bordj Omar Driss, *Algeria* **50 C7** 28 10N 6 40 E
Zaouiet Reggâne, *Algeria* **50 C6** 26 32N 0 3 E
Zaozhuang, *China* **35 G9** 34 50N 117 35 E
Zap Suyu = Zāb al Kabīr →, *Iraq* **44 C4** 36 1N 43 24 E
Zapadnaya Dvina = Daugava →, *Latvia* **9 H21** 57 4N 24 3 E
Západné Beskydy, *Europe* **17 D10** 49 30N 19 0 E
Zapala, *Argentina* **96 D2** 39 0S 70 5W
Zapaleri, Cerro, *Bolivia* **94 A2** 22 49S 67 11W
Zapata, *U.S.A.* **81 M5** 26 55N 99 16W
Zapolyarnyy, *Russia* **24 A5** 69 26N 30 51 E
Zaporizhzhya, *Ukraine* **25 E6** 47 50N 35 10 E
Zaporozhye = Zaporizhzhya, *Ukraine* **25 E6** 47 50N 35 10 E
Zara, *Turkey* **44 B3** 39 58N 37 43 E
Zaragoza, *Coahuila, Mexico* **86 B4** 28 30N 101 0W
Zaragoza, *Nuevo León, Mexico* **87 C5** 24 0N 99 46W
Zaragoza, *Spain* **19 B5** 41 39N 0 53W
Zarand, *Kermān, Iran* **45 D8** 30 46N 56 34 E
Zarand, *Markazī, Iran* **45 C6** 35 18N 50 25 E
Zaranj, *Afghan.* **40 D2** 30 55N 61 55 E
Zarasai, *Lithuania* **9 J22** 55 40N 26 20 E
Zarate, *Argentina* **94 C4** 34 7S 59 0W
Zard, Kūh-e, *Iran* **45 C6** 32 22N 50 4 E
Zāreh, *Iran* **45 C6** 35 7N 49 9 E
Zaria, *Nigeria* **50 F7** 11 0N 7 40 E
Zarneh, *Iran* **44 C5** 33 55N 46 10 E
Zarós, *Greece* **23 D6** 35 8N 24 54 E
Zarqā', Nahr az →, *Jordan* **47 C4** 32 10N 35 37 E
Zarrīn, *Iran* **45 C7** 32 46N 54 37 E
Zaruma, *Ecuador* **92 D3** 3 40S 79 38W
Żary, *Poland* **16 C8** 51 37N 15 10 E
Zarzis, *Tunisia* **51 B8** 33 31N 11 2 E
Zaskar →, *India* **43 B7** 34 13N 77 20 E
Zaskar Mts., *India* **43 C7** 33 15N 77 30 E
Zastron, *S. Africa* **56 E4** 30 18S 27 7 E
Zavāreh, *Iran* **45 C7** 33 29N 52 28 E
Zave, *Zimbabwe* **57 B5** 17 6S 30 1 E
Zavitinsk, *Russia* **27 D13** 50 10N 129 20 E
Zavodovski, I., *Antarctica* **5 B1** 56 0S 27 45W
Zawiercie, *Poland* **17 C10** 50 30N 19 24 E
Zāwiyat al Bayḑā = Al Bayḑā, *Libya* **51 B10** 32 50N 21 44 E
Zāyā, *Iraq* **44 C5** 33 33N 44 13 E
Zāyandeh →, *Iran* **45 C7** 32 35N 52 0 E
Zaysan, *Kazakstan* **26 E9** 47 28N 84 52 E
Zaysan, Oz., *Kazakstan* **26 E9** 48 0N 83 0 E
Zayü, *China* **32 D4** 28 48N 97 27 E
Zazafotsy, *Madag.* **57 C8** 21 11S 46 21 E
Zbarazh, *Ukraine* **17 D13** 49 43N 25 44 E
Zdolbuniv, *Ukraine* **17 C14** 50 30N 26 15 E
Zduńska Wola, *Poland* **17 C10** 51 37N 18 59 E
Zeballos, *Canada* **72 D3** 49 59N 126 50W
Zebediela, *S. Africa* **57 C4** 24 20S 29 17 E
Zeebrugge, *Belgium* **15 C3** 51 19N 3 12 E
Zeehan, *Australia* **62 G4** 41 52S 145 25 E
Zeeland □, *Neths.* **15 C3** 51 30N 3 50 E
Zeerust, *S. Africa* **56 D4** 25 31S 26 4 E
Zefat, *Israel* **47 C4** 32 58N 35 29 E
Zeil, Mt., *Australia* **60 D5** 23 30S 132 23 E
Zeila, *Somali Rep.* **46 E3** 11 21N 43 30 E
Zeist, *Neths.* **15 B5** 52 5N 5 15 E
Zeitz, *Germany* **16 C7** 51 2N 12 7 E
Zelenograd, *Russia* **24 C6** 56 1N 37 12 E
Zelenogradsk, *Russia* **9 J19** 54 53N 20 29 E
Zelienople, *U.S.A.* **78 F4** 40 48N 80 8W
Zémio, *C.A.R.* **54 A2** 5 2N 25 5 E
Zemun, *Serbia, Yug.* **21 B9** 44 51N 20 25 E
Zenica, *Bos.-H.* **21 B7** 44 10N 17 57 E
Žepče, *Bos.-H.* **21 B8** 44 28N 18 2 E
Zevenaar, *Neths.* **15 C6** 51 56N 6 5 E
Zeya, *Russia* **27 D13** 53 48N 127 14 E
Zeya →, *Russia* **27 D13** 51 42N 128 53 E
Zêzere →, *Portugal* **19 C1** 39 28N 8 20W
Zghartā, *Lebanon* **47 A4** 34 21N 35 53 E
Zgorzelec, *Poland* **16 C8** 51 10N 15 0 E
Zhabinka, *Belarus* **17 B13** 52 13N 24 2 E
Zhailma, *Kazakstan* **26 D7** 51 37N 61 33 E
Zhambyl = Taraz, *Kazakstan* **26 E8** 42 54N 71 22 E
Zhangaqazaly, *Kazakstan* **26 E7** 45 48N 62 6 E
Zhangbei, *China* **34 D8** 41 10N 114 45 E
Zhangguangcai Ling, *China* **35 B15** 45 0N 129 0 E
Zhangjiakou, *China* **34 D8** 40 48N 114 55 E
Zhangwu, *China* **35 C12** 42 43N 123 52 E
Zhangye, *China* **32 C5** 38 50N 100 23 E
Zhangzhou, *China* **33 D6** 24 30N 117 35 E
Zhanhua, *China* **35 F10** 37 40N 118 8 E
Zhanjiang, *China* **33 D6** 21 15N 110 20 E
Zhannetty, Ostrov, *Russia* **27 B16** 76 43N 158 0 E
Zhanyi, *China* **32 D5** 25 38N 103 48 E
Zhanyu, *China* **35 B12** 44 30N 122 30 E
Zhao Xian, *China* **34 F8** 37 43N 114 45 E
Zhaocheng, *China* **34 F6** 36 22N 111 38 E
Zhaotong, *China* **32 D5** 27 20N 103 44 E
Zhaoyuan, *Heilongjiang, China* **35 B13** 45 27N 125 0 E
Zhaoyuan, *Shandong, China* **35 F11** 37 20N 120 23 E
Zhashkiv, *Ukraine* **17 D16** 49 15N 30 5 E
Zhashui, *China* **34 H5** 33 40N 109 8 E
Zhayyq →, *Kazakstan* **25 E9** 47 0N 51 48 E
Zhdanov = Mariupol, *Ukraine* **25 E6** 47 5N 37 31 E
Zhecheng, *China* **34 G8** 34 7N 115 20 E
Zhejiang □, *China* **33 D7** 29 0N 120 0 E
Zheleznodorozhnyy, *Russia* **24 B9** 62 35N 50 55 E
Zheleznogorsk-Ilimskiy, *Russia* **27 D11** 56 34N 104 8 E
Zhen'an, *China* **34 H5** 33 27N 109 9 E
Zhengding, *China* **34 E8** 38 8N 114 32 E
Zhengzhou, *China* **34 G7** 34 45N 113 34 E
Zhenlai, *China* **35 B12** 45 50N 123 5 E
Zhenping, *China* **34 H7** 33 10N 112 16 E
Zhenyuan, *China* **34 G4** 35 35N 107 30 E
Zhetiqara, *Kazakstan* **26 D7** 52 11N 61 12 E
Zhezqazghan, *Kazakstan* **26 E7** 47 44N 67 40 E
Zhidan, *China* **34 F5** 36 48N 108 48 E
Zhigansk, *Russia* **27 C13** 66 48N 123 27 E
Zhilinda, *Russia* **27 C12** 70 0N 114 20 E
Zhitomir = Zhytomyr, *Ukraine* **17 C15** 50 20N 28 40 E
Zhlobin, *Belarus* **17 B16** 52 55N 30 0 E
Zhmerinka = Zhmerynka, *Ukraine* **17 D15** 49 2N 28 2 E
Zhmerynka, *Ukraine* **17 D15** 49 2N 28 2 E
Zhob, *Pakistan* **42 D3** 31 20N 69 31 E
Zhob →, *Pakistan* **42 C3** 32 4N 69 50 E
Zhodino = Zhodzina, *Belarus* **17 A15** 54 5N 28 17 E
Zhodzina, *Belarus* **17 A15** 54 5N 28 17 E
Zhokhova, Ostrov, *Russia* **27 B16** 76 4N 152 40 E
Zhongdian, *China* **32 D4** 27 48N 99 42 E
Zhongning, *China* **34 F3** 37 29N 105 40 E
Zhongtiao Shan, *China* **34 G6** 35 0N 111 10 E
Zhongwei, *China* **34 F3** 37 30N 105 12 E
Zhongyang, *China* **34 F6** 37 20N 111 11 E
Zhoucun, *China* **35 F9** 36 47N 117 48 E
Zhouzhi, *China* **34 G5** 34 10N 108 12 E
Zhuanghe, *China* **35 E12** 39 40N 123 0 E
Zhucheng, *China* **35 G10** 36 0N 119 27 E
Zhugqu, *China* **34 H3** 33 40N 104 30 E
Zhumadian, *China* **34 H8** 32 59N 114 2 E
Zhuo Xian = Zhuozhou, *China* **34 E8** 39 28N 115 58 E
Zhuolu, *China* **34 D8** 40 20N 115 12 E
Zhuozhou, *China* **34 E8** 39 28N 115 58 E
Zhuozi, *China* **34 D7** 41 0N 112 25 E
Zhytomyr, *Ukraine* **17 C15** 50 20N 28 40 E
Ziārān, *Iran* **45 B6** 36 7N 50 32 E
Ziarat, *Pakistan* **42 D2** 30 25N 67 49 E
Zibo, *China* **35 F10** 36 47N 118 3 E
Zichang, *China* **34 F5** 37 18N 109 40 E
Zielona Góra, *Poland* **16 C8** 51 57N 15 31 E
Zierikzee, *Neths.* **15 C3** 51 40N 3 55 E
Zigey, *Chad* **51 F9** 14 43N 15 50 E
Zigong, *China* **32 D5** 29 15N 104 48 E
Ziguinchor, *Senegal* **50 F2** 12 35N 16 20W
Zihuatanejo, *Mexico* **86 D4** 17 38N 101 33W
Žilina, *Slovak Rep.* **17 D10** 49 12N 18 42 E
Zillah, *Libya* **51 C9** 28 30N 17 33 E
Zima, *Russia* **27 D11** 54 0N 102 5 E
Zimapán, *Mexico* **87 C5** 20 54N 99 20W
Zimba, *Zambia* **55 F2** 17 20S 26 11 E
Zimbabwe, *Zimbabwe* **55 G3** 20 16S 30 54 E
Zimbabwe ■, *Africa* **55 F3** 19 0S 30 0 E
Zimnicea, *Romania* **17 G13** 43 40N 25 22 E
Zinder, *Niger* **50 F7** 13 48N 9 0 E
Zinga, *Tanzania* **55 D4** 9 16S 38 49 E
Zion National Park, *U.S.A.* **83 H7** 37 15N 113 5W
Ziros, *Greece* **23 D8** 35 5N 26 8 E
Zirreh, Gowd-e, *Afghan.* **40 E3** 29 45N 62 0 E
Zitácuaro, *Mexico* **86 D4** 19 28N 100 21W
Zitundo, *Mozam.* **57 D5** 26 48S 32 47 E
Ziwa Maghariba □, *Tanzania* **54 C3** 2 0S 31 30 E
Ziway, L., *Ethiopia* **46 F2** 8 0N 38 50 E
Ziyang, *China* **34 H5** 32 32N 108 31 E
Zlatograd, *Bulgaria* **21 D11** 41 22N 25 7 E
Zlatoust, *Russia* **24 C10** 55 10N 59 40 E
Zlín, *Czech Rep.* **17 D9** 49 14N 17 40 E
Zmeinogorsk, *Kazakstan* **26 D9** 51 10N 82 13 E
Znojmo, *Czech Rep.* **16 D9** 48 50N 16 2 E
Zobeyrī, *Iran* **44 C5** 34 10N 46 40 E
Zobia, *Dem. Rep. of the Congo* **54 B2** 3 0N 25 59 E
Zoetermeer, *Neths.* **15 B4** 52 3N 4 30 E
Zolochev = Zolochiv, *Ukraine* **17 D13** 49 45N 24 51 E
Zolochiv, *Ukraine* **17 D13** 49 45N 24 51 E
Zomba, *Malawi* **55 F4** 15 22S 35 19 E
Zongo, *Dem. Rep. of the Congo* **52 D3** 4 20N 18 35 E
Zonguldak, *Turkey* **25 F5** 41 28N 31 50 E
Zonqor Pt., *Malta* **23 D2** 35 51N 14 34 E
Zorritos, *Peru* **92 D2** 3 43S 80 40W
Zou Xiang, *China* **34 G9** 35 30N 116 58 E
Zouar, *Chad* **51 D9** 20 30N 16 32 E
Zouérate = Zouîrât, *Mauritania* **50 D3** 22 44N 12 21W
Zouîrât, *Mauritania* **50 D3** 22 44N 12 21W
Zoutkamp, *Neths.* **15 A6** 53 20N 6 18 E
Zrenjanin, *Serbia, Yug.* **21 B9** 45 22N 20 23 E
Zufār, *Oman* **46 D5** 17 40N 54 0 E
Zug, *Switz.* **18 C8** 47 10N 8 31 E
Zugspitze, *Germany* **16 E6** 47 25N 10 59 E
Zuid-Holland □, *Neths.* **15 C4** 52 0N 4 35 E
Zuidbeveland, *Neths.* **15 C3** 51 30N 3 50 E
Zuidhorn, *Neths.* **15 A6** 53 15N 6 23 E
Zula, *Eritrea* **46 D2** 15 17N 39 40 E
Zumbo, *Mozam.* **55 F3** 15 35S 30 26 E
Zumpango, *Mexico* **87 D5** 19 48N 99 6W
Zunhua, *China* **35 D9** 40 18N 117 58 E
Zuni, *U.S.A.* **83 J9** 35 4N 108 51W
Zunyi, *China* **32 D5** 27 42N 106 53 E
Zurbātīyah, *Iraq* **44 C5** 33 9N 46 3 E
Zürich, *Switz.* **18 C8** 47 22N 8 32 E
Zutphen, *Neths.* **15 B6** 52 9N 6 12 E
Zuwārah, *Libya* **51 B8** 32 58N 12 1 E
Zūzan, *Iran* **45 C8** 34 22N 59 53 E
Zverinogolovskoye, *Russia* **26 D7** 54 26N 64 50 E
Zvishavane, *Zimbabwe* **55 G3** 20 17S 30 2 E
Zvolen, *Slovak Rep.* **17 D10** 48 33N 19 10 E
Zwettl, *Austria* **16 D8** 48 35N 15 9 E
Zwickau, *Germany* **16 C7** 50 44N 12 30 E
Zwolle, *Neths.* **15 B6** 52 31N 6 6 E
Zwolle, *U.S.A.* **81 K8** 31 38N 93 39W
Żyrardów, *Poland* **17 B11** 52 3N 20 28 E
Zyryan, *Kazakstan* **26 E9** 49 43N 84 20 E
Zyryanka, *Russia* **27 C16** 65 45N 150 51 E
Zyryanovsk = Zyryan, *Kazakstan* **26 E9** 49 43N 84 20 E
Żywiec, *Poland* **17 D10** 49 42N 19 10 E
Zyyi, *Cyprus* **23 E12** 34 43N 33 20 E